ANNUAL REVIEW OF PSYCHOLOGY

ANNUAL REVIEW OF PSYCHOLOGY

PAUL H. MUSSEN, *Editor*

University of California, Berkeley

MARK R. ROSENZWEIG, *Editor*

University of California, Berkeley

VOLUME 23

1972

ANNUAL REVIEWS INC.
4139 EL CAMINO WAY
PALO ALTO, CALIFORNIA 94306, USA

ANNUAL REVIEWS INC.
PALO ALTO, CALIFORNIA, USA

© 1972 BY ANNUAL REVIEWS INC.
ALL RIGHTS RESERVED

Standard Book Number 8243–0223–0

Library of Congress Catalog Card Number 50–13143

FOREIGN AGENCY

Maruzen Company Limited,
6, Tori-Nichome, Nihonbashi
Tokyo

PRINTED AND BOUND IN THE UNITED STATES OF AMERICA BY
GEORGE BANTA COMPANY, INC.

PREFACE

Readers have noticed that, over the years, the volumes of the *Annual Review of Psychology* have gradually but consistently increased in size. The present volume is by far the largest in the 23-year history of the series. We are in the midst of a data explosion—although there are doubts about whether it is a knowledge explosion. The number of articles in each major area of psychology increases enormously each year, and consequently each reviewer's task becomes more difficult and more complicated. It is virtually impossible to review *everything* published in a year in fields as broad as social psychology, personality, or learning. While several of the chapters in the present volume encompass general areas (for example, human abilities, personality, and developmental), there is a clearly discernible trend toward chapters that focus on significant, selected *topics* within the field rather than overall reviews. But chapter topics are not so restricted that they will appeal only to a very limited number of readers.

The continued success and usefulness of the *Annual Review* depends upon each volume's being comprehensive (but reasonably brief), readable, and low priced.

To limit the size of the volume—and thus keep its price down—it is necessary to make specific page allotments for each chapter, based on the breadth of the topic and the amount of publication on that topic. In order to comply with strict space limitations, authors must be extremely selective in their coverage and may frequently find it necessary to condense or omit discussions of some highly relevant publications. The editors and the readers of the *Annual Review* are most grateful to the authors for providing such concise, well-reasoned reviews within the assigned space. Even so, some manuscripts that are submitted greatly exceed the number of allotted pages. In such cases the editors must recommend drastic cutting, although they and the authors find this extremely painful. Unhappily, in the future we shall have to hold even more rigidly to the page limits.

The majority of publications reviewed in this series is American. However, as editors we are concerned with increasing international coverage, and as a step in this direction we are beginning a series of chapters on psychological research in other countries. Designed to coincide with the meeting every third year of the International Congress of Psychology, the chapter will deal with psychology in the host country, with publication scheduled early in the year of the meeting. Since the meeting this year is in Tokyo, there is a chapter on psychological research in Japan.

In 1971 Dr. Lyle V. Jones completed his five-year term of membership on the editorial committee. Throughout his tenure we have drawn heavily on his extensive knowledge of current work in various fields of psychology. Professor Warren T. Norman has accepted the Board's invitation to fill this position for the next five-year period. Miss Jean Heavener, assistant editor, is our full collaborator in developing and producing this series. We also wish to thank Mrs. Dorothy Read for preparing the accurate and detailed subject index.

P. H. M.
M. R. R.

TOPICS AND AUTHORS
ANNUAL REVIEW OF PSYCHOLOGY
VOLUME 24 (1973)

CONTENTS

REPRINTS

The conspicuous number (175 to 193) aligned in the margin with the title of each review in this volume is a key for use in the ordering of reprints.

Reprints of most articles published in the *Annual Reviews of Psychology* and *Biochemistry* from 1961, and the *Annual Reviews of Microbiology* and *Physiology* from 1968, are now maintained in inventory. Beginning with July 1970, this reprint policy was extended to all other *Annual Reviews* volumes.

Available reprints are priced at the uniform rate of $1 each postpaid. Payment must accompany orders less than $10. The following discounts will be given for large orders: $5–9, 10%; $10–24, 20%; $25 and over, 30%. All remittances are to be made payable to Annual Reviews Inc. in U. S. dollars. California orders are subject to sales tax. One-day service is given on items in stock.

For orders of 100 or more, any *Annual Reviews* article will be specially printed and shipped within 6 weeks. Reprints which are out of stock may also be purchased from the Institute for Scientific Information, 325 Chestnut Street, Philadelphia, Pa. 19106. Direct inquiries to the Annual Reviews Inc. reprint department.

The sale of reprints of articles published in the *Reviews* has been expanded in the belief that reprints as individual copies, as sets covering stated topics, and in quantity for classroom use will have a special appeal to students and teachers.

DEVELOPMENTAL PSYCHOLOGY

LEWIS P. LIPSITT AND PETER D. EIMAS[1]

Brown University, Providence, Rhode Island

INTRODUCTION

Each succeeding annual chapter on Developmental Psychology in these volumes has reflected the increasing frustration, and indeed desperation, of the authors as they have sought to summarize and reflect on the year's advances in their field. It is perhaps time that it be stated explicitly that the task is virtually impossible, for the burgeoning research literature has become so terribly broad in scope, and some of it so greatly specialized, as to defy human appraisal within the constraints of space, time, and talent necessarily imposed on a volume such as this.

Following a cataloging and inspection of the year's research papers, review articles, and critical syntheses, and more than a dozen new volumes devoted entirely to issues and data in developmental psychology, the authors quickly concluded that they must be very selective in their coverage if they are to say anything more, about any of the work, than that an article was published on a particular topic. While we have attempted to be judicious in our selections, it goes without saying that those issues and those research advances closest to our hearts are the ones on which we have dwelt most, and exclusion of a paper, or even an entire research area, is more likely a reflection of our idiosyncratic fascinations this year than of the adequacy of the omitted contribution.

INFANT BEHAVIOR

It is clear from the number and variety of infant studies published, as well as the large number of books that have appeared dealing either entirely or in large part with infant behavior and development, that 1970 was a positive growth year, reflecting the burgeoning concern of our culture with the nature and welfare of young people. If there need to be banners carried by researchers dealing with different behavior phenomena or processes, or if various camps require ideologic separation, then Kagan (135) has provided the necessary rubrics for delineating the factions. In a paper on attention and

[1] Work on this review was supported in part by United States Public Health Service Grants HD 03911 and HD 05331, to Lewis P. Lipsitt and Peter D. Eimas respectively. The writers are indebted to Helen Haeseler, Jane Carlstrom, and Meredith S. Pandolfi for aid in assembling materials for this review, which is concerned primarily with the literature appearing in the year 1970.

psychological change in the young child, Kagan has indicated that one approach to the study of behavior change is through the mechanisms of conditioning. A second involves the study of "delayed appearance of species-specific behaviors after exposure to a narrow band of experience." Bird-song and children's language fall here, and it is argued that the development of such behaviors does not conform to conditioning principles. Such behavior, the author says, involves the ". . . establishment of and successive changes in cognitive structures not tied directly to behavior." (This view calls to mind a recent *Punch* cartoon showing a little girl returning from school and announcing to her parents "I'm not learning anything. I'm developing cognitive skills.") Kagan's metaphorical emphasis on "cognitive competence" is carried into a third type of developmental change, involving the acquisition of schemata defined as representations of experience, preserving the temporal and spatial relations of the original event. A schema, like an engram, ". . . was invented to explain the organism's capacity to recognize an event encountered in the past." It is supposed (as by Sokolov) that a cortical neuronal representation is acquired and that a matching of successive experiences against that model underlies recognition.

A series of experiments conducted by Kagan and his associates (e.g. 170, 171, 175) deals with differential reactions to stimuli differing in degree of "discrepancy" from an initial familiarization stimulus which provides the "schema." In general, it has been shown that children deploy visual attention (and direct smiles at) stimuli in a fairly orderly fashion relating to the test-stimulus discrepancy from the familiarized original: ". . . events that possessed a high rate of change in their physical characteristics, that were moderately discrepant from established schemata, and that activated hypotheses in the service of assimilation had the greatest power to recruit and maintain attention in the young child." In some instances an inverted-U function is obtained indicating avoidance of or disinterest in widely discrepant test stimuli.

While the basic behavioral phenomenon, to which J. McV. Hunt and colleagues (Greenberg et al 107; Uzgiris & Hunt 262) have also addressed themselves, is unquestioned, it must also be appreciated (and Kagan does appreciate this) that attentional behavior can be manifested by different behaviors (e.g. fixation, vocalization, quieting, thrashing, smiling, and autonomic changes), that different sense modalities must produce different schemata, that some types of attentional investments may be idiosyncratic to certain modalities, and that the state, not to mention the age, of the organism is an important determinant of the shape of "discrepancy" function obtained. Oddly, the *structure* of this type of theory is remarkably similar to the Hull and Spence variety. Numerous categories of response (response frequency in Hull, length of eye fixation in Kagan) are elicited differentially depending upon prior experience (stimulus trials in Hull, amount of familiarization in Kagan) which impresses upon the organism a "condition" (habit in Hull, schema in Kagan) which manifests itself across a range of generalization stimuli (other stimuli on the same physical continuum in Hull, variations on the original face in Kagan) depending upon the state of the organism (drive in Hull, wakefulness or arousal level in Kagan?). Whether eventual quantitative refinement of the basic postulates of the Kagan theory will withstand close empirical testing remains to be seen. The recent history of similar approaches suggests that a lot of mileage lies ahead.

In addition to the references already cited, a rather large number of studies appeared during the year concerned with the visual alertness and visual fixation behavior of young infants, particularly as these measures are affected by individual differences or temporary states of the babies. Moss & Robson (190) explored the relation between the amount of time infants spend in various state-conditions with the development of visual behavior. A group of 42 infants were observed at home at 1 and 3 months of age, followed shortly by a laboratory test of visual fixation time. Infants showing more quiet and awake states at 1 month and absence of irritability at 3 months looked longer at visual stimuli in the laboratory test. Interestingly, mothers' own ratings, at the time of laboratory test, of their babies' irritability showed the same correlations with fixation times as did the home observations. Lewis (151) has written on the role of individual differences in the measurement of early cognitive growth and presents data to indicate that the rate and amount of young infants' response decrement in a habituation procedure is predictive of later measures of cognitive development and central nervous system functioning. Habituation rate was related to such variables as age of infant, state at time of testing, the mother-infant interaction, and even socioeconomic status. Response-decrement rates also predicted learning task and concept formation ability at later ages, and 4-year IQ is found to be related to 1-year habituation. In general, the faster the response decrement under early habituation procedures, the more "efficient" is the individual alleged to be in later assessments. Lewis suggests, finally, that habituation rate may be a valuable early diagnostic tool for detecting subclinical nervous system dysfunctions, supporting a similar proposition by the Soviet investigator Bronshtein. Clearly, much more research should be done to evaluate the usefulness of responses obtained in experimental-manipulative tasks for purposes of predicting later intellectual and emotional responsivity. Typically, standardized developmental tests have been used for this purpose, and such psychometric devices tend to capitalize upon the elicitation of "milestone" behaviors which have already been acquired rather than on the *processes* by which the infant acquires or becomes able to manifest these behaviors (see Lipsitt 155). In two recent papers, Lipsitt (156, 157) has reviewed some of the progress recently made in the detailed exploration of behavioral plasticity of the child in the first year of life. Such processes must be documented longitudinally to understand precisely the manner in which proficiency in later complex learning situations depends upon the prior mastery of more fundamental learning tasks.

Even the premature infant can see patterned stimulation (182; see also

79). Miranda's study (182) shows that conceptional age, in addition to age since birth, is a determinant of visual selection. He compared 27 $3\frac{1}{2}$-day-old, normal full-term babies with 27 prematures, the latter tested at less than 38 weeks of conceptional age. Stimuli were presented in pairs, counterbalanced, and the infants' eyes were scored as looking left or right. Both premature and full-term infants resolved grating stimuli of $\frac{1}{2}$ inch and $\frac{1}{4}$ inch, fixating these patterns more frequently and longer than a plain gray stimulus. Both groups tended to prefer the less complex of paired stimuli.

Visual alertness of newborns was studied in the context of the mother-infant relationship by Korner & Thoman (146). The subjects were 40 crying and 24 sleeping infants in the second and third day of life. Six different types of intervention, involving vestibular and contact stimulation, in the upright position or not, were involved. A high reliability scale of visual alertness showed highly significant individual differences among the infants in alerting, with no differences due to sex or breast versus bottle feeding. In soothing the crying infant, vestibular stimulation produced a striking effect on alerting, while tactual contact by itself produced little alerting. In another study from the same research program, Korner (145) explored individual differences among 32 newborns with respect to frequency and duration of visual alertness, along with incidence of visual pursuit. High correlations were found among the three measures. In addition to this high intraindividual stability, great variance in visual alertness was found across infants. Among the conditions that showed no relationship to alerting behavior were sex, parity, birth-weight, conceptional age, and postnatal age within the two days studied. Assessments of activation or arousal were judged to be related to frequency and duration of visual alertness, but not to visual pursuit. For those who think that some babies are "visual responders" while others are "auditory responders," sensitivity to auditory stimuli was significantly related to the capacity for visual pursuit but not to frequency and duration of visual alertness.

An increasing number of studies is beginning to appear relating to visual behavior in infants older than neonates and younger than preschoolers. McGurk (172) studied eight children between 6 and 26 weeks of age, using stimuli representing abstract and facial objects presented in different orientations. After an initial study in which the children showed no discrimination among orientations as evidenced by spontaneous visual preference patterns, two other studies utilized a habituation procedure. Following habituation to an object in one orientation, tests were made with the same objects in other orientations. Magnitude analyses of attention-recovery responses showed that infants from 6 to 26 weeks perceive alterations in orientation of 180 degrees, but only beyond 20 weeks of age can infants discriminate an upright from an inverted facial object. As in so many recent studies, the author concludes that "infants are more sensitive to the spatial orientation of forms than has hitherto been believed to be the case." In a study of visually evoked cortical responses and infant pattern vision, Harter & Suitt (116) obtained evoked potentials from one infant, longitudinally from 21 to 155 days of age, in response to checkerboard patterns. During the first month of life, greatest response was to large-check patterns, with greatest response occurring to progressively smaller checks with increasing age. Another study of differential attentional behavior to different visual stimuli, in this case representations of human and humanoid faces, was presented by Carpenter et al (42). In addition, Messer et al (176) were able to show that fixation time and habituation rate relate to tempo of play in infants 13 months of age, with a striking sex reversal of correlation direction occurring; a high positive correlation occurred between number of play shifts and rate of habituation for boys, and this relationship was negative for girls. In a study of emotional concomitants of visual mastery in infants, Shultz & Zigler (244) showed that smiling and vocalization occurred earlier, within the age range between 8 and 18 weeks, in response to a simple stimulus rather than to a more complex one. Over successive testing sessions habituation of smiling, vocalizing, and visual fixation were noted.

Bower (22, 23) continues to dazzle the field with reports of enormously precocious neonatal feats of visual assimilation and discrimination. From the first study, Bower concludes that neonates extend their hands toward seen objects, and that they touch and occasionally grasp them. While this behavior appears to many as merely excited thrashing or fortuitous touching, Bower believes that he has documented it as indicative of true intentional behavior. The reader is directed to the original article for the procedures employed, which are too complicated for brief review, but it may be stated that the argument for neonate intentional behavior is based upon the fact that infants invariably cried when "reaching" for illusory objects, but none of them did when reaching for actual objects. In a second paper, Bower et al assert that while it is commonly assumed that "touch teaches vision" during development, recent studies show that in judgment situations vision functionally dominates touch.

Progress continues toward the further understanding of individual differences among very young infants and the stimulating circumstances that have an effect upon their neonatal status and subsequent course of development. An early 1970 publication edited by Ambrose (5) contains chapters by Levine on infantile stimulation, by Ginsburg on genotypic variables affecting response to postnatal stimulation, an article on imprinting and development of preferences by Bateson, chapters by Ainsworth and Bell and by David and Appell on mother-child interactions, a contribution by Bruner on growth processes in infancy, a new paper on conditioning in neonates and older infants by Papousek and Bernstein, and an article on social class and infant cognitive development by Kagan. On the subject of neonate-mother interaction, Thoman et al (257) have reported on a procedure developed for studying feeding patterns of mothers with their newborns. Automatic time measures of feeding interactions enabled recording without the presence of an observer. These measures enabled, for example, detection of differences in the behavior of primiparous and multiparous mothers with their two-day-olds. Primiparous mothers attended and persisted more than multiparas, but were less effective in facilitating the infant's food consumption. Such observations may be importantly relevant to later-observed patterns of behavior among first-borns and their siblings. In another study of newborn feeding behavior, Nisbett & Gurwitz (198) showed that heavier infants take more formula than do lighter babies, and that when sucking for formula is made difficult the heavier infants exert less effort to obtain food than do their lighter counterparts. A sex difference was found in that females responded more to a sweet nutritive food than males but worked with less effort to obtain the formula than males. The authors state that these findings parallel weight and sex differences found in human adults and that such individual differences are biologically determined. Murray & Campbell (191) have shown that olfactory thresholds measured by startle behavior and respiratory disruption reveal that the threshold is higher during regular sleep than during irregular or REM sleep, further supporting the importance of state in the determination of neonatal response to exteroceptive stimulation.

With the increasing concern of infant researchers for the study of state factors, apparatus and methodological innovations continue to be made along with the carrying out of studies that effect changes in state parameters through varying experiential circumstances (see Lipsitt 155). Besides a report on a new type of stabilimeter (152), a method for the study of sleep cycles and skin potential in newborns involving a simplified observation and recording system has been developed by Bell (11; see also Prechtl 211). Findings using the Bell method replicated ". . . essential features of quiet and active sleep cycles . . . reported previously to exist against the background of decreasing level of physiological arousal, as sleep proceeds." In 12 newborns, one half of the interfeeding sleep time was spent in the rapid eye movement stage. Skin potential declined rapidly during the transition from waking to sleep, and increased in variability during REM sleep. A manipulative study by Van den Daele (263) indicated that distressed infants cease their fretful behavior when rocked. Corroborating a similar finding of DeLucia (Reese & Lipsitt 215, pp. 414–15), infant response varied with rocking rate and infant state but additionally appeared to be independent of age of infant, sex, developmental level, and specific environmental antecedents. In a study of the effects of temperature and position on the sucking behavior of newborn infants (Elder 73), the behavior of 27 healthy, full-term infants showed that sucking pressure decreased as environmental temperature was increased, and sucking pressure increased from the third to the fifth day of life. Moreover, sucking pressure increased in the morning feeding relative to the afternoon recordings, again indicating that both state and diurnal factors are pertinent to behavioral assessments of infants.

A number of studies have capitalized upon the visual-fixation recording procedures developed by Fantz, as well as the stimulus familiarization effect of Cantor and his colleagues, to explore the effects of prior stimulus exposure (and thus memory) on the subsequent visual attentive behavior of infants. Fagan (78), for example, has demonstrated that infants in the age range from 3 to 6 months of age show differential fixation time on novel and familiar targets, with novel targets commanding more attention whether the tests of stimulus recognition are immediate or delayed. In a study of recovery of habituation in infants (Pancratz & Cohen 207), 32 4-month-old infants were given 10 visual familiarization trials with one stimulus followed by a retention interval, followed by presentation of both the familiar and novel stimulus. Males, but not females, habituated their fixation time over trials, differentiating between the novel and familiar stimuli when the posthabituation interval was 15 seconds, but neither sex did so for as long as 5 minutes. Another study of habituation in newborns, conducted by Moreau et al (187), demonstrated that in 2-day-old infants, habituation to somesthetic stimulation occurs earlier than habituation to auditory stimulation although the two types of stimulation were equally effective in eliciting responsivity initially. Moreover, rates of habituation of an autonomic and a motoric response to auditory stimulation were compared and showed that motoric habituation was faster, more stable, and independent of autonomic habituation to the same stimulus. Brackbill and her colleagues have added data to an ongoing research program relating to the interaction of stimulus and response during infant conditioning, through a study by Abrahamson et al (1), in which tactile, auditory, and temporal classical conditioning of sucking was attempted in three studies of normal human newborns. While conditioning to tactile and auditory conditioned stimuli occurred, no temporal conditioning was obtained. Following further in the tradition of Eastern European and Soviet studies of infant conditioning, Sameroff (226) carried out a study in Papousek's laboratory of non-nutritive sucking response to auditory stimulation in 1-, 2-, and 3-month-old infants. The 1- and 2-month-old infants showed ambiguous effects of auditory stimulation when paired with non-nutritive sucking opportunity, while the older infants produced reliable shortening of the sucking burst and other changes in sucking activity, presumably based upon the conditioning experience. While the effects of intrusion of auditory stimulation were found at all three ages, manifest in the increased sucking interval when tones were administered, the inhibition effect reported by Bronshtein (see 215, p. 37) wherein sucking bursts should be shortened when exteroceptive stimulation occurs, was found in 3-month infants, but not at younger ages.

In a new study from Brackbill's research program, Schwartz et al (236) have shown in two studies that infant vocalizations can be conditioned through the use of only one or two components of the traditionally employed composite social reinforcer involving the simultaneous presentation of auditory, tactile, and visual stimulation. Moreover, the components seem to be of relatively equal effectiveness in increasing conditioned response rate. A review by Fitzgerald & Porges (83) of one decade of infant conditioning research suggests that within a very short span of time it has been rather thoroughly established that neonates and older infants within the first year of life are highly conditionable, and that the research task in the future is one of examining closely and under sophisticated quantitative conditions the parameters controlling conditioned behavior at successive ages.

Perhaps because cardiac rate is relatively easily measured, numerous studies have appeared which illuminate the stimulus parameters controlling heart-rate change under various unconditioned stimulus conditions. Such studies are essential to an eventual understanding of the conditioned changes in cardiac activity resulting from cumulative experiential circumstances. In a study by Lewis et al (153), dealing with the heart rate of the fetus in the last trimester and its relationship to heart-rate measures within the entire first year of postnatal life, it was demonstrated, perhaps disappointingly, that no relationship exists between either maternal or fetal and later infant heart rate. The primary finding in this study was that both mean heart rate and variability show consistent decreases over the first year of life. A study by Brackbill (24) compared effects of three auditory conditions involving no sound, intermittent sound, or continuous sound on arousal level in infants, and indicated that level of arousal was diminished by the presentation of continuous sound while it was increased by intermittent sound, compared with the presentation of the no-sound condition. Arousal was measured through state ratings, respiration, heart rate, and motor activity. As in other studies reported recently (e.g. Graham & Jackson 104a), it could not be shown that response to discrete auditory stimulation related to initial arousal levels, including those inferred from heart rate. Another study in which the Law of Initial Value received scant support was that of Hutt & Hutt (125), in which the regression coefficients for control periods, using heart-rate as the dependent variable, did not differ from those in which auditory stimulation was administered. Another study involving heart rate examined a hypothesis previously presented by both Bronshtein and Luria that infants with nervous system damage either failed to habituate to exteroceptive stimulation or habituate more slowly than normal infant control groups. Comparable habituation findings were obtained for both groups, although latency of response was apparently greater for high-risk subjects (see 234). Longer latencies of response, moreover, were correlated with increased prematurity.

An interesting use of the cardiac response measure has been made by Campos et al (39), who tested infants younger and older than crawling age on a visual cliff apparatus. Those who did not yet crawl produced reliable cardiac deceleration when placed on top of the deep side of the cliff relative to crawling infants, but no differences were found on the shallow side. Supporting the original propositions of Walk and Gibson, fewer signs of distress were elicited on the deep side of the cliff at earlier ages, relative to post-crawling ages wherein more distress occurred to the deep side. It was thus apparent from this study that deep-side distress does not occur suddenly upon achievement of crawling behavior. Finally, cardiac responsivity was studied as a function of age by Graham et al (105), with the result that heart-rate change was curvilinearly related to age and, as in other studies reported earlier, was independent of prestimulus heart-rate differences. No cardiac deceleration to exteroceptive stimulation appeared at birth, but this mode of response increased from 6 to 16 weeks of age, thereafter lessening from 16 weeks to adulthood.

Several studies appeared in the literature during 1970 relating to maternal attachment behavior of infants and their reactions to separation from the mother. A study by Fleener & Cairns (86) involved the testing of 64 infants, aged 3 to 19 months, to determine the incidence at different ages of disruptive reactions upon maternal separation. The test utilized involved the departure and then return of the mother and another female, and the results showed that only the infants of 12 months and over showed a greater tendency to cry upon departure of the mother than of the other adult female. Moreover, crying upon separation was related to no other measure of maternal responsiveness or with the child's sex. Attachment, exploration, and separation in 1-year-old children were also tested by Ainsworth & Bell (3), who studied 56 infants exposed to a strange situation. The authors concluded that mother's presence encouraged exploratory behavior and her absence depressed such behavior and increased crying. Upon maternal reunion proximity-seeking and contact-maintaining behavior was increased but, interestingly, some subjects upon reunion actively resisted such contact. In a study of the development of object concepts as related to infant-mother-attachment, Bell (12) explored the relation between the development of person and object permanence and the attachment of infants to their mothers. Three hypotheses were confirmed: (a) babies tend to achieve the concept of person-permanency more quickly than object-permanency; (b) differences in the acquisition of person-permanency are related to attachment-behavior characteristics in the presence of the mother; and (c) acquisition of person-permanence may affect, but is at least related to, the development of object permanence. H. R. Schaffer, a long-time student of infant-mother attachment, has now co-authored an experimental study (Schaffer & Parry 231) which seeks to refine the documentation of the infant's ability to classify stimuli as familiar or unfamiliar. A short-term period of familiarization was administered to infants aged either 6, 9, or 12 months, the familiarization period being followed by a simultaneous discrimination task in which the familiar was paired with a novel stimulus. While the results indicated ability to visually discriminate at all three ages, "manipulative discrimination" took place only in the older two groups.

A very interesting brief review of infant-mother separation studies in a variety of mammals was published by Rheingold & Eckerman (216), along with data from two studies of their own, one conducted in a seminaturalistic setting with children from 1 to 5 years old, and the other a laboratory study with 10-month-old infants. The former study indicated clearly that the distance which young children will venture from their mothers becomes progressively longer with increasing age. The study of 10-month-olds showed—

surprisingly considering the generally held view that infants of this age are universally prone to "separation anxiety"—that all 24 infants in the study crept away from their mothers without fussing or crying and locomoted to another larger room, whether that room was empty or contained a toy visible from the starting point. The only effect of the toy inducement was to promote longer separation from the mother. The more toys available in the adjoining room, the longer the infants stayed away. Of further interest was the observation by Rheingold & Eckerman that when infants returned to home base they touched the mother only two-thirds of the time and on other occasions apparently just came to look; moreover, observations of emotionality could not substantiate that fear or relief from fear were factors in any of the traversals made by the infants. In connection with infantile expressions of fear, it is of interest to note here that Scarr & Salapatek (229) demonstrated in a longitudinal study of 91 infants that there are few interrelationships among infant expressions of fear of strangers, of heights, of mechanical objects, and toys, and moreover, that fear behavior is not predictable from measures of cognitive abilities as measured, for example, by object-permanence tests.

Two rather interesting studies were reported from the National Collaborative Project relating to the predictive power of the 8-month Bayley Scales, particularly when considered in connection with the socioeconomic origins of the child. In a study by Ireton et al (128), socioeconomic ratings produced higher correlation coefficients (.43 for males, .38 for females) than 8-month developmental scores with 4-year IQ, but in this sample of 536 children, 8-month mental scores also showed reliable correlations with 4-year IQ (.28 for males, .23 for females). Low mental scores were better predictors of low 4-year IQ than was low social status, but high social status was a better predictor of high 4-year IQ than was a high 8-month mental score. This finding of an interaction between infant mental status and socioeconomic condition was further substantiated in a study by Willerman et al (274) in which Bayley Mental and Motor scores, along with social class ratings, were related to 4-year Binet IQ in a sample of over 3000 children. For infants scoring in the upper quartile on the mental and motor tests at 8 months, the occurrence of low IQ (less than 80) at age 4 did not relate to social ratings. However, among infants scoring in the lowest quartiles on the mental and motor tests, social class did relate to a finding of low IQ. Specifically, retarded infants were seven times more likely to obtain IQs less than 80 at age 4 if they came from the lower socioeconomic range than if they came from a higher social class. Two papers relating to the usefulness of developmental test scores especially in unusual circumstances or in association with other considerations, are those of Thomas (258) and Erikson et al (75).

Heredity and Environment and Jensen

Arthur R. Jensen, the educational psychologist who wrote the controversial 1969 *Harvard Educational Review* treatise on the heritability of IQ, and thereby brought the nature-nurture issue into new focus, has now published a fascinating article (131) in which data from four classic studies of identical twins are reanalyzed. Apart from reminding us that one pair of identical twins of the Newman et al sample which were reared apart showed an IQ disparity of 24 points, this paper shows convincingly that the distribution of IQ differences found among identicals reared apart is essentially a chi square distribution, which permits the inference that the effects of environmental differences in this twin population are normally distributed, with a mean absolute difference of 6.6 IQ points (5.6 corrected for attenuation) and a twin-twin correlation of .824. Those who would take the 24-point difference out of context are cautioned that the exception, reflecting only normal variation of differences, does not constitute an "unusual event" when it is considered in the normal distribution context. As for the effects of environment on intellectual competence, Jensen notes that in such studies of twins reared apart ". . . there is always some uncertainty about the degree to which the nongenetic variance components are common to the separated twins." Again, "There is never truly random assignment of separated twins to their foster homes. Some separated twins are reared, for example, in different branches of the same family. And twins put out for adoption rarely go into the poorest homes." Nevertheless, Jensen believes that such twin-separation studies are the closest approximation found under natural conditions to the idealized experiment for estimating heritability of intelligence. Since, as Jensen points out, the environmental variation existing in these studies is not as great as it could possibly be (such an experiment would be cruel in the extreme), the meticulous statistical analysis provides no grounds on which to refute the proposition that in principle (i.e. under other conditions) the mean and standard deviation of the IQ disparity could be greater than 6.6 points (SD—6.2), and specific within-twin-pair differences could go greater than 24 IQ points.

That the issue is still very much alive and probably will remain so for some time is suggested by a letter in *American Psychologist* (118) from Hebb in which he suggests that many of Jensen's detractors have been dogmatic, emotional, and illogical, but that Jensen himself has used a "misleading" conception of heritability. The nub of Hebb's argument is that if 100 boys were reared in barrels and fed through the bung-hole until age 12, as Mark Twain proposed, their IQ variance would be essentially zero, due to the homogeneity of rearing conditions, thus making it appear as if heredity is all; such a statistic, however, would overlook the fact that all of the boys would probably have low IQs in direct consequence of the *environmental* conditions. In an as yet unpublished retort to the Hebb argument that heritability analyses overlook the latter half of the story, Jensen claims that it is Hebb's concept of heritability that is "confused," in fact is "nonsense." Heritability proportions always refer, he says, to specific populations, and Hebb has left consideration of the boys in the barrel the moment he starts comparing them with other boys (e.g. those reared under home conditions and predicted to have mean IQ of 100). Another determination of heritability is required for the analysis Hebb wants, an analysis of twin-pairs reared in barrels, in comparison with twin-pairs reared at home and with twin-pairs reared under disparate conditions: "In a population with such heterogeneous environments, consisting of homes and barrels, we should expect the value of h^2 (heritability) to be comparatively small, reflecting the greater variance due to the extreme environmental variation."

A very important volume published in 1970 on *Compensatory Education, a National Debate* (119) contains Jensen's current thinking on heritability, especially regarding racial differences in mental abilities, along with a chapter by Bereiter (15) on the educational implications of the Jensen debate, and a chapter by a geneticist (43) who concludes that "A review of present knowledge on interracial divergence in man makes it unlikely that a difference as large as the observed one is genetic." In the same volume is another chapter by Jensen (130) on the subject of so-called culture-fair testing. Other new works relating to these issues include a widely acclaimed article by Jinks & Fulker (132) comparing biometric, genetic, and other approaches to the analysis of human behavior; a book by Bulmer (35) on the biology of twinning in man and the methodology of twin research; and an article by Bresler (26) reporting a study with implications for developmental psychology in its demonstration that fetal loss is an increasing function of genetic dissimilarity of parents. Related to the latter finding, but interpretively difficult, is a study (275) by a psychologist-geneticist team of the National Collaborative Project in which the interracial offspring of white mothers obtained higher IQs at 4 years of age than interracial offspring of Negro mothers, which the authors suggest reflects that environmental factors play an important role in the lower intellectual performance of Negro children.

PERCEPTION

Research on perceptual processes of children is of such a diffuse and unprogrammatic nature, and the character of the stimulating conditions utilized is so varied, as to defy coherent organization or critical analysis. There are few theoretical or methodological "handles," and the research surveyor finds himself categorizing studies either on the basis of sensory modality investigated or on grounds that the study did or did not explore age differences. A third feature, that relating to whether the study required the subjects to match, compare, or adjust across modalities (or "organize sensorily"), then destroys the earlier categorizations.

Work has continued to document the progressive change in illusion effects with increased age. Barclay & Comalli (8) have shown that the Müller-Lyer illusion can be reduced with appropriate practice and that the training is more effective with normal adults than with either children or the aged. Using a method of production, Pressey & Sweeney (212) demonstrated that the Poggendorf illusion decreases with age, as has been previously shown with the method of adjustment. Increasing age significantly affects other forms of perceptual expertise as well. Girgus & Hochberg (101), in a study of two groups aged about 4 and 9 years, had their subjects view patterns moving continuously across a fixed aperture, and found that identification of those successively viewed was better with increased age. However, identification of simultaneously presented patterns was not related to age, and recognition errors were not greatly affected, suggesting that memory rather than perceptual acuity probably underlies the developmental effect. In another developmental study by Siegel & McBurney (246), 96 subjects varying from age 6 to adulthood were required to match grip pressure to numbers presented orally and lengths of lines. Matching ability increased systematically with age, and because response variability was not affected by age, the method holds considerable promise for psychophysical studies in which children's perceptual and cognitive skills are explored.

A number of studies have explored the question of form versus color saliency as determined by age. It is clear that a wide variety of techniques is possible and that the outcome may be as much related to methodology as to organismic factors. In a study by Harris et al (115), 100 children ranging from preschool to 3rd grade judged which of two figures matched a third that was the same color as one figure and the same form as another. For all ages, form matching was most likely with geometric figures and least for "nonsense" figures. Number of children "preferring" form and "strength" of preference increased with age, preferences had high test-retest reliability, and no sex differences occurred. In another study of form discrimination by Taylor & Wales (256), using matching-to-sample procedures, findings suggested that under age 4 the task is very difficult and the children respond on the basis of inappropriate criteria, but that by age 5 attention to correct discriminative cues is apparent and leads to correct performance. In an interesting attempt to produce shifts in children's attention to color and form dimensions, Gaines (94) trained color-dominant and form-dominant responders to go with or go against their dominant mode and compared these subjects with no-training controls. While no shift in the controls occurred over a 5-week period, both color and form selectors shifted over the same period through training. The author suggests that response set is as much a predisposing factor as developmental stage in determining children's selections of form or color alternatives. The term "form constancy" is questioned as a universally meaningful label by data presented by Kaess (134) through which he showed, in a study of 120 8-, 13-, and 18-year-olds, that the age trends were dissimilar for two different response analyses involving "form constancy."

That response set and contextual cues are developmentally pertinent to perceptual judgments and preferences was further substantiated by O'Reilly & Steger (201) and others. The former study required children aged 5 to 11 to judge a series of weights in a standard psychophysical paradigm using selected anchors as a frame of reference. All children over 6 could order the series appropriately as well as shift or alter their judgments as a whole (engage in transitivity behavior) with a change in the weight of the anchor point. Although the authors obtained proficient performance at ages lower than usual for such tasks, the 5-year-olds could not display either seriation or transitivity. The effects of anchoring were also studied by Salzinger et al (225) in children 3 to 6 years, using two types of verbal response class. The use of an ordinal scale (number) for judgment enabled the children to resist the anchor more than did the use of a nominal scale (color), and there were indications that the facility of the older children with numbers was relevant to the effect. Such mediationally determined enhancement of perceptual judgment was further explored by Katz et al (136), who employed a verbal distinctiveness pretraining condition prior to assessment of perceptual, discrimination learning, and recognition tests. The greatest facilitation took place in the younger of two groups (1st and 6th graders) with highly similar stimuli, while the older children's performance was affected little by the predifferentiation training. Perceptual judgment was more affected by pretraining than recognition tests.

The search and recognition behaviors of adults and children were further studied by Mackworth & Bruner (164), who used the well-known Mackworth eye-tracking technique to document visual fixation behavior of 20 6-year-olds and 20 adults when presented either sharp, blurred, or very blurred photographs. Presumably visual tracking of the sharp pictures involves comprehension seeking, while observation of the blurred pictures involves more casual inspection. Several differences were noted between the adults and children; using the adults as the standard, the children lacked adequate coverage of the sharp displays, their eye tracks were smaller, and they were less skillful in selecting informative areas in blurred scenes. Another avenue to the exploration of attention was through the documentation of autonomic responsivity by Clifton et al (47). These researchers took heart-rate measures on school-aged children who were induced to attend to, ignore, or make judgments about passively presented tactile stimuli. Greater heart-rate deceleration occurred under the attention condition, although the attended and ignored physical stimuli were identical. Auditory attention and preference was studied by Duke & Gullickson (68) in 48 preschoolers given 80 trials in a stimulus-choice task, the indicator response being a move of a lever in one of four directions. Stimulus complexity of the alternatives was defined by the number of components in each stimulus, dissimilarity of the components, and component patterning. Group results indicated general preference for increased complexity of auditory stimulation, but individual records revealed a tendency toward selection of stimulus variability (i.e. absence of consistent stimulus preferences). Where individual preferences did occur, a tendency toward selection of stimulus simplicity was present in some.

An interesting pair of studies was presented to compare adults and children with respect to visual information processing, under conditions of tachistoscopic stimulus viewing, by Haith et al (110) and Liss & Haith (158). In the first study, preschoolers and adults viewed geometric shapes for presentation durations from 5 to 40 msec, with the result that data on the 5-year-olds approximated those of adults, except that the children required about 5–10 msec longer for comparable identification proficiency. Because the results indicate excellent performance of children under conditions in which eye movements are not required, the authors conclude that "hypotheses about the development of visual operations in information processing can be tested without confounding the influence of age differences in visual scanning." In the second study, of 5- and 10-year-olds and adults, backward masking produced greater disruption of visual identification performance than forward masking, and disruption of both types of masking decreased with increasing age. Only in a location task requiring visual search was stimulus processing speed slower in the youngest group. In a study by Samuels (227) investigating the effect of associative connections between words on speed of word recognition, 4th graders were shown to have faster recognition speeds when a target word was preceded by a high associate or when an anticipated word was presented. Using an interesting delayed matching-to-sample technique, Williams et al (276) required subjects to choose from a selection of anagrams the one most resembling the stimulus word. Each choice was a particular type of word-recognition error, reflecting a match either on the basis of individual letters or overall shape. Nonreading kindergarteners showed no consistent error types; beginning readers matched on the basis of either first or last letter; and reading adults used complex strategies involving visual, aural, and shape matching.

Sensory-modality integration involving touch and vision has drawn several studies. Connolly & Jones (48) tested 5, 8, and 11-year-old children and a group of adults for ability in intra-modal and cross-modal matching, using straight lines presented either visually or kinesthetically. Analyzing results in terms of absolute errors and variance for the four combinations revealed that performance improved with age, that intra-modal matching was more accurate and less variable than cross-modal, and that visual-visual matching was less variable than all others. In agreement with this, Milner & Bryant (181) found that children aged 5 to 7 find visual-visual matching easiest of the four combinations of visual and tactual matching. DeLeon et al (61) studied the integration of visual and touch stimulation in the shape perception of preschool children, compared with use of one modality alone, and found that visual discrimination alone was superior to tactual discrimination and that the integrated use of both modalities resulted in no better performance than for visual alone.

DISCRIMINATION LEARNING AND TRANSFER

The study of discrimination learning and transfer-of-discrimination learning continues to occupy the research efforts of many child psychologists. Most studies were attempts to ascertain underlying mechanisms or to determine the role of developmental level with respect to the operation of processes assumed to be critical to the solution of discriminative learning tasks. There were other studies of a more purely empirical nature, and where at times the selection of independent variables for study appeared to be random.

As might be expected, original learning was found to be impeded by the presence of irrelevant dimensions, particularly when the stimulus values along these dimensions varied within trials (but see also Evans & Beedle 77). Sugimura (253) found that the speed of original learning in 5- and 6-year-old children was significantly retarded with an increase in the number of irrelevant dimensions from zero to two. Of notable interest in this same study was the fact that during reversal learning the detrimental effects of irrelevant stimulation were confined only to those children who had not received over-training on the original problem. Nolan & Pendarvis (199) also found that a second irrelevant dimension impeded original learning in nursery school children, but this did not occur when the most salient of three dimensions was relevant. House (123) compared the effects of varying amounts of redundant relevant and irrelevant information on the discriminative learning of retarded children. She found that redundant relevant information retarded performance more than did redundant irrelevant information. Inasmuch as the addition of redundant cues resulted in stimuli that were not well "integrated" (see Garner 97), the decrement in performance may have resulted from an overloading of the short-term memory store. Croll, Knauss & Duke (54) have also obtained evidence implicating active short-term memory processes in discriminative learning.

A number of other variables were investigated. For example, Etaugh (76) demonstrated in both retarded and normal children faster discriminative learning with stereometric stimuli than with planometric stimuli. However, the addition of haptic cues did not further facilitate learning, as might be predicted. In a successive discrimination in which four stimulus-response associations were acquired concurrently, Croll (51) found that intertrial intervals of 6, 11, or 16 seconds were equally better than an ITI of 1 second. Adequate explanation of these results is at present elusive just as for the results of a study by Berch (14), who investigated the effects of delays of reinforcement procedures. Essentially he found that a constant 16-second delay was more disruptive than a constant 2-second delay or a covariable 2- and 30-second delay. Spence (250) found that material rewards significantly interfered with verbal discrimination learning in 2nd and 3rd graders, presumably by acting as distractors. In two studies which compared three types of informative feedback on discriminative learning, the experimenter saying right or wrong, right or nothing, and wrong or nothing, Schroth (233) and Moffat & Motiff (183) found that the right-wrong condition resulted in faster acquisition and that the wrong-nothing condition was superior to the right-nothing condition.

In two studies of generalization responses in preschool children, Croll (52) and Dick & Landau (62) demonstrated that these children were often responsive to more than one attribute or dimension of the reinforced cue. Of particular interest in the Dick & Landau study was the breadth of the individual differences, some children being responsive to but a single attribute and others responsive to the maximum number of available component cues, three. Explanations of these individual differences, like so many other effects, remain a mystery. Perhaps different but unknown training histories resulted in different scanning responses, just as the nature of the stimulus property (i.e. absolute or relational) to which the response is associated can be strongly influenced by training as Yeh (279) demonstrated.

Two major theoretical models of discriminative learning and transfer in children, developed in the last decade by the Kendlers (139) and Zeaman & House (280), continue to dominate the field. A number of different transfer operations have been employed to test the validity of these models, but unfortunately there has been little or no agreement between proponents of these two models as to a common testing situation. Supporters of the Kendler developmental mediational model have most often used comparisons between reversal (RV) and extradimensional (ED) shifts either by measuring the relative rates of acquisition or by comparing the proportions of RV shifts in an optional shift situation across a number of developmental levels. On the other hand, supporters of attentional models have most often made comparisons between intradimensional (ID) shifts and ED shifts, though regrettably not always with subjects at different levels of development.

Several studies have been reported recently that used the optional shift paradigm. The most extensive study was that of the Kendlers (140), in which they tested children at 70, 94, and 142 months of age and college students. A significant increment, as predicted by their mediational model, was found in the percentage of RV shifts as a function of age. However, there is a possible confounding factor in the study in that the number of overtraining trials on the optional shift problem covaried with age. Tighe & Tighe (260) likewise found a reliable increase in the proportion of RV shifts with developmental level, although in this study only the difference between nursery school children and older children (1st, 3rd, and 5th graders) was significant. In addition, the Tighes found that perceptual pretraining and perceptual pretraining plus verbal labeling resulted in an increased number of RV shifts, although not always in the manner predicted by differentiation theory.

In a novel version of the optional shift paradigm, Campione (38) compared the probability of obtaining optional ID or ED shifts in preschool and 2nd-grade children. He found no reliable difference due to age; the percentage of ID shifts was approximately 65%. Tighe et al (259) found that dimensional preference did not influence the proportion of RV shifts, although it did affect the rate of original learning, but only if assessment of dimensional preference was made prior to the experiment and not at the conclusion of the experiment. The evidence from these and earlier studies indicates the necessity for more complex models of discriminative learning and transfer than presently exist; that is, developmental, situational, and training variables must all be considered as determining factors (see also Reese & Lipsitt 215, chapter 9).

In two closely related studies by Caron (41) and Dickerson, Wagner & Campione (65), the relative rates of RV and ED shift acquisition in preschool children were shown to be a function of the manner of presentation of the irrelevant visual dimension. With constant irrelevant stimulation within trials, ED shifts were acquired either faster or at the same rate as RV shifts, but with variable irrelevant stimulation within trials, RV shifts were learned more rapidly. These findings are more in accord with attentional models than with the developmental mediation model.

There were several other transfer studies of interest that used a variety of experimental paradigms. First, Sugimura (253) demonstrated the overtraining reversal effect and in addition found that the magnitude of this effect was related to the number of irrelevant dimensions, a finding readily interpretable by attentional models. Blank & Klig (18) found that preschool children learned intra- and cross-modal ID shifts faster than comparable ED shifts. Dickerson (63) showed that the attachment of distinctive verbal labels to either the relevant or irrelevant cues respectively facilitated or retarded later discriminative learning. Moreover, similar effects were obtained when the attachment of distinctive labels was to different stimuli along the same dimensions. Finally, Schaeffer & Ellis (230) demonstrated that explicit stimulus dimensions were not necessary for obtaining RV and nonreversal (really half-reversal) shift differences; without overtraining on the original task, RV shifts were acquired more slowly, whereas the converse was true after overtraining. Goulet & Williams (104) were also able to demonstrate faster RV shift acquisition compared with half-reversal acquisition, both in the absence of explicit conceptual categories or perceptual dimensions and without overtraining on the original problem. The discrepancy in the two studies may be a function of the extent of original learning; Goulet & Williams had a much more stringent criterion. The Goulet-Williams study also revealed that the superiority of the RV shifts may well have been a function of a nonmediational "response-switching" strategy.

Both oddity and probability learning, which might be considered more complex discriminative learning situations, received considerable attention. Croll (53) showed that very few preschool children were able to learn the oddity concept, possibly because of a strong stimulus perseveration strategy. Scott (239), on the other hand, using more distinctive stimuli, obtained virtually perfect oddity learning in children only slightly older, and Small (248) demonstrated improved oddity learning with the use of greater stimulus variation. Further confirmation that stimulus factors are strong determinants of oddity acquisition and transfer comes from two studies by Brown (30, 31). She found that oddity training was facilitated when the "vehicle dimension" was a preferred dimension and that greater transfer occurred when the vehicle dimension remained the same (ID shifts) than when it differed from the original training dimension (ED shift). In other studies of oddity, Dickerson & Girardeau (64) found that retarded children tended to respond to oddity as a stimulus characteristic independent of reinforcement, and Saravo, Bagby & Haskins (228) demonstrated the disruptive effects of a number of factors, e.g. reversal components.

Probability learning in children was found to be significantly affected by a wide range of variables. For a review of earlier work the reader is referred to Goulet & Goodwin (103). A greater tendency to maximize, that is, to select the more frequently reinforced alternative, was found to be related to age. Both younger and older boys (CA = 5 and 17 years) chose the more frequently reinforced alternative in an 80:20 situation than 9- or 13-year-old boys (Sullivan & Ross 254). Sex also produced reliable effects in that males tended to show more evidence of maximizing (Dusek & Hill 69, Sullivan & Ross 254). However, to date there does not appear to be a comprehensive theoretical model that can account parsimoniously for all or even most of the results. Explanations tend to revolve about the assumption that different response strategies (e.g. risk taking and problem solving) and the rejection of these strategies are differentially associated with such factors as age, sex, social class, and level of aspiration (Gruen, Ottinger & Zigler 108).

PAIRED-ASSOCIATE LEARNING

Recent and important innovations in the study of paired-associate learning (PAL) have been the exploration of the role of imagery in the formation of simple associations, and the attempt to understand how the role of imagery changes with developmental level. Reviews of the empirical findings and discussions of theoretical positions have been presented by Paivio (204), Palermo (206), Reese (213, 215), and Rohwer (218). A number of different experimental paradigms have been used to explore the effects of imagery. Paivio & Yuille (205) compared the rates of PAL when the stimulus and response items were either concrete or abstract nouns. Earlier research had demonstrated that concrete nouns produced greater amounts of reported imagery than do abstract nouns, as might be intuitively expected. As was true for adult subjects, children in grades 4 and 8 learned pairs of concrete nouns faster than pairs of abstract nouns. When only one member of the pair was a concrete noun, performance was better when the concrete noun occupied the stimulus position. More important was the finding that the magnitude of these effects was considerably smaller in children that those obtained previously with adult subjects; mediation by visual imagery does not appear to be as effective a mechanism in children as in adults.

Another paradigm has compared the acquisition of S-R pairs when the stimuli are presented pictorially as compared with aural presentations. As predicted, pictorial presentations improved performance and the degree of improvement was greater for older children (Dilley & Paivio 66). Another finding of interest was that when the S-R pair consisted of a picture in the stimulus position and a word in the response position, acquisition was faster when compared with the learning of picture-picture pairs, with the difference decreasing with age. It should be noted that Blue (21) was not able to replicate the faster acquisition of picture-word pairs with mental retardates (MA = 11 years) or CA- and MA-matched normal controls.

Reese (213) and Rohwer (218) have used pictorially presented stimulus and response items accompanied by different forms of elaboration, both verbal and pictorial in nature. These elaborations, such as embedding the stimulus and response in a sentence with a transitive verb accompanied (or not) by motion pictures of the same action sequence, are assumed to increase the amount and complexity of visual imagery over that which would be evoked by the same stimulus-response pairs in isolation. In general, the results of studies of this nature indicated that increases in visual imagery did improve performance over a wide range of developmental levels. However, at younger ages (4 or 5 years) verbal elaborations are more effective than visual, whereas the converse is true for older children (9 to 13 years). Confirming evidence has been obtained by Davidson & Adams (59) and Fuld (91), although Reese (214) was not able to replicate the greater effectiveness of visual imagery in older children. Of interest is a study by MacMillan (162), who found that verbal elaborations provided by the experimenter facilitated learning in retarded children, but that subject-produced elaborations were ineffective.

When the stimuli were presented in word form, either aurally or written, Levin (150) and Davidson, Schwenn & Adams (60) were unable to obtain any effect of verbal elaborations. However, Davidson et al and Schwenn & Davidson (238) were able to demonstrate that verbal elaborations significantly reduced the negative transfer invariably obtained in an A-B, A-C transfer paradigm. In addition, Gallagher (95) found that meaningful S-R pairs presented aurally facilitated performance in both retarded and MA-matched normal children (MA = 8.8 years). This finding was true for word pairs forming noun-verb, adjective-noun, or verb-noun pairs. The failure to find an effect of verbal elaborations with S-R pairs in verbal form is not explicable at present. It may well be that more attention will have to be given to the linguistic structure of the elaboration as compared with the potential imagery-inducing characteristics of the elaborations.

Despite the contradictory nature of some of the data, the weight of evidence supports the contention that visual imagery can be utilized by children to represent information and to mediate PAL. However, the development of effective visual mediators lags behind the development of effective verbal mediators, contrary to established developmental theory. Explanations of these effects are numerous and varied. Rohwer (218), basing his arguments on the assumptions that language is an earlier established, more coherent, and well-organized system for representing information than visual imagery, and that effective visual mediation requires the simultaneous storage of a verbal mediator, an age-related process, is able to account for much of the data. However, the reader will find counter-arguments and alternative explanations (e.g. the conceptual peg hypothesis of Paivio) in the papers by Paivio (204), Palermo (206), and Reese (213).

In a related study, Hollenberg (121) was able to demonstrate that visual imagery does not always facilitate performance. She found that children between the ages of 6 and 10 who were rated high on the ability to produce and utilize visual imagery did learn picture-nonsense syllable pairs more quickly than low-imagery-producing children, but that these same high-imagery children acquired concepts more slowly. As Hollenberg notes, Galton may have been correct when he concluded that an over-reliance upon visual imagery ("mental pictures") may be detrimental to the acquisition of the principles of abstract thought. A study by Hohn & Martin (120) confirms the finding that individual differences in imagery production become a reliable variable in predicting the rate of PAL.

A number of other variables were investigated within the context of PAL. For example, Kellas & Butterfield (137) obtained evidence that pretraining on the response items facilitated performance in 3rd-grade children. In addition, the magnitude of this facilitating effect was inversely related to the ease of pronunciability of the response items. In a second study by the same authors (138), response pretraining was found to facilitate the performance of retarded children (MA = 8 years), but not the performance of MA-matched normals beyond that which could be attributed to the simple warm-up effects. The latter finding is undoubtedly due to the fact that in this study the response items were meaningful words, hence both readily pronounceable and firmly established in the response repertoires of the normal children. In an attempt to measure cue selection in PAL by retarded and MA-matched normal children, Baumeister & Berry (9) found reliable evidence for cue selection in both groups which was limited mostly to the initial letter of the triconsonant stimuli. Backward associations were found to be reliably present in both normal and retarded children (Baumeister, Kellas & Gordon 10) and, as might be expected, the degree of free associative strength between stimulus and response affected the PAL of normal and retarded children (Gallagher & Reid 96).

In a study of transfer effects, Wilcox & Baumeister (273) compared the acquisition rates of normal and retarded children under four standard transfer conditions: A-B, C-D; A-B, A-C; A-B, C-B; and A-B, A-Br. They found greater negative transfer in the A-B, A-Br condition with the retarded subjects, which they attributed to a deficit in associative learning processes. However, this explanation cannot account for the fact that there was positive transfer in the A-B, C-B condition for the retarded subjects and negative transfer for the normal children. Finally, Cantor (40) showed that when 8th and 9th graders are required to learn concurrently both motor and verbal responses to random shapes, motor associative learning can be both facilitated and interfered with by the concomitant verbal response. Evidence was also presented that the verbal response functioned to mediate the acquisition of the motor response.

MEMORY

Interest in memory and related processes by developmental psychologists has continued to increase. Although the research has not reached the programmatic stage often enough, considerable progress is apparent. The studies under review attest to this fact as well as point to the very wide range of topics being studied.

Haith and his associates (111) have investigated short-term memory for very briefly presented visual information in 5-year-old children and adults. Either two, three, or four geometric forms were presented tachistoscopically for 150 msec. The number of correctly reported items asymptoted at slightly less than two items for the children, whereas the function was a montonically increasing one for adults. Further analyses revealed that increasing the amount of information to be processed may have "overloaded" the system and consequently lowered performance.

Whereas the study by Haith et al was concerned principally with storage problems, Hoving, Morin & Konick (124) investigated search processes in active memory. Using the procedures recently developed by Sternberg (251), they obtained evidence that the search processes of children and adults are remarkably similar. An exhaustive serial search strategy was used by kindergarten children, 4th graders, and adults. Although total reaction time decreased markedly with age, perhaps reflecting differential efficiencies in perceptual and motoric processes, the time to scan a single item was virtually constant across this wide range of developmental levels. In a related study, Morin, Hoving & Konick (188) required children 6 and 10 years of age and college students to indicate as rapidly as possible whether or not two stimuli were from the same set of stimuli. The stimulus sets were either familiar (e.g. all foods) or arbitrary (e.g. a single stimulus from each of four taxonomic categories) and were memorized prior to testing. The evidence supported the contention that the youngest children were deficient in their ability to encode stimuli and perhaps in their use of rehearsal. The youngest children also appeared to rely more on visual information than representationally encoded information. Calfee (37), in a study of short-term serial memory in young children, obtained results indicating a similarity between children and adults in the processes used in this type of task. For example, he found that the proportion of correctly recalled items decreased with the size of the sample, although the absolute number of items recalled increased. In addition, there were primacy and strong recency effects. Similar findings were obtained for retarded children, indicative of similar recall strategies. However, retarded children were found to be deficient in the organizational principles as compared with normal children. MacMillan (163) found in accord with the latter that older (MA = 8.5) retarded children were able to take advantage of imposed organizational features, whereas younger (MA = 6.0) were unable to do so.

Dornbush & Basow (67) investigated the short-term memory abilities for bisensory information in 1st, 3rd, 5th, and 9th graders. The amount of information recalled was a positive function of age, and more auditory information was recalled than visual information. Significantly more information was recalled from the first-reported channel than from the second. Moreover, the youngest children were unable to report virtually any information from the second channel. Whether this latter finding is a function of faster loss of information, the inability to store information from two channels simultaneously, or poorer recall strategies cannot be determined from the data.

tion of one or more of the assumed carriers of conservation, that is, the acquisition of the concepts of identity, compensation, or reversibility.

Whiteman & Peisach (271) attempted to induce conservation of both number and mass by manipulating experience with the principle of correspondence between the transformed and untransformed arrays; correspondence is closely related to, and perhaps identical with, the operation of reversibility. The subjects were lower-class black children from kindergarten and 3rd grade. The children were trained with varying numbers of situational supports which were intended to demonstrate and accentuate the correspondence between the original array and the transformed array, and which included manipulations such as matching colors, the use of guidelines, and the actual moving of the objects back to their original positions. As the number of supports increased there was a reliable increase in the percentage of conservation of number judgments and adequate verbal justification in older children. There was also some suggestion that perceptual experience (support) was more beneficial to the older children whereas motoric support produced more facilitation in younger children. Roll (220) demonstrated that reversibility training increased the likelihood of a conservation judgment in Latin American children, although he failed to find any increase in appropriate verbal explanations. Peters (210), in a similar study on number conservation in lower SES kindergarten children found that simple reversibility training did not facilitate the establishment of conservation. However, reversibility training plus additional visual cues or additional verbal explanations did result in improved performance on both immediate and delayed post-tests. In the same experimental vein, Halford & Fullerton (113) trained nonconserving 6-year-old children of low SES to use correspondence as a cue in a number of conservation tasks. Their training procedure differed in that it more closely resembled a discrimination learning situation, but without informative feedback. The children were required to judge whether a row of dolls would fit into a row of beds. There were five rows of dolls on each training trial, of which one matched the number of beds (and a standard set of dolls) in number and spacing and other rows might match in number but not spacing. The trained group produced more conservation judgments on both delayed and immediate tests. Verbal explanations were not obtained, with the result that Piagetians might argue that the results reflect not true conservation but rather pseudo-conservation. Be that as it may, it is of interest that this form of training, a discriminative procedure without feedback, permitted the development of at least some form of conservation, a finding difficult to accommodate within the structure of Piagetian theory. Christie & Smothergill (45) did a partial replication of the Gelman procedure (98) and failed to obtain any increment in conservation judgments on a number task in 4-year-old children. However, the reason for the failure was most likely that the authors used an inadequate training criterion on the discrimination task.

In other training studies, Lister (159) was able to demonstrate the concept of volume conservation in educationally subnormal children by use of a rather flexible and general training procedure. In addition, the ability to make conservation judgments was stable over time and almost always accompanied by appropriate verbal explanations. Overbeck & Schwartz (202) trained 5- to 8-year-old children on weight conservation. The training procedure consisted of reinforcement or nonreinforcement, with reinforcement defined as verification of the experimenter's explanatory statements by scale weightings, and active or passive participation by the child. Participation had no effect, in contradiction of Bruner's (33) views on the development of conservation, but reinforcement did enhance the occurrence of conservation judgments. Strauss & Langer (252) found no differential effects as a function of training procedures that used Bruner's methods of screening and conflict inducement on a conservation of continuous quantity task. However, the experimental children performed better than control subjects, with the greater change coming from children originally classified as being in a transitional stage with respect to quantity conservation. Finally, Waghorn & Sullivan (265) used film models to induce conservation of quantity and were successful. They interpreted their results as at least questioning the adequacy of Piaget's action-equilibrium model.

A number of other studies were reported that likewise cast at least some doubt upon the validity of the Piagetian explanation of the growth of conservation in children. Both Larsen & Flavell (148) and Schwartz & Scholnick (237) failed to find any evidence that conservation is mediated by development of the operation of compensation. Larsen & Flavell also found that the complexity of the question was related to success on tasks involving compensation judgments, especially when these tasks were difficult. Schwartz & Scholnick obtained evidence showing that the differential difficulty of comparison, identity, and equivalence judgments was related to stimulus conditions. On the basis of these data, they concluded that conservation is attained by recognizing the irrelevancy of some transformation to the judged quantity, and not by the development of one or more concrete operations. Other evidence contradictory to Piagetian theory comes from studies by Ford (87) and Murray (192). Murray found that the mode of stimulus presentation, whether by objects, pictures, or verbal description, was unrelated to the incidence of conservation judgments. Ford obtained evidence that distance conservation was not a necessary prerequisite for the development of a Euclidean coordinate system, as had been assumed by Piaget. In addition, there was little correspondence between predictive and perceptual judgments of waterline level. Although not a direct test of Piaget's developmental theory, Hall et al (114) found no relation between conservation of continuous quantity and a synthesis task that involved a transformation of pictorial representations of words into action. Data more compatible with Piaget's ideas come from a study by Peisach & Wein (209). They found, as might be expected, that the adequacy of the verbal explanations for conservation judgment covaried with the difficulty of the conservation task in lower and middle SES children from kindergarten, 1st, and 2nd grades.

In attempting to summarize these studies on conservation, we were impressed first that there was a wide variety of training procedures that were effective in promoting conservation in young children, and second that there is a growing body of data at least in partial contradiction of Piagetian theory. Given that theoreticians are rarely persuaded to abandon favored models by the weight of mere empirical evidence, especially if alternative models are not available, it is heartening to find that there were at least a few concerted efforts to present alternative analyses of the development of conservation [but see Brainerd (25) for the Piagetian viewpoint]. Halford (112) argues for a modified learning position. He attempts to demonstrate that what the child must acquire in order to conserve is the knowledge that a concept such as quantity is inextricably intertwined with (and even defined by) its relationship with at least two physical dimensions. For Halford, the concept of quantity cannot be understood until the child comprehends these relationships with the defining dimensions. Thus, the development of conservation is not related to the development of concrete operations, but rather is a process by which relationships are acquired, perhaps in a manner similar to discriminative learning. In a much more critical, but very readable, attack on Piagetian theory, Green & Laxon (106) argue that not only are many of Piaget's basic assumptions and even logic inappropriate, but also that a complete understanding of conservation development cannot occur without careful analyses of the child's linguistic knowledge and of the concept of identity. Green & Laxon present evidence for developmental changes in the child's understanding of the words "some," "more," and "less," the meanings of which must correspond to those of the experimenter if conservation judgments are to be obtained. In the writings of a number of workers in this area, one finds attempts to relate the conservation task to a discriminative learning task or what might be better termed a concept identification task. Halford considered this possibility but rejected the idea that the conservation task and concept identification (concept recognition in his terms) are equivalent tasks, on the grounds that if this analogy is accepted then the conservation task loses its special status; in a concept identification task, the concept is known, but is often not manifested because of the tendency to respond to irrelevant information. However, given the accumulating evidence, this model of conservation may not be inappropriate, and indeed one may want to question seriously theoretical models that place heavy reliance upon data from the various conservation situations.

Other studies have been reported that attempt to investigate cognitive abilities closely related to the concrete and formal operations of Piagetian theory. It has not always been the case that the tasks developed by Piaget and his co-workers have been used. Various experimenters often devise new instruments or situations in order to measure a particular subset of cognitive abilities. As a consequence, when results contradictory to established theory are obtained, the question arises regarding the validity of the test instrument. Resolution of this problem is always difficult, and it is perhaps worth noting that the criticism can be turned about to question the validity of the standard Piagetian tasks; primacy in the development of a test instrument does not always imply validity.

One such problem that purports to measure the development of concrete operations is that of class inclusion. Both Jennings (129) and Ahr & Youniss (2) reported work on this problem with children between the ages of 5 and 10 years. Unlike the earlier results of Wohlwill (277), Jennings did not obtain facilitation by presentation of the stimulus information in a verbal mode. Jennings' criterional measure was more stringent than that of Wohlwill; he required not only a correct judgment but also an adequate verbal explanation. It actuality, he found that a pictorial presentation of information facilitated performance, particularly in the older subjects. Ahr & Youniss showed that the errors on the class inclusion problem increased with increasing numerical differences between the two subordinate classes in younger children (CA = 6 and 8 years). Special training that involved correction of erroneous responses improved performance and led the authors to conclude that the inability of younger children to make correct judgments may be a performance and not a competence problem.

Another form of problem solving that has recently become popular not only with Piagetians but also with more behavioristically minded developmental psychologists is that which Haygood & Bourne (117) have called rule learning (or identification) and which Inhelder & Piaget (127) refer to as propositional thinking. The testing situation has often been similar to the usual concept identification paradigm, modified so that the concept involves multiple attributes (dimensions) and the positive and negative instances are defined by the rules of formal logic. However, other procedures have been used. Furth, Youniss & Ross (92), for example, use a methodology that presents the problem in symbolic form. After considerable tuition of 6- to 12-year-old children on the logical concepts of disjunction and conjunction, children were presented with values from a number of dimensions and were required to indicate whether these values were an instance (a "match") of the logical concept depicted in symbolic form. Their data indicated three distinct levels of ability. The lowest level was marked by repeated failure, inasmuch as symbols were treated as perceptual facts; the logical connective and negation signs were ignored and matches or mismatches were indicated almost exclusively on the basis of correspondence between the symbols and the attribute values. Level 2 subjects were in a transitional state, whereas Level 3 children were capable of successful propositional thinking, except in instances where the connective was negated. Furth and associates note that the age-level matches were in close agreement with Piaget's norms for the development of propositional thinking. Other variables such as the presence or absence of an attribute, affirmation or negation, and type of logical construct were found to interact with age. This paper should be consulted by readers interested in a lucid Piagetian analysis of this form of problem.

With the more typical concept identification paradigm, Johnson, Warner & Lee (133) found that enforced attention to the attribute values improved both disjunctive and biconditional rule learning in 1st-grade children. In a second experiment, enforced attention was demonstrated not only to improve performance but also to enhance the acquisition of an effective solution strategy, the truth-table strategy. King & Holt (142) showed that conjunctive rule learning was easier than disjunctive rule acquisition, as has been previously demonstrated [but see Furth et al (92) for some limitations on this effect], and that forced verbalization of the hypothesis for each response improved performance in 6-, 9-, and 12-year-old girls.

In other studies of propositional thinking, Seggie (240) found that by demonstrating the logical relationship between the individual attributes and a conjunctive concept, e.g. implication in the case of a relevant dimension, conjunctive rule learning was facilitated in both 12-year-old children and college students. Scholnick (232) obtained evidence that inferential judgments concerning a simple affirmative concept were strongly influenced by the presence or absence of a positive instance in a series of two-trial problems, in 5-, 7-, and 9-year-old children. Neimark (194, 197) measured the ability of children from third grade through college to understand the principles of class inclusion and exclusion (A, Ā), class intersection (A and B), and class union (A or B). Inclusion and exclusion were understood by a majority of children at all ages, as was class intersection with the exception of the youngest subjects. Class union, on the other hand, was not comprehended until the highest developmental level had been attained. Errors on the class union problem were largely a function of interpreting this problem as one of class intersection. Neimark argues that solution of the union problem requires the prior development of formal operations and that her age differences are in accord with Piaget's stage model. However, in another study (195) she was unable to find significant correlations among three tasks, assumed to be measuring formal operations. Mention should be made of the study by Leskow & Smock (149) that demonstrated marked changes in problem-solving strategy with a permutation task, as well as studies by Shapiro & O'Brien (241) and Roberge (217) that measured deductive reasoning in children. The former showed that the recognition of logical necessity was present by 6 to 8 years of age, but that having to test for logical necessity developed slowly with age, and the latter study showed that reversing the order of a set of logical premises did not affect performance.

A large number of studies concerned with the development of problem-solving strategies and cognition were reported that are difficult to classify both with respect to a common theoretical orientation and methodology, but that nevertheless provide new and often important findings. For example, Huttenlocher et al (126) investigated the negative equative construction (i.e. A is not as x as B) in adults and 3rd-grade children. Using this construction in a three-term-series problem, they obtained evidence that the difficulty of actually arranging items corresponds to the difficulty of reasoning about the items. This was taken as corroborating the contention that the solution strategy for this problem involves imagining the arrangements of items in accord with the instructions. Implementation of this mediational process is controlled by both the type of grammatical construction and the semantic markings of the adjectives. Bem (13) studied a similar task in which nursery-school children had to arrange objects to correspond to verbal instructions (e.g. make it so that the red block is on top of the blue block). She found, as previous evidence showed, that performance improved when the grammatical subject corresponded to the mobile block performance, rather than when the grammatical object was the mobile block. However, she also found that by special training during which the subject saw the outcome of object instructions prior to responding, performance was facilitated on later transfer tasks. As a consequence, Bem argued that the difficulty children have with the object construction is not in imagining how to turn the instruction into action, as assumed by Huttenlocher et al., but rather in failing to comprehend the desired end state. Thus there is now a comprehension deficiency to go along with production and mediational deficiencies. Determining which of these explanations is correct, if indeed either is correct (46), requires considerably more data.

The production of concepts and their nature was investigated by Elkind, Medvene & Rockway (74). Children 9 and 14 years old were asked to describe how pairs of pictorial stimuli were alike. The number of produced concepts was inversely related to the abstractness of the stimuli in younger children, whereas in older children the percentage of perceptual concepts was inversely related to the abstractness of the stimuli. These results indicate the greater plasticity of older children in that they were more capable of shifting from their dominant conceptual orientation. Miller, Kessel & Flavell (179), in an ingenious study that tapped development of the recursive nature of thinking (e.g. "He is thinking that she is thinking that he is thinking . . ."), showed that the improvement with age was stage-like in its progression. The growth of this ability was discussed within the framework of role-taking skills.

Working with a modified selection procedure in which children from the 2nd, 4th, 6th, and 8th grades and college students were required to determine which cell of a matrix was correct, Eimas (70) found that the amount of information in each response increased with developmental level as did the number of categorical responses and ideal focusing strategies. The saliency of the conceptual categories was also found to be related to the three response measures. Evidence was also obtained to substantiate qualitatively different levels of solution strategies that were correlated with age. Odom & Guzman (200) also found that stimulus properties reliably affected concept attainment. They found faster acquisition when the relevant dimension was defined by variation along a simple sensory continuum than when the relevant dimension was defined by constancy of stimulus values. The effect, however, was true only for kindergarten children and was in agreement with earlier work by Saltz & Sigel (224) on overdiscrimination in young children. Experience with each of two dimensions that were later combined to form a double classification problem was found by Darnell & Bourne (58) to significantly improve performance. Finally, development of a relatively simple problem-solving strategy (win-stay, lose-shift) was found to be related to age by Berman et al (16) and moreover, the lose-shift component was acquired more easily at all age levels from 4 to 10 years.

Recently there have been several attempts to analyze problem-solving situations into their component processes and to evaluate experimental manipulation of these processes on problem acquisition in children. For example, Eimas (71) showed that 1st- and 2nd-grade children were capable of using an ideal focusing strategy in the solution of the blank-trials problem, provided only that the relevant information was available for processing. This was accomplished by the use of memory aids, and the nearly perfect focusing was mirrored by greater coding, recoding, and retention of outcome information, all of which, together with the logical rule of intersection, were considered necessary for focusing to occur. Results showed that deficiencies in complex problem-solving situations may often be a function of the unavailability of relevant information and not of the absence of the necessary rules or operations, as has often been assumed. Further evidence that the use of simple memory supports facilitates problem solving comes from studies by Roodin & Gruen (221) and Sieber et al (245). The former study showed improved performance in making transitivity judgments by elimination of the requirement that the young children retain the individual premises in memory storage, while the latter study demonstrated improved performance on both puzzle and concept attainment tasks by the use of memory aids.

The data from these studies as well as the studies on conservation and logical thinking indicate that theoretical explanations of cognition and its development must consider the development not only of logical rules but also of efficient information processing strategies. It is heartening to note that several developmental psychologists have realized the deficiencies in developmental theories to date and have begun to consider new approaches which appear to hold considerable promise for the future. For example, Neimark (196), in outlining an information processing approach to thinking and its development, has translated many of Piaget's constructs into computer terminology, noting that such processes as attention must be given priority in the analyses of problem solving. Klahr & Wallace (143) attempted with some success to apply the processing model of Simon & Kotovsky (247) to the serial completion task in young children. In a second paper (144) these same authors outlined the processes necessary to solve a number of classification tasks in terms of an information processing model. Finally, Pascual-Leone (208) has developed a mathematical model that can account for response variability among a group of children at the same stage of intellectual development. There is considerable work to be accomplished in theoretical child psychology; indeed, most writers in this area have yet to consider in detail the nature of the transition from one level of performance to another or the role of language, in terms of modern linguistics, in problem solving and thought. However, there does appear the hope that we are moving to more precise, less global, and more data-bound models of thought and its development.

LANGUAGE

Acquisition of syntax.—Undoubtedly the main interest of psychologists and linguists concerned with language development has been the acquisition of syntax during the initial years of language development. The attempts to systematize the earlier findings were led by McNeill (173, 174). For more general coverage of the psycholinguistic literature the reader is referred to Miller & McNeill (178) and to Fillenbaum (81), as well as to an article by Bronowski & Bellugi (28), who have examined the basic nature of language and its relation to the way humans analyze their experience of the external world. McNeill (173, 174) has continued to be an active proponent of the viewpoint that language in man is largely a result of innate, species-specific capacities, and that syntactic development can best be understood within the framework of a transformational grammar. Additional evidence that a transformational grammar provides a meaningful mode of analysis comes from a chapter by Brown & Hanlon (32). They studied the emergence of eight different sentence types, all of which were simple active sentences: affirmative declaratives and interrogatives, negative declaratives and interrogatives, truncated affirmative and negative declaratives, and truncated affirmative and negative interrogatives. The order of emergence of these sentences was firmly related to the derivational complexity as defined by an adult transformational grammar. Brown & Hanlon also argued that the order of emergence could not be accounted for by sentence length, frequency of occurrence, or semantic differences [but see Watt (269) for criticism of the least effort principle in particular, and Bever (17) for an alternative explanation in terms of perceptual and cognitive strategies].

Bloom (20) has also studied syntactic development in three children, one between the ages of 21 and 24 months and the other two between 19 and 27 months. Bloom has made a significant contribution to the study of the earliest utterances of children in that she has carefully documented the environment in which an utterance occurred, thereby permitting a more careful analysis of the semantic component of each verbal string. As a consequence, a more realistic appraisal of the syntactic competence of her subjects was possible. For example, she noted that noun-noun constructions could occur in a variety of ways, that is, in a conjunctive, genitive, attributive, locative, or subject-object relation. From data of this nature, Bloom hypothesized that "It was necessary for the grammars to generate strings that specified inherent semantic relationships between lexical items and were often hierarchical in nature" (p. 115). Indeed, the grammatical models for her subjects, which are transformational models, are considerably more complex than the earlier pivot grammars (which incidentally are subsumed by her models) or the grammars proposed by McNeill (173, 174) in which the categories of the base strings are specified as optional elements. Bloom argues cogently that language development cannot be understood solely as a function of innate processes, but rather that a complete explanation of language development must include the principles of cognitive and perceptual development in addition to other forms of nonlinguistic experience (cf Bever 17).

In a study designed to test whether the grammaticality of a sentence influenced a young child's ability to imitate, Freedle, Keeney & Smith (88) presented both grammatical and ungrammatical sentences to children with a mean CA of 4.3 years. They found that the recall of free morphemes (nouns, verbs, or adjectives) was unaffected by sentence grammaticality, whereas the recall of articles (function words) and bound morphemes (inflections) of verbs but not of nouns was influenced by sentence grammaticality. It would seem that children imitate in a telegraphic manner not because they fail to appreciate the syntax of a sentence, but rather because of some as yet unknown process acting at the time of production. Although the results of the study by Freedle et al (88) also indicated that such factors as stress cannot be the sole causal agent for telegraphic imitation, this is not to say that stress exerts no influence. Indeed, Blasdell & Jensen (19) showed that children between 28 and 39 months imitated nonsense syllables reliably more often when they were marked with primary stress.

The study of syntactic development was not confined to the earliest years of childhood. With the publication of Carol Chomsky's monograph (44) on syntactic development between the ages of 5 and 10 years, evidence exists to reject the claim of some psycholinguistics that the acquisition of syntax is virtually complete by 5 years of age. Chomsky investigated the grammatical construction, "NP_1 V NP_2 to infinitive verb," where NP signifies a noun phrase and V signifies a verb. Usually NP_2 is the subject of the infinitive verb, e.g. "John told Mary to run." This illustrates the minimal distance principle (MDP) in that the NP most closely preceding the infinitive verb is the assigned subject of the infinitive verb. However, there are exceptions, e.g. "John promised Mary to run." In this example, John is the assigned subject of the infinitive verb "to run." In the case of the verb "ask," the MDP holds under some circumstances but not under others, e.g. in the context "John asked Mary to run," but not in the context "John asked Mary what to do." Intuitively one would expect children to have difficulty with the verb "promise," in that it violates a basic principle. In addition, one would expect children to take even longer to master the verb "ask," since in different contexts it may either agree or not agree with the MDP. The study confirmed these expectations; children had acquired an understanding of "promise" by approximately 9 years of age, whereas understanding of "ask" was not achieved by some children who were beyond 10 years of age. Chomsky also investigated the now famous construction, "John is easy to please." The construction was also acquired relatively late in that not all children until the age of 8 years fully understood that John was not the logical subject of the sentence, but rather was the object of the infinitival complement "to please."

Confirmation of several of these findings was obtained by Kessel (141) and by Cromer (55). Kessel, using the "clinical methodology" of Piaget, obtained similar age norms for the easy-eager distinction and somewhat earlier acquisition of the ask-tell distinction. Cromer investigated the sentence, "John is easy to see," and found that only children with a MA of almost 7 years were able to recognize the grammatical structure of the apparent subject "John." Moreover, these same children were able to transfer these deep structure rules to nonsense adjectives after a single presentation in a differentiating frame.

Semantic development.—In one of the few studies on the growth of meaning, Anglin (6) investigated the role of semantic features in determining meaning in children age 9 to 17 years, and in adults. A number of experimental procedures were used, including the sorting task of Miller (177), free and ordered recall, and an equivalence task. The same 20 words were used in all of the studies, and were drawn from four grammatical categories (nouns, verbs, adjectives, and prepositions). The words were selected in order to form a continuum of abstractness within each grammatical class. Abstractness was defined as a set of nested features that united the words but later revised to emphasize the number of shared features. For example, the nouns "boy" and "girl" are examples of the feature child. When "horse" is added to the list the unifying feature becomes animal. Inclusion of the noun "flower" changes the unifying feature to living thing or being. With each addition, the unifying feature appears, at least intuitively, to be more abstract. The sorting experiments indicated that adults use grammatical classes as a basis for sorting more reliably than do children, and that the extent to which two items are sorted together is inversely related to the abstractness of the unifying feature. The decrease in clustering with increasing abstractness was considerably more pronounced in children, although children did cluster opposites (e.g. boy-girl) as frequently as did adults. The recall tasks were less sensitive to the hierarchical structure of words, although the same general trends were obtained. Abstractness was inversely related to the degree of clustering and the children's clusters were less paradigmatic, more idiosyncratic, and smaller than adult clusters. Similar findings were obtained for the remaining measures. The evidence supported the contention that meaning develops slowly over time and the direction of this development is from concrete to abstract. The process of change is marked by the gradual accretion of features of ever-increasing generality.

Moran & Swartz (186) obtained free associates from 9-, 12-, and 15-year-old children. Each group was retested on the same list after a 1-year interval and again after a 2-year interval. The data indicated that there was a reliable tendency for these subjects to be consistent in their use of associative principles. Subjects who tended to use, for example, synonyms or contrasts, did so consistently over time. However, the same associates were not given at each testing. Rather it appeared that the cognitive dictionaries were organized by hierarchies of associative principles rather than by hierarchies of specific word-word associations. In a study with 4th, 6th, and 8th graders, Shepard (242) found that boys gave more paradigmatic associations than did girls, but when later asked to define the word, girls gave more complex definitions (i.e. that included both a function and a synonym). Apparently the two tasks tap different hierarchies of associative principles. Finally, in a study of meaning at a more complex level, Bugental, Kaswan & Love (34) investigated the perception of conflicting messages. In essence, they found that "joking" messages (criticism conveyed with a smile) were perceived more negatively by children than adults and that this effect was most apparent when the message source was a female.

Phonological development.—Friedlander (90) has argued for an increased emphasis on the study of speech perception and receptive listening behavior during the first year of life. As Friedlander notes, the past literature on the development of the phonological system deals almost exclusively with the production of speech and only rarely with the perception of speech. Why this should have been the case is not clear, since it is apparent that perceptual processing is necessary if a child is to be able to match his phonetic productions with those of the parental language. Recently, however, investigations of the infant's ability to perceive speech have been undertaken, and the evidence indicates that they are sensitive to the sounds of speech and capable of quite fine discriminations. For example. Moffitt (184), using synthetic speech stimuli, showed that 5-month-old infants were able to discriminate between /bah/ and/gah/. Eimas et al (72), also using synthetic speech stimuli, demonstrated that 1- and 4-month-old infants were able to discriminate the difference between /bah/ and /pah/. More importantly, they perceived the stimuli in very nearly a categorical manner, as do adults, and hence presumably in a linguistic mode as opposed to a purely acoustic mode.

Gilbert (99) has studied the perception (absolute identification) of vowels by 4-year-old children in a somewhat novel manner. The vowels to be identified were actually produced by the children. Two sets of vowel productions were obtained: one from a group of normal language users and one from a group of late language users. Spectrographic analyses revealed no reliable physical differences between the two sets of vowels, yet the identification scores were better for the vowels produced by the normal language users. This was true for both normal and late language users. The basis for this identification difference is not apparent, but its appearance supports the contention that the perception of speech is an extremely complex process and one not determined solely by the acoustical properties of the signal (154). Equally perplexing was a second study by Gilbert (100) showing that the ability to identify acoustic stimuli increased in difficulty as the stimulus

patterns more closely approximated speech signals. Finally, mention should
be made of a study by Hornby & Hass (122) indicating that preschoolers
tended to use contrastive stress in describing the single aspect of two pictures
that differed, whether it be the agent, action, or object.

  Language functions.—In a test of Luria's (160) model for language-
mediated control of voluntary behavior, Miller, Shelton & Flavell (180)
tested children between the ages of 3 and 5.3 years. The experimental task
was simply to press a rubber bulb in the presence of one visual stimulus and
to withhold responding in the presence of a second stimulus. At each age level
there were four treatment groups. One group received no instructions regarding verbalizing at the time of responding. Another was instructed to say
"squeeze" in the presence of the positive stimulus, while a third group was
instructed to say "don't squeeze" in the presence of the negative stimulus.
The fourth group received both verbal instructions. The data indicated that,
contrary to Luria's model, instructions did not interact with age. Indeed, at
no age level did verbal self-instructions facilitate performance, nor did the
instruction not to squeeze interfere with performance at the younger ages.
Perhaps most in contradiction to the model was the finding that the motoric
response tended to precede the verbal response.
  Language has been found in numerous earlier studies to mediate memorial
processes (see also the section on memory). Additional evidence for the role
of language comes from the following studies. First, Smith & Larson (249)
found that the ability to recognize a color improved with the ability to
communicate a description of the color to another person. Second, Rohwer &
Suzuki (219) showed that verbal strings of the form article-adjective-noun-
connective-article-adjective-noun were better recalled when the connective
was a verb than when it was a conjunction. Whether this result was a function of better visual imagery found to be associated with verbs, or whether it
was a function of better linguistic coding processes available to complete
sentences is an open question. Finally, Vanevery & Rosenberg (264) provided
evidence that the semantic structure influenced the recall of complete sentences. There was also evidence that semantically well integrated sentences
were recoded into larger chunks than were semantically poorly integrated
sentences.

BEHAVIOR MODIFICATION AND OPERANT STUDIES

  The increasing number of reported research investigations in which behavior modification techniques, adapted largely from the operant learning
laboratory, are deployed to the child guidance clinic, the institution for
mentally retarded, and even the ordinary classroom indicates clearly that
there is now a well-respected body of literature relating to these attempts,
and that specific studies can and do make contributions to the further understanding of psychological processes underlying the successful efforts. This
latter type of contribution does not go without saying, for the view is often

expressed by detractors that behavior modification "studies" are actually "clinical treatments" which simply borrow from the lab and lore of the operant conditioner, much as the engineer utilizes the physicist's principles to build his bridge, or as the internist uses the research of the pulmonary physiologist in treating the heart patient.

While the behavior modification "trainer" does capitalize upon the principles of reinforcement and diverse operant laboratory techniques for the purpose of bringing his "subject" under stimulus control, he also feeds back data that can (at least in principle) support or denigrate a presumed functional relationship. The veracity and generality of a theory or working set of behavior principles can be tried in applied settings in such a way as to make a substantive scientific contribution. Not all behavior modification "studies," of course, are of this variety, but some do fill the bill.

For example, Wasik (268), working with 20 culturally deprived 2nd graders, utilized successfully a behavior management procedure adapted from Premack's technique of reinforcing low-probability behaviors with opportunity to engage in higher-probability behaviors. When access to toys, games, and crafts was made contingent upon engaging in "desirable" behaviors such as cooperating, seeking support and assistance, and following directions, the children engaged in fewer undesirable behaviors such as aggression, resistance to authority, and annoyance of others. Withdrawal of the contingency condition resulted in reversion to former modes of behavior, but reinstituting the contingencies recaptured the effect.

Another study (27) has shown that attending behavior in the classroom can be markedly influenced through judicious application of teacher attention. The two most disruptive boys in a 2nd-grade classroom were studied in tandem. Following documentation of their baseline attending behavior, the teacher increased attention to one of the boys when his behavior was appropriate; this resulted in a sizable increase in the target subject's attending behavior and a concomitant but lesser increase in the second boy. In a second phase, the contingency was applied to the second child only, with comparable effect on the second child and a concomitant decline of attending in the first child. Withdrawal of reinforcement resulted in reduction of attending in both boys, but appropriate behavior was recovered in both boys when the contingency was applied to both. Another study facilitating "classroom attention" was reported by Packard (203), using a token reinforcement procedure.

That such behavior modification effects may not require external control by external contingencies is suggested by a study of Montgomery & Parton (185) in which the reinforcing effect of self-reward was demonstrated in elementary school children. A study with kindergarten children has also shown (166) that the systematic application by the teacher of reinforcement for desirable behavior tends to enhance children's social contacts with the teacher, relative to a control condition in which tokens were administered in comparable amounts but noncontingently. Apparently, children attend better, and perhaps more affectionately, to reinforcing agents who themselves behave according to detectable rules. Another study (161) has shown that school attendance in truant children can be significantly enhanced through the use of outside agents who control the reinforcers administered for school attendance, and that this procedure works better than ordinary school-attendance counseling.

Apparently, the phenomenon of children not attending to appropriate activities in the classroom is a problem frequently reported by teachers. Behavior modification experts have therefore addressed themselves to the behavioral analysis and amelioration of this condition. In another kindergarten study (235), reinforcement contingencies were applied to a group of five children who did not properly follow instructions (only 60% of the time as assessed in a baseline condition). When the teacher indulged the individual children with her attentions, the incidence of instructions followed rose to 78%. Upon withdrawal of the contingent attention condition, instruction following declined, but reinstitution of the procedure raised the level to 84%. The conclusion: consequences of instructed behavior determine the extent to which the instructions are followed. Interestingly, researchers seldom comment on the possibility that if the tasks in which the children were instructed were themselves more interesting, i.e. reinforcing, attending might thereby be enhanced without the necessity of an inordinate amount of teacher attention; the task itself, after all, is one of the consequences of following instructions!

In a special-purpose study by Craig & Holland (50), the classroom reinforcement of visual attending in deaf children was effected through the use of a light-flash reinforcer backed up by edibles or tokens. The application of modification techniques to specific behavior in the troubled child's repertoire apparently has a generalized effect on other nontarget behaviors, as was shown in a study by Wahler et al (266) of childhood stutterers. Stuttering children observed in clinic and home settings were found to present other management problems as well. When contingency procedures were applied to the secondary problems, both these and the stuttering behavior were reduced. Another study, this one of retarded children, showed that the training of positive social behavior in a circumscribed situation enhanced prosocial behavior toward other children (272).

Because the systematic application of behavior modification techniques in the classroom invariably presupposes that teacher expectations may be more nearly met under more favorable learning conditions, the issue of teacher expectation and its effect on student behavior is relevant to the success of behavior modification procedures. In that connection it is interesting to note that support has been obtained for the controversial Rosenthal & Jacobson position (222), which asserts that students' performances are influenced greatly by the prior expectations of the teachers. Brophy & Good (29) observed teacher-student contact in four 1st-grade classes, with the result that

... differential teacher behavior was observed which is not attributable to objective differences among the children and which is consistent with the hypothesis that differential teacher expectations function as self-fulfilling prophecies. The teachers demanded better performance from those children for whom they had higher expectations and were more likely to praise such performance when it was elicited. They were less likely to praise good performance from (poor) students when it occurred, even though it occurred less frequently.

Obviously, behavior modification expertise might be used beneficially to enhance the teacher's recognition and reinforcement of low-baseline, good performance in "poor" students.

While clinical interest in the utilization of operant procedures seems to be continuing strong, especially in relation to the autistic child, the number of empirical investigations reported may be waning. This is perhaps to be expected after an initial period of intense enthusiasm and a wave of innovations, but one does wonder whether there are only replications left to do until the next advance in the area. One nonreplication is a report of a very elaborate device (278) for the administration of aversive stimulation contingent upon self-injurious behavior. This helmet-like device protects the wearer's head from severe injury when the person strikes himself or throws himself at an object, and also delivers a shock to the arm. The authors claim thus far only that impressive changes occur in self-injurious autistics, and further studies will be required to determine whether self-punitive behavior can be suppressed through the administration of an alternative punishment.

Effective behavior-modification strategies with autistic children have been described by Sulzbacher & Costello (255) and Marshall & Hegrenes (167), but the nature of the procedures is such as to make difficult either a summary of the process or attribution of the obtained effects to specific details of the procedure. On the other hand, a study by Tramontana & Stimbert (261) successfully used the imitation behavior of the autistic child to combat echolalia and refusal to answer questions. Questions were asked of the subject, and then before inappropriate mimicking could occur, the correct answer was administered. Candy reinforcement of imitative responses to the prompt were administered and, after several sessions, were then faded out.

In a herculean study involving 45 autistic and 45 nonautistic boys from an institution for the retarded, Freitag (89) used a game to be played with an adult to compare these two groups with a third group of normal noninstitutional boys. The autistic children were shown to engage in less interpersonal contact and to be generally less responsive, spending less total time in the task. Analysis of results too elaborate for summary here have implications for previous findings of Zigler and colleagues (see Zigler 281); for example, the normal subjects spent more time in the game than did the institutionalized retardeds.

THEORETICAL YEARNINGS

Our predecessors in this series have regretted the failure to emerge from the field of child development a unifying theory, a system for putting the "whole child" back together again after so many years and such an abundance of studies in which the growing human has been broken into numerous developmental stages, processes, and behavior mechanisms. The regret seems to be that studies, for example, of the onset of smiling behavior, or of factors which conduce to appreciation of object permanency, or of the antecedents of adequate school performance, or of parental traits as they influence children's emotional responsivity, do not, when all is said and done, have much to do with the way in which organisms "get it all together."

It seems to us, on the contrary, that the human may not ever get it all together as the developmental scientist wishes. It is possible that the world view of the child investigator, whatever it may be, might never be realized, and that the perpetuation of the pursuit, while perhaps personally satisfying, constitutes a scientific labor worthy only of Sisyphus.

Human behavior consists, after all, of mechanisms and processes—sensory, learning, motivational, physiological, and other—all of which *can* in principle be understood, given the instigating hypotheses and the permitting technologies, methods, and analytic tools. That these processes get themselves together in diverse and fascinating ways in different people over the course of development should simply do honor to the devotees of individual differences in man. In turn, the vast array of unexplained individual differences in developing man should provide us with an inspiring perspective on the scope of the task before us in understanding the processes and mechanisms.

Yet, some attempts *were* made to get it all together, if not within the scope of a unified theory, then at least within the covers of a few books. Such a review as this could not close without at least a tip of the hat to the publication in 1970 of the much-awaited revision of Carmichael's *Manual of Child Psychology*, edited by Mussen (193). The contributors to this 2-volume work, too numerous to mention here, include some of the best talent in the field of child behavior and development, writing on topics in which their expertise is unquestioned (Piaget, writing on "Piaget's Theory," for example). Another publication worthy of special mention is an advanced level, and therefore unique, text on *Experimental Child Psychology*, edited by Reese & Lipsitt (215), to which 16 writers in addition to the editors contributed chapter material in their areas of special proficiency. Finally, there is the volume edited by Goulet & Baltes (102) with a title that at once giggles like a freshman at our petty specialities and yet encourages us like a severe taskmaster to get on with it: *Life-Span Developmental Psychology*.

LITERATURE CITED

1. Abrahamson, D., Brackbill, Y., Carpenter, R., Fitzgerald, H. E. 1970. Interaction of stimulus and response in infant conditioning. *Psychosom. Med.* 32:319–25
2. Ahr, P. R., Youniss, J. 1970. Reasons for failure on the class inclusion problem. *Child Develop.* 41:131–43
3. Ainsworth, M. D., Bell, S. M. 1970. Attachment, exploration, and separation: illustrated by the behavior of one-year-olds in a strange situation. *Child Develop.* 41:49–67
4. Allen, D. V. 1970. Acoustic interference in paired-associate learning as a function of hearing ability. *Psychon. Sci.* 18:231–33
5. Ambrose, A., Ed. 1969. *Stimulation in Early Infancy.* London: Academic. 289 pp.
6. Anglin, J. M. 1970. *The Growth of Word Meaning.* Cambridge: MIT Press. 108 pp.
7. Bach, M. J., Underwood, B. J. 1970. Developmental changes in memory attributes. *J. Educ. Psychol.* 61:292–96
8. Barclay, J. R., Comalli, P. E. Jr. 1970. Age differences in perceptual learning on the Müller-Lyer illusion. *Psychon. Sci.* 19:323–25
9. Baumeister, A. A., Berry, F. M. 1970. Single-letter cue selection in the paired-associate learning of normal children and retardates. *J. Exp. Child Psychol.* 9:400–10
10. Baumeister, A. A., Kellas, G., Gordon, D. 1970. Backward associations in paired-associate learning of retardates and normal children. *Child Develop.* 41:355–64
11. Bell, R. Q. 1970. Sleep cycles and skin potential in newborns studied with a simplified observation and recording system. *Psychophysiology* 6:778–86
12. Bell, S. M. 1970. The development of the concept of object as related to infant-mother attachment. *Child Develop.* 41:291–311
13. Bem, S. L. 1970. The role of comprehension in children's problem solving. *Develop. Psychol.* 2:351–58
14. Berch, D. B. 1970. Visual orientation in children's discrimination learning under constant, variable, and covariable delay of reinforcement. *J. Exp. Child Psychol.* 9:374–87
15. Bereiter, C. 1970. Genetics and educability: educational implications of the Jensen debate. See Ref. 119, 279–99
16. Berman, P. W., Rane, N. G., Bahow, E. 1970. Age changes in children's learning set with win-stay, lose-shift problems. *Develop. Psychol.* 2:233–39
17. Bever, T. G. 1970. The cognitive basis for linguistic structures. In *Cognition and the Development of Language*, ed. J. R. Hayes, 279–362. New York: Wiley. 370 pp.
18. Blank, M., Klig, S. 1970. Dimensional learning across sensory modalities in nursery school children. *J. Exp. Child Psychol.* 9:166–73
19. Blasdell, R., Jensen, P. 1970. Stress and word position as determinants of imitation in first-language learners. *J. Speech Hear. Res.* 13:193–202
20. Bloom, L. 1970. *Language Development: Form and Function in Emerging Grammars.* Cambridge: MIT Press. 270 pp.
21. Blue, C. M. 1970. Influence of mode of presentation, age, and intelligence on paired-associates learning. *Am. J. Ment. Defic.* 74:527–32
22. Bower, T. G. R., Broughton, J. M., Moore, M. K. 1970. The coordination of visual and tactual input in infants. *Percept. Psychophys.* 8:51–53
23. Bower, T. G. R., Broughton, J. M., Moore, M. K. 1970. Demonstration of intention in the reaching behaviour of neonate humans. *Nature* 228:679–81
24. Brackbill, Y. 1970. Acoustic variation and arousal level in infants. *Psychophysiology* 6:517–26
25. Brainerd, C. J. 1970. Continuity and discontinuity hypotheses in studies of conservation. *Develop. Psychol.* 3:225–28
26. Bresler, J. B. 1970. Outcrossings in Caucasians and fetal loss. *Soc. Biol.* 17:17 25
27. Broden, M., Bruce, C., Mitchell, M. A., Carter, V., Hall, R. V. 1970. Effects of teacher attention on attending behavior of two boys at adjacent desks. *J. Appl. Behav. Anal.* 3:199–203
28. Bronowski, J., Bellugi, U. 1970. Language, name, and concept. *Science* 168:669–73
29. Brophy, J. E., Good, T. L. 1970.

Teacher's communication of differential expectations for children's classroom performance: some behavioral data. *J. Educ. Psychol.* 61:365–74

30. Brown, A. 1970. The stability of dimensional preference following oddity training. *J. Exp. Child Psychol.* 9:239–52

31. Ibid. Transfer performance in children's oddity learning as a function of dimensional preference, shift paradigm and overtraining, 307–19

32. Brown, R., Hanlon, C. 1970. Derivational complexity and order of acquisition in child speech. See Ref. 17, 11–53

33. Bruner, J. S., Olver, R. R. 1966. *Studies in Cognitive Growth.* New York: Wiley. 343 pp.

34. Bugental, D. E., Kaswan, J. W., Love, L. R. 1970. Perception of contradictory meanings conveyed by verbal and nonverbal channels. *J. Pers. Soc. Psychol.* 16:647–55

35. Bulmer, M. G. 1970. *The Biology of Twinning in Man.* Oxford: Clarendon. 205 pp.

36. Bush, E. S., Cohen, L. B. 1970. The effects of relevant and irrelevant labels on short-term memory in nursery school children. *Psychon. Sci.* 18:228–29

37. Calfee, R. C. 1970. Short-term recognition memory in children. *Child Develop.* 41:145–61

38. Campione, J. C. 1970. Optional intradimensional and extradimensional shifts in children as a function of age. *J. Exp. Psychol.* 84:296–300

39. Campos, J. J., Langer, A., Krowitz, A. 1970. Cardiac responses on the visual cliff in prelocomotor human infants. *Science* 170:196–97

40. Cantor, J. H. 1970. Facilitating and interfering effects of stimulus naming on children's motor paired-associate learning. *J. Exp. Child Psychol.* 10:374–89

41. Caron, A. J. 1970. Discrimination shifts in three-year-olds as a function of shift procedure. *Develop. Psychol.* 3: 236–41

42. Carpenter, G. C., Tecce, J. J., Stechler, G., Friedman, S. 1970. Differential visual behavior to human and humanoid faces in early infancy. *Merrill-Palmer Quart.* 16: 91–108

43. Cavalli-Sforza, L. L. 1970. Problems and prospects of genetic analysis of intelligence at the intra- and interracial level. See Ref. 119, 111–23

44. Chomsky, C. 1969. *The Acquisition of Syntax in Children from 5 to 10.* Cambridge: MIT Press. 126 pp.

45. Christie, J. F., Smothergill, D. W. 1970. Discrimination and conservation of length. *Psychon. Sci.* 21: 336–37

46. Clark, H. H. 1969. Linguistic processes in deductive reasoning. *Psychol. Rev.* 76:387–404

47. Clifton, C. Jr., Clifton, R. K., Meyers, W. J., Miller, F. 1970. Cardiac responses to attended and ignored stimuli. *Psychon. Sci.* 18:361–62

48. Connolly, K., Jones, B. 1970. A developmental study of afferent-reafferent integration. *Brit. J. Psychol.* 61:259–66

49. Corsini, D. A. 1970. The effect of type of redundancy on retention in preschool children. *Psychon. Sci.* 19:117–18

50. Craig, H. B., Holland, A. L. 1970. Reinforcement of visual attending in classrooms for deaf children. *J. Appl. Behav. Anal.* 3:97–109

51. Croll, W. L. 1970. Children's discrimination learning as a function of intertrial interval duration. *Psychon. Sci.* 18:321–22

52. Croll, W. L. 1970. Generalization in a stimulus classification task: Stimulus selection within and among dimensions. *J. Exp. Child Psychol.* 9:227–38

53. Ibid. Response strategies in the oddity discrimination of preschool children, 187–92

54. Croll, W. L., Knauss, M. J., Duke, A. W. 1970. Sequential contiguity and short-term memory in children's discrimination learning. *J. Exp. Child Psychol.* 10:337–43

55. Cromer, R. F. 1970. 'Children are nice to understand': Surface structure clues for the recovery of a deep structure. *Brit. J. Psychol.* 61:397–408

56. Crowder, R. G. 1970. The role of one's own voice in immediate memory. *Cogn. Psychol.* 1:157–78

57. Crowder, R. G., Morton, J. 1969. Precategorical acoustic storage (PAS). *Percept. Psychophys.* 5:365–73

58. Darnell, C. D., Bourne, L. E. Jr. 1970. Effects of age, verbal ability, and pretraining with component concepts on the performance of chil-

dren in a bidimensional classification task. *J. Educ. Psychol.* 61:66–71

59. Davidson, R. E., Adams, J. F. 1970. Verbal and imagery processes in children's paired-associate learning. *J. Exp. Child Psychol.* 9:429–35

60. Davidson, R. E., Schwenn, E. A., Adams, J. F. 1970. Semantic effects in transfer. *J. Verb. Learn. Verb. Behav.* 9:212–17

61. DeLeon, J. L., Raskin, L. M., Gruen, G. E. 1970. Sensory-modality effects on shape perception in pre-school children. *Develop. Psychol.* 3:358–62

62. Dick, S., Landau, J. S. 1970. Attribute learning in preschool children: Mediation and selection mechanisms. *Psychon. Sci.* 21:105–7

63. Dickerson, D. J. 1970. Effects of naming relevant and irrelevant stimuli on the discrimination learning of children. *Child Develop.* 41:639–50

64. Dickerson, D. J., Girardeau, F. L. 1970. Oddity preference by mental retardates. *J. Exp. Child Psychol.* 10:28–32

65. Dickerson, D. J., Wagner, J. F., Campione, J. 1970. Discrimination shift performance of kindergarten children as a function of variation of the irrelevant shift dimension. *Develop. Psychol.* 3:229–35

66. Dilley, M. G., Paivio, A. 1968. Pictures and words as stimulus and response items in paired-associate learning of young children. *J. Exp. Child Psychol.* 6:231–40

67. Dornbush, R. L., Basow, S. 1970. The relationship between auditory and visual short-term memory and reading achievement. *Child Develop.* 41:1033–44

68. Duke, A. W., Gullickson, G. R. 1970. Children's stimulus selection as a function of auditory stimulus complexity. *Psychon. Sci.* 19:119–20

69. Dusek, J. B., Hill, K. T. 1970. Probability learning as a function of sex of the subject, text anxiety, and percentage of reinforcement. *Develop. Psychol.* 3:195–207

70. Eimas, P. D. 1970. Information processing in problem solving as a function of developmental level and stimulus saliency. *Develop. Psychol.* 2:224–29

71. Eimas, P. D. 1970. Effects of memory aids on hypothesis behavior and focusing in young children and adults. *J. Exp. Child Psychol.* 10:319–36

72. Eimas, P. D., Siqueland, E. R., Jusczyk, P., Vigorito, J. 1971. Speech perception in infants. *Science* 171:303–6

73. Elder, M. S. 1970. The effects of temperature and position on the sucking pressure of newborn infants. *Child Develop.* 41:95–102

74. Elkind, D., Medvene, L., Rockway, A. S. 1970. Representational level and concept production in children and adolescents. *Develop. Psychol.* 2:85–89

75. Erickson, M. T., Johnson, N. M., Campbell, F. A. 1970. Relationships among scores on infant tests for children with developmental problems. *Am. J. Ment. Defic.* 75:102–4

76. Etaugh, C. F. 1970. Factors in learning stereometric discriminations in children. *Percept. Mot. Skills* 30:614

77. Evans, R. A., Beedle, R. K. 1970. Discrimination learning in mentally retarded children as a function of irrelevant dimension variability. *Am. J. Ment. Defic.* 74:568–73

78. Fagan, J. F. 1970. Memory in the infant. *J. Exp. Child Psychol.* 9:217–26

79. Fantz, R. L. 1970. Visual perception and experience in infancy: issues and approaches. In *Early Experience and Visual Information Processing in Perceptual and Reading Disorders*, ed. F. A. Young, D. B. Lindsley, 351–81. Washington: Nat. Acad. Sci. 533 pp.

80. Felzen, E., Anisfeld, M. 1970. Semantic and phonetic relations in the false recognition of words by third- and sixth-grade children. *Develop. Psychol.* 3:163–68

81. Fillenbaum, S. 1971. Psycholinguistics. *Ann. Rev. Psychol.* 22:251–308

82. Firth, U. 1970. Memory coding for binary sequences in children. *Quart. J. Exp. Psychol.* 22:618–30

83. Fitzgerald, H. E., Porges, S. W. 1970. A decade of infant conditioning and learning research. *Merrill-Palmer Quart.* In press

84. Flavell, J. H. 1970. Developmental studies of mediated memory. In *Advances in Child Development and Behavior*, ed. H. W. Reese, L. P. Lipsitt, 182–211. New York: Academic. 265 pp.

85. Flavell, J. H., Friedrichs, A. G., Hoyt, J. D. 1970. Developmental changes in memorization processes. *Cogn. Psychol.* 1:324–40

86. Fleener, D. E., Cairns, R. B. 1970. Attachment behaviors in human infants: discriminative vocalization on maternal separation. *Develop. Psychol.* 2:215–23

87. Ford, L. H. 1970. Predictive versus perceptual responses to Piaget's water-line task and their relation to distance conservation. *Child Develop.* 41:193–204

88. Freedle, R. O., Keeney, T. J., Smith, N. D. 1970. Effects of mean depth and grammaticality on children's imitations of sentences. *J. Verb. Learn. Verb. Behav.* 9:149–54

89. Freitag, G. 1970. An experimental study of the social responsiveness of children with autistic behaviors. *J. Exp. Child Psychol.* 9:436–53

90. Friedlander, B. Z. 1970. Receptive language development in infancy: Issues and problems. *Merrill Palmer Quart.* 16:7–51

91. Fuld, P. A. 1970. Syntactical mediation of paired-associate learning as a function of age. *J. Exp. Child Psychol.* 10:248–56

92. Furth, H. G., Youniss, J., Ross, B. M. 1970. Children's utilization of logical symbols: An interpretation of conceptual behavior based on Piagetian theory. *Develop. Psychol.* 3:36–57

93. Gagné, R. M., Wiegand, V. K. 1970. Effects of a superordinate context on learning and retention of facts. *J. Educ. Psychol.* 61:406–9

94. Gaines, R. 1970. Children's selective attention to stimuli: stage or set? *Child Develop.* 41:979–91

95. Gallagher, J. W. 1970. Effect of meaningfulness of learning syntactic units. *Am. J. Ment. Defic.* 75:27–32

96. Gallagher, J. W., Reid, D. R. 1970. Effect of five free association strength values on paired-associate learning. *Am. J. Ment. Defic.* 75:33–38

97. Garner, W. R. 1970. The stimulus in information processing. *Am. Psychol.* 25:350–58

98. Gelman, R. 1969. Conservation acquisition: A problem of learning to attend to relevant attributes. *J. Exp. Child Psychol.* 7:167–87

99. Gilbert, J. H. 1970. Vowel productions and identification by normal and delayed children. *J. Exp. Child Psychol.* 9:12–19

100. Ibid. The learning of speechlike stimuli by children, 1–11

101. Girgus, J. S., Hochberg, J. 1970. Age differences in sequential form recognition. *Psychon. Sci.* 21:211–12

102. Goulet, L. R., Baltes, P. B., Eds. 1970. *Life-Span Developmental Psychology.* New York: Academic. 591 pp.

103. Goulet, L. R., Goodwin, K. S. 1970. Development and choice behavior in probabilistic and problem-solving tasks. See Ref. 84, 214–54

104. Goulet, L. R., Williams, K. G. 1970. Children's shift performance in the absence of dimensionality and learned representational response. *J. Exp. Child Psychol.* 10:287–94

104a. Graham, F. K., Jackson, J. C. 1970. Arousal systems and infant heart rate responses. See Ref. 84, 60–117

105. Graham, F. K. et al 1970. Cardiac orienting responses as a function of age. *Psychon. Sci.* 19:363–65

106. Green, R. T., Laxon, V. J. 1970. The conservation of number, mother, water and a fried egg chez l'enfant. *Acta Psychol.* 32:1–30

107. Greenberg, D., Uzgiris, I. C., Hunt, J. McV. 1970. Attentional preference and experience: III. Visual familiarity and looking time. *J. Genet. Psychol.* 117:123–35

108. Gruen, G., Ottinger, D., Zigler, E. 1970. Level of aspiration and the probability learning of middle- and lower-class children. *Develop. Psychol.* 3:133–42

109. Hagen, J. W., Meacham, J. A., Mesibov, G. 1970. Verbal labeling, rehearsal, and short-term memory. *Cogn. Psychol.* 1:47–58

110. Haith, M. M., Morrison, F. J., Sheingold, K. 1970. Tachistoscopic recognition of geometric forms by children and adults. *Psychon. Sci.* 19:345–47

111. Haith, M. M., Morrison, F. J., Sheingold, K., Mindes, P. 1970. Short-term memory for visual information in children and adults. *J. Exp. Child Psychol.* 9:454–69

112. Halford, G. S. 1970. A theory of the acquisition of conservation. *Psychol. Rev.* 77:302–16

113. Halford, G. S., Fullerton, T. J. 1970. A discrimination task which induces conservation of number. *Child Develop.* 41:205–13

114. Hall, V. C., Salvi, R., Seggev, L.,

Caldwell, E. 1970. Cognitive synthesis, conservation, and task analysis. *Develop. Psychol.* 2:423–28

115. Harris, L., Schaller, M. J., Mitler, M. M. 1970. The effects of stimulus type on performance in a color-form sorting task with preschool, kindergarten, first-grade, and third-grade children. *Child Develop.* 41: 177–91

116. Harter, M. R., Suitt, C. D. 1970. Visually-evoked cortical responses and pattern vision in the infant: A longitudinal study. *Psychon. Sci.* 18:235–37

117. Haygood, R. C., Bourne, L. E. Jr. 1965. Attribute- and rule-learning aspects of conceptual behavior. *Psychol. Rev.* 72:175–95

118. Hebb, D. O. 1970. A return to Jensen and his social science critics. *Am. Psychol.* 25:568

119. Hellmuth, J., Ed. 1970. *Disadvantaged Child: Compensatory Education, a National Debate.* Brainbridge Island, Wash.: Brunner, Mazel. 466 pp.

120. Hohn, R. L., Martin, C. J. 1970. Mediational styles: An individual difference variable in children's learning ability. *Psychon. Sci.* 18:348–49

121. Hollenberg, C. K. 1970. Function of visual imagery in the learning and concept formation of children. *Child Develop.* 41:1003–15

122. Hornby, P. A., Hass, W. A. 1970. Use of contrastive stress by preschool children. *J. Speech Hear. Res.* 13: 395

123. House, B. J. 1970. A decremental effect of redundancy in discrimination learning. *J. Exp. Child Psychol.* 10:403–12

124. Hoving, K. L., Morin, R. E., Konick, D. S. 1970. Recognition reaction time and size of the memory set: A development study. *Psychon. Sci.* 21:247–48

125. Hutt, C., Hutt, S. M. 1970. The neonatal evoked heart rate response and the law of initial value. *Psychophysiology* 6:661–68

126. Huttenlocher, J., Higgins, E. T., Milligan, C., Kauffman, B. 1970. The mystery of the "negative equative" construction. *J. Verb. Learn. Verb. Behav.* 9:334–41

127. Inhelder, B., Piaget, J. 1958. *The Growth of Logical Thinking.* New York: Basic Books. 356 pp.

128. Ireton, H., Thwing, E., Gravem, H. 1970. Infant mental development and neurological status, family socioeconomic status, and intelligence at age four. *Child Develop.* 41:937–45

129. Jennings, J. R. 1970. The effect of verbal and pictorial presentation on class-inclusion competence and performance. *Psychon. Sci.* 20:357–58

130. Jensen, A. R. 1970. Another look at culture-fair testing. See Ref. 119, 53–101

131. Jensen, A. R. 1970. IQs of identical twins reared apart. *Behav. Genet.* 1:133–46

132. Jinks, J. L., Fulker, D. W. 1970. Comparison of the biometrical, genetical, MAVA, and classical approaches to the analysis of human behavior. *Psychol. Bull.* 73:311–49

133. Johnson, P. J., Warner, M. S., Lee, D. R. 1970. Effects of enforced attention and stimulus phasing upon rule learning in children. *J. Exp. Child Psychol.* 9:388–99

134. Kaess, D. W. 1970. Form constancy and the perceptual task: A developmental study. *J. Exp. Psychol.* 83: 465–71

135. Kagan, J. 1970. Attention and psychological change in the young child. *Science* 170:826–32

136. Katz, P. A., Karp, B., Yalisove, D. 1970. Verbal mediation of children's perception: The role of response variables. *J. Exp. Psychol.* 85:349–55

137. Kellas, G., Butterfield, E. C. 1970. The interaction of pronunciability and response pretraining on the paired-associate performance of third-grade children. *J. Exp. Child Psychol.* 9:265–71

138. Kellas, G., Butterfield, E. C. 1970. Response familiarization and the paired-associate performance of noninstitutionalized retarded and normal children. *Am. J. Ment. Defic.* 75:81–87

139. Kendler, H. H., Kendler, T. S. 1970. Developmental processes in discrimination learning. *Hum. Develop.* 13:65–89

140. Kendler, T. S., Kendler, H. H. 1970. An ontogeny of optional shift behavior. *Child Develop.* 41:1–27

141. Kessel, F. S. 1970. The role of syntax in children's comprehension from ages six to twelve. *Monogr. Soc. Res. Child Develop.* 35:No. 139. 95 pp.

142. King, W. L., Holt, J. R. 1970. Conjunctive and disjunctive rule learn-

ing as a function of age and forced verbalization. *J. Exp. Child Psychol.* 10:100–11

143. Klahr, D., Wallace, J. G. 1970. The development of serial completion strategies: an information processing analysis. *Brit. J. Psychol.* 61:243–57

144. Klahr, D., Wallace, J. G. 1970. An information processing analysis of some Piagetian experimental tasks. *Cogn. Psychol.* 1:358–87

145. Korner, A. F. 1970. Visual alertness in neonates: individual differences and their correlates. *Percept. Mot. Skills* 31:499–509

146. Korner, A. F., Thoman, E. B. 1970. Visual alertness in neonates as evoked by maternal care. *J. Exp. Child Psychol.* 10:67–78

147. Lange, G. W., Hultsch, D. F. 1970. The development of free classification and free recall in children. *Develop. Psychol.* 3:408

148. Larsen, G. Y., Flavell, J. H. 1970. Verbal factors in compensation performance and the relation between conservation and compensation. *Child Develop.* 41:965–77

149. Leskow, S., Smock, C. D. 1970. Developmental changes in problem-solving strategies: Permutation. *Develop. Psychol.* 2:412–22

150. Levin, J. R. 1970. Factors related to the sentence facilitation of paired-associate learning: Some characteristics of verbs. *J. Educ. Psychol.* 61:431–39

151. Lewis, M. 1970. Individual differences in the measurement of early cognitive growth. In *Exceptional Infant*, Vol. 2, ed. J. Hellmuth. Bainbridge Island, Wash.:Brunner, Mazel. In press

152. Lewis, M., Wilson, L. 1970. An infant stabilimeter. *J. Exp. Child Psychol.* 10:52–56

153. Lewis, M., Wilson, C. D., Ban, P., Baumel, M. H. 1970. An exploratory study of resting cardiac rate and variability from the last trimester of prenatal life through the first year of postnatal life. *Child Develop.* 41:799–811

154. Liberman, A. M., Cooper, F. S., Shankweiler, D. P., Studdert-Kennedy, M. 1967. Perception of the speech code. *Psychol. Rev.* 74:431–61

155. Lipsitt, L. P. 1966. Learning processes of human newborns. *Merrill-Palmer Quart.* 12:45–71

156. Lipsitt, L. P. 1970. Developmental psychology. In *Contemporary Scientific Psychology*, ed. A. R. Gilgen, 148–82. New York: Academic. 328 pp.

157. Lipsitt, L. P. 1970. The experiential origins of human behavior. See Ref. 102, 285–303

158. Liss, P. H., Haith, M. M. 1970. The speed of visual processing in children and adults: Effects of backward and forward masking. *Percept. Psychophys.* 8:396–98

159. Lister, C. M. 1970. The development of a concept of volume conservation in ESN children. *Brit. J. Educ. Psychol.* 40:55–64

160. Luria, A. R. 1959. The directive function of speech in development and dissolution. *Word* 16:341–52

161. MacDonald, W. S., Gallimore, R., MacDonald, G. 1970. Contingency counseling by school personnel: an economical model of intervention. *J. Appl. Behav. Anal.* 3:175–82

162. MacMillan, D. L. 1970. Facilitative effect of verbal mediation on paired-associate learning by EMR children. *Am. J. Ment. Defic.* 74:611–15

163. Ibid. Effect of input organization on recall of digits by EMR children, 692–96

164. Mackworth, N. H., Bruner, J. S. 1970. How adults and children search and recognize pictures. *Hum. Develop.* 13:149–77

165. Mallory, S. A. G. 1970. Effect of stimulus presentation on free recall of reflective and impulsive Mexican-American children. *J. Psychol.* 76:193–98

166. Mandelker, A. V., Brigham, T. A., Bushell, D. Jr. 1970. The effects of token procedures on a teacher's social contacts with her students. *J. Appl. Behav. Anal.* 3:169–74

167. Marshall, N. R., Hegrenes, J. R. 1970. Programmed communication therapy for autistic mentally retarded children. *J. Speech Hear. Dis.* 35:70–83

168. Mathews, M. E., Fozard, J. L. 1970. Age differences in judgments of recency for short sequences of pictures. *Develop. Psychol.* 3:208–17

169. McBane, B. M., Zeaman, D. 1970. Dimensional control of retardate memory. *Psychon. Sci.* 19:104–5

170. McCall, R. B., Kagan, J. 1970. Individual differences in the infant's distribution of attention to stimu-

lus discrepancy. *Develop. Psychol.* 2:90–98

171. McCall, R. B., Melson, W. H. 1970. Complexity, contour, and area as determinants of attention in infants. *Develop. Psychol.* 3:343–49

172. McGurk, H. 1970. The role of object orientation in infant perception. *J. Exp. Child Psychol.* 9:363–73

173. McNeill, D. 1970. *The Acquisition of Language.* New York: Harper & Row. 183 pp.

174. McNeill, D. 1970. The development of language. See Ref. 193, 1:1061–1161

175. Melson, W. H., McCall, R. B. 1970. Attentional responses of five-month girls to discrepant auditory stimuli. *Child Develop.* 41:1159–71

176. Messer, S. B., Kagan, J., McCall, R. B. 1970. Fixation time and tempo of play in infants. *Develop. Psychol.* 3:406

177. Miller, G. A. 1969. A psychological method to investigate verbal concepts. *J. Math. Psychol.* 6:169–91

178. Miller, G. A., McNeill, D. 1969. Psycholinguistics. In *The Handbook of Social Psychology,* ed. G. Lindzey, E. Aaronson, 3:666–794. Reading: Addison-Wesley. 2nd ed. 978 pp.

179. Miller, P. H., Kessel, F. S., Flavell, J. H. 1970. Thinking about people thinking about people thinking about . . . : A study of social cognitive development. *Child Develop.* 41:613–23

180. Miller, S. A., Shelton, J., Flavell, J. H. 1970. A test of Luria's hypotheses concerning the development of verbal self-regulation. *Child Develop.* 41:651–65

181. Milner, A. D., Bryant, P. E. 1968. Cross-modal matching by young children. *J. Comp. Physiol. Psychol.* 71:453–58

182. Miranda, S. B. 1970. Visual abilities and pattern preferences of premature infants and full-term neonates. *J. Exp. Child Psychol.* 10:189–205

183. Moffat, G. H., Motiff, J. P. 1970. Effectiveness of different verbal reinforcement combinations on a discrimination-reversal problem in children. *Psychon. Sci.* 21:351–53

184. Moffitt, A. R. 1969. *Speech perception by 20–24-week old infants.* Presented at *Soc. Res. Child Develop.,* Santa Monica, Calif.

185. Montgomery, G. T., Parton, D. A. 1970. Reinforcing effect of self-reward. *J. Exp. Psychol.* 84:273–76

186. Moran, L. J., Swartz, J. D. 1970. Longitudinal study of cognitive dictionaries from ages nine to seventeen. *Develop. Psychol.* 3:21–28

187. Moreau, T., Birch, H. G., Turkewitz, G. 1970. Ease of habituation to repeated auditory and somesthetic stimulation in the human newborn. *J. Exp. Child Psychol.* 9:183–207

188. Morin, R. E., Hoving, K. L., Konick, D. S. 1970. Are these two stimuli from the same set? Response times of children and adults with familiar and arbitrary sets. *J. Exp. Child Psychol.* 10:308–18

189. Ibid. Short-term memory in children: Keeping track of variables with few or many states, 181–88

190. Moss, H. A., Robson, K. S. 1970. The relation between the amount of time infants spend at various states and the development of visual behavior. *Child Develop.* 41:509–17

191. Murray, B., Campbell, D. 1970. Differences between olfactory thresholds in two sleep states in the newborn infant. *Psychon. Sci.* 18:313–14

192. Murray, F. B. 1970. Stimulus mode and the conservation of weight and number. *J. Educ. Psychol.* 61:287–91

193. Mussen, P., Ed. 1970. *Carmichael's Manual of Child Psychology.* New York: Wiley. Vol. 1, 1519 pp.; Vol. 2, 872 pp.

194. Neimark, E. D. 1970. Development of comprehension of logical connectives: Understanding of "or." *Psychon. Sci.* 21:217–19

195. Neimark, E. D. 1970. A preliminary search for formal operations structures. *J. Genet. Psychol.* 116:223–32

196. Neimark, E. D. 1970. Model for a thinking machine: An information-processing framework for the study of cognitive development. *Merrill-Palmer Quart.* 16:345–68

197. Neimark, E. D., Slotnick, N. S. 1970. Development of the understanding of logical connectives. *J. Educ. Psychol.* 61:451–60

198. Nisbett, R. E., Gurwitz, S. B. 1970. Weight, sex, and the eating behavior of human newborns. *J. Comp. Physiol. Psychol.* 73:245–53

199. Nolan, J. D., Pendarvis, L. V. 1970. Effects of variable-irrelevant dimensions on the discrimination reversal learning of nursery school children. *J. Exp. Psychol.* 86:428–33

200. Odom, R. D., Guzman, R. D. 1970.

Problem solving and the perceptual salience of variability and constancy: A developmental study. *J. Exp. Child Psychol.* 9:156–65

201. O'Reilly, E., Steger, J. A. 1970. Children's use of context in judgment of weight. *Child Develop.* 41:1095–1101

202. Overbeck, C., Schwartz, M. 1970. Training in conservation of weight. *J. Exp. Child Psychol.* 9:253–64

203. Packard, R. G. 1970. The control of "classroom attention": A group contingency for complex behavior. *J. Appl. Behav. Anal.* 3:13–28

204. Paivio, A. 1970. On the functional significance of imagery. *Psychol. Bull.* 73:385–92

205. Paivio, A., Yuille, J. C. 1966. Word abstractness and meaningfulness, and paired-associate learning in children. *J. Exp. Child Psychol.* 4:81–89

206. Palermo, D. S. 1970. Imagery in children's learning: Discussion. *Psychol. Bull.* 73:415–21

207. Pancratz, C. N., Cohen, L. B. 1970. Recovery of habituation in infants. *J. Exp. Child Psychol.* 9:208–16

208. Pascual-Leone, J. A. 1970. A mathematical model for the transition rule in Piaget's developmental stages. *Acta Psychol.* 32:301–45

209. Peisach, E., Wein, N. 1970. Relationship of conservation explanations to item difficulty. *J. Genet. Psychol.* 117:167–80

210. Peters, D. L. 1970. Verbal mediators and cue discrimination in the transition from nonconservation to conservation of number. *Child Develop.* 41:707–21

211. Prechtl, H. F. R. 1969. Brain and behavioural mechanisms in the human newborn infant. In *Brain and Early Behaviour*, ed. R. J. Robinson, 115–31. London: Academic. 374 pp.

212. Pressey, A. W., Sweeney, O. 1970. Age changes in the Poggendorff illusion as measured by a method of production. *Psychon. Sci.* 19:99–100

213. Reese, H. W. 1970. Imagery and contextual meaning. *Psychol. Bull.* 73: 404–14

214. Reese, H. W. 1970. Imagery in children's paired-associate learning. *J. Exp. Child Psychol.* 9:174–78

215. Reese, H. W., Lipsitt, L. P. 1970. *Experimental Child Psychology*. New York: Academic. 782 pp.

216. Rheingold, H. L., Eckerman, C. O. 1970. The infant separates himself from his mother. *Science* 168:78–83

217. Roberge, J. J. 1970. The effect of reversal of premises on children's deductive reasoning ability. *J. Psychol.* 75:53–58

218. Rohwer, W. D. Jr. 1970. Images and pictures in children's learning: Research results and educational implications. *Psychol. Bull.* 73:393–403

219. Rohwer, W. D. Jr., Suzuki, N. 1970. The learning of verbal strings as a function of connective form class. *J. Exp. Child Psychol.* 9:20–28

220. Roll, S. 1970. Reversibility training and stimulus desirability as factors in conservation of number. *Child Develop.* 41:501–7

221. Roodin, M. L., Gruen, G. E. 1970. The role of memory in making transitive judgments. *J. Exp. Child Psychol.* 10:264–75

222. Rosenthal, R., Jacobson, L. 1968. *Pygmalion in the Classroom: Teacher Expectation and Pupils' Intellectual Development*. New York: Holt, Rinehart & Winston. 240 pp.

223. Ryan, S. M., Hegion, A. G., Flavell, J. H. 1970. Nonverbal mnemonic mediation in preschool children. *Child Develop.* 41:539–50

224. Saltz, E., Sigel, I. E. 1967. Concept overdiscrimination in children. *J. Exp. Psychol.* 73:1–8

225. Salzinger, S., Salzinger, K., Patenaude, J. 1970. Effect of verbal response class on shift in the preschool child's judgment of length in response to an anchor stimulus. *Develop. Psychol.* 2:49–57

226. Sameroff, A. J. 1970. Changes in the nonnutritive sucking response to stimulation during infancy. *J. Exp. Child Psychol.* 10:112–19

227. Samuels, S. J. 1970. Recognition of flashed words by children. *Child Develop.* 41:1089–94

228. Saravo, A., Bagby, B., Haskins, K. 1970. Transfer effects in children's oddity learning. *Develop. Psychol.* 2:273–82

229. Scarr, S., Salapatek, P. 1970. Patterns of fear development during infancy. *Merrill-Palmer Quart.* 16:53–90

230. Schaeffer, B., Ellis, S. 1970. The effects of overlearning on children's nonreversal and reversal learning using unrelated stimuli. *J. Exp. Child Psychol.* 10:1–7

231. Schaffer, H. R., Parry, M. H. 1970. The effects of short-term familiarization on infants' perceptual-motor

coordination in a simultaneous discrimination situation. *Brit. J. Psychol.* 61:559–69

232. Scholnick, E. K. 1970. Inference and preference in children's conceptual performance. *Child Develop.* 41:449–59

233. Schroth, M. L. 1970. The effect of informative feedback on problem solving. *Child Develop.* 41:831–37

234. Schulman, C. A. 1970. Heart rate response habituation in high-risk premature infants. *Psychophysiology* 6:690–94

235. Schutte, R. C., Hopkins, B. L. 1970. The effects of teacher attention on following instructions in a kindergarten class. *J. Appl. Behav. Anal.* 3:117–22

236. Schwartz, A., Rosenberg, D., Brackbill, Y. 1970. Analysis of the components of social reinforcement of infant vocalization. *Psychon. Sci.* 20:323–25

237. Schwartz, M. M., Scholnick, E. K. 1970. Scalogram analysis of logical and perceptual components of conservation of discontinuous quantity. *Child Develop.* 41:695–705

238. Schwenn, E. A., Davidson, R. E. 1970. Syntactical mediation and transfer. *J. Educ. Psychol.* 61:440–44

239. Scott, M. S. 1970. Transfer in nursery school children between two relational tasks. *Develop. Psychol.* 3:145

240. Seggie, J. L. 1970. The utilization by children and adults of binary propositional thinking in concept learning. *J. Exp. Child Psychol.* 10:235–47

241. Shapiro, B. J., O'Brien, T. C. 1970. Logical thinking in children ages six through thirteen. *Child Develop.* 41:823–29

242. Shepard, W. O. 1970. Word association and definition in middle childhood. *Develop. Psychol.* 3:412

243. Shuell, T. J., Keppel, G. 1970. Learning ability and retention. *J. Educ. Psychol.* 61:59–65

244. Shultz, T. R., Zigler, E. 1970. Emotional concomitants of visual mastery in infants: the effects of stimulus movement on smiling and vocalizing. *J. Exp. Child Psychol.* 10:390–402

245. Sieber, J. E., Kameya, L. I., Paulson, F. L. 1970. Effect of memory support on the problem-solving ability of test-anxious children. *J. Educ. Psychol.* 61:159–68

246. Siegel, A. W., McBurney, D. H. 1970.

Estimation of line length and number: A developmental study. *J. Exp. Child Psychol.* 10:170–80

247. Simon, H. A., Kotovsky, K. 1963. Human acquisition of concepts for sequential patterns. *Psychol. Rev.* 70:534–46

248. Small, M. Y. 1970. Children's performance on an oddity problem as a function of the number of values on the relevant dimension. *J. Exp. Child Psychol.* 9:336–41

249. Smith, E. E., Larson, D. E. 1970. The verbal loop hypothesis and the effects of similarity on recognition and communication in adults and children. *J. Verb. Learn. Verb. Behav.* 9:237–42

250. Spence, J. T. 1970. The distracting effects of material reinforcers in the discrimination learning of lower- and middle-class children. *Child Develop.* 41:103–11

251. Sternberg, S. 1969. Memory-scanning: Mental process revealed by reaction-time experiments. *Am. Sci.* 57:421–57

252. Strauss, S., Langer, J. 1970. Operational thought inducement. *Child Develop.* 41:163–75

253. Sugimura, T. 1970. The effect of number of stimulus dimensions on the overtraining reversal effect in preschool children. *Jap. J. Psychol.* 41:124–30

254. Sullivan, F. J., Ross, B. M. 1970. What is learned in probability learning. *Develop. Psychol.* 2:58–65

255. Sulzbacher, S. I., Costello, J. M. 1970. A behavioral strategy for language training of a child with autistic behaviors. *J. Speech Hear. Dis.* 35:256–76

256. Taylor, J. A., Wales, R. J. 1970. A developmental study of form discrimination in pre-school children. *Quart. J. Exp. Psychol.* 22:720–34

257. Thoman, E. B., Turner, A. M., Leiderman, P. H., Barnett, C. R. 1970. Neonate-mother interaction: effects of parity on feeding behavior. *Child Develop.* 41:1103–11

258. Thomas, H. 1970. Psychological assessment instruments for use with human infants. *Merrill-Palmer Quart.* 16:179–223

259. Tighe, L. S., Tighe, T. J., Waterhouse, M. D., Vasta, R. 1970. Dimensional preference and discrimination shift learning in children. *Child Develop.* 41:737–46

260. Tighe, T. J., Tighe, L. S. 1970. Op-

tional shift behavior of children as a function of age, type of pretraining, and stimulus salience. *J. Exp. Child Psychol.* 9:272–85

261. Tramontana, J., Stimbert, V. E. 1970. Some techniques of behavior modification with an autistic child. *Psychol. Rep.* 27:498

262. Uzgiris, I. C., Hunt, J. McV. 1970. Attentional preference and experience: II. An exploratory longitudinal study of the effect of visual familiarity and responsiveness. *J. Genet. Psychol.* 117:109–21

263. Van den Daele, L. D. 1970. Modification of infant state by treatment in a rockerbox. *J. Psychol.* 74:161–65

264. Vanevery, H., Rosenberg, S. 1970. Semantics, phrase structure, and age as variables in sentence recall. *Child Develop.* 41:853–59

265. Waghorn, L., Sullivan, E. V. 1970. The exploration of transition rules in conservation of quantity (substance) using film mediated modeling. *Acta Psychol.* 32:65–80

266. Wahler, R. G., Sperling, K. A., Thomas, M. R., Teeter, N. C., Luper, H. L. 1970. The modification of childhood stuttering: some response-response relationships. *J. Exp. Child Psychol.* 9:411–28

267. Walen, S. R. 1970. Recall in children and adults. *J. Verb. Learn. Verb. Behav.* 9:94–98

268. Wasik, B. H. 1970. The application of Premack's generalization on reinforcement to the management of classroom behavior. *J. Exp. Child Psychol.* 10:33–43

269. Watt, W. C. 1970. Comments on the Brown and Hanlon paper. See Ref. 17, 55–78

270. Weiner, B., Goodnow, J. J. 1970. Motor activity: effects on memory. *Develop. Psychol.* 2:448

271. Whiteman, M., Peisach, E. 1970. Perceptual and sensorimotor supports for conservation tasks. *Develop. Psychol.* 2:247–56

272. Whitman, T. L., Mercurio, J. R., Caponigri, V. 1970. Development of social responses in two severely retarded children. *J. Appl. Behav. Anal.* 3:133–38

273. Wilcox, S. J., Baumeister, A. A. 1970. Transfer of verbal paired associates in mentally retarded individuals and normal children as a function of interlist similarity. *J. Exp. Child Psychol.* 10:277–86

274. Willerman, L., Broman, S. H., Fiedler, M. 1970. Infant development, preschool IQ, and social class. *Child Develop.* 41:69–77

275. Willerman, L., Naylor, A. F., Myrianthopoulos, N. C. 1970. Intellectual development of children from interracial matings. *Science* 170:1329–31

276. Williams, J. P., Blumberg, E. L., Williams, D. V. 1970. Cues used in visual word recognition. *J. Educ. Psychol.* 61:310–15

277. Wohlwill, J. F. 1968. Responses to class-inclusion questions for verbally and pictorially presented items. *Child Develop.* 39:449–65

278. Yeakel, M. H., Salisbury, L. L. Jr., Greer, S. L., Marcus, L. F. 1970. An appliance for autoinduced adverse control of self-injurious behavior. *J. Exp. Child Psychol.* 10:159–69

279. Yeh, J. C. Wu 1970. Transposition and transfer of absolute responding as functions of learning-set training and stimulus similarity. *J. Exp. Child Psychol.* 10:57–66

280. Zeaman, D., House, B. J. 1963. The role of attention in retardate discrimination learning. In *Handbook of Mental Deficiency*, ed. N. R. Ellis, 159–223. New York: McGraw. 722 pp.

281. Zigler, E. 1963. Social reinforcement, environmental conditions, and the child. *Am. J. Orthopsychiat.* 33:614–23

DERIVED MOTIVES[1,2]

176

Robert C. Bolles and Seward A. Moot

University of Washington, Seattle

With almost any instrumental (operant) response, there are three classes of experimental manipulations that can affect its strength: 1. Associative. A response can be strengthened directly by making reinforcement contingent upon its occurrence or weakened by withdrawing contingent reinforcement. 2. Primary motivation. Response strength can be affected by manipulating the state of the organism, e.g. its deprivation, weight loss, hormonal and other biochemical conditions. 3. Acquired motivation. Response strength can be manipulated by presenting the organism with cues which predict either reinforcement or the absence of reinforcement. When appropriate behavioral effects are obtained with this class of procedures we may attribute them to learned or acquired motivation, i.e. "derived motives," or, to use a better label, "incentive motivation." Incentive motivation can be interpreted in other terms, of course, but we will attempt to demonstrate here the utility of describing incentive effects in terms of predictive cues.

The first class of behavior determinants, the purely associative ones, were historically the first to be propounded, and for a time they were the only ones we had to explain behavior. Then primary motivation factors were discovered, and although most psychologists were hard put to say just what "basic drives" were, there was little doubt that their discovery would ultimately lead to the explanation of a variety of behavioral phenomena and would permit us to relate these phenomena to the underlying physiological substrate. This worthy program is active enough to warrant review every other year. But it soon became apparent that the first two classes of be-

[1] Preparation of this chapter was supported by Research Grant GB-8035 from the National Science Foundation. Our review of the literature goes through March 1971. Two important secondary sources had been awaited but had not appeared by that date. These are Black & Prokasy's edited volume on classical conditioning (Appleton-Century-Crofts) and Brush's edited book on aversive behavior (Academic Press). Both works contain many relevant and valuable chapters, but we have not cited anything still in press. Primary sources in our area have been enriched by a new Academic Press journal, *Learning and Motivation*, which began in 1970.

[2] The following abbreviations will be used in this chapter: CS (conditioned stimulus); DP (direct placement in goal box); PREE (partial reinforcement extinction effect); R_F (frustration reaction); r_F (fractional anticipatory frustration reaction); S+ (cue indicating presence of reward or punishment); S− (cue indicating absence of reward or punishment); S^0 (cue without consistent relation to reward or punishment; zero contingency cue); US (unconditioned stimulus).

havioral determinants could not account for all that was known about instrumental behavior. Hence a third class of factors was hypothesized which would have both associative and motivational properties. Explanatory concepts of this third class have now become such powerful conceptual tools that theorists from several quarters have begun to question the necessity of the second class (8) and even the first class (5, 41, 63, 64, 122). Thus, if incentive motivation can explain so much of response strength variation, then perhaps the concept of reinforcement itself is redundant.

While incentive motivation has come to play an increasingly important role in behavior theory, it has also undergone substantial conceptual revision in the last few years (2). The theory of incentive motivation has traditionally incorporated two basic assumptions. One is that it is mediated by more or less peripheral responses, such as autonomic arousal reactions, which can be experimentally manipulated independently of the response systems to which they give incentive motivation. In the appetitive case there is the fractional anticipatory goal response (r_G) which has been tentatively identified as salivation or incipient consummatory movements; in the aversive case there are heart rate and other components of the fear reaction. Recent reviewers have concluded, however, that the appetitive mediators are central rather than peripheral, and that the peripheral events that have been monitored do not mediate instrumental behavior (7, 11, 98, 107). The search for the aversive mediators has been, if anything, even more discouraging. The heart rate conditioning literature has become so complex that it now seems doubtful that heart rate, or any other autonomic response, can provide a direct index of whatever it is that motivates avoidance behavior (99).

The second assumption constantly in the background of incentive theory is that the mediating emotional responses which provide incentive motivation are classically conditioned. Environmental or response-produced cues are the CS, the reinforcer is the US, and the mere contiguity of the two is sufficient to condition the mediator to the CS. This basic assumption of traditional two-factor theory has been critically examined in a very important paper by Rescorla & Solomon (98). They conclude that the evidence does not justify the postulation of two kinds of learning processes, namely, those hypothesized by Thorndike and Pavlov. They suggest instead that there are two kinds of effective training procedures. One involves contingent reinforcement; the other one—the one that concerns us here—subjects the animal to an invariant sequence of events regardless of its behavior. As a result of this latter procedure, cues which were initially ineffective become important if they predict important consequences, such as shock or food. The motivational effects of these cues can then be demonstrated outside of the original situation. The motivation, or mediation, subsequently seen in an instrumental situation is attributed to an unspecified "central process." Thus, Rescorla & Solomon give us an alternative to classically conditioned r_Gs and r_Es. We merely have to conceive of a noncontingent procedure in which different cues can be given different predictive values.

It is only necessary to add that the instrumental situation itself provides ample opportunity for establishing predictive cues. Thus, once the animal starts running in an alley, start box cues become predictive of goal box food and should therefore exercise a motivating effect upon the running response. For the moment we can forget about conditioning r_G to goal box stimuli and the generalization of this response down the alley; we can look instead at the extent to which alley cues predict food. We will adopt this kind of orientation here, looking first at the behavioral effects of cues to food, then we will move on to other kinds of predictors.

CUES TO FOOD

In the ordinary instrumental learning situation the discriminative stimuli (i.e. the cues in the presence of which the animal responds) become cues which predict food if, and to the extent that, the animal responds. These cues, therefore, become incentive motivation factors in the broad sense that that term is being used here. Classically, incentive motivation has been more narrowly defined as increased response strength when the conditions of reinforcement are improved. The effects of amount, quality, delay, and percentage of reinforcement are all well known, and have been reviewed recently in this series (7), so we do not need to review them.

We may note that the experimental literature has become somewhat simpler and more meaningful in a few respects. Thus, it has been shown that amount of reinforcement can affect performance in a discrimination task (123), a finding which has not been generally reported in the past. Amount of reinforcement also affects choice behavior (78), rate but not temporal distribution of fixed-interval responding (75), and only the post-reinforcement pause in fixed-ratio responding (88).

Generally, however, the research in this area has become increasingly complex and difficult to interpret. The results obtained by shifting the amount of reinforcement have led to a multitude of new findings and several new interpretations (e.g. 7, 40). More complexity has been introduced by the discovery that these incentive effects depend upon the amount of training. For example, it has been found that with a small amount of training, resistance to extinction increases with amount of reinforcement, but that this relationship is reversed with large amounts of training (87, 120). Indeed, the introduction of resistance to extinction as a routine dependent variable has led to innumerable complexities, because extinction effects are frequently different from acquisition-performance effects. Moreover, behavior in different parts of a runway are likely to show different functional relationships. The state in which this work now exists may be illustrated by a recent study (23) which shows that rats shifted from one amount of reinforcement to another amount and then extinguished show a residual effect of the first amount, but that this effect is limited to animals given a large number of training trials, and shifted downward, and this interaction is evident only in speed of running near the goal and is seen only on the first day of extinction. Where do we go from there?

Perhaps some of the complexities in this area arise because cues to food really are important determinants of behavior strength, but the predictive value of such cues is lessened when the animal's behavior intervenes between the food cue and the food. For example, goal box cues are highly predictive of food because the certainty of approaching and eating food puts such cues into a nearly fixed relationship with food. But start box cues are less informative because the relationship between them and food depends upon when and how the animal responds. Suppose we introduce a cue to food (S+) which bears a fixed relationship to food. A tone paired with food in the goal box has been shown to have a positive motivating effect upon running to the box when it is introduced on test trials in the start box (69, 129).

Suppose the response requirement is relaxed further, so that S+ is noncontingent, i.e. it predicts food independently of the animal's behavior. One attempt has been made to replicate the results of the just-cited experiments by using a procedure in which S+ is established noncontingently and in a separate situation (12). In this study a facilitating effect of S+ was found in extinction but not in acquisition performance.

Suppose the response requirement is relaxed entirely so that the S+ does not even call for the animal to approach and eat food. Evidence that S+ still has a motivating effect is shown by increased general activity as determined by direct observation (6) or by an electronic tambour type of device attached to the animal's cage (130–132). Reliable and dramatic effects are reported.

It has been known for some time that cues which are noncontingent predictors of food in one situation will help maintain discriminated operant behavior in another situation (15, 76). Bower & Grusec (14) showed that such cues can also be used to establish discriminative control, or at least that they facilitate this learning. This technique has now been used by Trapold and his students in an extensive series of experiments (112–119). Because this work has been reviewed elsewhere (11) we describe only one representative experiment (119). Rats were first trained to bar press for food on continuous reinforcement and then, with the bar withdrawn, different groups of animals were presented with cues signaling either noncontingent food or no food. Following this the bar was replaced and pressing was brought under the discriminative control of one of the cues. Animals for which the new discriminative stimulus had previously been a S+ acquired the discrimination more rapidly than controls, and the controls acquired it more rapidly than animals for which the discriminative stimulus had previously signaled no food. Comparable effects are obtained under a wide variety of experimental conditions. Comparable effects have also been obtained with thirsty animals and water reinforcement (74, 80).

It is clear then that the discriminative control of an instrumental response can be more readily established if discriminative cues (S+ and S−) are previously associated with reinforcement and nonreinforcement in a noncontingent situation. It would be nice if there was immediate transfer from noncontingent to contingent situations. It would also be nice if discriminative control of an instrumental response could be as readily established using noncontingent procedures as it can using the ordinary contingent porcedures. In other words, it would be convenient if it made no difference how the cue value of the discriminative cues was established, but Trapold's results do not quite support this conclusion.

For one thing, the transfer from noncontingent training to contingent test situations is never immediate or complete. Rather, the effect of cues established noncontingently is merely to facilitate acquisition of the subsequent discrimination. In most instances there is no evidence of immediate transfer. Another difficulty is that the noncontingent experience appears to be much less efficient than the comparable response-contingent effects (117). It appears to be necessary to use a large number of noncontingent trials—150 or more is common practice—while incentive motivation can be established in a response-contingent context in a mere handful of trials. A further difficulty is that Trapold's data often do not indicate if facilitated discrimination is due to transfer of a $S+$ effect, a $S-$ effect, or both. Other studies strongly suggest that transfer is due primarily to a $S-$ effect. Trapold concludes, rightly we think, that although there is considerable evidence of transfer of discriminative control from noncontingent to contingent situations, it may be premature to attribute the transfer to common motivational mechanisms (56). One reason for Trapold's reluctance to give a motivational interpretation is that he was unable to show differential response strength to cues signaling different amounts of reward (56). But other experimenters using similar techniques have reported positive results (42).

Another interesting noncontingent effect is the more rapid acquisition of a fixed-interval scallop following noncontingent food presentation on the same fixed interval (114, 131). The control animals in this case were on a variable interval schedule and so presumably had the same generalized incentive motivation but no temporal cues to food. These findings suggest first that the scallop is a motivational phenomenon, and second that it is mediated by internal temporal cues that predict food.

A technique that has become quite popular is the use of direct placement (DP) into a goal box which may be either baited with food or empty. The effects of the DP procedure are then examined in an instrumental situation in which the animal runs an alley to the goal box. This procedure had its inception in the latent learning (or extinction) studies in which the rationale was to condition (or extinguish) r_G independently of the instrumental response it was supposed to motivate. Although this latent learning effect (i.e. an upward shift in performance following a positive DP) has never been convincingly shown, the corresponding latent extinction effect has been frequently found. This asymmetry poses an additional problem for the argument that noncontingent reward is an effective way to produce incentive motivation.

A variety of motivational effects of DP have been demonstrated. The technique has now produced parallels to most of the motivational effects that have been produced with traditional contingent procedures. We will simply note these reports: (a) some of the sequence effects of alternating reinforcement and nonreinforcement (43); (b) a goal gradient obtained on the first running trial following DP (105); (c) an amount-of-reinforcement effect (22); (d) a contrast effect following a shift in amount of reinforcement (113); (e) an overlearning extinction effect (87), (f) various partial reinforcement extinction effects (54, 71). In this last case, the resistance to extinction of an instrumental running response was increased following DP in an empty goal box. This effect, however, seems to occur only if a small number of such DPs is given (54, 79).

This array of findings lends considerable support to the position that discriminative and motivational control of instrumental responding can be established with cues whose predictive value is acquired noncontingently. We still have some interpretive problems, though. One is that while the animal is learning to appreciate relevant cues, it also is likely to be responding—perhaps making postural and observing responses—in the presence of S+. There is some indication that such unauthorized responses may play an essential part in the subsequent utilization of S+ in the instrumental situation. The evidence comes from a comparison of different kinds of DP techniques. Some animals are placed with their face directly over the food dish while others are placed a few inches away so that they must approach it. Whenever this comparison has been made (86, 87, 115) it has been discovered that the animals which do just a little running show much more transfer to the instrumental running situation than animals which could start immediately to eat. If it should turn out that such responses are necessary, then of course the point of the noncontingent procedure is lost. And so too would be the force of a theoretical interpretation which emphasizes the predictive value of cues. We would have to return to response mediation.

Virtually all of the S+ literature involves cues to food and is concerned with their effects on hunger-motivated baseline behavior. But there is one study which shows positive transfer of a food S+ to thirst-motivated behavior (55), and there is some evidence for some kind of transfer of food cues to aversive situations (19, 46, 83), but these latter effects are not consistent and not easy to explain. Overmier & Bull (83) have provided a most helpful analysis of the difficulties.

Finally, let us consider a different function of the S+. In addition to asking if it motivates, depresses, or has some other incentive effect upon ongoing behavior, we may ask if it can also serve a reinforcing function when applied to a prior response.[3] Will S+ reinforce a response upon which its

___

[3] The distinction between reinforcing and motivating effects is based on temporal considerations. Specifically, if a cue affects the strength of a response which precedes it, we will call that a reinforcing effect (or punishing effect, depending upon the direction of the change). If a cue affects the strength of an ongoing response, we call that a motivating or depressing effect, depending upon the direction of change. If a cue

occurrence is contingent? It has been reported (73) that informative (as opposed to redundant) noncontingent cues to food are secondary reinforcers in the sense that they do maintain instrumental responding in the absence of primary reinforcement.

Another demonstration of a reinforcement effect used pigeons required to choose between two responses, one of which led to cues signaling a schedule of reinforcement while the other led to uninformative cues and the same reinforcement schedule (16). The animals showed rapid acquisition of the first response. We suspect that this is what secondary reinforcement is all about. It is not that a secondary reinforcer is paired with food or contiguous with food, or that it sets the occasion for food-reinforced behavior, but rather that it is a cue to food. We suggest further that one of the reasons secondary reinforcement has often been so difficult to demonstrate in the absence of primary reinforcement is that under these conditions the S+ is no longer a cue for food, and as it loses its cue value it loses reinforcing value. This conjecture is consistent with Wike's recent theoretical analysis of secondary reinforcement (128).

CUES TO WITHDRAWAL OF FOOD

In some contexts it may make sense to talk about cues to the absence of food, but we will be concerned here with the situation in which there are prior cues to food and the experimental treatment involves withdrawing food. We will ask first what the motivational effects of this treatment are on ongoing behavior.

Let us begin with the contingent case, so that the question becomes what happens to the strength of a response that takes an animal into the presence of S− cues which signal the withdrawal of food? The answer is plainly that the behavior collapses. Indeed, we cannot establish a contingent food-withdrawal cue very effectively simply because the baseline response loses strength during the course of establishing the negative value of the cue. Translated into more conventional terms, if reward is withdrawn, instrumental behavior extinguishes, and presenting cues that signal the loss of reward can only accelerate extinction. Another procedure that at least keeps the animal moving is provided by the discrimination learning situation in which one set of cues (S+) predicts food while a contrasting set of cues (S−) predicts no food. Again, the result is well known: the animal ultimately comes to respond entirely to S+ while responding to S− extinguishes. In both cases we are tempted to attribute extinction to the negative incentive effect of S− (97). But whatever we may think of the role of S in the extinction process, contingent procedures do not give the experimenter very

---

affects the strength of a response which is likely to start occurring, we call it an associative effect. These distinctions are easy to make in principle but hard to defend in practice. Most experimental procedures make it difficult to distinguish motivational and associative effects; a free-operant procedure can make all such distinctions impossible.

effective means of establishing an S−, or for investigating its behavioral effects.

One way to establish a S− noncontingently is to use direct placement (DP) of an animal in a goal box to which it has already learned to run, but which is now empty. The empty goal box thus becomes a noncontingent S−, the de-motivating affect of which can be seen upon returning the animal to the runway. This is the well-known latent extinction experiment.

A further parallel with the contingent case is discrimination training following experience in a different situation in which S− and S+ are established noncontingently. We have already cited a series of experiments by Trapold and his students making use of this paradigm, and we noted that they have repeatedly demonstrated a behavior-depressing effect of S−. Thus noncontingent procedures can be used for effectively establishing S− as well as S+. The behavioral effects appear to be qualitatively the same with contingent and noncontingent methods, but, as noted before, noncontingent methods appear not to be as effective as contingent methods, in terms of how many trials are required.

Frustration theory has become enormously popular; everyone today is some kind of a frustration theorist. We will discuss recent developments here briefly, partly because it is so popular and partly because part of the theory (we think the best part) overlaps with predictive cue theory. As it has been advanced by Amsel (1), frustration theory rests upon three basic assumptions, which will be taken up in the next three paragraphs.

The first assumption is that the withdrawal of reinforcement produces an immediate frustration reaction (R_F) which has a motivating effect upon ongoing behavior because it is a source of generalized drive (D). Over the years other theorists have hypothesized that frustration induces various kinds of specific behavior, including displacement and aggression. Amsel's proposal is interesting because it is perhaps the last vestige of Hullian drive theory, and it is still with us. Recently, however, it has been roundly criticized by Staddon (111). Staddon suggests that the increased speed in the second alley of the double runway apparatus, following withdrawal of reward in the first goal box, is due to the removal of a normally present inhibitory factor, namely, the post-reinforcement pause. He cites comparable effects in free-operant situations, along with the failure of reduced amount of reward and delay of reward to produce the effect (32, 59, 106), and some anomalous effects with drugs (57). Right or wrong, Staddon makes a good argument.

The second assumption in Amsel's theory is that a fraction of the primary R_F reaction is classically conditionable, just as other motivational mediators have been assumed to be, and that the classically conditioned fractional anticipatory form of the frustration reaction (r_F) is inherently aversive. That is, an animal is assumed to withdraw from, or make other competing responses to, stimuli which elicit r_F. The resulting depression of behavior is claimed to account for extinction and various kinds of discrimination learning effects (1). We see nothing wrong in the recognition of these effects, but the proposed mechanism seems questionable in view of Rescorla & Solomon's recent analysis of similar mechanisms (98). Amsel's account also seems to be much less parsimonious and much less certain than the principle that cues to withdrawal of reward are aversive. We will return to this point shortly.

The third assumption of frustration theory is that there are also stimulus consequences of r_F (s_F) which can enter into the associative control of behavior. If an instrumental response is subsequently reinforced, then the aversiveness of r_F and its consequences may be overcome, so that ultimately s_F becomes a source of associative strength for the response. The partial reinforcement extinction effect (PREE) can then be explained, but the hypothetical mechanisms require that there be a substantial number of trials. One difficulty for the theory is that the PREE can be demonstrated after very few acquisition trials (26, 27, 70, 72). Brooks (18) has attempted to rescue frustration theory from the dilemma by putting more emphasis on primary frustration and less on conditioned frustration, but this strategy cannot help Amsel's formulation.

Meanwhile, Capaldi (24, 25) has suggested an alternative account of the PREE. Basic to Capaldi's approach is the hypothesis that animals retain some representation of the consequences of their last response. Thus, if the last run was not rewarded, that information is available in some form (Capaldi calls it S^N, but has not yet proposed a mechanism) at the time of the next run. Then if this next run is rewarded, S^N will tend to become a cue to food, a $S+$. According to Capaldi, the intertrial interval, the goal gradient, where reward is given, the number of trials—indeed most of the parameters implicated in a frustration analysis—become irrelevant; the chief consideration is the number of times in training that nonreward is followed by reward. A good deal of recent work (24, 25) supports Capaldi's account. Oversimplifying to summarize, Capaldi has stripped the frustration explanation of the PREE of its burdensome mediating response mechanisms and simply stressed the fact that if rats can remember what happened last time, that information can be an $S+$ for food provided the reinforcement schedule is arranged appropriately. It should be noted that the DP technique has become a routine part of this recent research. It may also be noted that this is a difficult way to investigate $S+$ and $S-$ effects.

We have discussed only the motivating effects of $S-$ upon appetitive behavior. It is certainly possible to introduce $S-$ into an aversive situation, but the few experimenters who have done this (19, 46) have obtained conflicting results and have advanced no compelling reasons for expecting any particular pattern of results. We can only conclude that $S-$, like $S+$, has some effects upon ongoing avoidance behavior, but we are not sure what these are.

Finally, we may ask about the reinforcing effects of $S-$. We may expect from what has been said before that a response which produced $S-$ would be reduced in strength. That is, just as nonreward itself is aversive and/or punishing, so also should be the cues to nonreward. However, recent reviews of the history of the problem (62, 121) indicated that to that time these effects had not been convincingly demonstrated. Then Daly (33) reported a study in which rats were trained to run for 15 pellets and then shifted either to 1 or 0 pellets. On these trials a light cue accompanied the reduced or omitted reward. The animals were then trained on a new response, a hurdle jump, to turn off the light or to get out of the box. Learning to escape both kinds of S− was found. Daly (34) then duplicated these findings using a noncontingent (DP) procedure. These results convince us of what we knew all along, namely, that the cues to withdrawal (and also reduction) of reward are aversive.

To summarize the effects of S+ and S− for food, we can say that S+ has positive incentive and reinforcing values, while S− has negative incentive and reinforcing values. Additionally, both S+ and S− can be given their respective values by the use of either contingent or noncontingent procedures, although the contingent procedure for S− is not practical for some applications. There remains the fundamental question of whether the motivational and reinforcing effects produced with contingent and noncontingent procedures are the same or merely resemble each other.

CUES TO SHOCK

It ought to be possible to establish cues to aversive events other than shock, but few researchers seem to have made the attempt. Perhaps the reason is that shock is almost necessary for obtaining avoidance behavior. Thus, although it is easy to demonstrate escape from loud noise, bright light, cold temperature, etc, there is no corresponding avoidance literature. Perhaps shock is uniquely able to condition fear. In any case, we are limited to shock if we want to survey the range of different aversive procedures that are now available, so we will discuss the effects of a cue (S+) that predicts shock.

Consider first the case where S+ occurs as a consequence of the animal's behavior. Suppose we let a rat run into a box and give shock there so that the box becomes a S+. What will happen to the rat's tendency to run into the box? We should expect this approach behavior to collapse just as soon as the box begins to be established as a S+. This thought experiment suggests that a S+ for shock is a potent depressor of behavior. But it also suggests some serious limitations of the contingent procedure for establishing a S+. First, we are restricted in how strongly the S+ can be established; it can only become strong enough to abolish the behavior. Second, we would like to be able to control its strength, rather than let the animal's behavior do it. Third, the behavior will probably be lost so rapidly that we will not have a useful sample of it. And fourth, inherent in any contingent procedure is the problem that the motivating, reinforcing, and purely associative properties of the cue are difficult to separate experimentally.

Suppose then we present cues in a predictive relationship to shock independently of an animal's behavior in one situation, and then introduce these cues in a new situation where there is an established baseline of free-operant avoidance behavior. What we find is a dramatic, highly reliable strengthening of the avoidance response (20, 45, 58, 90, 92). Increasing the duration and intensity of shock increases the effect (68, 81). LoLordo (65) has reported that a noncontingent cue to loud noise also facilitates shock avoidance in dogs.

Rescorla & Solomon (98) attribute this facilitation of avoidance to an increment of fear elicited by S+. This argument is based upon two assumptions: first, that the fear reaction is classically conditioned to S+ as a result of its having been paired with shock; and second, that avoidance behavior is motivated by momentary fear level. Rescorla & Solomon themselves cite ample evidence for questioning both of these assumptions. At this point it seems preferable to give a purely descriptive account of the phenomenon, so we conclude that a noncontingently established S+ facilitates ongoing avoidance behavior and that a contingently established S+ leads to rapid extinction of the response upon which it is contingent.

In contrast with our scanty knowledge of the effects of food cues on avoidance behavior, a good deal is known about the effects of shock cues on appetitive behavior. A noncontingent S+ for shock produces a dramatic depression of ongoing behavior. Notice that there are two variants of this procedure. The older one is called conditioned suppression or conditioned emotional response; here the S+ is noncontingent and is the only predictor of shock (the predictive value of S+ may be maintained in the test situation by maintaining that contingency, or shock may be withheld and S+ presented alone). In the newer procedure, discriminated punishment, shock is response-contingent but only in the presence of an S+. The S+ is therefore not totally predictive of shock because the baseline response must also occur. We might expect on that account that less suppression would be found under discriminated punishment conditions than under conditioned suppression conditions. But remember that if punishment does work to weaken a contingent response, then the response in the discriminated punishment situation will be weakened both by the depressing (negative incentive) effect of cues to shock and by the direct punishing effect of the shock itself. Therefore, we might expect discriminated punishment to be more suppressing than conditioned suppression. The latter result was reported by Church, Wooten & Matthews (30), which would appear to settle the old question of whether punishment really works, but another report from the same laboratory (31) seems to throw the question wide open again.

In the customary punishment situation, too, there is not only the possibility of direct punishment of ongoing behavior by shock, but in addition, suppression by whatever cues are available in the situation to predict shock. A number of diverse studies from both punishment and conditioned suppression contexts (3, 28, 53, 101) shows that ongoing behavior will be suppressed in the presence of whatever cues predict shock whether they be explicit exteroceptive stimuli, implicit temporal stimuli, or internal response-produced stimuli. Perhaps that is all there is to it. The recent book by Campbell & Church (21) provides a fine background for many of these problems.

Then there is the question of whether S+ has a negative reinforcing effect in addition to its negative motivational effects. It is commonly assumed that termination of the CS in the avoidance situation is reinforcing. This may be true, but we cannot immediately accept the fact that animals learn to avoid as evidence that CS termination is reinforcing. The avoidance situation incorporates a host of other contingencies, and there is good reason to believe that several of them contribute to the strength of the avoidance response; CS termination is just one of many possible sources of reinforcement. We will have more to say about this problem shortly. When simpler situations are used the results are equivocal. Thus, some experimenters (4, 13) have been unable to obtain acquisition of a new response that was attributable to contingent termination of a previously established S+, but Dinsmoor (39) obtained positive results, perhaps because he gave more extensive training. A related question is whether a response-contingent S+ has a punishing effect. Seligman (100) has shown that it does. It can be concluded, therefore, that a S+ for shock positively motivates avoidance behavior, depresses appetitive behavior, and probably punishes any prior response that produces it.

Cues to the Nonoccurrence of Shock

An avoidance learning situation presents the animal subject with a multitude of stimulus patterns which change over time as different events are programed by the experimenter and by the animal's behavior. Some of these stimulus patterns are objectively more dangerous than others. Thus, if the animal has not moved since the CS came on several seconds ago, there will be a dangerous pattern which is highly predictive of shock. If the animal makes the required response and turns off the CS, there will be a relatively safe pattern which in most avoidance learning experiments predicts the absence of shock, at least for a short period of time. We may think of the former pattern as a S+ which serves to motivate the avoidance response, but we may also think of the latter pattern as a cue to the absence of shock, a S−, which serves to reinforce the avoidance response. In short, any set of S− cues which predicts the nonoccurrence of shock can be expected, by analogy with the cases we have already discussed, to have behavioral properties approximately opposite to those of a S+ for shock. For example, just as a response-contingent S+ is self defeating in the sense that it abolishes the behavior that produces it, so we can predict that a response contingent S−, such as the safety cues produced by avoidance, would be self-perpetuating in the sense that it would maintain the behavior that produces it. It should be noted that the prediction of no shock only makes sense against a background of earlier or more rapidly acquired cues to shock.

There is considerable evidence that S− does reinforce avoidance (10, 17, 29, 60, 94, 104, 125), and at least one writer (11) has proposed that for a large class of avoidance behaviors S− is the principal or only source of reinforcement. We will not discuss the problem of avoidance per se, except to note that some new concept, such as S−, is needed because the current literature bristles with problems which traditional two-factor theory cannot handle (11, 52).

In conclusion, a concept of a contingent S− promises to be useful; its main behavioral property is that it reinforces the response upon which its occurrence is contingent.

Let us turn now to the effects of a S− which is established independently of the animal's behavior. A procedure for doing this has been described by Rescorla & LoLordo (96). Dogs were first trained on free-operant avoidance. Then they were restricted to one side of the apparatus and presented with a series of shocks and stimulus configurations such that one, S+, predicted shock while another, S−, reliably predicted a period free from shock. The animals were then returned to the avoidance schedule and the cues introduced as brief probes from time to time. The S− produced a short, pronounced, highly reliable depression of the baseline avoidance behavior. Rescorla & LoLordo investigated various Pavlovian methods of establishing S− in the noncontingent phase of the experiment: discriminative inhibition, conditioned inhibition, and contrast. The comparability of results suggests that the sufficient condition for establishing S− is simply that it predict a period of time in which shock does not occur. This basic effect has now been replicated with a variety of subjects, response requirements, and other experimental parameters (36, 45, 82, 90, 92, 126).

Some additional findings: if the noncontingent experience is given prior to avoidance training, the latter is impaired and the subsequent S− effect disappears (84); if the noncontingent experience is given in a different apparatus, sometimes the S− effect is still there (45), but sometimes it is gone (37); the effectiveness of S− increases with how long a period of safety it predicts (35, 124, 127). The S− (as well as S+) effects can be obtained with curarized dogs (110) and rats (38). It has also been reported that the effectiveness of S− increases as the contrasting density of shocks in S+ is increased (93, 95).

Another twist: Moscovitch & LoLordo (77) report that a cue accompanying the termination of shock also comes to serve as a S−. Moreover, its effectiveness as an S− is governed by its predictive relationship to the next shock rather than its contiguity with the last shock. Again we see that it is the predictive value of cues that matters. Furthermore, recent reviewers (66, 109) suggest that the latter operation, i.e. pairing a cue with the termination of shock, does not establish the cue as a positive reinforcer. In spite of some recent reports which claim to show such an effect, both reviews indicate that until various procedural artifacts and control problems are properly handled, the "relief" effect remains to be demonstrated. It is not clear why a relief effect is so difficult to find when the conceptually similar safety effect is so easy.

Many of the basic findings in the present review, as well as much of its conceptual framework, are obviously due to Rescorla. The idea that cues which predict important consequences to the animal have a motivating (or depressing) effect upon ongoing behavior was originally his. Rescorla has always tied this idea to another one, namely, that the inhibitory effects of S— are due to Pavlovian inhibitory processes (91). Now if such processes exist, and if they are based upon a negative contingency between a cue and shock (the cue predicts the nonoccurrence of shock), and if the more familiar excitatory conditioning processes are based upon positive contingencies, then it should follow that zero conditioning requires zero contingency between cue and consequence. At the same time, both cues and consequences must be presented to the animal in order to control for their possible nonassociative effects. Rescorla therefore concludes (91) that the proper control for demonstrating the effects of zero Pavlovian conditioning is a "truly random" procedure in which cues and consequences are scheduled randomly in time. Rescorla's research generally incorporates such control groups.

Other writers have argued that while the truly random control procedure may provide an appropriate control for some purposes, it may not be adequate for others. Kremer & Kamin (61) report a significant degree of suppression when the zero contingency cue (S^0) is introduced as a probe in a conditioned suppression test. The implication is that although a lot of excitation may be conditioned to S+, some is also conditioned to S^0. Seligman (101, 102) has shown that in situations where the animal has no way to predict shock and no way to control it, which is what the truly random procedure entails, there can be a very high level of generalized fear, stress, and a good opportunity for the animal to acquire "learned helplessness" (67, 85, 103). Thus, the truly random procedure can produce a special kind of animal subject that is not comparable to an animal having a comparable amount of predictable shock.

In some situations, notably those involving avoidance baseline behavior, the truly random procedure appears to produce the same behavior effects as the customary control procedures for sensitization and pseudoconditioning (45, 126). In this case the question of which control to use does not become an issue. The problem arises in those situations, typically those involving appetitive baseline behavior, in which a S^0 constitutes the only control reference, and in which we would like to have some assurance that S^0 has not become, functionally, a S+. A further problem in this connection is that while S+ can be established in a few trials, S— can only be established slowly (126, 127). Hence as a cue becomes established under truly random conditions it may initially be excitatory and become neutral only later, when the slower conditioned inhibition processes come into play.

The next question is what are the motivational effects of a S— for shock on ongoing appetitive behavior. There are two kinds of studies. In one the effects of S— are determined against an uncontrolled background of S+ cues. The basic procedure is to train animals to bar press for food and then suppress this behavior with the usual conditioned suppression technique. It has been found that the new S+ suppresses less, or comes to suppress more slowly, if it had been previously established as a S— than if it had been previously established as a S⁰ (47–51, 89, 95, 108). None of these studies provides an entirely satisfactory answer to the original question, however. Thus, a series of experiments by Hammond (47–49) finds the effect after so few noncontingent trials that we cannot attribute it to S—. Some experimenters (50, 51, 89) have established the S— and S⁰ during the course of testing so that the S— undoubtedly became a cue to food while S⁰ did not. The two remaining studies (95, 108) do not suffer from these problems, but alas, they do not answer the question we would like to solve—is a S— for shock "good" in its own right, or does it merely inhibit the effects of S+ so that the total situation is not so bad? All of these tests were conducted in a conditioned suppression situation in which the baseline response was either dropping in strength or was already markedly below the normal level. They also included only a S⁰ control. Hence we cannot tell if the S— provided additional motivation for bar pressing, merely reduced the motivational effect of situational cues that had been paired with shock, or indeed if its effect was nonmotivational.

Another kind of study bearing on this issue tests for S— effects while controlling the background of S+ cues. Grossen (44) trained rats to bar press for food and then for separate groups established noncontingent S—, S+, or S⁰ cues for shock either in the same apparatus with the bar retracted or in a quite different apparatus. These groups were then returned to the bar-press situation, and each group got its cue introduced as a probe. The S+ invariably suppressed responding, S⁰ always had minimal effect on behavior, and S— had no effects upon the animals for which it had been established in the different situation. Hence S— did not seem to have any direct motivating effect upon appetitive behavior. The S— did increase bar pressing for animals for which it had been established in the same situation, i.e. animals which showed depression of the response baseline. All of the results are therefore consistent with the idea that a S— for shock makes no direct contribution to the motivation of appetitive behavior, but it does inhibit the depressing effect of S+ cues that are present in the test situation. The baseline behavior is reinstated, presumably, because S— depresses the competing avoidance behavior motivated by these S+ cues. The only motivating effect of S— for which there is substantial evidence then is that it depresses avoidance behavior.

Is there a reinforcing effect of S—? We started this discussion of S— by implicating it in the reinforcement of avoidance behavior. The main virtue of this hypothesis is that the logical alternatives to it are so unattractive. It was once widely believed that avoidance was reinforced by termination of S+, but the arguments against this position are now overwhelming (9, 52).

Another possibility is that avoidance is maintained by the motivating effects of S+ cues such as the CS. The troubles with this proposal are, first, that it requires something like reinforcement to get avoidance started, and second, that it requires the S+ to remain an S+ even though when the animal is avoiding consistently such cues are no longer cues to shock. To break out of this tangle we need to show that a noncontingent S− can reinforce avoidance behavior.

Unfortunately, there are only two relevant experiments and neither of them provides as powerful a test of reinforcement as we would like to have. Weisman & Litner (125), using differential reinforcement for high or low rates of response, were able to train rats to turn on a tone that had been previously established as a S−. Thus, their study does not show acquisition of a new response but only altered control of an old response. A further peculiarity of Weisman & Litner's procedure is that their animals were concurrently avoiding shock with the same response on a free-operant schedule. Thus, test conditions were appropriate for establishing the tone as a contingent S−. Rescorla (94) trained dogs to avoid shock by pressing either of two panels. Noncontingent S− and S⁰ were then established and these cues then introduced as consequences of responding on one or the other panel in a continuation of the avoidance program. Although there was no increase in overall response rate, there was a shift in preference for the panel that produced the S−. Again we have the baseline problem: we do not know if behavior was being reinforced by S− or punished by S⁰. Conditions were again those that should have made both cues contingent S−. Again there was no acquisition of a new response, only altered control over an old response. Such adjustments in behavior can be viewed as motivational. Moreover, the changes in response strength in both of these studies were rather small relative to the high level of baseline responding. The reinforcement effects found here hardly look substantial enough to account for the rapid acquisition of avoidance behavior found in a variety of situations. We appear to have the same dilemma we discovered in the case of cues to food, namely that the expected effect of a noncontingent cue exists, but it seems to be a poor facsimile of the sturdy behavior effect we attribute to contingent cues.

FINAL REMARKS

We can think of Pavlovian and Thorndikian procedures as presenting the animal with the possibility of ordering the stimulus events in its environment. The cue and the consequence in Pavlov's situation form an invariant sequence. In the instrumental situation the sequence is less certain because the animal's behavior must intervene. But there are many reasons for believing that in both kinds of learning situation the cues which bear a predictive relationship to important consequences are critically important determinants of behavior. They motivate ongoing behavior and they reinforce (or punish, depending upon what they predict) prior responses. Just as a descriptive scheme, such an organization provides a useful way to summarize a variety of experimental effects and procedures. Recent findings indicate that there is little effective transfer of such cues across motivational systems, except for the singular case of cues to shock which suppress appetitive behavior. However, there appear to be a number of well-documented and robust effects that can be found within a given motivational system. Cues to food motivate ongoing appetitive behavior (incentive motivation) and reinforce prior behavior (secondary reinforcement), while cues to the withdrawal of food depress ongoing appetitive behavior (extinction) and negatively reinforce prior behavior. Similarly, cues to shock motivate ongoing avoidance behavior (avoidance and punishment) and punish or negatively reinforce prior behavior, while cues to the nonoccurrence of shock depress avoidance behavior and perhaps reinforce it also.

We have organized this review about what we take to be the current trends in behavior theory. We believe such trends will prove to be more important in the long run than particular findings in particular research areas. We have organized the review about the concept of predictive cues. Some day we will know why predictive cues are such important behavioral determinants. Some day we will understand the underlying mechanisms. Some day we will discover the behavioral, cognitive, and neurological correlates, too. But in the meantime it is good to have a base to work from which does not constrain us with the heritage of Pavlovian and Thorndikian response mechanisms.

We have also organized the review about the concepts of motivation and reinforcement. Some day we will understand why these two concepts now seem so strangely overlapping and redundant. A day may come when one or both of these concepts will be gone. But in the meantime, we have attributed as much to the concept of motivation as we thought we reasonably could.

LITERATURE CITED

1. Amsel, A. 1967. Partial reinforcement effects on vigor and persistence, advances in frustration theory derived from a variety of within-subjects experiments. In *The Psychology of Learning and Motivation*, ed. K. W. Spence, J. T. Spence, 1–65. New York: Academic. 381 pp.
2. Appley, M. H. 1970. Derived motives. *Ann. Rev. Psychol.* 21:485–518
3. Azrin, N. H. 1956. Some effects of two intermittent schedules of immediate and non-immediate punishment. *J. Psychol.* 42:3–21
4. Baron, A. 1959. Functions of CS and US in fear conditioning. *J. Comp. Physiol. Psychol.* 52:591–93
5. Bindra, D. 1969. A unified account of classical conditioning and operant training. In *Nebraska Symposium on Motivation*, ed. W. J. Arnold,

D. Levine, 1–37. Lincoln: Univ. of Nebraska Press. 334 pp.
6. Bindra, D., Palfai, T. 1967. Nature of positive and negative incentive-motivational effects in general activity. *J. Comp. Physiol. Psychol.* 63:288–97
7. Bitterman, M. E., Schoel, W. M. 1970. Instrumental learning in animals: parameters of reinforcement. *Ann. Rev. Psychol.* 21:367–436
8. Bolles, R. C. 1967. *Theory of Motivation.* New York: Harper & Row. 546 pp.
9. Bolles, R. C. 1970. Species-specific defense reactions and avoidance learning. *Psychol. Rev.* 77:32–48
10. Bolles, R. C., Grossen, N. E. 1969. Effects of an informational stimulus on the acquisition of avoidance behavior in rats. *J. Comp. Physiol. Psychol.* 68:90–99

11. Bolles, R. C., Grossen, N. E. 1970. The noncontingent manipulation of incentive motivation. In *Current Issues in Animal Learning*, ed. J. H. Reynierse, 143–74. Lincoln: Univ. of Nebraska Press. 394 pp.

12. Bolles, R. C., Grossen, N. E., Hargrave, G. E., Duncan, P. M. 1970. Effects of conditioned appetitive stimuli on the acquisition of a runway response. *J. Exp. Psychol.* 85:138–40

13. Bolles, R. C., Tuttle, A. V. 1967. A failure to reinforce instrumental behavior by terminating a stimulus that had been paired with shock. *Psychon. Sci.* 9:255–56

14. Bower, G., Grusec, T. 1964. Effect of prior Pavlovian discrimination training upon learning an operant discrimination. *J. Exp. Anal. Behav.* 7:401–4

15. Bower, G., Kaufman, R. 1963. Transfer across drives of the discriminative effect of a Pavlovian conditioned stimulus. *J. Exp. Anal. Behav.* 6:445–48

16. Bower, G., McLean, J., Meacham, J. 1966. Value of knowing when reinforcement is due. *J. Comp. Physiol. Psychol.* 62:183–92

17. Bower, G., Starr, R., Lazarovitz, L. 1965. Amount of response-produced change in the CS and avoidance learning. *J. Comp. Physiol. Psychol.* 59:13–17

18. Brooks, C. I. 1969. Frustration to nonreward following limited reward experience. *J. Exp. Psychol.* 81:403–5

19. Bull, J. A. III 1970. An interaction between appetitive Pavlovian CSs and instrumental avoidance responding. *Learn. Motiv.* 1:18–26

20. Bull, J. A. III, Overmier, J. B. 1968. Additive and subtractive properties of excitation and inhibition. *J. Comp. Physiol. Psychol.* 66:511–14

21. Campbell, B. A., Church, R. M., Eds. 1969. *Punishment and Aversive Behavior*. New York: Appleton-Century-Crofts. 597 pp.

22. Campbell, P. E., Fixsen, D. L., Phillips, E. 1969. The reinstatement effect: Amount of noncontingent reward in the runway. *Psychon. Sci.* 14:228–29

23. Capaldi, E. D. 1970. Effect of an initial reward magnitude on subsequent resistance to extinction. *J. Exp. Psychol.* 86:283–87

24. Capaldi, E. J. A sequential hypothesis

25. Capaldi, E. J. An analysis of the role of reward and reward magnitude in instrumental learning. See Ref. 11, 357–89

26. Capaldi, E. J., Capaldi, E. D., Kassover, K. 1970. An instrumental partial reinforcement effect in the absence of any overt instrumental acquisition training. *Psychon. Sci.* 21:145–47

27. Capaldi, E. J., Waters, R. W. 1970. Conditioning and nonconditioning of small-trial phenomena. *J. Exp. Psychol.* 84:518–22

28. Carman, J. B. 1970. Effects of some stimulus probes upon negatively accelerated conditioned suppression responding. *Psychon. Sci.* 21:13–15

29. Cassady, M., Cole, M., Hall, M., Williams, T. 1971. The role of the CS and its relationship to the CR in avoidance conditioning. *Learn. Motiv.* 2:12–25

30. Church, R. M., Wooten, C. L., Matthews, T. J. 1970. Discriminative punishment and the conditioned emotional response. *Learn. Motiv.* 1:1–17

31. Church, R. M., Wooten, C. L., Matthews, T. J. 1970. Contingency between response and aversive event in the rat. *J. Comp. Physiol. Psychol.* 72:476–85

32. Daly, H. B. 1968. Excitatory and inhibitory effects of complete and incomplete reward reduction in the double runway. *J. Exp. Psychol.* 76:430–38

33. Ibid 1969. Learning of a hurdle-jump response to escape cues paired with reduced reward or frustrative nonreward. 79:146–57

34. Ibid 1969. Is instrumental responding necessary for nonreward following reward to be frustrating. 80:186–87

35. Denny, M. R., Weisman, R. G. 1964. Avoidance behavior as a function of nonshock confinement. *J. Comp. Physiol. Psychol.* 58:252–57

36. Desiderato, O. 1969. Generalization of extinction and inhibition in control of avoidance responding by Pavlovian CSs in dogs. *J. Comp. Physiol. Psychol.* 68:611–16

37. Desiderato, O. 1970. Transituational control of avoidance responding by Pavlovian CSs. *Psychon. Sci.* 19:11–13

38. DiCara, L. V., Miller, N. E. 1968. Changes in heart rate instru-

mentally learned by curarized rats as avoidance responses. *J. Comp. Physiol. Psychol.* 65:8–12

39. Dinsmoor, J. A. 1962. Variable-interval escape from stimuli accompanied by shocks. *J. Exp. Anal. Behav.* 5:41–48

40. Dunham, P. J. 1968. Contrasted conditions of reinforcement: a selective critique. *Psychol. Bull.* 69:295–315

41. Estes, W. K. 1969. Reinforcement in human learning. In *Reinforcement and Behavior*, ed. J. T. Tapp, 63–94. New York: Academic. 429 pp.

42. Flaherty, C. F., Davenport, J. W. 1969. Effect of instrumental response pretraining in classical-to-instrumental transfer of a differential reward magnitude discrimination. *Psychon. Sci.* 15:235–37

43. Franchina, J. J., Sparling, D. L., Chlipala, R. 1971. Effects of patterns of goal-box placements on the subsequent acquisition of instrumental response patterning. *J. Comp. Physiol. Psychol.* 74:84–89

44. Grossen, N. E. 1971. Effect of aversive discriminative stimuli on appetitive behavior. *J. Exp. Psychol.* 88:90–94

45. Grossen, N. E., Bolles, R. C. 1968. Effects of a classical conditioned 'fear signal' and 'safety signal' on nondiscriminated avoidance behavior. *Psychon. Sci.* 11:321–22

46. Grossen, N. E., Kostansek, D. J., Bolles, R. C. 1969. Effects of appetitive discriminative stimuli on avoidance behavior. *J. Exp. Psychol.* 81:340–43

47. Hammond, L. J. 1966. Increased responding to CS⁻ in differential CER. *Psychon. Sci.* 5:337–38

48. Hammond, L. J. 1967. A traditional demonstration of the active properties of Pavlovian inhibition using differential CER. *Psychon. Sci.* 9:65–66

49. Hammond, L. J. 1968. Retardation of fear acquisition by a previously inhibitory CS. *J. Comp. Physiol. Psychol.* 66:756–59

50. Hammond, L. J., Daniel, R. 1970. Negative contingency discrimination: Differentiation by rats between safe and random stimuli. *J. Comp. Physiol. Psychol.* 72:486–91

51. Hendry, D. P. 1967. Conditioned inhibition of conditioned suppression. *Psychon. Sci.* 9:261–62

52. Herrnstein, R. J. 1969. Method and theory in the study of avoidance. *Psychol. Rev.* 76:49–69

53. Holmes, P. A., Jackson, D. E., Byrum, R. P. 1971. Acquisition and extinction of conditioned suppression under two training procedures. *Learn. Motiv.* 2:305–11

54. Homzie, M. J., Gohmann, T., Hall, S. W. Jr. 1971. Runway performance in rats as determined by the predictive value of intertrial reinforcements. *J. Comp. Physiol. Psychol.* 74:90–95

55. Hyde, T., Trapold, M. A. 1967. Enhanced stimulus generalization of a food reinforced response to a CS for water. *Psychon. Sci.* 9:513–14

56. Hyde, T. S., Trapold, M. A., Gross, D. M. 1969. The facilitative effect of a CS for reinforcement upon instrumental responding as a function of reinforcement magnitude: a test of incentive motivation theory. *J. Exp. Psychol.* 78:423–28

57. Ison, J. R., Daly, H. B., Glass, D. H. 1967. Amobarbital sodium and the effects of reward and nonreward in the Amsel double runway. *Psychol. Rep.* 20:491–96

58. Kamano, D. K. 1970. Types of Pavlovian conditioning procedures used in establishing CS⁺ and their effect upon avoidance behavior. *Psychon. Sci.* 18:63–64

59. Karabenich, S. A. 1969. Effects of reward increase and reduction in the double runway. *J. Exp. Psychol.* 82:79–87

60. Katzev, R. D., Hendersen, R. W. 1971. Effects of exteroceptive feedback stimuli on extinguishing avoidance responses in Fischer-344 rats. *J. Comp. Physiol. Psychol.* 74:66–74

61. Kremer, E. F., Kamin, L. J. 1971. The truly random control procedure: associative or nonassociative effects in rats. *J. Comp. Physiol. Psychol.* 74:203–10

62. Leitenberg, H. 1965. Is time-out from positive reinforcement an aversive event? A review of the experimental literature. *Psychol. Rev.* 64:428–41

63. Levine, M. 1971. Hypothesis theory and nonlearning despite ideal S-R-reinforcement contingencies. *Psychol. Rev.* 78:130–40

64. Logan, F. A. 1969. *Fundamentals of Learning and Motivation.* Dubuque: Brown. 226 pp.

65. LoLordo, V. M. 1967. Similarity of different conditioned fear responses based upon different aversive

events. *J. Comp. Physiol. Psychol.*
64:154–58

66. LoLordo, V. M. 1969. Positive conditioned reinforcement from aversive situations. *Psychol. Bull.* 72:193–203

67. Maier, S. F. 1970. Failure to escape traumatic electric shock: Incompatible skeletal-motor responses or learned helplessness? *Learn. Motiv.* 1:157–69

68. Martin, L. K., Riess, D. 1969. Effects of US intensity during previous discrete delay conditioning on conditioned acceleration during avoidance extinction. *J. Comp. Physiol. Psychol.* 69:196–200

69. Marx, M. H., Murphy, W. W. 1961. Resistance to extinction as a function of the presentation of a motivating cue in the startbox. *J. Comp. Physiol. Psychol.* 54:207–10

70. McCain, G. 1968. The partial reinforcement effect after minimal acquisition: single pellet reward. *Psychon. Sci.* 13:151–52

71. McCain, G., Baewaldt, J., Brown, E. R. 1969. Extinction following a small number of goal-box replacements. *Can. J. Psychol.* 23:274–84

72. McCain, G., Brown, E. R. 1967. Partial reinforcement with a small number of trials: two acquisition trials. *Psychon. Sci.* 7:265–66

73. McCausland, D. F., Menzer, G. W., Demsey, T. K., Birkimer, J. C. 1967. Response-contingent and noncontingent informative and redundant secondary reinforcers. *Psychon. Sci.* 8:293–94

74. Mellgren, R. L., Ost, J. W. P. 1969. Transfer of Pavlovian differential conditioning to an operant discrimination. *J. Comp. Physiol. Psychol.* 67:390–94

75. Meltzer, D., Brahlek, J. A. 1968. Quantity of reinforcement and fixed-interval performance. *Psychon. Sci.* 12:207–8

76. Morse, W. H., Skinner, B. F. 1958. Some factors involved in the stimulus control of behavior. *J. Exp. Anal. Behav.* 1:103–7

77. Moscovitch, A., LoLordo, V. M. 1968. Role of safety in the Pavlovian backward fear conditioning procedure. *J. Comp. Physiol. Psychol.* 66:673–78

78. Neuringer, A. J. 1967. Effects of reinforcement magnitude on choice and rate of responding. *J. Exp. Anal. Behav.* 10:417–24

79. North, A. J., Carl, D. F. 1968. Acquisition and extinction with rewarded goal box placements interpolated among training trials. *Psychon. Sci.* 13:7–8

80. Ost, J. W. P., Mellgren, R. L. 1970. Transfer from Pavlovian differential to discriminative conditioning: Effect of amount of Pavlovian conditioning. *J. Comp. Physiol. Psychol.* 71:487–91

81. Overmier, J. B. 1966. Differential transfer of control of avoidance responses as a function of UCS duration. *Psychon. Sci.* 5:25–26

82. Overmier, J. B., Bull, J. A. III 1969. On the independence of stimulus control of avoidance. *J. Exp. Psychol.* 79:464–67

83. Overmier, J. B., Bull, J. A. III. Influence of appetitive Pavlovian conditioning upon avoidance behavior. See Ref. 11, 117–41

84. Overmier, J. B., Leaf, R. C. 1965. Effects of discriminated Pavlovian fear conditioning upon previously or subsequently acquired avoidance responding. *J. Comp. Physiol. Psychol.* 60:213–17

85. Overmier, J. B., Seligman, M. E. P. 1967. Effects of inescapable shock upon subsequent escape and avoidance responding. *J. Comp. Physiol. Psychol.* 63:28–33

86. Patten, R. L., Rudy, J. W. 1966. The effect on choice behavior of cues paired with noncontingent reward. *Psychon. Sci.* 6:121–22

87. Porter, J. J., Madison, H. L., Swatek, A. J. 1971. Incentive and frustration effect of direct goal placements. *Psychon. Sci.* 22:314–16

88. Powell, R. W. 1969. The effect of reinforcement magnitude upon responding under fixed-ratio schedules. *J. Exp. Anal. Behav.* 12:605–8

89. Reberg, D., Black, A. H. 1969. Compound testing of individually conditioned stimuli as an index of excitatory and inhibitory properties. *Psychon. Sci.* 17:30–31

90. Rescorla, R. A. 1966. Predictability and number of pairings in Pavlovian fear conditioning. *Psychon. Sci.* 4:383–84

91. Rescorla, R. A. 1967. Pavlovian conditioning and its proper control procedures. *Psychol. Rev.* 74:71–80

92. Rescorla, R. A. 1968. Pavlovian conditioned fear in Sidman avoidance

learning. *J. Comp. Physiol. Psychol.* 65:55–60

93. Ibid 1968. Probability of shock in the presence and absence of CS in fear conditioning. 66:1–5

94. Ibid 1969. Establishment of a positive reinforcer through contrast with shock. 67:260–63

95. Ibid. Conditioned inhibition of fear resulting from negative CS-US contingencies, 504–9

96. Rescorla, R. A., LoLordo, V. M. 1965. Inhibition of avoidance behavior. *J. Comp. Physiol. Psychol.* 59:406–12

97. Rescorla, R. A., Skucy, J. C. 1969. Effect of response-independent reinforcers during extinction. *J. Comp. Physiol. Psychol.* 67:381–89

98. Rescorla, R. A., Solomon, R. L. 1967. Two-process learning theory: Relationships between Pavlovian conditioning and instrumental learning. *Psychol. Rev.* 74:151–82

99. Schneiderman, N. Determinants of heart rate classical conditioning. See Ref. 11, 85–116

100. Seligman, M. E. P. 1966. CS redundancy and secondary punishment. *J. Exp. Psychol.* 72:546–50

101. Seligman, M. E. P. 1968. Chronic fear produced by unpredictable electric shock. *J. Comp. Physiol. Psychol.* 66:402–11

102. Seligman, M. E. P. 1969. Control group and conditioning: A comment on operationism. *Psychol. Rev.* 76:484–91

103. Seligman, M. E. P., Maier, S. F. 1967. Failure to escape traumatic shock. *J. Exp. Psychol.* 74:1–9

104. Seligman, M. E. P., Meyer, B. 1970. Chronic fear and ulcers in rats as a function of the unpredictability of safety. *J. Comp. Physiol. Psychol.* 73:202–7

105. Senkowski, P. C., Porter, J. J., Madison, H. L. 1968. Goal gradient effect of incentive motivation (K) manipulated through prior goal box placements. *Psychon. Sci.* 11:29–30

106. Sgro, J. A., Glotfelty, R. A., Moore, B. D. 1970. Delay of reward in the double alleyway: A within-subjects versus between-groups comparison. *J. Exp. Psychol.* 84:82–87

107. Shapiro, M. M., Mugg, G. J., Ewald, W. 1971. Instrumental preferences and conditioned preparatory responses in dogs. *J. Comp. Physiol. Psychol.* 74:227–32

108. Siegel, P. S., Domjan, M. 1971. Backward conditioning as an inhibitory procedure. *Learn. Motiv.* 2:1–11

109. Siegel, P. S., Milby, J. B. 1969. Secondary reinforcement in relation to shock termination. *Psychol. Bull.* 72:146–56

110. Solomon, R. L., Turner, L. H. 1962. Discriminative classical conditioning in dogs paralyzed by curare can later control discriminative avoidance responses in the normal state. *Psychol. Rev.* 69:202–19

111. Staddon, J. E. R. 1970. Temporal effects of reinforcement: A negative "frustration" effect. *Learn. Motiv.* 1:227–47

112. Trapold, M. A. 1966. Reversal of an operant discrimination by noncontingent discrimination reversal training. *Psychon. Sci.* 4:247–48

113. Trapold, M. A., Bell, J. E. 1964. Effect of noncontingent exposure to shifts in reward magnitude on subsequent instrumental runway performance. *Psychol. Rep.* 15:679–84

114. Trapold, M. A., Carlson, J. G., Myers, W. A. 1965. The effect of noncontingent fixed- and variable-interval reinforcement upon subsequent acquisition of the fixed-interval scallop. *Psychon. Sci.* 2:261–62

115. Trapold, M. A., Doren, D. G. 1966. Effect of noncontingent partial reinforcement on the resistance to extinction of a runway response. *J. Exp. Psychol.* 71:429–31

116. Trapold, M. A., Fairlie, J. 1965. Transfer of discrimination learning based upon contingent and noncontingent training procedures. *Psychol. Rep.* 17:239–46

117. Trapold, M. A., Lawton, G. W., Dick, R. A., Gross, D. M. 1968. Transfer of training from differential classical to differential instrumental conditioning. *J. Exp. Psychol.* 76:568–73

118. Trapold, M. A., Odom, P. B. 1965. Transfer of an operant discrimination and a discrimination reversal between two manipulandum-defined responses. *Psychol. Rep.* 16: 1211–21

119. Trapold, M. A., Winokur, S. 1967. Transfer from classical conditioning and extinction to acquisition, extinction, and stimulus generalization of a positively reinforced instrumental response. *J. Exp. Psychol.* 73:517–25

120. Traupmann, K., Porter, J. J. 1968. Free-operant extinction as a func-

tion of magnitude of reward and number of reinforcements. *Psychon. Sci.* 11:31–32

121. Wagner, A. R. 1969. Frustrative non-reward: A variety of punishment. See Ref. 21, 157–81

122. Walker, E. L. 1969. Reinforcement—"the one ring." See Ref. 41, 47–62

123. Waller, T. G. 1968. Effects of magnitude of reward in spatial and brightness discrimination tasks. *J. Comp. Physiol. Psychol.* 66:122–27

124. Weisman, R. G., Denny, M. R., Zerbolio, D. J. Jr. 1967. Discrimination based on differential nonshock confinement in a shuttle box. *J. Comp. Physiol. Psychol.* 63:34–38

125. Weisman, R. G., Litner, J. S. 1969. Positive conditioned reinforcement of Sidman avoidance behavior in rats. *J. Comp. Physiol. Psychol.* 68:597–603

126. Ibid 1969. The course of Pavlovian excitation and inhibition of fear in rats. 69:667–72

127. Ibid 1971. Role of the intertrial interval in Pavlovian differential conditioning of fear in rats. 74:211–18

128. Wike, E. L. Secondary reinforcement: Some research and theoretical issues. See Ref. 5, 39–84

129. Williams, J. L. 1970. Effects of the duration of a secondary reinforcer on subsequent instrumental responses. *J. Exp. Psychol.* 83:348–51

130. Zamble, E. 1967. Classical conditioning of excitement anticipatory to food reward. *J. Comp. Physiol. Psychol.* 63:526–29

131. Ibid 1969. Conditioned motivational patterns in instrumental responding of rats. 69:536–53

132. Zamble, E., Kirkwood, C. R. 1969. Discriminative classical conditioning of excitement anticipatory to food reward. *Psychon. Sci.* 16:252–53

THE NEUROPHYSIOLOGY OF LEARNING

RICHARD F. THOMPSON, MICHAEL M. PATTERSON, AND TIMOTHY J. TEYLER[1]

Department of Psychobiology, University of California, Irvine

The two major research strategies currently employed in neurophysiolog-ical studies of learning are correlational measures of neural processes during the course of learning in relatively intact animals and the use of simplified model biological systems to study mechanisms underlying learning-like phenomena. Both approaches are treated here. There are many excellent reviews and texts on various aspects of the neural basis of learning (1, 49, 75, 94, 101, 109, 117, 124, 134, 148, 161, 177–179, 181, 185, 194–196, 203, 207, 223). Unnecessary duplication is avoided here by a specific focus on electro-physiological studies of learning, particularly those done in the past 5 years. Ablation, stimulation, and chemical approaches will be noted only as they relate to the major topic. We thank the hundreds of scientists who responded to our request and apologize to the many whose work could not be included. Limitations of space exclude extensive coverage of even the most important articles. Related groups of studies must be referenced by selected recent or representative papers. This extreme constraint results in serious distortions of historical and even intellectual perspective.

NEURAL CORRELATES OF LEARNING

Learning has no specific definition. However, particular forms or proce-dures of learning such as classical and instrumental conditioning have rather precise operational definitions involving use of appropriate control condi-tions. Herein lies a critical issue. With a few notable exceptions, studies of neurophysiological correlates of learning fall in two categories, those with no controls and those with inadequate controls. In all fairness, the problem of proper controls has not yet been entirely resolved at the behavioral level (83, 139, 190, 206) and is more complex when dealing with neural correlates.

[1] This work was supported by Research Scientist Award MH 06650 from the National Institute of Mental Health; research grant NS 07661 from the National Institutes of Health; and research grant MH 19314 from the National Institute of Mental Health (Thompson); postdoctoral fellowships MH 34398 (Patterson) and MH 35534 (Teyler) from the National Institute of Mental Health; and a grant from the Graduate Division of the University of California, Irvine. We wish to acknowledge the UCLA Brain Information Service for their very helpful literature search connected with the project and express our thanks to Nancy M. Kyle for her invaluable assis-tance in the preparation of this manuscript. The review of literature for this chapter was concluded in January 1971.

Even in a simple classical conditioning paradigm where CS-US pairings are known to yield behavioral conditioning, a given index of neural activity that develops in close correlation with conditioning need have no necessary relevance to the conditioning process unless it is also shown *not* to develop in unpaired controls. The yoked control is generally considered adequate for instrumental avoidance conditioning. However, it does not provide control for the classical conditioning component that probably occurs in the brain. The differential control (206) is inadequate when measuring brain correlates because CS+ and CS− activate differing subsets of neurons. Furthermore, a different kind of learning may occur to the CS− (190).

In terms of procedures, learning studies can be divided into those in which the animal's behavior has no influence on stimulus presentation and those where it does. The former include habituation and classical conditioning; the latter, instrumental conditioning, can include all other forms of learning. This categorization is adopted here. Mechanisms of habituation will be covered in our discussion of model systems to follow. Possible habituation in sensory systems, presently an area of great controversy, has been treated at length in recent reviews (26, 246) and will not be discussed here.

Two basic kinds of electrical information are being recorded from the nervous system in relation to learning: extracellular single (or multiple) spikes; and "slow" potentials, ranging in duration from a few milliseconds to many seconds or minutes. The distinction depends in part on recording techniques and instruments and may under some conditions be arbitrary. The precise mechanisms of generation of most "slow" potentials remain unknown or debatable. However, recent work by several groups, most notably Verzeano and associates (76, 112, 221, 224, 231, 232) indicates that if both unit discharges and slower potentials are recorded from the same microelectrode in grey matter, there are consistent and reliable relations between the two, the smaller spikes occurring maximally at periods of maximum negative slope of the slower potential, and progressively larger spikes occurring progressively later. It is probable that in many instances the slow potentials and units share some common generators, i.e. neurons. In any event, it becomes possible to infer one type of activity from the other. Prior to Morrell's (161) comprehensive review, most studies of neural correlates of learning emphasized slow "grossly" recorded activity: EEG or evoked potentials (EP). In the past decade single and multiple unit recording techniques have been used more widely.

Classical Conditioning

Brainstem and diencephalon.—Neural activity in sensory and nonspecific systems has been recorded during conditioning in a number of studies. Following Morrell's (162) demonstration of sensory-sensory single unit conditioning, Chow, Lindsley & Gollender (44) attempted to modify single unit responses in cat lateral geniculate nucleus (LGN): a light spot CS was paired

with a light flash to the opposite eye. Unit response pattern changes seemed
CS specific, not generalizing, in some units showed specificity of inter-
stimulus interval (ISI), and were apparently independent of small eye
movements often elicited by noxious stimuli in paralyzed cats (43).

Galin (79) used a global integration of slow and fast neural activity as
a measure from several cat brain loci. Activity increases to the noise-burst
CS during extensive habituation were followed by marked decreases in both
background and evoked activity during pairing. Changes were most evident
in the inferior colliculus (IC), cochlear nucleus (CN), and trapezoid body.
Unfortunately, overt CRs were not recorded and no sensitization controls
utilized. Buchwald, Halas & Schramm (25) recorded integrated multiple
unit responses in various sensory areas during cat leg flexion conditioning to
tone and shock. Activity increases to the CS were observed during pairing
in IC, medial geniculate (MG), and medial lemniscus. Again, no unpaired
controls were utilized. Continuing this line of investigation, Halas and collaborators (88) have studied integrated multiple unit activity in CN and IC,
and have generally found increases in activity during CR elaboration. Recently Halas, Beardsley & Sandlie (89) measured multiple unit activity in
several brain areas simultaneously. An unpaired control group was used.
Activity increases to pairing were generally seen first in the nonspecific
systems, later in the specific sensory pathways, and finally in the auditory
cortex. Unfortunately, the criterion for conditioning was simply the observation of a change in activity during the CS. The activity constituting such a
change was unclear and the probability of such a change at random not
specified.

Several studies have been concerned with single unit activity in various
"nonspecific" structures. Bureš & Burešová (34) have recently provided an
excellent review of this literature, which indicates that single unit activity
often changes with conditioning. As noted (34), such plastic changes do not
implicate these neurons in the conditioning process, but show only that they
may be elements either within or in the output of a changing system. Attempting better localization of reinforcement processes, Bureš & Burešová
(33) paired an acoustic CS with direct microelectrode stimulation of the
measured cell. Of 128 thalamic, reticular formation (RF), hippocampal, and
neocortical neurons subjected to conditioning, only 17 showed stable CRs.
However, 14 of 17 IC units tested showed CRs. The difference in cellular
behavioral plasticity between IC and "nonspecific" structures seemed to lie
in the much greater preconditioning responsiveness to the CS of cells in the
IC. It was postulated that modification of a preformed connection with the
CS may constitute the initial stages of the formation of new responses. No
controls were run to determine response specificity to pairing.

Buchwald, Halas & Schramm (25), measuring RF multiple unit activity,
found pairing increases and extinction decreases. Similarly, Ellison, Humphrey & Feeney (65) found that dog's RF activity peaked during salivary

CRs. Extending these findings, Halas, Beardsley & Sandlie (89) found that "nonspecific" system multiple unit activity increases occurred prior to specific sensory system activity increases and also before overt CRs.

Most neural activity studies in subcortical systems have thus reported changes presumed to correlate with conditioning. However, Imig & Weinberger (106) have shown increases in multiple unit activity with bodily movement alone in the rat auditory system. Because conditioning situations can cause increases in muscular activity, it may be important to determine neural activity changes to the UR occurring independent of learning. In addition, Hall & Mark (90) paired a click CS with unavoidable shock US to produce a conditioned fear response (CER). Reliable increases were seen in the late evoked potential (EP) components to the CS, which were not due to freezing or other movement artifacts. Evoked potentials to a click also increased when a photic CS was used. They concluded that EP increases during pairing in aversive situations may be due to nonspecific sensitization and fear. Also utilizing aversive conditioning, Khachaturian & Gluck (123) found increases in EPs to a continuously presented light flash during leg flexion CR elaboration to a tone CS. No increases occurred during unpaired trials. They concluded that EP increases were not CS specific but due to a tonic activation. The activation was quite possibly analogous to Mark and Hall's CER effect, especially in view of the long (9 sec) ISI utilized, which would be expected to produce rather poor conditioning, hence long-lasting "fear" activation. Such fear reactions may be an inseparable part of aversive conditioning processes, but not necessarily an essential aspect in the formation of the final CR. Thus, large EP changes may occur in most classical aversive paradigms but would be lost with CR elaboration. Such EP magnitude changes would reflect the situation's aversiveness more closely than the conditioning process. On the other hand, certain EP changes may reflect CR formation and could be observed in sufficiently nonaversive situations, or with the correct control procedures. Schwartz, Stewart & Sunenshine (204) appear to corroborate Hall & Mark (90). Conditioning rabbit eyelid response and measuring subcortical EPs, they found no consistent correlation between EP amplitudes and CR performance, although reliable EP changes were observed in all animals. It was argued that the conditioning situation was not highly aversive, hence the effects of fear sensitization on the EP were not pronounced and any remaining EP changes not related to learning.

Limbic system.—Measuring single unit activity, Bureš & Burešová (33) found hippocampal neurons showing plasticity to tone CS paired with direct cellular polarization. Travis & Sparks (228) reported unit activity changes in globus pallidus and cingulate cortex. Hippocampal theta rhythms have also been studied and are generally assumed to be associated with orienting responses and CR performance (5, 109, 110). Adey (7) has recently characterized the hippocampus as playing a leading role in the interactions of the neocortical, subcortical, and limbic systems, with a major influence on consolidation of memory and recall. Such control functions have also been postulated by Gray & Ball (84), and by Komisaruk (133), who found a perfect correlation between theta rhythm and rhythmic activities such as vibrissa twitch in rats. In addition, Pickenhain & Klingberg (172) noted increases in hippocampal theta just prior to CR performance. However, Ellison, Humphrey & Feeney (65) found no correlation between dog theta and salivation CRs, although a small theta burst immediately followed CS onset which may have represented "memory readout" (5, 7, 109, 110). These data are generally supportive of hypotheses giving the hippocampus a major role in either memory storage and "readout" or behavioral response control (7, 51, 195).

Cerebral cortex.—Adám and others (2), Shulgina (208), and Travis & Sparks (228) have all shown cortical unit activity changes assumed to be due to CS-US pairing. No control paradigms were utilized, and in the Travis & Sparks (228) study, unit activity was measured only after extensive training. Kopytova & Rabinovich (135) were apparently able to establish unit CRs with simple temporal conditioning, a feat not previously reported in the American literature. Rabinovich & Polonskaya (186) described unit UR inhibition with CR elaboration despite continued motor UR performance. O'Brien & Fox (163) observed units in cat postcruciate cortex, finding increases in cellular firing in both paired and unpaired groups with significantly more firing during pairing. In contrast to several previous single unit studies (e.g. 34, 208), only cells showing initial response to the CS showed altered response during training. In a second paper (164) they concluded that the factor most important in predicting unit firing conditioning was initial CS responsiveness. Vassilevsky & Trubatchev (230) looked at unit spikes in somatosensory area I in curarized rabbits. They distinguish three types of neurons based on receptive fields: type I, local fields; type II, diffuse fields; type III, no distinct fields. Two effects of pairing a tone, light, or tactile CS with skin shock US were noted in the type I and II neurons: increases in diffuse firing rate with short latency after 2–30 trials and specialized, longer latency high frequency trains after 5–50 pairings. No controls were noted. It is possible that the diffuse response was analagous to the Mark & Hall (90) effect.

In studying single unit conditioning with direct cellular polarization as the US, Bureš & Burešová (33) found several parietotemporal units apparently showing modified responses with pairing. Caviedes & Bureš (39) hypothesized that direct stimulation of many cells should produce conditioned changes more easily than single unit polarization, and they utilized direct stimulation of sensorimotor cortex or tegmentum as the US. Evoked auditory CS potentials changed significantly in the US areas during pairing, but pseudoconditioning controls revealed that response changes to the cortical US and some of those to the tegmental US were due to nonassociative processes. Possibly the tegmental stimulation acted as an aversive US, mimicking a peripherally presented stimulus.

Reviews of the earlier literature on cortical EEG and EP changes during conditioning are provided by John (108, 109) and Morrell (161). Barrett (14) has provided a theoretical model of cortical functions, and Pribram (180) has developed an important theory concerning frontal cortex operation. Generally, initial CS-US pairings seem to produce widespread cortical EEG desynchronization related to the orienting reflex (129, 132). During conditioning, desynchronization decreases, leaving activity at only the primary sensory and motor response areas. Asratyan (12) has recently detailed the results of several Russian experiments studying various components of sensory and motor area EPs. During conditioning, EP development was characterized by a marked secondary component increase, a finding shared by Kalyozhnyi (115), and occasionally a new surface-negative wave developed with CR elaboration.

Popova (176) correlated EP activity in auditory cortex with CR performance. In agreement with earlier findings (12, 108, 109, 161) auditory cortex EPs, initially widespread in distribution, generally increased in amplitude and duration, then decreased with CR formation. Fleming (74) measured visual cortex EP activity during hindleg flexion conditioning and also found general increases followed by decreases in EP amplitude with CR elaboration. Late EP components appeared to correlate best with actual CR performance. In contrast, Galin (79) saw only decreases in cortical activity during conditioning, while Schwartz, Stewart & Sunenshine (204) found no correlation between EP amplitude and conditioning. Arutyunov & Polyakova (10) concluded that later EP components which typically show changes during training were due mainly to poly- and bi-sensory units allowing modality interaction, while early nonchanging components were due to monosensory units.

Investigating EP and single unit activity in motor cortex, Woody and associates (245) conditioned cat eyeblink to glabella tap. In initial investigations, EP characteristics in the facial nucleus to the US alone (243) and during conditioning (244) were delineated. Coronal-precruciate motor cortex EPs were then correlated with eyelid and facial nucleus activity. During conditioning, cortical EPs increased in amplitude and were well correlated with overt CR elaboration. From microelectrode stimulation and recording it was concluded that information about the CS reached the motor cortex prior to conditioning but that pairing selectively changed those cells projecting to the conditioned muscle. Unfortunately, a backward control was utilized and run only after paired trials. Siegel & Domjan (210) have recently shown that backward pairing may produce profound behavioral inhibition, which would complicate interpretation of Woody's findings.

General cortical excitability during conditioning has been investigated by Weinberger and collaborators (237). Recruiting responses (RR) were attenuated during initial CS-alone presentations, indicating cortical arousal (238) increasing with habituation. During conditioning, RRs were again attenuated after motor CR elaboration A discriminative stimulus (DS) also produced some RR attenuation. It was hypothesized that both the CS and DS produced arousal until differential conditioning was established, when the DS caused arousal only until it was recognized. Also exploring cortical activity and conditioning, Asato & Fleming (11) gave conditioning trials to cats only during periods of cortical synchrony, which produced faster conditioning than if trials were presented randomly. They argued that during synchrony, neurons responsible for formation of connections were more readily available to process information. However, an additional control group receiving trials only during periods of desynchronization is needed.

Recently, several studies have correlated conditioning and slow cortical dc potential shifts (SP) (e.g. 42, 52, 107, 175, 188, 189, 218). Several excellent reviews summarize various aspects of the SP and its relationships to conditioning (200, 201). Chiorini (42) suggested that SP activity may be due to a "diffuse" system associated with arousal level, while a local system would have to do with specific response development. Rowland (200) suggested SP as the physical analog of Hull's reaction potential (105).

Conditioning has repeatedly been shown to produce SP changes in sensory and motor cortices of various animals (e.g. 42, 52, 107), and it was postulated that SP shifts might be a necessary if not sufficient component for CR formation (28). However, Irwin & Rebert (107) found that small quantities of reinforcement (milk) delivered directly to the mouth produced no motor cortex SP shift to either CS or US despite 70% jaw movement CRs. Large rewards produced motor cortex SP shifts to both stimuli. Pseudo-conditioning controls showed no nonassociative effects. Thus, a fairly high level of motivation, or large reward, seems necessary to produce SP shifts. As pointed out by Irwin & Rebert (107), SP shifts may not be good indicators of cortical state, at least within present measurement techniques. It seems reasonable to assume that the potentials presently measured are not necessary for CR formation.

Instrumental Conditioning

Brainstem and diencephalon.—In the following sections we are concerned with instrumental conditioning, e.g. the animal's behavior directly modifies the receipt of reinforcement. Sparks & Travis (214) have investigated unit responses in the mesencephalic reticular formation (MRF) of well-trained squirrel monkeys engaged in a visual discrimination task. They observed four types of unit responses: 1. phasic increases in firing to relevant cues; 2. tonic increases in firing to relevant cues; 3. increased firing at response onset; and 4. increased firing associated with head and neck movements. Adey (4) has observed phasic MRF EPs from cats in a choice situation and a reversal of that habit that declined with practice.

Stimulation of the IC or MRF can serve as the cue controlling two-way avoidance behavior in the cat. Interestingly, transfer of training is seen from an animal initially trained on collicular stimulation and switched to MFR stimulation, but little transfer is seen from an animal initially trained on

MRF stimulation and switched to IC stimulation (45). Halas and associates (89) studied cells in cats trained on an avoidance task and found conditioned changes first in the mesencephalic and thalamic reticular formations. In an intriguing study, memory enhancement was seen with post-trial MRF stimulation in rats, suggesting that the MRF is involved in memory consolidation (48). Similarly, Majkowski and associates (154) report that cats can learn an active avoidance following a two-stage MRF lesion, but that it requires three to five times more trials than a normal cat. In the rat, however, two-stage MRF lesions did not interfere markedly with the ability to learn a two-way avoidance task or a maze task, but they did result in hyperactivity (122). Evidence has shown that the midline thalamic RF is involved in learning, as a cold block of midline thalamus produces a deficit in avoidance and alternation behaviors in the rat and cat (211).

Travis and associates (227, 228) studied cells of the globus pallidus during auditory discrimination training in squirrel monkeys. The pallidal units responded with an initial increase, decrease, or complex response to the CS+ onset, while showing a pronounced inhibition at CS+ offset. The units responded poorly to CS−. They suggest that the initial response reflected changes in set or anticipation, while the post CS+ inhibitory response was related to goal-directed motor activities. They also reported finding putamen units in monkeys trained on a discrimination task that fired on CS+ only if the subject responded to the threshold stimulus (213), and they contend that the putamen and basal ganglia are areas of sensorimotor integration and control.

John & Morgades (112) recorded units and local EPs in the lateral geniculate body of cats trained to bar press for food. They found a marked similarity between the EPs averaged from the LGN and the visual cortex, especially on trials in which the correct response subsequently occurred. These observations support John's view that slow wave potentials of the central nervous system may convey unique and vital information (109).

Stimulation of midline thalamus can serve as a CS for appetitive instrumental conditioning, as shown by Sakhilina & Merzhanova (202). They also recorded the recruiting responses evoked by thalamic stimulation and found that a specific waveform pattern developed in the motor-sensory cortex of cat in the region of the forepaw used to obtain food reinforcement. This response was distinct from recruiting responses seen in other cortical areas and, surprisingly, remained stable following behavioral extinction.

The positive reinforcing properties of stimulating the lateral hypothalamus (LH), particularly the median forebrain bundle of the rat, are well known (e.g. 248). Lateral hypothalamic stimulation during Sidman avoidance training has produced response facilitation in cat (36, 155). An impairment of two-way avoidance and signaled wheel-turn avoidance has been produced with concurrent LH stimulation (36), an interpretation being that LH stimulation enhances the performance of a well-learned response, but retards new learning by enhancing whatever response tendencies were dominant at the time of stimulation (155).

Medial hypothalamic stimulation, which can give rise to aggression and flight behaviors (193), has been shown to result in impaired delayed responding, as have lesions of the medial hypothalamus (167). Similarly, posterior hypothalamic stimulation has been shown to result in CER suppression (156) and impaired brightness discriminations (147). A comparison of the rate and asymptotic performance level under conditioning wherein the US was either a peripheral stimulus or a medial hypothalamic stimulation produced identical results (192). Wyrwicka & Dobrzecka (247) and Wada and associates (235) provide evidence against a homogeneous diencephalic motivational system from experiments in which the transfer from one diencephalic area to another was seen to be poor.

It has been long established that prefrontal cortical lesions result in deficits in delayed response (35, 167, 197). Hypotheses regarding the nature of the deficit have included dysfunctions of (a) acquisition, (b) storage, or (c) retrieval. It has also been shown that the same deficits are produced by lesions of the dorsomedial thalamic nucleus which projects to and from the prefrontal area (78). Recently Fuster (78) recorded units in the dorsomedial thalamus during a delayed response task with monkeys. At rest, units fired in bursts that were synchronized with cortical EEG. At arousal, when cortical EEG was desynchronized, the thalamic units displayed irregular firing. When the stimulus object was baited there appeared cortical EEG arousal and irregular thalamic firing. During a one-minute delay the EEG reverted to synchronization, the thalamus displayed bursting with the addition of rapid trains of thalamic firing, which was interpreted as possibly representing short-term storage. In a related study, Olds (167) stimulated prefrontal cortex and dorsomedial thalamus during various phases of the delayed response task in monkeys. Maximal disruption occurred when either prefrontal cortex or dorsomedial thalamus were stimulated during the delay period, leading Olds to conclude that the stimulation disrupted memory processes. Zornetzer & McGaugh (249) also propose a role in memory storage for the frontal cortex of rats and mice.

Miller and colleagues have demonstrated that visceral responses can be brought under a considerable degree of instrumental control. This finding has challenged the traditional view of the response systems conditionable by instrumental (skeletal) and classical (autonomic) techniques. Miller and associates have done an elaborate series of studies demonstrating that the instrumental changes were not mediated by movement, respiration, or other skeletal variables. They initially used lateral hypothalamic stimulation as a reinforcer in training curarized rats to increase their heart rate, vasomotor tone, intestinal contractions, and urine formation. Recent work has emphasized that the effect is not an exclusive result of using brain stimulation as the reinforcement or utilizing paralyzed subjects. Thus, work of Miller and associates has shown that autonomically innervated visceral response systems can be modified by instrumental procedures, and that these responses are probably not due to the mediating effects of skeletal activity (50, 160).

Limbic system.—Low-level stimulation of the septum in rats increases performance in one- and two-way avoidance (37), and interferes with acquisition of a passive-avoidance habit (120). These findings suggest that septal stimulation has the same behavioral effect as does a septal lesion (64). The effect is generally attributed to (*a*) an increase in emotionality and irritability (205); (*b*) an inability to inhibit dominant responses (120); (*c*) an increase in activity or competing responses (37, 205); or (*d*) the action of a "motivational amplifier" (68).

The hippocampus has long been thought to be involved in some aspect of response inhibition (51, 125, 152, 198) or in short-term or working memory (3, 51, 66, 165, 199). Routtenberg and associates (199) recorded hippocampal EEG during one-trial passive avoidance training followed by electroconvulsive shock (ECS). They found no differences between experimental and footshock-alone groups 24 hr after training, but they recorded an abnormal hippocampal EEG 4 to 6 hr after ECS which was correlated with degree of behavioral seizure and amount of memory deficit, and they concluded that the function of the hippocampus is related to working memory. Adey (3) has done extensive computer analyses of hippocampal EEG and finds a theta response (dominant frequency, 6 Hz) as a trained animal reaches a behavioral choice point. Lopes da Silva & Kamp (152), on the other hand, report that theta can be seen when an animal is receiving reinforcement, and they interpret this as representing a state of tension reduction. That the theta is not produced by skeletal movement has been shown by Dalton (46) in work on paralyzed dogs. Routtenberg (198) has recorded theta to novel stimuli in rats; this theta has shown habituation and has increased with food and water deprivation only to be "blocked" by eating or drinking. He sees theta as related to attentional processes and the "theta block" to organized response patterns. Olds & Hirano (165) and John & Morgades (112) have recorded unit activity in the hippocampus of behaving cats and found that most units that increased their firing rate to a CS alone increase even more to paired CS plus US, and that units which decrease firing to CS alone were attentuated or reversed to the CS plus US (165). Olds & Hirano (165) suggested that emotional and transient memory abides in the hippocampus. Electrical stimulation of the hippocampus has provided a wide range of effects, from the lack of deleterious effects of a hippocampal seizure discharge during the acquisition of an avoidance habit (184), to the facilitation of a discriminated bar press with low intensity post-trial stimulation (66), to the establishment of a discriminated instrumental response with hippocampal stimulation as the CS+ or CS− (64). Lesions of the hippocampus produce results that are not entirely consistent. However, many workers agree that a common feature of the hippocampal syndrome is a tendency to maintain a dominant response in the face of altered stimulus conditions (51, 126, 182).

Several studies have been concerned with the role of the hippocampus and entorhinal cortex in learning an instrumental response. Holmes & Adey (97) observed similar waveforms from the two structures in cats trained to approach concealed food. Specifically, the frequency of the EEG changed during learning, extinction, and relearning. Frequency analyses of the hippocampal EEG showed alterations in power spectra during the acquisition of a light/dark discrimination (63), a delayed response, and a T-maze problem (4). Adey (4) has described phase shift alterations in the hippocampal EEG in similar paradigms. Impedance measures similarly are reported to show reliable changes corresponding to various stages of conditioning (4). Adey interprets these findings in terms of (a) a neural phase comparator mechanism (4), and (b) the role of glia in the modulation of impedance and their role in the physical chemical changes underlying memory storage (6).

Cerebral cortex.—Extending earlier studies of the operant conditioning of units by central or peripheral reinforcers (161, 166), Fetz and colleagues have conditioned units in the motor cortex of awake monkeys. The units were reinforced for increasing their "spontaneous" rates by peripheral food or liquid reinforcements. The units decreased their rate of firing during subsequent nonreinforcement and could not be altered by noncontingent reinforcement (72).

Fox & Rudell (77), in an operant paradigm with milk reinforcement, have altered the waveform of a late component of a visual cortex EP to light flash. The significance of this alteration is unclear in that Fehmi and associates (71) have demonstrated, in an ingenious perceptual masking experiment, that the initial components of the EP convey all or enough of the sensory information to allow an animal to perform correctly on a visual discrimination. They trained monkeys on a visual discrimination to tachistoscopically presented CS+ and CS−. A blanking flash following either CS by 20 msec resulted in retroactive masking and a consequent increase in discrimination errors. By delaying the blanking flash, a portion of the afferent volley to the CS was "allowed passage" to the brain. If the first 15 msec of the EP was unblanked, the monkey's performance on the discrimination was unimpaired, suggesting that the initial portion of the EP carries the critical information.

Evarts (67) trained monkeys on a specific motor movement to light stimulation and recorded from cells of origin of the pyramidal tract in monkeys. He observed that these pyramidal tract cells fired prior to the occurrence of an electromyogram and that the latency of unit firing predicted the latency of the motor responses. Interestingly, the shortest pyramidal tract cell activity to the light cue in Evart's study was about 100 msec, yet in the chloralosed (221) or unanesthetized cat, visual responses can be detected 30–35 msec following stimulation, suggesting that a considerable amount of neural processing is occurring during the "missing" 70 msec. Several studies employing unit or multiple unit responses during instrumental training provide some information in this regard. Halas and associates (89) placed recording microelectrodes in subcortical and cortical structures in cats undergoing classical and instrumental avoidance conditioning. It is noteworthy that the order of structures showing "conditioning" was: medullary reticular formation, mesencephalic reticular formation, midline thalamus, subcortical auditory nuclei, and auditory cortex. Halas and associates suggest that the reticular formation is involved in the gating of information to cortical areas. In monkeys, Sparks & Travis (213) found units differentially responsive (increase or decrease in firing rate) to the cue associated with unavoidable shock and the cue associated with the opportunity to eat. These responses were observed in about 20% of the cells sampled from limbic areas, basal ganglia, and sensorimotor cortex. Another 10% responded nondifferentially in a complex manner to both stimuli, Unfortunately, one cannot rule out the role of sensitization, since unpaired controls were not employed. They suggested that the differentially responsive units belong to populations of units conveying information about the stimulus, and the nonspecific responding units convey information regarding the time of reinforcement. They further speculated that sensorimotor cortical excitability was being modified by the reticular formation. Others have implicated reticular formation influences on the cortical EP (4, 154, 214).

Cortical EP studies have tended to corroborate earlier observations of widespread initial EEG arousal to meaningful stimuli and a decrease in EP magnitude to the CS as the response strength grows (161). Klingberg & Pickenhain (130) observed the effect in rats trained on signaled avoidance tasks and further noted a startle response to the CS alone, the magnitude of which was directly related to the magnitude of the EP. Kitai and associates (128) trained cats on an appetitive classical conditioning paradigm which we will treat as instrumental as the cat does not receive the reinforcer unless it makes an instrumental response. They measured the visual cortex EPs during various phases of training. The EP decreased after several CS-US pairings, not to return until extinction was instituted. Asratyan (12, 13), in a classical alimentary conditioning paradigm (which has instrumental features), observed that as the behavioral response grew the initial component of the CS-evoked EP declined in magnitude.

A potentially more fruitful line of research has focused on changes in EP waveform rather than magnitude, and an attempt has been made to relate these brain wave "pattern" changes to behavioral change and brain loci. John and associates (114) have recorded EPs from lateral geniculate nucleus and visual cortex on chronic cats trained to obtain food by responding to a light flickering at frequency A and to avoid shock by responding to a light flickering at frequency B. Specific brain wave patterns were associated with stimuli A and B. Following training, a flickering light intermediate to A and B was presented as a test for generalization. To this intermediate frequency the animal sometimes responded as if it were A and at other times as if it were B. Interestingly, when the animal responded to the intermediate frequency as if it were A, the brain response was very similar to the brain response to A itself, and similarly, to B (111). John and colleagues presented data recorded from many brain areas showing similar waveforms which he interprets as supporting his unit comparator hypothesis referred to earlier

(113). The implications of these phenomena have been set forth in a stimulating book by John (109). Other studies as well have observed specific waveforms to the cues used in visual and auditory discriminations (12, 71, 130, 217).

Psatta and associates (183) report development of specific EP patterns in cats trained under various dosages of the anesthetic chloralose and tested when undrugged. The patterns of brain activity were most visible in the occipital cortex and reticular formation. Unfortunately, adequate conditioning controls were not used to rule out the possibility of sensitization.

On a different level of plastic change in the nervous system, Hirsch & Spinelli (96) raised cats from birth with one eye viewing only vertical lines and the other viewing only horizontal lines. At 10–12 weeks of age the visual cortical cells were tested for visual field orientations. The results are intriguing; the eye exposed to horizontal lines had only horizontal visual field cortical cells and the eye viewing vertical lines had only vertical visual fields. This, according to Hirsch & Spinelli, suggests that functional neuronal connections can be selectively and predictably modified by chronic environmental stimuli. For a general discussion of CNS change to chronically altered environmental conditions see Rosenzweig & Leiman (195).

Summary

Several conclusions regarding brain activity during learning can be drawn. During the initial phases of learning, the cortex is widely activated by the training stimuli. Later in training, cortical activity subsides to the primary sensory cortex associated with the stimuli and the motor cortex associated with the response. Such redistribution of cortical activity is usually preceded by activity increases in various brainstem "nonspecific" systems. Brain activity changes usually start prior to the appearance of the overt response. During conditioning, marked EP waveform similarities appear in many brain regions. The secondary EP components may reflect associative processes more closely than the primary components. However, in aversive situations, much of the change in EP activity may reflect nonspecific fear rather than learning. Similarly, slow potential shifts that often accompany learning may reflect motivational state rather than associative process. In addition, throughout the brain, behavior of some single cells can be modified, although successful conditioning in most units necessitates initial responsiveness to both conditioning stimuli.

Ten years have passed since Morrell's (161) review of the neurophysiology of learning. We had hoped that the large amount of research in the area over those years would allow us to compile a behavioral stereotaxic atlas of brain activity accompanying learning. This has not been possible. In fact, we still have only the barest outline of the neural correlates of learning. In our opinion, this dearth of data and paucity of substance is due mainly to the failure to utilize the necessary behavioral controls and well-delineated behavioral paradigms. Elegant neurophysiological recording techniques can tell us little about the neural basis of learning unless accompanied by correspondingly sophisticated behavioral techniques. The systematic investigation of brain activity accompanying learning necessitates the consistent use of behavioral systems in which the behavior can be accurately measured. Control procedures must be constantly utilized to rule out nonassociative activity in neural responses. The lack of such activity in overt behavior simply does not preclude its occurrence at neural levels.

We feel that a strong plea must be made for the adoption of a few behavioral situations in which to examine brain correlates of learning. Such standard preparations might include the following features: (a) one-session acquisition and extinction; (b) clearly and precisely quantifiable overt behavior; (c) some knowledge of the parametric features of the conditioning paradigm; (d) some knowledge of the neural elements involved in the response; and (e) adequate control procedures. A very few recent studies seem to be attempts at this type of analysis (25, 88, 89, 109, 165, 243–245). Hopefully they represent the beginnings of systematic inquiries.

<h3 style="text-align:center">BIOLOGICAL MODELS OF LEARNING</h3>

Simplified "model" biological systems, of great value in analysis of basic neural processes, are currently being used to study neural mechanisms of learning. There are at least three fundamental problems: 1. The behavioral properties of plasticity in the model system must correspond to those of intact higher vertebrates. Fortunately, simpler forms of learning such as habituation and classical and instrumental conditioning do seem to have common operational definitions and basic properties, at least for a wide range of vertebrates (18, 19, 127, 226). 2. Neural mechanisms underlying plasticity in the model system must be amenable to some degree of analysis. Thus, demonstrations of learning in even pieces of insects are of little value if the mechanisms are embedded in unknowable neuropile. 3. Mechanisms underlying plasticity in a model system must also be shown to hold for learning in the intact higher organism. This fundamental problem of inference is the greatest weakness of the model systems approach—there is no guarantee that the models will yield anything but interesting games quite irrelevant to an understanding of learning in higher vertebrates.

Habituation

All organisms and model systems show some forms of response decrement and/or increment to repeated stimulation. The extent to which such changes are habituation and sensitization has been determined in part by comparison with the parametric features of behavioral response habituation in higher vertebrates, e.g. decrement, spontaneous recovery, "dishabituation" or sensitization, etc (226). Two model systems, *Aplysia* and mammalian spinal cord, have been shown to exhibit most or all of these features.

Sympathetic ganglia and neuromuscular junctions of vertebrates exhibit

both increments (potentiation) and decrements (depression) following repeated activation, depending upon stimulus conditions; both appear to be
pre- rather than postsynaptic effects (116). Although these elementary forms
of plasticity do not correspond to habituation and sensitization, the underlying mechanisms may be related. A slow decremental analog of habituation
has been reported for the neuromuscular junctions between motor giant
axon and fast flexor muscle fibers in crayfish (21, 22). This slow decrement
differs from behavioral habituation in that it does not show potentiation of
habituation, is not proportional to stimulus frequency but occurs maximally
over a limited frequency range (1/min), and does not appear to show below-
zero habituation. It corresponds only in showing decrement, spontaneous
recovery, and "dishabituation." Although this cannot be considered a
legitimate example of habituation, the mechanism, apparently an alteration
in properties of the presynaptic terminals, may be of general significance.
Behavioral response habituation in crayfish cannot be accounted for by this
mechanism but involves decrements in central polysynaptic pathways (137,
138).

The monosynaptic reflex formed by IA fibers on motoneurons of mammalian spinal cord exhibits increments [post-tetanic potentiation (150)] and
decrements [low frequency depression (151)] analogous to sensitization and
habituation which appear due to presynaptic effects. Plasticity of the monosynaptic system resembles habituation in most properties, differing only in
time course and in not showing potentiation of habituation, below-zero
habituation, and of course generalization of habituation.

The giant synapse of the squid stellate ganglion also shows plasticity to
repeated stimulation if activated by a series of brief trains (102). It exhibits
decrement, spontaneous recovery, and the frequency effect, but does not
show "dishabituation" or other parametric features of habituation. The decrement appears to be the result of pre- rather than postsynaptic factors.

Aplysia has been a most productive model for analysis of habituation.
The phenomenon was described in earlier work by Tauc, Bruner & Kardel
(24, 119) and has been studied extensively by Kandel and associates (38
140, 173) and by Bruner & Tauc (23) and Bruner & Kehoe (21). Kandel's
group utilized the gill withdrawal reflex to tactile stimulation of the siphon
or mantle shelf mediated by identified motor neurons in the abdominal
ganglion. The behavioral response exhibits most of the characteristics of
habituation, although potentiation, generalization, and below-zero effects
were not prominant. The response plasticity was shown to be central and
appeared to be mediated by changes in amplitudes of excitatory synaptic
potentials of the gill motoneurons. One of these, L7, known to be mono-
synaptically activated by the siphon afferent, was studied in isolation. It
showed a profound low frequency depression to repeated monosynaptic
activation. This decrease was not due to gross changes in motor neuron input
resistance tested by intracellular hyperpolarization. Dishabituation from
stimulation of the head produced excitatory input to the motor neuron and

heterosynaptic facilitation (118) of the monosynaptic input, presumably via a pathway to the presynaptic terminals. Bruner & Kehoe (21) described habituation of a response mediated by the head ganglion—tentacular contraction to electrical or mechanical stimulation of the head. Essentially all parameters of habituation were found to occur for this polysynaptic system. When unitary, presumably monosynaptic, activation of motor neurons was examined, generalization did not occur, but potentiation of habituation was evident, and "dishabituation" could be obtained by an increased stimulus frequency to the habituated input.

A most interesting example of peripheral habituation has been described for *Aplysia* by Peretz (170). Following complete removal of the central nervous system, the gill withdrawal reflex still occurs and exhibits habituation, spontaneous recovery, frequency effect, potentiation of habituation, and dishabituation. It appears that at least three neural elements, sensory neurons, interneurons, and motor neurons, are present peripherally in this preparation. Finally, Sokolov and associates (212) report an interesting and persistent internal effect of repeated intracellular stimulation on responsiveness of a mollusk giant neuron.

Virtually all polysynaptic reflexes show habituation. Hindlimb flexion reflex of spinal mammal has been the most widely studied model system (87, 95, 117, 225, 226). We emphasize recent and analytic studies here. Thompson & Spencer (226) enumerated the nine "criteria" of habituation and demonstrated that habituation of the hindlimb flexion reflex of acute spinal cat exhibited all nine. Farel (69) recently demonstrated that hindlimb flexion of chronic spinal frog shows some of these features and exhibits prolonged habituation. Analytic studies in cat spinal cord have shown that the decrement in flexor response to repeated cutaneous stimulation does not involve alterations at cutaneous receptors, afferent volley, and muscle or neuromuscular junction or peripheral motor nerves. The gamma system does not play an essential role (216, 226). The decrement is a central process (see also 70). Alterations in motoneuron appear not to be involved (216, 240). Both behavioral and neural evidence (87, 216, 226) indicate that "dishabituation" is a superimposed sensitization process rather than a disruption of habituation. Alterations in excitability of afferent terminals, as would occur during presynaptic inhibition or excitation, have recently been ruled out, at least for spinal cutaneous afferents (86). Consequently, habituation and sensitization must involve interneuron mechanisms of plasticity (85, 236, 241). Recent evidence indicates that under appropriate conditions two categories of "plastic" interneurons can be distinguished, one ("type H"), having short latencies exhibits only habituation, and the other ("type S") shows sensitization and varying degrees of habituation (87).

There are at least three major theories of spinal habituation in terms of known synaptic processes: presynaptic inhibition acting on primary afferent terminals (93); postsynaptic inhibition of interneurons (236; 241); and "synaptic depression" (87, 99, 100, 216, 226). The first has been ruled out

(86). There is no direct evidence to distinguish the latter two. Postsynaptic inhibition of interneurons is postulated to develop via post-tetanic potentiation of other interneurons leading to increased tonic postsynaptic inhibition on interneurons of the flexor path (236, 241). The only evidence favoring this view concerns asymmetry of generalization of habituation of interneurons from stimulation of cut cutaneous nerve and skin (241). Although much has been made of this asymmetry (236), it is based on data from only three interneurons (241). Recent and more extensive studies (87) have demonstrated that generalization of habituation of interneurons activated by cut cutaneous nerve and skin tends, in fact, to be symmetrical. Consequently there is no evidence for postsynaptic inhibition. Further, there are *no* instances where an interneuron increases its activity during the development of pronounced response habituation, as required by the hypothesis. Synaptic depression is consistent with all known properties of flexor habituation. Similarly, sensitization could result from low frequency polysynaptic post-tetanic potentiation. "Low frequency potentiation" has been reported for hippocampal pyramidal cells (8) and monosynaptic connections of pyramidal tract fibers on spinal motoneurons (171). In recent reviews (87, 225) a wide range of behavioral and neural evidence was shown to be consistent with a "dual-process" view that the behavioral response to repeated stimulation is the net outcome of two inferred processes of habituation and sensitization for systems ranging from *Aplysia* ganglion to intact man (see also 222, 229, 239).

Classical Conditioning

Spinal conditioning has been one of the most controversial topics in psychology. There is no necessary reason why the spinal cord should not exhibit plasticity. Anatomically it is not a simple neural structure, but contains a very complex "isodendritic core" of interneurons resembling that of higher brain structures (187). In the original demonstration of spinal conditioning reported by Shurrager & Culler (209), the control necessary to demonstrate classical conditioning was run; a group given unpaired CS and US did not show conditioning. A subsequent study by Kellogg and associates (121) which failed to verify these results also failed to replicate essential features of the procedure. There are now several recent, well-controlled studies demonstrating classical conditioning of hindlimb flexion reflex in spinal carnivore; the phenomenon must be considered genuine. There are also several negative reports. Deese & Kellogg (47) replicated the conditions of the Shurrager & Culler experiment more closely but used long term chronic dogs (N = 2), daily training sessions, and whole limb response. Results were negative. Lloyd, Wikler & Whitehouse (149) used three adult chronic (at least 1 year) spinal dogs and a whole limb flexion response, with negative results. Pinto & Bromiley (174) used adult dogs; one group was prepared quite similarly to that of Shurrager & Culler. Only a few animals developed irregular "conditioned" responses. A major problem noted by these investigators was the occurrence of passive movement in the hind quarters from anterior struggling.

In terms of recent positive studies, Dykman & Shurrager (53) reported classical conditioning of acute or chronic spinal kittens, using whole limb flexion. Three control animals were tested for sensitization and showed none prior to conditioning. Buchwald & Schramm (27) paired tactile stimulation of skin and paw shock in acute spinal kitten and found development and increase of hindlimb movement. Animals given CS only also developed responses but the behavior was different. Buerger & Dawson (29, 30) demonstrated spinal conditioning in two separate experiments, using short term chronic spinal kittens. In the first study, conditioning animals showed a clear and significant increase in response over days, and unpaired sensitization control animals did not. These results were replicated in the second experiment. Additional animals trained following clamp of descending aorta (which destroys spinal interneurons) did not show conditioning. Fitzgerald & Thompson (73) demonstrated conditioning using adult acute cats immobilized with brainstem lesions. Although responsiveness of these preparations was markedly variable, the conditioning animals $(N=10)$ showed significant acquisition and extinction while unpaired controls $(N=10)$ did not. Finally, Patterson, Cegavske & Thompson (169) utilized acute adult cats spinalized under ether and paralyzed with Flaxedil. CS was weak shock to cutaneous nerve, US was strong shock to paw and response was reflex volley in flexor muscle nerve. Two replications, including 10 paired and 10 unpaired animals all given otherwise identical treatment, both demonstrated conditioning. This preparation rules out essential participation of the gamma system.

Classical conditioning has not been emphasized in studies of invertebrates. Most relevant are studies of "heterosynaptic facilitation" in cells of *Aplysia*. Kandel & Tauc (118, 119) first demonstrated the phenomenon: when two afferent nerves are stimulated together such that one (test) yields an EPSP and the other (priming) a train of spikes in a given neuron, certain identified and unidentified abdominal ganglion cells show a subsequent marked increase in the EPSP response. The investigators were careful to run the appropriate controls—unpaired stimulation—and found that in the giant cells the effect was not dependent on pairing. It is a form of sensitization. However, in three unidentified cells, pairing was critical. In more recent work (see 117) pairing was found to be occasionally more effective than unpaired stimuli but the differences were small and inconsistent. Von Baumgarten and associates (15, 16) examined the time parameter in certain identified cells showing heterosynaptic facilitation and report that maximum effects tend to occur with a test-priming interval of about 350 msec. However, pairing was not critical, only relatively more effective.

Instrumental Conditioning

Much recent work on instrumental conditioning in model systems has been stimulated by Horridge's ingenious leg position learning experiments in headless insects (103). The paradigm is instrumental avoidance using a yoked control (R = random), where response for shock avoidance requires maintenance of the leg position above a given point (P = position). Following the training session, both groups are run on shock-contingent response (testing session) and performance of the P and R groups compared. P preparations typically avoid shock much more during the second session than R preparations. Operationally this procedure fits the requirements of instrumental avoidance conditioning. Behavioral studies on this phenomenon in insects have been covered in several recent reviews (59, 61, 117, 223). The phenomenon differs from instrumental learning in intact higher vertebrates in several ways. In a very well controlled study, Eisenstein & Cohen (62) found that R animals learned much more poorly, if at all, in the testing session than did P animals in the training session. Further, if the ganglion was destroyed so that the preparation was purely leg with neuromuscular junctions, P legs "learned" in the training session and both P and R legs, "relearned" very rapidly in the testing session. The plasticity (i.e. difference between P and R in testing) is retained for 10 min following training but not for 45 min (9, 60).

Hoyle (104) refined the Horridge preparation by immobilizing the leg and recording neuromuscular junction potentials from a particular adductor muscle (ACAM) excited by a single axon in locust. An effect comparable to "leg lift" was produced by shocking the leg whenever spontaneous junction potentials fell below a given rate. As is true in the Horridge paradigm, when noncontingent shock is given first, subsequent contingent shock is ineffective—the discharge rate can no longer be altered. Palka (168) has recently questioned the generality and significance of this phenomenon—it apparently cannot be obtained from any other leg muscle of locust or from any leg muscle of cockroach.

Aranda & Luco (9) report alterations in both spontaneous and evoked activity of trained cockroach ganglia relative to control ganglia when testing is done immediately following the Horridge procedure, consistent with their earlier reports (153) of increased transmission through the ganglion following development of an antenna wiping response by the middle legs after removal of the normally used forelegs. Cycloheximide (20) and actinomycin D (82) increase leg position "learning" in P group headless roaches, but R group controls were not run. Nembutal appears to convert P group behavior to that of R group, but strychnine has no effect (58).

Several recent experiments have reported hind leg position "learning" in spinal toad (98) and rat (31). In a most interesting study, Buerger & Fennessy used the two hind legs of each spinal rat as the P and R groups, thus controlling for organismic variables, and were still able to achieve the effect, although it was less pronounced than with separate P and R animal conditions (32).

By stretching an analogy, entrainment of circadian rhythms may be construed as a form of operant conditioning (117). The studies of Strumwasser and associates (219, 220) and Lickey and associates (146) on one identified cell (R15) in the abdominal ganglion of *Aplysia* provide examples of this phenomenon. Strumwasser (219) first demonstrated by long-term intracellular recording that the cell showed maximum spike frequency at aquarium dawn, even when the ganglion was dissected out, and termed it a "parabolic burster." The cell's behavior, which can be entrained to light-dark cycles ranging from 10.5:10.5 to 13.5:13.5 hours even in the absence of the eyes (146) appears due to intrinsic postsynaptic mechanisms (220). Kandel and associates (see 117) report an interesting analog of operant conditioning for certain rhythmic cells of Aplysia abdominal ganglion. Both mixed polysynaptic and inhibiting monosynaptic inputs could briefly (usually 1–2 min) increase or decrease the bursting activity of L3 and L6 cells if delivered during spontaneous bursting or resting, respectively.

Studies of neural mechanisms underlying behavioral learning in sea slugs have made less progress. Lickey (145) has demonstrated a form of instrumental learning in Aplysia; they learn to reject forceps and accept food when presented on alternate trials and retain the discrimination for 4 days. Lee has reported a form of operant conditioning to water level for Aplysia (142). At the opposite extreme, much has been learned in neural terms about the escape swimming response of Tritonia (242). However, this fixed action pattern seems exceedingly resistant to learned modification (1). As noted by Abraham (1), although Aplysia and Tritonia have large identified neurons, and have yielded much valuable information on such elementary processes as fixed action patterns, circadian rhythms, and habituation, more complex learned behaviors, to the extent that they occur, likely involve the neuropile, which even in these simple beasts is enormously complex (143).

MECHANISMS AND MEMORY

The well-understood forms of synaptic actions, postsynaptic excitation, postsynaptic inhibition, and presynaptic inhibition, have time courses in the millisecond range, much too short to provide a direct substrate for even the simplest forms of learning. A quite different form of synaptic action, the slow synaptic potentials of autonomic ganglia (56, 57) recently elucidated by Libet and associates (131, 144), offer great promise as a potential model for central plasticity. Excitatory and inhibitory postsynaptic potentials lasting for seconds to minutes can be induced in ganglion cells. They differ fundamentally from fast synaptic potentials in not being generated by Na-K or Cl electrogenic ion pumps. Furthermore, the slow excitatory potential, mediated by a muscarinic action of ACh, apparently requires initial priming by another transmitter, dopamine. Following this initial priming, the ACh excitatory potential is enhanced for long periods. Such a mechanism could account very nicely for the temporal features of conditioning. It could also account for heterosynaptic facilitation in Aplysia: a persisting increase in responsiveness by postsynaptic actions that would not be distinguishable from presynaptic effects in terms of an absence of postsynaptic conductance change.

Post-tetanic potentiation (PTP) has been a popular candidate. As noted earlier marked potentiation can be achieved at relatively low frequencies of stimulation in certain brain systems (8, 171). Spencer and associates (215) described monosynaptic PTP that persisted for hours following prolonged tetanus, could not be disrupted by brief tetanus, eventually decayed, and could not be made permanent. Interneurons often respond repetitively to single activation; hence polysynaptic PTP could provide a temporary increase in activity through interneurons shared by CS and US in a conditioning paradigm. However, such a mechanism, while admirably suited to sensitization, cannot account for the temporal features of conditioning.

A traditional neural theory of learning ascribes formation of new connections to specific use and extinction or forgetting to disuse (54, 55). Any simple specific use hypothesis is in fundamental conflict with behavioral facts, as noted some time ago by Hebb (92) and Sharpless (207). Given that a stimulus elicits a response, repeated use leads to habituation, not conditioning; repeated use of CS-CR leads to extinction, not further conditioning; and further disuse after extinction leads to spontaneous recovery, not greater extinction. Tenotomy studies (17, 136), in which monosynaptic responses of motoneurons to tendon-sectioned muscles increased only if the spinal cord was not cut, were taken as evidence for the simple use hypothesis. However, in a recent and comprehensive analysis of this problem, Spencer & April (215) provide convincing evidence that increased synaptic effectiveness is associated with chronic *disuse*. Sharpless' suggestion in his classic review (207) that specific use leads to decreased responsiveness and specific disuse leads to increased responsiveness is thus further substantiated.

The failure of the specific use hypothesis must be contrasted with the more general long-term effects of overall use and disuse, particularly during postnatal development. The notable studies of Rosenzweig, Bennett & Diamond and others (see 194) have demonstrated beyond question that in rats reared in enriched environments, marked changes in brain develop relative to animals raised in standard laboratory environments. Impoverishment and deprivation during development yield opposite effects. Findings of consistent changes in brain anatomy, chemistry, and physiology as a function of degree and nature of stimulation during development support the general notion that "use improves" and may suggest possible substrates for learning, but they have not as yet provided specific mechanisms that can account for learning.

Chemical hypotheses of learning, treated in numerous recent reviews, will not be detailed here. A basic problem with most chemical theories concerns the manner in which chemical coding exerts influence on neural function. See Roberts (191) for a clear discussion. A memory molecule cannot exist in a vacuum. Although numerous alternative possibilities have been suggested, it still remains true that neurons influence one another primarily through synapses. A satisfactory molecular theory of learning must specify alterations at the level of the synapse.

Elucidation of the neural synaptic substrates of a particular form of learning will do no more than set the stage for an understanding of the neural basis of that aspect of learning. Analysis of learning at the brain-systems level, originally emphasized by Lashley (141), remains a fundamental problem. Gerard (80, 81) and Hebb (91) developed perhaps the first comprehensive systems analyses of brain function and learning. The distinction they both emphasized between short- and long-term aspects of learning has received overwhelming empirical support. There is no longer any question but what very recently learned behaviors are far more subject to interference and facilitation than are well-learned behaviors. As McGaugh has noted (157), there are many specific theories concerning the time dependent processes in learning and memory, ranging from dual or "multitrace" views (157, 158) to a single trace hypothesis (159). The issue remains a lively controversy. Electrophysiological theories of short-term memory depended on hypothetical reverberating circuits (91). Verzeano and associates (233, 234) have demonstrated that "reverberating" activity does in fact occur in neuronal networks of the brain, but the bridge to short-term memory has not been made. The important studies by Gerard and associates on consolidation of short-term postural asymmetry would seem to offer a possible model for analysis of this issue (40, 41).

Among the more comprehensive recent attempts at systems analysis of the brain and learning are the writings of John (109) and Pribram (179). As they and others have emphasized, we remain with the problems set by Lashley. Complex learning seems to involve widespread regions of the brain; yet the most complex learning done, human language acquisition, is represented in a particular region of the left temporal lobe. Our final conclusion is inevitable. Analysis of the neurophysiology of learning has only just begun.

ADDENDUM IN PROOF

After completing this review we learned of current research by Olds and associates, now in press, involving extensive on-line computer mapping of unit activity changes in the brain associated with a simple classically conditioned movement response (J. Olds, J. F. Disterhoft, M. Segal, C. L. Kornblith, and R. Hirsh: Learning centers of the rat brain mapped by measuring the latencies of conditioned unit responses. *J. Neurophysiol.*, in press). This approach appears to offer much promise—an unexpected result to date is that the posterior nucleus of the thalamus shows most marked short-latency learned increases in unit activity.

LITERATURE CITED

1. Abraham, F. 1971. *Neurobiology of Learning.* IBS Conf. Rep. 10. UCLA Brain Inform. Serv. 24 pp.
2. Adám, G., Adey, W. R., Porter, R. W. 1966. Interoceptive conditional response in cortical neurons. *Nature* 209:920–21
3. Adey, W. R. 1963. Computer analysis of hippocampal EEG activity and impedance in approach learning: Effects of psychotomimetic and hallucinogenic drugs. Pharmacology of conditioning, learning and retention. *Proc. Int. Pharmacol. Meet., 2nd,* 287–317
4. Adey, W. R. 1965. Electrophysiological patterns and cerebral impedance characteristics in orienting and discriminative behavior. *Int. Congr. Physiol. Sci., Lect. Symp. 23rd,* 324–39
5. Adey, W. R. 1967. Hippocampal states and functional relations with corticosubcortical systems in attention and learning. *Progress in Brain Research,* Vol. 27. *Structure and function of the limbic system,* ed. W. R. Adey, T. Tokizane, 228–45. Amsterdam: Elsevier. 489 pp.
6. Adey, W. R. 1969. Neural information processing; windows without and the citadel within. In *Cybernetics of the Central Nervous System,* ed. L. D. Proctor, 1–27. Boston: Little, Brown. 462 pp.
7. Adey, W. R. 1970. Spontaneous electrical brain rhythms accompanying learned responses. See Ref. 203, 224–42
8. Andersen, P., Lømo, T. 1970. Mode of control of hippocampal pyramidal cell discharges. In *The Neural Control of Behavior,* ed. R. E. Whalen, R. F. Thompson, M. Verzeano, N. M. Weinberger, 5–26. New York: Academic. 301 pp.
9. Aranda, L. C., Luco, J. V. 1969. Further studies on an electric correlate to learning. Experiments in an isolated insect ganglion. *Physiol. Behav.* 4:133–37
10. Arutyunov, V. S., Polyakova, A. G. 1970. Origin of the early component of associative cortical responses in cats. *Neurosci. Trans.* 12:23–31
11. Asato, H., Fleming, D. E. 1971. The relationship between EEG amplitude and the rate of classical conditioning. *Psychon. Sci.* 22:37–38

12. Asratyan, E. A. 1967. Electrophysiological manifestation of the well established and specialized conditioned reflexes. *Accad. Naz. Lincei Quad.* 109:93–99
13. Asratyan, E. A. 1967. The functional architecture of instrumental conditioned reflexes. *Cond. Reflex* 2: 258–72
14. Barrett, T. W. 1969. The cortex as interferometer: the transmission of amplitude, frequency and phase in cortical structures. *Neuropsychologia* 7:135–48
15. Baumgarten, R. J. von, Hukuhara, T. 1969. The role of the interstimulus interval in heterosynaptic facilitation in *Aplysia californica. Brain Res.* 16:369–81
16. Baumgarten, R. J. von, Jahan-Parwar, B. 1967. Time course of repetitive heterosynaptic facilitation in *Aplysia californica. Brain Res.* 4:295–97
17. Beránek, R., Hnik, P. 1959. Long-term effect of tenotomy on spinal monosynaptic response in the cat. *Science* 130:981–82
18. Bitterman, M. E. 1965. The CS-US interval in classical and avoidance conditioning. In *Classical Conditioning,* ed. W. F. Prokasy, 1–19. New York: Appleton-Century-Crofts. 421 pp.
19. Brogden, W. J. 1969. Acquisition of a conditioned avoidance response by cats, dogs, and rabbits. *J. Comp. Physiol. Psychol.* 68:343–47
20. Brown, B. M., Noble, E. P. 1968. Cycloheximide, amino acid incorporation and learning in the isolated cockroach ganglion. *Biochem. Pharmacol.* 17:2371–74
21. Bruner, J., Kehoe, J. 1970. Long-term decrements in the efficacy of synaptic transmission in molluscs and crustaceans. See Ref. 101, 323–59
22. Bruner, J., Kennedy, D. 1970. Habituation: Occurrence at a neuromuscular junction. *Science* 169: 92–94
23. Bruner, J., Tauc, L. 1965. Long-lasting phenomena in the molluscan nervous system. *Nervous and Hormonal Mechanisms of Integration. 20th Symp. Soc. Exp. Biol.,* 457–75. Cambridge Univ. Press
24. Bruner, J., Tauc, L. 1966. Habituation

at the synaptic level in *Aplysia*. *Nature* 210:37–39

25. Buchwald, J. S., Halas, E. S., Schramm, S. G. 1966. Changes in cortical and subcortical unit activity during behavioral conditioning. *Physiol. Behav.* 1:11–22

26. Buchwald, J. S., Humphrey, G. L. 1971. An analysis of habituation in the specific sensory systems. In *Progress in Physiological Psychology*, Vol. 5, ed. E. Stellar, J. Sprague. New York: Academic. In press

27. Buchwald, J. S., Schramm, S. G. 1965. A study of conditioning in chronically spinalized kittens. *The Physiologist* 8:125

28. Buerger, A. A. 1970. A possible biological analogue of the reinforcement control device in self-organizing systems. *Cond. Reflex* 5:52–61

29. Buerger, A. A., Dawson, A. M. 1968. Spinal kittens: Long-term increases in electromyograms due to a conditioning routine. *Physiol. Behav.* 3:99–103

30. Buerger, A. A., Dawson, A. M. 1969. Spinal kittens: Effect of clamping of the thoracic aorta on long-term increases in electromyograms due to a conditioning routine. *Exp. Neurol.* 23:457–64

31. Buerger, A. A., Fennessy, A. 1970. Learning of leg position in chronic spinal rats. *Nature* 225:751–52

32. Buerger, A. A., Fennessy, A. 1971. Long-term alteration of leg position due to shock avoidance by spinal rats. *Exp. Neurol.* 30:195–211

33. Bureš, J., Burešová, O. 1967. Plastic changes of unit activity based on reinforcing properties of extracellular stimulation of single neurons. *J. Neurophysiol.* 30:98–113

34. Bureš, J., Burešová, O. 1970. Plasticity in single neurones and neural populations. See Ref. 101, 363–403

35. Butter, C. M. 1969. Perseveration in extinction and in discrimination reversal tasks following selective frontal ablations in *Macaca mulatta*. *Physiol. Behav.* 4:163–71

36. Carder, B. 1970. Lateral hypothalamic stimulation and avoidance in rats. *J. Comp. Physiol. Psychol.* 71:325–33

37. Carder, B. 1971. Effects of septal stimulation on active avoidance in rats. *Physiol. Behav.* 6:503–6

38. Castellucci, V., Pinsker, H., Kupfermann, I., Kandel, E. R. 1970. Neuronal mechanisms of habituation and dishabituation of the gill-withdrawal reflex in *Aplysia*. *Science* 167:1745–48

39. Caviedes, E., Bureš, J. 1970. Changes in cortical and tegmental evoked responses to sensory stimuli reinforced by electrical stimulation of the area of recording. *Brain Res.* 19:249–61

40. Chamberlain, T. J., Halick, P., Gerard, R. W. 1963. Fixation of experience in the rat spinal cord. *J. Neurophysiol.* 26:662–73

41. Chamberlain, T. J., Rothschild, G. H., Gerard, R. W. 1963. Drugs affecting RNA and learning. *Proc. Nat. Acad. Sci.* 49:918–24

42. Chiorini, J. R. 1969. Slow potential changes from cat cortex and classical aversive conditioning. *Electroencephalogr. Clin. Neurophysiol.* 26:399–406

43. Chow, K. L., Lindsley, D. F. 1968. Influences of residual eye movements in single-unit studies of the visual system. *Brain Res.* 8:385–88

44. Chow, K. L., Lindsley, D. F., Gollender, M. 1968. Modification of response patterns of lateral geniculate neurons after paired stimulation of contralateral and ipsilateral eyes. *J. Neurophysiol.* 31:729–39

45. Colavita, F. B. 1970. The reticular formation and avoidance conditioning. *Physiol. Behav.* 5:1423–26

46. Dalton, A. J. 1969. Discriminative conditioning of hippocampal electrical activity in curarized dogs. *Comm. Behav. Biol.* 3:283–87

47. Deese, J., Kellogg, W. N. 1949. Some new data on the nature of "spinal conditioning." *J. Comp. Physiol. Psychol.* 42:157–60

48. Denti, A., McGaugh, J. L., Landfield, P. W., Shinkman, P. G. 1970. Effects of posttrial electrical stimulation of the mesencephalic reticular formation on avoidance learning in rats. *Physiol. Behav.* 5:659–62

49. Deutsch, J. A. 1969. The physiological basis of memory. *Ann. Rev. Psychol.* 20:85–104

50. DiCara, L. V. 1970. Learning in the autonomic nervous system. *Sci. Am.* 222:30–39

51. Douglas, R. J. 1967. The hippocampus and behavior. *Psychol. Bull.* 67:416–42

52. Durkovic, R. G., Cohen, D. H. 1968. Spontaneous, evoked and defensively conditioned steady potential

changes in the pigeon telencephalon. *Electroencephalogr. Clin. Neurophysiol.* 24:474–81

53. Dykman, R. A., Shurrager, P. S. 1956. Successive and maintained conditioning in spinal carnivores. *J. Comp. Physiol. Psychol.* 49:27–35

54. Eccles, J. C. 1961. The effects of use and disuse on synaptic function. In *Brain Mechanisms and Learning*, ed. J. F. Delafresnaye, A. Fessard, J. Konorski, 335–52. Oxford: Blackwell. 702 pp.

55. Eccles, J. C. 1970. *Facing Reality*, Chap. 2. New York: Springer

56. Eccles, R. M. 1952. Action potentials of isolated mammalian sympathetic ganglia. *J. Physiol.* 117:181–95

57. Eccles, R. M., Libet, B. 1961. Origin and blockade of the synaptic responses of curarized sympathetic ganglia. *J. Physiol.* 157:484–503

58. Eisenstein, E. M. 1965. Effects of strychnine sulfate and sodium pentrobarbital on shock-avoidance learning in an isolated prothoracic insect ganglion. *Proc. Am. Psychol. Assoc.*, 127–28

59. Eisenstein, E. M. 1967. The use of invertebrate systems for studies on the bases of learning and memory. See Ref. 185, 653–65

60. Eisenstein, E. M. 1970. The retention of shock avoidance learning in the cockroach, *P. americanna. Brain Res.* 21:148–50

61. Eisenstein, E. M. Learning in isolated insect ganglia: a survey of procedures and results including some theoretical speculations and suggested experiments. In *Experiments in Physiology and Biochemistry*, Vol. 4, ed. G. Kerkut. New York: Academic. In press

62. Eisenstein, E. M., Cohen, M. J. 1965. Learning in an isolated prothoracic insect ganglion. *Anim. Behav.* 13:104–8

63. Elazar, Z., Adey, W. R. 1967. Spectral analysis of low frequency components in the electrical activity of the hippocampus during learning. *Electroencephalogr. Clin. Neurophysiol.* 23:225–40

64. Ellen, P., Powell, E. W. 1966. Differential conditioning of septum and hippocampus. *Exp. Neurol.* 16:162–71

65. Ellison, G. D., Humphrey, G. L., Feeney, D. M. 1968. Some electrophysiological correlates of classical and instrumental behavior. *J.*

Comp. Physiol. Psychol. 66:340–48

66. Erickson, C. K., Patel, J. B. 1969. Facilitation of avoidance learning by posttrial hippocampal electrical stimulation. *J. Comp. Physiol. Psychol.* 68:400–6

67. Evarts, E. V. 1966. Pyramidal tract activity associated with a conditioned hand movement in the monkey. *J. Neurophysiol.* 29:1011–27

68. Fallon, D., Donovick, P. J. 1970. Low resistance to extinction in rats with septal lesions under inappropriate appetitive motivation. *J. Comp. Physiol. Psychol.* 73:150–56

69. Farel, P. B. 1971. Long lasting habituation in spinal frogs. *Brain Res.* 33:405–17

70. Farel, P. B., Thompson, R. F. 1971. Habituation and dishabituation in isolated frog spinal cord. *Behav. Biol.* In press

71. Fehmi, L. G., Adkins, J. W., Lindsley, D. B. 1969. Electrophysiological correlates of visual perceptual masking in monkeys. *Exp. Brain Res.* 7:299–316

72. Fetz, E. E. 1969. Operant conditioning of cortical unit activity. *Science* 163:955–58

73. Fitzgerald, L. A., Thompson, R. F. 1967. Classical conditioning of the hindlimb flexion reflex in the acute spinal cat. *Psychon. Sci.* 8:213–14

74. Fleming, D. E. 1967. Amplitude relationships between evoked potential components during trace conditioning. *Electroencephalogr. Clin. Neurophysiol.* 23:449–55

75. Fox, S. S. 1970. Evoked potential, coding, and behavior. See Ref. 203, 243–59

76. Fox, S. S., O'Brien, J. H. 1965. Duplication of evoked potential waveform by curve of probability of firing of a single cell. *Science* 147:888–90

77. Fox, S. S., Rudell, A. P. 1970. Operant controlled neural event: Functional independence in behavioral coding by early and late components of visual cortical evoked response in cats. *J. Neurophysiol.* 33:548–61

78. Fuster, J. M. 1971. Transient memory and neuronal activity in the thalamus. In *Behavioral Physiology of the Frontal Lobes*, ed. A. R. Luria, K. H. Pribram. New York: Academic. In press

79. Galin, D. 1965. Background and evoked activity in the auditory

pathway: Effects of noise-shock pairing. *Science* 149:761–63
80. Gerard, R. W. 1949. Physiology and psychiatry. *Am. J. Psychiat.* 106: 161–73
81. Gerard, R. W. 1961. The fixation of experience. See Ref. 54, 21–35
82. Glassman, E., Henderson, A., Cordle, M., Moon, H. M., Wilson, J. E. 1970. Effect of cycloheximide and actinomycin D on the behaviour of the headless cockroach. *Nature* 225: 967–68
83. Gormezano, I. 1965. Yoked comparisons of classical and instrumental conditioning of the eyelid response; and an addendum on "voluntary responders." See Ref. 18, 48–70
84. Gray, J. A., Ball, G. G. 1970. Frequency-specific relation between hippocampal theta rhythm, behavior, and amobarbital action. *Science* 168:1246–48
85. Groves, P. M., DeMarco, R., Thompson, R. F. 1969. Habituation and sensitization of spinal interneuron activity in acute spinal cat. *Brain Res.* 14:521–25
86. Groves, P. M., Glanzman, D. L., Patterson, M. M., Thompson, R. F. 1970. Excitability of cutaneous afferent terminals during habituation and sensitization in acute spinal cat. *Brain Res.* 18: 388–92
87. Groves, P. M., Thompson, R. F. 1970. Habituation: A dual process theory. *Psychol. Rev.* 77:419–50
88. Halas, E. S., Beardsley, J. V. 1970. Changes in neuronal activity in the cochlear nucleus as a function of classical and instrumental conditioning. *Psychon. Sci.* 18:161–63
89. Halas, E. S., Beardsley, J. V., Sandlie, M. E. 1970. Conditioned neuronal responses at various levels in conditioning paradigms. *Electroencephalogr. Clin. Neurophysiol.* 28:468–77
90. Hall, R. D., Mark, R. G. 1967. Fear and the modification of acoustically evoked potentials during conditioning. *J. Neurophysiol.* 30:893–910
91. Hebb, D. O., Ed. 1949. *The Organization of Behavior.* New York: Wiley. 183 pp.
92. Hebb, D. O. 1958. Alice in wonderland, or, psychology among the biological sciences. In *Biological and Biochemical Bases of Behavior,* ed. H. F. Harlow, C. N. Woolsey, 451–67. Madison: Univ. Wisconsin Press. 476 pp.

93. Hernández-Peón, R. 1960. Neurophysiological correlates of habituation and other manifestations of plastic inhibition (internal inhibition). In the *Moscow Colloquium on EEG of Higher Nervous Activity,* ed. H. H. Jasper, G. D. Smirnov. *Electroencephalogr. Clin. Neurophysiol. Suppl.* 13:101–14
94. Hernández-Peón, R., Sterman, M. B. 1966. Brian functions. *Ann. Rev. Psychol.* 17:363–94
95. Hinde, R. A. 1970. Behavioral inhibition. See Ref. 101, 3–40
96. Hirsch, H. V. B., Spinelli, D. N. 1970. Visual experience modifies distribution of horizontally and vertically oriented receptive fields in cats. *Science* 168:869–71
97. Holmes, J. E., Adey, W. R. 1960. Electrical activity of the entorhinal cortex during conditioned behavior. *Am. J. Physiol.* 199:741–44
98. Horn, A. L. D., Horn, G. 1969. Modification of leg flexion in response to repeated stimulation in a spinal amphibian (*Xenopus mullerei*). *Anim. Behav.* 17:618–23
99. Horn, G. 1967. Neuronal mechanisms of habituation. *Nature* 215:707–11
100. Horn, G. 1970. Changes in neuronal activity and their relationship to behavior. See Ref. 101, 567–606
101. Horn, G., Hinde, R. A., Eds. 1970. *Short-term Changes in Neural Activity and Behaviour.* Cambridge Univ. Press. 628 pp.
102. Horn, G., Wright, M. J. 1970. Characteristics of transmission failure in the squid stellate ganglion: A study of a simple habituating system. *J. Exp. Biol.* 52:217–31
103. Horridge, G. A. 1962. Learning leg position by the ventral nerve cord in headless insects. *Proc. Roy. Soc. B* 157:33–52
104. Hoyle, G. 1965. Neurophysiological studies on "learning" in headless insects. In *Physiology of the Insect Central Nervous System,* ed. J. W. Beament, J. Treherne, 203–32. New York: Academic. 277 pp.
105. Hull, C. L. 1951. *Essentials of Behavior.* New Haven: Yale Univ. Press. 145 pp.
106. Imig, T. J., Weinberger, N. M. 1970. Auditory system multi-unit activity and behavior in the rat. *Psychon. Sci.* 18:164–65
107. Irwin, D. A., Rebert, C. S. 1970. Slow potential changes in cat brain during classical appetitive conditioning

of jaw movements using two levels of reward. *Electroencephalogr. Clin. Neurophysiol.* 28:119–26

108. John, E. R. 1961. Higher nervous functions: Brain functions and learning. *Ann. Rev. Physiol.* 23:451–84

109. John, E. R. 1967. *Mechanisms of Memory.* New York: Academic. 468 pp.

110. John, E. R. 1967. Electrophysiological studies of learning. See Ref. 185, 690–704

111. John E. R. 1969. Neural correlates of learning and memory. *Symp. Brain Hum. Behav., 2nd Cent. Symp.* Loyola Univ. Med. Cent.

112. John, E. R., Morgades, P. P. 1969. Neural correlates of conditioned responses studied with multiple chronically implanted moving microelectrodes. *Exp. Neurol.* 23:412–25

113. John, E. R., Morgades, P. P. 1969. The pattern and anatomical distribution of evoked potentials and multiple unit activity elicited by conditioned stimuli in trained cats. *Comm. Behav. Biol. A* 3:181–207

114. John, E. R., Shimokochi, M., Bartlett, F. 1969. Neural readout from memory during generalization. *Science* 164:1519–21

115. Kalyozhnyi, L. V. 1969. Changes in evoked potential during different motivational reactions in rabbits. *Dokl. Acad. Nauk SSR* 189:898–901

116. Kandel, E. R., Castellucci, V., Pinsker, H., Kupfermann, I. 1970. The role of synaptic plasticity in the short-term modification of behavior. See Ref. 101, 281–322

117. Kandel, E. R., Spencer, W. A. 1968. Cellular neurophysiological approaches in the study of learning. *Physiol. Rev.* 48:65–134

118. Kandel, E. R., Tauc, L. 1965. Heterosynaptic facilitation in neurones of the abdominal ganglion of *Aplysia depilans. J. Physiol.* 181:1–27

119. Ibid. Mechanisms of heterosynaptic facilitation in the giant cell of the abdominal ganglion of *Aplysia depilans,* 28–47

120. Kasper, P. 1965. Disruption of position habit reversal by septal stimulation. *Psychon. Sci.* 3:111–12

121. Kellogg, W. N., Deese, J., Pronko, N. H., Feinberg, M. 1947. An attempt to condition the chronic spinal dog. *J. Exp. Psychol.* 37:99–117

122. Kesner, R. P., Fiedler, P., Thomas,

G. J. 1967. Functions of the midbrain reticular formation in regulating level of activity and learning in rats. *J. Comp. Physiol. Psychol.* 63:452–57

123. Khachaturian, Z. S., Gluck, H. 1969. The effects of arousal on the amplitude of evoked potentials. *Brain Res.* 14:589–606

124. Kimble, D. P., Ed. 1965. *Learning, Remembering, and Forgetting, Vol. I. The Anatomy of Memory.* Palo Alto: Science & Behavior. 451 pp.

125. Kimble, D. P. 1968. Hippocampus and internal inhibition. *Psychol. Bull.* 70:285–95

126. Kimble, D. P., Kirkby, R. J., Stein, D. G. 1966. Response perservation interpretation of passive avoidance deficits in hippocampectomized rats. *J. Comp. Physiol. Psychol.* 61:141–43

127. Kimble, G. A., Ed. 1961. *Hilgard and Marquis' Conditioning and Learning.* New York: Appleton-Century-Crofts. 590 pp.

128. Kitai, S. T., Cohen, B., Morin, F. 1965. Changes in the amplitude of photically evoked potentials by a conditioned stimulus. *Electroencephalogr. Clin. Neurophysiol.* 19: 344–49

129. Klingberg, F., Pickenhain, L. 1965. Electrophysiologische und verhaltensuntersuchungen uber die ausarbeitung eines bedinden abwehrreflexes auf elektrische reize ohne fluchtmoglichkeit bei ratten. *Acta Biol. Med. Ger.* 14:749–63

130. Ibid 1967. Dereinfluss des verhaltens auf die photisch ausgelöste rekrutierung. 19:267–83

131. Kobayashi, H., Libet, B. 1968. Generation of slow postsynaptic potentials without increases in ionic conductance. *Proc. Nat. Acad. Sci.* 60:1304–11

132. Kogan, A. B. 1960. The manifestations of processes of higher nervous activity in the electrical potentials of the cortex during free behavior of animals. See Ref. 93, 51–64

133. Komisaruk, B. R. 1970. Synchrony between limbic system theta activity and rhythmical behavior in rats. *J. Comp. Physiol. Psychol.* 70:482–92

134. Konorski, J. 1967. *Integrative Activity of the Brain.* Univ. Chicago Press. 531 pp.

135. Kopytova, F. V., Rabinovich, M. Y. 1969. Microelectrode investigations

of conditioned reflexes to time. *Neurosci. Trans.* 4:461–68

136. Kozak, W., Westerman, R. A. 1966. Basic patterns of plastic change in the mammalian nervous system. *Symp. Soc. Exp. Biol.* 20:509–44

137. Krasne, F. B. 1969. Excitation and habituation of the crayfish escape reflex: The depolarizing response in lateral giant fibers of the isolated abdomen. *J. Exp. Biol.* 50:29–46

138. Krasne, F. B., Roberts, A. 1967. Habituation of the crayfish escape response during release from inhibition induced by picrotoxin. *Nature* 215:769–70

139. Kremer, E. F., Kamin, L. J. 1971. The truly random control procedure: Associative or nonassociative effects in rats. *J. Comp. Physiol. Psychol.* 74:203–10

140. Kupfermann, I., Castellucci, V., Pinsker, H., Kandel, E. R. 1970. Neuronal correlates of habitation and dishabituation of the gill-withdrawal reflex in *Aplysia. Science* 167:1740–48

141. Lashley, K. S. 1929. *Brain Mechanisms and Intelligence.* Univ. Chicago Press. 335 pp.

142. Lee, R. M. 1969. *Aplysia* behavior: Effects of contingent water level variation. *Comm. Behav. Biol.* 4: 157–64

143. Lewis, E. R., Everhart, T. E., Zeevi, Y. Y. 1969. Studying neural organization in *Aplysia* with the scanning electron microscope. *Science* 165: 1140–43

144. Libet, B. 1970. Generation of slow inhibitory and excitatory postsynaptic potentials. *Fed. Proc.* 29:1945–56

145. Lickey, M. E. 1968. Learned behavior in *Aplysia vaccaria. J. Comp. Physiol. Psychol.* 66:712–18

146. Ibid 1969. Seasonal modulation and non-24-hour entrainment of a circadian rhythm in a single neuron. 68:9–17

147. Lindholm, E. P., Keesey, R. E. 1968. Discrimination learning as a function of the duration of rewarding hypothalamic stimulation. *Psychon. Sci.* 10:153–54

148. Lindsley, D. B., Lumsdaine, A. A., Eds. 1967. *Brain Function and Learning*, Vol. 4. Berkeley: Univ. California Press. 364 pp.

149. Lloyd, A. J., Wikler, A., Whitehouse, J. M. 1969. Nonconditionability of

flexor reflex in the chronic spinal dog. *J. Comp. Physiol. Psychol.* 68:576–79

150. Lloyd, D. P. C. 1949. Post-tetanic potentiation of response in monosynaptic reflex pathways of the spinal cord. *J. Gen. Physiol.* 33: 147–70

151. Lloyd, D. P. C., Wilson, V. J. 1957. Reflex depression in rhythmically active monosynaptic reflex pathways. *J. Gen. Physiol.* 40:409–26

152. Lopes da Silva, F. H., Kamp, A. 1969. Hippocampal theta frequency shifts and operant behavior. *Electroencephalogr. Clin. Neurophysiol.* 26: 133–43

153. Luco, J. V., Aranda, L. C. 1964. An electrical correlate to the process of learning. *Acta Physiol. Lat. Am.* 14:274–88

154. Majkowski, J., Sobieszek, A., Kowalski, J., Szwed, M. 1970. EEG and behavioral correlates of learning in cats with lesions in the mesencephalic reticular formation. *Brain Res.* 21:301–4

155. Margules, D. L., Stein, L. 1968. Facilitation of Sidman avoidance by positive brain stimulation. *J. Comp. Physiol. Psychol.* 66:182–84

156. Matisumiya, Y., Kling, J. W. 1970. Conditioned suppression based upon positively reinforcing intracranial stimulation. *Jap. Psychol. Res.* 12:26–35

157. McGaugh, J. L. 1966. Time-dependent processes in memory storage. *Science* 153:1351–58

158. McGaugh, J. L., Dawson, R. G. 1971. Modification of memory storage processes. *Behav. Sci.* 16:45–63

159. Melton, A. W. 1970. Short- and long-term postperceptual memory: Dichotomy or continuum? See Ref. 181, 3–5

160. Miller, N. E. 1969. Learning of visceral and glandular responses. *Science* 163:434–45

161. Morrell, F. 1961. Electrophysiological contributions to the neural basis of learning. *Physiol. Rev.* 41:443–90

162. Morrell, F. 1967. Electrical signs of sensory coding. See Ref. 185, 452–69

163. O'Brien, J. H., Fox, S. S. 1969. Single-cell activity in cat motor cortex.I. Modifications during classical conditioning procedures. *J. Neurophysiol.* 32:267–84

164. Ibid. Single-cell activity in cat motor

THE NEUROPHYSIOLOGY OF LEARNING 101

cortex. II. Functional characteristics of the cell related to conditioning changes, 285–96

165. Olds, J., Hirano, T. 1969. Conditioned responses of hippocampal and other neurons. *Electroencephalogr. Clin. Neurophysiol.* 26:159–66

166. Olds, J., Olds, M. E. 1961. Interference and learning in paleocortical systems. See Ref. 54, 153–87

167. Olds, M. E. 1966. Effects of electrical stimulation and electrocoagulation in cortex and thalamus on delayed response in monkeys. *Exp. Neurol.* 15:37–53

168. Palka, J. 1971. Discussion. In *Neurobiology of Learning,* ed. F. Abraham 8–9. Brain Inform. Conf. Rep. 10, UCLA. 24 pp.

169. Patterson, M. M., Cegavske, C., Thompson, R. F. 1971 Classical conditioning of the hindlimb flexor nerve response in the immobilized unanesthetized spinal cat. In preparation

170. Peretz, B. 1970. Habituation and dishabituation in the absence of a central nervous system. *Science* 169:379–81

171. Phillips, C. G., Porter, R. 1964. The pyramidal projection to motoneurons of some muscle groups of the baboon's forelimb. *Progress in Brain Research,* Vol. 12. *Physiology of Spinal Neurons,* ed. J. C. Eccles, J. P. Schade, 222–45. Amsterdam: Elsevier. 317 pp.

172. Pickenhain, L., Klingberg, F. 1967. Hippocampal slow wave activity as a correlate of basic behavioral mechanisms in the rat. See Ref. 5, 218–27

173. Pinsker, H., Kupfermann, I., Castellucci, V., Kandel, E. R. 1970. Habituation and dishabituation of the gill-withdrawal reflex in *Aplysia. Science* 167:1740–42

174. Pinto, T., Bromiley, R. B. 1950. A search for spinal conditioning and for evidence that it can become a reflex. *J. Exp. Psychol.* 40:121–30

175. Pinto-Hamuy, T., Bracchitta, H., Lagarrigue, I. 1969. Slow cortical potential (SCP) during habituation, conditioning and extinction in rabbit cortex. *Neuropsychologia* 7:335–47

176. Popova, N. S. 1969. Changes in auditory evoked potentials during defensive conditioning in dogs. *Neurosci. Trans.* 8:903–11

177. Pribram, K. H. 1967. Memory and the organization of attention. See Ref. 148, 79–122

178. Pribram, K. H., Ed. 1969. *On the Biology of Learning.* New York: Harcourt, Brace & World. 225 pp.

179. Ibid. The four R's of remembering, 191–225

180. Pribram, K. H. 1969. The primate frontal cortex. *Neuropsychologia* 7:259–66

181. Pribram, K. H., Broadbent, D. E., Eds. 1970. *Biology of Memory.* New York: Academic. 323 pp.

182. Pribram, K. H., Douglas, R. J., Pribram, B. J. 1969. The nature of nonlimbic learning. *J. Comp. Physiol. Psychol.* 69:765–72

183. Psatta, D. M., Ungher, J., Rogozea, R. 1969. Associated sensory-sensorial and avoidance conditioning under chloralose anaesthesia. *Rev. Roum. Neurol.* 6:109–17

184. Psatta, D. M., Ungher, J., Sirian, S. 1970. Effects of hippocampal stimulations on sensory versus motor conditioning. *Rev. Roum. Neurol.* 7:301–12

185. Quarton, G. C., Melnechuk, T., Schmitt, F. O., Eds. 1967. *The Neurosciences: A Study Program.* New York: Rockefeller Univ. Press. 962 pp.

186. Rabinovich, M. Y., Polonskaya, E. L. 1969. Interaction of conditioned stimuli at the level of individual neurons of the motor cortex. *Dokl. Akad. Nauk SSR* 184:150–63

187. Ramón-Moliner, E., Nauta, W. J. H. 1966. The isodendritic core of the brain stem. *J. Comp. Neurol.* 126:311–36

188. Rebert, C. S. 1969. *Learning, Motivation and Slow Potentials in Brain.* Prepared for Nat. Inst. Neurol. Dis. and Stroke, Nat. Inst. Health, U. S. Dep. HEW

189. Rebert, C. S., Irwin, D. A. 1969. Slow potential changes in cat brain during classical appetitive and aversive conditioning of jaw movements. *Electroencephalogr. Clin. Neurophysiol.* 27:152–61

190. Rescorla, R. A. 1967. Pavlovian conditioning and its proper control procedures. *Psychol. Rev.* 74:71–80

191. Roberts, E. 1966. Models for correlative thinking about brain, behavior and biochemistry. *Brain Res.* 2:109–44

192. Romaniuk, A. 1964. The formation of

defensive conditioned reflexes by direct stimulation of the hypothalamic "flight-points" in cats. *Acta Biol. Exp. (Warsaw)* 24:145–51

193. Ibid 1965. Representation of aggression and flight reactions in the hypothalamus of the cat. 25:177–86

194. Rosenzweig, M. R., Bennett, E. L., Diamond, M. C. Chemical and anatomical plasticity of brain: Replications and extensions (1970). In *Macromolecules and Behavior*, ed. J. Gaito. New York: Appleton-Century-Crofts. 2nd ed. In press

195. Rosenzweig, M. R., Leiman, A. L. 1968. Brain Functions. *Ann. Rev. Psychol.* 19:55–98

196. Rosner, B. S. 1970. Brain functions. *Ann. Rev. Psychol.* 21:555–94

197. Rosvold, H. E. 1968. The prefrontal cortex and caudate nucleus: A system for effecting correction in response mechanisms. In *Mind as a Tissue*, ed. C. Rupp, 21–38. New York: Harper & Row. 357 pp.

198. Routtenberg, A. 1968. Hippocampal correlates of consummatory and observed behavior. *Physiol. Behav.* 3:533–36

199. Routtenberg, A., Zechmeister, E. B., Benton, C. 1970. Hippocampal activity during memory disruption of passive avoidance by electroconvulsive shock. *Life Sci.* 9:909–18

200. Rowland, V. 1967. Steady-potential phenomena of cortex. See Ref. 185, 482–95

201. Rowland, V. 1968. Cortical steady potential (direct current potential) in reinforcement and learning. In *Progress in Physiological Psychology*, Vol. 2, ed. E. Stellar, J. M. Sprague, 1–77. New York: Academic. 326 pp.

202. Sakhilina, G. T., Merzhanova, G. K. 1966. Stable changes in the pattern of the recruiting response associated with a well established conditioned reflex. *Electroencephalogr. Clin. Neurophysiol.* 20:50–58

203. Schmitt, F. O., Ed. 1970. *The Neurosciences: Second Study Program.* New York: Rockefeller Univ. Press. 1068 pp.

204. Schwartz, M., Stewart, A., Sunenshine, H. 1969. Evoked responses to the CS during classical conditioning in the rabbit. *Comm. Behav. Biol.* 4:35–40

205. Schwartzbaum, J. S., Green, R. H., Beatty, W. W., Thompson, J. B. 1967. Acquisition of avoidance be-havior following septal lesions in the rat. *J. Comp. Physiol. Psychol.* 63:95–104

206. Seligman, M. E. P. 1969. Control group and conditioning: A comment on operationism. *Psychol. Rev.* 76:484–91

207. Sharpless, S. K. 1964. Reorganization of function in the nervous system —use and disuse. *Ann. Rev. Physiol.* 26:357–88

208. Shulgina, G. I. 1967. Investigation of the neuronal activity of the cerebral cortex at early stages of elaboration of a conditioned reflex. In *Sooremennye Problemy Electrofigiologii Centralmoj Nervnoj Systemy*, 296–308. Izdat. 'Nauka' Moskva

209. Shurrager, P. S., Culler, E. 1940. Conditioning in the spinal dog. *J. Exp. Psychol.* 26:133–59

210. Siegel, S., Domjan, M. 1971. Backward conditioning as an inhibitory procedure. *Learning and Motivation.* In press

211. Skinner, J. E., Lindsley, D. B. 1967. Electrophysiological and behavioral effects of blockade of the nonspecific thalamocortical system. *Brain Res.* 6:95–118

212. Sokolov, E. N., Pakula, A., Arakelov, G. G. 1970. The aftereffects due to an intracellular electric stimulation of the giant neuron "A" in the left parietal ganglion of the mollusk *Linnaea stagnalis.* See Ref. 181, 175–90

213. Sparks, D. L., Travis, R. P. Jr. 1967. Single unit activity during behavioral conditioning: Arousal effects. *Life Sci.* 6:2497–2503

214. Sparks, D. L., Travis, R. P. Jr. 1968. Patterns of reticular unit activity observed during the performance of a discriminative task. *Physiol. Behav.* 3:961–67

215. Spencer, W. A., April, R. S. 1970. Plastic properties of monosynaptic pathways in mammals. See Ref. 101, 433–74

216. Spencer, W. A., Thompson, R. F., Neilson, D. R. Jr. 1966. Decrement of ventral root electrotonus and intracellularly recorded postsynaptic potentials produced by iterated cutaneous afferent volleys. *J. Neurophysiol.* 29:253–74

217. Spinelli, D. N., Pribram, K. H. 1970. Neural correlates of stimulus response and reinforcement. *Brain Res.* 17:377–85

218. Stamm, J. S., Rosen, S. C. 1969.

Electrical stimulation and steady potential shifts in prefrontal cortex during delayed response performance by monkeys. *Acta Biol. Exp.* 29:385–99

219. Strumwasser, F. 1965. The demonstration and manipulation of a circadian rhythm in a single neuron. In *Circadian Clocks*, ed. K. Jürgen, J. Aschoff, 442–62. Amsterdam: North-Holland. 479 pp.

220. Strumwasser, F. 1967. Neurophysiological aspects of rhythms. See Ref. 185, 516–28

221. Teyler, T. J., Roemer, R. A., Thompson, R. F. 1971. Relations between gross and unit activity in pericruciate cortex of cat. *Physiol. Behav.* 6:375–79

222. Teyler, T. J., Roemer, R. A., Thompson, R. F. 1971. Habituation of the pyramidal response in unanesthetized cat. *Physiol. Behav.* In press

223. Thompson, R. F. 1967. *Foundations of Physiological Psychology.* New York: Harper and Row. 688 pp.

224. Thompson, R. F., Bettinger, L. A., Birch, H., Groves, P. M. 1969. Comparison of evoked gross and unit responses in association cortex of waking cat. *Electroencephalogr. Clin. Neurophysiol.* 27:146–51

225. Thompson, R. F., Groves, P. M., Teyler, T. J., Roemer, R. A. 1972. A dual-process theory of habituation: Theory and behavior. In *Habituation: Behavioral Studies and Physiological Substrates*, Vol. I, ed. H. V. S. Peeke, M. J. Herz. New York: Academic. In press

226. Thompson, R. F., Spencer, W. A. 1966. Habituation: A model phenomenon for the study of neuronal substrates of behavior. *Psychol. Rev.* 173:16–43

227. Travis, R. P. Jr., Hooten, T. F., Sparks, D. L. 1968. Single unit activity related to behavior motivated by food reward. *Physiol. Behav.* 3:309–18

228. Travis, R. P. Jr., Sparks, D. L. 1968. Unitary responses and discrimination learning in the squirrel monkey: The globus pallidus. *Physiol. Behav.* 3:187–96

229. Ursin, H., Wester, K., Ursin, R. 1967. Habituation to electrical stimulation of the brain in unanesthetized cats. *Electroencephalogr. Clin. Neurophysiol.* 23:41–49

230. Vassilevsky, N. N., Trubatchev, V. V. 1969. Neuronal mechanisms of the temporary connexion. *Electroencephalogr. Clin. Neurophysiol.* 27:447–51

231. Verzeano, M. 1970. Evoked responses and network dynamics. See Ref. 8, 27–55

232. Verzeano, M., Dill, R., Navarro, G., Vallecalle, E. 1970. The action of metrazol on spontaneous and evoked behavior. *Physiol. Behav.* 5:1099–1102

233. Verzeano, M., Laufer, M., Spear, P., McDonald, S. 1970. The activity of neuronal networks in the thalamus of the monkey. See Ref. 181, 239–71

234. Verzeano, M., Negishi, K. 1960. Neuronal activity in cortical and thalamic networks. *J. Gen. Physiol.* 43:177–95

235. Wada, J. A., Matsuda, M., Jung, E., Hamm, A. E. 1970. Mesencephalically induced escape behavior and avoidance performance. *Exp. Neurol.* 29:215–20

236. Wall, P. D. 1967. The laminar organization of dorsal horn and effects of descending impulses. *J. Physiol.* 188:403–23

237. Weinberger, N. M., Nakayama, K., Lindsley, D. B. 1968. Electrocortical recruiting responses during classical conditioning. *Electroencephalogr. Clin. Neurophysiol.* 24:16–24

238. Weinberger, N. M., Velasco, M., Lindsley, D. B. 1967. The relationship between cortical synchrony and behavioral inhibition. *Electroencephalogr. Clin. Neurophysiol.* 23:297–305

239. Wester, K. 1971. Habituation to electrical stimulation of the thalamus in unanesthetized cats. *Electroencephalogr. Clin. Neurophysiol.* 30:52–61

240. Wickelgren, B. G. 1967. Habituation of spinal motoneurons. *J. Neurophysiol.* 30:1404–23

241. Ibid. Habituation of spinal interneurons, 1424–38

242. Willows, A. O. D., Hoyle, G. 1969. Neuronal networks triggering a fixed action pattern. *Science* 166:1549–50

243. Woody, C. D., Brozek, G. 1969. Gross potential from facial nucleus of cat as an index of neural activity in response to glabella tap. *J. Neurophysiol.* 32:704–16

244. Woody, C. D., Brozek, G. 1969. Conditioned eye blink in the cat:

Evoked responses of short latency. *Brain Res.* 12:257–60

245. Woody, C. D., Vassilevsky, N. N., Engel, J. Jr. 1970. Conditioned eye blink: Unit activity at coronal precruciate cortex of the cat. *J. Neurophysiol.* 33:851–64

246. Worden, F. G. 1966. Attention and auditory electrophysiology. See Ref. **201,** 1:45–116

247. Wyrwicka, W., Dobrzecka, C. 1961. On the transfer of defensive conditioned reaction established to the electrical stimulation of the di-

encephalon in goats. *Bull. Acad. Pol. Sci.* 9:51–56

248. Wyrwicka, W., Dobrzecka, C., Tarnecki, R. 1960. The effect of electrical stimulation of the hypothalamic feeding centre in satiated goats on alimentary conditioned reflexes, type II. *Acta Biol. Exp.* 20:121–36

249. Zornetzer, S. F., McGaugh, J. L. 1970. Effects of frontal brain electroshock stimulation on EEG activity and memory in rats: Relationship to ECS-produced retrograde amnesia. *J. Neurobiol.* 1:379–94

THINKING[1,2]

178

LYLE E. BOURNE, JR.

University of Colorado, Boulder, Colorado

AND ROGER L. DOMINOWSKI

University of Illinois, Chicago Circle, Chicago, Illinois

Sometime, roughly 15 to 20 years ago, thinking, in one of its periodic resurgences, once again was legitimized as a topic in psychology. It is difficult to know exactly when it happened or who was responsible, but clearly Miller (159), Hovland (105), and Bruner (32) were major contributors. Since then, studies of cognitive or mental processes have become more and more common. Interest is still on the upswing, and it is not clear when or whether it will peak and, as history might be taken to suggest, again be suppressed. It is our opinion that psychology has reached a level of maturity, rigor, and technical capability that will permit deep and successful examination of complex behavioral phenomena, but the ultimate test, of course, is time.

Our task in this chapter is neither to review history nor to forecast the future. We aim simply to summarize the literature on human thinking of roughly the last 5 years and to try to determine what promising new theoretical ideas or significant empirical observations have been reported. The general plan is to evaluate progress since the field was last reviewed (206). Secondarily, and with less emphasis, we will attempt some conceptual analysis and interpretation of recent work.[3]

[1] For supplementary bibliographic material (143 references, 16 pages), order NAPS Document 01600 from ASIS National Auxiliary Publications Service, c/o CCM Information Corp.-NAPS, 909 Third Avenue, New York, NY 10022. Remit with your order $2.00 for microfiche or $5.00 for each photocopy.

[2] Preparation of this chapter was supported in part by research grant MH 14314 from the National Institute of Mental Health. The literature reviewed is taken primarily from the period beginning January 1965 and continuing through June 1970, although several more recent papers were cited because of their special significance.

[3] The selectivity of this summary needs to be clear. Various relevant topics are assigned to other chapters in the general plan for the *Annual Review*. Lest their absence in this chapter be taken as bias, we note at the outset that emphasis is to be placed on recent theoretical and experimental research in concept formation and problem solving. We have no doubts about the relevance of studies of decision making or creativity, of the involvement of social or developmental variables, or of the importance of naturalistic or clinical methodologies in the overall understanding of human thinking. These and other matters are taken up centrally in other chapters, however, and omitted here to avoid overlap and redundancy.

Theories of Thinking

As noted elsewhere (12), many theories of thinking have their roots in learning theory. This follows naturally from the near universal assumption that people mainly learn what and how to think. There would be no thinking without antecedent experience, practice, and memory.

Associative and Mediational Theory

The distinction often drawn (11, 120) between purely associative and mediational theory is based on whether there are any significant assumptions about the role of internal processes or mechanisms. Associative theories attempt to characterize behavior in terms of a person's performance (activity, responses) and his circumstances (stimulus or situation). An example is the statistical theory of Bourne & Restle (26), describing concept identification as a joint function of conditioning (associating) relevant cues to response categories and adapting (rendering ineffective) irrelevant cues.

Mediational theories are based on many of the same assumptions elaborated to include associative relations between implicit or hypothetical stimuli and responses. Representative examples are the positions of Maltzman (147, 148) and of Kendler & Kendler (119). Maltzman uses the hypothetical response hierarchy (any stimulus can trigger a set of responses ordered by associative strength) in analyses of mental set, originality, and thinking. The Kendlers interpret basic concept formation processes as a matter of strengthening the correct one of a set of possible mediational linkages. The activity of selecting and strengthening mediators is said to be the sum and substance of thought. It is almost universally assumed that mediational stimuli, responses, and associations are learned, the best developed argument being given by Mandler (150). Kendler & Kendler (119, 120) suggest that people begin (at birth) as essentially pure associative organisms and develop mediational ability by experience. The primary empirical evidence for this position comes from age-related change in the relative difficulty of (intradimensional) reversal and (extradimensional) nonreversal shifts in solution of concept problems (120–122, 142). The implications are that both purely associative and mediational models must be necessary in a complete account of behavior.

While there has been no shortage of experimental investigations of associative and mediational theory, the basic positions have not changed significantly in the last 5 years. Bourne (12) has presented an extention of the Bourne-Restle model to conceptual problems with partially relevant cues, but notes that unresolved difficulties arise for this model in nearly all cases of interproblem transfer, including solution shifts. Staats (188) has used mainly mediational constructs in a grandiose analysis of many major examples of thinking, including language.

Hypothesis Theory

The idea that people solve problems by formulating and testing hypotheses has as long and venerable a history as associative theory. In contrast to the associative and mediational positions, however, advances in hypothesis theory have been great in the past half decade. It is probably fair to say that this has become the predominant theory today, at least for behavior in conceptual tasks.

The current resurgence of interest in hypothesis theory can be traced to the work of Bruner, Goodnow & Austin (32), who provided the first thorough methodological analysis of performance in concept problems. Restle (180) made a major contribution to hypothesis theory by mathematically formalizing the description of several problem-solving strategies. His model has many interesting properties which have been the subject of empirical test. For example, mathematically the theory is indifferent to the number of hypotheses under consideration by a subject on any trial. This seems counter-intuitive, and there is some empirical evidence (140) to the contrary. As we will discuss momentarily, sampling assumptions have undergone considerable exploration and revision to accommodate more recent results. Later developments in hypothesis theory, to be considered next, have been primarily due to Bower & Trabasso (29) and Levine (139).

Bower-Trabasso model.—Bower & Trabasso propose that concept learning is a matter of selecting (or attending to) individual stimulus dimensions (e.g. color) and conditioning their values (e.g. red, green) to response categories in accord with informative feedback provided by the experimenter. In most of the tasks to which this model has been applied, the response system has been minimal (i.e. two categories corresponding to the two values of a relevant stimulus dimension), so that the conditioning component is trivial and problem solving is primarily a dimension search and selection process. There are some cases, however, with more complex response systems, in which the course of conditioning itself consumes a significant number of trials (176, 196).

Dimension selection follows basically three rules: (*a*) performance is representable as a two-state process, presolution (attending to an irrelevant dimension) and solution (attending to the relevant dimension); (*b*) a change from presolution to solution state can occur only on an error trial, errors leading subject to select a new dimension randomly and with replacement; and (*c*) the probability of selecting the relevant dimension, i.e. solving the problem, is constant over presolution trials. A unique contribution of the model is an analysis of cue saliency, the attention-getting value which determines probability of selection of a dimension (200).

Experimental evidence.—The Restle-Bower-Trabasso theory has generated many new ideas for research in concept learning. For example, a single unannounced shift in the correct stimulus-response assignments of a problem, made before subject committed his last error, had no effect on total trials or errors to eventual solution, as would be expected if subject solves on a single error trial (197, 199). Even more compelling is the observation

that repeated unannounced shifts, either reversing the correct S-R assignments or making a different dimension relevant in every other error trial,
had little effect on performance of adults (28, 29). Young children seem to
be adversely affected by these procedures, however (68). Trabasso (195) and
others (e.g. 81) have demonstrated the stationarity of response probabilities
prior to the solution state transition. Finally, in direct empirical checks,
Trabasso & Bower (198; see also 25) have confirmed that subjects have
notoriously poor memory for stimuli, responses, and feedback signals given
earlier in a sequence of trials.

But not all results are consistent with assumptions of the theory. Contrary to the model, the probability of selecting the relevant dimension is not
in general constant over presolution trials. Perhaps the clearest demonstration has been provided by Levine (136). His procedure was a kind of reception paradigm in which subject chose what he thought was the positive one
of two stimuli on each trial. Feedback on the correctness of his response was
given on the first and every fifth trial thereafter, the intervening blank trial
pairs representing a test of which and how many hypotheses subject had in
mind at the time. Data clearly indicate that the pool of hypotheses considered by subject to be still viable decreased in size, at least over the first
few feedback trials, and remained below the initial number throughout the
remainder of the problem. In an attempt to account for these and other results, Trabasso & Bower (199) introduced the notion of local consistency,
i.e. that subject samples from only those hypotheses that are consistent with
information provided on the immediate error trial, which is a set distinctly
smaller than the original pool. In contrast to the original sampling assumptions, local consistency of hypotheses gives the theoretical subject some
memory for previous events.

There are other sources of evidence contrary to the Bower-Trabasso
position. Suppes & Ginsberg (190) found response probabilities decidedly
nonstationary in certain concept problems, especially in the last half of the
trials. They suggested, however, that a three-state Markov process (presolution, partial solution, and solution) would handle the most important
results. Hypothesis revisions have been observed on correct response trials
(136, 191), and subjects are sensitive to new sources of information even
after a workable solution has been achieved (57, 95). Both results cast serious doubt on an error-trial-only learning principle.

White (212) has evidence of at least two types of problem solvers, hypothesis testers and associators (who depend largely on rote memorization);
deviant data, such as those reported above, may be partly a product of
heterogeneous subject samples. Finally, on an assumption that complex
multidimensional concept problems are solved as a set of independent unidimensional subproblems, Trabasso & Bower (199) extended the basic
model to an analysis of four-category problems with two relevant dimensions.
Neither the theorists' own data or other results (17) are consistent with this

extension, both showing evidence of greater memory and subproblem dependence than could be accommodated by the theory (but see 161).

Levine's theory.—In contrast to other models, Levine's position is highly specific and is based on direct probes and evaluations of subject's hypotheses rather than abstract assumptions. His supporting evidence comes primarily from a "blank trials" procedure, designed to reveal systematic response sequences (presumably based on subject's current hypotheses) at any point in a problem. The major differences between Levine's and other hypothesis theories lies in the assumptions about sampling and feedback effects. According to Levine (138, 139), subject samples subsets of hypotheses from the pool of possibilities (see also 178). To respond on any trial, he selects one from the subset as a working hypothesis, bases his category response on it, retains it on correct response trials, and rejects it on errors. At the same time, however, subject is monitoring the remaining hypotheses in his subset. Thus on a correct response trial, subject retains his working hypothesis but rejects other hypotheses in the subset which are disconfirmed by feedback. After an error, subject rejects both the working hypothesis and any other inconsistent hypothesis from the subset. He selects a new working hypothesis, either from the remaining possibilities or, if none, from a new subset. Thus, significant problem solving activities occur on both correct response and error trials.

The subject's functional subset of hypotheses is governed by the stimuli presented on outcome trials, i.e. trials with feedback. In simultaneous discrimination, where a positive and a negative stimulus are presented on each trial, subject is said to code verbally the values (e.g. "large," "black," etc) of the stimulus he thinks are positive. If feedback confirms his stimulus selection, he has a subset of (coded) hypotheses which contains the solution. If feedback contradicts his selection, all verbalized hypotheses are wrong. To achieve the subset with the correct hypothesis, subject must take the complement of his original coding. After confirmation, the coded subset is retained without further activity; after disconfirmation, subject must recode, which requires time and runs the risk of inaccuracies. This process continues until subject finds the correct hypothesis.

Levine's theory helps to clarify some previously unexplained results. While response probabilities often do hover around chance (presolution) until subject achieves solution, response latencies almost universally show a gradual decrease over a series of correct responses and especially over criterion trials (80). The apparent discrepancy between choice and latency data is relatively easily resolved on the idea that subject begins the criterion run with a subset containing the correct hypothesis, but has to narrow it down on successive trials. The theory is also consistent with evidence that the size of subject's hypothesis pool decreases across trials (79, 81, 137) and that both confirming and disconfirming feedback have significant effects on performance (24, 136).

The theory has other implications for the effects of temporal variables. Because information processing occurs after feedback, a relatively long inter-trial interval should and does yield faster problem solving than a brief interval (23). Moreover, subject should require more time after an error (to re-code and find the complement of his preceding hypothesis set) than after a correct response. Erickson et al (80) have observed longer response latencies after errors, but Bourne and co-workers (17) found no difference between conditions in which an optimal intertrial interval was contingent on correct responses or on errors. It might be, however, that these results are complicated by the mixture of subject types and strategies (212).

Information Processing Theory

Like the other headings in this section, information processing theory refers to a general approach to interpreting behavior, encompassing a variety of specific models, rather than a single, cohesive system. The models are grouped together mainly because they are all expressed in terms of operations on information. These operations, often referred to as the processes underlying behavior, are complexly organized and interrelated so as to convert input (information from one's environment) into a variety of possible outputs (or performances). Typically the models are explicitly programmed for computers, and tests are made by contrasting performance protocols of real subjects with those generated by the computer-model under logically equivalent informational circumstances.

Newell & Simon (165) have been particularly conscientious about testing the relevance of their theory to a variety of behaviors, having considered chess playing, theorem proving in logic and both sequential and class-type concept learning within the same general framework. In contrast, Hunt (108) has been concerned almost exclusively with concept formation. He divides a person's activities during a problem into two phases—the reception, classi-fication, and storage items of information and the scanning of storage (memory) for purposes of reorganization, formulating hypotheses, and searching for the unknown concept. Items of information are stored as clusters of attributes or values of stimulus dimensions and as stimulus-category assignments. The general idea is to reduce complex conceptual sys-tems to successively simpler subproblems. The form of solution eventually developed is a set of decision rules which correspond to the various combina-tions of values on relevant dimensions. The problem solver arrives at the right combinations by some strategy for testing attributes for their relevance to the difference between response categories against items of information stored in memory. The subject's strategy represents the major parameter of the theory and, over the period of development, at least eleven different attribute selection and test routines have been evaluated.

A basis for evaluating the power and generality of the information pro-cessing approach is provided by Gregg & Simon (93), who describe a family of models for simple concept identification subsuming the basic hypothesis theory of Bower & Trabasso. Indeed, they show how the Bower-Trabasso position may be derived from their theory. Each Gregg-Simon model is based on eight formalized assumptions about processes subjects use in deciding how to respond to stimuli. Five assumptions relate to stimulus characteristics and the experimental situation and three to subject's performance. Differences among the models arise from alternative assumptions of one sort or another, especially about hypothesis sampling. A particular set of processes and assumptions specifies a model that can be programmed and run on a computer to arrive at precise and objective predictions about a temporal sequence of responses. Gregg & Simon conclude that an information processing approach has the advantages of generality, predictive power, and testability over other forms of psychological theory. While their conclusion might be debated, the work of Gregg & Simon is the best example of an explicit application of information processing models to conventional laboratory work and of its point-for-point comparison to a competing theoretical analysis.

General Comment on Theories of Thinking

There is a characteristic which is common to all theories discussed here, indeed to psychological theories in general. They assimilate to a "cause and effect" deterministic idiom in which behavior is a mere byproduct of prior, more fundamental events and processes. While it is fashionable today to reject conceptual Behaviorism (and rightly so), most theorists still hold (sometimes tenaciously) to the definition of behavior, imposed by Watson, as publicly observable performance, or worse, bodily movement. On a descriptive level, this definition strips behavior of its intention, cognition, and competence attributes and characterizes it essentially in terms of physical responses. Theorizing then becomes the tortuous task of reconnecting behavior (qua performance) with its other logical attributes. These behavioral attributes enter in disguise as terms of the theory: (a) Cognition or knowledge is partly in the stimulus and partly in the hypothesis pool, or the divergent mediational response hierarchy, or list or cell structure that represents memory. (b) Intention or motivation may be supplied by (drive) stimuli or by an internal energizing mechanism. (c) Competence, skill, or know-how is a mediational response, an internalized symbolic analog of performance, or an information process of some sort. These semantically transformed attributes of behavior are then used to "explain" the impoverished performance-type concept of behavior.

Indeed, these theoretical constructs do help to make performance more intelligible but perhaps not for the reasons that are implied. Mediators, memories, drives, information processes, hypotheses, etc are rather less like underlying causes or determinants and more like properties of behavior. Some investigators (e.g. 158, 166) argue that implicitly or explicitly every complete behavior description makes some commitment about what a person knows, knows how to do, and wants to do, as well as his actual performance. The point is that we would not otherwise be able to distinguish a real behavior from an accident. In this system, what we generally accept as theoretical explanation is a case of fuller, more complete description. Knowledge, skill, and intention are taken to be behavioral, not physiological, quasi-physiological, mentalistic, representational, or some other kind of non-behavioral concept. Thinking, which corresponds primarily with the cognitive and competence parameters, is used as a term in behavior descriptions rather than in descriptions of hypothetical causative processes.

The product of this approach is a conception of behavior as a rule-following system with knowledge, skill, intention, performance, and achievement (the consequence of performance) as major parameters. Space prevents an elaboration of the theory, though the reader can be referred to several sources (14, 18, 166).

EXPERIMENTAL STUDIES OF THINKING

Determinants of Problem Difficulty

In simple terms, a person given a problem is asked to use the information provided to produce a solution meeting specified criteria. To assess the difficulty of a problem, one must examine the manner in which the problem solver is given information, the familiarity of the required solution, and the size of the problem (16).

Methods of presenting problems.—Gestalt theory implies that anagrams which are themselves words (e.g. present NIGHT, with solution THING) should be more difficult than nonsense anagrams, with word anagrams viewed as better organized and thus more resistant to reorganization. Although earlier results were inconclusive, positive findings were obtained by Beilin & Horn (7), and the predicted difference has been replicated with different problems and procedures (5, 6, 77, 78). The factor(s) responsible for this difference remains to be clearly specified. Using nonsense anagrams, both Hebert & Rogers (104) and Dominowski (65) found easily pronounced anagrams more difficult to solve than those hard to pronounce. Thus, one plausible but untested argument is that word anagrams are harder not because of some effect of denotative meaning but because they are easier to pronounce.

Displays which draw attention to a critical feature of the problem tend to facilitate solution. For example, anagrams which retain some of the structural features of the solution word are easier to solve than those which do not (60, 154). The "candle-box" problem requires the problem solver to affix a cardboard box to the wall as a support for a candle (in order that no wax drips on the table or floor). It has been reliably found that the problem is much more difficult when the box is presented filled with tacks (e.g. 74, 89). Glucksberg & Weisberg (92) suggested that the box-filled version is more difficult because subjects do not attend to the box as a separate object when that version is given. Consistent with their analysis, the difficulty of the box-filled version was greatly reduced when each object was separately labeled (i.e. the box was labeled "BOX") (see also 90, 91).

In a conceptual problem, information can be provided in a variety of ways. Some investigations have been concerned with variations among stimuli having the same logical status with respect to the concept. For example, a four-valued stimulus might be a geometric form varying in shape, size, color, and texture (a unitary figure) or a distributed figure such as a pair of forms each of which varies in two dimensions, or simply a sequence of plus and minus signs. Consistent with earlier studies (11), some researchers have found concepts easier to identify when unitary figures are used (134, 186). Differences favoring unitary figures have been found when the solution required that a stimulus possess all relevant attributes in order to belong to the concept, and there is evidence indicating that unitary figures encourage the adoption of a solution strategy advantageous for this type of concept but not necessarily for other concept types (126, 127, 210, 215).

Researchers periodically report that the particular dimension chosen as relevant affects the difficulty of the task. Two ideas have been advanced for such findings: that some dimensions are more salient than others because of differences in discriminability of their values, and that some dimensions will yield easier problems because of subjects' preferences for those dimensions, which may or may not be related to discriminability. Results are quite clear when the degree of separation of the values on the same dimension is varied; a concept based on color, for example, will be easier when the values are quite different than when the values are similar, though perfectly discriminable (42, 84, 185, 193). However, differences in preference among dimensions are not related in any simple way to differences in discriminability, and preferences for dimensions do not predict differences in difficulty of concepts based on the dimensions (42, 69, 111).

Solution familiarity.—The concept of a response hierarchy implies that the set of possible responses in a problem situation can be ordered in terms of strength (frequency, familiarity). Associative theory (e.g. 147) predicts that when the problem is presented, responses will be emitted in order of strength, i.e. from most frequent to least frequent. Research on the effects of solution familiarity has tended to support this prediction.

Studies of anagram solving have firmly established that problem difficulty is inversely related to the language frequency of the solution word (60, 61, 115, 152, 154). The predicted relationship between solution frequency and output order is further supported by research on a variety of verbal problems indicating that high-frequency solutions are generally given before those of lower frequency (47, 71, 72, 114, 151). With anagrams it has also been found that problems whose solutions contain letter sequences of higher frequency are easier (61, 97, 113, 153, 154, 202), although the effect is relatively small.

The effects of solution familiarity have been observed in conceptual tasks. Freibergs & Tulving (85) argued that the typical advantage associated with presentation of positive instances of a concept stems from subjects' lack of familiarity with negative instances, based on the finding that the difference in performance on the two instance types diminishes with practice. However, subsequent research (41) has demonstrated that it is more appropriate to consider differences in familiarity with appropriate inferential strategies rather than with the instances themselves. With simpler problems, training techniques which increase the familiarity of solutions facilitate performance, whether the solutions are words (47, 67, 78) or uses of objects (53; see also 72, 144).

When a problem requires only that the solution be selected from a set of alternatives presented, the relationship between solution familiarity and difficulty may be altered. If the problem solver is given information about the level of familiarity of the correct alternative, or if he has experienced a series of problems whose solutions have similar levels of familiarity, then problem difficulty is curvilinearly related to solution familiarity (59, 73, 116). The most familiar solution remains the easiest to find, but discovering a solution of intermediate familiarity is more difficult than selecting solutions which are the least familiar items in the set. When subject knows that the solution is an unfamiliar alternative, he selects low-frequency items at the outset. Maximum difficulty occurs with solutions of intermediate familiarity because, in the sets of alternatives which have been used, there are more alternatives of intermediate familiarity than of any other level. This curvilinear relationship is less likely to occur when a problem requires production of the solution (61, 62, 70, 76).

Problem Size

The following results illustrate the statement that problem difficulty increases with problem size. Increasing the number of switches available produces a linear increase in the difficulty of a problem requiring subject to produce a specified light pattern by locating relevant switches on a response panel (46). Solution time for problems requiring subjects to traverse complex verbal mazes "in their heads" increases linearly with the number of blind alleys (98). The likelihood that an object will be used in a particular (unusual) manner to solve a problem decreases when irrelevant or distracting functions for the object are possible (146, 209). The time needed to produce a particular word consistent with letter cues increases with the number of alternative words possible (31). Anagrams having repeated letters are easier than those without duplicated letters (203). Anagrams containing low-frequency letters (which allow fewer combinations) are easier than those with high-frequency letters (43).

Ronning (181) proposed that the alternatives in an anagram problem are the permutations of the anagram letters and found that problems for which more permutations could be ruled out (based on knowledge of English word structure) were easier. However, the notion that subjects solve anagrams by constructing different permutations of the letter set until a solution is reached is open to serious question (112); the reliable effect of word frequency (115) as well as subjects' reports (117) indicate that the dominant solution method is thinking of words based on a minimal amount of letter-sequence construction. Subsequent research indicated that Ronning's results are better interpreted in terms of variation in the number of alternate bases for word generation (62, 117).

Numerous studies have demonstrated that the difficulty of concept identification increases linearly with the number of relevant (e.g. 141) and irrelevant dimensions (e.g. 66, 118, 167), although the relationship may break down at higher levels (37, 213); the slope of the relationship increases with the difficulty of the conceptual rule (86, 103).

The impairment produced by increasing the number of irrelevant stimulus dimensions in conceptual tasks has been interpreted in terms of the number of value-category associations which must be adapted or in terms of the number of possible hypotheses to be considered. These interpretations must be qualified in at least two ways. First, the number of irrelevant dimensions affects only the attribute identification component of concept learning and not rule learning (27, 103). Second, even when the task does require only identification of the relevant attributes, if subjects adopt a strategy of eliminating attributes from an initially complex working hypothesis, then increasing the number of irrelevant dimensions will yield only a very slight increase in task difficulty (37). Increasing the number of values per dimension, which increases the size of the stimulus set, resulted in more efficient concept attainment, because subjects could more rapidly eliminate attributes as irrelevant (101).

Motivational and Ability Factors in Problem Solving

Investigators continue to be interested in identifying the correlates of problem-solving efficiency, but results vary in usefulness and clarity (149). In studies of sex differences the typical finding for "insight" problems is that males perform more efficiently than females (34, 35, 145). Sex differences are usually not observed with anagrams (157, 182). On conceptual tasks, the pattern of findings is complex, with females sometimes superior to (173, 175), not different from (134) or inferior to, males (132, 172). Some attempt has been made to specify what females and males do differently in problem situations, but the factors identified seem to apply as well within a sex group as between sexes (145).

Scores on intelligence tests are positively related to performance on anagrams (157) and on conceptual tasks (128, 132). In contrast, performance on an "insight" problem was found to be unrelated to either intelligence or several other ability measures (35), suggesting that solving insight problems might represent a unique kind of behavior not tapped by traditional measures of intelligence.

Many attempts have been made to distinguish intelligence and creativity, and creativity has been related to problem solving with intelligence controlled (208). A plethora of definitions and measures of creativity exists; in studies concerned with problem solving, the Remote Associates Test (156) has been used and has been assumed to index subjects' ability to shift attention rapidly on a symbolic level (utilize a wide variety of cues). As with intelligence, creativity test scores are positively related to anagram performance (64, 157) and to concept attainment (128, 132). A positive correlation was expected between creativity test scores and performance on an insight problem, but no relationship was observed (44). Using several reasoning problems and a different index of creativity (offering an innovative solution to an open-ended problem), Maier & Janzen (146) did observe a positive relationship between "creativity" and problem-solving efficiency. Based on these findings and the interpretations offered, it does appear that being able to utilize cues (information) in different ways and at a rapid rate is conductive to efficient problem solving, independent of the knowledge and skills tapped by intelligence tests.

Anxiety and stress.—Motivational level has been varied in two ways: by selecting subjects having different "chronic" motivational levels on the basis of scores on the Taylor Manifest Anxiety Scale, and by manipulating the amount of stress in the problem situation through instructions, incentives, shock, or failure. Clear expectations regarding motivational effects depend upon specifying the difficulty of the task and the effective motivational level, which is a joint function of subject's base level and that produced by the experimental situation. An interaction between task difficulty and motivational level has been demonstrated in various ways. For subjects undifferentiated with respect to anxiety (presumably having a moderate level), increasing motivation by offering incentives for superior performance impairs solution of a difficult version of a problem while having no effect on an easy version (88). With a concept-identification task of moderate difficulty, high-intelligence subjects exhibiting high levels of anxiety perform better than those with low anxiety, but this difference is reversed for subjects of low intelligence (50, 135). Increasing the number of irrelevant stimulus dimensions impairs concept attainment more for high-anxious subjects than for low-anxious subjects (75). When easy and difficult problems have been used with three levels of motivation, an inverted-U function has been obtained (189, 194).

A second reliable finding is that experimentally induced failure impairs subsequent problem solving (82, 83, 170). However, it cannot be determined at present whether this effect is best interpreted in terms of direct energizing of competing responses, the adoption of inappropriate solution strategies due to perception of the problems as more difficult than they are, or a lack of opportunity to learn relevant skills.

It may be more appropriate to consider individual differences in the tendency to become anxious in test situations rather than general anxiety when attempting to relate anxiety to problem solving (96, 157, 182, 214). Attempts to induce stress through ego-involving instructions have yielded impairment of problem solving (201), no effect (182), or complicated interactions (135). Requiring subjects to verbalize while working on a problem has been hypothesized to increase stress and thus impair performance (182), but verbalization can also facilitate performance by encouraging subject to work more carefully (48). Over all, the most consistent findings occur when investigators use tasks of varying difficulty levels, a result which can be expected on the basis of the Yerkes-Dodson law. As an example of the utility of this strategy, Dunn (75) found that increasing stress by associating concepts with shock magnified the effect of increased task difficulty for low-anxious subjects, but not for high-anxious subjects.

The Analysis of Concept Attainment

In this section, attention will be directed toward two aspects of conceptual tasks which have received recent emphasis and which not only have led to significant advances in our knowledge but also indicate the limitations of the formal theories, viz the importance of rules in the definition of concepts and the critical role played by solution strategies.

Conceptual rules.—Haygood & Bourne (99) made the elementary but important point that a concept is defined in terms both of certain stimulus attributes and of a rule connecting or integrating these attributes. For example, with geometric forms, having selected *red* and *circle* as the attributes of a concept, one can define different concepts by applying different rules (e.g. red *and* circle; red *or* circle; *if* red, *then* circle, etc). The separation of the rule and attribute components of concepts leads to the specification of three conceptual tasks, *attribute identification* (rule known, attributes unknown), *rule learning* or *identification* (attributes known, rule unknown), and *complete learning* (attributes and rule unknown).

Each unique conceptual rule involves a different assignment of the stimuli from some population to two categories, members (positive instances) and nonmembers (negative instances) of a concept. Table 1 illustrates the patterns of assignment for a number of familiar rules. Not all rules generate classes like these, of course; Azuma & Cronbach (4) and Uhl (204) have described and investigated certain quantitative scalar rules. Notice that the rules apply to logical descriptions of the stimuli (red, not red, square, not square) rather than to "physical" descriptions. With just two values per dimension (red or green, square or triangle), this distinction is trivial; but it becomes essential when more than two values per dimension exist (green squares and blue squares are alike in that they are both not-red squares). If subject learns a concept based on the logical stimulus descriptions, then an unambiguous prediction can be made concerning his behavior when a novel stimulus is presented (e.g. having learned the conditional rule, subject would classify a yellow hexagon as positive because it is a not-red not-square).

TABLE 1. Rules for Assigning Stimuli to Positive and Negative Categories

		Stimulus Classes[a]			Proportion Positive Instances		
	RS	RTr, RC	GS, BS	GTr, BTr, GC, BC	Two-valued Dimensions	Three-valued Dimensions	Verbal Description
Rule	TT	TF	FT	FF			
Affirmation	+	+	−	−	.50	.33	Red
Conjunction	+	−	−	−	.25	.11	Red and Square
Disjunction (inclusive)	+	+	+	−	.75	.55	Red and/or Square
Conditional	+	−	+	+	.75	.78	If Red, then Square
Biconditional	+	−	−	+	.50	.45	Red if and only if Square

[a] In defining stimulus classes, R =red, B =blue, G =green, S =square, C =circle, Tr =triangle, and T =true, F =false.

The various rules assign different proportions of the stimulus population to the positive and negative categories, and the homogeneity of both categories varies with the rule (22). The proportions of stimuli in the two categories vary also with the number of values per dimension, but not with the number of irrelevant dimensions. If the degree of stimulus uncertainty is an effective variable, one would expect these characteristics to affect rule difficulty. Increasing the amount of irrelevant information does increase the difficulty of attribute identification and complete learning since, with more stimulus attributes, there are more possible attribute combinations which might be relevant. In contrast, however, increasing the number of irrelevant dimensions does not affect rule learning (27, 103). Provided that some irrelevant stimulus dimensions exist, rule learning is easier than attribute identification (21, 54, 55, 99).

A consistent order of increasing difficulty has emerged from research: affirmational, conjunctive, inclusive disjunctive, and conditional, both for attribute identification and rule learning (21, 22, 86, 99, 109, 129, 164). The placement of the biconditional rule in this order is uncertain, with some studies indicating that it is the most difficult (21, 86, 99), while others show it to be easier than the conditional or disjunctive rule (129, 133). The reasons for this inconsistency are not apparent, although it may result from variation in the information characteristics of initial instances (87, 192). Differences in rule difficulty decrease with practice, implying that subjects eventually become equally facile with any rule (99). The improvement is found not only over problems based on the same rule, but also between rules. Interrule positive transfer depends on the similarity of rules in terms of the category assignments of the logical stimulus types (15, 21).

Sources of rule difficulty are partially identified with particular stimulus classes. Rule differences are smallest in terms of performance on TT instances. Disjunctives differ most from conjunctives on TF and FT instances; this implies that subjects are biased toward treating these classes as negative, or that subjects initially treat conceptual problems as conjunctive (108). The greatest difficulty with conditional and biconditional rules occurs with FF instances, which must be assigned with TTs to the positive category. Performance under the biconditional rule is most facilitated by prior training on the conditional rule for this reason (21).

Interrule positive transfer is directly related to the number of different rules which subject encounters during training (21). Both this fact and the general improvement found over problems have been attributed to the acquisition by subject of a "truth-table strategy" for solving rule-learning problems. Fully mastered, this strategy involves attending to the relevant stimulus dimensions (given in a rule-learning task), associating attribute combinations with the truth table classes (TT, TF, FT, FF), and associating each logical class with one of the two categories, positive or negative. With this strategy subject needs to observe the category of only one stimulus from each truth-table class in order to know the rule and be able to categorize all subsequent stimuli without error. While "naive" subjects rarely give evidence of this strategy, nearly everyone does after 12 successive problems on a variety of rules (15). Furthermore, there is evidence indicating that the truth-table strategy can be taught even to young children, leading to a marked improvement in their performance (13, 94).

Attribute-identification strategies.—The truth-table strategy is useful primarily in the discovery of a conceptual rule when the relevant attributes are known; other research has been directed toward the identification of strategies subjects use in finding the relevant attributes of a concept when the rule is known. The pioneering work was performed by Bruner, Goodnow & Austin (32), who described two main classes of strategies; *focusing*—a procedure for eliminating (irrelevant) attributes—and *scanning*—a procedure for trial-by-trial hypothesis testing.

It has been argued that the selection paradigm should yield more efficient concept attainment than the reception paradigm because it allows subject to obtain information directly related to his current hypothesis (107). Comparisons of the two methods have not been uniformly favorable to the selection paradigm (107, 143, 184), and the most sensible conclusion at this time is that selection subjects will do better only if they utilize strategies yielding a high rate of stimulus information (160, 184).

Bruner et al (32) reported that subjects using a focusing strategy were more efficient problem solvers than those using a scanning strategy. One of the difficulties with the early work was the rather loose criterion for deciding what strategy subject was using. Various attempts have been made to utilize quantitative indices, with somewhat mixed results. Bourne (9, 10), using the reception paradigm, found that the number of trials to solution was inversely related to the number of attributes included in subject's initial hypothesis, but Siegel (186) was unable to replicate this finding. With the selection paradigm, attention has been directed toward the manner in which subjects select stimuli; in the initial formulation focusers were described as selecting stimuli which differ in one or two attributes from the first positive instance. Byers (36) has pointed out that the assumption of a fixed focus is unnecessarily restrictive and has demonstrated that allowing for a shifting focus in the calculation of strategies improves the prediction of the data. However, in some studies increased use of focusing has been unrelated or inversely related to problem-solving efficiency (19, 184). In contrast, Byers, Davidson, & Rohwer (38) found that instructing subjects in the use of a conservative focusing strategy not only improved performance but also eliminated the usually detrimental effect of increasing the number of relevant dimensions.

Laughlin (126, 127) has developed rules for quantifying focusing and has related focusing to a considerable variety of variables (130, 133, 135). In a most interesting proposal, Laughlin (129) argued that differences in difficulty among conceptual rules (in an attribute-identification task) could be predicted by assessing the difficulties of the focusing strategies appropriate to the various rules, and he obtained results consistent with the predictions.

Positive versus negative instances.—It has been rather generally accepted that concept identification is accomplished more readily from presentation of positive rather than negative instances (187). Following Hovland's (105, 106) lead, much emphasis has been given to the relative information provided by positive and negative instances. The information value of an instance is inversely related to the proportion of stimuli which belong to its class, a variable which depends on the conceptual rule and the number of values per stimulus dimension (Table 1). With binary stimulus dimensions, positive and negative instances of an affirmative concept provide equivalent information, yet recent research has confirmed earlier findings that positive instances lead to better performance (63). While such findings are consistent with the view that inferring a concept from information concerning which attributes are not in the concept is more difficult than inference from positive instances, Brinley & Sardello (30) obtained evidence supporting an analysis stressing memory load. They argued that subjects given negative instances have to remember or generate the set of possible solutions while this set is contained in a positive instance (see also 137), and they found that when subjects had available a list of possible answers, the difference in effectiveness of positive and negative instances disappeared.

With the more complex rules, the findings are rather systematic and illustrate the point made earlier. Positive instances of conjunctive concepts are more informative and lead to better performance (22, 162); in a mixed sequence, efficiency increases with the proportion of positive instances (183). Investigation of other rules, however, leads to the generalization that identifying the relevant attributes of a concept is easier when information is presented in the form of instances of the smaller of the two classes, whether it is positive or negative. The only qualification on this generalization is an allowance for an initial bias for positive instances. Thus, negative instances lead to more efficient attainment with conditional concepts (22), and the percentage of positive instances is unrelated to performance with biconditional concepts (100). For disjunctive concepts, the advantage of positive instances is either markedly reduced (22) or strikingly reversed (41, 45), and increasing the percentage of negative instances in a sequence facilitates attainment (49). The easier inferential strategy is associated with positive instances of conjunctive concepts but with negative instances of disjunctive concepts, and the results convincingly support the argument that the difference in difficulty of inferential strategies accounts for the difference in performance rather than the positive or negative label (45). As a final point, Bourne & Guy (22) demonstrated that in a rule-learning task efficiency is directly related to the variety of instances presented (the opposite of that for attribute identification), with a mixed sequence consistently superior to either all-positive or all-negative instances for all rules.

Memory.—Since complete information about the concept to be identified is usually spread over a series of trials, memory for previous information must play an important role in concept attainment (58). In the reception paradigm subjects' hypotheses are generally consistent with available stimulus information but frequently inconsistent with prior information, the likelihood of an inconsistency increasing with the remoteness of the stimulus (20). Both perceptual and memory errors are more characteristic of less efficient solvers (20, 186). As might be expected from these findings, allowing prior information to remain in view facilitates concept attainment. Although display of the stimulus pattern is more important than display of feedback (23), it is clear that performance is most facilitated by the continued availability of both types of information (8, 23, 171, 174).

The tendency for subjects' hypotheses to be inconsistent with earlier (and no longer available) stimuli has been assumed to reflect forgetting of this information. However, measures of stimulus (and feedback) recall fail to substantiate this view. Stimulus recall typically shows a bowed serial-position curve (25, 39, 63, 198), leading to the paradox that subject's hypothesis is most likely to be inconsistent with the earliest stimulus in a series, which is best recalled. The data are consistent with the idea that naive subjects, at least on the early trials of the first problem, might attempt to solve by remembering "everything," but, as practice continues (both within a problem and over problems), they switch to a more efficient solution strategy for which only recall of selected information is appropriate (25).

Based on the finding that allowing subjects to use paper and pencil to keep a record of whatever they choose has virtually no effect on performance in the selection paradigm, it has been suggested that memory effects might be limited to the reception paradigm (129, 131). However, this view is incorrect, since making available the category designations of previously selected stimuli facilitates performance (19), even for subjects who have been instructed to use a focusing strategy (38).

Memory factors have been suggested as an explanation for the differences in difficulty observed among conceptual rules (51, 52). The argument is based on the findings that short-term forgetting increases with the information-processing difficulty of an interpolated task (177). Differences in rule difficulty are noticeably reduced when prior stimuli and their category designations are made available (19, 51, 52). However, the process of attribute identification when prior information is available might not be the same process used when this information is not available. For example, subjects might utilize strategies emphasizing positive instances when prior information is unavailable but make use of the highly informative comparison of positive and negative instances (211) when memory is artificially provided.

Based on the assumption that subjects solve concepts by comparing instances from the same category, Underwood (205) had proposed that efficiency would be inversely related to the degree of separation of same-category instances in a series. However, while it is true that attribute identification is facilitated by the successive occurrence of stimuli from the "same" category (variously defined, depending on the rule), there is no independent evidence indicating that degree of separation is an effective variable (66, 102). It has been shown that when only one attribute changes between successive stimuli (providing unambiguous information, whether the category changes or not), the advantage of successive occurrence of same-category instances is lost (1, 2). A discrepant result was reported by Peterson (168), who found no effects due to the type of series, the number of attributes changing, or their interaction. With this exception, the results suggest that stimulus sequences will vary in effectiveness, not because of differential forgetting of stimulus information but because of differences in the ambiguity of information provided by successive transitions in the series.

Concluding Statement

This literature review has been both selective and sketchy. Lest this coverage fail to reflect the resurgence of thinking and cognition as psychological concepts and the rapid pace of scientific developments in the area today, we note (not exhaustively) in conclusion the publication of several recent books and monographs whose contribution is impossible to summarize adequately. Research monographs: *Attention in Learning* (200), *Studies in Cognitive Growth* (33), and *Experiments in Induction* (110). Each outlines in detail a specific program of original research and its implications for human cognitive processes.

Conference reports: *Problem Solving* (124), *Analyses of Concept Learning* (123), *Approaches to Thought* (207), *Verbal Behavior and General Behavior Theory* (56), *Concepts and the Structure of Memory* (125), *Cognition and Affect* (3). Each volume summarizes the knowledge and deliberations of a group of recognized scientists on some general issues in thinking.

General books and textbooks: *Language and Thought* (40), *Cognition and Thought* (179), *Cognitive Psychology* (163), *Thinking* (155), *Abstraction and*

Concept Formation (169), *Human Conceptual Behavior* (11), and *The Psychology of Thinking* (18). These books typically review a broad segment of the current literature in greater detail than has been attempted in this chapter. In addition to these resource materials, a journal, *Cognitive Psychology*, under the editorship of Walter Reitman, was founded in 1970 to provide further space for original contributions. *Cognitive Psychology* should become the leading archive in the area.

Interest among psychologists in human cognitive processes is at an all-time high, if the sheer volume of current literature is any measure. Our review suggests that substantial progress is being made toward the solution of some of psychology's most intractable problems.

LITERATURE CITED

1. Anderson, R. C. 1966. Sequence constraints and concept identification. *Psychol. Rep.* 19:1295–1302
2. Anderson, R. C., Guthrie, J. T. 1966. Effects of some sequential manipulations of relevant and irrelevant stimulus dimensions on concept learning. *J. Exp. Psychol.* 72:501–4
3. Antrobus, J. S., Ed. 1970. *Cognition and Affect*. Boston: Little, Brown. 210 pp.
4. Azuma, H., Cronbach, L. J. 1966. Cue-response correlations in the attainment of a scalar concept. *Am. J. Psychol.* 79:38–49
5. Beilin, H. 1966. Solving words as anagrams: A re-examined issue examined. *Psychon. Sci.* 6:77–78
6. Beilin, H. 1967. Developmental determinants of word and nonsense anagram solution. *J. Verb. Learn. Verb. Behav.* 6:523–27
7. Beilin, H., Horn, R. 1962. Transition probability effects in anagram problem solving. *J. Exp. Psychol.* 63:514–18
8. Blaine, D. D., Dunham, J. L., Pyle, T. W. 1968. Type and amount of available past instances in concept learning. *Psychon. Sci.* 12:159–60
9. Bourne, L. E. Jr. 1963. Factors affecting strategies used in problems of concept-formation. *Am. J. Psychol.* 76:229–38
10. Bourne, L. E. Jr. 1965. Hypotheses and hypothesis shifts in classification learning. *J. Gen. Psychol.* 72:251–61
11. Bourne, L. E. Jr. 1966. *Human Conceptual Behavior*. Boston: Allyn & Bacon. 139 pp.

12. Bourne, L. E. Jr. 1968. Concept attainment. See Ref. 56
13. Bourne, L. E. Jr. 1969. *Development of conceptual rules: Some preliminary findings*. Tech. Rep. No. 81, Univ. Wisconsin Cent. Cognitive Learn.
14. Bourne, L. E. Jr. 1969. Concept learning and thought. See Ref. 207
15. Bourne, L. E. Jr. 1970. Knowing and using concepts. *Psychol. Rev.* 77:546–56
16. Bourne, L. E. Jr., Battig, W. F. 1966. Complex processes. *Experimental Methods and Instrumentation in Psychology*, ed. J. B. Sidowski. New York: McGraw. 803 pp.
17. Bourne, L. E. Jr., Dodd, D. H., Guy, D. E., Justesen, D. R. 1968. Response-contingent intertrial intervals in concept identification. *J. Exp. Psychol.* 76:601–8
18. Bourne, L. E. Jr., Ekstrand, B. R., Dominowski, R. L. *The Psychology of Thinking*. Englewood Cliffs: Prentice-Hall. In press
19. Bourne, L. E. Jr., Ekstrand, B. R., Montgomery, B. 1969. Concept learning as a function of the conceptual rule and the availability of positive and negative instances. *J. Exp. Psychol.* 82:538–44
20. Bourne, L. E. Jr., Goldstein, S., Link, W. E. 1964. Concept learning as a function of availability of previously presented information *J. Exp. Psychol.* 67:439–48
21. Bourne, L. E. Jr., Guy, D. E. 1968. Learning conceptual rules: I. Some interrule transfer effects. *J. Exp. Psychol.* 76:423–29

22. Ibid 1968. Learning conceptual rules: II. The role of positive and negative instances. 77:488–94

23. Bourne, L. E. Jr., Guy, D. E., Dodd, D. H., Justesen, D. R. 1965. Concept identification: The effects of varying length and informational components of the intertrial interval. *J. Exp. Psychol.* 69:624–29

24. Bourne, L. E. Jr., Guy, D. E., Wadsworth, N. 1967. Verbal-reinforcement combinations and the relative frequency of informative feedback in a card-sorting task. *J. Exp. Psychol.* 73:220–26

25. Bourne, L. E. Jr., O'Banion, K. 1969. Memory for individual events in concept identification. *Psychon. Sci.* 16:101–2

26. Bourne, L. E. Jr., Restle, F. 1959. Mathematical theory of concept identification. *Psychol. Rev.* 66:278–96

27. Bower, A. C., King, W. L. 1967. The effect of number of irrelevant stimulus dimensions, verbalizations, and sex on learning. *Psychon. Sci.* 8:453–54

28. Bower, G., Trabasso, T. 1963. Reversals prior to solution in concept identification. *J. Exp. Psychol.* 66:409–18

29. Bower, G., Trabasso, T. 1964. Concept identification. *Studies in Mathematical Psychology*, ed. R. C. Atkinson, Stanford Univ. Press. 414 pp.

30. Brinley, J. F., Sardello, R. J. 1970. Increasing the utility of negative instances in conjunctive concept identification. *Psychon. Sci.* 18:101–2

31. Broerse, A. C., Zwaan, E. J. 1966. The information value of initial letters in the identification of words. *J. Verb. Learn. Verb. Behav.* 5:441–46

32. Bruner, J. S., Goodnow, J. J., Austin, G. A. 1956. *A Study of Thinking.* New York: Wiley. 330 pp.

33. Bruner, J. S., Olver, R. R., Greenfield, P. M. 1966. *Studies in Cognitive Growth.* New York: Wiley. 343 pp.

34. Burke, R. J. 1965. Sex differences in recognizing the correct answer to a problem. *Psychol. Rep.* 17:532–34

35. Burke, R. J., Maier, N. R. 1965. Attempts to predict success on an insight problem. *Psychol. Rep.* 17:303–10

36. Byers, J. L. 1967. A note on the calculation of strategies in concept attainment. *Am. Educ. Res. J.* 4:361–66

37. Byers, J. L., Davidson, R. E. 1968. Relevant and irrelevant information in concept attainment. *J. Exp. Psychol.* 76:283–87

38. Byers, J. L., Davidson, R. E., Rohwer, W. D. Jr. 1968. The effects of strategy instructions and memory on concept attainment. *J. Verb. Learn. Verb. Behav.* 7:831–37

39. Calfee, R. C. 1969. Recall and recognition memory in concept identification. *J. Exp. Psychol.* 81:436–40

40. Carroll, J. B. 1964. *Language and Thought.* Englewood Cliffs: Prentice-Hall. 118 pp.

41. Chlebek, J., Dominowski, R. L. 1970. The effect of practice on utilization of information from positive and negative instances in identifying disjunctive concepts. *Can. J. Psychol.* 24:64–69

42. Clayton, K. N., Merryman, C. T., Leonard, T. B. III. 1969. Rate of concept identification and the noticeability of the relevant dimension. *Psychon. Sci.* 15:109–10

43. Cohen, J. L. 1968. The effect of letter frequency on anagram solution times. *Psychon. Sci.* 11:79–80

44. Danks, J. H., Glucksberg, S. 1966. Asymmetric transfer between the Remote Associates Test and functional fixedness. *Psychol. Rep.* 19:682

45. Davidson, M. 1969. Positive versus negative instances in concept identification problems matched for logical complexity of solution procedures. *J. Exp. Psychol.* 80:369–73

46. Davis, G. A. 1967. Detrimental effects of distraction, additional response alternatives and longer response chains in solving switch-light problems. *J. Exp. Psychol.* 73:45–55

47. Davis, G. A., Manske, M. E. 1968. Effects of prior serial learning of solution words upon anagram problem solving: II. A serial position effect. *J. Exp. Psychol.* 77:101–4

48. Davis, J. H., Carey, M. H., Foxman, P. N., Tarr, D. B. 1968. Verbalization, experimenter presence, and problem solving. *J. Pers. Soc. Psychol.* 8:299–302

49. Denney, N. W. 1969. The effect of varying percentage of positive and negative instances and instructions on conjunctive and disjunctive learning. *Psychon. Sci.* 17:193–94

50. Denny, J. P. 1966. Effects of anxiety and intelligence on concept formation. *J. Exp. Psychol.* 72:596–602

51. Denny, N. R. 1969. Memory and transformations in concept learning. *J. Exp. Psychol.* 79:63–68

52. Denny, N. R. 1969. Memory load and concept-rule difficulty. *J. Verb. Learn. Verb. Behav.* 8:202–5

53. DiVesta, F. J., Walls, R. T. 1967. Transfer of object-function in problem solving. *Am. Educ. Res. J.* 4: 207–16

54. DiVesta, F. J., Walls, R. T. 1967. Transfer of solution rules in problem solving. *J. Educ. Psychol.* 58: 319–26

55. DiVesta, F. J., Walls, R. T. 1969. Rule and attribute identification in children's attainment of disjunctive and conjunctive concepts. *J. Exp. Psychol.* 80:498–504

56. Dixon, T. R., Horton, D. L., Eds. 1968. *Verbal Behavior and General Behavior Theory.* Englewood Cliffs: Prentice-Hall. 596 pp.

57. Dodd, D. H., Bourne, L. E. Jr. 1969. A test of some assumptions of a hypothesis-testing model of concept identification. *J. Exp. Psychol.* 80: 69–72

58. Dominowski, R. L. 1965. Role of memory in concept learning. *Psychol. Bull.* 63:271–80

59. Dominowski, R. L. 1965. Problem difficulty as a function of relative frequency of correct responses. *Psychon. Sci.* 3:317–18

60. Dominowski, R. L. 1966. Anagram solving as a function of letter moves. *J. Verb. Learn. Verb. Behav.* 5:107–11

61. Dominowski, R. L. 1967. Anagram solving as a function of bigram rank and word frequency. *J. Exp Psychol.* 75:299–306

62. Ibid 1968. Anagram solving as a function of letter-sequence information. 76.78–83

63. Dominowski, R. L. 1968. Stimulus memory in concept attainment. *Psychon. Sci.* 10:359–60

64. Dominowski, R. L. 1968. *Anagram solving and creativity: Effects of letter moves and word frequency.* Presented at 9th Ann. Meet. Psychon. Soc., St. Louis, Mo.

65. Dominowski, R. L. 1969. The effect of pronunciation practice on anagram difficulty. *Psychon. Sci.* 16:99–100

66. Dominowski, R. L. 1969. Concept attainment as a function of instance contiguity and number of irrelevant dimensions. *J. Exp. Psychol.* 82:573–74

67. Dominowski, R. L., Ekstrand, B. R. 1967. Direct and associative priming in anagram solving. *J. Exp. Psychol.* 74:84–86

68. Douglass, H. J., Bourne, L. E. Jr. Chronological age and performance on problems with repeated presolution shifts. *Develop. Psychol.* In press

69. Downing, B. 1969. Discriminability and preference in concept identification. *Psychon. Sci.* 14:85–86

70. Duncan, C. P. 1961. Attempts to influence performance on an insight problem. *Psychol. Rep.* 9:35–42

71. Duncan, C. P. 1966. Problem solving within a verbal response hierarchy. *Psychon. Sci.* 4:147–48

72. Duncan, C. P. 1966. Effect of word frequency on thinking of a word. *J. Verb. Learn. Verb Behav.* 5:434–40

73. Duncan, C. P., Ed. 1967. Response hierarchies in problem solving. *Thinking: Current Experimental Studies.* Chicago: Lippincott. 503 pp.

74. Duncker, K. 1945. On problemsolving. *Psychol. Monogr.* 58:5 (Whole No. 2 70)

75. Dunn, R. F. 19 68. Anxiety and verbal concept lea rning. *J. Exp. Psychol.* 76:286–90

76. Edmonds, E. M., Mueller, M. R. 1969. Effect of word frequency restriction on anagram solution. *J. Exp. Psychol.* 79:545–46

77. Ekstrand, B. R., Dominowski, R. L. 1965. Solving words as anagrams. *Psychon. Sci.* 2:239–40

78. Ekstrand, B. R., Dominowski, R. L. 1968. Solving words as anagrams: II. A clarification. *J. Exp. Psychol.* 77:552–58

79. Erickson, J. R. 1968. Hypothesis sampling in concept identification. *J Exp. Psychol.* 76:12–18

80. Erickson, J. R., Zajkowski, M. M., Ehmann, E. D. 1966. All-or-none assumptions in concept identifications: Analysis of latency data. *J. Exp. Psychol.* 72:690–97

81. Erickson, J. R., Block, K. K., Rulon, M. J. 1970. Some characteristics of hypothesis sampling in concept identification. *Psychon. Sci.* 20:103–5

82. Feather, N. T. 1966. Effects of prior

success and failure on expectations of success and subsequent performance. *J. Pers. Soc. Psychol.* 3: 287–98

83. Feather, N. T., Saville, M. R. 1967. Effects of amount of prior success and failure on expectations of success and subsequent task performance. *J. Pers. Soc. Psychol.* 5: 226–32

84. Fredrick, W. C. 1968. Concept identification as a function of the number of relevant and irrelevant dimensions, presentation method, and salience. *Psychol. Rep.* 23:631–34

85. Freibergs, V., Tulving, E. 1961. The effect of practice on utilization of information from positive and negative instances in concept identification. *Can. J. Psychol.* 5:101–6

86. Giambra, L. M. 1969. Effect of number of irrelevant dimensions with ten concept types on the attribute identification task in the selection mode with exemplar and nonexemplar start cards. *Psychon. Sci.* 14:75–76

87. Giambra, L. M. 1970. Conditional and biconditional rule difficulty with attribute identification, rule learning, and complete learning task. *J. Exp. Psychol.* 86:250–54

88. Glucksberg, S. 1962. The influence of strength of drive on functional fixedness and perceptual recognition. *J. Exp. Psychol.* 63:36–41

89. Glucksberg, S. 1964. Functional fixedness: Problem solution as a function of observing responses. *Psychon. Sci.* 1:117–18

90. Glucksberg, S., Danks, J. H. 1967. Functional fixedness: Stimulus equivalence mediated by semantic-acoustic similarity. *J. Exp. Psychol.* 74:400–5

91. Glucksberg, S., Danks, J. H. 1968. Effects of discriminative labels and of nonsense labels upon availability of functions. *J. Verb. Learn. Verb. Behav.* 7:72–76

92. Glucksberg, S., Weisberg, R. W. 1966. Verbal behavior and problem solving: Some effects of labeling in a functional fixedness problem. *J. Exp. Psychol.* 71:659–64

93. Gregg, L. W., Simon, H. A. 1967. Process models and stochastic theories of simple concept formation. *J. Math. Psychol.* 4:246–76

94. Guy, D. E. 1969. A developmental study of performance on concep-

tual problems involving a rule shift. *J. Exp. Psychol.* 82:242–49

95. Guy, D. E., Van Fleet, F., Bourne, L. E. Jr. 1966. Effects of adding a stimulus dimension prior to a non-reversal shift. *J. Exp. Psychol.* 72: 161–68

96. Harleston, B. W., Smith, M. G., Arey, D. 1965. Test-anxiety, heart rate, and anagram solving. *J. Pers. Soc. Psychol.* 1:551–57

97. Harris, R., Loess, H. 1968. Anagram solution times as a function of individual differences in stored diagram frequencies. *J. Exp. Psychol.* 77: 508–11

98. Hayes, J. R. 1965. Problem topology and the solution process. *J. Verb. Learn. Verb. Behav.* 4:371–79

99. Haygood, R. C., Bourne, L. E. Jr. 1965. Attribute- and rule-learning aspects of conceptual behavior. *Psychol. Rev.* 72:175–95

100. Haygood, R. C., Devine, J. V. 1967. Effects of composition of the positive category on concept learning. *J. Exp. Psychol.* 74:230–35

101. Haygood, R. C., Harbert, R. L., Omlor, J. A. 1970. Intradimensional variability and concept identification. *J. Exp. Psychol.* 83:216–19

102. Haygood, R. C., Sandlin, J., Yoder, D., Dodd, D. 1969. Instance contiguity in disjunctive concept learning. *J. Exp. Psychol.* 81:605–7

103. Haygood, R. C., Stevenson, M. 1967. Effects of number of irrelevant dimensions in nonconjunctive concept learning. *J. Exp. Psychol.* 74: 302–4

104. Hebert, J. A., Rogers, C. A. Jr. 1966. Anagram solution as a function of pronounceability and difficulty. *Psychon. Sci.* 4:359–60

105. Hovland, C. I. 1952. A "communication analysis" of concept learning. *Psychol. Rev.* 59:461–72

106. Hovland, C. I., Weiss, W. 1953. Transmission of information concerning concepts through positive and negative instances. *J. Exp. Psychol.* 43: 175–82

107. Hunt, E. B. 1965. Selection and reception conditions in grammar and concept learning. *J. Verb. Learn. Verb. Behav.* 4:211–15

108. Hunt, E. B. 1967. Utilization of memory in concept learning systems. See Ref. 125

109. Hunt, E. B., Hovland, C. I. 1960.

Order of consideration of different types of concepts. *J. Exp. Psychol.* 59:220–25

110. Hunt, E. B., Marin, J., Stone, P. J. 1966. *Experiments in Induction.* New York: Academic. 247 pp.

111. Imai, S., Garner, W. R. 1965. Discriminability and preference for attributes in free and constrained classification. *J. Exp. Psychol.* 69:596–608

112. Johnson, D. M. 1966. Solution of anagrams. *Psychol. Bull.* 66:371–84

113. Johnson, D. M., Parrott, G. R., Stratton, B. P. 1967. Productive thinking: Produce one solution or many. *Proc. 75th Ann. Conv. APA* 2:299–300

114. Johnson, D. M., Parrott, G. L., Stratton, B. P. 1968. Production and judgment of solutions to five problems. *J. Educ. Psychol.* 59:1–21

115. Johnson, T. J., Van Mondfrans, A. P. 1965. Order of solutions in ambiguous anagrams as a function of word frequency of the solution words. *Psychon. Sci.* 3:565–66

116. Jurca, N. H., Duncan, C. P. 1969. Problem solving within a word-frequency hierarchy. *J. Verb. Learn. Verb. Behav.* 8:229–33

117. Kaplan, I. T., Carvellas, T. 1968. Effect of word length on anagram solution time. *J. Verb. Learn. Verb. Behav.* 7:201–6

118. Keele, S. W., Archer, E. J. 1967. A comparison of two types of information in concept identification. *J. Verb. Learn. Verb. Behav.* 6:185–92

119. Kendler, H. H., Kendler, T. S. 1962. Vertical and horizontal processes in problem-solving. *Psychol. Rev.* 69:1–16

120. Kendler, H. H., Kendler, T. S. 1969. Reversal-shift behavior: Some basic issues. *Psychol. Bull.* 72:229–32

121. Kendler, H. H., Kendler, T. S., Marken, R. S. 1969. Developmental analysis of reversal and half-reversal shifts. *Develop. Psychol.* 1:318–26

122. Kendler, T. S. 1964. Verbalization and optional reversal shifts among kindergarten children. *J. Verb. Learn. Verb. Behav.* 3:428–33

123. Klausmeier, H., Harris, C. 1966. *Analyses of Concept Learning.* New York: Academic. 272 pp.

124. Kleinmuntz, B., Ed. 1966. *Problem Solving: Research Method and Theory.* New York: Wiley. 406 pp.

125. Kleinmuntz, B., Ed. 1967. *Concepts and the Structure of Memory.* New York: Wiley. 286 pp.

126. Laughlin, P. R. 1965. Selection strategies in concept attainment as a function of number of persons and stimulus display. *J. Exp. Psychol.* 70:323–27

127. Ibid 1966. Selection strategies in concept attainment as a function of number of relevant problem attributes. 71:773–76

128. Laughlin, P. R. 1967. Incidental concept formation as a function of creativity and intelligence. *J. Pers. Soc. Psychol.* 5:115–19

129. Laughlin, P. R. 1968. Focusing strategy for eight concept rules. *J. Exp. Psychol.* 77:661–69

130. Ibid 1969. Information specification in the attainment of conditional concepts. 79:370–72

131. Laughlin, P. R., Doherty, M. A. 1967. Discussion versus memory in cooperative group concept attainment. *J. Exp. Psychol.* 58:123–28

132. Laughlin, P. R., Doherty, M. A., Dunn, R. F. 1968. Intentional and incidental concept formation as a function of motivation, creativity, intelligence, and sex. *J. Pers. Soc. Psychol.* 8:401–9

133. Laughlin, P. R., Jordan, R. M. 1967. Selection strategies in conjunctive, disjunctive, and biconditional concept attainment. *J. Exp. Psychol.* 75:188–93

134. Laughlin, P. R., McGlynn, R. P. 1967. Cooperative versus competitive concept attainment as a function of sex and stimulus display. *J. Pers. Soc. Psychol.* 7:398–402

135. Laughlin, P. R., McGlynn, R. P., Anderson, J. A., Jacobsen, E. S. 1968. Concept attainment by individuals versus cooperative pairs as a function of memory, sex, and concept rule. *J. Pers. Soc. Psychol.* 8:410–17

136. Levine, M. 1966. Hypothesis behavior by humans during discrimination learning. *J. Exp. Psychol.* 71:331–38

137. Levine, M. 1967. The size of the hypothesis set during discrimination learning. *Psychol. Rev.* 74:428–30

138. Levine, M. 1969. The latency-choice discrepancy in concept learning. *J. Exp. Psychol.* 82:1–3

139. Levine, M. 1970. Human discrimination learning: The subset-sampling

assumption. *Psychol. Bull.* 74:397–404

140. Levine, M., Yoder, R. M., Kleinberg, J., Rosenberg, J. 1968. The presolution paradox in discrimination learning. *J. Exp. Psychol.* 77:602–8

141. Looney, N. J., Haygood, R. C. 1968. Effects of number of relevant dimensions in disjunctive concept learning. *J. Exp. Psychol.* 78:169–70

142. Lowenkron, B. 1969. Nonoutcome trial behavior: A predictor of solution shift performance and the effects of overtraining. *J. Exp. Psychol.* 81:484–88

143. Lowenkron, B., Johnson, P. J. 1968. Yoked group comparisons of selection and reception paradigms of concept attainment: A biased procedure. *Psychol. Rep.* 23:1143–49

144. Maier, N. R., Burke, R. J. 1966. Test of the concept of "availability of functions" in problem solving. *Psychol. Rep.* 19:119–25

145. Maier, N., Casselman, G. 1970. Locating the difficulty in insight problem: Individual and sex differences. *Psychol. Rep.* 26:103–17

146. Maier, N. R., Janzen, J. C. 1969. Are good problem-solvers also creative? *Psychol. Rep.* 24:139–46

147. Maltzman, I. 1955. Thinking: From a behavioristic point of view. *Psychol. Rev.* 62:275–86

148. Ibid 1960. On the training of originality. 67:229–42

149. Maltzman, I. 1962. Motivation and the direction of thinking. *Psychol. Bull.* 59:457–67

150. Mandler, G. 1962. From association to structure. *Psychol. Rev.* 69:415–27

151. Manske, M. E., Davis, G. A. 1968. Effects of simple instructional biases upon performance in the Unusual Uses Test. *J. Gen. Psychol.* 79:25–33

152. Mayzner, M. S., Tresselt, M. E. 1958. Anagram solution times: A function of letter order and word frequency. *J. Exp. Psychol.* 56:376–79

153. Ibid 1962. Anagram solution times: A function of word transition probabilities. 63:510–13

154. Ibid 1966. Anagram solution times: A function of multiple-solution anagrams. 71:66–73

155. McGuigan, F. J. 1966. *Thinking Studies of Covert Language Processes.* New York: Appleton. 295 pp.

156. Mednick, S. A. 1962. The associative basis of the creative process. *Psychol. Rev.* 69:220–32

157. Mendelsohn, G. A., Griswold, B. B., Anderson, M. L. 1966. Individual differences in anagram-solving ability. *Psychol. Rep.* 19:799–809

158. Michel, T., Ed. 1969. *Human Action.* New York: Academic. 293 pp.

159. Miller, G. A. 1956. The magical number seven, plus or minus two: Some limits on our capacity for processing information. *Psychol. Rev.* 63:81–96

160. Murray, F. S., Gregg, R. E. 1969. Reception versus selection procedures in concept learning. *J. Exp. Psychol.* 82:571–72

161. Nahinsky, I. D., Penrold, W. C., Slaymaker, F. L. 1970. Relationship of component cues to hypotheses in conjunctive concept learning. *J. Exp. Psychol.* 83:351–53

162. Nahinsky, I. D., Slaymaker, F. L. 1970. Use of negative instances in conjunctive concept identification. *J. Exp. Psychol.* 84:64–84

163. Neisser, U. 1967. *Cognitive Psychology.* New York: Appleton. 351 pp.

164. Neisser, U., Weene, P. 1962. Hierarchies in concept attainment. *J. Exp. Psychol.* 64:640–45

165. Newell, A., Simon, H. A. 1967. Overview: Memory and process in concept formation. See Ref. 125

166. Ossorio, P. Meaning and symbolism. *Contemporary Experimental Psychology*, Vol. 3, ed. F. S. Reynolds. Chicago: Scott, Foresman. In press

167. Overstreet, J. D., Dunham, J. L. 1969. Effect of number of values and irrelevant dimensions selection and associative learning in a multiple-concept problem. *J. Exp. Psychol.* 79:265–68

168. Peterson, M. J. 1968. Concept identification as a function of the type of training series. *J. Exp. Psychol.* 78:128–36

169. Pikas, A. 1966. *Abstraction and Concept Formation.* Cambridge: Harvard Univ. Press. 303 pp.

170. Pishkin, V. 1965. Dimension availability with antecedent success of failure in concept identification. *Psychon. Sci.* 2:69–70

171. Pishkin, V. 1967. Availability of feedback-corrected error instances in concept learning. *J. Exp. Psychol.* 73:318–19

172. Pishkin, V., Rosenblum, E. S. 1966. Concept identification of auditory

dimensions as a function of age and sex. *Psychon. Sci.* 4:165–66

173. Pishkin, V., Shurley, J. T. 1965. Auditory dimensions and irrelevant information in concept identification of males and females. *Percept. Mot. Skills* 20:673–83

174. Pishkin, V., Wolfgang, A. 1965. Number and type of available instances in concept learning. *J. Exp. Psychol.* 69:5–8

175. Pishkin, V., Wolfgang, A., Rasmussen, E. 1967. Age, sex, amount, and type of memory information in concept learning. *J. Exp. Psychol.* 73:121–24

176. Polson, P. G., Dunham, J. L. A comparison of two types of theories of multiple-category concept identification. *J. Verb. Learn. Verb. Behav.* In press

177. Posner, M. I. 1965. Memory and thought in human intellectual performance. *Brit. J. Psychol.* 56:197–215

178. Reeve, B., Polson, P. G., Dunham, J. L. 1970. The size of focus samples in multiple-category concept identification. *Psychon. Sci.* 20:125–26

179. Reitman, W. R. 1965. *Cognition and Thought: An Information-Processing Approach.* New York: Wiley. 312 pp.

180. Restle, F. 1962. The selection of strategies in cue learning. *Psychol. Rev.* 69:320–43

181. Ronning, R. R. 1965. Anagram solution times: A function of the "Rule-out" factor. *J. Exp. Psychol.* 69:35–39

182. Russell, D. G., Sarason, I. G. 1965. Test anxiety, sex, and experimental conditions in relation to anagram solution. *J. Pers. Soc. Psychol.* 1:493–96

183. Schvaneveldt, R. W. 1966. Concept identification as a function of probability of positive instances and number of relevant dimensions. *J. Exp. Psychol.* 72:649–54

184. Schwartz, S. H. 1966. Trial-by-trial analysis of processes in simple and disjunctive concept-attainment tasks. *J. Exp. Psychol.* 72:456–65

185. Sechrest, L., Kaas, J. S. 1965. Concept difficulty as a function of stimulus similarity. *J. Educ. Psychol.* 56:327–33

186. Siegel, L. S. 1969. Concept attainment as a function of amount and form of information. *J. Exp. Psychol.* 81:464–68

187. Smoke, K. L. 1933. Negative instances in concept learning. *J. Exp. Psychol.* 16:583–88

188. Staats, A. W. 1968. *Learning, Language and Cognition.* New York: Holt, Rinehart & Winston. 614 pp.

189. Suedfeld, P., Glucksberg, S., Vernon, J. 1967. Sensory deprivation as a drive operation: Effects upon problem solving. *J. Exp. Psychol.* 75:166–69

190. Suppes, P., Ginsberg, R. 1963. A fundamental property of all-or-none models, binomial distribution of responses prior to conditioning, with application of concept formation in children. *Psychol. Rev.* 70:139–61

191. Suppes, P., Schlag-Rey, M. 1965. Observable changes in hypotheses under positive reinforcement. *Science* 148:661–62

192. Taplin, J. Effects of initial instance on attribute-identification of concepts using a selection procedure. *J. Exp. Psychol.* In press

193. Taylor, C. L., Haygood, R. C. 1968. Effects of degree of category separation on semantic concept identification. *J. Exp. Psychol.* 76:356–59

194. Tecce, J. J. 1965. Relationship of anxiety (drive) and response competition in problem solving. *J. Abnorm. Psychol.* 70:465–67

195. Trabasso, T. 1963. Stimulus emphasis and all-or-none learning of concept identification. *J. Exp. Psychol.* 65:395–406

196. Trabasso, T., Bower, G. 1964. Component learning in the four-category concept problem. *J. Math. Psychol.* 1:143–69

197. Trabasso, T., Bower, G. 1964. Presolution reversal and dimensional shifts in concept identification. *J. Exp. Psychol.* 67:398–99

198. Trabasso, T., Bower, G. 1964. Memory in concept identification. *Psychon. Sci.* 1:133–34

199. Trabasso, T., Bower, G. 1966. Presolution dimensional shifts in concept identification: A test of the sampling with replacement axiom in all-or-none models. *J. Math. Psychol.* 3:163–73

200. Trabasso, T., Bower, G. 1968. *Attention in Learning.* New York: Wiley. 253 pp.

201. Tramontana, J., Morris, J. B. 1969. Problem-solving ability as affected by mild stress versus minimal or no stress. *Psychol. Rec.* 19:295–300

202. Tresselt, M. E., Mayzner, M. S. 1965. Anagram solution times: A function of individual differences in stored diagram frequencies. *J. Exp. Psychol.* 70:606–10

203. Tresselt, M. E., Mayzner, M. S. 1968. Anagram solution times: A function of single- and double-letter solution words. *J. Verb. Learn. Verb. Behav.* 7:128–32

204. Uhl, C. N. 1966. Effects of multiple stimulus validity and criterion dispersion on learning of interval concepts. *J. Exp. Psychol.* 72:519–25

205. Underwood, B. J. 1952. An orientation for research on thinking. *Psychol. Rev.* 59:209–20

206. VandeGeer, J. P., Jaspars, J. M. 1966. Cognitive function. *Ann. Rev. Psychol.* 17:145–76

207. Voss, J. F., Ed. 1969. *Approaches to Thought.* Columbus, O.: Merrill. 337 pp.

208. Wallach, M. A., Kogan, N. 1965. *Modes of Thinking in Young Children.* New York: Holt, Rinehart & Winston. 357 pp.

209. Weisberg, R. W., Suls, J. M. 1969. Some factors influencing solution of the candle problem. *Proc. 77th Ann. Conv. APA* 4:77–78

210. Wells, H. 1965. Stimulus compounding and the attainment of conjunctive concepts. *Percept. Mot. Skills* 21:767–70

211. Wells, H. 1967. Facilitation of concept learning by a "simultaneous contrast" procedure. *Psychon. Sci.* 9:609–10

212. White, R. M. Jr. 1967. *Effects of some pretraining variables on concept identification.* PhD thesis. Univ. Colorado, Boulder. 49 pp.

213. Wolfgang, A. 1967. Exploration of upper limits of task complexity in concept identification of males and females in individual and social conditions. *Psychon. Sci.* 9:621–22

214. Zaffy, D. J., Burning, J. L. 1966. Drive and the range of cue utilization. *J. Exp. Psychol.* 71:382–86

215. Zippel, B. 1969. Unrestricted classification behavior and learning of imposed classifications in closed, exhaustive stimulus sets. *J. Exp. Psychol.* 82:493–98

INDIVIDUAL DECISION BEHAVIOR[1]

AMNON RAPOPORT

AND

THOMAS S. WALLSTEN

L. L. Thurstone Psychometric Laboratory, University of North Carolina, Chapel Hill, N. C.

Decision theory is a complex, somewhat ill-defined, body of knowledge developed by mathematicians, statisticians, economists, and psychologists attempting to prescribe how decisions should be made and to describe systematically what variables affect decisions. In organizing this paper, we have followed previous reviews whose emphases were primarily psychological (11, 32, 36, 174), an introductory textbook by Lee (86, see also 45, 202, and references there), an extensive bibliography by Edwards (37), and a long and well-organized chapter by Luce & Suppes (94). The latter provides an excellent technical presentation of algebraic and probabilistic theories of individual decision making, and critically discusses a few experimental studies which bear on the validity of these theories. It has made an important contribution in providing a perspective of the area and setting guidelines for research.

Classification.—Whereas the distinction between individual and group decision making is obvious, classification of decision tasks and of theories of individual decision making is not. Several have been proposed (33, 66, 74, 93, 94, 174). They differ from one another, the distinctions within some of them are sometimes slippery, and the resulting classes are not always collectively exhaustive. However, the usefulness of classifications is undeniable.

We shall maintain a distinction between *single-stage* and *multi-stage* tasks, depending on the number of decisions the decision maker (DM) is required to make. A single-stage (frequently called "static") decision task can be formally characterized by a triple (E, D, r), where E is a finite nonempty set of possible events ("states of nature"), D is a finite nonempty set of possible decisions or courses of action available to DM, and r is a reward or payoff uniquely associated with the joint occurrence of a decision and an event.

[1] *Acknowledgments*: This work was supported in part by PHS Research Grant No. MH-10006 from the National Institute of Mental Health and in part by a University Science Development Program Grant No. GU-2059 from the National Science Foundation. The present review covers the period from 1965 through the end of 1970. A few later papers are included, with no attempt to be exhaustive beyond 1970. We wish to thank those who made reprints and preprints available to us.

The DM together with his environment constitute a "system" that may be in one of several states. The state of the system, denoted by s, consists of selected variables that are assumed to affect DM's decision. These may include DM's utility function, financial status, or informational pattern. The latter is typically expressed as a probability distribution, objective or subjective, over the set of events, or, more generally, as a probability distribution over the rewards associated with each decision. Given that the system is in state s, DM chooses a course of action, receives the reward determined by the joint occurrence of his action and the event that obtains, and never makes another decision to which he might apply whatever he may have learned. It is frequently assumed that DM chooses his decision so as to optimize some objective criterion (payoff function) such as maximizing subjectively expected utility (SEU), minimizing regret, or whatever.

A multi-stage decision task can be roughly characterized by a quadruple (E, D, p, r), where E and D are abstractly defined as above, p associates with each pair (s, d) a probability distribution on E known as a transformation rule or a transition function, and r is now the reward associated with the transition from one state of the system to another. At the beginning of a stage (trial) of the process the system is in state s. DM then makes a decision d, the system moves to state s' (which may or may not be identical to s), selected according to the transformation rule, and DM receives the reward $r(s, d, s')$ associated with this transition. The process continues for N stages, and DM is assumed to maximize some criterion function, typically the total subjectively expected reward over all stages or the subjectively expected reward for the last stage only. The definition of "state" is quite arbitrary as before. When the state changes from one state to another, this change may or may not be affected by the previous history of the system.

SINGLE-STAGE DECISION MAKING

Classifications of theories of single-stage decision making depend upon the assumptions made about the characteristics of the system, such as the information that DM possesses, DM's response mechanism, or the nature of the task. Luce & Suppes (94) presented a useful three-way dichotomization of single-stage decision theories. The first is whether the theory employs algebraic or probabilistic tools. The second is whether each decision determines a reward with certainty or a probability distribution over the rewards (uncertainty). The third is whether the theory provides a complete ranking of all the available courses of action or merely specifies which one will be selected. We shall de-emphasize, but not abandon, the popular distinction between prescriptive (normative) and descriptive theories. This distinction is difficult to make precise (see e.g. 183), has philosophical connotations which are frequently misleading, and may be altogether unnecessary when, as sometimes happens (e.g. 11), it corresponds in a rough way to the distinction between algebraic and probabilistic theories.

ALGEBRAIC DECISION THEORIES

Algebraic decision theories have been mostly formulated as composition rules (see e.g. 80) that describe a particular functional relation, typically additive, multiplicative, or distributive, among scale values of stimulus dimensions. The major difficulty in evaluating such functional relations has been the absence of adequate independent procedures for measuring the relevant variables. Of the several approaches to this problem we feel that the most satisfactory and the one which may have the most profound impact on future developments in decision theory is the conjoint-measurement approach (e.g. 45, 95, 185), recently presented in an excellent book by Krantz, Luce, Suppes & Tversky (79). This approach seeks to determine whether measurement scales for the relevant variables may be constructed such that the proposed composition rule is satisfied, thus solving both problems simultaneously.

As with measurement in general (see e.g. 79, 207), conjoint-measurement requires formulation of a set of necessary and structural axioms concerning ordinal properties of an empirical relational structure, sufficient to establish two theorems. One is a representation theorem stating the existence of an isomorphism from the empirical into a numerical relational structure, and the other is a uniqueness theorem establishing the permissible transformations that also yield isomorphisms. The axioms may be regarded as a set of qualitative empirical laws. If they hold, scales of measurement, unique up to appropriate transformations, can be constructed.

Conjoint-measurement has led to or inspired the development of axiomatic theories of preference (79, 92, 186, 189), risk (22, 131), and choices involving time (74). These theories differ markedly from nonaxiomatic theories such as functional measurement (1, 163, 164), and the linear model (172, 174), both of which will be reviewed below.

Some methodological problems of testing.—In evaluating the experimental evidence concerning algebraic decision theories, it became apparent to us that experimentation has not caught up with theorizing. Some of the reasons for this lag may disappear as testable properties are exhibited in less technical terms (see e.g. 80). Beyond this, however, satisfactory experimental evaluations of the theories are very difficult. One consideration is that evaluating a theory by testing conditions which are only necessary rather than necessary and sufficient for its existence, as has been the case in most studies of SEU theory, may lead to the theory's rejection but not to its acceptance (186). A related problem is that axiomatic decision theories are constructed for large, often infinite, sets of elements, whereas any experimental test of necessity involves only a small, finite subset. For example, the Archimedean (one of the structural) axiom, which essentially says that certain infinite sets are at least countable, is laterally not testable as an isolated axiom (79).

Choice of stimulus elements is also crucial. It can be demonstrated that with a judicious selection one may considerably affect, though, of course, not uniquely determine, the chances of accepting or rejecting some algebraic model. Compare, for example, the probability values used in two experiments by Tversky (186, 188), both of which employed two-outcome gambles of the form (r, p), in which one could win a positive reward r with probability p and win nothing with probability $1-p$. In the former study, which supported SEU, the values used were $p = .2, .4, .6, .8$, whereas in the latter study, which rejected SEU, they were $p = 7/24, 8/24, 9/24, 10/24, 11/24$. It is tempting to say that in many cases failure to reject a decision model when it is wrong or accept it when it is "approximately" right may indicate as much about the design of the experiment as the adequacy of the model.

A related but more pervasive difficulty in experimentally testing algebraic theories is that of observational error. One major shortcoming of the axiom systems for single-stage decision making is the lack of any appropriate error theory, making it exceedingly difficult to determine whether a discrepancy between theory and data should be attributed to error or to inadequacies in the basic model.

Frequently every DM must be considered a separate experiment, as his subjective values may differ from those of others. Considerable amounts of data are needed to estimate individual parameters, and this may be difficult in a single-subject design. Subjects required to make hundreds of decisions about complex stimuli may become bored, and consequently tend to employ simplified decision policies. Evidence exists (130, 175) that choices among bets become less consistent, transitive, and single-peaked under experimental conditions fostering extremely high motivation to respond correctly.

A related motivational problem is whether subjects are required to make hypothetical or real choices. Slovic et al (175) found that imaginary incentives led subjects to employ simpler decision strategies than did real payoffs. Slovic (170) showed that when choices were hypothetical, subjects maximized gain and discounted losses, but when the choices had real consequences, subjects were considerably more cautious. Although hypothetical choices may depart from reality, real ones may alter the DM's financial status quo, and hence his decision behavior during the experiment (18). One may attempt to resolve this dilemma by explicitly accounting for behavior resulting from changes in the status quo [e.g. by assuming the Consistency Principle of Pfanzagl (114)]. Alternatively, one may randomly select some of the subject's choices during the experiment and genuinely play them at the end of the experimental session (e.g. 18, 186).

Subjectively Expected Utility

Theory.—The most general and influential theory for single-stage decision making asserts that DM behaves so as to maximize SEU. That is, ordinal properties of DM's decisions are assumed to satisfy certain necessary and structural axioms, such that one can construct subjective probability and utility functions from which SEU may be calculated to account for DM's decisions. These functions are inferred from behavior, not directly supplied by DM, and he is not assumed to consciously calculate SEU. If the axioms are satisfied, then the construction of subjective probability and utility functions consititutes a conjoint-measurement procedure (79).

Applying the finite additive conjoint-measurement approach, Tversky (186) presented an experimental procedure which yields simultaneous estimates of utilities and subjective probabilities from decisions. His study was concerned with two-outcome gambles of the form (r, p) described above. It employed the concept of a data matrix M, whose $M(r, p)$ entry is a measure of the worth of the gamble (r, p). A data matrix $M = R \times P$ is called "additive" if it is possible to rescale its cell entries $M(r, p)$ such that their order is preserved and that every rescaled entry can be expressed as a sum of its row and column components. Tversky (186) proved that for such gambles the SEU model holds if and only if M is additive and the utility of zero is equal to zero. Satisfactorily testing the additivity of the data matrix M provides a test of SEU theory independent of the measurement of subjective probability or utility. Moreover, unlike all previous evaluations of the SEU model [e.g. (18) as well as earlier studies reviewed in (11) and (32)], this provides a complete test which may lead to the model's acceptance rather than only to its rejection.

Opinion differs about what entities should be treated as primitives in a SEU model and what structural axioms should be assumed. The axiom system that currently seems most satisfactory is the *conditional* SEU theory of Luce & Krantz (92), presented in more detail in (79). (See also related work in 46, 115, and 116). The basic concept of the theory, that which differentiates it from others (e.g. 150, 194), is called "conditional decision." Decisions are conditional in the sense that they accept, as given, that a fixed non-null event will occur, which, when the decision is considered, delineates the universe of possible outcomes. Each conditional decision simply specifies what consequences are associated with each of the possible outcomes of this event. If D denotes the set of conditional decisions used in an experiment and if all pairs of them are presented, then the DM's decisions induce a binary relation of weak preference on D. This relation is axiomatized by a list of necessary and structural axioms, one of the latter, axiom 9, being particularly delicate, which are sufficient to establish the usual representation and uniqueness theorems. If the structural axioms of the conditional SEU theory are acceptable, the theorems assert that there exists a numerical scale of utility, unique up to a linear transformation, over the conditional decisions and a probability function over events, such that the utility of the union of a finite set of mutually disjoint conditional decisions equals their conditional expected utility.

Krantz et al (79) point out several undesirable features of Savage's

axiom system, long the most general and satisfactory formulation of uncon-
ditional SEU theory, which the conditional SEU theory handles more
successfully. The undesirability of these features has no experimental implications when the number of events and consequences is finite since, as
Luce & Krantz (92) show, their theory and that of Savage may be transformed into each other in this case.

Experiments.—Almost all the recent experiments concerned with SEU
have concentrated on testing one or more necessary axioms (postulates).
MacCrimmon (97) directly tested the normative implications of each of five
postulates. Unlike previous experiments, he studied not only the initial
responses of DMs to several decision problems, but also their behavior after
they were presented with arguments relevant to the postulates and were
given time to reflect upon their decisions. Although his procedure of employing experienced, practicing DMs rather than college undergraduates, focusing on the level of individual postulates, and allowing a systematic follow-up
on some normative implications of the postulates is commendable, it is
doubtful whether, as MacCrimmon asserted, it puts "the postulates to a
very severe test, perhaps more severe than would arise in most real-life
decision situations" (97 p. 4). That is because his subjects were presented
with hypothetical rather than real decision problems; their reward in no way
depended on the accuracy of their responses.

Transitivity was the first postulate to be tested by MacCrimmon. Of the
114 responses (three responses per each of 38 subjects) only eight violated
transitivity. Whereas MacCrimmon investigated whether preferences are
generally transitive, Tversky (188), in a manner similar to Becker & Brownson (10), asked whether systematic and predictable intransitivities can be
constructed, and under what experimental conditions. Given this question,
Tversky's (188) biased sampling procedure of using only those subjects
satisfying a predetermined criterion is legitimate. The results, however, are
not "interesting" unless the proportion of subjects included in the subset is
not too small.

In Tversky's (188) first experiment five two-outcome gambles of the form
(r, p) were employed. The values of p, displayed in a non-numerical form,
were 7/24, 8/24, 9/24, 10/24, and 11/24 for gambles A, B, C, D, and E,
respectively; the corresponding values of r were \$5.00, \$4.75, \$4.50, \$4.25,
and \$4.00. It was hypothesized that at least some subjects would choose
between adjacent gambles (e.g. A and B, B and C, etc) on the basis of r, but
that for gambles lying far apart in the chain (e.g. A and E) would choose
according to p, or according to the expected value (EV) of the gamble, which
increased monotonically in p. As predicted, the majority of subjects violated
transitivity. Violations were in the expected direction and in the predicted
locations. Similar results were obtained in a second experiment concerned
with preference between profiles rather than gambles.

To test the second postulate, the sure-thing principle, MacCrimmon employed the following four gambles—

A: 500% return with $p=.10$, bankruptcy with $p=.01$, and 5% return with $p=.89$;

B: 5% return for sure;

A': 500% return with $p=.10$, and bankruptcy with $p=.90$;

B': 5% return with $p=.11$, and bankruptcy with $p=.89$.

This will be recognized as the Allais paradox (see e.g. 103, 150). The sure-thing principle implies that a choice of A over B should lead to a choice of A' over B' and conversely, whereas, according to Allais, typical DMs frequently choose B over A and A' over B' and maintain such a choice even upon reflection. As anticipated by Allais, the sure-thing principle was significantly violated by slightly under 40% of MacCrimmon's subjects.

A second implication of the sure-thing principle concerns what MacCrimmon (97) called "risk versus uncertainty" and others (e.g. 10, 176) called "ambiguity." The experiment designed to test this implication was originally proposed by Ellsberg (43). In Ellsberg's paradigm a DM is confronted with two urns. Urn I contains 100 red or black balls; ambiguity is maximal in that the number of each color is not specified, nor is there provided a procedure whereby it can be determined. There is no ambiguity about Urn II which contains 50 red and 50 black balls. Four gambles are presented to DM, contingent on a draw from either Urn I or Urn II, where p is the probability of randomly drawing a red ball from a given urn, r is a prize, and the subscript denotes the urn used, namely,

R_I: r if red or 0 is black (Urn I, p and $1-p$ unknown)

B_I: 0 if red or r if black (Urn I, p and $1-p$ unknown)

R_{II}: r if red or 0 is black (Urn II, $p=1/2$)

B_{II}: 0 is red or r if black (Urn II, $p=1/2$).

It follows from the sure-thing principle that a choice of R_I over R_{II} implies a choice of B_{II} over B_I and conversely, regardless of the value of r. The results of Ellsberg's (43) interrogations were that many DMs exhibited a different preference pattern. They were indifferent between R_I and B_I and between R_{II} and B_{II}, but they preferred R_{II} to R_I and B_{II} to B_I. Ellsberg further claimed that even upon reflection DMs would tend to persist in these choices, thereby violating the sure-thing principle. The results reported by MacCrimmon partially supported this claim. Only 25% of his subjects showed the above preference pattern, and in the terminal interview most of these subjects indicated a wish to change their responses.

In a carefully designed experiment, Becker & Brownson (10) found that 16 of 34 graduate students of business conformed to Ellsberg's predictions, a considerably higher proportion than reported by MacCrimmon (97). In addition, Becker & Brownson (10) also provided three urns intermediate in ambiguity between I and II; call these Urns III, IV, and V, in decreasing order of ambiguity. When presented with Urns I, III, IV, and V, each of which paired with Urn II, 15 DMs who had exhibited "ambiguity aversion" in the first phase of the experiment offered to pay an average of 36¢, 27¢, 20¢, and 12¢, respectively, to draw from the preferred Urn II, showing systematic and predictable violations of the sure-thing principle.

The third postulate tested was the dominance principle. Of the 37 subjects who completed MacCrimmon's experiment, 12 violated it at least once, and 5 out of the 12 had multiple violations. Upon reflection, almost all subjects who had violated the postulate revised their decisions. Two additional postulates, Postulate 4, essentially asserting that subjective probabilities are independent of utilities, and Postulate 5, stating that DM should be able to construct an n-fold equivalent partition of the universal state, were also tested by MacCrimmon. The former was violated by the majority of the subjects, indicating strong dependence between tastes and beliefs. During the interview, however, almost all of these violations were attributed to "mistakes." The latter postulate was supported by all but five of the subjects.

In a series of card-guessing experiments, Irwin and his students (70–73) addressed themselves to the problem of the relationships between beliefs and values. Crucial to their experiments is a distinction between two types of values—independent outcome values (IOs), that do not depend upon the correctness of DM's response, and dependent outcome values (DOs), that are contingent on the correctness of DM's prediction. All of Irwin's experiments demonstrated a significant interaction between an IO of an event and the subjective probability or strength of expectancy of its occurrence, in contrast to Postulate 4. The most consistent finding (70, 71, 73) is that the percent predictions is higher if the IO is positive than if it is negative, with objective probability held constant. Irwin & Graae (70) found that differences in IO between a marked and a blank card had a significant effect on the mean percent bet on the preferred card when the two IOs of the pair had the same sign. Slovic (166), employing a different experimental procedure, obtained similar results. However, neither experiment showed strong and regular variation.

Preference and bidding data incompatible with any SEU theory have been reported in various studies (e.g. 88, 90, 172). Most used *duplex* gambles in which probabilities and outcomes are explicitly stated. A duplex gamble is described by four independent dimensions, probability of winning (p_W), amount to win (r_W), probability of losing (p_L), and amount to lose (r_L). DM wins r_W with probability p_W and nothing with probability $1 - p_W$, and loses r_L with probability p_L and nothing with probability $1 - p_L$. Slovic & Lichtenstein (172) showed an interaction between utility and subjective probability. Equally damaging to SEU was the finding that the choice pattern depended on the response mode. Subjects who had been asked to rate the attractiveness of each gamble on a bipolar rating scale assigned more weight to p_W than to any other dimension, whereas subjects who had been instructed to bid for each gamble, assigned somewhat heavier weight to r_L than to any other dimension.

If choices and bids are influenced differentially by payoff and probability dimensions, it might be possible to construct a pair of duplex gambles with the same EV such that DM would choose one of them but bid more for the other. Such a reversal is inconsistent with any SEU theory. This hypothesis was tested and confirmed (88, 90, 167).

A few experiments (186, 187, 196) rather than testing single postulates of the SEU theory, provided complete tests, which could lead either to its acceptance or rejection. The results of all three experiments were favorable to the SEU theory. In Tversky's (186) study subjects were presented with both riskless and risky options. To test strict additivity, which implies the SEU model, a logarithmic transformation was applied to the response data, minimum selling prices of the options. The transformed bids were submitted to a series of individual two-factor ANOVA tests. Only one of 33 tested interactions (11 subjects, three data matrices for each) reached significance; the transformed bids in 32 out of 33 experiments could be expressed as simple additive combinations of the options' components. Thus, within the margin of error afforded by ANOVA, the results supported the independence of utility and subjective probability.

In the case of riskless data strict additivity implies that the utility for money is identical to the actual money value. But the utilities of the commodities are determined only up to a common additive constant. Two models were proposed by Tversky (186) to determine that constant. One required the same utilities for risky and riskless choices, but not that subjective probabilities of complementary events sum to one. The other model had the latter requirement but utility was not assumed risk-invariant. Note that each of these two models contradicts the classical SEU theory (150, 194). The "subjective probability" function that Tversky derived need not be a probability measure (74). Contrary to the classical theory, the data supported one model but not the other, and conversely, although not both simultaneously.

A logarithmic transformation of the response data implies multiplicative rather than additive errors in ANOVA, which does not fit nicely into the otherwise very elegant procedures employed by Tversky. A second limitation of that transformation is that the ANOVA test, in determining the fit of the additive model, "gives the greatest importance to small, near-worthless responses. These, however, are just the responses given the least attention by the subjects" (163, p. 78). Presumbably this limitation will be removed when the problem of error receives a satisfactory solution.

Wallsten's (196) experiment addressed itself to two related questions. One concerned the assumption that DM's probability estimates are identical to their subjective probabilities inferred from SEU theory. The other was to provide a measurement-free test of SEU theory based on the principle of additivity. The analyses were based on indifferences between gambles rather than logarithmic transformations of bids, but the results were similar to those obtained by Tversky (186). Additivity, and therefore SEU theory, were sustained for each of the subjects. With regard to the former question, the analysis showed the probability estimates to be significantly different from the subjective probabilities for each subject. The discrepancies were very small, though statistically significant.

In a paper that preceded those of Tversky (186, 187) and Wallsten (196), Coombs et al (18) derived and tested measurement-free empirical implications of the SEU theory. In two experiments, the three frequently tested versions of the SEU theory, EV, EU, and SEV (11, 32), could not account for the responses of 12% or more of the subjects. SEU was inadequate in 10% or less of the cases in the first experiment and 5% in the second experiment.

Whether any version of SEU is supported or rejected depends on the experimental design (see our comments about testing above), the implicit assumptions made about error and, consequently, the criteria employed for acceptance or rejection. Since the criteria and designs vary from one study to another, the results reported by the various studies are not strictly comparable. Perhaps more important than the percentage of cases supporting SEU are the high correlations often obtained between subjects' bids and the EVs of the gambles. Tversky (186) reported a mean rank-order correlation of .99 between the risky bids and the additive solution obtained under SEU. The correlations dropped to about .92 when EV was substituted for the additive solution. A correlation of .94 was obtained between bids and EVs in Edwards' (38) experiment in Las Vegas using genuine gamblers, meaning that "about 88% of the job of explaining what the subjects did is taken care of simply by knowing the expected value of each bet" (38, p. 39). On the other hand, in an experiment designed to explore the effect that variations in EV have on a DM's choices among bets (89), the majority of subjects found EV irrelevant or of minor importance as a guide to making a single decision, even when the concept of EV was carefully explained and clearly displayed for them. It is not clear what the design features are of the experiment of Lichtenstein et al (89) that made EV less relevant than in the experiments of Tversky (186), Edwards (38), and Wallsten (196). It may be partly that in the former experiment the subjects played only one bet, which made the notion of long-run EV maximization less appealing, whereas in the latter studies they typically played more bets.

In addition to EV there have been other attempts to develop decision models which do not require the notions of utility and subjective probability (see e.g. 93, Chap. 13). One of these is based on the notion of regret, introduced by Savage (150) and critically discussed by Luce & Raiffa (93). Consider an option $G = (r, p; r', 1 - p)$, where one wins r with probability p and r' with probability $1 - p$. Suydam (180) and Myers, Suydam & Gambino (105) proposed two indexes to account for differences in strength of preference for one gamble of the form G over another with different payoffs. One is the difference in EV, x, and the other is the expected loss ratio y, also called the expected regret ratio by Lee (84, 85). Both indexes were suggested to be monotonically related to differences in strength of preference between two gambles and both appeared to have some merit. However, no meaningful comparison is possible, since in the studies of Suydam (180) and Myers et al (105), x and y values were strongly confounded. Lee (84) clarified the mathematical relationships between x and y and gave formulas for the construction of sets of gamble pairs orthogonal in x and y. Employing these formulas, he conducted two experiments (85) to assess the effects of x and y. Not surprisingly, the results showed that both indexes can affect preference strength, that the effects depend on the arbitrary choice of payoffs, and that there are strong determinants of preference strength other than x and y.

Is it possible to reconcile the inclusive and conflicting evidence which in some studies violates, sometimes systematically and predictably, almost every testable postulate of SEU, and in other studies sustains additivity and hence the SEU theory? In attempting to answer a similar question, Tversky (187) suggested that independence between utilities and subjective probabilities is supported in gambling experiments in which subjective probability is inferred from decisions while it is not supported in direct estimation studies, and that it is more likely to be supported when payoffs are contingent upon decisions than when they are not. The evidence from many studies (e.g. 70–73, 188) seems incompatible with this suggestion. Wallsten (196) suggested a somewhat different answer, based upon the intuitive concept of "simplicity." He argued that experiments supporting SEU theory typically employ very basic gambles; they involve simple events with the objective probabilities easily discriminable and quantifiable, and the outcomes, one of which is zero, are point or money values. Experiments that refute SEU theory, the argument goes, are in one way or another more complicated. Wallsten's conclusion is that "the psychological changes from simple to progressively more complicated situations is qualitative, not quantitative" (196, p. 30). His argument, however, may serve as a partial answer at best since it hinges on the notion of "simplicity," a satisfactory explication of which he has not offered. Moreover, if correct, the argument severely restricts the applicability of SEU theory to a very narrow, unacceptable class of experimental tasks. It seems then that the conflicting evidence pertaining to SEU theory is presently irreconcilable. Consequently, the basic experimental question should not be whether to accept or reject SEU theory as a whole, but rather to systematically discover the conditions under which it is or is not valid.

Additive Difference Model

Intransitivities in choice disconfirm the SEU theory and, more generally, any probabilistic theory of choice which implies some form of stochastic transitivity. To account for consistent intransitivities, which, as we have seen above, can be successfully generated in properly designed experiments

Morrison (104) and later Tversky (188) proposed the *additive difference model* (ADM). Formally, the ADM is defined on a product set $A = A_1 \times A_2 \times \cdots \times A_n$ of multidimensional alternatives with elements of the form $x = (x_1, \cdots, x_n)$ and $y = (y_1, \cdots, y_n)$, where x_i, $i = 1, \cdots, n$, is the value of alternative x on dimension i. The ADM is satisfied in a preference choice situation if there exist real-valued (utility) functions $u_1, \cdots, u_n$, and increasing continuous (difference) functions $\phi_1, \cdots, \phi_n$, defined on some real intervals such that alternative x is weakly preferred to y if and only if $\sum_{i=1}^{n} \phi_i[u_i(x_i) - u_i(y_i)] \geq 0$, where $\phi_i(-\delta) = -\phi_i(\delta)$ for all i.

Considered as a processing model, the ADM suggests that the two alternatives x and y are compared by first making intradimensional evaluations, and the results of these binary comparisons are then summed across the n dimensions to determine the preference. In other words, the ADM incorporates two fundamental assumptions (189): (*a*) *Intradimensional subtractivity*, in which each dimensionwise contribution is the value of the utility difference; and (*b*) *Interdimensional additivity*, in which the binary preference is a function of the sum of dimensionwise contributions. In the ADM the alternatives are represented in a dimensionally organized space, but the preference ordering need not coincide with any metric.

Tversky & Krantz (189) presented an axiomatic analysis of the ADM based on similarity rather than preference judgments. The axiomatic analysis reveals the testable ordinal assumptions that are necessary or sufficient for intradimensional subtractivity and interdimenional additivity to be satisfied. It does not tell, nor does it intend to, how to determine the difference functions ϕ_i. Besides Tversky's (188) experiments supporting a lexicographic semi-order model (which is a special case of the ADM), there have been no attempts to test the ADM.

Risk

Theory.—An alternative basic concept to SEU, that of risk, has been repeatedly proposed as a descriptive or an explanatory construct. This concept has appeared in studies of personality and social psychology (e.g. 78), perceived riskiness of gambles (19–23, 200), multi-stage gambling behavior (139), and portfolio selection in business (63, 99, 181, and many others). The reasons for its increasing popularity, particularly in management science, business, and economics, are the tremendous difficulties in applying SEU to situations consisting of many decision alternatives, and the mixed success (some will say failure) of SEU as a descriptive theory in experiments involving only a few variables. Also, intuition and experience suggest that risk may be an important factor in affecting the perception of, or preference between, gambles.

There is a psychologically important distinction between risk and preference which has not always been maintained. In the economic and business literature concerned with portfolio selection (63, 99, 181), once the risk of a portfolio has been determined, typically as a function of its mean and variance, minimization of risk has almost universally been assumed or prescribed. In the economic literature defining risk in terms of properties of the utility function (102, 132), and in the psychological literature discussing perceived riskiness (22, 131), the relationships between risk and preference have been assumed or shown to be more complicated. For example, the two studies of Slovic (168) and Slovic & Lichtenstein (172) taken jointly show that the probabilities p_W and p_L and the payoffs r_W and r_L combine differently to determine the attractiveness of duplex gambles, presumably directly related to preference between them, or the perceived riskiness of such gambles.

Three basic assumptions are common to the various approaches to the study of risk (131): (a) risk is a property of (risky) options which affects choices among them; (b) options can be ordered with respect to their riskiness; and (c) the risk of an option is related to the variance of its outcomes. In addition to its variance, other properties of an option have been suggested to partly represent its risk, namely, the probabilities of the option's components, the maximum loss or regret, the range of outcomes, or some combinations of these parameters. However, beyond these three assumptions there is no apparent agreement concerning the explication of risk, and there have been only a very few attempts to interrelate the various approaches, or to derive the assumptions about the nature of risk from more basic, testable principles.

One attempt is due to Pollatsek & Tversky (131), who formulated a theory of risk in terms of a triple $(S, *, \succsim)$, where S is a set of all probability distributions on the real line, interpreted as options with monetary outcomes, $*$ is a binary relation of convolution of probability distributions, i.e. of options, and $\succsim$ is a binary relation on S. They proposed four axioms, and proved a theorem which states that if these four axioms hold there exists a real-valued (risk) function R defined on the set of options S, such that for any two options A and B in S: 1. $A \succsim B$ if and only if $R(A) \geq R(B)$; 2. $R(A*B) = R(A) + R(B)$; and 3. R is a ratio scale. They further showed that if three additional axioms are satisfied, there exists a unique θ, $0 < \theta \leq 1$, such that for all options A and B in S, $A \succsim B$ if and only if $R(A) \geq R(B)$, where the risk of an option is expressible as a linear combination of its mean weighted by θ and its variance weighted by $1 - \theta$.

The latter result may be too restrictive if skewness or higher moments of the distribution of outcomes systematically affect perception of gambles' riskiness. In this case, the range of applicability of the theory may be restricted to symmetric or equally skewed options. Also, we suspect that some of the axioms tested singly may not be always empirically satisfied, in particular axiom A2, which implies that risk ordering is independent of DM's financial position, and axiom A6(ii), which states that the risk ordering between gambles is independent of the denomination of the payoffs, provided their expectations are zero.

Experiments.—In a series of studies, Coombs and his students (19–23) attempted to isolate and systematically investigate the variables that affect the perceived riskiness of two-outcome gambles. The study by Coombs & Meyer (23) used coin-tossing games which varied in two aspects: the denomination (c) of an unbiased coin involved in a single toss, and the number of simultaneous tosses (n) composing the complete game. Risk was manipulated by varying c and n. The results for gambles with zero EV, at an ordinal level, suggest that DMs' choices are mediated by a single-peaked preference function over a unidimensional risk scale, and that risk is a monotonically increasing function of c and n. Further results pertaining to gambles with positive rather than zero EV are reported by Coombs & Huang (21).

Basic to the works by Coombs & Huang (22) and Coombs & Bowen (19, 20) is a set of transformations defined on gambles of the form $G = (r, p; r', 1 - p)$, which are assumed to induce corresponding subjective transformations on the perceived riskiness of these gambles. Coombs & Huang (22) applied certain of those transformations to G, and used the conjoint-measurement data analysis procedures proposed by Krantz & Tversky (80) to consider four composition rules to measure the perceived riskiness of the transformed gambles. Only the distributive polynomial model was essentially supported. Pollatsek & Tversky (131) showed that this model is implied by their result that the risk of a gamble of the form G is expressible as a linear combination of its EV and variance, and consequently that Coombs & Huang's (22) distributive model reduces to theirs.

Coombs & Bowen (19) used two of the transformations employed in (22) plus an additional one. In their carefully designed experiment they showed that varying the odds of a gamble of the form G without changing the EV or the variance substantially changed the perceived risk, contrary to any theory, such as that of Pollatsek & Tversky, requiring perceived riskiness to be a function solely of its EV and variance. Moreover, the distributive polynomial model was clearly rejected in this study.

Other transformations of G obtained by combining two or more gambles were investigated by Coombs & Bowen (20). Their results were contrary to predictions derived from the model of Pollatsek & Tversky, but supportive of an as yet unpublished theory of Huang (see 20). Their experiment considered one special case, and since it appears that both theories cannot simultaneously be true, it is of interest to observe which, if either, holds in general.

It is not known whether the incompatible results of Coombs & Huang (22) and Coombs & Bowen (19, 20) are due to differences in the experimental procedure [Coombs & Huang (22) employed as subjects graduate students of psychology who completed the task in their homes] or whether they imply that the distributive polynomial model holds only under certain classes of transformations of gambles.

In attempting to determine the relative importance of p_W, p_L, r_W, and r_L, Slovic (168) had 32 subjects rate the perceived riskiness of 27 duplex gambles on a 10-point scale. The four risk dimensions had zero intercorrelations across the gambles. The data analysis consisted of correlating each subject's ratings with the levels of each risk dimension across the 27 gambles. Although the results indicate that p_L was the most important single determiner of perceived risk, the conclusion that "perceived risk was determined primarily by a gamble's probability of losing" (168, p. 223) is debatable (the average correlation was only .52). The low correlations reported between the ratings of perceived riskiness and the gambles' variances are difficult to interpret, since the report does not indicate that the EVs of the 27 gambles were controlled for in computing these correlations.

In summary, it seems that the concept of risk is psychologically meaningful but highly elusive. Expected value, variance, number of independent plays, probabilities of winning and losing, and other transformations of two-outcome gambles all affect the perceived riskiness of gambles in one way or another, making the development of a satisfactory theory of risk a very difficult task. Since the concept of risk, as that of utility, would appear to be highly idiosyncratic, perhaps a more promising experimental procedure is to shift from multiple-subject to single-subject designs.

Functional Measurement

Two major, nonaxiomatic approaches, the "correlational" and the "functional measurement" approach, have recently stimulated research on individual decision making. The former is characterized by its use of correlational statistics, whereas the latter primarily relies on ANOVA in describing the information integration process and in developing a substantive theory.

Theory.—Functional measurement (e.g. 1 and references there) is a numerical rather than an axiomatic approach to the study of composition rules in psychology. Like conjoint measurement it attempts simultaneously to scale the stimulus attributes and response measures and to determine the composition rule relating the two. Unlike conjoint measurement, however, it ordinarily assumes the representation of a qualitative empirical structure by a numerical structure. Its main features are reliance on factorial designs, quantitative response measures, and a monotone transformation for rescaling these measures.

Functional measurement has devoted special attention to decision tasks in which a simple algebraic model involving adding, averaging, subtracting, or multiplying the information input serves as the substantive theory (see e.g. 1, 2, 162–164). In its general form, this algebraic model is written as a weighted sum:

$$R = \sum w_i s_i + C \qquad\qquad 1.$$

where s and w are the "scale" value and "weight" value, respectively, of a piece of information, C is a constant representing such things as response bias and scaling factors, which will not be considered here, R is a theoretical response assumed to be on a continuous or numerical scale, and summation is over all relevant stimuli.

By differently interpreting "scale" and "weight," the additive model (Equation 1) may be applied to both single-stage (2, 163) and multi-stage (162) decision tasks under certainty or uncertainty. For example, consider a two-factorial design in which the rows correspond to stimuli $S_1, S_2, \ldots$ and the columns to other stimuli $T_1, T_2, \ldots$, and let the subjective values of S_i and T_j be denoted by s_i and t_j, respectively. Then the model equation is

$$R_{ij} = w_1 s_i + w_2 t_j \qquad \qquad 2.$$

where R_{ij} is the theoretical response to the stimulus pair (S_i, T_j), say a measure of its subjective worth, and w_1 (w_2) is the "weight" of the row (column) dimension. Two independence assumptions are made: (a) there are no contextual effects; and (b) w_1 (w_2) is invariant over all row (column) stimuli.

To understand the reliance of functional measurement on factorial designs and rescaling of the response measures, consider Equation 2. Since the equation implies that the row by column interaction is zero in principle and nonsignificant in practice, ANOVA can be used for testing goodness of fit. If the interaction is nonsignificant, the additive model is supported and the subjective values of S_i and T_j can be estimated by straightforward procedures. Significant interactions will occur if the model is violated or the response scale is invalid, perhaps because the overt responses only constitute an ordinal scale, or both. The approach then calls for transforming the response measures to eliminate the significant interaction term. This can be accomplished by carefully inspecting graphs of the data or by applying general computing routines such as Kruskal's (81). If no satisfactory transformation of the response data can be found, any discrepancy from the model must be due to more than a simple distortion of the response scale. Conversely, finding such transformation implies support for the model (163).

The advantages of functional measurement or "information integration theory," as it is frequently called when applied to decision making (2, 163), are many. It provides general and quite simple techniques, both for testing the additive model of Equation 1 and for scaling the stimulus variables at the level of the individual DM. When verified it provides interval scales both for the response and for the stimulus dimensions. More importantly, it provides a unified treatment of a wide range of single-stage decision making tasks.

Integration theory has its unsolved problems too. The first is that, like other algebraic approaches, it has not justified an explicit error theory. The results of ANOVA depend on the variability inherent in the data, whether from individuals or groups. Such dependence may mask real interactions and lead to the acceptance of a wrong hypothesis. For example, in an experiment by Shanteau & Anderson (164) the omission of subjects with significant individual interactions apparently reduced the error term in the group analysis sufficiently to allow a smaller real effect to manifest itself.

There is a second problem, the practical implications of which are not fully known, in the way ANOVA is employed to test the null hypothesis of no interaction. To the extent that monotonic transformations of response scales are used, it is either to satisfy the ANOVA's assumptions of normality and homogeneity of variance, or to eliminate significant interactions. Despite the confusion on this issue in the literature, there is no reason to expect that the same transformation will fulfill both conditions (91). Integration theory relies heavily on ANOVA in testing the validity of the proposed composition rule and even in estimating the contributions of the various treatment combinations. However, it also permits, indeed requires, transformations of the response data which, though decreasing interaction, do not necessarily increase the adequacy of the ANOVA.

To understand the relationships between SEU theory and integration theory, consider Equation 1 specialized for duplex bets (2, 163). Interpreting s_i to be the utility of r_i and w_i to be the subjective probability of p_i, $i = W, L$, Equation 1 is identical in form to the SEU model. What does this imply about the substantive relationships between the SEU theory and integration theory? Anderson & Shanteau (2) note two "basic differences." The first is that SEU theory includes a normative element, namely, the assumption that DM acts as though he is maximizing SEU, whereas integration theory does not impose any such postulate. This "basic difference," we think, is based on misunderstanding of SEU theory in its axiomatic form. Rather than assuming maximization of SEU, the theory derives it from more fundamental assumptions. Indeed, some of these assumptions such as transitivity and independence are implied by integration theory. A second and more specific difference is related to the interpretation of the weight value w_i. Anderson & Shanteau claim that the weight parameter is a more general concept than subjective probability. In addition to reflecting the reliability or likelihood of the informational stimulus, it may be affected by other variables such as "individual differences in probability preference," and "risk preference." However, placing no restrictions on the weight parameters has its disadvantages as well. For example, without demanding risk invariance, integration theory does not allow the straightforward measurement of utility of gambling, an important psychological concept in decision making, so elegantly performed by Tversky (186).

Experiments.—Experimental tests of SEU theory have demonstrated that with a judicious selection of stimulus elements and with an appropriate experimental design one may considerably affect the chances of supporting the whole theory or rejecting some of its testable axioms. An analogous situation holds for integration theory despite its nonaxiomatic formulation. There is no compelling evidence for purposeful, directed attempts to reject integration theory, as there has been for SEU theory (e.g. 71, 72, 188). For example, Equation 2, tested by Anderson & Shanteau (2) and Shanteau

(163), implies transitivity as well as independence between values (s scales) and beliefs (w scales). No tests of transitivity, however, were reported in these studies.

Equation 2 is seen to consist of two integration operations, namely, adding and multiplying. The former operation may be analyzed with a graphical test of parallelism or with standard ANOVA tests (see e.g. 1, 164). The multiplying operation requires another development, presented by Anderson (1) and summarized by Anderson & Shanteau (2), which extracts the Linear $\times$ Linear component of the $p_W \times r_W$ interaction and then tests the residual.

The evaluation of integration theory is based on separating and then testing both the adding and multiplying models. This method of analysis permits localization of any discrepancy from the theory, unlike tests of SEU. The adding model was tested by Shanteau & Anderson (164). They proposed a conflict model of preference judgment which assumed that the strength of an overt numerical response depended on the strengths of the competing responses. Identifying the subjective values of the alternatives with the strengths of the competing responses, the conflict model reduced to a subtractive model of preference. As such it implied that the interaction should be zero, so that ordinary ANOVA might be applied. Support for the model was moderate. The group results conformed to the prediction, but about 25% of the individual subjects exhibited significant interactions.

The adding model was further tested in an experiment by Anderson & Shanteau (2) employing duplex bets. Separate ANOVA tests were performed for the adding and multiplying models. The former was rejected for the group and individual data. However, discrepancies between observed and predicted results were small, unimportant for most interpretations. The multiplying model was supported in the group data but, as in Shanteau & Anderson's (164) experiment, 25% of the residual interactions of individual subjects were significant. None of the F ratios for individual subjects was large, and individual plots showed no systematic trends. Although the multiplying model was not strictly verified, Anderson & Shanteau (2) went ahead with estimating the subjective values of probability and money. The results closely resembled those reported by Tversky (186).

The results of Shanteau's (163) related study almost duplicated those of Anderson & Shanteau (2). The multiplying model worked very well for one-part and two-part bets both in the individual and group analyses. In fact, the fit with verbal bets was better than with the numerical bets of Anderson & Shanteau. Tests of the adding model revealed serious discrepancies which were not removed by simple response scale transformations.

When the worths of a multi-part bet and the worths of its components are judged separately, the adding model yields an additional prediction, namely, that the worth of the bet is equal to the sum of worths of its components. Similar predictions have been made and tested in numerous studies (e.g. 13, 64) employing Thurstonian scaling techniques and using multi-part riskless options, or commodity bundles. In testing the adding model on risky verbal options, Shanteau (163) found a clear subadditivity effect. The worth of two-part bets was judged to be less than the sum of worths of its two components. The same effect was found in a reanalysis of riskless response data reported in several studies (see 163).

The Linear Model

Theory.—The correlational approach to decision making requires numerical responses, but unlike functional measurement it assumes that responses are unique up to a linear transformation. When applied to individual decision making, the correlational approach has been mainly concerned with DM's policy of weighting various stimulus dimensions, placing less importance than Brunswik and his followers did on modeling the environment, but emphasizing the need to manipulate it experimentally. Several simple models have been developed to capture DM's policy, the most prominent of which is the *linear model*, postulating that DM's numerical responses constitute some linear combination of the available stimulus dimensions.

Let $A(G)$ denote the attractiveness of a duplex gamble to a particular DM. Then the model equation is $A(G) = \mu + w_1 p_W + w_2 r_W + w_3 p_L + w_4 r_L$, where the w's are the regression weights for the DM reflecting the relative importance of each dimension. The primary data analysis consists of correlating DM's numerical responses with each of the four dimensions across a set of gambles. Since the dimensions are uncorrelated, the correlations between the dimensions and DM's responses are directly proportional to the weights in the linear regression equation characteristic of this DM.

The special advantage of the linear model is that, if correct, it allows independent assessment of the relative effects of the various stimulus dimensions. The drawbacks are three. First, the assumption of interval scale response data seems untenable for many if not most decision tasks. Second, since the linear model does not specify ordinal properties (i.e. axioms) that the responses ought to satisfy, the interpretability of results favorable to the model is problematic. It is well known that two or more decision models may be algebraically equivalent yet suggestive of radically different underlying processes. Thirdly, and more seriously, given fallible data one may too easily accept the linear model when it is indeed invalid. It has been well demonstrated (206; see also 56, 174) that whenever predictor variables are monotonically related to a criterion variable, a simple linear combination of main effects will do a remarkably good job of predicting, even if interactions exist.

Experiments.—To test the linear model, several experiments have been conducted (88, 90, 107, 167, 170–173) in which subjects were asked to rate their strength of preference for playing a gamble, typically a duplex gamble, or to express their opinion about the gamble's attractiveness by stating their maximum buying price, minimum selling price, or simply a "fair price" for a gamble. The main impact of these experiments has been negative in rejecting the independence assumption of SEU theory. The results show that decision behavior may be strongly influenced by information processing considerations, and that biases due to these considerations may produce inconsistencies in subjective probability and utility functions derived from different types of responses (167).

These negative findings, however, do not necessarily imply support for the additive model approach. Studies designed to test the linear model have not always used goodness-of-fit tests to determine the significance of differences between the weights. The multiple correlations that have been reported between stimulus dimensions and DM's responses are not sufficiently high to exclude alternative, nonlinear models such as the ones studied by Einhorn (42). Moreover, various studies (2, 163, 186, 196, and especially 187) which compared the linear and SEU models all produced data incompatible with the linear model.

In discussing tests of SEU theory we have already mentioned several experiments inspired by the linear model. Results reported by Slovic & Lichtenstein (172) suggest that the requirement to bid for a duplex gamble directs subjects to attend more closely to the payoff dimensions r_L and r_W, whereas under rating instructions choices seem to be influenced more by the gamble's probabilities. Their study also suggested that r_L is relatively more important than r_W. In a similar experiment to that of Slovic & Lichtenstein (172), Slovic (169) found that ratings of duplex gambles were influenced primarily by p_W, whereas bids were most affected by r_L. To explain these results he proposed a two-stage model that was supported by his data.

It has been frequently suggested (32, 78) that the variance of a gamble exercises considerable influence in determining a gamble's attractiveness. Unfortunately, most of the experiments showing variance preference confounded the variance with the gamble's probabilities and payoffs. By using duplex gambles, Slovic & Lichtenstein (173) succeeded in separating variance from probabilities and payoffs. They concluded "that dispersion or variance, as manipulated here, is at best a minor determinant of bids and choices" (173, p. 653). Payne & Braunstein (107) demonstrated convincingly the importance of the risk dimensions p_W, p_L, r_W, and r_L, as opposed to the EV and variance in determining choices between gambles. They suggested that the EV and variance may be good predictors of choices among pairs of gambles simply because they usually correlate with the relevant variables. To substantiate this suggestion, the sources of information used by individual subjects should be identified and a model of information integration should be proposed and tested. It remains to be seen whether the information-processing model of choice proposed in a flow-chart form by Payne & Braunstein "appears more promising than those based on moments of the underlying distribution" (107, p. 17).

In discussing the merits of the axiomatic and numerical approaches to the study of composition rules in psychology, Krantz & Tversky (80) submit that these should be regarded as complementary rather than competing. When the numerical values of the dependent variable obey the proposed composition rule to a satisfactory degree of approximation, the dependent variable can be regarded as an adequate measure of the relevant psychological dimension. ANOVA or regression techniques may be applied routinely to test the validity of the proposed composition rule and to estimate the contribution of the various stimulus dimensions. If the proposed composition rule is not satisfied by the data, ordinal properties that are necessary for the composition rule to hold should be systematically tested as proposed and demonstrated by Krantz & Tversky (80), Tversky (186), and Coombs & Huang (22).

The assessment of the potential contributions of the axiomatic and numerical approaches to single-stage decision making should be based to some extent on practical considerations. Complementarity of the approaches is devoid of much operational meaning unless criteria for determining "a satisfactory degree of approximation" are provided. Here we cannot add much to what Green (56) has said in critically evaluating the numerical approach. Whether one accepts its first-order approximations "as good descriptions of reality or as fictions contributed by the method of analysis depends partly on one's purposes. If the goal is prediction in some practical situation, an adequate description will serve. But if the goal is to understand the process, then we must beware of analyses that mask complexities" (56, p. 98).

MULTI-STAGE DECISION MAKING

Multi-stage decision processes, and consequently theories of such processes, may be divided in several different ways depending upon the definition of "state," the characterization of the transformation rule, and the nature of the objective criterion. We have found it useful to distinguish between two classes of multi-stage decision tasks, *sequential* and *dynamic*. In the former class, a stage-to-stage change in the state of the system, if it occurs, does *not* depend on DM's previous decisions. Noncontingent probability learning, which will not be discussed in this review, revision of opinion (e.g. 36, 109, 174), and optional stopping (e.g. 34, 141) tasks fall in this class. In a dynamic decision task, stage-to-stage changes in the state of the system are directly affected by DM's previous decisions, as well as by the states of the system at the preceding stages.

The major difference between a sequential and dynamic decision system is that to maximize the objective criterion in the latter case, DM has to consider the effect of each of his decisions on the future states of the system and consequently on his future decisions. He also has to consider the duration of the process, i.e. the number of stages, which may or may not be known to him. In other words, he has to plan his sequence of decisions in advance. In a sequential decision task, however, decisions are mutually independent.

Presumably because of this difference, sequential decision theory is relatively less concerned with action selection at each stage than with the logically prior problem of diagnosis (e.g. 41, 109, 134), whereas in dynamic decision theory the emphasis is reversed.

SEQUENTIAL DECISION THEORY

Bayesian Revision of Opinion

Theory.—Diagnosis can be conceptualized as the process of revising a subjective probability distribution over a set of $m+1$ events $e_0, e_1, \ldots, e_m$ on the basis of some data. Formally, the events e_i, $i = 0, \cdots, m$, are probability distributions $f_i(x)$. Bayes' rule provides the mathematically appropriate way to combine the $f_i(x)$ with the prior probabilities, $p_0(e_i)$, after n observations of data $x_1, x_2, \ldots, x_n$ to obtain the posterior probabilities $p_n(e_i) = p(e_i | x_1, \ldots, x_n)$.

Bayes' rule has provided the starting point for a considerable amount of psychological research. Much of this can be traced to Edwards' (33) early exposition of dynamic decision theory, to the discussion by Edwards et al (40) of Bayesian statistics, and to a variety of related works by Savage, Raiffa, Schlaifer (see e.g. 133), and others. Relatively current reviews of work in this area are in (28, 29, 36, 39, 86, 109, 198). Slovic & Lichtenstein (174) present a comprehensive review, relating the Bayesian work to regression approaches to information processing.

The axiomatic method has not yet been extensively employed in sequential decision theory (but see 133). It may be noted that Savage (151, p. 307) feels it to be of limited usefulness in psychology. Rather, one class of theories has developed, altering it around Bayes' rule to yield a psychological model. It is relatively easy, and we think necessary, to view this class of theories critically. It is also somewhat unfair to the authors, because much of the original work was strictly empirical, designed to answer specific applied questions rather than ones of a general theoretical nature (e.g. 41, 69, 154). The subsequent theoretical development then was built upon this rather narrow empirical base. Nevertheless, it must ultimately be evaluated in a broad framework.

One form of Bayes' rule, which yields the posterior odds in favor of e_1 relative to e_0 given the data, now collectively denoted X_n, is

$$\Omega(e_1 | X_n) = L(X_n; e_1)\Omega(e_1) \qquad\qquad 3.$$

In this expression $\Omega(e_1 | X_n)$, the posterior odds, is the ratio $p(e_1/X_n)/p(e_0 | X_n)$, the likelihood ratio $L(X_n; e_1)$ is the ratio $p(X_n | e_1)/p(X_n | e_0)$, and $\Omega(e_1)$, the prior odds, is the ratio $p_0(e_1)/p_0(e_0)$. A considerable number of studies, to be reviewed in the empirical section, have compared DMs' numerical estimates in appropriate tasks to $p(e_i | X_n)$ or to $\Omega(e_i | X_n)$. The general but far from unanimous result has been that the estimates were monotonically related to these quantities (within most studies at least) but were too evenly distributed among the e_i; that is to say, they were conservative (36) relative to the predicted Bayesian values.

The conservative estimates have led to a descriptive model, which assumes that DMs treat $L(X_n; e_1)$ as if it were raised to a power $b < 1.0$ (36, 118). Theoretical attempts to understand conservatism then may be considered as attempts to understand why $b < 1.0$. Three alternatives have been offered: misperception of the diagnosticity of the data (i.e. of the implications of its likelihood ratio); misaggregation of the data; or simply a response bias (29, 36, 174). These concepts have been developed strictly within an empirical framework and will be returned to below.

Beyond discussing these, however, it is well to consider the basic model and how it relates to the psychological processes it purports to describe. Green (56), commenting on papers by Edwards (36) and Hoffman (65), raised the important but often overlooked distinction between descriptions and explanations. Without doubt, raising $L(X_n; e_1)$ to a power $b < 1$ often describes the subjects' *mean* responses, and for many specific applications this may be sufficient. Whether this also serves to explain the processes underlying these responses is another matter, and on this there is very little evidence. Equation 3 in log form is a linear expression; the comments made in the section above on Linear Models regarding the ease with which an additive model may be falsely accepted were also made by Green (56) and apply here. Green suggested that one way to cope with this problem is to pit the additive model against an alternative. This has been done within the optional stopping paradigm (121, 129), but not within an estimation one. [But see (65) for an example of this in a related estimation situation. Also see (52) and (174) for similar discussions.]

Another way to view Green's criticism is that the Bayesian model as presently constituted is very difficult to falsify. This, of course, is a serious deficiency. However, this problem arises not only because it is an additive model, but also because b is a completely free parameter. The value of b, commonly called the Accuracy Ratio (112), is obtained by taking the slope of the best fitting line relating subjects' likelihood ratios (inferred from their estimates) to Bayesian likelihood ratios, plotted on log-log graph paper. The slope is generally, but not always, less than one. Green (56) and Du-Charme (29) point out that the model offers no indication of why or when b should be less than one. Neither does it allow a priori prediction of the value of b. Furthermore, as will be seen in reviewing the empirical work, the Accuracy Ratio depends on various parameters of the task, thus disallowing predictions in one situation based on the value of b calculated in another. Predictions have been made in optional stopping experiments using "ball-park" values of b (34, 195), but this is unsatisfactory for reasons to be described later. Indeed, it appears as if very little can be done with the value of b, the Accuracy Ratio, beyond reporting it.

Leaving aside the question of possibly falsely accepting the linear model, with or without b, there is the problem of the relation between the response and the psychological process which gave rise to the response. Stated more generally, the problem is one of developing and testing the theory using unique scale values. To accept the modified form of Equation 3 as a description of the process on the basis of the evidence available is to accept the existence of an identity relation between the response and its underlying psychological dimension. Some authors (29, 30, 98, 124 and references there, 162, 197), are not prepared to do this, while others are (36, 109). Among the latter are a number who contend that at the least conditions can be arranged (through the use of proper scoring rules) such that the identity holds (see e.g. 26, 165, 178 and references there, 204).

Two approaches attempt to circumvent this problem while at the same time giving the model an appropriate test. With a single exception (190), the models developed around Bayes' rule have implicitly assumed that equal likelihood ratios are subjectively equal. Wallsten (197) has made the much weaker assumption that the response is a monotonic function of the ratio of the subjective probability of X_n given e_1 to the subjective probability of X_n given e_0. Letting ϕ_1 and ϕ_2 represent the subjective conditional likelihoods in the numerator and denominator of the ratio, respectively, this may be written as

$$R(e_1, e_0 \mid X_n) = f\left[\frac{\phi_1(X_n \mid e_1)}{\phi_2(X_n \mid e_0)}\right] \qquad 4.$$

where $R(e_1, e_0 \mid X_n)$ is the numerical response favoring e_1 on the basis of X_n. Taking logs within the domain of f makes it immediately apparent that Equation 4 implies an additive conjoint-measurement model, with the numerator and denominator of the ratio as the factors. Thus, the axioms of additive conjoint measurement are necessary for the likelihood ratio principle, and that principle is changed from one of assumption to one of empirical fact, subject to possible rejection. Furthermore, it is easily seen that Equation 3 is a special case of Equation 4. The use of conjoint-measurement techniques answers many of the criticisms discussed above and generates questions different in nature from the misperception-misaggregation controversy, such as concerning the relation between the ϕ_i, or the conditions under which the likelihood ratio principle does or does not hold. However, it is too early yet to determine whether the approach will ultimately be useful.

Another approach was developed by Shanteau (162) using functional measurement techniques. The subject gives a quantitative response in favor of e_i following the observation of each datum, x_k, $k = 1, 2, \cdots, n$. This response after n data R_n is assumed to equal the weighted sum of the scale values of the x_k. Letting w_k and s_k be the weight and scale value of x_k, respectively:

$$R_n = \sum_{k=0}^{n} w_k s_k \qquad 5.$$

where the term $w_0 s_0$ denotes an initial decision state. With each position in the data sequence as a factor and each of the possible values of x_k as a level (two in Shanteau's case), one may perform a factorial experiment and apply the methods of functional measurement discussed earlier. Certainly these methods will demonstrate whether the additive model implied by Equation 3 is incorrect within a level of n. Shanteau (162) assumed $\sum_{i=0}^{n} w_k = 1$ and $s_k = \{0, 1\}$, depending on whether x_k favors e_0 or e_1, making the expression a weighted average model in order to assess recency or primacy effects. Lathrop (83) also developed a factorial procedure to test the additive form of Equation 3 using the framework of conjoint measurement.

Experiments.—The experimental literature can be divided conveniently into four categories: (a) *conservatism*, concerned with the establishment and manipulation of the basic phenomenon behind the theorizing; (b) *explanations*, pertaining to the misaggregation, misperception, response bias controversy; (c) other *predictions* of the basic theories; and (d) *response scales*, concerning the relations between responses and their determinants.

Conservatism.—Experiments reviewed herein have incorporated a wide range of variations on either of two paradigms, depending on whether the task was a "simple laboratory" or a "complex real-world" task. The simple paradigm is represented, for example, in (112, 118). In the former study (112) subjects were faced with two large urns, each containing about 1000 black and white marbles. The ratio of black to white was 3:2 in urn B and 2:3 in urn W. The experimenter flipped a coin to select one urn, randomly sampled a fixed number of marbles from it, and showed the marbles but not the urn to the subjects. After each sample the subjects estimated the probability that urn B was being used; they were shown the urn after the final sample. In the latter study (118) subjects were asked to imagine the manipulations rather than experience them, a technique used in many other experiments. One might expect this difference in design to yield systematic differences in the results, and sufficiently fine grained analyses might show some, but none have been glaringly evident.

Analyses can be performed directly on subjects' responses, usually either odds or probability estimates, but often these are converted instead to log odds. Then log odds for trial $n-1$ are subtracted from those on trial n to obtain the DMs' *inferred log likelihood ratio*, assuming, of course, that the log of Equation 3 is an appropriate model for the responses. The ratio of the inferred value to the corresponding Bayesian value is the Accuracy Ratio, or b referred to above.

The aforementioned paradigms have been manipulated in terms of prior probabilities, sampling probabilities, use of hypotheses other than binomial (e.g. normal or multinomial), response methods, feedback, etc, but not, unless otherwise mentioned, in the use of asymmetrical hypotheses. Symmetrical binomial hypotheses have the advantage that y, the difference between the numbers of each kind of event, is linearly related to posterior log odds or log likelihood ratio, and therefore provides a convenient, simple independent variable. This, in turn, has the disadvantage of often leading experimenters to confound and ignore other independent variables which have subsequently been shown to have an effect on responses, such as sample proportions (9; also mentioned incidentally in 24) or the number of occurrences of the predominant event (129).

The complex paradigms were developed mainly to evaluate a class of man-machine systems for probabilistic information processing initially proposed by Edwards (33, 35, 41) and termed PIP. The basic idea of the system is to have DMs estimate likelihood ratios rather than posterior odds and to have these aggregated by a computer according to Bayes' rule. The paradigms usually involve simulated military problems, but that is not necessary for the main concepts which have been extended, e.g. to medical diagnosis (59, 76, 96).

Schum and his collaborators developed an extensive, complicated computer controlled experimental environment, in which highly trained subjects estimated $p(X_n|e_i)$ or $p(e_i|X_n)$ for each of up to eight e_i concerning an aggressor's possible strategies (69, 154, 161). In Schum et al (159) the data X_n, actually consisted of probability distributions over from 2 to 8 possible states in each of up to 25 data classes. An example of a data class is "Aggressor's Tactical Air Support Squadrons," with possible states being the presence of 0, 1, 2, or 3 squadrons. A modified Bayes' Rule (MBT) developed by Dodson (see 159) was applied to the sets of multinomial probability distributions to calculate optimal $p(e_i|X_n)$. MBT could also be used on the subjects' estimated $p(X_n|e_i)$ in the manner called for by the PIP system. [See (51) and (155) for subsequent improvements in MBT.] The other "real-world" paradigm was developed by Edwards et al (41) and will be discussed below.

With these simple and complex paradigms briefly outlined it is a simple matter to review the results. Generally in binomial and multinomial tasks subjects' posterior estimates favoring the more likely e_i increased with the likelihood ratio of a datum, as they should, but considerably less than the Bayesian values did (e.g. 17; 57; 113, Exp. II; 118, Exp. I; 160). Most of these studies presented subjects with data in batches of size greater than one. In Experiment I of Peterson & Swensson (113) samples contained one datum each and posterior estimates corresponded exactly to Bayesian values. However, Vlek (190) and Pitz et al (126) found subjects utterly insensitive to datum diagnosticity. Pitz et al (126) additionally reported that reanalysis of results of Phillips & Edwards (118) showed their subjects to be ignoring likelihood ratios and basing their responses only on y. When the data were generated by either of two normal distributions (30, 31), the mean or median estimated posterior odds varied appropriately with datum diagnosticity. The estimates appeared to be conservative relative to Bayesian odds only when the latter exceed 10:1.

Only one experiment that we are aware of is partially relevant to the question of effects of datum diagnosticity in the complex paradigm. Schum et al (159) found that when diagnosticity was varied by manipulating the multinomial probability distributions over data states the experienced subjects' posterior estimates decreased as reliability decreased, but were greater than Bayes' at high reliability and conservative only at the lowest levels. This result is distinctly contrary to others, but it may be argued that the task is one of cascading data over different levels in a hierarchy (51, 155) and thus is not directly comparable to the other experiments. It may be mentioned here that a very carefully controlled study involving perceptual unreliability of the data (156) also found subjects to be sensitive to the un-reliability, although not to the degree mathematically warranted (see also 177).

Leaving now the problem of the likelihood ratio of an individual datum, we turn to the effects of various properties of samples of data. Samples may vary in terms of their size, composition, and method of presentation of the elements. The latter will be taken up under *model predictions*.

Peterson et al (112) showed subjects 48 pieces of binary data in sequential samples of size 1, 4, 12, or 48, and found that the magnitude of the final $p(e_i | X_n)$ estimates was inversely related to sample size. In fact, subjects revised their estimates after each sample. The mean accuracy ratios after each were all less than one and were smaller for larger sample sizes. In other words, estimates were conservative, and increasingly so for larger samples. On the average larger samples are more diagnostic, and the results are probably due to both of these factors.

Thus, Pitz (120) and Vlek (190) both found that for samples of equal diagnosticity, measured by y, confidence was inversely related to sample size. However, contrary results were reported by Pitz (122), who had subjects give confidence estimates following each datum in a sample and found final estimates a slightly increasing function of sample size for equal values of y. He had one group give final estimates only, and these were invariant over sample size. Looking now at effects of variations in sample diagnosticity holding size constant, Vlek (190) and Green et al (57) using binomial hypotheses, Schum & Martin (160) using multinomial, and Du-Charme & Peterson (31) using normal hypotheses, found estimates to increase with diagnosticity, but not to the same degree as did the Bayesian values. The pattern of results is similar within complex simulation tasks (119, 152, 157).

Most of the studies discussed have used relatively naive subjects. The pattern of results appears to be different with highly experienced subjects. In the experiments of Schum and his colleagues (153, 158, 159) subjects' mean performance was virtually indistinguishable from optimal, although the correlations and the appendices of (158) indicate that intersubject variability was still fairly great. Strub (179) found experienced subjects to give considerably more extreme estimates than naive subjects and to make final decisions on the basis of less evidence. See Howell (69, pp. 19–21) for further discussion, (53) and (100) concerning some effects of feedback, and Goodman (54) for a powerful effect of a particular kind of experience.

To summarize, the phenomenon of conservatism is indeed pervasive, but by no means always present. After reviewing the large number of studies, we have come to believe that the emphasis on comparing human estimates with Bayesian values, although understandable, has been perhaps somewhat misplaced. The experimental model has been classical psychophysics in which responses are compared to objective measures of the stimuli. The difference, however, is that in most uses of psychophysics objective measures vary monotonically with physical characteristics of the stimuli, while in the present case otherwise identical stimuli often have different Bayesian values, and, conversely, different stimuli often have identical values. In most psychophysical work, DMs respond to characteristics of the stimuli which are conveniently summarized by the objective measures. Here, too, DMs differentially respond to characteristics of the data sets, but these are not always systematically related to the Bayesian probabilities. In addition to the evidence already reviewed, we will discuss below various manipulations which have effects on DMs but to which the Bayesian model is indifferent. Thus we think now that although conservatism certainly exists, it is at least as much dependent on the measures we have been using as on the DM's behavior, and that our theoretical understanding of human inference requires closer attention to aspects of the system other than just Bayesian probabilities. Two studies in this direction are (4, 193).

Explanations.—Regardless of our opinion concerning the theoretical status of conservatism, and largely because of its implications for applied problems, a literature has developed concerning its possible causes. It was previously mentioned that assuming the validity of the Bayesian model, explanations of conservatism and supporting evidence have been offered in terms of misperception of the data's diagnostic impact, misaggregation of data, or response bias. These will now be expanded.

Three forms of misperception have been considered. One assumes subjective sampling distributions to be flat relative to those generated by the probability distributions under the e_i. This was tested in two studies (111, 201) in which subjects estimated binomial sampling distributions $p(X_n | e_i)$, following which they estimated $p(e_i | X_n)$ in the usual manner. The median sampling distributions were too flat and the median posterior estimates were conservative, but on the average each subject's posterior estimate was fairly well predicted using his estimate of $p(X_n | e_i)$ in Bayes' rule. Vlek & Van der Heijden (191) report similar results for the average subject, but found virtually no relation between the two measures for individuals. It would be well to see distinct analyses for individual subjects.

Another possible type of misperception is to employ beliefs about the data generators that are incorrect in more than just parameter values. Lichtenstein & Feeney (87) used two circular normal distributions as the e_i, and found that calculations based on them predicted subjects' responses very poorly, but a considerably simpler (essentially additive) model correlated well with the responses. Vlek & Van der Heijden (192) used that model with Lichtenstein & Feeney's data to infer sampling distributions for individual subjects.

Yet another possible form of misperception is to discount the importance (likelihood ratio) of rare events when they occur. This was suggested by Vlek (190) and was evident in the analyses by Vlek & Van der Heijden (192). Beach (3) designed an experiment specifically to test this, in which identical likelihood ratios were composed of different values of $p(X_n|e_i)$. Although the ratios exerted primary control over posterior estimates, the magnitudes of their components were also quite influential in the manner suggested by Vlek. Indeed, Beach's results go further in showing that the unconditional probability of the data influences subjects' estimates, even when the data are not "rare." Contrary to Beach, Gettys & Manley (50) found no effect of sampling probability on posterior estimates in a binomial task. They suggest that the important difference was that in their experiment each problem involved a single datum and thus required no aggregation, while in Beach's study each problem involved three data.

The evidence that DMs misperceive various aspects of the data is compelling, but that does not imply that they accurately combine the disperate pieces of data according to Bayes' rule. Misaggregation as the major source of conservatism has been advocated primarily by Edwards and his colleagues (36, 41, 75) and by Schum and his colleagues (154, 157, 161).

Many of the studies already discussed may be interpreted to support this view, particularly DuCharme & Peterson (31) and Peterson & Swensson (113). Both studies found optimal posterior estimates following the first datum in a sequence, but conservative estimates following additional data. The extensive simulation experiment by Edwards et al (41) in a fictitious world of 1975 has also been offered as evidence in favor of the misaggregation hypothesis (and the PIP system based on that hypothesis). The subjects in the PIP condition evaluated the diagnostic impact of each datum separately, whereas others gave posterior estimates based on all the data. Combining the PIP subjects' responses according to Bayes' rule resulted in posterior values favoring the same hypotheses as did those of the other subjects, but to a considerably greater degree. Or in other words, subjects who had to aggregate data were consistently conservative relative to those who did not.

However, "objective truth" was not known, and consistently higher posterior odds does not mean consistently more accurate posterior odds, as Edwards et al (41) and Kaplan & Newman (75) pointed out, and thus are not necessarily an argument that misaggregation causes conservatism. To answer this criticism Phillips (117) ran a similar study in which objective values could be calculated. It turned out that likelihood ratio estimates were conservative relative to objective values, but not nearly to the degree that posterior odds estimates were, thus supporting both misperception and misaggregation.

The third possible cause of conservatism is that DMs simply have a bias against the use of extreme numbers, leaving "open the question of whether or not (humans) are Bayesian information processors" (29, p. 29). This hypothesis has the advantage of explaining why estimate errors are in a particular direction, and by its very nature virtually none of the evidence discussed can be taken to contradict it. The notion of a response artifact was put forward by Peterson (see 36) and in (191) and was cleverly demonstrated in a signal detection task (108). Additional support for the response bias explanation comes from an experiment by DuCharme (30) within a framework more similar to the other studies discussed.

Predictions.—It has already been mentioned that too few studies have addressed themselves to the adequacy of Bayes' rule as a processing model; virtually all have assumed it and then incorporated that assumption in the analyses. An exception is the study by Peterson (108), in which the model was substantiated. In addition, Shanteau's (162) data were compatible with an additive model, but the weighted averaging was superior to the Bayesian.

Studies which have looked at the sequential effects of data are partially relevant here. Relevant because, with the exception of stage-to-stage changes in information, the Bayesian model predicts absence of sequential effects, but only partially so because in some of the studies it cannot be determined whether the effect is simply in the particular response or in the actual processing. Pitz et al (126) found what they termed an "inertia effect." Subjects revised their estimates to a greater degree (in terms of inferred log likelihood ratio) following evidence which confirmed their currently favored hypothesis than following the same evidence when it infirmed their hypothesis. This was also reported by Dale (24). Pitz (122) reasoned that the subjects may have been "committed" to their previous decision. Alternatively, the inertia effect may have resulted from subjects' expecting, and therefore ignoring, occasional infirming data. Consequently, Pitz (122) manipulated the degree of commitment and found this to have the predicted effect, whereas the expectancy hypothesis was not supported. However, it cannot be determined in this experiment whether the act of commitment itself influenced the processing of the data. Brody (14) previously ran a similar study and found commitment to affect stated confidence, but not the amount of information required for a final decision, indicating that the effect was only on the estimates. Also, Peterson & DuCharme (110), particularly in Experiment II, found strong primacy effects perfectly compatible with the inertia effect.

Geller & Pitz (49) required subjects to predict which binary event would occur at each stage in a sequence, and following the event to guess which of two processes was generating the events and to rate their confidence. Decision times were also recorded, unknown to the subjects. A variety of complicated systematic sequential effects occurred, all of which may be taken as negative evidence for a Bayesian model. But in particular for the present discussion, support was obtained for the hypothesis that subjects occasionally expect disconfirming data. That is, following disconfirming-predicted data, subjects persisted in *increasing* their confidence (although their decision speed *decreased*), while following disconfirming-nonpredicted data subjects reduced their confidence (and speeds also decreased). The amount of confidence reduction depended upon whether the previous event was disconfirming or confirming, as did decision times, but the contingencies on prior events worked in the opposite directions. For related experiments reporting primacy and recency effects see (4, 126–128, 147, 163).

To summarize, there is no doubt that strong sequential effects exist in DMs' responses. Whether they can be taken as negative evidence for a Bayesian model of information processing, however, depends on where in the system the effects are assumed to occur, and on this there is no conclusive evidence. With the currently strong interest in and the potential usefulness of the Bayesian model of revision of opinion, it is to be hoped that theoretical development and subsequent experimentation will soon be forthcoming which will properly allow its validity to be tested. As with SEU theory, the question is not whether it is right or wrong, but under what conditions does it hold and in what ways is it violated.

Responses.—It has been mentioned often that there is a distinction between a response and that of which it is a measure. The distinction is difficult to make, however, without a theory which relates the unobservable process to observable behavior. If the theory is not rejected it can be used to evaluate the response (196). Indeed, we feel that strictly speaking it is only within the context of such a theory that the unobservable process is defined. Conjoint measurement and functional measurement are examples of this approach.

In the absence of detailed theories, one might look for certain qualitative or ordinal properties in the data. For example, two different measures of "subjective probability," such as confidence estimates and either decision speed or amount of information required prior to a decision, would be expected to move in the same directions under all circumstances. This was not the case in two previously described studies (14, 49), and it can only be concluded that the various responses were not measures of the same thing. There is no way to evaluate which measure is "best" without theoretical predictions against which to test them.

Additionally, if one is going to use identity scale properties of responses in data analysis, as has so often been done, one might expect responses on different scales to be identical under appropriate transformations. This expectation was supported in an interesting study by Wise (205), but was obviously not the case in two other studies (118, 203). Another (5) found high correlations between various kinds of probability estimates, but they were not identity transforms of one another since the slopes of the regression lines were not close to one. Beach & Wise (6–8) did find identity relations between responses on different scales, but unfortunately the response method was a between-subject variable and analyses were performed on group means. In two of the studies variability was quite great (7, 8) and in one not reported (6). Sanders (148) manipulated response as a within-subject variable, but although the main effect of this manipulation was insignificant, it interacted significantly with subjects. Thus, it is hard to say whether the mean results of the latter four experiments are representative of individuals.

Optional Stopping

Theory.—Instead of presenting the DM with a set of data and then asking him for a probability or an odds estimate favoring e_0 or e_1, one may charge him c_k units to observe each x_k. After observing x_k, DM has three decisions, called d_0, d_1, and w. The decision d_i, $i=0$, 1, that e_i is the correct event, is terminal. It is followed by payment to DM of the (possibly negative) amount r_{ij}, where e_j is the correct event, $j=0$, 1. The decision w is to wait and purchase an observation x_{k+1} at a cost of c_{k+1}. DM's objective criterion is the minimization of expected loss.

The number of available observations N may or may not be limited. Also, the cost of an observation may depend on the correct event as well as on the stage number, in which case it is denoted c_{jk} (and in which case the DM is not informed how much he has spent for data until after he makes a terminal decision, since that would immediately tell him which is the correct event). Alternatively, each observation may cost a fixed sum c, regardless of the correct event or the stage. Finally, there is no loss of generality, mathematically at least, in letting $r_{00}=r_{11}=0$, and in considering the r_{ij}, $i \neq j$, to be losses.

This is a general formulation, which has been treated in the statistical and operations research literature (see e.g. 12, 27; see also 141, which has summarized and extended some of this work for psychologists). It allows different assumptions about the parameters prior to deriving optimal policies minimizing expected loss. The optimal policy specifies, in general, two decision boundaries for each stage in terms of posterior probabilities δ, at or above which d_1 is made, and γ, at or below which d_0 is made, $\delta \geq \gamma$. Between δ and γ the decision w is made.

Extending some work by Blackwell & Girschik, Edwards (34) presented equations for the optimal policy in the case in which the number of observations is unlimited and the cost per observation is constant. The assumption of linear observation costs is probably never valid when considering utilities instead of values, but it may be close when small amounts of money are involved. Similarly, pressures of time and money will limit available observations to fewer than infinity, but infinity is sometimes a good approximation (141). The equations are transcendental, but tabular values are offered for various special conditions.

Failures of the model's predictions are difficult to evaluate. This is due in part to the insensitivity of EV to departures from the optimal model. Stopping boundaries widely discrepant from the optimal ones often lead to only small increases in expected loss (141, 199), and this lack of precision by the minimizing DM may be well compensated for by saved time and effort. Equally as serious, however, the predictions may be wrong because any of a number of assumptions may be violated. Utility may not be linearly related to money, utility of observation costs may not be constant over trials, and N may be subjectively very small and nonconstant. Such problems are not specific to Edwards' model, but they are typical of the sort encountered in any attempt to evaluate a normative model in descriptive terms.

One solution has been to develop predictions from the model independently of some or all scale values. For example, Pitz (121) pointed out that according to Edwards' (34) model, size of the data sample n at the terminal decision d_i is a random variable. In the symmetric binomial case where the posterior log odds are linearly related to y, the difference between the numbers of occurrences of each event, one may obtain $E(n|y)$ for each value of y. Thus, if DM terminates on the basis of posterior odds and independently of n, as the model predicts, regardless of how terminal y is determined and of whether it fluctuates over problems, the mean n given y should be insignificantly different from $E(n|y)$. Deviations may occur because the basic minimizing model is wrong, subjective log odds are not linear in y, N is subjectively small, or utility of information cost is nonconstant over trials, but not for any other reasons.

A stronger prediction, consistent with any minimization of expected loss model assuming $N = \infty$ and c_{jk} nondecreasing in k (141), is that DMs will terminate at a posterior odds greater than any previously available in the sequence (123, 129, 149, 195). A prediction requiring no assumptions about N and c_{jk} is that the sequence of data is irrelevant (127, 128, 149).

An alternative approach towards evaluating the descriptive power and the subsequent modification of the Bayesian model is presented by Rapoport & Burkheimer (141), some of whose findings have already been mentioned (see also 12 and 27). They presented the general expressions required to obtain numerical solutions for the optimal policy, as well as some other statistics when N is fixed and known to the subject, c_{jk} is free to vary, and $r_{ij} \neq r_{ji}$. They also suggested modifications of the basic model in the current spirit of psychophysics, i.e. quantizing the stimulus input, or having the response output depend on a probabilistic mechanism. However, the sensitivity problem previously discussed makes comparison of the various models difficult, and the problems of parameter estimation are still far from solved.

Virtually no models of optional stopping have developed outside of the Bayesian framework. However, Pitz (121) and Pitz et al (129) developed two simple models as alternatives to the normative. These models are quite specific to the particular experimental task and discussion of them will be deferred to the empirical section. Pitz (124) also presented an outline of a more general model existing as a computer program, the aim of which is to link specific notions about sequential processing with current conceptualizations of short-term memory. Although the model appears promising, it is not yet sufficiently developed to comment on further.

By way of summary, we believe that optimization models have been and will continue to be useful tools in the development of psychological theory, but these tools must be tempered by special consideration of problems more or less unique to psychology. This includes specification of the role in human decision making of psychological processes which are not relevant to statistical decision theory, such as memory and hypothesis formation. It also includes paying special attention to developing models in such a manner that their very existence and evaluation does not depend upon a level of uniqueness of measurement beyond that guaranteed by the theory.

Experiments.—What may be the most thorough yet least referred to empirical test of Edwards' (34) model and of certain parametric extensions of it was performed by Larsson (82), who ran the same subjects through six experiments, of which two will be mentioned here. In one, an interesting departure from the usual, subjects observed data relevant to two symmetric binomial e_i until they thought that choice of an e_i would lead to an expected loss of a prespecified value equal to αr_{ij} (recall $r_{00} = r_{11} = 0$, and for $i \neq j$, $r_{ij} = r_{ji} \neq 0$), where α is the error probability. Subjects knew that their loss would not be r_{ij}, but would be 1 öre (Swedish currency) for each observation deviant from the optimal number. Various preselected posterior probabilities $(1 - \alpha)$ were factorially crossed with various binomial parameters. These values along with the dependent variable, mean number of observations in each condition, allowed subjective $E(z)$, denoted as $h(z)$, to be calculated for each true $E(z)$ separately within levels of α for each subject, assuming the optimal model and utility linear in money (equation 3.1 in 82, or equation 12 or 13 in 34). There was considerable intersubject variability, but generally $h(z)$ was a linear function of $E(z)$ with slope much less than 1.0 and positive intercept. This is in accord with the conservatism findings.

However, $h(z)$ was also a decreasing function of α for each subject. In other words, within the framework of the optimal model these results show that perceived datum diagnosticity is inversely related to the level of risk, α, one is required to maintain. This might be considered strong negative evidence for the model, since most interpretations would entail independence of these two variables.

Larsson (82) instead chose to accept the relation. In a second experiment he used $h(z)$ in the optimal model to predict average number of observations purchased under 20 combinations of V, $V = r_{ij}/c$, $i \neq j$, and $E(z)$. Predictions were successful for two subjects, and two bought considerably less than predicted. In addition, subjects' terminal odds in a given condition varied considerably over replications, indicating that at the least a stochastic version of the model is more appropriate.

Edwards' (34) model was also specifically tested in (47, 121, 149, 195). All used symmetric binomial distributions as the e_i. Observations were unlimited in the latter two experiments, limited to $N = 48$ in the first, and to $N = 5$, 10, or 20 in the second. All studies agreed in finding that subjects relaxed their stopping odds as sample size n increased, clearly contrary to the specific model. Both Pitz (121) and Wallsten (195) included predictions based on considerations of conservatism, but they were not borne out. [But see (199), which did find evidence of conservatism.] Generally, subjects bought too many observations when only a few were needed, but not enough when a larger number were called for.

At least three explanations exist within the optimal model framework for these results. One is that subjects establish a critical stopping odds but subjective posterior odds increase with sample size, perhaps by a process analogous to the inertia effect discussed earlier. This was tested by Pitz & Barrett (125), who gave subjects varying amounts of free information after which they could purchase more. All else equal, subjects purchased less information following greater numbers of free items, supporting the hypothesis, but the magnitude of the effect was too small to completely explain the earlier results.

Alternative explanations are that N was subjectively small, i.e. subjects imposed their own limits on the amount of information available, or that the utility of the cost of an observation increased with number of observations. These have not been adequately tested, although Pitz noted more decisions following small samples when the number of items was less.

Pitz (121) pitted Edwards' (34) critical odds model against one specifying that subjects buy a fixed number of observations, as did Pitz et al (129), who also introduced a "World Series Model." According to the latter model, observations are purchased until a fixed number m of one kind occurs, and on the average it predicts lower terminal odds with increasing sample size. The critical odds model was evaluated by comparing appropriate dependent variables to $E(n|y)$ and $\text{Var}(n|y)$, respectively. The fixed sample size model was evaluated by comparing data to $E(y|n)$ and $\text{Var}(y|n)$, respectively, and the World Series Model was evaluated by comparing data to $E(k|m)$ and $\text{Var}(k|m)$, respectively, where k is the number of less frequent events. The data clearly violated the critical odds model and were closest to the World

Series Model. Similar results were found in Pitz (123), except that he also collected decision times and found them to depend on sample size, but not on parameters of the World Series Model. This model is specially tailored to the task of deciding between two binomial distributions, and the degree to which it describes behavior must be taken as an indication of the degree to which we are limited in generalizing from behavior in this task to others.

To summarize, the Bayesian model, assuming utility linear in money, N infinite, and c_{jk} invariant, clearly has been insufficient to explain the observed results. It is not yet possible to determine whether the model is wrong merely in assumptions about parameters or in more fundamental ways. But it does appear as if experiments should not be restricted to having DMs test hypotheses consisting of two binomial distributions [see (68) for examples where it is not], and should include more single-subject designs.

Dynamic Decision Theory

Many military, business, political, and control engineering decisions are made dynamically; DM's decision influences the environment, later information is contingent on the consequences of earlier decisions, and implications of any decision may reach far into the future. Considerable attention and effort has been devoted to the formulation and solution of dynamic decision problems in operations research, management science, and mathematical statistics (see e.g. 27, 67). Behavioral decision theorists, on the other hand, have rarely attempted to understand how people plan their behavior as a sequence of interrelated decisions over time, or of how they regulate or control well-defined segments of their environment. One possible reason is that single-stage and sequential decision processes are often considered more fundamental, and it may be argued that only by studying them may one learn about the qualitative laws that govern behavior.

Sequential decision tasks assume mutual independence between decisions. However, independence among successive decision situations is rather exceptional in real life (183), and severely limits our ability to investigate purposeful decision behavior over time, or the interplay between man and his environment. Moreover, mutual independence is difficult to achieve experimentally. The existence of various sequential dependencies in many decision experiments indicates that instructing subjects to maintain independence among successive decisions is no assurance that they will actually do so. If that is the case, is it not better to build dependencies into the models and the experimental situations and study them systematically?

Other more prosaic reasons for the relatively little research on dynamic decision making are the tremendous difficulties in characterizing "state," "stage," "transformation rule," and "criterion function," and in successfully delineating segments of the environment plus a sequence of decisions as a dynamic decision process. The mathematics required to derive the optimal policy is relatively new, unpleasantly complex, and yields numerical rather than analytical solutions in all but simple cases. Also, because of their complexity, dynamic decision experiments are difficult to design and implement without on-line computers. These problems are not insurmountable as the growing experimental research on dynamic decision making clearly indicates (e.g. 16, 77, 135–139, 142–144, 182–184).

Theory.—Dynamic decision theory emerged as an experimental science in 1962 with pioneering papers by Edwards (33) and Toda (182). Edwards (33) proposed to follow the methodology of signal detectability theory by defining an ideal dynamic DM, "comparable in nature, abstractness, and lack of realism to Tanner's ideal psychophysical observer" (33, p. 62), then comparing him in action with real DMs. Obviously discrepancies between optimal and actual decision behavior are bound to occur, but it is assumed that they will not be so large and unsystematic as to make the comparison meaningless. Moreover, if such differences are systematic across DMs, or for each DM across different tasks, they might be interpreted in terms of constraints imposed upon the DM (e.g. 135, 137, 183) or operating in the situation.

Dynamic decision theory then primarily compares real with optimal behavior, leading to modifiable "normative-descriptive" models (183). Mathematically, this yields constrained optimization models of behavior. For example, if an observed discrepancy is reasonably and meaningfully interpreted as due to a limitation on DM's information processing capability, such as his finite memory or his limited capability to project the effects of his decision into the future, this limitation may be incorporated into the model as an additional constraint. The optimal policy may then be derived under this constraint and compared to actual behavior. One may successively collect data, compare actual to optimal behavior, and improve the model so that, finally, decisions can be interpreted as optimal under given perceptual, intellectual, and cognitive constraints. Dynamic decision theory may prove useful only if discrepancies between optimal and actual decisions are small, systematic, and the constraints are psychologically interpretable.

Experiments.—A research methodology known as the "fungus-eater" approach was proposed by Toda (182) in a highly inspiring and imaginative paper in order to show how people plan, or how people individually and collectively "organize their behavior over time" (184, pp. 1–2). To realize this goal, Toda constructed a very simple environment, the planet Taros, and a very simple, single-minded robot, the fungus-eater. Defining the objective function to be the collection of uranium ore distributed over the surface of Taros, Toda solved for the optimal behavior of the robot under various assumptions about the cognitive, perceptual and physiological properties of the fungus-eater and about the structure of Taros. The mathematical problems which Toda has encountered are very close to those of dynamic programming (106), except the goal is descriptive rather than normative. "Indeed, who cares for the efficiency of a hypothetical robot on a hypothetical planet? Our primary concern is to investigate the *logic* of environment-organism interaction as reflected in the structure of the optimal behavior" (184, pp. 3–4). Toda has run subjects on a few "fungus-eater" experiments, comparing the data to the optimal policies, with encouraging results (184 and references there).

Other paradigms for dynamic decision making have been less imaginative but considerably easier to implement experimentally. We shall discuss only one, which bears on the single-stage theories of SEU and risk discussed above.

Rapoport and his associates (55, 139, 140, 142, 143) have studied gambling behavior in a multi-stage betting game (MBG) which resembles certain sequential investment processes. In the MBG DM is provided with some capital s, $s > 0$, and is required to allocate it over m alternatives, $m \geq 2$, each of which obtains with probability $p_i (p_i > 0, i = 1, \cdots, m, \sum_{i=1}^{m} p_i = 1)$. At each stage of the game DM allocates all of his capital over the m alternatives, betting the amount d_i on alternative i $(d_i \geq 0, \sum_{i=1}^{m} d_i = s)$. If alternative i obtains at a given stage, DM's starting capital for the next stage is $d_i r_i$, where r_i, $r_i > 0$, is the return for alternative i. The MBG is played for N stages and p_i and r_i are stationary. DM is paid in proportion to his capital at the end of stage N.

The problem in playing the MBG "rationally" is to choose an objective criterion and a betting policy optimal with respect to this criterion. Indeed, this is the same problem faced by single-stage theories for decision making under uncertainty. As we saw above, these theories suggest two main alternative criteria, the maximization of SEU and the minimization of risk. Rapoport (140) proved that if the risk of a multiple-outcome gamble is expressed as a linear combination of its EV and variance, and if the expectation level (EV divided by capital) is assumed fixed for each stage, the optimal betting policy to minimize the risk of the final gamble in MBG is a proportional betting policy. Adopting this policy, DM should bet a fixed proportion of his capital on any alternative i, independent of N, of the stage number, of the previous history of the gambling process, and of the amount of capital on hand. Rapoport & Jones (142) and Rapoport et al (143) showed that a maximization of SEU also yields a proportional betting policy when the utility function is concave, either linear, logarithmic, or power. In particular, when the utility function is logarithmic, the optimal betting policy prescribes probability matching, i.e. $d_i = p_i s$, for each stage.

Several MBG experiments have been conducted, with various values of p_i and N, fixing the number of alternatives at $m = 2$ (55, 142), $m = 3$ (190), $m = 4$ (143), and assuming $r_i = m$ for every i. The results thus far weakly support the logarithmic model as a first approximation only (55, 142, 143), show large and systematic individual differences (55, 139), and, in violation of any proportional betting policy, systematic effects of capital size and somewhat weaker effects of previous outcomes (55, 139, 142, 143). Of special interest are the capital size effects, which most single-stage and sequential decision experiments have attempted to eliminate rather than to study. As capital increased, about half of the subjects in the MBG experiments decreased the proportion bet on the most likely alternative, and for a few subjects the proportion of capital bet on the most likely alternative first decreased and then increased as capital size grew larger. The mean results reported by Rapoport et al (143), which conform to the betting behavior of the latter subgroup of subjects, may be due to averaging over subjects with different betting patterns.

A major difficulty in interpreting results from dynamic decision experiments is the low sensitivity associated with the optimal policies for a variety of dynamic decision tasks and objective criteria, such as the minimization of expected loss in deferred decision making (141) or in detection of change processes (15), and the minimization of risk or maximization of SEU in multi-stage gambling (139, 142, 143). Because of the low sensitivity of many decision models, a clear distinction between two goals must be maintained. One is the assessment of DM's performance relative to the optimal policy. The other goal, independent of the first, is the discovering of DM's decision policy.

OMISSIONS

Unlike the previous review papers by Edwards (32) and Becker & McClintock (11), we have not discussed the vast literature on group decision making. Lucid introductions to two-person and n-person game theory may be found in (25, 145, 146). The experimental literature has been reviewed in (11, 48, 58, 60), and three bibliographies have been compiled recently (61, 62, 101). Additionally, we have had to omit several major areas in individual decision making. For example, we have said nothing about probabilistic decision models (94), about methods for independently measuring utility (44) and subjective probability, nor about the increasing use and development of proper scoring rules for measuring subjective probability (178). We have touched far too little on the interesting applications of decision theory. These omissions should not be interpreted as a statement of our ranking of relative importance of topics, but rather as an indication of our theoretical biases in selecting from the voluminous research on decision processes which has appeared since 1965.

LITERATURE CITED

1. Anderson, N. H. 1970. Functional measurement and psychophysical judgment. *Psychol. Rev.* 77:153–70
2. Anderson, N. H., Shanteau, J. C. 1970. Information integration in risky decision making. *J. Exp. Psychol.* 84:441–51
3. Beach, L. R. 1968. Probability magnitudes and conservative revision of subjective probabilities. *J. Exp. Psychol.* 77:57–63
4. Beach, L. R., Hunt, E. B., Carter, W. B. 1970. Memory and decisions in a monitoring task. *Organ. Behav. Hum. Perform.* 5:238–44
5. Beach, L. R., Phillips, L. D. 1967. Subjective probabilities inferred from estimates and bets. *J. Exp. Psychol.* 75:354–59
6. Beach, L. R., Wise, J. A. 1969. Subjective probability and decision strategy. *J. Exp. Psychol.* 79:133–38
7. Ibid. Subjective probability estimates and confidence ratings, 438–44
8. Ibid 1969. Subjective probability revision and subsequent decisions. 81:561–65
9. Beach, L. R., Wise, J. A., Barclay, S. 1970. Sample proportions and subjective probability revisions. *Organ. Behav. Hum. Perform.* 5:183–90
10. Becker, S. W., Brownson, F. O. 1964. What price ambiguity? or the role of ambiguity in decision-making. *J. Polit. Econ.* 72:62–73
11. Becker, G. B., McClintock, C. G. 1967. Value: Behavioral decision theory. *Ann. Rev. Psychol.* 18:239–86
12. Birdsall, T. G., Roberts, R. A. 1965. Theory of signal detectability: Deferred-decision theory. *J. Acoust. Soc. Am.* 37:1064–74
13. Bock, R. D., Jones, L. V. 1968. *The Measurement and Prediction of Judgment and Choice.* San Francisco: Holden-Day. 370 pp.
14. Brody, N. 1965. The effect of commitment to correct and incorrect decisions in a sequential decision task. *Am. J. Psychol.* 78:251–56
15. Burkheimer, G. J., Rapoport, A. 1971. *Models for detection of change.* Psychom. Lab. Rep. 95, Univ. North Carolina, Chapel Hill
16. Carlson, J. A., O'Keefe, T. B. 1969. Buffer stocks and reaction coefficients: An experiment with decision making under risk. *Rev. Econ. Stud.* 36:467–84
17. Chinnis, J. O. Jr., Peterson, C. R. 1968. Inference about a nonstationary process. *J. Exp. Psychol.* 77:620–25
18. Coombs, C. H., Bezembinder, T. G. G., Goode, F. M. 1967. Testing expectation theories of decision making without measuring utility or subjective probability. *J. Math. Psychol.* 4:72–103
19. Coombs, C. H., Bowen, J. 1971. A test of VE-theories of risk and the effect of the central limit theorem. *Acta Psychol.* 35:15–28
20. Coombs, C. H., Bowen, J. 1971. Additivity of risk in portfolios. *Percept. Psychophys.* 10:43–46
21. Coombs, C. H., Huang, L. C. 1968. A portfolio theory of risk preference. *Mich. Math. Psychol. Progr. Tech. Rep. 68-5,* Ann Arbor, Mich.
22. Coombs, C. H., Huang, L. C. 1970. Polynomial psychophysics of risk. *J. Math. Psychol.* 7:317–38
23. Coombs, C. H., Meyer, D. E. 1969. Risk-preference in coin-toss games. *J. Math. Psychol.* 6:514–27
24. Dale, H. C. A. 1968. Weighing evidence: An attempt to assess the efficiency of the human operator. *Ergonomics* 11:215–30
25. Davis, M. 1970. *Game Theory.* New York: Basic Books. 208 pp.
26. de Finetti, B. 1970. Logical foundations and measurement of subjective probability. *Acta Psychol.* 34:129–45
27. DeGroot, M. H. 1970. *Optimal Statistical Decisions.* New York: McGraw. 489 pp.
28. De Zeeuw, G., Vlek, C. A. J., Wagenaar, W. A. 1970. Subjective probability theory, experiments, applications. *Acta Psychol.* 34:129–397
29. DuCharme, W. M. 1969. A review and analysis of the phenomenon of conservatism in human inference. *Interdisciplinary Progr. Appl. Math. Syst. Theory,* Syst. No. 46–5. Rice Univ., Houston, Texas
30. DuCharme, W. M. 1970. Response bias explanation of conservative human inference. *J. Exp. Psychol.* 85:66–74
31. DuCharme, W. M., Peterson, C. R. 1968. Intuitive inference about

normally distributed populations. *J. Exp. Psychol.* 78:269–75

32. Edwards, W. 1961. Behavioral decision theory. *Ann. Rev. Psychol.* 12:473–98

33. Edwards, W. 1962. Dynamic decision theory and probabilistic information processing. *Hum. Factors* 4:59–73

34. Edwards, W. 1965. Optimal strategies for seeking information: Models for statistics, choice reaction time, and human information processing. *J. Math. Psychol.* 2:312–29

35. Edwards, W. 1966. Introduction: Revision of opinions by men and man-machine systems. *IEEE Trans.* HFE-7:1–6

36. Edwards, W. 1968. Conservatism in human information processing. In *Formal Representation of Human Judgment*, ed. B. Kleinmuntz, 17–52. New York: Wiley. 273 pp.

37. Edwards, W. 1969. A bibliography of research on behavioral decision processes to 1968. *Univ. Mich. Hum. Perform. Cent. Memo. Rep. No. 7*

38. Edwards, W. 1969. Value and probability: The determinants of risky decisions. Unpublished manuscript

39. Edwards, W., Lindman, H., Phillips, L. D. 1965. Emerging technologies for making decisions. In *New Directions in Psychology II*, 261–325. New York: Holt, Rinehart & Winston. 422 pp.

40. Edwards, W., Lindman, H., Savage, L. J. 1963. Bayesian statistical inference for psychological research. *Psychol. Rev.* 70:193–242

41. Edwards, W., Phillips, L. D., Hays, W. L., Goodman, B. C. 1968. Probabilistic information processing systems: Design and evaluation. *IEEE Trans.* SSC-4:248–65

42. Einhorn, H. J. 1970. The use of non-linear, noncompensatory models in decision making. *Psychol. Bull.* 73:221–30

43. Ellsberg, D. 1961. Risk, ambiguity, and the Savage axioms. *Quart. J. Econ.* 75:643–69

44. Fishburn, P. C. 1968. Utility theory. *Manage. Sci.* 14:335–78

45. Fishburn, P. C. 1970. *Utility Theory for Decision Making.* New York: Wiley. 234 pp.

46. Fishburn, P. C. A mixture-set axiomatization of conditional expected utility. Unpublished manuscript

47. Fried, L. S., Peterson, C. R. 1969. Information seeking: Optional versus fixed stopping. *J. Exp. Psychol.* 80:525–29

48. Gallo, P. S. Jr., McClintock, C. G. 1965. Cooperative and competitive behavior in mixed-motive games. *J. Conflict Resolut.* 9:68–78

49. Geller, E. S., Pitz, G. F. 1968. Confidence and decision speed in the revision of opinion. *Organ. Behav. Hum. Perform.* 3:190–201

50. Gettys, C. F., Manley, C. W. 1968. The probability of an event and estimates of posterior probability based upon its occurrence. *Psychon. Sci.* 11:47–48

51. Gettys, C. F., Willke, T. A. 1969. The application of Bayes's theorem when the true data state is uncertain. *Organ. Behav. Hum. Perform.* 4:125–41

52. Goldberg, L. R. 1968. Simple models or simple processes? Some research on clinical judgments. *Am. Psychol.* 23:483–96

53. Goldstein, I. L., Emanuel, J. T., Howell, W. C. 1968. Effect of percentage and specificity of feedback on choice behavior in a probabilistic information-processing task. *J. Appl. Psychol.* 52:163–68

54. Goodman, B. C. 1970. Risky decisions by individuals and groups. *Univ. Mich. Hum. Perform. Cent. Tech. Rep. 21*

55. Gordon, L. R. 1970. *Effects of capital size in computer-controlled multistage betting games.* PhD thesis. Univ. North Carolina, Chapel Hill. 159 pp.

56. Green, B. F. Jr. 1968. Descriptions and explanations: A comment on papers by Hoffman and Edwards. See Ref. 36, 91–96

57. Green, P. E., Halbert, M. H., Robinson, P. J. 1965. An experiment in probability estimation. *J. Market. Res.* 5:266–73

58. Groennings, S., Kelley, E. W., Leiserson, M. A., Eds. 1970. *The Study of Coalition Behavior.* New York: Holt, Rinehart & Winston. 489 pp.

59. Gustafson, D. H. 1969. Evaluation of probabilistic information processing in medical decision making. *Organ. Behav. Hum. Perform.* 4:20–34

60. Guyer, M. 1967. A review of the literature on zero-sum and nonzero-sum games in social sciences. *Univ. Mich. Ment. Health Res. Inst. Commun. 220*

61. Guyer, M., Zabner, M. 1969. Experi-

mental games: A bibliography (1965–1969). *Univ. Mich. Ment. Health Res. Inst. Commun. 258*

62. Ibid 1970. Experimental games: A bibliography (1945–1964). Commun. 265

63. Hester, D. D., Tobin, J., Eds. 1967. *Risk Aversion and Portfolio Choice.* New York: Wiley. 180 pp.

64. Hicks, J. M., Campbell, D. T. 1965. Zero-point scaling as affected by social object, scaling method, and context. *J. Pers. Soc. Psychol.* 2: 793–808

65. Hoffman, P. J. 1968. Cue-consistency and configurality in human judgment. See Ref. 36, 53–90

66. Howard, R. A. 1968. The foundations of decision analysis. *IEEE Trans.* SSC-4:211–19

67. Howard, R. A. 1970. Decision analysis: Perspectives on inference, decision, and experimentation. *Proc. IEEE* 58:632–43

68. Howell, W. C. 1966. Task characteristics in sequential decision behavior. *J. Exp. Psychol.* 71:124–31

69. Howell, W. C. 1967. Some principles for the design of central systems: A review of six years of research on a command-control system simulation. *Wright-Patterson Air Force Base Rep. AMRL-TR-67-136*

70. Irwin, F. W., Graae, C. N. 1968. Test of the discontinuity hypothesis of the effects of independent outcome values upon bets. *J. Exp. Psychol.* 76:444–49

71. Irwin, F. W., Metzger, M. J. 1966. Effects of probabilistic independent outcomes upon predictions. *Psychon. Sci.* 5:79–80

72. Ibid 1967. Effects of independent outcome-values of past events upon subsequent choices. 9:613–14

73. Irwin, F. W., Snodgrass, J. G. 1966. Effects of independent and dependent outcome values upon bets. *J. Exp. Psychol.* 71:282–85

74. Jamison, D. 1970. *Studies in individual choice behavior.* PhD thesis. Harvard Univ., Cambridge, Mass. 209 pp.

75. Kaplan, R. J., Newman, J. R. 1966. Studies in probabilistic information processing. *IEEE Trans.* HFE-7: 49–63

76. Keeley, S. M., Doherty, M. E. The biologist as an intuitive statistician. *Bull. Math. Biophys.* In press

77. Kleiter, C. D. 1970. Trend-control in a dynamic decision making task. *Acta Psychol.* 34:387–97

78. Kogan, N., Wallach, M. A. 1967. Risk taking as a function of the situation, the person, and the group. In *New Directions in Psychology III,* ed. T. M. Newcomb, 111–281. New York: Holt, Rinehart & Winston. 289 pp.

79. Krantz, D. H., Luce, R. D., Suppes, P., Tversky, A. 1971. *Foundations of Measurement,* Vol. 1. New York: Academic. In press

80. Krantz, D. H., Tversky, A. 1971. Conjoint-measurement analysis of composition rules in psychology. *Psychol. Rev.* 78:151–69

81. Kruskal, J. B. 1965. Analysis of factorial experiments by estimating monotone transformations of the data. *J. Roy. Stat. Soc. A* 27:251–63

82. Larsson, B. 1968. *Bayes Strategies and Human Information Seeking.* Lund CWK Gleerup: Univ. Lund Press. 119 pp.

83. Lathrop, R. G. Riskless human decisions—a tutorial and a model. Unpublished manuscript

84. Lee, W. 1971. Preference strength, expected value difference, and expected regret ratio. *Psychol. Bull.* 75:186–91

85. Lee, W. The effects of expected value difference and expected regret ratio on preference strength. *Am. J. Psychol.* In press

86. Lee, W. 1971. *Decision Theory and Human Behavior.* New York: Wiley. In press

87. Lichtenstein, S., Feeney, G. J. 1968. The importance of the data-generating model in probability estimation. *Organ. Behav. Hum. Perform.* 3:62–67

88. Lichtenstein, S., Slovic, P. Reversals of preference between bids and choices in gambling decisions. *J. Exp. Psychol.* In press

89. Lichtenstein, S., Slovic, P., Zink, D. 1969. Effect of instruction in expected value on optimality of gambling decisions. *J. Exp. Psychol.* 79:236–40

90. Lindman, H. R. 1970. Inconsistent preferences among gambles. *Indiana Math. Psychol. Progr. Rep. 70-2.* Bloomington, Ind.

91. Luce, R. D. 1967. Remarks on the theory of measurement and its relation to psychology. Symposium: *Les Modèles et la Formalisation du Comportement, Paris 1965*

92. Luce, R. D., Krantz, D. H. Conditional expected utility. *Econometrica*. In press

93. Luce, R. D., Raiffa, H. 1957. *Games and Decisions*. New York: Wiley. 509 pp.

94. Luce, R. D., Suppes, P. 1965. Preference, utility, and subjective probability. In *Handbook of Mathematical Psychology*, Vol. 3, ed. R. D. Luce, R. R. Bush, E. Galanter, 249–410. New York: Wiley. 537 pp.

95. Luce, R. D., Tukey, J. W. 1964. Simultaneous conjoint measurement: A new type of fundamental measurement. *J. Math. Psychol.* 1:1–27

96. Lusted, L. B. 1968. *Introduction to Medical Decision Making*. Springfield, Ill.: Thomas. 271 pp.

97. MacCrimmon, K. R. 1968. Descriptive and normative implications of the decision-theory postulates. In *Risk and Uncertainty*, ed. K. Borch, J. Mossin, 3–32. New York: Macmillan. 455 pp.

98. Manz, W. 1970. Experiments on probabilistic information processing. *Acta Psychol.* 35:184–200

99. Markowitz, H. M. 1959. *Portfolio Selection*. New York: Wiley. 344 pp.

100. Martin, D. W., Gettys, C. F. 1969. Feedback and response mode in performing a Bayesian decision task. *J. Appl. Psychol.* 53:413–18

101. McClintock, C. G., Messick, D. M. 1966. Empirical approaches to game theory and bargaining: A bibliography. *Gen. Syst.* 11:229–38

102. Meyer, R. F., Pratt, J. W. 1968. The consistent assessment and fairing of preference functions. *IEEE Trans.* SSC-4:270–78

103. Morrison, D. G. 1967. On the consistency of preference in Allais' paradox. *Behav. Sci.* 12:373–83

104. Morrison, H. W. 1962. *Intransitivity of paired comparison choices*. PhD thesis. Univ. Michigan, Ann Arbor. 97 pp.

105. Myers, J. L., Suydam, M. M., Gambino, B. 1965. Contingent gains and losses in a risk-taking situation. *J. Math. Psychol.* 2:363–70

106. Nemhauser, G. L. 1966. *Introduction to Dynamic Programming*. New York: Wiley. 256 pp.

107. Payne, J. W., Braunstein, M. L. 1971. Preferences among gambles with equal underlying distributions. *J. Exp. Psychol.* 87:13–18

108. Peterson, C. R. 1968. Aggregating information about signal and noise. *Proc. 76th Ann. Conv. APA* 3:123–24

109. Peterson, C. R., Beach, L. R. 1967. Man as an intuitive statistician. *Psychol. Bull.* 68:29–46

110. Peterson, C. R., DuCharme, W. M. 1967. A primacy effect in subjective probability revision. *J. Exp. Psychol.* 73:61–65

111. Peterson, C. R., DuCharme, W. M., Edwards, W. 1968. Sampling distributions and probability revisions. *J. Exp. Psychol.* 76:236–43

112. Peterson, C. R., Schneider, R. J., Miller, A. J. 1965. Sample size and the revision of subjective probabilities. *J. Exp. Psychol.* 69:522–27

113. Peterson, C. R., Swensson, R. G. 1968. Intuitive statistical inferences about diffuse hypotheses. *Organ. Behav. Hum. Perform.* 3:1–11

114. Pfanzagl, J. 1959. A general theory of measurement—applications to utility. *Naval Res. Logistics Quart.* 6:283–94

115. Pfanzagl, J. 1967. Subjective probability derived from the Morgenstern-von Neumann utility concept. In *Essays in Mathematical Economics in Honor of Oskar Morgenstern*, ed. M. Shubik, 237–51. Princeton Univ. Press. 475 pp.

116. Pfanzagl, J. 1968. *Theory of Measurement*. New York: Wiley. 235 pp.

117. Phillips, L. D. 1966. Some components of probabilistic inference. *Univ. Mich. Hum. Perform. Cent. Tech. Rep. 1*, Ann Arbor, Mich.

118. Phillips, L. D., Edwards, W. 1966. Conservatism in a simple probability inference task. *J. Exp. Psychol.* 72:346–54

119. Phillips, L. D., Hays, W. L., Edwards, W. 1966. Conservatism in complex probabilistic inference. *IEEE Trans.* HFE-7:7–18

120. Pitz, G. F. 1967. Sample size, likelihood, and confidence in a decision. *Psychon. Sci.* 8:257–58

121. Pitz, G. F. 1968. Information seeking when available information is limited. *J. Exp. Psychol.* 76:25–34

122. Pitz, G. F. 1969. An inertia effect (resistance to change) in the revision of opinion. *Can. J. Psychol./Rev. Can. Psychol.* 23:24–33

123. Pitz, G. F. 1969. Use of response times to evaluate strategies of information seeking. *J. Exp. Psychol.* 80:553–57

124. Pitz, G. F. 1970. On the processing of information: Probabilistic and otherwise. *Acta Psychol.* 34:201–13

125. Pitz, G. F., Barrett, H. R. 1969. Information purchase in a decision task following the presentation of free information. *J. Exp. Psychol.* 82:410–14

126. Pitz, G. F., Downing, L., Reinhold, H. 1967. Sequential effects in the revision of subjective probabilities. *Can. J. Psychol.* 21:381–93

127. Pitz, G. F., Geller, E. S. 1970. Revision of opinion and decision times in an information-seeking task. *J. Exp. Psychol.* 83:400–5

128. Pitz, G. F., Reinhold, H. 1968. Payoff effects in sequential decision-making. *J. Exp. Psychol.* 77:249–57

129. Pitz, G. F., Reinhold, H., Geller, E. S. 1969. Strategies of information seeking in deferred decision making. *Organ. Behav. Hum. Perform.* 4: 1–19

130. Pollatsek, A. 1966. On the relation between subjectively expected utility theory and the psychophysics of gambling. *Mich. Math. Psychol. Progr. Tech. Rep. 66-1*, Ann Arbor, Mich.

131. Pollatsek, A., Tversky, A. 1970. A theory of risk. *J. Math. Psychol.* 7: 540–53

132. Pratt, J. 1964. Risk aversion in the small and in the large. *Econometrica* 32:122–36

133. Pratt, J. W., Raiffa, H., Schlaifer, R. 1965. *Introduction to Statistical Decision Theory* (Prelim. ed.) New York: McGraw

134. Raiffa, H. 1968. *Decision Analysis: Introductory Lectures on Choices under Uncertainty.* Reading, Mass.: Addison-Wesley. 309 pp.

135. Rapoport, A. 1967. Dynamic programming models for multistage decision making tasks. *J. Math. Psychol.* 4:48–71

136. Rapoport, A. 1967. Variables affecting decisions in a multistage inventory task. *Behav. Sci.* 12:194–204

137. Rapoport, A. 1968. Choice behavior in a Markovian decision task. *J. Math. Psychol.* 5:163–81

138. Rapoport, A. 1969. Effects of observation cost on sequential search behavior. *Percept. Psychophys.* 6: 234–40

139. Rapoport, A. 1970. Minimization of risk and maximization of expected utility in multistage betting games. *Acta Psychol.* 34:375–86

140. Rapoport, A. 1970. *Proportional Markov betting policies for multistage betting games.* Psychom. Lab. Rep. 84, Univ. North Carolina, Chapel Hill

141. Rapoport, A., Burkheimer, G. J. Models for deferred decision making. *J. Math. Psychol.* In press

142. Rapoport, A., Jones, L. V. 1970. Gambling behavior in two-outcome multistage betting games. *J. Math. Psychol.* 7:163–87

143. Rapoport, A., Jones, L. V., Kahan, J. P. 1970. Gambling behavior in multiple-choice multistage betting games. *J. Math. Psychol.* 7:12–36

144. Rapoport, A., Lissitz, R. W., McAllister, H. A. Search behavior with and without optional stopping. *Organ. Behav. Hum. Perform.* In press

145. Rapoport, An. 1966. *Two-Person Game Theory.* Ann Arbor: Univ. Michigan Press. 229 pp.

146. Rapoport, An. 1970. *N-Person Game Theory.* Ann Arbor: Univ. Michigan Press. 331 pp.

147. Roby, T. B. 1967. Belief states and sequential evidence. *J. Exp. Psychol.* 75:236–45

148. Sanders, A. F. 1968. Choice among bets and revision of opinion. *Acta Psychol.* 28:76–83

149. Sanders, A. F., ter Linden, W. 1967. Decision making during paced arrival of probabilistic information. *Acta Psychol.* 27:170–77

150. Savage, L. J. 1954. *The Foundations of Statistics.* New York: Wiley. 294 pp.

151. Savage, L. J. 1967. Difficulties in the theory of personal probability. *Phil. Sci.* 34:305–32

152. Schum, D. A. 1966. Prior uncertainty and amount of diagnostic evidence as variables in a probabilistic inference task. *Organ. Behav. Hum. Perform.* 1:31–54

153. Schum, D. A. 1966. Inferences on the basis of conditionally nonindependent data. *J. Exp. Psychol.* 72: 401–9

154. Schum, D. A. 1969. Concerning the simulation of diagnostic systems which process complex probabilistic evidence sets. *Wright-Patterson Air Force Base Rep. AMRL-TR-69-10*

155. Schum, D. A., DuCharme, W. M. Comments on the relationship between the impact and the reliability of evidence. *Organ. Behav. Hum. Perform.* In press

156. Schum, D. A., DuCharme, W. M.,

DePitts, K. E. 1971. Research on human multistage probabilistic inference processes. *Interdisciplinary Progr. Appl. Math. Syst. Theory*, Systems 46-11. Houston, Texas: Rice Univ.

157. Schum, D. A., Goldstein, I. L., Howell, W. C., Southard, J. F. 1967. Subjective probability revisions under several cost-payoff arrangements. *Organ. Behav. Hum. Perform.* 2: 84–104

158. Schum, D. A., Goldstein, I. L., Southard, J. F. 1965. The influence of experience and input information fidelity upon posterior probability estimation in a simulated threat-diagnosis system. *USAF Behav. Sci. Lab. Rep. AMRL-TR-65-25*

159. Schum, D. A., Goldstein, I. L., Southard, J. F. 1966. Research on a simulated Bayesian information-processing system. *IEEE Trans.* HFE-7:37–48

160. Schum, D. A., Martin, D. W. 1968. Human processing of inconclusive evidence from multinomial probability distributions. *Organ. Behav. Hum. Perform.* 3:353–65

161. Schum, D. A., Southard, J. F., Wombolt, L. F. 1969. Aided human processing of inconclusive evidence in diagnostic systems: A summary of experimental evaluations. *Wright-Patterson Air Force Base Rep. AMRL-TR-69-11*

162. Shanteau, J. C. 1970. An additive model for sequential decision making. *J. Exp. Psychol.* 85:181–91

163. Shanteau, J. C. 1970. *Component processes in risky decision judgments.* PhD thesis. Univ. California, San Diego. 95 pp.

164. Shanteau, J. C., Anderson, N. H. 1969. Test of a conflict model for preference judgment. *J. Math. Psychol.* 6:312–25

165. Shuford, E. H. Jr., Albert, A., Massengill, H. E. 1966. Admissible probability measurement procedures. *Psychometrika* 31:123–45

166. Slovic, P. 1966. Value as a determiner of subjective probability. *IEEE Trans.* HFE-7:22–28

167. Slovic, P. 1967. Influence of response mode upon the relative importance of probabilities and payoffs in risk taking. *Proc. 75th Ann. Conv. APA* 2:33–34

168. Slovic, P. 1967. The relative influence of probabilities and payoffs upon perceived risk of a gamble. *Psychon. Sci.* 1:223–24

169. Slovic, P. 1968. Consistency of choice among equally valued alternatives. *Proc. 76th Ann. Conv. APA* 3:57–58

170. Slovic, P. 1969. Differential effects of real versus hypothetical payoffs on choices among gambles. *J. Exp. Psychol.* 80:434–37

171. Slovic, P. 1969. Manipulating the attractiveness of a gamble without changing its expected value. *J. Exp. Psychol.* 79:139–45

172. Slovic, P., Lichtenstein, S. 1968. Relative importance of probabilities and payoffs in risk taking. *J. Exp. Psychol. Monogr.* 78:1–18

173. Slovic, P., Lichtenstein, S. 1968. Importance of variance preferences in gambling decisions. *J. Exp. Psychol.* 78:646–54

174. Slovic, P., Lichtenstein, S. Comparison of Bayesian and regression approaches to the study of information processing in judgment. In *Human Judgment and Social Interaction*, ed. L. Rappoport, D. A. Summers. New York: Holt, Rinehart & Winston. In press

175. Slovic, P., Lichtenstein, S., Edwards, W. 1965. Boredom-induced changes in preferences among bets. *Am. J. Psychol.* 78:208–17

176. Smith, V. L. 1969. Measuring nonmonetary utilities in uncertain choices: The Ellsberg urn. *Quart. J. Econ.* 83:324–29

177. Snapper, K. J., Fryback, D. G. 1971. Inferences based on unreliable reports. *J. Exp. Psychol.* 87:401–4

178. Staël von Holstein, C.-A.S. 1970. *Assessment and Evaluation of Subjective Probability Distributions.* Econ. Res. Inst. Stockholm Sch. Econ., Stockholm, Sweden. 229 pp.

179. Strub, M. H. 1969. Experience and prior probability in a complex decision task. *J. Appl. Psychol.* 53: 112–17

180. Suydam, M. M. 1965. Effects of cost and gain ratios, and probability of outcome on ratings of alternative choices. *J. Math. Psychol.* 2:171–79

181. Tobin, J. 1965. The theory of portfolio selection. In *The Theory of Interest Rates*, ed. F. H. Hahn, F. R. P. Brechling, 3–51. London: Macmillan. 364 pp.

182. Toda, M. 1962. The design of a Fungus-Eater: A model of human behavior in an unsophisticated environment. *Behav. Sci.* 7:164–83

183. Toda, M. 1968. Algebraic models in dynamic decision theory. In *Algebraic Models in Psychology*, ed. C. A. J. Vlek, 105–60. Leyden, The Netherlands: Psychol. Inst. Univ. Leyden. 303 pp.

184. Toda, M., Miyamae, H. 1967. *The theory and an experiment on a simple Fungus-Eater game*. Working paper 121, West. Manage. Sci. Inst., Los Angeles

185. Tversky, A. 1967. A general theory of polynomial conjoint measurement. *J. Math. Psychol.* 4:1–20

186. Ibid. Additivity, utility, and subjective probability, 175–201

187. Tversky, A. 1967. Utility theory and additivity analysis of risky choices. *J. Exp. Psychol.* 75:27–36

188. Tversky, A. 1969. Intransitivity of preferences. *Psychol. Rev.* 76:31–48

189. Tversky, A., Krantz, D. H. 1970. The dimensional representation and the metric structure of similarity data. *J. Math. Psychol.* 7:572–96

190. Vlek, C. A. J. 1965. *The use of probabilistic information in decision making*. Rep. 009–65, Psychol. Inst., Univ. Leiden, The Netherlands

191. Vlek, C. A. J., Van der Heijden, L. H. C. 1967. *Subjective likelihood functions and variations in the accuracy of probabilistic information processing*. Rep. E 017–67, Psychol. Inst., Univ. Leiden, The Netherlands

192. Vlek, C. A. J., Van der Heijden, L. H. C. 1969. Alternative data-generating models for probabilistic information processing. *Organ. Behav. Hum. Perform.* 4:43–55

193. Vlek, C. A. J., Van der Heijden, L. H. C. 1970. Aspects of suboptimality in a multidimensional probabilistic information processing task. *Acta Psychol.* 34:300–10

194. von Neumann, J., Morgenstern, O. 1947. *Theory of Games and Eco-nomic Behavior*. Princeton Univ. Press. 2nd ed. 641 pp.

195. Wallsten, T. S. 1968. Failure of predictions from subjectively expected utility theory in a Bayesian decision task. *Organ. Behav. Hum. Perform.* 3:239–52

196. Wallsten, T. S. 1970. *Subjects' probability estimates and subjectively expected utility theory: Their relationship and some limitations*. Psychom. Lab. Rep. 85, Univ. North Carolina, Chapel Hill

197. Wallsten, T. S. 1971. *Probabilistic information processing, Bayes' rule, and conjoint measurement*. Psychom. Lab. Rep. 98, Univ. North Carolina, Chapel Hill

198. Wendt, D., Ed. 1969. *Proceedings of a Research Conference on Subjective Probability and Related Fields*. Psychol. Inst., Univ. Hamburg, Germany. 49 pp.

199. Wendt, D. 1969. Value of information for decisions. *J. Math. Psychol.* 6:430–43

200. Wendt, D. 1970. Utility and risk. *Acta Psychol.* 34:214–28

201. Wheeler, G., Beach, L. R. 1968. Subjective sampling distributions and conservatism. *Organ. Behav. Hum. Perform.* 3:36–46

202. White, D. J. 1969. *Decision Theory*. Chicago: Aldine. 185 pp.

203. Winkler, R. L. 1967. The assessment of prior distributions in Bayesian analysis. *J. Am. Statist. Assoc.* 62:776–800

204. Ibid 1969. Scoring rules and the evaluation of probability. 64:1073–78

205. Wise, J. A. 1970. Estimates and scaled judgments of subjective probabilities. *Organ. Behav. Hum. Perform.* 5:85–92

206. Yntema, D. B., Torgerson, W. S. 1961. Man-computer cooperation in decisions requiring common sense. *IRE Trans.* HFE-2:20–26

207. Zinnes, J. C. 1969. Scaling. *Ann. Rev. Psychol.* 20:447–78

HUMAN ABILITIES

Leona E. Tyler

University of Oregon, Eugene, Oregon

INTRODUCTION

This review covers mainly the 3-year period from January 1, 1968, through December 21, 1970, although in a few instances an earlier reference is cited for some special reason, such as the fact that it is one of a series that needs to be considered as a whole. A few references from early 1971 that came to my attention before the manuscript's completion date are also included.

In order to keep the total length within the prescribed limits, it was necessary to exclude rather arbitrarily several categories of publications. Textbooks or revisions of textbooks on tests and measurements, methodological discussions, and studies of factors related to school achievement were ruled out. Reports on the characteristics of particular tests, old or new, were included only if they pointed toward new or significant generalizations about the abilities measured. A parallel sort of guideline was employed in dealing with studies in which the main focus was mental retardation or illness. Such studies were included only if they threw some light on the nature of mental abilities.

Even within these limits, not everything published has been cited. Minor reports based on small numbers have usually been omitted. Papers repeating the same information reported elsewhere have sometimes not been included. What I have attempted to bring together are the ideas and research evidence that have emerged during the 3-year period about the nature and extent of individual differences in ability and the factors to which such differences are related, as source or consequence.

If one were to attempt a general description of the "zeitgeist" of the period, he would characterize it as an era of revolt against the IQ-dominated technology that has prevailed throughout most of the twentieth century and the psychological concepts upon which it is based. In various ways investigators, educators, social commentators are casting about for new approaches, some new ways of ordering the complex data of individual differences.

One plausible reason for the emergence of this trend at this time is the transformation of the educational system, in the United States or elsewhere, from a mechanism for successive screenings into an institution to develop the abilities of all of our youth. The 1970 census figures show that more than three-fourths of the population in the 25–29 age group has had 4 years of high school or more, and almost one-sixth of the cohort has had at least 4 years of college.[1] As recently as 1940, only 37.8 percent had finished high school and only 5.8 percent had completed 4 years of college. In previous periods, intelligence test scores have been good predictors of the level a person would reach in the educational system and of social criteria related to this level. They no longer serve this screening function in today's schools; thus the increasing uncertainty as to whether they now serve any useful function at all. The whole system works differently these days.

In the series of studies sponsored by the Russell Sage Foundation on the place of testing in modern society, Goslin (90) summarized criticisms of ability tests—that they are unfair to some groups and individuals, that they are not good predictors of subsequent performance, that they may have the function of self-fulfilling prophecies, and that they exert unfavorable effects on thinking patterns, self-images, motivation, aspirations, and other things. Brim et al (22), however, in another Russell Sage study, analyzed the attitudes and opinions of secondary school students toward tests, and while they found many of these attitudes to be related to social class, they did not pick up any strong antitest feeling in any of the groups questioned.

A serious and searching attempt to reorient concepts and technology was reported by the Commission on Tests set up by the College Entrance Examination Board (41). It recommended that CEEB accept responsibility for three functions—distributive, credentialing, and educative—and that it recognize students as well as institutions as its clientele. This would lead to more emphasis on designing information systems by which students could locate suitable educational opportunities, and to a variety of changes in tests themselves to make them more diversified and diagnostic.

The best thinking of the decades of the 1950s and 1960s with regard to human abilities is represented by the 11 lectures in the Bingham Memorial series. These have been brought together in a book edited by Wolfle (237). The editor's introduction is a notable synthesis of ideas about ability under three main headings: (a) the nature of human ability and the reasons for its variability; (b) the structure of human ability; and (c) the methods of measuring, predicting, and fostering the development of human ability.

INTELLIGENCE

Several general discussions of intelligence and its measurement have appeared during this period. Butcher's (25) well-organized text includes experimental as well as correlational research, with chapters on problem solving and concept attainment, and on brains and machines, as well as the material typically covered in books on tests. It provides an overview of British and American research through 1967. Wiseman (236) and Tyler (211) have edited books of readings, making available some of the major state-

---

[1] *Chronicle of Higher Education*, February 15, 1971.

ments and research reports upon which current conceptions of intelligence rest. Burt (24) has provided another statement of his influential views that intelligence should be defined as "innate, general, cognitive ability," and that abilities can best be structured as a hierarchy with "g" at the top. Bouchard (18), after reviewing several theoretical concepts from a number of sources, has come out for a model based on information-processing theory.

Three longitudinal research reports confirm relationships that have consistently appeared in previous research. Härnquist (102, 103) analyzed changes in intelligence from 13 to 18 for 4616 Swedish school children, a 10 percent sample of all children born in 1948. The amount of change in individuals was related to education and home background, a relationship that was stronger for general intellectual level than for spatial or verbal components. Oden (171) reported results of the 1960 follow-up of Terman's gifted group at a time when the average age of the subjects was about 50. Their record of achievement was still very impressive. A comparison of the 100 most successful men with the 100 least successful indicated, as did a similar comparison in 1940, that the differentiating factors are home background, health and adjustment, and volitional traits such as ambition and integration, rather than initial intellectual level. Maxwell (155) reported on the 1969 status of Scottish subjects tested in 1947 at age 11.

NATURE-NURTURE CONTROVERSY

One of the most conspicuous trends was the resurgence of the nature-nurture argument. In the years just preceding this period, it had seemed that this area of research was no longer a field of controversy.

Many of the publications of the period covered here reflected the agreement that had been reached on concepts and principles. A symposium edited by Glass (86) provided a good summary of progress; the chapter by Vandenberg (213) brought together the evidence for the heritability of intelligence. Schoenfeldt (197) computed heritability ratios based on 524 twin pairs in the Project TALENT study and cited them as evidence for a significant genetic component in intelligence, special aptitudes, educational achievement, and special kinds of knowledge. Vandenberg (214) presented evidence from a twin study for a genetic factor in spatial abilities, of the sort involving perception of form and perspective. Jensen (129) summarized the results of studies of identical twins reared apart. It is a generally accepted fact that an individual's phenotypical level of ability results from a developmental process that involves the interaction of genetic with environmental determiners.

What stirred up the old arguments again was the conclusion presented in several papers by Jensen (123–127, 130) that race and socioeconomic differences may be determined to some extent by genetic factors. He stated flatly that compensatory education has failed. His main point, however, sometimes lost in the acrimonious exchanges, was that the pattern of

mental abilities may differ in different races and that Negroes and other
lower-class persons averaging lower on what most intelligence test items
measure appear to be equal to whites on the kind of associative memory
measured by digit span tests. He proposed that this ability to memorize
can be an educational asset; his critics interpreted his hypothesis as the
assignment of a second-class ability to the Black race. A strong statement
by the Society for the Psychological Study of Social Issues (202) repudiated
the Jensen position. The major part of the next two issues of the *Harvard
Educational Review* following the one in which the Jensen paper appeared
(125) were devoted to a discussion of the issues he had raised by psychologists and educators who disagreed with his conclusions. Evidence against the
Jensen hypothesis that IQ and rote memory are differently related to one
another in high and low status groups was presented by Humphreys &
Dachler (119) using data from the Project TALENT files. Jensen (128) replied that Project TALENT tests are not well designed to test this particular
hypothesis, and that his theory rests on considerable experimental evidence
besides the one investigation Humphreys & Dachler criticized. This paper
also presented a clear, brief statement of what Jensen's theory states: (*a*)
that there are two broad types of mental ability, Level I (associative and rote
learning) and Level II (abstract reasoning); (*b*) that Level II processes are
functionally dependent on Level I processes; and (*c*) that society's sorting
mechanisms work in such a way that socioeconomic groups tend to differ on
abilities at Level II, not on those at Level I. Predictably, Humphreys &
Dachler (120) replied to the Jensen reply, restating their major criticism
and denying that additional evidence refutes it.

A major share of the volume on the disadvantaged child edited by
Hellmuth (104) was devoted to the Jensen controversy. Jensen (130) contributed a statement about why he considers it important to pursue research on
race differences and suggested new kinds of evidence that might be sought.
Bereiter (14) brought the educational issues into focus, making a clear distinction often overlooked in the heat of argument, the distinction between
raising the IQ level of a group in the population (possible through education)
and eliminating individual differences in IQ in the population (not possible,
on the basis of any existing evidence). He recommended a systematic search
for heredity-experience interactions that might lead to desirable kinds of
development and proposed an attitudinal shift to a thoroughgoing pluralism
that would generate equal respect for all kinds of ability rather than evaluation in terms of a single prestige scale.

In a different sort of research attack on the role of hereditary factors
in race differences, Osborne & Gregor (173) computed separate heritability
ratios for spatial ability in Negroes and whites, based on twin differences,
and found them to be equal for the two groups, as Osborne, Gregor &
Miele (174) had already found for verbal abilities. Osborne & Miele (175)
obtained the same sort of results for measures of numerical ability. It is
not clear what these studies prove, however. The fact that environment

has no more influence on individual differences in one group than the other does not seem to tell us much about its influence on differences between the group means.

Correlational studies assessing environmental effects continue. Rosenberg & Sutton-Smith (187) found the spacing of children in the family to be related to cognitive development, differently for boys and girls. Dandes & Dow (48) also obtained the predicted low negative correlation between IQ and an index of family size and density. Mathis (154) found that a simple checklist of possessions and activities correlated significantly with scores on the General Aptitude Test Battery even with education partialed out. When Negroes and whites were matched on the environmental variable, differences in mean scores were severely reduced, suggesting an environmental explanation of the differences typically found. Tulkin (209) and Tulkin & Newbrough (210) broke down a total group of fifth and sixth-grade children into eight subgroups representing upper and lower socioeconomic levels, whites and Negroes, males and females, and demonstrated that environmental variables such as broken homes, maternal employment, and crowdedness of living quarters show a different relationship to scores on intelligence and achievement tests in the different subgroups. Race differences at the upper socioeconomic level disappeared when the environmental differences were controlled by covariance analysis. The authors concluded that discriminating analyses of environmental effects are necessary if any meaningful discussion of race differences is to occur.

SPECIAL STUDIES OF THE DISADVANTAGED

The continuing social concern about poverty and inequality has stimulated numerous investigations of the abilities of disadvantaged groups. Dreger & Miller (54) surveyed the research reported between 1959 and 1965, comparing Negroes with whites. They found the same gap between the means of the two groups that earlier research had reported, but noted that more attention was being paid in more recent studies to various complexities—interactions, uncontrolled factors, subtle effects. Kennedy (136) conducted a follow-up of the Southern Negro children tested in his normative study 5 years earlier. Results indicated that IQs tended to be quite stable. Correlations ranged from .60 to .89. The average IQ for the group was still 79. One of the most interesting of the general surveys was Bachman's (7) report on the first round of a continuing survey of 2213 tenth-grade boys in 87 high schools from all parts of the United States. Scores on the brief intelligence test and scores on the other tests highly correlated with intelligence were best predicted from socioeconomic level, race, and number of siblings. The race effect, however, arose largely from scores of respondents in Southern segregated schools. Blacks in integrated schools averaged only 3.3 IQ points below whites, when adjustment for differences in socioeconomic level had been made.

A matter of increasing concern to both researchers and appliers of psychological knowledge is whether tests used to assess abilities are really fair to disadvantaged groups. The guidelines sent out by the Equal Employment Opportunity Commission (69) and the statement by the Department of Labor (50) have made it obligatory for employers to consider this question. The American Psychological Association (3) published an official statement on the employment testing of minority groups.

Test fairness is a more complex matter than was at first recognized. Even if it can be shown that all items on a test are equally familiar to subjects from different subcultures, it may turn out that the validity coefficients are not the same. Furthermore, if the test is used for selection in the absence of adequate evidence about its predictive validity, it may unfairly eliminate members of the lower-scoring group who would have been fully capable of handling the job demands. These and other factors were pointed out in a book by Kirkpatrick et al (139), who presented results of five research studies illustrating the complexities and difficulties they discuss. Ruda & Albright (189) analyzed the subsequent history of 1034 applicants for office positions and found that while the intelligence test used differentiated between whites and Negroes, and between applicants hired and rejected, it was not a valid predictor of the turnover criterion. Mitchell et al (165) also produced evidence from employment records that the same test screened out twice as many Negroes as whites, but that it showed no validity in either group for predicting termination versus continuation.

In educational situations there seems to be a fair amount of evidence that intelligence tests do show similar validity for predicting achievement criteria in disadvantaged and advantaged groups in different kinds of schools (Cleary & Hilton 40; Cleary 39; Flaugher 76; Stanley 203). What bias there is tends toward overprediction rather than underprediction for disadvantaged subjects, so that if tests are used in selection, the disadvantaged are somewhat more likely to be chosen than their advantaged competitors. The commonly expressed view that time limits handicap Black testees was not supported by Dubin et al (57). Allowing more time and extra practice for high school subjects improved the scores of both racial groups and both socioeconomic groups about equally.

At a younger age level, Goolsby & Frary (89) found that the Metropolitan Readiness Test was somewhat more predictive of school achievement for Negro than for white school entrants and that the pattern of correlations between ability and achievement tests was somewhat different for the two groups.

The subject of culture-fair or status-fair tests was discussed in a comprehensive way by Jensen (124, reprinted in 104). He ended with a recommendation that the emphasis on measuring "g" be decreased and the spectrum of measured abilities extended. (Experimental work by Jensen and others attempting to identify special abilities related to school learning will be summarized in a later section of this review.)

Effects of Compensatory Education

The major national program attempting to increase the intelligence and general educability of children with environmental handicaps, Head Start, was evaluated in 1968 and 1969. The report of what is usually referred to as the Westinghouse-Ohio University Study (Cicirelli et al 36) quickly became a controversial document. The results indicated that summer Head Start programs had produced no demonstrable effect; full-year programs gave participants some advantage in grades one and two, especially in the case of Black children and those from the Southeast region, but the differences between experimental and control groups were not large enough to be of much practical significance. The report has given rise to a great deal of controversy (Smith & Bissell 201; Cicirelli et al 37; White 230; Campbell & Erlebacher 29, 30; Cicirelli 35; Evans & Schiller 71; Mendelsohn 161). The major questions critics raised concerned the advisability of making the study at all at the time it was done, the grossness of the evaluation design, the nature of the sampling and the way in which the matching of experimental and control subjects was accomplished, and the general suitability of the instruments used to measure the effects. Perhaps one of the most important consequences of the whole episode is an increasing sophistication about evaluation research. Zimiles (241) analyzed some of the considerations that have now become apparent, and Anderson (6) described graphically the complexities and difficulties a well-designed research project runs into, on the basis of her experience in conducting the longitudinal study Educational Testing Service is making of the early educational experiences of the disadvantaged.

There are, of course, other early education programs besides Head Start which are attempting to stimulate accelerated growth of intellectual abilities and thus reduce or eliminate the educational handicap of disadvantaged children in their later school careers. The conference report edited by Hess & Bear (106) provides a useful summary of major ideas in this research area, indicating what is being attempted and why. A follow-up of an experimental summer program at Peabody College has been in progress for some time. The report by Klaus & Gray (140) after 5 years showed that children who had participated in the preschool experience maintained their superiority over the controls on intelligence and achievement measures through the first two years of regular school, but a later follow-up after 7 years (Gray & Klaus 92) indicated that while the children in the experimental group were still significantly superior to controls in tested intelligence, no differences on achievement tests at the fourth grade level could be demonstrated. One benign research complication this investigation has identified is a "diffusion" effect. Children in the local control group and younger siblings of the children in the program, as well as the subjects themselves, seem to have benefited from it.

While there are many different hypotheses about what "disadvantage" means in mental development, and thus what it is that needs to be "compensated" for in compensatory education, the major division is probably between those who think of it in terms of linguistic development and those who base their hypotheses on Piaget's statements about the primacy of perceptual-motor development. Following the first of these approaches, Blank & Solomon (15, 16) have presented evidence for significant increases in IQ for 22 children who were given individual tutoring designed to stimulate them to use language in thinking. The idea that the natural language of Black children is deficient or pathological in some way and that compensatory education must overcome this linguistic "deprivation" has, however, come under searching criticism (Houston 115, 116). The first of these studies showed that Black children have at least two distinct "registers," and that the linguistic deficiencies to which previous researchers have referred appear only in the School Register. In the second paper, Houston has summarized the evidence against the basic propositions underlying the linguistic-cognitive deprivation theory and compensatory programs based on it. Baratz & Baratz (9) recommend that we replace the whole "social pathology" model with a "social differences" model as a basis for research on Negro-white ability and educability.

During this period, some attempts to accelerate the perceptual development of young children have involved tutoring in the home with toys. One study (Karnes et al 133) trained mothers to provide this experience for their own 3-year-olds. Another (Schaefer 192) made use of outside tutors who visited the homes. Hess et al (107) had earlier pointed to differences in the natural teaching styles of lower and middle class mothers, differences that presumably could to some extent be eliminated by coaching mothers in desirable practices. Providing assistance to mothers in stimulating the mental development of their children had been an important feature of the Peabody project (92, 140).

The influence of Piaget's ideas about the origins of intelligence can be seen in the increasing interest being shown in bringing intervention to bear on developmental handicaps at an earlier age than the preschool projects have done. Lambie & Weikart (143) and Meier et al (160) have described two such efforts at infant education.

One provocative study of perceptual development (Pollack 181) suggests the possibility that retinal pigmentation may be related to race differences in one type of perceptual ability in the early years.

CREATIVITY
GENERAL DISCUSSIONS

Research on creativity has flourished during the period under consideration. Dellas & Gaier (49) have summarized several kinds of research findings—research on divergent thinking indicating that its relationship to criteria of creative accomplishment is somewhat doubtful, research analyzing the relationship between what is measured by creativity and intelligence tests, and research on cognitive styles and personality and motivational characteristics related to creativity. They criticized much of this research on several counts. Cattell & Butcher's book (32) brings together, for the benefit of educational psychologists, the main ideas and research findings of the Cattell group. In England, Freeman et al (78) have synthesized findings on the relationship of creativity to intelligence and personality, and the effects of education and environmental influences on creative development. This publication also provides a comprehensive report on the validation of an interesting new test by McComisky, and links to the creativity research several other areas of interest to psychologists such as learning sets, intolerance of ambiguity, and deferred judgment or brainstorming. Tryk (207) summarized assessment research on creativity defined as a product, a process, and a capacity, pointing out the major problems. Albert (1) analyzed published work from 1927 to 1965, showing how interest in "genius" has declined while interest in "giftedness" has increased. Chambers (34) put together a multidimensional theory of creativity based on the thinking of a large number of writers and researchers.

Creativity and Intelligence

One often-explored research topic is the relationship of creativity to intelligence. In general, the conclusion that had been put forward in 1965 by Wallach & Kogan (217) that the two kinds of ability are somewhat independent of one another has been supported. Wallach & Wing (218), using with college students the same techniques Wallach & Kogan had employed with children, found near-zero correlations between creativity and intelligence measures. Aspects of both were related to academic achievement. Bowers (19) and Alzobaie et al (2) also found both intelligence and creativity measures to be related to school achievement. Ward (220) and Clark & Mirels (38) found creativity scores to be related to one another but not to intelligence, the latter report indicating that it was fluency that linked the creativity scores together.

An additional conclusion has emerged from several factor analyses in the United States, England, Ireland, and Australia, of the creativity-intelligence correlations (Cave 33; Hetrick et al 108; Ward 219; Fee 73; Dacey et al 47; Cropley 45). It is found that verbal and figural creativity scores are at least partially independent of one another. When a variety of commonly used creativity tests is included, two creativity factors tend to appear.

Several specific hypotheses that have enjoyed some popularity have not held up well under research testing. The Wallach & Kogan proposition that a free play rather than an evaluative set is necessary for assessing creativity was not substantiated by Williams & Fleming (233) or Boersma & O'Bryan (17). Mednick's idea that there is greater variation in creativity scores on the Remote Associates Test at the higher than at the lower ranges of intelligence was not confirmed by Ginsburg & Whittemore (85).

VALIDITY OF CREATIVITY TESTS

One persisting question has to do with the validity of commonly used creativity tests as predictors of reasonable criteria of creativity. Dewing (52) found some relationship between the Minnesota tests and teacher and peer ratings, and Torrance (205) showed that some of the scores derived from the same battery administered to high school seniors predicted adult creative achievement, as evaluated by a check list 7 years later. Goodman et al (87), however, were not able to demonstrate validity for creativity scores of employees in a research laboratory. In a different sort of investigation, the growth study being conducted by Educational Testing Service, Klein & Evans (141) showed that creative achievements at the seventh and ninth grade levels correlated significantly with similar achievements at the twelfth grade level, and that academic ability and accomplishment were predictive of creative accomplishment.

RELATIONSHIP TO OTHER FACTORS

Explorations of the relationship of creativity (or creativity test scores) to a variety of situational and psychological variables have continued during this period. Lichtenwalner & Maxwell (146) found that kindergartners who were firstborn or only children scored higher than those in other family positions, and that middle class children scored higher than lower class. Torrance et al (206), in a large-scale study of third, fourth, and fifth-graders, found monolinguals to be significantly higher than bilinguals on fluency and flexibility. The hypothesis that bilinguals would score higher on originality and elaboration was only weakly supported. In another study at the elementary school level. Pollert et al (182) presented evidence that scores on memory tests are related to creativity. McHenry & Shouksmith (157) reported that among 10-year-olds, creativity was related to suggestibility, as measured by willingness to accept suggestions about what figures looked like, and Bowers & Van Der Meulen (20) showed that hypnotic suggestibility was related to creativity in college subjects. Eisenman (64) found scores on creativity tests to be related to choice of college major. English majors scored significantly higher than business majors.

Relationships are appearing between creativity and other kinds of thinking that have heretofore not carried the "creative" label. Gibson et al (84) found tests of critical thinking to be related to measures of adaptive flexibility in undergraduates. In a novel series of experiments, Maier et al (150–153) identified consistent individual differences in the ability to use words previously memorized in writing creative stories. There seem to be three ways of dealing with this kind of problem-solving task: 1. using the pairs of words as learned (respecting associative bonds); 2. using only one member of each learned pair (fragmenting associative bonds); 3. making new groupings from the pair members (reorganizing the elements learned). Number 3 is the most creative type of performance, and its stability in individuals under different experimental conditions suggests that it depends upon ability rather than preferences or circumstances.

Ward (223) was interested in the relationship between children's rate of responding to creativity tests and the uniqueness of their responses, building upon a hypothesis Mednick had proposed earlier. He found that his creative boys differed from the noncreative mainly in the fact that they continued for a longer time to generate responses. Since original responses were most likely to occur toward the end of a series, these children scored higher than the others in originality as well as productivity. Ward suggested that this might reflect a motivational rather than a cognitive difference.

Cronbach (43), in commenting on the Wallach & Kogan research cited earlier, raised the question as to whether the so-called "high-creative" children, those whose fluency scores were much higher than their intelligence test scores, might really be more maladjusted that creative, in that they are less able to inhibit the expression of ideas by automatically screening them for quality. In England, Hudson (117), who in his earlier book and in this one avoided the "creativity" label and talked instead about "convergent vs divergent thinkers," reported some interesting anecdotal evidence supporting Cronbach's surmise. When by some ingenious instructions he encouraged the boys who had been lower on divergent thinking to say anything that came into their minds, striking increases in the number of responses, many of them obscene, violent, or both, occurred. Hudson comes up with some new ideas about what the convergent-divergent distinction signifies. Domino (53) showed that boys singled out as creative on the basis of both teacher nomination and test scores had mothers who differed significantly from the norm on several scales of a personality test.

EXPERIMENTAL ATTEMPTS TO INCREASE CREATIVITY

Several kinds of experimental manipulation have been found to affect creativity test scores. In two kindergarten samples, Goodnow (88) demonstrated that active handling of objects produced more nonstandard uses than did looking alone. Krop et al (142) found that 20 college students decreased their level of divergent thinking but not convergent thinking after viewing a stressful film. Ward (222) increased the number of divergent responses in creative but not in noncreative children (identified by test scores) by putting them into a "cue-rich" environment. He suggested that the use of environmental cues may be one of the strategies that enables children labeled "creative" to get their high scores. Piers & Morgan (180) increased the number of responses to an Alternate Uses test by giving fifth-graders free association training, but found that the increase did not transfer to another creativity test, Pattern Meanings.

One of the main reasons for conducting such experiments is the interest many educators have in fostering creativity through school experiences. A book edited by Michael (162) contains chapters suggesting how this may be done at all educational levels. Two English reports point in opposite directions with regard to the significance of one educational variable. Haddon & Lytton (101) compared two informal primary schools with two more formal ones and found, as they expected, that scores for divergent thinking were higher in the schools with the informal atmosphere and organization. A similar study at the secondary level by Lytton & Cotton (149) showed very little difference between formal and informal schools. It is not clear what this disparity arises from, whether the more advanced developmental level, the greater selectivity of secondary schools, or some other factor is involved.

DIFFERENTIATION AND STRUCTURE
GUILFORD'S S-I MODEL

By far the most coherent and comprehensive theory about the differentiation and organization of abilities is Guilford's three-dimensional Structure-of-Intellect Model. Progress has continued during this period in elaborating and clarifying its concepts, obtaining research data in support of hypotheses derived from it, and applying it to new groups and new problems.

Guilford himself has brought out several important general statements. One book (96) is a collection of 18 papers that have appeared over the years during which the S-I model was taking shape. A handbook chapter (97) combines a clear statement of what the model is with brief descriptions of many of the factors, including test examples and some thoughts about the relationship of the model to information-processing theory and the work of Piaget. A chapter by Guilford & Tenopyr (99) continues the translation of the theory into information-processing terms, and goes on to equate creativity with problem-solving and to show how creative thinking involves any or all of the separate abilities rather than just a selected few. Guilford & Hoepfner's book (98) provides an up-to-date and integrated account of a 20-year research program in the course of which 98 abilities have been differentiated. Michael (163) explained how the S-I model can provide a basis for unified theories of ability, learning, and teaching, thus making possible better predictions that lead to better placement of students in educational situations. (Research on aptitude-treatment-interactions is summarized in a later section of this review.) Varela (215) made an interesting suggestion that the well-known cube representing the S-I model be replaced by a cylinder to bring factors between which relationships have been demonstrated closer together.

Several factor analytic studies have filled in additional cells of the three-dimensional model. Hoepfner & O'Sullivan (112) analyzed scores high school subjects obtained on six tests of behavioral cognition thought to indicate social intelligence. The ability was fairly well differentiated from IQ. Brown et al (23) found evidence for the six separate semantic memory abilities hypothesized from the S-I model, again based on a factor analysis of scores obtained from high school students. Dunham et al (61) demonstrated the existence of the abilities one would expect to be related to concept learning, abilities having to do with the cognition, production, and memory of class concepts. Hoepfner et al (111) located ten information-transformation abilities along with six other factors needing to be differentiated from them.

Another line of S-I research has been the extension of the system to new kinds of populations. Sitker & Meyers (200) found the same six-factor pattern in groups of Negro and White 4-year-olds. In the context of the race comparisons on intelligence mentioned in a previous section, it is of some interest that in this study the typical middle class superiority appeared only on CMU (Cognition of Semantic Units). Carlson & Meyers (31) came out with the same factor structure in 9-year-old retarded children whose mental age was 4 that had previously been identified in normal preschool children.

In an attempt to apply the S-I system to a teaching situation, Dunham & Bunderson (60) presented concept problems to high school learners under two kinds of instruction, Decision-Rule Instruction and No-Rule Instruction. Performance was better under the Decision-Rule condition, but it was interesting to note that different abilities were related to performance under the two conditions: Associative Memory and Induction when no rules were provided, but General Reasoning and Induction when decision rules were given. In exploring the relationship of S-I abilities to the learning of tenth-grade geometry, Caldwell et al (26) found higher validities for a composite of S-I tests than for combinations of commercial prognostic tests, and the time required to administer the S-I tests was much shorter than the other battery required. A further report on the project (Caldwell et al 27) indicated, however, that there was considerable shrinkage in both multiple R's upon cross-validation.

While the S-I model has dominated this research area, there have been other proposals for the classification of mental abilities. Schlesinger & Guttman (196) showed that correlations between intelligence and achievement tests could be accounted for by using a facet analysis model dividing the test space into three sectors—Figural, Numerical, and Verbal—in which the distance of a test point from the origin indicates whether it involves rule-inferring (most central), rule applying (intermediate), or school achievement (outer). Bratfisch & Ekman (21) classified the tests in a battery by having 31 persons who had taken them judge how similar each pair of tests was. The structure based on such judgments turned out to agree very closely with the structure based on an earlier factor analysis of correlations for a much larger group. If this result is confirmed, it could be an economical way of analyzing ability structures.

MEASUREMENT OF APTITUDES

Some research on vocational aptitudes continues, although such efforts have not constituted a major focus during this period. The Employment Service continued to develop its General Aptitude Test Battery (GATB). Showler & Droege (198) retested clients who had taken the tests after 1, 2, and 3 years and found that the stability coefficients were high (.73 to .90). The validity of the tests for predicting occupational criteria seems to be more problematical. Droege (55) carried on a large-scale follow-up of high school testees 2 years after graduation. Validities for occupational criteria were low (mostly in the .20s), with predictions of academic standing for college-goers ranging somewhat higher. Bemis (13) summarized results for a large number of validity studies over a 20-year period. These studies indicate that the median coefficient for single aptitude predictions is .22. Multiple correlations for batteries of tests ran somewhat higher. A current project of the GATB group is the development of a nonreading edition of the battery (Droege et al 56).

In the area of motor skills, Hinrichs (110) corroborated Fleishman's earlier finding that during the course of learning, task specific factors increase in importance. Hilsendager et al (109) carried out a factor analysis that produced factors similar to those Fleishman had reported.

In Sweden mechanical aptitude was discussed by Ekvall (65), who presented factor analytic evidence for the existence of two factors often noted in similar studies in this country, Spatial Ability and Mechanical Knowledge. The usual sex differences also appeared. Grant & Bray (91) obtained respectable validity coefficients for five aptitude tests used to select minority as well as nonminority trainees for positions as telephone installers and repairmen.

Georgas et al (83) reported correlations with a typing criterion for the Minnesota Clerical Test (including a special section using Greek names) similar in magnitude to those ordinarily obtained in this country (about .4).

Music aptitude tests still interest musicians, although little is being published about them primarily for the benefit of psychologists. Lehman (144) published a survey of available tests without attempting critical analysis. Wing (235) brought the evidence about his tests up to date in a second edition of a book first published in 1948. Shuter (199) presented a comprehensive review of what is known about musical talent, summarizing most of the research that has been done on it to date.

PATTERNS OF ABILITY IN DIFFERENT POPULATION GROUPS

The idea that it is the patterning of mental abilities that most clearly differentiates one cultural group from another was restated during this period by Lesser & Stodolsky (145), who had earlier presented interesting evidence with regard to differences between White, Negro, Jewish, and Oriental children. Studies by others have not provided much corroboration as yet. Barnes (10), comparing Negroes with whites in two socioeconomic classes found the same pattern to be present in all four groups of 8-year-old boys. As usual, the upper socioeconomic groups scored higher on all tests. Moore et al (166), who tested Negro and white applicants for refinery jobs, found Negroes lower on all five tests, although the difference was larger for nonverbal than for verbal scores.

The finding, contrary to what many people assume to be true, that Negroes are less handicapped on verbal than on performance tests, was corroborated in a study by Caldwell & Smith (28) of 420 Negro children in the South. The verbal IQ was significantly higher than the performance IQ. Wysocki & Wysocki (238) obtained the same sort of result in testing white and Negro veterans, the racial difference turning out to be greater on the performance than on the verbal tests. In one respect the Wysocki results fit in with Jensen's theory, discussed elsewhere in this review, in that Negroes scored significantly higher than whites on the Digit Span test.

Two investigators report a difference that appears to be in the opposite direction. Baughman & Dahlstrom (11) made an intensive study of Negro and white children in a rural area of the South. On the Primary Mental Abilities tests, Negroes scored lower on V (Verbal) than on P (Perceptual). Willard (231) found that disadvantaged Negro children scored a little higher on the Culture-Fair Test than on an individual intelligence test that was more verbal in nature. It is clear that the final word on pattern differences between Negroes and whites has not yet been said.

PATTERNS OF ABILITY IN DIFFERENT COUNTRIES

Cross-cultural comparisons on ability tests are of considerable interest. Vernon (216), after beginning with an overview of research concerned with environmental influences on mental growth, presented the results of investigations he has made of the patterning of mental test scores in Jamaica, East Africa, Canada, and Alaska, in which he attempted to relate the deficiencies of disadvantaged groups to particular environmental factors. This proved to be difficult to do. It appears, however, that the overall deficit is related to the number of adverse conditions a group encounters. Two analyses of African data (Irvine 122; El-Abd 66) suggest that the basic factor pattern is similar from place to place. The factors that usually show up in British and American studies appeared in Africa also, although there are a few that seem to be peculiar to the particular cultural setting, such as "male educational aptitude." MacArthur (156), applying British theories that postulate a hierarchical organization of mental abilities to data from Northern Canadian native youth, concluded that abilities higher in the hierarchy are more similar from one cultural group to another than are those lower down. The size and nature of the "g" factor derived from the correlations was similar for Eskimos, Indians, and whites. With regard to the more limited factors, Eskimos and Indians were superior to whites on some, lower than whites on others.

Some of the most stimulating suggestions about the origins of the kinds of cultural differences that show up on ability tests can be found in some work reported by Hudson (118) having to do with the perception of pictures by Africans as compared with white Europeans and Americans. His results, experimental and descriptive, indicate that most Africans, even those with considerable schooling, do not interpret two-dimensional representations three-dimensionally. The cues Europeans use for depth perception are assimilated by Africans to a flat picture. Thus they may "see" something quite different from what the maker of a test expected them to "see." African responses to pictures also differ in several other ways from those of most Europeans. Deregowski (51) explored some of these differences in school children using an ingenious experimental procedure. Interesting corroboration of the hypothesis that there may be basic perceptual differences between national groups came from a report by Guthrie et al (100) that Vietnamese helicopter technicians trained in the United States did not perceive pictures three-dimensionally, and were confused by size differences between objects and their representations on the test that they were given.

Such findings suggest the ironic conclusion that in trying to produce "culture-free" or "culture-fair" tests by using picture items rather than verbal items, psychologists may have been creating the maximum "disadvantage" for many of the groups tested. The fact that it is often on perceptual and spatial tests that disadvantaged groups do most poorly fits in with this possibility. It warrants further attention.

INTELLIGENCE AND LEARNING

In spite of the fact that "learning ability" is often used as a synonym for "intelligence," it has been clear to researchers for a long time that these are not equivalent terms. While scores on intelligence tests are good general predictors of success in school, they do not correlate at all with many criteria of learning, in school or out. Because of the widespread interest during the past few years in reducing the educational gap between the less and more favored groups in our society, the relationship between intelligence and other kinds of learning ability has become a problem of concern to several theorists and investigators.

One of these major attempts was that of Jensen and his associates, referred to in an earlier section. The controversy over his conclusion that racial differences may be determined partially by heredity tended to obscure the major purpose of this research undertaking to locate learning abilities on which groups low in socioeconomic status are not inferior to middle and upper class groups and to utilize these abilities in the design of educational programs. More recent statements of the Jensen theory and research results than those cited in the earlier section (Jensen & Rohwer 132; Jensen 131;

Keogh & MacMillan 137; Rohwer 186) have pointed out weaknesses in the theory as originally stated and led to modifications. The first point at which research results did not confirm hypotheses derived from the initial theory was with regard to the dependence of Level II ability (intelligence or conceptual learning) on Level I abilities (rote memory or associative learning). The higher correlations between the two varieties of ability for upper social levels than for lower levels predicted by the theory have not been consistently found. The second complication arose out of the fact that results from learning experiments involving Paired Associates do not follow the same pattern as those from experiments involving Digit Span. Rohwer (186) has proposed a more complex two-dimensional model for the classification of learning abilities. One dimension contrasts Acquisition with Recall-Application. The other has Formal Conceptual Activity at one extreme, Imaginative Conceptual Activity at the other.

Jensen's proposition that Digit Span is an indicator of an ability of some importance in its own right has received confirmation in results reported by Whimbey et al (228, 229), who showed that a Digit Span test correlated .77 with a test of mental addition and that Digit Span scores of a group of college students were correlated with a pretraining test of syllogistic reasoning, though not with scores after training.

Another influential theoretical formulation about the nature of intelligence distinguishes between fluid and crystallized intelligence. It has been given a clear statement in two papers by Horn (113, 114). Fluid intelligence is determined by neural-physiological factors and incidental learning. It declines with brain damage and with aging. Crystallized intelligence reflects acculturation. It increases with education and experience and holds up well throughout adult life. Ability tests measure both aspects to differing degrees, along with other unrelated things, such as sensory modality factors, motivational tendencies, and strategies.

A somewhat different theoretical approach contends that intelligence is primarily the product or effect rather than the cause of learning. Wesman (227) has elaborated in some detail the consequences of two simple propositions: (a) that intelligence is an attribute, not an entity; and (b) that intelligence is the summation of the learning experiences of the individual. Gagné (79) also views mental ability as a product of cumulative learning in which various skills form a transfer hierarchy ranging from stimulus-response connections through chains, motor and verbal, multiple discriminations, concepts, and simple rules, to complex rules.

Gagné's theory can be regarded as a more complex version of Jensen's two-level theory, or it can be seen in relationship to Piaget's theory of distinct stages, each built on the preceding one. Dudek et al (59) and O'Bryan & MacArthur (170) have explored the relationships between Piaget-type tasks and mental ability tests of various sorts.

Roberts (185) presented a synthesis of research results on the problem of learning abilities. He concluded that there are several dimensions of ability and of learning tasks and that the stage of practice should be considered in exploring relationships. Some abilities relate more closely to early parts of a learning process, others to later parts. His conclusion that more research is needed is one that all the persons cited in this section would support.

APTITUDE-TREATMENT INTERACTION

The fact that a number of able research workers have become simultaneously interested in ability differences, the learning process, and the improvement of education has led to an accelerating attack on the problem of aptitude-treatment interaction (ATI). General discussions of the importance of combining the "two disciplines of scientific psychology," as Cronbach has for years been recommending, have been published by Owens (176), Vale & Vale (212), and Feldman & Hass (74). But by far the most comprehensive and penetrating review of the whole field is to be found in a monograph by Cronbach & Snow (44). After discussing the nature and history of the problem and the statistical and methodological difficulties it involves, the authors presented a summary of much of the work on record, including their own. The results, to date, are not impressive. Evidence for significant interactions is scarce and fragmentary. What has been accomplished, however, is a clearing away of the underbrush, so to speak, the preparation of the terrain for the charting of new and more effective lines of ATI research based on coherent theories.

Three experimental studies, more recent than those included in Cronbach's review, show some interaction effects, though not large enough to be important practically (Games & Bechtoldt 80; Keislar & Stern 135; King et al 138). Tobias (204) failed to find the hypothesized interactions.

The identification of differences between natural groups in the population with regard to the relationships between ability, achievement, and environmental variables is a related line of research. Tulkin & Newbrough (210) reported some significant triple interactions between sex, race, and social class. Cultural variables relate to ability in some subgroups, but not in others. Olson et al (172) added to the growing body of evidence that the relationships between ability and achievement differ for boys and girls. In a particularly interesting report, Farnham-Diggory (72) discussed an interaction between race and type of task with regard to the kinds of training most effective in increasing young children's ability to carry out cognitive synthesis. Jensen's research involving interactions between race and method of learning has been cited in an earlier section.

DEVELOPMENT OF ABILITIES

A number of longitudinal studies have continued the search for aspects of early development predictive of intellectual ability at a later time. A Hawaiian study (Werner et al 226; Werner 225; Pearson 179) corroborates previous findings from other parts of the world that correlations between children's intelligence test scores and indices of parents' educational level increase with age. Moore (167) in London reported similar results. He also noted correlations with ordinal position, and stimulus quality and emotional climate of the home. Infant tests ordinarily do not predict later intelligence well, but Willerman & Broman (232) and Ireton et al (121) discovered that scores on the Bayley scale at 8 months were significantly related to IQ at 4 years for children at lower socioeconomic levels. Parental status was more predictive at upper levels. Garber & Ware (81), analyzing home character-istics found that the only aspects predictive of intellectual development were: (a) expectations for child's schooling; and (b) learning materials in the home. Palmer (178) reported some dissonant findings. For a large group of Negro preschool boys there was no consistent correlation between intellec-tive tests and indices of parental socioeconomic status.

Several of these investigators reported sex differences in the pattern of correlations. Bayley (12), reporting on a follow-up of subjects in the Berkeley Growth Study at age 36, analyzed the sex differences in some de-tail. For males, intelligence level is related positively to introspective, thoughtful behavior, negatively to lack of control. For females, the positive correlation with introspective, thoughtful behavior also appears, but the highest negative correlations are with conventional, bland, anxious char-acteristics. All correlations are much lower for females than males.

Rees & Palmer (183) combined the data from five major longitudinal studies, looking for parental and environmental variables related to increases or decreases in mental test performance over the years. They turned up mostly low, nonsignificant correlations. Socioeconomic status differences and some sex differences appeared.

A perennial question, never completely settled, is whether abilities be-come more differentiated during the course of development from infancy to adulthood. Dye & Very (62) added to the positive evidence. Their factor analysis produced a larger number of factors at the eleventh grade than at the tenth grade level. As in some previous studies, females turned out to be less differentiated than males. At the college level, Lunneborg & Lunneborg (148) reported that retests of seniors on tests they had taken at the precollege level showed that the deviations from the predicted gain were correlated, though not highly, with the amount of course work taken in different subject-matter fields. Here again, males were more differentiated than females.

Another perennial set of research questions has to do with age changes in adults. The fact that longitudinal studies have typically pointed to smaller declines than have cross-sectional studies has focused attention on environ-mental trends affecting succeeding age cohorts differently. Green (93) re-ported that in standardizing a Spanish version of the Wechsler Adult In-telligence Scale, the apparent decline with age disappeared when covariance adjustments for education and urban-rural residence were made. Green & Reimanis (94) repeated a previous longitudinal study with the Wechsler test at a Veterans Administration hospital and found that there had been no decline for men who were under 65 at the time of the first testing.

Tuddenham & Blumenkrantz (208), using the GATB, indicated that only a very slight decline had occurred over a 20-year period. Schaie & Strother (193, 194) reported in detail one of the most comprehensive studies ever carried out, designed to examine both age and cohort differences over the entire adult life span from 21 to 75. As expected, cohort differences were larger than age differences, and the trends were different for different special abilities. A special analysis of results for a highly intelligent aged group (195) indicated that all special abilities declined from 70 on. Fozard (77), studying veterans with the GATB, found that tests of cognitive ability were most sensitive to socioeconomic differences, tests of psychomotor functioning most sensitive to age differences. Ross (188) reported decreasing differentiation of abilities with age in adults.

Noncognitive Components of Ability

During this period there has been a resurgence of interest in this research topic. Some of it is related to the attempt to explain ethnic and socioeconomic differences as differences in test motivation. Straightforward attempts to improve test performance by persuading testees to try harder or by changing the format of the test, or the race of the examiner (Nitardy et al 169; Ward et al 224; Costello 42) have, as in previous years, produced few significant results. However, investigators starting with more subtle concepts of motivation (Zigler & Butterfield 240; Katz 134) have found some evidence for motivational differences between deprived and nondeprived groups. Hertzig et al (105) came up with some evidence that a major difference between Puerto Rican and middle-class nondisadvantaged children may lie in the disposition to respond to cognitive demands with "non-work" rather than "work" responses.

Another category of research has to do with cognitive styles and the ways in which they control what we observe and measure as ability. Field independence vs field dependence (DuBois & Cohen 58; Eagle & Goldberger 63; Gruenfeld & Arbuthnot 95; Gardner et al 82) appear to be related both to abilities and to social characteristics. Reflection-impulsivity (Ward 221; Mumbauer & Miller 168; Yando & Kagan 239; Reppucci 184; Meichenbaum & Goodman 159), especially in young children, is related to a variety of specific performances. Cropley & Field (46) indicated that science achievement is related to category width preference as well as to abstract thinking and intelligence. Baird & Bee (8) demonstrated that young children could be induced to shift toward a more mature style but not to a less mature style if given appropriate rewards.

One growing and coherent body of work has been demonstrating that scores on a biographical inventory can be used to predict many criteria at least as accurately as typical ability measures do. Results have been reported for creative achievement (Schaefer & Anastasi 191; Anastasi & Schaefer 5; Schaefer 190) and for success in science and engineering (Owens 177; Ellison et al 67). One promising feature of this technique is that while scores predict school success, they are not correlated with race (Ellison et al 68). Some correlations reported by Lipp et al (147) suggest that the scale on the California Psychological Inventory labeled Intellectual Efficiency may actually measure intelligence rather than a noncognitive aspect of personality. Wing & Wallach (234) showed that a differently constituted student body would be found in selective colleges if real life accomplishments rather than grades and test scores were the bases of selection.

EMERGING CONCEPTS

Out of the research and thinking of our time are appearing evidences of a more complex and sophisticated conceptualization of human abilities than we have previously employed. It might be labeled a pluralistic approach to individual differences. Various aspects of the emerging theory have been emphasized in general statements and discussions. Anastasi (4), in her Tryon memorial lecture, brought together factor analytic evidence for the increasing differentiation of abilities in children with age, showed how the pattern relates to education, socioeconomic level, and what is emphasized in different cultures, and called attention to problem-solving styles and strategies. Mischel (164) began by accepting as fact the specificity and inconsistency we constantly run into in our search for stable global traits and rejecting the prevailing "genotype-phenotype" interpretation. What he arrived at is a new approach to personality research, using concepts like "alternatives," some incompatible with one another, and "strategies," replaceable and modifiable on the basis of experience. Mehler & Bever (158) postulated mental structures as the bases for performance. They pointed out that not to demonstrate a structure in an experimental or test situation does not prove its nonexistence. Failure to perform may be an indicator of lack of the requisite expressive capacity rather than lack of ability. Escalona (70) discussed at some length the ideas and concepts that have come out of the intensive study of individual infants and their later development. She postulates an intermediate variable, "experience patterns," between the causal organismic and environmental variables on the one hand and the developmental outcome variables on the other.

Fischer (75) has proposed a new definition of intelligence as "the effectiveness, relative to age peers, of the individual's approaches to situations in which competence is highly regarded by the culture," and explored its implications for testing procedures. Accepting this definition leads to an emphasis on description rather than measurement, and on systematic variations in conditions and instructions, something like the Rorschach procedure for "testing the limits." The aim should be to understand the person's meanings and frames of reference rather than simply to measure his performance under standard conditions.

Undoubtedly we shall see more discussions along these lines in the years just ahead. A transformation of the science and technology of individual differences may be on the horizon.

LITERATURE CITED

1. Albert, R. S. 1969. Genius: present-day status of the concept and its implications for the study of creativity and giftedness. *Am. Psychol.* 24:743–53
2. Alzobaie, A. J., Metfessel, N. S., Michael, W. B. 1968. Alternative approaches to assessing the intellectual abilities of youth from a culture of poverty. *Educ. Psychol. Meas.* 28:449–55
3. American Psychological Association Task Force on Employment Testing of Minority Groups. 1969. Job testing and the disadvantaged. *Am. Psychol.* 24:637–50
4. Anastasi, A. 1970. On the formation of psychological traits. *Am. Psychol.* 25:899–910
5. Anastasi, A., Schaefer, C. E. 1969. Biographical correlates of artistic and literary creativity in adolescent girls. *J. Appl. Psychol.* 53:267–73
6. Anderson, S. B. From textbooks to reality: social researchers face the facts of life in the world of the disadvantaged. See Ref. 104, 226–37
7. Bachman, J. G. 1970. *Youth in Transition, Vol. 2: The Impact of Family Background and Intelligence on Tenth-Grade Boys.* Ann Arbor: Survey Res. Center
8. Baird, R. R., Bee, H. L. 1969. Modification of conceptual style preference by differential reinforcement. *Child Develop.* 40:903–10
9. Baratz, S. S., Baratz, J. C. 1970. Early childhood intervention: the social science basis of institutional racism. *Harvard Educ. Rev.* 40:29–50
10. Barnes, K. 1970. Patterns of WISC scores for children of two socioeconomic classes and races. *Child Develop.* 41:493–99
11. Baughman, E. E., Dahlstrom, W. G. 1968. *Negro and White Children.* New York: Academic
12. Bayley, N. 1968. Behavioral correlates of mental growth: birth to thirty-six years. *Am. Psychol.* 23:1–17
13. Bemis, S. E. 1968. Occupational validity of the General Aptitude Test Battery. *J. Appl. Psychol.* 52:240–44
14. Bereiter, C. 1970. Genetics and educability: educational implications of the Jensen debate. See Ref. 6, 279–99
15. Blank, M., Solomon, F. 1968. A tu-torial language program to develop abstract thinking in socially disadvantaged preschool children. *Child Develop.* 39:379–89
16. Ibid. 1969. How shall the disadvantaged child be taught? 40:47–61
17. Boersma, F. J., O'Bryan, K. 1968. An investigation of the relationship between creativity and intelligence under two conditions of testing. *J. Personality* 36:341–48
18. Bouchard, T. J. Jr. 1968. Current conceptions of intelligence and their implications for assessment. In *Advances in Psychological Assessment*, ed. P. McReynolds, 1:14–33. Palo Alto: Science and Behavior Books
19. Bowers, J. 1969. Interactive effects of creativity and IQ on ninth-grade achievement. *J. Educ. Meas.* 6:173–77
20. Bowers, K. S., van der Meulen, S. J. 1970. Effect of hypnotic susceptibility on creativity test performance. *J. Pers. Soc. Psychol.* 14:247–56
21. Bratfisch, O., Ekman, G. 1969. Subjective and objective intelligence factors. *Psychol. Rep.* 25:607–20
22. Brim, O. G., Glass, D. C., Neulinger, J., Firestone, I. J. 1969. *American Beliefs and Attitudes about Intelligence.* New York: Russell Sage Found.
23. Brown, S. W., Guilford, J. P., Hoepfner, R. 1968. Six semantic-memory abilities. *Educ. Psychol. Meas.* 28:691–717
24. Burt, C. 1969. What is intelligence? *Brit. J. Educ. Psychol.* 39:198–201
25. Butcher, H. J. 1968. *Human Intelligence: Its Nature and Assessment.* London: Methuen
26. Caldwell, J. R., Michael, W. B., Schrader, D. R., Meyers, C. E. 1970. Comparative validities and working times for composites of structure-of-intellect tests and algebra grades and composites of traditional test measures and algebra grades in the prediction of success in tenth-grade geometry. *Educ. Psychol. Meas.* 30:955–59
27. Caldwell, J. R., Schrader, D. R., Michael, W. B., Meyers, C. E. 1970. Structure-of-intellect measures and other tests as predictors of success in tenth-grade modern geometry. *Educ. Psychol. Meas.* 30:437–41

28. Caldwell, M. B., Smith, T. A. 1968. Intellectual structure of Southern Negro children. *Psychol. Rep.* 23:63–71

29. Campbell, D. T., Erlebacher, A. How regression artifacts in quasi-experimental evaluations can mistakenly make compensatory education look harmful. See Ref. 6, 185–210

30. Ibid. Reply to the replies, 221–25

31. Carlson, D. C., Meyers, C. E. 1968. Language, memory, and figural ability hypotheses in retardates of mental age 4. *Am. J. Ment. Defic.* 73:105–12

32. Cattell, R. B., Butcher, H. J. 1968. *The Prediction of Achievement and Creativity.* Indianapolis: Bobbs-Merrill

33. Cave, R. L. 1970. A combined factor analysis of creativity and intelligence. *Multivar. Behav. Res.* 5:177–91

34. Chambers, J. A. 1969. Beginning a multidimensional theory of creativity. *Psychol. Rep.* 25:779–99

35. Cicirelli, V. G. The relevance of the regression artifact problem to the Westinghouse-Ohio evaluation of Head Start: a reply to Campbell and Erlebacher. See Ref. 6, 211–15

36. Cicirelli, V. G. et al 1969. *The impact of Head Start. An evaluation of the effects of Head Start on children's cognitive and affective development.* Washington, D. C.: Clearinghouse Fed. Sci. Tech. Inform., US Dep. Commerce, Nat. Bur. Stand., Inst. Appl. Tech. PB 184–328

37. Cicirelli, V. G., Evans, J. W., Schiller, J. S. 1970. The impact of Head Start: a reply to the report analysis. *Harvard Educ. Rev.* 40:105–29

38. Clark, P. M., Mirels, H. L. 1970. Fluency as a pervasive element in the measurement of creativity. *J. Educ. Meas.* 7:83–86

39. Cleary, T. A. 1968. Test bias: prediction of grades of Negro and white students in integrated colleges. *J. Educ. Meas.* 5:115–24

40. Cleary, T. A., Hilton, T. L. 1968. An investigation of item bias. *Educ. Psychol. Meas.* 28:61–75

41. College Entrance Examination Board. 1970. *Report of the Commission on Tests. I. Righting the Balance.* New York: CEEB

42. Costello, J. 1970. Effects of pretesting and examiner characteristics of young disadvantaged children. *Proc. 78th Ann. Conv. APA*, 309–10

43. Cronbach, L. J. 1968. Intelligence? Creativity? A parsimonious reinterpretation of the Wallach-Kogan data. *Am. Educ. Res. J.* 5:491–511

44. Cronbach, L. J., Snow, R. E. 1969. *Individual Differences in Learning Ability as a Function of Instructional Variables.* Stanford Univ. Sch. Educ.

45. Cropley, A. J. 1968. A note on the Wallach-Kogan Tests of Creativity. *Brit. J. Educ. Psychol.* 38:197–200

46. Cropley, A. J., Field, T. W. 1969. Achievement in science and intellectual style. *J. Appl. Psychol.* 53:132–35

47. Dacey, J., Madaus, G., Allen, A. 1969. The relationship of creativity and intelligence in Irish adolescents. *Brit. J. Educ. Psychol.* 39:261–66

48. Dandes, H. M., Dow, D. 1969. Relation of intelligence to family size and density. *Child Develop.* 40:641–45

49. Dellas, M., Gaier, E. L. 1970. Identification of creativity: the individual. *Psychol. Bull.* 73:55–73

50. US Dep. Labor. 1968. Validation of employment tests by contractors subject to the provisions of Executive Order 11246. *Fed. Regist.* 33: Whole No. 186

51. Deregowski, J. B. 1968. On perception of depicted orientation. *Int. J. Psychol.* 3:149–56

52. Dewing, K. 1970. The reliability and validity of selected tests of creative thinking in a sample of seventh-grade West Australian children. *Brit. J. Educ. Psychol.* 40:35–42

53. Domino, G. 1969. Maternal personality correlates of sons' creativity. *J. Consult. Clin. Psychol.* 33:180–83

54. Dreger, R. M., Miller, K. S. 1968. Comparative psychological studies of Negroes and whites in the United States: 1959–1965. *Psychol. Bull. Monogr. Suppl.* 70 (2):1–58

55. Droege, R. C. 1968. GATB longitudinal validation study. *J. Couns. Psychol.* 15:41–47

56. Droege, R. C., Showler, W., Bemis, S., Hawk J. 1970. Development of a nonreading edition of the General Aptitude Test battery. *Meas. Eval. Guid.* 3:45–53

57. Dubin, J. A., Osburn, H., Winick, D. M. 1969. Speed and practice: effects on Negro and white test

performances. *J. Appl. Psychol.* 53:19–23

58. DuBois, T. E., Cohen, W. 1970. Relationship between measures of psychological differentiation and intellectual ability. *Percept. Mot. Skills* 31:411–16

59. Dudek, S. Z., Lester, E. P., Goldberg, J. S. 1969. Relationship of Piaget measures to standard intelligence and motor scales. *Percept. Mot. Skills* 28:352–62

60. Dunham, J. L., Bunderson, C. V. 1969. Effect of decision-rule instruction upon the relationship of cognitive abilities to performance in multiple-category concept problems. *J. Educ. Psychol.* 60:121–25

61. Dunham, J. L., Guilford, J. P., Hoepfner, R. 1969. The cognition, production, and memory of class concepts. *Educ. Psychol. Meas.* 29: 615–38

62. Dye, N. W., Very, P. S. 1968. Growth changes in factorial structure by age and sex. *Genet. Psychol. Monogr.* 78:55–88

63. Eagle, M., Goldberger, L. 1969. Field dependence and memory for social vs. neutral and relevant vs. irrelevant incidental stimuli. *Percept. Mot. Skills* 29:903–10

64. Eisenman, R. 1969. Creativity and academic major: business versus English majors. *J. Appl. Psychol.* 53:392–95

65. Ekvall, G. 1969. *The Construct Validity of Mechanical Aptitude Tests.* Stockholm: Swedish Counc. Personnel Admin.

66. El-Abd, H. A. 1970. The intellect of East African students. *Multivar. Behav. Anal.* 5:423–33

67. Ellison, R. L., James, L. R., Carron, T. J. 1970. Prediction of R & D performance criteria with biographical information. *J. Ind. Psychol.* 5:37–57

68. Ellison, R. L., James, L. R., Fox, D. G., Taylor, C. W. 1970. *The Identification of Talent among Negro and White Students from Biographical Data.* Washington, D. C.: Off. Educ., Bur. Res. Final Rep. Project 9-H-033

69. Equal Employment Opportunity Commission. 1966. *Guidelines on Employment Testing Procedures.* Washington, D. C.: EEOC

70. Escalona, S. K. 1968. *The Roots of Individuality.* Chicago: Aldine

71. Evans, J. W., Schiller, J. How preoccupation with possible regression artifacts can lead to a faulty strategy for the evaluation of social action programs: a reply to Campbell and Erlebacher. See Ref. 6, 216–20

72. Farnham-Diggory, S. 1970. Cognitive synthesis in Negro and white children. *Monogr. Soc. Res. Child Develop.* 35(2):1–84, Ser. 135

73. Fee, F. 1968. An alternative to Ward's factor analysis of Wallach and Kogan's 'creativity' correlations. *Brit. J. Educ. Psychol.* 38:319–21

74. Feldman, C. F., Hass, W. A. 1970. Controls, conceptualization, and the interrelation between experiment and correlational research. *Am. Psychol.* 25:633–35

75. Fischer, C. T. 1969. Intelligence defined as effectiveness of approaches. *J. Consult. Clin. Psychol.* 33:668–74

76. Flaugher, R. L. 1970. *Testing Practices, Minority Groups, and Higher Education: a Review and Discussion of the Research.* Princeton: Educ. Test. Serv.

77. Fozard, J. L. 1970. Age and socioeconomic status influences on performance on ability tests. *Proc. 78th Ann. Conv. APA,* 687–88

78. Freeman, J., Butcher, H. J., Christie, T. 1968. *Creativity: A Selective Review of Research.* London: Soc. Res. Higher Educ.

79. Gagné, R. M. 1968. Contributions of learning to human development. *Psychol. Rev.* 75:177–91

80. Games, P. A., Bechtoldt, H. P. 1969. Role of five abilities in the learning of two paired associates tasks. *Proc. 77th Ann. Conv. APA,* 167–68

81. Garber, M., Ware, M. B. 1970. Relationship between measures of home environment and intelligence scores. *Proc. 78th Ann. Conv. APA,* 647–48

82. Gardner, R. W., Lohrenz, L. J., Schoen, R. A. 1968. Cognitive control of differentiation in the perception of persons and objects. *Percept. Mot. Skills* 26:311–30

83. Georgas, J. G., Bramos, I., Bakirdgis, I. 1968. The Minnesota Clerical Test in Greece. *Personnel Psychol.* 21:79–83

84. Gibson, J. W., Kibler, R. J., Barker, L. L. 1968. Some relationships between selected creativity and crit-

ical-thinking measures. *Psychol. Rep.* 23:707–14

85. Ginsburg, G. P., Whittemore, R. G. 1968. Creativity and verbal ability: a direct examination of their relationship. *Brit. J. Educ. Psychol.* 38:133–39

86. Glass, D. C., Ed. 1968. *Genetics.* New York: Rockefeller Univ. Press and Russell Sage Found.

87. Goodman, P., Furcon, J., Rose, J. 1969. Examination of some measures of creative ability by the multitrait-multimethod matrix. *J. Appl. Psychol.* 53:240–43

88. Goodnow, J. J. 1969. Effects of active handling, illustrated by uses for objects. *Child Develop.* 40:201–12

89. Goolsby, T. M., Frary, R. B. 1970. Validity of the Metropolitan Readiness Test for white and Negro students in a Southern city. *Educ. Psychol. Meas.* 30:443–50

90. Goslin, D. A. 1968. Standardized ability tests and testing. *Science* 159:851–55

91. Grant, D. L., Bray, D. W. 1970. Validation of employment tests for telephone company installation and repair occupations. *J. Appl. Psychol.* 54:7–14

92. Gray, S. W., Klaus, R. A. 1970. The early training project: a seventh-year report. *Child Develop.* 41:909–24

93. Green, R. F. 1969. Age-intelligence relationships between ages sixteen and sixty-four: a rising trend. *Develop. Psychol.* 1:618–27

94. Green, R. F., Reimanis, G. 1970. The age-intelligence relationship—longitudinal studies can mislead. *Indian Geront.* 6:1–16

95. Gruenfeld, J., Arbuthnot, J. 1969. Field independence as a conceptual framework for prediction of variability in ratings of other. *Percept. Mot. Skills* 28:31–44

96. Guilford, J. P. 1968. *Intelligence, Creativity, and Their Educational Implications.* San Diego: Knapp

97. Guilford, J. P. 1968. The structure of intelligence. In *Handbook of Measurement and Assessment in Behavioral Sciences,* ed. D. K. Whitlas, 215–60. Reading: Addison-Wesley

98. Guilford, J. P., Hoepfner, R. 1971. *The Analysis of Intelligence.* New York: McGraw

99. Guilford, J. P., Tenopyr, M. L. 1968. Implications of the structure-of-intellect model for high school and college students. In *Teaching for Creative Endeavor,* ed. W. B. Michael, 25–45. Bloomington: Indiana Univ. Press

100. Guthrie, G. M., Brislin, R., Sinaiko, H. W. 1970. *Some Aptitudes and Abilities of Vietnamese Technicians: Implications for Training.* Arlington: Inst. Def. Anal.

101. Haddon, F. A., Lytton, H. 1968. Teaching approach and the development of divergent thinking in primary schools. *Brit. J. Educ. Psychol.* 38:171–80

102. Härnquist, K. 1968. Relative changes in intelligence from 13 to 18: I. Background and methodology. *Scand. J. Psychol.* 9:50–64

103. Härnquist, K. 1968. Relative changes in intelligence from 13 to 18: II. Results. *Scand. J. Psychol.* 9:65–82

104. Hellmuth, J., Ed. 1970. *Disadvantaged Child, Vol. 3: Compensatory Education: a National Debate.* New York: Brunner, Mazel. 466 pp.

105. Hertzig, M. E., Birch, H. G., Thomas, A., Mendez, O. A. 1968. Class and ethnic differences in the responsiveness of preschool children to cognitive demands. *Monogr. Soc. Res. Child Develop.* 33(1):1–69 Ser. 117

106. Hess, R. D., Bear, R. M., Eds. 1968. *Early Education.* Chicago: Aldine

107. Hess, R. D., Shipman, V., Brophy, J., Bear, R. M. 1968. *The Cognitive Environments of Urban Preschool Children.* Univ. Chicago, Grad. Sch. Educ.

108. Hetrick, S. H., Lilly, R. S., Merrifield, P. R. 1968. Figural creativity, intelligence, and personality in children. *Multivar. Behav. Res.* 3:173–87

109. Hilsendager, D., Karnes, E., Spiritoso, T. 1969. Some dimensions of physical performance. *Percept. Mot. Skills* 28:479–87

110. Hinrichs, J. R. 1970. Ability correlates in learning a psychomotor task. *J. Appl. Psychol.* 54:56–64

111. Hoepfner, R., Guilford, J. P., Bradley, P. A. 1970. Information-transformation abilities. *Educ. Psychol. Meas.* 30:785–802

112. Hoepfner, R., O'Sullivan, M. 1968. Social intelligence and IQ. *Educ. Psychol. Meas.* 28:339–44

113. Horn, J. L. 1968. Organization of abilities and the development of intelligence. *Psychol. Rev.* 75:242–59

114. Horn, J. L. 1970. Organization of data on life-span development of human abilities. In *Life-Span Developmental Psychology: Research and Theory*, ed. L. R. Goulet, P. B. Baltes, 423–66. New York: Academic

115. Houston, S. H. 1969. A sociolinguistic consideration of the black English of children in northern Florida. *Language* 45:599–607

116. Houston, S. H. 1970. A re-examination of some assumptions about the language of the disadvantaged child. *Child Develop.* 41:947–63

117. Hudson, L. 1968. *Frames of Mind.* London: Methuen

118. Hudson, W. 1967. The study of the problem of pictorial perception among unacculturated groups. *Int. J. Psychol.* 2:90–107

119. Humphreys, L. G., Dachler, H. P. 1969. Jensen's theory of intelligence. *J. Educ. Psychol.* 60:419–26

120. Ibid. Jensen's theory of intelligence. A rebuttal, 432–33

121. Ireton, H., Thwing, E., Gravem, H. 1970. Infant mental development and neurological status, family socioeconomic status, and intelligence at age four. *Child Develop.* 41:937–45

122. Irvine, S. H. 1969. Factor analysis of African abilities and attainments: constructs across cultures. *Psychol. Bull.* 71:20–32

123. Jensen, A. R. 1968. Social class, race, and genetics: implications for education. *Am. Educ. Res. J.* 5:1–42

124. Jensen, A. R. 1968. Another look at culture-fair testing. *Proc. West. Reg. Conf. Test. Prob.*, 50–104. Berkeley: Educ. Test. Serv.

125. Jensen, A. R. 1969. How much can we boost IQ and scholastic achievement? *Harvard Educ. Rev.* 39:1–123

126. Jensen, A. R. 1969. Intelligence, learning ability, and socioeconomic status. *J. Spec. Educ.* 3:23–35

127. Jensen, A. R. 1968. Patterns of mental ability and socioeconomic status. *Proc. Nat. Acad. Sci.* 60:1330–37

128. Jensen, A. R. 1969. Jensen's theory of lntelligence: a reply. *J. Educ. Psychol.* 60:427–31

129. Jensen, A. R. 1970. IQ's of identical twins reared apart. *Behav. Genet.* 1:133–46

130. Jensen, A. R. Can we and should we study race differences? See Ref. 6, 124–57

131. Jensen, A. R. 1971. Hierarchical theories of intelligence. In *On Intelligence*, ed. B. Dockrell, 119–90. London: Methuen

132. Jensen, A. R., Rohwer, W. D. Jr. 1970. *An Experimental Analysis of Learning Abilities in Culturally Disadvantaged Children.* OEO Final Rep. 2404

133. Karnes, M. B., Teska, J. A., Hodgins, A. S., Badger, E. D. 1970. Educational intervention at home by mothers of disadvantaged infants. *Child Develop.* 41:925–26

134. Katz, I. 1970. Experimental studies of Negro-white relationships. *Advan. Exp. Soc. Psychol.* 5:71–117

135. Keislar, E. R., Stern, C. 1970. Differentiated instruction in problem solving for children of different mental ability levels. *J. Educ. Psychol.* 61:445–50

136. Kennedy, W. A. 1969. A follow-up normative study of Negro intelligence and achievement. *Monogr. Soc. Res. Child Develop.* 34(2):1–40, Ser. 126

137. Keogh, B. K., MacMillan, D. 1970. Social class, IQ, and motivational effects on digit recall tests. *Proc. 78th Ann. Conv. APA*, 643–44

138. King, F. J., Roberts, D., Kropp, R. P. 1969. Relationship between ability measures and achievement under four methods of teaching elementary set concepts. *J. Educ. Psychol.* 60:244–47

139. Kirkpatrick, J. J., Ewen, R. B., Barrett, R. S., Katzell, R. A. 1968. *Testing and Fair Employment.* New York Univ. Press

140. Klaus, R. A., Gray, S. 1968. The early training project for disadvantaged children: a report after five years. *Monogr. Soc. Res. Child Develop.* 33(4):1–66, Ser. 120

141. Klein, S. P., Evans, F. R. 1969. Early predictors of later creative achievements. *Proc. 77th Ann. Conv. APA*, 153–54

142. Krop, H. D., Alegre, C. E., Williams, C. D. 1969. Effect of induced stress on convergent and divergent thinking. *Psychol. Rep.* 24:895–98

143. Lambie, D. Z., Weikart, D. P. Ypsilanti Carnegie infant education project. See Ref. 6, 362–404

144. Lehman, P. R. 1968. *Tests and Measurements in Music.* Englewood Cliffs: Prentice-Hall.

145. Lesser, G., Stodolsky, S. S. 1969. Equal opportunity for maximum

development. In *Harvard Educational Review; Equal Educational Opportunity*, 126–38. Harvard Univ. Press

146. Lichtenwalner, J. S., Maxwell, J. W. 1969. The relationship of birth order and socioeconomic status to the creativity of preschool children. *Child Develop.* 40:1241–47

147. Lipp, L., Erikson, R., Skeen, D. 1968. Intellectual efficiency: a construct validation study. *Educ. Psychol. Meas.* 28:595–97

148. Lunneborg, C. E., Lunneborg, P. W. 1969. Deviations from predicted growth of abilities for male and female college students. *J. Educ. Meas.* 6:165–72

149. Lytton, H., Cotton, A. C. 1969. Divergent thinking abilities in secondary schools. *Brit. J. Educ. Psychol.* 39:188–90

150. Maier, N. R. F., Burke, R. J. 1968. Studies in creativity: II. Influence of motivation in the reorganization of experience. *Psychol. Rep.* 23:351–61

151. Maier, N. R. F., Janzen, J. C. 1969. Are good problem-solvers also creative? *Psychol. Rep.* 24:139–46

152. Maier, N. R. F., Julius, M., Thurber, J. A. 1967. Studies in creativity: I. Individual differences in the storing and utilization of information. *Am. J. Psychol.* 80:492–519

153. Maier, N. R. F., Thurber, J. A., Julius, M. 1968. Studies in creativity: III. Effect of overlearning on recall and usage of information. *Psychol. Rep.* 23:363–68

154. Mathis, H. I. 1968. Relating environmental factors to aptitude and race. *J. Couns. Psychol.* 15:563–68

155. Maxwell, J. 1969. *Sixteen Years On: a Follow-up of the 1947 Scottish Survey*. Univ. London Press

156. MacArthur, R. 1968. Some differential abilities of Northern Canadian native youth. *Int. J. Psychol.* 3:43–51

157. McHenry, R. E., Shouksmith, G. A. 1970. Creativity, visual imagination and suggestibility: their relationship in a group of 10-year-old children. *Brit. J. Educ. Psychol.* 40:154–60

158. Mehler, J., Bever, T. G. 1968. The study of competence in cognitive psychology. *Int. J. Psychol.* 3:273–80

159. Meichenbaum, D., Goodman, J. 1969. Reflection-impulsivity and verbal control of motor behavior. *Child Develop.* 40:785–97

160. Meier, J. H., Segner, L. L., Grueter, B. B. An education system for high-risk infants: a preventive approach to developmental and learning disabilities. See Ref. 6, 405–44

161. Mendelsohn, R. Is Head Start a success or failure? See Ref. 6, 445–63

162. Michael, W. B., Ed. 1968. *Teaching for Creative Endeavor*. Bloomington: Univ. Indiana Press

163. Michael, W. B. 1969. Implications of the structure-of-intellect model for selection and placement of college students. *Educ. Psychol. Meas.* 29:391–401

164. Mischel, W. 1969. Continuity and change in personality. *Am. Psychol.* 24:1012–18

165. Mitchell, M. D., Albright, L. E., McMurry, F. D. 1968. Biracial validation of selection procedures in a large southern plant. *Proc. 76th Ann. Conv. APA*, 575–76

166. Moore, C. L., MacNaughton, J. F., Osburn, H. G. 1969. Ethnic differences within an industrial selection battery. *Personnel Psychol.* 22:473–82

167. Moore, T. 1968. Language and intelligence: a longitudinal study of the first eight years. Part II. Environmental correlates of mental growth. *Hum. Develop.* 11:1–24

168. Mumbauer, C. C., Miller, J. O. 1970. Socioeconomic background and cognitive functioning in preschool children. *Child Develop.* 41:471–80

169. Nitardy, J. R., Peterson, C. D., Weiss, D. J. 1969. Differential influence of test format variables on ability test performance. *Proc. 77th Ann. Conv. APA*, 139–40

170. O'Bryan, K. G., MacArthur, R. S. 1969. Reversibility, intelligence, and creativity in nine-year-old boys. *Child Develop.* 40:33–45

171. Oden, M. H. 1968. The fulfillment of promise: 40-year follow-up of the Terman gifted group. *Genet. Psychol. Monogr.* 77:3–93

172. Olson, G. M., Miller, L. K., Hale, G. A., Stevenson, H. W. 1968. Long-term correlates of children's learning and problem-solving behavior. *J. Educ. Psychol.* 59:227–32

173. Osborne, R. T., Gregor, A. J. 1968. Racial differences in heritability

estimates for tests of spatial ability. *Percept. Mot. Skills* 27:735–39

174. Osborne, R. T., Gregor, A. J., Miele, F. 1968. Heritability of Factor V: Verbal comprehension. *Percept. Mot. Skills* 26:191–202

175. Osborne, R. T., Miele, F. 1969. Racial differences in environmental influences on numerical ability as determined by heritability estimates. *Percept. Mot. Skills* 28:535–38

176. Owens, W. A. 1968. Toward one discipline of scientific psychology. *Am. Psychol.* 23:782–85

177. Owens, W. A. 1969. Cognitive, noncognitive, and environmental correlates of mechanical ingenuity. *J. Appl. Psychol.* 53:199–208

178. Palmer, F. H. 1970. Socioeconomic status and intellective performance among Negro preschool boys. *Develop. Psychol.* 3:1–9

179. Pearson, C. 1969. Intelligence of Honolulu preschool children in relation to parent's education. *Child Develop.* 40: 647–50

180. Piers, E. V., Morgan, F. T. 1970. Free association as creativity training in children. *Proc. 78th Ann. Conv. APA*, 303–4

181. Pollack, R. H. 1969. Some implications of ontogenetic changes in perception. In *Studies in Cognitive Development*, ed. D. Elkind, J. H. Flavell, 365–407. New York: Oxford Univ. Press

182. Pollert, L. H., Feldhusen, J. F., Van Mondfrans, A. P., Treffinger, D. J. 1969. Role of memory in divergent thinking. *Psychol. Rep.* 25:151–56

183. Rees, A. H., Palmer, F. H. 1970. Factors related to change in mental test performance. *Develop. Psychol.* 3(2):1–57

184. Reppucci, N. D. 1969. Individual differences in the consideration of information among two-year-old children. *Proc. 77th Ann. Conv. APA*, 257–58

185. Roberts, D. M. 1968–69. Abilities and learning: a brief review and discussion of empirical studies. *J. Sch. Psychol.* 7:12–21

186. Rohwer, W. D. Jr. 1970. Mental elaboration and proficient learning. In *Minnesota Symposia on Child Psychology*, 4:220–60. Minneapolis: Univ. Minn. Press

187. Rosenberg, B. G., Sutton-Smith, B. 1969. Sibling age spacing effects upon cognition. *Develop. Psychol.* 1:661–68

188. Ross, J. E. 1970. Simplification of human abilities with age in four social class groups. *Proc. 78th Ann. Conv. APA*, 685–86

189. Ruda, E., Albright, L. E. 1968. Racial differences on selection instruments related to subsequent job performance. *Personnel Psychol.* 21:31–41

190. Schaefer, C. E. 1969. The prediction of creative achievement from a biographical inventory. *Educ. Psychol. Meas.* 29:431–37

191. Schaefer, C. E., Anastasi, A. 1968. A biographical inventory for identifying creativity in adolescent boys. *J. Appl. Psychol.* 52:42–48

192. Schaefer, E. S. 1969. A home tutoring program. *Children* 16:59–61

193. Schaie, K. W., Strother, C. R. 1968. The effect of time and cohort differences upon age changes in cognitive behavior. *Multivar. Behav. Res.* 3:259–94

194. Schaie, K. W., Strother, C. R. 1968. A cross-sequential study of age changes in cognitive behavior. *Psychol. Bull.* 70:671–80

195. Schaie, K. W., Strother, C. R. 1968. Cognitive and personality variables in college graduates of advanced age. In *Human behavior and aging: recent advances in research and theory*, ed. G. A. Talland, 281–318. New York: Academic

196. Schlesinger, I. M., Guttman, L. 1969. Smallest space analysis of intelligence and achievement tests. *Psychol. Bull.* 71:95–100

197. Schoenfeldt, L. F. 1968. The hereditary components of the Project TALENT two-day test battery. *Meas. Eval. Guid.* 1:130–40

198. Showler, W. K., Droege, R. C. 1969. Stability of aptitude scores for adults. *Educ. Psychol. Meas.* 29: 681–86

199. Shuter, R. 1968. *The Psychology of Musical Ability.* London: Methuen

200. Sitker, E. G., Meyers, C. E. 1969. Comparative structure of intellect in middle and lower class four-year-olds of two ethnic groups. *Develop. Psychol.* 1:592–604

201. Smith, M. S., Bissell, J. S. 1970. Report analysis: the impact of Head Start. *Harvard Educ. Rev.* 40:51–104

202. Society for Psychological Study of Social Issues 1969. Statement by

SPSSI on current IQ controversy: heredity versus environment. *Am. Psychol.* 24:1039–40

203. Stanley, J. C. 1971. Predicting college success of the educationally disadvantaged. *Science* 171:640–47

204. Tobias, S. 1969. Effect of creativity, response mode, and subject matter familiarity on achievement from programmed instruction. *J. Educ. Psychol.* 60:453–60

205. Torrance, E. P. 1969. Prediction of adult creative achievement among high school seniors. *Gifted Child Quart.* 13:223–29

206. Torrance, E. P., Wu, J. J., Gowan, J. C., Aliotti, N. C. 1970. Creative functioning of monolingual and bilingual children in Singapore. *J. Educ. Psychol.* 61:72–75

207. Tryk, H. E. Assessment in the study of creativity. See Ref. 8, 34–54

208. Tuddenham, R. D., Blumenkrantz, J. 1968. Age changes on AGCT: a longitudinal study of average adults. *J. Consult. Clin. Psychol.* 32:659–63

209. Tulkin, S. R. 1968. Race, class, family, and school achievement. *J. Pers. Soc. Psychol.* 9:31–37

210. Tulkin, S. R., Newbrough, J. R. 1968. Social class, race, and sex differences on the Raven (1956) Standard Progressive Matrices. *J. Consult. Clin. Psychol.* 32:400–6

211. Tyler, L. E., Ed. 1969. *Intelligence: some recurring issues.* New York: Van Nostrand

212. Vale, J. R., Vale, C. A. 1969. Individual differences and general laws in psychology. *Am. Psychol.* 24:1093–1108

213. Vandenberg, S. G. The nature and nurture of intelligence. See Ref. 86, 3–58

214. Vandenberg, S. G. 1969. A twin study of spatial ability. *Multivar. Behav. Res.* 4:273–94

215. Varela, J. A. 1969. Elaboration of Guilford's S-I model. *Psychol. Rev.* 76:332–36

216. Vernon, P. E. 1969. *Intelligence and Cultural Environment.* London: Methuen

217. Wallach, M. A., Kogan, N. 1965. *Modes of Thinking in Young Children.* New York: Holt, Rinehart & Winston. 357 pp.

218. Wallach, M. A., Wing, C. W. Jr. 1969. *The Talented Student.* New York: Holt, Rinehart & Winston

219. Ward, J. 1967. An oblique factorization of Wallach and Kogan's 'creativity' correlations. *Brit. J. Educ. Psychol.* 37:380–82

220. Ward, W. C. 1968. Creativity in young children. *Child Develop.* 39:737–54

221. Ibid. Reflection-impulsivity in kindergarten children, 867–74

222. Ward, W. C. 1969. Creativity and environmental cues in nursery school children. *Develop. Psychol.* 1:543–47

223. Ward, W. C. 1969. Rate and uniqueness in children's creative responding. *Child Develop.* 40:869–78

224. Ward, W. C., Kogan, N., Pankove, E. 1970. Motivation and ability in children's creativity. *Proc. 78th Ann. Conv. APA*, 285–86

225. Werner, E. E. 1969. Sex differences in correlations between children's IQs and measures of parental ability and environment ratings. *Develop. Psychol.* 1:280–85

226. Werner, E. E., Honzik, M. P., Smith, R. S. 1968. Prediction of intelligence and achievement at ten years from twenty months pediatric and psychologic examinations. *Child Develop.* 39:1063–75

227. Wesman, A. G. 1968. Intelligent testing. *Am. Psychol.* 23:267–74

228. Whimbey, A., Fischhof, V., Silikowitz, R. 1969. Memory span: a forgotten capacity. *J. Educ. Psychol.* 60:56–58

229. Whimbey, A. E., Ryan, S. F. 1969. Role of short-term memory and training in solving reasoning problems mentally. *J. Educ. Psychol.* 60:361–64

230. White, S. H. The national impact study of Head Start. See Ref. 6, 163–84

231. Willard, L. S. 1968. A comparison of Culture-Fair Test scores and individual intelligence test scores of disadvantaged Negro children. *J. Learn. Disabil.* 1:584–89

232. Willerman, L., Broman, S. H. 1970. Infant development, preschool IQ, and social class. *Child Develop.* 41:69–77

233. Williams, T. M., Fleming, J. W. 1969. Methodological study of the relationship between associative fluency and intelligence. *Develop. Psychol.* 1:155–62

234. Wing, C. W., Wallach, M. A. 1971.

College Admissions and the Psychology of Talent. New York: Holt, Rinehart & Winston

235. Wing, H. 1968. *Tests of Musical Ability and Appreciation.* Cambridge Univ. Press

236. Wiseman, S., Ed. 1967. *Intelligence and Ability: Selected Readings.* Harmondsworth: Penguin Books

237. Wolfle, D., Ed. 1969. *The Discovery of Talent.* Harvard Univ. Press

238. Wysocki, B. A., Wysocki, A. C. 1969. Cultural differences as reflected in Wechsler-Bellevue Intelligence (WBII) Test. *Psychol. Rep.* 25:95–101

239. Yando, R. M., Kagan, J. 1970. The effect of task complexity on reflection-impulsivity. *Cognitive Psychol.* 1:192–200

240. Zigler, E., Butterfield, E. C. 1968. Motivational aspects of changes in IQ Test performance of culturally deprived nursery school children. *Child Develop.* 39:1–14

241. Zimiles, H. Has evaluation failed compensatory education? See Ref. 6, 238–45

INSTRUCTIONAL PSYCHOLOGY[1]   181

ROBERT GLASER AND LAUREN B. RESNICK

University of Pittsburgh
Pittsburgh, Pennsylvania

INTRODUCTION

In increasing numbers, experimental psychologists are turning their enterprise to analyses and investigations of the instructional process. Evidence of the trend is quite clear. For example, the 1950 yearbook of the National Society for the Study of Education on learning and instruction (4) did not list Hull, Skinner, Spence, or Tolman in its index; the 1964 yearbook on the same topic (147) lists them in abundance, and the yearbook itself contains many chapters written by experimental psychologists (cf 125). Also, for the first time in 1969 a chapter on instructional psychology appeared in the *Annual Review of Psychology* (113). This trend appears to be unique not only to psychologists interested in learning, but also to developmental psychologists, social psychologists, and others. The increasing involvement of psychologists of such varied training and points of view with questions heretofore the preserve of "educational psychology" portends a change in the nature of psychological concern for instructional processes. There are many reasons for this surge of interest: the increasing prestige that has come from working on socially relevant as well as purely disciplinary problems; the new adventuresomeness of psychology in investigating more complex and implicitly cognitive behaviors; and the conviction that the interaction between task-oriented and discipline-oriented research will be mutually beneficial for society and for psychological science.

A related trend is inherent in the notion that psychological analysis is appropriate to the development of procedures for optimizing learning, as distinguished from the theoretical or empirical description of learning. Skinner (e.g. 296) has made this point in his work on a technology of teaching, and Bruner (38) has contrasted the nature of a theory of instruction with a theory of learning. Bruner points out that a theory of learning is descriptive, whereas a theory of instruction is prescriptive, in the sense that it sets forth rules concerning or specifying the most effective way of achieving knowledge or mastering skills. A theory of learning describes, after the fact, the conditions under which some behavior was acquired. A theory of in-

[1] The preparation of this review was carried out under the auspices of the Learning Research and Development Center at the University of Pittsburgh, supported in part by funds from the United States Office of Education, Department of Health, Education and Welfare. We wish to acknowledge the assistance of John Caruso, who conducted an extensive and thoughtful search and classification of the literature for this review.

struction is a normative theory in that it sets up a criterion and then states the conditions for meeting it. Groen & Atkinson (134) and Atkinson & Paulson (9) have indicated one possible way of going from a description of the learning process to a prescription for optimizing learning. They consider the optimization task to be clearly distinguished from finding the appropriate theoretical description in the first place. Nevertheless, a fundamental aspect of prescriptive procedures for the optimizing of learning is some description or hypothesis of the underlying learning processes involved. If one can employ statistical learning theory models, then the optimization methods of Atkinson & Paulson (9) seem to follow. However, such mathematical descriptions are not readily forthcoming for complex cognitive tasks, and optimization rules are required on the basis of our current knowledge and ability to model the learning process and describe its mechanisms.

Regardless of the kind of descriptive theory with which one works, certain characteristics of prescriptive theory for the optimization of learning seem reasonable to consider. They are: (a) a description of the state of knowledge to be achieved; (b) description of the initial state with which one begins; (c) actions which can be taken, or conditions that can be implemented to transform the initial state; (d) assessment of the transformation of the state that results from each action; and (e) evaluation of the attainment of the terminal state desired. Put another way: (a) analysis of the task properties of a knowledge domain; (b) diagnosis of the characteristics of the learner; (c) design of the instructional environment; (d) assessment of specific instructional effects; and (e) evaluation of generalized learning outcomes. We concentrate in this review on the first three of these concerns.

As increased progress is made toward contact between scientific endeavors and technological developments in education, a number of issues are emerging and problems for study are taking shape. In the past few years, certain areas have become more clearly defined, and in this review we attempt to identify these areas and provide a characterization and momentary definition of the field of instructional psychology. Also, it should be pointed out that in our effort to characterize emerging areas in some depth, our reporting of the literature is often illustrative rather than exhaustive, and we have paid little attention to certain standard areas such as programmed instruction, discovery learning, transfer studies, concept acquisition and rule learning, and instructional models and media. Nor, in the space allotted to us, have we been able to examine in detail the implications of certain burgeoning areas of psychology of apparent relevance for research on instruction such as imagery, memory organization, and perceptual learning, although our interpretations throughout are influenced by our understanding of theory and data in these and related domains.

THE ANALYSIS OF TASKS

As psychologists have turned their attention to instructional problems, they have been faced with the necessity of studying behavior with respect to tasks considerably more complex than those typically studied in the laboratory. This, in turn, has required the development of new ways of analyzing tasks and specifying the content of learning. Emphasis in the psychology of learning has in the past been upon *how* learning occurs, i.e. learning processes, and techniques for determining the content and properties of *what* is learned are not well worked out. Tasks in the learning laboratory have, for the most part, been selected according to what is convenient and manageable for experimental and theoretical analysis. Concentration on tasks artificially constructed for experimental purposes has meant that few learning psychologists have, until recently, confronted the problem of analyzing complex tasks in terms that allow access to psychological theory and data and yet still preserve some fidelity to the real-life character of the tasks themselves.

For the psychologist concerned with instructional processes, however, the problem of task analysis is a central one. Analytic description of what is to be learned facilitates instruction by attempting to define clearly what it is that an expert in a subject matter domain has learned; for example, what it is that distinguishes a skilled reader from an unskilled one. When this analysis identifies classes of behaviors whose properties as learning tasks are known or can be systematically studied, then inferences concerning optimal instructional processes can be formulated and tested. The analysis of instructional tasks by either rational or experimental means is a relatively new enterprise and comprises a set of activities that appears to be an important part of instructional psychology. It should be pointed out, however, that this enterprise is still relatively undefined, and that we review studies here which are not necessarily instructionally oriented, but which are illustrative of how the properties of complex tasks, particularly school-like tasks, can be analyzed.

Task analysis, as the term is used here, is characterized by the description of tasks in terms of the demands they place on such basic psychological processes as attention, perception, and linguistic processing. Further, since the individual's capacities change over time, task analyses reflect current knowledge and assumptions on the part of psychologists concerning the processes available at different stages of learning or development.

Implicit in the work of many individuals concerned with instruction is a distinction between the subject matter structure as it has been organized by the scientists and scholars in a discipline and the way in which structures in the discipline ought to be formulated for students just acquiring knowledge about that discipline (e g 38, 102, 109, 121, 122, 314). The organizations employed by the expert are not necessarily the structures most useful in facilitating the learning of an individual at a particular developmental level or at a particular level of sophistication in the subject matter. Since advanced knowledge structures may not be good structures for elementary learning, research related to instruction needs to concentrate on the determination of units, structures, and sequences which serve to facilitate learning for the novice.

CATEGORIES OF LEARNING AND LEARNING HIERARCHIES

Taxonomies.—One way of describing tasks is through the use of a taxonomy of behavior categories into which tasks can be sorted. A set of such categories can be useful in facilitating identification of psychologically isomorphic tasks—tasks that, although differing in specific subject matter content, share similar characteristics with respect to optimal conditions for learning. Taxonomies have been a particular feature of attempts to apply the psychology of learning to instructional problems (103, 109, 214, 222). Certain of these attempts grew out of the requirements for technical training in the military (221).

Need for a taxonomy was documented in the book edited by Melton (214) entitled *Categories of Human Learning.* In addition to discussing the role of taxonomies in the development of a science, Melton points out that the need for a technology of human learning has highlighted the issues surrounding the taxonomy of learning processes:

> When one is confronted with a decision to use massed or distributed practice, to insist on information feedback or not to insist on it, to arrange training so as to maximize or minimize requirements for contiguous stimulus differentiation, etc., and discovers that the guidance received from experimental research and theory is different for rote learning, for skill learning, and for problem solving, taxonomic issues become critical and taxonomic ambiguities become frustrating, to say the least (p. 327).

Taxonomies can be established (*a*) on the basis of the different learning conditions required for different classes of tasks, and/or (*b*) on the basis of inferred processes which underlie the performance of the tasks. A major effort in categorizing tasks according to learning requirements has been made in the widely read book by Gagné, written in 1965 (104) and revised in 1970 (109). In the revised edition, Gagné modifies his description of eight varieties of learning that are differentiated from each other in terms of the conditions required to bring them about. In a detailed presentation, he attempts to show that each variety of learning begins with a different state of the organism and ends with a different capability for performance. Furthermore, the conditions that influence learning, i.e. the external, independent variables in the situation, are not necessarily the same for each of the varieties of learning.

Hierarchies of learning tasks.—In the new edition, Gagné gives increasing prominence to his notion of learning hierarchies (102) as the basic theoretical conception in this book. The theory states that the defining aspect of the eight types of learning is that they are arranged in hierarchical order, i.e. the simpler types being prerequisite states for learning the more complex types. The conditions for chaining, for example, require that the individual has previously learned stimulus response connections available to him so that they can indeed be chained. In general, with respect to the eight varieties of learning, the prerequisite conditions are such that problem solving requires learned rules as prerequisites; rules, since they consist of a chain of two or more concepts, require concept learning as a prerequisite; concept learning requires the discrimination of properties of objects or events, and hence multiple discriminations are prerequisite; and prerequisite to discrimination learning are the simpler types of learning. The new edition treats learning hierarchies as a potential tool for instructional technology, particularly in connection with the design of instructional sequences and curricula. Questions of learning readiness and intellectual development are discussed briefly with relevance to hierarchical analysis.

Present conceptions of learning hierarchies, based on some years of experimentation with them, are of current interest. Gagné himself (107) has made some clarifications concerning the question of what are the entities (capabilities) that make up a learning hierarchy; the answer given is that they are "intellectual skills," what some writers have called cognitive strategies, and not entities of verbalizable knowledge. They answer the question "what the individual can do" and avoid statements about "what the individual knows." "I mean that what learning hierarchies describe is, in computer language, subroutines of a program; what they do not describe is the facts or propositions retrievable from memory as verbalizable statements" (107, p. 4). Certain failures of instructional sequences based on learning hierarchy analysis to show evidence of positive transfer from one level of the hierarchy to the next have occurred (e.g. 218); these failures are attributed to the fact that the hierarchy component described what the learner needed to know rather than the intellectual operations that he could perform. Thus, Gagné explicitly excludes verbalizable knowledge from consideration and makes little contact in his present formulation with the large amount of work going on in meaningful verbal learning and the organization of memory.

Various approaches to the validation of hypothesized hierarchical sequences are discussed by Gagné (107) and Resnick & Wang (255). The approaches have been of two kinds, studies of transfer relationships and psychometric studies of hierarchical ordering. Transfer studies postulate that two tasks are hierarchically related when one task produces positive transfer to the other, i.e. learning the subordinate task as a prerequisite results in fewer trials to learn the superordinate task. The original studies by Gagné and his colleagues (111, 112) constructed hierarchies for a sequence of instruction on a limited topic and investigated transfer effects between various skill levels in the course of acquiring the terminal behavior. Studies of such relatively extensive instructional sequences are rare (e.g. 218); however, carefully controlled studies of two- or three-step transfer hierarchies are beginning to appear. Such studies indicate significant positive transfer effects which have implications for curriculum design and for the psychological analysis of the acquisition of complex behavior. A study by Resnick, Siegel & Kresh (254) showed that subjects who learned the tasks in optimal order (i.e. the simpler task first, then the more complex) learned the complex task in fewer trials than subjects who began with the complex task. In addition, the subjects who succeeded in learning the complex task first showed evidence of having acquired the simpler task. This latter finding is quite significant from an instructional point of view, since it implies that all students need not go through a learning sequence step by small step, but that certain students can take large leaps and learn the subordinate skills in the process.

Psychometric studies (62, 327) have employed Guttman scaling techniques or similar procedures to investigate the sequenced dependencies among tasks in a hypothesized hierarchy. Scaling data indicate the extent to which performance on lower order tasks can reliably be predicted from information concerning performance on higher order tasks: i.e. tasks are hierarchically related when all individuals who can perform the higher-order task can also do the lower-order one, and those who fail the lower-order task reliably fail the higher-order one. Psychometric data of this kind are of only suggestive utility for instructional purposes, since many tasks might display the relationships just described without the lower-order tasks necessarily providing positive transfer in the learning of the higher-order ones. Thus, psychometric procedures must be viewed primarily as a heuristic means of searching for task relations which can then be tested by transfer experiments.

However, another use of psychometrically validated hierarchies can be considered. Once ordering of component behaviors is established, a hierarchical structure provides a space in which individuals can be placed with respect to their level of knowledge. Each sequential objective can define a test exercise which an individual can pass or fail and by which his placement at the appropriate point in an instructional sequence can be determined. Passing an objective implies that the individual should be further tested on the next superordinate objective; failing implies that he should be tested on subordinate objectives in order to determine whether lack of competence is the result of inadequate performance on prerequisite subobjectives or the result of inadequate instruction on the new objective. Such a structure provides a decision tree for the application of tailored testing procedures where an individual's prior performance determines his next test exercise (82, 127).

Of special interest for psychological and instructional theory is the question of what a prerequisite relationship between tasks might mean. In general terms, the lower-order task is said to be a component of the higher-order task. However, there are several possible relationships that might exist between component and superordinate tasks. The lower-order task might be one of a number of components of the more complex task, each of which can be acquired independently of the others, but all of which must be combined to produce the higher-order performance. Alternatively, the lower-order tasks may themselves be hierarchically related to one another, constituting a sequenced progression leading to increasingly complex performance. Lower-order tasks may also be competencies which facilitate the learning of the more complex task but are dropped out in the more "skillful" performance, or the lower-order tasks might function as heuristics for discovering or inventing procedures for carrying out the more complex task. Research along these lines, investigating the acquisition of complex performance, would be especially relevant for instructional psychology.

The use and implications of learning hierarchy concepts for the design of curriculum sequences is currently undergoing examination (107, 252, 256). A recent monograph (256) applies behavior analysis procedures to the problem of designing a sequence of learning objectives that might provide an optimal match for the child's "natural" sequence of acquisition of mathematical skills and concepts. Tasks involved in children's learning of the concept of number are analyzed in detail. These include seriation, comparison of sets, counting, the correspondence of numbers and objects, and addition and subtraction. In the first part of the analyses, competent performance in the tasks representing these objectives is described by informal use of a technique similar to protocol analysis (228). In the second part, a separate hierarchical analysis of the prerequisite behaviors is carried out for each of the component stages in performance. Analysis of this kind appears to provide a basis for teaching a given component task. The detailed analysis does not become part of the formal curriculum but provides information about the learning difficulty of the various tasks, e.g. demands made on memory and perceptual functioning, which assists in identifying instructional requirements and which makes curriculum design more amenable to experimental study.

THE EXPERIMENTAL ANALYSIS OF TASKS

We turn now to experiments that directly attempt to determine what is learned in the case of specific tasks. Studies have appeared with increasing frequency which are designed to analyze the nature of complex cognitive performances. Studies of this kind impress us as capable of discovering the properties of tasks that are likely to influence the way in which the tasks are learned. Although this instructional concern is not explicit in all of the studies we mention, exemplary studies are considered here which involve analysis of reading and spelling tasks, reasoning and language processing tasks, arithmetic tasks, and classification tasks.

Reading and spelling.—Gibson (117–120) has suggested that once a child begins the progression from spoken language to written language there are three phases involved which are roughly sequential: learning to differentiate graphic symbols; learning to decode letters to sound; and using progressively higher orders of structure. In the first phase, a child must learn to differentiate written characters from one another. Gibson's experiments lead to the conclusion that what children learn as they improve in their ability to discriminate letter-like forms are the dimensions of difference which are critical for distinguishing one letter from another. These include such characteristic features as whether the straight segment of a letter is horizontal, vertical, or oblique; whether its curved section is closed, open vertically, or open horizontally; whether there are line intersections, cyclical changes or symmetry, etc. Experiments show that letters which are differentiated by many of these features are generally less confused in the course of learning than letters which are differentiated by only a few of them. These findings suggest strategies for the grouping and sequencing of stimuli in discrimination training in order to optimize the learning of letters.

Other work (300) suggests that the recognition of letters and words is based upon at least two kinds of information. One is the distinctive features of the individual letters. The second is statistical information or sequential dependencies among the letters—for example, information which indicates that the final letter of an English sequence *an* is probably *d*, *t* or *y*. The combined featural and statistical information serves to permit identification of a particular sequence of letters. It is proposed that a reader uses such statistical information about probabilities of occurrence of particular letters, and that this permits him to identify letters and words which he may not be able to identify when the letter is given in isolation.

In decoding letters to sound, a question that arises is what graphemic units need to be discriminated so that they can be associated with particular sounds which the child has already learned to hear and reproduce. Gibson (117, 119) suggests that the smallest components in written English are "spelling patterns." A spelling pattern is a cluster of graphemes which in a given environment of letters has an invariant pronunciation according to the rules of English. Experiments in word perception show that these patterns function as units which children learn and which facilitate the decoding process. The suggestion for instruction is that material designed to teach reading should enhance the opportunity to detect these correspondence rules in the structure of English orthography. Once detected, use of these structures can be reinforcing to the student in the sense that uncertainty is reduced and faster processing of the word occurs.

The structure of English orthography and its relation to sounds has been studied in detail by Venezky (322) on the basis of an analysis of the spellings and pronunciation of 20,000 most common English words. Orthographic structures are differentiated in terms of spelling patterns, as mentioned above, and the systematic influences of graphemic environments, i.e. the position of graphemes, stress in pronunciation, and functional units of meaning (morphemic boundaries). Venezky concerns himself primarily with the print to sound translation, emphasizing that it is this translation which is the language skill unique to beginning reading. Interesting insights for the re-examination of reading instruction are provided. For example, an alternative is suggested to the usual procedure, common to almost all new "linguistic" approaches to teaching reading, of presenting only a single value of each letter early in instruction. The alternative approach is based upon early discrimination of graphemic environments which may allow the learner to generalize more readily to new words because he discriminates the different rules involved. For example, short and long pronunciation of the letter *a* might be taught simultaneously, with emphasis on the role of the final *e* in modifying pronunciation of the first vowel.

Also considered are different requirements for instruction when the learning of spelling to sound patterns are based primarily on orthographic convention or on phonological habits. For example, initial *c* has different pronunciations in the words *cent* and *caught*; similarly, medial *n* is differently pronounced in *anchor* and *vanity*. The choice between soft and hard *c* in the first two words is primarily dependent on conventions of orthography; thus, learners would need to be directly taught the two different pronunciations for *c* and when to employ each. The difference between *n* in the last two words, however, is primarily phonological; since native speakers of English would perform the phonological changes as part of their learned speech, they would not have to be taught to do so when learning to read.

Related problems of sound to print and print to sound translation are examined in a paper by Carol Chomsky (51) which considers English orthography from the point of view of phonological theory within the framework of transformational linguistics (52). Carol Chomsky's general point is that the conventional spelling of words corresponds "more closely to an underlying abstract level of representation within the sound system of the language than it does to the surface phonetic form that the words assume in the spoken language" (51, p. 288). Like the syntactic structures of transformational grammar, phonological theory from a transformational view describes general rules by which abstract underlying forms are converted into particular phonetic realizations. The argument is that, viewed in this way, English spelling appears more regular than a purely phonetic criterion might indicate. Consider such words as anxious-anxiety; courage-courageous; critical-criticize; revise-revision; illustrate-illustrative. What is common to these pairs of words is not their surface form, i.e. their phonetic representation, because they are pronounced differently. Rather, what is common is an underlying form that can be called a "lexical spelling," to which the orthography corresponds quite closely.

The suggestion is that the mature reader seeks and recognizes not the surface grapheme-phoneme correspondences, but rather the correspondences of written symbols to the abstract lexical spelling of words. "Letters represent segments in lexical spelling, not sounds. It is the phonological rule system of the language, which the reader commands, that relates the lexical segments to sounds in a systematic fashion" (51, p. 296). In order to progress to the more complex stages of reading and spelling, a child must abandon the assumption of surface grapheme-phoneme regularities and come to use this hypothesized transformational system. Poor readers may be characterized by not being able to make this crucial transition. In practice, this shift could be aided by discussing word families with children to bring out the variety of pronunciations that are associated with individual spellings, considering, for example, such words as major-majority, history-historical-historian, nature-natural. In this way the child would learn that orthography bears an indirect rather than a direct relation to his pronunciation. In general, the basic mechanism implied by Carol Chomsky is that the development of this sort of competence depends on recognizing the relationships between a learned stratum of vocabulary "including Latinate forms and a network of affixes which account for a large portion of surface phonetic variations" (pp. 299–300). The acquisition of literacy from this point of view may extend over a longer period of time than ordinarily assumed, and is closely interwoven with other aspects of the child's linguistic development.

Reasoning and language processing.—A further example of the interaction between the structural properties of language and task performance is provided by the work of Clark (54). This analysis demonstrates that the principal difficulties inherent in certain reasoning problems may be due to the form of the language in which the problems are stated. The language in which the problems are stated requires that the person store and search through the information in a certain way; certain processes used in understanding language make the information more or less available and accessible, and more or less difficult to match with congruent information in memory. Thus, Clark's theory states that certain linguistic principles which describe the structure of language can be used as a basis for predicting or accounting for aspects of problem-solving behavior.

The reasoning tasks studied and analyzed are two-term and three-term series problems. A three-term series problem consists of two propositions and a question: e.g. "If John is better than Dick, and Pete is worse than Dick, then who is best?" A two-term series problem is of the form: "If John is better than Pete, then who is worse?" The wording of these problems is critical. For example, most research has shown that the three-term problem given above is easier to solve than the following one: "If Dick is worse than John, and Dick is better than Pete, then who is best?" The difference occurs even though both problems present the same information, at least superficially. Clark proposes an explanation based on psycholinguistic principles of how the language of the problems is understood and how the structure of the language influences problem solution. Experimental data support this explanation, and application of the theory to similar experiments with children suggests developmental changes in the ability to comprehend relational propositions. Studies of this kind raise questions concerning the form of verbal problems presented in the course of instruction and suggest variables which might influence the teachability of reasoning abilities.

Problem solving in the context of natural language also has been investigated in algebra word problems (240). Using as a point of reference computer programs capable of solving such problems, solution processes were studied in high school and college students. Of particular interest were the individual differences observed in subject protocols. These differences were apparent in (a) the use of direct transformations of the information contained in a problem in contrast to the use of auxiliary information that went beyond the information presented; and (b) in primary reliance on either physical-spatial or verbal representations of the problem situation.

Studies by Huttenlocher et al (156, 157) investigate how the structure of the verbal statement of a relationship—the way in which the subject, object, and relation between them are verbally described—influences understanding of the statement. For relational statements such as, "The red block is under the green block," the question asked was how the performance of a child in placing blocks is influenced by the relation between the verbal statement and the extralinguistic situation it describes. With 6- to 9-year-olds, it is clear that the task is easier when the movable block is the subject rather than the object of the instructor's statement. While there were improvements with age, the difference in difficulty between the two kinds of statements showed no marked developmental changes. One implication from these findings is that the requirements of a task influence what the child tries to understand from a particular statement, and the form of the instructor's statement must be appropriately coordinated with the extralinguistic situation in order for it to be readily understood (see also 330, 331).

A study by Frase (96) examines the structure of large segments of text material and how this structure might influence inferential processes which in turn control learning and retention of the text information. Experimental text passages were designed so that the depth of inferential reasoning from certain primary assertions could be quantified. Frase predicted that the retention of facts in a passage would be a function of the number of encounters with these facts that occurred in the course of an inductive reasoning chain established by task requirements. In scanning a passage for information necessary to draw required conclusions, text which is not relevant to the conclusion to be drawn will receive only minimal processing by the reader and these items will not be remembered. High-level inferences which engage the reader in more encounters and re-encounters with certain items of information were predicted to cause greater retention for these items.

As hypothesized, experimental results showed that when the structure of a passage predicted that a certain text item would be a component of a problem solution, the item was higher in recall than for items which according to predictions would not be used. Requiring an individual to analyze a text more deeply enhanced the retention of text information but had little effect on the retention of deeper inferences that could be drawn from the text.

Arithmetic tasks.—The structure of the task in drill and practice in simple arithmetic problems has been studied by Suppes et al (315, 317, 318). The main feature of the analysis identified structural characteristics that contributed to the difficulty of a problem. Analysis of the data obtained indicated that the number of steps required to solve a problem was most important for analysis of the processes underlying performance. The number of steps required was analyzed into three classes of processes: (*a*) transformation—transforming the problem into a standard equational form where the unknown stands by itself as the only term to the right of the equal sign; (*b*) operation—the number of arithmetic operations that must be performed; and (*c*) memory—the number of digits that must be held in memory. Operations and memory steps enter into problem processing after transformation has taken place. In analyzing a problem, the total number of transformation, operation, and memory steps are determined (although some students will solve a problem by a shorter or longer method). Thus, for example, the problem $25 + 26 = 17 + \_\_$ has a maximum of 14 steps, namely, one transformation step, 6 operation steps, and 7 memory steps; in contrast, the problem $5 + 0 = \_\_$ has a minimum of 0 steps. Total number of steps in a problem, plus two magnitude variables, the magnitude of the largest number and the magnitude of the smallest number, were entered into regression equations to predict problem difficulty. In general, the findings indicated that compared with the influence of magnitude variables, the number of steps was the aspect of the structure of the problem that most influenced problem solution. Particularly critical was the way in which the structure of the problem required the use of memory.

Further studies of arithmetic problem solving by Suppes and Groen (133, 316) explored alternate solution processes for addition of single digit numbers with sums up to 18. It was hypothesized that for a given problem, different solution "models" would require a different number of steps, and therefore should take different amounts of time to solve. For example, $2 + 7 = \_\_$ could be solved by incrementing by 2 (two steps) and then incrementing by 7 (seven steps) for a total of nine steps in all. Alternatively, the problem could be solved by setting a counter equal to 7 (one step) and then incrementing by 2 for a total of three steps. On the basis of latency data for problems of this kind, Groen and Suppes suggest that first-grade children typically use the model of setting the counter equal to the higher of the two addends, regardless of its position, and then incrementing by the smaller.

Classification tasks.—Two recent articles by Klahr & Wallace (180, 181) report information processing analyses, using computer simulation methods, of classification tasks drawn from the Piagetian literature. In the earlier study, Klahr & Wallace (180) analyze seven tasks, ranging from simple sorting on the basis of perceptual features to hierarchical classification and class inclusion problems. They identify a set of fundamental processes that constitute the "building blocks" out of which computer routines capable of performing each of the tasks can be assembled. These processes include such functions as noticing a value (feature) of an object, identifying values common to two objects, and finding all objects with a given value. No empirical test of the adequacy of this analysis is reported, although several tests are suggested. Among these the most interesting is one that involves teaching subjects all of the hypothesized fundamental processes and then determining whether they are able to solve the classification problems. An interesting extension of this notion is predicting, through computer simulation or logical analysis, the kinds of errors that would be made by subjects lacking particular processes. It would then be possible to match these predictions with errors actually made by subjects whose repertoire lacked the particular processes under study.

In the second study, Klahr & Wallace (181) undertake a more detailed analysis of one of the tasks considered earlier (class inclusion). This analysis employs a new method of describing information processing models of cognition, the "production system," proposed by Newell & Simon (229). A production system is comprised of a collection of independent rules, each consisting of an action and the conditions appropriate for performing that action. Using production systems, models can be set up to examine the effects of addition or deletion of particular processes on overall performance capabilities. Such models may be particularly useful in suggesting the effects upon performance of new capabilities acquired either through developmental growth or instruction.

No summary of this area of task analysis seems possible at this time. The studies we have chosen to define the field come from a variety of sources and only some of them have an explicit instructional orientation. What is especially striking, however, is their convergence on the analysis of performance in terms of the interactions between task structure variables and the learning and information processing capacities of the individual. Such an emphasis seems to us to be crucial for an instructional psychology which seeks to explicate the conditions under which educationally relevant learning takes place.

EARLY EDUCATION

The past 5 years have witnessed an increasing involvement of psychologists in programs of educational intervention, particularly in the areas of early childhood and compensatory education. This movement of psychologists into the field of education has coincided with an increase in concern with the ways in which intellectual development might best be enhanced in young children, particularly those from "disadvantaged" backgrounds. As a result, large numbers of developmental psychologists have begun to study problems of "instruction"—the deliberate fostering of intellectual development. In this section we will review the recent psychological literature on early educational intervention. In a subsequent section we will consider a body of basic resarch literature on the training of basic cognitive abilities, including Piagetian concepts, which provides a relevant empirical basis for discussion of some of the issues raised with respect to educational intervention.

Most of the publishing in the general area of early education continues to be analytic and theoretical rather than experimental or empirical. A number of conferences resulting in publications (37, 70, 144, 203, 243), together with collections of reprinted or invited articles (50, 74), have provided forums for the contrast of various points of view concerning early education. These nonempirical and review writings are of several types: (*a*) discussion of the psychological rationale for early intervention programs (e.g. 72, 155, 185, 335); (*b*) proposals based on various psychological theories and some data, for the character of optimal intervention programs (e.g. 243); (*c*) analysis of existing programs in psychological terms (e.g. 77, 153, 185); (*d*) discussions of social and family variables (e.g. maternal teaching styles, 145, 146) which are believed to provide the explanation for observed difficulties in educating certain groups of children. More empirical studies, often circulating only in mimeographed form, have been either evaluative reports on relatively extended intervention programs (e.g. 132, 173, 182, 242, 332), or reports of brief studies designed to support a theoretical position concerning the appropriate form of early intervention (e.g. 26, 27, 334).

CONTENT OF PRESCHOOL INSTRUCTION

One of the more striking characteristics of the psychological literature on early educational intervention is its attention to questions of content as well as method of instruction. Virtually all psychologists currently addressing the problem of early education accept cognitive development as a major goal of intervention efforts. As if to highlight the shift in emphasis from an earlier concern with socio-emotional development, the Social Science Research Council conference on early education, which led to publication of the book by Hess & Bear (144), focused explicitly on "the environmental conditions facilitating *mental* growth . . ." (p. 223).

Although there is a general consensus that cognitive skills are a primary concern, there is considerable disagreement both on the kinds of cognitive skills to be taught and the methods of teaching to be used. Maccoby & Zellner (203), in a book reviewing the work of ten different sponsors of federally funded Follow Through programs (for primary grade children who are "graduates" of Head Start), distinguished between two major theoretical positions which provided bases for programs they studied: reinforcement learning theory (in the tradition of B. F. Skinner) and cognitive development theory (derived in large part from Jean Piaget). While this distinction appears to work reasonably well with respect to motivation and incentives (203, Chapter 4), it does not seem to adequately represent the variety of empirical and theoretical bases for content selection of the various intervention programs. In particular, the dichotomy is incapable of adequately describing the work of those who seek to apply behavioral analysis to Piagetian and related tasks in the course of defining curriculum, nor does it account for all varieties of language and perceptual development emphases. The following discussion reviews some of the varying views of what constitutes appropriate curriculum content for the early educational period.

Enrichment.—The earliest view—and perhaps still the most dominant in terms of actual practice in the field—is derived from an analysis of the "deficits" observable in the cognitive-academic repertoires of disadvantaged children as they enter school. Analysis of these handicaps typically leads to a general enrichment model for intervention (e.g. 72, 182, 220), with heavy emphasis on language development. Programs that derive curriculum from this point of view typically emphasize self-concept and motivational variables as well as strictly cognitive skills (see especially 182).

Language training.—The emphasis on language in the enrichment programs is derived both from direct observation of differences in the language performance of disadvantaged and middle-class children, and from an initial acceptance of verbally loaded IQ scores as a measure of success of intervention. On the whole, these programs have not developed detailed theories of the nature of language development itself, nor very detailed proposals as to what language skills to focus on and how to best teach these skills. Much more detailed work in the area of language instruction has been done by Cazden (48), Bereiter & Engelmann (23, 24, 236), Blank & Solomon (25–27), and Risley, Reynolds & Hart (258). Several language development programs are also described in a monograph edited by Brottman (37).

Cazden (48), basing her work on current theories concerning the acquisition of grammar, compared the effects of two forms of language training for children under $3\frac{1}{2}$ years: (*a*) "expansion," in which the tutor, in the context of a game, systematically expanded the child's grammatically incomplete sentences into complete sentences with the same referential meaning; and (*b*) "modeling" or "expatiation," in which the tutor provided many well-formed sentences, not necessarily expansions of the child's statements, as models of grammatical speech. Contrary to expectations, modeling—the provision of a rich variety of verbal stimulation—proved more effective than expansion of children's speech, at least in the intensive one-to-one tutorial situation studied.

Blank & Solomon (26) have developed a tutorial language program aimed at developing abstract thinking. The child is required to answer questions and follow verbal instructions in a process aimed at developing selective attention, categorization and class exclusion, imagery and prediction of future events, verbal mediation, cause and effect and sequential reasoning, awareness of possessing language, and separation of the word from its referent. Comparisons of IQ gains for tutored and untutored children (including those who had an equivalent number of sessions with an adult who did not use the special techniques develped by Blank & Solomon) showed significantly higher gains for the tutored children.

Bereiter & Engelmann's (23, 24, 236) language training program differs from Cazden's and Blank's in both the specificity with which learning objectives are stated and sequenced and the approach to instruction. Objectives for the language curriculum are derived from an analysis of the language necessary to profit from instruction. The result is an English curriculum focusing on sentence frames that convey basic information (e.g. "This is a ball"; "This ball is not red"); logical operators (e.g. "all," "only," "some," "maybe"); and basic concepts (shapes, sizes, colors, etc) with an emphasis throughout on processes of careful description and logical deduction. The curriculum material is organized into a sequenced and scripted program which is used in small group, direct teaching sessions. The program, now available commercially, has been widely used with disadvantaged preschool children. Results of trials have been reported both by the authors of the program (23, 236) and by other investigators (174, 333). IQ gains of 10 to 30 points in a year have been reported.

Risley and his colleagues (258) have used modeling and systematic reinforcement procedures to develop a variety of language competencies in disadvantaged 3- and 4-year-old children. Assessment of the training procedures is made by collecting samples of the children's language behavior in the course of regular school activities, rather than through the use of tests. Among the skills developed in these experiments are rate and grammatical character of spontaneous speech, appropriate timing of talking, verbal social skills (such as "good morning"), narration skills, immediate and delayed imitation of verbal statements of varying lengths and forms, and accurate description of one's own behavior. One of the training methods was structured so that social reinforcement from the teacher and access to play materials were contingent upon successively longer and more complex verbalizations by the child. Other training was conducted in individual or small group sessions, all of which used systematic social or material reinforcement of appropriate language behavior.

The problem of assessing language development in children has continued to trouble the field. As mentioned, there has been continued reliance on IQ measures, particularly the verbally loaded Stanford-Binet and Peabody tests. Recently, the Illinois Test of Psycholinguistic Abilities (ITPA) has also been widely used. A paper by Stern (306) discusses some of the problems inherent in measuring language development and describes some specific tests. A much more extended consideration of language assessment problems is given by Cazden (49), who discusses various kinds of goals for language development, including both affective and cognitive goals, and considers measurement strategies, including naturalistic observation, special testing situations, and standardized tests.

Piaget-derived curricula.—Concurrent with the general increase of interest over the past decade in the work of Jean Piaget has been an increased search for the relevance of Piaget's theories and data to questions of instruction (e.g. 8, 19, 77, 101, 293, 313). In the area of early childhood education, two individuals, Stendler-Lavatelli (305) and Kamii (172), have been particularly active in attempting to derive the outlines of a curriculum structure from Piaget's work. Stendler-Lavatelli has outlined a set of activities designed to teach conservation of number and continuous quantities, relativity of perspective, and seriation and classification skills. The proposed program has been implemented on an experimental basis, but no data on effectiveness have been reported. Over a period of several years, Kamii and her collaborators have elaborated a curriculum stressing both socio-emotional and cognitive objectives. Socio-emotional objectives include the development of curiosity and intrinsically motivated involvement in learning, of which more will be said below. Cognitive objectives are elaborated in detail for four domains: physical knowledge (knowledge of the physical characteristics of objects); social knowledge (facts concerning social organization and convention, reactions of people, language labels, etc); logico-mathematical knowledge (classification, seriation, elementary number concepts); and representation (pictures, words, symbols, images). Emphasis throughout is on the development of active processing of information, consonant with Piaget's view of intelligence and learning as an adaptive and "constructive" process rather than on receptive acquisition of facts. Operationally speaking, this appears to imply reliance on manipulative games and activities rather than on verbal instruction. Development of perceptual skills is explicitly minimized as an objective, since perception is seen as a process of receiving information through the senses rather than constructing reality through actions. Elsewhere Kamii (171) has discussed problems of evaluation in preschool education, and has described methods of measuring socio-emotional, perceptual-motor, and cognitive objectives drawn from a Piagetian framework.

Early academic training.—A few individuals have emphasized the possibility and desirability of simply moving the typical primary grade curriculum into the preschool. Moore (223) has developed a method of teaching reading and writing by permitting the child to explore an especially responsive electric typewriter. Fowler (89, 90) has used game-like activities in the teaching of reading to 2- and 3-year-olds. Staats (302, 303) has reported on a program of early teaching of alphabet and word recognition and simple arithmetic using a few minutes a day of carefully programmed and systematically reinforced practice. Finally, the Bereiter-Englemann program, in addition to special work in language as described above, begins direct instruction in reading and arithmetic with 4-year-olds, using programmed small group lessons characterized by active oral responding. Kindergarten children taught by this method have achieved first- and second-grade level scores on reading and arithmetic tests (23, 236)

An approach that bridges pre-academic and academic concerns is that of Resnick (252, 256). Resnick's approach to the analysis of subject matter has been mentioned in an earlier section of this review. The method has been applied to a variety of early school learning objectives and also to objectives derived from the Piagetian analysis of cognitive development, with the aim of identifying successively simpler prerequisites that could be incorporated into a preschool curriculum. This work has yielded a set of hierarchically sequenced curricula stressing the development of the number concept and basic classificatory concepts. The validity of these sequences is being tested both in a series of laboratory experiments (255, 327) and in classroom trials (328).

Perceptual skill development.—A few psychologists have seen the preschool period as one in which a major task is the development of perceptual organization and integration. Several psychologists (e.g. 77, 153, 185) have analyzed the Montessori program, with particular reference to its stress on perceptual or sensory development and the shaping of attention. In accord with these analyses, one preliminary empirical study has demonstrated a differential improvement in performance as opposed to verbal aspects of intelligence on the part of children in a Montessori preschool program (309).

Apart from Montessori, for whom perceptual training is indirect, a function of her view of how conceptual intelligence develops, the observation of perceptual deficit has most often occasioned attempts at using with preschool children perceptual motor programs originally developed for special and remedial education of older children. A carefully sequenced program designed explicitly for preschool children has been developed by Rosner (269, 271). Results of controlled trials of the visual training program have demonstrated its effectiveness in raising scores on WPPSI performance subtests, the Gesell Copyforms, and the Rutgers Drawing Test at least to age norms after 6–8 weeks of intensive tutoring (270, 273).

Cognitive "socialization."—In contrast to theories that attempt to identify specific cognitive content as the appropriate emphasis of the preschool, Hess (143, 146) and Maccoby (202), among others, have suggested that the primary goals of preschool education fall in the realm of establishing basic strategies for dealing with information, habits of attention, and reflective "styles" of cognitive behavior. Hess' ideas are based on his own studies and those of others (see 100) concerning differences in cognitive and linguistic behavior of middle- and lower-class parents toward their children. Hess argues that it is not that disadvantaged children have not learned anything prior to school, but rather that they have learned the wrong things (with respect to school expectations). The job of the compensatory school then is to "resocialize" the child into modes of thinking that are more compatible with the demands of the school.

Some empirical support for the emphasis on general cognitive socialization as opposed to the training of specific skills or knowledge is perhaps offered by the findings of two intervention studies. Weikart (333) compared the effects of three preschool curricula: (a) the "cognitively oriented curriculum" of the Ypsilanti Perry Preschool Project (see 332), built in part on Piagetian principles, and incorporating language training similar to that advocated by Cazden (48) and sociodramatic play of the kind developed by Smilansky (298); (*b*) the Bereiter-Engelmann language training program described above; and (*c*) (as a control group) a traditional nursery school program incorporating projects designed to develop cognitive skills and information. To the investigator's surprise, there were no significant differences among the three groups on most of the criteria, and all three showed large gains in Stanford-Binet IQ (e.g. mean gains from 27.5 to 30.2 points for the 3-year-olds).

Palmer (242) trained 2- and 3-year-olds over a period of 8 months in a tutorial setting (2 hours per week) using a structured curriculum which emphasized basic vocabulary and logical concepts assumed to mediate later learning. In addition to a no-treatment control group, there was also a treated control group (later renamed the "discovery" group) comprised of children who had an equivalent number of unstructured sessions, using the same materials but with no particular concept taught. The discovery group performed as well as the structured training group on most measures, with both these groups showing significantly better performance than the untreated control group.

These findings have led the investigators to conclude that the primary role of a specific curriculum is to provide teachers (not children) with a focus and guidelines—i.e. there is no particular curriculum that is the optimal one for early development. Against these conclusions it is necessary to consider the finding of Blank & Solomon, cited above, in which children who experienced an equal amount of one-to-one interaction with a teacher, but with no attempt to tutor, did not benefit as much as children in a special tutorial language program. No clear conclusion concerning the importance of specific curriculum objectives can be drawn at this time. However, it may be useful to point out some considerations that are likely to influence the way in which future evidence is interpreted.

First, the distinction, drawn earlier in this section, between content of instruction and method of instruction is an important one in this context. Blank & Solomon's program is less a "curriculum" than a method of interacting with children, guided by relatively general statements as to the objectives of instruction; there is no particular set of terms or skills to be taught in a given session. Their findings suggest that a carefully defined methodology of instruction may be important to the learning of cognitive strategies even if the particular content to which it is applied is subject to considerable variation.

A second consideration concerns the types of measurements made in assessing learning outcomes. Where measures of general intelligence are used—as was the case in each of the three studies under consideration here—differences in specific content are less likely to matter. However, where measures of specific skills or information are used, results are likely to differentiate between the children who have been taught the content assessed and those who have not. Where assessment of specific curriculum objectives is used as the basis for evaluating a program, a burden lies with the investigator or program developer to justify those behaviors taught as being of particular importance to the child's development. Where such justification can be made and accepted by others, specific as opposed to general assessment may represent the more powerful measurement effort, since results of the tests can be used not only to compare treatments, but also to suggest places in which a particular treatment program might benefit from revision or improvement.

METHODS OF PRESCHOOL INSTRUCTION

Direct instruction versus environmental design.—The distinction between general and specific assessment has as its instructional parallel the question of whether education should be concerned with the design of total learning environments or with the development of specific teaching components. Most work concerned with optimizing learning has focused on strategies of lesson design; that is, on determining efficient ways of teaching specific learning objectives such as organizing sequences, stimulus conditions, and feedback conditions (see 6, 113). By contrast, developmental psychologists addressing themselves to the problems of early education have frequently tended to focus attention on the design of total environments that would foster learning of the various kinds considered appropriate to the preschool and early primary years (e.g. 44, 143). The environmental approach is particularly marked among those concerned with intervention during infancy and the years up to 3 (e.g. 70, 334), and this in turn has led to a special interest in working directly with the mother or other primary caretaker of the child in order to modify the home environments (e.g. 130, 175, 286, 287, 333). Recently a number of preschool programs have also incorporated parent-training components.

Earliest compensatory education efforts focused on providing an environment for the disadvantaged child that would replicate key features of the middle-class home (cf. 311). Arguments against such direct replication have been several: preschools provide group rather than the more or less one-to-one interaction of the middle-class home; children spend a very brief portion of their lives in the preschool so that more efficient means of instruction are required; methods that are optimal at one stage of development (e.g. 1–3 years) may no longer be optimal at a later stage. Today it seems to be generally accepted that any educational program is "artificial" in the sense that it sets out to reach specifiable goals and seeks to optimize attainment of those goals through careful planning (e.g. 335). Thus, even the environmental design advocates recognize the need for specifying clear points of intervention. Differences between environmental design and direct instruction advocates center largely around (*a*) whether instructional intervention should take place throughout the child's time in school or only during specified (and relatively brief) periods; and (b) whether instructional exchanges should be largely child- or largely teacher-initiated.

Kohlberg (184), Hunt (153, 155), Elkind (77), and others have argued, largely on the basis of Piagetian stage theory, that a critical aspect of instructional design is finding a way of matching new cognitive demands to the child's current level of competence. Each of these writers has implied that, in the absence of detailed scientific knowledge concerning optimal matches of instruction to development, permitting children to choose their own tasks from among a variety available to them may be the most effective procedure. They have pointed to the Montessori program as an example of a workable model of such free choice by children. A number of other early education models have also stressed free choice of tasks and, concomitantly, intrinsic motivation for performing these tasks. One of the effects of the emphasis on free choice and intrinsic motivation is a concern with designing a total environment in which tasks available and environmental responses to the child are those that will optimally foster learning. To date, no comparisons of free choice versus prescription by the teacher for the same set of tasks have been made.

Two programs represent the direct instruction point of view in its present form. Bereiter & Engelmann (24), in accord with their emphasis on the teaching of specific cognitive skills which have been identified as missing in the repertoire of disadvantaged children, have argued that the instructional designer's concern should not be with total environments but with a limited period of time each day in which intensive and carefully sequenced direct instruction is given. The Bereiter-Engelmann and Engelmann-Becker (see 203) programs have paid primary attention to developing the lesson materials and teacher-training materials for implementing this direct instructional approach. Staats (303) also proposes very brief periods of carefully programmed instruction. Underlying each of these programs is a theory of intellectual development that can best be described as cumulative and hierarchical (cf. 106). The assumption is that cognitive competence is acquired through the combination of simple behaviors into successively more complex performances. Attainment of a new level of cognitive development depends upon the prior or simultaneous acquisition of specific simpler competencies. The implication that the behaviors constituting readiness for school learning, like school tasks themselves, are specific, identifiable, and teachable; hence, the emphasis on direct instruction in the preschool period.

It is generally true that programs stressing the learning of specific cognitive objectives have been concerned with the design of individual lessons, while programs concerned with generalized cognitive development have stressed environmental concerns. The split is not strictly between "behaviorists" and "cognitivists," however. For example, Sheldon White (335), in a discussion of the various points of view represented in the Hess & Bear book, points out that Baer & Wolf (14), behaviorists whose paper stressed the systematic programming of social reinforcement contingencies in the nursery school, and Moore (223), who is adamantly committed to learning entirely via feedback from the task itself, both "converge on situations arranged so that the environment reacts instantly and appropriately to what the child does . . ." (335, p. 214). It is interesting too that Moore's goals are limited to a specifiable set of basic communication skills (reading, writing, typing, etc) and that he, like Bereiter and Staats, chooses to invest heavily in the design of only a very brief portion of the child's school day (about half an hour). In a further blurring of the behaviorist-cognitivist distinction, Blank & Solomon (25–27) use limited and intensive time periods but advocate a dialogue which follows the child's line of interest wherever consonant with the broad goals of the curriculum.

Motivation.—Some discussion proceeds around the issue of the appropriate forms of reinforcement for early intervention programs. The debate centers around "intrinsic" versus "external" reinforcement, with a related issue in some discussions of whether children should be free to choose their own tasks in an early educational environment or whether tasks should be assigned to them by adults. Maccoby & Zellner's book (203) on the points of view of the various Follow Through program sponsors provides a general overview of the theoretical and ethical issues that are being discussed by psychologists actively engaged in broad-scale intervention efforts. On the whole, the protagonists in this debate line up much as they do on the environmental design versus direct instruction issue, although there are exceptions. Baer & Wolf (14), for example, argue that the behavior of adults in a child's environment has reinforcing characteristics regardless of whether these are intended or not, and that the issue is not, therefore, whether or not to use external reinforcement, but whether or not to use it consciously, for desirable ends, rather than haphazardly for unplanned and possibly counterproductive ends. Their article reviews a series of studies on the effects of adult social reinforcement contingencies on preschool children in nursery school programs. Dependent variables in these studies have been largely social behaviors rather than cognitive, but there are a few studies (e.g. 43, 258, 289) in which social reinforcers or token economies have been used to shape cognitive and academic behaviors in preschool children.

    Proponents of the use of intrinsic motivation argue that (*a*) children engage naturally in exploration of their environment, and that external reinforcers are unnecessary; (*b*) children permitted to select their own tasks will choose tasks that represent an optimal match with current levels of cognitive development and that practice on such optimally matched tasks is spontaneous, the organism being biologically programmed to engage in processes of adaptation and accommodation mediated by such practice (77, 155); (*c*) reliance on external reinforcers will produce children who engage in learning behavior only when the external reinforcers are present and, presumably, optimally programmed. Conclusive evidence from either observational or experimental studies for the validity of these arguments is lacking at the present time, however.

As we have noted for some other issues, this debate is characterized by more talk than experimentation. Small-scale, tightly controlled empirical studies usually demonstrate the effectiveness of one or another kind of reinforcer in controlling behavior and ignore other motivational variables that might be operating concurrently. Intervention studies are often more eclectic, claiming to employ both intrinsic and extrinsic forms of reinforcement, but the research reports on these programs do not attempt to separate the effects of the different forms. Current theories of reinforcement (e.g. 17, 87) suggest that the distinction between intrinsic and extrinsic reinforcement is an artificial one, and that reinforcement from both sources controls behavior in similar ways. This new view suggests that debates concerning internal versus external reinforcement may be fruitless and that a more profitable line of research for instructional psychology will be the interaction of self-produced and externally provided reinforcers in learning.

Timing.—Since by cultural tradition deliberate education of any kind prior to the age of 5 or 6 is unusual, any proposals for intensive educational intervention earlier than that time necessarily raise the question of whether such early education is appropriate or not. Several psychologists (e.g. 45, 70, 155), arguing by analogy to the literature on early stimulation in animals (e.g. 268, 290), and frequently citing the work of Bloom (28) on the development of IQ, have argued that intelligence is particularly "plastic" during the years prior to 5, and that the basic foundations of intellectual development are established by this time. On this basis, they argue for the particular importance of the preschool years for intellectual as well as social development, and hence for the desirability of systematic early intervention. The strongest advocates of the "critical period" argument have advocated not only preschool but infancy intervention (e.g. 45, 286).

Evidence for plasticity of human infant development is given in the work of Burton White (334), in which the onset of visually coordinated grasping was accelerated by 2 months through the use of special visual and motor stimulation of the infant beginning at 6 days of age. Earlier studies with institutionalized children also provide evidence for the effectiveness of modified rearing conditions in significantly improving the general responsiveness and skillfulness of such children (e.g. 71, 295). These studies suggest that massive environmental enrichment for children living in severely restricted environments can have strong and lasting effects on general development. This parallels the findings for various species of animals in which general enrichment of living conditions improves later performance on learning tasks. However, in neither case have the specific aspects of the treatment that are effective been parceled out. Further, despite fairly widespread acceptance of the idea that preschool and infancy years are particularly susceptible to educational influence, there have been no recent studies which have attempted to determine whether particular skills are really acquired more easily at earlier than later ages.

THE LIMITS OF INSTRUCTIONAL INTERVENTION— BIOLOGICAL AND CULTURAL FACTORS

The increase of interest in early instructional programs, and particularly in their potential for counteracting the effects of relatively adverse environmental conditions, has brought forward a series of questions concerning the general effectiveness of instruction—or any form of deliberate intervention—in altering the biologically and culturally determined course of intellectual development. Two key questions or points of argument can be identified in the general discussion of how effective intensive instructional efforts are likely to be. These are: (a) the role of heredity in limiting the individual's likely level of learning or academic achievement; and (b) the extent to which passage through the normative stages of cognitive development (typically defined in Piagetian terms) can be accelerated by instruction.

Hereditary limitations on instruction.—Although there is no one today who seriously claims that either environmental factors alone or hereditary factors alone can account for the individual's characteristics, there remains lively discussion, and in some quarters bitter controversy, over the character of the heredity-environment interaction. In current debate, an article by Arthur Jensen (165), arguing that most of the difference in IQ between blacks and whites is a function of heredity, forms a frequent point of reference, together with the work of theorists whom Jensen himself challenged—most notably Hunt (154, 155) and his notion of plasticity of intelligence. Jensen's article entitled How Much Can We Boost IQ and Scholastic Achievement? begins with the sentence, "Compensatory education has been tried and it apparently has failed" (165, p. 2). The article thus constitutes an explicit attack on compensatory education as a means of remedying the gap in educational achievement.

The empirical heart of Jensen's argument lies in his estimates of "heritability" of IQ, i.e. the proportion of the variance in IQ scores that can be attributed to heredity. These estimates are based on application of an analysis of variance model (developed at some length in the text) to previously published data from a number of studies of IQ correlations for individuals with varying degrees of kinship. After an extended discussion of the kinds of environmental factors that may account for that portion of the variance in IQ that is environmentally determined, Jensen briefly reviews the empirical evidence concerning social class and particularly race differences in measured intelligence. No direct application of heritability estimates is made to these differences. Rather, a series of detailed arguments against the plausibility of environmental causality and in favor of hereditary causality are presented.

Criticisms of Jensen's position have come from a variety of authors, and Jensen has replied to some (166). The arguments are extremely varied and complex, and a complete summary is impossible here. The nature of some of the most important criticisms, however, should be mentioned. One line of argument challenges Jensen's view of how environmental factors operate in modifying intelligence (73, 154, 308). Both Hunt and Stinchcombe stress the cumulative and long-range effects of environment, arguing that initially small differences in environment can result in very large divergences in eventual capability. Hunt also cites evidence from animal research suggesting that environmental variables can directly affect the physiological characteristics of the individual, thus both reiterating his own views concerning the plasticity of intelligence and challenging Jensen's implicit notion that the effects of heredity are fixed once the child is born.

A second set of questions concerns Jensen's definition of heritability (67, 154) and the quantitative models used in estimating it (67, 81, 192). Both Hunt and Crow argue that heritability estimates for particular traits are specific to the environment in which they are measured and that prediction from existing data may be impossible when the environment is radically changed. Light & Smith (192) and Fehr (81) examine Jensen's mathematical model and his parameter estimates in some detail. Light & Smith conclude that under several different assumptions (one of which accepts both Jensen's model and his parameter estimates) most or all of the observed IQ differences between races can be attributed to environmental effects. They also argue, as does Deutsch (73), that accurate estimation of heritability depends upon random allocation of members of the groups being compared to the various environments, and that in the case of blacks and whites, this assumption is not met. Deutsch points out, in elaboration of this argument, that the assumption that the environment of a middle-class black is the same as that of a middle-class white is false.

With respect to the implications of this controversy for compensatory education, it seems appropriate to point out, as have Deutsch and Hunt in their responses to Jensen, that compensatory education has not really been extensively tried; that is, high quality programs have not been offered to the same children beginning in preschool and continuing for at least several years of schooling. For an adequate test of the effects of instructional intervention, these effects must be allowed to cumulate, much as the negative effects of environmental deprivation cumulate over time. Short-term intervention, even when striking improvements in cognitive performance are demonstrated, simply does not permit the testing of a cumulative intervention hypothesis.

Accelerating cognitive development.—The question of whether early deficits can be compensated for by intervention prior to entering school is generally seen as quite separate from the issue of accelerating "natural" development. Proponents of early intervention have argued that the limits of capacity of the young child for learning have never been systematically explored, and that these limits can only be determined by early and cumulative intervention seeking to accelerate acquisition of basic cognitive processes (e.g. 88, 155). The implication of these arguments is that, since learning is cumulative, earlier learning of important components of intelligent behavior will permit earlier learning of the next level of complexity, and that higher ultimate intellectual performance will thereby be fostered. Critics and skeptics (e.g. 259) raise the question of whether competencies acquired particularly early are stable (i.e. does relative advantage persist over an extended period), but the evidence is typically drawn from cases of early intervention in which there was no follow-up training building on the initial achievements. A more fundamental question that has been raised is whether earlier stimulation will lead only to faster growth, but not necessarily to qualitatively richer growth, i.e. whether the character of terminal performance is changed or only its rate of acquisition (165, p. 103).

An article by Kohlberg (184) develops a point of view widely shared by developmental psychologists of Piagetian persuasion. Kohlberg argues that while environmental influences are crucial in intellectual development, it is general experience rather than specific encounters that produce changes in basic capabilities. This position leads to considerable pessimism concerning the probable effectiveness of direct instructional intervention, at least in influencing development of the basic intellectual structures. The position thus conincides with the hereditarians' position concerning the likely limited effect of early and compensatory educational intervention. Nevertheless, attempts to directly instruct children in tasks involving the fundamental cognitive structures defined by Piaget have continued to increase (see discussion of this literature in the next section). And, as we have seen, there continue to be attempts to design both content and method of intervention programs on the basis of Piagetian cognitive theory.

INSTRUCTION IN PIAGETIAN CONCEPTS

In this section, we consider research on direct instruction of tasks drawn from Piagetian and related literature on cognitive development. Such research has been characterized by the intensive study of tasks that are considered to be representative of certain stages in the development of intelligence. In the Piagetian theory of intelligence, two milestones of cognitive development normally occur during the school years. These are the entrance into the stage of "concrete operations," at around the age of 7, and the entrance into the stage of "formal operations," at the onset of adolescence. These stages are thought to mark major qualitative changes in the modes of thinking available to the child, and consequently in the kinds of specific learning of which he is capable. Evidence that acquisition of the modes of thought characterizing these stages could be significantly accelerated as a result of instruction would, then, be of major significance with respect to both educational practice and our scientific understanding of the origins and functioning of intelligence. Work on the possibility of training operational thinking has concentrated almost exclusively on the acquisition of concrete operations. Only a tiny minority of studies have been concerned with teaching formal operations.

It is possible at this time to note a significant shift in the balance of evidence concerning trainability of functions. After reviewing available training studies in 1963, Flavell (85) stated:

> Probably the most certain conclusion is that it can be a surprisingly difficult undertaking to manufacture Piagetian concepts in the laboratory. Almost all the training methods reported impress one as sound and reasonable and well-suited to the educative job at hand. And yet most of them have had remarkably little success in producing cognitive change . . . Further, there is more than a suspicion from present evidence that when one does succeed in inducing some behavioral change through this or that training procedure, it may not cut very deep (p. 377).

In 1968 Kohlberg (184) echoed Flavell's conclusion, stating that:

> These studies suggest that direct teaching of conservation through verbal instruction and reinforcement or through provision of observations of examples of conservation (e.g., weighing masses changed in shape on a balance) do not lead to the formation of a general or stable concept of conservation. Little change is induced by such methods (p. 1031).

Since Kohlberg's article, however, a significant number of studies have appeared which, taken together with a smaller number of earlier successful training studies, offer grounds for considerable optimism concerning the possibility of developing operational thinking through instruction, providing that the proper instructional strategies can be discovered. The shift was noted by Flavell & Hill in 1969 (86) and has since been further documented with respect to conservation concepts, in particular by Brainerd & Allen (34).

INSTRUCTION IN CONSERVATION

The bulk of the training work on Piagetian concepts has centered on the various concepts of conservation. Training studies typically begin with a pretest on one or more dimensions of conservation (number, continuous quantity, discontinuous quantity, length, weight, substance, volume, and area). Nonconserving and sometimes transitional subjects are then divided into training and control groups, with training offered on one or more conservation concepts by one or more training methods. Comparisons of post-test scores for the training and nontraining groups constitute the major dependent variable. Brainerd & Allen (34) have reviewed the great bulk of the literature on conservation training. Of 18 studies they reviewed (considering only studies that employed control groups), 12 report successful training of conservation responses. Of the 6 studies reporting no success, 3 are by a single author, and all but one (216) appeared prior to 1967. By contrast, half of the successful studies appeared after 1967. Brainerd & Allen conclude that, "conservation of at least four of the first-order quantitative invariants can be accelerated by appropriate training procedures" (34, p. 139).

Additional credence is lent to this conclusion by the results of 11 studies published in the 1968–70 period that Brainerd & Allen did not review. Nine of these studies reported successful induction of conservation in experimental as compared with control group subjects (20, 137, 138, 189, 193, 225, 238, 246, 265). Only two (136, 310) reported little or no effect of training.

In evaluating the success of short-term training studies, many psychologists will likely raise the question of whether a generalized and stable concept of conservation has been induced; i.e. one that reflects the child's achievement of a generally higher level cognitive structure, rather than a specific set of responses to test questions. Three tests of achievement of such a general concept have been proposed: (a) retention of conserving responses over an extended period of time; (b) transfer of conservation to quantitative dimensions on which no training was offered; and (c) resistance to "counter-suggestion," i.e. attempts to persuade the child that conservation does not hold.

Retention.—Of the successful training studies reviewed (including both those reviewed by Brainerd & Allen and the more recent ones), six (115, 138, 246, 294, 325, 326) reported delayed post-tests of periods of 2 to 4 weeks. In each case the advantage of trained subjects over untrained control subjects was retained over this period, thus indicating effects that are not specific to the immediate conditions of training.

Delayed tests of several months have been reported in four studies. Rothenberg & Orost (275) trained number conservation and found retention of effects after 3 months. Kingsley & Hall (179) found 4-month retention of effects after training on length and weight conservation. Bearison (20) showed 7-month retention of the effects of training on liquid quantity. Lister (193) trained retarded children (9 to 15 years old) on volume conservation and showed retention on a 5-month delayed post-test. However, Lister used no control group for the delayed post-test, since the original control group had been trained in the intervening period, in a form of replication of the initial experiment. It is of significance that each of these studies demonstrating long-term retention of training effects also found transfer to at least one conservation dimension on which no training was offered (see below for further discussion).

Transfer.—Brainerd & Allen (34), following other investigators, distinguish between specific transfer (transfer to tests of the same conservation dimension but using different materials than the ones used in training) and nonspecific transfer (transfer to a new dimension). Brainerd & Allen report no failures to find specific transfer when it has been tested for. Of the more recent studies, Overbeck & Schwartz (238) did find a failure of transfer from continuous to discrete materials in a weight conservation study. On the other hand, Lumsden & Kling (200) found that children pretrained on the concept of "bigger," using blocks, were more likely to conserve size using clay materials than children not so trained.

The picture is more mixed for nonspecific transfer. Brainerd & Allen report more failures than successes in producing transfer to dimensions on which no training was offered, and they conclude that Piagetian predictions are generally upheld concerning the ineffectiveness of short-term instruction for a generalized concept of conservation. Two of the more recent studies call this conclusion into question, however. Lister (193) trained volume conservation and found reliable transfer to conservation of weight and substance (as well as to displacement volume). Bearison (20) trained kindergarteners on continuous (liquid) quantity conservation and showed strong transfer effects to discontinuous quantity, number, length, mass, continuous area, and discontinuous area (in that order of strength of transfer). In addition, Rothenberg & Orost (275) found some transfer from number training to discontinuous quantity conservation. Kingsley & Hall (179) also found transfer from weight training to substance, although there is some question about whether this represents really nonspecific transfer since the concepts are almost identical (cf. 34, p. 137). Since each of these studies also demonstrated long-term retention effects (see above), they offer relatively strong support for the possibility of both generalized and stable training effects.

Resistance to counter-suggestion.—The idea that trained conservers might be less resistant to attempts to extinguish conservation judgments than "natural" conservers was first presented by Smedslund (297). Smedslund trained children to conserve weight and then presented them with trials on which the experimenter surreptitiously removed a piece of material from one piece of plasticene as he changed its shape. All of the trained conservers stopped giving conservation responses, while only half of the natural conservers did so. Several other investigators have since attempted to replicate Smedslund's finding. Roll (265) found equally strong resistance to counter-suggestion regarding number conservation in both natural and trained conservers; this is in agreement with an earlier finding of Wallach & Sprott (325) concerning number conservation. Brison (36) found substance conservation to be highly resistant to extinction for both groups. Kingsley & Hall (179) and Smith (301), on the other hand, have both reported almost uniform extinction of conservation of weight under counter-suggestion conditions, again for both natural and trained conservers. Thus, although there are apparent differences in the resistance of different concepts of conservation to extinction, there does not appear to be any reliable difference between natural and trained conservers. Resistance to extinction as a criterion of an operational conservation concept is thus of questionable validity.

Content and method of training.—A great variety of procedures have been used in attempts to train conservation, and attempts to summarize or identify critical features are bound to result in conclusions open to challenge and debate. Much of the research in this area, it is important to point out, has been less interested in exploring instructional variables than in using instruction as a means of isolating the critical components of the conservation concept itself. Thus, there has been rather more attention to the conceptual content of training than to instructional method variables. The assumption behind such a research strategy for isolating the components of conservation is that if a hypothesized underlying process is trained, and this results in successful learning of conservation, then the trained process is crucial to the conservation concept. Theories concerning the crucial bases of conservation have varied widely (see 324), and training procedures used by different investigators have been based on: "reversibility" (the recognition that the reverse of any action can be performed, thus returning the objects to their original state); multiple classification (see discussion of classification training below); linguistic mediators; discrimination among various dimensions of quantity; and the concepts of addition, subtraction, and equivalence. Brainerd & Allen argue convincingly that the component common to all of the successful training studies they reviewed was reversibility, although reversibility training was often embedded in other kinds of experiences. The study by Bearison (20), that has thus far shown the greatest degree of transfer and retention of all conservation training experiments, embedded reversibility experience in extended use of standard units for measuring liquid quantity. Measurement training, it may be noted, accords well with the conclusion drawn by Wallach (324), that conservation depends on the recognition of an "indicator property" which retains the same value after transformation (of shape or arrangement) as before.

Even among studies training some form of reversibility (a content variable) one may note different degrees of success in training—as measured by percentages of trained subjects who learned to conserve, length of retention, and range of generalization. Hence, it is necessary to search beyond the conceptual content in accounting for training effects, and to consider certain instructional strategy variables. No analysis of instructional strategies in conservation training comparable to Brainerd & Allen's analysis of conceptual content has been attempted. Such an analysis, now that a significant body of successful training studies exists, might represent a significant contribution not only to our understanding of the instructional process, but also to an explication of the general role of deliberate instruction in cognitive development.

Instruction in Classification Skills

The research literature is rich in studies showing changes in children's performance on classification and concept formation tasks with age. However, attempts at instruction on these tasks or their components have been infrequent. In general, there has been less attention to training in this domain than there has been in conservation, and such research as there is, is not so strictly dominated by Piagetian definition of the tasks. Non-Piagetian research on the training of classification and concept attainment skills is included here because it generally shares the Piagetian concern with qualitative rather than strictly quantitative changes in intellectual competence.

When a child sorts a set of objects into a limited set of categories, established by himself or by the experimenter, two component abilities are presumably required: the generalized ability to impose structure on a stimulus field characterized by complexity and variability; and the ability to recognize specific dimensions of similarity and difference among the objects. This distinction between strategies for structuring variability and specific dimensions of categorization is a useful one to maintain in reviewing research on instruction in classificatory behavior. It is useful because the possibility of extensive and sustained training effects in the area of classification skills will probably depend upon discovering optimal interactions between generalized, structure-oriented, and specific, dimension-oriented training. Although training of both kinds may well be needed, a clear conceptual distinction at the outset should help in interpretation and development of instructional strategies.

General classification strategies.—Of the various investigators of variables in the acquisition of classification skills, the Clarkes, of the University of Hull in England, have been the most explicit in recognizing the distinction between generalized strategies and specific dimensions. In an extended series of studies they have been concerned with demonstrating the acquisition of generalized classification skills in the course of specific short-term training and practice. In each of several studies, nursery school children (56, 57) or older mentally retarded subjects (58) were given training on sorting and matching tasks using geometric figures. Gains in performance were shown for a sorting task in which pictures or words were sorted into conceptual classes such as "human beings," "furniture," or "animals." Since the perceptual dimensions trained (various aspects of shape, size, and orientation) were irrelevant to the transfer task categories, transfer had to be due to the child having acquired a generalized skill in classificatory behavior rather than a set to discriminate a specific dimension. A subsequent study by the Clarkes (57) showed that the complexity of forms used in training (i.e. the number of relevant and irrelevant dimensions present) rather than the difficulty of the discrimination (i.e. how fine the differences were on the relevant dimension) was the significant factor in producing transfer.

Transfer from verbal training, in which subjects sorted verbs into categories of types of activity, has also been demonstrated in tasks involving dissimilar stimuli and dimensions (57, 59), particularly when the training words are presented in clusters rather than randomly (59). This latter finding suggests the development through instruction of a generalized tendency to search for and establish clusters. A study (231) carried out on Nigerian Ibo children of 11 and 12 years of age demonstrated an effect similar to that of the Clarkes. Okonji trained his subjects on grouping and regrouping wooden blocks that differed in color, form, and size. He demonstrated significant pre- to post-test gains on a transfer task in which subjects sorted models of animals on dimensions such as domestic versus nondomestic, carnivorous versus noncarnivorous, reptile versus nonreptile, etc.

Several investigators have studied methods of training strategies of concept attainment. Osler & Scholnick (237, 288) found that a combination of "dimensional" training (discrimination of the dimension to be used in the transfer problems) and "inferential" training (experience in using feedback in a discrimination problem) produced significant transfer to a set of concept attainment problems in 5-year-olds. Stern & Keislar (176, 307) successfully trained second-grade children in a simple hypothesis testing strategy by having them verbalize both their hypotheses and what was learned from positive and negative feedback on successive trials. In these latter studies, only very specific transfer from training to test problems was demonstrated, since both the attributes and the form in which the problem was presented remained the same on the test series as it had been in training. Anderson (5), however, has trained a more generalized skill, that of varying only a single dimension at a time in selecting instances for testing in a concept attainment task. Subjects were bright first graders. Training problems used a variety of dimensions (e.g. cards differing in form, color, and number; leaves with different structures; switches, some of which turned on buzzers and some of which did not, etc), and transfer was demonstrated to problems involving a number of dimensions not previously encountered.

Double classification skills.—The ability to attend simultaneously to two dimensions of classification, that is to engage in multiplicative classification, is generally considered to be one of the key abilities associated with the stage of concrete operations (159), and in fact has been hypothesized to be one of the bases for the development of conservation (cf. 294). There have been fewer attempts to train double classification skills than there have been to train conservation. However, a series of studies by Jacobs & Vandeventer should be especially noted, both because of its success in producing transfer to a widely recognized normative intelligence test (Raven's Progressive Matrices), and because the series of studies taken as a whole illustrates very well the iterative sequence of trial and revision that characterizes most successful instructional development.

Following two unsuccessful training attempts that used remedial self-instruction on the test items themselves (160, 161), Jacobs & Vandeventer (163) developed a training strategy in which the experimenter showed the child a series of matrices, asked him questions designed to direct his attention to the similarities of shapes or colors in the rows and columns, and required him to infer what kind of object and what color were missing from the matrix. Testing was on items similar in format to the training matrices; half used the same dimensions as the training matrices, half used transfer dimensions of shading and size. On both the trained and the transfer items, trained subjects showed greater pre- to post-test gains than control subjects, and this advantage was retained on a 4-month delayed post-test. However, experimental subjects did not do better than control subjects on the Raven's test, for which the number and fineness of perceptual discriminations were greater.

In the most recent study of the series (162), training was extended to include experience in searching for bases of classification and to include four rather than only two dimensions of classification. On the post-test, 12 dimensions of classification were used. Training on four dimensions produced greater learning across the universe of dimensions than did training on only two dimensions, but the two-dimensional training was better than no training at all. On a three-month retention test, the effects for both the two- and the four-dimension training groups still remained. What is more, administration of the Raven's test at this time showed a significant advantage for the extended four-dimension training over the control group. Thus, the training procedure developed iteratively over a period of several years, ultimately succeeded in producing transfer to a standardized intelligence test.

Class-inclusion relations.—For Piaget (159), the ability to comprehend relations of class inclusion and the quantifiers, all, some, and none, is a central aspect of operational classificatory structure, paralleling the achievement of conservation in the development of operational mathematical concepts. Nevertheless, there has been nothing paralleling the research interest in conservation for this classification concept.

The most extensive report of an attempt to train class inclusion is by Kohnstamm (186), who undertook to show that earlier work of Piaget and Morf on attempting to teach this skill had not exhausted all of the pedagogical possibilities. Kohnstamm worked with 5-year-old Dutch children. Two initial training attempts, using a correction procedure on test-like items, yielded no marked success. A third training attempt was then made, this time using a set of blocks differing only in size and color. Of 20 children trained this way, 16 learned to answer class inclusion questions about the blocks successfully, and, after five "warmup" questions, this transferred to nearly complete success with pictures using a variety of different classes. On a 2- to 3-week delayed post-test, the skill was maintained, and, further, it transferred to verbally presented problems which had not previously been experienced by these children. From the point of view of instructional theory, the significant aspect of Kohnstamm's third and successful training method is that by use of the blocks the learning problem was simplified for the child. He now had to deal only with the class inclusion logic and not with coordinating knowledge about a variety of different classes (e.g. animals, pets, cars, flowers, things to eat with, people, etc). Once the logical structure had been acquired in this simplified environment, experience with a few "lead-in" pictorial questions was enough to permit transfer to a wide variety of classes. Two other studies (1, 340) have shown more limited improvement on class-inclusion tasks through training.

The validity of Kohnstamm's results has been questioned by Pascual-Leone & Bovet (244), who argue that since Kohnstamm's test problems were phrased in exactly the same way as the training problems, his results can be ascribed to acquisition of a "learning set" for problems of that kind rather than to the acquisition of concrete operational structures. Pascual-Leone & Bovet argue that in order to conclude that the operational mechanisms had been affected, it would be necessary to present test problems in different forms, to require verbal justifications, to use counter-suggestion techniques, and to test for transfer to other classification tasks associated with the stage of concrete operations. Independently recognizing some of these objections, Lasry & Laurendeau (188) replicated Kohnstamm's training procedure and included requirements for verbal justification together with a problem that contained elements of counter-suggestion in the post-test. The training group for this study was 4- to 6-year-old French Canadian children. Kohnstamm's results were replicated for problems of the kinds he had used, although the rate of success was lower when criteria of verbal justification were applied or counter-suggestion problems were used. Kohnstamm (187) has collected reports of his and Lasry's experiments, together with Pascual-Leone & Bovet's critique and further commentary of his own, in a small book that is an illustration of the tension between Piagetian theory and pedagogic experiments which seek to facilitate the acquisition of specific cognitive skills.

INSTRUCTION ON OTHER PIAGETIAN TASKS

Conservation and classification concepts represent the major abilities studied by investigators interested in the acquisition and instruction of Piagetian concepts. However, scattered studies involving instruction in other abilities have been reported, and these will be mentioned briefly. Three tasks associated with the stage of concrete operations have been studied. E. V. Proscura (see 148) taught 3- to 6-year-old children to seriate. Nelson, Zelniker & Jeffrey (227) taught 5- to 7-year-olds a concept of proportionality; and Beilin, Kagan & Rabinowitz (21) trained 7-year-old children to represent the water level of jars tilted at various angles. In each study, trained subjects performed better than control groups, although there were differences in degree of transfer, and age of subjects tended to interact with training methods.

Only three studies attempting to train children on tasks associated with the stage of formal rather than concrete operations have been identified. These include two studies by Fischbein, Pampu & Manzat: in one (83) they trained 9-year-olds to make correct predictions concerning the color of marble likely to be drawn from a bag containing various proportions of two different colors; in the other (84) they trained 10- to 14-year-olds to estimate the number of permutations possible for sets of different sizes. Wiegand (338) used Gagne's procedure to generate a hierarchy of "learning sets" leading to the ability to perform a task similar to Inhelder & Piaget's (158) "Hauling

Weight on an Inclined Plane" task. Twelve-year-olds learned the training task by taking tests on the behaviors in the hierarchy, beginning with the simpler ones and progressing to the more complex, and were then able to perform the Piagetian task as well.

THE EFFECT OF SCHOOLING ON THE ACQUISITION OF OPERATIONAL THINKING

It is generally believed that the concrete and formal operational stages are achieved independently of formal education, on the basis of the child's general experience in his culture. There have been relatively few tests of this assumption, largely because there are so few unschooled children in Western societies, and because comparisons with children in the developing nations confound differences in schooling with differences in general cultural experience. The closing of schools in Prince Edward County, Virginia, in response to school integration demands provided a unique opportunity to test the effects of schooling in a Western, if largely rural and ill-educated, population. Mermelstein & Shulman (217) found no differences on tests of conservation between 9-year-olds who had never been to school and children of similar social background who had attended school. These results are in accord with earlier findings of Goodnow (129), which showed that unschooled Hong Kong children did as well as European children of the same age on conservation tasks, although they performed less well on tasks involving combinatorial reasoning and on Raven's Progressive Matrices. In addition, a study by Almy (3) compared performance on Piagetian tasks of urban American second-graders having different types and lengths of science instruction, and found that type or length of science program did not systematically effect performance on the Piagetian tasks.

Findings of the kind just cited tend to support the view that formal schooling is of limited importance in children's attainment of operational thinking. A rather different picture emerges, however, from a study comparing children with different degrees and kinds of schooling in New Guinea (249). In this study, a battery of science concept tests based on Piagetian tasks were administered to children of various ages (8–18) and school experience in three culturally distinct regions. Across the regions there were weak associations of performance on these tasks with calendar age, but relatively strong associations with number of years in school (which is only slightly correlated with age in areas where formal education has only recently been introduced and children begin first grade at very different ages). In addition, comparison of special subgroups of children revealed that children in schools in which a modern mathematics program stressing measurement and estimation activities was used performed better on conservation tasks than children without such a special program, and also better than children in a modern mathematics program which stressed concepts of number only. Furthermore, children whose education had been primarily in native languages, rather than English, did not perform as well as English-language educated children. Apparently in very primitive cultures the basal experience is not sufficient to produce spontaneous development of basic Piagetian concepts, while in even relatively deprived Western cultures (e.g. Prince Edward County), or in poor but urbanized cultures (Hong Kong), the incremental effect of schooling is slight. The effect of urbanization on acquisition of these concepts is supported in a study by Poole (248), who compared 10- and 11-year-old village, market-town, and urban children of the Hausa tribe in Northern Nigeria on a set of Piagetian concept tasks. Urban children generally performed better than more rural children, although not as well as an age-comparable sample of English children, on measurement, spatial conservation, and mechanical tasks.

LEARNING AND INDIVIDUAL DIFFERENCES

Throughout the entire short history of modern psychology, two of its major fields, the measurement of individual differences and the experimental psychology of learning, have had only fleeting contact. Throughout the years the importance of coordination between the two fields has been recognized, but sustained work has been conducted by only a few (see 124). The requirements of a psychology of instruction appear to make coordination between the two fields mandatory, with changes in traditional practices being required in each field. Basic problems revolve around the issues inherent in adapting educational alternatives (learning conditions) to individual differences, both those apparent at the beginning of a course of instruction and those that appear during learning.

The literature of learning theory has shown an increasing concern for the proposition that research on individual differences in learning is of fundamental importance for future progress. There is a growing commitment to the explanation of the individual case, particularly at the urging of Skinner and his associates (e.g. 292), and this commitment is not restricted only to operant kinds of investigations (e.g. 105, 151, 229). In fact, there may be every reason to believe that theories which are most amenable to incorporating individual difference parameters will emerge as the most powerful theories of learning. From the point of view of education, there is a long-standing desire to design instructional systems that are "individualized" and provide educational alternatives for the various needs and talents of the learner. Educators have employed various kinds of ungraded and track systems, but the degree of adaptation has never been enough to force answers to the underlying problem of the interaction of individual differences with instructional variables. Various patterns of adapting to individual differences that can be identified in past and present educational practices have been described by Cronbach (63).

Aptitude-Treatment Interaction

As a consequence of the above influences, educational psychologists and others have recently combed their studies for evidence of interaction between individual differences and learning variables. To some extent, this work was heralded by the book by Cronbach & Gleser (64) which was concerned with the development of a decision-theory model for the selection and placement of personnel into various "treatments." The word "treatment" was given a broad meaning, referring to what was done with an individual in an institutional setting, e.g. for what job an applicant should be trained in industry, to what therapeutic method a patient should be assigned, and, in education, to which particular educational program or instructional method should a student be assigned or given the opportunity to select.

Individual difference variables are useful in adapting to treatment only when measures of individual differences and treatment can be shown to interact. The point is made by the distinction between two types of significant interaction effects in the analysis of variance, called "ordinal" and "disordinal" interactions (199). Given an aptitude measure with two treatments, if one plots performance for each treatment group with achievement on one axis and aptitude on another, then a significant interaction effect is called ordinal when the treatment lines do not cross, i.e. when one method is consistently better at all aptitude levels. A disordinal interaction occurs when the treatment lines cross, and this has been interpreted as evidence for aptitude treatment interaction; that is, students should be assigned differentially to alternate treatments to obtain optimal instructional payoff (33, 126).

A comprehensive review by Bracht (31, 32) reports a detailed survey and analysis of ATI (aptitude-treatment interaction) studies, as the field has come to be called. Bracht carefully assessed each of 90 studies for significance of disordinal interaction. The results of this survey are quite striking. In the 90 studies, 108 individual difference treatment interactions were examined or identified. Of these, only five were identified as significant disordinal interactions. Only one of these five involved individual difference measures of the kind commonly studied with respect to education (e.g. under- and over-achievement). The others studied personalogical variables of various kinds (e.g. need affiliation, social environment). Two general conclusions that can be drawn from this survey are these: (a) Although IQ scores and similar measures of general ability and achievement were used as the individual difference variable in a large number of studies, no evidence was found to suggest that such individual differences were useful variables for differentiating alternative treatments for subjects in a homogeneous age group, although the measures correlated substantially with achievement in most school related tasks. (b) In most of the experiments reported, the analysis of interaction effects was often an afterthought rather than a carefully planned part of the experiment. Alternate treatments do not seem to have been generated by systematic analysis of the kinds of psychological processes called upon in particular treatments, and individual differences were not assessed in terms of these same processes.

Somewhat earlier than the Bracht study, an extensive and thoughtful analysis of the many ramifications of the ATI problem appeared in an informal report by Cronbach & Snow (65). The authors of this report consider their work somewhat preliminary and caution the reader about the tentative nature of many of their boldest statements. The report presents a general perspective on the ATI problem from an educational, methodological, and social-philosophical context. It discusses previous work on the structure of abilities, and poses the problem of how abilities and individual differences might be conceptualized so that the selection of variables for ATI research could be more systematically made than it has been in the past. In this regard, reference is made to the work of Witkin, Guilford, Guttman, Vernon, and Catell. With respect to ATI research, the conclusion of the report is similar to Bracht's: few or no ATI effects have been solidly demonstrated; the frequency of studies in which disordinal interactions have been found is low; and the empirical evidence is often not very convincing in the studies that do claim to show such interactions.

These negative results raise significant questions about this area of research. Perhaps generally accepted aptitude constructs are not a productive way of measuring those individual differences that interact with different instructional methods because these measures come out of a psychometric, selection-oriented tradition which does not relate to the processes of learning and performance. Or perhaps, as Cronbach & Snow suggest, the conceptualization of dimensions of instructional methods is inadequate; gross analyses are employed which characterize instructional techniques in terms of relative difficulty, degree of structure, degree of inquiry, amount of self-direction, etc, but these are not operational enough to make contact with learning variables that have been investigated or with the specific requirements of educational practice.

PROCESS CONSTRUCTS AS INDIVIDUAL DIFFERENCES

One approach that seems likely to be fruitful for future research is the conceptualization of individual difference variables in terms of the process constructs of contemporary theories of learning and performance. In the reported results of a symposium entitled *Learning and Individual Differences* (105), there is an impressive consensus in this direction, although the papers presented approach this basic theme in various ways. In his comments on the conference, Melton writes:

> We know that we can manipulate experimentally the extent to which response integration, stimulus differentiation and coding, and a variety of mediational processes, may be involved in new learning. We also know that to look at any new learning without an attempt to assess the status of the habit systems of the learner with respect to the availability of these pre-established response integration, stimulus differentiation, and mediational habits, is to be blind to the nature of the processes that are under investigation. If this is so, then it seems self-evident that the analysis of individual differences variables must carry this multi-process analysis of the learning process to the analysis of individual performance differences (215, p. 247).

Glanzer suggests a shift from the term "individual differences" to the term "individual performance" and writes as follows:

> Most work on individual differences has a futile air about it. A set of measurements shows that one individual is worse than another on some measure. In some cases these measurements might help predict performance on a criterion task. The measurements could therefore be used for purposes of selection. They do not, however, give a basis for doing anything about the performance. They do not tell how the subject should be trained to improve his performance. They do not tell how the situation should be changed to make the criterion performance easier. Since they do not give a basis for doing anything about the performance, they do not give a basis for the understanding or analysis of the performance (123, p. 148).

Jensen (164) elaborates on the theme of basic processes as individual differences by making a distinction between phenotypes and genotypes, phenotypes being described in terms of task characteristics, and the genotypes being the basic processes which cause patterns of intercorrelations among the phenotypes. The primary task of research on individual differences consists of discovering these genotypes, which hopefully will be limited as compared with phenotypic variation. He tentatively suggests that one might imagine that the genotypes look something like the constructs of Hullian theory.

There is little research along these lines; however, a recent exemplary set of studies on individual differences and paired-associate learning by Rohwer (261, 263, 264) can serve to illustrate a possible direction. Rohwer has studied a process he calls "mental elaboration," following along the lines of the variety of sources that now suggest that subjects recode or transform the materials presented to them by elaborating the content (e.g. 30, 241, 251). For example, before noun pairs are initially presented, subjects can be given two kinds of instructions: to read aloud the words as they appear, or to construct and say aloud a sentence containing the two words as they appear. In the latter activity the subject is engaged in mental elaboration; that is, he is elaborating the word pairs into sentences. [Verbal elaboration can be contrasted with visual elaboration, the latter referring to the effect of visual or imagery instructions in facilitating learning (e.g. 30, 241, 251).] Rohwer has studied the various syntactic and semantic variables which influence the facilitating effect of such verbal elaboration and has also studied individual differences with respect to age, race, and socioeconomic status (SES).

Rohwer's findings with respect to age differences in the use of elaborative activity of this kind as a means of acquiring information are of interest. When both verbal and visual elaboration is provided, 8-year-olds are more proficient learners than 4-year-olds, but only verbal elaboration facilitates learning in 4-year-olds. A combination of verbal and visual forms of elaboration adds a detectable increment to the performance produced by verbal forms alone in 4-year-olds but adds nothing for the 8-year-olds (261, 263). These findings suggest that during the age interval from 4 to 8, children increasingly begin to generate their own forms of mental elaboration in response to presented materials. It is also suggested that a preference and a capacity for the use of visual representation develops later than verbal modes for representing and storing information. Such a finding runs counter to the usual claim that the pictorial (ikonic) forms of representation develop earlier than verbal (symbolic) forms (39). Rohwer explains this by theorizing that at earlier ages language is a coherent, organized system and imagery is not.

With respect to individual differences that appear within homogeneous age groups, a model is proposed of possible relationships between elaborative cognitive processes and ethnic and SES differences in performance (263, 264). In effect, the model classifies tasks along two dimensions: one dimension designates the kind of conceptual ability likely to be elicited by a task, either formal or imaginative; the second dimension refers to the type of terminal behavior demanded, either acquisition-production or recall-application. Formal conceptual activity is elicited by tasks that require the processing of relatively explicit rules. Imaginative conceptual activity, on the other hand, involves the invention of ad hoc ways of processing and transforming information and does not require the application of highly formalized rules and conventions. Acquisition-production behaviors require principally the acquisition of new information or skills; recall-application refers to the recall of information or the exercise of skills previously acquired. The suggestion is that individual differences in task performance can be conceptualized in terms of these dimensions, assuming that individuals differ in the kind of conceptual activity to which they are predisposed and the kind of task they are better at performing.

Various tasks used in experiments on learning and on standardized tests can be categorized by being placed in the four quadrants of the space defined by the two dimensions of this model. Rohwer reports that in terms of this scheme, differences in favor of high-SES white samples over low-SES black samples have been reported for all tasks except those located in the quadrant characterized by the acquisition-production and imaginative conceptual activity. The implication is that culturally disadvantaged populations will differ from advantaged populations on recall-application tasks and on tasks that require formal conceptual activity (formal concepts being acquired during early environmental encounters), but not on acquisition tasks that require imaginative conceptual activity. Rohwer's model leads him to a different interpretation of his data than that derived from the model proposed by Jensen (165) to account for somewhat similar data. Jensen postulated two kinds of learning abilities, associative and conceptual, and interpreted the data as suggesting that high- and low-SES groups differ in performance on conceptual learning tasks but not on associative learning tasks. Rohwer suggests that conceptual processing is generally involved in performance, but that its nature depends upon past learning and the type of task performed.

In general, Rohwer's work supports the increasing amount of evidence in the psychological literature indicating that learning of all varieties proceeds best when the conditions of learning elicit conceptual activity in the learner, and that individual differences will occur with respect to certain kinds of conceptual processes. Further, if elaborative conceptual activities facilitate learning in general, then it would be fruitful to train children in elaborative techniques of learning. Rohwer's studies (264) indicate that substantial improvement in PA learning and performance was produced by elaboration training, and that elaboration training improved the performance of low-SES black children to a level commensurate with that of the high-SES white children.

Rohwer's conceptualization scheme is tentative at best; however, his work suggests a line of research on individual differences involving a variety of cognitive processes. Such studies would attempt to identify the kinds of processes required by various tasks and the characteristics of an individual's performance of these processes. The conditions required to learn a task could then be adapted to these individual characteristics, or the individual might be taught how to more effectively engage in these processes. Some cognitive processes which seem likely candidates for this kind of work have been suggested in a recent chapter on cognitive development in education (262); they include attention, behavioral tempo, perceptual abilities, language processes, and conceptual proficiencies. Along these lines, a study by Dunham & Bunderson (76) investigated the relationship of cognitive abilities to performance in multiple-category concept problems, and their findings suggest that individual differences in reasoning and memory interact with different characteristics of problem-solving tasks.

COGNITIVE STYLES AS AN INDIVIDUAL DIFFERENCE VARIABLE

Attempts at individualized models of education have been criticized for being too exclusively concerned with relating individual differences to rate of learning, achievement outcomes, initial subject matter competence, etc, and neglecting attention to differences in cognitive style or personality characteristics that influence the learning process.

The work that seems pertinent to this problem has been brought together in a review by Kagan & Kogan (170). These authors indicate that one of the themes of their chapter comes from the fact that the work and insights of personality theorists have demonstrated not only that motives and conflicts affect perceptual and problem-solving performance, but also that cognitive as well as motivational factors strongly influence responses to traditional projective and objective personality tests. Following up this point of view, "personality variables" are discussed in terms of individual differences in the cognitive processes involved in problem solving, namely, encoding, memory, generation of hypotheses, evaluation, and deduction.

In discussing individual differences in the encoding process, Kagan & Kogan refer to research on the available language resources in children for labeling events to which attention should be paid; the role of set and perception; susceptibility to distraction and cognitive interference in tasks contain-

ing conflicting cues; the effects of developmental change and cultural background on the relative dominance of a sensory modality as the locus of control in encoding; and the selectivity of attention in infants and young children.

In the category of memory the authors consider, among other things, the
negative relation between anxiety and the quality of immediate recall. The
favored interpretation of this relationship is that anxiety creates distracting
stimulation which deflects attention from relevant incoming information and
thus impairs memory. Another example of individual differences in memory
process is what is called the cognitive control of "leveling-sharpening"; this
refers to the degree to which an individual holds a changing image in memory.
Levelers are so named because they merge new stimuli with previously
presented ones; sharpeners, in contrast, retain a high degree of separation
between memory of previous stimuli and current information. Thus, an
image being remembered remains discrete for the sharpeners but tends to lose
its articulation for levelers.

Under the category of hypothesis generation for problem solution, the
most solid research reported concerns the sorting and grouping of concepts.
Presumably the ability to generate hypotheses is influenced by preferences
for particular conceptual categorizations. The work reported, however, seems
only peripherally related to this category. The fourth category, evaluation,
concerns the degree to which an individual pauses to evaluate the quality of
his cognitive products in the course of problem solving. Some people accept
and report the first hypothesis available and act on it; others devote a long
period of time to study and reflection, and censor many hypotheses. This
dimension of individual difference is reported as being apparent as early as 2
years of age. An excellent review is given of the great amount of work on
reflection-impulsivity generated by Kagan and his associates. The last
category, the deductive phase, concerns the implementation of hypotheses;
this involves deduction of conclusions by which a problem is solved. Prominent in this discussion is reference to the individual differences in deductive
problem solving reported in the study of ethnic differences by Lesser, Fifer &
Clark (190).

Evaluation of this extensive review and discussion of individual variation
in cognitive processes is made by Kagan & Kogan (170) themselves:

> Few systematic conclusions flow easily . . . Inquiry into variation and cognitive
> functioning has not had the beneficial guidance of strong theory and, on occasion,
> has become empirically barbaric. The movement began in a revolutionary atmo-
> sphere and, like many revolutions, has constructed its principles a posteriori, rather
> than a priori. The subsequent fabric of generalizations has more intuitive appeal
> than logical coherence or commandingness (p. 1351).

With respect to the term "cognitive style," the authors conclude:

> Although the names applied to theoretical constructs for 'style' often have an
> exotic quality, it is possible that the phenomena they serve touch more familiar

dynamic themes. Anxiety over error, attention distribution, expectancy of success or failure, and vulnerability to distraction are central to many of the test procedures utilized (p. 1352).

Two recent studies investigate analytic versus global ("relational") cognitive style with respect to learning variables. Davis & Klausmeier (68), using a concept identification task, found that high-analytic subjects made fewer errors in identifying the concepts to be learned than did low-analytic subjects, but the study failed to find significant interactions between differences in analytic cognitive style and training conditions. A study by Peters (246) investigated ATI effects in the context of training in the conservation of number. Individual differences were measured with respect to language comprehension and preferred categories of sorting behavior. The various treatment conditions involved cued and noncued guided discovery and verbal instructions. Results indicated that while all the experimental groups were superior to a nontrained group, there was little evidence of ATI's when degree of final learning was the dependent variable. However, regression equations to predict performance at different stages of learning indicated a change in the regression weights attributed to the individual difference measures over the course of learning. The pattern of this change suggested that those subjects who enter training with high-analytic scores and low-verbal scores should be assigned to the verbal treatment, while high-language, low-analytic subjects should be assigned to the cue-discrimination treatment to maximize their performance. Subjects who had an inclination for the use of cue discrimination seemed to benefit from the verbal statement of the rule, while those who had greater command of the verbal requirements of the task benefited from training in making the required discriminations. This particular suggestion argues for a compensatory notion of instruction in contrast to the usual adaptive-matching notion of ATI studies.

Aptitude Training as a Means of Adapting to Individual Differences

The notion that it is possible, by specifically exercising aptitudes that are weak in an individual's repertoire, to enhance his ability to profit from instruction, suggests the possibility of direct training of aptitude or cognitive styles thought to be called upon in instruction. It suggests, in other words, a strategy that treats aptitudes as dependent rather than control variables, and seeks to influence them through instructional intervention. Only a limited number of studies of this kind exist, but they warrant discussion here since they represent a potentially powerful means of adapting to individual differences in the entering characteristics of learners.

Cognitive style variables.—There have been several attempts to modify implusive children's behavior in the direction of greater reflectivity. Yando & Kagan (344) found that when first-grade children were placed with experienced reflective teachers, the children became more reflective during the school year than those placed with implusive teachers. The practical im-

plication for school instruction is the notion of tailoring the tempo of the
teacher to the tempo of the child, so that impulsive behavior is influenced by
the presence of a reflective model. This work has been followed up in a study
by Debus (69), which explores the modifiability of an impulsive conceptual
tempo in the context of Bandura's (16) notions of social modeling. The findings of the study lend support to the modifiability of the behavior of impulsive students through teacher influence. A set of studies by Meichenbaum (212, 213) investigates the controlling function of self-speech upon
impulsive behavior (cf. 194, 201). The results of these studies suggest the
possibility of training children in a self-guidance procedure whereby impulsive children are taught to covertly talk to themselves and in this way
modify their cognitive styles.

Perceptual abilities.—It is widely recognized that perceptual processes
are implicated in a variety of cognitive tasks, ranging from simple discriminations to complex performances such as reading. In the field of special
education, extensive attention has been given to learning disabilities of a
perceptual character (both visual and auditory), which are widely thought to
underlie difficulties in reading and other school subjects for many children.
Perceptual training programs have been developed to cope with deficits in
this area, and a modest literature on the effects of training in both auditory
and visual skills exists, primarily in the special education journals. We cite
here a few illustrative studies that examine the effects of training on perceptual aptitude tests, or that demonstrate a relationship between training a
perceptual skill and learning some academic skill.

In the first category, Brinkmann (35) found differential improvement in
scores on the Space Relations subtest of the Differential Aptitude Tests
following approximately 3 weeks of programmed instruction in a special
approach to geometry which stressed perceptual rather than formal-logical
aspects of the subject matter. Girls reached a terminal level of performance
equal to that of the boys in a perceptual skill in which girls are generally
assumed to have less ability. The visual training programs of Rosner, described in the section on early education, are also examples of successful
training of perceptual aptitudes as measured by commonly accepted
tests.

In the second category of studies, those measuring effects of perceptual
training on academic performance, Raven & Strubing (250) compared second
graders trained for 12 days on one of two Frostig visual training units with an
untrained control group on learning of a subsequently presented science
unit on relativity of position and motion. Both of the Frostig training groups
performed significantly better than the control group. A study by Elkind &
Deblinger (78) examined the effects of nonverbal perceptual training exercises designed to promote "decentration" (defined in Piagetian terms) administered to inner-city children over a period of 15 weeks. Dependent variables were several subtests of the California Achievement Test, together

with perceptual tests developed earlier by Elkind on the basis of Piagetian perceptual theory. Comparing pre- to post-test gains, trained subjects showed greater improvement than control subjects on the California Word Form and Word Recognition subtests and on Elkind's Picture Integration Test. There was, however, no effect on general reading scores, reading comprehension, or other nonperceptual components of reading. Rosner (272) studied the effects of auditory training on reading skills, using as dependent variables both a new test of auditory perception based on phonic analysis tasks (274) and a word decoding test. After about 50 small group instructional periods of 20 minutes each, spread over about 13 weeks, trained subjects showed significantly higher auditory perception scores than untrained subjects. Further, their decoding scores were higher than those of matched control subjects in the same classrooms, thus indicating a transfer from trained auditory perception to reading performance.

These three studies, although each quite limited in scope, illustrate the kind of research which is needed to directly test the relationship between the improvement of perceptual skills through direct instruction and the effect of such instructionally improved perceptual skills on some aspect of academic performance. Considerably more work in this area is required, both to confirm the effectiveness of such training and explicate its characteristics, and to explore the extent to which instructionally improved perceptual skills produce concomitant gains in the performance of complex academic tasks.

Effects of schooling on intelligence and aptitude tests.—We have noted earlier a number of early childhood intervention studies that used changes in IQ scores as a major dependent variable. This use of IQ derives in part from the paucity of other accepted measures for the preschool years, and in part from the well-established predictive validity of IQ measures for traditional school achievement. Stein & Susser (304) have done a general review of studies on the effects of early schooling and social milieu change. They conclude that special intervention programs for children can indeed result in a measureable increase in IQ scores for initially low IQ groups, but that the advantages gained from 1- or 2-year intervention programs are generally not self-sustained; that is, in the absence of continuing special programs in the early school grades, children from the preschool programs do not maintain their advantage over children who did not attend these programs. It is not that the treated children decline in IQ, but rather that the untreated ones increase upon entrance to school, thus suggesting that it is school experience itself, rather than any particular form of it or any particular timing of it, that produces the increase.

Such an interpretation is supported by the findings of Zigler & Butterfield (345), who demonstrated that a significant portion of IQ gain from special intervention programs could be attributed to motivational and social factors (on which entrance to school is likely to have large influence) rather than to cognitive factors. The Zigler & Butterfield study compared fall and spring IQ scores for tests administered both under standard conditions and "optimal" conditions designed to increase motivation to respond correctly. Subjects were children of nursery school age, some attending and some not attending special preschool classes. Optimal testing conditions produced significant increases in IQ scores over standard conditions, and this difference was greater in the fall than in the spring (at which time the school experience had presumably overcome some of the motivational deficits). Further, correlational analyses showed that for the nursery groups, the larger a child's increase from standard to optimal testing in the fall (i.e. the larger his motivational deficit), the larger his gains in IQ over the school year for tests administered under standard conditions. This correlation did not hold for children not attending school, thus indicating the school's role in overcoming initial motivational handicaps. The results of this study, in addition to demonstrating a significant motivational component in IQ scores which can lead to systematic underestimation of IQ among certain groups of children, suggest that caution should be applied in interpreting all claims of IQ improvement from compensatory intervention. In general, unless pretests are administered only after considerable attention to developing social comfort in the testing situation, and unless motivational conditions are carefully managed, only very dramatic increases in IQ can be interpreted as demonstrating changes in cognitive competence.

Two studies have appeared recently which investigate the effects of secondary school experience on the development of verbal, quantitative, and spatial aptitudes. Both conclude that differential schooling leads to differential development of these aptitudes in students. Meuris (219) conducted separate factor analyses for a battery of verbal, spatial, and numerical tests for Belgian students in the first year and the last year of secondary school. There was more differentiation (i.e. the general factor accounted for less of the variance) in the older than in the younger group. In addition, in the terminal year, classical students did better on the verbal tests, but science students were better on the numerical and spatial tests, although the classical students had excelled on both sets of tests in the inital year. A Canadian study (177) performed separate factor analyses at grades 7, 9, and 11 and found increasing differentiation of factors with increasing school experience. While less clear with respect to the effects of school than the Meuris study, because there was no comparison of students receiving markedly different educational programs, this study nonetheless suggests that increased learning experiences lead to progressive differentiation of aptitudes—again an effect of learning upon aptitudes, rather than aptitudes upon learning.

GENERAL COMMENT ON THE NATURE OF APTITUDES AND INDIVIDUAL DIFFERENCES

It is striking that our search for research on the training of aptitudes and abilities as psychometrically defined has yielded far fewer studies than we were able to review in the section on training Piagetian concepts. This observation invites reflection on why the Piagetian definition of intelligence has stimulated so much more instructional research than has the psychometric one. Piagetian theory is not concerned with differential prediction, but with explication of developmental changes in thought structures and the influence of these structures on performance. This emphasis has suggested a variety of specific performances on which to focus instructional attention, and also a set of hypotheses concerning the optimal character of instructional attempts.

By contrast, most psychometric tests of intelligence, for which items have been chosen because of their predictive power rather than their relationship to observed or hypothesized intellectual processes, offer few concrete suggestions as to what to train. It is generally recognized that highly specific training, geared to the particular items on a test, is likely to raise test scores but destroy the predictive validity of the test; and since the test has no other strong theoretical basis (construct validity) to which to appeal, the results of such training are seen to be of little significance. However, there are a few cases in which increases in test performance appear to reflect generalized capability rather than item-specific performance. These are the instances in which underlying processes mediating successful performance on the tests have been hypothesized and trained (as in the perceptual training studies, for example), or where the entering level of general performance is unusually low and a broad-based instructional program has been applied (as in some of the early intervention studies).

We have noted earlier that attempts to identify aptitude-treatment interactions on the basis of psychometrically defined aptitudes and broadly characterized treatments have yielded little of interest. The few studies with significant findings were those in which both treatments and aptitudes were characterized in terms of the specific processes called upon in instruction and available to the learner. Again, with respect to training, we note that abilities defined with respect to behavioral process rather than predictive power seem more amenable to instructional intervention. Thus, it appears that successful attempts to adapt instruction to individual differences will depend upon a line of research on process variables in instruction and performance that is only now beginning to emerge.

BEHAVIOR MODIFICATION

Reinforcement and feedback have long been considered key variables in the instructional process. Recent journals in educational and instructional psychology have contained sections on this subject which typically have reviewed either laboratory studies on the effects of various types or scheduling of reinforcers or feedback variables in programmed instruction, concept learning, motor skills, and other laboratory tasks (e.g. 6, 113). This kind of research on reinforcement effects has continued; however, during the past 4 or 5 years, a major new trend in the study of reinforcement variables in instruction has emerged. This is "applied behavior analysis," more popularly referred to as "behavior modification," and we shall limit our discussion here to this topic.

Behavior modification represents a direct application of principles and methods of the behavioral laboratory to socially relevant problems (15). Much of the research relevant to instruction in this area bears the stamp of operant orientation and methodology: single-subject reversal designs rather than large-sample control group designs; direct observation of the behavior being studied; emphasis on experimental control of behavior through manipulation of schedules and contingencies of reinforcement.

A recent paper by Wolf & Risley (342) has outlined the major characteristics of behavior modification research in the operant tradition. The authors emphasize that applied behavior analysis carries the strategies and practices of laboratory research directly into field settings, rather than extrapolating principles from laboratory studies and applying them without direct testing in the new environment. The paper illustrates the characteristics of reversal and multiple baseline designs in applied settings. Statistics for assessing the significance of multiple baseline effects have been proposed by Revusky (257); Gottman, McFall & Barnett (131) have also proposed analyses for research employing an essentially similar design called the "multiple time series."

Reinforcement in the Classroom

The earliest applications of systematic reinforcement contingencies occurred in the context of clinical psychology, and behavior therapy is now a well-established speciality within that branch of psychology. Educational applications are more recent, and in fact were concentrated until only 3 or 4 years ago in various special classrooms in which educational and behavioral problems could not be easily distinguished. A recent review by Hanley (141) brings together most of the research on behavior modification in classrooms—special and normal—up to about 1968. Beginning in 1968 a new journal, the *Journal of Applied Behavior Analysis*, became the focus of most of the controlled research on applied reinforcement relevant to education, although studies continue to appear in *Behavior Research and Therapy*, *Exceptional Children*, and related journals. A recent article by O'Leary & Drabman (233) reviews classroom token reinforcement research. A number of "guidebooks" for teachers interested in applying behavior modification techniques have appeared during the past few years (e.g. 42, 150, 204, 207, 211). There are also some recent collections of readings on behavior modification in education (80, 260).

The most common treatment variables for classroom behavior modification studies have been social reinforcement [praise and other forms of attention from the teacher (e.g. 53, 140, 142, 289, 291, 319, 329)]; token economies [points or counters which can later be exchanged for tangible reinforcers or used as access to desired activities (e.g. 43, 128, 233, 239, 321, 337)]; and "contracts" [agreements with the student that desirable activities or material objects will be made available as soon as he has completed a specified amount of work (e.g. 205, 299)]. Recently, a few studies have appeared which examine the effects of self-administered rather than teacher-administered reinforcement (169, 198).

Punishment has been studied relatively little in educational settings, partly as a consequence of the operant stress on positive reinforcement, partly because of concerns of educators and those working with them that punishment could be badly misused by untrained or insensitive teachers. There are a few exceptions. Madsen et al (206) showed that a mild "punisher" (i.e. a teacher's command to "sit down" when a child left his seat) actually functioned as a reinforcer. Children were out of their seats more under this condition than when out-of-seat behavior was ignored and in-seat behavior praised. At the same time, Thomas, Becker & Armstrong (319) showed that a well-controlled classroom would become disruptive when the teacher increased her rate of contingent disapproval and eliminated praise statements. Further study of the function of reprimands (232, 234) has shown that different kinds of reprimands (e.g. "loud" and "quiet") produce different effects. McAllister et al (209) found that negative verbal comments were sometimes useful in establishing conditions under which praise would be more effective.

With respect to dependent variables, the bulk of classroom behavior modification studies have focused not on learning or academic performance but on decreasing disruptive behavior and its obverse, increasing attention to task. A nondisruptive and hard-at-work class is, of course, highly reinforcing to a teacher, and this probably accounts for some of the emphasis on these variables by behavioral researchers who have often been faced with the task of convincing teachers that reinforcement strategies were worthwhile. These variables have also been easier to study during the early period of behavior modification research because the same unit of behavior is observed repeatedly and measurement procedures directly analogous to those used in the operant laboratory could, therefore, be applied. By contrast, the use of learning outcomes as dependent variables requires attention to a variety of new measurement and scaling problems. Although it seems logical enough that at least some minimal level of attention to the task at hand is required for learning to take place, the extent of this relationship has never been adequately demonstrated in the classroom setting. For this reason, studies that use some measure of learning outcome are of the most direct interest to the field of instructional psychology.

Most studies that have examined learning outcomes have used general academic achievement, as measured by standardized tests or school grades, as the measure of learning (e.g. 53, 55, 60, 208, 320, 341). Some have measured the number of academic tasks completed but without directly assessing learning outcomes from this practice (e.g. 198, 230). Specific reinforcement effects have been shown for the learning of spelling (22, 346), history and geography (128), current events information (321), reading (336), following instructions (289), and oral language (258). Subjects in these studies have ranged from preschoolers through secondary school students, and have included retarded and normal children, middle-class and lower-class, black and white, delinquents and normal achievers. In addition, reinforcement systems of several major types have been used—tokens, social reinforcement, contingency contracting. Thus, considerable generality of the reinforcement effect for school learning outcomes has been demonstrated. However, there has been only slight attention to the problem of whether and how systematic reinforcement programs can be terminated and the behavior maintained by contingencies existing in the natural environment (253).

Modeling and Observational Learning

The major full-length works in the field of behavior modification have continued to stress therapeutic rather than educational applications. Of these, a book by Bandura (16) is significant for instructional psychology, despite its essentially clinical orientation, because of the range of techniques of behavior modification other than directly administered reinforcement that it considers. It is also exceptionally cogent in its discussion of the ethical concerns that are sometimes raised regarding the use of behavior modification techniques. In this book and in a recent paper (17), Bandura discusses in detail a wide range of studies in the use of modeling and vicarious and self-reinforcement processes as a means of modifying behavior.

Modeling or observational learning is the process of acquiring new responses by imitating or simply observing the behavior of another individual. In contrast with the acquisition of new responses through differential reinforcement of successive approximations, the accepted behavioral formulation, learning through observation need not involve direct reinforcement of the learner, and need not, in fact, involve overt performance of the new behavior until the test situation, sometimes considerably delayed from the acquisition phase. Bandura reviews both the various theoretical conceptions of how modeling works and a range of laboratory and applied studies demonstrating its effectiveness in facilitating the performance of behaviors already in the individual's repertoire, inhibiting inappropriate responses, and developing novel responses. It is with the role of modeling processes in the development of novel responses, not previously available to the individual, that instructional psychology will be most directly concerned.

Central to the role of modeling as an instructional process is the notion that complex behaviors are developed primarily by the combination of components already in the learner's repertoire. Observation of the model's performance leads, according to Bandura's formulation, to the establishment of "representational schemes"—imagery and verbal encoding—which on a subsequent occasion provide ". . . a basis for self-instruction regarding the manner in which component responses must be combined and sequenced to produce new patterns of behavior" (16, p. 141). A number of studies have shown that when several different models are observed, a generalized class of behaviors rather than a specific direct imitation of the model can be learned.

In Bandura's theory, as in much current psychological theory, a distinction is made between learning and performance. Learning is assumed to occur as the model is observed and symbolic mediators are generated. The extent of learning depends on the learner's level of attention to the model and on the degree to which the model's performance makes the characteristics of the behavior to be learned highly discriminable. In learning, reinforcement plays an indirect role, largely through the activation of appropriate attentional and mediational processes. Performance, on the other hand, is governed by the laws of reinforcement; the individual is more likely to perform the new behavior when he is reinforced for doing so, or expects to be so reinforced. This expectation can be fostered through observation of reinforcement contingencies applied to the model's performance. Vicarious reinforcement of this kind is an important factor in observational learning. Thus modeling theory does not deny the importance of reinforcement variables in the modification of behavior. But it does direct attention to other aspects of the instructional intervention, and it suggests strongly that the learning process can be considerably shortened by making use of the human being's capacity to learn through symbolic processes, i.e. from being shown what to do and observing the effects of performance by others. A continuing debate between operant and mediational interpretations of modeling and observational learning is illustrated in the discussion by Gewirtz (116) of one of Bandura's papers.

Most research on modeling has studied the acquisition of social rather than cognitive behaviors. The major exceptions lie in the development of language. An outstanding example of the use of modeling, in conjunction with a carefully designed differential reinforcement program, is the work of Lovaas and his associates (195–197) in training language and related conceptual behaviors in autistic children. Cazden's (48) work has demonstrated the usefulness of a general modeling approach in language instruction for disadvantaged children. Several other studies have demonstrated the role of models in modifying syntactic productions of children (18, 191, 266). In another domain, a study by Sullivan (312) found the viewing of films of adults conserving liquid and substance improved conservation performance of first graders. Finally, a study by Rosenthal, Zimmerman & Durning (267) used modeling procedures to modify children's information seeking strategies. Modeling principles have also been used recently in the development of programs to train teachers in skills that combine significant social and cognitive behaviors. McDonald & Allen (210, Chap. 4) showed that provision of videotaped models of effective teaching behaviors enhanced acquisition of those behaviors to some degree. However, the model's effectiveness was greatest when the trainees viewed it along with an experimenter who pointed out both the appropriate behaviors of the model and the occasions (student responses) suitable for those behaviors.

An interesting extension of the concept of modeling is learning from verbal instructions, i.e. from being *told* what to do. Bandura calls instructions "verbal models," as opposed to the more widely studied "behavioral models" (films, puppets, or live performers of the behavior). Instructions, he points out, have both an instigational function (getting performance started and perhaps setting the subject to process information in a particular way) and a modeling function (describing the action required). Little work along these lines has been done up to this time. A great deal of activity has occurred, however, in the investigation of the retention of verbal information as a function of the processing requirements of written prose. This research is discussed in the next section.

LEARNING FROM WRITTEN PROSE

Over the past 10 years there has been a pronounced increase in the number of studies concerned with the question of how learning takes place from written materials. This work has concentrated on meaningful prose material of reasonable paragraph length typical of the kind of material employed in textbooks and everyday written communication, in contrast to the more artificial materials of traditional verbal learning experiments, or the specifically designed sentences and short paragraphs of the more recent psycholinguistic studies. The typical experimental procedure in these studies is to vary the characteristics of written text or the instructions to the learner and to assess the influence of these conditions upon how the material is attended to, processed, and retained.

Impetus for work in this area has been provided by Rothkopf and Ausubel. Rothkopf summarized his work in 1965 (276) and more recently in 1970 (279). Frase (97) also has recently summarized the findings in this area; and Anderson (7) has discussed the role of attentional processes in verbal learning and instruction, and has related this research to an analysis of prompting techniques as described in the literature on programmed instruction. The work of Ausubel (10, 11) on meaningful verbal learning has been influential and has also stimulated studies on learning from written materials which continue to appear in the literature.

Rothkopf (279) had developed the concept of mathemagenic activities to refer to those behaviors that "give birth to learning." More specifically, this concept is related to the distinction between nominal and effective stimuli. Nominal stimuli are transformed by mathemagenic activities such as set, habits of attention, information and cognitive processing, rehearsal, etc., and such activities determine the nature of effective stimuli in instructional situations. Mathemagenic activities with respect to written materials consist of (a) the relatively overt activities of attending to and scanning the text, and (b) the more internal processes accompanying reading. Some work has been carried out on the former (e.g. 75, 139, 323), primarily concerned with the operant analysis of attending behavior, but this work has been been sparse. Most investigators have addressed themselves to the second type of behavior along the lines described below.

The position of questions in text.—Recent studies (40, 92) have confirmed the earlier finding (e.g. 276, 277, 280) that adjunct questions administered shortly after the text segment to which they are relevant affect mathemagenic activities. In general, students learn most when the questions come after the material to which they relate rather than before, although questions in either position are superior to no questions at all in promoting learning. Postquestions have both specific and general facilitative effects in contrast to prequestions, which facilitate only the retention of question-relevant information. The reason for this seems to be that the students in prequestion conditions tend to spend their reading time in looking for the question-relevant prose content; on the other hand, since students in postquestion conditions do not know which information may turn out to be relevant, reading and processing skills (mathemagenic activities) are encouraged which result in more careful inspection of the entire text. A recent study on the effect of prequestions on delayed retention (245) has indicated that the specific facilitating effect of prequestions holds up in measures of 7-day delayed retention, and that there is inferior retention of question-irrelevant information. In this study a control group was employed that used the time available to other groups for dealing with prequestions for studying the text itself. Results showed that in terms of the total amount of knowledge acquired, the time spent on prequestions might just as profitably have been used for extending the time for attending to the actual text.

The frequency of questions.—Since embedded questions can interact with the text to restrict the range of effective stimuli, studies have been carried out to investigate whether learning is further facilitated by using more frequent questions placed closer to the related material, hence increasing their selective effect (91, 226). Frase investigated the effect of the location and frequency of adjunct questions upon retention of prose material. It was found that frequent prequestions decreased overall retention and that retention increased with the frequency of postquestions. It was concluded that while frequent postquestioning either shaped or elicited appropriate reading skills, frequent prequestions interfered with the continuity of the prose materials and inhibited learning both relevant and incidental information. The differential effect of postquestions and prequestions, the former facilitating both relevant and incidental learning and the latter having their primary effect on specific information, was further substantiated.

Type of question.—A study by Frase (93) compared the effect of general prequestions (e.g. "When were the men in the paragraph born?") with more specific prequestions (e.g. "When was Jack born?") on learning from a text passage. It was predicted that general questions would require subjects to process more information than more specific questions and hence that more would be learned. Contrary to this prediction, retention was lowest with general questions. It appeared that the effect of specific questions was to direct the student to particular portions of the text and to the appropriate associations between different parts of the text; general questions did not force the subject to respond to larger segments of text.

Oral questioning.—Since it has been shown that text-embedded questions exert significant influence on learning, a recent study (281) questioned whether the delivery of adjunct oral questions by a teacher could promote more effective study of written instructional materials than written adjunct questions embedded in the text. The findings of the study indicated that the oral questions involving social contact resulted in slightly higher performance than the written adjunct questions embedded in the text.

Structural characteristics of text material.—Recent studies, particularly those by Frase (94–96, 98, 99), have been concerned with the structural characteristics of text material and their influence upon learning and retention, e.g. the study by Frase described in the earlier section on task analysis (96). In another study (94), the text passages were designed so that subjects had to search for the name of an object which had a particular set of attributes. In the written material, different planets were the objects to which certain attributes (i.e. distance from earth, terrain, atmospheric color, etc) were assigned. For half the subjects, the material was organized in terms of the objects (planets) with the attributes varying; for the other half, the paragraph was arranged by attributes so that each attribute had to be assigned to a particular object as the passage was read. In the first condition, subjects had to enter the attributes into memory while they searched for its object; in the second condition, each object was held in memory as search proceeded for its attribute. Retention tests indicated that, as predicted, the group which read the sentences organized by object name retained more attributes than the group which read the same sentences organized by attribute; the latter group retained more object names. Apparently, changing the organization of the material resulted in different patterns of search and influenced what words were entered into memory and rehearsed in the course of reading.

Other studies (96, 98) confirm the general finding that memory of text information improves with an increase in the amount of processing of the text required. The amount of processing is influenced by the number of problems to be solved from the text or by the difficulty (amount of information required) of a problem. A study by Rothkopf (278) indicates that repeated exposures to text passages result in the progressive modification of mathemagenic or text inspection behaviors, and suggests further investigation of changes in reading habits over prolonged exposure to texts with particular organizational structures.

"Organizers."—Ausubel (10, 11) has emphasized that, in the context of meaningful prose material, prior "organizers" or previously learned correlative information influence retention. The theoretical position involved asserts that meaningful learning and retention are dependent upon more general cognitive structures under which the ideas represented in newly presented information can be subsumed. Appropriately organized material facilitates this subsumption process, which enhances learning and retention.

A number of studies report work along these lines (2, 41, 135). A study by Gagné (108) confirms Ausubel's notions that a context in which there is a superordinate arrangement, i.e. the material is presented with an introductory general topic sentence, facilitates recall of facts to a greater extent than does a coordinate context (i.e. related information but without a topic sentence). The coordinate context, in turn, leads to greater recall than unrelated context. A follow-up study by Gagné & Wiegand (114) investigated whether the influence of a superordinate topic sentence is exerted during the learning phase or whether it has its organizing effect during the retrieval phase, or both. Results indicate that a topic sentence improves the remembering of facts when it is presented just before a retention test, implying that the locus of effect for the organizing function of a topic sentence occurs in the retrieval phase of the remembering process.

Classical verbal learning variables.—A large number of studies have investigated the classical variables of verbal learning in the context of meaningful prose. The variables studied include retroactive inhibition (66, 167, 343), retroactive facilitation (12), proactive effects (13), isolation effects (47, 108), repeated presentation (152), and delay of feedback (224). The general impression obtained from these investigations is that what is required at the present time is a selective review to pull together the various findings and theoretical interpretations.

A series of studies have investigated the effects of word associations on reading behavior (283–285). The findings indicate that the strength of the associative relationship between words influences reading speed, recall, and guessing behavior on multiple choice tests. The speed of word recognition is facilitated or retarded depending upon the association strength existing between word pairs presented. The associative strength between adjective-noun pairs influences learning to read the second word of the pair, assuming that the reader can read the first word. This effect seems to be all or none in the sense that even minimum amounts of word association training compared to none produce significant increases in reading attainment—a finding which lends support to the general practice followed by some teachers of introducing new reading words in the context of a sentence and having the student repeat the reading of the sentence aloud.

Very little work seems to have been undertaken on the learning and recall of prose as a function of linguistic variables (46, 168, 183, 282).

Summary comments.—The work that has been reported in this section has barely scratched the surface of the problem of how people learn from texts. The learning and retention of facts have been studied, but not many studies ask how these facts are organized by the reader. Making inferences and drawing conclusions from written passages has been little studied. The trainability of text-processing behaviors and their generalizability over different materials need to be investigated. A task analysis of reading comprehension tests seems called for, particularly to study their relationship to habits of text processing. A nagging impression that one gets in reading the literature as it grows in this area is that it could become another insular activity like the traditional field of verbal learning. If this is to be prevented, researchers must live down their past habits of empiricism untempered by theoretical analysis, the neglect of processes which can account for individual variation, and the retreat to artificial laboratory tasks such as arbitrary verbal associations. So far, however, the increased attention to learning from written materials is an exemplary trend in attempts to close the gaps that exist between our knowledge of learning and the processes of everyday school instruction.

SOME INTERESTING ITEMS

In the period covered by this review, the following items of interest have appeared and should be called to the attention of the reader:

(a) Two small volumes have appeared entitled *Soviet Studies in the Psychology of Learning and Teaching Mathematics* (178). The editors point out that materials have been prepared for 15 volumes, and the contemplated series represents a collection of translations from the Soviet literature of the past 25 years on research in the psychology of mathematical instruction. Included in the present volumes are methods of teaching mathematics which appear to be directly influenced by psychological research. One is impressed with the fact that the lead-off chapter in Volume I is entitled "Fifty Years of Soviet Instructional Psychology." Some additional Soviet work in developmental psychology relating to early learning and education is reported in a *Handbook of Contemporary Soviet Psychology* (61).

(b) A book by Estes (79) gives critical attention to the relationship between learning theory and research concerned with mental development—normal development with special attention to individual difference in learning abilities and types of deviation from the norm which define mental retardation. A wide variety of learning theories and learning phenomena are examined. The book occasionally expresses some hope for substantial advances in the training of mentally retarded on the basis of theoretical and experimental analyses of learning. For example, investigations associated with the operant conditioning position and with contemporary discrimination learning theories have had some striking successes in the training of the mentally retarded. In the main, however, the conclusion of the book is that contacts between learning theory and the empirical study of mental development have been sparse and unsystematic. The relative isolation of the two disciplines, learning theory and the science of mental development, is reminiscent of the relationship between learning and instruction in general.

(c) Not referenced in other reviews is a volume appearing in 1968 entitled *Learning Research and School Subjects* (110). In this volume, chapters on concept learning, perceptual learning, mathemagenic activities, and transfer of training are considered with respect to teaching and instruction. A final chapter considers the question of values in educational programs.

(d) A new book by Olson (235) entitled *Cognitive Development: The Child's Acquisition of Diagonality* impresses us as an outstanding and unique example of an experimental and theoretical inquiry of intellectual development, complemented by investigation of the effects of instruction on the formulation of early concepts. According to the author, educational theorists require

> ... a description of development complemented by an account of the process involved in the child's selection and utilization of the information he encounters in his experience and in instruction. This aspect necessarily involves an account of the nature and effects of instruction on this development. Instruction is one of the major concerns of this monograph, as well as one of the major research tools used in elucidating the process of intellectual development" (p. xv).

(e) Among a flurry of books interpreting Piaget for those interested in education and instruction (8, 19, 77, 85, 313), two volumes were of special interest to us. The first (247) is comprised of two texts by Piaget, one dating from 1965 entitled "Education in Teaching since 1935," and the other dating from 1935 entitled "The New Methods [of education]: Their Psychological Foundations." The second, by Furth (101), is entitled *Piaget for Teachers* and also consists of two parts. Part one gives a description of Piaget's ideas on thinking and intelligence; part two consists of an explication of the author's ideas for a school designed for the teaching of thinking. Examples of exercises for such teaching are given. Of particular interest is the author's concern that the preoccupation of society with teaching specialized skills that represent criteria of scholastic success (e.g. reading 1) might detract from work in the early grades that has more to do with thinking.

(f) In the present climate of research and development in instruction it is becoming increasingly difficult to make the traditional separation between work on learning, psychometrics, and the evaluation of learning outcomes. Two books reflect this trend. One, the result of a symposium edited by Wittrock & Wiley (339), considers the theory and practice of the evaluation in instruction together with instructional variables. The second is a sizable handbook by Bloom, Hastings & Madaus with chapters by other authors (29) on formative and summative evaluation of student learning. It discusses the use of evaluation for instructional decisions and describes evaluation techniques for assessing learning in a wide variety of educational domains.

(g) An interesting volume of papers has been collected by Holtzman (149) on computer-assisted instruction, testing, and guidance. The papers are substantive and coverage is broad. Topics include system design, language processing, instructional design, and optimizing learning. Specific exemplary programs of work accomplished are also described. Another book on computer-assisted instruction reports the work of a specific project directed by Suppes on arithmetic teaching (318). A book of readings, edited by Atkinson & Wilson (9a), which reflects current trends in research and development in computer-assisted instruction, has also been published.

LITERATURE CITED

1. Ahr, P. R., Youniss, J. 1970. Reasons for failure on the class inclusion problem. *Child Develop.* 41:131–43
2. Allen, D. I. 1970. Some effects of advance organizers and level of question on the learning and retention of written social studies material. *J. Educ. Psychol.* 61:333–39
3. Almy, M. 1970. *Logical Thinking in Second Grade.* New York: Teachers Coll. Press. 216 pp.
4. Anderson, G. L., Ed. 1950. *Learning and Instruction. The 49th Yearbook of the NSSE.* Part I. Univ. Chicago Press. 352 pp.
5. Anderson, R. C. 1965. Can first graders learn an advanced problem-solving skill? *J. Educ. Psychol.* 56:283–94
6. Anderson, R. C. 1967. Educational psychology. *Ann. Rev. Psychol.* 18:129–64
7. Anderson, R. C. 1970. Control of student mediating processes during verbal learning and instruction. *Rev. Educ. Res.* 40:349–69
8. Athey, I. J., Rubadeau, D. O., Eds. 1970. *Educational Implications of Piaget's Theory.* Waltham: Ginn-Blaisdell. 378 pp.
9. Atkinson, R. C., Paulson, J. A. 1972. An approach to the psychology of instruction. *Psychol. Bull.* In press
9a. Atkinson, R. C., Wilson, H. A., Eds. 1969. *Computer-Assisted Instruction: A Book of Readings.* New York: Academic. 362 pp.
10. Ausubel, D. P. 1963. *The Psychology of Meaningful Verbal Learning: An Introduction to School Learning.* New York: Grune & Stratton. 255 pp.
11. Ausubel, D. P. 1968. *Educational Psychology: A Cognitive View.* New York: Holt, Rinehart & Winston. 685 pp.
12. Ausubel, D. P., Stager, M., Gaite, A. J. H. 1968. Retroactive facilitation in meaningful verbal learning and retention. *J. Educ. Psychol.* 59:250–55
13. Ibid 1969. Proactive effects in meaningful verbal learning and retention. 60:59–64
14. Baer, D. M., Wolf, M. M. 1968. The reinforcement contingency in preschool and remedial education. See Ref. 144, 119–29
15. Baer, D. M., Wolf, M. M., Risley, T. R. 1968. Some current dimensions of applied behavior analysis. *J. Appl. Behav. Anal.* 1:91–97
16. Bandura, A. 1969. *Principles of Behavior Modification.* New York: Holt, Rinehart & Winston. 677 pp.
17. Bandura, A. 1971. Vicarious and self-reinforcement processes. See Ref. 126a, 228–78
18. Bandura, A., Harris, M. B. 1966. Modification of syntactic style. *J. Exp. Child Psychol.* 4:341–52
19. Beard, R. M. 1969. *An Outline of Piaget's Developmental Psychology for Students and Teachers.* New York: Basic Books. 139 pp.
20. Bearison, D. J. 1969. Role of measurement operations in the acquisition of conservation. *Develop. Psychol.* 1:653–60
21. Beilin, H., Kagan, J., Rabinowitz, R. 1966. Effects of verbal and perceptual training on water level representation. *Child Develop.* 37:317–29
22. Benowitz, M. L., Busse, T. V. 1970. Material incentives and the learning of spelling words in a typical school situation. *J. Educ. Psychol.* 61:24–26
23. Bereiter, C. 1968. A nonpsychological approach to early compensatory education. See Ref. 74, 337–46
24. Bereiter, C., Engelmann, S. 1966. *Teaching Disadvantaged Children in the Preschool.* Englewood Cliffs, N. J.: Prentice-Hall. 312 pp.
25. Blank, M. 1972. The wrong response: Is it to be ignored, prevented, or treated? See Ref. 243. In press
26. Blank, M., Solomon, F. 1968. A tutorial language program to develop abstract thinking in socially disadvantaged preschool children. *Child Develop.* 39:379–89
27. Ibid 1969. How shall the disadvantaged child be taught? 40:47–61
28. Bloom, B. S. 1964. *Stability and Change in Human Characteristics.* New York: Wiley. 237 pp.
29. Bloom, B. S., Hastings, J. T., Madaus, G. F. 1971. *Handbook on Formative and Summative Evaluation of Student Learning.* New York: McGraw-Hill. 923 pp.
30. Bower, G. H. 1971. Mental imagery and associative learning. In *Strategies in Organization in Learning,* ed. L. Gregg. New York: Wiley. In press
31. Bracht, G. H. 1969. *The relationship of treatment tasks, personological vari-*

ables, and dependent variables to apti-tude-treatment interaction. PhD dissertation. Univ. Colorado, Boulder. 221 pp.

32. Bracht, G. H. 1970. Experimental factors related to aptitude-treatment interactions. Rev. Educ. Res. 40:627–45

33. Bracht, G. H., Glass, G. V. 1968. The external validity of experiments. Am. Educ. Res. J. 5:437–74

34. Brainerd, C. J., Allen, T. W. 1971. Experimental inductions of the conservation of "first-order" quantitative invariants. Psychol. Bull. 75:128–44

35. Brinkmann, E. H. 1966. Programed instruction as a technique for improving spatial visualization. J. Appl. Psychol. 50:179–84

36. Brison, D. W. 1966. Acceleration of conservation of substance. J. Genet. Psychol. 109:311–22

37. Brottman, M. A., Ed. 1968. Language remediation for the disadvantaged preschool child. Monogr. Soc. Res. Child Develop. 33:No. 8

38. Bruner, J. S. 1964. Some theorems on instruction illustrated with reference to mathematics. See Ref. 147, 306–35

39. Bruner, J. S. 1966. On cognitive growth: I, II. In Studies in Cognitive Growth, ed. J. S. Bruner et al, 1–67. New York: Wiley. 343 pp.

40. Bruning, R. H. 1968. Effects of review and testlike events within the learning of prose materials. J. Educ. Psychol. 59:16–19

41. Ibid 1970. Short-term retention of specific factual information in prose contexts of varying organization and relevance. 61:186–92

42. Buckley, N. K., Walker, H. M. 1970. Modifying Classroom Behavior: A Manual of Procedure for Classroom Teachers. Champaign, Ill.: Research Press. 124 pp.

43. Bushell, D. Jr., Wrobel, P. A., Michaelis, M. L. 1968. Applying "group" contingencies to the classroom study behavior of pre-school children. J. Appl. Behav. Anal. 1:55–61

44. Caldwell, B. M. 1967. What is the optimal learning environment for the young child? Am. J. Orthopsychiat. 37:8–21

45. Caldwell, B. M. 1968. The fourth dimension in early childhood education. See Ref. 144, 71–81

46. Carroll, J. B. 1968. On learning from being told. Educ. Psychol. 5:5–11

47. Cashen, V. M., Leicht, K. L. 1970. Role of the isolation effect in a formal educational setting. J. Educ. Psychol. 61:484–86

48. Cazden, C. B. 1968. Some implications of research on language development for preschool education. See Ref. 144, 131–42

49. Cazden, C. B. 1971. Evaluation of learning in preschool education: Early language development. See Ref. 29, 345–98

50. Chandler, C. A., Lourie, R. S., Peters, A. D. 1968. In Early Child Care—The New Perspectives, ed. L. L. Dittmann. New York: Atherton. 385 pp.

51. Chomsky, C. 1970. Reading, writing and phonology. Harvard Educ. Rev. 40:287–309

52. Chomsky, N., Halle, M. 1968. The Sound Pattern of English. New York: Harper & Row. 470 pp.

53. Clark, C. A., Walberg, H. J. 1968. The influence of massive rewards on reading achievement in potential urban school dropouts. Am. Educ. Res. J. 5:305–10

54. Clark, H. H. 1969. Linguistic processes in deductive reasoning. Psychol. Rev. 76:387–404

55. Clark, M., Lachowicz, J., Wolf, M. 1968. A pilot basic education program for school dropouts incorporating a token reinforcement system. Behav. Res. Ther. 6:183–88

56. Clarke, A. M., Cooper, G. M. 1966. Transfer in category learning of young children: Its relation to task complexity and overlearning. Brit. J. Psychol. 57:361–73

57. Clarke, A. M., Cooper, G. M., Clarke, A. D. B. 1967. Task complexity and transfer in the development of cognitive structures. J. Exp. Child Psychol. 5:562–76

58. Clarke, A. M., Cooper, G. M., Henney, A. S. 1966. Width of transfer and task complexity in the conceptual learning of imbeciles. Brit. J. Psychol. 57:121–28

59. Clarke, A. M., Cooper, G. M., Loudon, E. H. 1969. A set to establish equivalence relations in pre-school children. J. Exp. Child Psychol. 8:180–89

60. Cohen, H., Filipczak, J., Bis, J. 1968. CASE project: Contingencies applicable to special education. In Re-

search in Psychotherapy, ed. J. Shlien, 34–41. Washington: Am. Psychol. Assoc. 618 pp.

61. Cole, M., Maltzman, I., Eds. 1969. *A Handbook of Contemporary Soviet Psychology.* New York: Basic Books. 887 pp.

62. Cox, R. C., Graham, G. T. 1966. The development of a sequentially scaled achievement test. *J. Educ. Meas.* 3:147–50

63. Cronbach, L. J. 1967. How can instruction be adapted to individual differences? See Ref. 105, 23–39

64. Cronbach, L. J., Gleser, G. C. 1965. *Psychological Tests and Personnel Decisions.* Urbana: Univ. Illinois. 2nd ed. 347 pp.

65. Cronbach, L. J., Snow, R. E. 1969. *Individual differences in learning ability as a function of instructional variables.* Final Rep. Sch. Educ., Stanford Univ. Contract No. OEC 4-6-061269-1217, US Off. Educ.

66. Crouse, J. H. 1970. Transfer and retroaction in prose learning. *J. Educ. Psychol.* 61:226–28

67. Crow, J. F. 1969. Genetic theories and influences: Comments on the value of diversity. *Harvard Educ. Rev.* 39:301–9

68. Davis, J. K., Klausmeier, H. J. 1970. Cognitive style and concept identification as a function of complexity and training procedures. *J. Educ. Psychol.* 61:423–30

69. Debus, R. L. 1970. Effects of brief observation of model behavior on conceptual tempo of impulsive children. *Develop. Psychol.* 2:22–32

70. Denenberg, V. H., Ed. 1970. *Education of the Infant and Young Child.* New York: Academic. 140 pp.

71. Dennis, W., Sayegh, Y. 1965. The effect of supplementary experiences upon the behavioral development of infants in institutions. *Child Develop.* 36:81–90

72. Deutsch, M., et al 1967. *The Disadvantaged Child.* New York: Basic Books. 400 pp.

73. Deutsch, M. 1969. Happenings on the way back to the forum: Social science, IQ, and race differences revisited. *Harvard Educ. Rev.* 39: 523–57

74. Deutsch, M., Katz, I., Jensen, A. R., Eds. 1968. *Social Class, Race and Psychological Development.* New

York: Holt, Rinehart & Winston. 423 pp.

75. Doran, J., Holland, J. G. 1971. Eye movements as a function of response contingencies measured by blackout technique. *J. Appl. Behav. Anal.* 4:11–17

76. Dunham, J. L., Bunderson, C. V. 1969. Effect of decision-rule instruction upon the relationship of cognitive abilities to performance in multiple-category concept problems. *J. Educ. Psychol.* 60:121–25

77. Elkind, D. 1970. *Children and Adolescents—Interpretive Essays on Jean Piaget.* New York: Oxford Univ. Press. 160 pp.

78. Elkind, D., Deblinger, J. A. 1969. Perceptual training and reading achievement in disadvantaged children. *Child Develop.* 40:11–19

79. Estes, W. K. 1970. *Learning Theory and Mental Development.* New York: Academic. 223 pp.

80. Fargo, G., Behrns, C., Nolen, P., Eds. 1970. *Behavior Modification in the Classroom.* Belmont, Calif.: Wadsworth. 344 pp.

81. Fehr, F. S. 1969. Critique of hereditarian accounts of "intelligence" and contrary findings: A reply to Jensen. *Harvard Educ. Rev.* 39: 571–80

82. Ferguson, R. L. 1971. *Computer assistance for individualizing measurement.* No. 1971/8, Learn. Res. Develop. Center, Univ. Pittsburgh

83. Fischbein, E., Pampu, I., Manzat, I. 1970. Comparison of ratios and the chance concept in children. *Child Develop.* 41:377–89

84. Fischbein, E., Pampu, I., Manzat, I. 1970. Effects of age and instruction on combinatory ability in children. *Brit. J. Educ. Psychol.* 40:261–70

85. Flavell, J. H. 1963. *The Developmental Psychology of Jean Piaget.* New York: Van Nostrand. 472 pp.

86. Flavell, J. H., Hill, J. P. 1969. Developmental psychology. *Ann. Rev. Psychol.* 20:1–56

87. Fowler, H. 1971. Implications of sensory reinforcement. See Ref. 126a, 151–95

88. Fowler, W. 1962. Cognitive learning in infancy and early childhood. *Psychol. Bull.* 59:116–52

89. Fowler, W. 1965. A study of process and method in three-year-old twins

and triplets learning to read. *Genet. Psychol. Mongr.* 72:3–89

90. Fowler, W. 1968. The effect of early stimulation in the emergence of cognitive processes. See Ref. 144, 9–36

91. Frase, L. T. 1968. Effect of question location, pacing, and mode upon retention of prose material. *J. Educ. Psychol.* 59:244–49

92. Frase, L. T. 1968. Some data concerning the mathemagenic hypothesis. *Am. Educ. Res. J.* 5:181–89

93. Frase, L. T. 1968. Some unpredicted effects of different questions upon learning from connected discourse. *J. Educ. Psychol.* 59:197–201

94. Ibid 1969. Cybernetic control of memory while reading connected discourse. 60:49–55

95. Ibid. Paragraph organization of written materials: The influence of conceptual clustering upon the level and organization of recall, 394–401

96. Frase, L. T. 1969. Structural analysis of the knowledge that results from thinking about text. *J. Educ. Psychol. Monogr.* 60:6, Part 2

97. Frase, L. T. 1970. Boundary conditions for mathemagenic behaviors. *Rev. Educ. Res.* 40:337–47

98. Frase, L. T. 1970. Influence of sentence order and amount of higher level text processing upon reproductive and productive memory. *Am. Educ. Res. J.* 7:307–19

99. Frase, L. T., Silbiger, F. 1970. Some adaptive consequences of searching for information in a text. *Am. Educ. Res. J.* 7:553–60

100. Freeberg, N. E., Payne, D. T. 1967. Parental influence on cognitive development in early childhood: A review. *Child Develop.* 38:65–87

101. Furth, H. G. 1970. *Piaget for Teachers.* Englewood Cliffs, N. J.: Prentice-Hall. 163 pp.

102. Gagné, R. M. 1962. The acquisition of knowledge. *Psychol. Rev.* 69:355–65

103. Gagné, R. M. 1965. The analysis of instructional objectives for the design of instruction. In *Teaching Machines and Programed Learning, II: Data and Directions,* ed. R. Glaser, 21–65. Washington, D. C.: NEA. 831 pp.

104. Gagné, R. M. 1965. *The Conditions of Learning.* New York: Holt Rinehart & Winston. 308 pp.

105. Gagné, R. M., Ed. 1967. *Learning and Individual Differences.* Columbus, O.: Merrill. 265 pp.

106. Gagné, R. M. 1968. Contributions of learning to human development. *Psychol. Rev.* 75:177–91

107. Gagné, R. M. 1968. Learning hierarchies. *Educ. Psychol.* 6:1–9

108. Gagné, R. M. 1969. Context, isolation, and interference effects on the retention of fact. *J. Educ. Psychol.* 60:408–14

109. Gagné, R. M. 1970. *The Conditions of Learning.* New York: Holt, Rinehart & Winston. 2nd ed. 407 pp.

110. Gagné, R. M., Gephart, W. J., Eds. 1968. *Learning Research and School Subjects.* Itasca, Ill.: Peacock. 268 pp.

111. Gagné, R. M., Mayor, J. R., Garstens, H. L., Paradise, N. E. 1962. Factors in acquiring knowledge of a mathematical task. *Psychol. Monogr.* 76:7, Ser. No. 526

112. Gagné, R. M., Paradise, N. E. 1961. Abilities and learning sets in knowledge acquisition. *Psychol. Monogr.* 75:14, Ser. No. 518

113. Gagné, R. M., Rohwer, W. D. Jr. 1969. Instructional psychology. *Ann. Rev. Psychol.* 20:381–418

114. Gagné, R. M., Wiegand, V. K. 1970. Effects of a superordinate context on learning and retention of facts. *J. Educ. Psychol.* 61:406–9

115. Gelman, R. 1969. Conservation acquisition: A problem of learning to attend to relevant attributes. *J. Exp. Child Psychol.* 7:167–87

116. Gewirtz, J. L. 1971. The roles of overt responding and extrinsic reinforcement in "self-" and "vicarious-reinforcement" phenomena and in "observational learning" and imitation. See Ref. 126a, 279–309

117. Gibson, E. J. 1965. Learning to read. *Science* 148:1066–72

118. Gibson, E. J. 1968. Perceptual learning in educational situations. See Ref. 110, 61–86

119. Gibson, E. J. 1969. *Principles of Perceptual Learning and Development* New York: Appleton-Century-Crofts. 537 pp.

120. Gibson, E. J. 1970. The ontogeny of reading. *Am. Psychol.* 25:136–43

121. Gilbert, T. F. 1962. Mathetics: The technology of education. *J. Mathetics* 1:7–73

122. Ibid 1962. Mathetics: II. The design of teaching exercises. 2:7–56

123. Glanzer, M. 1967. Individual performance, R-R theory and perception. See Ref. 105, 141–59

124. Glaser, R. 1967. Some implications of previous work on learning and individual differences. See Ref. 105, 1–18

125. Glaser, R. 1969. Learning. In *Encyclopedia of Educational Research*, ed. R. L. Ebel, 706–33. New York: Macmillan. 4th ed. 1522 pp.

126. Glaser, R. 1970. Individual differences in learning. In *Individualized Curriculum and Instruction. Proc. 3rd Invitational Conf. Elem. Educ.*, ed. K. A. Neufeld, 17–31. Edmonton: Univ. Alberta. 223 pp.

126a. Glaser, R., Ed. 1971. *The Nature of Reinforcement*. New York: Academic. 379 pp.

127. Glaser, R., Nitko, A. J. 1971. Measurement in learning and instruction. In *Educational Measurement*, ed. R. L. Thorndike, 625–70. Washington, D. C.: Am. Counc. Educ. 768 pp.

128. Glynn, E. L. 1970. Classroom applications of self-determined reinforcement. *J. Appl. Behav. Anal.* 3: 123–32

129. Goodnow, J. J. 1962. A test of milieu effects with some of Piaget's tasks. *Psychol. Monogr.* 76: Whole No. 555

130. Gordon, I. J. 1971. Early child stimulation through parent education. In *Readings in Research in Developmental Psychology*, ed. I. J. Gordon, 146–54. Glenview, Ill.: Scott, Foresman. 351 pp.

131. Gottman, J. M., McFall, R. M., Barnett, J. T. 1969. Design and analysis of research using time series. *Psychol. Bull.* 72:299–306

132. Gray, S. W., Klaus, R. A. 1970. The early training project: A seventh-year report. *Child Develop.* 41:909–24

133. Groen, G. J. 1967. *An investigation of some counting algorithms for simple addition problems*. Tech. Rep. 118, Inst. Math. Stud. Soc. Sci., Stanford Univ.

134. Groen, G. J., Atkinson, R. C. 1966. Models for optimizing the learning process. *Psychol. Bull.* 66:309–20

135. Grotelueschen, A., Sjogren, D. D. 1968. Effects of differentially structured introductory materials and learning tasks on learning and transfer. *Am. Educ. Res. J.* 5:191–202

136. Halford, G. S. 1970. A classification learning set which is a possible model for conservation of quantity. *Aust. J. Psychol.* 22:11–17

137. Halford, G. S. 1970. A theory of the acquisition of conservation. *Psychol. Rev.* 77:302–16

138. Halford, G. S., Fullerton, T. J. 1970. A discrimination task which induces conservation of number. *Child Develop.* 41:205–13

139. Hall, R. V., Lund, D., Jackson, D. 1968. Effects of teacher attention on study behavior. *J. Appl. Behav. Anal.* 1:1–12

140. Hall, R. V., Panyan, M., Rabon, D., Broden, M. 1968. Instructing beginning teachers in reinforcement procedures which improve classroom control. *J. Appl. Behav. Anal.* 1:315–22

141. Hanley, E. M. 1970. Review of research involving applied behavior in the classroom. *Rev. Educ. Res.* 40:597–625

142. Hart, B. M., Reynolds, N. J., Baer, D. M., Brawley, E. R., Harris, F. R. 1968. Effect of contingent and non-contingent reinforcement on cooperative play of a preschool child. *J. Appl. Behav. Anal.* 1:73–76

143. Hess, R. D. 1968. Early education as socialization. See Ref. 144, 1–8

144. Hess, R. D., Bear, R. M., Eds. 1968. *Early Education: Current Theory, Research and Action*. Chicago: Aldine. 272 pp.

145. Hess, R. D., Shipman, V. C. 1965. Early experience and the socialization of cognitive modes in children. *Child Develop.* 36:869–86

146. Hess, R. D., Shipman, V. C. 1968. Maternal influences upon early learning: The cognitive environments of urban preschool children. See Ref. 144, 91–103

147. Hilgard, E. R., Ed. 1964. *Theories of Learning and Instruction. The 63rd Yearbook of the NSSE*, Part I. Univ. Chicago Press. 430 pp.

148. Holowinsky, I. Z. 1970. Seriation actions in preschool children. *J. Learn. Disabil.* 3:34–35

149. Holtzman, W. H., Ed. 1970. *Computer-Assisted Instruction, Testing, and Guidance*. New York: Harper & Row. 402 pp.

150. Homme, L., Csanyi, A. P., Gonzales, M. A., Rechs, J. R. 1969. *How to Use Contingency Contracting in the Classroom*. Champaign, Ill.: Research Press. 130 pp.

151. Horowitz, F. D. 1969. Learning, developmental research and individual differences. In *Advances in Child Development and Behavior*, ed. H. W. Reese, L. P. Lipsitt, 4:83–126. New York: Academic. 333 pp.

152. Howe, M. J. A. 1970. Repeated presentation and recall of meaningful prose. *J. Educ. Psychol.* 61:214–19

153. Hunt, J. M. 1968. Revisiting Montessori. In *Early Childhood Education Rediscovered: Readings*, ed. J. L. Frost, 102–27. New York: Holt, Rinehart & Winston. 594 pp.

154. Hunt, J. M. 1969. Has compensatory education failed? Has it been attempted? *Harvard Educ. Rev.* 39: 278–300

155. Hunt, J. M. 1969. *Challenge of Incompetence and Poverty—Papers on the Role of Early Education*. Urbana: Univ. Illinois Press. 289 pp.

156. Huttenlocher, J., Eisenberg, K., Strauss, S. 1968. Comprehension: Relation between perceived actor and logical subject. *J. Verbal Learn. Verbal Behav.* 7:527–30

157. Huttenlocher, J., Strauss, S. 1968. Comprehension and a statement's relation to the situation it describes. *J. Verbal Learn. Verbal Behav.* 7:300–4

158. Inhelder, B., Piaget, J. 1958. *The Growth of Logical Thinking from Childhood to Adolescence*. New York: Basic. 356 pp.

159. Inhelder, B., Piaget, J. 1964. *The Early Growth of Logic in the Child*. New York: Norton. 302 pp.

160. Jacobs, P. I. 1966. Programmed progressive matrices. *Proc. 74th Ann. Conv. APA*, 263–64

161. Jacobs, P. I., Vandeventer, M. 1968. Progressive matrices: An experimental developmental, nonfactorial analysis. *Percept. Mot. Skills* 27: 759–66

162. Jacobs, P. I., Vandeventer, M. 1969. *The learning and transfer of double-classification skills: A replication and extension. ETS Res. Bull. 69–88*. Princeton, N. J.: Educ. Test. Serv.

163. Jacobs, P. I., Vandeventer, M. 1971. The learning and transfer of double-classification skills by first-graders. *Child Develop.* 42:149–59

164. Jensen, A. R. 1967. Varieties of individual differences in learning. See Ref. 105, 117–35

165. Jensen, A. R. 1969. How much can we boost IQ and scholastic achievement? *Harvard Educ. Rev.* 39:1–123

166. Ibid. Reducing the heredity-environment uncertainty: A reply, 449–83

167. Jensen, L., Anderson, D. C. 1970. Retroactive inhibition of difficult and unfamiliar prose. *J. Educ. Psychol.* 61:305–9

168. Johnson, R. E. 1970. Recall of prose as a function of the structural importance of the linguistic units. *J. Verbal Learn. Verbal Behav.* 9:12–20

169. Johnson, S. M. 1970. Self-reinforcement versus external reinforcement in behavior modification with children. *Develop. Psychol.* 3:147–48

170. Kagan, J., Kogan, N. 1970. Individual variation in cognitive processes. In *Carmichael's Manual of Child Psychology*, ed. P. H. Mussen, 1:1273–1365. New York: Wiley. 3rd ed. 1519 pp.

171. Kamii, C. K. 1971. Evaluation of learning in preschool education: Socio-emotional, perceptual-motor, and cognitive-development. See Ref. 29, 281–344

172. Kamii, C. K. 1972. An application of Piaget's theory to the conceptualization of a preschool curriculum. See Ref. 243. In press

173. Karnes, M. B., Hodgins, A. S., Stoneburner, R. L., Studley, W. M., Teska, J. A. 1968. Effects of a highly structured program of language development on intellectual functioning and psycholinguistic development of culturally disadvantaged three-year-olds. *J. Spec. Educ.* 2:405–12

174. Karnes, M. B., Hodgins, A. S., Teska, J. A. 1969. *Research and Development Program in Preschool Disadvantaged Children*. Urbana, Ill.: Inst. Res. Except. Child. Vol. 1

175. Karnes, M. B., Teska, J. A., Hodgins, A. S., Badger, E. D. 1970. Educational intervention at home by mothers of disadvantaged infants. *Child Develop.* 41:925–35

176. Keislar, E. R., Stern, C. 1970. Differentiated instruction in problem solving for children of different

mental ability levels. *J. Educ. Psychol.* 61:445–50

177. Khan, S. B. 1970. Development of mental abilities: An investigation of the "differentiation hypothesis." *Can. J. Psychol./Rev. Can. Psychol.* 24:199–205

178. Kilpatrick, J., Wirszup, I., Eds. 1969. *Soviet Studies in the Psychology of Learning and Teaching Mathematics.* Univ. Chicago. Vol. 1, 216 pp.; Vol. 2, 128 pp.

179. Kingsley, R. C., Hall, V. C. 1967. Training conservation through the use of learning sets. *Child Develop.* 38:1111–26

180. Klahr, D., Wallace, J. G. 1970. An information processing analysis of some Piagetian experimental tasks. *Cognitive Psychol.* 1:358–87

181. Klahr, D., Wallace, J. G. 1972. Class inclusion processes. In *Information Processing in Children*, ed. S. Farnham-Diggory. New York: Academic. In press

182. Klaus, R. A., Gray, S. W. 1968. The early training project for disadvantaged children. A report after five years. *Monogr. Soc. Res. Child Develop.* 33: No. 4

183. Koen, F., Becker, A., Young, R. 1969. The psychological reality of the paragraph. *J. Verbal Learn. Verbal Behav.* 8:49–53

184. Kohlberg, L. 1968. Early education: A cognitive-developmental view. *Child Develop.* 39:1013–62

185. Kohlberg, L. 1968. Montessori with the culturally disadvantaged: A cognitive-developmental interpretation and some research findings. See Ref. 144, 105–18

186. Kohnstamm, G. A. 1963. An evaluation of part of Piaget's theory. *Acta Psychol.* 21:313–56

187. Kohnstamm, G. A. 1967. *Piaget's Analysis of Class Inclusion: Right or Wrong?* The Hague: Mouton. 153 pp.

188. Lasry, J. C., Laurendeau, M. 1969. Apprentissage empirique de la notion d'inclusion. *Hum. Develop.* 12:141–53

189. Lefrancois, G. 1968. A treatment hierarchy for the acceleration of conservation of substance. *Can. J. Psychol./Rev. Can. Psychol.* 22:277–84

190. Lesser, G. S., Fifer, G., Clark, D. H. 1965. Mental abilities of children from different social-class and cultural groups. *Monogr. Soc. Res. Child Develop.* 30: No. 4

191. Liebert, R. M., Hanratty, M., Hill, J. H. 1969. Effects of rule structure and training method on the adoption of a self-imposed standard. *Child Develop.* 40:93–101

192. Light, R. J., Smith, P. V. 1969. Social allocation models of intelligence: A methodological inquiry. *Harvard Educ. Rev.* 39:484–510

193. Lister, C. M. 1970. The development of a concept of volume conservation in ESN children. *Brit. J. Educ. Psychol.* 40:55–64

194. Lovaas, O. I. 1961. Interaction between verbal and nonverbal behavior. *Child Develop.* 32:329–36

195. Lovaas, O. I. 1967. A behavior therapy approach to the treatment of childhood schizophrenia. In *Minnesota Symposia on Child Psychology*, ed. J. P. Hill, 1:108–59. Minneapolis: Univ. Minnesota. 239 pp.

196. Lovaas, O. I., Berberich, J. P., Perloff, B. F., Schaeffer, B. 1966. Acquisition of imitative speech by schizophrenic children. *Science* 151:705–7

197. Lovaas, O. I., Freitas, L., Nelson, K., Whalen, C. 1967. The establishment of imitation and its use for the development of complex behavior in schizophrenic children. *Behav. Res. Ther.* 5:171–81

198. Lovitt, T. C., Curtiss, K. A. 1969. Academic response rate as a function of teacher- and self-imposed contingencies. *J. Appl. Behav. Anal.* 2:49–53

199. Lubin, A. 1961. The interpretation of significant interaction. *Educ. Psychol. Meas.* 21:807–17

200. Lumsden, E. A., Kling, J. K. 1969. The relevance of an adequate concept of "bigger" for investigations of size conservation: A methodological critique. *J. Exp. Child Psychol.* 8:82–91

201. Luria, A. R. 1961. *The Role of Speech in the Regulation of Normal and Abnormal Behavior.* New York: Liveright

202. Maccoby, E. E. 1968. Early learning and personality: Summary and commentary. See Ref. 144, 191–202

203. Maccoby, E. E., Zellner, M. 1970. *Experiments in Primary Education: Aspects of Project Follow-Through.*

New York: Harcourt, Brace & Jovanovich. 132 pp.
204. MacDonald, W. S. 1971. *Battle in the Classroom: Innovations in Classroom Techniques.* Scranton, Pa.: Int. Textbooks
205. MacDonald, W. S., Gallimore, R., MacDonald, G. 1970. Contingency counseling by school personnel: An economical model of intervention. *J. Appl. Behav. Anal.* 3:175–82
206. Madsen, C. H. Jr., Becker, W. C., Thomas, D. R., Koser, L., Plager, E. 1968. An analysis of the reinforcing function of "sit-down" commands. In *Readings in Educational Psychology*, ed. R. K. Parker, 265–78. Boston: Allyn & Bacon. 605 pp.
207. Madsen, C. H. Jr., Madsen, C. K. 1970. *Teaching Discipline: Behavioral Principles Toward a Positive Approach.* Boston: Allyn & Bacon
208. Martin, M., Burkholder, R., Rosenthal, T. L., Tharp, R. G., Thorne, G. L. 1968. Programming behavior change and reintegration into school milieu of extreme adolescent deviates. *Behav. Res. Ther.* 6:371–83
209. McAllister, L. W., Stachowiak, J. G., Baer, D. M., Conderman, L. 1969. The application of operant conditioning techniques in a secondary school classroom. *J. Appl. Behav. Anal.* 2:277–85
210. McDonald, F. J., Allen, D. W. 1967. *Training effects of feedback and modeling procedures on teaching performance.* Tech. Rep. No. 3. Center Res. Develop. Teach., Stanford Univ.
211. Meacham, M., Wiesen, A. 1969. *Changing Classroom Behavior: A Manual of Precision Teaching.* Scranton, Pa.: Int. Textbooks
212. Meichenbaum, D. H. 1971. *The nature and modification of impulsive children: Training impulsive children to talk to themselves.* Res. Rep. No. 23, Dep. Psychol., Univ. of Waterloo
213. Meichenbaum, D., Goodman, J. 1969. Reflection-impulsivity and verbal control of motor behavior. *Child Develop.* 40:785–97
214. Melton, A. W., Ed. 1964. *Categories of Human Learning.* New York: Academic. 356 pp.
215. Melton, A. W. 1967. Individual differences and theoretical process variables: General comments on the conference. See Ref. 105, 238–52
216. Mermelstein, E., Meyer, E. 1969. Conservation training techniques and their effects on different populations. *Child Develop.* 40:471–90
217. Mermelstein, E., Shulman, L. S. 1967. Lack of formal schooling and the acquisition of conservation. *Child Develop.* 38:39–52
218. Merrill, M. D. 1965. Correction and review on successive parts in learning a hierarchical task. *J. Educ. Psychol.* 56:225–34
219. Meuris, G. 1970. The structure of primary mental abilities of Belgian secondary school students. *J. Educ. Meas.* 7:191–97
220. Miller, J. O. 1970. Disadvantaged families: Despair to hope. In *Psychology and the Problems of Society*, ed. F. F. Korten, S. W. Cook, J. I. Lacey, 179–97. Washington, D. C.: Am. Psychol. Assoc. 459 pp.
221. Miller, R. B. 1962. Task description and analysis. In *Psychological Principles in System Development*, ed. R. Gagné, 187–228. New York: Holt, Rinehart & Winston. 560 pp.
222. Miller, R. B. 1965. Analysis and specification of behavior for training. In *Training Research and Education*, ed. R. Glaser, 31–62. New York: Wiley. 596 pp.
223. Moore, O. K., Anderson, A. R. 1968. The responsive environments project. See Ref. 144, 171–89
224. More, A. J. 1969. Delay of feedback and the acquisition and retention of verbal materials in the classroom. *J. Educ. Psychol.* 60:339–42
225. Murray, F. B. 1968. Cognitive conflict and reversibility training in the acquisition of length conservation. *J. Educ. Psychol.* 59:82–87
226. Natkin, G., Stahler, E. 1969. The effects of adjunct questions on short and long-term recall of prose materials. *Am. Educ. Res. J.* 6:425–32
227. Nelson, K. J., Zelniker, T., Jeffrey, W. E. 1969. The child's concept of proportionality: A re-examination. *J. Exp. Child Psychol.* 8:256–62
228. Newell, A. 1968. On the analysis of human problem solving protocols. In *Calcul et formalisation dans les sciences de l'homme*, ed. J. C. Gardin, B. Jaulin, 146–85. Presses Universitaires de France
229. Newell, A., Simon, H. A. 1971. *Human Problem Solving.* Englewood Cliffs, N. J.: Prentice-Hall

230. Nolen, P. A., Kunzelmann, H. P., Haring, N. G. 1967. Behavioral modification in a junior high learning disabilities classroom. *Except. Child.* 34:163–68

231. Okonji, M. O. 1970. The effect of special training on the classificatory behavior of some Nigerian Ibo children. *Brit. J. Educ. Psychol.* 40:21–26

232. O'Leary, K. D., Becker, W. C. 1968. The effects of the intensity of a teacher's reprimands on children's behavior. *J. Sch Psychol.* 7:8–11

233. O'Leary, K. D., Drabman, R. 1971. Token reinforcement programs in the classroom: A review. *Psychol. Bull.* 75:379–98

234. O'Leary, K. D., Kaufman, K. F., Kass, R. E., Drabman, R. S. 1970. The effects of loud and soft reprimands on the behavior of disruptive students. *Except. Child.* 37:145–55

235. Olson, D. R. 1970. *Cognitive Development: The Child's Acquisition of Diagonality.* New York: Academic. 220 pp.

236. Osborn, J. 1968. Teaching a teaching language to disadvantaged children. *Monogr. Soc. Res. Child Develop.* 33: No. 8

237. Osler, S. F., Scholnick, E. K. 1968. The effect of stimulus differentiation and inferential experience on concept attainment in disadvantaged children. *J. Exp. Child Psychol.* 6:658–66

238. Overbeck, C., Schwartz, M. 1970. Training in conservation of weight. *J. Exp. Child Psychol.* 9:253–64

239. Packard, R. G. 1970. The control of "classroom attention": A group contingency for complex behavior. *J. Appl. Behav. Anal.* 3:13–28

240. Paige, J. M., Simon, H. A. 1966. Cognitive processes in solving algebra word problems. In *Problem Solving: Research, Method and Theory*, ed. B. Kleinmuntz, 51–119. New York: Wiley. 406 pp.

241. Paivio, A. 1970. On the functional significance of imagery. *Psychol. Bull.* 73:385–92

242. Palmer, F. H. 1972. Minimal intervention at age two and three and subsequent intellective changes. See Ref. 243. In press

243. Parker, R. K., Ed. 1972. *Conceptualizations of Preschool Curricula.* Boston: Allyn & Bacon. In press

244. Pascual-Leone, J., Bovet, M. C. 1966. L'apprentissage de la quantification de l'inclusion et la theorie operatoire. *Acta Psychol.* 25:334–56

245. Peeck, J. 1970. Effect of prequestions on delayed retention of prose material. *J. Educ. Psychol.* 61:241–46

246. Peters, D. L. 1970. Verbal mediators and cue discrimination in the transition from nonconservation to conservation of number. *Child Develop.* 41:707–21

247. Piaget, J. 1969. *Science of Education and the Psychology of the Child.* Transl. D. Coltman. New York: Viking. 186 pp.

248. Poole, H. E. 1968. The effect of urbanization upon scientific concept attainment among Hausa children of Northern Nigeria. *Brit. J. Educ. Psychol.* 38:57–63

249. Prince, J. R. 1968. The effect of Western education of science conceptualization in New Guinea. *Brit. J. Educ. Psychol.* 28:64–74

250. Raven, R. J., Strubing, H. 1968. The effect of visual perception units on achievement in a science unit: Aptitudinal and substantive transfer in second grade children. *Am. Educ. Res. J.* 5:333–42

251. Reese, H. W. 1970. Imagery in children's learning: A symposium. *Psychol. Bull.* 73: No. 6

252. Resnick, L. B. 1967. *Design of an early learning curriculum.* Working Paper 16. Learn. Res. Develop. Center, Univ. Pittsburgh

253. Resnick, L. B. 1971. Applying applied reinforcement. See Ref. 126a, 326–33

254. Resnick, L. B., Siegel, A. W., Kresh, E. 1971. Transfer and sequence in learning double classification skills. *J. Exp. Child Psychol.* 11:139–49

255. Resnick, L. B., Wang, M. C. 1969. Approaches to the validation of learning hierarchies. *Proc. 18th Ann. West. Reg. Conf. Test. Probl.* Princeton, N. J.: Educ. Test. Serv.

256. Resnick, L. B., Wang, M. C., Kaplan, J. 1970. *Behavior analysis in curriculum design: A hierarchically sequenced introductory mathematics curriculum.* Monogr. 2, Learn. Res. Develop. Center, Univ. Pittsburgh

257. Revusky, S. H. 1967. Some statistical treatments compatible with individual organism methodology. *J. Exp. Anal. Behav.* 10: 319–30

258. Risley, T., Reynolds, N., Hart, B. 1970. Behavior modification with disadvantaged preschool children. In *Behavior Modification: The Human Effort*, ed. R. Bradfield, 123–57. San Rafael, Calif.: Dimensions Publ.

259. Robinson, H. B., Robinson, N. M. 1968. The problem of timing in pre-school education. See Ref. 144, 37–51

260. Roden, A., Klein, R., Hapkiewicz, W., Eds. 1971. *Behavior Modification in Educational Settings*. Springfield, Ill.: Thomas. In press

261. Rohwer W. D. Jr. 1970. Images and pictures in children's learning. *Psychol. Bull.* 73:393–403

262. Rohwer, W. D. Jr. 1970. Implications of cognitive development for education. See Ref. 170, 1379–1454

263. Rohwer, W. D. Jr. 1970. Mental elaboration and proficient learning. In *Minnesota Symposia on Child Psychology*, ed. J. P. Hill, 4:220–60. Minneapolis: Univ. Minnesota

264. Rohwer, W. D. Jr. 1971. Learning, race and school success. *Rev. Educ. Res.* 41:191–210

265. Roll, S. 1970. Reversibility training and stimulus desirability as factors in conservation of numbers. *Child Develop.* 41:501–7

266. Rosenthal, T. L., Whitebook, J. S. 1970. Incentives versus instructions in transmitting grammatical parameters with experimenter as model. *Behav. Res. Ther.* 8:189–96

267. Rosenthal, T. L., Zimmerman, B. J., Durning, K. 1971. Observationally-induced changes in children's interrogative classes. *J. Pers. Soc. Psychol.* In press

268. Rosenzweig, M. R., Krech, D., Bennett, E. L., Diamond, M. C. 1968. Modifying brain chemistry and anatomy by enrichment or impoverishment of experience. In *Early Experience and Behavior: The Psychobiology of Development*, ed. G. Newton, S. Levine, 258 98. Springfield, Ill.: Thomas. 785 pp.

269. Rosner, J. 1969. *The design of an individualized perceptual skills curriculum*. Working Paper 53. Learn. Res. Develop. Center, Univ. Pittsburgh

270. Ibid 1970. *Visual analysis training and the copying skills of 4-year-old children* (Mimeo)

271. Ibid 1971. *The design board program.* No. 1971/7

272. Rosner, J. 1971. Phonic analysis training and beginning reading skills. *Elem. Sch. J.* In press

273. Rosner, J., Levine, S., Simon, D. 1971. *Effects of design board training on the performance scale and subtests on the WPPSI*. Presented at Ann. Meet. AERA, New York, 1971

274. Rosner, J., Simon, D. P. 1971. The auditory analysis test: An initial report. *J. Learn. Disabil.* In press

275. Rothenberg, B. B., Orost, J. H. 1969. The training of conservation of number in young children. *Child Develop.* 40:707–26

276. Rothkopf, E. Z. 1965. Some theoretical and experimental approaches to problems in written instruction. In *Learning and the Educational Process*, ed. J. D. Krumboltz, 193–221. Chicago: Rand McNally. 277 pp.

277. Rothkopf, E. Z. 1966. Learning from written materials: An exploration of the control of inspection behavior by test-like events. *Am. Educ. Res. J.* 3:241–49

278. Rothkopf, E. Z. 1968. Textual constraint as function of repeated inspection. *J. Educ. Psychol.* 59:20–25

279. Rothkopf, E. Z. 1970. The concept of mathemagenic activities. *Rev. Educ. Res.* 40:325–36

280. Rothkopf, E. Z., Bisbicos, E. 1967. Selective facilitative effects of interspersed questions on learning from written material. *J. Educ. Psychol.* 58:56–61

281. Rothkopf, E. Z., Bloom, R. D. 1970. Effects of interpersonal interaction on the instructional value of adjunct questions in learning from written material. *J. Educ. Psychol.* 61:417–22

282. Sachs, J. S. 1967. Recognition memory for syntactic and semantic aspects of connected discourse. *Percept. Psychophys.* 2:437–42

283. Samuels, S. J. 1968. Effect of word associations on reading speed, recall, and guessing behavior on tests. *J. Educ. Psychol.* 59:12–15

284. Ibid 1969. Effect of word associations on the recognition of flashed words. 60:97–102

285. Samuels, S. J., Wittrock, M. C. 1969. Word-association strength and learning to read. *J. Educ. Psychol.* 60:248–52

286. Schaefer, E. S. 1970. Need for early and continuing education. See Ref. 70, 61–82
287. Schaefer, E. S., Aaronson, M. 1972. Infant education research project: Implementation and implications of a home tutoring program. See Ref. 243. In press
288. Scholnick, E. K., Osler, S. F., Katzenellenbogen, R. 1968. Discrimination learning and concept identification in disadvantaged and middle-class children. *Child Develop.* 39:15–26
289. Schutte, R. C., Hopkins, B. L. 1970. The effects of teacher attention on following instructions in a kindergarten class. *J. Appl. Behav. Anal.* 3:117–22
290. Scott, J. P. 1968. *Early Experience and the Organization of Behavior.* Belmont, Calif.: Brooks/Cole. 177 pp.
291. Sibley, S. A., Abbott, M. S., Cooper, B. P. 1969. Modification of the classroom behavior of a disadvantaged kindergarten boy by social reinforcement and isolation. *J. Exp. Child Psychol.* 7:203–19
292. Sidman, M. 1960. *Tactics of Scientific Research.* New York: Basic Books. 428 pp.
293. Sigel, I. E. 1969. The Piagetian system and the world of education. In *Studies in Cognitive Development: Essays in Honor of Jean Piaget*, ed. D. Elkind, J. H. Flavell, 465–89. New York: Oxford Univ. Press. 503 pp.
294. Sigel, I. E., Roeper, A., Hooper, R. H. 1966. A training procedure for acquisition of Piaget's conservation of quantity: A pilot study and its replication. *Brit. J. Educ. Psychol.* 36: 301–11
295. Skeels, H. M. 1965. Effects of adoption on children from institutions. *Children* 12:33–34
296. Skinner, B. F. 1968. *The Technology of Teaching.* New York: Appleton-Century-Crofts. 271 pp.
297. Smedslund, J. 1961. The acquisition of conservation of substance and weight in children: III. Extinction of conservation of weight acquired "normally" and by means of empirical controls on a balance scale. *Scand. J. Psychol.* 2:85–87
298. Smilansky, S. 1968. *The Effects of Sociodramatic Play on Disadvantaged Preschool Children.* New York: Wiley. 164 pp.
299. Smith, D. E. P., Brethower, D., Cabot, R. 1969. Increasing task behavior in a language arts program by providing reinforcement. *J. Exp. Child Psychol.* 8:45–62
300. Smith, F. 1969. The use of featural dependencies across letters in the visual identification of words. *J. Verbal Learn. Verbal Behav.* 8: 215–18
301. Smith, I. D. 1968. The effects of training procedures upon the acquisition of conservation of weight. *Child Develop.* 39:515–26
302. Staats, A. W. 1968. *Learning Language and Cognition: Theory, Research and Method for the Study of Human Behavior and Its Development.* New York: Holt, Rinehart & Winston. 614 pp.
303. Staats, A. W., Brewer, B. A., Gross, M. C. 1970. Learning and cognitive development: Representative samples, cumulative-hierarchical learning, and experimental-longitudinal methods. *Monogr. Soc. Res. Child Develop.* 35: No. 8
304. Stein, Z., Susser, M. 1970. Mutability of intelligence and epidemiology of mild mental retardation. *Rev. Educ. Res.* 40:29–67
305. Stendler-Lavatelli, C. 1968. A Piaget-derived model for compensatory preschool education. See Ref. 153, 530–44
306. Stern, C. 1968. Evaluating language curricula for preschool children. *Monogr. Soc. Res. Child Develop.* 33:49–61
307. Stern, C., Keislar, E. R. 1967. Acquisition of problem solving strategies by young children, and its relation to mental age. *Am. Educ. Res. J.* 4:1–12
308. Stinchcombe, A. L. 1969. Environment: The cumulation of effects is yet to be understood. *Harvard Educ. Rev.* 39:511–22
309. Stodolsky, S. S., Karlson, A. L. 1970. *Differential outcomes of a Montessori curriculum. Report.* Univ. Chicago
310. Strauss, S., Langer, J. 1970. Operational thought inducement. *Child Develop.* 41:163–75
311. Strodtbeck. F. L. 1964. The hidden curriculum of the middle class home. In *Urban Education and Cultural Deprivation*, ed. C. W. Hunnicutt, 15–31. Syracuse Univ. Press. 126 pp.

312. Sullivan, E. V. 1967. Acquisition of conservation of substance through film modeling techniques. In *Recent Research on the Acquisition of Substance*, ed. D. W. Brison, E. Sullivan, 11–23. Ontario: Ont. Inst. Stud. Educ.
313. Sullivan, E. V. 1967. Piaget and the school curriculum—A critical appraisal. *Ont. Inst. Stud. Educ. Bull. 2*
314. Suppes, P. 1966. Mathematical concept formation in children. *Am. Psychol.* 21:139–50
315. Suppes, P. 1967. Some theoretical models for mathematics learning. *J. Res. Develop. Educ.* 1:5–22
316. Suppes, P., Groen, G. 1967. Some counting models for first-grade performance data on simple addition facts. In *Research in Mathematics Education*, ed. J. M. Scandura, 35–43. Washington, D. C.: Nat. Counc. Teachers Math. 125 pp.
317. Suppes, P., Hyman, L., Jerman, M. 1967. Linear structural models for response and latency performance in arithmetic on computer-controlled terminals. See Ref. 195, 160–200
318. Suppes, P., Jerman, M., Brian, D. 1968. *Computer-Assisted Instruction: Stanford 1965–66 Arithmetic Program.* New York: Academic. 385 pp.
319. Thomas, D. R., Becker, W. C., Armstrong, M. 1968. Production and elimination of disruptive classroom behavior by systematically varying teacher's behavior. *J. Appl. Behav. Anal.* 1:35–45
320. Tyler, V. O. Jr. 1967. Application of operant token reinforcement to academic performance of an institutionalized delinquent. *Psychol. Rep.* 21:249–60
321. Tyler, V. O. Jr., Brown, G. D. 1968. Token reinforcement of academic performance with institutionalized delinquent boys. *J. Educ. Psychol.* 59:164–68
322. Venezky, R. L. 1967. English orthography: Its graphical structure and its relation to sound. *Reading Res. Quart.* 2:75–106
323. Walker, H. M., Buckley, N. K. 1968. The use of positive reinforcement in conditioning attending behavior. *J. Appl. Behav. Anal.* 1:245–50
324. Wallach, L. 1969. On the bases of conservation. See Ref. 293, 191–219
325. Wallach, L., Sprott, R. L. 1964. Inducing number conservation in children. *Child Develop.* 35:1057–71
326. Wallach, L., Wall, A. J., Anderson, L. 1967. Number conservation: The roles of reversibility, addition-subtraction, and misleading perceptual cues. *Child Develop.* 38:425–42
327. Wang, M. C., Resnick, L. B., Boozer, R. 1971. The sequence of development of some early mathematics behaviors. *Child Develop.* In press
328. Wang, M. C., Resnick. L. B., Schuetz, P. A. 1970. *PEP in the Frick elementary school: Interim evaluation report of the primary education project, 1968–69.* Working Paper 57. Learn. Res. Develop. Center, Univ. Pittsburgh
329. Ward, M. H., Baker, B. L. 1968. Reinforcement therapy in the classroom. *J. Appl. Behav. Anal.* 1:323–28
330. Wason, P. C. 1961. Response to affirmative and negative binary statements. *Brit. J. Psychol.* 52:133–42
331. Wason, P. C. 1965. The contexts of plausible denial. *J. Verbal Learn. Verbal Behav.* 4:7–11
332. Weikart, D. P., Deloria, D. J., Lawser, S. A., Wiegerink, R. 1970. *Longitudinal results of the Ypsilanti Perry Preschool Project. Report.* High/Scope Educ. Res. Found., Ypsilanti, Michigan
333. Weikart, D. P., Lambie, D. Z. 1970. Early enrichment in infants. See Ref. 71, 83–107
334. White, B. L. 1968. Informal education during the first month of life. See Ref. 144, 143–69
335. White, S. H. 1968. Some educated guesses about cognitive development in the pre-school years. See Ref. 144, 203–14
336. Whitlock, C. 1966. Note on reading acquisition: An extension of laboratory principles. *J. Exp. Child Psychol.* 3:83–85
337. Whitlock, C., Bushell, D. Jr. 1967. Some effects of "back-up" reinforcers on reading behavior. *J. Exp. Child Psychol.* 5:50–57
338. Wiegand, V. K. 1970. *A study of subordinate skills in science problem solving.* Presented at AERA Ann. Meet., Minneapolis
339. Wittrock, M. C., Wiley, D. C., Eds. 1970. *The Evaluation of Instruction:*

Issues and Problems. New York: Holt, Rinehart & Winston. 494 pp.

340. Wohlwill, J. F. 1968. Responses to class-inclusion questions for verbally and pictorially presented items. *Child Develop.* 39:449–65

341. Wolf, M. M., Giles, D. K., Hall, R. V. 1968. Experiments with token reinforcement in a remedial classroom. *Behav. Res. Ther.* 6:51–64

342. Wolf, M. M., Risley, T. R. 1971. Reinforcement: Applied research. See Ref. 126a, 310–25

343. Wong, M. R. 1970. Retroactive inhibition in meaningful verbal learning. *J. Educ. Psychol.* 61:410–15

344. Yando, R. M., Kagan, J. 1968. The effect of teacher tempo on the child. *Child Develop.* 39:27–34

345. Zigler, E., Butterfield, E. C. 1968. Motivational aspects of changes in IQ test performance of culturally deprived nursery shool children. *Child Develop.* 39:1–14

346. Zimmerman, E. H., Zimmerman, J. 1962. The alteration of behavior in a special classroom situation. *J. Exp. Anal. Behav.* 5:59–60

SOCIAL ETHOLOGY

JOHN H. CROOK AND J. D. GOSS-CUSTARD

Department of Psychology, University of Bristol, United Kingdom

INTRODUCTION

THE HISTORICAL BASIS AND RECENT DEVELOPMENT OF SOCIAL RESEARCH IN ETHOLOGY

The expansion of ethology in the last few years and its entry into the guarded purlieus of neighboring disciplines provides strong testimony for the significance of the biological approach to the behavioral sciences that owes so much to the provocative ideas of Konrad Lorenz (125–129) and N. Tinbergen (193, 194). Ethological methods and ideas are of growing importance to the development of a number of study areas and in some cases may even foreshadow major reorganizations of whole sciences. In particular it now seems quite probable that in psychology the conceptual basis for the subject may move progressively away from older analogies—in which behavioral processes were conceived in terms of physical models—to a more fundamentally biological orientation based upon interrelated physiological and evolutionary analyses. The link between animal and man is now too effectively established to allow the absurd dichotomy between the human and animal behavioral sciences to perpetuate itself much longer.

Ethological approaches to the ontogeny of behavior are currently making a major impact on theoretical interpretations of human behavioral development (Bowlby 19). In anthropology and sociology ethological ideas are once more discussed (Tiger & Fox 190, Fox 63, Reynolds 159, Jolly 103, Morris 137, Chapple 26), provoking a widening perspective within these hitherto narrowly conceived disciplines. The fences between subjects are coming down as the interpenetration of system processes previously studied in isolation is appreciated and their interlocking in complex patterns of temporal change increasingly perceived. We are faced at present with a much wider and more revolutionary development of our subject than the perpetual shifting about between varying degrees of interest in the "comparative psychology" of the "behaviorist" American school and the "classical ethology" (see Klopfer & Hailman 106) of the European founding fathers. Indeed, the present more global expansion of the subject is in large measure a consequence of the extent to which these historically and culturally separated approaches to animal behavior have become linked, if not yet fused. In particular, by approaching both subjects from the unremittingly empirical orientation of a Cambridge experimental biologist, Robert Hinde (90) has largely succeeded in providing a synthesis that will probably prove to be an historical landmark. Other outstanding textbooks tend also to reinforce this view (Barnett 14, Marler & Hamilton 132, Altman 3, Manning 131). It is interesting to reflect that these books are the first generation of texts designed to instruct university students at all levels in ethology.

The need for a biological education in psychology is made explicit in Hodos & Campbell's article (93) which points out that many papers in so-called comparative psychology suffer from serious logical defects based upon an inadequate comprehension of the difficulties of evolutionary inference, from confusions between phylogenetic scales and phylogenetic trees and between homology and homoplasy (Simpson 178), and from a misuse of typological thinking. The clarification of such issues lies in the very groundwork of ethology. Ethology, however, is by no means confined to "evolutionary psychology," as J. P. Scott (171) seems to imply in his review of 1967. Both the classical ethology of Lorenz and Tinbergen and the modern ethology of Hinde attempt to provide comprehensive answers to three interrelated questions concerning causality and one concerning the function of behavior. A given behavior can be examined from the point of view of its physiological (i.e. proximate) causation, its ontogeny (developmental causation), and its evolutionary (i.e. ultimate) causation in terms of the natural selection of genetic factors. In addition, ethology attempts to answer questions concerning the function of a particular behavior in a given social and ecological environment.

The fact that animal behavior has been a field of study shared by several sciences, each tending to emphasize contrasting scholastic viewpoints, has led, as Jaynes (100) says, "sometimes to competition, sometimes amalgamation, sometimes an antipaty eroding truth into loyalty and sometimes, fortunately, a division of labour benefiting all." The classical framework of ethology is no longer sufficient to comprise certain developments in the subject. In particular this applies to research into the relations between social behavior, social dynamics of groups, population dynamics, and ecology in which the old approach to communication focusing on dyads and a simple Darwinian view of historical change needs updating through more effective concepts and analyses. Jaynes' brief examination of the history of ethological ideas is important here because too many students have been educated to believe that ethology came into being with Konrad Lorenz, and they have been instructed neither to carry out deeper reading into the history of the subject nor to read Lorenz's own early papers in which he makes clear his personal debt to other thinkers. Fortunately, R. B. Martin's able translations (129) of Lorenz's most important early works, including the seminal "Kumpan paper," make this ignorance no longer excusable. Tinbergen's historically important book of 1951 has been reissued recently.

Jaynes' (100) historical reevaluation of ethology makes a number of important points. Both "Comparative Psychology" and "Ethology" are terms that originated in France in the 1830s as a consequence of divisive debates between Baron Cuvier and E. Geoffroy Saint-Hilaire. Here began the conflict between a laboratory based anatomical and (later) experimental approach to behavior and a naturalistic, observational, synthesizing and (later) evolutionary perspective. For historical reasons [which include the preempting of the term "Ethology" for use as a science of human character by J. S. Mill in 1843; see Nash (145) for an instructive excerpt], the founding of ethology in 1859 by Saint-Hilaire's son, Isidore, as the study of living things in their natural environment, was followed by very slow progress. By contrast, the politically powerful Cuvier tradition was maintained by P. Flourens, who, in a rewrite of an earlier textbook, coined the term "Comparative Psychology" in which human and animal behavior are both examined from the standpoint of a mechanistic neurology. Flourens, an overinfluential figure, was antagonistic to the Darwinian evolutionary theory, so it is not surprising that the term "comparative" in this discipline had little of the connotation of a phylogenetic analysis of behavior in a modern biologically acceptable sense. Indeed the problems posed by Hodos & Campbell (93) seem to stem from this very time.

In spite of the brilliance of much comparative psychology, especially following its translation to the New World, the subject floundered into a narrow scholastic decadence under J. B. Watson's "Behaviorism" and never achieved an appreciation of the importance of naturalistic observation (even though Watson himself did do some effective field study of birds, and Yerkes and his students initiated vigorous captivity and field studies of primates). Comparative psychology in recent years has confined itself almost exclusively to highly controlled experimental testing of a range of alternative learning theories and animal training methodologies which, although of a certain intellectual interest and even of practical value when applied to the basic therapy of the educationally subnormal, lack the breadth endowed by a firm base in biology. When linked with physiology, however, this orientation was able to provide an effective and important corrective to the excesses of Lorenzian theorizing and thus to assist in opening the way to modern experimental ethology (Lehrman 123).

The early ethology could easily have disappeared at a tender age. The term was unfortunately coined at almost the same time as Haeckel adopted the name "Oecology" for the study of living things in their environment. A differential emphasis on the *behavior* of an animal on the one hand and an animal's *relations with the habitat* on the other only emerged with clarity much later in spite of the fact that these contrasting but interrelated perspectives were made explicit as early as 1902 (213). The survival of early ethology was mainly due to Alfred Giard (71), a biologist of wide interests and professor of the Evolution of Organic Beings at the Sorbonne around 1900. Unfortunately, Giard also espoused Lamarkianism, and with the dismissal of this evolutionary theory, ethology once more fell under a fog if not actually a cloud. Only among certain underestimated sociologists working in Brussels (see below) did it retain a certain influence.

Curiously, the students of animal behavior who were responsible for the reemergence of ethology in its classical phase seem to have been little aware of its earlier intellectual history. Lorenz (129), in the introduction to the new collection of his papers, remarks on his almost total ignorance of both earlier controversies and those contemporaneous with his early researches in the late 1920s and early 1930s. Although he of course knew the work of his paternal mentor, Oscar Heinroth, he was then unaware of workers such as Watson, Yerkes, McDougall, and Lloyd-Morgan and therefore uninformed on their divergent viewpoints. Likewise, G. P. Baerends told Jaynes (100) that neither he, Tinbergen, nor Lorenz knew the origin of the term Ethology nor its history, even at the time when it began to be used as a designation for their work. The pleasing truth seems to be that the founding fathers of classical ethology were all more in love with their animals than with the art of competition in controversy. They were, as Lorenz says, "starers at animals," pure observers whose theories only gradually crystallized as an almost inductive necessity from the mountains of acutely perceptive observations they collected Indeed the direct intellectual ancestors of the Lorenzian school—Charles Darwin, the Peckhams, C O. Whitman, E. Selous, D. Spalding, and O. Heinroth—were all primarily observers in the tradition of natural history and all zoologists in the Geoffroy Saint-Hilaire sense. Only gradually did experimentation join observation in ethology, primarily through the influence of D. Spalding, H. S. Jennings, and N. Tinbergen. The authors responsible for Lorenz's development as a theoretician were primarily Wallace Craig and Oscar Heinroth, whose motivation theories backed by direct observation of appetitive, aversive, and consummatory behavior in relation to the performance of fixed action patterns led to Lorenz's formulation of the famous hydraulic model (see 126) and Tinbergen's attempt to present this in neurophysiological terms (193).

The history of classical ethology and its modern derivative has been amply explored by Klopfer & Hailman (106). They examine the pre-Lorenzian discussions of mental evolution in animals, stressing the contribution of authors such as Darwin, Romanes, William James, Lloyd-Morgan, and Julian Huxley. The studies discussed in Jaynes' examination, however, are not mentioned, nor are the ideas of Emile Waxweiler and Raphael Petrucci, to which we must return shortly.

Apart from a new precision in the description of animal behavior, the prime contributions of classical ethology lay (a) in the provision of a provocative model of behavior motivation which steered clear of vitalism without accepting the environmentalist approach of the mechanists in comparative psychology (Lorenz 126); (b) in the renewal of studies on early behavioral development and the Lorenzian formulation of the imprinting problem; and (c) in the use of ethographic material in the analysis of animal communication (Tinbergen 192) and in the study of the evolution of behavior in neo-Darwinian terms (196, 197). Currently the reexamination of the Lorenzian model of motivation has led to a voluminous literature based primarily on neurophysiological and behavior-endocrinological studies (see

90). It is regrettable that Lorenz (127) himself has failed to take such developments adequately into account when making major pronouncements on the nature of animal and human aggression as if it were motivated in the same manner as, say, sexual behavior. By using a theoretical framework virtually indistinguishable from his views in the 1930s, he has only succeeded in presenting a confusing and overauthoritative popular book which, through the pens of lesser minds, has been followed by a thoroughly misleading literature on the subject with antiliberal political overtones (e.g. 8; for critical comment see 35, 89). These views on motivation have furthermore permeated both popular and, to a degree, academic discussion of another issue—namely the nature of social processes in higher vertebrates and man. While some authors (e.g. Eibl-Eibesfeldt 56) on the whole affirm a traditionalist Lorenzian position, others seek to break out of what has become an unacceptably narrow framework.

In classical ethology the focus on courtship and agonistic behavior led to a treatment of social interaction mainly in terms of reciprocal interactions occurring in dyads between whose members stereotyped, usually species specific, signals were given (e.g. 194). The species specificity of such patterns supported the view that they could be broadly considered as innate, and hence a direct consequence of processes of neo-Darwinian selection. When society is treated as a network of such interactions, then social organization likewise appears to be a direct product of natural selection and adapted through genetic change to the habitat conditions that molded it. A number of recent otherwise excellent studies have taken this limited position. Research in which the intraspecific adaptability of social structure (e.g. group size, composition, and dispersion) is more apparent (see 58, 78, 162) indicates, however, that far from being a fixed species-specific property, social structure is a "dynamic system expressing the interactions of a number of factors within both the ecological and social milieux that influence the spatial dispersion and grouping tendencies of populations within a range of lability allowed by the behavioral tolerance of the 'species' " (36). The shortfall of the classical approach was due to a neglect of group processes other than dyadic interaction, a lack of interest in contrasting patterns of dispersion and group composition, and a fixation on neo-Darwinian explanation in accounting for historical change in social life. Yet had classical ethologists read more widely, such interests might have been incorporated at a much earlier date. As a consequence, popular modern ethology might present a rather different face than the overemphasized Lorenzian position allows it to do today.

The older ethology of Giard had in fact been taken up by an important though short-lived school of sociology directed by Emile Waxweiler at the Instituts Solvay in Brussels between 1900 and World War I. Furthermore, the approach of this school focused upon exactly the kind of social problem that classical ethology was to neglect (64). The work of Waxweiler (212) and his colleague Raphael Petrucci (157) stems from an earlier study of animal sociology by A. Espinas (57), who worked in the tradition of Auguste Comte. As Klopfer & Hailman (106) indicate, Espinas' work (like that of Kropotkin 111) failed to make the impact it can now be seen to have merited, perhaps because the *Zeitgeist* of the period emphasized an extreme individualism while both these authors often focused on cooperative or altruistic behavior. Crook (37) points out that Espinas' views were far from simply interaction-ist, for he attempted to account for the continuity and durability of societies in a set of principles that had a markedly cybernetic flavor. In addition, he showed how different forms of animal society were related to ecological con-ditions.

Petrucci and Waxweiler also emphasized the link with ecology. Indeed, Petrucci sought to explain society in terms of the direct action of ecology rather than in terms of adaptation through natural selection. Waxweiler furthermore considered sociology to be a mere part of the social ethology of the animal kingdom as a whole, an important part nevertheless, since the properties of human social systems were unique and distinctive. In redis-covering these viewpoints, Crook (37) stressed their relevance to the modern ethology of social organization, the absence of any discussion of the ques-tions they raised in the literature of animal behavior, and the fact that apart from W. M. Wheeler (214) no ethologist with biological training appears to have been aware of the work of these authors. While biologists of the period were preoccupied with the mechanist-vitalist conflict, sociologists and an-thropologists were excessively nervous of biology, suspecting without justi-fication a biological takeover bid for their sciences. In any case, Waxweiler's school came to a premature end with the invasion of Belgium by the Ger-mans in World War I. As we have seen, when ethology finally reappeared in its classical form, social analysis took a markedly interactionist form with little emphasis on the environment as a factor molding the form of animal society.

Although Degeener in 1918 (51) had published a kind of taxonomy of social structure, and Allee (2) had formulated a number of general perspec-tives for comparative study, it was left to Julian Huxley (96) to recommend a focus on the adaptive significance of social organizations, specifically the mating systems of birds, in relation to ecology. In America significant con-tributions to social analysis were made by authors interested in population dynamics (e.g. Calhoun 24) and the descriptive study of social behavior (e.g. 30, 169, 170). Nevertheless, it was not until E. Cullen's (46) work with N. Tinbergen's gull group in Oxford (197) and Crook's (32) weaver studies that broad-based ecological approaches to comparative ethology got under way. At the same time the social significance of the work of Lack (118, 120, 121) on avian population dynamics became apparent, and the modern interest in the links between evolutionary ecology (119, 152) and ethology, so well introduced in Klopfer's (105) book of 1962, was born.

In the last few years, studies that emphasize the relations between individuals in groups, intergroup interactions, and the role of social factors in population dynamics (e.g. 28, 188, 221) have begun to form a major new orientation in ethology distinct from the classical concern with patterns of dyadic interaction. Crook (39) has termed this field of study *Social Ethology*, thus distinguishing it from physiologically oriented ethology which stems historically from the classical work on motivation. Nevertheless, the links between social and physiological ethology remain very close, particularly in the endocrinology of social interaction and in developmental studies. In this paper we review briefly the current state of social ethology—the history and orientation of which we trust we have now made clear.

CURRENT PERSPECTIVES IN SOCIAL ETHOLOGY

Social ethology is concerned with the description of social structures, their significance as adaptive and adaptable systems, and the relations between individuals within such systems. In addition, it sets social structure within a temporal dimension so that the nature of phase changes in structure become apparent (135) and subject to analysis in terms of seasonal determinants acting upon individuals. Structure represents a single frame in the running film of social dynamics. Change in social structure through time consists of several laminated processes with different rates of operation. Environmental change (cold weather or food dispersion, for example) may effect social relations directly (e.g. "proximate" factors), while the indirect effects of longer term environmental change on learned traditions of social interaction come about more slowly. Genetic selection within society comes about more slowly still under the influence of selective pressures or "ultimate" factors. Lack (119–121) has viewed animal dispersion patterns primarily as an adaptive relation between social behavior and the distribution of life-essential commodities (food, cover, nest holes, water sources, sleeping sites etc.) in the environment. He views dispersion as the means whereby individuals so space themselves as to maximize their effective genetic contribution to succeeding generations. The behavior whereby this is achieved is thus interpreted in terms of the natural selection of individuals.

Wynne-Edwards (221, 222), by contrast, has argued that many if not all dispersion patterns are primarily adaptations to reduce the risk of overexploitation of resources. The density of a population thus tends to be at an optimum with respect to supply rather than incurring recurrent shortages. For invoking group selection to explain many examples in his case presentation, and also for his attribution of remarkable capacities and powers of foresight to animals, Wynne-Edwards has been criticized by many (see appendix to 120, also 33, 143). Generally, effects of social behavior on numbers are now considered to be a consequence of individuals competing for ownership of limited essential commodities, rather than involving mechanisms evolved specifically to regulate population density (e.g. 140). Wynne-Edwards' arguments have led to important researches showing that territorial and individual distance behavior may produce much socially mediated mortality (see Watson & Moss 211; also 52, 108, 202, and certain studies discussed below.) In addition, social relations between individuals may be markedly affected by their numerosity, as the voluminous literature for and against the regulation of animal numbers by physiological responses to density-dependent stress has shown.

Much current social ethology involves comparative studies of social structure and communication behavior in relation to habitat features. Such correlational patterns as emerge permit inference to the evolutionary processes concerned (e.g. 146, 177). Such work cannot be more than suggestive, however, and a number of other lines of research (22) can be used to evaluate hypotheses based solely on correlational analysis.

1. Studies of function. Following important studies of the functions of behavior patterns in gulls—showing for instance that egg shell removal is a vital part of the camouflaging of the nest by black-headed gulls (200), Patterson (155) has demonstrated that the location of a nest site within a colony is of major importance in the reproductive success of the same species.

2. Longitudinal studies of populations over many years reveal the essential links between social and population dynamics. Coulson's (31) research demonstrates clearly that not only is the obtaining of a central site in a kittiwake colony prognostic of high reproductive success throughout life, but that a low rate of divorce is similarly important. Long-term studies of populations also reveal which factors are important in the control of numbers. Thus while in some rodent studies ecological factors such as food shortage are crucial, in others emigration contingent upon aggressive encounters relieves population pressure before stress symptoms appear. Where emigration is not possible or fails to lower density sufficiently, then the classical effects of population stress indeed appear and may lead to catastrophic mortality with effects lasting over the following generation (see Archer 7). The relations between factors extrinsic and intrinsic to a sociodemographic system remain an area of lively debate, and a range of long-term and experimental studies of diversity of animals is clearly needed (Chitty 27).

3. The manner in which competition and cooperation operate within groups to produce patterns of social dispersion requires direct analysis of social interaction. A major requirement for biological success is not only that an individual adapt effectively to the norms of its group throughout its behavioral development, but also that in competition with rivals for essential commodities it should achieve considerable success. Deferment of maturity makes sense if males can only obtain females at a later age when strong enough to do so. Such a process has important effects on social organization leading to the formation of various types of male exclusion from reproductive groups and the formation of all-male groups. Likewise, cooperative behavior may either maintain an animal's social position in the face of competition or enable it to succeed in replacing a rival. Among primates complex processes of social subterfuge have developed, probably as learned responses to pressures in a given structure. Only in geese, certain other

avian groups, certain carnivores, and primates are long-term sexual bonds and social affiliations of long duration established. The dynamics of such groups and their ecological significance are a focus of growing interest (see last section of review).

In our critical account of a necessarily brief selection of recent publications in these areas, we divide social ethology under two headings: Socioecology, under which perspectives 1 and 2 above will be discussed from an evolutionary viewpoint, and Social Dynamics, which treats only the third perspective.

SOCIOECOLOGY

Social adaptations to the environment.—In a Darwinian evolutionary sense, the fitter individual is the one that rears more young than its contemporaries to reproductive adulthood. If the capacities which enable the parent to achieve this are passed on to its young, the line or genotype will gradually come to predominate in the population. Hence, natural selection distinguishes between the abilities of individuals to contribute to the gene pool of succeeding generations (see for instance 218). One would therefore expect to find adaptations which maximize the number of young an individual can produce. There is now a considerable amount of comparative and experimental evidence which suggests, for instance, that the average clutch size of nidicolous birds corresponds to that which enables the parents to rear the greatest number of young to fledgling (e.g. 120, 164). On general evolutionary grounds, one might expect that the prime components of social systems could be viewed in this light as well.

There are two means by which the number of offspring reaching maturity may be increased. First, the number of eggs laid or births achieved during an individual's lifetime may be increased by either producing larger clutches or litter sizes or by reproducing more frequently. Second, the amount of time and energy the parent devotes to each young may be increased so that the chances of each young being reared are maximized. These two methods will to some extent be incompatible: the greater the number of young produced the smaller the amount of time and energy that can be devoted to each of them. Presumably natural selection favors the compromise between these two strategies that proves most successful, as the findings from studies of avian reproductive rates seem to suggest (120). Obviously, healthy parents are necessary, and those that survive the longest, *ceteris paribus*, will be able to breed most frequently. Hence, adaptations aiding individual survival as well as the successful production of young are expected to evolve, and many such adaptations involve social behavior.

Both these requirements seem to be affected by the same kind of ecological variables. In conjunction with the gross nature of the habitat, two factors appear particularly important determinants of social structure, and their individual effects will be considered separately. One is predation, which may be particularly severe on the relatively helpless young. The other is the abundance and dispersion of a population's resources, principally that of the food supply. The resources available to a population set a limit to population growth which means that, at least at certain times of the year, some individuals may be dying or failing to breed through lack of some essential commodity, particularly food (e.g. 120, 209). Hence a premium for survival and reproduction is placed on possession of the limiting commodity, and this may generate intense competition between individuals. This has profound effects on the social structure since it is largely through social behavior that competition for a limited resource is expressed.

Several kinds of studies are used in investigating the adaptiveness of social structures. Descriptive field studies are at some stage essential since only field work can yield an adequate account of the social structure as a whole. Also field studies are required to identify the naturally occurring selective agents. In addition, many important ideas on the adaptiveness of social structures have been made by induction from extensive comparative studies of groups of birds and mammals in the field. Crook's (32, 33) and Lack's studies (121) on avian social systems and Crook & Gartlan's (42) studies of primate social systems provide examples.

Tests of ideas on the adaptiveness of particular features are made in a number of ways, and some of the most common may be mentioned. A frequent procedure is to utilize the naturally occurring variability between individuals. For instance, it is sometimes possible to compare the survival or breeding success of individuals that vary in respect to the feature being examined (e.g. 95, 155), although controlling for confounding factors in such studies may be difficult.

Predictions about the occurrence of certain features in particular ecological conditions may be tested by reference to a number of well-studied populations. However, comparative data from several populations of the same species may not exist, or the species ecology may not vary enough between populations for major contrasts in the social structure to be expected. Since either or both of these conditions are common, most workers usually employ interspecific comparisons using data drawn from a group of closely related species (e.g. 146, 151). Many hypotheses are testable by either laboratory or field experiment. For instance, Tinbergen, Impekoven & Frank (201) have used field experiments to test the hypothesis that the prey of certain avian predators are able to increase their safety by spacing themselves out. Similarly, Krebs et al (110) have shown in the laboratory that individuals within flocks of foraging great tits (*Parus major*) may be able to locate food faster than do solitary hunting birds. In this section we rely on material obtained by all these approaches to research.

Studies of the selection pressures influencing social structure have been made on a number of classes, particularly on birds and mammals. Because they are relatively easy to study in the field, a great deal of attention has been given to primates and more recently to ungulates as well. In this section we review the extensive literature on birds and, after a brief discussion of contrasts, refer the reader to other reviews of the work carried out on primates. This is because the main concepts in vertebrate socioecology have developed within ornithology.

AVIAN SOCIAL STRUCTURE

Social adaptations to food exploitation.—The food supply of populations may vary considerably in overall density and in spatial and temporal patterning of abundance. Thus the food of some wading birds on estuaries, for instance, may be relatively uniformly dispersed and fluctuate little in density over long periods (Goss-Custard 74). In contrast the food of many fish-eating birds may be extremely patchily distributed and wholly unpredictable in its place of occurrence in huge areas of ocean (11, 177). Such vastly different kinds of food supply require quite different adaptations for their efficient exploitation.

Many of these adaptations are of an individual or a social nature. For example, apart from the effect of nutritional quality in determining diet (see 69), birds may select the size of prey that yields them the greatest return per unit time (87, 104, 147, 163). Similarly, birds appear able to learn the specific characteristics of camouflaged prey so that they are able to locate these with an enhanced efficiency once they have discovered the first few (45, 49, 191). Again, birds seem to have the capacity to locate and remain for disproportionately long periods in the densest parts of food gradients (75, 165, 179).

There appear to be a number of ways in which an individual may benefit from the close proximity of conspecifics in situations where the food supply is so dispersed that it is difficult to find. For instance, one advantage accruing to flocks of great tits (*Parus major*) may be that the birds which first locate a food clump reveal its existence to other members of the group, so that in effect a greater area is being searched per unit time. Krebs, Mac-Roberts & Cullen (110) tested this idea experimentally using captive birds and found that each bird in a flock of four searching for concealed prey obtains its first food item faster than does a single individual presented with the same task.

This kind of mutual benefit may be found in other situations as well. Avian food supplies often occur in widely scattered patches of local abundance which may continually change their location. Clearly, the birds using such a food supply must be able to range widely to find the currently available sites. Their chances of finding such sites may be greatly increased if they are able to utilize the knowledge obtained by other individuals. For instance, birds that respond to conspecifics feeding on the ground may locate food faster than those which do not, especially if the food supply iteslf is difficult to spot from afar (32, 121, 143, 207). This "local enhancement" might well explain, for example, the rapid congregation of finches on patches of grain (32, 147) and seabirds on surfacing schools of fish (10).

This idea was extended by Ward (207) to account for the huge communal roosts formed in Africa by the granivorous weaverbird *Quelea quelea*. He proposed that the main function of the roost is to increase the area over which mutual benefits may be derived from social feeding. It seems likely that birds who found a good feeding place one day would return to it on the next, while those that found only poor feeding areas would not. The less successful birds may find the good food sources more rapidly than they would on their own by joining departing birds which, by flying straight away from the roost, indicated they were flying to good feeding areas. The idea has not yet been tested but has been convincingly applied to a number of other species by Zahavi (223).

Fisher (61) had already proposed a similar explanation for colonial nesting, and Horn (95) successfully applied the hypothesis to colonies of nesting Brewer's blackbird (*Euphagus cyanocephalus*). In fact, it seems that the hypothesis may be applied in general to nesting colonies and to communal roosts. Comparative studies show that colonies and roosts occur in species which feed socially on patches of food which may change in their location, usually unpredictably (33, 121, 223).

Horn (95) also presents a model which suggests a further advantage of colonial nesting in the Brewer's blackbird. He compares the average distance flown by parents on foraging forays when the nests are dispersed evenly in the area within which food occurs to the distance flown when the nests are concentrated in a colony at the center. The model suggests that the distance flown by each bird, and therefore the time and energy expended in travel, is least if all the nests are placed centrally in a colony. Horn's model argues for locating the nest in the center of an individual's home range rather than for coloniality per se. Centrality will give rise to coloniality only when several birds share the same home range, as happens when all the individuals in a population range over a limited area bounded by unsuitable habitat. While applicable to the Brewer's blackbird for which Horn develops the model, these conditions may be met only seldom in other species since it would seem more usual for the individual home ranges to be much smaller than the range occupied by the population as a whole.

While birds that nest or roost communally may be able to benefit from the successful foraging of other birds, there are obvious disadvantages to social foraging as well. The accumulation of birds on locally rich feeding sites may lead to competition of various kinds. "Direct competition" occurs when encounters over individual food items take place, as when one bird supplants another that has found a food item (e.g. 43, 124), while "indirect competition" occurs when one animal takes food that would later be found by another or disturbs its food supply in some way (Goss-Custard 74).

Presumably, these disadvantages are more than outweighed by the advantages provided by the more rapid location of food that communal foraging permits. In some circumstances such disadvantages as exist may be relatively slight, as when the grain food supply of some finches (147) is doomed to destruction, whether or not birds feed on it, by falls of snow or agricultural practice. In some cases the effects of competition may be minimized by an appropriate dispersal strategy away from the roost or colony (84, 85). In other circumstances, however, some birds are clearly at a disadvantage when large numbers of individuals locate a food patch. The females in flocks of *Quelea quelea*, for instance, are subordinate to the males and hence have difficulty in obtaining their food (41, 207). Presumably, however, the chances that such females might find another patch of food on their own are slight enough that it still is advantageous for them to stay on the one being exploited by the main flock.

It could be argued that the first bird to find a patch of food might gain by defending it against others, thereby ensuring itself a food supply that lasts longer than would otherwise be the case. However, it would probably be uneconomic or simply impracticable to do so. Where all the food of a population is localized in a few places, there may be very large numbers of birds attempting to feed at each site, so that the defense of a part or the whole of such a food source would be extremely difficult. Furthermore, during the breeding season the nest and food source may be widely separated so that the bird must spend much of its time away from the food and hence would not be able to defend it. Finally, a food source may be so mobile or transient that nothing is gained by attempting to defend it since it will disappear anyway, however great the numbers of birds which feed on it.

On the other hand, where the food supply is such that it can be economically defended, one might expect territories to evolve since they could ensure an uncompeted and undisturbed supply for the owner and, during the breeding season, for its young as well. The notion of "economic defendability" in influencing whether or not territories evolve was stressed by Brown (20). Whereas a mobile or transient food source might not merit defense, a more evenly dispersed and dependable food supply may. Zahavi (224) has demonstrated experimentally in the white wagtail the importance of the food being predictable in determining whether or not territories will form.

The prediction derived from this line of argument is that there should be a correlation between the nature of the food supply on the one hand and the dispersion system of the birds on the other, and this has been largely substantiated by a number of authors. Both Crook (32, 33) and Lack (121) show that, in general, birds that nest colonially or birds that roost communally outside the breeding season feed socially on temporally and spatially variable foods. By contrast, feeding territories occur both during and outside the breeding season in species exploiting more evenly dispersed and dependable food supplies. Similar correlations emerge from intraspecific comparisons. Many birds form territories in the breeding season but occur in flocks at other times of year, and these changes correlate with a change in food dispersion from an evenly dispersed supply to one that is patchy in distribution.

Social adaptations to predation

(a) Adaptations in the breeding season:

Colony nesting, and the spacing that occurs between nests within a colony, may reduce the risk of eggs, young, and sitting adults being taken by predators. Colonies are generally sited in positions that makes them invulnerable to attack, at least by some predators. For instance, sea-bird colonies are often sited on offshore islands where no ground predators occur. Additional behavioral mechanisms may then exist to reduce the risk to eggs and young from other predators, particularly birds, that can reach the colony. Several birds attacking together may be more successful than one in driving away predators (113). Horn (95) notes that flying avian predators are driven away by mass attacks from Brewer's blackbird colonies and that mobbing may also distract predators that enter the colony, and hence reduce the risk of nests being destroyed. In addition to deterring and distracting potential predators, a colony may also enable approaching predators to be detected more effectively since many pairs of eyes are likely to detect the danger sooner than one. The first bird to notice the predator then alerts the rest of the group by alarm calls and thus the chances of individuals being taken by surprise are reduced. Furthermore, by being in a colony the breeding population is concentrated into a much smaller number of predator home ranges than would be the case if the nests were widely dispersed over a much greater area. Along with highly synchronous breeding (155), this may have the effect of reducing the total number of nests destroyed simply because the small number of predators exploiting the colony will be limited in the number of prey they can take. While these arguments have been supported to various extents by field observation and experiment (95, 113, 155), they may be countered by the claim that predators may more easily find a conspicuous colony and, having found the first nest, return to the colony later to find others (113). Hence at present it is not clear whether colony nesting in itself in all cases improves the chances of the birds bringing off young.

The alternative strategy is to spread the nests more evenly through the habitat. Crook (32) shows that weaverbird nests sited in homogeneous vegetation which provides no protection from predators are usually widely spaced in territories. He argues that if a predator finds one nest, there is little clue as to the whereabouts of others. Also it seems that the spacing-out of nests within a colony may reduce the chances of eggs being discovered by predators (i.e. 45, 195, 201). Spacing out camouflaged nests to a much greater degree than occurs within colonies may further improve their safety, especially if the parents adopt suitably cryptic behavior when approaching or leaving the nest. Krebs (109), for instance, showed that in great tits the farther a nest is from its neighbor the safer it is from weasels. Similarly, Murton & Isaacson (141, 142) found good evidence in the wood pigeon (*Columba palumbus*) that nests at high densities were more likely to be predated by jay (*Garrulus glandarius*) and magpies (*Pica pica*) than were nests at low densities.

Hence there may be two broad dispersion strategies open to birds for increasing the safety of their nests from predators. One is nesting in colonies in places inaccessible to many predators, associated with mechanisms for group defense against those that reach the colony. The second involves the development of cryptic nests in vegetation which may or may not hinder some predators, associated with antipredator responses to predators near the nest, such as sitting still (e.g. 95) or performing distraction displays (176). Which of these two strategies is likely to evolve in a particular instance may depend on other factors, as discussed below.

(b) Adaptation outside the breeding season:

Outside the breeding season the release of birds from the fixed point of the nest site influences the kind of strategy that is most likely to be effective against predators. While solitary individuals may not attract predators' attention as much as groups, spacing seems less likely to reduce predation on adults than on nests. Spacing of nests is thought to be favored as a result of the tendency of predators to search in the vicinity of their first find (45, 201). While those eggs, and often young, in the nests near to the one that has just been predated cannot escape, adults are able to do so.

On the other hand, there are a number of ways in which clumping or forming flocks may be an adaptation to predation. A clumped dispersion may reduce the chances of individual prey in open habitats being detected and pursued by a visually searching predator (206). It may also be the inevitable result of prey attempting to reduce their "domain of danger" from attacks by predators (83). Flocks and communal roosts may also be able to detect an approaching predator sooner than an individual and hence reduce the chances of surprise attacks being successful (118). Thus wagtails (*Motacilla a. alba*) roosting in a group are much more difficult to catch by hand than are solitary roosting individuals (223). Once discovered, groups may deter attacks or enable harassing of the predator to take place (193). A group may also present a predator with so many stimuli that it is less able to single out one for pursuit; this might delay the attack and allow the prey more time to escape. However, all these suggestions require further investigation.

Combined effects of adaptations to predation and food exploitation.—It seems that in birds both spacing and congregation may be adaptations to exploit the food efficiently and to reduce the risk of predation. Assuming that the dispersion patterns have the effects that have been postulated for them, we may examine the combined influence that predation and the food supply are thought to have as selection pressures on the social system.

Reviews of avian social systems emphasize the primary role of the food supply in dictating the system that will evolve (33, 121). There are several reasons for this. First, there is now considerable evidence that food shortage may often act as an important mortality agent in birds. This means that, at least at certain times of the year, the food supply is so sparse that the feeding activities of one bird may influence the chances of another collecting adequate food: hence competition occurs. This may place a premium on efficient social and asocial adaptations to locating and exploiting the food supply. Furthermore, during the breeding season, the clutch size of many birds may be determined by the amount of food the parents can collect, and this again suggests adaptations would arise to collect the food efficiently. In contrast, except during the breeding season when eggs and young may be vulnerable, predation generally seems to a less important pressure.

The second reason is that in many situations being either spaced out or in colonies would seem equally effective ways of reducing predation risk, whereas the requirement of efficient exploitation of the food more clearly seems to favor only one of them. For example, birds feeding in a forest on a more or less uniformly dispersed insect prey would seem able to reduce predation either by forming a colony in an innaccessible site or by having overdispersed cryptic nests. However, the even distribution of the food would seem to favor the spacing-out of pairs, because it involves the birds in the least expenditure of time and energy in traveling to collect food for the young (95). Anyway, this kind of food supply probably obviates the need for individuals to benefit from the success of others in locating food.

The third reason, which relates rather closely to the last one, is that comparative surveys show that avian dispersion systems tend to correlate rather closely with the nature of the food supply (32, 121, 223). In statistical terms, a large proportion of the variance in social systems seems to be accountable in terms of variations in the food supply, and there are good reasons for thinking these relationships to be causal. However, we must admit that thorough attempts to relate social structure to ecological factors which might influence the pattern of predation, such as the cover provided by the habitat, have not been attempted.

Of course, this is not to say that predators have not acted as important selection pressures on avian social systems. For instance, it is very common for socially feeding birds to form flocks which appear unnecessarily compact or well integrated for exploiting a patchy food supply. Overwintering wading birds may forage widely over their estuarine, coastal, and inland feeding sites. The strong influence of the weather and tide in determining which habitat and which site within each habitat is the best for feeding provides many of these birds a rather widespread and, in effect, variable food supply (e.g. 73). Some individuals of some species do form small feeding territories during the winter, but these are readily vacated if the conditions are such that feeding elsewhere is beneficial. Hence, in general the food supply seems such that a fluid dispersion system in which individuals can range widely and congregate on highly suitable feeding areas seems desirable. However, there would seem to be nothing in the food supply itself which requires the birds to feed in the often extremely compact flocks that form within a feeding area and which are maintained as the birds forage over large distances. On the other hand, predation may act as a sufficient selection pressure to bring the animals together into persistent groups, as long as this is consistent with efficient feeding (Goss-Custard 74).

There are other cases, however, where the relative influence of the food supply and predation is uncertain. Birds feeding at sea obviously have to nest on land, so the nests are inevitably placed some distance from the feeding grounds. Most such birds nest in colonies rather than spreading their nests more evenly along the coastline. Colonies tend to occur on islands or other sites inaccessible to small mammal predators. However, as we have seen, the colony may provide protection against aerial predators as well as provide an "information center" in the sense of Zahavi (223), through which unsuccessful birds can locate the food found by the more successful ones; therefore both factors may be involved. Similarly, red grouse (*Lagopus scotticus*) occupy large feeding territories on heather moors, and their cryptic nests are well spaced. The food supply is relatively uniform and competition occurs for possession of territories (101, 208, 210). Territoriality here may both reduce the chances of predation and provide a better food source. Coloniality, however, would seem maladaptive, both because of the even dispersion of the food and because colony sites inaccessible to ground predators seem rare. In cases like this, one can at present only say that both predation and the food supply may act together in favoring the territorial habit.

Adaptations to mating.—As was noted earlier, an individual may increase the number of offspring it rears by producing more young and by spending more time and energy looking after them. So far we have discussed social adaptations which increase the chances of survival of an individual and its progeny. Social adaptations which increase the number of eggs per individual may now be considered.

In the majority of birds, monogamous pairs form during the breeding season and both parents take part in rearing the young. In nidicolous species, it seems the average number of eggs laid is that which yields the greatest number of fledged young (118, 120); laying too few eggs means that the food-collecting capacity of the parents is not fully utilized, while laying too many eggs results in each chick receiving too little food for proper growth.

In some species, however, polygamy has evolved so that one male holds a territory in which two or more females fertilized by him rear their young. As Armstrong (9) first pointed out, this seems to occur in situations where the food supply is so abundant that females may rear their young successfully with little or no help from the males. The advantage of polygamy to those males which are relatively free from having to provide food for their young is obvious: the more females they fertilize the greater will be their contribution to the gene pool of succeeding generations. Certainly polygamy does not occur simply because there is a shortage of males (151, 175, 204, 225), although in some cases the slower rate of maturing of the males may contribute to the inbalance in the sex ratio of breeding adults. However, in general one male can only acquire several females when others fail to obtain any at all. One would thus expect to find that polygamy gives rise to competition between males for the available females, and characters which enhance the success with which males compete with each other would be expected to evolve. Furthermore, one would also expect females to have developed mechanisms with which to select the best males, since each clutch involves her in an investment of considerable time and energy and may, indeed, constitute a sizeable proportion of her total reproductive effort (133, 153). Given the obvious importance of both males and females of optimizing their mating strategies, it is not surprising that the consequences of sexual selection for animal social systems seem to have been profound.

The nature of sexual selection and its consequences for sexual dimorphism and mating systems have been considered by several authors (especially 62, 97, 133, 153) since the original formulation by Darwin (48). Sexual selection appears to operate in two ways, and both very often have been involved in the evolution of a single feature. First, intrasexual selection favors structural and behavioral characters that enhance a male's chances of competing successfully with other males. Secondly, some features which appear nonfunctional in combat may have evolved by intersexual selection in which the female's preference for certain characteristics determines the evolution of male behavior and adornments.

Intrasexual selection in birds seems to have favored increased male size enhanced allaesthetic characteristics, and aggressiveness. Intersexual selection seems to have particularly favored the dramatic male plumage and displays that occur particularly among promiscuous birds. Many such species gather on arenas or leks where the males compete for females, e.g. the ruff and blackcock. Presumably, displaying communally increases the chances that females will find the males. Predation, however, acts as a counter-selection pressure against bright coloration, especially in species where the male holds a feeding territory and collects some food for the young. Clearly, too conspicuous a male foraging on his own would be vulnerable to predation or would too easily give the location of its nests away to predators (see 175).

Intersexual selection may also operate in more subtle ways. In addition to being fertilized, a female needs to ensure that her young stand the best chances of survival. One would thus expect her to select a male that seemed most likely to help her do this. If her sensory capabilities permit, one would expect a female to select the fittest male since she is thereby likely to produce young that are more fit, on the average, than females mating with poorer males (62, 153).

In species where the male plays an extensive role in rearing young, one would also expect a female to select a mate likely to provide the best care for her young (153). For instance, female weaverbirds in selecting mates may be attracted as much by the location of the nest and colony in relation to food or defense against predation as by anything else (41).

Orians (153) develops a model which portrays the circumstances in which females are likely to select males that already have one or more females in their territory instead of nearby unmated males. In a heterogeneous habitat where the likelihood of the parents raising young depends on the quality of the habitat, some males will possess good territories while others will occupy poor ones. Clearly the female's best policy is to settle in the best territory. However, as the number of females settling in the best territories increases, the reproductive success of each of them is likely to fall for several reasons: the food may decline; more predators may be attracted to the area; and if the male does to a limited extent help care for the young, each brood will receive less help. Hence a point is reached—the "polygamy threshold" (205) —where newly settling females would do better by joining unmated males in their poor territories.

Of course, these arguments apply in cases where the clutchsize is not primarily determined by the amount of food or protection that both parents can provide for their young. If the interests of the female have had the strong influence during evolution that we expect on theoretical grounds, we would at first glance anticipate finding polygamy only in those species where male care of the young would not enable a female to rear more offspring. If this were not the case, monogamy might be expected to evolve, since a female would presumably select a monogamous male in preference to a polygamous one because she would be able to rear a greater brood of young with his help than she would without it.

These conditions are certainly met in many promiscuous species where only the female looks after the large nidifugous brood and where the clutch size does not appear limited by the amount of care that can be provided for the young. In other cases, however, it is not clear that factors other than parental care always limit clutch size. For instance, many nidicolous and polygynous tropical birds have very small clutches (180, 181), and one would suppose that the addition of male help would enable a larger brood to be reared. On the other hand, it is possible that mating with a polygynous male and rearing fewer young each breeding season may be in the long run a better strategy than mating with a monogamous male. The short-term loss in reproductive capacity for the female may be more than compensated by the fact that by mating with such males she is more likely to leave male offspring which in their turn will fertilize many females and thus contribute disproportionately to the gene pool (134).

Grades of avian social systems.—So far we have examined, to some extent in isolation, various ways in which particular dispersion patterns may be adaptive as survival, rearing, and mating strategies. Of course, in reality the whole range of adaptations shown by an individual will determine its success and form an interacting complex such that a shift in one adaptation may have effects on the functioning of others. Ideally the complex should be viewed as a whole (32, 196). Each feature is one aspect of a whole collection of characteristics that are in a very broad sense adaptive. Huxley (see 32) coined the term "grade" to refer to the characteristic life styles of species adapted to a particular biotype. Correlations between ecology and the system of co-adaptations comprising social structure have now been recognized in many groups of birds. Particularly noteworthy is the work of Tinbergen (198, 199), E. Cullen (46), J. M. Cullen (47), Stonehouse (184), Crook (32, 33), Immelmann (98, 99), Orians (151), and Nelson (146); and Lack (121) has recently published an important review. Rather than review such comprehensive studies, we refer the reader to them.

PRIMATE SOCIAL STRUCTURE

Comparative studies of mammalian (particularly primate) social structures suggest that, as in birds, the three factors of resource distribution, predation, and mating requirements have together molded the form that social systems take (38, 40, 42, 53, 58, 70, 76, 114, 115, 220). Of course there are striking differences in the effects that such factors produce. In particular, many primates are dispersed in long-lasting and relatively stable groups within which the number of mature males and the sex ratio may vary. The development of such groups in primates and their absence in birds seems related to two fundamental differences between avian and mammalian biology.

Among mammals, males generally provide much less care to their offspring than do most birds. For obvious reasons, only the females provide food for the young prior to weaning. Furthermore, although there are notable exceptions (e.g. marmosets, gibbons), the male usually plays little part in grooming and carrying the young even though he is physically able to do so. Usually the male only contributes indirectly, as by deterring predators or defending a territory. A second contrast between birds and many mammals is the lengthy period of dependence of the slowly developing young mammal on its parent. In contrast to the short development period of young birds, in primates the growth periods of successive litters may overlap. The advantage of the infants staying with the parents long after they have become physically capable of leading an independent existence presumably lies with the benefits they can derive from the parents' superior knowledge of the local environment. The young animal's chances of survival may be greatly enhanced if this knowledge enables it, for example, to locate new sources of food, scarce water holes (5), or safe sleeping sites sooner or more certainly than it would be able to do on its own.

While this factor may account for stable groups comprising mothers and young, it fails to account for the widespread occurrence of at least one mature male in primate groups; knowledge of the habitat would seem to depend primarily on age rather than sex (76). Since solitary males could easily join a group of females and young for short periods for mating purposes, the adaptive significance of the males' continuous association with the group needs to be sought elsewhere.

One possibility is that intrasexual selection favors males that form a continuous association with several females, i.e. take a harem. Such males may thereby ensure themselves exclusive use of at least a proportion of the available females which may come into estrus throughout much of the year.

However, it is not clear whether a male would actually increase the number of fertilizations he achieves by taking a harem, since by staying with females he has already fertilized he will be failing to find others that are in estrus (Goss-Custard et al 76).

The second possibility is that by staying with his females and young the male may be able to improve their chances of survival and hence his own reproductive success. For example, unaccompanied females and young may be very vulnerable to attacks by predators or unable to compete successfully with other animals for limited resources such as safe sleeping sites or food. If the male's presence reduces the severity of such risks, natural selection would be expected to favor those males that form long-lasting relationships with their females and young. The fact that one male may be able to care for several litters at once may account for the widespread occurrence of groups comprising one mature male and several females and young [for example: *Erythrocebus patas* (79); *Papio hamadryas* (116); *Theropithecus gelada* (34)].

Mating with males that contribute to the rearing of their young is also clearly to the advantage of the female. Being fertilized by such males increases the female's own chances of survival and those of her young. Furthermore, those males that prove most successful in sexual competition with other males, and also have well-developed tendencies to care for their young, may be particularly preferred by the females. Hence both intra- and intersexual selection seem likely to be involved in the evolution of "one-male" groups.

Caring for the young and the necessity for survival involve primates in social strategies in relation to their ecology similar to these discussed for birds. Predation and the predictability and dispersion of the food supply seem to have had the same profound effects on social structure, although the causal links appear rather different. Since these have been reviewed extensively in recent months, we refer readers to the following sources. The socioecology of primate groups and the role of sexual selection is discussed further in reviews by Crook (38) and Goss-Custard et al (76). In a further paper, Crook (40) generates hypothetical relationships between defendability of home ranges, their resource contents, and the supportable group size. Denham (53) likewise examines the role of ecological factors in the evolution of primate social systems. Reviews of comparable material on ungulates are provided, for example, by Jarman (personal communication; see also 39) and Estes (58).

SOCIAL DYNAMICS

An individual is born into a social structure, but not necessarily one consisting of sociable creatures. Within such a structure the manner in which his innate and acquired characteristics enable him to fit the prevailing social environment and to cope with direct competition for environmental resources (e.g. food, water, sleeping perch), social supports (e.g. potential mate, spouse), or socioenvironmental commodities (e.g. territory with food value as well as being a mating area) determine his life trajectory with respect to reproductive success over a lifetime and longevity. The ways in which an individual optimizes the chances of high reproductive success or minimizes the effects of social misfortune comprise strategies that can become exceedingly complex in advanced animals.

The dynamics of relationships between members of a set of individuals, expressed in terms of the outcomes of interindividual encounters, reciprocities, and facilitations, comprise the forces that maintain a particular phase of social structure as a constrained organization. We consider the main processes going on in the maintenance of social structures to be as follows:

1. Competitive dynamics leading to territorial spacing, dominance rankings, or the exclusion of certain individuals or classes of individuals from breeding communities.

2. Integrative dynamics comprising the effects of social facilitation, behavioral copying, follow-up responses, and the simple control of individual and group affect to prevent group disintegration.

3. Bonding dynamics comprising behavior that bonds individuals in dyads, polygynous mating units, or multi-individual groups of more or less constant composition for short or long periods of time. Under this head fall not only the bonding effects of mutual courtship in some species (note: courtship by no means always leads to long-term pairing), but also the elaborate bonding processes (for example in geese, wolves, and primates) that maintain intimate relationships between individuals in groups at a far more complex level of cooperative behavior than that achieved in, say, starling flocks which depend only on the integrative behavior mentioned above. Bonding dynamics also include the elaborate cases of social subterfuge so far only studied in primates (see below), the apparent function of which is to reduce the socially disintegrative effects of competition in tightly organized groups. These behaviors involve high degrees of skill in the manipulation of others which are clearly dependent on social learning.

In any given case the type of dynamic interplay between individuals that accounts for a social structure is likely to involve at least the first two and probably also the third of the processes described above. The complexity of vertebrate societies increases to the degree to which all three processes are present and cofunctional. Stability of social organization, much like the stability of ecological communities, is a consequence of an internal complexity involving a diversity of processes acting sometimes antagonistically and sometimes in synergy. While complexity is a feature particularly of carnivore and primate social interaction, the exact difference between the social control processes in these two taxa and, say, the societies of artiodactyla or pinnepeds requires further elucidation.

An overlapping perspective on these problems has been emphasized by T. Sebeok in a continuing series of valuable contributions to the zoosemiotics of behavioral interaction (172–174). For Sebeok, as for Altman (4), the line

between zoosemiotics and social organization is "gossamer-thin," zoosemiotics being the communication aspect of organization and one inevitably present in all social dynamics.

In this paper we concern ourselves only with the dynamics and social
consequences of bonding and, for reasons of space, simply list some of the
key studies in competitive and integrative dynamics. In competitive dynamics valuable studies have appeared in the analysis of territory and spacing (6, 12, 44, 58, 86, 102, 109, 130, 146, 224); in research on competition for
mates in polygynous mating systems in birds (94, 95, 112, 151, 204, 205); in
analyzing hierarchy and role in goose society (107, 158) and in primates and
other mammals (1, 15, 29, 38, 40, 53–55, 68, 76, 116, 122, 167, 182, 185, 187).
The complexity of hierarchies and the unsuitability of the dominance terminology in modern primate studies has become a major issue (Gartlan 66,
67). The fact that status ranking may differ with the commodity for which
competition occurs (41, 161) disposes of any idea that dominance is a unitary
phenomenon. Studies of integrative dynamics focus, for example, on social
mimicry and other mechanisms of integration in bird flocks (59, 98, 99, 117,
138, 139, 183) and on problems of behavioral synchronization (77) in particular vocal duetting (156, 189).

Dynamics of Bonding

Although probably mediated by relatively automatic signal systems
derived from innate motor components, and lacking the flexibility of much
avian and mammalian bonding behavior, the relations between mouthbreeding fish and their young continue to attract attention (13, 150, 215, 216).
Wickler (217) has discussed apparent analogies between the social system of
such species and those of primates. The mouthbreeding behavior itself has
been reviewed (149) and shown to occur in 53 fish genera in four orders of
Osteichthyes (8 families) inhabiting marine, brackish, or fresh water. It appears to have been derived in evolution from the increased security gained by
young taken into the mouth in situations unfavorable to nesting and necessarily involves the cessation of feeding by the parent performing the activity.
In *Betta* species the behavior may have developed from a prior behavior in
which eggs were placed orally in a bubble nest, in cichlids from mouthing
and transferring behavior. Associated signal changes increasing efficiency in
egg pickup and in fertilization involve the evolution of colorful tassels, false
eggs on anal fins, etc.

In a review of some aspects of long-term pair bonding in birds, with
special reference to zebra finches, Butterfield (23) defines a pair bond as
reciprocal mutual attachment between two heterosexual sexually mature
organisms between which aggressive tendencies are largely suppressed. In
the zebra finch, which pairs for life, the original selection of a mate in pair
formation has genetic consequences over several broods. The complex visual
characteristics of the male have been selected to assist and maintain con-

specific mating especially under conditions of sympatry with close taxonomic relatives. It follows that marked dimorphism is not only a characteristic of polygynous birds but may also be an adaptation to long-term bonding, at least in certain species. In laboratory tests Butterfield examined the strength of a bird's tendency to "rejoin" another in a specially constructed Skinner box. She found that males work hard to see their mate on the far side of a one-way window, less hard for other females, and hardest of all when the spouse has another male with her on the far side of the screen. Females did not work to see males. This might be attributed to the male's role of searcher when the pair get separated in the wild, the female remaining still awaiting his approach (see further 98, 99). The physiological basis of long-term pair bonds in these birds has been discussed by several authors (e.g. Farner 60).

Bonding between parents and offspring to form an integrated clan-like social unit occurs in a limited number of bird species in a variety of taxonomic families (33) and appears to be a consequence of particular tropical conditions favoring assistance of the parents at the nest by relatives. Such altruistic behavior, discussed by Hamilton (82) from the genetical viewpoint, has the consequence that the behavior of an individual aids in the transference of at least some of its own genes to the next generation through increasing the survival and reproduction of kin under conditions when the individual is not itself breeding. Brown (21) contributes a useful field study of altruistic behavior in a flock of about 14 Mexican jays (*Alpheocoma ultramarina*.). Few quantitative data on such behavior had been available previously, and although the flock was not completely banded throughout the study, important new facts emerge.

For the psychologist recent studies on bonding and affiliation in primates are of particular significance. The numerous papers of Harlow, Mason, and Hinde and their collaborators on the mother-infant relation have yielded major advances in understanding this basic bonding system, demonstrating how the presence of other siblings and "aunts" may also be significant to the development of the baby. Hinde's recent review (91) of problems in this area will be an important spur to further research.

Kummer shows how the formation of harems in hamadryas baboon troops is intimately related to the protective roles adopted by young males in relation to juvenile females. This relation initiates bond formation and the creation of a harem nucleus even though the female is still too young for mating behavior. The hamadryas male in his prime is nevertheless an intolerant animal, rarely letting his females move more than a few meters from him. This is not true of other baboon social systems with a structural similarity to those of the hamadryas. In the patas monkey (79, 81) the "one-male groups" are widely dispersed. The male commonly sits rather distantly from his females, acting more as a sentinel than as an "overlord," and the females indeed can, in conjunction, dominate him. In laboratory observations the very different character of the male patas from that of the hamadryas was confirmed. In the gelada baboon, females (34) in large herds may wander up to some 200 yards from the male, but they look at him periodically and close in on him to move off with him when he begins a march. Gelada harems do not appear to form in the same way as in the hamadryas, but details are as yet lacking.

In multimale troop structures intersexual bonding is of relatively short duration, but the extent to which mates remain together at the height of the female's estrus seems to vary between species. The laboratory studies of R. Michael and his colleagues and also Saayman (166) analyze in depth the endocrinal and behavioral basis of pairing in macaques and baboons.

Jane van Lawick-Goodall's important monograph (72) on the chimpanzee emphasizes the long-term duration of the tie between mother and offspring. Goodall points out that the open society of chimps necessitates a close maternal-child link. This includes a particularly lengthy suckling period (3–4 1/2 years) and a drawn-out weaning. Mother-child bonds endure well into adult life. Rejection of the infant by the mother in weaning is less severe than in baboons, macaque, or langurs.

Chimpanzees are promiscuous and consorting between particular oppositely sexed animals does not apparently involve aggression between the male and others of his sex. Indeed even a subordinate male is allowed to copulate with the female of a consorting male. However, surprisingly little has yet been published on the sexual relations of these animals and further details are awaited with interest.

Affiliations between animals which are often kin are common in primate groups. Friendships between adult males may allow a group of them to act as controllers of social behavior, "policing" the quarrels of others and maintaining prior access to estrous females (Hall & De Vore 80). Young males may form the leaders of a branch troop when Japanese macaque groups split (Sugiyama 186). The role of kinship is not always analyzed in such studies and is likely to be even more important than currently realized. Wilson (219), for example, reports that when juvenile male rhesus on Cayo Santiago Island move from one troop into the all-male periphery of another, their entering there is assisted by adoption by older animals usually relatives and often brothers. The importance of affiliation based on kinship was emphasized by Vandenbergh (203), who attributed the instability of groups of rhesus introduced on small islands off Puerto Rico to an absence of long-term matrilineal kinship links among the populations utilized in the introductions.

Bonding between the sexes in one-male group-living primates may be of long duration. As Crook (40) has stressed, these social structures are rearing units, and the bonds maintaining the adult relationship appear important for the security and growth of the young. In certain ecologies, where multimale troops rather than harem type reproductive units are favored, the whole troop functions as a rearing unit and the specificity of long-term bonding between individuals is not pronounced. Probably shifts between multimale and one-male reproductive units have not been infrequent in Cercopithecoid social history, and some five steps seem to be required in either evolutionary direction.

COHESION AND TENSION IN PRIMATE GROUPS

The importance of group maintenance in higher primates lies, as we have just seen, not only in protection against predation but in the fact that the group comprises the social unit that provides the physical and psychological security necessary for the rearing of socially and ultimately reproductively effective young.

Within such groups, however, the advantages of altruism never entirely replace those of biological self-interest, so that cooperation and competition coexist uneasily in the social dynamics maintaining such groups. This is particularly apparent in large multimale troops in which the competition for positions of social advantage is at all times either active or latent. This accounts for the concern of earlier authors with dominance as the prime social mechanism structuring monkey society. Gartlan (66, 67), Rowell (161), and Bernstein & Sharpe (18) have shown very clearly how inadequate the dominance terminology and conceptual approach had become. They have attempted in various ways to interpret primate social structure in terms of "roles."

Gartlan (67), following Bernstein & Sharpe (18), takes a functional view of role which he derives from observations of contrasts in behavior between age-sex classes of vervet monkeys studied on Lolui Island in Lake Victoria, Uganda. His social role profiles of these classes comprise the percentage contribution of each class to a variety of behavioral categories (the roles) characteristic of the group as a whole. The differences between the classes are shown to have differing functional value to the life of the group. While the identification of social roles in this manner allows quantitative comparison between both populations of the same species and those of different species, it remains unclear as to how useful the term "role" is here, since it is arbitrarily assigned to categories extracted from behavioral description. Furthermore, the interpretation fails to make clear whether the "function" of the behavior is in relation to some feature of the group such as cohesion or in relation to long-term survival values of individuals or species. The flexibility of the role behavior in relation to local environment and group traditions suggests that the way in which such behavioral differentiation "functions" has yet to be made clear.

Hinde (91), in a discussion of the problems raised by this study, points out that the term "role" can be used with respect to the behavior of different individuals or age-sex classes in relation to one another. Thus the several age/sex categories may have different "roles" with respect to an infant or infants collectively. While this use of the term, like Gartlan's, is a consequence of the predictability of behavior with respect to age/sex categorization, it is clearly a contrasting usage. A further variation follows from the use of the term to indicate the contribution of an individual—a "partner," "consort," "mother," or any other named category derived from some classification of group members—to the consequences of a specified pattern of dyadic interaction. Thus Hinde & Atkinson (92) attempt to assess the "roles" (i.e. relative contributions) of the social partners in maintaining mutual proximity through a study of mother-infant relations (rhesus monkeys). They show that at first the mother plays the major role in maintaining proximity with her infant, whereas after a certain age the infant's behavior tends to ensure proximity.

Aldrich-Blake (1) constructed histograms showing the contributions of individuals in groups to a range of activities such as grooming, aggression, mounting, play, sitting with, etc, representing all the behavior sampled and not simply those categories designated as roles. He grouped the information by classes to show the frequency with which each class took part in each behavior, and then plotted histograms for hypothetical average individuals of each class. His analysis of field data on *Cercopithecus mitis* in Budongo forest, Uganda, shows that while mature males, infants, and babies are groomed more than they groom, adults other than mature males groom more than they are groomed. The averaged data can also be presented in behavior profiles for the average individual of each class. It is also possible to examine the relations between individuals or between classes by analyzing the affinities between individuals or between classes. It remains unclear whether any advantage would be gained by describing the behavior of an individual or class analyzed in this way as its "role" within the group as a whole or not. At the purely descriptive level the term is not necessary to the analysis.

The term "role," however, may be of use in the comparison of regularities in group structure when groups of the same or differing species are compared and also in the comparison of the state of the same group through time. It may also be useful as a way of indicating the position of the individual in a group without necessarily having to describe its complete behavioral repertoire. Bernstein (17), in describing the behavior of capuchins, showed that although no clear-cut hierarchies could be established, certain males became "control" animals which approached and terminated cases of intragroup disturbance and acted protectively when the group was faced by external danger. Similarly, in baboon and macaque troops control animals, often in association with "friends," function in the same way, although in this case the "alpha" male is usually also the dominant, at least by some criteria, animal of the troop. Most such troops have a "despot" or "alpha animal" readily distinguishable from others; indeed should a male disappear he is usually replaced after a period of instability by another. Such an animal is performing a "role" in the sense of Sarbin (168) and Nadel (144); it occupies a given slot in a social structure.

The role here is not a fixed behavioral characteristic of the individual but rather is defined by the social position occupied by the individual in the context of a social structure characteristic of the species. The control animal or alpha male role is a particularly clear case. Classification of other roles becomes more arbitrary but can be based upon analysis of the behavioral contribution of the individual to the repertoire of behavior shown by the group as a whole, using methods like those of Gartlan and Aldrich-Blake. Thus in macaque groups the control animal role, the secondary male role, and peripheral females are commonly distinguishable. The boundaries between one role and another may in some cases be marked by clear-cut discontinuities. In other cases the ranking of the behavior criteria may show a gradient of differentiation—say along a dominance-subordination continuum.

Individuals may be variously categorized with respect to their social position in a group structure. Thus an animal of a given sex and age-group category occurs in a type of group of characteristic composition (viz multimale or one-male) and affiliates with other individuals, often kin, in the course of a day's activities. In addition, it has relative priority of access with respect to food or (if male) to estrous females, a priority that places it in a status hierarchy. This status, however, may be affected by the presence or absence of affiliated individuals or (in females) by its reproductive condition. As Rowell (161) points out, dominance ranking according to one criterion may differ from that according to another. A sufficiently detailed analysis of the behavior of individuals in a group will reveal the unique features of each individual's "social position." Where a number of individuals (say subordinate males) behave similarly, one may say that they all play the same role (36).

An advantage of this approach is that it allows description of the sequence of role changes shown by an individual in the course of a given period of time. If sufficient information were available, the complete "life trajectory" of an individual could be worked out. The course followed would be the consequence of the interaction of numerous factors including the roles and dominance status of close adult kin, learning from punishment and reward in relation to competitive situations, and observational learning from the behavior of others.

Crook (36) argued that at least three types of factors interact in the social sorting process. First, competitive interaction with respect to commodities (food, females, sitting places, etc) results in agonistic encounters and the gradual establishment of a social hierarchy that allocates prior access to the more dominant individuals. In cohesive groups high behavioral constraint may force some young males into isolation (148). A second process is the tendency of large groups to split up, as affiliated individuals tend to wander separately, no longer following the dictates of the leaders (65, 136, 186). It is of great interest here that the Japanese researchers have recorded cases of solitary males taking over such branch groups as "leaders," thereby totally altering their social role. Thirdly, aging affects the role an animal occupies. Thus the sexual maturing of males is often followed by their expulsion of juveniles from one-male groups or their exclusion to a "periphery" of multimale ones. The experience of old hamadryas baboons as leaders seems responsible for the fact that they are attended to and followed by other animals after they have ceased to be sexually active (25, 116).

These aspects of group dynamics suggest that the imposition of behavioral constraint by the presence of assertive mature adults is avoided by subordinates. While some, probably of low dominance matrilineal lines, always remain low rankers, others seek solitude only to assert themselves socially once an opportunity offers. Likewise when a control animal dies or is ill, cooperative competition by a group of lower-ranking affiliated animals may lead to a marked change in their rank over others formerly dominant to them. It follows that during the life of an individual he may occupy a number of contrasting social positions within the structure of the society into which he is born. The use of a role terminology seems likely to prove useful in describing the dynamics of such changes. Indeed such a process seems likely to be a prefigurement of the emergence of control (political) structures in Man (16).

Reynolds (160) describes the process of role change among females consequent upon changes in consort relations and estrus cycles in a captive rhesus colony. The consort roles of both sexes only appear in the breeding seasons of these animals, and then the female's dominance rank (dependent rank) is commonly related to that of her male consort. The consortship varies in duration from a few days to an association that can last well into pregnancy. Reynolds shows how in a change from subordinate to dominant role the overt behavior changes from a repertoire characteristic of low rank to one found in high rank. In particular he recorded that while the death of an animal in a key role in his group had ramifying and widespread effects, eventually the social structure reverted as if by some process of social homeostasis to a "social structure phenotype" characteristic of the species.

Another consequence of behavioral constraint is that individuals appear to perform social subterfuge (36) in order either to ease their tense relations with other more dominant individuals or, more directly, in order to initiate a change in rank. Affiliation with and male care of young in Japanese monkeys may permit a rise in social rank when the infant receiving attention is kin to high-ranking animals. Likewise, young mature Barbary macaque males spend much time in caring for babies and appear to use them as "buffers" in reducing the likelihood of an aggressive encounter with senior males (50). This phenomenon, like the Japanese case, may be of local occurrence, and certainly the use of babies by the feral Barbary macaques on Gibraltar (F. Burton, personal communication) takes a different form from that in the Middle Atlas mountains of North Africa.

Cooperative and competitive processes within cohesive primate groups form the basis for an elaborate dynamics of social interaction which is as yet little understood. The importance of matrilineal kinship, of affiliation, of role change, and of social subterfuge seems likely to be confirmed. Such concepts, largely derived from the work of social anthropologists and social psychologists, are likely to be of importance in the ever-growing debate concerning the social history of man from a biological standpoint. That the behavior of higher primates prefigures that of Man is no longer in doubt, but the extent and nature of the resemblance awaits further analysis.

LITERATURE CITED

1. Aldrich-Blake, F. P. G. 1970. *The ecology and behavior of the Blue Monkey, Cercopithecus mitis stuhlmanni.* PhD thesis. Bristol Univ. Library

2. Allee, W. C. 1931. *Animal Aggregations, a Study in General Sociology.* Univ. Chicago Press

3. Altman, J. 1966. *Organic Foundations of Animal Behavior.* New York: Holt, Rinehart & Winston

4. Altmann, S. A., 1967. The structure of primate social communication. In *Social Communication Among Primates*, ed. S. A. Altmann. Univ. Chicago Press

5. Altmann, S. A., Altman, J. 1970. Baboon ecology: African field research. *Bibl. Primatol.* 12:1–220

6. Anderson, P. K., Hill, J. L. 1965. *Mus musculus*, experimental induction of territory formation. *Science* 148: 1753–55

7. Archer, J. 1970. Effects of population density on behavior in rodents. See Ref. 37, 169–210

8. Ardrey, R. 1967. *The Territorial Imperative.* London: Collins

9. Armstrong, E. A. 1955. *The Wren.* London: Collins

10. Ashmole, N. P. 1963. The regulation of numbers of tropical oceanic birds. *Ibis* 103b:458–73

11. Ashmole, N. P., Ashmole, M. J. 1967. Comparative feeding ecology of sea birds of a tropical oceanic island. *Bull. Peabody Mus. Natur. Hist.* 24:1–131

12. Assem, J. van den 1967. Territory in the three-spined stickleback, *Gastevosteus aculeatus* L. An experimental study in intra-specific competition. *Behav. Suppl.* 16:1–164

13. Barlow, G. W., Green, R. F. 1970. The problems of appeasement and of sexual roles in the courtship behavior of the blackchin mouthbreeder, *Tilapia melanotheron* (Pisces: Cichlidae). *Behavior* 36:1–2, 84–115

14. Barnett, S. A. 1963. *A Study in Behavior.* London: Methuen

15. Beilharz, R. G., Cox, D. F. 1967. Social dominance in swine. *Anim. Behav.* 15(1)117–22

16. Benedict, B. 1969. Role analysis in animals and men. *Man* 4(2):203–14

17. Bernstein, I. S. 1966. Analysis of a key role in a Capuchin (*Cebus albifrons*) group. *Tulane Stud. Zool.* 13(2):49–54

18. Bernstein, I. S., Sharpe, L. G. 1966. Social roles in a rhesus monkey group. *Behavior* 26:91–104

19. Bowlby, J. 1969. *Attachment and Loss,* Vol. 1, ed. M. Masud, R. Khan. Int. Psycho-anal. Libr. London: Hogarth

20. Brown, J. L. 1964. The evolution of diversity in avian territorial systems. *Wilson Bull.* 76:160–69

21. Brown, J. L. 1970. Cooperative breeding and altruistic behavior in the Mexican jay, *Aphelocoma ultramarina. Anim. Behav.* 18(2):366–78

22. Brown, J. L., Orians, G. H. 1970. Spacing patterns in mobile animals. *Ann. Rev. Ecol. System.* 1:239–62

23. Butterfield, P. A. 1970. The pair bond in the zebra finch. See Ref. 37, 249–78

24. Calhoun, J. 1952. The social aspects of population dynamics. *J. Mammal.* 33(2):139–59

25. Chance, M. R. A. 1967. Attention structure as the basis of primate rank orders. *Man* 2(4):503–18

26. Chapple, F. D. 1970. *Culture and Biological Man.* New York: Holt, Rinehart & Winston

27. Chitty, D. 1967. What regulates bird populations? *Ecology* 48:698–701

28. Christian, J. J. 1963. Endocrine adaptive mechanisms and the physiological regulation of population growth. In *Physiological Mammalogy*, Vol. 1, ed. W. Mayer, R. van Gelder. London: Academic

29. Cole, D. D., Shafer, J. N. 1966. A study of social dominance in cats. *Behaviour* 27:1–2, 39–53

30. Collias, N. E. 1950. Social life and the

individual among vertebrate animals. *Ann. NY Acad. Sci.* 51(6): 1074–92

31. Coulson, J. C., 1968. Differences in the quality of birds nesting in the centre and on the edges of a colony. *Nature (London)* 217:478–79

32. Crook, J. H. 1964. The evolution of social organisation and visual communication in the weaver birds (Ploceinae). *Behav. Suppl.* 10:1–178

33. Crook, J. H. 1965. The adaptive significance of avian social organizations. *Symp. Zool. Soc. London* 14: 181–218

34. Ibid 1966. Gelada baboon herd structure and movement: a comparative report. 18:237–58

35. Crook, J. H. 1968. The nature and function of territorial aggression. In *Man and Aggression*, ed. M. F. Ashley-Montagu. New York: Oxford Univ. Press

36. Crook, J. H. 1970. Sources of cooperation in animals and man. *Soc. Sci. Inform.* 9(1):27–48

37. Crook, J. H. 1970. Social behavior and ethology. In *Social Behaviour in Birds and Mammals*, ed. J. H. Crook. London: Academic

38. Ibid. The socio-ecology of primates, 103–66

39. Crook, J. H. 1970. Social organisation and the environment, aspects of contemporary social ethology. *Anim. Behav.* 18:197–209

40. Crook, J. H. 1971. Sexual selection, dimorphism and social organisation in the primates. In *Sexual Selection and the Descent of Man*, ed. B. Campbell. Chicago: Aldine. In press

41. Crook, J. H., Butterfield, P. Gender role in the social system of *Quelea*. See Ref. 37, 211–48

42. Crook, J. H., Gartlan, J. S. 1966. Evolution of primate societies. *Nature (London)* 210:1200–3

43. Crook, J. H., Ward, P. 1968. The *Quelea* problem in Africa. In *Birds as Pests*, ed. R. K. Murton, E. N. Wright. London: Academic

11. Crowcroft, P., Rowe, F. P. 1963. Social organisation and territorial behavior of wild house mice. *Proc. Zool. Soc. London* 140:517–31

45. Croze, H. 1970. Searching image in carrion crows. *Z. Tierpsychol.* Suppl. 5

46. Cullen, E. 1957. Adaptations in the kittiwake to cliff-nesting. *Ibis* 99: 275–302

47. Cullen, J. M. 1960. Some adaptations in the nesting behavior of terns. *Proc. 12th Int. Ornithol. Congr.* 12: 153–57

48. Darwin, C. 1871. *The Descent of Man and Selection in Relation to Sex.* London: Murray

49. Dawkins, M. Perceptual changes in chicks: another look at the 'Searching Image' concept. *Anim. Behav.* In press

50. Deag, J., Crook, J. H. 1971. Social behavior and "agonistic buffering" in the wild Barbary macaque, *Macaca sylvana. Folia Primatol.* In press

51. Degeener, P. 1918. *Die Formen der Vergesellschaftung im Tierreiche.* Leipzig: Verlag

52. Delius, J. D. 1965. A population study of skylarks, *Alauda arvensis. Ibis* 107:465–92

53. Denham, W. W. 1971. Energy relations and some basic properties of primate social organisation. *Am. Anthropol.* 73:77–95

54. DeVore, I. 1965. Male dominance and mating behavior in baboons. In *Sex and Behavior*, ed. F. A. Beach. New York: Wiley

55. Dickson, D. P., Barr, G. R., Weickert, D. A. 1967. Social relationship of dairy cows in a feed lot. *Behaviour* 29:2–4, 195–203

56. Eibl-Eibesfeldt, I. 1970. *Ethology, the Biology of Behavior.* New York: Holt, Rinehart & Winston

57. Espinas, A. 1878. *Des Societes Animales.* Paris: Bailliere

58. Estes, R. D. 1966. Behavior and life history of the wildebeest (*Connochaetes taurinus*, Burchell). *Nature* 212:999–1000

59. Evans, S. M. 1970. Some factors affecting the flock behavior of red avadavats (*Amandava amandava*) with particular reference to clumping. *Anim. Behav.* 18:762–67

60. Farner, D. S. 1967. The control of avian reproductive cycles. *Proc. 14th Int. Ornithol. Congr.*, 107–33

61. Fisher, J. 1954. Evolution and bird sociality. In *Evolution as a Process*, ed. J. Huxley et al. New York: Collier

62. Fisher, R. A. 1958. *The Genetic Theory of Natural Selection.* New York: Dover

63. Fox, R. 1967. In the beginning: aspects of hominid behavioral evolution. *Man* 2:415–33

64. Frost, H. H. 1960. The functional so-

ciology of Emile Waxweiler and the Institut de Sociologie: Solvay. *Acad. Roy. Belg., Cl. Lett., Mem.* 53:5

65. Furuya, Y. 1963. On the Gagyusan troop of Japanese monkeys after the first separation. *Primates* 4, 1:116–18

66. Gartlan, J. S. 1964. Dominance in East African monkeys. *Proc. East Afr. Acad.* 2:75–79

67. Gartlan, J. S. 1968. Structure and function in primate society. *Folia Primatol.* 8:89–120

68. Gartlan, J. S., Brain, C. K. 1968. Ecology and social variability in *Cercopithecus aethiops* and *C. mitis.* In *Primates: Studies in Adaptation and Variability,* ed. P. Jay. New York: Holt, Rinehart & Winston

69. Gardarsson, A., Moss, R. 1970. Selection of food by Icelandic ptarmigan in relation to its availability and nutritive value. See Ref. 209, 47–72

70. Gautier, J. P., Gautier-Hion, A. 1969. Les Associations poly-specifiques chez les Cercopithecidae du Gabon. *Terre et Vie* 2:164–201

71. Giard, A. 1905. L'evolution des sciences biologiques. *Rev. Sci.* 5: 193–205

72. Goodall, J. van L. 1968. The behavior of free living chimpanzees in the Gombe stream reserve. *Anim. Behav. Monogr.* 1(3):161–311

73. Goss-Custard, J. D. 1969. The winter feeding ecology of the redshank *Tringa totanus. Ibis* 111:338–56

74. Goss-Custard, J. D. 1970. Feeding dispersion in some over-wintering wading birds. See Ref. 37, 3–36

75. Goss-Custard, J. D. 1970b. Response of redshank (*Tringa totanus* L.) to spatial variations in the density of their prey. *J. Anim. Ecol.* 39:91–113

76. Goss-Custard, J. D., Dunbar, R. I. M., Aldrich-Blake, F. P. G. Survival, mating and rearing strategies in the evolution of primate social structure. *Folia Primatol.* In press

77. Hall, J. R. 1970. Synchrony and social stimulation in colonies of the black headed weaver *Ploceus eucullatus* and Viellot's black weaver, *Melanopteryx nigerrimus. Ibis* 112(1):93–104

78. Hall, K. R. L. 1963. Variations in the ecology of the chacma baboon, *Papio ursinus. Symp. Zool. Soc. London* 10:1–28

79. Hall, K. R. L. 1965. Behavior and ecology of the wild patas monkey, *Erythrocebus patas,* in Uganda. *J. Zool.* 148:15–87

80. Hall, K. R. L., DeVore, I. 1965. Baboon social behavior. In *Primate Behavior,* ed. I. DeVore. New York: Holt, Rinehart & Winston

81. Hall, K. R. L., Mayer, B. L. 1967. Social interactions in a group of captive patas monkeys (*Erythrocebus patas*). *Folia Primatol.* 5:213–36

82. Hamilton, W. D. 1963. The evolution of altruistic behavior. *Am. Natur.* 97:354–56

83. Hamilton, W. D. 1969. Paper read to Ann. Conf. Assoc. Study Anim. Behav. To be published in *J. Theor. Biol.*

84. Hamilton, W. J. III, Gilbert, W. M., Heppner, F. H., Planck, R. J. 1967. Starling roost dispersal and a hypothetical mechanism regulating rhythmical and animal movement to and from dispersal centres. *Ecology* 48:825–33

85. Hamilton, W. J. III, Watt, K. E. F. 1970. Refuging. *Ann. Rev. Ecol. System.* 1:263–86

86. Henshaw, J. 1970. Consequences of travel in the rutting of reindeer and caribou (*Rangifer tarandus*). *Anim. Behav.* 18:256–58

87. Hinde, R. A. 1959. Behavior and speciation in birds and lower vertebrates. *Biol. Rev.* 34:85–128

88. Hinde, R. A. 1961. Behavior. In *Biology and Comparative Physiology of Birds,* ed. H. J. Marshall, 2:373–411. New York, London: Academic

89. Hinde, R. A. 1967. The nature of aggression. *New Society.*

90. Hinde, R. A. 1969. *Animal Behavior.* New York: McGraw. 2nd ed.

91. Hinde, R. A. Some problems in the study of the development of social behavior. In *The Biopsychology of Development,* ed. E. Tobach. New York: Academic. In press

92. Hinde, R. A., Atkinson, S. 1970. Assessing the roles of social partners in maintaining mutual proximity, as exemplified by mother-infant relations in rhesus monkeys. *Anim. Behav.* 18:169–76

93. Hodos, W., Campbell, C. B. G. 1969. Scala Naturae: Why there is no theory in comparative psychology. *Psychol. Rev.* 76(4):337–50

94. Hogan-Warburg, A. J. 1966. Social behavior of the ruff, *Philomachus pugnax* L. *Ardea* 54:109–229

95. Horn, H. S. 1968. The adaptive significance of colonial nesting in the Brewer's blackbird (*Euphagus cyanocephalus*). *Ecology* 49:682–94

96. Huxley, J. S. 1923. Courtship activities in the red throated diver (*Colymbus stellatus* Pontopp) together with a discussion of the evolution of courtship in birds. *J. Linn. Soc.* 35:253–92

97. Huxley, J. S. 1938. The present standing of the theory of sexual selection. In *Evolution: Essays Presented to Prof. E. S. Goodrich*, ed. G. DeBeer. Oxford Univ. Press

98. Immelmann, K. 1962. Beitrage zu einer vergleichenden Biologie australischer Prachtfinken (Spermestidae). *Zool. Jahrb. Syst.* 90:1–196

99. Ibid 1967. Verhaltensökoligische Studien an afrikanischen und australischen Estrildiden. 94:1–67

100. Jaynes, J. 1969. The historical origins of "Ethology" and "Comparative Psychology." *Anim. Behav.* 4:601–6

101. Jenkins, D., Watson, A., Miller, G. R. 1963. Population studies on red grouse (*Lagopus L. scoticus*). *J. Anim. Ecol.* 36:97–122

102. Jenkins, T. M. Jr. 1969. Social structure, position choice and microdistribution of two trout species (*Salmo tratta* and *S. gaidneri*) resident in mountain streams. *Anim. Behav. Monogr.* 2, 2:57–124

103. Jolly, C. J. 1970. The seed eaters: a new model of hominid differentiation based on a baboon analogy. *Man* 5:5–26

104. Kear, J. 1962. Food selection in finches with special reference to interspecific differences. *Proc. Zool. Soc. London* 138:163–204

105. Klopfer, P. H. 1962. *Behavioral Aspects of Ecology*. New Jersey: Prentice-Hall

106. Klopfer, P., Hailman, J. P. 1967. *An Introduction to Animal Behavior. Ethology's First Century*. New York: Prentice-Hall

107. Klopman, R. B. 1968. The agonistic behavior of the Canada goose. *Behavior* 30:287–319

108. Krebs, J. R. 1970. Regulation of numbers in the great tit (*Aves Passereformes*). *J. Zool.* 162:317–34

109. Krebs, J. 1970. *A study of territorial behavior in the Great Tit, Parus major*. LDPhil. thesis. Univ. Oxford

110. Krebs, J. R., MacRoberts, M. H., Cullen, J. M. Flocking and feeding in the great tit, *Parus major*, an experimental study. In preparation

111. Kropotkin, P. 1902. *Mutual Aid—A Factor of Evolution*. London: Heinemann

112. Kruijt, J. P., Bossema, I., de Vos, H. J. 1970. Factors underlying choice of mate in black grouse. *Proc. 15th Int. Ornithol. Congr., The Hague*. In press

113. Kruuk, H. 1964. Predators and antipredator behavior of the blackheaded gull (*Larus ridibundus*). *Behav. Suppl.* 11:1–129

114. Kruuk, H. 1966. Clan system and feeding habits of spotted hyaenas (*Crocuta crocuta* Erxlebe). *Nature* 209:1257–58

115. Kühme, W. von 1965. Freilandstudien zur Sociologie des Hyänenhundes (*Lycaon pictus lupinus* Thomas, 1902). *Z. Tierpsychol.* 22:495–541

116. Kummer, H. 1968. Social organisation of hamadryas baboons. *Bibl. Primatol.* 6:1–189

117. Kunkel, P. 1967. Displays facilitating sociability in waxbills of the genera *Estrilda* and *Laganosticta*. *Behaviour* 29:2-4, 237–61

118. Lack, D. 1954. *The Natural Regulation of Animal Numbers*. Oxford

119. Lack, D. 1965. Evolutionary ecology. *J. Anim. Ecol.* 34:223–31

120. Lack, D. 1966. *Population Studies of Birds*. Oxford

121. Lack, D. 1968. *Ecological Adaptations for Breeding in Birds*. London: Methuen

122. Le Boeuf, B. J., Peterson, R. S. 1969. Social status and mating activity in elephant seals. *Science* 163:91–93

123. Lehrman, D. S. 1953. A critique of Konrad Lorenz's theory of instinctive behavior. *Quart. Rev. Biol.* 28:337–63

124. Lockie, J. D. 1956. Winter fighting in feeding flocks of rooks, jackdaws and carrion crows. *Bird Study* 3:180–90

125. Lorenz, K. 1935. Der Kumpan in der umwelt des Vogels. *J. Ornithol.* 83:137–214, 289–413

126. Lorenz, K. 1950. The comparative method in studying innate behavior patterns. *Symp. Soc. Exp. Biol.* 4:221–68

127. Lorenz, K. 1963. *Das Sogennante Bose*. G. Borotha-Schoeler. Vienna: Verlag

128. Lorenz, K. 1966. *Evolution and Modi-*

fication of Behaviour. London: Methuen

129. Lorenz, K. 1970. *Studies in Animal and Human Behavior.* London: Methuen

130. Mackintosh, J. H. 1970. Territory formation by laboratory mice. *Anim. Behav.* 18:177–83

131. Manning, A. 1967. *An Introduction to Animal Behaviour.* London: Arnold

132. Marler, P. R., Hamilton, W. J. 1966. *Mechanisms of Animal Behavior.* New York: Wiley

133. Maynard, S. J. 1962. Sexual selection. In *A Century of Darwin,* ed. S. A. Barnett. London: Heinemann

134. McClaren, I. A. 1967. Seals and group selection. *Ecology* 48:104–10

135. McBride, G. 1964. A general theory of social organisation and behavior. *Univ. Queensl. Pap., Vet. Sci.* 1:75–110

136. Mizuhara, H. 1964. Social changes of Japanese monkey troops in the Takasakiyama. *Primates* 5:27–52

137. Morris, D. 1967. *The Naked Ape.* London: Jonathan Cape

138. Moynihan, M. 1960. Some adaptations which help to promote gregariousness. *Proc. 12th Int. Ornithol. Congr., Helsinki, 1958,* 523–41

139. Moynihan, M. 1968. Social mimicry, character convergence versus character displacement. *Evolution* 22:315–31

140. Murton, R. K. 1967. The significance of endocrine stress in population control. *Ibis* 109:622–33

141. Murton, R. K., Isaacson, A. J. 1962. The functional basis of some behavior in the wood pigeon *Columba palumbus. Ibis* 104:503–21

142. Murton, R. K., Isaacson, A. J. 1964. Productivity and egg predation in the wood pigeon. *Ardea* 52:30–47

143. Murton, R. K., Isaacson, A. J., Westwood, N. J. 1966. The relationships between wood pigeons and their clover food supply and the mechanism of population control. *J. Appl. Ecol.* 3:55–96

144. Nadel, S. F. 1957. *The Theory of Social Structure.* Glencoe, Ill.: Free Press

145. Nash, R. H. 1969. *Ideas of History,* Vol. 2 (Dutton Paperback Original)

146. Nelson, J. B. 1970. The relationship between behavior and ecology in the Sulidae with reference to other sea birds. *Oceanogr. Mar. Biol. Ann. Rev.* 8:501–74

147. Newton, I. 1967. The adaptive radia-

tion and feeding ecology of some British finches. *Ibis* 109:33–98

148. Nishida, T. 1966. A sociological study of solitary male monkeys. *Primates* 7:141–204

149. Oppenheimer, J. R. 1970. Mouthbreeding in fishes. *Anim. Behav.* 18:493–503

150. Oppenheimer, J. R., Barlow, G. W. 1968. Dynamics of parental behavior in the black chinned mouthbreeder, *Tilapia melanotheron* (Pisces: Cichliden). *Z. Tierpsychol.* 25:889–914

151. Orians, G. H. 1961. The ecology of blackbird (*Agelaius*) social systems. *Ecol. Monogr.* 31:285–312

152. Orians, G. H. 1962. Natural selection and ecological theory. *Am. Natur.* 96:257–63

153. Ibid 1969. On the evolution of mating systems in birds and mammals. 103:589–603

154. Orians, G. H. The adaptive significance of mating systems in the Icteridae. *Proc. 15th Int. Ornithol. Congr., The Hague, 1970.* In press

155. Patterson, I. J. 1965. Timing and spacing of broods in the black headed gull. *Ibis* 107:433–39

156. Payne, R. B., Skinner, N. J. 1970. Temporal patterns of duetting in African barbets. *Ibis* 112:173–83

157. Petrucci, R. 1906. Origine polyphylétique, homotypie et noncomparabilité directe des sociétés animales. *Institut Solvay. Travaux de l'Institut de Sociologie. Notes et Memoires,* fasc. 3. Bruxelles: Misch et Thon

158. Raveling, D. G. 1970. Dominance relationships and agonistic behavior of Canada geese in winter. *Behaviour* 37:291–319

159. Reynolds, V. 1968. Kinship and the family in monkeys, apes and man. *Man* 3:209–23

160. Ibid 1970. Roles and role change in monkey society: the consort relationship of rhesus monkeys. 5(3):449–65

161. Rowell, T. E. 1966. Hierarchy in the organization of a captive baboon group. *Anim. Behav.* 14(4):420–43

162. Rowell, T. E. 1967. Variability in the social organisation of primates. In *Primate Ethology,* ed. D. Morris. London: Weidenfeld & Nicholson

163. Royama, T. 1966. Factors governing feeding rate, food requirement and brood size of nestling great tits *Parus major major. Ibis* 111:11–16

164. Royama, T. 1969. A model for the global variation of clutch size in birds. *Oikos* 20:562–67

165. Royama, T. 1970. Factors governing the hunting behavior and selection of food by the great tit, *Parus major* L. *J. Anim. Ecol.* 39:619–68

166. Saayman, G. S. 1970. The menstrual cycle and sexual behavior in a troop of free ranging chacma baboons (*Papio ursinus*). *Folia Primatol.* 12:81–110

167. Sadlier, R. M. F. S. 1970. The establishment of a dominance rank order in male *Peromyscus maniculakis* and its stability with time. *Anim. Behav.* 18(1):55–59

168. Sarbin, T. R. 1954. Role theory. In *Handbook of Social Psychology*, ed. G. Lindzey. Cambridge, Mass: Addison-Wesley

169. Scott, J. P. 1945. Social behavior, organisation and leadership in a small flock of domestic sheep. *Comp. Psychol. Monogr.* 18(4):1–29

170. Scott, J. P. 1950. The social behavior of dogs and wolves; an illustration of sociobiological systematics. *Ann. NY Acad. Sci.* 51(6):1009–21

171. Scott, J. P. 1967. Comparative psychology and ethology. *Ann. Rev. Psychol.* 18:65–86

172. Sebeok, T. A., Ed. 1968. *Animal Communication: Techniques of Study and Results of Research*. Bloomington: Indiana Univ. Press

173. Sebeok, T. A. 1970. Zoosemiotic structures and social organisation. In *Linguaggi rella Societa e rella tecnica*. Milano: Edizioni di Comunita

174. Sebeok, T. A., Ramsay, A., Eds. 1969. *Approaches to Animal Communication*. The Hague: Mouton et Cie

175. Selander, R. K. 1965. On mating systems and sexual selection. *Am. Natur.* 99:129–41

176. Simmons, K. E. L. 1955. The nature of the predator-reactions of waders towards humans; with special reference to the role of the aggressive—escape—and brooding drives. *Behaviour* 8:130–73

177. Simmons, K. E. L. 1970. Ecological determinants of breeding adaptations and social behavior in two fish-eating birds. See Ref. 37, 37–77

178. Simpson, G. G. 1961. *Principles of Animal Taxonomy*. New York: Columbia Univ. Press

179. Smith, J. N. M., Dawkins, R. The

hunting behavior of individual great tits in relation to spatial variations in their food density. *Anim. Behav.* In press

180. Snow, D. 1962. A field study of the black and white manakin, *Manacus manacus*, in Trinidad. *Zoologica* (*NY*) 47:65–104

181. Ibid. A field study of the golden headed manakin, *Pipra erythrocephala*, in Trinidad, 183–98

182. Southwick, C. H. 1967. An experimental study of intra-group agonistic behavior in rhesus monkeys (*Macaca mulatta*). *Behaviour* 28:1–2, 182–209

183. Sparks, J. 1964. Flock structure of the red avadavat with particular reference to clumping and allopreening. *Anim. Behav.* 12:125–36

184. Stonehouse, B. 1960. The king penguin *Aptenodytes patagonica* of South Georgia. I. Breeding behavior and development. *Sci. Rep. Falkland Isl. Depend. Surv.* 23:1–181

185. Struhsaker, T. T. 1967. Social structure among vervet monkeys (*Cercopithecus aethiops*). *Behavior* 29:83–121

186. Sugiyama, Y. 1960. On the division of a natural troop of Japanese monkeys at Takasakiyama. *Primates* 2:109–46

187. Sugiyama, Y. Social organisation of Hanuman langurs. See Ref. 4, 221–36

188. Thiessen, D. D. 1964. Population density and behavior: a review of theoretical and physiological contributions. *Tex. Rep. Biol. Med.* 22:266–314

189. Thorpe, W. H. 1967. Vocal imitation and antiphonal song and its implications. *Proc. 14th Int. Ornithol. Congr.*, *Oxford*, 245–69

190. Tiger, L., Fox, R. 1966. The zoological perspective in social science. *Man* 1:76–81

191. Tinbergen, L. 1960. The dynamics of insect and bird populations in pine woods. *Arch. Neerl. Zool.* 13:259–472

192. Tinbergen, N. 1939. On the analysis of social organisation among vertebrates, with special reference to birds. *Am. Midl. Natur.* 21:210–33

193. Tinbergen, N. 1951. *The Study of Instinct*. Oxford: Clarendon

194. Tinbergen, N. 1953. *Social Behavior in Animals*. London: Methuen

195. Tinbergen, N. 1956. On the functions of territory in gulls. *Ibis* 98:401–11
196. Ibid 1959. Behavior, systematics and natural selection. 101:138–330
197. Tinbergen, N. 1959. Comparative studies of the behavior of gulls (Laridae): a progress report. *Behaviour* 15:1–70
198. Tinbergen, N. 1964. On adaptive radiation in gulls (*Tribe Larine*). *Zool. Meded.* 39:209–23
199. Tinbergen, N. 1967. Adaptive features of the black headed gull (*Larus ridibundus*). *Proc. 14th Int. Ornithol. Congr.*, 43–59
200. Tinbergen, N., Brockhuysen, G. S., Feekes, F., Houghton, J. C. W., Kruuk, H., Szule, E. 1962. Egg shell removal by the black headed gull (*Larus ridibundus* L.): A behavioral component of camouflage. *Behaviour* 19:74–117
201. Tinbergen, N., Impekoven, M., Frank, P. 1967. An experiment on spacing-out as a defence against predation. *Behavior* 28:307–21
202. Tompa, F. S. 1964. Factors determining the numbers of song sparrows, *Melospeza melodia* (Wilson) on Mandarte Island, B. C. Canada. *Acta Zool. Fenn.* 109:1–68
203. Vandenbergh, J. G. 1967. The development of social structure in free-ranging rhesus monkeys. *Behaviour* 29:179–94
204. Verner, J. 1964. Evolution of polygamy in the long-billed marsh wren. *Evolution* 18:252–61
205. Verner, J., Willson, M. F. 1966. The influence of habitats on mating systems of North American passerine birds. *Ecology* 47:143–47
206. Vine, I. 1971. Risk of visual detection and pursuit by a predator and the selective advantage of flocking behavior. *J. Theor. Biol.* 30:405–22
207. Ward, P. 1965. Feeding ecology of the black-faced dioch *Quelea quelea* in Nigeria. *Ibis* 107:173–214
208. Watson, A. 1967. Population control by territorial behavior in red grouse. *Nature* 215:1274–75
209. Watson, A., Ed. 1970. *Animal populations in Relation to their Food Resources.* Brit. Ecol. Soc. Symp. 10. Oxford: Blackwell
210. Watson, A., Jenkins, D. 1968. Experiments on population control by territorial behavior in red grouse. *J. Anim. Ecol.* 37:595–614
211. Watson, A., Moss, R. 1970. Dominance, spacing behavior and aggression in relation to population limitation in vertebrates. See Ref. 209, 167–220
212. Waxweiler, E. 1906. Esquisse de sociologie. See Ref. 157, fasc. 2
213. Wheeler, W. M. 1902. "Natural History," "Oecology" or "Ethology"? *Science* 15:971–76
214. Wheeler, W. M. 1939. Animal Societies. In *Essays in Philosophical Biology.* New York: Russell
215. Wickler, W. 1962. Zur Stammesgeschichte funktionelle Korrelierter Organ—und Verhaltensmerkmale: Ei-Attrapen und Maulbruten bei Afrikanischen Cichliden. *Z. Tierpsychol.* 19:129–64
216. Wickler, W. 1965. Neue Varianten des Fortpflanzungsverhaltens afrikanscher Cichliden (Pisces : Perciformes). *Naturwissenschaften* 52: 219
217. Wickler, W. 1969. Zur Soziologie des Brobantbuntbarsches, *Tropheus Moorei* (Pisces : Cichlidae). *Z. Tierpsychol.* 26:967–87
218. Williams, G. C. 1966. *Adaptation and Natural Selection: A Critique of Some Current Evolutionary Thought.* Princeton Univ. Press
219. Wilson, A. P. 1968. *Social behavior of free ranging rhesus monkeys with an emphasis on aggression.* PhD thesis. Univ. California, Berkeley
220. Woolpy, J. H. 1968. The social organization of wolves. *Natur. Hist. N Y* 77:46–55
221. Wynne-Edwards, V. C. 1962. *Animal Dispersion.* Edinburgh: Oliver & Boyd
222. Wynne-Edwards, V. C. 1970. Feedback from food resources to population regulation. See Ref. 209, 413–27
223. Zahavi, A. 1971. The function of pre-roost gatherings and communal roosts. *Ibis* 113:106–9
224. Ibid. The social behavior of the white wagtail *Motacilla alba alba* wintering in Israel, 203–11
225. Zimmerman, J. L. 1966. Polygyny in the dickcissel. *Auk* 83:534–46

AUDITION[1]

183

J. Donald Harris

Departments of Speech and Psychology
University of Connecticut, Storrs

INTRODUCTION

The last general review of audition in this series was that by Lawrence (116), for which the references closed as of April 1967. There is then ostensibly a need to review the field for the past 4 years. Fortunately much of this has been accomplished by other series, particularly by Grinnell (80) and by Eldredge & Miller (60). Green & Henning (78) provided a review in depth of binaural hearing, and Raab (170) reviewed microelectrode studies of the auditory nervous system. Another of his very thought-provoking general surveys of the present status of auditory theory was provided by Davis (50). This review will generally avoid citing references covered in the above papers.

A number of books have appeared that are of great help to the busy reader. First of all should be mentioned a handbook on otology (11) bound in six volumes; chapters on anatomic-physiological advances, on oto-audiologic testing, on psychological and physiological acoustics, each by a world-recognized authority, go far beyond the usual textbook on otology. Vinnikov & Titova (215) extend the material of two earlier books emphasizing electron microscopy of the sensory epithelia of the cochlea. Rauch (173) summarized his and other studies on biochemistry of the ear; similar material on the same topic edited by Papparella (152), one of the Henry Ford Hospital symposia, will be even more widely used.

In response to current general concern with noise pollution, a symposium of the American Association for the Advancement of Science was held on the physiological, neurophysiological, and endocrinological effects of noise (218), together with another book on the same topic (145), Kryter's distillation of his 30-year preoccupation with the same general problem (113), and a much more superficial text (25) for the layman. Kryter's treatment

---

[1] The following abbreviations are used in this chapter: AER (auditory-evoked response); AP (action potential); 2A-FC (2-alternative forced-choice); CF (characteristic frequency); CM (cochlear microphonic); dBA (decibels measured through the standard A filter); EP (endocochlear potential); LSO (lateral superior olivary nuclei); MLD (masking level difference); MSO (medial superior olivary nuclei); OCB (olivocochlear bundle); S/N (signal-to-noise); SP (summating potential); SPL (sound pressure level); TSD (theory of signal detection); V (vertex); VCN (ventral cochlear nucleus).

is by far the most useful of these books, with an especially complete bibliography. He also satisfactorily reviews the topic of psychological loudness, as well as of annoyance and of noise as such. The problem of noise is of course involved heavily with industry and with public transportation. One monograph (26) describes a field study of 1000 persons in industry on whom 4000 audiograms were taken. The 200-page appendix is a store-house of information. A symposium was held composed of the best minds in the country bearing on the whole problem of transportation noises and community acceptance (38).

Publishing events of the first water were the appearance of Tobias' (209) edited collection of in-depth chapters on a variety of themes in psychological and physiological acoustics. An equally exciting collection came from a symposium on frequency selectivity and periodicity pitch contributed to by international authorities (162). A textbook of psychoacoustics appeared (119), treating the physics of sound; the psychoacoustics of absolute and differential thresholds, masking, auditory fatigue, spatial localization, and speech intelligibility; and a section on audiometers and hearing aids. Most of the references are quite out of date, and in fact a bibliography is entirely lacking. The title is misleading in that no material from physiological acoustics is presented.

This review concentrates on the anatomy and physiology of the whole auditory system from pinna to cortex, emphasizing function. It is not too much to say that new methods for examining structure and function, such as scanning electron microscopy, laser interferometry, the acoustic hologram, the Mössbauer effect for detection of displacement, and new computer techniques for extracting and displaying almost overwhelming amounts of information from a single nerve cell, to give a few examples, have caused a revolution in the past 4 years in our concepts of the ear and hearing. Another information explosion, in the biochemistry of the cochlea, is occurring, quite beyond this reviewer's ability to summarize or even, properly speaking, to read.

In addition, a brief overview is given here of studies in the hearing of animals, and of some recent papers in human signal detection and masking, two psychoacoustic areas in which real advances have recently been made. Reasons are given for thinking it premature at this time to review the equally burgeoning psychoacoustic areas of binaural hearing, frequency effects, and loudness, which are adequately treated elsewhere in current books and chapters.

THE CONDUCTION SYSTEM

Outer Ear and Eardrum

The pinna.—Psychologists have speculated since 1900 that the auricle is more than a vestigial structure, that in fact it reduces front-back confusions in localization and aids in angular discrimination at high frequencies, especially in the vertical plane. Quite recently these notions have been corroborated and quantified, and several more uses for the auricle have been un-covered. Although one does not obtain true reflections from a surface whose width is less than about 1/4 the wavelength of incident sound, which would limit such an action of the auricle to very high frequencies (1/4 wavelength at 10 kHz is about 1/3 inch), nevertheless refraction and scattering of sound at lower frequencies can sum in the auricle to yield an appreciable gain. Berland & Nielsen (13) found amplification up to 10 dB in the frequency range 2–5 kHz at the entrance to the external auditory meatus, which they show to be due to the auricle. This effect is quite variable; Erber (63) showed it was reduced for adult males as compared with women or children of either sex. This effect, somewhat surprisingly, is fairly independent of the direction from which the sound comes. One sees in Berland & Nielsen's data that the amplification is greatest when the sound source in a free field is at the 0° and 45° azimuths, but when Shaw (185) mounted five drivers in a special holder, each driver oriented in a different way to the opening of the meatus, there were negligible differences among acoustic sources in the sound pressure levels (SPLs) measured at the canal opening.

The problem of specifying an artificial pinna, an idea now coming to the fore in several applications, must take into account not only such data as Erber's on dimensions which differ among subpopulations, but as Wodak (223) points out, also the linear standoff from the head and the angle the anterior surface of the pinna makes with the skull. Several groups have used a variant of the plaster-cast method for creating exact copies of the auricle of a person to be used in research. Bauer et al (9) and Shaw & Teranishi (186) used rubber-like materials so that the pinna had not only the dimension of an actual ear but also approximated its texture. The pinna of Fisher & Freedman (71) was of an unyielding substance and could not flatten against the skull to accept any but the larger circumaural cushions. In an attempt to create as simply as possible the acoustic conditions of a real auricle, Teranishi & Shaw (206) used models consisting of shallow cylindrical cavities to represent the concha and fitted with rectangular flanges to rep-resent the pinna itself. Agreement was good with real-ear data up to 7 kHz for sound at any angle of incidence. For some types of standardization, such an artificial ear would be especially useful because of its ease and repeat-ability of construction. It would not be useful for a researcher using certain types of earphone.

Bystrenin (28) directly investigated the effect of the pinnae on direc-tionality by providing a subject with tubes three cm long as extensions of the meati and fitted on the outer ends with artificial pinnae. Under these conditions the sound shadow of the head itself is minimized and effects can be pretty well ascribed to the auricle. When he oriented the pinnae down-ward, sounds seemed depressed in space, and when backward, sounds in front seemed to the rear. Cancura (32) noted that in listening to high tones in a free field, the minimum audible pressure was fainter as the subject moved the head (and thereby the pinnae); this was explained on the basis of sampling the field for the optimum standing wave pattern of all those created by the pinna when it moves.

In further studies on localization in the vertical dimension, Butler (27, 178) showed that the pinnae contributed importantly to such verticality sensitivity as we do possess. Fisher & Freedman (71) discuss the pinna problem thoroughly, both the monaural and binaural condition, and give incontrovertible evidence of the transformation of complex acoustic stimulation which the pinna provides. They go so far as to introduce the notion that the usual earphone lateralization experiment is quite a misleading prediction of what the human can do with such stimuli as, for example, the cocktail party effect.

Feldmann & Steinmann (67) explored another function of the auricle, the reduction of wind noise. They quantified the spectrum of wind noise as from 20–3000 Hz, using a dummy head with realistic auricles and ear canal with microphones for eardrums, but it depended in intensity and frequency composition both on the wind velocity and the angle of incidence. At some angles a tilt to the spectrum was seen. An air turbulence at the meatal entrance due to the wind prevented a sharp rise at 2–4 kHz due to ear canal resonance, and thus acted to enhance signal/noise ratio under some conditions of signal detection in wind. The rather peculiar shape of the pinna was seen as ideally suited to create such turbulence.

The ear canal.—Bauer et al (9) went to great lengths to create a simulated external auditory meatus. A passage resembling the configuration of an average canal was constructed of machined (i.e. reproducible) parts, and an acoustical impedance-matching network was added to present the same impedance load to an earphone as does the average eardrum/middle ear. It is understood that this model is commercially available. Hantman's (86) design looks like a real canal, but it is a teaching device for the outer and middle ear rather than a working tool. Shaw & Teranishi (186) built up a complete rubber outer ear comparable to that of Bauer et al, also with varying acoustic impedance networks, and compared its response to that of real ears from 1–15 kHz and over different angles of incidence of sound. Responses were measured at various points with a probe microphone. The artificial system aped the real-ear system through 7 kHz.

A problem arises when dummy heads such as these are used to initiate two-channel information to a pair of earphones worn by a subject, perhaps in a different room than the anechoic space containing the dummy head, and perhaps after the information is stored on magnetic tape. If an ear canal is used in recording, then when the subject listens, his own canal must be operative, and the 15-dB bandpass filter of the canal is represented twice at 3–5 kHz. Thus, while an artificial head fitted with ear canals may appear best and be in fact necessary for certain purposes, as for instance the determination of the attenuation of earmuffs etc, yet for other purposes such as the storing of information on magnetic tape, the pinnae of Fisher & Freedman (71) mated directly to microphones in the plane of the cavum concha would be ideal. It is understood that these latter pinnae are available commercially.

Standard artificial ear.—Since many psychologists use earphones in their work, yet probably should not take valuable time to become acoustically very sophisticated, it is important to know that true artificial ears are being developed, based upon accurate measurements of the acoustic impedance presented by the average ear. Heretofore, it has only been possible to state that the earphone, at the voltage used in the experiment, developed a certain SPL in one of two cylindrical cavities standardized in this country for mating an earphone to a microphone. But these simple cavities do not well predict what SPL that earphone may generate at the eardrum, which is what the experimenter wishes to know. With a true artificial ear, eardrum SPL could be reliably inferred. The International Standards Association (1) has specified such a tool, based largely on the work of the National Physical Laboratory (53), and a design based on comparable ideas and measurements was released by Zwislocki (230). Bauer et al (9) have offered their system for standardization.

Until a model is both standardized and commercially available, one will have to depend upon the simple acoustic couplers. But a caution appears here: even though a set of several earphones may on the surface look exactly or at least nearly alike, when they are each energized to create the same SPL at the microphone in a closed acoustic coupler, they nevertheless may not sound equally loud when applied to the ear. Differences of impressed voltage of as much as 12 dB may need to be introduced for the outputs of two such phones at the same frequencies to sound equally loud (195). Here the experimeter will remain uncertain as to the SPL at his subject's eardrum unless (*a*) he can provide a probe tube microphone reading as a real-ear response under the earphone, as is almost universally done now in good animal work; or (*b*) he must himself obtain some standard earphone [see Ref. (2) for the data for several standard earphones in this and other countries] and himself loudness-balance his own earphone against it, preferably by one of the newer techniques (87), in order to be able to specify his SPL even in terms of a simple coupler. It is to be hoped that Bauer's or Zwislocki's or the British design for a valid artificial ear, or all three, will shortly solve these dilemmas and uncertainties.

THE MIDDLE EAR

The eardrum.—In the quarter-century since the classic study of Wilska, experimenters have puzzled over the almost incredibly small eardrum displacements at human threshold. The problem has been the extrapolations demanded over many orders of magnitude of intensity and over several octaves from low to high frequencies. Tonndorf & Khanna (210) with a laser interferometer are the latest to have corroborated Wilska; they have extended his estimate of movement at threshold down to the order of 10^{-11} cm. These submicroscopic displacements, existing also at the stapes, offer even graver difficulties than before to those who envision such infinitesimal movements (about 1/10 billionth of an inch) as creating any shear stress on a stereocilia about a million times larger (10^{-5} cm) than the applied displacement.

Otologists have long been puzzled by the low-tone losses in cases of relatively slight cuts or tears in the eardrum, more especially when some data on cat (154) showed relatively little loss. McArdle & Tonndorf (124) showed that in the earlier experiments the pre-perforation control was not the normal condition, in that the bulla was left open to receive the round window electrode. Now in this condition, the acoustic wave could penetrate to the middle ear and the long wavelengths tend to reduce eardrum movement by phase cancellation; thus the pre-perforation output was already reduced, and perforation itself could not reduce the output much more. But when the bulla was closed, perforation then did have a phase-cancellation effect at those low frequencies for which the phase on both sides of the eardrum was approximately equal, and the cochlear microphonic (CM) did drop off at low frequencies below 1 kHz at the rate of about -10 dB/octave.

In patients with the eardrum and ossicles removed, this phase cancellation is known to operate on the oval and round windows simultaneously, with consequent minimized movement of the basilar membrane and reduced hearing. Gaudin (74) has recently taken up this problem with new materials; he shows two surgical ways to isolate the round window with a sponge of silicone elastomer.

Wever's experiment had apparently disproved Helmholtz's conception of a pressure amplification by the eardrum itself acting as a catenary lever, but Tonndorf & Khanna (211) have reopened the matter and studied by time-averaged holograms the movements of the typmanic membrane simultaneously over its whole surface. The holograms show that the membrane does not move as a stiff plate, hinged above the annulus, but obeys the mechanism of curved membranes and itself contributes to a transformer action by a factor of about 2. But as the curvature of the membrane increases from the anterior process of the manubrium toward the umbo, the effective lever ratio of the ossicles was said to be reduced from the anatomical 2.2 (in the cat this ratio is much greater than in man) to approximately 1.4. And finally, since in the holograms the whole eardrum was seen to add its contribution, it is clear that the areal ratio of the eardrum to the oval window should consider 100% of the eardrum area rather than the 70% suggested by Békésy and Wever, and the areal ratio was thus computed as 34.6. Tonndorf & Khanna now combine these three factors ($2 \times 1.4 \times 34.6$) to yield 39.7 dB as the transformer action of the whole middle ear. This figure corresponds exactly to an independent estimate of the contribution of the whole middle ear in the cat (212) and validates their measurements and assumptions.

The response of the eardrum as revealed by holography is of even further interest. Tonndorf & Khanna (211) show that for constant SPL its volume displacement is the same for all frequencies up to about 1.5 kHz. At about 3 kHz the displacement pattern begins to break up into quasi-independent subpatterns, their complexity increasing with frequency, and at about 7 kHz the eardrum itself is seen not to contribute, serving merely as a baffle for the manubrium. In some of the holograms the area anterior to the manubrium can be seen to be moving out of phase with the area posterior to the manubrium.

The ossicles and the middle ear transformer action.—El-Mofty & El-Serafy (62) studied the ossicular chain in representative mammals from Africa and developed a comparative theme. Much of this material goes beyond the measurements, lever action, and areal rations of mammals as given by Kirikae (106).

In the human ear, acoustic impedance constants (resistance, compliance, reactance, and absolute impedance) can now be measured or calculated with commercially available impedance bridges. Burke et al (24) have provided norms using two types of acoustic impedance bridge.

In the human, of course, the intense interest in the ossicular chain stems from the recent dramatic successes in reconstructive surgery. Upon removal of the stapes, for example, artificial stapes are usually inserted, but some surgeons wherever possible reintroduce the patient's own bone. Glaninger (76), however, looks toward the creation of stapes banks; all ten of his patients accepted refrigerated and lyophilized stapes. Heretofore, such transplants had usually been rejected.

A seeming discrepancy has always existed in that while the middle ear seems to transmit all low frequencies equally well, the audiogram seems to indicate the low frequencies (below about 1 kHz) are filtered out at the rate of -12 dB/octave. Khanna & Tonndorf (105) point out that the flat characteristic of the middle ear at low frequencies applies only to constant SPL, that is, displacement. But it can be shown that for constant SPL the mechanoacoustic *power* in the stimulus also falls off at the rate of -12 dB octave. Thus the audiogram in terms of power, not displacement, would in fact be a flat, not a low-band reject filter, and the ear would be interpreted as very efficient for low frequencies rather than very inefficient. Of course, as long as we continue to measure the stimulus with the usual microphone sensitive to SPL (linearly related to particle displacement) the question is perhaps academic.

Muscle reflexes.—Cancura (33) arranged in the cadaver a recording of the movements of fluid in response to stapes displacement. When tensile forces were applied to the muscles, reduction of fluid movements could be shown. A load of 50g on the tensor tympani exerted a damping of 8 dB, and of 10 dB for a load of 10g on stapedius, at frequencies lower than 1 kHz only. The two are synergistic in effect, as preceding research had shown, but antagonistic in their mechanical action. A slight improvement in transmission existed at 2 kHz in consequence of the tilt of the frequency spectrum from the increased stiffness. This novel approach corroborates previous studies on the effect on other response indications of loading the muscles.

McRobert et al (130) developed a new technique for measuring the attenuation of low-frequency tones due to contraction of the middle ear muscles in contralateral remote masking.

Djupesland (56, 57) shows how a knowledge of the stimuli which differentially activate the stapedius (sound of 80 dB sensation level) and the tensor tympani (burst of air to the orbit or lifting the eyelid) together with the characteristic response of each muscle on the impedance bridge, can help in diagnosis of middle ear disorders.

It has long been known that the stapedius is an exceptionally fast-acting muscle, and that its motor units are smaller than in most other skeletal muscles. Teig (205) counted nerve and muscle fibers in stapedius or rabbit and corroborated the small ratios. He also arranged threshold stimulation of the stapedial twig of the VIIth nerve and observed latency and other response indexes of individual motor units.

Using an impedance meter to register stapedius activity, Bates et al (8) concluded that if the reflex were indeed conditionable to a light flash, it was uncertain at best.

Sato & Ono (184) measured the movement of the stapes in response to stapedius contraction, and showed some adaptation over a 2-min period for stimulation of 2 kHz at 120 SPL. This reflex is often said not to adapt. Tietze (208), however, also showed adaptation up to $\frac{1}{2}$ after 10 sec at 1.5 kHz, reaching a plateau after about 20 sec. Even with large inter-subject variability, a formula for the average adaptation curve could be written.

Numbers of workers have studied movements of the eardrum in consequence of reflex action, by registering changes in air pressure in the ear canal. But when the system is sensitive enough to record threshold movement the record is almost swamped by noise, principally the pulse. Neergaard & Rasmussen (144) reduced this noise as much as possible, and averaged over several reflexes with the oscilloscope. They were able to show some eardrum movement on contraction of the stapedius alone. Some had thought that the action of the stapedius in moving the stapes downward and backward could hardly have an appreciable effect on the eardrum. The solution in the animal to the problem of noise while recording pressure changes due to eardrum movement was suggested by Miyahara et al (140), who introduced the recording tube not into the meatus, but into the middle ear through a small hole in the bulla, thus avoiding complications due to pulse, respiration, and head (mainly jaw) movement.

Feldman (66) adds another patient to the literature who showed no change in impedance to sound transmission in consequence of cutting the tendon of the tensor tympani. Thus, while as we now see the stapedius can affect tympanomanometry, the tensor tympani does not appreciably affect impedance measures.

The full story on the physiology of the human middle ear muscles has not as yet been written, neither the type and range of stimuli which will activate or habituate them, nor their mechanical effects on, for example, threshold, dynamic range, or appearance of distortion. Large species differences, even among one class such as rodents, and still more across classes, render animal research of little predictive value. Techniques of research on these problems in the human are now fairly well developed, however, and we should see a number of reports on the effects of these reflexes on a wide variety of situations such as the intelligibility of speech, remote masking, localization of sounds, auditory fatigue, and the perception of one's own voice.

THE COCHLEA

The sensory epithelium.—An important round-table conference on the cochlear epithelia was held (164) with M. Portmannas as moderator and including Engstrom and Spoendlin, authors of two recent books on the subject. Topics emphasized were the influence of noise, ototoxic drugs, etc., on the hair cells and their intricate neural supply.

The dimensions of the basilar and tectorial membranes in squirrel, monkey, cat, and rat were given by Igarishi et al (96), information needed for computing, for example, neural innervation density per millimeter either linear or areal. The latter computations were provided for the human in a long and important monograph by Bredberg (20). The taper of the basilar membrane is such that the density of the outer hair cell population is less per square millimeter toward the apex, though it is actually greater per linear distance.

Lim (120, 121) has provided some dramatic three-dimensional views of the hair cells and related structures using the scanning electron microscope. The reality is such that one seems to be taking a fantastic voyage up the cochlear canal. We must be nearing an absolutely final anatomical view of the whole scala media when individual hair cells can be counted as present or absent.

The endocochlear potential (EP) and the cochlear microphonic (CM).— These topics were extensively reviewed by Eldredge & Miller (60), who provisionally concluded that the metabolic energy for a +80 mV EP is provided by the stria vascularis which maintains the K^+ gradient and pumps Na^+ out of endolymph into the blood, and that the cochlear microphonic (CM) is actually an ac ripple on this larger dc current. This possibility is not contradicted by numbers of experiments which show that EP and CM do not always covary (see e.g. 39, 166) since the two electricities have two different sources of metabolism: the EP the capillaries in the stria, while the hair cells are bathed in perilymph and receive their supplies from

blood vessels at their base (115). Thus a malfunctioning stria could result
in a reduced EP, but the cyclic modulation of the hair cells could still be
normal. The presence of a normal stria vascularis and a normal EP in deaf
guinea pigs (197) seems to support this interpretation, but a puzzling observation was made by Brown & Ruben (21), who found a normal EP (50–
120 mV) in ten mice with atrophied organ of Corti and of stria vascularis.
What had maintained this EP?

The cochlear microphonic (CM) and summating potential (SP).—Eldredge
& Miller (60) agree with Whitfield that the dc drift of the CM on the face
of the oscilloscope, known as the SP, is actually an expression of some vector
of three nonlinear processes in (*a*) the middle ear, (*b*) the traveling wave,
and (*c*) the mechano-electric generation of the CM, and is no important
potential in its own right.

The CM and the traveling wave.—Since Békésy's classic demonstration
that CM at a point on the cochlear partition is proportional to displacement
of the basilar membrane at that point, many workers have sought to trace
the genesis and development of the traveling wave up the cochlea by picking
up the CM at selected points. Nordmark et al (148) stimulated the guinea
pig with two tones an octave apart and picked up CM at two turns in the
guinea pig. As is always found, a certain frequency reached maximum CM
at some point on the partition after some time on the tapped delay line, but
they noted that all lower frequencies reached that point with the same latency. Only after the wave to a certain frequency reaches its point of maximum effect does it slow up and dissipate. Honrubia & Ward (95) picked up
CM and SP from the first turn of the guinea pig, cat, monkey, and again
showed that low frequencies (32–2500 Hz), which from Békésy's widely
publicized tuning curves are often thought of as acting on only the apical
half of the cochlea, are heavily represented in the basal half as well. Such
studies tell us that the traveling wave is very broadly tuned, and that the
specification of a point of maximal response on the basilar membrane is
probably not connected to the most obvious feature of the wave.

Johnstone et al (99) used the Mössbauer technique to measure the movements of the basilar membrane in the live guinea pig, the sensitivity being
such as to measure displacement to a few Angstrom units. Cobalt[57] is diffused
onto a small spot in a 5-μ stainless steel foil, then a square of 100 μ is cut and
mounted on the membrane. Movement at that spot, for constant stapes
displacement across frequencies, is measured and plotted together with data
from other spots. At one typical spot, a maximum amplitude of 0.0055 Å at
17 kHz was computed (extrapolated down from 60–70 dB SPL), which fell
off to 0.000025 Å at 0.5 kHz, but fell off at higher frequencies at the rate of
95 dB/octave. Tuning peaks by this method correspond more closely than
by some other methods to the sharpness of tuning exhibited by some primary neurons.

Laszlo et al (114) replicated earlier studies on the traveling wave in the guinea pig, using paired differential electrodes up and down the canals, taking extreme care with the control and measurement of the acoustic event at the eardrum. They point out that others had used the round window CM as the reference, or had inferred SPL from closed coupler measurements, and they offer slightly revised tuning curves and travel times.

Since the half-dozen experiments to date on CM as an index of the traveling wave all had resort to considerable interpolation of the state of affairs between, e.g. the first and second turn, Kohllöffel (111) inserted an array of no less than 20 pairs of electrodes in the first turn alone. His data are correspondingly more complete in this region, though no major reinterpretation is called for.

Tonndorf pointed out a decade ago that there were in fact three waves engendered by stapes motion: the traditional Békésy longitudinal wave, but also a longitudinal shear wave and a radial shear wave, each with its own dynamics. The traveling wave, indeed, is powerless to shear the stereocilia if the whole scala media simply moves up and down; only if some structures move differentially will the hair cell create CM. Khanna, Sears & Tonndorf (104) now point out by computer simulation that the longitudinal shear wave, which could itself move the stereocilia, is not at all coterminous with the traveling wave; for tones of up to 1–2 kHz, for example, there is little shear until the traveling wave nearly approaches its maximum displacement. Thus the "tuning" of the longitudinal shear is much more pronounced for any medium or low frequency. At 5 kHz the two wave patterns coincide.

It is possible that the radial shear wave is even more sharply localized; after all it is a radial displacement between the tectorial membrane and the reticular lamina which looks optimal for affecting the stereocilia.

Legouix (118) has continued to attack the problem of frequency resolution throughout the cochlea by differential recording of CM at various cochlear turns in response to acoustic transients of varied frequency and duration. His important results tend to show that the frequency resolution is not to periodicity as such, but to the slope of attack of the stapes—a slower excursion inward of the stapes activates a larger region and is picked up farther apicalward, while greater impedance is offered to a quicker excursion and the energy is dissipated through an early shunt to the round window, leaving more apical regions unperturbed. Aran & Delaunay (5) bear on the same problem by computer-averaging whole-nerve response to trains of filtered clicks.

Scattered data from several studies on the latency of the first spike of a first-order auditory neuron seem to show a differential delay in the case of fibres with lower characteristic frequencies; data here would begin to quantify the speed of the traveling wave.

The CM and the action potential (AP).—The direct question, whether the CM initiates AP by electrical initiation of the generator potential (the nerve cell's precursor to the propagated impulse) cannot now be answered.

There is no evidence whatsoever of any chemical substance massively and almost instantaneously released by the hair cells when their stereocilia are levered, nor of any esterase which would likewise massively and almost instantaneously remove it. If our ear were built up on any such chemical mediation as the eye or the nose, for example, we would be half deaf for about 5 minutes every time the telephone rang, and the phone and door bell would sound alike, as a sharply peak-clipped white noise. On the other hand, the EP battery across each hair cell is one-sixth of a volt, indeed a large biopotential, while according to Whitfield we have no real idea of the CM which a single hair cell can generate. Recall further that about four-fifths of all primary neurons are attached without arborizing to the inner hair cells, about 8–12 nerves per hair cell. Now an electric field generated by a hair cell would be more likely to stimulate whatever tissue were nearby, let us say 8–12 Type 1 nerve endings, than that a droplet of chemical would be divided by one-eighth to one-twelfth and thereafter stimulate all 8–12 endings. The general thought at the moment is that chemical process is directly involved, but the writer would be surprised if consideration in favor of an all-electric process should turn out to be suppositious nonsense.

Knothe et al (110) found the latency between CM and AP to be unchanged at 0.85 and 1.03 msec when strychnine was applied, and felt this negative result implied a cholinergic stimulation of AP. On the other hand, Honrubia & Ward (95) adopt an electromechanical hypothesis in setting up their electrical analog of the cochlea.

Darrouzet & Guilhaume (49) reported a dissociation of CM and AP in two types of mice, one strain with degenerated hair cells in the basal turn, and one with degeneration in the apical turn. The basal defects showed no CM. But normal AP is thought to arise as the result of the synchronization of nerve response in the first 0.5 msec in the first turn only, where this strain was defective. Possibly a closer look at the latency of the AP in this strain of mouse would be in order.

Teas & Henry (204) picked up whole VIIIth nerve responses to 2 and 6 kHz tone pips. Neural responses were enhanced at a repetition rate of 10/sec, indicating integration over a duration of 100 msec. For the 2 kHz burst at 2/sec, a weak background noise enhanced rather than reduced the output to the tone. However, when maximum enhancement was achieved at 10/sec for 6 kHz, it was reduced (masked?) by noise. Psychologists will look for the behavioral correlates of these facilitory and inhibitory effects.

Finck (68) attempted to infer some aspects of VIIIth nerve activity by combining the data on sensitivity, characteristic frequency, and response area of his many single neurons in hamster. The data tend to corroborate the principle of greater sensitivity in physical regions of greater neural density.

CM and AP in man.—Finck et al (70) put an electrode on the round window of six patients and found CM which yielded threshold visual detection on their oscilloscope. The SPL of the threshold CM, when plotted as a cochleagram, aped the behavioral audiogram. Even if so, this is known not to be the case with all animals.

While otologic surgeons have occasionally studied CM and AP on the operating table with an electrode through the middle ear on the promontory of the cochlea, Sohmer & Feinmesser (188) inserted an electrode simply into the external auditory meatus and used an averaging computer to tease AP out of system noise. This success has been duplicated by several others. Yoshie and his colleagues (225–227) have used both clicks and pure tones. Coats & Dickey (43) give specific instructions for inserting a needle electrode in the skin of the ear canal. They recovered averaged AP of 1–4 mV as compared with 60 mV in cat at the same location, with only moderately loud clicks (55–65 dB SPL). Surprisingly, the AP overloads at a sensation level lower than that at which the CM overloads. Spreng & Keidel (191, 192) have found that electrodes on the hard palate and on the mastoid bone may yield a usable CM and AP. This recalls early results with animals in which CM and AP could be found in spots throughout the whole calvarium.

THE AUDITORY CENTRAL NERVOUS SYSTEM

Direct stimulation.—The electrophonic effect so well documented a decade and more ago has been revived (165, 169) to include not only the usual ac stimuli in the audiofrequency range but also amplitude modulation of high carrier frequencies. It is possible that this effect also underlies the "hearing" of electromagnetic waves (97), but here it is theoretically possible for the CNS to be directly stimulated. In the latter case all that could possibly be experienced would be some sort of noise, since for hearing of, say, speech, the stimulus would have to be impossibly transformed from the acoustic code to the drastically different code in the neural stream from the brainstem. (Those who dream the deaf could hear by picking up sound with a microphone and delivering it to a sheaf of electrodes in the cortex, as might be done to some extent in vision, should be disabused of this hope).

Clark (40) has reviewed attempts in France and in this country to insert one or more electrodes in the cochlea to stimulate the auditory nerve directly. Some word discrimination has been achieved on the basis largely of low-tone effects. Clark compared fans of electrodes in the auditory nerve of the cat, but had better success with the array placed in the cochlea where the nerves are more tonotopically arrayed. His criteria were the correspondence between the two placements as compared with an actual acoustic stimulus, when he recorded responses by pickup electrodes in the superior olivary complex.

Gerken (75) trained cats to respond behaviorally to electrical stimulation applied through chronic electrodes at various auditory sites from the brainstem to the midbrain. Prior to training, there were observable gross responses to these stimuli. Evidence of interaction between the electric and an actual acoustical stimulus was obtained in only one electrode out of four. Certainly, the cats could distinguish parameters of the electric stimuli as intensity, duration, and repetition rate; and features of our acoustic world, if transformed and delivered as in these cats, could be expected eventually to shape behavior.

Anatomy of brain stem nuclei and their connections.—Two outstanding publications in this field deserve special attention, the complementary studies of Osen (151) and of Van Noort (214). Careful histological techniques have identified 9 cell regions in the cochlear nucleus of cat (Osen) rather than the classic 13 of Lorente de No, and the destinations of three of these have so far been elucidated: 1. an area of so-called "octopus cells" in the most caudal part of the ventral nuclei connects by way of the intermediate acoustic stria of Held to the retro-olivary and medial pre-olivary nuclei; 2. an area of small spherical cells in the most dorsal part of the ventral nuclei receives from all frequencies and goes to both lateral superior olivary nuclei (LSO); and 3. an area of large spherical cells in the most rostral part of the ventral nuclei receives *only from low and middle frequencies* and goes to both medial superior olivary nuclei (MSO).

Van Noort (214), among other achievements in his excellent monograph, has traced the origin and destination of three bundles of second-order fibers of distinctively small, medium, and large diameter from regions in the ventral cochlear nucleui to nuclei in the superior olivary complex. Some of these can be identified with the tracts described by Osen.

On the basis of Osens' and Van Noort's studies as well as others it now seems desirable to speak of nine cochlear nuclei rather than three (dorsal, anteroventral, posteroventral), just as the division into three was an advance over the earlier one ("cochlea nucleus"). Similarly it is no longer justified to speak of the "superior olivary complex"; enough is known of the distinctive histology and separate connections of each of half a dozen nuclei in this region that each should be mentioned specifically wherever possible. Again, we see that the trapezoid body has no true organization but is merely a structural convenience to group together several tracts of second-order fibers each of distinct import.

It has been known for some years that each bipolar cell in the crescent-shaped MSO receives precise tonotopic innervation of second-order fibers from both sides, and Osen shows that only the low and middle frequencies are represented; but it appears that the S-shaped LSO likewise receives precise tonotopic layouts from both sides, and Osen shows furthermore that these represent all frequencies. Another major difference between MSO and LSO is that the LSO receives its contralateral supply as third-order fibers, all the second-order fibers relaying in the "nucleus of the trapezoid body" next to the receiving LSO. Both MSO and LSO outputs split and send half their output up each lateral lemniscus, where their destinations are at present obscure.

The studies of Osen and Van Noort are of especial interest in view of the excellent review by Raab (170) of the complex activities found at the lowest level of the brainstem. We now push even below the inferior colliculus the site of important integrative and interpretative functions of the auditory nervous system. Mast (133), for example, found 20% of single fibers in the middle layers of the dorsal cochlear nucleus to be sensitive only to ipsilateral stimulation, but any spontaneous activity could be inhibited by contralateral stimulation. These cells were also sensitive to small differences in interaural intensity, and thus may play a role in localizing sound even though they do not go to bilateral layouts in MSO or LSO. Likewise in the ventral cochlear nucleus, Rupert & Moushegian (182) found very complicated patterns of response activity (interspike intervals, perstimulus time histograms).

Boudreau & Tsuchitani (18) contribute a longish paper in their series on single-cell activity in the LSO. The ipsilateral supply to LSO is certainly from spherical cells in the anteroventral cochlear nucleus, excitatory in nature; and an entirely inhibitory supply converges tonotopically ultimately from the contralateral ventral cochlear nucleus (VCN). This inhibitory supply originates in the contralateral VCN, crosses the midline to the nucleus of the trapezoid body, relaying in a synapse adapted for fast transmission, and goes to the nearby LSO. Thus a cell in LSO receives an ipsilateral excitatory and a contralateral inhibitory supply, the latter with some time delay which is reduced as far as possible.

Boudreau & Tsuchitani show that the excitatory response area of all fibers falls off from the unit's characteristic frequency (CF) at the rate of over 100 dB/octave for frequencies lower, and over 200 dB/octave for frequencies higher, than CF. Thresholds at CF for units tuned to the CF region ranged over about 30 dB SPL. Input-output functions (number of spikes to a 200-msec tone per 5-dB SPL increase) were not remarkable, being monotonic over a 15–80 dB range. Now when contralateral acoustic stimulation was added, these characteristics all changed. As the SPL was raised over threshold for a contralateral tone, the output of the cell had its ipsilateral stimulus threshold progressively raised, its input-output function flattened, and its maximum output reduced, perhaps to zero. The output of the cell at its CF was reduced most when the intensity was about the same in both ears; if anything, the inhibition was stronger, so that if the excitatory tone was at 80 dB above its threshold, the inhibitory tone need be only 55 dB above its threshold for the cell to cease to fire.

A striking fact was that of the 116 units from 64 cats, only 7 had CF less than 4 kHz; thus the LSO is essentially a high-frequency nucleus, in contrast to the moon-shaped medial superior olivary nucleus (MSO) which Osen (151) has shown to be a low and middle frequency nucleus. The other contrast between MSO and LSO is that the contralateral input is inhibitory in LSO, excitatory in MSO.

The relevance for behavior of these facts will be unknown till the crucial behavioral studies are done, but it may be noted that the MSO is often mentioned as ideally laid out to increase neural flow to the midbrain when the acoustic stimulus is in the median sagittal plane and thus the MSO is strongly implicated by inference in localization of sounds in space. But we also know that our best localization is to high-frequency transients, which the MSO may not even carry. It is at least possible that the LSO operates as a null instrument for these stimuli, so that head movements in locating and tracking such high-frequency transients are designed maximally to reduce neural upflow rather than enhance it.

One further important fact appears, that the LSO does not participate in a "neural sharpening" of cochlear patterns. For ipsilateral stimulation this is clearly seen; and for binaural stimulation, the neural locus of maximum activiation is not at the cells with CF at stimulus frequency but represents two peaks of activity, one at a frequency lower than the CF, the other at a higher frequency.

Secondary acoustic connections.—Many workers see that a concentration on the main afferent pathways needs to be tempered with a consideration of other influences for a round picture of auditory activity. Antonelli & Calearo (4) give a useful summary of how the reticular formation affects auditory integration. Rossi et al (181) traced a fiber tract from the cerebellum to the cochlear nuclei and to superior olivary nuclei (retro- and pre-olivary nuclei). Mitra & Snider (139) stimulated the nucleus fastigii in the cerebellum and found single-unit responses in the thalamus (medial geniculate) and auditory cortex of cat. Electrical stimulation of the cerebellum and acoustic stimulation combined to influence the response.

Auditory cortex.—Diamond et al (55) with degeneration techniques have gone over the relations among auditory cortical areas in cat. Generally, each subdivision directly connects with every other. Efferents to several specific nonauditory cortical areas were also documented. In monkey, Symmes (201) trained animals to respond to sound, then ablated the lateral frontal cortex. Relatively severe behavioral deficit ensued. Electrical stimulation of this area gave a (transitory) augmentation to the sound-evoked potential from the ipsilateral auditory cortex. Evidently the frontal cortex participates in primate acoustic-evoked behavior.

In five patients with temporal cortices exposed during surgery, Celesia & Puletti (37) picked up click-evoked activity from the primary auditory area, a first positive wave of 2–20 mV with a latency of 12–22 msec, and a second of 30–75 mV with a latency of 23–55 msec. Kern et al (102) showed that a dural electrode in guinea pig gave a sound-evoked negative wave from the vertex after 25 msec, which was swamped by myogenic potentials if the electrode was on the unopened skull. This dural electrode vertex was varied with frequency, but was not compared with behavioral thresholds for these animals. These authors (103) showed that when myogenic responses were minimized by curarization, an electrode simply on the skull could yield three averaged waves, one of latency 1–2 msec and arising probably from first-order fibers, a second of latency 3–5 msec, probably from the inferior colliculus, and a third of latency 13–19 msec, said to be a cortical response. When an electrode was placed on the dura over the primary cortical area, a large response was obtained with latency 6–16 msec. This response could be evoked by clicks or tone bursts only, whereas the vertex dural response could be evoked as well from photic stimuli.

Miller et al (137) approached the functional significance of the auditory-evoked intradural cortical potential in monkey by taking four steps: they first established its latency as about 15 msec, then trained the animals to release a lever on auditory cue and established the total reaction time from acoustic cue to response. Then the animals were found to react when the stimulating electrode in the cortex was energized. Not only were the animals able to transfer from the acoustic to the electric cue, but the latency of behavioral response to the electric cue was 15 msec shorter—just the time previously found for the relay from eardrum to cortex. Rosenfeld et al (180) found in the human that a late component of the averaged auditory-evoked response (AER) from the vertex could be changed by classic instrumental conditioning even without oscilloscopic (visual) feedback, just as is possible with numerous autonomic functions.

A good review of the AER to 1968 is given by Price (167); see also Keidel & Spreng (101). Eldredge & Miller (60) give the neurological reasons for considering that the components of the vertex (V) potential of the AER at least up to 250 msec are generated only in primary auditory cortex. The V potential has thus come within the last few years to serve many laboratories and clinics as a test of the intactness of the cochlea, VIIIth nerve, and of all primary auditory CNS tissue including the cortex. Rapin et al (171), for example, regard it as a powerful audiometric tool even in the face of brain damage. Its value in audiometry is of course due to the lack of necessity for voluntary cooperation as in infants and children (e.g. 199, 202) or even in the fetus (183). Several have confirmed that threshold AER can come very close to the voluntary threshold when a lengthened latency at and near threshold is taken into account (10, 125). Burian et al (23) point out that SPLs which yield no observed AER may yet influence the AER to later louder sound and thus be useful in audiometric surveys. In handling certain types of hearing loss, as from rubella with brain damage (171), Meniere's with recruitment (109), and presbycusis (213), where normal threshold AER may be found but with an early overload in the input-output function, the AER has been of great help.

There is a linear relation between the peak-to-peak amplitude vs dB SPL up to the point of overload, but the maximum amplitude falls off from 2–8 kHz and the input-output slope approaches 0 at 8 kHz (3). Rau (172) found the slope to obey Steven's power law—the output is a power function of the stimulus with an exponent of 0.28. The slopes maintained here may of course be modified by habituation or the attention of the subject.

The AER definitely habituates. Fruhstörfer et al (73) found at the click rate of 1/sec the AER reaches asymptote after only 3 stimuli. Furthermore, habituation can be confounded with other response-diminishing processes (see e.g. 177). Whereas Fruhstörfer et al (73) found habituation to be less rapid and less pronounced at a stimulus rate of 3/sec, most workers now recommend a rate no more rapid than 1/sec. Rau (172) found that to use 4/sec would reduce the slope of the input curve to .14 or even lower.

Onishi & Davis (150) recommend tone bursts of any rise-time less than 30 msec, and any stimulus duration longer than 30 msec. In order not to confound "on" effects with "off" effects (193), Spreng (190) recommends pulse durations of at least 300 msec (see also 137).

Moore & Reneau (142) point out that radio telementry is suited to transmit such information from the unrestrained child. Agreement was found among thresholds by behavioral audiogram, direct recording, and telemetry.

Clark & Dunlop (41) placed an active electrode in the nasopharynx as close to the base of the skull as possible, and recorded an auditory-evoked response with a latency of 42 msec and lasting to 85 msec. This location may best tap regions of activity between N_1 and the V potential.

The corticofugal pathways.—Efferent pathways and their effects have been well reviewed to 1968 (64, 79), but a few papers should be mentioned. Kaneko & Daly (100) showed that the upper radial fibers in the tunnel of Corti were efferent, since acetycholinestrase activity was found, while the lower tunnel radials were afferent. Kittrell & Dalland (107) lean to the position that electrical stimulation of the crossed olivocochlear bundle (OCB) results in an augmentation, though slight, of the CM. In their data it was increased by 2 dB at 1 kHz, falling off slowly at lower and higher frequencies. The effect of electrical stimulation of OCB on the primary neuron response is less controversial. Dayal (51) has further found that AP latency to sound stimulation is lengthened upon electrical OCB stimulation, while Daigneault et al (46) decentralized the cochlea (VIIIth nerve cut) and found changes in N_1, N_2 which they ascribed to the missing OCB. They could simulate some of these changes by direct injection of acetycholine into the vascular system of the ear.

In spite of the effects of electrically stimulating the crossed or uncrossed OCB on cochlear electricities, no clear-cut experiment has shown that an ear's primary nerve output has been altered in any way by acoustic stimulation of the other ear (crossed OCB) (159). The experiment of Klinke et al (108), sometimes mentioned as demonstrating such an effect, used an electrode in the cochlear nucleus (thus possibly on second-order or third-order fibers) where an abundance of binaural sound effects has been observed.

However, Zöllner & Stange (228, 229) showed that the time-course of adaptation of round window AP to repetitive acoustic clicks was reduced when the cells of the cochlear nucleus were selectively destroyed by neomycin sulphate, presumed to have been because of reduction of efferent control to the ipsilateral ear.

Holstein et al (93) showed that a prior generalization was incorrect that habituation did not occur below the thalamus. They inserted electrodes in cochlear nucleus, inferior colliculus, and medial geniculate. Although habituation to trains of tone bursts (each 1.5 sec duration, 1 every 5 sec) decreased regulaily up the system, it was in fact apparent even at the lowest level. And this is what one would expect considering the corticofugal pathways to the cochlear nuclei (see 45) for a pathway from ipsilateral superior olive to cochlear nucleus, and from such results as those of Swisher (200), who in a series of 45 patients with temporal lobe damage found that excision of the lobe immediately sensitized the patients to intensity differences, apparently by removing corticofugal control.

Pfalz (160) delivered electrical shocks to spots on the basilar membrane and picked up the compound action potential (AP) with a gross electrode in the ventral cochlear nucleus (VCN) of guinea pig. This VCN-AP could be reduced, as much as 100%, by an acoustic stimulus at the contralateral eardrum. There was a bilateral tonotopic layout in VCN—electrical stimulation of the basal, or apical, turn could best be inhibited by pure tones of high or low frequency respectively. While the latency of inhibition from the moment of acoustic stimulation was as short as 5 msec (loud high tones), it was as long as 80 msec (weak low tones), and commonly required 80–100 msec to reach its maximum. For continuous tones, inhibition declined (adapted) exponentially over a period of seconds; here a curious phenomenon occurred, in that the reduction in inhibition rather abruptly accelerated for all frequencies at SPLs above about 85 dB SPL. When the contralateral tone was turned off, inhibition declined exponentially but persisted for perhaps 200–300 msec.

A striking finding was a strictly linear relation between the percentage of inhibition found in AP amplitude for any acoustic stimulus, and the increase in latency to maximum intensity. It may be that the chief effect of the inhibitory process, rather than to reduce the AP amplitude, is to shift the neural tuning by some constant amount and allow some sort of autocorrelation function.

To explain the dispersion of latencies, Pfalz mentions from the literature three efferent pathways known to exist: 1. from one cochlear nucleus through both superior olives to the VCN of the other side; 2. from one cochlear nucleus through both lateral lemnisci to both inferior colliculi, and thence corticofugally, to both superior olives and the VCN of the other side; and 3. from one cochlear nucleus up the contralateral afferent path to the medial geniculate and thence corticofugally to the VCN of the same side.

THE EAR AND HEARING IN ANIMALS

Lower orders.—For the tympanic organ of the cricket, Suga (198) has determined threshold SPLs at 60 dB for the region 20–30 kHz, but responses from 5–150 kHz exist; for the sensory hairs, threshold was at 80 dB SPL for sounds below .5 kHz, but responses existed up to 1.5 kHz. Apparently many insects have evolved two separate acoustic-sensitive systems. The Orthoptera, prey of bats, has a so-called T fiber which receives strong ipsilateral flow, and also contralateral flow, weak in excitatory but strong in inhibitory effect (McKay 129). There was (*a*) little habituation, and (*b*) tuning to the frequency of a bats' call—i.e. all the properties required of a warning system to pulsed high frequency.

Van Bergeijk (12) and Dekle (52) provide general reviews on the evolution of mammalian hearing. A half-dozen recent papers on hearing in fish from several laboratories have appeared, most recently emphasizing the differences in pressure vs particle velocity sensitivity: in a so-called far-field, SPL and particle velocity are equal, while in a near-field, velocity exceeds SPL by up to 35 dB. Cahn et al (29) took behavioral audiograms in fish *Haemulon sciurus* and found that at 400 Hz the fish were truly sensitive with their ears, not the lateral-line systems (see also 65, 149, 217).

A careful study of the anatomy of the ear of the sea turtle and its adaptation to hearing in both air and water is available (82). The reptile, as an example of the earliest ear with the possibility of differential frequency display over some distance across a sensory epithelium, is of especial interest (132, 153). Wever (219) summarizes his many studies on types of lizard ear in which the place principle seems to be initiated. Manley (131) in the caiman determined the characteristic frequencies from 70–2900 Hz of single neurons in the cochlear nucleus. At this stage of phylogeny the tonotopic layout parallels the bird's, while the sensitivity curve of all neurons and the number of neurons in each frequency range are similar in some ways to warm-blooded creatures. Konishi (112) shows that the bird's ear is far superior to most mammals in time-locking to clicks at fast repetition rates. The birds single auditory neuron will fire at each click at 500 clicks/sec while in cat, for example, the response to stimuli at that rate will drop off to only 50% of responses. The pitch discrimination of the pigeon was determined by Price et al (168), the Weber fraction being about .025 from 1–4 kHz. Perhaps other birds could more closely approach the differential sensitivity of the cat and human. Scattered throughout a volume of essays presented to W. H. Thorpe on the occasion of his retirement (91) may be found many facts concerning the hearing of birds and the effects which specific sounds may have not only directly on their behavior but on their physiology. For example, in the budgerigar (a small parrot) specific male vocal behavior promotes gonatotropin secretions in both sexes, together with full ovarian activity in females and testicular activity in males, as well as inducing sexually active females to assume the posture of soliciting-for-copulation. Some notion of the auditory discriminations necessary in this species may be had from the fact that at least 10 specific sounds yield specific behaviors: the ehh, nest-defense ehh, squacks, chedelees, whedelees, tuk-tuk, loud warble, soft warble, loud-plus-soft components warble, and a nest entrance note. The notion of vocal-endocrinological feedback initiating and modulating long-term behavior adds a new dimension to studies of the hearing of animals. One-microvolt cochleagrams were provided by Peterson & Heaton (155) for a low order of mammal, Edentata (armadillo, sloth, anteater), together with other indices to cochlear activity.

As part of Wever's broad survey of the hearing of all orders, Wever & Herman (220) give CM on the tenrec, a hedgehog-like insectivore. The opossum (174) and hedgehog (175) were studied. The rodent continues to be well covered, represented by the mouse (14, 16, 81, 189), the gerbil (69), chinchilla (135, 136, 196), rat (44), kangaroo rat (22), guinea pig (39), and bat (84, 85, 127). Hall (85) especially compares the cochlea and cochlear nuclei in bat, cat, whale, and man.

Hertzler et al (90) compared several electrophysiological outputs in raccoon, from cochlear microphonic to gross cortical evoked activity, with previous behavioral audiograms on the same specimens (224). Rose et al (179) provided an audiogram for the beagle based on the computer-averaged AER to tone pulses, with threshold values slightly lower than for the 1-microvolt cochleagram for this breed provided by Peterson et al (156).

Dallos (47) has found that the helicotrema acts as a very low band-reject filter, in that animals with relatively small helicotremas (guinea pigs, kangaroo rats) fall off in CM below 100 Hz at the rate of -12 dB/octave, whereas in animals with relatively large openings the fall-off is less (-6 dB/octave), though the effect of the helicotrema size is negligible at 200^+ Hz.

Two papers (161, 207) have studied the discrimination of intensity in rats.

Three papers on the pinniped appeared. Møhl (141) determined both airborne and waterborne behavioral thresholds on one seal. In this species the airborne and waterborne discrepancy is less than in man at relevant frequencies. Wever and his colleagues (126) took CM in dolphin and completed studies determining that the meatus and tympanic membrane do not contribute to waterborne hearing in this species. Hall (83) studied the basilar membrane, VIIIth nerve, and auditory nervous system in several species of whale.

Mitchell et al (138) report behavioral thresholds on three species of lemur. Rather remarkable is the broad frequency range (1–40 kHz) through which the median threshold are flat ±5 dB. Hoffman et al (92) subdivided the auditory cortex of monkey with the use of the AER to tone pulses, and Dalton et al (48) and Bragg & Dreher (19) gave behavioral thresholds.

Two groups have done extensive research on the evolution of hearing among primates from protosimian to man. A comprehensive summary by Masterton, Heffner & Ravizza (134) appeared in 1969. CM or behavioral audiograms reported for specific species include tree shrews (88, 157), bush baby (89, 157), and marmoset; the capuchin, squirrel, and rhesus monkeys; and chimpanzee (157).

SOME PHENOMENA OF HUMAN HEARING

Binaural hearing.—A total of 42 interesting important papers recently appeared in this reviewer's cumulative file on various aspects of binaural hearing. However, the psychological aspects of binaural hearing were fully treated by Green & Henning (78), and the physiological aspects by Grinnell (80) and Eldredge & Miller (60), while Raab (170) extensively reviewed studies on single nerve units responding to binaural as well as monaural inputs. It is probably premature at this time to structure the field again.

Frequency effects.—The area of frequency analysis by psychoacoustic studies up to 1963 has been well reviewed by Nordmark (147), including his own important study in 1968 (146). He summarizes his reasons for proposing that the auditory system performs frequency analysis by sensitivity to time differences at high as well as at low frequencies, rather than using time at lows and resorting to a place principle at some transitional frequency region. Small (187) brings the subject of periodicity pitch up to 1966.

Ward (216) summarizes for the musician what is known of the psychology of hearing as affected by frequency: jnd, pitch scaling, musical scales, vibrato, timbre, absolute pitch, diplacusis, binaural effects, consonance, and distortion products. On balance it would seem that a great deal is known, but actually psychoacoustics has hardly begun to formulate experimentally, let alone treat the great questions of musical hearing for complex acoustic patterns which are of first (artistic) concern to musicologists (222).

The topics of frequency analysis and the generation of pitch will be dominated for a decade by the proceedings of the Driebergen Symposium (162). Thirty-four of the world's foremost experimentalists on these topics met for formal and informal presentations on: cochlear function (Keidel, Johnstone, Honrubia, Kohllöffel, Legouix, Kupperman); the auditory pathway (Whitfield, Kallert, Klinke, Møller); VIIIth nerve-fiber activity (de Boer, Rose, Hind); combination tones (Dallos, Goldstein); pitch perception (Ritsma, Smoorenburg, Terhardt, Bilsen, Wilson, Fourcin, Pollack, Cardozo, Henning, van den Brink); and frequency analysis and masking (Zwicker, Plomp, Schügerl, Carterette, Zwislocki, Scharf, and Pols). This volume will for some time be a touchstone by which to determine whether a paper on frequency analysis goes significantly beyond the facts and concepts in current theory. To judge by the flow of papers in this area, probably at least 3 years more should elapse before another review would be useful.

Signal detection.—The Theory of Signal Detection (TSD) did psychoacoustics a great favor when it provided a means of quantifying changes in a listener's criterion in YES-NO judgments, a problem which had led Jastrow in 1890 to abandon the YES-NO format and to invent the Method of Right and Wrong Cases, the modern version of which is called the Method of 2-Alternative Forced-Choice (2A-FC) judgment. Most psychoacoustic studies since Seashores's work about 1904 have used some variant of 2A-FC. Jeffress (98) correctly concludes that one should use either TSD when a YES-NO judgment must be employed, sensitivity being reported in d', or one should use 2A-FC and report threshold in percent correct judgments. It should be said that where a criterion cannot be well verbalized for the subject, the ABX method or some variant ordinarily can be devised to avoid simple YES-NO reports.

TSD has looked at detectability of a signal as affected by such parameters as energy, amplitude, duration, bandwidth, frequency uncertainty, temporal uncertainty, and cueing signal (see 98 for studies reviewed through 1964). A valuable body of knowledge on specifics was obtained, but this lode has lately proved rather unproductive.

One problem concerns the personality of subjects in simple psychoacoustic tasks. Stephens (194) found that a 2A-FC method significantly reduced the variance by a few dB at 250 Hz as compared with the usual audiometric Method of Serial Exploration (Limits), and that the reduction by the use of 2A-FC was greater in neurotics; non-neurotics showed negligible differences. In the overall results for the 2A-FC method, variance was greater in extraverts than in introverts. Thus the 2A-FC method yielded smallest variance in stable introverts and largest in neurotic extraverts.

Campbell has tried strenuously to adapt the virtues of TSD to the practice of audiometry. He has found that subjects really do not always pay attention to the differences in their sensations between two successive time periods, as assumed in TSD, but effectively judge 'present' or 'absent' on the basis of the first interval alone (30). Campbell & Moulin (31) applied TSD to the clinic, and found it necessary to recommend restructuring subjects' criteria before TSD would be applicable. Barr Hamilton et al (7) compared 2A-FC with Békésy audiometry, working out a procedure to take about the same time for both, with encouraging results: threshold by TSD was significantly more sensitive. Of course, with 2A-FC we are back to Jastrow.

Lindner (122) questioned whether a detection criterion, either strict or lax, had any effect on the signal-to-noise ratio (S/N) at which subject not only could detect the signal but also identify some feature of the stimulus (whether $f = 500$ or 1100 Hz). The detection performance varied with the criterion in the fashion predicted by TSD, but the recognition S/N did not. Thus TSD was not able to specify the criterion for recognition.

Taylor & Forbes (203) presented low-frequency noise bursts to subject for monaural detection. Now with another identical burst to the other ear, in diotic fashion, performance was even better than that of an ideal energy detector. However, if the noise to the opposite ear was from another noise generator, though identically filtered and timed, no improvement over the monaural condition existed. This was true only for bandwidths less than 1.6 kHz, and the likelihood is that phase effects introduce something like binaural unmasking with the signal in phase, the physiological noise out of phase and the introduced noises out of phase.

Pfafflin (158) tested whether subject was disrupted in S/N when either signal levels or noise levels varied from trial to trial during a block of trials. Either for YES-NO or 2A-FC trials, $p(c)$ and d' were not changed with random changes in signal level, but were with such changes in noise level. It seemed that one variable in TSD is short-term memory for noise.

Mulligan et al (143) found that the regularity of a six-category rating scale procedure in monaural detection was such that it could predict the psychometric function from a knowledge of the masking noise. In this experiment an especially interesting item appeared, namely, evidence that critical bandwidth changes with S/N, decreasing as S/N increases, the rate of decrease depending on frequency. This is only one of several hints that the "critical bandwidth of the ear" is too static a concept.

Masking.—Ehmer & Ehmer (59) worked over the patterns of pure-tone-on-tone masking using the residual-masking method to avoid beats. The data differ only in second order of magnitude from Ehmer's earlier curves which remain the classic picture to date. Elliott (61) argues persuasively that it takes time for the development of steady-state patterns capable of such effects as well as of other phenomena. Bilger & Melnick (15) showed that masking patterns do not necessarily remain stable—the masking of a tone (0.5 kHz) by a band of noise (0.2–4 kHz) reduced over a 2-min tracking period, the amount depending on whether subject adjusted the tone or the noise. Evidently masking is influenced, as of course it must be, by any peripheral or central event which changes over time the relative neural activities to two separate sounds, either tones or noise. Homick et al (94) feel that the perception of order and the temporal aspects of masking are alike.

In the matter of backward masking, Babkoff & Sutton (6) found somewhat less pronounced effects than usual, and felt that their results could be explained simply on the basis of intensity at the periphery converting to time in the CNS. On the other hand, Pollack (163) had shown that forward and backward masking were probably two separate mechanisms.

Carterette (36) constructed infinitely sharp-shouldered filters by computer and used them as maskers for pure tones. Just at the edge of the shoulders a slight peak could be observed, which seemed to be the analogue of Mach bands in vision, he argues that this tends to show laterally inhibiting neural nets in the cochlea, such as are well known in the retina.

Green (77) found that the masking by a sine wave and of a noise, each adjusted to mask a signal by, say, 40 dB, will when added together yield a masker of 63⁺ dB. Green states that additivity rather than occlusion means that the two maskers generate two different processes. This sounds correct, but does not readily accord with Coats' (42) position that the amount of masking by any stimulus on any other stimulus is related to the degree of 'overlap' within neural units responding to masked and masking stimuli.

Masking level differences (MLD) ('release from masking') were studied by Carhart et al (34) for speech with 37 binaural listening conditions. Maskers were amplitude-modulated white noise and speech; homophasic, antiphasic, and time-delayed conditions were used; and three masker levels were employed. Lateralization judgments as well were demanded. This important experiment showed that MLD and lateralization involve two different neurological mechanisms. This had in fact been the conclusion of a previous study (35).

MLD does not continue to grow at the lower frequencies, as it would if phase cancellation were all that need be considered. Dolan (58) found that at 150 Hz vs 300 Hz his data could be explained by the intrusion of more intense internal noise. McFadden (128) tested the growth of masking with increase in spectrum level, in an MLD condition and in a non-MLD condition. The growth of masking differed, depending on overall level, but an explanation is at hand in the decades-old concept of the relative importance of uncorrelated internal noise, and the experiment, while formally elaborate, is in reality trivial. Wightman (221) arranged a truly original condition in which a single pure tone is binaural and is at once both signal and masker. As a masker, the tone was always diotic; as a signal, it was either diotic or 180° out of phase at the two ears. The masker was either continuous or was gated on and off with the signal. Under some conditions the signal-out-of-phase was less detectable (*negative* MLD!), this effect reaching the surprising extent of 10 dB for short-duration gated signals.

Zwislocki (231, 232) presented a rather complete picture of central masking, the shift in threshold of tones in one ear as a result of relatively weak tones in the other. The most striking results were the times necessary to establish this effect, its decay curve over time and the critical frequency band within which the effect is seen. Blegvad (17) must have been dealing with central masking when he found that low-level noise in one ear raised Békésy thresholds at 1–4 kHz in the other ear, either for continuous or pulsed tones, but more so for continuous tones. Blegvad's explanation in terms of efferents is only one, rather unlikely, possibility.

The truth is that with a few exceptions psychoacoustic experiments in the realm of masking are not so fruitful as neurophysiological experiments. The latter are usually carried out for other stated reasons, but contain observations almost by the way as to how the neural response to one stimulus is facilitated, inhibited, its temporal pattern changed perhaps quite drastically, its input-output altered or even distorted, etc. by the presence at some point in relative time of a second acoustic stimulus. The words mask, masker, masked are indeed misnomers—the masked stimulus may have as much effect on the masker as the converse. What we see in the fuller picture is rather an interplay of excitatory and inhibitory influences, some corticopetal, some corticofugal, now monaural, now binaural, now waxing, now waning, the vector of all of which on some final common path determines the response, its magnitude, latency, and temporal pattern. The time has come in masking especially, though in some other psychoacoustic fields likewise, for those who wish to understand the working of the auditory system, to design psychoacoustic experiments to determine the relevance for our experiential world of what we see in neurophysiology, rather than as in the past to seek in the animal the basis for psychoacoustic phenomena.

Popular interest in noise pollution.—A spate of generally trivial but popular-interest reports is appearing even in reputable journals on the effects of noise from tractors, outboard motors, small and large airplanes, home appliances, rock and roll music, and other common noise polluters. We take up only rock and roll music here. Flugrath (72) determined that the acoustic spectrum of ten rock and roll bands was essentially that of a steady-state noise with maximum output at 2 kHz, so that from published curves of damage risk criteria for octave-bands of white noise and a knowledge of exposure pattern and duration one should be able to predict the hazard to hearing of such music. Interpretation of the music in such fashion led to the statement that several of the ten bands exceeded damage risk criteria. Lebo & Oliphant's (117) conclusions thus were validated, that the music groups they measured unmistakably did exceed criteria. Dey (54), in one of the better-controlled experiments, arranged exposures to rock and roll music for up to 2 hr and measured temporary threshold shift after 2 min in 15 young adults. A level of 100 dBA was fairly innocuous, but when the level reached 110 dBA, 16% of subjects sustained a temporary threshold shift after 2 min of 40+ dB, considered generally a danger signal of impending permanent loss. Now Rintelmann & Borns (176) had shown, working with music at the level of 105 dBA, that only 5% of rock and roll musicians exhibited permanent loss attributable to their music. Thus one may conclude that the quieter bands may be harmless, but if the amplification/reverberation condition reaches 110 dBA, a sizable fraction of persons would be adversely affected, probably permanently; while a 120-dBA level, at which some music groups have registered, would create havoc with most audiograms.

A study by Lipscomb (123), who found cochlear damage in guinea pigs after 88 hr exposure to rock and roll music at 122 dBA, has led to a public banning of that species from certain New York City discotheques.

LITERATURE CITED

1. Anon. 1970. An IEC artificial ear, of the wide band type, for the calibration of earphones used in audiometry. 1 rue de Varembe, Geneva, Switzerland: Bureau Central de la Commission Electrotechnique Internationale.
2. Anon. 1970. ANSI S3. 1969. Specifications for audiometers. New York: Nat. Standards Inst., 1430 Broadway
3. Antinoro, F., Skinner, P. H., Jones, J. J. 1969. Relation between sound intensity and amplitude of the AER at different stimulus frequencies. *J. Acoust. Soc. Am.* 46:1433–36
4. Antonelli, A. R., Calearo, C. 1968. On the influence of the reticular activation system upon the auditory function. *Acta Otolaryngol.* 65:625–30
5. Aran, J. M., Delaunay, J. 1969. Neural responses of the end organ of the guinea pig. VIIIth Nerve action potentials evoked by click and tone pips (filtered clicks) of different frequencies. *Rev. Laryngol. (Bordeaux)* 90:598–614
6. Babkoff, H., Sutton, S. 1968. Monaural temporal masking of transients. *J. Acoust. Soc. Am.* 44:1373–78
7. Barr Hamilton, R. M., Bryan, M. E., Tempest, W. 1969. Application of signal detection theory of audiometry. *Int. Audiol.* 8:138–46
8. Bates, M. A., Loeb, M., Smith, R. P., Fletcher, J. L. 1970. Attempts to condition the acoustic reflex. *J. Aud. Res.* 10:132–35
9. Bauer, B. B., Rosenheck, A. J., Abbagnaro, L. A. 1967. External-ear replica for acoustical testing. *J. Acoust. Soc. Am.* 42:204–7
10. Beagley, H. A., Kellogg, S. E. 1969. A comparison of evoked response and subjective auditory thresholds. *Int. Audiol.* 8:345–53
11. Berendes, J., Link, R., Zöllner, F., Eds. 1964. *Hals-Nasen-Ohren-Heilkunde. Ein Kurzgefasstes Handbuch in Drei Banden.* Stuttgart: Georg Thieme
12. Bergeijk, W. A. Van 1967. The evolution of vertebrate hearing. *Contrib. Sens. Physiol.* 2:1–49
13. Berland, O., Nielsen, T. E. 1969. Sound pressure generated in the human external ear by a free sound field. *Sound* 3:78–81

14. Berlin, C. I., Majeau, D. A., Steiner, S. 1969. Hearing and vocal output in normal, deaf and infant mice. *J. Aud. Res.* 9:318–31
15. Bilger, R. C., Melnick, W. 1968. Shifts in masking with time. *J. Acoust. Soc. Am.* 44:941–44
16. Birch, L. M., Warfield, D., Ruben, R. J., Mikaelian, D. D. 1968. Behavioral measurements of pure tone thresholds in normal CBA-J mice. *J. Aud. Res.* 8:459–68
17. Blegvad, B. 1967. Contralateral masking and Bèkèsy audiometry in normal listeners. *Acta Otolaryngol.* 64:157–65
18. Boudreau, J. C., Tsuchitani, C. 1970. Cat superior olive S-segment cell discharge to tonal stimulation. *Contrib. Sens. Physiol.* 4:144–213
19. Bragg, V. C., Dreher, D. E. 1969. A shock-avoidance technique for determining audiologic thresholds in the cebus monkey. *J. Aud. Res.* 9:270–77
20. Bredberg, G. 1968. Cellular pattern and nerve supply of the human organ of Corti. *Acta Otolaryngol. Suppl.* 236:10–135
21. Brown, P. G., Ruben, R. J. 1969. The endocochlear potential in the Shaker-1 (Sh-1/Sh-1) mouse. *Acta Otolaryngol.* 68:14-20
22. Brown, P. G., Webster, D. G. 1968. Cochlear microphonics and endocochlear potential from the basal and third turns of the kangaroo rat cochlea. *J. Aud. Res.* 8:420–26
23. Burian, K., Gestring, G. F., Hruby, S. 1968. Die Interaktion sensorischer reize im rahmen der objektiven Horschwellenbestimmung. *Arch. Klin. Exp. Ohr. Nas. Kehlkopfheilk* 192:116–23
24. Burke, K. S., Herer, G. R., McPherson, D. L. 1971. Middle ear impedance measurement. *Acta Otolaryngol.* 70:29–34
25. Burns, W. 1969. *Noise and Man.* Philadelphia: Lippincott
26. Burns, W., Robinson, D. W. 1970. *Hearing and Noise in Industry.* London: Her Majesty's Stationary Office
27. Butler, R. A. 1970. The effect of hearing impairment on locating sound in the vertical plane. *Int. Audiol.* 9:117–26
28. Bystrenin, V. A. 1970. Importance of the auricular conchae for hearing

orientation in the sagittal plane (Russian). *Vestn. Otorinolaringol.* 32:71–74 (see *Excerpta Med.* 1970, Sect. 11:4271)

29. Cahn, P. H., Siler, W., Wodinsky, J. 1969. Acousto lateralis system of fishes: tests of pressure and particle velocity sensitivity in grunts, *Haemulon sciurus* and *Haemulon parrai*. *J. Acoust. Soc. Am.* 46:1572–78

30. Campbell, R. A. 1969. Context and sequence effects with an adaptive threshold procedure. *J. Acoust. Soc. Am.* 46:350–55

31. Campbell, R. A., Moulin, K. K. 1968. Signal detection audiometry: An exploratory study. *J. Speech Hear. Res.* 11:402–10

32. Cancura, W. 1967. Ueber die Bedeutung der ohrmuschel für die Wahrnehmung besonders hoher Töne. *Mschr. Ohrenheilk.* 101:497–502

33. Ibid 1970. Der Einfluss der binnenohrmuskulatur auf die Schallubertragung im mittelohr. 104:3–46

34. Carhart, R., Tillman, T. W., Greetis, E. S. 1969. Release from multiple maskers: effects of interaural time disparities. *J. Acoust. Soc. Am.* 45:411–18

35. Carhart, R., Tillman, T. W., Johnson, K. R. 1968. Effect of interaural time delays on masking by two competing signals. *J. Acoust. Soc. Am.* 43:1223–30

36. Carterette, E. C. 1969. Mach bands in hearing. *J. Acoust. Soc. Am.* 45:986–98

37. Celesia, G. G., Puletti, F. 1969. Auditory cortical areas of man. *Neurology* 19:211–20

38. Chalupnik, J. D., Ed. 1970. *Transportation Noises: A Symposium on Acceptability Criteria.* Seattle: Univ. of Washington Press

39. Chambers, A. H., Terrien, T. F., Schultz, C. E. 1968. Effect of anoxemia on cochlear AC and endolymphatic potentials of the guinea pig. *J. Aud. Res.* 8:237–50

40. Clark, G. M. 1970. A neurophysiological assessment of the surgical treatment of deafness. *Int. Audiol.* 9:103–9

41. Clark, G. M., Dunlop, C. W. 1970. Extracranial auditory responses from the base of the skull. *Laryngoscope* 80:1834–47

42. Coats, A. C. 1967. Physiological masking in the peripheral auditory system. *J. Neurophysiol.* 30:931–48

43. Coats, A. C., Dickey, J. R. 1970. Non-

surgical recording of human auditory nerve action potentials and cochlear microphonics. *Ann. Otol. Rhinol. Laryngol.* 79:844–52

44. Coltheart, M., Irvine, D. 1968. The slope of ROCs in the rat. *J. Aud. Res.* 8:167–70

45. Comis, S. D., Davies, W. E. 1969. Acetylcholine as a transmitter in the cat auditory system. *J. Neurochem.* 16:423–29

46. Daigneault, E. A., Brown, R. D., Pruett, J. 1968. Cochlear round window recorded responses to acetylcholine and click stimulation following decentralization. *Acta Otolaryngol.* 66:10–16

47. Dallos, P. 1970. Low-frequency auditory characteristics: species dependence. *J. Acoust. Soc. Am.* 48:489–99

48. Dalton, L. W. Jr., Taylor, H., Henton, W., Allen, J. N. 1969. Auditory thresholds in the rhesus monkey using a closed system helmet. *J. Aud. Res.* 9:178–82

49. Darrouzet, J., Guilhaume, A. 1967. A propos d'une absence de potentiel microphonique: étude histologique de l'organe de Corti de la souris. *Rev. Laryngol.* (*Bordeaux*) 88:813–33

50. Davis, H. 1968. Mechanism of the inner ear. *Ann. Otol. Rhinol. Laryngol.* 77:644–55

51. Dayal, V. S. 1968. The effects of olivocochlear bundle stimulation on latency of action potential. *Laryngoscope* 78:1590–96

52. Dekle, T. G. 1969. Evolution of the ear. *Laryngoscope* 79:638–51

53. Delany, M. E., Whittle, L. S., Cook, J. P., Scott, V. 1967. Performance studies on a new artificial ear. *Acustica* 18:231–37

54. Dey, F. L. 1970. Auditory fatigue and predicted permanent hearing defects from rock and roll music. *New Engl. J. Med.* 282:467–70

55. Diamond, I. T., Jones, E. G., Powell, T. P. S. 1968. The association connections of the auditory cortex of the cat. *Brain Res.* 11:560–79

56. Djupesland, G. 1969. Observations of changes in the acoustic impedance of the ear as an aid to the diagnosis of paralysis of the stapedius muscle. *Acta Otolaryngol.* 68:1–5

57. Djupesland, G. 1969. Use of impedance indicator in diagnosis of middle ear pathology. *Int. Audiol.* 8:570–78

58. Dolan, T. R. 1968. Effect of masker

spectrum level on masking level differences at low signal frequencies. *J. Acoust. Soc. Am.* 44:1507–12

59. Ehmer, R. H., Ehmer, B. J. 1969. Frequency pattern of residual masking by pure tones measured on the Békésy audiometer. *J. Acoust. Soc. Am.* 46:1445–48

60. Eldredge, D. H., Miller, J. D. 1971. Physiology of hearing. *Ann. Rev. Physiol.* 33:281–310

61. Elliott, L. 1967. Development of auditory narrow-band frequency contours. *J. Acoust. Soc. Am.* 42:143–53

62. El-Mofty, A., El-Serafy, S. 1967. The ossicular chain in mammals. *Ann. Otol. Rhinol. Laryngol.* 76:903–9

63. Erber, N. P. 1968. Variables that influence sound pressures generated in the ear canal by an audiometric earphone. *J. Acoust. Soc. Am.* 44:555–62

64. Euler, C. Von, Skoglund, S., Soderberg, U., Eds. 1968. *Structure and Function of Inhibitory Neuronal Mechanisms.* Int. Symp. Ser. Vol. 10. Oxford: Pergamon. 563 pp.

65. Fay, R. 1969. Behavioral audiogram for the goldfish. *J. Aud. Res.* 9:112–21

66. Feldman, A. S. 1967. A report of further impedance studies of the acoustic reflex. *J. Speech Hear. Res.* 10:616–22

67. Feldmann, H., Steinmann, G. 1968. Die Bedeutung des äusseren Ohres für das Hören im Wind. *Arch. Klin. Exp. Ohr. Nas. Kehlkopfheilk.* 190:69–85

68. Finck, A. 1968. Analysis of single unit response areas in the cochlear nerve. *J. Aud. Res.* 8:207–13

69. Finck, A., Goehl, H. 1968. Vocal spectra and cochlear sensitivity in the Mongolian gerbil. *J. Aud. Res.* 8:63–69

70. Finck, A., Ronis, M. L., Rosenberg, P. E. 1969. Some relationships between audiometry and cochlear microphonics in man. *J. Speech Hear. Res.* 12:156–60

71. Fisher, H. G., Freedman, S. J. 1968. The role of the pinna in auditory localization. *J. Aud. Res.* 8:15–26

72. Flugrath, J. M. 1969. Modern day rock and roll music and damage risk criteria. *J. Acoust. Soc. Am.* 45:704–11

73. Fruhstörfer, H., Soveri, P., Jarvilehto, T. 1970. Short term habituation of the auditory evoked response in man. *EEG Clin. Neurophysiol.* 28:153–61

74. Gaudin, E. 1968. Die porose elastomere für Hörverbesserung bei Schadigunge des tympanalsystems. *Arch. Klin. Exp. Ohr. Nas. Kehlkopfheilk.* 192:351–57

75. Gerken, G. M. 1970. Electrical stimulation of the subcortical auditory system in behaving cat. *Brain Res.* 17:483–97

76. Glaninger, J. 1968. Freie transplantation konservierter menschicher gehorknochelchen. *Mschr. Ohrenheilk.* 102:609–23

77. Green, D. M. 1967. Additivity of masking. *J. Acoust. Soc. Am.* 41:1517–25

78. Green, D. M., Henning, G. B. 1969. Audition. *Ann. Rev. Psychol.* 20:105–28

79. Gribenski, A. 1968. L'Innervation efferente de la cochlée et son role. *Ann. Oto-Laryngol.* 85:511–23

80. Grinnell, A. D. 1969. Comparative physiology of hearing. *Ann. Rev. Physiol.* 31:545–80

81. Hack, M. H. 1968. The developmental Preyer reflex in the SH-1 mouse. *J. Aud. Res.* 8:449–58

82. Hadžiselimović, H., Andelić, M. 1967. A contribution to the knowledge of the ear in the sea turtle. *Acta Anat.* 66:460–77

83. Hall, J. G. 1967. Hearing and primary auditory centers of the whales. *Acta Otolaryngol. Suppl.* 224:244–50

84. Hall, J. G. 1969. The cochlea and the cochlear nuclei in the bat (*Plecotus auritus*). *Acta Otolaryngol.* 67:350–53

85. Ibid. The cochlea and the cochlear nuclei in the bat, 490–500

86. Hantman, I. 1968. An ear manikin. Teaching and training device. *Arch. Otolaryngol.* 88:407–12

87. Harris, J. D. 1970. An efficient monaural procedure for the psychoacoustic calibration of earphones. *J. Acoust. Soc. Am.* 47:1048–54

88. Heffner, H. E., Ravizza, R. J., Masterton, B. 1969. Hearing in primitive mammals. III. Tree shrew (*Tupaia glis*). *J. Aud. Res.* 9:12–18

89. Ibid. Hearing in primitive mammals. IV. Bush baby (*Galaga senegalensis*), 19–23

90. Hertzler, D. R., Saunders, J. C., Gourevitch, G. R., Herman, P. N. 1970. Cochlear and neural activity in the auditory system of the raccoon. *J. Aud. Res.* 10:155–63

91. Hinde, R. A. 1969. *Bird Vocalizations: Their Relations to Current Problems in Biology and Psychology.* Cambridge: Univ. Press

92. Hoffman, J. P., Walker, J. V., Wodin, L. R., Kayoda, S., Massopust, L. C. Jr. 1969. Evoked responses in the auditory cortex of the cebus monkey. *J. Aud Res.* 9:89–99

93. Holstein, S. B., Buchwald, J. S., Schwafel, J. A. 1969. Progressive changes in auditory response patterns during repeated tone during normal wakefulness and paralysis. *Brain Res.* 16:133–48

94. Homick, J. L., Elfner, L. F., Bothe, G. G. 1969. Auditory temporal masking and the perception of order. *J. Acoust. Soc. Am.* 45:712–18

95. Honrubia, V., Ward, P. H. 1969. Cochlear potentials inside the cochlear duct at the level of the round window. *Ann. Oto. Rhinol. Laryngol.* 78:1189–1200

96. Igarishi, M., Mahon, R. G. Jr., Konishi, S. 1968. Comparative measurements of cochlear apparatus. *J. Speech Hear. Res.* 11:229–35

97. Ingalls, C. E. 1967. Sensations of hearing in electromagnetic fields. *NY State J. Med.* 67:2992–97

98. Jeffress, L. A. Masking. See Ref. 209, 87–114

99. Johnstone, B. M., Taylor, K. J., Boyle, A. J. 1970. Mechanics of the guinea pig cochlea. *J. Acoust. Soc. Am.* 47:504–9

100. Kaneko, Y., Daly, J. F. 1968. Acetylcholinesterase on the nerve endings of outer hair cells and the tunnel radial fibers. *Laryngoscope* 78:1566–81

101. Keidel, W. D., Spreng, M. 1970. Recent status and problems of objective audiometry in man. *J. Franc. Otorhinolaryngol.* 19:45–60

102. Kern, E. B., Cody, D. T. R., Bickford, R. G. 1969. Vertex response thresholds to pure tones in guinea pigs. *Arch. Otolaryngol.* 90:315–25

103. Kern, E. B., Cody, D. T. R., Bickford, R. G. 1969. Neurogenic components of the averaged response evoked by clicks in guinea pigs. *Mayo Clin. Proc.* 44:886–99

104. Khanna, S. M., Sears, R. E., Tonndorf, J. 1968. Some properties of longitudinal shear waves: a study by computer simulation. *J. Acoust. Soc. Am.* 43:1077–84

105. Khanna, S. M., Tonndorf, J. 1969.

106. Kirikae, I. 1960. *The Structure and Function of the Middle Ear.* Univ. of Tokyo Press

107. Kittrell, B. J., Dalland, J. I. 1969. Frequency dependence of cochlear microphonic augmentation produced by olivocochlear bundle stimulation. *Laryngoscope* 79:228–38

108. Klinke, R., Boerger, G., Gruber, J. Studies on the functional significance of efferent innervation in the auditory system: afferent neuronal activity as influenced by contralaterally applied sound. *Pfluegers Arch.* 302:165–75

109. Knight, J. J., Beagley, H. A. 1969. Auditory evoked response and loudess function. *Int. Audiol.* 8:382–86

110. Knothe, J., Seidel, P., Flach, M. 1969. Die latenzeit des summenaktionspotentials (SAP) der cochlea, ihre exakts messung und die wirkung von strychnin auf die lange der latenzzeit. *Arch. Klin. Exp. Ohr. Nas. Kehlkopfheilk.* 193:121–27

111. Kohllöffel, L. U. E. 1970. Longitudinal amplitude and phase distribution of the cochlear microphonic (guinea pig) and spatial filtering. *J. Sound Vib.* 11:325–34

112. Konishi, M. 1969. Time resolution by single auditory neurones in birds. *Nature (London)* 222:566–67

113. Kryter, K. D. 1970. *The Effects of Noise on Man.* New York: Academic

114. Laszlo, C. A., Gannon, R. P., Milsum, J. H. 1970. Measurement of the cochlear potentials of the guinea pig at constant sound-pressure level at the eardrum. I. Cochlear-microphonic amplitude and phase. *J. Acoust. Soc. Am.* 47:1063–70

115. Lawrence, M. 1967. Electric polarization of the tectorial membrane. *Ann. Otol. Rhinol. Laryngol.* 76:287–312

116. Lawrence, M. 1968. Audition. *Ann. Rev. Psychol.* 19:1–26

117. Lebo, C. P., Oliphant, K. P. 1968. Music as a source of acoustic trauma. *Laryngoscope* 77:1211–18

118. Legouix, J. P. 1969. Étude experimentale de l'influence de la dureé du stimulus sur les réponses cochléaires

aux signaux transitoires. *Int. Audiol.* 8:591–94

119. Lehmann, R. 1969. *Éléments de Physio et de Psychoacoustique.* Paris: Dunod

120. Lim, D. J. 1969. Three dimensional observation of the inner ear with the scanning electron microscope. *Acta Otolaryngol. Suppl.* 255:38

121. Lim, D. J., Lane, W. C. 1969. Cochlear sensory epithelium. A scanning electron microscopic observation. *Ann. Otol. Rhinol. Laryngol.* 78:827–41

122. Lindner, W. A. 1968. Recognition performance as a function of detection criterion in a simultaneous detection-recognition task. *J. Acoust. Soc. Am.* 44:204–11

123. Lipscomb, D. M. 1969. Ear damage from exposure to rock and roll music. *Arch. Otolaryngol.* 90:545–55

124. McArdle, F. E., Tonndorf, J. 1968. Perforations of the tympanic membrane and their effects upon middle ear transmission. *Arch. Klin. Exp. Ohr. Nas. Kehlkopfheilk.* 192:145–62

125. McCandless, G. A., Lentz, W. E. 1968. Amplitude and latency characteristics of the auditory evoked response at low sensation levels. *J. Aud. Res.* 8:273–82

126. McCormick, J. G., Wever, E. G., Palin, J. 1970. Sound conduction in the dolphin ear. *J. Acoust. Soc. Am.* 48:1418–28

127. McCue, J. J. G. 1969. Signal processing in the bat (*Myotis lucifugus*). *J. Aud. Res.* 9:100–7

128. McFadden, D. 1968. Masking-level differences determined with and without interaural disparities in masker intensity. *J. Acoust. Soc. Am.* 44:212–23

129. McKay, J. M. 1969. The auditory system of Homorocoryphus (tettigonioidea, orthoptera). *J. Exp. Biol.* 51:787–802

130. McRobert, H., Bryan, M. E., Tempest, W. 1969. The effect of middle ear muscle contractions on sound transmission through the human ear. *Int. Audiol.* 8:557–62

131. Manley, G. A. 1970. Frequency sensitivity of auditory neurons in the Caiman cochlear nucleus. *Z. Vergl. Physiol.* 66:251–56

132. Ibid. Comparative studies of auditory physiology in reptiles. 67:363–81

133. Mast, T. E. 1970. Binaural interaction and contralateral inhibition in dorsal cochlear nucleus of the chinchilla. *J. Neurophysiol.* 33:108–15

134. Masterton, B., Heffner, H., Ravizza, R. 1969. The evolution of human hearing. *J. Acoust. Soc. Am.* 45:966–85

135. Miller, J. D. 1970. Audibility curve of the chinchilla. *J. Acoust. Soc. Am.* 48:513–23

136. Miller, J. D., Luz, G. A. 1970. A 'learning-set' procedure for sound quality discrimination by chinchillas. *J. Aud. Res.* 10:136–46

137. Miller, J. M., Moody, D. B., Stebbins, W. C. 1969. Evoked potentials and auditory reaction time in monkeys. *Science* 163:592–94

138. Mitchell, C., Gillette, R., Vernon, J., Herman, P. 1970. Pure-tone auditory behavioral thresholds in three species of lemurs. *J. Acoust. Soc. Am.* 48:531–35

139. Mitra, J., Snider, R. S. 1969. Cerebellar modification of unitary discharges in auditory system. *Exp. Neurol.* 23:341–52

140. Miyahara, T., Kawata, T., Morizono, T., Sueta, T. 1967. Pressure changes in the middle ear cavity following acoustic stimulation in the cat. *Otol. Fukuoka*, Suppl. 1, 13:165–75

141. Møhl, B. 1968. Auditory sensitivity of the common seal in air and water. *J. Aud. Res.* 8:27–38

142. Moore, E. J., Reneau, J. P. 1969. Averaged electroencephalic responses to sound stimuli obtained by direct method recording and radio telemetry. *Int. Audiol.* 8:639–50

143. Mulligan, B. E., Adams, J. C., Mulligan, M. J., Burwinkle, R. E. 1968. Prediction of monaural detection. *J. Acoust. Soc. Am.* 43:481–86

144. Neergaard, E. B., Rasmussen, P. E. 1967. Extratympanic phonometry. *Acta Otolaryngol. Suppl.* 224:372–75

145. Nitschkoff, S., Kriwizkaja, G. 1969. *Larmbelastung, Akustischer Reize und Neurovegatitive Storungen.* Leipzig: Georg Thieme. 312 pp.

146. Nordmark, J. O. 1968. Mechanisms of frequency discrimination. *J. Acoust. Soc. Am.* 44:1533–40

147. Nordmark, J. O. 1970. Time and frequency analysis. See Ref. 209, 57–83

148. Nordmark, J. O., Glattke, T. J., Schubert, E. D. 1969. Waveform preservation in the cochlea. *J. Acoust. Soc. Am.* 46:1587–88

149. Offutt, G. C. 1968. Auditory response in the goldfish. *J. Aud. Res.* 8:391–400

150. Onishi, S., Davis, H. 1968. Effects of duration and rise time of tone bursts on evoked V potentials. *J. Acoust. Soc. Am.* 44:582–91

151. Osen, K. K. 1969. The intrinsic organization of the cochlear nuclei in the cat. *Acta Otolaryngol.* 67:352–59

152. Papparella, M. N. 1970. *Biochemical Mechanisms in Hearing and Deafness.* Springfield, Ill.: Thomas

153. Patterson, W. C., Evering, F. C., McNall, C. L. 1968. The relationship of temperature to the cochlear response in a poikilotherm. *J. Aud. Res.* 8:439–48

154. Payne, M. C. Jr., Githler, F. J. 1951. Effects of perforations of the tympanic membrane on cochlear potentials. *Arch. Otolaryngol.* 54:666–74

155. Peterson, E. A., Heaton, W. C. 1968. Peripheral auditory responses in representative edentates. *J. Aud. Res.* 8:171–84

156. Peterson, E. A., Pate, W. E., Wruble, S. D. 1966. Cochlear potentials in the dog: I. Differences with variation in external-ear structure. *J. Aud. Res.* 6:1–11

157. Peterson, E. A., Wruble, S. D., Ponzoli, V. I. 1968. Auditory responses in tree shrews and primates. *J. Aud. Res.* 8:345–55

158. Pfafflin, S. M. 1968. Detection of auditory signal in restricted sets of reproducible noise. *J. Acoust. Soc. Am.* 43:487–90

159. Pfalz, R. K. J. 1969. Absence of a function for the crossed olivocochlear bundle under physiological conditions. *Arch. Klin. Exp. Ohr. Nas. Kehlkopfheilk.* 193:89–100

160. Pfalz, R. K. J. 1969. The ventral cochlear nucleus: the significance of the crossed, inhibitory pathways towards the nucleus for directional hearing. *Advan. Oto-Rhino-Laryngol.* 16:1–94

161. Pierrel, R., Sherman, G., Blue, S., Hegge, F. W. 1970. Auditory discrimination: a three-variable analysis of intensity effects. *J. Exp. Anal. Behav.* 13:17–35

162. Plomp, R., Smoorenburg, G. F., Eds. 1970. *Frequency Analysis and Periodicity Detection in Hearing.* Leiden: Sijthoff

163. Pollack, I. 1964. Interaction of forward and backward masking. *J. Aud. Res.* 4:63–67

164. Portmann, M. 1967. Symposium on the sensory cell of Corti's organ. *Acta Otolaryngol. Suppl.* 63. 71 pp.

165. Prasch, G., Siegl, H. 1969. Gehorseindrucke durch einwirkung von tonfrequenten wechselstromen und amplituden modulierten hochfrequenzstromen. *Arch. Klin. Exp. Ohr. Nas. Kehlkopfheilk.* 194:516–21

166. Pražma, J. 1969. Passive ion transport through the Reissner membrane. *Acta. Otolaryngol.* 68:53–61

167. Price, L. L. 1969. Cortical-evoked response audiometry. In *Audiometry for the Retarded,* ed. R. T. Fulton, L. L. Lloyd, 210–37. Baltimore: Williams and Wilkins

168. Price, L. L., Dalton, L. W. Jr., Smith, J. C. 1967. Frequency DL in the pigeon as determined by conditioned suppression. *J. Aud. Res.* 7:229–39

169. Puharich, H. K., Lawrence, J. L. 1969. Hearing rehabilitation by means of transdermal electrotherapy in human hearing loss of sensorineural origin. Preliminary report. *Acta. Otolaryngol.* 67:69–83

170. Raab, D. 1971. Audition. *Ann. Rev. Psychol.* 22:95–118

171. Rapin, I., Graziani, L., Lyttle, M. 1969. Summated auditory evoked responses for audiometry. Experience in 51 children with congenital rubella. *Int. Audiol.* 8:371–76

172. Rau, R. M. 1968. Über die Abhängigkeit der objektiv ermittelten Intensitätsfunktion des menschlichen Gehors von der Tonfolgefrequenz. *Arch. Klin. Exp. Ohr. Nas. Kehlkopfheilk.* 190:133–45

173. Rauch, S. 1964. *Biochemie des Hororgans.* Stuttgart: Georg Thieme

174. Ravizza, R. J., Heffner, H. E., Masterton, B. 1969. Hearing in primitive mammals. I. Opossum (*Didelphus virginianus*). *J. Aud. Res.* 9:1–7

175. Ibid. Hearing in primitive mammals. II. Hedgehog (*Hemiechinus auritus*), 8–11

176. Rintelmann, W. F., Borns, J. F. 1968. Noise-induced hearing loss and rock and roll music. *Arch. Otolaryngol.* 88:377–85

177. Roeser, R. J., Price, L. L. 1969. Effects of habituation on the auditory evoked response. *J. Aud. Res.* 9:306–13

178. Roffler, S. K., Butler, R. A. 1968. Factors that influence the localiza-

tion of sound in the vertical plane. *J. Acoust. Soc. Am.* 43:1255–59

179. Rose, D. E., Lambert, P. D., Morgan, R. J., Garner, R. J. 1970. Auditory acuity in the beagle measured by EEG evoked potential. *J. Aud. Res.* 10:151–54

180. Rosenfeld, J. P., Rudell, A. P., Fox, S. S. 1969. Operant of neural events in humans. *Science* 165:821–23

181. Rossi, G., Cortesina, G., Robecchi, M. G. 1967. Cerebellifugal fibres to the cochlear nuclei and superior olivary complex. *Int. Audiol.* 6:375–79

182. Rupert, A. L., Moushegian, G. 1970. Neuronal responses of kangaroo rat ventral cochlear nucleus to low frequency tones. *Exp. Neurol.* 26:84–102

183. Sakabe, N., Arayama, T., Suzuki, T. 1969. Human fetal evoked response to acoustic stimulation. *Acta Otolaryngol. Suppl.* 252:29–36

184. Sato, R., Ono, Y. 1969. The displacement of the stapes by the reflex of the human stapedius muscle. *Acta Otolaryngol.* 68:509–13

185. Shaw, E. A. G. 1969. Hearing threshold and ear-canal pressure levels with varying acoustic field. *J. Acoust. Soc. Am.* 46:1502–14

186. Shaw, E. A. G., Teranishi, R. 1968. Sound pressure generated in an external-ear replica and real human ears by a nearby point source. *J. Acoust. Soc. Am.* 44:240–49

187. Small, A. M. Jr. Periodicity pitch. See Ref. 209, 3–54

188. Sohmer, H., Feinmesser, M. 1967. Cochlear action potentials recorded from the external ear in man. *Ann. Otol. Rhinol. Laryngol.* 76:427–35

189. Soliman, S. M. 1969. The auditory evoked response of mice with different brain weights. *J. Aud. Res.* 9:338–51

190. Spreng, M. 1969. Problems in objective cerebral audiometry using short sound stimulation. *Int. Audiol.* 8:424–29

191. Spreng, M., Keidel, W. D. 1967. Separierung von Cerebroaudiogramm (CAG), Neuroaudiogramm (NAG) and Otoaudiogramm (OAG) in der objektiven Audiometrie. *Arch. Klin. Exp. Ohr. Nas. Kehlkopfheilk.* 189:225–46

192. Spreng, M., Keidel, W. D. 1970. Recent status results and problems of objective audiometry in man. Part 2. *J. Franc. Otorhinolaryngol.* 19:55–60

193. Spychala, P., Rose, D. E., Grier, J. B. 1969. Comparison of the 'on' and 'off' characteristics of the acoustically evoked response. *Int. Audiol.* 8:416–23

194. Stephens, S. D. G. 1969. Auditory threshold variance, signal detection theory and personality. *Int. Audiol.* 8:131–37

195. Stewart, K. C., Burgi, E. J. 1970. Loudness balance study of selected audiometer earphones. *U. S. Pub. Health Serv.*, Nat. Center for Health Statistics, Publ. No. 1000-2-No. 40

196. Strother, W. F. 1967. Hearing in the chinchilla (*Chinchilla lanigera*): I. Cochlear potentials. *J. Aud. Res.* 7:145–55

197. Suga, F., Hattler, K. W. 1970. Physiological and histopathological correlates of hereditary deafness in animals. *Laryngoscope* 80:80–104

198. Suga, N. 1968. Neural responses to sound in a Brazilian mole cricket. *J. Aud. Res.* 8:129–134

199. Suzuki, T., Origuchi, K. 1969. Averaged evoked response audiometry (ERA) in young children during sleep. *Acta Otolaryngol. Suppl.* 252:19–28

200. Swisher, L. P. 1967. Auditory intensity discrimination in patients with temporal lobe damage. *Cortex* 3:179–93

201. Symmes, D. 1967. Behavioral and electrophysiological studies on auditory functions of the frontal lobe in monkeys, *J. Aud. Res.* 7:335–51

202. Taguchi, K., Picton, T. W., Orpin, J. A., Goodman, W. S. 1969. Evoked response audiometry in newborn infants. *Acta Otolaryngol. Suppl.* 252:5–17

203. Taylor, M. M., Forbes, S. M. 1969. Monaural detection with contralateral cue. I. Better than energy detection performance by human observers. *J. Acoust. Soc. Am.* 46:1519–26

204. Teas, D. C., Henry, G. B. 1969. Auditory nerve responses as a function of repetition rate and background noise. *Int. Audiol.* 8:147–63

205. Teig, E. 1969. Tension and contraction velocity of single motor units of the stapedius muscle. *Acta Physiol. Scand.* 76:16A–17A

206. Teranishi, R., Shaw, E. A. G. 1968. External-ear acoustic models with simple geometry. *J. Acoust. Soc. Am.* 44:257–63

207. Terman, M. 1970. Discrimination of auditory intensities by rats. *J. Exp. Anal. Behav.* 13:145–60

208. Tietze, G. 1969. Zeitverhalten des akustischen reflexes bei reizung mit dauertonen. *Arch. Klin. Exp. Ohr. Nas. Kehlkopfheilk*, 193:43–52

209. Tobias, J. V. 1970. *Foundations of Modern Auditory Theory*, Vol. I. New York: Academic

210. Tonndorf, J., Khanna, S. M. 1968. Submicroscopic displacement amplitudes of the tympanic membrane (cat) measured by a laser interferometer. *J. Acoust. Soc. Am.* 44:1546–54

211. Tonndorf, J., Khanna, S. M. 1970. The role of the tympanic membrane in middle ear transmission. *Ann. Otol. Rhinol. Laryngol.* 79: 743–53

212. Tonndorf, J., Khanna, S. M., Fingerhood, B. J. 1966. The input impedance of the inner ear in cats. *Ann. Otol. Rhinol. Laryngol.* 75: 752–63

213. Tyberghein, J., Forrez, G. 1969. Cerebral evoked potentials and presbycusis. *Int. Audiol.* 8:377–81

214. Van Noort, J. 1969. *The Structure and Connections of the Inferior Colliculus.* Assen, Holland: Van Gorcum

215. Vinnikov, Y. A., Titova, L. K. 1964. *The Organ of Corti.* New York: Consultants Bureau

216. Ward, W. D. Musical perception. See Ref. 209, 407–47

217. Weiss, B. A. 1969. Lateral-line sensitivity in the goldfish. *J. Aud. Res.* 9:71–75

218. Welch, B. L., Welch, A. S., Eds. 1970. *Psychological Effects of Noise.* New York: Plenum

219. Wever, E. G. 1967. Tonal differentiation in the lizard ear. *Laryngoscope* 77:1962–73

220. Wever, E. G., Herman, P. N. 1968. Stridulation and hearing in the tenrec, *Hemicentetes semispinosus. J. Aud. Res.* 8:39–42

221. Wightman, F. L. 1969. Binaural masking with sine wave maskers. *J. Acoust. Soc. Am.* 45:72–78

222. Wing, H. 1968. *Tests of Musical Ability and Appreciation.* New York: Cambridge Univ. Press. 2nd ed.

223. Wodak, E. 1967. Uber die Stellung und Form der menschlichen Ohrmuschel. *Arch. Klin. Exp. Ohr. Nas. Kehlkopfheilk.* 188:331–36

224. Wollack, C. H. 1965. Auditory thresholds in the raccoon (*Procyon lotor*). *J. Aud. Res.* 5:139–44

225. Yoshie, N. 1968. Auditory nerve action potential responses to clicks in man. *Laryngoscope* 78:198–215

226. Yoshie, N., Ohashi, T. 1969. Clinical use of cochlear nerve action potential responses in man for differential diagnosis of hearing losses. *Acta Otolaryngol. Suppl.* 252:71–87

227. Yoshie, N., Yamaura, K. 1969. Cochlear microphonic responses to pure tones in man recorded by a nonsurgical method. *Acta Otolaryngol. Suppl.* 252:37–69

228. Zöllner, F., Stange, G. 1967. Augmentation of the compound action potential of the acoustic nerve by isolated damage of central auditory pathway. *Int. Audiol.* 6:369–74

229. Zöllner, F., Stange, G. 1971. Efferente Summenaktionspotentiale am Nervus Cochlearis des Meerschweinchens bei kontralateraler Beschallung. *Arch. Klin. Exp. Ohr. Nas. Kehlkopfheilk.* 197:331–50

230. Zwislocki, J. J. 1970. An acoustic coupler for earphone calibration. Special Report, Laboratory of Sensory Communication, Syracuse Univ.

231. Zwislocki, J. J., Buining, E., Glantz, J. 1968. Frequency distribution of central masking. *J. Acoust. Soc. Am.* 43:1267–71

232. Zwislocki, J. J., Damianopoulos, E. N., Buining, E., Glantz, J. 1967. Central masking: some steady-state and transient effects. *Percept. Psychophys.* 2:59–64

COLOR VISION

184

P. L. WALRAVEN

Institute for Perception TNO, Soesterberg, The Netherlands

The previous review on color vision by Ripps & Weale (187) gave a useful outline of the field; this review will follow the same general format. Some elements of Alpern's review (6) on the distal mechanisms of vertebrate color vision are also included. For a long time color vision was a field for psychophysicists. Therefore theories of color vision were developed to explain certain aspects of color perception without taking into account "what is really going on" in the retina and the visual nervous system. What color vision theory must do, after all, is explain and describe how and what we see, in terms of what we call color. Objective studies of biochemistry and physical absorption of visual pigments, of the electrophysiological activity in the retina, lateral geniculate nucleus and higher centers do restrict the possibilities for a theory, but they leave much room for speculation. However, these objective data are not suitable as a basis for color vision theory without the reports of observers, often called subjective data. Both objective and subjective data must be explained. Altogether color vision is a fascinating topic for study. The tremendous amount of literature reflects this. Only by strict selection and limitation could this review be kept within prescribed length.

GENERAL REFERENCES

The excellent book by Cornsweet (43) is a useful general reference. It is not only a guide and introduction to the field, but also a source of much enjoyable reading for experts. Introductions such as those by Weale (246) and Le Grand (123) are worth mentioning here. For a more penetrating introduction, the text of an "Enrico Fermi" course (179) is recommended. Brindley's book has appeared in a second edition (29). MacAdam (133) has assembled a number of color classics ranging from Plato to Le Gros Clark into a fascinating book.

A critical analysis of present theory, written in a provocative style, is provided by Sheppard (199). This book is useful since it points out that conclusions long taken for granted are now open for criticism. However, Sheppard himself is somewhat trapped by the complexity of color vision, as indicated by Hurvich & Jameson (98) in an essay review. In a review paper by Autrum (16) on color vision in man and animals, the emphasis is on the color vision of insects. He cannot be blamed for that.

Color vision deficiency has been surveyed by Verriest (230), and a new approach to color blindness is presented in a book by Cruz-Coke (45). Surveys on the photophysiology and the physics of vertebrate color vision are given by Ripps & Weale (188) and Ruddock (189), respectively. For a good insight into the recent research on the retina, an assembly of papers edited by Ashton (15) is recommended.

The appearance of survey papers in *Color Engineering* is an encouraging sign. These papers provide knowledge outside the narrow world of specialists and contribute to practical applications. Examples of such papers include the description of color vision mechanisms by Boynton (25), the discussions of metamerism by Nimeroff (162) and Allen (4, 5), the history of the Munsell system by Nickerson (160), and the ideal color space by Judd (109). Nimeroff (163) has also written a booklet on colorimetry. This topic is covered in references by Wyszecki (251) in the series of Optical Resource Letters.

The proceedings of the first congress of the Association Internationale de la Couleur in Stockholm in 1969 (178) are an important source of information. The congress of course covered much more than color vision. The proceedings make clear how interdisciplinary is the study of color.

Objective Studies

Absorption of the ocular media.—In two studies on the yellow pigment of the human lens an interesting result is reported. Contrary to common belief the pigment concentration is found not to increase with age. Cooper & Robson (41) tried to explain the changes in overall density which they observed by supposing that a new pigment appeared in later life, which they were not able to extract. The report of Mellerio (144) suggests the explanation: the density per unit pathlength is constant, but the pathlength increases significantly with age. The absolute density values given are in good correspondence with other findings (Wyszecki & Stiles 252).

The absorption in fish eyes has also been discussed in some recent reports (28, 134, 153).

The early receptor potential (ERP).—Not much progress has been made in understanding this very rapid electrical response to an intense light flash. It was already known that in a mixed retina like the frog's, the ERP seems to be generated almost exclusively by the cone system. This is confirmed in the studies by Goldstein & Berson (66, 67). In normal human and macaque retinae it was estimated that the rods contributed only 20–40 percent to the total ERP response. In a study of subjects with a loss of rod or cone function this was confirmed (19). A new issue was raised in this study by the observation that loss of rod function (in retinitis pigmentosa) accompanies the shortening of cone ERP recovery by a factor of five. Concerning the origin of the rod ERP, Hagins & Rüppel (81) gave conclusive evidence that these voltages arise as displacements of charge in the plasma membranes at the outer segments.

Receptors, pigments, and waveguides.—The common distinction between rods and cones on the grounds of morphological differences has often been questioned. However, new data have come from an unexpected source to support the concept that there are two distinct classes of visual receptor cells. Using the method of autoradiographic labeling of proteins, Young (255) has uncovered a difference in the behavior of the disc structure of rods and cones. In the outer segments of mature rods the disc structure is continually renewed by a process of repeated disc assembly at the base of the outer segment. At the apex of the outer segment the discs are destroyed. The cones, on the contrary, behave completely differently. The new protein simply diffuses into the existing disc structure, and evidently no new discs are produced. Another important conclusion from this study is that a specific retinal dysfunction resulting from a failure of the disc renewal mechanism may be expected and is indeed observed.

Another difference between rods and cones is now becoming clear. That is, that the absorption curves of primate cone pigments are definitely narrower than those of rod pigments. Most pigments follow Dartnall's rule; that is, their action spectra are identical, apart from a translation parallel to the abscissa axis if this axis is scaled in frequencies. The absorption curves of cone pigments are narrower, compared to most of the other pigments plotted in this way. This should prove that retinal is not the prosthetic group of cone pigment. Le Grand (124) applies Dartnall's rule to these narrower action spectra and shows that the rule remains valid.

The density of human cone pigments had been a matter of dispute. Though earlier microspectrophotometric (33, 137) and densitometric (193, 247) reports never mentioned a value above 0.3, the recent report of Dobelle, Marks & MacNichol (52) suggests much higher values (> 0.7). This finding probably ends the dispute over whether the self-screening hypothesis, which needs high density values (92), could explain deviations in color-matching data after bleaching (30, 219), changes in the Stiles-Crawford effect after bleaching (238), and the second Stiles-Crawford effect (239). A tetrachromatic hypothesis like that suggested by Ingling (104), in which a low density is assumed, is then not necessary.

The primaries derived from the absorption data of Marks, Dobelle & MacNichol (137), particularly for the shortwave receptors, do not fit with the primaries derived from color mixture data or with data on the confusion loci of dichromats (234). This is a warning not to use these curves as the fundamental response curves of the three-color mediating systems, but to use them merely as an indication of the existence of three different pigments.

The microspectrophotometric experiments of Liebman strongly demonstrate the power of this method (128). Though the error typically present in these measurements is much greater than that in measurements on extracted pigments, the experiments can be repeated many times on the same type of cone. Another important advantage is that pigments can be measured which represent minority populations (e.g. 0.5 percent of total pigment). Moreover, the cell type is identified together with the pigment. Liebman's measurements on the turtle pigment reveal an interesting property of this retina. Despite the presence of colored oil drops, which normally would indicate that only one type of visual pigment was present (117, 171), three different cone pigments are actually found (127).

Friedman & Kuwabara (62) found, on the basis of data obtained from infrared interference microscopic examination of single photoreceptors in the frog before and after bleaching, measurable photoreceptor outer-segment swelling coupled with a decrease of index of refraction. These findings have been confirmed by Enoch (54), who interpreted them as having implications on waveguide properties. These may change at high bleaching levels, resulting in the change of efficiency of transmission of the waveguide as a function of wavelength. They could also be a source of error in fundus reflectometry determinations. Snyder & Hall (203) suggest that one photopigment can give pigment responses in different parts of the spectrum, due to different waveguide properties of the three types of receptors. This idea fails, however, because the spectral absorption of the receptors is not very dependent upon the direction of light.

S potentials.—A lucidly written article by Rushton (194) reviews the literature before 1968. Since then Brown & Murakami (32) were able to separate the rod and cone contribution to the S potential solely by examining the waveform. Steinberg extended this work and proved in a series of papers (209–212) that in the cat retina the S potentials of the L type reveal a Purkinje shift and also that rod and cone inputs are added independently in one L-type unit. This latter finding is in correspondence with Gouras' (68) report of rod and cone independence in the monkey's electroretinogram.

In contrast, Maksimova & Maksimov (136), measuring the fish retina, report that an L-type cell which has been saturated by input of one receptor cannot respond to excitation of another receptor type. The conclusion seems justified in that for some fishes only one receptor type contributes to one L-type unit (121), so no mixing of the output of different types of receptors occurs at or before this level. The authors suggest that the discrepancy among various reports on the matter of multiple input to L units might result either because there are different types of L units or because deterioration of the preparation causes measurement of two or more L units at the same time.

The origin of the S potentials seems to have to be found. In several types of fish (113, 114, 249) and in the cat (212) the old hypothesis that the horizontal cells are the generators of S potentials is now confirmed by intracellular dye injection. In this procedure the microelectrode is inserted into the cell, the intracellular potentials are measured, and then a dye is electrophoretically injected which stains the cell for later histological identification. Most of the work has been done on L-type units, which give a hyperpolarizing response to light. Kaneko (113) suggests that the C type, which changes its response polarity according to wavelength, also comes from the horizontal cells. No histological differences were seen between cells giving either the C- or the L-type response.

The electroretinogram (ERG).—Up to now many ERG experiments on selective adaptation have shown only very limited wavelength selectivity. Sternheim & Riggs (214) announced some effects with the alternating barred pattern method, but the results have not yet been published. However, Padmos & Van Norren (169) showed that with improved stimulus and recording techniques selective adaptation proved clearly demonstrable and that the results of both ERG and psychophysical experiments with strong colored backgrounds are the same. This opens a way of deriving the three fundamental response curves from ERG data. Contrary to the hypothesis of Alfieri & Solé (3), it is concluded that the differences in adaptation are mainly due to the fact that different proportions of scotopic and photopic activity are evoked by the various wavelengths.

Gouras (72) describes some basic principles of electroretinography and emphasizes that they provide a valuable link with those molecular and biochemical events in vision which are at the root of many inherited and acquired retinal abnormalities. The clinical applications of ERG methods to the problem of color blindness are discussed by Van Lith (228). While the protanope can be easily identified by his depressed sensitivity on the red side of the spectrum, the deuteranope cannot be identified since hardly any change in absolute and relative sensitivity can be found. A new application of the Stiles-Crawford effect is described by Sternheim & Riggs (214). It was only under conditions designed to elicit photopic stimulation that a decrease in efficiency of evoking a criterion response was observed. Thus the Stiles-Crawford effect serves as an indicator of whether or not the measured electrical activity was initiated by cones.

Though not directly related to color vision, the reviews of Brown (31) and Dowling (53) are worth mentioning since they discuss the relations between retinal structures and the different components of the ERG.

Electroretinography provides a valuable tool for the study of animal retinas. In the last few years the spectral sensitivity of many animals has been investigated: the baboon (2), the octopus (83), the goldfish (34), a teleost fish (164), the frog (61), and the hooded rat (205). Most of the authors used chromatic adaptation in order to detect the extent to which more than one system contributed to the overall sensitivity function. The isolated cone systems are often compared with a Dartnall pigment. The described correspondence does not seem very convincing in view of the experimental error (61).

A technique that is now used frequently records simultaneously electrical responses from the eye and the scalp. Recent advances in stimulus and recording techniques (13) make the comparison of the signals more appropriate and suggest that this technique may become a valuable tool for clinical diagnosis (12, 131). The representation of the retina on the visual cortex can be investigated (14), together with retinal interaction effects (189). Riggs & Sternheim (185) compared wavelength discrimination functions at different stages of the visual system and concluded that an enhancement of discrimination takes place somewhere between ganglion cell and striate cortex.

One very important observation with respect to the ERG a wave has recently been made by Hagins et al (80). They studied the late receptor potential—generally accepted to be identical with the P III or a wave—in isolated rat retina, directly at the site of the outer segment of the rods. Flashes of light produce a photocurrent in the outer segments, which reduces transiently the steady dark current. The action of light is local within 12μ of the point of light absorption, and the electrical effects of the photocurrent are large enough to permit detection of single photons by the visual system. So this a-wave, like the photocurrent, is the primary effect of light absorption by the pigment.

Ganglion cell.—Working with the macaque, Gouras (69–71) partially isolated and identified blue, green, and red cone mechanisms at the level of the retinal ganglion cells. The spectral sensitivities which he measured for these mechanisms were about the same as those determined on the basis of human psychophysics. He distinguished two main classes of cells. The transient brisk firing cells with synergistic red and green input he called phasic cells. Cells which have excitatory input from one of the three cone mechanisms and inhibitory input from another cone mechanism he called tonic, because their response was maintained for a long time. By antidromic stimulation of the optic tract, Gouras (71) found that phasic cells have a conduction velocity twice that of tonic cells. Some other findings combined with these led him to postulate that the group of tonic cells is probably identical with Polyak's (177) monosynaptic midget system.

In a series of three articles, Michael (147–149) described the properties of the all-cone retina of the ground squirrel. Twenty-five percent of the cells had an opponent color response composed of a blue (460 nm) and a green (525 nm) mechanism. Red-green receptor inputs were not found, and the nonopponent cells seemed to get their input exclusively from the green cones. Both Gouras and Michael found a center-surround type of organization of the receptive fields. In the ground squirrel, however, 25 percent of the cells had a clear directional movement sensitivity.

With the discovery of "double-opponent" color cells in the goldfish retina, Daw (46) provides new evidence on the cellular basis of color contrast. These cells gave an "on" response to green light and an "off" response to red light in the periphery of the receptive field, and an "on" response to red light and an "off" response to green light in the center (or vice versa). The double-opponent type of cell constitutes half of the ganglion cells found on the goldfish retina. However, in the primate visual system, indications are that only an extremely small fraction of cells have similar properties (93). Two other studies on nonmammalian color vision have shown that most of the frog's ganglion cells receive input from at least two photopic mechanisms (195) and that the plaice besides rods, has several cone mechanisms which may interact in a color-opponent way.

Lateral geniculate nucleus (LGN).—Comparison of behavioral and electrophysiological experiments between macaque and squirrel monkeys by De Valois & Jacobs (48) supports the hypothesis that at the level of the LGN, nonopponent cells are brightness (or, rather whiteness) coders and spectral opponent cells are hue coders. Compared with the macaque, which has a color vision very similar to normal human trichromats, the squirrel monkey has a relative paucity of opponent cells. In addition, its nonopponent system has much less sensitivity to longer wavelengths, and the ratio of opponent to nonopponent cell spectral sensitivity is minimal near 500 nm. This is all in accordance with behavioral data on hue discrimination, spectral sensitivity, and saturation, which classifies the squirrel monkey as identical with protanomalous trichromats.

Using presumed spectral absorption of pairs of photopigments, Abramov (1) was able to predict the output of single cells in LGN. In this analysis the R-G (red-green) opponent system was assumed to be constituted of 535 nm and 570 nm cone mechanisms, and the Y-B (yellow-blue) system of 445 nm and 570 nm cone types. Because of the somewhat arbitrary choice of underlying receptor mechanisms, one may ask how much the prediction depends on the various possible interactions at the LGN level. (Note: One must keep in mind that the nomenclature Red-Green and Yellow-Blue applies only to the colors corresponding to the spectral regions of maximal sensitivity which lie on each side of the neutral point of the cell. The naming of the presumed three cone types in the human as blue, green, and red is often used as shorthand to denote wavelengths of maximal absorption and is not to be confused with De Valois' nomenclature.)

Until now the function of the LGN in primate vision is still rather obscure, the main characteristics of cells in LGN being about the same as at the ganglion cell level. De Valois & Pease (49) examined the responses of single units in the monkey LGN to different portions of figures which differed from their background in color and brightness. Border enhancement was found in the response to luminance figures but not in the response to color figures. In situations in which a very striking brightness contrast is seen perceptually, the cells do not show the corresponding changes in firing rate across the whole pattern. The lateral inhibitory mechanisms found in the retina and geniculate can thus account for luminance border enhancement, but not entirely for simultaneous brightness or color contrast, for which other cortical processes of some sort must be responsible. In the work of Hull (95) a corticofugal influence was established by cooling the cortical projection areas. The effect of cooling made clear that the cortical input to LGN could be either facilitation or inhibition, depending on the cell under study. How much color vision can be altered by cortical influence cannot be determined from this paper. The weak color vision which the cat is known to possess (47) is confirmed electrophysiologically by Pearlman & Daw (170). They gave evidence for the existence of a small fraction of opponent cells associated with 450 nm and 556 nm cone mechanism.

Cortex.—To our knowledge, after the early work of Lennox-Buchtal (125) and Motokawa et al (156) no work had been published on color coding in single cortical cells of primates until the paper of Gouras (73). Most of the cells described by Gouras have a phasic firing character and show on- and off-discharges with a very low spontaneous activity. By means of chromatic adaptation, three cone mechanisms could be identified. The major finding of the paper is that many cells which apparently have something to do with color coding receive excitatory inputs from two of three cone mechanisms (either at light-on or light-off, depending on the cone mechanism) with no sign of mutual inhibition of cone inputs. This is in clear contrast to the macaque LGN where the cells generally are excited or inhibited by a cone mechanism. Moreover, it has never been demonstrated that more than two cone mechanisms feed into one LGN cell, while a part of the cortical cells receive input of three cone mechanisms. Gouras' work has been performed with flashing light, so no relation with movement-sensitive cells is established.

Visual evoked potential (VEP).—The interpretation of the scalp-recorded electrical responses to monochromatic stimuli remains a difficult affair. The variances in measurement due to electrode position and subject differences are sizable. It is even suggested that the dispute on whether or not the waveform changes with stimulus wavelength (36, 37, 115, 140, 200) can be resolved by dividing all subjects in two classes: coders and noncoders. Ripps' & Weale's expectation in their 1969 review that "it may soon be possible to determine spectral sensitivities of mechanisms which contribute to the evoked potential" has not yet been fulfilled. A reliable determination of the overall spectral sensitivity (141, 186) seems quite difficult and still cannot compete with retinographically determined sensitivity in terms of variability.

The dominance of long wavelength stimuli in the recorded pattern is described by Ciganek & Shipley (37) and May & Siegfried (141). As far as the clinical value of the VEP is concerned, the remarkable feature is that while ERG measurements cannot reveal deutan abnormalities, the VEP does show deviations from the normal patterns in these cases (115, 130, 172, 200).

Regan (181) tried rather unsuccessfully to correlate flicker threshold and the minimum in the fundamental evoked potential. Massopust et al (138) measured evoked responses at the surface of the visual cortex of the squirrel monkey. They showed differences in response to a red and a blue stimulus, which were dependent upon the place on the visual cortex. This paper may suggest that the proportions of rod and cone projections to the cortex may vary with location.

No work on evoked potentials and color perception has any obvious relation to findings at the single cell level in retina, LGN, or cortex. Regan measured the VEP due to sinusoidally modulated light (180). Chromatic adaptation produced marked changes in the curve of response amplitude versus stimulus modulation frequency. The changes depended strongly on the color, but little on the intensity of the adapting light. Lateral interactions whose propagation speeds were color dependent are supposed.

SUBJECTIVE STUDIES

Threshold, color naming.—Schmidt-Clausen (198) measured the effectiveness of short flashes compared to continuous light as a function of background luminance. The Blondel-Rey formula proved to be correct for the achromatic threshold, but not for the chromatic threshold. The author presents formulas which describe the deviations as a function of wavelength.

Hargroves & Hargroves (84) reviewed the work done with flashing lights from 1711 to 1969; their paper makes quick access to the relevant literature possible.

Color naming is recognized as a useful tool for studying color discrimination. It is possible to obtain quite reliable results with this technique (26, 106). Applied to color defective subjects, significant information about color recognition and discrimination can be obtained. In this way Scheibner & Boynton (196) showed that in most cases of very strong red-green deficiency there still is residual color discrimination. This result is confirmed by Iinuma et al (100). Using the color-naming procedure, Kaiser (111) showed that with 12' stimuli color naming remains constant, with retinal illuminance multiplied by time constant, for time up to 50 msec. With decrease in total energy caused by shortening the duration, the degree of artificial tritanopia increased. Ingling et al (105) found that even for 3' flashes the central fovea is not dichromatic but tends toward tritanopia. Siegel & Siegel (202) deny this tendency in a color-naming study in which duration and surround luminance were varied. With their conclusion that blue receptors are apparently scarce but not entirely lacking in the central fovea, they confirm the conclusions of Walraven (237) and Weitzman & Kinney (248) in earlier studies of the same kind. The small field dichromacy during fixation is a foveal Troxler effect which turns the blue-yellow system off. Hurvich (97) points to the possibility that maximal absorption in the very center of the fovea of the macular pigment may account for differences between "small field tritanopia" anywhere in the retina and in the central fixation area. Anyhow, Wald (236) appears to be alone in his suggestion that the very center of the fovea lacks blue sensitive cones.

Color recognition of flashes during voluntary eye movements was found to be best when the flash is presented during steady fixation, poorer just before a saccade and still poorer after a saccade (122). The poorest recognition of red and green test flashes occurs when the flash arrives precisely in the middle of a saccade, and 40 to 80 msec later for blue test flashes. When the test flashes are presented immediately following a saccade, changes in hue somewhat analogous to the Bezold-Brücke shift are seen. These color shifts are mostly toward the "yellower" wavelengths and are due, according to Richards (182), to an increase in neural activity desaturating principally the red and green color channels.

In a series of studies, Connors (38–40) examined the luminance requirements for hue perception as a function of size and duration of the targets. His findings repeat and extend the earlier studies by Bouman & Walraven (24). The results show both that there is great variability in color naming near threshold and that for a small brief stimulus the luminance-exposure-time relationship for chromatic threshold approaches Bloch's law. The earlier finding of small photochromatic intervals at both ends of the spectrum (24) was confirmed by Connors (39) as well as by Graham & Hsia (74) and Novakova (165). The photochromatic interval appears to increase with retinal eccentricity (207).

Because rods and long-wave cones interact to produce color sensations, it is clear that the rods can be as much a part of the human color-producing systems as the cones (135). This seems to agree with data from a blue cone monochromat, where such interaction also took place (22). However, although these "rods" have the action spectrum of rhodopsin (176), they have the directional sensitivity and the dark adaptation curve of normal red and green cones (7).

Bouman (23) has stressed the point that achromatic vision is not limited to the rods, nor is chromatic vision limited to the cones. The same view is expressed in a series of papers by Stabell & Stabell (208), who studied the magnitude of the photochromatic interval. Bouman (23) considers the possibility that cones have connections with a chromatic and an achromatic transmission system. Analyzing the dependence of the achromatic zone as a function of wavelength, the following interesting postulation is given: the cones of the human retina are organized in distinct units which are called "human ommatidia." Such an ommatidium contains one blue, two or three of both red and green cones, and an eccentricity-dependent number of rods. Single quantum hits in two receptors lead to a scotopic response, but double hits in one receptor are needed to give photopic perceptions. Two red cones can therefore produce an achromatic perception; that is, scotopic vision can thus be mediated by cones. Multiple hits per rod produce white, by which the rods contribute to photopic vision. Interaction of the red, green, and blue cones and the rods in the ommatidia, and groups of ommatidia in recipient units, lead to red-white-green and yellow-white-blue channels. The tendency toward dichromacy and monochromacy with increasing eccentricity is due to the fact that the red-green channel and the yellow-blue channel are more and more inundated by white signals from the rods.

Sperling & Harwerth (206), in a well executed study with rhesus monkeys, assume three spectral information channels to describe the increment threshold spectral sensitivity with white and colored backgrounds. These three spectra are: (a) subtraction of the red from the green absorption spectrum; (b) subtraction of the green from the red absorption spectrum; and (c) the blue absorption spectrum.

A color effect that has not yet been explained is the following: When one compares the hue impression of an array of little pinholes with a homogenous field of the same wavelength, the hue of the pinholes is shifted somewhat toward green in the red-green region of the spectrum (191).

Turning to the applied side of the topic, we may note that Michon et al (150) prove by reaction time experiments that fluorescent orange is the most conspicuous color, and it is therefore recommended for safety clothing for people who work on or near the road. Mortimer (154), in a study of vision in traffic, reports that red as a flashing light gets more attention, measured by reaction time, than green or amber.

Spatial and temporal effects.—Chromaticity information is transmitted by narrower spatial and temporal frequency bands than is luminance. This conclusion can be deduced from the results of studies of Van der Horst et al (223–225) and Munker (158). Color transfer functions are derived which show that the spatial passband for yellow-blue is smaller than for red-green, indicating the effect of small field tritanopia. Neither the spatial nor the temporal transfer functions show a peak at some frequency, as the well-known De Lange curves do for brightness vision. In color transfer functions there is a monotonic increase of the amplitude with increasing frequency. This was confirmed by Hilz & Cavonius (89). Moreover, a regular motion of the test pattern, which normally enhances visibility (229), never enhances the visibility of color gratings. This suggests that such inhibitory effects as occur in brightness vision, and which are the sources of Mach bands, are very weak or missing in the mechanisms of color vision. This agrees with the fact that color Mach bands do not occur. Hilz & Cavonius (90) measured visual acuity for color gratings in which the bars differed in wavelength. The chromatic acuity with the greatest wavelength difference never reaches achromatic acuity, but corresponds only to an acuity reached with a luminance contrast of 30–50 percent.

Next to the tritanopic effect of small fields there exists a deterioration of color discrimination as a function of a luminance which resembles also tritanopia (44, 254). In this case one has to be careful because this is a pseudo trita-effect (240).

Guth & Eastman made the unexpected finding that for luminance contrasts between 0.1 and 0.4 a colored object may be more but may be also less visible than a corresponding neutral object, depending on the color combinations (78).

Koenderink, Van de Grind & Bouman (118) describe the chromatic transfer function in the framework of the scaling-ensemble model. Such a scaling ensemble is a group of scalers with common scaling factor that provide an effective compression of the dynamic range of the input signals. The model predicts Weber's law, Bloch's law, and the mentioned transfer functions for moving sinusoidal bar patterns.

Green (76) determined flicker characteristics of the separate color-receptive systems by measuring the modulation thresholds for sinusoidal flicker of one color superimposed on a background of a complementary color. The red and green mechanisms have frequency response with about equal peak sensitivity but differing in shape, but the blue sensitive system has a reduced flicker fusion frequency.

A phase shift greater for blue and green than for red has been found by Ercoles & Salvi by analysis of the response to sinusoidally modulated light of different spectral composition (55).

Foveal grating acuity for blue is always found to be lower than for other chromatic illuminants; according to Pokorny et al (175) this must be attributed to neural rather than dioptric factors. Also the vernier acuity performance is worse under blue light, even when this light is corrected for refraction (59). The reduction of visual acuity for a blue grating by applying a yellow background is about a factor of six (75).

Bartley & Ball (17), still continuing their research on the effects of intermittent stimulation, show that the appearance of spectral wavelengths changes, in particular around 500 nm. In this case a strong desaturation occurs. Other wavelengths may produce supersaturation. Induced hue changes are grouped around two neutral points. Wavelengths below 500 nm are altered to a more violet hue perception, wavelengths above 500 nm to more yellow hue perception. These results resemble the Bezold-Brücke shift. The desaturation at 500 nm is explained by Walters (243) as due to interaction of rods and cones. The Bezold-Brücke shift itself is of neural rather than pigment origin (42). The effect increases if the field size of the stimulus decreases (227). The brightness-gain of the Brücke-Bartley effect is accompanied by a hue shift (226), and this can be explained by the Bezold-Brücke effect.

Von Campenhausen (231) has shown, in contrast to earlier reports, that the colors of Benham's top are independent of the spectral composition of metameric light mixtures. This is a very fortunate finding, because the earlier reports were in conflict with the trichromatic theory. The author supposes that the colors are caused by phase sensitive lateral retinal inhibition.

Kilmer & Kilmer (116), discussing Lettvin's hypothesis (126) on central facts of color phenomena, developed a rotating disc experiment to test

Lettvin's rules on the Land effect. A new color effect showed up to which Lettvin's rules did not apply, and the authors are not able to explain it.

Ishak (107) confirms the present belief (232) that the operation of the Stiles-Crawford effect underlies the color stereoscopic effect wherein some colors appear to stand out in front of others, but he thinks that the chromatic difference of magnification might also play a role.

Adaptation.—The blue process always plays a peculiar role. This appears also in a study of positive visual after-images. After exposure to bright white light the perceived color sequence is generally white, then greenish, desaturated red and purple, and finally blue (168). Apparently there is a basic difference in the after functioning between the blue process and those processes mediating the red and green sensations. It is also rather remarkable that sometimes the after-image appears more saturated than any spectral color.

Studies on changes in hue due to a change in something other than the stimulus wavelength are numerous. They are indeed important for the development of color vision theory. In this connection it is worth mentioning the study of Gestrin & Teller (64), which followed up the reports of De Valois and Walraven (50). The latter showed that after an intense red bleach to one eye, the wavelength necessary to produce the best subjective yellow in the contralateral eye was displaced toward green for a period of several minutes. In the follow-up study, pressure sufficient to cause pressure blindness was applied to the bleached eye at the termination of the bleaching light. In this case no displacement is observed. The results show that the interocular hue effect depends on the continuity of the signal from the bleached retina.

One must be very careful, therefore, with a haploscopic matching technique. Heinrich (87) and Valberg (222) studied simultaneous contrast, or in other words, color induction with this technique. Heinrich shows that with increasing luminance in the surrounding field, the central color shifts along a nearby straight line in the chromaticity diagram. The distance of this shift is proportional to surrounding luminance. Valberg indicates that changing the luminance of the inducing color only changes the brightness of the induced colors. It has no influence at all on purity in terms of the Luther-Nyberg color solid. These two studies warn against simply plotting appearances as color points in the chromaticity diagram. It is legitimate to plot these data in the diagram as long as one is cautious in drawing conclusions about attributes of color perception. The chromaticity diagram never was designed for this.

The change in brightness is dependent only upon the luminance of the surrounding field, not on the wavelength (157). The study of Nayatani (159) on color induction is made with the two test fields in one eye. This is more realistic compared with practical viewing situations, but the interpretation is complicated by the successive contrast in addition to the simultaneous contrast. Other extensive measurements are made by Fedorova et al (57) and Takasaki (218).

Sternheim explains the chromatic contrast effects in terms of selective lateral inhibition and the concept of opponent-response induction (213). Wagner (235) treats the adaptive color shift produced by a change of chromatic adaptation on a colorimetric basis. Color shifts are due to changes in lateral neuronal connections.

Evans & Swenholt (56) call attention to the fact that the relative luminance of a color at the threshold between gray content and apparent fluorescence is not much affected by the luminance of the surround, but greatly affected by its chromaticity. The continuum of color perceptions of a color stimulus seen against a variety of backgrounds is four dimensional.

Krauskopf, measuring increment thresholds during chromatic adaptation (120), found the critical duration for the red and green systems to be different. Moreland (152) concludes that the site of the generation of the blue arcs is more proximal than the photoreceptor layer and more distal than the ganglion axon layer. The small diffuse variety of ganglion cell is the most probable site of arc generation.

An after-effect now well known is the McCollough effect: when one looks alternately at red vertical and green horizontal stripes, vertical and horizontal white stripes appear greenish and pink respectively. Hypotheses explaining this effect include contour detecting cells found in the human visual system (85). Experiments varying the angular separation of the adapting pattern support this notion (58). Hajos (82) states that the effect is not primarily dependent on stimulation by closed contours, but that the effect can be obtained when stimulation patterns comply with the size of the receptive fields of color detectors in the lateral geniculate nucleus.

A new after-effect is a motion-contingent one. When one views green stripes moving up, and red stripes moving down for several hours, followed by white stripes moving up or down, a pink after-effect is seen when the stripes are moving up, and green when the white stripes move down (88). Such after-effects do not transfer from one eye to the other (216).

Colorimetry, color theory.—One of the fundamentals of colorimetry is the additivity of luminances: Abney's law. A very extensive and well-documented paper by Guth et al (79) now presents an overwhelming body of evidence demonstrating that Abney's law is not even approximately valid for direct brightness matches or threshold judgments involving bichromatic mixtures. Since flicker photometry is additive, these authors suggest on the basis of this evidence that brightness matching and threshold observations are mediated by both the opponent and the nonopponent systems, and flicker observations are dependent upon the nonopponent system itself. Boynton & Kaiser (27) indicate that when the criterion of a minimally distinct border between two precisely juxtaposed fields is used rather than the usual criterion of equal brightness, the additivity law holds. In fact, the same flicker fusion criterion is used here, if according to Fourier analysis the spatial step-function is considered as a composition of spatial frequencies!

Large field colorimetry has its own problems. The rods play a role here too, and nonadditivity has been observed (132). Equivalent luminances were determined for these circumstances by Kowaliski (119). Miller (151) has tested the consistency between color-matching data and spectral sensitivity measurements using the two-color threshold technique. Except for $\lambda > 650$ nm the consistency could be established.

What emerges from the tremendous amount of literature is that most of the authors adhere to one kind or another of trichromatic opponent theory of color vision. The idea is that the light is absorbed by three kinds of pigments in three kinds of cones, the pigment having maximal absorption in different parts of the spectrum. The messages from the receptors are recoded into opponent responses in two chromatic channels and one brightness channel. Jameson & Hurvich (108) and Richter (184) derive opponent responses as linear relations with the absorption curves of the photopigments. Some authors, like Bouman (23) and Sperling (206), think of these responses as differences between outputs of receptors; others, such as Shklover (201), Matveev (139), and Meessen (143), assume logarithmic or other nonlinear transformations before recoding takes place. The processes depend also on the state of adaptation. The influence of the rods is taken into account by Bouman (23) as contributing to the brightness and to the whiteness. Hough (91) and Ruddock (190) think along the same line, considering that rod signals are colorimetrically neutral; more specifically, supported by Trezona (221), they suppose that the rod and blue cones share their input before recoding takes place. Walraven supposes that normal color vision is a combination of tritanopic and deuteranopic vision (240); Judd & Yonemura suggest, following the Müller theory, that it is a combination of tritanopic and protanopic vision (110). Hassenstein (86) presents another variation by assuming that the green system is antagonistic to a combined action of blue and red systems.

Summarizing, all these proposals are variations of the trichromatic opponent concept, and much work is still to be done to make a choice between all these variations. The concept is a good start for the description of just noticeable color differences, and thus for the development of the line elements in brightness-color space (see 220). Richter (184) makes an attempt —and it seems well done—to include the Munsell space as well within this framework.

Burnham et al (35), Indow & Matsushima (103), and Stone & Coles (215) applied the powerful method of multidimensional scaling to the spacing of colors, as for example in the Munsell system. In view of the success of the method in other fields of research, this approach certainly has to be continued in order to determine the perceptual attributes of color.

Color vision defects.—There is a continuous stream of studies evaluating existing color blindness tests, and new methods are appearing.

Ikeda & Urakubo (101) used the fact that color defectives have a lower fusion frequency for color-flicker as a testing technique. Normals can be distinguished from defectives, protans from deutans, but dichromats cannot be separated from anomalous subjects.

Fujii & Ikeda (63, 94) apply the two-color threshold method of De Vries and Stiles. They report that differentiation of normals from color defectives and the discrimination of protanopes from deuteranopes was easily made. However, Watkins (244) doubts that the increment threshold curve can be diagnostic for deutans because of the large variability observed in normals. Nevertheless, for groups of ten normals, ten deuteranomals, and five deuteranopes, the mean threshold was significantly different between groups. The π_4 mechanism of the deuteranomals appeared to be shifted about 10 nm towards the red end of the spectrum, confirming earlier findings (242). As was expected, the π_5 mechanism is lacking in the protanope. In protanomaly its sensitivity is considerably reduced in the long wavelengths (245).

Alpern & Torii (9, 11) state that in protanomaly and deuteranomaly the absorption spectrum of at least one of the cone pigments must be abnormal. They suggest two possibilities for protanomaly (10): (a) the anomalous pigment is a diluted normal red pigment; (b) its absorption spectrum is similar to that of the normal green pigment, but shifted slightly toward the long wave end of the spectrum. Two possible hypotheses are also suggested for deuteranomaly (11): (a) the anomalous pigment is a diluted normal red pigment; (b) its absorption spectrum is similar to that of the normal red pigment but shifted slightly toward shorter wavelengths. They favor the second possibility. Unfortunately Alpern & Torii do not consider the possibility that both a shift and a dilution may occur. The green curve might be shifted toward the long wavelength, as Watkins (244) suggested, and the red pigment might be diluted, as Walraven & Leebeek (241) suggested. This would explain a large part of the huge chromatic Stiles-Crawford effect in anomalous trichromacy (241).

Because the different anomaloscope match in anomalous trichromatism is due to a λ_{max} shift in pigment, a correlation between anomaloscope matches and red-green photometric matches is not expected. Although earlier results in the literature contradicted this, it seems (250) that these results were obtained due to a procedural accident.

Richards & Luria (183) claim that deuteranomals can, as with color normals, be divided into two classes. Hurvich et al (99), however, question the existence of two classes of normals. This hypothesis is based upon a bimodal distribution of the spectral locus of unique green. In their opinion this bimodality vanishes if a neutral state of adaptation is guaranteed in the experimental conditions. Pickford (173) also supposes more than one kind of deuteranomaly, and Linksz & Waaler (129) find a correlation between the two classes of normals and their anomaloscope quotient, although in a direction they did not predict. Obviously, things are not as simple as sometimes anticipated.

Although there is some variability in the luminosity curves among deuteranopes, Alpern, Mindel & Torii (8) and Richards & Luria (183) conclude that all the deuteranopes they studied were completely lacking the green pigment. Therefore they question the hypothesis that deuteranopes have both the normal red and the normal green pigment and that the nerves from the two kinds of cones are "fused." The latter view has been very popular because the confusion lines of deuteranopes at the CIE diagram seem to converge very near $x = 1.0$, $y = 0.0$. This point is the theoretical convergence point for such a fusion deuteranope.

Nimeroff (161) recently has written a tremendously elucidating paper on this topic which clears up a long-standing error. He has shown from the literature, including some from Russian sources, and from his own measurements that although there is a considerable spread, the convergence points have a weighted mean of $x = 1.54$ and $y = -0.54$. This is not at all close to the theoretical value for the fusion deuteranope. However, it agrees completely with the hypothesis that the deuteranope has lost the normal green system. The deuteranopic confusion center is then assumed to be the fundamental green primary point. Thus Rushton's view no longer contradicts the psychophysical data that in addition to cyanolabe the protanope has only the pigment chlorolabe (192) and the deuteranope only the pigment erythrolabe (193). It seems it is now time to remove from the handbooks the wrong confusion center of the deuteranopes, which has so long obscured the issue.

Vos & Walraven (233) have derived a value for the theoretical deuteranopic confusion point from several kinds of psychophysical data, including the Bezold-Brücke effect, the different Weber fractions for the three fundamental systems, and the absolute sensitivities of protanopes and deuteranopes. Their value is $x = 1.40$, $y = -0.40$, which is within the permissible range of Nimeroff's data.

The derivation of the color-sensitive mechanisms in the eye by analysis of the data of abnormal retinae has been fruitful. Blackwell & Blackwell (21), however, are puzzled by the sensitivity curves of patients with abnormal macular development. Analysis leads to too narrow sensitivity curves. Pokorny, Smith & Swartley (176) reproduce protan functions in normal observers by superposition of a red field on the bipartite anomaloscope field.

Although they are rare, differences in defects between the two eyes in one person occur. De Vries-De Mol & Went (51) present a family study of a male subject with extreme deuteranomaly in the right eye and normal anomaloscope setting in the left eye. Nimeroff (161) reports a subject with a deuteranopic left eye and a protanopic right eye.

Schmidt (197) made a detailed examination of a tritanomalous daughter and her tritan father.

A tremendous number of studies have been made on acquired color deficiencies occurring as a result of many diseases. Two extensive recent studies are those by François & Verriest (60) and Pinckers (174).

It seems unbelievable, but Imamura (102) claims that by application of electric stimuli between the temporal areas, color blindness can be treated. Both protanopes and deuteranopes are reported to react favorably. If these results can be replicated, they will pose a problem for the photochemical explanation of dichromacy.

The fact that color defects are scarcer in relatively underdeveloped societies was confirmed for the town of Ticul, Yucatán, Mexico (65) and for New Zealand's Maoris and "islanders" (77); the difference was less pronounced for the population in Madhya Pradesh (20). In Yucatán no color vision abnormalities were detected in the several hundred females tested.

ANIMAL BEHAVIOR

Humphrey (96) found by repeated measurements highly consistent hue preferences in monkeys. The order of preference was blue, green, white, yellow, orange, red. Color preferences in the pecking response of newly hatched ducks were determined by Oppenheim (167).

Daw & Pearlman (47) investigated the ability of cats to distinguish colors at mesopic and photopic levels. At both levels cats were found able to distinguish red from cyan. These results suggest that cats have more than one type of cone. This is confirmed with recording at the LGN. When cats are not trained to discriminate between wavelengths, color appears to be an irrelevant dimension in comparison with intensity (145).

Nuboer (166) found that the rabbit could discriminate spectrally different lights; at 496 nm the rabbit could discriminate a wavelength difference of 30 nm, pointing to a "blue" and "green" sensitive system in their retina. According to Nuboer, one of the most prominent functions of the rabbit's visual system is to detect moving objects. During twilight these objects will be illuminated by diffuse sky light. The energy spectrum of this light has its maximum at shorter wavelengths. The energy spectrum of the setting sun, on the other hand, lacks these shorter wavelengths. Objects exposed to direct illumination will therefore reflect almost exclusively light of longer wavelengths, whereas their shadows will reflect light of shorter wavelengths. The biological value of the described dichromatic color vision may be an adaptation to twilight color contrast.

Recent data have shown that the tree shrew is a dichromat. From the results of training experiments after removal of the posterior neocortex it is concluded that color vision in this species can be mediated by the tectum (204).

From behavioral measures of spectral sensitivity following chromatic adaptation in the goldfish it was possible to derive the absorption curves of three pigments (253).

Mote & Goldsmith (155) showed that in the compound eye of the cockroach *Periplaneta*, two color receptors are in the same ommatidium. The most recent findings on the ability of honeybees to distinguish between hues, and to memorize colors and color combinations are presented by Mazokhin (142). Menzel (146) has studied the honeybee's memory of spectral colors. They were presented with 444 and 590 nm as stimuli, and one frequency was reinforced with a sucrose solution. Specimens rewarded once lose preference in a few days, but after three rewards the preference lasts for more than a fortnight.

Kaiser (112) investigated the optomotor reaction of the flesh fly *Phormia regina Meig* on viewing rotating striped patterns in various spectral colors. The spectral sensitivity of the light-adapted animal differs somewhat from its spectral sensitivity at threshold. The difference is too small to interpret these findings in terms of a Purkinje shift. The fly failed to respond to a rotating striped pattern in pairs of different colors of equal animal-subjective brightness. Even within the context of these results Kaiser does not conclude that the *Phormia* is color-blind.

Bernhard et al (18) suggest that modifications of the tracheoles beneath photoreceptors of the compound eye of the butterfly *Heliconius erato* produce an increase in reflection of red light resulting in similar increases in the sensitivity of the eye to red light. The spectral sensitivity is similar to that of the moth, with differences solely to internal reflections rather than differing arrays of photopigment. Swihart & Gordon, on the other hand, suggest the presence of a photopigment with maximum absorption in the red part of the spectrum. They base their conclusion on a careful evaluation of the ERG and conclude that the response to red color is physiological rather than physical (217).

ACKNOWLEDGMENTS

I thank my associates P. Padmos and D. van Norren for their help in preparing the material about objective studies, and both Miss M. H. Frederiks and Miss H. de Groot for their assistance and literature search.

LITERATURE CITED

1. Abramov, I. 1968. Further analysis of the response of LGN cells. *J. Opt. Soc. Am.* 58:574–79
2. Adams, C. K., Bryan, A. H., Jones, A. E. 1968. Electroretinographic determination of the spectral sensitivity of the baboon (*Papio anubis*). *Vision Res.* 8:1399–1405
3. Alfieri, R., Solé, P., Scioldo-Zürcher, P. 1967. Harmonic analysis of the electroretinogram. *Proc. ISCERG Symp., 6th, Erfurt.* Advan. electrophysiol. pathol. of visual syst., 305–18
4. Allen, E. 1968. Metamerism—A study in dimension. *Color Eng.* 6(6):38–43
5. Ibid 1969. Some new advances in the study of metamerism: Theoretical limits of metamersim: An index of metamerism for observer differences. 7(1):35–40
6. Alpern, M. 1968. Distal mechanisms of vertebrate color vision. *Ann. Rev. Physiol.* 30:279–318
7. Alpern, M., Lee, G. B., Maaseidvaag, F., Miller, S. S. 1971. Colour vision in blue-cone 'monochromacy.' *J. Physiol.* 212:211–33
8. Alpern, M., Mindel, J., Torii, S. 1968. Are there two types of deuteranopes? *J. Physiol.* 199:443–56
9. Alpern, M., Torii, S. 1968. Prereceptor colour vision distortions in protanomalous trichromacy. *J. Physiol.* 198:549–60
10. Alpern, M., Torii, S. 1968. The luminosity curve of the protanomalous fovea. *J. Gen. Physiol.* 52:717–37
11. Ibid. The luminosity curve of the deuteranomalous fovea, 738–49
12. Armington, J. C. 1969. Electrophysiology of the human visual system. *Arch. Environ. Health* 19:598–604
13. Armington, J. C. 1970. Simultaneous electroretinograms and evoked potentials. *Am. J. Optom.* 47:450–58
14. Armington, J. C., Marsetta, R., Schick, A. M. L. 1970. Stimulus alternation and low level response. *Vision Res.* 10:227–36
15. Ashton, N., Ed. 1970. Recent research on the retina. *Brit. Med. Bull.* 26, No. 2
16. Autrum, H. 1968. Colour vision in man and animals. *Naturwissenschaften* 55:10–18
17. Bartley, S. H., Ball, R. J. 1969. Effects of intermittent photic input on brightness, hue, saturation, visual acuity and stereopsis. *Am. J. Optom.* 46:315–18
18. Bernhard, C. G., Boëthius, J., Gemne, G., Struwe, G. 1970. Eye ultrastructure, colour reception and behaviour. *Nature (London)* 226:865–66
19. Berson, E. L., Goldstein, E. B. 1970. Recovery of the human early receptor potential during dark adaptation in hereditary retinal disease. *Vision Res.* 10:219–26
20. Bhargava, R. P., Rajani, P. 1968. Incidence of color blindness in Madhya Pradesh. *Indian J. Med. Sci.* 22:88–90
21. Blackwell, H. R., Blackwell, O. M. Spectral sensitivity mechanisms derived from studies of abnormal retinae. See Ref. 178, 131–38
22. Blackwell, H. R., Blackwell, O. M. 1957. Blue mono-cone monochromacy: A new color vision defect. *J. Opt. Soc. Am.* 47:338
23. Bouman, M. A. 1969. My image of the retina. *Quart. Rev. Biophys.* 2:25–64
24. Bouman, M. A., Walraven, P. L. 1957. Some color-naming experiments for red and green monochromatic lights. *J. Opt. Soc. Am.* 47:834–39
25. Boynton, R. M. 1968. Mechanisms of colour vision. *Color Eng.* 6(5):43–46
26. Boynton, R. M., Gordon, J. 1965. Bezold-Brücke hue shift measured by color-naming technique. *J. Opt. Soc. Am.* 55:78–86
27. Boynton, R. M., Kaiser, P. K. 1968. Vision: The additivity law made to work for heterochromatic photometry with bipartite fields. *Science* 161:366–68
28. Bridges, C. D. B. 1969. Yellow corneas in fishes (letter to the editors). *Vision Res.* 9:435–36
29. Brindley, G. S. 1970. *Physiology of the Retina and Visual Pathway.* London: Arnold. 2nd ed.
30. Brindley, G. S. 1955. A photochemical reaction in the human retina. *Proc. Phys. Soc. B* 68:862–70
31. Brown, K. T. 1968. The electroretinogram: its components and their origins. *Vision Res.* 8:633–77
32. Brown, K. T., Murakami, M. 1968. Rapid effects of light and dark adaptation upon the receptive field organization of S-potentials and late receptor potentials. *Vision Res.* 8:1145–71

33. Brown, P. K., Wald, G. 1964. Visual pigments in single rods and cones of the human retina. *Science* 144: 45–52

34. Burkhardt, D. A. 1968. Cone action spectra: evidence from the goldfish electroretinogram. *Vision Res.* 8: 839–53

35. Burnham, R. W., Onley, J. W., Witzel, R. F. 1970. Exploratory investigation of perceptual color scaling. *J. Opt. Soc. Am.* 60:1410–20

36. Ciganek, L., Ingvar, D. H. 1969. Colour specific features of visual cortical responses in man evoked by monochromatic flashes. *Acta Physiol. Scand.* 76:82–92

37. Ciganek, L., Shipley, T. 1970. Color evoked brain responses in man (letter to the editors). *Vision Res.* 10:817–19

38. Connors, M. M. 1968. Luminance requirements for hue perception in small targets. *J. Opt. Soc. Am.* 58:258–63

39. Ibid 1969. Luminance requirements for hue identification in small targets. 59:91–97

40. Ibid 1970. Luminance requirements for hue perception and identification for a range of exposure durations. 60:958–65

41. Cooper, G. F., Robson, J. G. 1969. The yellow colour of the lens of man and other primates. *J. Physiol.* 203:411–17

42. Coren, S., Keith, B. 1970. Bezold-Brücke effect: Pigment oi neural locus? *J. Opt. Soc. Am.* 60:559–62

43. Cornsweet, T. N. 1970. *Visual Perception.* New York:Academic

44. Cornu, L., Harlay, F. 1969. Modifications de la discrimination chromatique en fonction de l'éclairement. *Vision Res.* 9:1273–87

45. Cruz-Coke, R. 1970. *Color Blindness. An Evolutionary Approach.* Springfield, Ill.: Thomas

46. Daw, N. W. 1968. Colour-coded ganglion cells in the goldfish retina: extension of their receptive fields by means of new stimuli. *J. Physiol.* 197:567–92

47. Daw, N. W., Pearlman, A. L. 1970. Cat colour vision: evidence for more than one cone process. *J. Physiol.* 211:125–37

48. De Valois, R. L., Jacobs, G. H. 1968. Primate color vision. *Science* 162: 533–40

49. De Valois, R. L., Pease, P. L. 1971. Contours and contrast: Responses of monkey lateral geniculate nucleus cells to luminance and color figures. *Science* 171:694–96

50. De Valois, R. L., Walraven, J. 1967. Monocular and binocular aftereffects of chromatic adaptation. *Science* 155:463–65

51. De Vries-De Mol, E. C., Went, L. N. 1971. Unilateral colour vision disturbance. A family study. *Clin. Genet.* 2:15–27

52. Dobelle, W. H., Marks, W. B., MacNichol, E. F. Jr. 1969. Visual pigment density in single primate foveal cones. *Science* 166–1508:10

53. Dowling, J. E. 1970. Organization of vertebrate retinas. The Jonas M. Friedenwald Memorial Lecture. *Invest. Ophthalmol.* 9:655–80

54. Enoch, J. M. Personal communication

55. Ercoles, A. M., Salvi, G. 1969. Influence of spectral composition of a mixture on the response to sinusoidally modulated light. *Atti Fond. Giorgio Ronchi* 24:93–101

56. Evans, R. M., Swenholt, B. K. 1969. Chromatic strength of colors. III. Chromatic surrounds and discussion. *J. Opt. Soc. Am.* 59:628–34

57. Fedorova, V. I. 1968. Changes in hue, saturation and brightness of spectral stimuli as a result of chromatic adaptation. *Am. J. Optom.* 45:595–604

58. Fidell, L. S. 1970. Orientation specificity in chromatic adaptation of human "edge-detectors." *Percept. Psychophys.* 8:235–37

59. Foley-Fisher, J. A. 1968. Measurements of vernier acuity in white and coloured light. *Vision Res.* 8: 1055–65

60. Francois, J., Verriest, G. 1968. Nouvelles observations de déficiences acquises de la discrimination chromatique. *Ann. Oculist.* 201:1097–1114

61. Frank, R. N. 1970. Electroretinographic response from the green rods of the isolated, perfused frog retina. *Vision Res.* 10:1102–7

62. Friedman, E., Kuwabara, T. 1968. The retinal pigment epithelium. IV. The damaging effects of radiant energy. *Arch. Ophthalmol.* 80:265–79

63. Fujii, T., Ikeda, M. 1969. Color vision tester devised on the principle of the two color threshold method. I. Construction of the apparatus. *Jap. J. Ophthalmol.* 23:783–89

64. Gestrin, P. J., Teller, D. Y. 1969. In-

terocular hue shifts and pressure blindness. *Vision Res.* 9:1267–71

65. Giles, E. et al 1968. Hydrogen cyanide and phenylthiocarbamide sensitivity, mid-phalangeal hair and color blindness in Yucatán, Mexico. *Am. J. Phys. Anthropol.* 28:203–12

66. Goldstein, E. B., Berson, E. L. 1970. Rod and cone contributions to the human early receptor potential. *Vision Res.* 10:207–18

67. Goldstein, E. B., Berson, E. L. 1969. Cone dominance of the human early receptor potential. *Nature (London)* 222:1272–73

68. Gouras, P. 1966. Rod and cone independence in the electroretinogram of the dark-adapted monkey's perifovea. *J. Physiol.* 187:455–64

69. Gouras, P. 1968. Cone receptive field organization of monkey ganglion cells. *Fed. Proc.* 27: 637

70. Gouras, P. 1968. Identification of cone mechanisms in monkey ganglion cells. *J. Physiol.* 199:533–47

71. Ibid 1969. Antidromic responses of orthodromically identified ganglion cells in monkey retina. 204:407–19

72. Gouras, P. 1970. Electroretinography: Some basic principles. *Invest. Ophthalmol.* 9:557–60

73. Gouras, P. 1970. Trichromatic mechanisms in single cortical neurons. *Science* 168:489–92

74. Graham, C. H., Hsia, Y. 1969. Saturation and the foveal achromatic interval. *J. Opt. Soc. Am.* 59:993–97

75. Green, D. G. 1968. The contrast sensitivity of the colour mechanisms of the human eye. *J. Physiol.* 196:415–29

76. Green, D. G. 1969. Sinusoidal flicker characteristics of the color-sensitive mechanisms of the eye. *Vision Res.* 9:591–601

77. Grosvenor, T. 1970. The incidence of red-green color deficiency in New Zealand's Maoris and "islanders." *Am. J. Optom.* 47:445–50

78. Guth, S. K., Eastman, A. A. 1970. Chromatic contrast. *Am. J. Optom.* 47:526–34

79. Guth, S. L., Donley, N. J., Marrocco, R. T. 1969. On luminance additivity and related topics. *Vision Res.* 9:537–75

80. Hagins, W. A., Penn, R. D., Yoshikama, S. 1970. Dark current and photocurrent in retinal rods. *Biophys. J.* 10:380–412

81. Hagins, W. A., Ruppel, H. 1971. Fast photoelectric effects and the properties of the vertebrate photoreceptors as electric cables. *Fed. Proc.* 30:64–68

82. Hajos, A. 1968. Psychophysiologische Probleme bei 'Farbkonturen' und 'Konturfarben.' *Stud. Psychol.* 10: 254–66

83. Hamasaki, D. I. 1968. The ERG-determined spectral sensitivity of the octopus. *Vision Res.* 8:1013–21

84. Hargroves, J. A., Hargroves, R. A. 1971. Bibliography of work on flashing lights (1711–1969). *Vision Res.* Suppl. 2

85. Harris, C. S., Gibson, A. R. 1968. Is orientation-specific color adaptation in human vision due to edge detectors, afterimages, or 'dipoles'? *Science* 162:1506–7

86. Hassenstein, B. 1967/1968. Modellrechnung zur Datenverarbeitung beim Farbensehen des Menschen. *Kybernetik* 4:209–23

87. Heinrich, F. Der Einflusz der Umfeld-Leuchtdichte beim farbigen Simultankontrast. See Ref. 178, 229–36

88. Hepler, N. 1968. Color: A motion-contingent aftereffect. *Science* 162: 376–77

89. Hilz, R., Cavonius, C. R. 1970. Sehschärfe bei Farbunterschieden ohne Helligkeitsunterschiede. *Vision Res.* 10:1393–98

90. Hilz, R., Cavonius, C. R. 1970. Wavelength discrimination measured with square-wave gratings. *J. Opt. Soc. Am.* 60:273–77

91. Hough, E. A. 1968. The spectral sensitivity functions for parafoveal vision. *Vision Res.* 8:1423–30

92. Howett, C. L. 1968. Variation of absorptance-curve shape with changes in pigment concentration. *J. Res. Nat. Bur. Stand. A* 72:309–40

93. Hubel, D. H., Wiesel, T. N. 1968. Receptive fields and functional architecture of monkey striate cortex. *J. Physiol.* 195:215–43

94. Hukami, K., Ikeda, M., Fujii, T. 1969. Color vision tester device on the principle of the two-color threshold method. II. Clinical experiment. *Jap. J. Clin. Ophthalmol.* 23:887–91

95. Hull, E. M. 1968. Corticofugal influence in the macaque lateral geniculate nucleus. *Vision Res.* 8:1285–98

96. Humphrey, N. 1971. Colour and

brightness preferences in monkeys. *Nature* 229:615–17

97. Hurvich, L. M. Is the central fixation area of the fovea blue-blind? See Ref. 178, 49–57

98. Hurvich, L. M., Jameson, D. 1969. Human color perception. An essay review. *Am. Sci.* 57:143–66

99. Hurvich, L. M., Jameson, D., Cohen, J. D. 1968. The experimental determination of unique green in the spectrum. *Percept. Psychophys.* 4:65–68

100. Iinuma, I., Kawaguchi, M., Kawanami, T. 1969. Evaluation of the Rayleigh equation in anomaloscopy. *Folia Ophthalmol. Jap.* 20:163–68

101. Ikeda, M., Urakubo, M. 1968. Flicker HTRF as test of color vision. *J. Opt. Soc. Am.* 58:27–31

102. Imamura, T. 1968. Color perception training of selectively stimulating frequency currents for color blindness. IV. *Jap. J. Clin. Ophthalmol.* 22:57–66

103. Indow, T., Matsushima, K. 1969. Local multidimensional mapping of Munsell color space. *Acta Chromatica* 2:16–24

104. Ingling, C. R. Jr. 1969. A tetrachromatic hypothesis for human color vision. *Vision Res.* 9:1131–48

105. Ingling, C. R. Jr., Scheibner, H. M. Boynton, R. M. 1970. Color naming of small foveal fields. *Vision Res.* 10:501–11

106. Ishak, I. G. H., Bouma, H., Van Bussel, H. J. J. 1970. Subjective estimates of colour attributes for surface colours. *Vision Res.* 10:489–500

107. Ishak, I. G. H., Said, F. S., Abd-Elsala, F. 1969. Colour stereoscopy. *Opt. Acta* 16:69–74

108. Jameson, D., Hurvich, L. M. 1968. Opponent-response functions related to measured cone photopigments (letter to the editor). *J. Opt. Soc. Am.* 58:429–30

109. Judd, D. B. 1970. Ideal color space. *Color Eng.* 8(2):37–52

110. Judd, D. B., Yonemura, G. T. 1969. CIE 1960 UCS diagram and the Müller theory of color vision. *J. Res. Nat. Bur. Stand. A* 74:23–30

111. Kaiser, P. K. 1968. Color names of very small fields varying in duration and luminance. *J. Opt. Soc. Am.* 58:849–52

112. Kaiser, W. 1968. Zur Frage des Unterscheidungsvermögens für Spektralfarben: Eine Untersuchung der Optomotorik der königlichen Glanzfliege Phormia regina Meig. *Z. Vergl. Physiol.* 61:71–102

113. Kaneko, A. 1970. Physiological and morphological identification of horizontal, bipolar and amacrine cells in goldfish retina. *J. Physiol.* 207:623–33

114. Ibid 1971. Electrical connexions between horizontal cells in the dogfish retina. 213:95–105

115. Kaneko, H. et al 1967. Clinical application of VEP (VEP by monochromatic color flicker stimuli). *Proc. ISCERG Symp., 6th, Erfurt: Advan. electrophysiol. pathol. of visual syst.*, 113–23

116. Kilmer, E., Kilmer, W. 1968. Temporal reversal of Land effect colour rules. *Nature* 218:883

117. King-Smith, P. E. 1969. Absorption spectra and function of the coloured oil drops in the pigeon retina. *Vision Res.* 9:1391–99

118. Koenderink, J. J., Van de Grind, W. A., Bouman, M. A. 1971. Foveal information processing at photopic luminances. *Kybernetik* 8:128–44

119. Kowaliski, P. 1969. Equivalent luminances of colors. *J. Opt. Soc. Am.* 59:125–30

120. Krauskopf, J. 1969. Variation of critical duration of red and green cone receptors with chromatic adaptation. *J. Opt. Soc. Am.* 59:504

121. Laufer, M., Millán, E. 1970. Spectral analysis of L-type S-potentials and their relation to photopigment absorption in a fish (*Eugerres plumieri*) retina. *Vision Res.* 10:237–51

122. Lederberg, V. 1970. Color recognition during voluntary saccades. *J. Opt. Soc. Am.* 60:835–42

123. Le Grand, Y. 1970. *An Introduction to Photobiology. The Influence of Light on Life.* London: Faber & Faber

124. Le Grand, Y. 1969. Photopigments des cones humains. *Doc. Ophthalmol.* 26:257–63

125. Lennox-Buchtal, M. A. 1962. Single units in monkey (*Cercocebus torquatus atys*) cortex with narrow spectral responsiveness. *Vision Res.* 2:1–15

126. Lettvin, J. 1967. The colors of colored things. *Mass. Inst. Technol. Quart. Progr. Rep.* 87:193–229

127. Liebman, P. A., Entine, G. 1968. Visual pigments of frog and tadpole. *Vision Res.* 8:761–75

128. Liebman, P. A., Granda, A. M. 1971. Microspectrophotometric measurements of visual pigments in two species of turtle, *Pseudemys scripta* and *Chelonia mydas. Vision Res.* 11: 105–14

129. Linksz, A., Waaler, G. H. M. 1968. Naming of groups with normal colour vision. *Nature* 218:687–88

130. Liske, E., Kislin, B. 1968. Flashing color and the electroencephalogram in color-deficient subjects. *Neurology* 18:9–15

131. Lodge, A. et al 1969. Newborn infants' electroretinograms and evoked electroencephalographic responses to orange and white light. *Child Develop.* 40:267–93

132. Lozano, R. D., Palmer, D. A. 1969. Large-field color matching and adaptation (letter to the editor). *J. Opt. Soc. Am.* 58:1653–56

133. MacAdam, D. L., Ed. 1970. *Sources of Color Science.* Cambridge, Mass., London: MIT press

134. McCandless, R. L., Hoffert, J. R., Fromm, P. O. 1969. Light transmission by corneas, aqueous humor and crystalline lenses of fishes. *Vision Res.* 9:223–32

135. McCann, J. J., Benton, J. L. 1969. Interaction of the long-wave cones and the rods to produce color sensations. *J. Opt. Soc. Am.* 59:103–7

136. Maksimova, Ye. M., Maksimov, V. V. 1969. Saturation of S potentials of the fish retina. The L type reaction. *Biophysics* 14:772–81

137. Marks, W. B., Dobelle, W. H., MacNichol, E. F. Jr. 1964. Visual pigments of single primate cones. *Science* 143:1181–83

138. Massopust, L. C. Jr., Wolin, L. R., Kadoya, S. 1969. Differential color responses in the visual cortex of the squirrel monkey. *Vision Res.* 9: 465–73

139. Matveev, A. B. 1969. On some psychophysiological operational characteristics of color perception, described by a nonlinear model. *Probl. Fiziol. Opt.* 15:19–26

140. May, J. G., Forbes, W. B., Piantanida, T. P. 1971. The visual evoked response obtained with an alternating barred pattern: Rate, spatial frequency and wavelength. *Electro-*

141. May, J. G., Siegfried, J. B. 1970. Spectral sensitivity of the human VER obtained with an alternating barred pattern. *Vision Res.* 10: 1399–1410

142. Mazokhin, G. 1968. Color vision of the honey bee and the color tints of plants. *Nauka Zhiznedeiatel.* 35(3): 58–63

143. Meessen, A. 1968. Structural model of the retina, relating the observed trichromatic and opponent-color responses. *J. Opt. Soc. Am.* 58:702–3

144. Mellerio, J. 1971. Light absorption and scatter in the human lens. *Vision Res.* 11:129–41

145. Mello, N. K. 1968. Color generalization in cat following discrimination training on achromatic intensity and on wavelength. *Neuropsychology* 6:341–54

146. Menzel, R. 1968. Das Gedächtnis der Honigbiene für Spektralfarben. I. Kurzzeitiges und langzeitiges Behalten. *Z. Vergl. Physiol.* 60:81–102

147. Michael, C. R. 1968. Receptive fields of single optic nerve fibers in a mammal with an all-cone retina. I. Contrast-sensitive units. *J. Neurophysiol.* 31:249–56

148. Ibid. Receptive fields of single optic nerve fibers in a mammal with an all-cone retina. II. Directionally selective units, 257–67

149. Ibid. Receptive fields of single optic fibers in a mammal with an all-cone retina. III. Opponent color units, 268–82

150. Michon, J. A., Eernst, J. T., Koutstaal, G. A. 1969. Safety clothing for human traffic obstacles. *Ergonomics* 12:61–70

151. Miller, S. 1970. Psychophysical spectral-sensitivity measurements and color-matching data. *J. Opt. Soc. Am.* 60:1404–6

152. Moreland, J. D. 1969. Retinal topography and the blue-arcs phenomenon. *Vision Res.* 9:965–76

153. Moreland, J. D., Lythgoe, J. N. 1968. Yellow corneas in fishes (letter to the editors). *Vision Res.* 8:1377–80

154. Mortimer, R. G. 1969. Research in automotive rear lighting and signaling system. *Eng. Publ. 3303 General Motors Corp.*

155. Mote, M. I., Goldsmith, T. H. 1971. Compound eyes: Localization of the

two color receptors in the same ommatidium. *Science* 171:1254–55

156. Motokawa, K., Taira, N., Okuda, J. 1962. Spectral responses of single units in the primate visual cortex. *Tohoku J. Exp. Med.* 78:320–37

157. Mount, G. E., Thomas, J. P. 1968. Relation of spatially induced brightness changes to test and inducing wavelengths. *J. Opt. Soc. Am.* 58:23–27

158. Munker, H. Die Ubertragung der Farbinformationen im visuellen Kanal. See Ref. 178, 213–18

159. Nayatani, Y. Estimation of color induction by simultaneous color contrast. See Ref. 178, 219–28

160. Nickerson, D. 1969. History of the Munsell color system. *Color Eng.* 7(5):42–51

161. Nimeroff, I. 1970. Deuteranopic convergence point. *J. Opt. Soc. Am.* 60:966–69

162. Nimeroff, I. 1968. A survey of papers on degree of metamerism. *Color Eng.* 6(6):44–46

163. Nimeroff, I. 1968. Colorimetry. *Nat. Bur. Stand. Monogr.* 104

164. Northmore, D. P. M., Muntz, W. R. A. 1970. Electroretinogram determinations of spectral sensitivity in a teleost fish adapted to different wavelengths. *Vision Res.* 10:799–816

165. Novakova, O. 1970. Some remarks on the amplitude of the photochromatic interval. *Atti. Fond. Giorgio Ronchi* 25:402–4

166. Nuboer, J. F. W. 1971. *Visual acuity, spectral sensitivity and spectral discrimination in the rabbit.* PhD thesis. Univ. of Utrecht

167. Oppenheim, R. W. 1968. Color preferences in the pecking response of newly hatched ducks (*Anas platyrhynchos*). *J. Comp. Physiol. Monogr. Suppl.* 66:No. 3, part 2

168. Padgham, C. A. 1968. Measurements of the colour sequences in positive visual after-images. *Vision Res.* 8:939–49

169. Padmos, P., Van Norren, D. 1971. Cone spectral sensitivity and chromatic adaptation as revealed by human flicker-retinography. *Vision Res.* 11:27–42

170. Pearlman, A. L., Daw, N. W. 1970. Opponent color cells in the cat lateral geniculate nucleus. *Science* 167:84–86

171. Pedler, C., Boyle, M. 1969. Multiple oil droplets in the photoreceptors of the pigeon. *Vision Res.* 9:525–28

172. Perry, N. W., Childers, D. G., Dawson, W. W. 1969. Human cortical correlates of color with monocular, binocular and dichoptic vision. *Vision Res.* 9:1357–66

173. Pickford, R. W. 1968. A pedigree showing variability in deuteranomaly. *Vision Res.* 8:469–74

174. Pinckers, A. J. L. G. 1971. *Verworven stoornissen van de kleurzin. Een klinisch onderzoek.* PhD thesis. Nijmegen

175. Pokorny, J., Graham, C. H., Lanson, R. N. 1968. Effect of wavelength on foveal grating acuity. *J. Opt. Soc. Am.* 58:1410–14

176. Pokorny, J., Smith, V. C., Swartley, R. 1970. Threshold measurements of spectral sensitivity in a blue monocone monochromat. *Invest. Ophthalmol.* 9:807–13

177. Polyak, S. L. 1941. *The Retina.* Univ. Chicago Press

178. *Proc. 1st AIC (Int. Colour Assoc.) Congr.,* Stockholm, Sweden, June 1969, "Color 69." 2 vols. Göttingen: Musterschmidt (1970)

179. *Proc. Int. Sch. Phys. "Enrico Fermi,"* course 43: Processing of the optical data by organisms and by machines, Varenna, 1968. New York: Academic (1969)

180. Regan, D. 1968. Chromatic adaptation and steady-state evoked potentials. *Vision Res.* 8:149–58

181. Ibid 1970. Evoked potentials and psychophysical correlated changes in stimulus colour and intensity. 10:163–78

182. Richards, W. 1970. Color shifts following rapid eye movements. *J. Exp. Psychol.* 84:399–403

183. Richards, W., Luria, S. M. 1968. Recovery and spectral sensitivity curves for color-anomalous observers. *Vision Res.* 8:929–38

184. Richter, K. New opponent colour concept. See Ref. 178, 403–17

185. Riggs, L. A., Sternheim, C. E. 1969. Human retinal and occipital potentials evoked by changes of the wavelength of the stimulating light. *J. Opt. Soc. Am.* 59:635–40

186. Ripps, H., Vaughan, H. G. Jr. 1969. The spectral sensitivity of evoked potentials from the retina and cortex of nocturnal and diurnal monkeys. *Vision Res.* 9:895–907

187. Ripps, H., Weale, R. A. 1969. Color vision. *Ann. Rev. Psychol.* 20:193–216

188. Ripps, H., Weale, R. A. 1970. The photophysiology of vertebrate colour vision. *Photophysiology* 5:127–68

189. Ruddock, K. H. 1971. The physics of colour vision. *Contemp. Phys.* 12:229–56

190. Ruddock, K. H. 1971. Parafoveal colour vision responses of four dichromats. *Vision Res.* 11:143–56

191. Ruddock, K. H. 1969. Cone vision under small field conditions. *Opt. Acta* 16:391–98

192. Rushton, W. A. H. 1963. A cone pigment in the protanope. *J. Physiol.* 168:345–59

193. Ibid 1965. A foveal pigment in the deuteranope. 176:24–37

194. Rushton, W. A. H. S-potentials. See Ref. 179, 256–69

195. Scheibner, H., Baumann, Ch. 1970. Properties of the frog's retinal ganglion cells as revealed by substitution of chromatic stimuli. *Vision Res.* 10:829–36

196. Scheibner, H. M., Boynton, R. M. 1968. Residual red-green discrimination in dichromats. *J. Opt. Soc. Am.* 58:1151–58

197. Schmidt, I. 1970. On congenital tritanomaly. *Vision Res.* 10:717–43

198. Schmidt-Clausen, H. J. 1968. *Uber das Wahrnehmen verschiedenartiger Lichtimpulse bei veränderlichen Umfeldleuchtdichten.* PhD thesis. Darmstadt

199. Sheppard, J. J. Jr. 1968. *Human Color Perception. A Critical Study of the Experimental Foundation.* New York: Elsevier

200. Shipley, T., Jones, R. W., Fry, A. 1968. Spectral analysis of the visually evoked occipitogram in man. *Vision Res.* 8:409–31

201. Shklover, D. A. A new uniform color space. See Ref. 178, 312–19

202. Siegel, M. H., Siegel, A. B. 1971. Color name as a function of surround luminance and stimulus duration. *Percept. Psychophys.* 9:140–44

203. Snyder, A. W., Hall, P. A. V. 1969. Unification of electromagnetic effects in human retinal receptors with three pigment colour vision. *Nature* 223:526–28

204. Snyder, M., Killackey, H., Diamond, I. T. 1969. Color vision in the tree

shrew after removal of posterior neocortex. *J. Neurophysiol.* 32:554–63

205. Sokol, S. 1970. Cortical and retinal spectral sensitivity of the hooded rat. *Vision Res.* 10:253–62

206. Sperling, H. G., Harwerth, R. S. 1971. Red-green cone interactions in the increment-threshold spectral sensitivity of primates. *Science* 172:180–84

207. Spillman, L., Seneff, S. 1971. Photochromatic intervals as a function of retinal eccentricity for stimuli of different size. *J. Opt. Soc. Am.* 61:267–70

208. Stabell, B., Stabell, U. 1969. Chromatic rod and cone activities as a function of the photochromatic interval. *Scand. J. Psychol.* 10:215–19

209. Steinberg, R. H. 1969. Rod and cone contributions to S-potentials from the cat retina. *Vision Res.* 9:1319–29

210. Ibid. Rod-cone interaction in S-potentials from the cat retina, 1331–44

211. Ibid. The rod after-effect in S-potentials from the cat retina, 1345–55

212. Steinberg, R. H., Schmidt, R. 1970. Identification of horizontal cells as S-potential generators in the cat retina by intracellular dye injection. *Vision Res.* 10:817–20

213. Sternheim, C. E. 1970. Chromatic contrast and visual sensitivity: Evidence for disparate mechanisms. *J. Opt. Soc. Am.* 60:694–99

214. Sternheim, C. E., Riggs, L. A. 1968. Utilization of the Stiles-Crawford effect in the investigation of the origin of electrical responses in the human eye. *Vision Res.* 8:25–33

215. Stone, L. A., Coles, G. J. 1971. Dimensions of color vision revisited. *J. Psychol.* 77:79–87

216. Stromeyer, C. F., Mansfield, R. J. W. 1970. Colored aftereffects produced with moving edges. *Percept. Psychophys.* 7:108–14

217. Swihart, S. L., Gordon, W. C. 1971. Red photoreceptor in butterflies. *Nature* 231:126–27

218. Takasaki, H. 1969. Von Kries coefficient law applied to subjective color change induced by background color. *J. Opt. Soc. Am.* 59:1370–76

219. Terstiege, H. 1966. *Untersuchungen zum Persistenz- und Koeffizientensatz.* PhD thesis. Berlin

220. Trabka, E. A. 1968. On Stiles' line element in brightness-color space and the color power of the blue. *Vision Res.* 8:113–34

221. Trezona, P. W. 1970. Rod participation in the "blue" mechanisms and its effect on colour matching. *Vision Res.* 10:317–32

222. Valberg, A. Simultaneous colour contrast. Basic relations represented in a colour space of related colours. See Ref. 178, 237–46

223. Van der Horst, G. J. C. 1969. Fourier analysis and color discrimination. *J. Opt. Soc. Am.* 59:1670–76

224. Ibid. Chromatic flicker, 1213–17

225. Van der Horst, G. J. C., Bouman, M. A. 1969. Spatiotemporal chromaticity discrimination. *J. Opt. Soc. Am.* 59:1482–88

226. Van der Horst, G. J. C., Muis, W. 1969. Hue shift and brightness enhancement of flickering light. *Vision Res.* 9:953–63

227. Van der Wildt, G. J., Bouman, M. A. 1968. The dependence of Bezold-Brücke hue shift on spatial intensity distribution. *Vision Res.* 8:303–13

228. Van Lith, G. H. M. 1968. Electroretinography in colour blindness. *Ophthalmologica* 156:16–18

229. Van Nes, F. L. 1969. Enhanced visibility by regular motion of retinal images. *Am. J. Psychol.* 81:367–74

230. Verriest, G. 1969. Les déficiences de la vision des couleurs. *Bull. Soc. Franc. Ophtalmol.* 69, No. 11

231. Von Campenhausen, C. 1969. The colors of Benham's top under metameric illuminations. *Vision Res.* 9:677–82

232. Vos, J. J. 1966. The color stereoscopic effect (letter to the editors). *Vision Res.* 6:105–7

233. Vos, J. J., Walraven, P. L. 1971. On the derivation of the foveal receptor primaries. *Vision Res.* 11:799–818

234. Wagner, H. G. Zur Bestimmung der grünen Grundvalenz. See Ref. 178, 59–66

235. Wagner, H. G. 1968. Valenzmetrische Untersuchungen der Farbumstimmung. *Farbe* 17:229–84

236. Wald, G. 1967. Blue-blindness in the normal fovea. *J. Opt. Soc. Am.* 57:1289–1301

237. Walraven, P. L. 1962. On the mechanisms of colour vision. PhD thesis. Univ. of Utrecht

238. Walraven, P. L. 1966. Recovery from the increase of the Stiles-Crawford effect after bleaching. *Nature* 206:311–12

239. Walraven, P. L., Bouman, M. A. 1960. Relation between directional sensitivity and spectral response curves in human cone vision. *J. Opt. Soc. Am.* 50:780–84

240. Walraven, P. L., Bouman, M. A. 1966. Fluctuation theory of colour discrimination of normal trichromats. *Vision Res.* 6:567–86

241. Walraven, P. L., Leebeek, H. J. 1962. Chromatic Stiles-Crawford effect of anomalous trichromats. *J. Opt. Soc. Am.* 52:836–37

242. Walraven, P. L., Van Hout, A. M. J., Leebeek, H. J. 1966. Fundamental response curves of a normal and a deuteranomalous observer derived from chromatic adaptation data. *J. Opt. Soc. Am.* 56:125–27

243. Walters, J. W. 1970. An investigation of rod-cone interaction as a possible mechanism for explaining the desaturation found in intermittent 510 nm monochromatic light. *Diss. Abstr. Int.* 30(11B) 5269–70

244. Watkins, R. D. 1969. Foveal increment thresholds in normal and deutan observers. *Vision Res.* 9:1185–96

245. Ibid. Foveal increment thresholds in protan observers, 1197–1204

246. Weale, R. A. 1968. *From Sight to Light.* Edinburgh: Oliver & Boyd

247. Weale, R. A. 1965. Vision and fundus reflectometry: A review. *Photochem. Photobiol.* 4:67–87

248. Weitzman, D. O., Kinney, J. A. S. 1969. Effect of stimulus size, duration, and retinal location upon the appearance of color. *J. Opt. Soc. Am.* 59:640–43

249. Werblin, F. S., Dowling, J. E. 1969. Organization of the retina of the mudpuppy, *Necturus masculosus.* II. Intracellular recording. *J. Neurophysiol.* 32:339–55

250. Wildman, K. N., Baker, H. D. 1970. The spurious correlation between anomaloscope matches and red-green photometric matches (research note). *Vision Res.* 10:1305–6

251. Wyszecki, G. 1969. Optical Resource Letter on colorimetry. *J. Opt. Soc. Am.* 59:123–25

252. Wyszecki, G., Stiles, W. S. 1967. *Color Science. Concepts and Methods,*

Quantitative Data and Formulas. New York: Wiley

253. Yager, D. 1969. Behavioral measures of spectral sensitivity in the goldfish following chromatic adaptation. *Vision Res.* 9:179–86

254. Yonemura, G. T., Kasuya, M. 1969. Color discrimination under reduced angular subtense and luminance. *J. Opt. Soc. Am.* 59:131–35

255. Young, R. W. 1971. An hypothesis to account for a basic distinction between rods and cones. *Vision Res.* 11:1–5

PERSONALITY

185

JEROME L. SINGER AND DOROTHY G. SINGER[1]

City University of New York, New York
Manhattanville College, Purchase, New York

INTRODUCTION

The study of the human personality is at once the most exciting and the most baffling and frustrating area in psychology. Just a year's work spreads before one a vast amount of research involving ingenious experimental manipulations, subtle interaction effects, and complicated statistical analyses. A series of books, all attempting to integrate a variety of personality theories, are available, yet they scarcely use identical operational systems and sometimes do not even overlap on major theoretical issues. Suddenly the psychology of the human personality changes from a fleshed-out, complex, well-developed structure, and one is left instead staring at the grin of the Cheshire cat. Is there indeed such a thing as the personality, and can it be studied in any systematic and satisfying fashion?

Thousands of students who flock to take courses in psychology are convinced that there is indeed "a personality," a self, and a set of enduring, if complex, dispositions which differentiate one person from another and which also give each of us some sense of uniqueness as well as commonality with the human race. They come to hear what psychologists have learned about our complicated inner feelings, our doubts, our fantasies, and our joys and excitements. The very intensity of their search suggests the importance of the subject matter of personality as a central field in psychology.

Our research methods and formulations and our approach to presenting the scientific material all too often let the students down. They are quickly "turned off" by the seeming triviality and artificiality of most of the research in the area to which they are exposed. They are curious about their dreams and daydreams, their boredom or excitement, their doubts and confusions about their sexuality, their struggle with values and aspirations, their awareness of their own jealousies, hatreds, and also of their creative impulses. All too often we tell them about pigeons pressing bars, or make them play Prisoner's Dilemma games, or have them fill out relatively trivial questionnaires. It is not the role of the scientific investigator to develop his discipline along lines that will appease his students. Still we must try to understand why it is that students much prefer to read books by R. D. Laing,

[1] Support for the senior author from NIMH Grant MH 10956–07 is herewith acknowledged. The authors are indebted to David Schwartz, Michele Maceli, and Violet Levine for abstracting and clerical services.

Erich Fromm, or Rollo May, or fictionalized case studies such as "I Never Promised You a Rose Garden" rather than the texts or journal readings that are often assigned. It is too easy to dismiss this trend by saying that students prefer "easy to read, watered-down popular psychology." The "semipopular" writings of psychoanalysts and humanists offer the students a sense of the ongoing personality and its complexity, and it is just in that sphere where scientific psychology has made its smallest contribution.

This problem of the discrepancy between what genuinely seems the major problem in the study of personality and the actual research that goes on is raised in a scholarly yet passionate article by Carlson (31). Carlson has analyzed hundreds of journal articles and has shown statistically that a vast majority are carried out on psychology students largely male; that most of the studies are experimental; almost invariably they involve a time span of a single session with the subject; and rarely do they examine in any detail the sex differences and the *meaning* of these differences on the measures employed in any given study. There are three major approaches to understanding personality, all of which are essential in this particular area of inquiry: (*a*) the study of the common characteristics of all individuals in personality dispositions such as emotion, motivation, and imaginative characteristics, etc; (*b*) the study of the ways in which individuals differ from each other along dimensions of that type or the determination of which dimensions are the major ones in defining personality differences; and (*c*) the ways in which individuals are unique and generate complex individual qualities which afford them a feeling of being independent personalities.

Carlson's review of 226 articles indicates that 57% of the studies published in the two major journals of personality disregarded subject variables and showed a "generalist" bias. Forty-three percent of the studies examined group differences but generally limited these differences to only one dimension such as repression-sensitization, birth order, or level of anxiety. Carlson did not find a single article in this group that carried out any extended examination or even a limited one into the way in which personality variables were organized in a given individual. She writes:

> We cannot study the organization of personality because we know at most only one or two 'facts' about any subject. We cannot study the stability of personality, nor its development over epochs of life, because we see our subjects for an hour. We cannot study the problems or capacities of the mature individual, because we study late adolescence. We cannot study psychosexuality, because we avoid looking at distinctive qualities of masculinity and femininity as a focal problem. We cannot study how persons strive for their important goals because we elect to induce motivational sets. . . . We cannot study development and the power of friendship— nor the course of true love—because we choose to manipulate interpersonal attraction. . . . Personality psychology would seem to be paying an exorbitant price in potential knowledge for the security afforded by preserving norms of convenience and methodological orthodoxy. Must these important, unanswered questions be left to literature and psychiatry? (31, p. 207)

Carlson's paper is more than a polemic, however; it points the way toward approaches which involve the use of the subjects' own curiosity, introspective tendencies, and their own natural behavior as part of any ongoing research. Carlson proposes alternatives to the employment of deception, and he lists a variety of unobtrusive observational techniques, as well as studies of persons in situations in which they can be followed systematically over longer periods of time.

In organizing this review, one realizes that in the preceding decade a significant change in the *Zeitgeist* of American psychology has occurred. This has to do with the revival of interest in central phenomena such as imagery, dreams, and affects. While one could not say that the 1960s show a very large quantity of research in those areas, it was in that decade that such private processes were again perceived as central questions for psychology. Compared with the previous 40 years, the amount of research carried on during the late 1960s on subjects such as dreams, emotions, and imagery has shown a steeply increasing gradient. To the extent that these "inner experiences" are close indeed to what we often think of as the private or unique aspects of our personalities, we might want to devote some attention in this review to the degree to which theory and research in the past year or so in the psychology of personality reflects this trend.

The 1960s also witnessed a tremendous flowering in the behavior modification approaches and saw them spread from treatment of individual phobias through establishment of token economies in hospitals, residential centers, and eventually into even broader settings such as schools or social agencies. The unquestioned effectiveness of many of the behavior modification techniques in individual cases and in control of certain socially disruptive behavior patterns, the fact that these techniques are relatively susceptible to systematic study and evaluation, and the increasing imagination and flexibility applied to these techniques in a variety of settings poses a serious question that must be faced by personality theorists who have emphasized the importance of complex intrapsychic dynamics as the basic personality variables. We are thus faced with a curious situation: on the one hand, in the past decade we saw a great increase in psychologists' capacity to study the inner experiences of individuals through imagery and affect; and at the same time there has been a remarkable refinement in our capacity to use reinforcement and systematic modeling and conditioning procedures, all oriented towards overt performance as a means of modifying behavior (12). The fact that the behavior modification methods rely heavily on the subjects' capacity to generate imagery (e.g. desensitization, implosion, symbolic mediation modeling, or aversive counter-conditioning through imagery) suggests that an important confluence of trends from the cognitive and social learning approaches is under way (210). Can the work of the past year or so give us any clues as to how these trends may perhaps come together to enrich our understanding of the psychology of personality in the coming decade?

SOME RECENT TEXTBOOKS

A quick review of recent textbooks on personality (33, 81, 102, 136, 144, 154, 170) suggests that while most take note of the issue raised by Carlson, none is really written from that viewpoint. Closest perhaps is the volume by Janis and associates (102), but this book suffers from lack of integration between its separate sections. Hall & Lindzey's (81) revision is again impressive and human-oriented, but it seems still not up to date. It gives insufficient attention to the modern cognitive-social influence of Lewin through Heider, Festinger, Zajonc, Deutsch, Zimbardo, and Cartwright, among others, or to the cognitive affective theories of McClelland, Atkinson, Kelley, and Tomkins and the social learning viewpoint of Rotter, Mischel, and Bandura.

Viewed strictly as a teachable undergraduate text, Mischel's (154) new volume seems better organized, more clearly presented, and the most effective new work. While it carries a social learning, behaviorist orientation, it presents the major issues in the field in a succinct and remarkably pointed fashion so that the more humanistically oriented instructor can use the book to good advantage. One might wish for more material on emotion, imagery, and fantasy, but on the whole the book points up the critical questions in personality with impressive clarity.

THEORETICAL DEVELOPMENTS

While in the 1940s and 1950s personality theory was dominated by drive, concepts, and psychoanalytic models oriented around energy discharge or drive satisfaction, the 1960s have been increasingly characterized by a shift away from drive models towards a view of man as an information processing and image making creature. This change is perhaps not as well reflected in the texts as it ought to be, but certainly it seems increasingly characteristic of more general theoretical papers of psychology and of recent books and reexaminations of theories of perception and emotion. Neisser's (163) *Cognitive Psychology*, while not oriented towards personality issues, has opened the way towards a reexamination of much of the data that is employed in personality research from the standpoint of a cognitive orientation. The emergence of ego-psychology has forced psychoanalytic investigators to examine much more thoughtfully the nature of the cognitive functions. This is clearly indicated in the collection of papers honoring David Rapaport (93). Papers in this book such as that by the late George Klein on peremptory ideation (119), or by Paul (169) on the concept of schema in memory theory, signalize the greater attention being paid to information processing by the analytically oriented theorists. An even more recent paper by Klein (118) raises deeper doubts concerning the nature of psychoanalytic relations of the ego in view of information processing constructs.

The cognitive model of man naturally has its roots in the work of Lewin

(128) and Tolman (229). An early formulation that was somewhat neglected was made by Rotter (183) and is also to be found in the somewhat less precise psychotherapeutic theories of Kelly (114). Rotter's influence can be found in the social learning views by Bandura (13) and Mischel (152, 154). During the 1960s the small but influential volume by Miller, Galanter & Pribram (150) generated considerable reexamination of the way man steers himself in his environment, physical as well as social. Lewin's influence has made a strong impact on social psychological personality research through the developments by Heider (85) and Festinger (62) which have generated views of the importance of cognitive consistency and attitudinal balance in the way man orients himself and appraises situations. The integration of the cognitive with conceptions of man's emotions and differentiated affect system is also a part of this development and is manifested in work such as that of Schacter (191), McClelland (141), Kelley (Attribution Theory) (112), Lazarus (124), Tomkins (230), and Zajonc (254).

Of all of these, Tomkins' position is the most ambitious in its attempt to integrate the image-making capacity of man with a differentiated affect system that serves as the basic motivational structure. Tomkins' theory comes closest to being a major new personality theory that deserves examination alongside those listed by Hall & Lindzey, but its influence is only recently being felt in empirical research, particularly in studies of emotion.

A series of recent symposia have also brought together investigators who are applying cognitive constructs to the examination of research questions that bear ultimately on personality (4, 103, 197, 209). As Jessor & Feshbach (103) point out, a cognitive position actually makes it possible also to examine in detail the nature of a variety of stimulus situations and should not be misconstrued as primarily an intrapsychic position. Indeed the nature of cognitive appraisal makes it necessary that we examine the interactions between the type of plans or images that a person brings to a situation and the complex environmental situations that confront him, so that we can ultimately make better prediction of the interaction of the initial expectations brought to a situation with the complex demands of the social structure.

Research examples also of cognitive approaches to the control of aggression and of a variety of other motivations are presented in the collections of Singer (209) and Zimbardo (256). The last named describes a series of ingenious experiments involving elaborations of balance theory in social psychology as a mechanism by which subjects can control a great variety of physiological and social responses. What is perhaps lacking in Zimbardo's work (as he himself admits) is sufficient emphasis on predisposing personality characteristics. As Wallach has noted (238), the future research in personality requires that we take into account the complex internal differentiation of predispositions which the subject brings to a situation. We cannot rely solely on one dimensional measurement in relating individual differences to a specific situation under investigation. This means that if we are to make statements about personality-environmental interactions, at the very least we ought to have some combination of moderator variables—e.g. High and Low Repression-Sensitization, High and Low External Locus of Control, High and Low Introversion-Extraversion, High and Low Anxiety, etc—in some combination (200) before we move on to any form of experimental manipulation.

EMOTIONS AND PERSONALITY

The healthy outcome of the more cognitively oriented theorizing in the 1960s has been, intriguingly enough, the revival of interest in emotion and affect as fundamental motivational characteristics of human behavior. This is an important step because theories of personality have paid surprisingly little attention to the experiences of excitement, surprise, or joy, as well as fear or anger. The recent findings that there are centrally controlled "joy" or aversive control mechanisms in the brain (41, 165) have made it all the more important that we recognize the nature of man's capacity for self-reward and punishment through a differentiated affect system. The affects, as experienced, undoubtedly are critical in motivation, but in addition (we shall see from reviewing some of the empirical research in a moment) the affects also play a critical role in communication of reinforcing (negative or positive) stimulation from one's social environment. That is to say, in making judgments about our own behavior or others, we are constantly on the lookout for indications that others approve, are happy, sad, interested, or angry, and that communication of our affects through facial or bodily gestures may influence the interaction possibilities in a situation.

A major publication in the last year was *Feelings and Emotions*, edited by Magda Arnold (5). This volume reflects more emphasis on the integration of cognitive and emotional factors than was the case in earlier symposia on emotion. This is evident in Pribram's (173) chapter on feelings as monitors, in which he relates the notion of emotion to the concept of hierarchy of plans and of images. One might also call attention to the extremely condensed but insightful paper by Tomkins (232) which attempts to specify the innate activators of nine separate affects, which Tomkins feels are essentially highly differentiated systems, that man as a species has developed through natural selection. He proposes that the affects are by themselves functions of the information-processing capacities of the organism so that the different affects are aroused as a consequence of the rate of stimulation increase, stimulation persistence, and stimulation decrease. In effect, this proposal involves an appraisal of a variety of situations and of the organism's capacity to deal rapidly and effectively with new stimulus information. In this sense it represents an integration of an information-processing system with a complex emotional structure which communicates positive or aversive information to the organism.

Papers by Schacter (191) on the social contexts of evaluation of emotion, and by Arieti (3), written from a psychiatric point of view signaling the increasing awareness of the cognitive role in emotion, also are part of this trend. Especially valuable is the paper by Lazarus, Averill & Opton (124), which carries the cognitive perspective on emotion into the description of a series of empirical studies. For these authors the appraisal of the situation is a key feature of emotion; each particular emotion presumably being related to a different evaluation. Arnold (6) also emphasizes this point of view and attempts to trace out the different patternings within the brain itself which might account for a differentiated affect system.

Darwin's famous studies in 1872 suggested that the face plays a central role in affect and emotion, as well as in motivation. This notion has been strongly revived in recent years through the influence of Tomkins (230). Izard (98) has moved on to carry out a series of significant studies that make it clear that the human face indeed is "wired" to present a series of emotions and that these can be discriminated across cultural groups. For example, Izard (97, 98) proposes the hypothesis that emotions provide a common basis of subjective experiences and expressive behaviors, and that these experiences and expressions tend to generate a set of labels or symptoms which have universal meaning. This hypothesis was tested by indicating that subjects from different cultures are able to match pictured representations of the fundamental emotions and verbal labels of these emotions with a high degree of uniformity. Free response labeling of the emotional expressions and of attitudes toward the emotion also showed substantial cultural consistency. A second major hypothesis was that there are a limited number of fundamental emotions, and that the closer one comes to representing one of these in pure form, the greater the likelihood of recognition, even when complex emotions are represented on stimulus pictures. It was clear that although there were important cultural differences, a considerable number of similarities emerged. Izard also proposed that similarity across cultures would decrease as one moved from facial behavior which, according to Tomkins, is an intrinsic component of the emotion itself, to gross bodily response gestures or peripheral responses, and finally to instrumental acts. Emotional labeling should be most closely linked to facial expression across cultures.

Another investigator who has pursued a similar line with somewhat different means has been Ekman. An impressive series of careful investigations (45–50) have also suggested the comparability of facial representation of the basic emotions across cultural groups. These emotions are happiness, anger, sadness, disgust, surprise, and fear. Ekman and collaborators (50) were able to show that facial expressions were judged relatively comparable by a group of Caucasian and Oriental subjects. Indeed, it was possible to show that preliterate cultures, only minimally exposed to Western civilization influences, also were capable of identifying the same fundamental emotional expressions represented on photographs. By the use of very clever graphic techniques, Ekman's group (46) has also been able to demonstrate that important discrepancies between a conscious intended emotion and an emotion which the subject was trying to conceal could be detected by comparing a facial expression with postural and leg movements. Ekman & Friesen (45) have sought to classify nonverbal behavior systematically in relation to their communication intent and have carried out mappings of the possible range of muscular activity and facial expression. Most recently Ekman, Friesen & Tomkins (49) have developed an instrument entitled the Facial Affect Scoring Technique, which consists of a large series of photographs that have been carefully tested for reliability and examined for their capacity to evoke single emotions. We are now in a much better position to move towards careful research on the subtleties of affective communication via the face.

An important personality dimension that has often been noted in connection with affective communication has been degree of control over overt expression of emotion. A most interesting study on the evaluation of a slap-stick movie by subjects encouraged to laugh concurrently or to inhibit laughter was carried out by Leventhal & Mace (127). The major results of their two experiments suggest that people with high control over the onset and termination of their own expressive behavior (in this case laughter) are able to discount their own laughter when making cognitive evaluations of their response to a stimulus. This would suggest that some degree of differentiation takes place at the cognitive level in persons who have already mastered certain kinds of affective control. Lanzetta & Kleck (122) also found in quite a different study that the subjects who themselves showed considerable control over their emotions as expressed facially, and whose nonverbal behavior could not be discriminated by others, were themselves better at discriminating nonverbal affective behavior. The authors propose that "the person who has been given training by a socializing agent in the inhibition of his affect displays should be sensitive to these displays in other individuals." The relationships between this type of control and the kind of cognitive differentiation of field dependence-independence described by Witkin and his collaborators seems an especially intriguing possiblity for future research.

A study by Carlson & Levy (32) carries the notions of Tomkins concerning basic idioaffective polarities a step farther toward empirical tests in a series of experiments. Tomkins developed a polarity scale (231), an instrument designed to test the difference between idioaffective postures that are part of the socialization of affect in the individual. The humanist posture is characterized as involving an orientation toward an interest in people and an openness to new experience manifested also in a willingness to "taste" things. By contrast, the normative orientation implies a maintenance of safe distance from potential unpleasantness (an olfactory orientation), a somewhat contemptuous rejection of unpleasant experiences, and a tendency to review external situations as negatively affective loaded in general. Using a sample of Black male and female college students, Carlson & Levy found that the "tasters" were much more likely to indicate interpersonal and socially oriented interests, whereas the "smellers" were much more likely to emphasize interests and values and individual "virtues." When the same subjects were given an opportunity to rate photographs for pleasantness-unpleasantness of facial expression, the subjects who were high on a combination of personal orientation and "taste" differed strikingly from those high on social orientation and "smell." Combining the social-personal dimension, and the taste-smell dimension, led to clear indications that the humanistic subjects who construed themselves in interpersonal terms are more likely to see another person experiencing pleasant emotions.

An unusually interesting study that relates cognitive and affective variables was reported by Witkin, Lewis & Weil (252). They studied affective reactions of patients in psychotherapy under conditions where both patients' level of psychological differentiation (as measured by the Witkin rod and frame test) and therapists' level of differentiation were known. This study, while involving only a small number of subjects, is especially noteworthy because it is one of the few that meets some of the criteria for personality research raised by Carlson. It establishes a fundamental predisposition that the subject brings to the session; it measures subjects over a relatively longer period than one experimental hour; and it examines the organization of personality dimensions within a given individual. For example, the investigators propose that shame, since it is more oriented towards the reaction of others, would correspond to a more field-dependent orientation (since it is known that field-dependent persons are more likely to examine the faces of others). Guilt, in contrast, is more likely to be based on an individual's independent judgment against his own internalized moral standards. A series of predictions were made concerning the references to shame and guilt, manifestations of diffuse or specific anxieties, and to the patterns of communications and interaction between patients and therapists.

On the basis of ratings of taped protocols over 20 sessions of psychotherapy, there was ample evidence that the patients differentiated by their cognitive styles also differed rather remarkably in their language, references to symptoms and problems, amount of communication at different stages of a session or treatment, and also in their pattern of interaction with therapists of like or differing cognitive style. For example, the combination of a field-dependent patient with a field-independent therapist produced more interactions than the combination of field-independent patient and field-independent therapist. A recent study by Gates (73) has also yielded evidence that field-independent subjects are more likely to emit negative-toned affective communications, and to differ in conditionability in a verbal conditioning experiment.

Studies of Specific Affective and Cognitive Dimensions

Anxiety.—Anxiety continues to play a significant role as a means of dividing subjects and proposing individual differences in performance based on some theoretical construct. A major new trend in the work with anxiety has been a shift towards new instruments which attempt to differentiate anxiety as a persisting predisposition (trait) and anxiety as a momentary reaction to a stress (state) (215, 216). Efforts are under way to examine more precisely the differential internal characteristics of anxiety which must be studied in combination with other variables in order to produce a predicted result (55, 137, 202). A careful reexamination of the literature by Saltz (184) has also emphasized the necessity of taking into account different stressors in the situations which lead to differential reactions in persons ordinarily classified as high or low on manifest anxiety scales. There is also an increasing interest in combining either stress reactions or measures of manifest anxiety with measures of introversion-extroversion as a basis for making predictions about specific response patterns (67, 200).

An important paper by Epstein (53) reflects again the move towards a somewhat more cognitive view of the nature of anxiety. Epstein concludes that all the theories of anxiety yield the following commonality: all describe anxiety in relation to primary overstimulation, cognitive incongruity, and response availability. He proposes that all three conditions yield somewhat different feeling states, but all three have one thing in common: they produce a high state of diffuse arousal. It should be noted that this formulation is not dissimilar from that of Tomkins (230) or of Izard & Tomkins (99), who describe anxiety as one of the major affects (they use the term fear-terror) which is aroused by a relatively steep increase in "density of neural firing," or in other words, unassimilable information. Epstein attempts to relate anxiety to general arousal level which overlap considerably since both are a function of intensity, rate of stimulation, expectancy, and opportunity for motor discharge, as well as the preceding excitatory state of the organism. Epstein proposes that fear and anxiety are attempts to provide defenses which prevent the occurrence of the more intolerable extreme levels of arousal. He elaborates at some length on the issue of stimulus uncertainty as a factor in anxiety, and it is quite clear from analysis, his emphasis on expectancy, and the series of experimental studies described that the role of cognition will play an increasingly important part in any future studies of anxiety. As Epstein notes, the initial level of arousal of the individual, as measured for example by his scores on state and trait anxiety scales, and the degree of uncertainty in a given situation would both have to be determined to predict an anxiety reaction to a complex stimulus. Again, it is clear that multivariate procedures and the use of moderator variables would be critical for any future research testing some of these notions concerning anxiety.

Thus, Hamilton (82) was able to show that there were two major personality dimensions, repression—sensitization and submissiveness, which were primarily important in differentiating between a group of subjects who used different methods for resolving cognitive inconsistencies. One can hope that the extensive development of the state-trait anxiety measure (215, 216) will lend itself to combinations with a variety of other scales for future research that will give a more complex description of the characteristics subjects bring to experimental situations or (hopefully) to the naturalistic situations that may be the subjects of future research. Spielberger's work also gives greater emphasis to cognitive factors (74, 215).

A number of studies involving extensive physiological measurement have appeared which indicate the role of expectancy and of uncertainty. For example, Epstein & Clarke (54) found among other things that there was an increase in deceleration of heart rate immediately before the impact of a noxious stimulus, which served later to reduce heart rate immediately following the impact. A similar result was obtained by Elliott, Bankart & Light (51), who found that heart rate fell in anticipation of a shock while Palmar conductance tended to increase. Epstein & Roupenian (56) also noted that the group with the greatest expectation of receiving a shock showed the least arousal during the anticipatory period, while for both Palmar conductance and heart rate the group showing the least expectation of the shock showed the greatest impact effect. Epstein & Fenz (55) also classified subjects on the basis of an analysis of the Taylor Manifest Anxiety Scale into those showing predominantly striated muscle tension and those showing predominantly autonomic arousal. Differences emerged between the subjects with respect to habituation to a loud noise.

An intriguing difference in physiological responsiveness as a function of the social stimulus valve emerged in a study by Goldstein and co-workers (76). These investigators found that adolescents whose problems were family centered showed much greater physiological reactivity during family interviews than did youngsters whose behavior difficulties extended beyond the home. Parental physiological reactivity paralleled that of the children.

The attribution theory of Kelley was strongly supported in an ingenious study (223) which demonstrated that insomniacs were able to get to sleep more rapidly if they could attribute their restlessness to the effects of a pill rather than to their habitual difficulty. Subjects who believed their normal restlessness was persisting despite a presumed relaxation pill (actually a placebo) had even greater trouble sleeping than usual.

Although much of the research on test anxiety as one phase of the general study of anxiety has originated in the Hull-Spence drive theory, more recent emphasis has also been upon the cognitive components related to test anxiety. This is well exemplified in a recent review of a number of studies of test-anxiety in children by Sarason (187). His exploration of a large number of studies leads to the conclusion that persons differing in assessed test anxiety differ largely with respect to the degree to which they attend to environmental stimuli and how they employ these cues in problem solving. Sarason cites a particularly interesting study which he carried out with a sample of juvenile delinquents (188). The study involved a television modeling procedure and a comparison of high and low anxious adolescents. The results made it clear that the manner of presentation made quite a difference in the ways in which the test-anxious subjects used the cue (70, 189). Shimkunas (202) also emphasizes the role of cognitive factors such as expectancy in the performance of anxious adult subjects.

A study by Messer (148) examined anxiety in children along with a cognitive stylistic variable, Kagan's reflective-impulsive dimension (108). Messer was able to demonstrate that decision time in a cognitive task was increased for both impulsive and reflective children by induced anxiety, with the result that the impulsive children then showed fewer errors because of the "greater delay in responding." There is also support from a study by Martens & Landers (137) of the well-known "inverted-U" hypothesis for subjects low, medium, or high in trait anxiety on the Children's Manifest-Anxiety Scale.

Aggression.—Aggression continues to be a subject of serious concern to investigators of personality, although the enormity of the problem as evidenced in the dramatic instances of violence that have occurred in wars, insurrections, and in individual acts of private citizens still remains largely beyond the scope of investigation in a more formal sense. A series of books which have appeared attest to the fact that psychologists can address themselves in a very careful and effective fashion to the technical problems of studying aggression and its relationship to personality factors (19, 61, 111, 143, 166, 209). Berkowitz (19), for example, reexamines the whole question of frustration and aggression and relates the aggressive response to the "dashing of hopes" or to a breakdown in expectation. Megargee & Hokanson's (143) collection of papers includes Megargee's investigation of under-controlled and overcontrolled personality types and extreme violence. Hokanson also presents an important study of aggression as a learned response in relation to a particular target which can be tension-reducing under specific circumstances, but which can also show an increased likelihood or recurrence during threat. Hokanson (143) also cites evidence that counter-responses towards others can have physical tension-reducing characteristics. These data, as well as very interesting work on the control of aggression in nursery school groups by Brown & Elliot (28) and the research program of Bandura and various collaborators (13), all point to social learning and inter-personal orientation as a central feature of aggressive behavior. This social learning point of view is especially well presented in a brief but thoughtful examination of the nature of aggression by Kaufmann (111). Kaufmann deals quite effectively with the limitation of the widely held views of aggression as the drive or periodically built up instinct, and points out very carefully the ways in which it is most usefully viewed as a learned behavior. The physiological underpinnings of aggressive reactions are especially well summarized by Moyer (159), and the key role of a brain structure such as amygdala is examined. The possibilities of chemical and electrophysiological control of aggressive response are dealt with in this thoughtful review. Important reviews of literature on alternatives to aggression through the development of altruistic responses are also presented by Staub (219) and by Kaufmann (111).

During 1969 and 1970, public pressure on popular media led to sharp reductions in the television presentation of fictional violence. This public concern also led to the establishment of a special National Institute of Mental Health committee which has now funded approximately 25 studies on various aspects of television violence. In 1971, however, a major review (211) appeared which questioned whether the emphasis on fictional violence in television might be given too much weight as a factor leading to overt aggressive behavior in children and adults. The outcome of such studies is far from certain, and one must examine more fully the role of news reports of violence and the general modeling effect of the war itself on the response of individuals. An important question raised is whether personality differences that precede the viewing situation itself may play a role in the degree to which either an increase or reduction in aggression follows the viewing of aggressive material in television. Biblow (20), for example, found that children who were first aroused to anger and then shown either an aggressive, benign, or nonfantasy television presentation differed considerably in their subsequent behavior depending on whether they were initially predisposed toward imaginative play or not. High-fantasy children showed a reduction in aggressive behavior following both aggressive and benign presentations, while low-fantasy children showed a trend toward increased aggression following only the aggressive film. Important differences in mood evoked by the different types of film also were in evidence, suggesting that one is dealing largely with an effect on mood rather than with a specific drive-arousing or drive-reducing effect.

A major study appearing in 1971 was that of Feshbach & Singer (61). This investigation is one of the most carefully controlled experiments on the effects of extended television viewing of violence on boys' overt aggressive behavior. Especially important is the fact that actual aggressive behavior as well as aggressive play behavior were studied, and that the initial hostility level of the subjects was taken into account and was examined in relation to the response to a steady diet of aggressive or nonaggressive television programs. In general, the data suggest that there was a reduction in overt aggressive behavior for the children who viewed the predominant television diet of violence. This reduction was especially strong for the boys initially highly aggressive. The authors interpret their results not so much in terms of a traditional catharsis hypothesis, but rather in terms of a cognitive support hypothesis: the boy who does not or cannot engage in self-generated fantasy needs the external support provided by the vicarious fantasy experience of watching violence on television. In contrast to the high-manifest-aggression boys whose "need" for cognitive support stems from the strength of their aggressive tendencies, the "need" of the low-fantasy subjects stems from their lack of adequate cognitive resources. This would be especially true for low-fantasy-aggression boys with strong manifest aggressive tendencies. The experimental effects tend to be the strongest for this group.

A grim and dramatic opportunity to test the role of participation directly or vicariously in hostile activities in the reduction of subsequent hostile aggressive fantasy was carried out by Shallit (199). This author studied a group of Israeli troops who were tested on various projected techniques measuring aggressive fantasy just prior to the 1967 Six-Day War, and then immediately following the war, and finally a year after the war. All indices of fantasy hostility were lower in 1967 immediately after the war or following years. The results seem to support those of Singer (206) which dealt with the reduction of aggression for highly aroused and involved subjects after exposure to hostile humor.

Much of the accumulating data on the role of aggression in personality seems to suggest that aggression is largely a learned response, primarily triggered by observation of others' aggressive behavior (57, 203, 227). Shortell et al (203), for example, were led to conclude that the critical role in instigation to aggression was played by the subject's perception of the opponent's aggressive intent. A well-executed study on the possible learning milieu producing subsequent aggressive behavior in children was carried out by Deur & Parke (42). These authors, using a reinforcement paradigm with young children, found considerable evidence of the fact that while punishment may indeed suppress aggressive behavior in children, inconsistent reward and punishment for aggressiveness lead the aggressive behavior to be more resistant to extinction.

There seems to be considerable increase in clarity in our approach to the study of individual aggressive behavior. Yet most of these studies examine predominantly one, or at most two, interacting variables: generally a situationally induced variable and perhaps one other predisposition variable such as the original level of aggression or fantasy predisposition. Clearly, we need studies which will take into account combinations of such variables as imaginative predisposition, general aggressive tendency, expectations of a given situation, perception of aggression in others in the situation, and so forth. In addition, one needs to examine evidence for persisting trends of aggressive behavior as against single actions. The relationship of aggressive overt responses to emotional arousal or the affect of anger still needs further study.

We seem as yet far from understanding what prompted the incredible cold-blooded killings during the My-Lai incident. A series of studies by Baron (15–17) addresses some of the questions raised in indicating that aggressive attacks in an experimental situation are greater when the subjects are angered than when they are relatively unaroused. The degree of aggressive response is sharply *reduced* by evidence of *pain and suffering* on the part of the victim, despite previous level of anger arousal or degree of aggressive-victim similarity. Finally, it was found that even a high expectation of retaliation failed to reduce aggression that had been influenced by the observation of a model's aggressive behavior. It remains to be seen, however, whether the impact of a generalized model (such as the overall military, for example) will override the screams and apparent pain of the victim to lead the aggressor to an increase or persistence of aggressive responses. This has yet to be tested. Does the My-Lai situation provide an answer?

Cognitive styles, imaginativeness, and fantasy.—Fruitful and intriguing work continues in the area of delineation of styles of information processing and organization which seem to have important correlates for the personality manifestations of individuals. This work, unfortunately, is fragmented, in the sense that individual investigators make up their own cognitive styles based on specific operations which they rarely relate directly to the cognitive styles that others are working with, or else they fail to attempt any kind of a general theoretical integration of the different styles which might lead to some more formal researches bringing together the different approaches.

The major cognitive style thus far delineated is Witkin's psychological differentiation or field independence-dependence (248–252). Studies continue to emerge offering some support or in general indicating the value of this significant notion of how individuals organize their experience (38, 100, 125, 139, 151, 193). Witkin has fairly recently provided a very thorough review of some of the major cross-cultural research bearing on cognitive style (248), which when added to his earlier paper (249) rounds out an impressive body of data indicating the value of this dimension for extended exploration. The reliability of the cognitive style across a time period received further support for a group of alcoholics (100) and in a longitudinal study of 28 male subjects over a 10-year period (193). Relationships between the measure of psychological differentiation and other important stylistic variables need to be clarified further, and subjects indeed ought to be chosen for their scores on combinations of style variables. An example of this approach is to be found in a study by Crego (38), who combined field-independence with two other major styles: Byrne's repression-sensitization and Rotter's internal-external control of reinforcement.

Other styles for which work has been done during this period include a number of studies of repression sensitization (11, 69). Weissman & Ritter (243), for example, report that high sensitizers are more open to a variety of experiences than middle groups or repressors, and they are less bound by rigid rules of society; they are less defensive but more anxious, less controlling over impulses, more rebellious and questioning, less satisfied with life, and more likely to experience frustration in interpersonal living (on the basis of their self report). Yet these authors found that sensitizers do not differ from middle scorers ("normals") on a measure of ego strength. These results certainly seem consistent with the report by Schimek (193), who has measured what he calls intellectualization (a score based on ratings of Rorschach protocols which, however, are geared towards the sensitization-repression dimension). Schimek's measure indicates a good deal of similarity between intellectualizers and sensitizers in the sense that there is interest in intellectual activity, competence, openness to new experience, pleasure in exploring and playing with ideas and fantasies, etc. Pathological tendencies include a tendency to depressive moods, self doubting, and aloofness or distrust. Schimek's measure is also associated with Witkin's field-independence with the indication that those few subjects who show discrepancies between their intellectualization scores and the field-independence measure also showed greatest conflict in their life situations. Hamilton (82) found that sensitizers tended to be more aware of inconsistencies in material presented and responded by efforts to go along with the threat rather than to avoid or deny the existing incongruities.

A rather complex study by Shevrin, Smith & Fritzler (201) attempted to pin down some of the physiological concomitants of attention for subjects classified as repressive or non-repressive on ratings also drawn from the Rorschach test. They found that for subliminal stimulus presentation, repressive subjects tended to have smaller amplitudes on an EEG measure and fewer subliminal verbal associates. The authors are led into some rather elaborate post hoc reasoning to deal with the findings of differences for the supraliminal and subliminal stimuli for the two groups. Andrew (2), employing her own method of measuring repression-sensitization, applied this to the rather novel situation of recovery from surgery. The evidence indicated that persons who scored at the intermediate levels on the R-S dimension showed the most adaptive reactions, particularly when provided with information about the operation.

Some other styles that were the subject of research during this period may be mentioned briefly. Grove & Eisenman (80), for instance, studied complexity-simplicity. Bronson (27) found rather striking differences in young children during a longitudinal study in the role played by their fear of novelty. Following a group of 30 boys and 30 girls over a period of 8 years, Bronson found that the predisposition to fearfulness in novel situations manifested in boys as early as 6 months of age was consistently predictive of fear reactions over the 8-year period. This style was not in evidence for girls in the sample, however. This is an extremely important finding and merits considerable further work because of its wide implications. Still another dimension studied in children and manifested at relatively early ages has been the tendency towards imaginative predisposition (20, 68, 77, 175). These investigators found that children showed early a tendency to engage in varied degrees of make-believe play. Such sociodramatic play can lead to greater concentration and enjoyment during spontaneous play and can aid in coping with frustration and the effects of aggressive television shows. Meichenbaum & Goodman (146) have shown that teaching children to talk to themselves can also aid in controlling excessive impulsivity.

There has been some further work on the style of augmenters and reducers in respect to response to pain (156). At some point this dimension ought to be related more closely to measures such as repression-sensitization, field-dependence, internal vs external locus of control, and related aspects of personality.

The introversion-extraversion dimension, particularly as it is related to the processing of stimuli from long-term memory for the projection of fantasies and the dependence upon stimulation from the outside world, has become a more central part again of descriptions of personality structure. The significance of man's imagery was emphasized in recent publications by Natsoulas (162), Paivio (168), Rohwer (181), Horowitz (94), Singer (208), and Segal (197). The continuity between dreams and daydreams as active processes manifesting the ongoing problem solving orientation of man—his creativity, reaction time, and time experience—was also brought out in a series of recent publications (65, 115, 120, 125, 180, 192, 210, 233, 244). These authors have all emphasized the adaptive function of imagining and fantasy behavior for children and adults and their role in the structure of personality.

Sarbin & Juhasz (190) have attempted reexamination of the linguistic use of imagination with the view of indicating more precisely what we mean when we talk of man's imagery. These authors emphasize the active role of imitation and role taking in the production of imaginative behavior, and they attempt to dispel the notion of man as a passive screen across whose "mind" images flit. Their emphasis is strongly on the *as if* quality of man's ability to act. They report on research in which a variety of tasks requiring production of imagery for their solution turn out to show a significant correlation with performance measures of imagery and role taking ability. This view of imagery and fantasy capacity as involving aspects of accommodation to the outside, and assimilation of the imitated material as well as projection on to the future of alternative possibilities, has also been stressed by Singer (207, 208). Clinical studies such as the one by Chethik & Fast (34) on fantasy in emotionally disturbed children also call attention to the degree to which fantasy behavior has positive adaptive aspects.

The emphasis on centrally emitted stimuli and imagery, day-dreaming, and imagery processes has also been heightened by new avenues of research relating to increased attentional control and central feedback processes in which there is increased evidence of the value of imagery techniques in effecting autonomic brain processes. Especially dramatic have been the findings of Kamiya (109) and his various collaborators on the operant control of the EEG alpha rhythm. Examples of the importance of meditation and controlled imagery in producing increased hypnotic susceptibility and related states are presented by Maupin (138) and by Tart (226). The importance of the dimension of hypnotizability, which has been increasingly studied not so much as a mysterious trance state but as a capacity to focus attention, has also been examined in relation to imagery capacity and to the availability of external sensory stimulation (24, 131, 225, 247). Preliminary work on the important uses of various types of meditation in imagery in controlling particularly EEG states has been reported by Green, Green & Walters (79). They also describe, in addition to their research on creative imagery, samples of remarkable control of heart rate as well as alpha, theta, and delta rhythms on the EEG by specially trained subjects and by Japanese Zen masters or Indian yogis.

An excellent new review of the entire issue of the relationship of hypnotic states to altered states of consciousness, including various types of meditation experiences and the effects of various psychedelic drugs, has just been published by Barber (14). Barber's work is especially valuable because of its freedom from any burden of excessive theoretical elaboration. It focuses on hypnosis and related altered states of consciousness as examples of extremely concentrated attention and other capacities that are part of a normal adult behavioral repertory, but which emerge only under special circumstances of restricted sensory stimulation.

The relation of personality variables of various types to the tendency to engage in considerable daydreaming, imagery, or related fantasy processes has not been really extensively studied. In general, the data seem to agree in suggesting that attention to one's own inner processes and openness to novel experience or to fantasy play a role in this respect (70, 79, 190, 222, 226, 243).

Some rather remarkable findings that imply an ultimate relationship between introversive processes and the hemispheric dominance in the brain have been described by Bakan (8, 9). Bakan's emphasis has been on the shift in direction of gaze of an individual when he is required to answer questions that call for processing of long-term memory material of an imaginative nature [a technique originally proposed by Day (40)]. The necessity for elimination of external stimulation during the processing of daydreamlike material had been demonstrated experimentally by Singer, Greenberg & Antrobus (212). Bakan found that subjects were either predominantly right or left lookers in about 70% of their responses to certain questions. A study of individuals showing either left or right eye movement indicated that left movers (persons characterized by considerable dominance presumably of the right brain hemisphere) indicate a greater hypnotic susceptibility, higher production of alpha in the EEG, greater control over alpha with training, more capability in verbal than in quantitative scores on SATs. They are more likely to choose classical-humanist college major subjects than right movers. Left movers report more vivid imagery than right movers, are more likely to prefer "warm" colors (e.g. red and yellow), music, and religion, and are more prone to asthma, while right movers are more prone to migraine headaches.

Bakan goes on to speculate that predominance of movement to the left may reflect greater dominance of the right hemisphere of the brain which presumably controls the more "non-verbal, emotional, analogic and subjective" modes of thought and response, while the left hemisphere may be more specific in controlling "verbal, rational, digital and objective" reactions. How do results like these tie in with the large body of data on field-dependence-independence of Witkin? What other connections can we perceive with styles or predispositions? Mobbs (155) noted that introverts spent much less time looking over at the experimenter's face while engaging in an imaginative task. A study by Singer, Greenberg & Antrobus (212) indicated that men use a shift of eye focus in order to "gate out" irrelevant visual input when processing their daydreams or related long-term memory material, while female subjects employed some more central gating technique under the same conditions.

We seem on the threshold in all of these studies of penetrating more deeply into longstanding and intriguing cognitive styles which play a rather important role in determining how much attention is paid to processing relatively internal material or external material and how these relative preferences may govern a whole set of interactions with the environment. Libby's (129) findings of stylistic differences in patterns of foreperiod delay in reaction time for adolescents and the many findings of reflectiveness-impulsivity in young children (see below) also point to the fact that some form of introversion-extraversion of a Jungian sort is still with us (200). It should be studied as part of the predispositions for information-processing which are brought along to situations by experimental subjects.

ACHIEVEMENT AND COPING BEHAVIORS

Early childhood.—Looking ahead in the 1970s, one can anticipate a tremendous acceleration in research on early childhood, spurred no doubt by the day care or comprehensive child care center movements. Of special interest even now is the effect of substitute care on the cognitive or emotional development of children and their subsequent school achievement or coping behaviors. A controlled study by Caldwell et al (30) found that children reared in a day care setting showed, if anything, a "slight rise" in developmental level. The importance of the mother, or of a nurturing adult, in fostering exploratory behavior or achievement motivation and self-reinforcing tendencies is stressed in studies of infants (1) and in retrospective reports of adolescents (86, 87).

Evidence of the importance of early predispositional styles such as reflectiveness-impulsivity in the achievement and information-processing behavior of children continues to appear. Reppucci (179) demonstrated that in children as young as 27 months, individual differences in sustained involvement, consideration of information, and formation of plans were evident. Maw & Maw (140) reported that boys who showed considerably more curiosity in spontaneous situations gave indications of higher self-esteem than those low in curiosity. Messer (149) found that impulsive boys studied in first and then third grade were decidedly inferior in achievement and language skills and seemed to miss important cues for reading development. A complex study by Reali & Hall (178) led to the conclusion that while the two stylistic groups did not differ in response to success or failure experiences, the reflectives took more time in decision making. This result was further borne out by Drake (43), who found longer eye fixations on a standard to be characteristic of reflective children. Adults in general were more reflective, but reflective adults showed a more complex and abstraction-oriented search pattern than did the impulsive adults.

The importance of identification patterns with same-sex figures or figures of differentiated social experience in generating self-esteem and achievement behavior is brought out in studies by Ozehosky & Clark (167). Girls exposed to more female models show higher self-esteem than boys at an early age (5), while children in desegregated schools show higher self-concepts and achievement than those in segregated schools. The susceptibility of the younger child to influence in learning tasks under praise or criticism is evident in a study by Spear (214), who compared first and fifth graders. Criticism has especially negative effects.

Attribution and achievement motivation.—Relatively new developments in the theory of achievement motivation and of motivation viewed as a cognitive appraisal process rather than as a function of drive are evident in a series of studies (66, 110, 177, 213, 234, 239, 240). Attribution theory emphasizes the importance that a person's appraisal of the causality relationships in different situations plays in determining his subsequent achievement. Weiner & Kukla (239), for example, conducted six experiments which related achievement motivation to causal ascription. Evaluation of achievement outcome was positively related to the amount of effort expended, but inversely related to level of ability. The writers found, too, that when individual differences in locus of causality were examined they were related to level of achievement needs. The results also indicated that individuals high in resultant achievement motivation were more likely to take personal responsibility for success than individuals low in achievement motivation. In the last of their six experiments, risk preference behavior and Atkinson's theory of achievement motivation were construed in attribution theory language. It was contended that cognitions about causality mediate between level of achievement needs and performance. Further work in attribution theory was also carried out by Raynor (177), who found in two studies, for example, that students high in Need Achievement and low in Test Anxiety received higher grades when they conceived a good grade in a particular college course to be related to their own future career success.

Smith & Winterbottom (213) found that college students with unrealistic expectations concerning grades attribute their difficulties to academic factors rather than to personal concerns. They tend also to be defensive, dependent on parents, and lacking in positive motivation for academic work. Other characteristics of high achievers involved relatively less alienation, distrustfulness, egocentricity, and anxiety than low achievers (174) in a study conducted with an upper middle class predominantly Jewish group. Turner (235) also found an identification variable of importance in the development of achievement motivation. His data suggest that occupation of father rather than class status or community background is the major determinant of need achievement in males. The degree of the father's entrepreneurial role, as evidenced by freedom from supervision of others, authority over others, decision-making obligations, and coordinating activities, was critical in establishing an achievement-oriented family structure.

On the whole, the pattern of studies suggests that a cognitive approach involving one's images and plans of the future and one's attributions of causality or images plays a key role in providing incentives for school or career achievement. The importance of opportunities for increased awareness, critical thought, and exploration of imagery as the means of maintaining academic orientation and combating alienation are stressed in a number of investigations (37, 52, 117, 158, 204).

Altruism.—Still a relatively fresh subject for personality researchers is the problem of altruism and benevolent behavior. A comprehensive review by Krebs (121) yielded the following general conclusions: 1. Most research examines the effect of temporary states rather than personality traits of the benefactor. 2. Both positive affective states associated with success and competence, and negative affective states associated with harming another result in altruistic behavior. 3. Research examining the effect of temporary states of the recipients suggests that the basic altruism-eliciting attribute of recipients is their dependency. The trait as well as the state of dependency can elicit altruism. 4. Interpersonal attractiveness of the recipient relates to altruism. 5. A fairly consistent increase in altruism with age is found in children. 6. Social class differences indicate that members of the working class and entrepreneurial middle class tend to behave in accord with the norm of reciprocity, while bureaucratic middle classes are more socially responsible. 7. In relation to recipients, the research demonstrates that the receipt of favors results in a general disposition toward altruism in some situations, although in research analyzed in the category of social norms, a state variable is assumed. 8. Although altruism does not consistently relate to sex in children, adult males have been found to act *less* altruistically toward highly (versus lowly) dependent others, especially if they seem threatening. Altruistic females act *more* altruistically toward highly dependent others.

Schwartz, Clausen & Clausen (195) replicated the Darley and Latane study of bystander aid to a seizure victim and examined the effects of: (*a*) number; (*b*) competence of bystanders; (*c*) information appropriate for action; and (*d*) ascription of responsibility upon helping by males and females. The factorial experiment involved 179 subjects. Speed of helping dropped significantly for females but not for males when other bystanders were present. Reporting also decreased but direct help was unaffected. Speed of helping dropped significantly further when another bystander was medically competent. In this condition reporting increased while direct help decreased. Among females disposed to accept rationales for denying responsibility, affects were particularly strong. Information-action and ascription of responsibility to the self were associated with faster and more direct help.

Staub and associates, working with children, have performed some recent experiments dealing with sharing behavior, children's actions in witnessing distress, the influence of nurturance in modeling children's attempts to help, and use of role playing and induction in children's learning in helping and sharing behavior (217–220). These studies, too complex for detailed presentation, spell out step by step the key predispositional and situational variables that contribute to altruistic responses in children. They point especially to the practical possibilities for training children in benevolent behavior.

Baldwin & Baldwin (10) attempted to study the development of children's cognitive understanding of interpersonal relationships and the development of concepts of kindness. A Kindness Picture-Story Measure was administered to 110 undergraduates and the children from kindergarten, second, fourth, sixth, and eighth grades. The data lend support to Piaget's findings of changes in maturity of cognitive understanding between 5 and 7 years of age. In five of the ten kinds of situations, significant increases in movement toward adult-like judgments came at this age period.

Attempting to compare development of moral attitudes between white and Negro boys, Harris (83) found, in an individually administered Piaget-type interview with 200 subjects, that "maturity" of moral attitudes was positively related to social class, white race, and vocabulary skills. Weisbroth (241) also attempted to study relationships of moral judgment with both sex and parental identification. Using 37 males and 41 females—white, middle class, college graduates, ages 21 to 39—the author found that there was no significant difference in moral judgment on Kohlberg's test between the sexes. Identification with both parents significantly related to high moral judgment in males, while identification with the father is significantly related to high moral judgment in females. Work with preadolescents (161) showed that girls who were more honest and altruistic (according to peer ratings) had warm intimate interactions with their mothers and high self-esteem. Boys' honesty (situational) was negatively correlated with gratifying relationships with parents and peers and self-esteem, but altruism was associated with good personal ego strength. Thus we see that girls who have high moral judgment tend to identify with their fathers, while girls who are altruistic tend to have intimate relationships with their mothers. Bryan & London (29) concerned themselves with modeling behavior, and concluded that family constellations which support expressions of affect, including empathic responses and helping behavior, would most likely raise children with concern for others. Families stressing competitive practices and status would attenuate helping.

A series of studies in 1970 also explored cultural factors in authoritarianism (253) and a variety of relationships between acquiescence, conformity, and anxiety level (36, 59, 72, 243, 257). To the growing list of studies on father-absence and its effect on personality variables, Numbauer & Gray (164) add an investigation of resistance to temptation in Negro boys and girls. They report that boys in father-absent families are more likely to yield to temptation than are girls from such families.

Trust.—Another dimension that has proved to be of increasing interest to personality researchers has been that of trust. Rotter (182) has led the way in exploring the possibility of a generalized expectancy for interpersonal trust as a major personality predisposition. Rotter and Stein, in an unpublished study, did find some evidence for a relation between their measure of interpersonal trust and the maladjustment as measured by the Incomplete Sentences Blank. In general, Rotter's data suggest that interpersonal trust in college students bears significant relations to parental attitudes, with the father playing a key role, and that it is not simply a function of low intelligence or gullibility. Strong support for the validity of the construct comes from an experiment by Boroto (23), who found that subjects who surreptitiously peeked at the experimenters' papers or at some "filthy pictures" scored far lower on the Rotter Trust Scale than did subjects who did not do so. More than half of the "peekers" later denied doing so, another indication of the validity of the trust construct. Interesting sex differences in cheating behavior were also reported by Jacobson, Berger & Millham (101), with men generally proving less likely to cheat.

The use of experimental games such as the Prisoner's Dilemma Game in a series of studies has not justified broad generalizations from behavior in the games to measures of trust or other personality variables (37, 135, 198, 221). Johnson (104, 105) found that role reversal more than self-presentation led to meaningful attitude change. More trust also emerged with reversal in another study by Johnson & Dustin (106). Johnson contends that most studies which involve bargaining games involve strategies and competitive choices that cannot be translated easily into behavior outside the laboratory. He urges more conflict resolution and trust research in actual consultation or T-group situations.

The importance of establishing open intentions and of compliant initiatives in developing cooperation and trust in experimental games was also found in several studies (142, 228). The evidence seems clear from experimental social interaction studies that the conditions needed to generate trustworthiness and positive interaction are increasingly well understood within these artificial structures. What we seem to need are increasing applications of these procedures to bargaining in more natural daily situations (e.g. labor disputes). From the standpoint of personality research, it is impressive to note how little effort is made to establish individual consistencies over time in response to these situations or how infrequently several combined personality trait measures are studied in relation to the experimental-created situation. An interesting step towards developing theory, and a method that may yield evidence on traits or generalized expectancies such as trust or authoritarianism, can be found in a study by Kelley & Stahelski (113). Using an attribution approach, they studied cooperation and competition in subjects with high and low scores in authoritarianism. They were able to show that the expectations of cooperation and competition from others in these contrasting groups lead to their own behavior reflecting their expectations of others. They propose a cognitive theory of how personality predisposition influences the information one looks for and the feedback one gets from his social environment. They extend the view to explain the mechanism of projection hitherto explained chiefly in psychodynamic terms. This approach suggests the beginnings of a much-needed extension of attribution theory and trust research to the area of psychopathology, where clinicians so often talk of the profound lack of early-established trust in schizophrenics. Can we ever begin to bring some of these notions together through formal research? One can also begin to think of applying these notions to the development of innovative social leadership in community work (123) or in response to real life stress (2).

SELF-CONCEPT, SELF-ESTEEM, AND SEX ROLE

Research and theory on self ought to stand at the center of personality research. Indeed, it is the awareness of self, the effort at differentiation of self, and the desire to see continuities in one's being that motivate so much popular interest in the psychology of personality or in abnormal psychology. The volume of research produced on self-esteem, sex-role identity, and development of self-concepts is quite extensive indeed, but it lacks any clear focus or major theoretical model which can help in unifying the material. This year did see the publication of a very well-written, lucid presentation of the major issues in Gergen's *The Concept of Self* (75). This short but excellent text deserves wide use by undergraduate students in clarifying how psychology can begin to make a contribution to studying the interactions of environmental circumstances and persisting memories and guiding images which provide the feeling of a sense of self. Gergen explores the definition of self, self-conception from a sociocognitive point of view, social comparison as a form of self-definition, multiple roles and role playing, social attraction, power, influence, and self-alienation. An example of Gergen's thoughtful yet simply presented approach is in his discussion of self in a complex society:

> To be maximally adaptive in a multiplex social environment is to be maximally vulnerable to experiences of self-alienation. In order to relate successfully over a wide range of relationships, it is virtually impossible to bind our behavior to a limited set of self-conceptions. Self-alienation, then, may be viewed as a necessary by-product of successful adaptation in a complex social world (p. 70).

Family structure and self development.—Most of the research during the past year on the role of the family constellation in the development of self-concepts has dealt with issues of sex-role and identity. Of special interest was the influence of father absence or presence in the family because of heightened awareness that so many poor and minority group families are matriarchal. Santrock (185), for example, employed both doll play and interviews with mothers to generate behavior ratings on preschool boys and girls from father-present and father-absent homes. The data yielded some strong sex difference. Father-absent boys were significantly more feminine, less aggressive, and more dependent than their father-present counterparts, but no significant differences emerged between father-absent and father-present preschool girls. The maternal interview proved to be a more discriminative device than the doll play interview in revealing sex-typed behaviors. Father-absent girls with older female siblings only, were significantly more dependent; father-present girls with older male siblings only, and father-absent girls with older male siblings only, were significantly more aggressive than father-absent girls with older female siblings only. Father-absent boys with older male siblings only were significantly more masculine than father-absent boys with older female siblings only. Father-absent boys with a father substitute were significantly less dependent than father-absent boys with no father substitute.

The significance of peer-orientation of parents (92) of ordinal position as well as family constellation and the availability of various positive role models for sex role and self-esteem are strongly supported in a series of studies (39, 91, 196), with indications that persisting patterns were well established by age 5. The importance of viewing the over-all family interaction pattern and availability of surrogate parents, or sociocultural milieu, is stressed in studies and reviews of the literature on male sex-role development (21, 22, 96). It is especially clear that most of the impact of father-absence on self-development is upon the male child, but the precise effects seem to vary widely for cultural groups.

Sex role, identification, and self-esteem in adolescence.—Studies with older children and adolescents continue to focus primarily upon the male role, or at least the data emphasize its importance. Connell & Johnson (35), for instance, found male adolescents with high sex-role identification also have greater feelings of self-esteem than either other men or women (irrespective of their sex-role identification). For the early adolescent, it would appear that the male role has value as a basis for self-esteem beyond that of the female role, regardless of whether the role is accepted by a male or female. Approaches to measurement of sex-role differentiation of the more general style of cognitive differentiation have relied heavily on human figure drawing methods (133, 224, 237). The work of Faterson & Witkin (60) is especially noteworthy because it is longitudinal, comparing subjects at ages of 8 and 13 for one group and 10, 14, 17, and 24 in another. They found an increase between ages 8 and 14 of the articulation of body concept, with little change thereafter and remarkable individual stability in differentiation evident over a 14-year span.

A number of studies with college students have continued to explore identification and role model patterns in relation to self-esteem and perception of sex role (18, 95, 176, 194, 236, 246). The question of comparable measurement methods and well-established behavioral and situational samplings remains a knotty problem in this area of research. So many of the methods depend on inventory and self-report scales that are often stereotyped (171) and subject to social-desirability or other test-taking measures of ideal self that seem especially vulnerable to social stereotype (171, 194). These measurement problems, whether in questionnaire or projective test form, make it difficult to interpret some studies which report that moderate hallucinogenic drug users have reasonably high degrees of self-acceptance (160), or that Haight-Ashbury drug users are less defensive about body boundaries (84). Unless a sufficient network of behavioral correlates surround a given score, it is difficult indeed to establish any generality for the many one-variable studies in this area.

Some of the many experimental variables introduced in relation to self-esteem have included similarity and attraction (90); compliance and anxiety in opinion and behavior change (126); receptivity and influencibility (255); acquiescence (44); behavioral consequences of induced self-esteem (78); social comparison and self-consistency (157); the effects of self-esteem and perceived performance on attributions of causality (63); the relationships of self-esteem and competence (88); and personality integration (25). In general, these investigators found that subjects tend to perceive others as similar in degree of self-esteem and to attribute positive characteristics to those high in self-esteem. Self-esteem is associated with "activity" in peer ratings (245), but it is also attributed to internal sources. Efforts at influencing young people or changing attitudes must take into account levels of self-esteem. The subtle interrelations of attractiveness of others, self-esteem, and linking of self to "ideal personality" are brought out in a study by Sapperfield & Balogh (186), using the choice of attractive photographs. An especially interesting study is that of Kiesler & Baral (116), who found that male dating choices of more or less attractive girls by college men were influenced by temporary raising or lowering of their self-esteem. Perhaps we need more studies that move out of the laboratory into the daily choice situations people face, to show how their persisting trend toward self-esteem or the temporary fluctuation in this variable affect their behavior. Ludwig (132) has provided a good review of the issue of the correlates and measurement of self-concept and has shown that self-ratings of esteem do vary with positive and negative feedback and that high self-esteem is associated with low overt aggressive behavior.

Some attempts to carry the study of self-esteem into work with pathological groups is reported by Jordan & Kempler (107) and Platman & Plutchik (171). The former divided subjects into hysterical and nonhysterical personalities and assigned them to groups receiving academic or sexual threat or a no-threat control. Physiological, perceptual, and behavior ratings were employed. Although the galvanic skin response did not differentiate between threat conditions, the psychological measures lend support to the authors' view that anxiety over inadequacy and over sex-role competence especially are significant factors in the hysteric's personality organization. Platman & Plutchik (171) found that when depressive patients were rated on various self-images, the depressed state was correlated highly with "least liked self." No discrimination on their scales emerged for manic patients.

Some attempts have also been made to relate minority group status and segregated or desegregated school experience to measures of self-concept (130). Powell & Fuller (172) assessed the effects of school desegregation and self-concept of junior high students in parochial and public segregated and desegregated schools. In all, 149 Negro students from desegregated schools and 175 Negro students from segregated schools were given a Self-Concept Scale and a Powell-Fuller Socio-Familial questionnaire. Results indicated that of the 617 subjects tested, higher scores on self-control were found by Negroes in segregated or predominantly (80%) Negro schools. Family stability, educational and occupational level of parents, and aspirational level of students were found to be related to self-esteem. These results are somewhat contradictory of findings reported with much younger children (167). Nor do they agree with those of a study by Singer (205) in which there were indications from self-drawings and other measures that experiences in unsegregated schools were more associated with higher self-awareness and acceptance for Black children.

BIRTH ORDER AND AFFILIATIVE TENDENCIES

The powerful effect of birth order in our society continues to be explored, although we still have insufficient evidence about the causal role involved in creating such consistent differences, especially between only children or first-born males and others. Is it the anxiety of new parents, the lack of competitiveness, or the overprotection that occasions the greater achievement motivation and the affiliative drive under anxiety of the initial child? An intriguing study with small samples by Weiss (242) indicates that first-born male infants show more rapid heart beats and higher respiration both in stress and later resting conditions than are found in later-born infants. This early indication of higher anxiety in first borns is remarkably like the findings for young adults differing in birth order.

Since affiliation under anxiety is one of the main dividing lines between first and later borns some clarification of the theory of affiliation and conformity ought to be incorporated into future studies. Mehrabian & Ksionzky

(145) represent affiliative characteristics in terms of a two-dimensional framework. Persons can be characterized by the extent to which they generally expect interactions with others to be positively reinforcing and negatively reinforcing. Four categories of affiliation are described and are related to existing measures of affiliative tendency. Conformity behavior in a related model is then expressed as a function of affiliative characteristics and target attributes. Bragg & Allen (26) used a form of role theory applied to the problem of birth order and conformity to a same sex peer group. Subjects were 73 male and female college students from two-sibling families. Results demonstrated that highest conformity was found for later-born females with same sex sibling, and least conformity for later-born males with same sex sibling. In the case of first borns, no difference in conformity emerged as a function of sex of their sibling. In a study by Forbes (64), first-born or only children when confronted with stress also preferred to affiliate themselves with others, confirming the now well-established finding. MacDonald (134), using 81 males and 99 females in an anxiety affiliation experiment, found that first borns reduced their anxieties more under enforced conditions, while later borns reduced their anxiety more in social isolation than in affiliation. First borns reduced their anxiety later than later borns in affiliation, but it was those first borns who did not want to affiliate that accounted for this difference; i.e. first borns in enforced affiliation reduced their anxiety more than first borns in self-selected affiliation. The link between anxiety and affiliation was especially pronounced in first-born males. Although achievement is often shown to be higher for first-born males, Exner & Sutton-Smith (58), in a study of Peace Corps volunteers, found that first-born or only siblings were more successful in teaching math and sciences, while second and third borns were more successful in teaching English. Thus one would have to look more closely at the particular characteristics of the experience provided by ordinal birth position before making any firm generalization about achievement or vocational direction.

SEX DIFFERENCES

In 1970 the Women's Liberation movement reached its highest point of influence and has had salutary effects in forcing psychologists to look more squarely at their own prejudices and blind spots in research. The review by Carlson (31), cited earlier, points out the degree to which research has neglected the female or the special quality of sex differences in reported findings. Space limitation prevents any detailed review of the recent developments in sex-difference research, although surprisingly few specific studies appeared this year. At least most of the papers reviewed this year made clear the sex composition of their groups and called attention to specific differences.

A well-organized, clear review by Garai (71) does present the major findings of some 30 studies that bear on sex differences in mental health and personality. The evidence he presents leads him to conclude that women suffer more from worries, fears, and anxiety-repressive psychosomatic symptoms such as headaches, backaches, insomnia, and high blood pressure than men, who are more likely to show skin disorders or peptic ulcers. Men's anxieties center more around occupational adancement or failure, while women are generally more anxious about interpersonal involvements. "Hapiness" for both groups is similarly related to occupational (men) or interpersonal relations (women). Whether such a finding will be sustained in the coming decade with women moving ever more actively into careers remains to be seen.

Surveying a range of reports, Garai also notes that while men around the world commit suicide three times as frequently as women, women's *attempts* outnumber those of men four to one. The psychological data support the greater achievement drive in men and affiliation motivation in women. While men tend to deny mental problems and illness, women are much more ready to seek help. Garai feels that the overall pattern suggests that women attain their sexual identity through intimacy with men, whereas men's identity is formed more through occupational goal attainment or "creative" endeavors. It remains to be seen whether more extensive research can clarify the origins of these gross differences which, like the much-discussed sex differences in Field-Dependence and Field-Independence reported so often by Witkin and his collaborators, remain an intriguing problem for personality research. Meanwhile, Helson (89) has continued her useful study of career development in women. Mischel (153) also has provided a fine review of sex-typing as a function of socialization.

A study by Mendelsohn & Gall (147) supports an earlier investigation by these authors in indicating that the "interpersonal context plays a far more significant role for female subjects than for male subjects" (147, p. 350). The study makes it clear that sex of experimenter and subject are critical variables in determining many experimental outcomes. One would hope that the 1970s may indeed show a fuller flowering of creative research on just what the psychological factors are that promote sex differences, how these differences lead to diverse information processing and affective styles, and whether changing occupational and educational opportunities for women will lead to a blurring of the psychological distinctions between the sexes in the future.

A FINAL WORD

Viewing the year's research against the perspective of the previous decade provides us with a clear indication that the model of personality that guides research has changed significantly. The earlier emphasis was on fundamental drives and on drive-reduction or hydraulic energy models strongly influenced by psychoanalysis. This model has yielded to a view of man as an information-processing creature whose emotions, fantasies, and dreams, as well as his self-concept, are part of his search for certainty, balance, and novelty in his environment. This newer model seems very liberating to the investigator. It remains to be seen, however, whether in the 1970s personality psychologists can meet the challenge of Carlson (31) and move to study persons in their natural environments over extended periods, to study the interrelationships of cognitive or affective styles within a person, and to carry out some type of analysis of the various environments in which people find themselves. Only then can we begin to estimate more accurately the variances contributed by longstanding predispositions and by specific situations.

LITERATURE CITED

1. Ainsworth, M. D., Bell, S. M. 1970. Attachment, exploration, and separation: Illustrated by the behavior of one-year-olds in a strange situation. *Child Develop.* 41:49–67
2. Andrew, J. M. 1970. Recovery from surgery, with and without preparatory instruction for three coping styles. *J. Pers. Soc. Psychol.* 15: 223–26
3. Arieti, S. 1970. Cognition and feeling. See Ref. 5, 135–43
4. Antrobus, J. S., Ed. 1970. *Cognition and Affect.* Boston: Little-Brown
5. Arnold, M., Ed. 1970. *Feelings and Emotions.* New York: Academic
6. Ibid. Perennial problems in the field of emotion, 169–85
7. Aronson, S. R. 1970. *A comparison of cognitive vs. focused-activities techniques in sensitivity group training.* PhD thesis. Univ. Connecticut
8. Bakan, P. 1969. Hypnotizability, laterality of eye movements and brain assymetry. *Percept. Mot. Skills* 28:927–32
9. Bakan, P. 1971. The eyes have it. *Psychol. Today* 4:64–69
10. Baldwin, C. P., Baldwin, A. L. 1970. Children's judgments of kindness. *Child Develop.* 41:29–47
11. Baker, R. P., King, H. H. 1970. The relationship between the repression-sensitization scale and the incomplete sentences blank. *J. Proj. Tech. Pers. Assess.* 34: 492–96
12. Bandura, A. 1969. *Principles of Behavior Modification.* New York: Holt, Rinehart & Winston
13. Bandura, A., Walters, R. 1963. *Social Learning and Personality Development.* New York: Holt, Rinehart & Winston
14. Barber, T. X. 1970. *L.S.D., Marijuana, Yoga and Hypnosis.* Chicago: Aldine
15. Baron, R. A. 1971. Magnitude of victim's pain cues and level of prior anger arousal as determinants of adult aggressive behavior. *J. Pers. Soc. Psychol.* 17:236–41
16. Baron, R. A. 1971. Exposure to an aggressive model and apparent probability of retaliation from the victim as determinants of aggressive behavior. *J. Exp. Soc. Psychol.* 7. In press
17. Baron, R. A. Aggression as a function of magnitude of victim's pain cues, level of prior anger arousal, and aggressor-victim similarity. *J. Pers. Soc. Psychol.* In press
18. Bell, A. P. 1970. Role modelship and interaction in adolescence and young adulthood. *Develop. Psychol.* 2:123–28
19. Berkowitz, L. 1969. *Roots of Aggression.* New York: Atherton
20. Biblow, E. 1970. *The role of fantasy in the reduction of aggression.* PhD thesis. City Univ. of New York
21. Biller, H. B. 1970. Father absence and the personality development of the male child. *Develop. Psychol.* 2:181–201
22. Biller, H. B., Singer, D. L., Fullerton, M. E. 1969. Sex-role development and creative potential in kindergarten boys. *Develop. Psychol.* 1: 291–96
23. Boroto, D. R. 1970. *The Mosher Forced Choice Inventory as a predictor of resistance to temptation.* Master's thesis. Univ. Connecticut
24. Bowers, K. S., van der Meulen, S. J. 1970. Effect of hypnotic susceptibility on creativity test performance. *J. Pers. Soc. Psychol.* 14: 247–56
25. Bowles, S., Wright, L. 1970. Personality integration in preadolescent males. *Develop. Psychol.* 2:151

26. Bragg, B. W., Allen, V. L. 1970. Ordinal position and conformity: A role theory analysis. *Sociometry* 33:371–81

27. Bronson, G. W. 1970. Fear of visual novelty: Developmental patterns in males and females. *Develop. Psychol.* 2:33–40

28. Brown, P., Elliott, R. 1970. Control of aggression in a nursery school class. See Ref. 143, 101–7

29. Bryan, J. H., London, P. 1970. Altruistic behavior by children. *Psychol. Bull.* 73:200–11

30. Caldwell, B. M., Wright, C. M., Honig, A. S., Tannenbaum, J. 1970. Infant day care and attachment. *Am. J. Orthopsychiat.* 40:397–412

31. Carlson, R. 1971. Where is the person in personality research? *Psychol. Bull.* 75:203–19

32. Carlson, R., Levy, N. 1970. Self, values and affects: Derivations from Tomkin's polarity theory. *J. Pers. Soc. Psychol.* 16:338–45

33. Carson, R. C. 1969. *Interaction Concepts of Personality.* Chicago: Aldine

34. Chethik, M., Fast, I. 1970. A function of fantasy in the borderline child. *Am. J. Orthopsychiat.* 40:756–65

35. Connell, D. M., Johnson, J. E. 1970. Relationship between sex-role identification and self-esteem in early adolescents. *Develop. Psychol.* 3:268

36. Costanzo, P. R. 1970. Conformity development as a function of self-blame. *J. Pers. Soc. Psychol.* 14:366–74

37. Cottle, L. J., Edwards, C. N., Pleck, J. 1970. The relationship of sex role identity and social and political attitudes. *J. Pers.* 38:435–52

38. Crego, C. A. 1970. A pattern analytic approach to the measure of modes of expression of psychological differentiation. *J. Abnorm. Psychol.* 76:194–98

39. Davids, A., Holden, R., 1970. Consistency of maternal attitudes and personality from pregnancy to eight months following childbirth. *Develop. Psychol.* 2:364–66

40. Day, M. E. 1964. An eye movement phenomenon relating to attention, thought and anxiety. *Percept. Mot. Skills* 19:443–46

41. Delgado, J. M. R., Roberts, W. W., Miller, N. E. 1954. Learning motivated by electrical stimulation of the brain. *Am. J. Physiol.* 179:587–93

42. Deur, J., Parke, R. 1970. Effects of inconsistent punishment on aggression in children. *Develop. Psychol.* 3:403–11

43. Drake, D. M. 1970. Perceptual correlates of impulsive and reflective behavior. *Develop. Psychol.* 2:202–14

44. Eisenman, R., Townsend, T. D. 1970. Studies in acquiescence: I, social desirability; II, self-esteem; III, creativity; IV, prejudice. *J. Proj. Tech. Pers. Assess.* 34:45–54

45. Ekman, P., Friesen, W. V. 1969. The repertoire of nonverbal behavior: Categories, origins, usage, and coding. *Semiotica* 1:49–98

46. Ekman, P., Friesen, W. V. 1969. Nonverbal leakage and clues to deception. *Psychiatry* 32:88–106

47. Ekman, P., Friesen, W. V. 1971. Constants across cultures in the face and emotion. *J. Pers. Soc. Psychol.* 17:124–29

48. Ekman, P., Friesen, W. V., Ellsworth, P. 1971. *Emotions in the Human Face: Guidelines for Research and a Review of Findings.* New York: Pergamon

49. Ekman, P., Friesen, W. V., Tomkins, S. S. 1971. Facial affect scoring technique: A first validity study. *Semiotica* 3. In press

50. Ekman, P., Sorenson, E. R., Friesen, W. V. 1969. Pan-cultural elements in facial displays of emotion. *Science* 164:86–88

51. Elliott, R., Bankart, B., Light, T. 1970. Differences in the motivational significance of heart rate and palmar conductance. *J. Pers. Soc. Psychol.* 14:166–72

52. Elson, A., Elson, M. 1970. Educating teacher and children on law: An approach to reduce alienation in inter-city schools. *Am. J. Orthopsychiat.* 40:870–78

53. Epstein, S. 1972. The nature of anxiety with emphasis upon its relationship to expectancy. In *Anxiety: Current Trends in Theory and Research,* ed. C. D. Spielberger. New York: Academic. In press

54. Epstein, S., Clarke, S. 1970. Heart rate and skin conductance during experimentally induced anxiety: Effects of anticipated intensity of noxious stimulation and experience. *J. Exp. Psychol.* 84:105–12

55. Epstein, S., Fenz, W. D. 1970. Habituation to a loud sound as a function of manifest anxiety. *J. Abnorm. Psychol.* 75:189–94
56. Epstein, S., Roupenian, A. 1970. Heart rate and skin conductance during experimentally induced anxiety: The effect of uncertainty about receiving a noxious stimulus. *J. Pers. Soc. Psychol.* 16:20–38
57. Epstein, S., Taylor, S. P. 1967. Instigation to aggression as a function of degree of defeat and perceived aggressive intent of the opponent. *J. Pers.* 35:267–89
58. Exner, J. E. Jr., Sutton-Smith, B. 1970. Birth order and hierarchical vs. innovative role requirements. *J. Pers.* 38:581–87
59. Ezekiel, R. S. 1970. Authoritarianism, acquiesence, and field behavior. *J. Pers.* 38:31–42
60. Faterson, H. F., Witkin, H. A. 1970. Longitudinal study of development of the body concept. *Develop. Psychol.* 2:429–38
61. Feshbach, S., Singer, R. 1971. *Television and Aggression.* San Francisco: Jossey-Bass
62. Festinger, L. 1961. *A Theory of Cognitive Dissonance.* Palo Alto, Calif.: Stanford Univ. Press
63. Fitch, G. 1970. Effects of self-esteem, perceived performance, and choice on causal attributions. *J. Pers. Soc. Psychol.* 16:311–15
64. Forbes, G. 1970. Fraternity and sorority membership and birth order: Sex differences and problems of reliability. *J. Soc. Psychol.* 82:277–78
65. Foulkes, D. 1970. *Longitudinal studies of dreams in children.* Presented at Am. Acad. Psychoanal., New York City
66. Franken, R. E., Morphy, D. R. 1970. Effects of fortuitous success on goal setting behavior of individuals high and low in achievement motivation. *Percept. Mot. Skills* 30:855–64
67. Fremont, T., Means, G. 1970. Anxiety as a function of task performance feedback and extraversion-introversion. *Psychol. Rep.* 27:455–58
68. Freyberg, J. T. 1970. *Experimental enhancement of imaginative play of kindergarten children in a poverty area school.* PhD thesis. City Univ. of New York
69. Gaines, L. S., Fretz, B. R. 1970. Ego

strength, social impression value of stimuli, and self-reference language. *J. Proj. Tech. Pers. Assess.* 3:428–31
70. Ganzer, V. J., Sarason, I. G., Green, C. T., Rinke, C. 1970. Effects of model's and observer's hostility on Rorschach, interview and test performance. *J. Proj. Tech. Pers. Assess.* 34:302–15
71. Garai, J. C. 1970. Sex differences in mental health. *Genet. Psychol. Monogr.* 81:123–42
72. Gardner, R. A. 1970. The use of guilt as a defense against anxiety. *Psychoanal. Rev.* 57:124–36
73. Gates, D. 1970. *Verbal conditioning, transfer and operant level (speed style) as functions of cognitive style.* PhD thesis. City Univ. of New York
74. Gaudry, E. Spielberger, C. D. 1970. Anxiety and intelligence in paired-associate learning. *J. Educ. Psychol.* 61:386–91
75. Gergen, K. J. 1971. *The Concept of Self.* New York: Holt, Rinehart & Winston
76. Goldstein, M. J., Rodnick, E. H., Judd, L. L., Gould, E. 1970. Galvanic skin reactivity among family groups containing disturbed adolescents. *J. Abnorm. Psychol.* 75:57–67
77. Gottlieb, S. 1968. *Modeling effects on fantasy.* PhD thesis. City Univ. of New York
78. Graf, R., Hearne, L. 1970. Behavior in a mixed motive game as a function of induced self-esteem. *Percept. Mot. Skills* 31:511–17
79. Green, E., Green, A. M., Walters, E. D. 1970. Voluntary control of internal states: Psychological and physiological. *J. Transpers. Psychol.* II:1–26
80. Grove, M., Eisenman, R. 1970. Personality correlates of complexity-simplicity. *Percept. Mot. Skills* 31:387–94
81. Hall, C. S., Lindzey, G. 1970. *Theories of Personality.* New York: Wiley. 2nd ed.
82. Hamilton, D. L. 1970. Personality attributes related to response preferences in resolving inconsistency. *J. Pers.* 38:134–45
83. Harris, H. 1970. Development of moral attitudes in white and Negro boys. *Develop. Psychol.* 2:376–83
84. Hartung, J. R., McKenna, S. A., Baxter, J. C. 1970. Body image and

defensiveness in an L.S.D.-taking subculture. *J. Proj. Tech. Pers. Assess.* 34:316–23

85. Heider, F. 1958. *The Psychology of Interpersonal Relations.* New York: Wiley

86. Heilbrun, A. B. 1970. Perceived maternal child-rearing experience and the effect of vicarious and direct reinforcement of males. *Child Develop.* 41:253–62

87. Heilbrun, A. B., Norbert, N. 1970. Maternal child-rearing experience and self-reinforcement effectiveness. *Develop. Psychol.* 3:81–87

88. Helmreich, R., Aronson, E., Lefan, J. 1970. To err is humanizing-sometimes: Effects of self-esteem, competence, and a pratfall on interpersonal attraction. *J. Pers. Soc. Psychol.* 16:259–64

89. Helson, R. 1970. Sex-specific patterns in creative literary fantasy. *J. Pers.* 38:344–63

90. Hendrick, C., Page, H. A. 1970. Self-esteem, attitude similarity, and attraction. *J. Pers.* 38:588–601

91. Herbert, E., Gelfand, D., Hartmann, D. 1969. Imitation and self-esteem as determinants of self-critical behavior. *Child Develop.* 40:421–30

92. Hollander, E. P., Marcia, J. E. 1970. Paternal determinants of peer-orientation and self-orientation among pre-adolescents. *Develop. Psychol.* 2:292–302

93. Holt, R., Ed. 1967. *Motives and Thought: Psychoanalytic Essays in Honor of David Rapaport.* New York: Int. Univ. Press

94. Horowitz, M. J. *Image Formation and Cognition.* New York: Appleton-Century-Crofts

95. Horricks, J., Weinberg, S. 1970. Psychological needs and their development during adolescence. *J. Psychol.* 74:51–69

96. Houston, H. S. 1970. Familial correlates of sex-role development in boys: An exploratory study. *Personality* 1:303–17

97. Izard, C. 1968. The emotions as a culture-common framework of motivational experience and communicative cues. *Tech. Rep. No. 30, Contract Nonr 2149, NR 171-609, Offi. Naval Res.*

98. Izard, C. 1971. *The Face of Emotion.* New York: Appleton-Century-Crofts

99. Izard, C., Tomkins, S. S. 1966. Affect and behavior: Anxiety as a nega-tive affect. In *Anxiety and Behavior,* ed. C. D. Spielberger, 81–125. New York: Academic

100. Jacobson, G. R., Pisani, V. D., Berenbaum, H. L. 1970. Temporal stability of Field-Dependence among hospitalized alcoholics. *J. Abnorm. Psychol.* 76:10–12

101. Jacobson, L. I., Berger, S. E., Millham, J. 1970. Individual differences in cheating during a temptation period when confronting failure. *J. Pers. Soc. Psychol.* 15:48–56

102. Janis, I. L., Mahl, G. F., Kagan, J., Holt, R. R. 1969. *Personality.* New York: Harcourt, Brace & World

103. Jessor, R., Feshbach, S., Eds. 1967. *Cognition, Personality and Clinical Psychology.* San Francisco: Jossey-Bass

104. Johnson, D. W. 1971. Effectiveness of role reversal: Actor or listener. *Psychol. Rep.* 28:275–82

105. Johnson, D. W. 1967. Use of role reversal in intergroup competition. *J. Pers. Soc. Psychol.* 7:135–41

106. Johnson, D. W., Dustin, R. 1970. The initiation of cooperation through role reversal. *J. Soc. Psychol.* 82:193–203

107. Jordan, B. T., Kempler, B. 1970. Hysterical personality: An experimental investigation of sex-role conflict. *J. Abnorm. Psychol.* 75:172–76

108. Kagan, J., Moss, H. A., Sigel, I. E. 1963. Psychological significance of styles of conceptualization. *Monogr. Soc. Res. Child Develop.* 28 No. 86, whole No. 2:73–112

109. Kamiya, J. 1969. Operant control of the EEG alpha rhythm and some of its reported effects on consciousness. In *Altered States of Consciousness,* ed. C. Tart, 507–17. New York: Wiley

110. Kates, S. L., Barry, W. T. 1970. Failure avoidance and concept attainment. *J. Pers. Soc. Psychol.* 15:21–27

111. Kaufmann, H. 1970. *Aggression and Altruism.* New York: Holt, Rinehart & Winston

112. Kelley, H. H. 1967. Attribution theory in social psychology. *Neb. Symp. Motiv.* 15:192–240

113. Kelley, H. H., Stahelski, A. J. 1970. Social interaction basis of cooperators' and competitions' beliefs about others. *J. Pers. Soc. Psychol.* 16:66–91

114. Kelly, G. 1955. *The Psychology of*

Personal Constructs, 2 vol. New York: Norton

115. Khatena, J. 1969. Onomatopeia and images: Preliminary validity study of a test of originality. *Percept. Mot. Skills* 28:335–38

116. Kiesler, S. B., Baral, R. L. 1970. The search for a romantic partner: The effects of self-esteem and physical attractiveness on romantic behavior. In *Personality and Social Behavior*, ed. K. J. Gergen, D. Marlow, 155–65. Reading, Mass.: Addison-Wesley

117. Kirtley, D., Harless, R. 1970. Student political activity in relation to personal and social adjustment. *J. Psychol.* 75: 253–56

118. Klein, G. S. 1969–1970. The emergence of ego psychology: The ego in psychoanalysis: A concept in search of identity. *Psychoanal. Rev.* 56: 511–25

119. Klein, G. S. 1967. Peremptory ideation: Structure and force in motivated ideas. See Ref. 93, 78–128

120. Klinger, E. 1969. Development of imaginative behavior: Implications of play for a theory of fantasy. *Psychol. Bull.* 72:277–98

121. Krebs, D. L. 1970. Altruism—an examination of the concept and a review of the literature. *Psychol. Bull.* 73:258–302

122. Lanzetta, J. T., Kleck, R. E. 1970. Encoding and decoding of nonverbal affect in humans. *J. Pers. Soc. Psychol.* 16:12–19

123. Lao, R. C. 1970. Internal-external control and competent and innovative behavior among Negro college students. *J. Pers. Soc. Psychol.* 14: 263–70

124. Lazarus, R., Averill, J. R., Opton, E. M. 1970. Towards a cognitive theory of motivation. See Ref. 5, 207–32

125. Lefcourt, H. M., Siegel, J. M. 1970. Predisposition to fantasy and situational variations as determinants of attention in reaction time tasks. *J. Consult. Clin. Psychol.* 34:415–24

126. Lehmann, S. 1970. Personality and compliance: A study of anxiety and self-esteem in opinion and behavior change. *J. Pers. Soc. Psychol* 15:76–86

127. Leventhal, H., Mace, W. 1970. The effect of laughter on evaluation of a slapstick movie. *J. Pers.* 38: 16–30

128. Lewin, K. 1935. *A Dynamic Theory of Personality*. New York: McGraw-Hill

129. Libby, W. I. 1970. Reaction time and remote association in talented male adolescents. *Develop. Psychol.* 3: 285–97

130. Lightfoot, O. B., Foster, D. L. 1970. Black studies, Black identity, formation and some implications for community psychiatry. *Am. J. Orthopsychiat.* 40:751–55

131. London, P., McDevitt, R. A. 1970. Effects of hypnotic susceptibility and training on responses to stress. *J. Abnorm. Psychol.* 76:336–48

132. Ludwig, D. J. 1970. Evidence of construct and criterion-related validity for the self-concept. *J. Soc. Psychol.* 80:213–33

133. Ludwig, D. J. 1969. Self-perception and the Draw-A-Person Test. *J. Proj. Tech. Pers. Assess.* 33:257–61

134. MacDonald, A. P. Jr. 1970. Anxiety, affiliation and social isolation. *Develop. Psychol.* 3:242–54

135. Mac Donald, A. P. Jr., Kessel, V. S., Fuller, J. B. 1970. *Self-disclosure and two kinds of trust*. Presented at Rehabil. Res. Train. Center, West Virginia Univ.

136. Maddi, S. 1968. *Personality Theories: A Comparative Analysis*. Homewood, Ill.: Dorsey

137. Martens, R., Landers, D. M. 1970. Motor performance under stress: A test of the inverted-U hypothesis. *J. Pers. Soc. Psychol.* 16:29–37

138. Maupin, E. W. 1965. Individual differences in response to a Zen meditation exercise. *J. Consult. Psychol.* 29:139–45

139. Mausner, B., Graham, J. 1970. Field-Dependence and prior reinforcement as determinants of social interaction in judgment. *J. Pers. Soc. Psychol.* 16:486–93

140. Maw, W., Maw, E. 1970. Self-concepts of high and low curiosity boys. *Child Develop.* 41:123–29

141. McClelland, D. G. 1965. Toward a theory of motive acquisition. *Am. Psychol.* 20:321–33

142. McClintock, C., Nuttin, J., McNeel, S. 1970. Sociometric choice, visual presence and game playing behavior. *Behav. Sci.* 15:124–31

143. Megargee, E. I., Hokanson, J. E., Eds. 1970. *The Dynamics of Aggression*. New York: Harper & Row

144. Mehrabian, A. 1968. *An Analysis of Personality Theories*. Englewood Cliffs, N.J.: Prentice Hall

145. Mehrabian, A., Ksionzky, S. 1970. Models for affiliative and conformity behavior. *Psychol. Bull.* 74: 110–26

146. Meichenbaum, D. H., Goodman, J. 1971. Training impulsive children to talk to themselves. *J. Abnorm. Psychol.* 77:115–26

147. Mendelsohn, G. A., Gall, M. D. 1970. Personality variables and the effectiveness of techniques to facilitate creative problem solving. *J. Pers. Soc. Psychol.* 16:346–51

148. Messer, S. B. 1970. The effect of anxiety over intellectual performance on reflection-impulsivity in children. *Child Develop.* 41:723–35

149. Messer, S. B. 1970. Reflection-impulsivity: Stability and school failure. *J. Educ. Psychol.* 61:487–90

150. Miller, G. A., Galanter, E., Pribram, K. 1960. *Plans and the Structure of Behavior.* New York: Holt, Rinehart & Winston

151. Minard, J. G., Mooney, W. 1969. Psychological differentiation and perceptual defense: Studies of the separation of perception from emotion. *J. Abnorm. Psychol.* 74:131–39

152. Mischel, W. 1968. *Personality and Assessment.* New York: Wiley

153. Mischel, W. 1970. Sex-typing and socialization. In *Carmichael's Manual of Child Psychology,* ed. P. H. Mussen, 3–72. New York: Wiley

154. Mischel, W. 1971. *Introduction to Personality.* New York: Holt, Rinehart & Winston

155. Mobbs, N. A. 1968. Eye contact in relation to Social Introversion-Extraversion. *J. Soc. Clin. Psychol.* 7:305–6

156. Morgan, A. H., Lezard, F., Prytulak, S., Hilgard, E. R. 1970. Augmenters, Reducers and their reaction to cold pressor pain in waking and suggested hypnotic analgesia. *J. Pers. Soc. Psychol.* 16:5–11

157. Morse, S., Gergen, K. J. 1970. Social comparison, self-consistency and the concept of self. *J. Pers. Soc. Psychol.* 16:148–56

158. Mosher, R., Sprinthall, N. 1970. Psychological education in secondary schools: A program to promote individual and human development. *Am. Psychol.* 25:911–24

159. Moyer, K. 1971. The physiology of aggression and the implications for aggression control. See Ref. 209, 61–92

160. Mukherjee, B. N., Scherer, S. E. 1970. A multivariate study of self-ideal congruence among drug users and nonusers when social desirability factor is controlled. *Personality* 1: 333–54

161. Mussen, P., Rutherford, E., Harris, S., Keasey, C. B. 1970. Honesty and altruism among preadolescents. *Develop. Psychol.* 3:169–94

162. Natsoulas, T. 1970. Concerning introspective "knowledge." *Psychol. Rev.* 73:89–111

163. Neisser, U. 1967. *Cognitive Psychology.* New York: Appleton-Century-Crofts

164. Numbauer, C. C., Gray, S. N. 1970. Resistance to temptation in young Negro children. *Child Develop.* 41: 1203–7

165. Olds, J. A., Milner, P. 1954. Positive reinforcement produced by electrical stimulation of septal area and other regions of rat brain. *J. Comp. Physiol. Psychol.* 47:419–27

166. Olweus, D. 1970. Aggression from the perspective of personality psychology. *Rep. Inst. Psychol.* No. 2. Bergen: Univ. Norway

167. Ozehosky, R., Clark, E. 1970. Children's self-concept and kindergarten achievement. *J. Psychol.* 75:185–92

168. Paivio, A. 1970. On the functional significance of imagery. *Psychol. Bull.* 73:385–92

169. Paul, I. H. 1967. The concept of schema in memory theory. See Ref. 93, 218–58

170. Pervin, L. A. 1970. *Personality.* New York: Wiley

171. Platman, S. R., Plutchik, R. 1970. Self-concepts associated with mania and depression. *Psychol. Rep.* 27: 399–406

172. Powell, G., Fuller, M. 1970. Self-concept and school desegregation. *Am. J. Orthopsychiat.* 40:303–4

173. Pribram, K. 1970. Feelings as monitors. See Ref. 5, 41–54

174. Propper, M. M., Clark, E. 1970. Alienation: Another dimension of underachievement. *J. Psychol.* 75:13–18

175. Pulaski, M. A. S. 1970. Play as a function of toy structure and fantasy predisposition. *Child Develop.* 41:531–37

176. Rappaport, A., Payne, D., Steinmann, A. 1970. Perceptual differences between married and single college women from the concepts of self, ideal woman and man's ideal

woman. *J. Marriage Fam.* 32:441–42

177. Raynor, J. O. 1970. Relationships between achievement-related motives, future orientation, and academic performance. *J. Pers. Soc. Psychol.* 15:28–33

178. Reali, N., Hall, V. 1970. Effect of success and failure on the reflective and impulsive child. *Develop. Psychol.* 3:392–402

179. Reppucci, N. D. 1970. Individuald ifferences in the consideration of information among two-year-old children. *Develop. Psychol.* 2:240–46

180. Richardson, A. 1969. *Mental Imagery.* New York: Springer

181. Rohwer, W. D. Jr. 1970. Images and pictures in children's learning. *Psychol. Bull.* 73:393–403

182. Rotter, J. 1971. Generalized expectancies for interpersonal trust. *Am. Psychol.* 26:443–52

183. Rotter, J. 1954. *Social Learning and Clinical Psychology.* New York: Prentice-Hall

184. Saltz, E. 1970. Manifest anxiety. *Psychol. Rev.* 77:568–73

185. Santrock, J. W. 1970. Paternal absence, sex-typing and identification. *Develop. Psychol.* 2:264–72

186. Sapperfield, B., Balogh, B. 1970. Perceived attractiveness of social stimuli as related to their perceived similarity to self. *J. Psychol.,* 74:105–11

187. Sarason, I. G. 1972. Experimental approaches to test anxiety: Attention and the uses of information. See Ref. 53

188. Sarason, I. G., Ganzer, V. J. 1969. Developing appropriate social behaviors of juvenile delinquents. In *Behavioral Counseling: Cases and Techniques*, ed. D. Krumholtz, C. C. Thoresen, 178–93. New York: Holt, Rinehart & Winston

189. Sarason, I. G., Ganzer, V. J. 1971. Effects of delay interval, test anxiety and test instructions on serial learning. *Personality.* In press

190. Sarbin, T. R., Juhasz, J. B. 1970. Toward a theory of imagination. *J. Pers.* 38:52–76

191. Schacter, S. 1970. The assumption of identity and peripheralist-centralist controversies in motivation and emotion. See Ref. 5, 111–21

192. Schaefer, C. E. 1969. Imaginary companions and creative adolescents. *Develop. Psychol.* 1:747–49

193. Schimek, J. G. 1968. Cognitive style

and defenses: A longitudinal study of intellectualization and field dependence. *J. Abnorm. Psychol.* 73:575–80

194. Schludermann, S., Schludermann, E. 1970. Personality correlations of adolescent self-concepts and security-insecurity. *J. Psychol.* 74:85–90

195. Schwartz, S. H., Clausen, G., Clausen, G. T. 1970. Responsibility, norms, and helping in an emergency. *J. Pers. Soc. Psychol.* 16:299–310

196. Sears, R. R. 1970. Relation of early socialization experience to self-concepts and gender role in middle childhood. *Child Develop.* 41:267–90

197. Segal, S. J. 1971. *Imagery: Current Cognitive Approaches.* New York: Academic

198. Sermat, V. 1970. Is game behavior related to behavior in other interpersonal situations? *J. Pers. Soc. Psychol.* 16:92–109

199. Shallit, B. 1970. Environmental hostility and hostility in fantasy. *J. Pers. Soc. Psychol.* 15:171–74

200. Shapiro, K. J., Alexander, I. E. 1969. Extraversion-introversion, affiliation and anxiety. *J. Pers.* 37:387–406

201. Shevrin, H., Smith, W. H., Fritzler, D. E. 1970. Subliminally stimulated brain and verbal responses of twins differing in repressiveness. *J. Abnorm. Psychol.* 76:39–46

202. Shimkunas, A. M. 1970. Anxiety and expectancy change: The effects of failure and uncertainty. *J. Pers. Soc. Psychol.* 15:34–42

203. Shortell, J., Epstein, S., Taylor, S. P. 1970. Instigation to aggression as a function of degree of defeat and the capacity for massive retaliation. *J. Pers.* 38:313–28

204. Sindos, L. K. 1970. A program for the encouragement, motivation, and education of the high school dropout. *Am. J. Orthopsychiat.* 10:512–19

205. Singer, D. G. 1967. Reading, writing and race relations. *Transaction* 4:27–31

206. Singer, D. L. 1968. Aggression arousal, hostile humor, and catharsis. *J. Pers. Soc. Psychol. Monogr. Suppl.* 8

207. Singer, J. L. 1966. *Daydreaming.* New York: Random House

208. Singer, J. L. 1970. Drives, affects, and daydreams: The adaptive role of spontaneous imagery or stimulus-independent mentation. See Ref. 4, 131–58

209. Singer, J. L., Ed. 1971. *The Control of Aggression and Violence: Cognitive and Physiological Factors.* New York: Academic

210. Singer, J. L. 1971. Imagery and daydream techniques in psychotherapy. In *Current Topics in Clinical and Community Psychology, Vol. 3,* ed. C. D. Spielberger. New York: Academic. In press

211. Singer, J. L. 1971. The influence of violence portrayed in television or motion pictures upon overt aggressive behavior. See Ref. 290, 19–60

212. Singer, J. L., Greenberg, S., Antrobus, J. S. 1971. Looking with the mind's eye: Experimental studies of ocular motility during daydreaming and mental arithmetic. *Trans. NY Acad. Sci.* In press

213. Smith, C. P., Winterbottom, M. T. 1970. Personality characteristics of college students on academic probation. *J. Pers.* 38:379–91

214. Spear, P. S. 1970. Motivational effects of praise and criticism on children's learning. *Develop. Psychol.* 3:124–32

215. Spielberger, C. D., Gorsuch, R. L., Lushene, R. E. 1970. *STAI Manual for the State-Trait Anxiety Inventory.* Palo Alto, Calif.: Consulting Psychologists

216. Spielberger, C. D. 1972. Anxiety as an emotional state. In *Anxiety: Current Trends in Theory and Research,* ed. C. D. Spielberger. New York: Academic. In press

217. Staub, E. 1969. A child in distress: The effect of focusing responsibility on children on their attempts to help. *Develop. Psychol.* 2:152–53

218. Staub, E. 1970. A child in distress: The influence of age and number of witnesses on children's attempts to help. *J. Pers. Soc. Psychol.* 14:130–40

219. Staub, E. 1971. The learning and unlearning of aggression: The role of anxiety, empathy, efficiency and prosocial values. See Ref. 209, 94–124

220. Staub, E., Sherk, L. 1970. Need for approval, children's sharing behavior, and reciprocity in sharing. *Child Develop.* 41:243–52

221. Stein, D. K. 1970. *Expectation and modeling in sensitivity groups.* PhD thesis. Univ. Connecticut

222. Stein, K. B., Lenrow, P. 1970. Expressive styles and their measurement. *J. Pers. Soc. Psychol.* 16:656–64

223. Storms, M. D., Nisbett, R. E. 1970. Insomnia and the attribution process. *J. Pers. Soc. Psychol.* 16:319–28

224. Summers, D. L., Felker, D. W. 1970. Use of the It Scale for children in assessing sex-role preference in preschool Negro children. *Develop. Psychol.* 2:330–34

225. Sutcliffe, J. P., Perry, C. W., Sheehan, P. W. 1970. Relation of some aspects of imagery and fantasy to hypnotic susceptibility. *J. Abnorm. Psychol.* 76:279–87

226. Tart, C. T. 1970. Increases in hypnotizability resulting from a prolonged program for enhancing personal growth. *J. Abnorm. Psychol.* 75:260–66

227. Taylor, S. P., Epstein, S. 1967. Aggression as a function of the interaction of the sex of the aggressor and the sex of the victim. *J. Pers.* 35:474–86

228. Tedesch, J., Bonoma, T., Lindskold, S. 1970. Threateners reactions to peer announcement of behavioral compliance on defiance. *Behav. Sci.* 15:171–79

229. Tolman, E. C. 1932. *Purposive Behavior in Animals and Men.* New York: Century

230. Tomkins, S. S. 1962, 1963. *Affect, Imagery, Consciousness,* 2 vols. New York: Springer

231. Tomkins, S. S. 1965. Affect and the psychology of knowledge. In *Affect, Cognition, and Personality,* ed. S. S. Tomkins, C. E. Izard, 72–97. New York: Springer

232. Tomkins, S. S. 1970. Affect as the primary motivational system. See Ref. 5, 101–10

233. Torrance, E. P. 1969. Originality of imagery in identifying creative talent in music. *Gifted Child Quart.* 13:3–8

234. Tseng, M. S., Carter, A. R. 1970. Achievement motivation and fear of failure as determinants of vocational choice, vocational aspiration and perception of vocational prestige. *J. Couns. Psychol.* 17:150–56

235. Turner, J. 1970. Entrepreneurial environments and the emergence of achievement motivation in adolescent males. *Sociometry* 33:147–65

236. Vogel, S., Broverman, I. K., Broverman, D. M., Clarkson, F. E., Rosenkrantz, P. S. 1970. Maternal employment and perception of sex roles among college students. *Develop. Psychol.* 3:384–91

237. Vroegh, K. 1970. Lack of sex-role differentiation in preschooler's figure drawings. *J. Proj. Tech. Pers. Assess.* 34:38–40

238. Wallach, M. 1967. Thinking, feeling, and expressing: Toward understanding the person. See Ref. 103, 141–72

239. Weiner, B., Kukla, A. 1970. An attributional analysis of achievement motivation. *J. Pers. Soc. Psychol.* 15:1–20

240. Weiner, B., Potepan, P. A. 1970. Personality characteristics and affective reactions toward exams of superior and failing college students. *J. Educ. Psychol.* 61:144–51

241. Weisbroth, S. P. 1970. Moral judgment, sex and parental identification in adults. *Develop. Psychol.* 2:396–402

242. Weiss, J. H. 1970. Birth order and physiological stress response. *Child Develop.* 41:461–70

243. Weissman, H., Ritter, K. 1970. Openness to experience, ego strength and self description as a function of repression and sensitization. *Psychol. Rep.* 26:859–64

244. Wheeler, J. 1969. *Temporal Experience and Fantasy.* PhD thesis. City Univ. of New York

245. White, W., Richmond, B. 1970. Perception of self and of peers by economically deprived Black and advantaged white fifth graders. *Percept. Mot. Skills* 30:533–34

246. Whittaker, D. 1970. College student needs and identity as indicated by their self-reported, peak experiences. *Am. J. Orthopsychiat.* 40:345–46

247. Wickramasekera, I. 1970. Effects of sensory restriction on susceptibility to hypnosis: A hypothesis and more preliminary data. *J. Abnorm. Psychol.* 76:69–75

248. Witkin, H. A. 1967. A cognitive style approach to cross-cultural research. *Int. J. Psychol.* 2:233–50

249. Witkin, H. A. 1965. Psychological differentiation and forms of pathology. *J. Abnorm. Psychol.* 70: 317–36

250. Witkin, H. A., Dyk, R. B., Faterson, H. F., Goodenough, D. R., Karp, S. A. 1962. *Psychological Differentiation.* New York: Wiley

251. Witkin, H. A. et al 1954. *Personality Through Perception.* New York: Harper

252. Witkin, H. A., Lewis, H. B., Weil, E. 1968. Affective reactions and patient-therapist interactions among more differentiated and less differentiated patients early in therapy. *J. Nerv. Ment. Dis.* 146:193–207

253. Yang, K. 1970. Authoritarianism and evaluation of appropriateness of role behavior. *J. Soc. Psychol.* 80: 171–81

254. Zajonc, R. B. 1968. Cognitive theories in social psychology. In *The Handbook of Social Psychology*, ed. G. Lindzey, E. Aronson, 1:320–411. New York: Addison-Wesley. 2nd ed.

255. Zellner, M. 1970. Self-esteem, reception and influenceability. *J. Pers. Soc. Psychol.* 15:87–93

256. Zimbardo, P. G. 1969. *The Cognitive Control of Motivation.* Glenview: Scott, Foresman

257. Zimmerman, S. F., Smith, K. H., Pedersen, D. M. 1970. The effect of anticonformity appeals on conformity behavior. *J. Soc. Psychol.* 81: 93–103

BRAIN FUNCTIONS 186

C. BLAKEMORE, S. D. IVERSEN, AND O. L. ZANGWILL

Departments of Physiology and Experimental Psychology,
University of Cambridge, England

The authors propose to cover three main topics in this review: first, sensory processing, with special reference to the visual and auditory systems; second, recent advances in the anatomy and physiology of the motor system and their relevance to the organization of behavior; third, asymmetry of cerebral hemisphere function in man, dealing with both the effects of unilateral brain injury and studies of patients who have undergone commissurotomy.

SENSORY PROCESSING

In this section it would be impossible to cover all the literature of the past few years, for this is an area of intense and productive research. We shall concentrate on activity in single neurons in the visual and auditory pathways. Wherever possible we have chosen to discuss topics that are related to human perception.

VISUAL SYSTEM

Perhaps because vision is our dominant sense, we understand the visual stimulus better than that for any other sensory system. The coding properties of neurons cannot possibly be sorted out if the stimulus itself cannot be adequately described. There have been many useful reviews in this area in the last few years (e.g. 49, 50, 78, 177).

Analysis of contrast, shape, and movement.—The major function of the relay of visual information at the lateral geniculate nucleus of the thalamus (LGN), if there is a special purpose, remains obscure. The neurons of the LGN in the cat and the monkey usually have receptive fields with antagonistic centers and surrounds (166, 192, 198, 347) like those of the retina. If the central part of the receptive field produces a response when a spot of light is shone on it, illumination of the surrounding retinal region will produce a response when the light is turned off. In addition to these on-center cells there are also off-center cells whose responses to illumination of center and surround are the other way round. Simultaneous illumination of center and surround by a diffuse light is not as effective as illumination of the center alone. This antagonism between center and surround, which serves to enhance the response to small objects with distinct borders, is said by Hubel

& Wiesel (166) to be more marked in the LGN than in the retina. However, Campbell, Cooper & Enroth-Cugell (66), using moving grating patterns of dark and light bars, found little attenuation of the response with large bar-widths.

Kozak, Rodieck & Bishop (198) and Kinston, Vadas & Bishop (192) describe rarer classes of LGN cell. They include: (a) units with large receptive fields without inhibitory surrounds; (b) units responding to movement of an object into (centripetal) or out of (centrifugal) the middle of the receptive field, whether the object is black or white; (c) binocular neurons with receptive fields in both eyes; (d) cells with receptive fields stretching into the ipsilateral hemifield; and (e) units responding more to one direction of image motion than any other (direction-selective units). The wide occurrence of direction-selective neurons in visual systems is well reviewed by Grüsser & Grüsser-Cornehls (152).

Singer & Creutzfeld (305) have evidence that on-center cells are inhibited by off-center and vice versa. This arrangement would reduce spontaneous activity and improve the signal for a sudden change in intensity.

It is now usually accepted that most, if not all, cells in the cat's visual cortex are specifically sensitive to the orientation of dark or bright bars of light and black-white edges (65, 167, 170, 272). However, automated methods of plotting the receptive fields with small moving spots often produce very "diffuse" maps covering enormous retinal areas (311). Hubel & Wiesel, however, found that most cells respond only weakly, if at all, to flashing or moving spots and that the receptive fields that can be plotted with small moving spots often do not predict the neurons' responses to more complicated shapes.

According to conventional dogma, so-called "simple" cells early in the cortical hierarchy receive input from a small number of LGN cells with their concentric receptive fields in a row on the retina (154). Many simple cells with identical preferred orientation send messages to a "complex" cell with a larger receptive field but equally strict orientational specificity. A few complex cells provide excitatory and inhibitory inputs to each "hypercomplex" cell. "Lower-order hypercomplex" cells require their oriented target to be of a particular length and sometimes a specific width. "Higher-order hypercomplex" units have dual preferred orientations, being excited both by one orientation and by the perpendicular to it. Evidence for this sequential arrangement comes from measurements of the latency of each class to electric shock of the optic tract (86).

This hierarchical neuronal network is arranged in a columnar form. Within columns or sheets of cortical tissue all cells have the same preferred orientation (167, 168, 170). Simple cells occur mainly in and around layer IV, where geniculate fibers terminate. Complex and hypercomplex cells occur in the deeper and more superficial layers.

The monkey area 17 is very similarly organized (173), the major differences being: (a) some cells are specific for the color of the oriented target;

(b) in layer IV there are many units with monocular, concentric receptive fields that probably are cells but could be geniculate fibers; (c) the receptive fields are on the average smaller and the orientation specificity more acute; (d) the orientation columns are probably smaller; (e) there are overlapping columnar systems for eye dominance (which eye is particularly effective), direction selectivity (which direction of movement is preferred), and possibly for the color and form of the target; (f) the hierarchical layering is even more pronounced; (g) there are no higher-order hypercomplex cells.

Wurtz (352) has confirmed many of these findings in alert, conscious monkeys and has shown, in virtuosic experiments, that the same response is caused by movement of a target across the stationary eye as by an eye movement across the target (353).

Single neurons in the human occipital lobe have, with considerable technical difficulty, been studied for brief periods (232). Some at least are orientation-selective and so far none is color-specific.

Visual cortical units in the cat can be influenced by vestibular stimulation, clicks (24, 184), loud tones (312), and shocks to the skin (162). Horn & Hill (163) found that a few cortical neurons change their preferred orientation slowly after the cat is tilted to one side, as if to correct, at least partially, for the rotation of the eye. This finding gives a role for the large vestibular input to the cortex but is rather hard to interpret since the neurons even showed shifts in the repeated estimates of preferred orientation when the cat was held stationary.

Apart from the classical occipital and parietal visual areas, the Clare-Bishop area of the lateral suprasylvian gyrus in the cat receives a considerable visual projection both from the LGN and from the visual cortical areas. Hubel & Wiesel (174) and Wright (351) have plotted receptive fields for neurons in this region. In general they are remarkably similar to those in the visual cortex, but there are no simple or higher-order hypercomplex cells. Most of them are complex with very large receptive fields. There are many direction-selective units and some that respond merely to movement in any direction.

The inferotemporal cortex receives considerable projection from the visual cortex, and its involvement in visual function is clear. Gross, Bender & Rocha-Miranda (151) found that some of the cells there have very exact requirements. Half responded to light and dark bars, while half were direction-selective. Some needed colored stimuli, and a few signaled the overall light level. Many were inhibited by their "optimal" stimulus. One neuron was found to respond better to a silhouette of a monkey's hand than to anything else that was tried. The receptive fields were very large, all including the fovea, and often stretching many degrees into the ipsilateral hemifield.

Gross visual inputs, as well as other sensory stimuli, can probably influence many cortical neurons in the so-called association areas through the generalized thalamotelencephalic system (60), but cells responding to precise visual stimuli, as well as other modalities, have been described in association cortex of the cat. In the anterior portion of the middle suprasylvian gyrus, two-thirds of all neurons respond to light (107), and they are of three types: 1. S-cells, having uniform, large off or on-off receptive fields, some of which extend more than 10° into the ipsilateral hemifield; 2. M-cells, which respond specifically to movement and to clicks, and have very large receptive fields; 3. E-cells, which respond to moving edges at particular orientations but are probably not as orientation-specific as cells in the visual cortex.

Analysis of color.—Color-coded receptive fields are very common in the LGN of the monkey (2, 98, 99, 347). De Valois used diffuse flashes of colored light to demonstrate excitation by some colors and inhibition by others. Experiments with adaptation to strong-colored lights and stimulation with color mixtures proved that probably most cells have connections with only two of the three cone types. These cells could account for the perceptual phenomenon of successive color contrast. Wiesel & Hubel (347) plotted the receptive fields in detail, with these findings: 1. Most cells have concentric, opponent-color receptive fields. If the center responds to red or blue light, the surround responds in the opposite fashion to green light. The center response can be on or off. If the center is sensitive to green light, the surround prefers red. 2. A second class of cells has the same spectral sensitivity in center and surround, both being connected to at least two classes of cone. 3. Another small group of cells has no obvious surround but shows opponent-color responses within the whole receptive field. Many cells have connections with rods as well as cones, and their spectral sensitivities demonstrate a Purkinje shift when they are dark-adapted.

Until very recently all the evidence has suggested that cells in the cat's LGN all have connections to rods, with peak absorption at 400 nm, and only one class of cone, with peak absorption at 556 nm (84). However, Pearlmen & Daw (270) found three cells in layer B that also received signals from a second class of cone, with peak absorption at 450 nm. In two of these neurons the center gave blue on-responses and green off-responses, and the surround produced blue off- and green on-responses. These double opponent-color cells could account for the perceptual phenomenon of simultaneous color contrast.

In the monkey visual cortex only a tiny proportion of orientational cells are also color-specific, having opponent-color responses or simply preferring targets of one color (173). Many of the color-specific cells have connections with all three cone types (148).

Binocular interaction.—After a period when it was unfashionable to emphasize the role of the cat's LGN in binocular interaction, it has recently been found that most, if not all, neurons have a receptive field in both eyes, but in one of them it is almost purely inhibitory (291). It is suggested that this interaction may express itself in the perceptual phenomenon of binocular rivalry.

Wholesale binocular combination occurs in the visual cortex. Most of the neurons in the cat area 17 can be driven by a similar target shown to either eye (20, 58, 167, 311). If more subtle subliminal effects are considered, all cortical units in the cat have connections with both eyes (157).

When both eyes are stimulated simultaneously, the targets must be rather precisely positioned for facilitation to occur. Inappropriate positioning causes occlusion of the response (20, 183, 271). In other words, each neuron responds to images at a particular retinal disparity and therefore responds best for an object at a specific distance from the eyes. The optimal disparity varies enormously from cell to cell, so different neurons respond to objects at different distances (20, 183, 260). This could be the neural basis of stereoscopic vision. Hubel & Wiesel (175) have found similar "binocular depth cells" in area 18 of the monkey. They can scarcely be stimulated at all through one eye alone.

Hubel & Wiesel's orientation columns fall into two classes according to their binocular organization (36). In a constant depth column all units (as well as having identical preferred orientation) have their receptive fields at the same retinal disparity. In a constant direction column the disparity varies from cell to cell, but all the receptive fields are superimposed on the contralateral retina. Hence each depth column is surveying a slab of visual space at a specific distance from the eyes. Each direction column is viewing a tube of visual space extending out from the contralateral eye. These columns may be involved in the encoding of visual space and the control of eye movements.

Intercortical connections in the corpus callosum.—The border region between areas 17 and 18 is joined to the same area of the other hemisphere by fibers running in the corpus callosum. This border region represents the central vertical meridian of the visual field, and it has been suggested (72, 172) that the interconnections serve to bind the two halves of the visual field together. In the normal cat the receptive fields of neurons in the 17/18 border straddle the midline of the visual field and intrude into the ipsilateral hemifield (35, 172, 212), and many fibers in the splenium of the corpus callosum have receptive fields like those of cortical cells, with all of them clustered around the midline (29, 172).

If the optic tract in the cat is cut on one side, visually evoked responses can still be recorded in the 17/18 border of the ipsilateral occipital lobe in the cat. The neurons have their receptive fields very near the middle of the visual field (72, 330). When the optic chiasma is split sagitally, some binocular neurons can still be found in this area 17/18 region. They have their receptive fields just inside the temporal half of each retina (30). Blakemore (35) has suggested that these cells receiving interhemispheric input may not only be concerned in binding together the two halves of the visual field, but may also play a part in stereoscopic vision in the midline of the field. Objects directly behind or in front of the fixation point have images falling just inside the nasal or temporal retina in both eyes. Interhemispheric connections may be necessary to produce binocular neurons sensitive to these disparities.

Maturation of visual cortex in early life.—Very young kittens have cortical neurons virtually indistinguishable from those of the adult cat (169). However, if one eye is covered even for just a few days within the critical period of about 4–8 weeks of age, there is a dramatic loss of binocularity in the cortex (128, 176). It is as if there is competition between the two eyes for synaptic sites on cortical neurons and the uncovered eye wins most of them. Much the same thing happens if one eye is given an artificial squint by cutting one of the extraocular muscles (171). The cats are virtually blind for any visual shape discrimination in the eye that loses its cortical connections, and there is only a little recovery over a period of months or years (100, 127). Closure of both eyes in early life leads to almost total blindness, but strangely the cortex is less obviously abnormal than in the case of unilateral closure (346).

Hirsch & Spinelli (161) have shown that the visual experience of a kitten can alter the properties of its cortical neurons in startling ways. Kittens reared with one eye viewing vertical lines and the other horizontal lines were found to have a modified distribution of orientation-selective neurons in the cortex. Cells with oriented receptive fields were virtually all monocular, and the preferred orientation of each one closely matched the orientation of the lines experienced by its eye. Blakemore & Cooper (37) found that kittens reared with normal binocular viewing of horizontal or vertical stripes have the distribution of preferred orientations in the cortex markedly biased towards the experienced angle. The kittens also had considerable perceptual deficits, particularly for patterns of the orientation that they had not seen in early life.

AUDITORY SYSTEM

Naturally occurring sounds, vocalizations, and other noises of communication are generally mixtures of tones that change in time in a complicated fashion. Without some knowledge of the biologically important sounds for the animal, or a good deal of inspired guesswork, it would be very difficult to sort out the critical auditory features to which higher auditory neurons probably respond. However, there has been considerable success in the last few years. Recently several useful reviews have appeared (e.g. 97, 111, 150, 344). We shall discuss a few recent papers under headings relevant to auditory perception.

Analysis of frequency.—Neurons with distinct optimal or characteristic frequencies have been described at every level up to and including the auditory cortex. Whitfield (344) provides an excellent summary of the earlier studies.

Recently the responses to tones of neurons in the cochlear nuclei of the cat (133), rat (246), and kangaroo rat (250) have been described. In the last case the characteristic frequencies range from below 500 Hz to about 13 kHz. In some cells the tuning is very broad, suggesting the convergence of signals from a large portion of the basilar membrane.

In the superior olivary complex of the cat (251, 325) and the dog (141) there is a distinct tonotopic arrangement, at least in some of the nuclei. This tonal mapping is retained in the cat's nuclei of the lateral lemniscus (4). Some cells maintain their response to a steady tone, but many give only on-responses. This trend towards phasic discharges is just as pronounced in the auditory system as in the visual pathway. The lateral lemniscal cells often have their impulses phase-locked to the stimulus for tones below 1 kHz. This phase locking (presumably an inevitable consequence of the transduction process) is gradually lost in passage through the auditory pathway. Some cells in this nucleus are distinctly inhibited by frequencies on either side of their characteristic frequency. Lateral inhibition presumably serves, among other things, to sharpen up the tuning curves. In general some neurons at high levels in the pathway have tuning curves narrower than, or as narrow as, any that can be found in lower nuclei.

In the cat's inferior colliculus there is still a tonotopic map and large variation in bandwidth. The firing patterns during a tone burst range from tonic discharge to transient on-responses, but the general pattern is one of an initial burst followed by a period of silence (132).

Cells in the cat's medial geniculate body (which receives independent projections from inferior colliculus and lower nuclei) generally show the same initial excitation, followed by inhibition and rebound (5).

In the cat's primary auditory cortex there is general agreement that some cells are incredibly narrow in their tuning, while others are almost as broad as the audible spectrum (1, 110, 112, 134, 145, 263, 345). Only about 60% of cells respond to tones, many with transient on- or off-responses. Evans, Ross & Whitfield (112) have challenged the idea that there is functional tonotopic mapping in the primary auditory cortex (AI). Goldstein, et al (144) also concluded that there is only a very crude tonotopic map, but they were a little hesitant to dismiss the whole idea.

Gerstein & Kiang (134), Onishi & Katsuki (263), and Abeles & Goldstein (1) have assembled good evidence for a system of columns in the auditory cortex. The cells in a single perpendicular electrode stab usually have very similar characteristic frequencies with any broad tuning curves covering the range of characteristic frequencies for nearby narrowly tuned units.

Spatial localization.—The simplest kinds of auditory space perception depend, for low and medium frequency tones and some complex sounds, on a comparison of the arrival times or phase relationships of sounds at the two ears. For high frequency tones and other complex sounds, difference of intensity at the two ears is the vital cue. There are elegant neural mechanisms to detect interaural differences of intensity and timing.

There is binaural convergence on single cells as early as the dorsal cochlear nucleus in the chinchilla (235). Twenty percent of neurons are binaurally influenced, mainly excited by the ipsilateral ear and inhibited by the contralateral (over the same frequency band). These so-called E-I cells act as detectors of interaural intensity difference. A change in average intensity hardly influences them, but a change in intensity at one ear produces an enormous change in response. Very similar E-I cells are found in the superior olivary complex of the cat (46, 341) and dog (141, 142). Many neurons in the superior olive are excited by both ears (so-called E-E cells) and they register a general change in intensity at both ears.

All the papers referred to above make reference to low-frequency neurons that are sensitive to interaural phase difference. Such cells show distinct binaural facilitation, occlusion, or both, and require very specific timing of the inputs to the two ears to show this interaction. Typically, if the relative phase of a tone is shifted in the two ears, the cells show a series of response maxima at various interaural delays. The periodicity of this pattern matches the frequency of the tone. The optimum interaural delay nearest to synchrony is usually the same whatever the frequency of the tone, the average intensity, and sometimes the relative intensity at the two ears. It is also the same for clicks. This is called the *characteristic delay*. Surely these cells must be involved in auditory spatial localization.

E-E and E-I cells and neurons with characteristic delays are also found in the dorsal nucleus of the lateral lemniscus (53), inferior colliculus (132), medial geniculate body (5, 8), and AI cortex of the cat (54, 110, 153). Evans (110) reports that 46 percent of cortical cells have a preference for the position of real sound sources, 31 percent needing very specific location of the sound. The majority prefer sounds in the contralateral auditory field, and about 4 percent respond specifically to midline stimuli. About 10 percent of cells only respond to an auditory stimulus if it falls within the visual field and if the unanesthetized cat is actually looking at the object. Brugge et al (54) have analyzed in detail the responses of cortical cells to changes of overall intensity, interaural intensity, and timing. They also examined nine cells in the second auditory cortex (AII) in the anterior ectosylvian gyrus. There were no obvious differences between neurons in AI and AII.

Responses to complex sounds.—The fact that 20 percent of auditory cortical neurons in the cat can be aroused only by finger clicks, jangling keys, and other complex sounds, and never by a single tone (110) is a sure sign that the cortex is abstracting other more specific features of the auditory input.

The responses of neurons to sounds varying in frequency is sometimes not predictable from their responses to steady tones. In the cochlear nucleus (109), inferior colliculus (257), and the cortex (345) of the cat, and in the inferior colliculus (319) of the bat, many cells respond asymmetrically to rising and falling tones. Whitfield & Evans have analyzed this property in detail. Ten percent of cortical cells will respond well to gliding tones but not at all to steady ones. Some are excited by a gliding tone plus a steady tone but not to either alone (120). Even more exciting is the fact that many of the cells that respond to frequency modulation are direction selective: they respond if the tone is increasing in frequency but not if it is decreasing, or vice versa.

Another form of auditory direction selectivity has been demonstrated recently for cells in the cat's inferior colliculus (7) and medial geniculate body (8). These neurons respond to a change in the interaural delay for trains of clicks presented to the two ears, but only for a change in one direction. So they respond to a noisy object moving laterally from one side of the cat's auditory field to the other, but not in the reverse direction. The neuronal connections necessary to explain this complexity of response are formidable. Finally, Winter and his colleagues (349) have reported that some neurons in the AI cortex of the squirrel monkey are driven specifically by particular complex vocalizations from the natural repertoire of the animal's communication sounds. These fascinating findings are probably just a hint of the feature-abstracting properties of higher auditory neurons.

GENERAL PRINCIPLES OF SENSORY SYSTEMS

Lateral inhibition.—Apart from the obvious function of compensating for any divergence in a neural projection and limiting activity to one set of cells, lateral inhibition may have another important consequence: it will sharpen the tuning curves of neurons for any sensory modality that is topographically mapped in the neuronal layer in question. Surround inhibition in the retina makes ganglion cells more specific for the spatial positioning of light. Perhaps mutual inhibition in the visual cortex, where neighboring columns encode similar orientations, serves to sharpen the tuning of the cells for orientation. This may be a clue to the reason for topographic mapping and columnar organization.

Lateral inhibition probably occurs in every sensory system. It has, for example, been reported in the somatosensory system (22), in particular at the thalamus and cortex of the cat (70, 147, 247) and the monkey (248, 343). Lateral inhibition in the auditory system has already been discussed, and its involvement in sharpening of tuning curves (22) and in direction selectivity is clear. It is of great interest that mutual inhibition between neighboring neurons has recently been reported in the olfactory bulb (106, 284) and the olfactory (prepyriform) cortex (31), and also in the motor cortex (185).

Direction selectivity.—The examples of direction selective neurons in various parts of the visual system of vertebrates and invertebrates are legion (152). It seems clear that the differential detection of change is a fundamental property of sensory systems. Direction-selective detectors for changes in spatial position of the stimulus have also been reported in the auditory system, for moving sound sources (7, 8), and in the somatosensory system for moving objects on the skin (147, 249).

Direction selectivity in the frequency domain is also a common property in the auditory system (345). Direction selectivity may be due to an asymmetric distribution of excitation and inhibition along a particular receptor surface or stimulus domain.

Columnar organization.—There is now overwhelming evidence that the basic multicellular functional unit in the cortex is a column, block, or sheet of neurons, running from surface to white matter. Every cell in a column responds to the same submodality, although there may be much variation in properties for other stimulus qualities. Thus the column as a whole generalizes for many stimulus properties while perfectly preserving information about a specific quality.

For example, in the primary somatosensory cortex all the cells in a single column respond either to light cutaneous stimulation or to deep pressure and manipulation of joints (247–249). In the cat's secondary somatosensory cortex there is a similar columnar grouping of specific mechanoreceptive and nonspecific neurons (70).

In the visual cortex there are many overlapping columnar subdivisions for orientation and eye dominance (168, 173), for distance and visual direction (36, 175), and possibly for direction of movement, target form, and color (173).

In the auditory cortex there are certainly narrow columns in which the characteristic frequencies are in register. There may also be similar binaural interaction in each column (1).

Finally, in the motor cortex, focal stimulation has revealed columns of cells, each column being responsible for a particular kind of movement involving one or many muscles (e.g. 16).

If columns are laid out in a topology related to the particular stimulus characteristic for which the columns are specific, then lateral inhibition between neighboring columns will lead to an automatic increase in tuning and selectivity for that particular stimulus quality. Columnar mapping and lateral inhibition may be fundamental to the action of the brain.

MOTOR SYSTEMS

The decision to include a review of motor systems reflects sentiments expressed by Sperry:

> An analysis of our current thinking will show that it tends to suffer generally from a failure to view mental activities in their proper relation, or even in any relation, to motor behavior. The remedy lies in further insight into the relationship between the sensori-associative functions of the brain on the one hand and its motor activity on the other. In order to achieve this insight, our present one-sided pre-occupation with the sensory avenues to the study of mental processes will need to be supplemented by increased attention to the motor patterns, and especially to what can be inferred from these regarding the nature of the associative and sensory functions (310).

The basic anatomy and physiology of the motor system are reviewed because we consider it imperative that functional models of the learning process be consistent with the working of the normal motor system.

This review is global and of necessity limited, but recent symposia and reviews provide detailed information on (a) disease of the basal ganglia— *Handbook of Clinical Neurology*, Volume 6 (332); (b) the pyramidal tract (Wiesendanger 348); (c) the red nucleus (Massion 234); (d) electrophysiology of the cerebellum (Eccles, Ito & Szentagothai 108); (e) neurophysiological studies of normal and abnormal motor activities (Yahr & Purpura 355); (f) the thalamus in relation to motor activities (Purpura & Yahr 282); (g) cerebrocerebellar interactions in the motor system (Evarts & Thach 118).

CORTICOSPINAL ORGANIZATION

The motor neurons of the spinal cord are innervated by two descending systems, the corticospinal (or pyramidal) and the subcorticospinal (or extrapyramidal), with differential terminal distribution in the spinal grey matter (199, 220). More recently the functional significance of this anatomical organization has been sought.

The extrapyramidal system.—In both cat and monkey the subcorticospinal pathways are divided into ventromedial and lateral systems on the basis of their respective terminal distribution to the ventral/medial and dorsal/lateral parts of the spinal internuncial zone (203). The interneurons project to motor neurons where similar organization reflects the muscle innervation pattern (315, 316). In the cat (201) and the monkey (210, 211) after pyramidectomy, interruption of the ventromedial system results in severe impairment of axial and proximal limb movement, as contrasted with impairment of distal extremities after lesions to the lateral system. The cortex projects to the sites of origin of the subcorticospinal pathways, and the topographical division within the subcorticospinal system is paralleled by organization in the motor cortex. The rostral precentral motor cortex is primarily concerned with head, trunk, and proximal limbs and the caudal parts with distal limb movements. A similar organization has been noted in the projections to the cerebellum from the cortex (118) and to the extrapyramidal system from the cerebellum. The emerging picture is of a centromedial system exerting general control over movements, i.e. erect posture, integration of trunk and limbs and progression, with a lateral system superimposing control and independent use of the extremities, especially the hands. After discrete lesions, the impairments reflect alterations in the grading of innervation, in the stopping and starting of muscular contractions and in the flow of movement from one muscle group to the next.

The pyramidal system.—The corticospinal system largely mimics the subcorticospinal system, and Kuypers & Brinkman (202) have shown different sites of origin in the precentral motor cortex of corticospinal projections to the dorsolateral and ventromedial portions of the internuncial zone. In addition, the corticospinal pathways control fractionated distal movements, e.g. of the fingers. Lawrence & Hopkins (209) have shown that both the corticospinal fibers and dexterous finger movements, which are absent at birth in the monkey and normally develop in the first few weeks, fail to develop if the motor cortex is removed soon after birth. After adult bilateral pyramidal section, monkeys are able to sit upright, stand, walk, run, and make placing reactions. The ability to use the extremities is initially absent, but although some recovery of discrete hand movements occurs, the dexterity afforded by discrete finger movement does not. An impairment of axial musculature is only seen if the pyramidal section results in deep tegmentum damage (210). These findings support anatomical claims that in higher primates mono-synaptic corticospinal pathways terminate on motoneurons innervating distal muscles (220, 274); that the squirrel monkey, which is less dexterous, has few such fibers (155); and that the cat which, lacks direct cortico-motoneuronal connections, also lacks separate movement of the digits (200). Partial sparing of the pyramids results in rapid recovery of limb movement and limited finger movement, but the patterns of recovery and the location of the lesion do not suggest strict somatotopic localization in the pyramid of the monkey, which is in agreement with earlier electrophysiological findings. The importance of the pyramidal system for dexterous behavior is illustrated by the effect of pyramidal section on various components of choice reaction responses. Laursen (208) trained monkeys with the right hand in a chained operant situation to gain access to a handle which had to be turned to the left if it was at 29°C and to the right if at 25°C. Left pyramidectomy increased only the latency of the choice reaction.

Interactions between pyramidal and extrapyramidal systems.—After damage to the corticospinal pathways, the changes in tone of the component muscle groups depend on which part of the cortico-subcortical projection is disrupted (143). The corticospinal fibers innervate both alpha and gamma motoneurons, and after pyramidal section the lack of correspondence between the hypokinesia and paralysis suggests that differential activation of tonic and phasic mechanisms of the cord is possible. The changes are not accounted for simply by the loss of either "inhibitory" or "facilitatory" systems, but rather by an imbalance.

The tonic and phasic interactions of the pyramidal and extrapyramidal systems have long been of concern to experimental neurologists, and the difficulty in unraveling these interactions by means of brain lesions is infamous. Denny-Brown and Mettler are largely responsible for the success of such studies, and as both have recently published reviews (87, 236) further comment is unnecessary. In view of the anatomical complexity at the subcortical level, it is not surprising that the use of discrete lesions has not added definitively to our understanding of the system.

Recent anatomical work referred to earlier, indicating hitherto unsuspected specificity in the projections of the two systems to the spinal cord, has encouraged extension of dissociation studies to that level. The results have defined some aspects of movement and tone control more clearly than before, and in general it seems that pyramidal lesions produce more specific disorder of movement than of tone and that the reverse is true of the extrapyramidal system. Even so, in the opinion of Goldberger (143), there is "no lesion affecting motor systems, which, if studied carefully, results in a change either in tone or in movement alone."

The relationship between the motor cortex and motoneurons.—The motor cortex has, in addition to corticospinal pathways, wide projections to the extrapyramidal nuclei and hence to the spinal cord. Although much is known both anatomically and physiologically about these extrapyramidal projections, the functional relationship of motor cortex to motoneuron activity is best understood in the corticospinal pathway. This is true especially in the primates, where the monosynaptic nature of the projection aids interpretation of electrophysiological results of movements of the different body parts.

It was clear from early studies involving mapping that the parameters of the electrical stimulus used influences the results obtained. Hines (159) had difficulty in eliciting discrete responses and suggested that although a particular muscle was not the only muscle represented at a specific cortical site, it was the one predominantly represented there. Therefore, weak stimulation should permit restriction of responses to single muscles. Woolsey et al (350), using unifocal 60 Hz/s alternating current, were able to elicit a large range of minimal muscular responses.

Similar studies by Chang et al (71) failed to obtain evidence of minute localization, and in working on the representation area of the muscles of the ankle joint it was noted that with equal stimuli not all the muscles were equally available. This subsequently became the principle of "differential accessibility" (Liddell & Phillips, 216, 217), which now dominates theories of motor cortex organization. Mapping experiments continued, using a variety of stimulus parameters. Liddell & Phillips (216–218), using a 5 msec single rectangular cathodal pulse of 1.0 mA, found a small area eliciting contralateral thumb and index finger movement. With increasing amplitude, the finger area grew larger and adjacent areas gave toe responses, until at 5 mA all these parts moved together from sites widely dispersed on the Rolandic area. The impression was that certain muscles held preferential representation, and Phillips exploited the monosynpatic pathway to forelimb muscle motoneurons in the baboon in the pursuit of this problem (204, 205). The motonuerons were identified by antidromic stimulation of nerves innervating forearm muscles, and the motor cortex was mapped with focal anodal stimulation to determine the size of the field producing monosynaptic excitation of the motoneurons. Both very discrete (1 mm^2) and very wide (8 $\times$ 2.5 mm) field sizes were found, and these values were substantiated by studies in which excitation was plotted as a function of stimulus strength (274). The preferential representation and the large fields suggest that finesse of voluntary movement does not depend "on a fine grained anatomical mosaic at the head of the corticospinal outflow; it must, instead, require a marvelously subtle routing of activity in the outer cortical layers to pick up in significant functional groups, the required corticofugal neurons, which are scattered and intermingled with unwanted ones which may be suppressed" (Phillips, 273).

Mapping experiments have been greatly refined by the development of discrete microstimulation of pyramidal cells (317). Using cathodal currents of 10 μA for 0.2 msec, Asanuma & Sakata (15) report radially arranged points of low threshold and a preponderance of 1 mm² fields for monosynaptic activation of motoneurons. The larger fields seen by Landgren et al (204, 205) were probably a reflection of the large surface stimulating current used.

Although mapping experiments seek the finest level of motor representation, the final output of the motoneurons is reintegrated onto the muscle groups necessary for posture, locomotion, or voluntary movement. Preston and his collaborators (278) have examined in cat and baboon the contrasting pattern of excitation and inhibition of extensor and flexor muscles in the limbs after stimulation of the motor cortex. In the baboon, they relate differences in the cortical representation of extensor muscles in the hind and forelimb (350) and their pattern of inhibition and facilitation after cortical stimulation to the emergence of bipedal locomotion which releases the forelimb for dexterous movement. There is some controversy as to whether such segmental organization is mediated by direct corticospinal influence on motoneurons or through interneurons associated with segmental reflex systems (221). However, although the activation of gamma motoneurons by cortical stimulation and the role of the muscle spindles in segmental reflexes may be noted (149, 215, 314), space does not permit comment on this particular controversy.

The relationship between motor cortex output and its afferent input.—The motor cortex receives somesthetic and kinesthetic information via the ventral posterolateral thalamic nucleus (VPL), although the stronger lemniscal input is to the postcentral gyrus (Somatic I). It may be noted that the Group I afferents (from muscle spindles) are included in the kinesthetic projection but do not synapse on pyramidal tract neurons (PTNs) (265). The specific thalamic nuclei, posterior nuclei (164), and the nucleus center median (59, 60) have been reported to convey auditory and visual input to the motor cortex. The existence of polysensory projections to the motor cortex (32) may appear incongruous, but it has been known for many years. In early mapping experiments, Woolsey suggested that in the cat the nomenclature MsI, MsII, SmI, SmII be used for the motor and sensory cortical areas indicating the preponderant but not exclusive nature of the input/output relationships.

In addition, the cerebellum projects to the motor cortex via the red nucleus and the venterolateral (VL) nucleus of the thalamus; the caudate nucleus projects via the midline thalamic nuclei, and the pallidum via the VL. These three input systems are interrelated and in turn receive descending motor projections and therefore constitute feedback loop systems of immense anatomical complexity. Massion (234) has recently reviewed the red nucleus, and Evarts & Thach (118) have reviewed the cerebrocerebellar connections.

Currently there is a great deal of electrophysiological work on these intricate circuits, admirably reviewed in two books edited by Purpura and Yahr (282, 355). Attempts to relate sensory input to the output of the motor cortex have been made at the pyramidal neuron itself. Brooks and his colleagues (51, 52) have pioneered microelectrode studies of the Ms cortex of the cat, which contains pyramidal tract neurons and also receives somesthetic, visual, and auditory information via the ventroposterolateral, ventrolateral, and posterior nuclei of the thalamus (6, 59). However, it is not clear whether these projections are direct or mediated by adjacent cortical areas (9). Electrode penetrations were made in the pericruciate gyrus, and stimulation of the medullary pyramid was used to identify the cells as PTNs. The stimulus specificity was determined and peripheral receptive fields of the cells were then plotted. The results indicated that there was somatotopic representation and that neurons responding to a body part such as the hind limb were arranged in columns of 0.1–0.4 mm diameter, although the size of their receptive fields and the effective stimulus varied.

The radial columns were dominated (75 percent) by cells showing either local receptive fields (e.g. part of the paw) or stockinglike fields (limb), and these seemed to provide a framework for cells with wider receptive fields (e.g. half body) and in some cases polysensory sensitivity. These characteristics contrast with those of the radial columns of cells in SmI of the cat which also receive kinesthetic and somesthetic input but which tend to show restricted receptive fields and stimulus specificity within a column—features presumably related to a discriminative function (247).

Weldt et al (342) have discussed the properties of the Ms neurons in terms of the building blocks of integration which could mediate many of the inbuilt placing reactions seen in the cat's normal motor repertoire. This contention has been strengthened by Asanuma et al (16), who, using similar techniques, have demonstrated that when a PTN with a local receptive field in the paw of the cat is stimulated, it activates the appropriate paw muscles to carry the receptive field towards the stimulus. On the other hand, Sakata & Miyamoto (290) report a preponderance of aversive movements, stimulation of a PTN carrying the limb away from the object with which the receptive field is in contact. Motor cortex inhibits input on classical sensory pathways, and Ghez & Lenzi (138) report <35 percent reduction in lemniscal responses in the cat as a conditioned paw response is made. Clearly we are some distance from understanding the full significance of the input/output relationships of the motor reflex arc.

The task is to relate these intricacies of organization to the final motor output of the system. Lesions are powerful tools for studying functional involvement in the CNS, but the singular lack of discrete high-order motor deficits such as hypokinesia, hyperkinesia, rigidity, tremor, etc. after lesions to the component parts of these feedback systems has been disappointing. Recently, however, some progress has been made in explaining the role of extrapyramidal structures in postural mechanisms through the study of Parkinson's disease, a condition associated with basal ganglia disease and in particular with cell loss in the nigrostriatal pathway and depletion of the neurotransmitter dopamine (DA), which occurs in high concentration on this pathway. The spectrum of motor disturbances varies widely in these patients but tremor is a common feature. Poirier et al (275) and Bedard et al (21) have shown that in monkeys large ventromedial tegmentum lesions produce marked tremor. The lesion interrupts ascending cerebellar fibers, the connections of the red nucleus, and the nigrostriatal pathway, resulting in loss of DA (276).

The significance of damage to both the ascending monoaminergic neurons of the substantia nigra and the rubrocerebellar-thalamic loop is emphasized by the therapeutic value of both DOPA therapy and VL lesions in Parkinsonian patients. In more recent studies, ventromedial tegmental lesions which spare the monoaminergic fibers failed to produce tremor, which was then elicited by Harmaline, a drug interfering with monoamine metabolism (206). It is interesting that only in monkeys and man, where a parvocellular-red nucleus and a rubro-olivo-cerebellar loop exist, can a Parkinson-like syndrome be induced.

The Role of Motor Systems in Conditioned Behavior

Motor responses may be changed by the procedurally defined processes of conditioning. Much is known about the discriminative and reinforcement mechanisms involved, but a more challenging and rather neglected question concerns the relation between the normal properties of the motor system and learning. Particularly in question is the way in which widely separate areas of the CNS, which are involved in the learning process, correlate with the motor system to produce what we call a conditioned response. Weldt et al (342) demonstrated how building blocks in the Ms cortex could subserve the stimulus response pattern of instinctive placing reactions, but it remains to be explained how the cat could be trained to make a placing reaction to one visual stimulus and not to another.

Semmes, Mishkin & Cole (299) have shown that if conditioned responses to somesthetic stimuli are learned, forebrain structures outside the sensory receiving and motor areas are required, although intuitively one would suppose that a cortical interaction of lemniscal input and pyramidal output would be sufficient. They found that monkeys with the motor, somatosensory, and parietal cortex intact, but with all other cortex plus hippocampus and amygdala removed, were impaired in learning "certain basic discrimination strategies" in somesthetic tasks. The suggestion is that either a descending projection from the cortex or a particular structure involved in such strategies as response suppression, position shift, and stimulus comparison—or perhaps a combination of these factor—were disrupted by the lesion.

Electrophysiological studies.—Motor skills are acquired by the reinforcement of patterns of motor activity, which may be closely or remotely related to patterns of "involuntary" behavior. The overall patterning of activity in the various parts of the motor system during skilled movement is unknown, but during the past 5 years, Evarts (115), using the electrophysiological techniques pioneered by Jasper for recording in unanesthetized animals, has asked some very specific questions about what is going on in the PTNs of the monkey during spontaneous voluntary movement and trained skilled movement. He has found PTN activity to be correlated with arm movement in a monkey reaching for food, with some neurons showing phasic increases in firing with movement and others showing tonic discharge even in the absence of movement (113). Luschei et al (225) have reported similar phasic and tonic responses in PTNs when a monkey presses a key on a variable interval schedule (VI 32 sec) for food.

To specify more precisely the latency of PTN activity in relation to movement, Evarts (114) subsequently trained monkeys to release a key when a light flashed. Although the latency of the motor cortex response to a light flash has been shown to be 30 msec, the pyramidal cells did not fire until 100 msec (a delay of 70 msec) and the responses occurred at 180–200 msec. As Evarts remarks: "what sequence of neural events takes place during the 70 msec delay? An answer to this question would provide useful clues as to mechanisms of sensorimotor integration."

Evarts' technique also lends itself to the analysis of the eye-hand coordination behaviors which have been analyzed with split-brain preparations (129). Such tasks involve the integration of midbrain/cortical systems concerned with eye movement and discrete motor responses, and it would be interesting to compare the latency and activity of PTNs and neurons in Area 8, which if stimulated produce saccadic eye movements (287) and which have been shown to fire after initiation of eye and head movements (33, 34).

In more recent experiments, Evarts has tried to discover which element of the motor response is primarily coded by the PTN activity. Monkeys are trained to move a handle back and forth by extension and flexion of the wrist. PTN activity is recorded for free movement, when extension and flexion are opposed by varying weights (<400 g) (115, 116), and when a fixed posture is held (117). Contrary to expectation, force and in particular rapidly changing force (Fd/Ft), rather than displacement or position per se, relates most closely to patterns of PTN activity.

Kitai et al (194) have shown that in primates which have both a cerebro-olivo-cerebellar and a cerebro-pontine-cerebellar pathway, the fibers of the pathways arise from cells in different layers of the motor cortex. The olivary projection comes from cells in the superficial layers, the pontine from both deep PTNs and the superficial cells. The pathway from the cerebellum to the motor cortex projects to the deep PTNs, and it would be interesting, in Evarts' study, to know whether both superficial and deep PTNs responded before movement and with what latency. It is possible that the 70 msec is occupied with a reafferent pathway including the cerebellum and that the cerebellum actually initiates the pattern of activity in the PTNs.

Anatomical studies.—Supporting evidence for this idea has been presented by Evarts & Thach (118) in their review of the anatomical and electrophysiological connections of the cerebellum. Certain anatomical features are related to the classical functions of the cerebellum, notably the intermediate zone to regulation of motonueron response to corticospinal discharge (108), and the midline system to adjustment and correction of motor output following initiation (165). Most emphasis is given to the anatomy of the lateral cerebellar zone, and it is suggested that its organization is in keeping with a role in the initiation of voluntary movement, a suggestion made long ago by Holmes on clinical grounds.

The pathways involve the projection from the nonsensorimotor cortex to the lateral cerebellum and the reafferent pathway from the Purkinje cells to the motor cortex directly or via the red nucleus to the VL of the thalamus. Thach (322) has shown that the Purkinje cells of the cerebellum are activated when monkeys perform conditioned arm movements, but clearly the relationship between activity in the cerebellum-VL nucleus and PTNs should now be explored. The suggestion is that "certain parts of the cerebral 'association' cortex discharge over the several different pathways open to them (principally the cerebropontine relay) into lateral portions of the cerebellum which in turn activates the motor PTNs in the cerebrum." Cerebellar lesions impair the initiation of voluntary movements, and similar symptoms are frequently part of the Parkinson syndrome, which is thought to reflect abnormality of the olivo-cerebello-VL pathway. Red nucleus lesions in the cat impair conditioned flexion response without affecting unconditioned flexion of the same limb to shock (306). Large lesions of the medial thalamus have also been reported to impair initiation of conditioned responses in rats (327, 328). There is some evidence that cerebellar lesions in man impair the selection of appropriate motor patterns, e.g. patients cannot flex one finger to appose it with the thumb—all four fingers flex. Marr (38, 233) has recently described a model of cerebellar functioning which is consistent with a memorizing device capable of initiating motor actions and maintaining voluntary postures initially organized elsewhere.

NEUROPSYCHOLOGICAL STUDIES

The final challenge is to discover how programmed motor and sensory responses become related. It is now well established that cortical association areas in proximity to the primary sensory areas are concerned in higher levels of perceptual analysis and that lesions of these areas impair visual (244), auditory (256), and somesthetic (245) discrimination. This appears to be due to defective perceptual processing rather than to inability to condition response strategies (180). Association cortex projects to the lateral cerebellar zone (118), but it is seldom suggested that the connection between the perceptual and motor systems is straightforward. Transcortical pathways to the motor cortex have also been discounted (103, 285). However, the hippocampus is a structure which on the basis of electrophysiological (3, 181) and neuropsychological (104, 105) evidence has been implicated in associative processes. The hippocampus is not involved in perceptual analysis (242), yet it has polysensory input, access to motor systems (333), and connections with those parts of the limbic system and hypothalamous supposedly concerned with reinforcement. These properties (which, except for reinforcement, resemble the sensory/motor representation in the cerebellar cortex) have been used by Olds (262) to construct a model memorizing system in the various differentiated cell layers of the hippocampus. In microrecording experiments Hirano et al (160) have compared midbrain and hippocampal responses during classical conditioning of auditory positive and negative stimuli for food presentation and have found contrasting activity in these two sites to habituation, conditioning, and extinction procedures. Hippocampal units do not respond to novel stimuli but do show clear discrimination between the stimuli, which is still apparent after midbrain skeletal and motivational responses have been extinguished. Lesions to the hippocampus in various species impair maze learning, response discrimination, and extinction (178). Epileptic seizures in the hippocampus prevent learned avoidance behavior, timing behavior (231), and organized defense reactions (10). Flynn & Wasman (123) found that although avoidance learning proceeds during seizures, the responses do not appear until after-discharge terminates. In man, bilateral medial temporal lesions impair associative learning and memory in the visual, auditory, and somesthetic modalities without apparently impairing discriminative functions (239) but, interestingly enough, do not appear to impair skilled motor learning (76). It is possible that the latter depends upon cerebellar rather than temporal lobe mechanisms. In this connection, it is perhaps unfortunate that so little attention has been paid to skilled motor behavior in experimental animals, and it would be interesting to pursue studies of cerebellar lesions with some of the excellent behavioral techniques now available.

In view of these various considerations, it seems likely that the hippocampus plays a crucial role in the programming of acquired sensory-response patterns, but there remains the problem of where the subsequent interactions and access to the motor system occur. An extrapyramidal site seems most likely and is supported by anatomical evidence. But the importance of the corticospinal pathway for dexterous distal limb movements strongly suggests that if fine movement is demanded, the final common pathway is in the motor cortex with a preceding site of integration in the cerebellum, to which the hippocampus projects (119), or in the VL nucleus of the thalamus.

The failure of some experimental studies to demonstrate impaired discrimination behavior after hippocampal lesions might be thought to weaken this hypothesis. However, retention of preoperatively acquired discrimination strategies is frequently tested in such experiments, and it is possible that the hippocampus is maximally involved in the coding of new response strategies rather than in control of trial-to-trial responding. Acquisition of the discriminative strategy might well be a more sensitive test for hippocampal damage. Indeed, the chronic electrophysiological studies have stressed the changing rather than stable pattern of activity as the discrimination strategy is achieved (3).

Little attention is paid to such behavioral variables, but it is reasonable to suppose that different brain mechanisms are involved in different learning conditions and at different stages of learning. For example, the errorless discrimination paradigm (321), in which the negative stimulus is gradually increased in intensity, achieves perfect discrimination without the animal ever having responded to the negative stimulus. But this is presumably achieved in a way different from simultaneous discrimination in which both stimuli at full intensity are present and which demands the elimination of one response in favor of the other.

The principal hippocampal efferent pathway, the fornix, projects to the mamillary body and thence to the anterior thalamic and pontine nuclei. However, the fornix does not seem to mediate the motor involvement referred to above. On the basis of both lesion and anatomical studies, Votaw (333, 334) contends that these effects are mediated *via* hippocampal association cortex pathways.

The association cortex projects to the three extrapyramidal loop systems described above. The inferotemporal cortex, for example, project to the tail of the caudate nucleus and putamen, which project topographically to the substantia nigra and pallidum (281, 320). Access to the motor system could then occur either directly via the VL nucleus or descending subcortical pathways (255). The caudate also projects independently to the midline thalamic nuclei. The basal ganglia seem to be involved in conditioned motor responses. Caudate nucleus neurons fire during voluntary movement (195). Stimulation of the caudate nucleus arrests conditioned lever pressing (196), and striatal lesions in rats impair well-trained passive avoidance responses and the acquisition of active avoidance and escape responses (193). Cryogenic lesions in the caudate reduce the ability of monkeys to track a moving light with the hand (47), surgical lesions prevent the adaptation of a reaching response distorted with prisms (45), and lesions of the tail of caudate impair visual discrimination retention (102). Globus pallidus neurons fire during conditioned arm movements (85), and lesions of this structure in cats impair avoidance behavior (207). Stimulation of the midline thalamic nuclei alters cortically induced movement (219), whereas lesions disturb avoidance behavior (328); both the hippocampus and medial thalamic sites show correlated electrical activity during avoidance behavior (329).

Finally, there is one aspect of cortical control over motor functions which is not related to the learning process per se. This is the role of the frontal cortex in controlling general levels of motor readiness. Lesions of the frontal cortex produce a range of behavioral deficits, many of which suggest general disinhibition of unconditioned (55) and conditioned (243) response tendencies rather than difficulty in acquiring new conditioned responses as such. The impairment has been localized to the orbitofrontal cortex and characterized by means of extinction tests (62) and go/no go visual and auditory discrimination tasks (179). Furthermore, it is known that these frontal areas project to the basal ganglia and that lesions of the head of the caudate nucleus produce similar impairments (288). The pathways by which the frontal cortex brings about change in response output and the nature of the change itself remain puzzling, as both anterior and posterior cortex project to the caudate and hence to the globus pallidus and substantia nigra (320), albeit to topographically distinct parts of these structures. Furthermore, limbic mechanisms may be involved in the frontal system (63, 182, 226).

The hope is that this combination of fact and hypothesis will in the end justify Sherrington's belief that "by combining methods of comparative psychology . . . with the methods of experimental physiology investigation may be expected ere long to furnish new data of importance toward the knowledge of movement as an outcome of the workings of the brain."

ASYMMETRY OF CEREBRAL HEMISPHERE FUNCTION

The concept of cerebral dominance, originally defined in terms of handedness and speech lateralization, has been widened to take into account evidence of hemispheric asymmetry in relation to a wide variety of nonlinguistic skills, in particular visual and spatial. In addition to more precise statistical analysis of the *sequelae* of unilateral hemisphere lesions, the introduction of radical neurosurgical techniques, in particular hemispherectomy and commissurotomy, has given fresh impetus to the analysis of differential hemisphere function. Further, the recent growth of studies on unilateral asymmetries in the normal individual, particularly in the acoustic sphere, is forging a link between issues of hemisphere dominance and more conventional areas of experimental psychology.

ANATOMICAL ASYMMETRIES

Morphological differences between the hemispheres have been claimed for at least a century, but few if any have stood the test of time. However, Geschwind & Levitsky (137) have recently produced evidence of left-right asymmetries in the posterior temporal region that may prove to have an important bearing on differential hemisphere function. They claim that the planum temporale, which lies immediately behind Heschl's gyrus and forms part of the conventional speech area, is larger on the left in 65 percent of 100 adult brains examined at necropsy and smaller in only 11 percent. Comparable findings have also been reported at necropsy in the brains of young infants (Geschwind 135). Correlations with handedness and speech lateralization are still to be undertaken. Differences in cerebro-vascular blood supply have been adduced by Carmon & Gombos (69) as a possible determinant of cerebral dominance.

HANDEDNESS AND CEREBRAL DOMINANCE

Handedness.—The origins of handedness and its relation to speech lateralization continue to attract interest. Annett (11, 13), a strong proponent of the genetical view, has drawn attention to the fact that when handedness is classified in terms of right, left, and 'mixed,' the percentages of these three groups are in binomial proportions. This she regards as fully compatible with a genetical model according to which both handedness and speech lateralization are determined by two alleles, one usually dominant and the other imperfectly recessive. This model prescribes that heterozygotes may be right, left, or ambilateral, but as a rule develop right handedness and left speech dominance. Annett (12) has also shown that both the distribution of hand preferences and relative manual speed between the ages of $3\frac{1}{2}$ and 15 years remain surprisingly constant and that there is a linear relation between degrees of preference and degrees of relative manual skill.

On the other hand, emphasis has been placed on acquired factors in handedness by Collins (73, 74) on the basis of genetic studies in mice, and by Provins (279, 280), who has repeatedly shown that the potential skill level of the nonpreferred hand is as high as that of the preferred. Provins therefore regards handedness as secondary to the acquisition of skill, which he considers to require only a minimal level of general intelligence and motor capacity. Oldfield (261), however, has pointed out that handedness originates essentially with regard to bimanual coordination and is not primarily a matter of the speed, agility, and precision of unimanual acts. He considers it to be intimately bound with the expression of intention and volitional control.

Dominance in sinistrals.—Luria (222) and Gloning et al (139, 140) have assembled additional evidence that the incidence of aphasia from unilateral brain damage in sinistrals is higher than in dextrals and that its course is usually more transient. This is in keeping with the now widely held view that the lateralization of language in sinistrals is less complete than in dextrals and that in at least some cases bilateral representation exists. There is also evidence that in sinistral patients the incidence and severity of defects in reading, writing, and calculation—though not in expressive speech—are less if the hemisphere affected is ipsilateral to the preferred hand (140). While handedness is now regarded as a very uncertain guide to speech lateralization in persons who are not fully right handed, attempts to establish dominance by methods other than the Wada test (intracarotid sodium amylobarbitone) must be viewed as unproved. The possible value of unilateral electroconvulsive treatment (ECT) in this connection, however, is being explored (277).

Somatosensory Asymmetries

Primary sensory function.—The apparent asymmetries in somatosensory representation disclosed by Semmes et al (300) in their well-known studies of the effects of focal unilateral brain wounds have led to the suggestion that somatosensory function is more focally represented in the left than in the right hemisphere, with consequent specialization of the former for fine sensorimotor skill and of the latter for multimodal coordination of the kind appropriate to spatial orientation (298). This view is undeniably attractive but the findings of Corkin et al (77) render it somewhat implausible. Using essentially the same methods as those of Semmes et al, these workers find lasting sensory loss to be associated exclusively with lesions of the post-central gyrus in either hemisphere. Further, their data provide no evidence for diffuse somatosensory function, at all events with regard to contralateral sensory input. Doubt has likewise been cast on the existence of lateral asymmetries in somatosensory discrimination, reported by some earlier authors who claimed that they bear a relation to handedness and presumptive hemisphere dominance (68, 121).

Higher-order asymmetries.—Here again the evidence is conflicting. Whereas some studies of complex tactile discrimination have shown greater impairment from right-sided than from left-sided lesions (75, 90, 91), others have failed to show significant differences between the effects of broadly equivalent lesions of the two hemispheres (258, 283, 301). Studies using complex stereognostic tasks in commissurotomy patients, however, do appear to indicate that performance is better with the left hand, suggesting a degree of right hemisphere superiority (214).

Visual Field Asymmetries

Evidence of greater efficiency of the right binocular visual field for verbal and of the left for nonverbal information was first reported by Kimura (189) and regarded by her as further evidence of 'dual' functional asymmetry, i.e. verbal information being processed by the left and non-verbal by the right hemisphere. Unfortunately, this evidence has been extremely difficult to assess. Such differences as may exist are influenced by general differences in visual efficiency between the two eyes (266, 354) and between the nasal and temporal halves of each monocular field (230) and perhaps also by ocular dominance (230). Directional reading habits may also play a part, though almost certainly a less important one than was at one time conjectured (228, 229, 264). The actual structure of the letters used in a stimulus array may also affect efficiency (124, 125). Nevertheless, the work of Hines et al (158), who used an analog of the dichotic listening paradigm, and of McKeever & Huling (228, 229), who paid particular attention to the control of fixation, has shown that in the case of verbal material at least there is convincing evidence of right field (i.e. left hemisphere) superiority.

Ear Difference Effects

The earlier work of Milner and Kimura, using the dichotic stimulation technique, brought out a differential effect of left and right temporal lobe excisions on the recall of verbal and nonverbal input respectively. Thus digits or words gave a right ear advantage and musical passages a left ear advantage. Asymmetries in the same direction, though of much lesser magnitude, were subsequently ascertained in a normal population (187, 188, 190, 302). These findings have given rise to an extensive literature [see Richardson & Knights (286) for bibliography] which it is impossible to summarize in full. The present review will be limited to work on handedness and speech lateralization, the basis of differential ear advantage, and the effects of cerebral lesions on dichotic performance.

Handedness and speech lateralization.—An interaction between ear channel and handedness in the recall of dichotically presented digits has been found in several studies (56, 79–81, 190, 227, 293, 294, 358). In general, left-handers also show a left-ear advantage, though this is appreciably smaller than the right-ear advantage shown by right-handers; indeed in one study only 40 percent of left-handed subjects showed reversed ear advantage. They are also likely to show greater variability. These findings are not surprising if one bears in mind that even among left-handers aphasia appears to result very much more frequently from lesions of the left than of the right cerebral hemisphere (222, 357) and that in some a degree of bilateral speech representation may well exist. Among sinistrals, too, lack of significant ear difference or even a bias towards the left ear in the perception of melodies has been reported (79, 227). Kimura (190, 197) has reviewed the relation between ear advantage and cerebral dominance and stresses the comparatively early age (5 years) at which ear advantage becomes apparent. She also finds evidence of a sex difference, right-ear advantage for verbal input being established earlier in girls than in boys, whereas boys appear superior to girls in identifying nonverbal sounds (left-ear advantage).

The basis of ear differences.—Let us consider right-ear advantage first. It has become clear that this does not depend on linguistic or semantic factors, as was at first supposed. Indeed, nonsense speech material gives a right-ear advantage equal to or only slightly less than that given by words or digits, (79, 81, 190, 303). In consequence, interest has focused increasingly on the properties of the speech signal which endow it with right-ear (and presumably left hemisphere) advantage (82, 83, 254, 303, 318). A significant right-ear advantage has been found for plosives (stop consonants), whether initial of final, though not for steady-state vowels (82, 303, 318). Its magnitude varies between 2 and 22 percent and is usually greater for initial than for final consonants. The effect does not depend on order of report of the signals (82, 294, 303). Significant and independent right-ear advantage for the articulatory or initial stop consonants has been clearly established (303, 318). Fricatives, too, give significant right-ear advantage (82, 83), greater when formant transitions are present. Indeed, there is evidence that the laterality effect generally is largely attributable to formant transitions (254). While not all phonemes give a right-ear advantage, it is significant that no phoneme has been shown to give an advantage to the left ear.

Left-ear advantage for nonspeech sounds has been less intensively studied. Originally established for tonal sequences (302), it was later found to characterize common environmental sounds (80). Spellacy (309) has found a significant left-ear advantage for complex sound patterns though not for rhythm, timbre, or pitch (see also 313). On the other hand, Darwin (82) reports that sounds that can be reliably distinguished on the basis of overall pitch contour alone give a clear left-ear advantage, whether the pitch is carried on a verbal or nonverbal timbre. Using musically trained subjects and carefully controlled conditions, McDonough (227) was able to replicate Kimura's findings for melody and contends that the major component is time-relation variability, i.e. a variability of rhythm rather than pitch.

Some workers (Oxbury, Oxbury & Gardiner 269; Kinsbourne 191) have contended that attentional bias plays an important part in creating ear difference effects and operates primarily through ear-order effects. This view, however, has been strongly criticized (82, 254, 292, 318) and certainly fails to explain a large number of observations. At the same time, it cannot be denied that the distribution of attention between two concurrent auditory inputs may play some part in the genesis of asymmetry (323) or that the two hemispheres may differ in their attentional "readiness" to respond to and process different classes of auditory information.

While ear differences are revealed for the most part only under dichotic stimulation, lateral asymmetry has recently been reported under certain conditions of monaural stimulation (17-19, 252, 253, 304).

Effects of cerebral lesions.—Kimura's original findings in cases of unilateral temporal lobe excision were (a) an overall impairment of digit recall after dominant (left) temporal lobe excision, and (b) an additional impairment of digit recall at the ear contralateral to the lesion. She explained these findings in terms of the greater functional efficacy of the pathway from the contralateral ear to the dominant hemisphere as compared with that of the ipsilateral pathway, together with inhibition of the ipsilateral signal on dichotic stimulation. The overall deficit is commonly thought to represent loss of the normal 'dominance effect,' whereas the additional unilateral loss is attributed directly to the lesion (lesion effect). As has been pointed out, however, it is difficult to know how to account for the lesion effect from this model, at least in its present form (308).

Oxbury & Oxbury (267) have reanalyzed the Milner-Kimura data and point out that the deficit is greater in cases in which the whole of Heschl's gyrus had been included in the excision and that this occurs regardless of whether input to the right ear is reported first or second. They also note that right temporal lobectomy will affect performance only if Heschl's gyrus is included.

Goodglass (146) has reported pronounced loss on dichotic digits tests in children with long-standing brain damage, sometimes amounting to virtual failure to report input from the ear contralateral to the lesion. He comments on the similarity of the effect to the familiar visual or tactile extinction with bilateral simultaneous stimulation. In adults with unilateral brain damage of recent origin (including cases with aphasia), he and his colleagues (296, 308) find a unilateral right-ear decrement for tonal sequences and a severe bilateral deficit for digits associated with left hemisphere lesions, and a unilateral left-ear decrement for digits and bilateral decrement for tonal sequences with right-hemisphere lesions. A modification of Kimura's model to allow for the incidence of gross extinction effects is proposed (308).

In commissurotomy cases, there is noteworthy failure to report digits from the left ear on dichotic—though not on monaural—stimulation (241, 307). This again suggests extinction of signals from the ear ipsilateral to the dominant hemisphere. On the other hand, cases of agenesis of the corpus callosum show no pronounced ear asymmetry (57, 295); nor is there evidence of gross unilateral extinction in cases of right hemispherectomy (57, 80).

Observations by Vignolo (331) raise the interesting possibility that defects in recognition of common environmental sounds following unilateral cerebral lesion differ according to the hemisphere affected. Although right-sided lesions lead to failure in perceptual discrimination, left-sided lesions appear to produce defect in the associative and semantic sphere. These findings he relates to the existing evidence of cerebral asymmetry in auditory recognition.

Visual Perception

Although it is always perilous to infer the localization of functions from that of lesions, there is an increasing body of evidence linking right-sided cerebral lesions with disturbances in various aspects of visual performance. This evidence comes mainly from the comparative study of deficits produced by approximately equivalent lesions of the two hemispheres and is supported by recent evidence from the study of commissurotomy cases. The latter appears to show that in the matching of visual material not readily specified in linguistic terms, the right hemisphere exhibits a decisive superiority (213, 324).

Form and pattern perception.—Earlier work led Milner to conclude that "the right temporal lobe aids in rapid visual identification." This claim, however, has proved controversial. Warrington & James (336) report findings on tachistoscopic number recognition in patients with unilateral brain damage, first determining detection thresholds at corresponding points in the left and right half-fields to control for amblyopic defects. They were unable to confirm Kimura's earlier finding (186) of impaired number estimation from right-sided temporal lobe damage, except in the contralateral half-fields in which detection thresholds were significantly elevated. On the other hand, there was definite impairment with right parietal lesions that could not be ascribed to amblyopia. Rubino (289), on the other hand, has reported a clear-cut inferiority in the identification of meaningless patterns in patients with right temporal excisions as compared with those with comparable left temporal excisions. Irrespective, however, of the role of the temporal lobe per se, there is abundant evidence that higher-order perceptual tasks (e.g. the discrimination of overlapping figures or effecting "visual closure") are more adversely affected by right-sided than by left-sided lesions of closely comparable location and extent (94, 258, 259).

Facial recognition.—Difficulty in recognizing individuals by sight, unaccompanied by other signs of visual agnosia, has long been known and ascribed to occipito-parietal or temporoparietal lesions, often bilateral though as a rule predominantly or even exclusively right-sided. These observations have generated a series of inquiries designed to elucidate this bizarre disorder (28, 92, 95, 326, 337, 356). For the most part, photographs or line drawings of faces, familiar or unknown, have been used, together with immediate recognition or matching tests of varying difficulty. Broadly, the results show beyond reasonable doubt that impairment in facial recognition is much more closely linked with lesions of the right than of the left hemisphere. There is also a suggestion that whereas recognition of strange (i.e. novel) faces is maximally impaired by right parietal lesion, that of well-known faces is maximally impaired by right temporal lesion (337). Tzavaras et al (326), in contradistinction to De Renzi and his associates (92, 94, 95), find no correlation between performance on face-recognition tests and on comparable recognition tests using other types of complex visual material. Therefore, they are led to conclude that there may be "an autonomous defect of human visual recognition." Although this might appear far-fetched, the work of Yin (356) lends some credence to their view. It is also noteworthy that recent studies of commissurotomy patients appear to have established a "predilection" of the right hemisphere for the selection and matching of photographs of human faces (324).

Color recognition.—Color anomia may appear together with alexia as a highly circumscribed syndrome which has been ascribed to "disconnection" between the striate cortex of the right hemisphere and the speech areas (136, 268). It may also appear in a context of more general aphasia, though the color-naming defect may be surprisingly outspoken. In tests involving visual memory for colors, patients with left hemisphere lesions (especially those with aphasia) commonly, though not invariably, perform worse than those with comparable right hemisphere lesions (96). None the less, precise hue-matching (Farnsworth-Munsell 100 Hue Test) is actually performed less effectively by patients with right-sided than by those with left-sided lesions (297). Results of color-matching tests with commissurotomy patients are eagerly awaited but preliminary findings seem to favor a special role of the right hemisphere (324).

Stereopsis.—Loss of depth perception from unilateral cerebral lesion has very occasionally been reported in the neurological literature and in such cases the lesion appears to have been invariably right-sided. But there are, of course, a great many negative cases. Carmon & Bechtoldt (67), using a method which requires the subject to locate a form in depth by binocular disparity clues alone (Julesz stereograms), have established significant deficit in patients with right hemisphere lesions as compared with those having left hemisphere lesions or compared with healthy control subjects. These observations have been confirmed (27).

Visuoconstructional ability.—Disability in drawing, copying, assembly, and constructional tasks carried out primarily under visual control occurs with posterior lesions of either cerebral hemisphere, but its nature apears to vary somewhat with the laterality of the lesion [see Warrington (335) for review]. Dramatic evidence of superior capacity by commissurotomy patients (especially in the early postoperative period) to copy designs or assemble mosaics with the left than with the right hand has been adduced by Bogen (39, 40). This provides strong evidence for the view put forward some years ago that the right hemisphere is dominant for certain visuospatial functions. At the same time, studies of visuoconstructional activity in patients with broadly comparable lesions of the two hemispheres (23, 64, 89, 258, 283, 338) have given more equivocal results, and much appears to depend on the precise requirements of the task and the degree to which it is sensitive to perceptual, executive, or linguistic deficit. By and large, tasks depending narrowly on fine visuospatial analysis and which minimize the executive component appear most sensitive to right hemisphere damage (23, 64, 89, 126, 258, 283), whereas tasks which place stress on the programming of action appear most sensitive to left hemisphere damage, especially when there is associated aphasia (23, 156, 335). It should also be borne in mind that whereas visuoconstructional defects are maximal with posterior parietal lesions, they may appear to some extent with lesions elsewhere, at all events in the right hemisphere (23, 25, 26, 258).

Visual maze learning.—Using a stylus maze given in the form of a visual test, Newcombe (258, 259) found that patients with long-standing penetrating brain wounds involving the upper posterior parietal or occipitoparietal areas show very poor performance. On the other hand, they perform relatively well on perceptual 'closure' tests, on which patients with posterior temporal or low temporoparietal lesions do very poorly. This suggests a certain dissociation between synthetic visual perception and visuospatial skill.

Hemispheric specialization.—Lévy-Agresti & Sperry (214) have reaffirmed the view that while the left hemisphere is primarily specialized for language, the right hemisphere is equally specialized for skills presupposing synthetic visual capacity (see also 39). The implication is that in skilled visuoconstructional activity, right hemisphere capacities are normally channeled through the left (dominant) hemisphere and right hand. It has been further suggested by Lévy-Agresti & Sperry that a possible reason for cerebral lateralization is a basic incompatibility between language functions on the one hand and synthetic perception on the other; this raises interesting possibilities regarding the course of cerebral lateralization in childhood and has prompted the claim that the complete or partial lateralization of speech to the right hemisphere in some sinistrals depresses the growth of visuoconstructional ability (213).

MATERIAL-SPECIFIC MEMORY DEFICITS

Verbal deficits.—It has been known for some years that defect in verbal learning, retention, and recall is characteristic of patients who have undergone left anterior temporal lobectomy. The nature of this defect has been studied by Corsi (cf Milner 239), using a simplified form of the Peterson and Peterson technique and the Hebb recurring digits task. His findings indicate that there is abnormally rapid decline in the accuracy of recall, the extent of which appears to vary with the medial extent of the excision. Milner (239) is therefore led to conclude that the left medial temporal region plays an important part in the consolidation phase of verbal learning. An apparently specific defect in short-term acoustico-verbal memory associated with left temporal or temporoparietal lesions has also been claimed by Luria and his associates (223, 224), and by Warrington & Shallice (340), who describe a remarkable case of brain injury in which learning capacity and long-term memory are said to be unaffected.

In patients with long-standing unilateral brain wounds, Newcombe (258) reports less efficient verbal registration and verbatim recall performance with left temporoparietal injury. Her findings appear to conflict with earlier observations suggesting that the verbal memory deficit following left temporal lobectomy undergoes virtually complete remission within 4 years of operation. Greater sensitivity of verbal memory to left-sided than to right-sided hemisphere dysfunction is also indicated in recent studies of the effects of unilateral electroconvulsive therapy (122, 277).

Visual deficits.—There is abundant evidence linking some aspects of memory loss for diagrammatic and pictorial material, particularly of the kind difficult to specify verbally, e.g. meaningless designs, photographs of faces, with right hemisphere lesions (88, 92, 186, 237, 238, 336). These findings are readily compatible with recent commissurotomy studies which suggest that visual material unsuited to verbal analysis or description is better identified through the right hemisphere (324). Conversely, experiments in which the material can be readily named, e.g. pictures of animals or common objects, indicate greater deficit from left-sided hemisphere lesions (42, 93, 94). Memory for colors likewise seems to show a left hemisphere superiority, even if the stimuli employed are variants of the same hue and consequently difficult to name individually (44, 48, 88). While the localization of visual memory deficits within the hemisphere is uncertain, there is a suggestion that the temporal lobe is an especially important site (88, 239, 339) and that the extent of damage to the underlying hippocampus may be an important factor in governing its severity (239).

REACTION-TIME STUDIES

The assumption that extent of brain damage—and by implication the degree of general psychological impairment—can be inferred from simple reaction time measurements has been widely held in Italian neuropsychology. However, evaluation of brain scan estimates of lesion size by Boller et al (43) throws some doubt upon this assumption, particularly in the case of the left hemisphere. While significant correlations have been obtained between the volume of a brain lesion calculated from its scan image and simple auditory and visual reaction times in the case of the right hemisphere, in the case of the left hemisphere reaction time and scan volume are not found to be correlated. At the same time there is a suggestion that the data in cases of left hemisphere lesion without aphasia resemble those from the cases of right hemisphere lesion. Therefore, while reaction time appears to rise in direct proportion to lesion volume in nonaphasic cases, lesions affecting the language areas do not appear significantly to affect reaction time. In any case, it cannot necessarily be assumed that 'general' intellectual impairment obeys a mass-action principle. Dimond (101) has reported experiments in which signals are directed exclusively to the temporal or nasal half-fields in normal subjects and simple response times, using either the ipsilateral or the contralateral hand, recorded. With single signals he finds no significant differences between the hands, but with two simultaneous signals, combined reaction times are lowest when pairs of signals are directed to different hemispheres, one through either eye. However, when both signals are directed to the same hemisphere through different eyes, a significant increase in response times is found. This is thought to indicate that the information received by each hemisphere must be analyzed separately before interhemispheric transfer takes place. Perhaps this also can be related to the observation of Gazzaniga (129) that in commissurotomy patients there is no increase of reaction time for the right hand to a two-choice visual discrimination task presented to the right field when a comparable task is simultaneously presented in the left field. Some degree of independent processing would appear self-evident.

LANGUAGE AND COMMUNICATION

The predominant relation of language to the dominant (normally left) cerebral hemisphere may be considered established. None the less, many issues remain. For instance, the extent to which the right hemisphere may participate in speech, actually or potentially, is a problem of great importance not only for neurological theory but also for re-education in aphasia.

Effects of right hemisphere lesions on language.—Two studies have failed to reveal appreciable linguistic defect in groups of patients with right-sided brain damage. Boller (41) compared the performance of patients with right brain lesions and nonaphasic patients with left brain lesions on some simple tests of comprehension, fluency, and object-naming. No differences between the two groups emerged. Newcombe (258) found no significant differences in the performance of a group of World War II veterans who had sustained missile wounds of the right hemisphere and that of a closely matched healthy control group on tests of vocabulary, spelling, arithmetic, fluency, and object-naming. On the other hand, Archibald & Wepman (14), in keeping with earlier reports, found that 8 out of 37 right-handed patients with unilateral right-sided brain damage due to cerebrovascular accident displayed minor dysphasic signs: they made significantly more errors on the Wepman-Jones Language Modalities Test for Aphasia than either a nonaphasic brain-damaged or a healthy control group. While this might appear to indicate right hemisphere language deficit, the authors are careful to point out that the presence of speech errors could have been due to either bilateral involvement or to general mental deterioration, involving decreased attention to the task in hand.

Commissurotomy studies.—The work of Gazzaniga & Sperry (131) has shown convincingly that, at least in some commissurotomy patients, the right hemisphere possesses rudimentary powers cf oral comprehension. Nouns in particular are fairly readily understood. More recent work has shown that some commissurotomy patients further possess the capacity to discern whether an action picture flashed to the right hemisphere is appropriately described by an affirmative or negative sentence (130). At the same time, there is still little or no evidence to suggest that the minor hemisphere can appreciate syntax or the meaning of a proposition (129, 130).

The issue of "right hemisphere speech" proper, i.e. speech generated exclusively by the disconnected right hemisphere in association with subcortex, has been debated extensively. Instances of speech responses thought to have been generated by the right hemisphere in commissurotomy patients have been cited by Butler & Norrsell (61), Levy & Sperry (213), and Milner & Taylor (240), and by Levy & Sperry (213) for writing responses. Dr. R. W. Sperry's laboratory also has data as yet unpublished which further support this contention. On the other hand, Gazzaniga (129,

130) has argued that what might appear to be right hemisphere speech is really due to transfer of information to the dominant hemisphere either by subtle 'cross-cueing' or through its encoding in some preverbal form that permits its transfer via the midbrain to the left hemisphere speech areas. This whole matter urgently awaits clarification.

LITERATURE CITED

1. Abeles, M., Goldstein, M. H. Jr. 1970. Functional architecture in cat primary auditory cortex: columnar organization and organization according to depth. *J. Neurophysiol.* 33:172–87

2. Abramov, I. 1968. Further analysis of the responses of LGN cells. *J. Opt. Soc. Am.* 58:574–79

3. Adey, W. R. 1961. Studies of hippocampal electrical activity during approach learning. In *Brain Mechanisms and Learning*, ed. J. F. Delafresnaye, 577–88. Oxford: Blackwell

4. Aitkin, L. M., Anderson, D. J., Brugge, J. F. 1970. Tonotopic organization and discharge characteristics of single neurons in nuclei of the lateral lemniscus of the cat. *J. Neurophysiol.* 33:421–40

5. Aitkin, L. M., Dunlop, C. W. 1968. Interplay of excitation and inhibition in the cat medial geniculate body. *J. Neurophysiol.* 31:44–61

6. Albe-Fessard, D., Guiot, G., Lamarre, Y., Arfel, G. 1966. Activation of thalamocortical projections related to tremorogenic processes. See Ref. 282, 237–54

7. Altman, J. A. 1968. Are there neurons detecting direction of sound source motion? *Exp. Neurol.* 22:13–25

8. Altman, J. A., Syka, J., Shmigidina, G. N. 1970. Neuronal activity in the medial geniculate body of the cat during monaural and binaural stimulation. *Exp. Brain Res.* 10:81–93

9. Amassian, V. E., Weiner, H. Monosynaptic and polysynaptic activation of pyramidal tract neurons by thalamic stimulation. See Ref. 282, 255–82

10. Andy, O. J., Akert, K. 1955. Seizure patterns induced by electrical stimulation of hippocampal formation in the cat. *J. Neuropathol. Exp. Neurol.* 14:198–213

11. Annett, M. 1967. The binomial distribution of right, mixed and left handedness. *Quart. J. Exp. Psychol.* 29:327–33

12. Annett, M. 1970. The growth of manual preference and speed. *Brit. J. Psychol.* 61:545–58

13. Annett, M. 1970. Handedness, cerebral dominance and the growth of intelligence. In *Specific Reading Disability: Advances in Theory and Method*, ed. D. J. Bakker, P. Satz, 61–78. Rotterdam Univ. Press

14. Archibald, J. M., Wepman, J. M. 1968. Language disturbance and nonverbal cognitive performance in eight patients following injury to the right hemisphere. *Brain* 91:117–30

15. Asanuma, H., Sakata, H. 1967. Functional organization of a cortical efferent system examined with focal depth stimulation in cats. *J. Neurophysiol.* 30:35–54

16. Asanuma, H., Stoney, S. D. Jr., Abzug, C. 1968. Relationship between afferent input and motor outflow in cat motorsensory cortex. *J. Neurophysiol.* 31:670–81

17. Bakker, D. J. 1969. Ear asymmetry with monaural stimulation. *Cortex* 5:36–41

18. Bakker, D. J. 1970. Ear asymmetry with monaural stimulation: relations to lateral dominance and lateral awareness. *Neuropsychologia* 8:103–18

19. Bakker, D. J., Boeihenga, J. 1970. Ear-order effects on ear asymmetry with monaural stimulation. *Neuropsychologia* 8:385–87

20. Barlow, H. B., Blakemore, C., Pettigrew, J. D. 1967. The neural mechanism of binocular depth discrimination. *J. Physiol.* 193:327–42

21. Bedard, P., Larochelle, L. L., Parent, A., Poirier, L. J. 1969. The nigrostriatal pathway: A correlative study based on neuroanatomical and neurochemical criteria in the cat and the monkey. *Exp. Neurol.* 25:365–77

22. Békésy, G. von 1967. *Sensory Inhibition*. Princeton Univ. Press

23. Benson, D. F., Barton, M. I. 1970. Disturbances of constructional ability. *Cortex* 6:19–46

24. Bental, E., Dafny, N., Feldman, S. 1968. Convergence of auditory and visual stimuli on single cells in the primary visual cortex of unanesthetized unrestrained cats. *Exp. Neurol.* 20:341–51

25. Benton, A. L. 1968. Differential behavioural effects of frontal lobe disease. *Neuropsychologia* 6:53–60

26. Benton, A. L., Ed. 1969. Constructional apraxia: Some unanswered questions. In *Contributions to Clinical Neuropsychology*. Chicago: Aldine

27. Benton, A. L., Hécaen, H. 1970. Stereoscopic vision in patients with unilateral cerebral disease. *Neurology* 20:1084–89

28. Benton, A. L., Van Allen, M. W. 1968. Impairment in facial recognition in patients with cerebral disease. *Cortex* 4:344–58

29. Berlucchi, G., Gazzaniga, M. S., Rizzolatti, G. 1967. Microelectrode analysis of transfer of visual information by the corpus callosum. *Arch. Ital. Biol.* 105:583–96

30. Berlucchi, G., Rizzolatti, G. 1968. Binocularly driven neurons in visual cortex of split-chiasm cats. *Science* 159:308–10

31. Biedenbach, M. A., Stevens, C. F. 1969. Synaptic organization of cat olfactory cortex as revealed by intracellular recording. *J. Neurophysiol.* 32:204–14

32. Bignall, K. E., Singer, P. 1967. Auditory, somatic and visual input to association and motor cortex of the squirrel monkey. *Exp. Neurol.* 18:300–12

33. Bizzi, E. 1967. Discharge of frontal eye field neurons during eye movements in unanaesthetized monkeys. *Science* 157:1588–90

34. Bizzi, E., Schiller, P. H. 1970. Single unit activity in the frontal eye fields of unanaesthetized monkeys during eye and head movement. *Exp. Brain Res.* 10:151–58

35. Blakemore, C. 1969. Binocular depth discrimination and the nasotemporal division. *J. Physiol.* 205:471–97

36. Ibid 1970. The representation of three-dimensional visual space in the cat's striate cortex. 209:155–78

37. Blakemore, C., Cooper, G. F. 1970. Development of the brain depends on the visual environment. *Nature* 228:477–78

38. Bloomfield, S., Marr, D. 1970. How the cerebellum may be used. *Nature* 227:1224–28

39. Bogen, J. E. 1969. The other side of the brain. I. Dysgraphia and dyscopia following cerebral commissurotomy. *Bull. Los Angeles Neurol. Soc.* 34:73–105

40. Bogen, J. E., Gazzaniga, M. S. 1965. Cerebral commissurotomy in man: minor hemisphere dominance for certain visuospatial functions. *J. Neurosurg.* 23:394–99

41. Boller, F. 1968. Latent aphasia: right and left "non-aphasic" brain damaged patients compared. *Cortex* 4:245–56

42. Boller, F., De Renzi, E. 1967. Relation between visual memory defects and hemispheric locus of lesion. *Neurology* 17:1052–58

43. Boller, F., Howes, D., Patten, D. M. 1970. A behavioural evaluation of brain scan estimates of lesion size. *Neurology* 20:852–59

44. Boller, F., Spinnler, H. 1967. Visual memory for colours in patients with unilateral brain damage. *Cortex* 3:395–405

45. Bossom, J. 1965. The effect of brain lesions on prism-adaptation in monkey. *Psychon. Sci.* 2:45–46

46. Boudreau, J. C., Tsuchitani, C. 1968. Binaural interaction in the cat superior olive S segment. *J. Neurophysiol.* 31:442–54

47. Bowen, F. P. 1969. Visuomotor deficits produced by cryogenic lesions of the caudate. *Neuropsychologia* 7:59–65

48. Brewer, W. F. 1969. Visual memory, verbal encoding and hemispheric localization. *Cortex* 5:145–51

49. Brindley, G. S. 1970. Central pathways of vision. *Ann. Rev. Physiol.* 32:259–68

50. Brindley, G. S. 1970. *Physiology of the Retina and Visual Pathway.* London: Edward Arnold. 2nd ed.

51. Brooks, V. B., Rudomin, P., Slaynan, C. L. 1961. Sensory activation of neurons in the cat's cerebral cortex. *J. Neurophysiol.* 24:286–301

52. Ibid. Peripheral receptive fields of neurons in the cat's cortex, 302–25

53. Brugge, J. F., Anderson, D. J., Aitkin, L. M. 1970. Responses of neurons in the dorsal nucleus of the lateral lemniscus of cat to binaural tonal stimulation. *J. Neurophysiol.* 33:441–58

54. Brugge, J. F., Dubrovsky, N. A., Aitkin, L. M., Anderson, D. J. 1969. Sensitivity of single neurons in auditory cortex of cat to binaural tonal stimulation; effects of varying interaural time and intensity. *J. Neurophysiol.* 32:1005–24

55. Brutowski, S. 1965. Functions of prefrontal cortex in animals. *Physiol. Rev.* 45:721–46

56. Bryden, M. P. 1970. Laterality effects in dichotic listening: relations with handedness and reading ability in children. *Neuropsychologia* 8:443–50

57. Bryden, M. P., Zurif, E. B. 1970. Dichotic listening performance in a case of agenesis of the corpus callosum. *Neuropsychologia* 8:371–77

58. Burns, B. D., Pritchard, R. 1968. Cortical conditions for fused binocular vision. *J. Physiol.* 197:149–71

59. Buser, P. Subcortical controls of pyramidal activity. See Ref. 282, 323–44

60. Buser, P., Bignall, K. E. 1967. Nonprimary sensory projections on the cat neocortex. *Int. Rev. Neurobiol.* 10:111–65

61. Butler, S. R., Norrsell, U. 1968. Vocalization possibly initiated by the minor hemisphere. *Nature* 220:793–94

62. Butter, C. M., Mishkin, M., Rosvold, H. E. 1963. Conditioning and extinction of a food-rewarded response after selective ablations of frontal cortex in rhesus monkeys. *Exp. Neurol.* 7:65–75

63. Butters, N. 1968. The effect of caudate and septal nuclei lesions on resistance to extinction and delayed alternation. *J. Comp. Physiol. Psychol.* 65:397–403

64. Butters, N., Barton, M. 1970. Effect of parietal lobe damage on the performance of reversible operations in space. *Neuropsychologia* 8:205–14

65. Campbell, F. W., Cleland, B. G., Cooper, G. F., Enroth-Cugell, C. 1968. The angular selectivity of visual cortical cells to moving gratings. *J. Physiol.* 198:237–50

66. Campbell, F. W., Cooper, G. F., Enroth-Cugell, C. 1969. The spatial selectivity of the visual cells of the cat. *J. Physiol.* 203:223–35

67. Carmon, A., Bechtoldt, H. P. 1969. Dominance of the right hemisphere for stereopsis. *Neuropsychologia* 7:29–39

68. Carmon, A., Bilstrom, D. E., Benton, A. L. 1969. Thresholds for pressure and sharpness on the right and left hands. *Cortex* 5:27–35

69. Carmon, A., Gombos, G. H. 1970. A physiological vascular correlate of hand-preference. Possible implications with respect to hemispheric cerebral dominance. *Neuropsychologia* 8:119–28

70. Carreras, M., Andersson, S. A. 1963. Functional properties of neurons of the anterior ectosylvian gyrus of the cat. *J. Neurophysiol.* 26:100-26

71. Chang, H. T., Ruch, T. C., Ward, A. A. 1947. Topographical representation of muscles in motor cortex of monkeys. *J. Neurophysiol.* 10:39–56

72. Choudhury, B. P. Whitteridge, D., Wilson, M. E. 1965. The function of the callosal connections of the visual cortex. *Quart. J. Exp. Physiol.* 50:214–19

73. Collins, R. L. 1968. On the inheritance of handedness: I. Laterality in mice. *J. Hered.* 59:9–12

74. Ibid 1969. On the inheritance of handedness: II. Selection of sinistrality in mice. 60:117–19

75. Corkin, S. 1965. Tactually-guided maze-learning in man: Effects of unilateral cortical excisions and bilateral hippocampal lesions. *Neuropsychologia* 3:339–51

76. Ibid 1968. Acquisition of motor skill after bilateral medial temporal lobe excision. 6:255–65

77. Corkin, S., Milner, B., Rasmussen, T. 1970. Somatosensory thresholds. Contrasting effects of post-central gyrus and posterior parietal lobe excisions. *Arch. Neurol.* 23:41–58

78. Creutzfeldt, O., Sakmann, B. 1969. Neurophysiology of vision. *Ann. Rev. Physiol.* 31:499–544

79. Curry, F. K. W. 1967. A comparison of left-handed and right-handed subjects on verbal and non-verbal dichotic listening tasks. *Cortex* 3:343–52

80. Ibid 1968. A comparison of the performance of a right hemispherectomised subject and twenty-four normals on four dichotic listening tasks. 4:144–53

81. Curry, F. K. W., Rutherford, D. R. 1967. Recognition and recall of dichotically presented verbal stimuli by right- and left-handed persons. *Neuropsychologia* 5:119–26

82. Darwin, C. J. 1969. *Auditory perception and cerebral dominance.* PhD thesis. Univ. Cambridge

83. Darwin, C. J. 1971. Ear differences in the recall of fricatives. *Quart. J. Exp. Psychol.* 23:46–62

84. Daw, N. W., Pearlman, A. L. 1969. Cat colour vision: one cone process or several. *J. Physiol.* 201:745–64

85. Delong, M. R. 1971. Activity of pallidal neurons during movement. *J. Neurophysiol.* 34:414–27

86. Denney, D., Baumgartner, G., Adorjani, C. 1968. Responses of cortical neurones to stimulation of the visual afferent radiations. *Exp. Brain Res.* 6:265–72

87. Denny-Brown, D. The fundamental organization of motor behaviour. See Ref. 355, 415–44

88. De Renzi, E. 1968. Nonverbal memory and hemispheric side of lesion. *Neuropsychologia* 6:181–90

89. De Renzi, E., Faglioni, P. 1967. The relationship between visuo-spatial impairment and constructional apraxia. *Cortex* 3:327–42

90. De Renzi, E., Faglioni, P., Scotti, G. 1968. Tactile spatial impairment and unilateral cerebral damage. *J. Nerv. Ment. Dis.* 146:468–75

91. De Renzi, E., Faglioni, P., Scotti, G. 1970. Hemispheric contribution to exploration of space through the visual and tactile modality. *Cortex* 6:191–203

92. De Renzi, E., Faglioni, P., Spinnler, H. 1968. The performance of patients with unilateral brain damage in face recognition tasks. *Cortex* 4:17–33

93. De Renzi, E., Spinnler, H. 1966. The influence of verbal and non-verbal defects on visual memory. *Cortex* 2:332–36

94. De Renzi, E., Spinnler, H. 1966. Visual recognition in patients with unilateral cerebral disease. *J. Nerv. Ment. Dis.* 142:515–25

95. De Renzi, E., Spinnler, H. 1966. Facial recognition in brain-damaged subjects—an experimental approach. *Neurology* 16:145–52

96. De Renzi, E., Spinnler H. 1967. Impaired performance on colour tasks in patients with hemispheric damage. *Cortex* 3:194–217

97. de Reuck, A. V. S., Knight, J., Eds. 1968. *Hearing Mechanisms in Vertebrates.* Ciba Found. Symp. London: Churchill

98. De Valois, R. L. 1965. Analysis and coding of color vision in the primate visual system. *Cold Spring Harbor Symp.* 30:567–79

99. De Valois, R. L., Abramov, I., Mead, W. R. 1967. Single cell analysis of wavelength discrimination at the lateral geniculate nucleus in the macaque. *J. Neurophysiol.* 30:415–33

100. Dews, P. B., Wiesel, T. N. 1970. Consequences of monocular deprivation on visual behaviour in kittens. *J. Physiol.* 206:437–55

101. Dimond, S. J. 1970. Hemispheric refractoriness of control and reaction time. *Quart. J. Exp. Psychol.* 22:610–17

102. Divac, I., Rosvold, H. E., Szwarcbart, M. K. 1967. Behavioral effects of selective ablation of the caudate nucleus. *J. Comp. Physiol. Psychol.* 63:184–96

103. Doty, R. W., Giurgea, C. Conditioned reflexes established by coupling electrical excitations of two cortical areas. See Ref. 3, 133–51

104. Douglas, R. J. 1967. The hippocampus and behaviour. *Psychol. Rev.* 67:416–42

105. Douglas, R. J., Pribram, K. H. 1966. Learning and limbic lesions. *Neuropsychologia* 4:197–220

106. Doving, K. B. 1970. Experiments in olfaction. In *Taste and Smell in Vertebrates*, ed. G. E. W. Wolstenholme, J. Knight, 197–225. Ciba Found. Symp. London: Churchill

107. Dow, B. M., Dubner, R. 1969. Visual receptive fields and responses to movement in an association area of cat cerebral cortex. *J. Neurophysiol.* 32:773–84

108. Eccles, J. C., Ito, M., Szentagothai, J. 1967. *The Cerebellum as a Neuronal Machine.* Berlin: Springer-Verlag

109. Erulkar, S. D., Butler, R. A., Gerstein, G. L. 1968. Excitation and inhibition in cochlear nucleus. II. Frequency-modulated tones. *J. Neurophysiol.* 31:537–48

110. Evans, E. F. Cortical representation. See Ref. 97, 272–95

111. Evans, E. F. 1971. Central mechanisms relevant to the neural analysis of simple and complex sounds. *Pattern Recognition in Biological and Technical Systems*, 328–43. Berlin: Springer Verlag

112. Evans, E. F., Ross, H. F., Whitfield, I. C. 1965. The spatial distribution of unit characteristic frequency in the primary auditory cortex of the cat. *J. Physiol.* 179:238–47

113. Evarts, E. V. 1965. Relation of discharge frequency to conduction

velocity in pyramidal tract neurons. *J. Neurophysiol.* 28:216–28

114. Ibid 1966. Pyramidal tract activity associated with a conditioned hand movement in the monkey. 29:1011–27

115. Evarts, E. V. Representation of movements and muscles by pyramidal tract neurons of the precentral motor cortex. See Ref. 355, 215–53

116. Evarts, E. V. 1968. Relation of pyramidal tract activity to force exerted during voluntary movement. *J. Neurophysiol.* 31:14–27

117. Ibid 1969. Activity of pyramidal tract neurons during postural fixation. 32:375–85

118. Evarts, E. V., Thach, W. T. 1969. Motor mechanisms of the C.N.S.: Cerebro-cerebellar interrelations. *Ann. Rev. Physiol.* 31:451–98

119. Fanardjian, V. V., Donhoffer, H. 1964. An electrophysiological study of cerebello-hippocampal relationships in the unrestrained cat. *Acta Physiol. Acad. Sci. Hung.* 24:321–33

120. Feher, O., Whitfield, I. C. 1966. Auditory cortical units which respond to complex tonal stimuli. *J. Physiol.* 182:39P

121. Fennell, E., Satz, P., Wise, R. 1967. Laterality differences in the perception of pressure. *J. Neurol. Neurosurg. Psychiat.* 30:337–40

122. Fleminger, J. J., de Horne, D. J., Nott, P. N. 1970. Unilateral electroconvulsive therapy and cerebral dominance: effect of right- and left-sided electrode placement on verbal memory. *J. Neurol. Neurosurg. Psychiat.* 33:408–11

123. Flynn, J. P., Wasman, M. 1960. Learning and cortically evoked movements during propogated hippocampal after-discharges. *Science* 131:1607–8

124. Fudin, R. 1969. Recognition of alphabetical arrays presented in the right and left visual fields. *Percept. Mot. Skills* 29:15–22

125. Ibid 1970. Letter structure factors in the recognition of alphabetical arrays presented in the right and left visual fields. 31:555–59

126. Gainotti, G., Tiacci, C. 1970. Patterns of drawing disability in right and left hemisphere patients. *Neuropsychologia* 8:379–84

127. Ganz, L., Fitch, M. 1968. The effect of visual deprivation on perceptual behaviour. *Exp. Neurol.* 22:638–60

128. Ganz, L., Fitch, M., Satterberg, J. A.

1968. The selective effect of visual deprivation on receptive field shape determined neurophysiologically. *Exp. Neurol.* 22:614–37

129. Gazzaniga, M. S. 1970. *The Bisected Brain.* New York: Appleton-Century-Crofts

130. Gazzaniga, M. S., Hillyard, S. A. 1971, Language and speech capacity of the right hemisphere. *Neuropsychologia* 9:278–80

131. Gazzaniga, M. S., Sperry, R. W. 1967. Language after section of the cerebral commissures. *Brain* 90:131–48

132. Geisler, C. D., Rhode, W. S., Hazelton, D. W. 1969. Responses of inferior colliculus neurons in the cat to binaural acoustic stimuli having wide-band spectra. *J. Neurophysiol.* 32:960–74

133. Gerstein, G. L., Butler, R. A., Erulkar, S. D. 1968. Excitation and inhibition in cochlear nucleus. I. Tone-burst stimulation. *J. Neurophysiol.* 31:526–36

134. Gerstein, G. L., Kiang, N. Y.-S. 1964. Responses of single units in the auditory cortex. *Exp. Neurol.* 10:1–18

135. Geschwind, N. Feb. 1969. Paper presented at National Hospital, Queen Square, London

136. Geshwind, N., Fusillo, M. 1966. Colour-naming defects in association with alexia. *Arch. Neurol.* 15:137–46

137. Geschwind, N., Levitsky, W. 1968. Human brain: left-right asymmetries in temporal speech region. *Science* 161:186–87

138. Ghez, C., Lenzi, G. L. 1970. Modulation of afferent transmission in the lemniscal system during voluntary movement in the cat. *Brain Res.* 24:542 (Abstr.)

139. Gloning, I., Gloning, K., Haub, G., Quatember, R. 1969. Comparison of verbal behaviour on right-handed and non-right-handed patients with anatomically verified lesion of one hemisphere. *Cortex* 5:43–52

140. Gloning, K., Quatember, R. 1966. Statistical evidence of neuropsychological syndrome in left-handed and ambidextrous patients. *Cortex* 2:484–88

141. Goldberg, J. M., Brown, P. B. 1968. Functional organization of the dog superior olivary complex: an anatomical and electrophysiological study. *J. Neurophysiol.* 31:639–56

142. Ibid 1969. Response of binaural neu-

rons of dog superior olivary complex to dichotic tonal stimuli: some physiological mechanisms of sound localization. 32:613–36

143. Goldberger, M. E. 1969. The extra-pyramidal systems of the spinal cord. II. Results of combined pyramidal and extra-pyramidal lesions in the macaque. *J. Comp. Neurol.* 135:1–26

144. Goldstein, M. H. Jr., Abeles, M., Daly, R. L., McIntosh J. 1970. Functional architecture in cat primary auditory cortex: tonotopic organisation. *J. Neurophysiol.* 33:188–97

145. Goldstein, M. H. Jr., Hall, J. L. II, Butterfield, B. O. 1968. Single-unit activity in the primary auditory cortex of unanesthetized cats. *J. Acoust. Soc. Am.* 43:444–55

146. Goodglass, H. 1967. Binaural digit presentation and early bilateral brain damage. *Cortex* 3:295–306

147. Gordon, G., Manson, J. R. 1967. Cutaneous receptive fields of single nerve cells in the thalamus of the cat. *Nature* 215:597–99

148. Gouras, P. 1970. Trichromatic mechanisms in single cortical neurons. *Science* 168:489–92

149. Granit, R., Keller, J.-O. The effects of stretch receptors on motoneurons. See Ref. 355 3–28

150. Grinnell, A. D. 1969. Comparative physiology of hearing. *Ann. Rev. Physiol.* 31:545–80

151. Gross, C. G., Bender, D. B., Rocha-Miranda, C. E. 1969. Visual receptive fields of neurons in inferotemporal cortex of the monkey. *Science* 166:1303–6

152. Grüsser, O.-J., Grüsser-Cornehls, U. 1969. Neurophysiologie des Bewegungssehens. Bewegungsempfindliche und richtungsspezifische Neurone im visuellen System. *Ergeb. Physiol.* 61:178–265

153. Hall, J. L. II, Goldstein, M. H. Jr. 1968. Representation of binaural stimuli by single units in primary auditory cortex of unanaesthetized cats. *J. Acoust. Soc. Am.* 43:456–61

154. Hammond, P. 1971. Chromatic sensitivity and spatial organization of cat visual cortical cells: cone-rod interaction. *J. Physiol.* 213:475–94

155. Harting, J. K., Noback, C. R. 1970. Corticospinal projections from the pre-post central gyri in the squirrel monkey. *Brain Res.* 24:322–38

156. Hécaen, H., Assag, G. 1970. Compari-son of constructive deficits following right and left hemisphere lesions. *Neuropsychologia* 8:289–303

157. Henry, G. H., Bishop, P. O., Coombs, J. S. 1969. Inhibitory and subliminal excitatory receptive fields of simple units in cat striate cortex. *Vision Res.* 9:1289–96

158. Hines, D., Satz, P., Schell, B., Schmidlin, S. 1969. Differential recall of digits in left and right visual half-fields under free and fixed order of recall. *Neuropsychologia* 7:13–22

159. Hines, L. 1947. Significance of the precentral motor cortex. In *The Precentral Motor Cortex*, ed. P. C. Bucy. Illinois Univ. Press

160. Hirano, R., Best, P. J., Olds, J. 1970. Units during habituation, discrimination learning and extinction. *Electroencephalogr. Clin. Neurophysiol.* 28:127–35

161. Hirsch, H. V. B., Spinelli, D. N. 1970. Visual experience modifies distribution of horizontally and vertically oriented receptive fields in cats. *Science* 168:869–71

162. Horn, G. 1965. The effect of somaesthetic and photic stimuli on the activity of units in the striate cortex of unanaesthetized unrestrained cats. *J. Physiol.* 179:263–77

163. Horn, G., Hill, R. M. 1969. Modifications of receptive fields of cells in the visual cortex occurring spontaneously and associated with bodily tilt. *Nature* 221:186–88

164. Hotta, T., Kameda, K. 1963. Interactions between somatic and visual or auditory responses in the thalamus of the cat. *Exp. Neurol.* 8:1–13

165. Houk, J., Henneman, E. 1967. Feedback control of skeletal muscles. *Brain Res.* 5:433–51

166. Hubel, D. H., Wiesel, T. N. 1961. Integrative action in the cat's lateral geniculate body. *J. Physiol.* 155:385–98

167. Ibid 1962. Receptive fields, binocular interaction and functional architecture in the cat's visual cortex. 160:106–54

168. Ibid 1963. Shape and arrangement of columns in the cat's striate cortex. 165:559–68

169. Hubel, D. H., Wiesel, T. N. 1963. Receptive fields of cells in striate cortex of very young visually inexperienced kittens. *J. Neurophysiol.* 26:994–1002

170. Ibid 1965. Receptive fields and functional architecture in two non-

striate visual areas (18 and 19 of the cat). 28:229–89

171. Ibid. Binocular interaction in striate cortex of kittens reared with artificial squint, 1041–59

172. Ibid 1967. Cortical and callosal connections concerned with the vertical meridian of visual fields in the cat. 30:1561–73

173. Hubel, D. H., Wiesel, T. N. 1968. Receptive fields and functional architecture of monkey striate cortex. J. Physiol. 195:215–43

174. Ibid 1969. Visual area of the lateral suprasylvian gyrus (Clare-Bishop area) of the cat. 202:251–60

175. Hubel, D. H., Wiesel, T. N. 1970. Cells sensitive to binocular depth in area 18 of the macaque monkey cortex. Nature 225:41–42

176. Hubel, D. H., Wiesel, T. N. 1970. The period of susceptibility to the physiological effects of unilateral eye closure in kittens. J. Physiol. 206: 419–36

177. Imbert, M. 1970. Aspects récents de la physiologie des voies visuelles primaires chez les vertébrés. J. Physiol. Paris 62:3–59

178. Iversen, S. D. 1971. Brain lesions and memory in animals. In Physiological Bases of Memory, ed. J. A. Deutsch. New York: Academic. In press

179. Iversen, S. D., Mishkin, M. 1970. Perseverative interference in monkeys following selective lesions of the inferior prefrontal convexity. Exp. Brain Res. 11:376–86

180. Iversen, S. D., Weiskrantz, L. 1967. The acquisition of conditional discriminations in baboons following temporal and frontal lesions. Exp. Neurol. 19:78–91

181. John, E. R. 1966. Neural processes during learning. In Frontiers in Physiological Psychology, ed. R. W. Russell, 149–84. New York: Academic

182. Johnson, T. N., Rosvold, H. E., Mishkin, M. 1968. Projections from behaviourally-defined sectors of the prefrontal cortex to the basal ganglia, septum, and diencephalon of the monkey. Exp. Neurol. 21:20–34

183. Joshua, D. E., Bishop, P. O. 1970. Binocular single vision and depth discrimination. Receptive field disparities for central and peripheral vision and binocular interaction on peripheral single units in cat striate cortex. Exp. Brain Res. 10:389–416

184. Jung, R., Kornhuber, H. H., Da Fonseca, J. S. 1963. Multisensory convergence on cortical neurons: neuronal effects of visual, acoustic and vestibular stimuli in the superior convolutions of the cat's cortex. Progr. Brain Res. 1:207–40

185. Kameda, K., Nagel, R., Brooks, V. B. 1969. Some quantitative aspects of pyramidal collateral inhibition. J. Neurophysiol. 32:540–53

186. Kimura, D. 1963. Right temporal-lobe damage. Arch. Neurol. 8:264–71

187. Kimura, D. 1963. Speech lateralisation in young children as determined by an auditory test. J. Comp. Physiol. Psychol. 56:899–902

188. Kimura, D. 1964. Left-right differences in the perception of melodies. Quart. J. Exp. Psychol. 16:355–58

189. Kimura, D. 1966. Dual functional asymmetry of the brain in visual perception. Neuropsychologia 4: 275–86

190. Kimura, D. 1967. Functional asymmetry of the brain in dichotic listening. Cortex 3:163–78

191. Kinsbourne, M. 1970. The cerebral basis of lateral asymmetries in attention. Acta Psychol. 33:193–201

192. Kinston, W. J., Vadas, M. A., Bishop, P. O. 1969. Multiple projection of the visual field to the medial portion of the dorsal lateral geniculate nucleus and the adjacent nuclei of the thalamus of the cat. J. Comp. Neurol. 136:295–316

193. Kirby, R. J., Kimble, D. P. 1968. Avoidance and escape behaviour following striatal lesions in the rat. Exp. Neurol. 20:215–27

194. Kitai, S. T., Oshima, T., Provini, L., Tsukahara, N. 1969. Cerebrocerebellar connections mediated by fast and slow conducting pyramidal tract fibres of the cat. Brain Res. 15:267–71

195. Kitsikis, A., Angyan, L., Buser, P. 1970. Relation between movements and unit activity in the basal ganglia in monkey. Brain Res. 24:543 (Abstr.)

196. Kitsikis, A., Rougeul, A. 1968. The effect of caudate stimulation on conditioned motor behaviour in monkeys. Physiol. Behav. 3:831–37

197. Knox, C., Kimura, D. 1970. Cerebral processing of non-verbal sounds in boys and girls. Neuropsychologia 8:227–37

198. Kozak, W., Rodieck, R. W., Bishop, P. O. 1965. Responses of single units

in lateral geniculate nucleus of cat to moving visual patterns. *J. Neurophysiol.* 28:19–47

199. Kuypers, H. G. J. M. 1960. Central cortical projections to motor and somato-sensory cell groups. *Brain* 83:161–84

200. Kuypers, H. G. J. M. 1963. The organization of the "motor system." *Int. J. Neurol.* 4:78–91

201. Kuypers, H. G. J. M. 1964. The descending pathways to the spinal cord, their anatomy and function. *Progr. Brain Res.* 2:178–202

202. Kuypers, H. G. J. M., Brinkman, J. 1970. Precentral projections to different parts of the spinal intermediate zone in the rhesus monkey. *Brain Res.* 24:29–48

203. Kuypers, H. G. J. M., Fleming, W. R., Farinholt, J. W. 1962. Subcorticospinal projections in the rhesus monkey. *J. Comp. Neurol.* 118:107–36

204. Landgren, S., Phillips, C. G., Porter, R. 1962. Minimal synaptic actions of pyramidal impulses on some alpha motoneurones of the baboon's hand and forearm. *J. Physiol.* 161:91–111

205. Ibid. Cortical fields of origin of the monosynaptic pyramidal pathway to some alpha motoneurones of the baboon's hand and forearm, 112–25

206. Larochelle, L., Bedard, P., Boucher, R., Poirier, L. J. 1970. The rubro-olivo-cerebello-rubral loop and postural tremor in the monkey, *J. Neurol. Sci.* 11:53–64

207. Laursen, A. M. 1963. Conditioned avoidance behaviour of cat with lesions in globus pallidus. *Acta Physiol. Scand.* 57:81–89

208. Laursen, A. M. 1970. Selective increase in choice latency after transection of a pyramidal tract in monkeys. *Brain Res.* 24:544–45 (Abstr.)

209. Lawrence, D. G., Hopkins, D. A. 1970. Bilateral pyramidal lesions in infant rhesus monkeys. *Brain Res.* 24:543–44 (Abstr.)

210. Lawrence, D. G., Kuypers, H. G. J. M. 1968. The functional organization of the motor system in the monkey. I. Effects of bilateral pyramidal lesions. *Brain* 91:1–14

211. Ibid. The functional organization of the motor system in the monkey. II. Effects of lesions of the descending brain-stem pathways, 15–36

212. Leicester, J. 1968. Projection of the visual vertical meridian to cerebral cortex of the cat. *J. Neurophysiol.* 31:371–82

213. Lévy, J., Sperry, R. W. 1969. *Lateral Specialization and Cerebral Dominances in Commissurotomy Patients.* Presented at Int. Congr. Psychol., 19th, London

214. Lévy-Agresti, J., Sperry, R. W. 1968. Differential perceptual capacities in major and minor hemispheres. *Proc. Nat. Acad. Sci.* 61:1151

215. Lewis, M. McD., Porter, R. 1971. Lack of involvement of fusiform activation in movements of the foot produced by electrical stimulation of monkey cerebral cortex. *J. Physiol.* 212:707–18

216. Liddell, E. G. T., Phillips, C. G. 1950. Thresholds of cortical representation. *Brain* 73:125–40

217. Liddell, E. G. T., Phillips, C. G. 1951. Overlapping areas in the motor cortex of the baboon. *J. Physiol.* 112:392–99

218. Liddell, E. G. T., Phillips, C. G. 1952. The cortical representation of motor units. *Brain* 75:510–25

219. Liles, S. L., Davis G. D. 1970. Interrelations of caudate nucleus and thalamus in alteration of cortically induced movement. *J. Neurophysiol.* 32:564–73

220. Lui, C. N., Chambers, W. W. 1964. An experimental study of the corticospinal system in the monkey (Macaca mulatta). The spinal pathways and preterminal distribution of degenerating fibres following discrete lesions of the pre- and postcentral gyri and bulbar pyramid. *J. Comp. Neurol.* 123:257–84

221. Lundberg, A. 1964. Supraspinal control of transmission in reflex paths to motoneurons and primary afferents. *Progr. Brain Res.* 12:197–221

222. Luria, A. R. 1970. *Traumatic Aphasia: Its Syndromes, Psychology and Treatment.* The Hague: Mouton

223. Luria, A. R., Karasseva, T. A. 1968. Disturbances of auditory speech memory in focal lesions of the deep regions of the temporal lobe. *Neuropsychologia* 6:97–104

224. Luria, A. R., Sokolov, E. N., Klimkowski, M. 1967. Towards a neurodynamic analysis of memory disturbances with lesions of the left temporal lobe. *Neuropsychologia* 5:1–11

225. Luschei, E. S., Johnson, R. A., Glickstein, M. 1968. Responses of neu-

rones in the motor cortex during performance of a simple repetitive arm movement. *Nature* 217:190–91

226. McCleary, R. A. 1966. Response-modulating functions of the limbic system: Initiation and suppression. *Progr. Physiol. Psychol.* 1:209–72

227. McDonough, S. H. 1970. Hearing tunes, separately and together. *Med. Res. Counc. Speech Commun. Res. Unit Rep. No. 6*, Edinburgh

228. McKeever, W. F., Huling, M.D. 1970. Left-central hemisphere superiority in tachistoscopic word-recognition performances. *Percept. Mot. Skills* 30:763–66

229. McKeever, W. F., Huling, M. D. 1970. Lateral dominance in tachistoscopic word recognition of children at two levels of ability. *Quart. J. Exp. Psychol.* 22:600–4

230. McKinney, J. P. 1967. Handedness, eyedness and perceptual stability of the left and right visual fields. *Neuropsychologia* 5:339–44

231. MacLean, P. D. 1957. Chemical and electrical stimulation of hippocampus in unrestrained animals. *Arch. Neurol. Psychiat.* 78:128–42

232. Marg, E., Adams, J. E., Rutkin, B. 1968. Receptive fields of cells in the human visual cortex. *Experientia* 24:348–50

233. Marr, D. 1969. A theory of cerebellar cortex. *J. Physiol.* 202:437–70

234. Massion, J. 1967. The mammalian red nucleus. *Physiol. Rev.* 47:384–436

235. Mast, T. E. 1970. Binaural interaction and contralateral inhibition in dorsal cochlear nucleus of the Chinchilla. *J. Neurophysiol.* 33:108–15

236. Mettler, F. Cortical subcortical relations in abnormal motor functions. See Ref. 355, 445–97

237. Milner, B. 1968. "Memory" in Alterations of perception and memory in man: Reflections on methods. In *Analysis of Behavioural Change*, ed. L. Weiskrantz, 268–375. New York: Harper and Row

238. Milner, B. 1968. Visual recognition and recall after right temporal excision in man. *Neuropsychologia* 6:191–209

239. Milner, B. 1970. Memory and the medial temporal regions of the brain. In *Biology of Memory*, ed. K. H. Pribram, D. E. Broadbent, 29–50. New York: Academic

240. Milner, B., Taylor, L. B. 1970. Somaesthetic thresholds after commissural section in man. *Neurology* 20:378

241. Milner, B., Taylor, L. B., Sperry, R. W. 1968. Lateralised suppression of dichotically presented digits after commissural section in man. *Science* 161:184–86

242. Mishkin, M. 1954. Visual discrimination performance following partial ablations of the temporal lobe. II. Ventral surfaces vs hippocampus. *J. Comp. Physiol. Psychol.* 47:187–93

243. Mishkin, M. 1964. Perseveration of central sets after frontal lesions in monkeys. In *The Frontal Granular Cortex and Behaviour*, ed. J. M. Warren, K. Akert, 219–41. New York: McGraw-Hill

244. Mishkin, M. 1971. Cortical visual areas and their interaction. In *The Brain and Human Behaviour*, ed. A. G. Karczmar. Berlin: Springer-Verlag. In press

245. Moffet, A., Ettlinger, G., Morton, H. B., Piercy, M. F. 1967. Tactile discrimination performance in the monkey: the effect of ablation of various subdivisions of posterior parietal cortex. *Cortex* 3:59–96

246. Moller, A. R. 1969. Unit responses in the cochlear nucleus of the rat to pure tones. *Acta Physiol. Scand.* 75:530–41

247. Mountcastle, V. B. 1957. Modality and topographic properties of single neurons of cat's somatic sensory cortex. *J. Neurophysiol.* 20:408–34

248. Mountcastle, V. B., Powell, T. P. S. 1959. Neural mechanisms subserving cutaneous sensibility, with special reference to the role of afferent inhibition in sensory perception and discrimination. *Bull. Johns Hopkins Hosp.* 105:201–32

249. Mountcastle, V. B., Talbot, W. H., Sakata, H., Hyvärinen, J. 1969. Cortical neuronal mechanisms in flutter-vibration studied in unanaesthetized monkeys. Neuronal periodicity and frequency discrimination. *J. Neurophysiol.* 32:452–83

250. Moushegian, G., Rupert, A. L. 1970. Response diversity of neurons in ventral cochlear nucleus of kangaroo rat to low-frequency tones. *J. Neurophysiol.* 33:351–64

251. Moushegian, G., Rupert, A. L., Langford, T. L. 1967. Stimulus coding by medial superior olivary neurons. *J. Neurophysiol.* 30:1239–61

252. Murphy, E. M., Venables, P. H. 1969. Effects of ipsilateral and contralateral shock on ear-asymmetry and

in the detection of two clicks. *Psychon. Sci.* 17:914–15

253. Murphy, E. M., Venables, P. H. 1970. Ear asymmetry in the threshold of fusion of two clicks: a signal detection analysis. *Quart. J. Exp. Psychol.* 22:288–300

254. Myers, T. F. 1970. Asymmetry and attention in phonic decoding. *Acta Psychol.* 33:158–77

255. Nauta, W. J. H., Mehler, W. R. 1966. Projections of the lentiform nucleus in the monkey. *Brain Res.* 1:3–42

256. Neff, W. D. 1961. On the relationships between physical, physiological and psychological variables. In *Sensory Communication*, ed. W. A. Rosenblith, 803–5. MIT Press

257. Nelson, P. G., Erulkar, S. D., Bryan, J. S. 1966. Responses of units of the inferior colliculus to time-varying acoustic stimuli. *J. Neurophysiol.* 29:834–60

258. Newcombe, F. 1969. *Missile Wounds of the Brain; A Study of Psychological Deficits.* Oxford Neurol. Monogr., Oxford Univ. Press

259. Newcombe, F., Russell, W. R. 1969. Dissociated visual perceptual and spatial deficits in focal lesions of the right hemisphere. *J. Neurol. Neurosurg. Psychiat.* 32:73–81

260. Nikara, T., Bishop, P. O., Pettigrew, J. D. 1968. Analysis of retinal correspondence by studying receptive fields of binocular single units in cat striate cortex. *Exp. Brain Res.* 6:353–72

261. Oldfield, R. C. 1969. Dominance and hemisphere. Presented at Int. Congr. Neurol., 9th, New York City. *Med. Res. Counc. Speech Commun. Res. Unit. Rep. No. 16,* Edinburgh

262. Olds, J. 1970. The behaviour of hippocampal neurons during conditioning experiments. In *The Neural Control of Behaviour*, ed. R. E. Whalen, R. F. Thompson, M. Verzeano, N. M. Weinberger, 257–93. New York: Academic

263. Onishi, S., Katsuki, Y. 1965. Functional organization and integrative mechanism on the auditory cortex of the cat. *Jap. J. Physiol.* 15:342–65

264. Orbach, J. 1967. Differential recognition of Hebrew and English words in right and left visual fields as a function of cerebral dominance and reading habits. *Neuropsychologia* 5:127–34

265. Oscarsson, O. 1966. The projection of group I muscle afferents to the cat cerebral cortex. In *Muscular Afferents and Motor Control*, 307–16. New York: Wiley

266. Overton, W., Wiener, M. 1966. Visual field position and word recognition threshold. *J. Exp. Psychol.* 71:249–53

267. Oxbury, J. M., Oxbury, S. M. 1969. Effects of temporal lobectomy on the report of dichotically presented digits. *Cortex* 5:3–14

268. Oxbury, J. M., Oxbury, S. M., Humphrey, N. K. 1969. Varieties of colour anomia. *Brain* 92:847–60

269. Oxbury, S., Oxbury, J., Gardiner, J. 1967. Laterality effects in dichotic listening. *Nature* 214:742–43

270. Pearlman, A. L., Daw, N. M. 1970. Opponent colour cells in the cat lateral geniculate nucleus. *Science* 167:84–86

271. Pettigrew, J. D., Nikara, T., Bishop, P. O. 1968. Responses to moving slits by single units in cat striate cortex. *Exp. Brain Res.* 6:373–90

272. Ibid. Binocular interaction on single units in cat striate cortex: simultaneous stimulation by single moving slit with receptive fields in correspondence, 391–410

273. Phillips, C. G. 1966. Changing concepts of the precentral motor area. In *Brain and Conscious Experience*, ed. J. C. Eccles, 389–421. Berlin: Springer-Verlag

274. Phillips, C. G., Porter, R. 1964. The pyramidal projection to motoneurones of some muscle groups of the baboon's forelimb. *Progr. Brain Res.* 12:222–42

275. Poirier, L. J., Sourkes, T. L., Bouvier, G., Carabin, S. 1966. Striatal amines, experimental tremor and the effect of harmaline in the monkey. *Brain* 89:37–52

276. Poirier, L. J., Singh, P., Boucher, R., Bouvier, G., Olivier, A., Larochelle, L. 1967. Effect of brain lesions on striatal monoamines in the cat. *Arch. Neurol.* 17:601–8

277. Pratt, R. T. C., Warrington, E. K., Halliday, A. M. 1971. Unilateral ECT as a test for cerebral dominance, with a strategy for treating left-handers. *Brit. J. Psychiat.* 119:78–83

278. Preston, J. B., Shende, M. C., Vemura, K. The motor cortex: Pyramidal system. See Ref. 355, 61–74

279. Provins, K. A. 1967. Motor skill,

handedness and behaviour. *Aust. J. Psychol.* 19:137–50

280. Provins, K. A., Glencross, D. J. 1968. Handwriting, typewriting and handedness. *Quart. J. Exp. Psychol.* 20:282–89

281. Purpura, D. P., Frigyesi, T. L., Mallian, M. Intrinsic synaptic organization and relations of the corpus striatum. See Ref. 355, 117–204

282. Purpura, D. P., Yahr, M. D., Eds. 1966. *The Thalamus.* New York: Columbia Univ. Press

283. Ratcliff, G. 1970. *Aspects of disordered space perception.* PhD thesis. Univ. of Oxford

284. Reese, T. S., Brightman, M. W. Olfactory surface and central olfactory connexions in some vertebrates. See Ref. 106, 115–49

285. Reitz, S. L. 1969. Effects of serial disconnection of striate and temporal cortex on visual discrimination performance in monkeys. *J. Comp. Physiol. Psychol.* 68:139–46

286. Richardson, D. M., Knights, R. M. 1970. A bibliography on dichotic listening. *Cortex* 6:236–40

287. Robinson, D. A., Fuchs, A. F. 1969. Eye movements evoked by stimulation of frontal eye fields. *J. Neurophysiol.* 32:637–48

288. Rosvold, H. E. 1970. The prefrontal cortex and caudate nucleus: A system for effecting correction in response mechanisms. In *Mind as a Tissue,* ed. D. Rupp, 21–38. New York: Harper and Row

289. Rubino, C. A. 1970. Hemispheric lateralization of visual perception. *Cortex* 6:102–30

290. Sakata, H., Miyamoto, J. 1968. Topographical relationship between the receptive fields of neurons in the motor cortex and the movements elicited by focal stimulation in freely moving cats. *Jap. J. Physiol.* 18:489–507

291. Sanderson, K. J., Darian-Smith, I., Bishop, P. O. 1969. Binocular corresponding receptive fields of single units in the cat dorsal lateral geniculate nucleus. *Vision Res.* 9: 1297–1303

292. Satz, P. 1968. Laterality effects in dichotic listening. *Nature* 218:277–78

293. Satz, P., Achenbach, K., Fennell, E. 1967. Correlations between assessed manual laterality and predicted speech laterality in a normal population. *Neuropsychologia* 5:295–310

294. Satz, P. 1965. Achenbach, K., Pattishall, E., Fennell, E. 1965. Ear asymmetry and handedness in dichotic listening. *Cortex* 1:377–96

295. Saul, R., Sperry, R. W. 1968. Absence of commissurotomy symptoms with agenesis of the corpus callosum. *Neurology* 18:307

296. Schulhoff, C., Goodglass, H. 1969. Dichotic listening: side of brain injury and cerebral dominance. *Neuropsychologia* 7:149–60

297. Scotti, G., Spinnler, H. 1970. Colour imperception in unilateral hemisphere damaged patients. *J. Neurol. Neurosurg. Psychiat.* 33:22–28

298. Semmes, J. 1968. Hemispheric specialization: A possible clue to mechanism. *Neuropsychologia* 6:11–26

299. Semmes, J., Mishkin, M., Cole, M. 1968. Effects of isolating sensorimotor cortex in monkeys. *Cortex* 4: 301–27

300. Semmes, J., Weinstein, S., Ghent, L., Teuber, H.-L. 1969. *Somatosensory Changes After Penetrating Brain Wounds in Man.* Cambridge, Mass.: Commonwealth Fund

301. Semmes, J., Weinstein, S., Ghent, L., Teuber, H.-L. 1963. Correlates of impaired orientation in personal and extrapersonal space. *Brain* 86: 747–72

302. Shankweiler, D. 1966. Effects of temporal-lobe damage on perception of dichotically presented melodies. *J. Comp. Physiol. Psychol.* 62:115–19

303. Shankweiler, D., Studdert-Kennedy, M. 1967. Identification of consonants and vowels presented to left and right ears. *Quart. J. Exp. Psychol.* 19:59–63

304. Simon, J. R. 1967. Ear preference in a simple reaction time task. *J. Exp. Psychol.* 75:49–55

305. Singer, W., Creutzfeldt, O. D. 1970. Reciprocal lateral inhibition of on- and off-centre neurones in the lateral geniculate body of the cat. *Exp. Brain Res.* 10:311–30

306. Smith, A. M. 1970. Effects of visual area lesions on conditioned forebrain flexion responses in the cat. *Brain Res.* 24:549 (Abstr.)

307. Sparks, R., Geschwind, N. 1968. Dichotic listening in man after section of neocortical commissures. *Cortex* 4:3–16

308. Sparks, R., Goodglass, H., Nickel, B. 1970. Ipsilateral versus contralateral extinction in dichotic listening

from hemisphere lesions. *Cortex* 6: 249–60

309. Spellacy, F. 1970. Lateral preferences in the identification of patterned stimuli. *J. Acoust. Soc. Am.* 47: 574–78

310. Sperry, R. W. 1952. Neurology and the mind-brain problem. *Am. Sci.* 40:291–312

311. Spinelli, D. N., Barrett, T. W. 1969. Visual receptive field organization of single units in the cat's visual cortex. *Exp. Neurol.* 24:76–98

312. Spinelli, D. N., Starr, A., Barrett, T. W. 1968. Auditory specificity in unit recordings from cat's visual cortex. *Exp. Neurol.* 22:75–84

313. Spreen, O., Spellacy, F. J., Reid, J. R. 1970. The effect of inter-stimulus interval and intensity on ear asymmetry for nonverbal stimuli in dichotic listening. *Neuropsychologia* 8:245–50

314. Steg, G. 1964. Efferent muscle innervation and rigidity. *Acta Physiol. Scand.* 61 Suppl. 225:96

315. Sterling, P., Kuypers, H. G. J. M. 1967. Anatomical organization of the brachial root spinal cord of the cat. I. The distribution of dorsal root fibres. *Brain Res.* 4:1–15

316. Ibid. Anatomical organization of the brachial root spinal cord of the cat. II. The motoneuron plexus, 16–32

317. Stoney, S. D., Jr., Thompson, W. D., Asanuma, H. 1968. Excitation of pyramidal tract cells by intracortical microstimulation: Effective extent of stimulating current. *J. Physiol.* 31:659–69

318. Studdert-Kennedy, M., Shankweiler, D. 1970. Hemispheric specialization for speech perception. *J. Acoust. Soc. Am.* 48:579–94

319. Suga, N. 1969. Classification of inferior collicular neurones of bats in terms of responses to pure tones, FM sounds and noise bursts. *J. Physiol.* 200:555–74

320. Szabo, J. 1970. Projections from the body of the caudate nucleus in the rhesus monkey. *Exp. Neurol.* 27:1–15

321. Terrace, H. S. 1963. Errorless discrimination learning in the pigeon: effects of chlorpromazine and imipramine. *Science* 140:318–19

322. Thach, W. T. 1968. Discharge of purkinje and cerebellar nuclear neurons during rapidly alternating arm movements in the monkey. *J. Neurophysiol.* 31:785–97

323. Treisman, A., Geffen, G. 1968. Selective attention and cerebral dominance in perceiving and responding to speech messages. *Quart. J. Exp. Psychol.* 20:139–50

324. Trevarthen, C. 1971. Paper presented at Dep. Psychol., Univ. of Edinburgh

325. Tsuchitani, C., Boudreau, J. C. 1966. Single unit analysis of cat superior olive S-segment with tonal stimuli. *J. Neurophysiol.* 29:684–97

326. Tzavaras, A., Hecaen, H., Le Bras, H. 1970. Le probleme de la specificité du déficit de la reconnaissance du visage humain lors de lésions hémisphériques unilatérales. *Neuropsychologia* 8:403–16

327. Vanderwolf, C. H. 1962. Medial thalamic functions in voluntary behaviour. *Can. J. Psychol.* 16:318–30

328. Ibid 1963. Effects of medial thalamic lesions on previously established fear motivated behaviour. 17:183–87

329. Vanderwolf, C. H., Heron, W. 1964. Electroencephalographic waves with voluntary movement. *Arch. Neurol.* 11:379–95

330. Vesbaesya, C., Whitteridge, D., Wilson, M. E. 1967. Callosal connections of the cortex representing the area centralis. *J. Physiol.* 191:79–80P

331. Vignolo, L. A. Auditory agnosia. See Ref. 26, 172–208

332. Vinken, P. J., Bruyn, G. W., Eds. 1969. Diseases of the basal ganglia. *Handbook of Clinical Neurology*, Vol. 6. Amsterdam: North-Holland

333. Votaw, C. L. 1958. Certain functional and anatomical relations of the cornu ammonis of the macaque monkey. I. Functional relations. *J. Comp. Neurol.* 112:353–82

334. Ibid 1960. Certain functional and anatomical relations of the cornu ammonis of the macaque monkey. II. Anatomical relations. 114:283–93

335. Warrington, E. K. 1969. Constructional apraxia. In *Handbook of Clinical Neurology*, Vol. 4, ed. P. J. Vinken, A. W. Bruying. Amsterdam: North-Holland

336. Warrington, E. K., James, M. 1967. Tachistoscopic number estimation in patients with unilateral cerebral lesions. *J. Neurol. Neurosurg. Psychiat.* 30:468–74

337. Warrington, E. K., James, M. 1967. Disorders of visual perception in patients with localised cerebral lesions. *Neuropsychologia* 5:253–66

338. Warrington, E. K., James, M., Kinsbourne, M. 1966. Drawing disability in relation to laterality of lesion. *Brain* 89:53–82

339. Warrington, E. K., Rabin, P. 1970. A preliminary investigation of the relation between visual perception and visual memory. *Cortex* 6:87–96

340. Warrington, E. K., Shallice, T. 1969. The selective impairment of auditory verbal short term memory. *Brain* 92:885–96

341. Watanabe, T., Liao, T., Katsuki, Y. 1968. Neuronal response patterns in the superior olivary complex of the cat to sound stimulation. *Jap. J. Physiol.* 18:267–87

342. Weldt, C., Aschoff, J. C., Kameda, K., Brooks, V. B. Intracortical organisation of cats' motor sensory neurons. See Ref. 355, 255–88

343. Werner, G., Whitsel, B. L. 1968. Topology of the body representation in somatosensory area I of primates. *J. Neurophysiol.* 31: 856–69

344. Whitfield, I. C. 1967. *The Auditory Pathway.* London: Arnold

345. Whitfield, I. C., Evans, E. F. 1965. Responses of auditory cortical neurons to stimuli of changing frequency. *J. Neurophysiol.* 28: 655–72

346. Wiesel, T. N., Hubel, D. H. 1965. Comparison of the effects of unilateral and bilateral eye closure on cortical unit responses in kittens. *J. Neurophysiol.* 28:1029–40

347. Ibid 1966. Spatial and chromatic interactions in the lateral geniculate body of the rhesus monkey. 29: 1115–56

348. Wiesendanger, M. 1969. The pyrami-

dal tract. Recent investigations of its morphology and functions. *Ergeb. Physiol.* 61:72–136

349. Winter, P. 1971. Response properties of auditory cortical cells. *Brain Res.* In press

350. Woolsey, C. N., Settlage, P. H., Meyer, D. R., Sencer, W., Hamuy, T. P., Travis, A. M. 1952. Patterns of localization in precentral and "supplementary" motor areas and their relation to a concept of a premotor area. *Res. Publ. Assoc. Res. Nerv. Ment. Dis.* 30:238–64

351. Wright, M. J. 1969. Visual receptive fields of cells in a cortical area remote from the striate cortex in the cat. *Nature* 223:973–75

352. Wurtz, R. H. 1969. Visual receptive fields of striate cortex neurons in awake monkeys. *J. Neurophysiol.* 32:727–42

353. Ibid. Comparison of effects of eye movements and stimulus movements on striate cortex neurons of the monkey. 32:987–94

354. Wyke, M., Chorover, S. L. 1965. Comparison of spatial discrimination in the temporal and nasal sectors of the monocular visual field. *Percept. Mot. Skills* 20:1037–45

355. Yahr, M. D., Purpura, D. P., Eds. 1967. *Neurophysiological Basis of Normal and Abnormal Motor Activities.* New York: Raven Press

356. Yin, R. K. 1970. Face recognition by brain-injured patients: a dissociable ability. *Neuropsychologia* 8: 395–402

357. Zangwill, O. L. 1967. Speech and the minor hemisphere. *Acta Neurol. Psychiat. Belg.* 67:1013–20

358. Zurif, E. B., Bryden, M. P. 1969. Familiar handedness and left-right differences in auditory and visual perception. *Neuropsychologia* 7: 179–87

EFFECTS OF CHEMICAL AND PHYSICAL TREATMENTS ON LEARNING AND MEMORY

187

MURRAY E. JARVIK[1]

Departments of Pharmacology and Psychiatry, Albert Einstein College of Medicine, Bronx, New York

Departments of Pharmacology and Psychiatry, UCLA School of Medicine, Los Angeles, California

U. S. Veterans Administration, Brentwood, California

The search for the engram has played a prominent role in physiological psychology since the days of Franz & Lashley (53). There has been a growing optimism in recent years that subcellular and particularly molecular mechanisms involved in and responsible for memory storage will be revealed and controlled (64).

The problem can be stated very simply. For some organisms certain experiences leave an aftereffect which manifests itself in changed behavior at a later time. This change in behavior indicates that learning has occurred and has left a memory trace somewhere, presumably in the brain but not necessarily. Examples of experiences with long-lasting aftereffects are visible trauma, immunological reactions (23), drug tolerance and dependence (87), adaptive enzyme formation (110), sensory adaptation, habituation (170), and associative learning, including conditioning and perceptual learning (100). All of these phenomena involve plastic changes in various tissues. This review will concern itself mainly with associative learning where two sets of stimuli become interdependent because of spatial and temporal contiguity. The possibility that similar cellular and biochemical mechanisms, such as protein synthesis or modifications of neurohumoral transmission, underlie all of these phenomena is an important guiding principle in present-day drug research.

Newer histological and neurochemical techniques, such as histochemical fluorescence (54), offer great promise of contributing to the resolution of memory problems. Only when all the anatomical and chemical links in the information chain are specified will experimenters be certain that an engram

[1] I am indebted to Larry Squire for his very helpful criticism, and to Dr. Ellen Gritz, Miss Nancy Porter, and Miss Nina Schneider for their invaluable editorial assistance. I appreciate the help from numerous colleagues whose work is mentioned and from others who I hope will not feel offended because their names were omitted. This review covers mainly the period from 1965 to 1971.

has been found or, more importantly, can be destroyed by an amnesic treatment. Such identification is surely the goal of biological memory experiments (Lashley 113, Rosenzweig & Leiman 162) and may involve synaptic knobs, dendritic processes, membranous thickening, or macromolecular synthesis. In any case, the anatomical engram will have to be tied to a behavioral correlate. Thus, the use of psychological methods will always be needed for investigation in this field. This review will consider the ways in which various chemical and physical treatments have been used in recent years to reveal the nature of the memory trace. These include electrical stimulation of the nervous system, surgery, and drugs, particularly those implicating neurohumors and macromolecules. Other reviews have dealt with different aspects of the physiological basis of memory and learning Deutsch 36, (John 91, Kumar et al 109).

ELECTROCONVULSIVE SHOCK, BEHAVIORAL EFFECTS

The memory-impairing actions of electroconvulsive shock (ECS) were first noted in humans (201), but most of the experimental work on the amnesic effects of this agent has been with rodents. During the past decade there has been a burgeoning of ECS amnesia studies following the development of rapid, simple, one-trial learning procedures for rodents (123). Although the physiological effects of ECS are diffuse and poorly understood, it is by far the most popular treatment because it is easy to control and highly effective.

RETROGRADE AMNESIA FROM ECS IN HUMANS

The contrast between the paucity of human ECS amnesia studies and the plethora of such animal investigations is striking. It is evident that retrograde amnesia is more difficult to demonstrate in humans than in animals. Summarizing his work and that of his colleagues of the past 13 years, Cronholm (26) indicated that brief retrograde amnesia (RA) can be induced in man by ECS. Patients were less likely to remember a number given 5 sec before ECS than 15 sec before ECS, and a number given 60 sec earlier was apt to be remembered best. Furthermore, the longer one waited to test patients, the more likely it was that the number could be recalled. This indicates a diminishing anterograde postictal effect of ECS which is distinct from the RA effect. However, the short gradient of RA seemed to remain quite stable between 1 and 36 hr after ECS. Electroconvulsive shock also produced a marked increase in forgetting or anterograde amnesia in these patients.

Williams (195) describes a study in which patients were given ECS 11–17 min after learning pairs of words and retested 3 hr later. They remembered fewer items than a control group not given ECS. Another group was retested 3 weeks later and they remembered as much as the control group. This temporary memory defect, so commonly seen, could be attributed to postictal confusional impairment of retrieval. It is unfortunate that the patients were not given ECS at different times following learning to reveal whether a gradient of RA also existed. Accelerated forgetting similar to that following ECS may also be observed in animals following a variety of drugs and other procedures (Barondes 6, Geller & Jarvik 60, Swanson et al 182). Whether it is due to impaired consolidation of long-term memory or to increased sensitivity to interference are unanswered questions of great importance.

The problem of localizability of unilateral ECS applied to the scalp remains unresolved. Levy (118) reported that orientation and memory showed less impairment in patients receiving unilateral ECS therapy than bilateral. He felt that the bilateral treatments, however, produced a slightly greater relief of psychiatric depression, but that the differences were not striking. Other studies indicate that unilateral ECS produces less anterograde memory defect but seems to be just as effective in the treatment of depression as bilateral ECS (Bidder et al 12, Cronin et al 27). The very high electrical resistance of the skull makes it surprising to find localized effects. Perhaps the current entering through the foramina is responsible for lateralized effects.

There are very few other studies with humans indicating that RA can occur from either electrically or naturally induced seizures. Bickford et al (11) indicated that electrical stimulation of the temporal lobes in humans produces RA. Some studies of temporal lobe epilepsy or petit mal have indicated that events immediately preceding these seizures are more apt to be forgotten than those occurring much earlier (57). Blumer & Walker (13) cite case histories of patients exhibiting RA in temporal lobe epilepsy. The rule often cited by Williams (195), and frequently attributed to Teuber, that there is not retrograde amnesia without anterograde amnesia seems to be widely verified and implies that an amnesic treatment impairs learning and also accelerates forgetting or impairs consolidation. Since ECS is still widely used, particularly in the therapy of depression, more careful studies are both possible and highly desirable.

ELECTROCONVULSIVE SHOCK AND MEMORY IN ANIMALS

The work on ECS and memory in animals has produced controversy concerning both facts and interpretations. These have been reviewed by Dawson & McGaugh (33), Lewis et al (119) and Spevack & Suboski (173). It is now well established that learning of a variety of tasks is followed by a period of decreasing susceptibility to the disruptive effects of ECS as measured by subsequent performance. Such a retention deficit has most often been called RA. A similar phenomenon has been seen with spreading cortical depression, drugs, asphyxia, hypothermia, localized brain stimulation, and other treatments (89). Questions have been raised concerning the generality of the phenomenon of RA and whether retention, rather than registration or retrieval, is primarily affected by ECS.

Clearly, many types and maybe most types of memory are highly resistant to impairment by ECS (135). On the other hand, whatever produces the immobility of the passive avoidance response to punishment in many species of animals seems especially sensitive to the retrograde amnesic actions of ECS. McGaugh (123) prefers the term "inhibitory avoidance" to "passive avoidance" although there is real doubt that "freezing" truly represents avoidance. Jarvik & Geller (90) shocked animals in the usually safe compartment of the step-through apparatus and found that shocked animals had less of a tendency to step out of this compartment than non-shocked controls. Electroconvulsive shock produced a retrograde "facilitation" of this deficient active avoidance response. A parsimonious description of the passive "avoidance" response would be an inhibitory motor response to stimuli associated with punishing shock, quite analogous to the "conditioned emotional response" (CER) of Hunt & Brady (78). The conditioned stimuli are relatively specific to the situation with the degree of generalization dependent upon the discriminability of the cues involved (Kopp et al 105, Aron et al 4). Although the classically conditioned response of diminished movement may at times be maladaptive, the conditioned stimuli are discriminated, otherwise the animal would be in a continuous state of fear.

Even in the case of active avoidance tasks, ECS-produced RA has been reported (Duncan 44, Thompson & Dean 187, Agranoff & Davis 1) though, strangely enough, not frequently in recent years for rodents. In fact, Suboski & Weinstein (181) have demonstrated a biphasic gradient resembling the Kamin effect for ECS in an active avoidance situation. Animals were given 30 massed trials followed at 1 min, 1 hr, and 16 hr by either ECS or a retest. Animals given ECS were retested 24 hr later. Electroconvulsive shock-treated animals were impaired at 1 min relative to controls, suggesting that ECS decreased mobility. Both groups of animals were most impaired at 1 hr. This unexpected increasing susceptibility to ECS with time after learning is certainly not compatible with a monotonically increasing consolidation of the trace. Obviously, replication of this unusual and important finding is needed.

Although punishing electric foot shock is easy to control and therefore popular, other types of reinforcement have been used. Appetitive tasks have been shown to be sensitive to post-trial ECS (183). For example, a one-trial, water-rewarded task showed a somewhat steeper gradient to ECS (up to 30 min) than a passive avoidance task (72). Pinel (150) showed that in a one-trial water-reward situation ECS produced RA if given within 60 sec of training. It is fair to assume that different classes of reinforcement or conditioned stimuli may trigger different types of physiological mechanisms. Thus, ingestion or even the sight of food will start a digestive process that lasts for hours; punishment will also set off neurohumoral and endocrine discharges of long duration. Operationally, these and other progressive covert processes might well contribute to the memory of the original learning. Paradoxically, both foot shock (185) and ECS (134) increase norepinephrine turnover, although their behavioral effects are antagonistic.

The shape of the ECS gradient of RA has been a matter of some dispute. It is now evident that the early upward slope is quite variable depending upon the training situation and the criterion of learning. The longest gradients appear to be obtained in a step-through passive avoidance task Amnesic effects of less than 1 min seem to occur in step-down tasks (especially if the platform is placed away from the wall), in appetitive types of tasks (Pinel 150, Herz & Peeke 73), and in choice types of passive avoidance tasks (149). Preconditioning may influence the speed of consolidation when conditioning finally occurs. For example, in one series of reports, rats which were familiarized with a step-down apparatus failed to show RA from ECS, whereas animals that were naive to the situation did exhibit such an effect (Lewis et al 119, Miller 130).

Geller & Jarvik (60) failed to observe a familiarization effect. Lewis et al (119) used a step-down test whereas Geller & Jarvik used a step-through test. It may be that rodents have to get used to the absence of thigmotaxic stimulation from walls. Rodent species differences do not seem to account for discrepancies between earlier reports (Chorover & Schiller 21, Kopp et al 105). Rats and mice behave similarly in a step-through apparatus; a long gradient of susceptibility to ECS (at least 1 hr) can be obtained from both species (167). Very likely differences in interpretation could result from variations in arbitrary cut-off points used as measures of learning. Short cut-off will lead to the erroneous conclusion that amnesia did not occur in animals who would have shown an effect if longer latency measures were used. This may explain in part the short amnesic gradients of some investigators (Chorover & Schiller 21, Paolino et al 147).

One method of evaluating the mechanism of ECS-induced amnesia is to study its interaction with other treatments. Administration of ECS with drugs has been tried sparingly. It was found that anticonvulsant drugs of the hydantoin family could prevent convulsions and amnesic effects of ECS (192). McGaugh & Hart (125) found that pretreatment with subconvulsive doses of analeptics can antagonize the amnesic effects of ECS, presumably by speeding consolidation. On the other hand, convulsant doses of the same drugs produce powerful amnesic effects. One might speculate that the subconvulsant doses produce selective disinhibition of inhibitory synapses which ordinarily function to slow consolidation; whereas convulsions induced by excessive disinhibition in turn produce widespread inhibition of protein synthesis. Cotman et al (24) found that ECS inhibited protein synthesis though not nearly as much as the amounts of cycloheximide necessary to cause RA. Incidentally, Bennett & Edelman (8) found that spreading cortical depression decreased cortical protein synthesis, but they concluded that the effect was a nonspecific secondary diversion of energy sources or amino acids.

The permanence of ECS-induced amnesia has been a subject of recurring debate. Again the nature of the training procedure employed seems to be responsible for differences. Most investigators have found relatively long-lasting amnesia varying from days to weeks. Multiple retention or extinction tests can prevent recovery from amnesia which might otherwise occur (Pfingst & King 149, King & Glasser 102). Of course, the passive avoidance response itself will decay with the passage of time (60), and forgetting thus might act to mask any tendency towards recovery from ECS-induced amnesia.

Recovery from amnesia indicates either recovery from impairment of a retrieval ability or some capacity for spontaneous restrengthening of a weakened trace. Under the same training conditions, amnesia can be temporary if conditioning is strong, and permanent if conditioning is weak. Also, the strength of the amnesic treatment can influence permanence. Thus, high intensity ECS may produce a permanent amnesia whereas low intensity ECS can cause a temporary amnesia (Pagano et al 145, Hughes et al 76). Perhaps this recovery of an incompletely obliterated trace is due to the same process responsible for the increase in probability of a response attributed to incubation or rehearsal. Kohlenberg & Trabasso (104) also showed that disinhibition produced by ECS disappears with the passage of time. They used a drinking task, although it might well be that disinhibition of thirst is different than memory of pain. On the other hand, many investigators continue to find relatively permanent or long-lasting RA (Zornetzer & McGaugh 200, Geller & Jarvik 59), usually explained as a retention deficit. In humans, the spontaneous increase in the probability of emitting a partially forgotten response with the passage of time, sometimes called reminiscence, has been attributed either to rehearsal (138) or dissipation of inhibition (106). Similar mechanisms possibly occur in rodents.

If animals are tested at different times following a training trial that is followed after 20 sec by ECS, there is an apparent growth of amnesia, or a gradual decrease in passive avoidance latencies from 1 to 6 hr (60). This might be due to dissipation of postictal depression or else be a manifestation of decay of short-term memory. Hughes et al (76) found a growth of amnesia over 24 and 42 days. McGaugh & Landfield (127) found amnesia immediately present with a 5 sec training-ECS interval, but with a 20 sec delay for ECS, amnesia took time to develop. It is surprising that memory loss should appear to increase after the cessation of the amnesic treatment. If the effect is not an artifact, it may represent some continuing aspect of the treatment which is responsible for its effectiveness, or else some acceleration of normal forgetting. Indeed, a progressive loss of memory has been demonstrated with inhibitors of protein synthesis (6).

Reactivation of the susceptible phase of memory consolidation has been demonstrated by a number of experimenters, although others have had difficulty in producing this phenomenon. Manipulation of either the unconditioned or conditioned stimulus sometimes potentiates the amnesic action of ECS. Schneider & Sherman (168) showed that a second foot shock, given at a time when ECS no longer would be expected to have effects, enabled ECS then to produce RA. Misanin et al (132) reported that ECS could be effective 24 hr after training if there was reactivation of the original conditioning. Davis & Klinger (32) could obtain amnesia in fish 24 hr after training with KCl, puromycin, or acetoxycycloheximide if the fish were replaced for a brief period in the training environment just prior to injection. A similar effect could be obtained with ECS (31). However, some investigators have had difficulty in replicating this reactivation-potentiation phenomenon (Dawson & McGaugh 33, Jamieson & Albert 88). The paradoxical aspect of these findings is that one might expect the reactivated trace to be stronger than the o.iginal one because of the double reinforcement. If the strength of the trace is what determines its susceptibility, then such memories ought to be more rather than less resistant to ECS. More replications are needed to clarify this point

Although a single foot shock followed by ECS results in RA, repeated pairings of foot shock and ECS do not (136). Carbon dioxide produces similar results; that is, single treatments are more effective than repeated ones. Balancing the relative cumulative amnesic and punishing shocks in different situations may be a difficult algebraic problem. Apparently ECS-induced amnesia is never complete even when it appears so, because amnesic animals show marked savings upon relearning when compared with controls (59). The trace is weakened but not obliterated. Perhaps on repeated trials the ability of foot shock effects to cumulate may be superior to the ability of ECS amnesic effects to cumulate even though the latter may predominate on the first trial.

Events occurring during the conditioning-ECS interval may modify the amnesic effects of ECS. For example, detaining the animals in the test apparatus will not only produce amnesic effects of its own, but it markedly potentiates the amnesic actions of ECS (Davis 30, Robustelli et al 161). Any procedure that tends to weaken the trace appears to make it more susceptible to further weakening by ECS. Thus, a flashing light during the interval potentiates the action of ECS (131). Incidents occurring at any time during the retention interval might be expected to produce an interfering effect of some type. Positive "interference" or facilitation is apt to occur only when the degree of similarity between the original stimuli and intruding events is great. This relationship was proposed years ago in Osgood's retroaction surface model of interference (129). Similarity is determined by the relative position of stimuli on a generalization gradient and is of utmost importance in the matching reaction so necessary to demonstrate the existence of memory.

If ECS can interact with foot shock and other conditions to produce a relatively permanent nonamnesic change in the animal's behavior, such impairment might be difficult to differentiate from a memory defect even though the engram remains intact. Indeed, Aron et al (4) have demonstrated that ECS alone could produce aversion to light for as long as 4 weeks following its administration. Similarly, a long-lasting disinhibition might impair performance on a passive avoidance test and be interpreted as amnesia. The crucial factor in deciding whether retrograde amnesia has occurred is to determine whether the association between the foot shock and the situational cues has been disrupted If a foot shock-ECS combination produces greater activity in whatever situation an animal is placed, then the effect of ECS cannot be ascribed solely to amnesia.

The possibility that incubation of fear may account for ECS-induced amnesia was first proposed by Irwin et al (84). Incubation of fear was a concept utilized years ago by Denny & Ditchman (34) to explain the deteriorating performance of animals in an active avoidance task. Ultimately the fear disappears and the performance improves again (96). On the other hand, in a passive avoidance task an increase in fear would tend to improve performance, and indeed this has been noted, particularly in the step-through apparatus used in our laboratories. Spevack & Suboski (173) have contended that incubation does not represent strength of the memory trace per se and that ECS acts entirely upon incubation and not upon consolidation of memory. At this stage of our knowledge it is difficult to prove that incubation is independent of memory although this is a distinct possibility. Perhaps if some measure of learning other than response latency were used, incubation and memory could be dissociated.

There appear to be situations in which incubation does not occur in passive avoidance learning (158). Although Pinel & Cooper (152) showed a remarkable correlation between incubation and ECS gradient effects, Pinel (150, 151) seems to have found a passive avoidance situation in which little or no incubation occurs but where nevertheless ECS produces a fairly long gradient of amnesia (up to 1 hr). With such a dissociation it is difficult to attribute the action of ECS to an arrest of incubation. Incubation apparently does not occur in positively reinforced situations where ECS is nonetheless effective (72). Furthermore, even though the ECS and incubation curves were identical in Pinel & Cooper's study, there are many investigations which show that varying the amnesic treatment can shift the gradient considerably (Dorfman et al 42, Paolino et al 148, Bohdanecky et al 14, Ray & Barrett 156).

If ECS does arrest incubation in some situations, it would be interesting to reveal the mechanism whereby it does so, whether incubation and consolidation are identical or not. It appears, surprisingly enough, that in the passive avoidance test the arrest is permanent (61), and the animal is maintained at the level of freezing tendency which it had at the time of ECS. One possible explanation is that incubation of fear represents a real increase in the strength of the conditioned response or the probability of emission of the conditioned response, and that ECS stops this growth. Alternatively, incubation could represent the dissipation of some disinhibiting influence and ECS stabilizes this process. Perhaps the amnesic effects of ECS could be better understood if the underlying neurophysiological and biochemical actions of the ECS treatment were made clearer, so we will next consider findings on this subject.

NEUROPHYSIOLOGICAL AND BIOCHEMICAL EFFECTS OF ECS

It has generally been assumed that ECS is associated with a cerebral electrical storm, as is epilepsy. However, Chorover & DeLuca (20) indicated that preceding ECS with foot shock may considerably modify the cerebral electrical response. The electrocorticograms of convulsed rats, without foot shock, all showed hypersynchronous, bilaterally symmetrical, epileptiform activity of a grand mal type. Remarkably, ECS following foot shock in some rats produced no detectable electrocorticographic seizure activity and little change from pre-ECS amplitude and frequency, although the motor seizure was quite strong. There was, however, a significant latency of up to 5 min for such motor seizures accompanying an apparently normal electrocorticogram.

The implication in these findings of Chorover & DeLuca is that the convulsive seizure movements are not necessarily mediated by the brain but perhaps by some lower center. The absence of seizure activity in the electrocorticogram following ECS tended to occur most frequently when the animal had been exhibiting pronounced signs of locomotor inhibition, anxiety, or fear for a considerable period of time. It would be important to follow up this important finding with studies that attempt to correlate the electroencephalographic reaction to the electrical current applied to the head with the presence or absence of subsequent amnesia. Further evidence for dissociation of cerebral electrical activity and motor activity has been found in day-old chicks (116). The electroencephalographic changes following ECS were associated with RA, but not with behavioral convulsions (115).

Can surgical extirpation localize the region where ECS produces amnesia? Hostetter (75) demonstrated that lesions of the hippocampus could attenuate ECS-produced amnesia. This investigator used a passive avoidance test with a water approach baseline. One problem with this study is that the lesion may have tended to increase latencies slightly and this retardation could have been markedly potentiated by ECS. Sick animals have high latencies in all types of tests.

It is clear that ECS produces an enormous range of biochemical changes, and the problem is to determine which are connected with retrograde amnesic actions. Naturally, biogenic amines and especially catecholamines have been implicated in ECS action. ECS increases homovanillic acid excretion, which suggests an increase in dopamine synthesis (46). Essman (48) reported that ECS increased brain 5-HT levels. Brain tyrosine hydroxylase activity also increases after FCS (134). This effect may be the basis of the previously shown increase in turnover of norepinephrine. Significant elevations of 5-HT, norepinephrine, and DOPA have been reported following ECS in rats (74). These findings were not confirmed, however, by Glowinski & Axelrod (66), who instead found an increase in turnover.

Matussek & Ladisich (121) did not find a potentiating effect of ECS and desmethylimipramine (both antidepressive treatments) upon motor activity, and they concluded that ECS could not cause an increase in norepinephrine turnover. However, they assumed that desmethylimipramine acts solely through an adrenergic mechanism. They did, however, show that there was a change in the distribution of norepinephrine and its metabolites following administration of ECS twice daily for 4 days. Ladisich et al (111) found that ECS increased norepinephrine turnover, while Pryor et al (155) showed a slight increase in monoamine oxidase activity following ECS. The problem is to dissociate the primary effects of ECS on the brain from secondary effects of stress and motor activity. The use of peripherally acting agents, such as d-tubocurarine and norepinephrine combined with ECS, might help to answer this question. Whether or not ECS produces its amnesic effects by inhibiting synthesis of protein or of RNA or by influencing biogenic amine action or cholinergic transmission is still a major problem for investigation. The strong amnesic effects of ECS certainly have to be reconciled with the prevalent chemical theories of memory (Flexner 50, Deutsch 36, Glassman 64).

Brain Stimulation and Learning

One of the problems with ECS is that the path of the electrical current is not well defined. The locus of action could be approached by placement of electrodes in the brain itself. Effects of brain stimulation on behavior have been ably reviewed by Doty (43). Kesner & Doty (98) found that passive avoidance in cats could be disrupted by certain types of brain stimulation but not by others. Amnesia was produced by electrical after-discharges initiated in the dorsal hippocampus or amygdala but not from the septum, fornix, or ventral hippocampus. Furthermore, tonic-clonic seizures initiated in the frontal cortex or chronic seizures from stimulation in the mesencephalic reticular formation did not produce amnesia. Here again is evidence that motor convulsions may be dissociated from other actions of ECS.

Post-trial hippocampal electrical stimulation facilitated active avoidance learning and this facilitation could be antagonized by 1 mg/kg of atropine (47). Unfortunately, every correct response was followed by hippocampal stimulation, thereby possibly reinforcing the rewarding effect of avoiding the shock. The atropine might have been nonspecific, since it impairs discrimination performance. Post-trial hippocampal stimulation facilitated maze learning in rats if spaced trials were used (176). With massed trials, hippocampal stimulation produced disruption.

It may be that the retrograde amnesia of pain following anterior limbic system stimulation (103) really involved the same mechanisms as those implicated in hippocampal stimulation. Passive avoidance retention was impaired when post-trial electrical stimulation was applied to the hippocampus immediately following learning. Several studies have indicated that the high sensitivity of the hippocampus to such stimulation was seen when similar stimulation applied to adjacent areas did not produce retrograde amnesia. Shinkman & Kaufman (171) demonstrated that post-trial hippo-

campal seizures produced retrograde amnesia if they were induced immediately after learning but not if delayed 30 sec.

RA could be produced by stimulation of either the anterior or posterior
regions of the cerebrum (160), but the tendency to produce full tonic-clonic
seizures was greater from stimulation in the posterior regions. On the other
hand, transcorneal ECS was more effective in producing RA than transpineal (167). Stimulation of the caudate nucleus will produce RA in a passive avoidance situation (199), as will stimulation of the frontal region when
certain current levels are exceeded (200). Stimulation of the frontal region
did not cause the severe convulsions which were obtained with transpineal or
even transcorneal electrical stimulation. Zornetzer & McGaugh (200)
speculate that spinal mechanisms might be involved in the motor components of seizures, just as Chorover & DeLuca (20) suggested.

Delayed response performance in monkeys was impaired when electrical
stimulation was applied to the principal sulcus of the frontal lobe during the
first few seconds of an 8-sec delay (175). No effect was seen when stimulation
was applied during the intertrial interval or early during cue presentation,
but some effect was seen when it was applied during the final second of the
cue presentation or during the last 4 sec of the 8-sec delay. These results are
compatible with a retrograde amnesia or consolidation interpretation. These
findings are particularly significant since the animal was motivated for a
positive incentive, and no incubation function was been shown in this type
of test.

Stimulation of the reinforcing brain areas certainly influences learning,
particularly when stimuli used are unconditioned stimuli (Stein & Wise 177,
Briese & Olds 18, Olds 140). For example, post-trial electrical stimulation of
the mesencephalic reticular formation improved performance of rats but
slowed learning (35). Proactive effects of brain stimulation may resemble
actions produced by drugs when levels of arousal are influenced. However,
brain stimulation may play the same role as ECS in disrupting memory
when applied after learning.

It should be borne in mind that localizing the point of maximal effectiveness of electrical stimulation in the brain, of course, does not localize the
engram. However, much useful information can be gained from such experiments, particularly if they are combined with lesions. It would be surprising,
for example, if the engram for the one-trial passive avoidance test was localized very sharply, since abnormal activity and evoked responses can be
obtained from wide regions of the brain following punishing shock (20).

Brain lesions can produce retrograde amnesia, but most extirpation
studies have not systematically varied the time between training and surgery. Uretsky & McCleary (188), however, showed that a combined en-
torhinal-fornix lesion which had the effect of isolating the hippocampus produced a deficit on a one-way active avoidance task in cats. Landfield et al
(112) found that the hippocampal theta rhythm was highly correlated with
the period during which the animal was sensitive to amnesic treatments.
This occurred only if the lesion was introduced 3 hr after training and not

if an 8-day interval intervened. Thus, these results are compatible with a consolidation theory of memory.

DRUGS AND LEARNING

After surveying the psychopharmacological literature of the last century, one gets the distinct impression that learning and memory are psychological functions which are not very sensitive to drugs. At least, no drugs have been found which specifically affect either learning or memory without also influencing or being capable of influencing other psychological processes such as motivation, arousal, attention, sleep, and motor activity. Only posttrial drug administration eliminates the possibility of an action upon acquisition, but few studies have successfully demonstrated post-trial drug effects. This selective resistance of learning and memory argues for mechanisms utilizing chemical processes very different from those subserving the functions just mentioned or dependent upon physical processes.

If chemistry does underlie the associative process in learning, the most likely chemical candidates for a key role are amines (99), acetylcholine (36), and macromolecular synthesis (64). The pharmacological properties of brain structures underlying various psychological functions have been reviewed recently (133) and are believed to critically involve the neurotransmitter actions of various brain amines. Drug resistance to learning may occur in part because other more basic subsidiary processes such as consciousness or respiration are very much more drug sensitive. It is difficult to devise stratagems which circumvent the hierarchy of sensitivities which shield various phases of memory. The most direct approach to putative memory centers is through the skull with cannulae and electrodes, in order to spare the more primitive and generally more drug-sensitive vital centers (140). Alternatively, a temporal dissection may be used by applying treatment systematically before, during, or after a registration, retention, or retrieval period.

PREACQUISITION DRUG ADMINISTRATION

There have been remarkably few papers dealing with the influence of drugs upon registration or the acquisition of a habit (Russell 163, Steinberg & Tomkiewicz 178). Acquisition studies are very difficult, time-consuming, expensive, and risky. Also, drugs seem to have relatively little specific effect upon the associative aspects of learning. Thus, costly negative types of experiments inhibit their own replication. The last comprehensive review of drugs and learning was by McGaugh & Petrinovich (128).

A wide variety of substances will impair acquisition of a conditioned avoidance response in rodents (41). These include sedative-hypnotics, phenothiazines, narcotic analgesics, hallucinogenics, analeptics, and sympathomimetic stimulants. Some of the stimulants such as amphetamine have also been shown to facilitate acquisition of a habit, frequently by reducing freezing behavior in an active avoidance or appetitive situation. The sedative-hypnotic depressants such as the barbiturates or the benzodiazepine derivatives have the reputation of impairing learning and accelerating extinction. They might act by impairing motivation or perception, particularly of unconditioned stimuli. For example, chlordiazepoxide administered prior to learning preferentially attenuates the effects of negative incentives (49). Pentobarbital given both pre- and post-trial impaired imprinting in chicks (17); a post-trial drug administration produced both anesthesia and RA.

Anesthesiologists have long been interested in agents capable of producing amnesia without loss of consciousness. In one recent study (157), methoxyflurane was used to induce in human subjects a state characterized by perseveration, loss of memory of recent and past events, delayed response to simple verbal command, and impaired ability to focus eyes or distinguish color. After direct current cardioversion was administered, the investigators reported that amnesia for the procedure occurred, but they give no evidence other than subjective evaluation. Other recent reports indicate that diazepam given in very high intravenous doses before treatment results in memory loss for cardioversion (94). Such reports indicate that some of the amnesic effects of anesthetic and preanesthetic agents are proactive and probably are produced by impairment of registration or production of rapid forgetting. More adequate analysis of such actions would be highly desirable.

Though one might expect impairment of learning by sedative-hypnotic agents (128), in some circumstances such agents promote rather than impair functioning. For example, punishing shock apparently can facilitate visual discrimination learning at low levels and impair it at high levels, but with sodium amobarbital, shock facilitates learning at both levels (52). Presumably the drug shifts the arousal curve downward sufficiently to eliminate the disruptive effect of excessive arousal.

Weiss & Laties (190), in their incisive review of magnesium pemoline studies, leave the reader with the general impression that most of the studies with this drug were either inadequate or inaccurate. The conclusion that this agent facilitates memory probably is not justified. Doses of magnesium pemoline which facilitate conditioned avoidance and active avoidance responses have no facilitating effect on a passive avoidance response (196). Similarly, Kulkarni (108) showed that acquisition of conditioned avoidance in a lever-pressing situation can be facilitated by amphetamine and furthermore that the increased learning persists. Both pemoline and magnesium pemoline have been reported to improve learning in a shuttle box for mice (10). Magnesium pemoline also has a stimulating effect comparable with that obtained with caffeine and methylphenidate (141).

Pemoline seems to be a central stimulant resembling amphetamine in many, but not all, of its actions, and such drugs can ordinarily facilitate both learning and performance in situations where depression of activity resulting from inhibition or fatigue might otherwise cause impairment. However, the ability of a drug to facilitate learning by disinhibiting or arousing a subject should not be disparaged. Both acquisition and retrieval of memory traces are known to be influenced by potentially drug sensitive factors such as drive, state, arousal, and stimulus configurations. Even indirect drug actions on associative mechanisms can furnish the basis for therapeutic application.

Research on the facilitating effects of analeptics on memory has been greatly stimulated by the persevering work of McGaugh and his collaborators (124). Strychnine administered to rats during postnatal development in a rich environment facilitated maze learning and impaired those raised in laboratory cages (114). Rats raised without drugs were intermediate. That strychnine should make poor rats even poorer was rather surprising and emphasizes the situational dependence of this drug effect. Krivanek & McGaugh (107) have demonstrated an anterograde temporal gradient of facilitation with pentylenetetrazol in mice, indicating a possible action on acquisition and bolstering the consolidation hypothesis.

In rabbits, pentylenetetrazol given 15 min before classical conditioning of the nictitating membrane facilitated such learning and also respiration rate discrimination but did not influence heart rate conditioning (45). Since the drug was active both at the time of and following learning, it is not certain whether the primary influence was on acquisition or retention.

Amphetamine, which directly or indirectly seems to stimulate adrenergic receptors and thereby involve catecholamines, produces disinhibiting effects similar in many respects to those of septal lesions (139). Both treatments impair learning and performance of passive avoidance, whereas they facilitate active avoidance learning and performance. Prenylamine, a drug that presumably can selectively deplete catecholamines, depresses activity and not surprisingly interferes with learning of an avoidance response (69). Reserpine, though a nonselective depletor, does the same thing. The results of all these experiments are compatible with the hypothesis that catecholamines are necessary for arousal and therefore learning.

Lints & Harvey (120) conclude that 5-hydroxytryptamine (5-HT) helps to inhibit the effects of a painful stimulus and that depletion of 5-HT by brain lesions increases sensitivity to electric shock. Similar effects have been shown by Tenen (184), who found that p-chlorophenylalanine (PCPA), which decreases brain 5-HT, also increases sensitivity to shock and may modulate pain perception. One would expect 5-HT levels to influence both acquisition and performance of avoidance and escape tasks if it truly has analgesic properties.

There is a large older literature on the effects of hormones upon learning. However, for some reason this literature has fallen out of favor in recent years. ACTH 1–10, an analog of ACTH, delayed the rate of extinction of a pole jumping response in thyroidectomized rats (39). Thyroxin also delayed extinction. Unfortunately, no euthyroid controls were used in the experiment. Thyroidectomized animals might be expected to extinguish faster than normals because of their low metabolic rate. Cortisone did not affect acquisition of an avoidance response but facilitated extinction (15). Adrenalectomy alone produced no change in avoidance acquisition when animals were maintained on saline or deoxycorticosterone. Results by Weiss and colleagues (191) indicate that adrenocortical steroids inhibit excitatory activity, and therefore adrenalectomy produces more inhibitory activity in animals, a very paradoxical effect. Hypophysectomized animals, on the other hand, show less fear in a passive avoidance situation.

Facilitation of learning by injections of yeast RNA extracts have been obtained in at least two well-controlled experiments, one in rats (29) and the other in chicks (172). Although it is highly unlikely that this RNA reaches the brain, nevertheless it is possible that it might produce some secondary effect upon the liver or other structures and thereby stimulate the organism. Perhaps there is some relationship between these findings and the reputation of purines (caffeine, uric acid) as facilitators of learning.

Nakajima (137) found that actinomycin D injected into the hippocampus of rats impaired both learning and retention of a spatial task in a T-maze. Cortical injection did not produce impairment. The deficit was associated with spike discharges as well as inhibition of RNA synthesis.

Facilitation of learning with TCAP has sometimes been observed. However, Davenport (28) indicated that tricyanoaminopropene (TCAP) is an effective antithyroid agent and can cause long-lasting impairment of learning but no facilitation. The reputed ability of this compound to stimulate RNA and protein synthesis also has been questioned. Otis & Pryor (143) could not find any enhancement of learning of a pole climbing test by TCAP in rats (see also 179). Furthermore, Gurowitz et al (70) found that TCAP actually impaired passive avoidance learning. Contradictory findings like these and others should make investigators hesitate before leaping into print with spectacular findings.

Treatments During the Retention Interval

Treatments other than ECS capable of selectively influencing retention which were investigated during recent years included administration of analeptic drugs, spreading cortical depression, carbon dioxide, heating and cooling, and inhibitors of protein synthesis. It is not known whether a common mechanism such as inhibition of macromolecular synthesis, impairment of cholinergic transmission, or neuronal depolarization might underlie the amnesic effects. These treatments have been reviewed by Jarvik (89). Results with post-trial pentylenetetrazol (PTZ) combinations (101) supported the findings of Bohdanecky et al (14) that chemical convulsant treatments appear to have longer temporal gradients than ECS; this raises problems for the concept that amnesic treatments halt and preserve the effects of incubation (152). Simple heating and cooling have been reported to produce retrograde amnesia (86), although Kane & Jarvik (97) found an effect of diathermy heating only when convulsions were induced. The fact that some chemically induced gradients differ from those generated by ECS at least shows that incubation and all forms of retrograde amnesia do not have identical temporal functions.

There is a limited number of studies reporting amnesia from nonconvulsive post-trial drug administrations. Amobarbital produced a retrograde amnesic effect in animals that were trained to avoid one arm of a T maze (178). Similarly, post-trial injections of pentobarbital impaired performance of rats in a Hebb-Williams maze (56). All injections were given 2 min after feeding in the goal box. No other time intervals were used, so that a temporal gradient was not demonstrated. Anesthetic drugs may also produce facilitation when given after learning (197), and nitrous oxide given to humans after a learning task enhances subsequent retention by reducing interference-induced forgetting. Thus, a drug such as a barbiturate may cause retrograde amnesia either by impairing consolidation or by speeding forgetting. Alternatively, it may sometimes improve remembering by decreasing interference.

Palfai & Cornell (146) found no effect of post-trial injections of either 50 mg/kg pentobarbital or 5 mg/kg chlorpromazine in a passive avoidance situation, whereas PTZ seizures effectively produced retrograde amnesia. Similarly, Osborn et al (142) found that barbiturate anesthesia in humans did not produce retrograde amnesia.

The discrepancy of results discussed in the last two paragraphs with each other and with earlier reports is hard to explain, but it may rest on the finding of Winters (198) that the excitement stage of pentobarbital anesthesia is very brief. Perhaps subjects must be kept in this stage for a sufficiently long period to obtain amnesic effects.

Chlorpromazine given 1/2 min after shock retarded extinction of a one-trial passive avoidance response, whereas the same drug given 2 or 10 min later did not (92). Chlorpromazine given before training also impairs acquisition of this response. Unfortunately, neither dose nor time gradients were obtained in this experiment. Clearly more work is needed to clarify and establish this effect.

A visual discrimination task with rats given PTZ resulted in a reverse gradient of facilitation, with the least facilitation occurring when the drug was given immediately after the training trial and the greatest 10 min later (77). This complex gradient is difficult to understand. It is unfortunate that longer time intervals were not used to see whether the shape of gradient would change with a decrease again over longer time intervals.

Retrograde facilitation is as important as RA in providing evidence for a consolidation process, as McGaugh & Krivanek (126) have demonstrated. Post-trial administration of 1 mg/kg of picrotoxin facilitated maze learning in emotionally reactive male rats in the Hebb-Williams maze (56) as did post-trial injections of nicotine bitartrate (0.8 mg/kg). Post-trial injections of nicotine (0.8 mg/kg) improved learning of a Hebb-Williams maze but not of a shuttle box test (55). Nicotine is a cholinergic agonist with powerful catecholamine releasing properties. The central stimulation it produces, however, might well have something in common with that produced by the analeptics, PTZ, strychnine, and picrotoxin, if they all facilitate learning. A careful analytical comparison of their actions would be desirable.

A most unusual finding was a report of facilitation of memory by heavy water (117). Fish were trained to discriminate between a red and green light. Thereafter one experimental group was kept in different concentrations of deuterium oxide and controls in normal water. Retention was found to be significantly better in the heavy water fish. The authors speculate that the "memory molecules" might have been stabilized by replacing hydrogen with deuterium bonds. By the same token one might expect that heavy water fish would have greater difficulty in learning a new task. Extension of this work would be clearly desirable.

Two inhibitors of protein synthesis that operate by different mechanisms, puromycin and cycloheximide, have been shown to interfere in a time-dependent manner with what appears to be consolidation of memory (5). Both of these agents, as well as the congener acetoxycycloheximide, produce their greatest effects when given in close temporal proximity to the learning experience (Geller et al 62, 63; Swanson et al 182). Cycloheximide and iso-cycloheximide both produced comparable decrements in general activity in mice, but only the former inhibited protein synthesis and impaired memory (169).

There have been very few studies indicating a clear-cut effect of drugs upon retention in man. Stone et al (180) found that chlorpromazine showed the decay of visual short-term memory. This action was not obtained with scopolamine or pentobarbital. Hurst et al (80) showed that d-amphetamine could facilitate delayed recall of low competition paired-associate lists in students. Such experiments are not easy to perform, but the practical implications are very great.

TREATMENTS ENCOMPASSING THE RETEST

The third stage of memory is retrieval or the re-elicitation of information gained on the learning trial. The aftereffects of the learning experience may also manifest themselves in totally new behavior which would not have occurred without the experience. The freezing response in passive avoidance is an example of this. The response depends upon the subject's perception of some stimulus aspects of the original situation, the familiar stimulus generalization gradient. There is either a cue for a memory trace or it appears spontaneously as, for example, endogenous interference in memory (153). The important scanning mechanism whereby a cue such as a conditioned stimulus elicits an appropriate memory trace and response remains a mystery. Some type of resonance, suggested years ago by Lashley (113) as interference patterns, or more recently by Pribram (154) as holograms, may indeed lie at the basis of the extremely rapid selective retrieval from a huge store of memories. Olds (140) suggests a random access computer analogy, utilizing a gridwork in the hippocampus. The discovery of the physical basis of the retrieval mechanism remains one of the great challenges of physiological psychology.

Once a response has been stably learned, there is no a priori reason for thinking it must be distinguishable from an unlearned response. For example, despite nearly 20 years of concern with the hypothesis that drugs will selectively impair conditioned versus unconditioned responses (25), the fact has not been adequately demonstrated. The response-producing potential of conditioned and unconditioned stimuli must be equated before relative drug susceptibility can be assessed. In older studies of phenothiazine attenuation of conditioned responses, learning actually appears to be irrelevant whereas stimulus control is the important variable. Very likely chlorpromazine could more easily disrupt the weak auditory conditioned stimulus than the strong punishing electric unconditioned stimulus (Dews & Morse 40, Gollub & Brady 67).

On the other hand, it is possible and even plausible that the associative stimulus-response bonds involved in a learned response are different from those which are innately present. In many, though not all, instances they must be continually reinforced or else they extinguish. Extinction involves an abrupt change in reinforcement with consequent response attenuation. Older drug studies have been used as an argument against the interference theory of extinction (79) because extinction of active responses was more rapid under depressant drugs and slower under stimulant drugs. However, the nature of the reinforcement and the response have not been systematically varied with drugs. For example, if the response is prevented during extinction of a conditioned avoidance response, amobarbital no longer facilitates extinction (95). The real problem is that the percentage of reinforcements of an instrumental act is a function of the nature and speed of response, and unless these are controlled one cannot assume that a drug is directly affecting the associative processes involved in extinction.

Unfortunately, performance on a retrieval trial, sometimes misleadingly called a retention test, is the only presently available index of learned changes which may have occurred during retention. The actual learning experience in a one-trial situation, lacking a response, gives no measure of its effectiveness. At least one more trial is necessary to indicate both how much learning has taken place and how much has been retained (58). In multiple-trial learning procedures a succession of registration, retention, and retrieval trials may be quickly superimposed upon one another and the performance resulting from this complex interaction, particularly if massed, is considered a single learning experience (Agranoff et al 2, Barondes 6, McGaugh 122, Overton 144).

Phenothiazines are known to impair performance of a conditioned avoidance response (CAR), possibly by extra-pyramidal depression because of dopamine blockage (3). However, phenothiazines will disinhibit animals that have already learned a passive avoidance response, indicating that motor depression is not the only explanation of the impairing effects of chlorpromazine upon conditioning (85).

Tryptaminergic, as well as adrenergic and cholinergic systems, have been implicated in learning. An injection of PCPA, which blocks synthesis of 5-HT, enhanced the performance of rats in a conditioned avoidance task, but chronic administration of the same drug impaired performance (165). Perhaps these results are related to the modulation or reduction of pain perception by 5-HT suggested by Lints & Harvey (120).

The cholinergic system seems a likely one to be implicated in learning (37). For years scopolamine has been considered an amnesic agent (68) but its actions are primarily anterograde. Anticholinesterases have also been shown to impair and facilitate performance of a spatial task, depending upon the retention interval (Wiener & Deutsch 194, Deutsch & Wiener 38). Surprisingly, the behavioral effects of physostigmine were antagonized by methoscopolamine, a peripherally acting anticholinergic agent which had no effect when administered alone (174).

Drugs may influence learning by altering internal states, but by the same token they may also act as stimuli (144). This is not surprising since most unconditioned stimuli such as food, water, and electric shock also result in changes in internal states. By some criteria, food and water, which are chemical substances, may act as drugs. They also have external stimulus properties as well. Drugs have to be administered somehow and the act of administration may furnish cues. The drugged state may act as a cue to the subject and result in state-dependent learning or dissociative learning (144).

A nondrug condition that possibly causes dissociation or can act as conditional stimulus is spreading cortical depression (166). Some investigators have even found that the postictal condition induced by ECS may produce state dependence (186). Sedative-hypnotic drugs such as barbiturates seem to be capable of producing state-dependent learning relatively easily. A symmetrical dissociation exists when learning occurs in a nondrugged state and is transferred upon retest to the nondrugged but not to the drugged state, and conversely when learning that occurs in the drugged state is transferred to the drugged state. However, generally speaking, learning under a drug influence is poorer than in a sober state, and dissociation theory would require that retest performance of this poorly learned material be better under a drug than without it. This type of drug-facilitated performance is difficult to demonstrate although it has been done in some experiments (9).

Anticholinergic drugs apparently can give a certain degree of state-dependent learning. State-dependent learning with phenothiazines appears to be relatively weak. Sachs (164) has reported that abnormal brain electrolyte concentrations can cause state-dependent learning. State-dependent learning has been reported also with a variety of other drugs including amphetamine, morphine, and nicotine (144).

A somewhat different situation is the deliberate training of animals to use drugs as discriminative stimuli. Animals may be conditioned, for example, to differentiate anticholinergic drugs from sedative depressants. This technique may be used to place drugs along a stimulus continuum. Overton (144) has classified centrally acting drugs for discriminative control into three categories. Drugs with strong control are anesthetics and sedative-hypnotics. Drugs with moderate control are cholinergic and anticholinergic drugs, morphine, convulsants, and amphetamine. Weak control drugs include phenothiazines and imipramine. Peripherally acting drugs such as quaternary amines do not seem to acquire response control. Thus the order of ability of drugs to exercise stimulus control seems to be the same as to produce dissociation. Even though the drugs are used as conditioned stimuli, their reinforcing actions may play a role since the drugs with the strongest control are also the pleasantest to humans. Discrimination of internal drug states by animals has great potential as a screening device and also as a means of classification.

Sometimes a single administration of a drug can have effects lasting months or even years. Cochin & Kornetsky (22) showed tolerance following a single injection of morphine lasting for nearly a year. A mixture of amphetamine and amobarbital prevented habituation in an exploratory maze the first time it was administered (178). When animals were retested as much as 3 months later, a persistence of effect was noticed even though they had only a 3 minute experience the first time. Furthermore, the control animals which received only saline on the two trials showed an increase in activity at the beginning of the test period and then a steep decline, showing that there was an influence of the first trial upon the second albeit they were separated by months. These long-lasting "hit and run" effects resemble learning and may possibly involve the same mechanisms.

Protein synthesis is still given a major role in chemical theories of memory. Cycloheximide, an inhibitor of protein synthesis, not only causes rapid loss of memory (6) but produces retrograde amnesia when given post-trial (Geller et al 62, 63). Although the actions of puromycin were first attributed to its ability to inhibit protein synthesis (50), more recently the reversibility of these actions with saline washes and various drugs makes it more likely that the effect is upon retrieval. There is a strong relationship between the levels of peptidyl-puromycin in the brain and impairment of performance (51). Furthermore, parenteral administration of imipramine, tranylcypromine, and d-amphetamine reduces this impairment, suggesting that the peptidyl-puromycin complex is interfering with the function of adrenergic sites (159). It would be useful to have independent measures of central adrenergic function such as arousal or general activity.

Further support for the role of macromolecular synthesis in learning comes from a group of articles published in the *Proceedings of the National Academy of Sciences*, apparently a popular vehicle for this type of research. The North Carolina group (93), following up their earlier work, have now localized the increased RNA synthesis associated with learning. There was increased incorporation of uridine in the limbic system in trained but not yoked mice. The group at Oregon (7) found that there was increased leucine-H^3 in the hippocampus and entorhinal cortex for rats learning a one-way active avoidance task. Hydén & Lange (82) reported that rats trained on the reversal of handedness showed increased protein synthesis in pyramidal neurons of the hippocampus. In a rejoinder to a criticism of this experiment by Bowman & Harding (16), they reported that newly synthesized RNA in a learning task is characterized by a high proportion of adenine and uracil whereas this does not occur in purely stress situations (83). Hydén & Lange (81) also reported that a brain-specific acid protein, S-100, increases in the hippocampus in rats trained to transfer handedness in retrieving food pills from glass tubes. These results, while potentially very important, should be subjected to the scrutiny of replication in other laboratories.

NEGATIVE FINDINGS

The absence of a drug effect upon learning or discriminative performance in the presence of effects on other functions is surely evidence for selectivity of action. In a situation where an animal had to make a dichotomous simultaneous discrimination, chlorpromazine (CPZ) had relatively little effect, even when marked ataxia was present (193). Thus, motor impairment could be fairly marked without much effect upon discrimination, and this is a finding also consistent with those of Glick et al (65). They found that neither CPZ nor pentobarbital affected accuracy on a delayed matching test with monkeys, even though marked effects upon relative response frequency were obtained.

A number of studies have indicated that hypoxia or anoxia is ineffective in producing amnesia in situations where other treatments do work (Cherkin 19, Vacher et al 189). Even though anoxia results in unconsciousness, it spares memory processes, but memory processes are susceptible to treatments such as cycloheximide which do not produce unconsciousness; hence, unconsciousness and impairment of memory must have different mechanisms of action.

A number of skilled sensory motor acts in humans are remarkably unresponsive to phenothiazines and imipramine, although objective physiological measures are affected (71). It may be just as important to determine functions that are highly resistant to drugs as those which are susceptible, because these functions would have to be controlled either by parts of the brain or by peripheral structures which are not susceptible to these agents. This resistance may thus tell us something about the mechanisms or the barriers surrounding them.

CONCLUSION

The reason that the cerebral processes underlying learning and memory are not as well understood as other physiological functions, such as digestion or blood circulation, is that a good in vitro preparation of the brain has not been devised. Therefore, the brain of the learning animal has to be observed with implanted instruments while it is conscious and in a moving organism, or else direct methods of observation must be used.

The picture that emerges from this survey is that cerebral processes underlying learning and memory are very well insulated from the outside world. The scalp, skull, and meningeal layers that protect the brain from external physical assault also offer an obstacle to refined research. Pressure, temperature, vibration, and electromagnetic radiation can be used to surmount this barrier for experimental purposes only with the greatest of difficulty. On the other hand, electrical currents can get through with somewhat greater ease although localization is rather limited. The effectiveness of ECS and the availability of the EEG depend upon this permeability to electricity. Although ionizing radiation penetrates to the brain easily, it also seems to preferentially disrupt mesenchymal structures. Of course, the barrier can be transcended surgically, and brain lesions can still tell us a great deal about brain function, although their temporal limitations and irreversibility restrict the kind of information they can yield. Implantation of devices such as electrodes and catheters continues to offer great promise both for localization of function and circumvention of the blood brain barrier.

The consequences of learning are not grossly observable in the brain. Either prolonged environmental changes are needed to induce measurable modifications in brain structure (162), or else sensitive trace methods must be employed to detect change from a brief learning experience. Micro-electrode recordings continue to offer great promise.

Nevertheless, there are chemicals that can be administered parenterally and that can pass the blood brain barrier; their promise in the study of chemical mechanisms underlying learning and memory is great. Others must be put directly into the brain. Useful agents include inhibitors of biosynthetic processes such as actinomycin D, cycloheximide, and puromycin, blocking agents such as scopolamine, and potentiating agents such as physostigmine or tranylcypromine. Unfortunately, many drugs with strong action on behavior act by mechanisms as yet unidentified. These include sedative hypnotics, anesthetics, narcotic analgesics, and hallucinogens; nonlearning effects must be factored out. If an agent were available which was both specific and effective in influencing memory and the relevant biological process, the task of the investigator of the biological basis of memory would be much easier.

The likelihood of such an agent is remote because learning is protected not only by physical barriers but also by the greater susceptibility of other functions to various treatments. Thus arousal, motivation, activity, and perception may easily be impaired by low levels of drugs which do not impair learning or retrieval. Higher levels of drugs may render the animal inactive or unconscious. The way around this impasse is either temporal or spatial. Post-trial treatments may influence retention and spare registration or retrieval. Local application of drugs to the memory centers may conceivably act selectively on memory, but only the beginnings of such an approach are in evidence. Drugs that selectively localize of their own accord in learning centers have not yet been identified. Optimism is nevertheless warranted by the evolution of better implantation techniques and of more selective drugs.

LITERATURE CITED

1. Agranoff, B. W., Davis, R. E. 1968. The use of fishes in studies on memory. In *The Central Nervous System and Fish Behavior*, ed. D. Ingle, 193–201. Univ. Chicago press
2. Agranoff, B. W., Davis, R. E., Lim, R., Casola, L. 1968. Biological effects of antimetabolites used in behavioral studies. In *Psychopharmacology: A Review of Progress, 1957-67*, ed. D. Efron, 909–17. Washington, D.C.: Pub. Health Serv. Publ. No. 1836. 1342 pp.
3. Anden, N. E., Carlsson, A., Haggendal, J. 1969. Adrenergic mechanisms. *Ann. Rev. Pharmacol.* 9: 119–34
4. Aron, C., Glick, S. D., Jarvik, M. E. 1969. Long-lasting proactive effects of a single ECS. *Physiol. Behav.* 4:785–89
5. Barondes, S. H. 1970. Cerebral protein synthesis inhibitors block long term memory. *Int. Rev. Neurobiol.* 12: 177–205
6. Barondes, S. H. 1968. Effect of inhibitors of cerebral protein synthesis on "long term" memory in mice. See Ref. 2, 905–8
7. Beach, G., Emmens, M., Kimble, D. P., Lickey, M. 1969. Autoradiographic demonstration of biochemical changes in the limbic system during avoidance training. *Proc. Nat. Acad. Sci. USA* 62:692–96
8. Bennett, G. S., Edelman, G. M. 1969. Amino acid incorporation into rat brain proteins during spreading cortical depression. *Science* 163: 393–95
9. Berger, B. D., Stein, L. 1969. Asymmetrical dissociation of learning between scopolamine and Wy 4036, a new benzodiazepine tranquilizer. *Psychopharmacologia* 14:351–58
10. Bianchi, C., Marazzi-Uberti, E. 1969. Acquisition and retention of a conditioned avoidance response in mice as influenced by pemoline, by some of its derivatives and by some CNS stimulants. *Psychopharmacologia* 15:9–18
11. Bickford, R. G., Mulder, D. W., Dodge, H. W. Jr., Svien, H. J., Rome, H. P. 1958. Changes in memory function produced by electrical stimulation of the temporal lobe in man. *Assoc. Res. Nerv. Ment. Dis.* 36:227–43
12. Bidder, T. G., Strain, J. J., Brun-schwig, L. 1970. Bilateral and unilateral ECT: follow-up study and critique. *Am. J. Psychiat.* 127:737–45
13. Blumer, D., Walker, A. E. 1969. Memory in temporal lobe epileptics. In *The Pathology of Memory*, ed. G. A. Talland, N. C. Waugh, 65–74. New York: Academic. 322 pp.
14. Bohdanecky, Z., Kopp, R., Jarvik, M. E. 1968. Comparison of ECS and flurothyl-induced retrograde amnesia in mice. *Psychopharmacologia* 12:91–95
15. Bohus, B., Lissak, K. 1968. Adrenocortical hormones and avoidance behavior of rats. *Int. J. Neuropharmacol.* 7:301–6
16. Bowman, R. E., Harding, G. 1969. Protein synthesis during learning. *Science* 164:199–200
17. Bradford, J. P., MacDonald, G. E. 1969. Imprinting: pre- and post-trial administration of pentobarbital and the approach response. *J. Comp. Physiol. Psychol.* 68:50–55
18. Briese, E., Olds, J. 1964. Reinforcing brain stimulation and memory in monkeys. *Exp. Neurol.* 10:493–508
19. Cherkin, A. 1971. Memory consolidation in the chick: resistance to prolonged post-training hypoxia. *Commun. Behav. Biol.* 5:325–30
20. Chorover, S. L., DeLuca, A. M. 1969. Transient change in electrocorticographic reaction to ECS in the rat following footshock. *J. Comp. Physiol. Psychol.* 69:141–49
21. Chorover, S. L., Schiller, P. H. 1965. Short-term retrograde amnesia in rats. *J. Comp. Physiol. Psychol.* 59:73–78
22. Cochin, J., Kornetsky, C. 1964. Development and loss of tolerance to morphine in the rat after single and multiple injections. *J. Pharmacol. Exp. Ther.* 145:1–10
23. Cohn, M. 1970. Anticipatory mechanisms of individuals. In *Control Processes in Multicellular Organisms*, ed. G. E. W. Wolstenholme, J. Knight, 255–303. London: Churchill. 424 pp.
24. Cotman, C., Banker, G., Zornetzer, S., McGaugh, J. L. 1971. Electroshock effect on brain protein synthesis: relation to brain seizures and retrograde amnesia. *Science*. In press
25. Courvoisier, S., Fournel, J., Ducrot,

R., Kolsky, M., Koetschet, P. 1953. Propiétés pharmacodynamiques du chlorhydrate de chloro-3 (dimethylamine-3-propyl)-10 phenothiazine 4650 RP. *Arch. Int. Pharmacodyn. Ther.* 92:305–61

26. Cronholm, B. 1969. Post-ECT amnesias. See Ref. 13, 81–89

27. Cronin, D. et al 1970. Unilateral and bilateral ECT: a study of memory disturbance and relief from depression. *J. Neurol. Neurosurg. Psychiat.* 33:705–13

28. Davenport, J. W. 1970. Cretinism in rats: enduring behavioral deficit induced by tricyanoaminopropene. *Science* 167:1007–9

29. Davidson, A. B., Cook, L. 1970. Yeast ribonucleic acid: analysis of effects on pole-climb avoidance behavior. *Psychopharmacologia* 16: 399–408

30. Davis, R. E. 1968. Environmental control of memory fixation in goldfish. *J. Comp. Physiol. Psychol.* 65:72–78

31. Davis, R. E., Hirtzel, M. S. 1970. Environmental control of ECS-produced retrograde amnesia in goldfish. *Physiol. Behav.* 5:1089–92

32. Davis, R. E., Klinger, P. D. 1969. The environmental control of amnesic effects of various agents in goldfish. *Physiol. Behav.* 4:269–71

33. Dawson, R. G., McGaugh, J. L. 1969. Electroconvulsive shock effects on a reactivated memory trace; further examination. *Science* 166:525–27

34. Denny, M. R., Ditchman, R. E. 1962. The locus of maximal "Kamin effect" in rats. *J. Comp. Physiol. Psychol.* 55:1069–70

35. Denti, A., McGaugh, J. L., Landfield, P. W., Shinkman, P. G. 1970. Effects of post-trial electrical stimulation of the mesencephalic reticular formation on avoidance learning in rats. *Physiol. Behav.* 5:659–62

36. Deutsch, J. A. The cholinergic synapse and the site of memory. *Science.* In press

37. Deutsch, J. A. 1969. The physiological basis of memory. *Ann. Rev. Psychol.* 20:85–104

38. Deutsch, J. A., Wiener, N. I. 1969. Analysis of extinction through amnesia. *J. Comp. Physiol. Psychol.* 69:179–84

39. Dewied, D., Pirie, G. 1968. The inhibitory effect of ACTH 1–10 on extinction of a conditioned avoidance response: its independence of

thyroid function. *Physiol. Behav.* 3:355–58

40. Dews, P. B., Morse, W. H. 1961. Behavioral pharmacology. *Ann. Rev. Pharmacol.* 1:145–74

41. Domino, E. F., Caldwell, D. F., Henke, R. 1965. Effects of psychoactive agents on acquisition of conditioned pole jumping in rats. *Psychopharmacologia* 8:285–89

42. Dorfman, L. J., Bohdanecka, M., Bohdanecky, Z., Jarvik, M. E. 1969. Retrograde amnesia produced by small cortical stab wounds in the mouse. *J. Comp. Physiol. Psychol.* 69:324–28

43. Doty, R. W. 1969. Electrical stimulation of the brain in behavioral context. *Ann. Rev. Psychol.* 20: 289–320

44. Duncan, C. P. 1949. The retroactive effect of electroshock on learning. *J. Comp. Physiol. Psychol.* 42:32–44

45. Elliott, R., Schneiderman, N. 1968. Pentylenetetrazol: facilitation of classical discrimination conditioning in rabbits. *Psychopharmacologia* 12:133–41

46. Engel, J., Hanson, L. C. F., Roos, B. E., Strömbergsson, L. E. 1968. Effect of electroshock on dopamine metabolism in rat brain. *Psychopharmacologia* 13:140–44

47. Erickson, C. K., Patel, J. B. 1969. Facilitation of avoidance learning by post-trial hippocampal electrical stimulation. *J. Comp. Physiol. Psychol.* 68:400–6

48. Essman, W. B. 1968. Electroshock-induced retrograde amnesia and brain serotonin metabolism: effects of several antidepressant compounds. *Psychopharmacologia* 13: 258–66

49. Feldman, R. S. 1968. The mechanism of fixation prevention and "dissociation" learning with chlordiazepoxide. *Psychopharmacologia* 12:384–99

50. Flexner, L. B. 1967. Dissection of memory in mice with antibiotics. *Proc. Am. Phil. Soc.* 111:343–46

51. Flexner, L. B., Gambetti, P., Flexner, J. B., Roberts, R. B. 1971. Studies on memory: distribution of peptidylpuromycin in subcellular fractions of mouse brain. *Proc. Nat. Acad. Sci.* 68:26–28

52. Fowler, H., Goldman, L., Wischner, G. J. 1968. Sodium amytal and the shock-right intensity function for visual discrimination learning. *J.*

Comp. Physiol. Psychol. 65:155–59

53. Franz, S. I., Lashley, K. S. 1917. The retention of habits by the rat after destruction of the frontal portion of the cerebrum. *Psychobiology* 1:3–18

54. Fuxe, K. 1965. Evidence for the existence of monoamine neurons in the central nervous system. IV. Distribution of monoamine nerve terminals in the central nervous system. *Acta Physiol. Scand.* 247:37–85

55. Garg, M. 1969. The effect of nicotine on two different types of learning. *Psychopharmacologia* 15:408–14

56. Garg, M., Holland, H. C. 1969. Consolidation and maze learning: a study of some strain-drug interactions. *Psychopharmacologia* 14:426–31

57. Geller, M., Geller, A. 1970. Brief amnesic effects of spike-wave discharges. *Neurology* 20:1089–95

58. Geller, A., Jarvik, M. E. 1970. The role of consolidation in memory. In *Biochemistry of Brain and Behavior*, ed. R. E. Bowman, S. P. Datta, 245–78. New York: Plenum. 364 pp.

59. Geller, A., Jarvik, M. E. 1968. Electroconvulsive shock induced amnesia and recovery. *Psychon. Sci.* 10:15–16

60. Ibid. The time relations of ECS induced amnesia. 12:169–70

61. Geller, A., Jarvik, M. E., Robustelli, F. 1970. Permanence of a long temporal gradient of retrograde amnesia induced by electroconvulsive shock. *Psychon. Sci.* 19:257–59

62. Geller, A., Robustelli, F., Barondes, S. H., Cohen, H. D., Jarvik, M. E. 1969. Impaired performance by post-trial injections of cycloheximide in a passive avoidance task. *Psychopharmacologia* 14:371–76

63. Geller, A., Robustelli, F., Jarvik, M. E. 1970. A parallel study of the amnesic effects of cycloheximide and ECS under different strengths of conditioning. *Psychopharmacologia* 16:281–89

64. Glassman, E. 1969. The biochemistry of learning: an evaluation of the role of RNA and protein. *Ann. Rev. Biochem.* 38:605–46

65. Glick, S. D., Goldfarb, T. L., Robustelli, F., Geller, A., Jarvik, M. E. 1969. Impairment of delayed matching in monkeys by chlorpromazine and pentobarbital. *Psychopharmacologia* 15:125–33

66. Glowinski, J., Axelrod, J. 1966. Effects of drugs on the disposition of H^3-norepinephrine in the rat brain. *Pharmacol. Rev.* 18:775–85

67. Gollub, L. R., Brady, J. V., 1965. Behavioral pharmacology. *Ann. Rev. Pharmacol.* 5:235–62

68. Goodman, L. S., Gilman, A., Eds. 1970. *The Pharmacological Basis of Therapeutics.* New York: Macmillan. 4th ed. 1794 pp.

69. Gregory, K. 1968. The action of the drug prenylamine (segontin) on exploratory activity and aversive learning in a selected strain of rats. *Psychopharmacologia* 13:22–28

70. Gurowitz, E. M., Gross, D. A., George, R. 1968. Effects of TCAP on passive avoidance learning in the rat. *Psychon. Sci.* 12:293–94

71. Heimann, H., Reed, C. F., Witt, P. N. 1968. Some observations suggesting preservation of skilled motor acts despite drug-induced stress. *Psychopharmacologia* 13:287–98

72. Herz, M. J. 1969. Interference with one-trial appetitive and aversive learning by ether and ECS. *J. Neurobiol.* 1:111–22

73. Herz, M. J., Peeke, H. V. 1968, ECS-produced retrograde amnesia: permanence vs. recovery over repeated testing. *Physiol. Behav.* 3:517–21

74. Hinesley, R. K., Norton, J. A., Aprison, M. H. 1968. Serotonin, norepinephrine and 3,4-dihydroxyphenylethylamine in rat brain parts following electroconvulsive shock. *J. Psychiat. Res.* 6:143–52

75. Hostetter, G. 1968. Hippocampal lesions in rats weaken the retrograde amnesic effect of ECS. *J. Comp. Physiol. Psychol.* 66:349–53

76. Hughes, R. A., Barrett, R. J., Ray, O. S. 1970. Training to test interval as a determinant of a temporally graded ECS-produced response decrement in rats. *J. Comp. Physiol. Psychol.* 71:318–24

77. Hunt, E. B., Bauer, R. H. 1969. Facilitation of learning by delayed injections of pentylenetetrazol. *Psychopharmacologia* 16:139–46

78. Hunt, H. F., Brady, J. V. 1951. Some effects of electroconvulsive shock on a conditioned emotional response (anxiety). *J. Comp. Physiol. Psychol.* 44:88–98

79. Hunt, H. F. 1961. Methods for studying the behavioral effects of drugs. *Ann. Rev. Pharmacol.* 1:125–44

80. Hurst, P. M., Radlow, R., Chubb, N. C., Bagley, S. K. 1969. Effects of d-amphetamine on acquisition, persistence and recall. Am. J. Psychol. 82:307–19

81. Hydén, H., Lange, P. W. 1970. Brain-cell protein synthesis specifically related to learning Proc. Nat. Acad. Sci. USA 65:998–904

82. Hydén, H., Lange, P. W. 1968. Protein synthesis in the hippocampal pyramidal cells of rats during a behavioral test. Science 159:1370–73

83. Ibid 1969. Protein synthesis during learning. 164:200–1

84. Irwin, S., Kalsner, S., Curtis, A. 1964. Direct demonstration of consolidation of one-trial learning. Fed. Proc. 23:102

85. Iwahara, S., Iwasaki, T., Hasegawa, Y. 1968. Effects of chlorpromazine and homofenazine upon a passive avoidance response in rats. Psychopharmacologia 13:320–31

86. Jacobs, B. L., Sorenson, C. A. 1969. Memory disruption in mice by brief post-trial immersion in hot or cold water. J. Comp. Physiol. Psychol. 68:239–44

87. Jaffe, J. H. 1970. Drug addiction and drug abuse. See Ref. 68, 276–313

88. Jamieson, J. L., Albert, D. J. 1970. Amnesia from ECS: the effect of pairing ECS and footshock. Psychon. Sci. 18:14–15

89. Jarvik, M. E. 1968. Consolidation of memory. See Ref. 2, 885–90

90. Jarvik, M. E., Geller, A. 1970. The role of consolidation in memory. See Ref. 58, 245–77

91. John, E. R. 1967. Mechanisms of Memory. New York: Academic. 468 pp.

92. Johnson, F. N. 1969. The effects of chlorpromazine on the decay and consolidation of short-term memory traces in mice. Psychopharmacologia 16:105–14

93. Kahan, B., Krigman, M. R., Wilson, J. E., Glassman, E. 1970. Brain function and macromolecules. VI. Autoradiographic analysis of the effect of a brief training experience on the incorporation of uridine into mouse brain. Proc. Nat. Acad. Sci. USA 65:300–3

94. Kahler, R. L., Burrow, G. N., Felig, P. 1967. Diazepam induced amnesia for cardioversion. J. Am. Med. Assoc. 200:997–98

95. Kamano, D. K. 1968. Joint effect of amobarbital and response prevention of CAR extinction. Psychol. Rep. 22:544–46

96. Kamin, L. J. 1957. The retention of an incompletely learned avoidance response. J. Comp. Physiol. Psychol. 50:457–60

97. Kane, J., Jarvik, M. E. 1970. Amnesic effects of heating in mice. Psychon. Sci. 18:7–8

98. Kesner, R. P., Doty, R. W. 1968. Amnesia produced in cats by local seizure activity initiated from the amygdala. Exp. Neurol. 21:58–68

99. Kety, S. S. 1970. The biogenic amines in the central nervous system: their possible roles in arousal, emotion and learning. In The Neurosciences, ed. F. O. Schmitt, 324–35. New York: Rockefeller Univ. In press

100. Kimble, G. A. 1961. Hilgard and Marquis Conditioning and Learning. New York: Appleton-Century-Crofts. 2nd ed. 590 pp.

101. Kincaid, J. P. 1967. A comparison of the retrograde amnesic effects of metrazol and electroconvulsive shock. Psychon. Sci. 8:387–88

102. King, R. A., Glasser, R. L. 1970. Duration of electroconvulsive shock-induced retrograde amnesia in rats. Physiol. Behav. 5:335–39

103. King, R. A., Glasser, R. L., Flanagan, R. 1970. Retrograde amnesia following anterior limbic system stimulation. Proc. Ann. Conv. Am. Psychol. Assoc. 5:223–24

104. Kohlenberg, R., Trabasso, T. 1968. Recovery of a conditioned emotional response after one or two electroconvulsive shocks. J. Comp. Physiol. Psychol. 65:270–73

105. Kopp, R., Bohdanecky, Z., Jarvik, M. E. 1966. Long temporal gradient of retrograde amnesia for a well-discriminated stimulus. Science 153:1547–49

106. Krech, D., Crutchfield, R. S., Livson, N. 1969. Elements of Psychology New York: Knopf. 2nd ed. 864 pp.

107. Krivanek, J., McGaugh, J. L. 1968. Effects of pentylenetetrazol on memory storage in mice. Psychopharmacologia 12:303–21

108. Kulkarni, A. S. 1968. Facilitation of instrumental avoidance learning by amphetamine: an analysis. Psychopharmacologia 13:418–25

109. Kumar, R., Stolerman, I. P., Steinberg, H. 1970. Psychopharmacology. Ann. Rev. Psychol. 21:595–628

110. Kuntzman, R. 1969. Drugs and en-

zyme induction. *Ann. Rev. Pharmacol.* 9:21–36

111. Laidisich, W., Steinhauff, N., Matussek, N. 1969. Chronic administration of electroconvulsive shock and norepinephrine metabolism in the rat brain. II. 7-H³-NE metabolism after intracisternal injection with and without the influence of drugs in different brain regions, and by 7-H³-NE uptake in vitro. *Psychopharmacologia* 15:296–304

112. Landfield, P. W., McGaugh, J. L., Tusa, R. J. Theta rhythm: a correlate of post-trial memory storage processes in the rat. In preparation

113. Lashley, K. S. 1951. The problem of serial order in behavior. In *Cerebral Mechanisms in Behavior*, ed. L. A. Jeffress, 112–46. New York: Wiley. 311 pp.

114. LeBoeuf, B. J., Peeke, H. V. 1969. The effect of strychnine administration during development on adult maze learning in the rat. *Psychopharmacologia* 16:49–53

115. Lee-Teng, E. 1970. Retrograde amnesia gradients by subconvulsive and high convulsive transcranial currents in chicks. *Proc. Nat. Acad. Sci. USA* 65:857–65

116. Lee-Teng, E. 1969. Retrograde amnesia in relation to subconvulsive and convulsive currents in chicks. *J. Comp. Physiol. Psychol.* 67:135–39

117. Lehr, E., Wenzel, M., Werner, G. 1970. Zur biochemie des gedächtnisses. I. Einflub von schwerem wasser auf das gedächtnis von fischen. *Naturwissenschaften* 57:521–24

118. Levy, R. 1968. Clinical evaluation of unilateral electroconvulsive therapy. *Brit. J. Psychiat.* 114:459–63

119. Lewis, D. J., Miller, R. R., Misanin, J. R. 1969. Selective amnesia in rats produced by electroconvulsive shock. *J. Comp. Physiol. Psychol.* 69:136–40

120. Lints, C. E., Harvey, J. A. 1969. Altered sensitivity to footshock and decreased brain content of serotonin following brain lesions in the rat. *J. Comp. Physiol. Psychol.* 67:23–31

121. Matussek, N., Ladisich, W. 1969. Chronic administration of electroconvulsive shock and norepinephrine metabolism in the rat brain. III. Influence of acute and chronic electroshock upon drug induced behavior. *Psychopharmacologia* 15:305–9

122. McGaugh, J. L. 1968. Drug facilitation of memory and learning. See Ref. 2, 891–904

123. McGaugh, J. L. 1966. Time-dependent processes in memory storage. *Science* 153:1351–58

124. McGaugh, J. L., Dawson, R. G. 1971. Modification of memory storage processes. *Behav. Sci.* 16:45–63

125. McGaugh, J. L., Hart, J. T. Strychnine attenuation of retrograde amnesia induced by electroconvulsive shock. In preparation

126. McGaugh, J. L., Krivanek, J. A 1970. Strychnine effects on discrimination learning in mice: effects of dose and time of administration. *Physiol. Behav.* 5:1437–42

127. McGaugh, J. L., Landfield, P. W. 1970. Delayed development of amnesia following electroconvulsive shock. *Physiol. Behav.* 5:1109–13

128. McGaugh, J. L., Petrinovich, L. F. 1965. Effects of drugs on learning and memory. *Int. Rev. Neurobiol.* 8:139–96

129. McGeogh, J. A., Irion, A. L. 1962. *The Psychology of Human Learning*. New York: Longmans. 596 pp.

130. Miller, R. R. 1970. Effects of environmental complexity on amnesia induced by electroconvulsive shock in rats. *J. Comp. Physiol. Psychol.* 71:267–75

131. Miller, R. R., Mesanin, J. R., Lewis, D. J. 1969. Amnesia as a function of events during the learning-ECS interval. *J. Comp. Physiol. Psychol.* 67:145–48

132. Misanin, J. R., Miller, R. R., Lewis, D. J. 1968. Retrograde amnesia produced by electroconvulsive shock after reactivation of a consolidated memory trace. *Science* 160:554–55

133. Morgane, P. J. 1969. Neural regulation of food and water intake. *Ann. NY Acad. Sci.* 157:531–1216

134. Musacchio, J. M., Julou, L., Kety, S. S., Glowinski, J. 1969. Increase in rat brain tyrosine hydroxylase activity produced by electroconvulsive shock. *Proc. Nat. Acad. Sci. USA* 63:1117–19

135. Nachman, M. 1970. Limited effects of electroconvulsive shock on memory of taste stimulation. *J. Comp. Physiol. Psychol.* 73:31–37

136. Nachman, M., Meinecke, R. O. 1969. Lack of retrograde amnesia effects of repeated electroconvulsive shock

and carbon dioxide treatments. *J. Comp. Physiol. Psychol.* 68:631–36

137. Nakajima, S. 1969. Interference with relearning in the rat after hippocampal injection of actinomycin D. *J. Comp. Physiol. Psychol* 67:457–61

138. Norman, D. A. 1969. *Memory and Attention.* New York: Wiley. 201 pp.

139. Novick, I., Pihl, R. 1969. Effect of amphetamine on the septal syndrome in rats. *J. Comp. Physiol. Psychol.* 68:220–25

140. Olds, J. 1969. The central nervous system and the reinforcement of behavior. *Am. Psychol.* 24:114–32

141. Orzack, M. H., Taylor, C. L., Kornetsky, C. 1968. A research report on the anti-fatigue effects of magnesium pemoline. *Psychopharmacologia* 13:413–17

142. Osborn, A. G., Bunker, J. P., Cooper, L. M., Frank, G. S., Hilgard, E. R. 1967. Effects of thiopental sedation on learning and memory. *Science* 157:574–76

143. Otis, L. S., Pryor, G. T. 1968. Lack of effect of TCAP on conditioned avoidance learning in rats. *Psychon. Sci.* 11:95–96

144. Overton, D. A. 1968. Dissociated learning in drug states (state dependent learning). See Ref. 2, 918–30

145. Pagano, R. R., Bush, D. F., Martin, G., Hunt, E. B. 1969. Duration of retrograde amnesia as a function of electroconvulsive shock intensity. *Physiol. Behav.* 4:19–21

146. Palfai, T., Cornell, J. M. 1968. Effect of drugs on consolidation of classically conditioned fear. *J. Comp. Physiol. Psychol.* 66:584–89

147. Paolino, R. M., Quartermain, D., Levy, H. M. 1969. Effect of electroconvulsive shock duration on the gradient of retrograde amnesia. *Physiol. Behav.* 4:147–49

148. Paolino, R. M., Quartermain, D., Miller, N. E. 1966. Different temporal gradients of retrograde amnesia produced by carbon dioxide anesthesia and electroconvulsive shock. *J. Comp. Physiol. Psychol.* 62:270–74

149. Pfingst, B. E., King, R. A. 1969. Effects of post-training electroconvulsive shock on retention-test performance involving choice. *J. Comp. Physiol. Psychol.* 68:645–49

150. Pinel, J. P. J. 1969. A short gradient of ECS-produced amnesia in a one-trial appetitive learning situation. *J. Comp. Physiol. Psychol.* 68:650–55

151. Ibid 1970. Two types of ECS-produced disruption of one-trial training in the rat. 72:272–77

152. Pinel, J. P. J., Cooper, R. M. 1966. The relationship between incubation and ECS gradient effects. *Psychon. Sci.* 6:125–26

153. Postman, L. 1969. Mechanisms of interference in forgetting. See Ref. 13, 195–210

154. Pribram, K. H. 1969. The neurophysiology of remembering. *Sci. Am.* 220:73–86

155. Pryor, G. T., Otis, L. S., Uyeno, E. 1966. Chronic electroshock: effects on brain weight, brain chemistry and behavior. *Psychon. Sci.* 4:85–90

156. Ray, O. S., Barrett, R. J. 1969. Disruptive effects of electroconvulsive shock as a function of current level and mode of delivery. *J. Comp. Physiol. Psychol.* 67:110–16

157. Reier, C. E., Hamelberg, W. 1969. Conscious analgesia and amnesia for cardioversion. *J. Am. Med. Assoc.* 210:2052–54

158. Riddell, W. I., Herman, T. 1968. Incubation in one-trial passive avoidance learning: a cautionary note. *Psychon. Sci.* 12:335–36

159. Roberts, R. B., Flexner, J. B., Flexner, L. B. 1970. Some evidence for the involvement of adrenergic sites in the memory trace. *Proc. Nat. Acad. Sci. USA* 66:310–13

160. Robins, A. B., Thomas, G. J. 1968. Retrograde amnesia produced by localized electrical stimulation of brain through chronically implanted electrodes. *Psychon. Sci.* 12:291–92

161. Robustelli, F., Geller, A., Jarvik, M. E. 1968. Potentiation of the amnesic effect of electroconvulsive shock by detention. *Psychon. Sci.* 12:85–86

162. Rosenzweig, M. R., Leiman, A. L. 1968. Brain functions. *Ann. Rev. Psychol.* 19:55–98

163. Russell, R. W. 1964. Psychopharmacology. *Ann. Rev. Psychol.* 15:87–114

164. Sachs, E. 1962. *The role of brain electrolytes in learning and retention.* PhD thesis. Univ. Rochester

165. Schlesinger, K., Schreiber, R. A., Pryor, G. T. 1968. Effects of *p*-chlorophenylalanine on condi-

tioned avoidance learning. *Psychon. Sci.* 11:225–26

166. Schneider, A. M. 1967. Control of memory by spreading cortical depression: a case for stimulus control. *Psychol. Rev.* 74:201–15

167. Schneider, A. M., Malter, A., Advokat, C. 1969. Pretreatment effects of a single ECS and footshock plus ECS on step-down latencies of trained and untrained rats. *J. Comp. Physiol. Psychol.* 68:627–30

168. Schneider, A. M., Sherman, W. 1968. Amnesia: a function of the temporal relation of footshock to electroconvulsive shock. *Science* 159:219–21

169. Segal, D. S., Squire, L. R., Barondes, S. H. 1971. Cycloheximide: its effects on activity are dissociable from its effects on memory. *Science* 172:82

170. Sharpless, S. K. 1964. Reorganization of function in the nervous system— use and disuse. *Ann. Rev. Physiol.* 26:357–88

171. Shinkman, P. G., Kaufman, K. P. 1970. Time-dependent disruption of CER formation by post-trial hippocampal seizure. Proc. *Ann. Conv. Am. Psychol. Assoc.* 5:217–18

172. Siegel, R. K. 1967. Yeast ribonucleic acid: effects on avoidance behavior of the neonate domestic chick. *Psychopharmacologia* 12:68–77

173. Spevack, A. A., Suboski, M. D. 1969. Retrograde effects of electroconvulsive shock on learned responses. *Psychol. Bull.* 72:66–76

174. Squire, L. R., Glick, S. D., Goldfarb, J. 1971. Relearning at different times after training as affected by centrally and peripherally acting cholinergic drugs in the mouse. *J. Comp. Physiol. Psychol.* 74:41–45

175. Stamm, J. S. 1969. Electrical stimulation of monkeys' prefrontal cortex during delayed-response performance. *J. Comp. Physiol. Psychol.* 87:535–46

176. Stein, D. G., Chorover, S. L. 1968. Effects of post-trial electrical stimulation of hippocampus and caudate nucleus on maze learning in the rat. *Physiol. Behav.* 351:787–91

177. Stein, L., Wise, C. D. 1969. Release of norepinephrine from hypothalamus and amygdala by rewarding medial forebrain bundle stimulation and amphetamine. *J. Comp. Physiol Psychol.* 67:189–98

178. Steinberg, H., Tomkiewicz, M. 1968.

Drugs and Memory. See Ref. 2, 879–84

179. Stern, W. C., Heise, G. A. 1970. Failure of TCAP to facilitate acquisition of double alternation in rats. *Physiol. Behav.* 5:449–52

180. Stone, G. C., Callaway, E., Jones, R. T., Gentry, T. 1969. Chlorpromazine slows decay of visual short-term memory. *Psychon. Sci.* 16:229–30

181. Suboski, M. D., Weinstein, L. 1969. An ECS-maintained Kamin effect in rats. *J. Comp. Physiol. Psychol.* 3:510–13

182. Swanson, R., McGaugh, J. L., Cotman, C. 1969. Acetoxycycloheximide effects on one-trial inhibitory avoidance learning. *Commun. Behav. Biol.* 4:239–45

183. Tenen, S. S. 1965. Retrograde amnesia from electroconvulsive shock in a one-trial appetitive learning task. *Science* 148:1248–50

184. Tenen, S. S. 1967. The effects of *p*-chlorophenylalanine, a serotonin depletor, on avoidance acquisition, pain sensitivity and related behavior in the rat. *Psychopharmacologia* 10:204–19

185. Thierry, A. M., Javoy, F., Glowinski, J., Kety, S. S. 1968. Effects of stress on the metabolism of norepinephrine, dopamine and serotonin in the central nervous system of the rat. I. Modifications of norepinephrine turnover. *J. Pharmacol. Exp. Ther.* 163:163–71

186. Thompson, C. I., Neely, J. E. 1970. Dissociated learning in rats produced by electroconvulsive shock. *Physiol. Behav.* 5:783–86

187. Thompson, R., Dean, W. 1955. A further study on the retroactive effect of ECS. *J. Comp. Physiol. Psychol.* 48:488–91

188. Uretsky, E., McCleary, R. A. 1969. Effect of hippocampal isolation on retention. *J. Comp. Physiol. Psychol.* 68:1–8

189. Vacher, J. M., King, R. A., Miller, A. T. Jr. 1968. Failure of hypoxia to produce retrograde amnesia. *J. Comp. Physiol. Psychol.* 66:179–81

190. Weiss, B., Laties, V. G. 1969. Behavioral pharmacology and toxicology. *Ann. Rev. Pharmacol.* 9:297–326

191. Weiss, J. M., McEwen, B. S., Silva, M. T. A., Kalkut, M. F. 1969. Pituitary-adrenal influences on fear responding. *Science* 163:197–99

192. Weissman, A. 1967. Drugs and memory and learning. *Ann. Rep. Med. Chem.*, 279-87

193. White, O. A., Suboski, M. D. 1969. Resistance of one-trial discriminated avoidance to chlorpromazine. *Psychopharmacologia* 16:25-29

194. Wiener, N. I., Deutsch, J. A. 1968. The temporal aspects of anticholinergic and anticholinesterase induced amnesia for an appetitive habit. *J. Comp. Physiol. Psychol.* 66:613-17

195. Williams, M. 1969. Traumatic retrograde amnesia and normal forgetting. See Ref. 13, 75-80

196. Wimer, C., Donner, S., Martin, D. 1968. Magnesium pemoline: effects on active and passive avoidance conditioning in mice. *Psychon. Sci.* 12:23-24

197. Wimer, R. E. 1968. Bases of a facilitative effect upon retention resulting from post-trial etherization. *J. Comp. Physiol. Psychol.* 65:340-42

198. Winter, W. D. 1969. Neurophysiological classification of psychoactive drugs. In *Sleep, Physiology and Pathology: A Symposium*, ed. A. Kales, 298-307. Philadelphia: Lippincott. 360 pp.

199. Wyers, E. J., Peeke, H. V. S., Williston, J. S., Herz, M. J. 1968. Retroactive impairment of passive avoidance learning by stimulation of the caudate nucleus. *Exp. Neurol.* 22: 350-66

200. Zornetzer, S., McGaugh, J. L. 1969. Effects of electroconvulsive shock upon inhibitory avoidance: the persistence and stability of amnesia. *Commun. Behav. Biol.* 3:173-80

201. Zubin, J., Barrera, S. E. 1941. Effect of electroconvulsive therapy on memory. *Proc. Soc. Exp. Biol. Med.* 48: 596-97

ATTITUDES AND OPINIONS[1]

188

MARTIN FISHBEIN AND ICEK AJZEN[2]

Department of Psychology, University of Illinois at Urbana-Champaign

In a less than exhaustive search of the literature covered by this review, over 750 articles related to attitudes and opinions were uncovered. At the same time, numerous books and original chapters have appeared. Bem (29) and Zimbardo & Ebbesen (357) have written introductory monographs that will appeal to undergraduates, and Triandis (317) has provided a more general introduction to attitude and attitude change that will also be useful in undergraduate teaching. Somewhat more specialized but equally valuable are Cronkhite's (68) book on persuasive speech, Scheibe's (263) analysis of beliefs and values, and Greenwald, Brock & Ostrom's (111) collection of original theoretical contributions.[3]

This review will concentrate on theoretical and methodological problems at the expense of a more detailed survey of research findings. Our decision to proceed in this manner was guided not only by our conviction that these problems deserved the attention of attitude researchers, but also by our knowledge that a number of reviews covering the content of the area were available. The recent edition of the *Handbook of Social Psychology* (181) contains a number of excellent chapters relevant to the attitude area, as do the two additional volumes in the Berkowitz series of *Advances in Experimental Social Psychology* (32). Berscheid & Walster (34) have written a monograph on interpersonal attraction, and Sherwood, Barron & Fitch (280) have reviewed dissonance theory. The current status of cognitive consistency theories can be found in a valuable sourcebook by Abelson et al (1). Finally,

---

[1] This review covers material published between June 1, 1968 [where Sears & Abeles (271) ended their review] through December 31, 1970. Unlike our predecessors we have, with very few exceptions, decided not to review unpublished manuscripts or preprints of articles. Further, as will soon become obvious, we have heeded the Editorial Committee's admonition to "present a critical discussion of the current status of research in the field, rather than encyclopedic coverage of many papers." Thus when many articles were relevant for a given point or line of research, we tried to cite the two or three that we felt were the best examples.

[2] We are indebted to our colleagues Gerald L. Clore, Alice H. Eagly, Patrick R. Laughlin, Harry C. Triandis, and Nancy A. Wiggins for their critical comments on an earlier draft of this paper.

[3] Many other useful books published during our time period were given advance publicity by Sears & Abeles (271) in the 1969 *Annual Review of Psychology*, and space limitations prevent our mentioning them again here.

several reviews of all or parts of the attitude change literature are also available (e.g. 10, 62, 130, 178, 197, 226, 291). McGuire's (198) chapter is a particularly valuable overview of the general area of attitude and attitude change.

Our attempt to organize and structure the literature in the area has been guided by our conception of the relationships between beliefs, attitudes, intentions, and behaviors. The bare essentials of this conception can be stated as follows. A person learns or forms beliefs about an object. These beliefs influence his attitude toward the object. Consistent with Thurstone's (315) position, attitude is viewed as a compound in which the elements are beliefs and the affective value of the compound (i.e. attitude) is some function of the affective value of the constituent beliefs. This attitude constitutes a predisposition to respond in a generally favorable or unfavorable manner with respect to, or in the presence of, the object. It follows that an attitude is related to the totality of the person's intentions or behaviors with respect to the object, just as it is related to the totality of his beliefs about the object. However, any single belief, intention, or behavior may have little or no relation to attitude. Similarly, there is no reason to expect that any specific belief will be related to any specific intention or behavior. In contrast, it is expected that a given intention will, under most circumstances, be highly related to the corresponding behavior.

The above description is admittedly brief and has omitted feedback loops at various stages of the process. For example, an attitude once established may influence the formation of new beliefs. Similarly, performance of a particular behavior may lead to new beliefs about the object, which may in turn influence the attitude. These relationships will be discussed in greater detail in the appropriate sections below.

Considering that it is now 110 years since Herbert Spencer (298) first employed the term attitude in the psychological literature, it is somewhat incredible that the one thing on which most investigators agree is that "there exists no commonly accepted definition of the (attitude) concept" (Elizur 84, p. 36; see also 109, 163, 198). This review will attempt to show that many of the apparent inconsistencies and controversies in the attitude area are largely pseudoproblems created by this conceptual ambiguity.

SOME BASIC CONCEPTUAL AND METHODOLOGICAL PROBLEMS

In addition to a lack of agreement on the definition of attitude, different noncorrelated operations can be found for the same concept, and the identical operation is often given different conceptual labels. For example, "distraction" has often been manipulated by delayed voice feedback, performance of an irrelevant task, noise, visual displays, anticipation of a noxious experience, etc. At other times these same manipulations have been labeled effort (358), fear (128), stress (288), and arousal (65). Such practices are likely to result in what appear to be inconsistent findings. For example, two studies (98, 129) investigating the effects of "arousal" in a communication and persuasion paradigm reported contradictory results, but one study was concerned with the effects of a drug (epinephrine), while the other manipulated the volume of the persuasive message. Moreover, one study used a Likert-type opinionnaire while the other used an evaluative semantic differential to measure "attitude change." While multiple operations of a given concept may increase the generality of a conclusion beyond the specific details of any one experiment (18, 19), frequent reports of inconsistencies point to the possibility that the different manipulations and different labels employed are far from equivalent.

This relative neglect of the exact nature of the variables under investigation is in contrast to an overwhelming concern with the mechanics of independent variable manipulations. Perhaps it is a sign of the times that Aronson & Carlsmith's (19) chapter on Experimentation in Social Psychology turned out to be a guide for deceiving and manipulating subjects. The essential ingredients of a social psychological experiment are said to be of an "artistic, intuitive, ephemeral nature" (p. 1), and part of being a good experimental social psychologist presumably "involves learning to say 'whoops' convincingly" (p. 45). Furthermore, "it is extremely important for all subjects to be brought to the identical point by the manipulation of the independent variable" (p. 46) even if different procedures are necessary to accomplish this. While this recommendation cannot be rejected out of hand, it is obvious that it is justifiable only when the means employed are objective, i.e. communicable. This is the minimal prerequisite for replication which, unfortunately, is all too often found to be impossible (e.g. 60). This concern with the mechanics of manipulation has come at the expense of attending to what is being manipulated, and it has led to a widespread neglect of the reliability and validity of dependent variables (114, 219, 321). Further, the use of deception often associated with this approach has itself created new kinds of problems (268, 306).

Aronson & Carlsmith's (19) argument that the source of ideas for experiments or hypotheses "is not terribly important" (p. 37) reflects much current research in which an isolated but appealing hypothesis is selected on some intuitive basis. Even in the face of a large number of negative findings, some investigators will continue their attempts to confirm this "true" hypothesis rather than reject it. Usually each new study spots a procedural weakness in the preceding study that "if corrected" would confirm the "true" hypothesis or explain the inconsistency. Theoretical and substantive issues are de-emphasized, and the result is an accumulation of nomological studies designed to test intuitive hypotheses about the effects of procedural variations. Research of this kind has tended to be noncumulative and has failed to produce a systematically integrated body of knowledge (168, 200).

Another set of problems is related to the statistical treatment and interpretation of data. One cannot fail to be impressed by the widespread mistreatment of data, abuse of statistical procedures, and the frequency with which invalid conclusions are drawn. For example, factorial experimental designs are frequently analysed by simple t-tests. This is particularly inexcusable when an appropriate analysis of variance would yield nonsignificant findings.[4]

Frequently, nonsignificant results fail to deter an investigator. If the results were close to significance, he may simply discuss the effects as if they were significant, pointing to mean differences in the expected directions. The APA publication manual, however, states that "Such results are most economically interpreted as a function of chance and should be reported as nonsignificant" (p. 13). Another practice is to manipulate data until a significant result is obtained. This can usually be accomplished post hoc by combining conditions, subdividing the sample and doing internal analyses, transforming the dependent variables, applying different (and usually weaker) statistical tests to the results, etc. For an exchange concerning the use of many of these techniques, see (24, 25) and (251).

Even when data analyses are appropriate, the conclusions drawn are often unwarranted or clear overgeneralizations. A good illustration of the latter problem can be found in Barber & Silver's (25) excellent critique of experimenter bias effects. Other examples of how different investigators can reach different conclusions on the basis of the same set of data can be found in the exchanges between Deutscher (73) and Ajzen et al (6), or Schuchman & Perry (283) and Bauer (26).

Although these problems cannot be resolved overnight, we can draw the reader's attention to some recommended practices which, if followed, might alleviate a number of the difficulties noted above. First, concerning multiple operations and labels, Gulliksen (114) has recently reviewed procedures that can be used to determine the equivalence of measures. Similarly, new factor analytic (142) and analysis of variance (156) techniques have been developed for analyzing multitrait-multimethod matrices. Path analysis has also been used in this context (e.g. 331) and has redirected attention to problems of measurement reliability and stability (e.g. 37, 123, 331). One interesting outcome of this latter approach has been the conclusion that panel data do not provide an adequate basis for causal inferences (e.g. 78, 331) despite earlier claims to the contrary (352).

Despite repeated warnings by Cronbach and others (e.g. 67), the widespread use of change or difference scores in the attitude literature has hardly diminished. Since these scores tend to lead to invalid conclusions, we can only join in recommending that this practice be discontinued. In most cases, scores of this type can be avoided by using post-test only designs, by including both pre- and post-test scores in an analysis of variance, or by other means.

While the 5 percent significance level is an arbitrary convention, its utility is evidenced by the literature. Much contradiction and controversy

[4] When the overall analysis of variance does justify individual mean comparisons, the relative advantages of different procedures have been discussed by Petrinovich & Hardyck (229) and Davis (70).

might have been avoided if findings not reaching this criterion had been rejected. For an excellent defense of the significance requirement see (340). It appears desirable that research reports also include estimates of the percent of variance accounted for by the experimental effects (97, 322). A table for estimating the proportion of variance has been provided by Friedman (97). Fleiss (95) has discussed alternative estimation procedures.

Given the various problems discussed above, we were not surprised to find that even a careful reading of summaries and abstracts of articles could not provide an accurate picture of the field. In this review we have attempted to examine actual procedures and findings, and we have not relied on an author's own conclusions. In particular, whenever an appropriate analysis of the data showed nonsignificant results, the findings were considered to be negative. Some authors may therefore find that their work has been given an interpretation in this review that differs from their own.

THE SOCIAL PSYCHOLOGY OF THE PSYCHOLOGICAL EXPERIMENT

Continued concern with problems of demand characteristics, experimenter bias, evaluation apprehension, etc reflects an awareness of problems related to the internal and external validity of experiments. To a large extent, these problems fall into three broad categories: 1. The subject forms hypotheses to explain the sequence of experimental events that he observes. These hypotheses may be related to the purpose of the experiment or to contingencies between his own behavior and other events. 2. The subject forms beliefs that the experimenter expects or would like him to behave in certain ways. 3. The subject is or is not willing to meet the perceived expectations of the experimenter.

Demand characteristics, evaluation apprehension, experimenter bias, etc have typically been viewed as variables that affect behavior only in research settings. However, when viewed as related to the formation of beliefs about the situation, about the consequences of behavior, about the expectations of other people, and as related to motivational factors, these "biasing" variables are simply specific instances of the kinds of variables that influence behavior in general. Indeed, the present classification is based upon Dulany's (77) analysis of the determinants of human behavior. Page (e.g. 224) has made similar distinctions.

There seems to be little doubt that experimental manipulations may affect hypotheses that are being formed about the purpose of the experiment (e.g. 102, 224, 225, 289). For example, variations in communicator credibility (225) and in the unanimity of disagreeing majorities in a conformity situation (102) were found to influence subjects' beliefs that the experiment was concerned with persuasion. Evidence from verbal conditioning experiments makes it clear that subjects also form hypotheses about the contingencies between their own behavior and reinforcing events (e.g. 77, 224). There is also abundant evidence for experimenter bias effects (e.g. 24, 25, 251, 252). It can be argued that these effects influence the subject's beliefs about what is expected of him. Available evidence indicates that these biases are not likely to occur unless there is an intentional influence attempt by the experimenter (24, 25, 99). Finally, evidence suggests that the experimental setting can influence a subject's willingness to perform what he perceives is expected of him. For example, when evaluation apprehension is produced by the experiment, subjects will tend to respond in a direction of favorable self presentation, whether this is consistent or inconsistent with their perceptions of the experimenter's expectations (e.g. 290).

A number of factors have been found to influence the above effects. These include: volunteering which may increase the likelihood of belief formation and of motivation to meet the experimenter's perceived expectations (138, 139, 254); overall suspicion (306); use of a pretest (254); and the subjects' sophistication [e.g. previous experience in experiments, knowledge of psychology, time of semester at which the experiment is conducted (see 135, 224)]. None of the factors discussed however, have consistently produced significant results (e.g. 27, 90, 102, 332), probably because different experimental settings vary in the extent to which they allow beliefs and hypotheses to be formed. Since available evidence clearly demonstrates the existence of demand characteristics, experimenter bias, and evaluation apprehension (e.g. 25, 77, 224, 252, 290), little can be gained by further demonstrations of these effects. Research should now be directed at investigating the formation of beliefs about behavioral contingencies and about expectations of the experimenter, as well as at variables influencing the subject's motivation to meet the perceived expectations.

One other methodological issue that has been raised concerns the use of role playing (96). Empirical comparisons indicate that role playing may reproduce some of the more obvious, but perhaps not the subtle, effects of a traditional experiment (e.g. 335, 339).

Defining Beliefs, Attitudes, and Behavioral Intentions

Most investigators are not concerned with distinctions between beliefs, attitudes, opinions, and intentions. The prevailing view seems to be that these distinctions are not warranted since these variables have not been shown to behave differently (198). In practice, therefore, many investigators intuitively select variables and particular operations that seem to fit the purposes of their investigations. In the literature reviewed, we found almost 500 different operations designed to measure "attitude." They ranged from standard attitude scales (e.g. Likert, Thurstone, Guttman, the Semantic Differential, and others) to indices across various verbal items that may or may not have been subjected to some selection procedure (e.g. factor analysis), to single statements of feeling, knowledge, or intentions, to single behaviors and physiological measures. Indices across verbal items have been based on weighted or unweighted sums or averages, difference scores, similarity measures, squared differences, differences between differences, etc.

While it would be desirable to have general laws that would hold across any kind of dependent measure of "attitude," the great diversity of such measures makes this highly unlikely. For example, changes in a person's judgment that a given action is justifiable may not be accompanied by any change in his judgment of how good or bad that action is, who should engage in the action, or any other evaluation of the behavior. Similarly, a manipulation that is shown to affect a person's judgment that an object has a given attribute may not have any effect on other judgments concerning the object, such as: attributions of other characteristics to the object, liking for the object, willingness to perform various behaviors toward it, or the actual performance of such behaviors. Since minute differences in independent variable manipulations have sometimes been shown to greatly affect the outcome of an experiment (e.g. 69, 153), we may expect the same to be true for such gross variations in the dependent measures.

A review of the literature strongly supports this contention. Over 200 of the studies reviewed employed more than one dependent measure of an "attitudinal" variable, and about 70 percent obtained different results when different measures of "attitude" were used (e.g. 212, 276, 287). It is worth noting that since the different variables were all viewed as "attitudes," there was usually no expectation that different results would be obtained.

Some studies reported individual items as well as sums or averages across these items and here, too, different results were frequently obtained (e.g. 152, 189, 276). Some investigators did not bother to compute a summary index but merely reported individual analyses of each separate item (e.g. 132, 169). Since significant results are usually obtained only for one or two of the items, it appears to be unjustified to take this as evidence in support of the hypothesis. Equally unjustified is the common practice of obtaining a summary index without any analysis that supports the equivalence of the component measures. As many studies have shown, the component items may yield completely different results (see e.g. 63). Clearly, when the single label "attitude" is attached to all of these different and unrelated measures, results of different studies, as well as generalizations about attitude, have to appear contradictory and confusing. One step that seems imperative if this dilemma is to be resolved is to establish a meaningful classification of the great diversity of "attitudinal" measures commonly in use. One classification that has repeatedly been proposed is the age-old trilogy of affect, cognition, and conation. While many social psychologists appear to agree with such a classification, they seldom make use of it in their research.

Attitude.—Many of the dependent variables that have been used can be seen as measures that attempt to place the subject along a bipolar dimension of *affect* with respect to a given object. Indeed, all standard attitude scales (e.g. Thurstone, Likert and Guttman scales and the evaluative dimension of the Semantic Differential) arrive at a single number designed to index this general evaluation or feeling of favorableness toward the object in question. Other dependent measures that also appear to assess the subject's location on the affective dimension are the subject's self rating of liking for the object (e.g. "like-dislike"), of his favorability with respect to the object (e.g.

"favorable-unfavorable," "approve-disapprove"), or his evaluation of the object on a single "good-bad" scale (e.g. 104, 119, 295). Although published data concerning the evaluative nature of other single items are available (218), it cannot be assumed that such items will prove to measure affect under all circumstances; items may take on different meanings with respect to different concepts (e.g. 218) or for different subjects (e.g. 337).

Since there is widespread agreement that affect is an essential part of the attitude concept and that Thurstone, Likert, and Guttman scales and the evaluative dimension of the Semantic Differential are measures of attitude, we suggest that the term "attitude" only be used with reference to a person's location on the affective dimension vis-à-vis a given object. When studies have obtained more than one such measure of attitude toward the same object, the results were almost always identical. Evidence for the convergent validity of standard attitude scales and other affective measures continues to accumulate (e.g. 23, 94, 222, 261).[5]

Beliefs.—Another set of dependent variables are the subject's perception that an object or person has certain characteristics, qualities, or attibutes, or is related to some other concept, object, or person. Similar to these are measures of the subject's judgment that a given behavior, policy, or strategy has certain characteristics or leads to certain goals, values, or other outcomes (e.g. 27, 136, 169). Typically, judgments of this kind are elicited in one of three ways. First, the relationship between object and concept may be presented in the form of a statement and the subject is asked to make some judgment such as "agree-disagree," "true-false," "yes-no," "very much-not at all," "likely-unlikely," "probable-improbable," etc. The judgment may also be a rating of the probability of the relationship in terms of percentages or some other rating scale. Second, an object may be presented and the subject rates the degree to which that object is related to some other object or concept. For example, a stimulus person may be rated on one or more bipolar adjective scales, an event may be rated as justified or unjustified, etc. A third technique is to present the object and let the subject indicate relations to other concepts in a free response format. Sentence completion tasks, free association paradigms, etc, are examples. For a further discussion of some of these techniques see Triandis (317).

Underlying all of these judgments seems to be a common dimension of probability. In our view, it is this kind of judgment that has typically been regarded as *cognition* or belief. Indeed, use of the subjective probability concept in relation to beliefs has increased in recent years (e.g. 11, 68, 94, 116, 155, 263, 328, 348). We would recommend use of the label "belief" in those cases where the measure employed can be interpreted as placing the

---

[5] Upshaw and his associates (223, 320, 321) have demonstrated that conditions can be created under which single-item self-rating scales and Thurstone scales will yield different results.

subject along a dimension of subjective probability involving an object or behavior and some related concept.

In contrast to measures of attitude which always attempt to assess the same underlying dimension of affect, measures of beliefs with respect to the same object are not necessarily related to each other and may yield quite different results. Each belief regarding the given object links that object with a different concept and thus constitutes a different probability dimension. Thus it is hardly surprising that in many studies where two or more beliefs with respect to a given object have been measured, completely different results have emerged. For example, Bean et al (27) measured beliefs that "there are drawbacks to the way the president is presently elected" and "the president should be elected by Congress." They found only a low correlation between these two beliefs, and identical statistical analyses of the two items yielded completely different results. Similarly, Byrne & Griffitt (53) obtained measures of beliefs about another person's intelligence, morality, adjustment, and knowledge of current events, and again identical statistical analyses yielded different results for each item. Clearly, if it is possible to obtain conflicting results of this kind within a single study, little comparability can be expected across investigations that differ not only with respect to the measures of beliefs employed but also with respect to other characteristics.

Behavioral intentions.—The third general class of variables is assessed by the subject's indication of his intention or his willingness to engage in various behaviors with respect to or in the presence of a given person or object (e.g. 8, 35, 232). Measures of this type usually present the subject with a stimulus person or object and with one or more behaviors that could be performed vis-à-vis that person or object. The subject indicates his willingness to perform the behavior(s) on scales such as: "would-would not," "willing-unwilling," "intend-not intend," "will try-will not try," etc. Again, a probability dimension can be seen to underlie these judgments, but the probability dimension now links the subject to some behavior with respect to an object. Responses of this kind have usually been classified as *conation* or behavioral intention. It is thus our recommendation that the term "behavioral intention" be used when the measure employed can be interpreted as placing the subject along a subjective probability dimension involving a relation between himself and some action. As in the case of beliefs, different intentions will represent different probability dimensions and thus will not necessarily be highly related.

The distinction between attitude, beliefs, and intentions can be further clarified by a consideration of the relations between these classes of variables. Virtually all standard attitude instruments obtain a score that is based on a variety of beliefs or intentions. However, not every belief or intention with respect to the attitude object will meet the criteria of a particular scaling technique. Once a satisfactory set of items has been selected, the score based on these items is interpreted as an index locating the individual along an affective dimension with respect to the object, i.e. as an attitude. Indeed, there is strong evidence that when at least minimal attention has been paid to the construction of the index, significant relations have been obtained between the index and some standardized measure of attitude (e.g. 23, 188, 309). However, there may be little relation between single items and an index across such items. Thus, if a single belief or intention is to be used as an index of attitude, evidence has to be provided for a high correlation between responses to that item and some standard measure of attitude.

In sum, when the judgment called for implies an underlying dimension of subjective probability between an object and some concept, the label "belief" should be applied. When the judgment can be interpreted as a judgment of subjective probability linking the person and some behavior, the concept "behavioral intention" should be used. In the absence of appropriate evidence, such judgments should not be taken as measures of attitude, irrespective of the investigator's intuition regarding their affective nature. The concept "attitude" should only be employed where there is strong evidence that the obtained measure places an individual along a dimension of affect.

ATTITUDE MEASUREMENT

Before turning to substantive issues, a brief survey of recent publications in the area of attitude measurement may be in order, although there have been relatively few new developments. Due to space limitations, we have decided to restrict our review to a few selected issues that we found most interesting.

While in our earlier discussion we have defined attitude as a single affective dimension, belief and intention as probability dimensions, and a person's location on these dimensions as his attitude, belief, or intention, respectively, it should be clear that other characteristics of these dimensions may also be considered. It has been recognized for some time that in addition to a person's location on a dimension, his acceptance of adjacent locations can also be indexed (e.g. 277). Mortensen & Sereno (209) have shown that such indices of latitudes of acceptance and rejection can be obtained on graphic scales. With respect to the related own categories procedure for the measurement of involvement, Reich (237) has suggested use of the information theory measure of uncertainty as a more exact index.

A considerable part of Scott's (269) chapter on attitude measurement in the new edition of the *Handbook of Social Psychology* is devoted to measures of homogeneity, differentiation, etc. Other attempts to develop and utilize measures of this kind can be found in various sources (e.g. 94, 210, 270). In addition to providing descriptive indices of the cognitive and conative domains, these measures can be particularly useful in accounting for the differential effects of persuasive communication or other manipulations on individuals who have the same attitude score.

There appears to be some question about the degree to which judgments of preference or choice can be used as measures of a single dimension of affect. It has been shown that under certain conditions, assumptions of transitivity in preference judgments (319) and of linear combinations in information integration (e.g. 83) may be unwarranted. This is particularly true when stimuli can be evaluated in terms of a set of multidimensional attributes. It has been suggested that these problems may be overlooked when group data instead of individual data are analyzed (83, 319). For most practical purposes, however, the assumptions of transitivity and linearity seem to be reasonable (e.g. 14, 249).

Early multidimensional approaches were concerned primarily with cognitive domains in terms of similarity space. Recent developments of particular interest to the attitude area are attempts to relate the similarity space to preference judgments (108, 341). An excellent survey of some of the multidimensional techniques has been provided by Wiggins (336). Also useful is Green & Carmone's (108) comparison of a number of nonmetric unfolding techniques. Two new developments, the Carroll & Chang (56) model and Guttman's (265) smallest space analysis are also noteworthy. Examples of applications of these models are reported by Wish, Deutsch & Biener (341) and by Robinson & Hefner (242), respectively.

Readers interested in other issues and problems of attitude measurement are directed to Summers' (308) collection of 36 papers, including 9 original contributions. Particularly noteworthy are chapters on indirect measurement techniques (162), on uses of the pupil response as a measure of attitude (342), and an introduction to multidimensional scaling (255). We are also delighted to note that Green's (107) excellent and now classic chapter on attitude measurement has appeared as a separate publication. The manifold uses of the semantic differential are exhibited in Snider & Osgood's (297) collection of 52 articles, one of which (337) is an original contribution concerning individual differences in underlying semantic dimensions (337). Of related interest is Kuusinen's (167) attempt to use the semantic differential as a measure of denotative structure. Two new collections of scales that have been used in research on social and political attitudes have been presented (243, 244).

Problems related to standard attitude scaling continue to attract research. Studies have been published dealing with response biases and response sets (e.g. 74, 100, 326), and with the influence of a judge's opinion on his judgments (e.g. 166, 234, 320). Studies showing the differential effects of perspective on content and self-rating scales (e.g. 223, 321) are an interesting application of this work. Some new developments in Guttman scaling procedures have appeared (e.g. 214, 313), and work has continued on the development of indirect and unobtrusive measures (e.g. 44, 66, 281, 343). Interesting lines of research are reported on the use of nonverbal cues as indicants of attitude (e.g. 48, 201), and on the accuracy of perceiving nonverbal communication (e.g. 171, 203).

Turning to an examination of the literature in terms of its contents, we shall first consider problems related to the formation of beliefs, attitudes, and intentions. We shall then deal with attempts to produce changes in these variables, and finally we shall review some studies that have examined the relations between these variables and overt behavior.

BELIEFS

While the centrality of the belief concept has been stressed by several investigators (e.g. 68, 221, 246, 263), relatively little research in the attitude area has focused on belief formation. In fact, much of the information about this process comes to us in the form of incidental data collection or manipulation checks. In a typical study, the subject is exposed to a complex situation about which he holds few beliefs. After exposure he will have formed beliefs about some of the objects in the situation. Assuming that in the course of the experiment two stimuli (X) and (Y) have appeared and a third stimulus (Z) has not, the subject's beliefs can be elicited by asking him to make one of three probability judgments:

1. (O) said (X is Y)
2. (X) is (Y)
3. (X) is (Z)

That is, a subject may be asked to recall whether in the context of the experiment someone related (X) and (Y), whether he in fact believes that (X) is (Y), or he may be asked to make some inference (Z) about (X).

BELIEFS THAT (O) SAID (X IS Y)

While a distinction between the first two categories is often important, and while separate measurements of these two types of beliefs can easily be obtained, many studies confound this distinction by not making it clear to the subject which of these two judgments he is expected to make. This frequently occurs when a single "information" or "reception" test is administered after a persuasive communication, or with respect to various manipulation checks. It is often not clear whether the subject's judgment indicates his ability to recall or recognize what he was told, or his belief that what he was told is true. Two studies (220, 359) separately analyzed clear recall and structured "reception" or "learning" measures, and the different measures yielded contradictory results. For example, a visual distractor influenced responses to a multiple choice test but did not significantly affect recall (220). In at least 13 studies, authors' descriptions of multiple choice or other types of structured tests made it impossible to determine which of these measures was obtained, and the results of these studies tended to be inconsistent. For example, one study (356) found a positive relationship between acute self esteem and "reception," while another (258) reported a negative relationship. Similarly, a significant effect of communicator credibility on "reception" was found in one study (129) but not in another (128).

In contrast, consistent findings were obtained in studies where it was quite clear that the subject's task was to recall or recognize what the experimenter or a communicator said. As might be expected, recall was influenced by drug-produced arousal (98) and by some (e.g. 115, 359) but not all (e.g. 220, 358) types of distractors. However, it was not influenced by communicator credibility (147, 148) or attractiveness (292), and no difference was found in a subject's ability to recall information that was consistent or inconsistent with his own position (e.g. 43, 143, 187). Although many studies investigated the effects of individual difference variables on "reception," we found only one study that had a clear measure of recall, and its results were ambiguous. Although a low negative correlation was obtained between authoritarianism and recall, authoritarianism was not significant in an analysis of variance (148).

It thus appears that clear measures of recall are relatively uninfluenced by the subject's beliefs or attitudes, and it is doubtful that personality variables will be found to have consistent effects on recall. One possible exception is Steiner's (301) finding that subjects were less likely to recall negative than positive evaluations of themselves, although Holmes (134) only found a tendency for subjects to recall more pleasant than unpleasant experiences.

Beliefs that (X) is (Y)

In addition to forming beliefs of the type "O said (X is Y)," the subject may actually come to believe that (X) is related to (Y) with a certain probability. Evidence concerning formation of beliefs on the basis of information contained in oral or written communications is scarce since, as mentioned earlier, "reception" and "learning" tests frequently do not distinguish between recall of message content (i.e. reception) and the subject's own beliefs (i.e. acceptance of message content). In contrast, there is abundant evidence that beliefs of the type (X) is (Y) are formed on the basis of direct observation. For example, subjects were found to report veridically the attractiveness of a female experimenter (287), and in another study (204) they formed accurate beliefs about the amount of information a confederate revealed about himself.

Other evidence of relevance to the notion that subjects form beliefs on the basis of observation comes from studies dealing with the role of awareness in verbal conditioning of attitudes. Almost without exception, studies published in recent years indicate that conditioning does not occur unless the subject forms beliefs about the relationship between conditioned and unconditioned stimuli[6] (e.g. 72, 141, 180, 224).

[6] The occurrence of a conditioned response in the presence of contingency awareness does not necessarily imply that the subject was aware of the experimenter's expectations and that he behaved in accordance with them (e.g. 355). The distinction here is between "hypothesis of the distribution of reinforcement" and "behavioral hypothesis" (77), or more recently, between "contingency awareness" and "demand awareness" (e.g. 224). This latter type of awareness requires an inference on the part of the subject. Once this inference is made, the subject may or may not be motivated to comply with what he believes to be the expectations of the experimenter.

While the above studies provide evidence that belief formation occurs on the basis of observation, the actual process whereby beliefs are formed has been investigated more directly in the framework of mathematical models dealing with learning and decision making (e.g. 263, 294). A review of this body of research is beyond the scope of the present paper, but its relevance for belief formation should be recognized. Jones et al (151) utilized this approach in the attitude area and found that subjects formed beliefs about the trial-by-trial success of another person such that the predicted probability of success on trial n was a function of the proportion of successes on trials 1 through $n-1$.

INFERENCES

The above discussions indicate that in the course of an experiment subjects tend to form beliefs that reflect the things they hear or see, and under most circumstances the beliefs formed tend to be fairly veridical. In the period reviewed there is practically no evidence to support the notion that the subject's own beliefs, attitudes, or personality characteristics have any systematic effects on his beliefs about events occurring within the experimental setting. This should not be taken to mean that all types of beliefs are unaffected by variables of this kind. In fact, the most characteristic feature of inferences is that in addition to the stimulus situation per se, the individual uses residues of past experience to make his judgments. Inferential beliefs can be seen as falling along a continuum in terms of minimal to maximal use of such experiential residues. At one extreme the beliefs may be almost entirely self-generated. For example, Miller's (205) subjects were asked to "record their impressions" of a stranger on an adjective preference scale. The only information they had about the stranger was his or her photograph. On the other extreme are those judgments that are based almost exclusively on observable features of the stimulus. For instance, McEwen & Greenberg (194, 195) varied the intensity of modifiers and verbs included in a message. In one study subjects were asked to rate the potency of the speaker's language and in the other the extremity of his position. In both cases the appropriate inference was made.

There is abundant evidence that inferences are influenced by the person's attitude. In fact, many indirect measures of attitude (e.g. the own categories procedure, error choice tests) are based on the assumption that responses to certain statements are primarily determined by the subject's own attitude. Brigham & Cook (44) have recently validated a new measurement technique by showing that subjects' attitudes were related to their judgments of the effectiveness of arguments. In an unrelated context, Greenwald's (110) subjects believed that arguments they agreed with were more valid than arguments they disagreed with.

Attitude researchers have paid surprisingly little attention to a considerable body of literature on human judgment that deals directly with inference processes. Slovic & Lichtenstin (294) have pointed out that more than 600 studies concerned with information utilization in human judgment and decision making have appeared in the last 10 years; they discussed various regression models, Bayesian analyses, and Anderson's (14) functional measurement. The regression approach has frequently been employed in studies on cue utilization. A typical study might ask the subject to judge a person's intelligence on the basis of various cues such as his grade point average, aptitude test scores, credit hours attempted, etc. Multiple regression analyses result in estimate of the weights placed on the different cues in making inferences. These "objective" weights have sometimes been compared with the subject's own estimate of each cue's importance (e.g. 307), and the results indicate little correspondence. Attempts have also been made to compare the predictive utility of linear and nonlinear or configural combinatory models (e.g. 338). In general, even when evidence for configurality was obtained, the linear model accounted for most of the variance in the data. These and other questions are similar to some of the issues that have been raised within the attitude area. While a review of this body of literature is clearly beyond the scope of the present paper, its importance for an understanding of inferential belief formation can hardly be underestimated, and it is to be hoped that more attention will be paid to it.

In contrast to cue utilization and Bayesian approaches, functional measurement has often been applied in the attitude area. Most research conducted has dealt with evaluative judgments, and some recent studies will be discussed below. At least one investigation, however, has applied this approach to belief judgments. Himmelfarb & Senn (131) had their subjects judge the social status of people described in terms of income, occupation, and education. Contrary to the author's expectations, evidence for discounting of inconsistent information, previously reported with respect to evaluative judgments (e.g. Anderson & Jacobson 15), was not found. These results indicate that judgments along a probability dimension may yield different results than similar judgments along an affective dimension. Support for this conclusion comes from the results obtained in studies by Heise (122, 124) in which he regressed the evaluative, potency, and activity ratings of subjects, verbs, and objects in isolation onto similar ratings of each word in the context of a sentence. Different regression models were required to fit the data for each type of judgment. Wyer & Schwartz (351) also obtained different results for similar types of judgments along different belief dimensions.

One implication of these findings is that different combination rules seem to be necessary for judgments involving attitudes and various belief dimensions. This has apparently been recognized by investigators in the cue utilization area who have been concerned with discovering the appropriate combination rule for the judgment under consideration, while most research in the attitude area seems to assume that the same laws will hold across a wide variety of evaluative and probability judgments.

Belief attribution.—Inferential belief formation has also been studied within the mainstream of attitude research. Some of this research has been stimulated by a renewed interest in Heider's (121) "naive analysis of action" which has come to be called "attribution theory" (Kelley 158). The term "attribution" has been used to describe almost any kind of inference, but consistent with recent trends, it will be used here only with reference to inferences about stable dispositions of people based on information about or direct observation of their actions. While various theoretical papers on attribution processes have appeared (e.g. 150, 158, 302), few of the recently published studies seem to be direct extensions or tests of the underlying theory. Instead, most of these studies seem to be based on intuitive hypotheses, and their relationships to a systematic theory of attribution are usually left unstated, although there are some notable exceptions (e.g. 4, 151, 160, 275, 330).

The value of attribution theory as a guide to research can be seen with reference to studies on the attribution of responsibility for negative or positive actions. Shaver (273, 274) failed to replicate Walster's (324) earlier finding that attribution of responsibility for an auto accident was related to the severity of the accident's outcomes. However, in comparison to a dissimilar driver, a driver described as similar to the subject in terms of "attitudes, values, and feelings about the world," was perceived to be less responsible and more conscientious. This was interpreted as the subject's attempt to dissociate himself from a person who had caused an accident, but it may also be interpreted as the result of differential attraction to the driver, produced by the manipulation of perceived similarity.

Landy & Aronson (170 also investigated attribution of responsibility for an auto accident, manipulating attractiveness of victim and of defendant directly through positive and negative descriptions. In contrast to Shaver's findings, neither of these manipulations had a significant effect on the perceived guilt of the driver, although the proposed sentence (i.e. years imprisonment) was significantly smaller for the attractive than the non-attractive defendant. The victim's attractiveness was found to be related to sentencing only after the data from two studies had been pooled. In a somewhat related study, a pupil was reported to have been struck by a positively or negatively described teacher (276). Attractiveness of the teacher was found to be unrelated to his perceived responsibility (i.e. how much he was to blame for the incident), but consistent with Landy & Aronson's results, sentencing (i.e. whether he should be dismissed or supported) was more severe for the unattractive teacher.

These inconsistent findings with respect to attribution of responsibility are not surprising when it is realized that "responsibility" can be interpreted in terms of association, commission, foreseeability, intentionality, and justification (Heider 121, Shaw & Reitan 275). The importance of these "levels of causality" was demonstrated by Shaw and his associates (e.g. 275), who showed that these levels interacted with the severity of positive or negative outcomes in determining perceived responsibility. The level of causality was left ambiguous in the other studies, and thus it is conceivable that the dependent measure of "responsibility" may have been interpreted in terms of instrumentality (i.e. is the outcome the result of the actor's behavior?), foreseeability, intentionality, or justification. Since the effect of outcome intensity and other variables such as attractiveness will depend on level of causality, inconsistent findings are to be expected whenever these levels are neither manipulated nor made an explicit part of the dependent variable measure.

In support of the differential effects of outcome intensity, Breznitz & Kugelmass (42) found that the relative rating of a child's returning £1000 was more positive than returning £100, but less positive than returning £1. Similarly, a subject's imagined pride or shame for the performance of another person was related to the degree of that person's success, i.e. to outcome intensity (330). More importantly, felt pride or shame was influenced by information about the other person's ability and motivation. i.e. by levels of causality.

Several studies have examined internal versus external attribution of responsibility for success cr failure. One fairly consistent finding is that success is usually attributed more to internal than external causes (e.g. 305, 330). However, it appears that manipulation of the ability variable interacts differentially with actual success or failure in determining internal versus external attribution, depending upon whether such attributions are made to one's self (88) or to other people (330). Jones et al (151) also found differential attributions to self and others. In comparison to a series of descending successes, a series of ascending successes led to attributions of less ability and intelligence in others but to greater self attributions of ability and confidence. These results suggest that, contrary to recent analyses (28, 302), the process of self attribution may not be identical to the process whereby attributions are made to other people.

While the research reviewed above is in some way concerned with attributions to self and to others, the central issues of attribution theory have often been neglected. Attribution theory deals primarily with specifying the conditions under which attributions to a person will or will not be made. It has been suggested that levels of causality, the actor's perceived decision freedom, prior probability of his behavior, and perceived consequences of the behavior all affect the likelihood that an attribution will be made (4, 121, 150, 302). It is to be hoped that future research on attribution processes will be concerned with some of these central issues, or at least show awareness of them, so that an integrated and theoretically relevant body of knowledge may emerge.

Syllogistic reasoning.—Another approach to the inference process, and perhaps the most promising new development, is the increased utilization of subjective probability models. Holt and Watts (137, 329) have continued research on McGuire's (196) probabilistic model of syllogistic reasoning. Probability theory has been used in studying relationships among beliefs, and in the tradition of McGuire's work, the effects of change in one belief on changes in related beliefs have been examined (348, 349). Generally speaking, the relationships between objective probabilities (derived from probability theory) held reasonably well with respect to measures of subjective probabilities

Cronkhite (68) has developed a "paradigm of persuasion" that is phrased in terms of subjective probabilities and incorporates some notions from Toulmin (316), McGuire (196), and Fishbein (91). Although as yet untested, it is noteworthy as a first step toward an integration of these approaches. The development of viable probability formulations within the attitude area is admittedly still in its infancy, but some interesting applications have already emerged. For example, with respect to two elements, A and B, Wyer (346) has used probability notions to define a continuum ranging from redundancy $[p(AB) > p(A)p(B)]$ to inconsistency $[p(AB) < p(A)p(B)]$. As Wyer has noted, this measure of logical inconsistency can be varied independently of evaluative inconsistency. This approach defies belief explicitly in terms of a probability dimension and directs research to the consideration of relationships between different beliefs. Further, since probability theory specifies a complex pattern of interrelations between beliefs, it points out that a given experimental manipulation will tend to have differential impacts on a set of such beliefs. This makes it clear that unless the relationships between different beliefs employed in a given study are known, a general prediction is unlikely to be confirmed with respect to all beliefs although it may hold for some.

While this approach provides a useful and content-free theoretical framework in which systematic research on the formation, integration, and change of beliefs can be studied, it must be recognized that laws of objective probability may not always hold with respect to beliefs, i.e. subjective probabilities. For example, the revision of subjective probabilities upon the receipt of new information tends to be conservative in comparison to Bayesian predictions (81). In the context of attitude research, there is evidence that syllogistic reasoning can be influenced by wishful thinking and other factors (e.g. 137, 196).

Trait inferences.—Despite such difficulties, probability formulations may find useful applications in various areas. For example, Warr & Smith (328) compared the predictive power of six probability models of trait inferences. Specifically, they attempted to predict the conditional probability of trait C given traits A and B. In terms of the criteria employed, all models were highly successful although slight differences in predictive power were obtained. Research of this kind leads to a consideration of one final approach to inferential belief formation, namely, trait inferences. Initial impetus to work on trait inferences has come from Asch's (22) studies of impression formation and Bruner & Tagiuri's (47) discussion of person perception. Again, most of the relevant research has been conducted outside the attitude area and no attempt will be made to cover it in detail. Recent contributions and reviews are available (e.g. 120, 327).

Of particular interest is a series of studies stimulated by Peabody's (227) distinction between evaluative and descriptive aspects in trait inferences. Arguing that these two aspects had been confounded in previous trait inference studies, he used a procedure that orthogonally manipulated the evaluative and descriptive similarity of adjective pairs. Consider, for example, the positive trait "cautious" and an inference to the dimension defined by the endpoints "bold" (positive) and "timid" (negative). Peabody argued that if trait inferences were based on evaluative consistency, a person who was described as cautious should also be judged as bold. But if inferences follow descriptive consistency, he should be judged as timid. Contrary to expectations based on theories of affective or evaluational consistency, Peabody (227) found that trait inferences were determined more by descriptive than evaluative similarity. Further, a factor analysis of the total set of trait inferences failed to reveal a clearly evaluative factor, which he took as further support for the dominance of the descriptive aspect. More recently, however, it has been argued that Peabody may have underestimated the importance of evaluative similarity (80, 89, 228, 250). For example, where a multidimensional scaling approach was used and where the data were similarity indices between Peabody's traits (250), and when responses to an adjective check list containing the same traits were factor analyzed (80), clear evaluative dimensions were obtained. Extending Peabody's procedure, Felipe (89) found descriptive consistency for some inferences and evaluative consistency for others. He concluded that inferences are likely to follow descriptive similarity whenever this is possible, i.e. when the traits share some degree of denotative meaning. In the absence of denotative similarity, inferences are likely to be based on evaluative similarity. It must be realized that a precise test of Felipe's conclusion is difficult since no agreed-upon instrument for the measurement of denotative meaning is currently available, although Osgood's (217) recent work on semantic feature analysis may provide a solution to this problem.

When a gross distinction between descriptive and evaluative similarity of traits is made, a large number of studies provide incidental data that seem to support Felipe's (89) conclusion. For example, in many investigations of the relationship between similarity and attraction, subjects have been asked to make inferences about the characteristics or traits of a hypothetical stranger, as well as to indicate their attraction to the stranger. Sometimes these questions were treated as filler items and their results were not reported. Whenever results were reported, however, consistent findings seemed to emerge. At least six studies utilizing Byrne's Interpersonal Judgment Scale (49) have reported results on the four "filler" belief items: intelligence, knowledge of current events, morality, and adjustment (50–53,

189, 236). In five of the studies that reported these results, relatively extensive protocols were used for the similarity manipulation. This is in contrast to most other studies where a short 10- or 12-item opinion survey was usually employed. In the sixth study (50), a political candidate was described as holding a liberal or conservative position on six social issues. In all six studies, a positive relationship was found between similarity and beliefs about the other's intelligence. Other inferences were made consistently only when the information provided about the stranger was descriptively similar to the judgment required. Thus, beliefs about the other's knowledge of current events were formed only when the information dealt with political issues (50), or a variety of opinions about social issues (51, 189). Beliefs about the other's adjustment were formed in the study that provided information about his repression-sensitization profile (53). The only other study (51) reporting an effect on adjustment seems rather trivial since the subject himself was rated as maladjusted by the other person. Finally, judgements of morality were affected by information about a candidate's stand on six issues (50) and, again, in the trivial case where the subject himself was called immoral by the "stranger" (51).

Similar conclusions emerge from other experiments dealing with interpersonal attraction. For example, in two studies subjects provided information about themselves and a confederate gave positive or negative personality evaluations of the subjects, ostensibly on the basis of the information. The confederate who made positive evaluations was rated as higher in social sensitivity (184) and as more intelligent and doing a better job (287). In contrast, when the subject merely overheard the confederate saying that he did or did not like the subject (169), the confederate who expressed liking received higher ratings of kindness and friendliness, but no differential inferences were made with respect to eight other traits, including intelligence and sensitivity. Thus, there is again little evidence that trait inferences follow evaluative consistency. Finally, some indirect support for the relative weakness of evaluative inferences comes from studies that have used balance theory to predict inferences about (350) or learning of (179, 233, 257) interpersonal relationships. These studies found only weak support for predictions based on notions of affective balance.

In sum, it appears that the distinction between descriptive and evaluative similarity, or more generally between cognitive and affective consistency, is one of the fundamental issues in the area and characterizes two basic processes of inferential belief formation. Our review has dealt with at least three kinds of inference processes (i.e. attribution, syllogistic reasoning, and trait inferences) in each of which both evaluative and descriptive aspects seem to play an important role. It has to be recognized that the relative importance of evaluative and descriptive aspects may vary with the kind of inference process under consideration. One challenge for future research is to further our understanding of the factors that underlie these different inference processes.

ATTITUDES

Whatever the basis for belief formation, there seems to be widespread agreement that a person's attitude toward an object is related to his beliefs about it. Evidence for this general proposition continues to accumulate. Significant relationships were reported between attitude and a set of beliefs about the attitude object when the evaluations associated with the beliefs were taken into account. This relationship held whether the object was a person (e.g. 94, 314), an issue (e.g. 188, 309), or a behavior (e.g. 8, 140).

Attitude is generally perceived to be a function of the affect associated with the beliefs a person holds about the object. It is usually assumed that these affective values combine in some fashion to form the person's overall attitude. One question that has attracted considerable interest concerns the exact nature of this combinatory process. Weighted summation and weighted averaging models have frequently been suggested. Working with such a linear model, two variables have to be estimated: the affective value or evaluation of each concept believed to be related to the attitude object, and the weight assigned to each of these affective values in forming the overall attitude. For example, a person may be described in terms of three personality traits such as *frank*, *considerate*, and *reliable*. The subject is then asked to indicate his overall attitude toward the person. Evaluation of each trait is based either on normative data or is provided directly or indirectly by the subject's responses. In contrast, there is no general agreement as to the nature of the weights or how they should be measured. One approach would be to obtain least squares estimates through multiple regression analyses. This approach has been taken in cue utilization studies, but less frequently in research on attitude formation. Weights estimated by least squares or other analytic procedures are generally considered to reflect the trait's importance, relevance, or salience, but as we saw previously, a subject's own estimates of the importance he places on the information do not correspond with empirically determined weights. More consistent with our earlier definition of beliefs, several investigators (e.g. 8, 94, 116, 140, 155, 347) have viewed the weight as the strength of the belief, i.e. the subjective probability that the person has the trait in question.

Regardless of the interpretation given to the weights, the weighted evaluations of the traits may be added or averaged, and this controversy continues to attract the attention of several investigators (e.g. 11, 13, 345). Typically, studies concerning this issue compare the overall attitude toward two persons, each described by a different set of traits varying in size. The traits in the smaller set have a higher average evaluation but a lower sum than the traits in the larger set. Originally it was assumed that an averaging model was supported when the attitude based on the smaller set was more positive than the attitude based on the larger set, while a difference in the opposite direction was taken as evidence for a summation model. Unfortunately, it has not always been realized that this paradigm does not permit an adequate test of the summation versus averaging controversy. Anderson (13) has again pointed out that results which appear to support a summation model can be explained in terms of his averaging model when the subject's initial attitude toward the person is appropriately weighted relative to the new information. By the same token, a summation model could account for results apparently in support of an averaging process by also taking the subject's initial attitude into account. Moreover, even without the addition of an initial attitude, it can be shown that a summation model will account for apparent averaging phenomena when each trait is differentially weighted. Consider, for example, the traits *frank, considerate*, and *reliable* with evaluations of 1.5, 2.3, and 2.0 respectively. If Person A were described as *considerate* and *reliable*, and the weights of these two traits were .8 and .6 respectively, a weighted summation model would predict an attitude of 3.0 (Attitude = 2.3(.8)+2.0(.6)). If the third trait *frank* were now added, the usual prediction from a summation model would be an increment in attitude. However, assuming that the new information influences the weights of the original two traits, a decrement may occur. In our example, the subject may perceive *frank* to be inconsistent with *considerate* and hence may place a weight of .4 on both pieces of information while maintaining his initial weight of .6 for *reliable*. Thus, the summation prediction would be 2.3(.4)+2.0(.6)+1.5(.4) = 2.7. It should thus be obvious that conclusive evidence concerning the averaging versus summation controversy cannot be derived from studies that compare sets of traits selected to differ only in terms of their additive or mean affective values while neglecting the weights placed on the traits.

When the "weights" referred to in our example are replaced by subjective probabilities, i.e. the subject's beliefs, it becomes clear that providing new information may have several effects: First, if the new information is perceived to be inconsistent with the subject's prior beliefs, it may reduce his subjective probability that his prior information is true and/or that the new information is accurate. Second, if the new information is perceived to be redundant with prior beliefs, its contribution to the overall attitude may only be a fraction of its value in isolation. One attempt to incorporate redundancy into a summation model is Wyer's (345) use of conditional probabilities. Elsewhere, Wyer (346) has used probability notions to study the effects of redundancy, inconsistency, and novelty on attitude formation. Wyer (344) and Schmidt (266) have shown that attitude polarization decreases with redundancy. It has been suggested that information coming from a highly credible source is weighted more heavily than information coming from a low credibility source. Rosenbaum & Levin (247) supported this notion by showing that information from a credible source led to more polarized attitudes.

Just as interactive effects may occur with respect to belief strength, it has also been argued that the affective value of one piece of information may interact with that of another. Indeed, there is considerable evidence that affective values of words in isolation differ from their affective values in various contexts (e.g. 104, 122). Research on impression formation has typically dealt with primacy or recency effects resulting from different orders of presentation by differentially weighting the affective value of information according to the order in which it was presented (e.g. 12). Attempting to support Asch's (22) notion of directed impression, Chalmers (57) has recently proposed a "change in meaning" model which is essentially an alternative weighting procedure whereby the affective value of new information is weighted in terms of the affective value of preceding information. Differences in final attitudes obviously can be accounted for by assuming changes in subjective probabilities, affective values, or both. To determine the changes that actually occur, future research must permit the investigator to assess both types of changes simultaneously.

In the above discussion we have suggested that, consistent with general expectancy-value notions, the affective value of each piece of information be weighted by the information's subjective probability. Although there is no agreement concerning adding versus averaging, or other combinatory principles, a weighted linear model is usually found to predict the overall attitude fairly accurately. It has sometimes been argued that each piece of information should also be given a weight for its importance, salience, or relevance (e.g. 116, 347). Despite the intuitive plausibility of this position, recent studies that have obtained measures of importance or relevance in addition to belief strength have consistently found that adding these weights to an expectancy-value model attenuates the prediction of attitude (11, 116, 155, 347).[7]

Parenthetically it may be noted that measures of importance have sometimes been used in place of affective values (e.g. 117). This practice may perhaps be traced to a misunderstanding of Rosenberg's (248) use of the term "value importance" for the evaluation of goals or end states in his expectancy-value model. Clearly, when measures of importance are substituted for evaluations, negative findings cannot be taken as evidence against an expectancy-value model. In the same vein, measures of recall have sometimes been inappropriately substituted for measures of the subject's beliefs (e.g. 11), and beliefs reported by subjects have sometimes been eliminated because they were not part of the information given to them by the experimenter or because the content of a belief statement was unfamiliar to the subject (295). Needless to say, the subject's attitude is a function of what he actually believes, whether it is true or not, given to him by the experimenter or not, and whether he was or was not familiar with it prior to exposure.

[7] This is not meant to imply that "importance" is an irrelevant variable in studies of attitude and opinion. Like measures of other aspects of the cognitive structure, measures of belief importance can be useful in explaining differential change between two subjects with the same attitudes (e.g. 347).

INTERPERSONAL ATTRACTION

In contrast to an informational basis for attitude formation, several other variables have been suggested as antecedents of interpersonal attraction: similarity of values, beliefs, or personality traits; complementarity of need systems; reciprocity of liking; high ability or competence. Aronson (18) has pointed out that most of these factors can be loosely summarized under a general reinforcement, reward-cost, or exchange framework. However, he argued that neither a general theory of this type nor an encyclopedic listing of the antecedents of attraction are likely to be very fruitful. Instead he suggested the development of "mini-theories" of attraction, and in keeping with this recommendation, he proposed a "gain-loss" theory (18, 20). The central hypothesis of the theory is that " . . . a gain in esteem is a more potent reward than invariant esteem, and similarly, the loss of esteem is a more potent 'punishment' than invariant negative esteem" (20, p. 156). Four hypotheses were suggested as possible bases for this "gain-loss" effect: discernment, anxiety, effectance, and contrast. The contrast hypothesis is apparently untested, and the discernment hypothesis was not supported (169). To test the anxiety hypothesis, subjects were positively or negatively evaluated by a beautiful or ugly experimenter (287). Both main effects and the interaction were significant. In the positive evaluation condition, the beautiful experimenter was liked better than the ugly experimenter. However, the predicted difference was not significant in the negative evaluation condition. Moreover, in an experiment unrelated to the gain-loss theory, a main effect of praise versus criticism by an experimenter was found, but no effect of, or interaction with, whether the experimenter was a "good-looking blonde female" or "a bearded male" was obtained (180). In order to test the effectance hypothesis, Sigall (285) had "involved" and "uninvolved" subjects evaluate confederates who changed their opinions to varying degrees in the direction advocated by the subject. On two of the three attraction measures, a main effect of amount of change was found, and, consistent with his hypothesis, a significant interaction was obtained showing that involved subjects preferred the confederate who had changed to a large degree, irrespective of whether his final position agreed with that of the subject or not. Uninvolved subjects preferred the confederate who changed little but agreed with them to the confederate who changed a lot but still disagreed. Unfortunately, no data were collected on the effects of large shifts to agreement for uninvolved subjects. No significant effects were found for the third measure of attraction. Further, another study, unrelated to the gain-loss theory, varied subjects' involvement and the amount of change by different confederates. Neither a main effect of involvement nor an interaction between involvement and amount of change was obtained (36).

In sum, results of studies relevant to explanations of the gain-loss effect are neither consistent nor very encouraging. This is not at all surprising when the original gain-loss phenomenon is re-examined. The predicted effect on attraction was found only with gain but not with loss (20). In a second study, the gain effect but no loss effect was noted when the dependent variable was belief change, and neither gain nor loss effects were obtained for attraction (286). Further, no support for either a gain or a loss effect on attraction was found in another study (312). The obvious moral to this story is that studies designed to test hypotheses attempting to explain unreliable phenomena are themselves likely to lead to nonsignificant or inconsistent findings. These inconsistencies are not atypical for much of the literature dealing with interpersonal attraction. Many hypotheses in this area are based largely on the experimenter's intuition. While they are often interesting and apparently reasonable, the evidence suggests that more often than not our intuition is inaccurate. For example, a series of studies have tested the hypothesis that under certain conditions a given act will "humanize" the actor and thus make him more attractive (e.g. 125, 144, 267). The humanizing events have included such things as asking for a favor, giving a flower, or spilling coffee. These manipulations were expected to interact with the size of the favor requested (144), the formality of the situation (267), and the actor's competence (e.g. 125). None of these studies supported the predicted interaction effects on attraction, and results concerning main effects were inconsistent. With respect to requests for a favor, for example, one study found increased attraction following the request (144) while another found decreased attraction (31). Neither study supported the predicted interaction with a second manipulated variable (size of request or degree of the actor's dependence on the subject). The latter study, however, indicated that the effect of the request on attraction may depend upon its legitimacy. Consistent with this, an illicit plea for help or an illicit favor led to lowered attraction (175), and compliance with a legitimate request and noncompliance with an illegitimate request led to greater attraction than vice versa (186). Taken together, these studies indicate that a more systematic approach taking intentionality into account may help explain the obtained inconsistencies. In support of this notion, more consistent findings were usually obtained in studies of ingratiation (152, 184, 212) where attempts were made to systematically vary the ingratiator's perceived intent.

While there is lack of support for many of the intuitive hypotheses concerning interactive effects on attraction, there is considerable evidence that main effects are usually obtained when another person is described in a positive or negative fashion (e.g. 154), behaves favorably or unfavorably (9), agrees or disagrees with the subject (282), or when he positively or negatively evaluates the subject (e.g. 184, 287).

SIMILARITY AND ATTRACTION

A positive relationship between attraction and similarity of beliefs, values, attitudes, personality characteristics, interests, etc. has been found consistently. In the period covered by our survey more than 35 publications have again demonstrated that this relationship holds. Unfortunately, with few exceptions (e.g. 55, 58, 59, 199, 213, 314), these studies have demonstrated little else. One of the more interesting developments is the successful attempt to account for previous failures to demonstrate greater attraction when the similarity manipulation involved important rather than unimportant information (55, 58, 59). The results showed that this effect was obtained only when different numbers of important and unimportant items were included within the same description, i.e. when importance was a relative variable.

Underlying much of the similarity-attraction research is the assumption that similarity is related to attraction because it has reinforcement value (49). Many studies have included one or two variables in addition to the similarity manipulation in an apparent attempt to show that reinforcement leads to attraction. For example, subjects have been rewarded or punished by the other person, the experimenter, or a third person via evaluations, bonus points, or aversive stimuli (e.g. 51, 85, 86). Almost without exception, these variables have shown the expected main effect on attraction and no interaction with similarity. However, we fail to see how these results provide direct support for the claim that the effect of similarity is due to its reinforcement value.

A second attempt to test the reinforcement explanation has involved including personality variables in addition to the similarity manipulation. It has been argued that the reinforcement value of similar beliefs, personality traits, etc should interact with personality characteristics such as need for approval (86), anxiety or insecurity (103, 236), and self-esteem (e.g. 16, 113). Unfortunately, none of these personality variables interacted significantly with similarity to determine attraction, nor did other personality variables such as dogmatism (106) or repression-sensitization (53). The evidence concerning personality variables, therefore, seems to argue against a reinforcement interpretation of the similarity effect.

A third approach that has attempted to demonstrate the reinforcement value of similar beliefs or personality traits has utilized operant and classical conditioning paradigms. It is argued that if similarity is in fact reinforcing, it should be possible to use similar and dissimilar beliefs or traits as positive and negative reinforcers in these conditioning paradigms. In a number of studies subjects learned a visual discrimination task and were reinforced with belief statements with which they had previously agreed or disagreed. The results did indeed show that subjects acquired the correct reponses. However, several studies (e.g. 54, 238) demonstrated that this learning occurred only when the belief statements served as discriminant stimuli (i.e. as indicants that the subject had made a correct or incorrect response) and when subjects were aware of this contingency. For example, Reitz & Douey (238) found a conditioning effect using pro- and antireligious belief statements with pro- and antireligious subjects but not with subjects unselected for their religiosity. While these findings can be interpreted as support for the reinforcement effect of similarity, a simpler explanation is that belief statements with which subjects agree or disagree can serve as discriminant stimuli.

Such statements have also been used as unconditioned stimuli in classical conditioning paradigms. For example, statements were paired with nonsense figures and photographs of strangers; affective conditioning occurred, but only for aware subjects (261). These results, however, may be due to either similarity or the affective values of the unconditioned stimuli since these two aspects were confounded. In an attempt to separate similarity and affective value, Stalling's (300) subjects rated personality traits as "pleasant" or "unpleasant" and as "like me" or "unlike me." He used these ratings to construct four sets of unconditioned stimuli that represented the four orthogonal combinations of affective value and similarity. It may be noted that Stalling encountered considerable difficulty in constructing all four sets for each subject since most subjects perceived traits to be both positive and similar or negative and dissimilar (r = .88). The classical conditioning paradigm was utilized with those subjects for whom all four lists could be constructed, and the results showed only a main effect of affective value. The main effect of similarity was not significant nor was its interaction with the affective value.

These findings strongly suggest an alternative interpretation of the similarity-attraction relationship, and one that is consistent with our previous discussion of an informational basis for attitude formation. This interpretation assumes that the information used to describe the other person carries evaluative implications and hence allows the subject to form an attitude toward the person. Since similar beliefs or personality traits tend to be evaluated more positively than dissimilar ones (300), the subject will come to hold a more favorable attitude toward a similar than a dissimilar stranger. Some evidence supporting this notion has been reported by several investigators. It was shown that the effect of manipulated similarity on attraction was reduced to nonsignificance when trait evaluations were treated as a covariate (199), and that the correlation between similarity and attraction was reduced when trait evaluations were partialled out (314). Similarity in the form of sharing a fictitious taste trait led to different degrees of attraction depending upon the trait's frequency of occurrence and its desirability (146). Thus there seems to be little or no evidence that similarity per se leads to interpersonal attraction. Indeed, a field study clearly showed that reciprocal friendship pairs were no more likely to hold similar beliefs than were nonreciprocated friendship pairs or random pairs (172).

In sum, there is abundant evidence that under most circumstances similarity will be related to attraction, and further demonstrations of this relationship are clearly unnecessary. More research is needed to determine the factors underlying this relationship, and to separate the effects of similarity and the affective value of similar and dissimilar information.

OTHER SOURCES OF ATTITUDE

There is continued interest in classical and operant conditioning as a basis for attitude formation. Most studies have reported conditioning effects although, as mentioned previously, there is little or no evidence for conditioning without awareness (e.g. 72, 141, 180, 224, 261). The basis for attitude formation may therefore again be informational rather than automatic conditioning. Recent statements of the positions taken by three of the more active conditioning theorists can be found in Staats (299) and Lott & Lott (182).

A final line of research on attitude formation is the work of Zajonc (354) on the relation between frequency of exposure and affect. Hypotheses underlying this research are that novel stimuli produce response competition which leads to tension and therefore to negative affect. Motivation to reduce the tension leads to exploratory behavior and repeated exposure lowers response competition, therefore reducing tension and increasing positive affect. Experimental as well as correlational data have been reported in support of various links in this chain (e.g. 119, 190, 354). However, Boucher & Osgood (38) have pointed out that the semantic satiation hypothesis may account for the finding of increased affect in some of the experimental studies. They also argued that the correlational data could be accounted for equally well by a "Pollyanna" hypothesis, i.e. positively evaluated words are used more frequently. Irrespective of the direction of the relationship, one of the more interesting aspects of this work is the demonstration that exploratory or approach behavior is often inversely related to positive affect. Thus, the frequent equation of the attitude dimension with an approach-avoidance dimension seems untenable.

In conclusion, we agree with Aronson (18) that little is to be gained by continuing to compile an inventory of variables that might possibly affect attraction or attitude in general. It seems obvious that the intuitive approach has failed and that a more systematic theoretical integration of the area is called for. What we have tried to show throughout our discussion is that much of the research can be viewed within the framework of an informational basis for attitude formation, i.e. that attitudes are formed on the basis of beliefs. This view implies that the effects of an experimental manipulation on attitude or attraction can best be understood in terms of its impact on the subject's beliefs and/or the affective values of these beliefs.

BEHAVIORAL INTENTIONS

Attitudes have often been viewed as determinants of intentions and behavior. As mentioned earlier, there is clear evidence for a strong relationship between attitude and indices based on heterogeneous sets of intentions. However, there is also clear evidence that attitude may not be related to any given intention.

For example, Nemeth (212) found a correlation of .008 between liking for a person and volunteering to distribute questionnaires for him. Two studies of the subject's attraction toward the experimenter and his intention to take part in additional research with the experimenter yielded different results for the attraction and intention measures (144, 287). Novak & Lerner (213) manipulated perceived similarity with another person and either indicated or did not indicate that the other person was emotionally disturbed. While subjects were always more attracted toward the similar than the dissimilar person, they were more willing to interact with the dissimilar normal than with the similar disturbed.

Clearly then behavioral intentions have to be investigated in their own right. A review of the literature indicates that the study of intentions has been badly neglected, but a recent book on intentional behavior (260) and a review of classical theories of volition (165) are relevant. A notable contribution to the study of intentions is the work of Triandis and his associates (232, 317, 318) on interpersonal intentions using the Behavioral Differential. Different factors of behavioral intentions have been identified, and while there is some consistency in factor structures across different studies (e.g. 232, 318), it is important to note that the factors and factor loadings obtained are affected both by the subjects who make the judgments and the stimuli that are being judged. Thus, relationships between different behavioral intentions may vary from situation to situation, and it cannot be assumed that a given intention will always be representative of the same factor. Further, consistent with earlier arguments, attitudes tend to be differentially related to the factors that emerge within a given study (e.g. 232, 318).

Triandis has manipulated stimulus attributes such as race, sex, age, status, etc in factorial designs and has investigated the relative importance of these attributes as factors influencing different dimensions of behavioral intentions. Although in a less systematic fashion, other investigators (e.g. 202, 212, 241, 310) have also examined the effects of different stimulus attributes on one or more intentions. As might be expected, whenever more than one intention was measured, the same attributes tended to have different effects on different intentions. Indeed, the race versus belief-similarity controversy in reference to "prejudice" was resolved when it was realized that race and belief similarity have different effects on different measures of prejudice (i.e. on attitudes and different dimensions of behavioral intentions) (e.g. 230, 241, 310).

Two recent studies have shown that just as variations in attributes of the stimulus person affect interpersonal intentions, situational variations also have an influence. Using modified forms of the S-R anxiety inventory, Sandell (262) investigated situational effects on intentions to drink various beverages, and Bishop & Witt (35) investigated situational effects on intentions to engage in different leisure time activities. This approach yields estimates of the amount of variance in intentions accounted for by situations, behaviors, and individual differences, as well as by the various interactions between these variables. In both studies, more than 80 percent of the variance was accounted for by interactions. Further support for the influence of situational variables on intentions can be found in several recent studies (e.g. 8, 46, 75, 325).

In an attempt to understand the relationship between attitude and behavior, Fishbein and his associates (5, 7, 8, 93) have used a modified version of Dulany's (77) "theory of propositional control" to predict intentions and behavior.[8] According to the modified version, behavioral intentions are a function of two components, one attitudinal and the other normative. The relative weights of these components may vary with individual differences, situational variables, and the behavior under consideration. In contrast to most previous work, the attitudinal component in this formulation is the attitude toward the behavior itself, rather than the attitude toward the object of the behavior.[9] Consistent with an expectancy-value notion, this attitude toward the behavior is seen as a function of the subject's beliefs about the consequences of performing the behavior and his evaluation of those consequences. The normative component refers to the perceived expectations of relevant others (i.e. normative beliefs) and the subject's motivation to comply with these expectations. The motivation to comply has so far proved to be the weakest link in the formulation, and it has sometimes been omitted from research reports (e.g. 8).

Several studies have provided considerable support for this model. For example, behavioral intentions of players in different Prisoner's Dilemma games were predicted (5, 8). Strong relationships were found between predicted and obtained measures of intentions ($R \sim .80$ for the total sample). More importantly, consistent with expectations, the relative weights of the two components varied with the situation. Under a cooperative motivational orientation intentions were primarily determined by the normative component while the attitudinal component was more important under a competitive orientation. [For a more detailed review of research based on the model, see (7).]

The importance of normative influences on intentions has also been demonstrated in a study showing that the relationship between attitude and intentions was influenced by the subject's expectation that other people would or would not be aware of his action (325). Similarly, Bronfenbrenner (46) reported that children's intentions varied with their expectations that either peers or parents would be aware of their responses.

In view of the fact that intentions to engage in any given behavior with respect to an object are relatively independent of attitudes toward that object, and since, as we shall see below, intentions tend to be highly related to overt behaviors, more systematic research on behavioral intentions is clearly desirable.

[8] For a more extensive discussion of the relationships between Dulany's original model and the modified version, see (93).

[9] It is worth noting that Rokeach's (246) attitude toward the situation can also be viewed as an attitude toward a behavior.

CHANGING BELIEFS, ATTITUDES, AND INTENTIONS

Given that people have beliefs, attitudes, and intentions, a question of considerable interest concerns the ways in which changes in these variables can be produced. Indeed, most previous reviews and surveys of the attitude area (e.g. 198, 271) have focused on this problem. Our review has devoted more than the usual amount of space to processes underlying the formation of beliefs, attitudes, and intentions, and the present section will emphasize the relevance of these processes for an understanding of the problems associated with attempts to bring about change. While this approach does not permit a detailed content analysis of the area, it seems unlikely that any review would improve upon McGuire's summary (198). Further several recent reviews of more specific problem areas are also available (e.g. 17, 130, 176, 178, 197, 226, 291). Most of these reviews reflect the general state of the field in that they are organized around independent variables and manipulations while paying relatively little attention to the dependent variables. We hope to show that some of the problems and apparent contradictions in the area may be due to this neglect.

COMMUNICATION AND PERSUASION

Attempts to produce changes in beliefs, attitudes, or intentions have generally taken the form of manipulating information or manipulating behavior. The first approach involves providing the subject with some information concerning a particular topic, usually in the form of a persuasive communication. Any such message can be described as a series of belief statements, i.e. statements that link some object with another object or property. However, messages designed to change beliefs, attitudes, and intentions usually take very different forms. In order to clarify these differences, it is first necessary to distinguish between two types of belief statements: (a) those that link the attitude object to some other object, concept, value, or goal; and (b) those that provide "support" or "evidence" for this link. Further, a belief about the attitude object may be the conclusion of a given communication, or it may merely be a statement contained in the message.

A message designed to change a belief, such as "Drinking is detrimental to family life," will usually make the belief the implicit or explicit conclusion of the persuasive communication. In order to support this conclusion, the message usually contains several additional belief statements such as "Seventy-five percent of heavy drinkers have serious marital problems." Persuasion is typically measured in terms of change in the conclusion. Although seldom recognized, this paradigm involves two stages in the persuasion process. It is first assumed that acceptance of the supporting beliefs (i.e. the evidence) will increase acceptance of the conclusion. For this to occur a prior assumption has to be met, namely that the evidence itself has been accepted. Unfortunately, most studies of belief change have not bothered to measure the subject's acceptance of the supporting beliefs nor have they tested the assumption that there is a relationship between acceptance of this evidence and acceptance of the conclusion (e.g. 128, 129, 147, 220, 288). Clearly, these assumptions may not always be justified. We have seen previously that probability theory specifies a complex pattern of conditional probabilities between beliefs. Changes in the conclusion as a result of accepting other beliefs will in part be determined by these conditional probabilities (348, 349). Thus, even when there is equal acceptance of the evidence presented in two messages, differential acceptance of their conclusions (i.e. differential "persuasion") may be observed.

A message designed to change an attitude usually attempts to provide information that links the attitude object to several other concepts that are positively or negatively evaluated. For example, a message designed to change a person's attitude toward drinking might present the above conclusion that "Drinking is detrimental to family life," as well as statements such as "Drinking leads to auto accidents," and "Drinking results in liver ailments." Supportive evidence for each of these beliefs may also be presented. Most investigators are in agreement that a person's attitude is some function of the affective value associated with the beliefs he holds about the object. It is assumed that acceptance of these beliefs about drinking will lead to a change in the subject's attitude toward drinking. Again, however, this assumption is not always justified. Although the person's post-communication attitude will be a function of his beliefs about drinking and their affective values, the subject will have other beliefs about drinking besides those contained in the message. Unfortunately, while many investigators recognize that a person's prior beliefs (or attitudes) may influence his acceptance of the belief statements contained in the message (e.g. 41, 239, 259), they neglect the fact that accepting some of the beliefs in the message may in turn change some of the subject's prior beliefs. As we saw previously, "new" and "old" information may interact in different ways, and acceptance of "new" information may influence either the strength or affective value of previously held beliefs. Similarly, previously held beliefs may not only influence acceptance, but also the affective value of "new" beliefs that are accepted. Thus accepting new information about an object may lead to attitude change in some studies but not in others. Again, it is unfortunate that most studies of attitude change have neither tested the assumption that acceptance of beliefs (about drinking, for example) in the message will lead to attitude change, nor have they bothered to measure acceptance of those beliefs (e.g. 115, 192, 284, 333). Further, we know of no published study that has examined effects of a message on prior beliefs *not* contained in the communication.

A message designed to influence intentions is usually distinguishable from the previous messages in that it will also include a specific recommendation such as "Heavy drinkers should obtain medical treatment," or "You should stop drinking." Here it is assumed that acceptance of the prior information in the message (e.g. belief statements about drinking and evidence for them) and/or attitude change the message was designed to produce will increase acceptance of the recommendations. Our earlier discussion of behavioral intentions suggests, however, that acceptance of beliefs about drinking contained in the message, or a change in attitude toward drinking, may be unrelated to the intention to stop drinking. Although attitudes toward acts may be related to intentions to perform the act, this need not be the case, since normative factors may also influence intentions. In a recent study, Ajzen (5) demonstrated that messages designed to change either the subject's attitude toward the act of cooperating, or his normative beliefs about cooperation (i.e his belief that his partner expected him to cooperate), were differentially effective in changing intentions to cooperate under different conditions. Intentions of cooperatively oriented subjects were changed by normative but not by attitudinal messages, while the reverse was true for competitively oriented subjects.

The attitude relevant to intention formation is the subject's attitude toward *his* engaging in the action. While the subject may accept the message and believe that drinking leads to bad consequences, he may not believe that he is a heavy drinker or that *his* drinking will lead to those consequences. Similarly, even if he did believe that his drinking would lead to bad consequences, he might not accept the implicit or explicit statement that abiding by the recommendations will prevent these undesirable consequences. Again the main point to be made is that there are several assumptions underlying the expectation that a persuasive communication will lead to changes in intentions. These assumptions are usually not made explicit, they are seldom tested, and measures of acceptance of beliefs in the message and/or attitude change are rarely obtained (e.g. 87). A recent study demonstrates the importance of some of these assumptions. Rogers & Thistlethwaite (245) found that smokers intended to smoke less only when they were led to believe that quitting or cutting down smoking reduces a smoker's susceptibility to lung cancer. When quitting or cutting down smoking was said to be an ineffective means for reducing the probability of lung cancer, smokers showed little change in intentions. Nonsmokers whose behavior does not lead to the unpleasant consequence of lung cancer were relatively unaffected by this belief manipulation.

In conclusion, persuasive communications can be designed to change beliefs, attitudes, or intentions. The term "persuasion" will be reserved for acceptance of a conclusion (belief change), acceptance of a recommendation (change in intention), or a change in attitude brought about by a message. We have tried to show that a persuasive communication primarily consists of a series of supportive arguments designed to produce persuasion. This part of the message will be referred to as the "supportive message" and the arguments it contains as "supportive beliefs." Although ill acknowledged, there is an implicit assumption that acceptance of the supportive beliefs will increase persuasion. Unfortunately, little effort has been made to measure acceptance of the supportive message or to substantiate the assumption that its acceptance increases persuasion.

The question of reception.—While relatively little attention has been paid to acceptance of supportive beliefs, considerable effort has been expended in trying to determine whether these beliefs were "received." It has been argued (e.g. McGuire 197) that to be effective a message must, at a minimum be attended to and comprehended. However, a subject's reception of supportive beliefs is no guarantee that he has accepted them, and it is his acceptance of these supportive beliefs, and not his reception of them, that is assumed to influence persuasion. Similarly, although a subject may be unable to recognize or recall a given supportive belief, he may nevertheless accept it. Further, the message may have indirect effects on beliefs not contained in the message, and these effects would obviously not be revealed by any reception test where such beliefs would be regarded as "errors." Thus, there seems to be little value in continuing to rely on measures of reception as a basis for understanding the persuasive effects of a communication. This discussion indicates that persuasion is generally unrelated to reception, but that it may be related to acceptance of supportive beliefs. As mentioned earlier, it is often impossible to tell whether a given "learning" or "reception" test is a measure of reception or of acceptance. Therefore, such tests may or may not be found to correlate with persuasion and the results appear to be inconsistent. When a clear measure of reception was obtained, however, there was no evidence that recall of either the supportive message or of the conclusion or recommendation was related to persuasion (e.g. 220). It should therefore be obvious that the process of persuasion cannot be understood without measuring acceptance of supportive beliefs. Although not measuring acceptance of supportive beliefs, studies on logical syllogisms have provided some support for this argument by showing that acceptance of a minor premise led to a corresponding change in acceptance of the logically related conclusion (e.g. 137, 329, 348).

Variables influencing persuasion.—So far only problems related directly to the message and its contents have been discussed. The basic paradigm in most communication and persuasion research involves exposing all subjects to the same message while measuring or manipulating one or more other variables. Thus many studies have varied communicator credibility (e.g. 133, 147, 206, 239), others have manipulated distraction (e.g 115, 220, 359), external fear or arousal (e.g. 127, 207, 288), or involvement (e.g. 239, 259, 272). A number of studies have measured individual difference variables such as self-esteem (e.g. 79, 173, 177), anxiety (e.g. 173, 207, 333), dogmatism (e.g. 11, 206), or birth order (e.g. 127, 128). These variables have been assumed to mediate the persuasive effects of the communication. For example, it has been argued (e.g. McGuire 197) that personality variables such as self-esteem and anxiety are differentially related to the subject's reception of the message and his yielding to what is comprehended. Similarly, manipulations of arousal, distraction, external fear, etc are also expected to reduce comprehension and increase yielding. Research on fear appeals fits this same general paradigm. The constant message is usually a set of recommendations, and the high or low fear appeals can be viewed as an additional manipulation, although here the manipulation is usually contained within the message itself (e.g. 87, 138, 207). Again it is expected that anxiety produced by the message will reduce comprehension and increase yielding.

By assuming a multiplicative relation between reception and yielding, McGuire (197) has postulated a curvilinear effect of such variables on persuasion. An adequate test of this theory obviously requires separate measures of reception, yielding, and persuasion. It should be recalled, however, that reception is usually found to be unrelated to persuasion. Further, yielding as conceptualized by McGuire cannot be measured directly but must be estimated from the measures of reception and persuasion.

We have suggested a different model of the persuasion process which involves acceptance of supportive beliefs and persuasion. While reception of supportive beliefs can be measured, the crucial factor in persuasion is their acceptance. Unfortunately, it is acceptance of the supportive message that has traditionally been ignored. We have tried to show that the processes linking acceptance of the supportive message to persuasion differ for attempts to change beliefs, attitudes, and intentions. To understand the effects on persuasion of manipulations such as communicator credibility or distraction, a number of stages in the persuasion process must be considered. First, the manipulation may or may not influence acceptance of the supportive message. Second, even when the manipulation has differential effects on acceptance of supportive beliefs, their acceptance may be unrelated to persuasion, i.e. to acceptance of a conclusion, acceptance of a recommendation, or attitude change. In addition, a communication may have indirect effects by changing the subject's prior beliefs not contained in the message. These indirect effects may also influence persuasion and may or may not be related to the manipulation. Needless to say, a large body of conflicting findings must result from this accumulation of confounding factors: different types of messages, different dependent variables, different assumptions linking the supportive message to the dependent measures of persuasion, and failure to measure acceptance of supportive beliefs or indirect effects of the message.

Thus, it is hardly surprising to find that communicator credibility increased persuasion in some studies (e.g. 147, 193, 206, 225) but not in others (e.g. 64, 133, 239) or that interactions with other variables were sometimes obtained (e.g. 192, 284, 288). For example, McCroskey (192) found no main effect of credibility but a significant interaction with whether or not evidence was contained in the message Credibility increased attitude change only when statements about the attitude object were not supported by additional evidence Similarly, distraction increased persuasion in some studies (e.g. 220, 289, 359), decreased persuasion in others (115, 323), had no effect on persuasion (207), or interacted with other variables (258). Studies of external fear and/or arousal sometimes found greater persuasion under high arousal (127), no difference between high and low conditions (98), or, most frequently, interactions with other variables (e.g. 129, 207, 288). For example, Hendrick and his associates found that while females were more persuaded under low than under high "arousal," males were not affected in one study (129) and arousal interacted with birth order in the other (128). Equally inconsistent findings were reported in research on fear appeals. Some studies found no differences between high and low fear messages (87, 207), although one study (245) found a main effect of fear on intention but not on belief. In two other studies the fear appeal had no main effects, but it did significantly interact with volunteering (138, 139). While volunteers changed more under high fear, nonvolunteers either showed no difference (139) or the opposite effect (138). The results are no more consistent when individual difference variables are considered. For example, chronic self-esteem was found to have a low negative correlation with persuasion in one study (177) and no relationship in others (e.g. 11, 356). Several studies reported no main effects of self-esteem, but interactions with other variables (e.g. 79, 173).

While we could continue to list studies investigating other independent variables, the results are essentially the same, namely a general lack of consistency. It is obvious that this situation will not improve until more attention is paid to the dependent variable being studied, to the assumptions that link the supportive message with the dependent measure of persuasion, to acceptance of the supportive message, and to indirect effects of the persuasive communication.

REFERENT INFLUENCE

Some of these confounding factors are not present when a conclusion, recommendation, or an attitude is simply stated or attributed to some referent without providing any supportive information (e.g. 64, 191, 259, 264). Studies that have contrasted experimental groups (irrespective of other manipulations) with a control group have generally found significant referent influence (e.g. 41, 64, 264). Effects of other manipulations such as prestige of the referent (e.g. 41, 64), message discrepancy (41, 259), etc, however, have yielded inconsistent results. This again may be partially attributable to the fact that, as before, different dependent variables have been studied. For example, referent prestige significantly affected attitudes in three studies (41, 191, 264), while two studies dealing with beliefs (64, 293) showed no significant effects of this variable. Similarly, discrepancy was found to be linearly related to belief change (259) but curvilinearly to attitude change (41). While these differential effects on beliefs and attitudes are probably incidental, they do point to the necessity of paying more attention to the dependent variable under study.

ANTICIPATORY CHANGE

The above approach is related to research in which the subject is led to believe that he will be exposed to a communication and anticipatory changes are investigated. Papageorgis (226) has distinguished between disguising the purpose of the communication, forewarning the subject that the communication is designed to change his opinion, and providing information about the position advocated in the communication. In the period reviewed, three studies (64, 71, 145) investigated anticipatory change and all three provided information about the position that was to be advocated. In only one case (64) was there conclusive evidence that mere expectation of exposure produced anticipatory change, and even here the effects did not occur unless the subject was also told that the study was concerned with opinion change. In two of these studies (71, 145) subjects also anticipated that they would or would not have to defend their own positions. Both studies found anticipatory change toward the subject's own position rather than toward the position advocated in the anticipated message. Similarly, Greenwald (110) found anticipatory change toward the position subjects expected to role-play even when this position was opposed to their own. Along these same lines, subjects expecting to distribute leaflets against air pollution were found more negative toward pollution than were subjects who did not expect to perform this behavior (164). Finally, subjects about to make a decision expressed more consistent beliefs with respect to stimuli involved in the anticipated choice than with respect to stimuli not involved in the anticipated choice (215).

BEHAVIORALLY PRODUCED CHANGES IN BELIEFS, ATTITUDES, AND INTENTIONS

These considerations concerning anticipated behavior lead us directly to the second major approach in the study of persuasion, i.e. the manipulation of actual behavior. Early research on the effects of behavior of beliefs, attitudes, and intentions was conducted primarily in the context of studies concerned with interracial contact and role-playing. While these lines of research continue (e.g. 10, 62, 230, 304), most recent investigations have been stimulated by dissonance theory. One of the theory's more interesting implications was that the performance of certain behaviors would be followed by changes in "cognitions" only under certain conditions. This implication pointed to an important problem, and subsequent research has provided strong evidence for the conditional nature of behaviorally produced changes in beliefs, attitudes, and intentions. Unfortunately, as Sears & Abeles (271) indicated in their previous review of the area, the initial promise of dissonance theory has not been realized, and conditions that were expected to produce dissonance and concomitant "cognitive" changes have not been found to do so consistently. Our review of the recent literature indicates that little additional progress has been made: the conditions under which behavioral performance will change beliefs, attitudes, or intentions are still largely unknown.

Choice behavior.—Several studies have continued to investigate post-decisional changes in attitudes vis-a-vis chosen and unchosen alternatives (e.g. 39, 112, 118, 208). This particular paradigm may have certain methodological problems (219). Regression effects cannot be ruled out since subjects typically choose between two highly attractive alternatives or between one attractive and one relatively unattractive option. Differential regression effects can be expected for the chosen and unchosen alternatives in the two conditions. Thus changes in evaluations that have been taken as indications of dissonance reduction or postdecisional regret may be confounded with regression effects, especially when changes in both alternatives are combined into a single index. These problems again emphasize the difficulty of interpreting change scores, and also they make it obvious that studies of this kind require a no-choice control group.

In addition to the effects of choice difficulty, investigators have also looked at variables such as the absolute attractiveness of the choice alternatives (112), involvement (105), confidence (112), time of measurement (40), "salience," i.e. leaving or removing photos of the choice alternatives during ratings (40), and telling or not telling subjects that a reward was contingent upon their choice and actually rewarding or not rewarding them (39). Generally speaking, these studies have found nether consistent nor significant effects, although auxiliary data analyses sometimes have led to apparently significant findings. In a systematic investigation of choice processes, Harris (118) made use of a no-choice control group. He concluded that there was very little evidence for postdecisional dissonance reduction and, perhaps more importantly, he found no differences between experimental and control groups. Using a somewhat different procedure, Mittelstaedt (208) did obtain some support for dissonance predictions. His subjects first chose between either their third and fourth, or their third and fifth ranked options. Later, all subjects chose between their second and third ranked alternatives. Consistent with expectations, more of the subjects in the 3–4 group than in the 3–5 group chose the third alternative when confronted with the 2–3 choice.

Forced compliance.—Another series of studies investigated effects of behavior on beliefs, attitudes, and intentions within the "forced compliance" paradigm. In most studies subjects are induced to perform some "counterattitudinal" behavior under various conditions. One behavior frequently studied is writing or recording a counterattitudinal essay. It may be noted parenthetically that most of these studies have had beliefs as their dependent variables (e.g. 30, 60, 256, 278). In contrast, studies dealing with other behaviors have usually tended to measure attitudes (e.g. 60, 101, 174). Dissonance theory predicts more dissonance arousal and therefore more change under conditions of insufficient justification. For example, early studies varied magnitude of payment, assuming that a large monetary reward would increase justification for the behavior and thus lead to less change in beliefs or attitudes. A large number of studies attest to the difficulty of obtaining this effect consistently. Partly in response to this difficulty, investigators have turned to other variables that were expected to interact with reward magnitude, and mediate the dissonance effect.

Studies using counterattitudinal essays, for example, have looked at freedom to participate (136, 278, 279), time of payment (256, 279), audience position (211), audience awareness that the subject is not presenting his own views (126), reason given for the assigned task (61), and time of measurement (69). To be sure, some of these variables were found to interact with reward magnitude. For example, the three studies that manipulated subjects' freedom to participate, as well as reward magnitude, reported the same significant interaction. A negative relationship between reward magnitude and change (i.e. a dissonance effect) was found in the choice condition, while a positive relationship (i.e. an incentive effect) was found in the no-choice condition. Unfortunately, this cannot be taken as an indication that dissonance effects will always be obtained under high choice conditions. In fact, most studies attempt to convince the subject that his participation is voluntary. Yet these studies often do not produce the predicted effect of reward magnitude (e.g. 60, 61, 211). Much the same conclusions are reached with the other variables that were expected to interact with reward magnitude. Indeed, Collins and his associates (60, 126) have found it all but impossible to develop a paradigm that will consistently produce a negative relationship between reward magnitude and amount of change, irrespective of the counterattitudinal behavior involved.

The discussion so far has centered around effects of reward magnitude on changes produced by counterattitudinal essays. Many other behaviors and variables have been investigated, and while these manipulations have sometimes supported dissonance theory predictions, the overall pattern of results is ambiguous and inconclusive. For example, freedom to participate (which was found to be an important variable in some of the studies discussed above) has often been found to produce neither a main effect nor an interaction with other variables (e.g. 30, 101, 303). Part of the problem is that most recent studies are basically attempts to account for previously obtained inconsistent or negative findings. Many of the variables mentioned above were studied in attempts to explain the inconsistent effects of reward manipulations. While studies of this kind may sometimes be useful and necessary, it is unfortunate that, as in this case, they all too often result in an accumulation of reactive nomological studies that are much more concerned with methodological details than with theoretical issues (168, 200). Indeed, it appears that recent research investigating behavioral effects on beliefs, attitudes, or intentions within the dissonance framework has not significantly advanced our understanding of the conditions under which such effects will be observed. This state of affairs may reflect shortcomings of dissonance theory, the reactive nature of much of the research, or the unusually weak methodology that has tended to characterize this body of research. It is perhaps in this area, more than anywhere else, that one encounters misuse of statistics, incomplete experimental designs, conclusions based on nonsignificant findings, partial and internal data analyses, etc.

While it is doubtful that greater methodological rigor would make up for the general shortcomings of reactive nomological research, it might at least serve to eliminate some of the apparent inconsistencies. In any event, it seems obvious that new approaches in this area are called for. A possible step in this direction is Bem's (28) analysis of self-persuasion. While Bem's approach has implications beyond its use as an alternative explanation of dissonance phenomena, its major impact to date has been to generate studies designed to demonstrate that the interpersonal replication technique can or cannot reproduce earlier dissonance findings (21, 30, 76, 153, 231). Much of the controversy has revolved around the question of the amount of information about the "true" subjects' initial attitudes that should be given to observers in the interpersonal replication procedure. Unfortunately, even when Bem's procedures were followed (e.g. 76, 153, 231), it was just as difficult to replicate his initial findings as it has been to replicate dissonance effects with "true" subjects.

Although relatively few studies (e.g. 164) have examined the other implications of Bem's self-persuasion theory, Steiner (302) has incorporated some of these ideas in his recent monograph on perceived freedom. One major implication of Steiner's position is that performance of a behavior will influence a person's beliefs, attitudes, or intentions to the extent that he perceives he had decision freedom in performing the behavior. In his discussion of variables that are likely to influence perceived decision freedom, Steiner included many of the variables that have been studied in dissonance research. While it is too early to know whether this approach will solve the problems that have arisen, it is to be commended as a theoretical reorientation which can lead to new lines of research that are more than mere reactions to inconsistent or nonsignificant findings. Moreover, his approach like Bem's relates this area of research to attribution processes in general and thus provides a bridge to an emerging body of theory that may contribute to the understanding of behaviorally produced changes in beliefs, attitudes, and intentions.

Interpersonal contact.—As mentioned earlier, behavioral impact also continues to be studied in the framework of interpersonal contact. Here, too, it has been recognized (10, 62, 230) that coming into contact with other people will produce changes in interpersonal beliefs and attitudes only under certain conditions. Again numerous variables have been suggested as possible mediators, but as in the case of dissonance research, results have been disappointing. For example, in an ingenious experiment, Cook (62) attempted to optimize five characteristics of interpersonal contact situations that have frequently been assumed to produce favorable attitude change. Even under these optimal conditions he was only able to obtain significant attitude change in 8 of 23 subjects. Other studies have found positive effects of inter-personal contact (132), negative effects (157), interactions only (216), or no effects at all (292).

One problem with much of the interpersonal contact research is that it has neglected the immediate effects of contact on a person's beliefs. Inter-personal contact may or may not lead to the formation of new beliefs or to changes in old beliefs about the persons encountered. Similarly, it may or may not lead to new beliefs or to changes in old beliefs about the con-sequences of engaging in various behaviors with respect to those persons. Just as the communication and persuasion literature has failed to investigate the acceptance of supportive beliefs, research on interpersonal contact has failed to investigate the direct effects of an interpersonal contact situation on the kinds of beliefs described above. Different interpersonal situations may be more or less conducive to forming beliefs about the other's char-acteristics or about the consequences of engaging in some behavior with respect to that person. It seems clear that the immediate effects of the inter-personal contact experience on beliefs will have to be understood (or at least assessed) before a more general understanding of the influence of contact on interpersonal attitudes and intentions can be achieved.

This review of the literature concerned with producing changes in beliefs, attitudes, or intentions has made it clear that our understanding of these processes and the variables that influence them is still very limited. How-ever, even if we knew how to produce changes in beliefs, attitudes, or inten-tions, we would still be faced with a problem of greater practical significance, namely, the implications of such changes for behavior.

BEHAVIOR

Based on psychodynamic theorizing, it has often been assumed that as a defensive reaction subjects will reduce their attention to, or comprehension of, unpleasant, inconsistent, or threatening material. We have already seen that a person's position on an issue has little effect on his recall of a message, and that his attitude toward a person has little effect on his recall of what that person said or did. Similarly, it was noted that balanced or consistent relationships were not always easier to learn than unbalanced or inconsistent relationships. It should be noted, however, that balanced relations are not always judged to be more pleasant than unbalanced ones (3), thus confound-ing the effect of attitude on learning. Contrary to the assumption of a linear relation between evaluation and learning of material, it has usually been found (e.g. 183, 199) that positive and negative stimuli are learned and recalled better than neutral stimuli. Similarly, children had more factual knowledge about liked and disliked than about neutral countries (149). These results suggest that familiarity as well as evaluation may be responsi-ble for the obtained results, especially since as we saw earlier, frequency and affect tend to be associated. An effect of familiarity but not of evaluation on learning of CVC pairs was found when the subject's own ratings of familiarity and evaluation were used to construct the pairs (2). However, when normative data were used to construct the pairs, both main effects were obtained. In any event, there seems to be little evidence for a consistent relation between attitude and learning or recall.

Perhaps of greater relevance to the attitude-behavior relationship is the research on selective exposure to information. It has often been assumed that individuals will prefer and expose themselves to supportive rather than nonsupportive information. Recent studies (e.g. 45, 143, 253) have again demonstrated that there is little evidence to support this general hypothesis. In a search for mediating factors, investigators have considered variables such as prestige of the source (185), type of message, controversiality of the topic (235), anticipated defense of own position (71), familiarity with (45) and utility (45, 253) of the information, dogmatism (253), and the subject's confidence in his own position (185, 253). The predicted interactions were found only for source prestige (185) and topic controversiality (235): subjects preferred supportive information when it came from a high prestige source or when the issue was controversial. Overall, however, it appears that other factors are more important than attitudes in determining choice of information. For example, in a carefully executed study, Brock, Albert & Becker (45) found a preference for information which had high utility or which was unfamiliar to the subject, irrespective of the information's supportiveness.

ATTITUDES AND BEHAVIOR

Just as there is little evidence for the influence of attitude on exposure to new information, there is a growing awareness among investigators that attitudes tend to be unrelated to overt behaviors (e.g. 73, 82, 198, 334, 357). Indeed, a cursory inspection of the recent literature appears to support this conclusion. Of some 24 studies investigating the influence of a given manipulation on "attitudes" and "behavior," 19 reported different results, 2 reported the same effects, and 3 reported no effects at all. For example, Nemeth (212) varied whether a confederate helped or did not help the subject and whether the help was "voluntary" or "compulsory." At the end of the experiment, the confederate tried to enlist the subject's help in distributing questionnaires for a private project. Dependent variables were liking for the confederate (attitude), the number of questionnaires taken for distribution (intention), and the number of questionnaires received through the mail (behavior). The manipulations had different effects for all three dependent variables: there were no significant effects on behavior, a significant effect of voluntariness on intention, and a significant main effect of helping as well as a significant interaction on attitude. Further, he found no correlation between attitude and intention.

Similarly, in about 60 studies that measured or manipulated "attitude," 15 reported a positive relationship with "behavior," 15 reported no relation, and the remainder found relations under some conditions but not under others. For example, one study obtained a correlation of .73 between a general measure of attitude toward encountering a snake and a graded measure of approach behavior toward snakes (23); another found a high correlation between attitude toward another person and volunteering to help him in an informal situation and virtually no relationship in a formal situation (267); and a third reported a positive relation between similarity of players in a Prisoner's Dilemma game and altruistic behavior (i.e. choices that did not shock the opponent) under one condition and a negative relation in a different condition (85).

Various explanations have been offered for the low "attitude-behavior" relationship. Perhaps most widely accepted is the view that "attitude" is a complex concept consisting of cognition, affect, and conation and that measurement of any one component is insufficient for the prediction of behavior. However, we have seen earlier that indices across sets of beliefs (i.e. cognition) or across sets of intentions (i.e. conation) are highly correlated with measures of attitude (i.e. affect), and thus such indices are unlikely to improve prediction of behavior. For example, Ostrom (222) constructed Thurstone, Likert, and Guttman scales from items that were previously judged as representative of cognition, affect, and conation. These scales showed high convergent but little discriminant validity. Although Ostrom (222) argued that his conative scales were superior, correlations with self-reports of various behaviors were mostly nonsignificant, and the conative scales did not predict behavior significantly better than did the other scales.

More recently it has been suggested that prediction of behavior requires that situational characteristics, personality variables, norms, motivation, etc be taken into account, in addition to "attitude" (e.g. 82, 325, 334). Thus, we again find attention shifting to mediating variables in order to account for inconsistent or nonsignificant findings. Wicker (334) has pointed out that factors of this type have frequently been discussed, but they have seldom been systematically investigated. One exception is the work of Warner and his associates (e.g. 325), who argued that the size of the attitude-behavior relationship is contingent upon normative pressures and the degree of social distance implied by the behavior. Prejudiced and unprejudiced whites were asked to sign and mail a pledge that committed the subject to one of eight behaviors varying in social distance. The pledge was or was not to be made public. Even though the manipulations were found to have some influence on the relation between attitude and behavior, the results were not always consistent with predictions. Further, the response rate was low (less than 25%), yielding somewhat limited and perhaps biased data, and the analyses performed made interpretation difficult. In another study testing a mediation hypothesis, Tarter (311) found that attitude-behavior consistency did not vary as a function of whether the subject had an individualistic or collectivistic orientation.

Thus, although the influence of attitude on behavior may be mediated by other variables, little is known at present about the conditions under which a relationship between attitude and behavior will be obtained.

Indeed, in a useful review of over 30 studies investigating the "attitude-behavior" relationship, Wicker (334) concluded that "it is considerably more likely that attitudes will be unrelated or only slightly related to overt behaviors than that attitudes will be closely related to actions" (p. 65). In contrast, in a theoretical reanalysis of the attitude-behavior relationship, Fishbein (92) concluded that attitudes do predict behavior, provided that (a) the attitude measure is appropriate for the type of criterion being predicted, and (b) that the criterion is itself methodologically acceptable. He argued that the apparent inconsistency in findings is due to a lack of concern with the exact nature of the behavioral criterion on the one hand, and the now familiar failure to distinguish between beliefs, attitudes, and intentions on the other. Moreover, he argued that the validity of any given behavior as a criterion in tests of the attitude-behavior relationship cannot be taken for granted. An arbitrarily selected behavior may be of little relevance for the attitude under consideration, and thus there may be no theoretical basis for predicting a relationship between the two.

Fishbein (92) distinguished between several behavioral criteria. One frequently used criterion is the single observation of a single act. Recording of the behavior may be either dichotomous (e.g. the subject does or does not contribute money to charity) or continuous (e.g. the amount of money contributed). Another criterion in frequent use is an index based on repeated observations of the same single act (e.g. behavior across several trials in an experiment). Here a distinction can be made between repeated observations under homogeneous or heterogeneous conditions. Another type of criterion in less frequent use is an index based on single or repeated observations of different behaviors, i.e. a multiple act criterion. Consistent with earlier discussions throughout this paper, Fishbein (92) argued that traditional measures of attitude toward a given object should be related to multiple act criteria, but that there is no necessary correspondence between such measures of attitude and any single behavior. The best predictor of a single act (single or repeated observations) should be the person's intention to perform that specific act. It is worth noting, however, that various factors may at times attenuate the intention-behavior relation. More complete discussions of these factors can be found in Fishbein (92) and Ajzen & Fishbein (7). As we saw earlier, behavioral intentions (and thus the corresponding overt behaviors) can be predicted from the person's attitude toward the act and his normative beliefs.

A reanalysis of the literature in the light of these distinctions reveals that most studies with data bearing on the attitude-behavior relationship have used a single observation of a single act (e.g. 135, 212, 240, 325) or repeated observations of a single act (e.g. 8, 85, 140, 159, 180, 296) as their criterion. The great majority of these studies have measured or manipulated attitude toward an object or person (e.g. 180, 296, 325). Consistent with the above arguments, the general pattern of results is one of nonsignificance, although on a few occasions and under certain conditions a significant finding was obtained. In contrast, a small number of studies using single act criteria have obtained measures of behavioral intentions (5, 8, 159, 161), attitude toward the act (e.g. 5, 8, 140), or normative beliefs (5, 8, 240). Here, almost without exception, significant relations with behavior were obtained. Finally, a few studies have used multiple act criteria (e.g. 23, 33, 353), and in all cases general measures of attitude were found to be significantly related to these criteria.

In conclusion, it appears that inconsistent and nonsignificant findings concerning the attitude-behavior relationship can be understood when proper attention is given to the "attitudinal" predictors and to the behavioral criteria. It should be clear that there is no reason to expect traditional measures of general attitudes to be consistently related to any given behavior. The discussion above suggests that if the investigator's major aim is to understand and predict the performance of some specific behavior, one way to approach this problem is to consider behaviorial intentions and their determinants. It may be desirable for many purposes, however, to be able to employ a general attitude measure in order to predict one or more specific behaviors. While this is an important problem in its own right, it is unlikely to be resolved by an approach that assumes that the "true" inherent relationship between attitude and behavior is moderated by other variables. Indeed, as we saw in our discussion of behavioral impact, the search for mediating variables in response to a failure to demonstrate an assumed "true" relationship can easily lead to an accumulation of reactive nomological studies that provide little substantive information.

CONCLUSION

Reviewing the recent literature has confirmed our initial impression that the attitude area is characterized by a great deal of conceptual ambiguities and methodological deficiencies. We knew at the outset that investigators tend to pay little attention to their dependent variables, and we also expected to find inadequate analyses and unwarranted conclusions. What we did not anticipate, but what we are now convinced may be one of the most serious problems, is that a large proportion of research in the attitude area is basically reactive and nomological in nature. A relatively small number of assumptions or hypotheses continue to persist in the face of repeated failures to support their validity. Instead of questioning these assumptions, investigators will discover weaknesses in previous studies and hypothesize that by making a few changes they can strengthen the procedures and increase the probability of confirming the "true" hypothesis. As Meehl (200) has pointed out,

in this fashion a zealous and clever investigator can slowly wend his way through a tenuous nomological network, performing a long series of related experiments which appear to the uncritical reader as a fine example of 'an integrated research program,' *without ever once refuting or corroborating so much as a single strand of the network* (200, p. 114).

It is painfully obvious that what are required at this point in time are not additional studies of this type but rather serious reconsiderations of basic assumptions and thoughtful theoretical reanalyses of the problems confronting the field.

One step which could encourage such a reorientation, and which at the same time would alleviate the "information" explosion, would be for journal editors to adopt a more stringent editorial policy. At the very least, we would hope that articles will be rejected if they fail to meet APA standards. But beyond this basic requirement, an article should be more than a quasi-methodological treatment of pseudoproblems created by conceptual ambiguities or procedural weaknesses of some prior study which should never have been published in the first place.

LITERATURE CITED

1. Abelson, R. P. et al, Eds. 1968. *Theories of Cognitive Consistency: A Sourcebook.* Chicago: Rand McNally
2. Abramson, Y., Tasto, D. L., Rychlak, J. F. 1969. Nomothetic vs. idiographic influences of association value and reinforcement value on learning. *J. Exp. Res. Pers.* 4:65–71
3. Aderman, D. 1969. Effects of anticipating future interaction on the preference for balanced states. *J. Pers. Soc. Psychol.* 11:214–19
4. Ajzen, I. 1971. Attribution of dispositions to an actor: Effects of perceived decision freedom and behavioral utilities. *J. Pers. Soc. Psychol.* 18:144–56
5. Ajzen, I. 1971. Attitudinal vs. normative messages: An investigation of the differential effects of persuasive communications on behavior. *Sociometry* 34:263–80
6. Ajzen, I., Darroch, R. K., Fishbein, M., Hornik, J. A. 1970. Looking backward revisited: A reply to Deutscher. *Am. Sociol.* 5:267–73
7. Ajzen, I., Fishbein, M. 1970. *Attitudinal and normative variables as predictors of specific behaviors: A review of research generated by a theoretical model.* Presented at Attitude Res. Consum. Behav. workshop, Univ. Illinois, Urbana
8. Ajzen, I., Fishbein, M. 1970. The prediction of behavior from attitudinal and normative variables. *J. Exp. Soc. Psychol.* 6:466–87
9. Albert, S., Dabbs, J. M. Jr. 1970. Physical distance and persuasion. *J. Pers. Soc. Psychol.* 15:265–70
10. Amir, Y. 1969. Contact hypothesis in ethnic relations. *Psychol. Bull.* 71: 319–42
11. Anderson, L. R. 1970. Prediction of negative attitude from congruity, summation, and logarithm formulae for the evaluation of complex stimuli. *J. Soc. Psychol.* 81:37–48
12. Anderson, N. H. 1965. Primacy effects in personality impression formation using a generalized order effect paradigm. *J. Pers. Soc. Psychol.* 2:1–9
13. Ibid 1968. Application of a linear-serial model to a personality-impression task using serial presentation. 10: 354–62
14. Anderson, N. H. 1970. Functional measurement and psychophysical judgment. *Psychol. Rev.* 77:153–70
15. Anderson, N. H., Jacobson, A. 1965. Effect of stimulus inconsistency and discounting instructions in personality impression formation. *J. Pers. Soc. Psychol.* 2:531–39
16. Archibald, W. P. 1970. Self-esteem and balance with impersonal attitude objects. *Psychon. Sci.* 21: 363–64
17. Aronson, E. 1969. The theory of cognitive dissonance: A current perspective. See Ref. 32, 4:1–34
18. Aronson, E. 1970. Some antecedents of interpersonal attraction. In *Nebraska Symposium on Motivation,* ed. W. J. Arnold, D. Levine, 143–73. Lincoln: Univ. Nebraska Press
19. Aronson, E., Carlsmith, J. M. 1968. Experimentation in social psychology. See Ref. 181, 2:1–79
20. Aronson, E., Linder, D. 1965. Gain and loss of esteem as determinants

of interpersonal attractiveness. *J. Exp. Soc. Psychol.* 1:156–71

21. Arrowood, A. J., Wood, L., Ross, L. 1970. Dissonance, self-perception, and the perception of others: A study in *cognitive* cognitive dissonance. *J. Exp. Soc. Psychol.* 6:304–15

22. Asch, S. E. 1946. Forming impressions of personality. *J. Abnorm. Soc. Psychol.* 41:258–90

23. Bandura, A., Blanchard, E. B., Ritter, B. 1969. Relative efficacy of desensitization and modeling approaches for inducing behavioral, affective, and attitudinal changes. *J. Pers. Soc. Psychol.* 13:173–99

24. Barber, T. X., Silver, M. J. 1968. Fact, fiction, and the experimenter bias effect. *Psychol. Bull. Monogr.* 70:1–29

25. Ibid. Pitfalls in data analysis and interpretation: A reply to Rosenthal, 48–62

26. Bauer, R. A. 1970. Self-confidence and persuasibility: One more time. *J. Market. Res.* 7:256–58

27. Bean, J. R., Calder, B. J., Frey, R., Krovetz, M. L., Reisman, S. R. 1970. Demand characteristics and three conceptions of the frequently deceived subject. *J. Pers. Soc. Psychol.* 14:185–94

28. Bem, D. J. 1968. Attitudes as self-descriptions: Another look at the attitude-behavior link. See Ref. 111, 197–215

29. Bem, D. J. 1970. *Beliefs, Attitudes, and Human Affairs.* Belmont, Calif.: Brooks/Cole

30. Bem, D. J., McConnell, H. K. 1970. Testing the self-perception explanation of dissonance phenomena: On the salience of premanipulation attitudes. *J. Pers. Soc. Psychol.* 14:23–31

31. Berkowitz, L. 1969. Resistance to improper dependency relationships. *J. Exp. Soc. Psychol.* 5:283–94

32. Berkowitz, L., Ed. 1969, 1970. *Advances in Experimental Social Psychology*, Vol. 4, 5. New York: Academic

33. Berkowitz, L., Knurek, D. A. 1969. Label-mediated hostility generalization. *J. Pers. Soc. Psychol.* 13:200–6

34. Berscheid, E., Walster, E. H. 1969. *Interpersonal Attraction.* Reading, Mass.: Addison-Wesley

35. Bishop, D. W., Witt, P. A. 1970. Sources of behavioral variance during leisure time. *J. Pers. Soc· Psychol.* 16:352–60

36. Blake, B. F., Tesser, A. 1970. Interpersonal attraction as a function of the other's reward value to the person. *J. Soc. Psychol.* 82:67–74

37. Blalock, H. M. Jr. 1970. Estimating measurement error using multiple indicators and several points in time. *Am. Sociol. Rev.* 35:101–11

38. Boucher, J., Osgood, C. E. 1969. The Pollyana hypothesis. *J. Verb. Learn. Verb. Behav.* 8:1–8

39. Brehm, J. W., Jones, R. A. 1970. The effect on dissonance of surprise consequences. *J. Exp. Soc. Psychol.* 6:420–31

40. Brehm, J. W., Wicklund, R. A. 1970. Regret and dissonance reduction as a function of postdecision salience of dissonant information. *J. Pers. Soc. Psychol.* 14:1–7

41. Brewer, M. B., Crano, W. D. 1968. Attitude change as a function of discrepancy and source of influence. *J. Soc. Psychol.* 76:13–18

42. Breznitz, S., Kugelmass, S. 1968. The moral judgment of positive acts. *J. Soc. Psychol.* 76:253–58

43. Brigham, J. C., Cook, S. W. 1969. The influence of attitude on the recall of controversial material: A failure to confirm. *J. Exp. Soc. Psychol.* 5:240–43

44. Brigham, J. C., Cook, S. W. 1970. The influence of attitude on judgments of plausibility: A replication and extension. *Educ. Psychol. Meas.* 30:283–92

45. Brock, T. C., Albert, S. M., Becker, L. A. 1970. Familiarity, utility, and supportiveness as determinants of information receptivity. *J. Pers. Soc. Psychol.* 14:292–301

46. Bronfenbrenner, U. 1970. Reaction to social pressure from adults vs. peers among Soviet day school and boarding school pupils in the perspective of an American sample. *J. Pers. Soc. Psychol.* 15:179–89

47. Bruner, J. S., Tagiuri, R. 1954. The perception of people. See Ref. 181, 2:634–54

48. Bugental, D. E., Kaswan, J. W., Love, L. R. 1970. Perception of contradictory meanings conveyed by verbal and nonverbal channels. *J. Pers. Soc. Psychol.* 16:647–55

49. Byrne, D. 1969. Attitudes and attraction. See Ref. 32, 4:35–89

50. Byrne, D., Bond, M. H., Diamond, H. J. 1969. Response to political

candidates as a function of attitude similarity-dissimilarity. *Hum. Relat.* 22:251–62

51. Byrne, D., Ervin, C. R. 1969. Attraction toward a Negro stranger as a function of prejudice, attitude similarity, and the stranger's evaluation of the subject. *Hum. Relat.* 22:397–404

52. Byrne, D., Ervin, C. R., Lamberth, J. 1970. Continuity between the experimental study of attraction and real-life computer dating. *J. Pers. Soc. Psychol.* 16:157–65

53. Byrne, D., Griffitt, W. 1969. Similarity and awareness of similarity of personality characteristics as determinants of attraction. *J. Exp. Res. Pers.* 3:179–86

54. Byrne, D., Griffitt, W., Clore, G. L. 1968. Attitudinal reinforcement effects as a function of stimulus homogeneity-heterogeneity. *J. Verb. Learn. Verb. Behav.* 7:962–64

55. Byrne, D., London, O., Griffitt, W. 1968. The effect of topic importance and attitude similarity-dissimilarity on attraction in an intrastranger design. *Psychon. Sci.* 11:303–4

56. Carroll, J. D., Chang, J. J. 1970. Analysis of individual differences in multidimensional scaling via an N-way generalization of "Eckart-Young" decomposition. *Psychometrika* 35:283–319

57. Chalmers, D. K. 1969. Meanings, impressions, and attitudes: A model of the evaluation process. *Psychol. Rev.* 76:450–60

58. Clore, G. L., Baldridge, B. 1968. Interpersonal attraction: The role of agreement and topic interest. *J. Pers. Soc. Psychol.* 9:340–46

59. Clore, G. L., Baldridge, B. 1970. The behavior of item weights in attitude-attraction research. *J. Exp. Soc. Psychol.* 6:177–86

60. Collins, B. E., Ashmore, R. D., Hornbeck, F. W., Whitney, R. E. 1970. Studies in forced compliance: XIII & XV. In search of a dissonance-producing forced compliance paradigm. *Rep. Res. Soc. Psychol.* 1:11–23

61. Collins, B. E., Helmreich, R. L. 1970. Studies in forced compliance II: Contrasting mechanisms of attitude change produced by public-persuasive and private-true essays. *J. Soc. Psychol.* 81:253–64

62. Cook, S. W. 1969. Motives in a conceptual analysis of attitude-related behavior. See Ref. 18, 179–231

63. Cook, T. D., Burd, J. R., Talbert, T. L. 1970. Cognitive, behavioral and temporal effects of confronting a belief with its costly action implications. *Sociometry* 33:358–69

64. Cooper, J., Jones, R. A. 1970. Self-esteem and consistency as determinants of anticipatory opinion change. *J. Pers. Soc. Psychol.* 14:312–20

65. Corfield, V. K. 1969. The role of arousal and cognitive complexity in susceptibility to social influence. *J. Pers.* 37:554–66

66. Cox, K. K. 1969. Changes in stereotyping of Negroes and whites in magazine advertisements. *Public Opin. Quart.* 33:603–6

67. Cronbach, L. J., Furby, L. 1970. How should we measure "change"—or should we? *Psychol. Bull.* 74:68–80

68. Cronkhite, G. 1969. *Persuasion: Speech and Behavioral Change.* New York: Bobbs-Merrill

69. Crano, W. D., Messé, L. A. 1970. When does dissonance fail? The time dimension in attitude measurement. *J. Pers.* 38:493–508

70. Davis, D. J. 1969. Flexibility and power in comparison among means. *Psychol. Bull.* 71:441–44

71. Deaux, K. K. 1968. Variations in warning, information preference, and anticipatory attitude change. *J. Pers. Soc. Psychol.* 9:157–61

72. DeNike, L. D., Leibovitz, M. P. 1969. Accurate anticipation of reinforcement in verbal conditioning. *J. Pers.* 37:158–70

73. Deutscher, I. 1969. Looking backward: Case studies on the progress of methodology in sociological research. *Am. Sociol.* 4:35–41

74. Dillehay, R. C. 1969. Sincerity and dogmatism: A reassessment and new data. *Psychol. Rev.* 76:422–24

75. Dillehay, R. C., Bruvold, W. H., Siegel, J. P. 1969. Attitude, object label, and stimulus factors in response to an object. *J. Pers. Soc. Psychol.* 11:220–23

76. Dillehay, R. C., Clayton, M. L. 1970. Forced-compliance studies, cognitive dissonance, and self-perception theory. *J. Exp. Soc. Psychol.* 6:458–65

77. Dulany, D. E. 1968. Awareness, rules, and propositional control: A confrontation with S-R behavior theory. In *Verbal Behavioral and S-R Behavior Theory*, ed. D. Horton, T.

Dixon, 340–87. New York: Prentice-Hall

78. Duncan, O. D. 1969. Some linear models for two-wave, two-variable panel analysis. *Psychol. Bull.* 72:177–82

79. Eagly, A. H. 1969. Sex differences in the relationship between self-esteem and susceptibility to social influence. *J. Pers.* 37:581–91

80. Edwards, A. L. 1969. Trait and evaluational consistency in self-description. *Educ. Psychol. Meas.* 29:737–52

81. Edwards, W. 1968. Conservatism in human information processing. In *Formal Representation of Human Judgment*, ed. B. Kleinmuntz, 17–52. New York: Wiley

82. Ehrlich, H. J. 1969. Attitudes, behavior, and the intervening variables. *Am. Sociol.* 4:29–34

83. Einhorn, H. J. 1970. The use of nonlinear, noncompensatory models in decision making. *Psychol. Bull.* 73:221–30

84. Elizur, D. 1970. *Adapting to Innovation.* Israel: Jerusalem Academic Press

85. Epstein, Y. M., Hornstein, H. A. 1969. Penalty and interpersonal attraction as factors influencing the decision to help another person. *J. Exp. Soc. Psychol.* 5:272–82

86. Ettinger, R. F., Nowicki, S. Jr., Nelson, D. A. 1970. Interpersonal attraction and the approval motive. *J. Exp. Res. Pers.* 4:95–99

87. Evans, R. I., Rozelle, R. M., Lasater, T. M., Dembroski, T. M., Allen, B. P. 1970. Fear arousal, persuasion and actual versus implied behavioral change: New perspective utilizing a real-life dental hygiene program. *J. Pers. Soc. Psychol.* 16:220–27

88. Feather, N. T. 1969. Attribution of responsibility and valence of success and failure in relation to initial confidence and task performance. *J. Pers. Soc. Psychol.* 13:129–44

89. Felipe, A. I. 1970. Evaluative versus descriptive consistency in trait inferences. *J. Pers. Soc. Psychol.* 16:627–38

90. Fillenbaum, S., Frey, R. 1970. More on the "faithful" behavior of suspicious subjects. *J. Pers.* 38:43–51

91. Fishbein, M., Ed. 1967. A behavior theory approach to the relations between beliefs about an object and the attitude toward that object. In *Readings in Attitude Theory and Measurement*, 389–400. New York: Wiley

92. Fishbein, M. The prediction of behaviors from attitudinal variables. In *Advances in Communication Research*, ed. K. K. Sereno, C. D. Mortensen. New York: Harper, Row. In press

93. Fishbein, M. The search for attitudinal-behavioral consistency. In *Behavioral Science Foundations of Consumer Behavior*, ed. J. Cohen. Glencoe, Ill.: Free Press. In press

94. Fishbein, M., Landy, E., Hatch, G. 1969. Some determinants of an individual's esteem for his least preferred co-worker. *Hum. Relat.* 22:173–88

95. Fleiss, J. L. 1969. Estimating the magnitude of experimental effects. *Psychol. Bull.* 72:273–76

96. Freedman, J. L. 1969. Role-playing: Psychology by consensus. *J. Pers. Soc. Psychol.* 13:107–17

97. Friedman, H. 1968. Magnitude of experimental effect and a table for its rapid estimation. *Psychol. Bull.* 70:245–51

98. Friedman, P. H., Buck, R., Allen, V. L. 1970. Arousal, anxiety, aggression, and attitude change. *J. Soc. Psychol.* 82:99–108

99. Gallo, P. S. Jr., Dale, I. A. 1968. Experimenter bias in the Prisoner's Dilemma game. *Psychon. Sci.* 13:340

100. Gibbins, K. 1968. Response sets in the semantic differential. *Brit. J. Soc. Clin. Psychol.* 7:253–63

101. Glass, D. C., Mayhew, P. 1969. The effects of cognitive processes on skin conductance reactivity to an aversive film. *Psychon. Sci.* 16:72–73

102. Glinski, R. J., Glinski, B. C., Slatin, G. T. 1970. Nonaivety contamination in conformity experiments: Sources, effects, and implications for control. *J. Pers. Soc. Psychol.* 16:478–85

103. Goldstein, J. W., Rosenfeld, H. M. 1969. Insecurity and preference for persons similar to oneself. *J. Pers.* 37:253–68

104. Gollob, H. F. 1968. Impression formation and word combination in sentences. *J. Pers. Soc. Psychol.* 10:341–53

105. Gordon, A., Glass, D. C. 1970. Choice ambiguity, dissonance, and defensiveness. *J. Pers.* 38:264–72

106. Gormly, A. V., Clore, G. L. 1969. Attraction, dogmatism, and attitude similarity-dissimilarity. *J. Exp. Res. Pers.* 4:9-13

107. Green, B. F. 1969. *Attitude Measurement.* Reading: Addison-Wesley

108. Green, P. E., Carmone, F. J. 1969. Multidimensional scaling: An introduction and comparison of nonmetric unfolding techniques. *J. Market. Res.* 6:330-41

109. Greenwald, A. G. 1968. On defining attitude and attitude theory. See Ref. 111, 147-70

110. Greenwald, A. G. 1969. The openmindedness of the counterattitudinal role player. *J. Exp. Soc. Psychol.* 5:375-88

111. Greenwald, A. G., Brock, T. C., Ostrom, T. M. 1968. *Psychological Foundations of Attitudes.* New York: Academic

112. Greenwald, H. J. 1969. Dissonance and relative versus absolute attractiveness of decision alternatives. *J. Pers. Soc. Psychol.* 11:328-33

113. Griffit, W. B. 1969. Personality similarity and self-concept as determinants of interpersonal attraction. *J. Soc. Psychol.* 78:137-46

114. Gulliksen, H. 1968. Methods for determining equivalence of measures. *Psychol. Bull.* 70:534-44

115. Haaland, G. A., Venkatesan, M. 1968. Resistance to persuasive communications: An examination of the distraction hypothesis. *J. Pers. Soc. Psychol.* 9:167-70

116. Hackman, J. R., Anderson, L. R. 1968. The strength, relevance, and source of beliefs about an object in Fishbein's attitude theory. *J. Soc. Psychol.* 76:55-67

117. Hansen, F. 1969. Consumer choice behavior: An experimental approach. *J. Market. Res.* 6:436-43

118. Harris, R. J. 1969. Dissonance or sour grapes? Post-"decision" changes in ratings and choice frequencies. *J. Pers. Soc. Psychol.* 11:334-44

119. Harrison, A. A. 1968. Response competition, frequency, exploratory behavior, and liking. *J. Pers. Soc. Psychol.* 10:363-68

120. Hastorf, A. H., Schneider, D. J., Polefka, J. 1970. *Person Perception.* Reading: Addison-Wesley

121. Heider, F. 1958. *The Psychology of Interpersonal Relations.* New York: Wiley

122. Heise, D. R. 1969. Affectual dynamics in simple sentences. *J. Pers. Soc. Psychol.* 11:204-13

123. Heise, D. R. 1969. Separating reliability and stability in test-retest correlation. *Am. Sociol. Rev.* 34: 93-101

124. Heise, D. R. 1970. Potency dynamics in simple sentences. *J. Pers. Soc. Psychol.* 16:48-54

125. Helmreich, R., Aronson, E., LeFan, J. 1970. To err is humanizing—sometimes: Effects of self-esteem, competence, and a pratfall on interpersonal attraction. *J. Pers. Soc. Psychol.* 16:259-64

126. Helmreich, R., Collins, B. E. 1968. Studies in forced compliance: Commitment and magnitude of inducement to comply as determinants of opinion change. *J. Pers. Soc. Psychol.* 10:75-81

127. Helmreich, R., Hamilton, J. 1968. Effects of stress, communication relevance, and birth order on opinion change. *Psychon. Sci.* 11:297-98

128. Hendrick, C., Borden, R. 1970. Effects of extraneous fear arousal and birth order on attitude change. *Psychon. Sci.* 18:225-26

129. Hendrick, C., Shaffer, D. R. 1970. Effects of arousal and credibility on learning and persuasion. *Psychon. Sci.* 20:241-43

130. Higbee, K. L. 1969. Fifteen years of fear arousal: Research on threat appeals: 1953-1968. *Psychol. Bull.* 72:426-44

131. Himmelfarb, S., Senn, D. J. 1969. Forming impressions of social class: Two tests of an averaging model. *J. Pers. Soc. Psychol.* 12:38-51

132. Hofman, J. E., Zak, I. 1969. Interpersonal contact and attitude change in a cross-cultural situation. *J. Soc. Psychol.* 78:165-71

133. Hollender, J. W. 1969. Conflict in defensive males as a function of diagnostic expertise and undesirable personality interpretations. *J. Exp. Res. Pers.* 4:51-56

134. Holmes, D. S. 1970. Differential change in affective intensity and the forgetting of unpleasant personal experiences. *J. Pers. Soc. Psychol.* 15:234-39

135. Holmes, D. S., Appelbaum, A. S. 1970. Nature of prior experimental experience as a determinant of performance in a subsequent experiment. *J. Pers. Soc. Psychol.* 14:195-202

136. Holmes, J. G., Strickland, L. H. 1970. Choice freedom and confirmation of

incentive expectancy as determinants of attitude change. *J. Pers. Soc. Psychol.* 14:39–45

137. Holt, L. E. 1970. Resistance to persuasion on explicit beliefs as a function of commitment to and desirability of logically related beliefs. *J. Pers. Soc. Psychol.* 16:583–91

138. Horowitz, I. A. 1969. Effects of volunteering, fear arousal, and number of communications on attitude change. *J. Pers. Soc. Psychol.* 11: 34–37

139. Horowitz, I. A., Gumenik, W. E. 1970. Effects of the volunteer subject, choice, and fear arousal on attitude change. *J. Exp. Soc. Psychol.* 6:293–303

140. Insko, C. A., Blake, R. R., Cialdini, R. B., Mulaik, S. A. 1970. Attitude toward birth control and cognitive consistency: Theoretical and practical implications of survey data. *J. Pers. Soc. Psychol.* 16:228–37

141. Insko, C. A., Cialdini, R. B. 1969. A test of three interpretations of attitudinal verbal reinforcement. *J. Pers. Soc. Psychol.* 12:333–41

142. Jackson, D. N. 1969. Multimethod factor analysis in the evaluation of convergent and discriminant validity. *Psychol. Bull.* 72:30–49

143. Janis, I. L., Rausch, C. N. 1970. Selective interest in communications that could arouse decisional conflict: A field study of participants in the draft-resistance movement. *J. Pers. Soc. Psychol.* 14:46–54

144. Jecker, J., Landy, D. 1969. Liking a person as a function of doing him a favor. *Hum. Relat.* 22:371–78

145. Jellison, J. M., Mills, J. 1969. Effect of public commitment upon opinions. *J. Exp. Soc. Psychol.* 5:340–46

146. Jellison, J. M., Zeisset, P. T. 1969. Attraction as a function of the commonality and desirability of a trait shared with another. *J. Pers. Soc. Psychol.* 11:115–20

147. Johnson, H. H., Scileppi, J. A. 1969. Effects of ego-involvement conditions on attitude change to high and low credibility communicators. *J. Pers. Soc. Psychol.* 13:31–36

148. Johnson, H. H., Torcivia, J. M., Poprick, M. A. 1968. Effects of source credibility on the relationship between authoritarianism and attitude change. *J. Pers. Soc. Psychol.* 9:179–83

149. Johnson, N. B., Middleton, M. R., Tajfel, H. 1970. The relationship between children's preferences for and knowledge about other nations. *Brit. J. Soc. Clin. Psychol.* 9:232–40

150. Jones, E. E., Davis, K. E. 1966. From acts to dispositions: The attribution process in person perception. See Ref. 32, 2:219–66

151. Jones, E. E., Rock, L., Shaver, K. G., Goethals, G. R., Ward, L. M. 1968. Pattern of performance and ability attribution: An unexpected primacy effect. *J. Pers. Soc. Psychol.* 10:317–40

152. Jones, E. E., Stires, L. K., Shaver, K. G., Harris, V. A. 1968. Evaluation of an ingratiator by target persons and bystanders. *J. Pers.* 36:349–85

153. Jones, R. A., Linder, D. E., Kiesler, C. A., Zanna, M., Brehm, J. W. 1968. Internal states or external stimuli: Observers' attitude judgments and the dissonance-theory self-persuasion controversy. *J. Exp. Soc. Psychol.* 4:247–69

154. Jones, S. C., Shrauger, J. S. 1970. Reputation and self-evaluation as determinants of attraction. *Sociometry* 33:276–86

155. Kaplan, K. J., Fishbein, M. 1969. The source of beliefs, their saliency, and prediction of attitude. *J. Soc. Psychol.* 78:63–74

156. Kavanagh, M. J., MacKinney, A. C., Wolins, L. 1971. Issues in managerial performance: Multitrait-multimethod analyses of ratings. *Psychol. Bull.* 75:34–49

157. Kawwa, T. 1968. A survey of ethnic attitudes of some British secondary school pupils. *Brit. J. Soc. Clin. Psychol.* 7:161–68

158. Kelley, H. H. 1967. Attribution theory in social psychology. In *Nebraska Symposium on Motivation.* ed. D. Levine, 192–241. Lincoln: Univ. Nebraska Press

159. Kelley, H. H., Stahelski, A. J. 1970. Errors in perception of intentions in a mixed-motive game. *J. Exp. Soc. Psychol.* 6:379–400

160. Ibid. The inference of intentions from moves in the Prisoner's Dilemma game, 401–19

161. Kelley, H. H., Stahelski, A. J. 1970. Social interaction basis of cooperators' and competitors' beliefs about others. *J. Pers. Soc. Psychol.* 16: 66–91

162. Kidder, L. H., Campbell, D. T. 1970. The indirect testing of social attitudes. See Ref. 308, 333–85

163. Kiesler, C. A., Collins, B. E., Miller, N. 1969. *Attitude Change.* New York: Wiley

164. Kiesler, C. A., Nisbett, R. E., Zanna, M. P. 1969. On inferring one's beliefs from one's behavior. *J. Pers. Soc. Psychol.* 11:321–27

165. Kimble, G. A., Perlmuter, L. C. 1970. The problem of volition. *Psychol. Rev.* 77:361–84

166. Koslin, B. L., Pargament, R. 1969. Effects of attitude on the discrimination of opinion statements. *J. Exp. Soc. Psychol.* 5:245–64

167. Kuusinen, J. 1969. Affective and denotative structures of personality ratings. *J. Pers. Soc. Psychol.* 12:181–88

168. Lackenmeyer, C. W. 1970. Experimentation—A misunderstood methodology in psychological and social-psychological research. *Am. Psychol.* 25:617–24

169. Landy, D., Aronson, E. 1968. Liking for an evaluator as a function of his discernment. *J. Pers. Soc. Psychol.* 9:133–41

170. Landy, D., Aronson, E. 1969. The influence of the character of the criminal and his victim on the decisions of simulated jurors. *J. Exp. Soc. Psychol.* 5:141–52

171. Lanzetta, J. T., Kleck, R. E. 1970. Encoding and decoding of nonverbal affect in humans. *J. Pers. Soc. Psychol.* 16:12–19

172. Laumann, E. D. 1969. Friends of urban men: An assessment of accuracy in reporting their socioeconomic attributes, mutual choice, and attitude agreement. *Sociometry* 32:54–69

173. Lehmann, S. 1970. Personality and compliance: A study of anxiety and self-esteem in opinion and behavior change. *J. Pers. Soc. Psychol.* 15:76–86

174. Lepper, M. R., Zanna, M. P., Abelson, R. P. 1970. Cognitive irreversibility in a dissonance-reduction situation. *J. Pers. Soc. Psychol.* 16:191–98

175. Lerner, M. J., Lichtman, R. R. 1968. Effects of perceived norms on attitudes and altruistic behavior toward a dependent other. *J. Pers. Soc. Psychol.* 9:226–32

176. Leventhal, H. 1970. Findings and theory in the study of fear communications. See Ref. 32, 5:119–86

177. Levonian, E. 1968. Self-esteem and opinion change. *J. Pers. Soc. Psychol.* 9:257–59

178. Levonian, E. 1968. Interpretation of published results relating personality to opinion change. *Psychol. Bull.* 69:388–89

179. Lewit, D. W., Shanley, P. J. 1969. Prejudice and the learning of biracial influence structures. *Psychon. Sci.* 17:93–95

180. Lichtenstein, E., Craine, W. H. 1969. The importance of subjective evaluation of reinforcement in verbal conditioning. *J. Exp. Res. Pers.* 3:214–20

181. Lindzey, G., Aronson, E., Eds. 1968, 1969. *The Handbook of Social Psychology,* Vol. 1–5. Reading: Addison-Wesley. 2nd ed.

182. Lott, A. J., Lott, B. E. 1968. A learning theory approach to interpersonal attitudes. See Ref. 111, 67–88

183. Lott, A. J., Lott, B. E., Walsh, M. L. 1970. Learning of paired associates relevant to differentially liked persons. *J. Pers. Soc. Psychol.* 16:274–83

184. Lowe, C. A., Goldstein, J. W. 1970. Reciprocal liking and attributions of ability: Mediating effects of perceived intent and personal involvement. *J. Pers. Soc. Psychol.* 16:291–97

185. Lowin, A. 1969. Further evidence for an approach-avoidance interpretation of selective exposure. *J. Exp. Soc. Psychol.* 5:265–71

186. Luginbuhl, J. E. R. 1970. The effect of legitimacy of a request and compliance versus noncompliance on the evaluation of others. *J. Pers.* 38:482–92

187. Malpass, R. S. 1969. Effects of attitude on learning and memory: The influence of instruction-induced sets. *J. Exp. Soc. Psychol.* 5:441–53

188. Mascaro, G. F. 1970. Correspondence between evaluative expectations and attitudes. *Aust. J. Psychol.* 22:115–25

189. Mascaro, G. F., Lopez, J. A. 1970. The effects of delayed judgmental similarity on evaluative attraction. *Psychon. Sci.* 19:229–30

190. Matlin, M. W. 1970. Response competition as a mediating factor in the frequency-affect relationship. *J. Pers. Soc. Psychol.* 16:536–52

191. McCarrey, M. W., Chagnon, G. 1968. Intensity of assertion and the congruity principle. *J. Soc. Psychol.* 76:69–74

192. McCroskey, J. C. 1970. The effects of evidence as an inhibitor of counter

persuasion. *Speech Monogr.* 37: 188–94

193. McCroskey, J. C., Mehrley, R. S. 1969. The effects of disorganization and nonfluency on attitude change and source credibility. *Speech Monogr.* 36:13–21

194. McEwen, W. J., Greenberg, B. S. 1969. Effects of communication assertion intensity. *J. Commun.* 19: 257–65

195. Ibid 1970. The effects of message intensity on receiver evaluations of source, message, and topic. 20:340–50

196. McGuire, W. J. 1960. A syllogistic analysis of cognitive relationships. In *Attitude Organization and Change*, ed. M. J. Rosenberg et al, 65–111. New Haven: Yale Univ. Press

197. McGuire, W. J. 1968. Personality and susceptibility to social influence. In *Handbook of Personality Theory and Research*, ed. E. F. Borgatta, W. W. Lambert, 1130–87. Chicago: Rand McNally

198. McGuire, W. J. 1969. The nature of attitudes and attitude change. See Ref. 181, 3:136–314

199. McLaughlin, B. 1970. Similarity, recall, and appraisal of others. *J. Pers.* 38:106–16

200. Meehl, P. E. 1967. Theory testing in psychology and physics: A methodological paradox. *Phil. Sci.* 34:103–15

201. Mehrabian, A. 1969. Significance of posture and position in the communication of attitude and status relationships. *Pyschol. Bull.* 71:359–72

202. Mehrabian, A. 1970. When are feelings communicated inconsistently? *J. Exp. Res. Pers.* 4:198–212

203. Mehrabian, A., Reed, H. 1968. Some determinants of communication accuracy. *Psychol. Bull.* 70:365–81

204. Miller, A. G. 1969. Amount of information and stimulus valence as determinants of cognitive complexity. *J. Pers.* 37:141–57

205. Miller, A. G. 1970. Role of physical attractiveness in impression formation. *Psychon. Sci.* 19:241–43

206. Miller, G. R., Baseheart, J. 1969. Source trustworthiness, opinionated statements, and response to persuasive communication. *Speech Monogr.* 36:1–7

207. Millman, S. 1968. Anxiety, comprehension, and susceptibility to social influence. *J. Pers. Soc. Psychol.* 9:251–56

208. Mittelstaedt, R. 1969. A dissonance approach to repeat purchasing behavior. *J. Market. Res.* 6:444–46

209. Mortensen, C. D., Sereno, K. K. 1970. The influence of ego-involvement and discrepancy on perceptions of communication. *Speech Monogr.* 37: 127–34

210. Murdock, P., VanBruggen, Y. O. 1970. Stability, generality, and change of category width. *J. Per.* 38:117–23

211. Nel, E., Helmreich, R., Aronson, E. 1969. Opinion change in the advocate as a function of the persuasibility of his audience: A clarification of the meaning of dissonance. *J. Pers. Soc. Psychol.* 12:117–24

212. Nemeth, C. 1970. Effects of free versus constrained behavior on attraction between people. *J. Pers. Soc. Psychol.* 15:302–11

213. Novak, D. W., Lerner, M. J. 1968. Rejection as a consequence of perceived similarity. *J. Pers. Soc. Psychol.* 9:147–52

214. Ofshe, R., Ofshe, L. 1970. A comparative study of two scaling models: Paired comparisons and scalogram analysis. *Sociometry* 33:409–26

215. O'Neal, E., Mills, J. 1969. The influence of anticipated choice on the Halo effect. *J. Exp. Soc. Psychol.* 5: 347–51

216. Osbell, J. M., Sherrill, K. S. 1969. Racial attitudes and the metropolitan context: A structural analysis. *Public Opin. Quart.* 33:46–54

217. Osgood, C. E. 1970. Speculations on the structure of interpersonal intentions. *Behav. Sci.* 15:237–54

218. Osgood, C. E., Suci, G. J., Tannenbaum, P. H. 1957. *The Measurement of Meaning.* Urbana: Univ. Illinois Press

219. Oshikawa, S. 1968. The theory of cognitive dissonance and experimental research. *J. Market. Res.* 5:429–30

220. Osterhouse, R. A., Brock, T. C. 1970. Distraction increases yielding to propaganda by inhibiting counterarguing. *J. Pers. Soc. Psychol.* 15:344–58

221. Ostrom, T. M. 1968. The emergence of attitude theory: 1930–1950. See Ref. 111, 1–32

222. Ostrom, T. M. 1969. The relationship between the affective, behavioral, and cognitive components of at-

titude. *J. Exp. Soc. Psychol.* 5:12–30

223. Ostrom, T. M., Upshaw, H. S. 1968. Psychological perspective and attitude change. See Ref. 111, 217–42

224. Page, M. M. 1969. Social psychology of a classical conditioning of attitudes experiment. *J. Pers. Soc. Psychol.* 11:177–86

225. Page, M. M. 1970. Role of demand awareness in the communicator credibility effect. *J. Soc. Psychol.* 82:57–66

226. Papageorgis, D. 1968. Warning and persuasion. *Psychol. Bull.* 70·271–82

227. Peabody, D. 1967. Trait inferences: Evaluative and descriptive aspects. *J. Pers. Soc. Psychol. Monogr.* 7:4; Whole No. 644

228. Peabody, D. 1970. Evaluative and descriptive aspects in personality perception: A reappraisal. *J. Pers. Soc. Psychol.* 16:639–46

229. Petrinovich, L. F., Hardyck, C. D. 1969. Error rates for multiple comparison methods: Some evidence concerning the frequency of erroneous conclusions. *Psychol. Bull.* 71:43–54

230. Pettigrew, T. F. 1969. Racially separate or together? *J. Soc. Issues* 25:43–69

231. Piliavin, J. A., Piliavin, I. M., Loewenton, E. P., McCauley, C., Hammond, P. 1969. An observer's reproductions of dissonance effects: The right answers for the wrong reasons? *J. Pers. Soc. Psychol.* 13:98–106

232. Posavac, E. J., Triandis, H. C. 1968. Personality characteristics, race and grades as determinants of interpersonal attitudes. *J. Soc. Psychol.* 76:227–42

233. Press, A. N., Crockett, W. H., Rosenkrantz, P. S. 1970. Cognitive complexity and the learning of balanced and unbalanced social structures. *J. Pers.* 37:541–53

234. Rambo, W. W. 1969. Own-attitude and the aberrant placement of socially relevant items on an equal appearing interval scale. *J. Soc. Psychol.* 79:163–70

235. Ray, M. L. 1968. Biases in selection of messages designed to induce resistance to persuasion. *J. Pers. Soc. Psychol.* 9:335–39

236. Reagor, P. A., Clore, G. L. 1970. Attraction, test anxiety, and similarity-dissimilarity of test performance. *Psychon. Sci.* 18:219–20

237. Reich, J. W. 1969. Attitudes and cognitive discrimination: A methodological note. *J. Soc. Psychol.* 78:219–25

238. Reitz, W. E., Douey, J. 1968. Role of homogeneity and centrality of attitude domain on reinforcing properties of attitude statements. *J. Exp. Res. Pers.* 3:120–25

239. Rhine, R. J., Severance, L. J. 1970. Ego-involvement, discrepancy, source credibility, and attitude change. *J. Pers. Soc. Psychol.* 16:175–90

240. Ritter, E. H., Homes, D. S. 1969. Behavioral contagion: Its occurrence as a function of differential restraint reduction. *J. Exp. Res. Pers.* 3:242–46

241. Robinson, J. E., Insko, C. A. 1969. Attributed belief similarity-dissimilarity versus race as determinants of prejudice: A further test of Rokeach's theory. *J. Exp. Res. Pers.* 4:72–77

242. Robinson, J. P., Hefner, R. 1968. Perceptual maps of the world. *Public Opin. Quart.* 32:273–80

243. Robinson, J. P., Rusk, J. G., Head, K. B. 1968. *Measures of Political Attitudes.* Inst. Soc. Res. Univ. Michigan, Ann Arbor

244. Robinson, J. P., Shaver, P. R. 1969. *Measures of Social Psychological Attitudes.* Inst. Soc. Res., Univ. Michigan, Ann Arbor

245. Rogers, R. W., Thistlethwaite, D. L. 1970. Effects of fear arousal and reassurance on attitude change. *J. Pers. Soc. Psychol.* 15:227–33

246. Rokeach, M. 1968. *Beliefs, Attitudes and Values.* San Francisco: Jossey-Bass

247. Rosenbaum, M. E., Levin, I. P. 1969. Impression formation as a function of source credibility and the polarity of information. *J. Pers. Soc. Psychol.* 12:34–37

248. Rosenberg, M. J. 1956. Cognitive structure and attitudinal affect. *J. Abnorm. Soc. Psychol.* 53:367–72

249. Rosenberg, S. 1968. Mathematical models of social behavior. See Ref. 181, 1:179–244

250. Rosenberg, S., Olshan, K. 1970. Evaluative and descriptive aspects in personality perception. *J. Pers. Soc. Psychol.* 16:619–26

251. Rosenthal, R. 1968. Experimenter expectancy and the reassuring nature of the null hypothesis decision pro-

cedure. *Psychol. Bull. Monogr.* 70:30–47

252. Rosenthal, R., Rosnow, R. L., Eds. 1969. *Artifact in Behavioral Research.* New York: Academic

253. Rosnow, R. L., Gitter, A. G., Holz, R. F. 1969. Some determinants of postdecisional information preferences. *J. Soc. Psychol.* 79:235–45

254. Rosnow, R. L., Suls, J. M. 1970. Reactive effects of pretesting in attitude research. *J. Pers. Soc. Psychol.* 15:338–43

255. Ross, J. 1970. Multidimensional scaling of attitudes. See Ref. 308, 279–93

256. Rossomando, N. P., Weiss, W. 1970. Attitude change effects of timing and amount of payment for counter attitudinal behavior. *J. Pers. Soc. Psychol.* 14:32–38

257. Rubin, Z., Zajonc, R. B. 1969. Structural bias and generalization in the learning of social structures. *J. Pers.* 37:310–24

258. Rule, B. G., Rehill, D. 1970. Distraction and self-esteem effects on attitude change. *J. Pers. Soc. Psychol.* 15:359–65

259. Rule, B. G., Renner, J. 1968. Involvement and group effects on opinion change. *J. Soc. Psychol.* 76:189–98

260. Ryan, T. A. 1970. *Intentional Behavior: An Approach to Human Motivation.* New York: Ronald

261. Sachs, D. H., Byrne, D. 1970. Differential conditioning of evaluative responses to neutral stimuli through association with attitude statements. *J. Exp. Res. Pers.* 4:181–85

262. Sandell, R. G. 1968. Effects of attitudinal and situational factors on reported choice behavior. *J. Market. Res.* 5:405–8

263. Scheibe, K. E. 1970. *Beliefs and Values.* New York: Holt

264. Schleifer, S., Dunn, S. W. 1968. Relative effectiveness of advertisements of foreign and domestic origin. *J. Market. Res.* 5:296–99

265. Schlesinger, I. M., Guttman, L. 1969. Smallest space analysis of intelligence and achievement tests. *Psychol. Bull.* 71:95–100

266. Schmidt, C. F. 1969. Personality impression formation as a function of relatedness of information and length of set. *J. Pers. Soc. Psychol.* 12:6–11

267. Schopler, J., Thompson, V. D. 1968. Role of attribution processes in mediating amount of reciprocity

for a favor. *J. Pers. Soc. Psychol.* 10:243–50

268. Schultz, D. P. 1969. The human subject in psychological research. *Psychol. Bull.* 72:214–28

269. Scott, W. A. 1968. Attitude measurement. See Ref. 181, 2:204–73

270. Scott, W. A. 1969. Structure of natural cognitions. *J. Pers. Soc. Psychol.* 12:261–78

271. Sears, D. O., Abeles, R. P. 1969. Attitudes and opinions. *Ann. Rev. Psychol.* 20:253–88

272. Sereno, K. K. 1968. Ego-involvement, high source credibility, and response to a belief-discrepant communication. *Speech Monogr.* 35:476–81

273. Shaver, K. G. 1970. Redress and conscientiousness in the attribution of responsibility for accidents. *J. Exp. Soc. Psychol.* 6:100–10

274. Shaver, K. G. 1970. Defensive attribution: Effects of severity and relevance on the responsibility assigned for an accident. *J. Pers. Soc. Psychol.* 14:101–13

275. Shaw, M. E., Reitan, H. T. 1969. Attribution of responsibility as a basis for scanctioning behavior. *Brit. J. Soc. Clin. Psychol.* 8:217–26

276. Shepherd, J. W., Bagley, A. J. 1970. The effects of biographical information and order of presentation on the judgment of an aggressive action. *Brit. J. Soc. Clin. Psychol.* 9:177–79

277. Sherif, M. 1970. On the relevance of social psychology. *Am. Psychol.* 25:144–56

278. Sherman, S. J. 1970. Effects of choice and incentive on attitude change in a discrepant behavior situation. *J. Pers. Soc. Psychol.* 15:245–52

279. Ibid. Attitudinal effects of unforeseen consequences. 16:510–20

280. Sherwood, J. J., Barron, J. W., Fitch, H. G. 1969. Cognitive dissonance: Theory and research. In *The Study of Attitude Change,* ed. R. V. Wagner, J. J. Sherwood, 56–86. Belmont, Calif.: Brooks/Cole

281. Shotland, R. L., Berger, W. G., Forsythe, R. 1970. A validation of the lost-letter technique. *Public Opin. Quart.* 34:278–81

282. Shrauger, J. S., Jones, S. C. 1968. Social validation and interpersonal evaluations. *J. Exp. Soc. Psychol.* 4:315–23

283. Schuchman, A., Perry, M. 1969. Self-confidence and persuasibility in

marketing: A reappraisal. *J. Market Res.* 6:146–54

284. Siegal, E. R., Miller, G. R., Wotring, C. E. 1969. Source credibility and credibility proneness: A new relationship. *Speech Monogr.* 36:118–25

285. Sigall, H. 1970. Effects of competence and consensual validation on a communicator's liking for the audience. *J. Pers. Soc. Psychol.* 16:251–58

286. Sigall, H., Aronson, E. 1967. Opinion change and the gain-loss model of interpersonal attraction. *J. Exp. Soc. Psychol.* 3:178–88

287. Ibid 1969. Liking for an evaluator as a function of her physical attractiveness and nature of the evaluations. 5:93–100

288. Sigall, H., Helmreich, R. 1969. Opinion change as a function of stress and communicator credibility. *J. Exp. Soc. Psychol.* 5:70–78

289. Silverman, I., Regula, C. R. 1968. Evaluation apprehension, demand characteristics, and the effect of distraction on persuasibility. *J. Soc. Psychol.* 75:273–81

290. Silverman, I., Shulman, A. D. 1970. A conceptual model of artifact in attitude change studies. *Sociometry* 33:97–107

291. Simons, H. W., Berkowitz, N. N., Moyer, R. J. 1970. Similarity, credibility, and attitude change: A review and a theory. *Psychol. Bull.* 73:1–16

292. Singer, S. 1969. Factors related to participant's memory of a conversation. *J. Pers.* 37:93–109

293. Sistrunk, F. 1969. A comparison of the socially influenced behavior of college students and college-age dropouts. *Psychon. Sci.* 15:214–15

294. Slovic, P., Lichtenstein, S. Comparison of Bayesian and regression approaches in the study of information processing in judgment. In *Human Judgments and Social Interaction*, ed. L. Rappoport, D. A. Summers. New York: Holt. In press.

295. Smith, D. D. 1968. Dogmatism, cognitive consistency, and knowledge of conflicting facts. *Sociometry* 31: 259–77

296. Smith, E. W. L., Dixon, T. R. 1968. Verbal conditioning as a function of race of the experimenter and prejudice of the subject. *J. Exp. Soc. Psychol.* 4:285–301

297. Snider, J. G., Osgood, C. E. 1969. *Semantic Differential Technique.* Chicago: Aldine

298. Spencer, H. 1862. *First Principles.* New York: Burt

299. Staats, A. W. 1968. Social behaviorism and human motivation: Principles of the attitude-reinforcer-discriminative system. See Ref. 111, 33–66

300. Stalling, R. B. 1970. Personality similarity and evaluative meaning as conditioners of attraction. *J. Pers. Soc. Psychol.* 14:77–82

301. Steiner, I. D. 1968. Reactions to adverse and favorable evaluations of one's self. *J. Pers.* 36:553–63

302. Steiner, I. D. 1970. Perceived freedom. See Ref. 32, 5:187–248

303. Stimpson, D. V. 1970. The influence of commitment and self-esteem on susceptibility to persuasion. *J. Soc. Psychol.* 80:189–95

304. Streltzer, N. E., Loch, G. V. 1968. Influence of emotional role-playing on smoking habits and attitudes. *Psychol. Rep.* 22:812–20

305. Streufert, S., Streufert, S. C. 1969. Effects of conceptual structure, failure, and success on attribution of causality and interpersonal attitudes. *J. Pers. Soc. Psychol.* 11: 138–47

306. Stricker, L. J., Messick, S., Jackson, D. N. 1969. Evaluating deception in psychological research. *Psychol. Bull.* 71:343–51

307. Summers, D. A., Taliaferro, J. D., Fletcher, D. J. 1970. Subjective vs. objective description of judgment policy. *Psychon. Sci.* 18:249–50

308. Summers, G. F. 1970 *Attitude Measurement.* Chicago: Rand McNally

309. Szalay, L. B., Windle, C., Lysne, D. A. 1970. Attitude measurement by free verbal associations. *J. Soc. Psychol.* 82:43–55

310. Tan, A. L., de Vera, G. 1970. A test of the belief congruence theory of prejudice. *Cornell J. Soc. Relat.* 5:166–71

311. Tarter, D. E. 1969. Toward prediction of attitude-action discrepancy. *Soc. Forces* 47:398–405

312. Taylor, D. A., Altman, I., Sorrentino, R. 1969. Interpersonal exchange as a function of rewards and costs and situational factors: Expectancy confirmation-disconfirmation. *J. Exp. Soc. Psychol.* 5:324–39

313. TenHouten, W. D. 1969. Scale gradient analysis: A statistical method for constructing and evaluating Guttman scales. *Sociometry* 32:80–98

314. Tesser, A. 1969. Trait similarity and trait evaluation as correlates of attraction. *Psychon. Sci.* 15:319-20

315. Thurstone, L. L. 1927. Attitudes can be measured. *Am. J. Sociol.* 33:529-54

316. Toulmin, S. 1959. *The Uses of Argument.* England: Cambridge Univ. Press

317. Triandis, H. C. 1971. *Attitude and Attitude Change.* New York: Wiley

318. Triandis, H. C., Fishbein, M., Hall, E., Shanmagam, A. V., Tanaka, Y. 1968. Affect and behavioral intentions. In *Contributions to Psychology*, eds. A. K. P. Sinha, H. K. Misra, A. K. Kanth, K. S. Rao, 28-52. New Delhi: Inst. Soc. Psychol. Res.

319. Tversky, A. 1969. Intransitivity of preferences. *Psychol. Rev.* 76:31-48

320. Upshaw, H. S. 1969. The personal reference scale: An approach to social judgment. See Ref. 32, 4:315-71

321. Upshaw, H. S., Ostrom, T. M., Ward, C. D. 1970. Content vs. self-rating in attitude research. *J. Exp. Soc. Psychol.* 6:272-79

322. Vaughan, G. M., Corballis, M. C. 1969. Beyond tests of significance: Estimating strength of effects in selected ANOVA designs. *Psychol. Bull.* 72:204-13

323. Vohs, J. L., Garrett, R. L. 1968. Resistance to persuasion: An integrative framework. *Public Opin. Quart.* 32:445-52

324. Walster, E. 1966. Assignment of responsibility for an accident. *J. Pers. Soc. Psychol.* 3:73-79

325. Warner, L. G., DeFleur, M. L. 1969. Attitude as an interactional concept: Social constraint and social distance as intervening variables between attitudes and action. *Am. Sociol. Rev.* 34:153-69

326. Warr, P. B., Coffman, T. L. 1970. Personality, involvement and extremity of judgment. *Brit. J. Soc. Clin. Psychol.* 7:108-21

327. Warr, P. B., Knapper, C. 1968. *The Perception of People and Events.* New York: Wiley

328. Warr, P. B., Smith, J. S. 1970. Combining information about people: Comparisons between six models. *J. Pers. Soc. Psychol.* 16:55-65

329. Watts, L. E., Holt, W. A. 1970. Logical relationships among beliefs and timing as factors in persuasion. *J. Pers. Soc. Psychol.* 16:571-82

330. Weiner, B., Kukla, A. 1970. An attributional analysis of achievement motivation. *J. Pers. Soc. Psychol.* 15:1-20

331. Werts, C. E., Linn, R. L. 1970. Path analysis: Psychological examples. *Psychol. Bull.* 74:193-212

332. Wessler, R. L., Strauss, M. E. 1968. Experimenter expectancy: A failure to replicate. *Psychol. Rep.* 22:687-88

333. Wheatley, J. J., Oshikawa, S. 1970. The relationship between anxiety and positive and negative advertising appeals. *J. Market. Res.* 7:85-89

334. Wicker, A. W. 1969. Attitudes vs. actions: The relationship of verbal and overt behavioral responses to attitude objects. *J. Soc. Issues* 25:41-78

335. Wicker, A. W., Bushweiler, G. 1970. Perceived fairness and pleasantness of social exchange situations: Two factorial studies of inequity. *J. Pers. Soc. Psychol.* 15:63-75

336. Wiggins, N. Individual differences in human judgment: A multivariate approach. See Ref. 294

337. Wiggins, N., Fishbein, M. 1969. Dimensions of semantic space: A problem of individual differences. See Ref. 297, 183-93

338. Wiggins, N., Hoffman, P. J. 1968. Three models of clinical judgment. *J. Abnorm. Psychol.* 73:70-77

339. Willis, R. H., Willis, Y. A. 1970. Role playing vs. deception: An experimental comparison. *J. Pers. Soc. Psychol.* 16:472-77

340. Winch, R. F., Campbell, D. T. 1969. Proof? No. Evidence? Yes. The significance of tests of significance. *Am. Sociol.* 4:140-43

341. Wish, M., Deutsch, M., Biener, L. 1970. Differences in conceptual structures of nations: An exploratory study. *J. Pers. Soc. Psychol.* 16:361-73

342. Woodmansee, J. H. 1970. The pupil response as a measure of social attitudes. See Ref. 308, 514-33

343. Wrightsman, L. S. 1969. Wallace supporters and adherence to "law and order." *J. Pers. Soc. Psychol.* 13:17-22

344. Wyer, R. S. Jr. 1968. The effects of information redundancy on evaluation of social stimuli. *Psychon. Sci.* 13:245-46

345. Wyer, R. S. Jr. 1969. A quantitative comparison of three models of impression formation. *J. Exp. Res. Pers.* 4:29–41

346. Wyer, R. S. Jr. 1970. Information redundancy, inconsistency, and novelty and their role in impression formation. *J. Exp. Soc. Psychol.* 6:111–27

347. Wyer, R. S. Jr. 1970. The prediction of evaluations of social role occupants as a function of the favorableness, relevance and probability associated with attributes of these occupants. *Sociometry* 33:79 96

348. Wyer, R. S. Jr. 1970. Quantitative prediction of belief and opinion change: A further test of a subjective probability model. *J. Pers. Soc. Psychol.* 16:559–70

349. Wyer, R. S. Jr., Goldberg, L. 1970. A probabilistic analysis of relationships among beliefs and attitudes. *Psychol. Rev.* 77:100–20

350. Wyer, R. S. Jr., Lyon, J. D. 1970. A test of cognitive balance theory implications for social inference processes. *J. Pers. Soc. Psychol.* 16:598–618

351. Wyer, R. S. Jr., Schwartz, S. 1969. Some contingencies in the effects of the source of a communication on the evaluation of that communication. *J. Pers. Soc. Psychol.* 11:1–9

352. Yee, A. H., Gage, N. L. 1968. Techniques for estimating the source and direction of causal influence in panel data. *Psychol. Bull.* 70:115–26

353. Yukl, G. 1970. Leader LPC scores: Attitude dimensions and behavioral correlates. *J. Soc. Psychol.* 80:207–12

354. Zajonc, R. B. 1968. Attitudinal effects of mere exposure. *J. Pers. Soc. Psychol. Monogr.* 9:1–27

355. Zanna, M. P., Kiesler, C. A., Pilkonis, P. A. 1970. Positive and negative attitudinal affect established by classical conditioning. *J. Pers. Soc. Psychol.* 14:321–28

356. Zellner, M. 1970. Self-esteem, reception, and influenceability. *J. Pers. Soc. Psychol.* 15:87–93

357. Zimbardo, P., Ebbesen, E. B. 1969. *Influencing Attitudes and Changing Behavior.* Reading: Addison-Wesley

358. Zimbardo, P., Ebbesen, E. B. 1970. Experimental modification of the relationship between effort, attitude, and behavior. *J. Pers. Soc. Psychol.* 16:207–13

359. Zimbardo, P., Snyder, M., Thomas, J., Gold, A., Gurwitz, S. 1970. Modifying the impact of persuasive communications with external distraction. *J. Pers. Soc. Psychol.* 16:669–80

PERSONNEL SELECTION   189

DOUGLAS W. BRAY AND JOSEPH L. MOSES[1]

American Telephone and Telegraph Company, New York City

The field of personnel selection has received a great deal of attention in the 3-year period covered by this review—January 1, 1968, through December 31, 1970.[2] In some respects it has been a period of discovery—the recent discovery, as noted by Campbell (30), of minority and disadvantaged groups has undoubtedly changed the complexion of the field. The specter of personnel selection by civil legislation has evoked considerable interest by parties both within and outside the profession. This in many ways has served as an impetus not only to discover new techniques but also to critically examine current practices concerning the full utilization of the disadvantaged, blacks, women, the elderly, and other special groups.

At the same time, some serious questions have been raised concerning personnel research strategies. A highly simplified, but rather typical, personnel selection research strategy frequently follows this format: Give job applicants an aptitude test of some sort, hire some of them, get ratings of job performance, correlate test scores with performance ratings, add more tests, use elaborate statistical methods, hopefully arriving at a degree of prediction which, in light of the selection ratio, is of some practical usefulness. The adequacy of this model, although vastly superior to the still all too common buy test-use test-no research approach, has in the past 3 years been questioned increasingly. The forces influencing the model in the direction of greater sophistication were already apparent in 1969, or even before, as noted by Owens & Jewell (155). They have intensified in the intervening years.

Perhaps chief among these forces was the pressure, legal and otherwise, for fair employment practices. The demand for unbiased selection methods focused on testing and consequently placed personnel psychologists in an unaccustomed limelight. Such attention proved to be embarrassing, not only because testers had ignored minority groups but, as importantly, because the quality of research done even on the majority group left much to be desired.

Faced with renewed interest and pressures regarding selection practices, the general tenor of response has been disappointing. To some extent the

[1] The helpful contributions of James R. Huck are gratefully acknowledged.

[2] Articles appearing before and after this period are included where they provide continuity.

response to those challenges has been to turn inward. There seems to be, for example, a renewed interest in methodology for methodology's sake. The growing interest in using moderator variables, multitrait analysis, and computer technology represent, in part, ways of salvaging our traditional models.

On the other hand, some fundamental issues concerning personnel selection practices were called to our attention. For example, it became quite clear that there was little unanimity concerning the proper way to validate a test in the first place.

Such heightened concerns about test validation led naturally to the "criterion problem," a recurring problem through the years because few researchers directly face up to this issue. A little progress was noted. For example, supervisory ratings, one of the most easily obtained criteria measures, again were convincingly discredited, which no doubt will discourage few from using them in the future. An implicit point also under fire was whether criteria used in various test validation studies were actually pertinent to the test validated.

Another important issue in the past 3 years is related to criteria for selection in a different way. This is the question of how long after selection a criterion measure should be taken. This concern, as well as a somewhat newer interest in developmental changes in employees, has led to even more urgent pleas for longitudinal studies than was true previously.

There is a heightened awareness that selection procedures do not operate in a vacuum but are part of a system. The appropriateness of a particular selection standard depends not only on the way the job is structured, but upon the type and duration of training, as well as other factors. A systems view of selection appears to be increasing in prominence. Perhaps we may one day see a cohesive theory of man and woman at work.

While it seems clear that the classical selection model is giving way to a "fairness" model, with specific attention to the selection of special groups, there seems to be little effort to associate selection systems with overall manpower requirements. It is quite possible that we will be faced with severe manpower needs in the years to come; many, for example, cite the critical shortage of qualified managers in the next generation. Obviously we need to look at mobility patterns as they effect employment practices. Most of all, there is a strong probability that we may move from selection systems per se to placement systems. To do so will require serious integration of existing systems, an area which is still in an embryonic stage.

The distal end of the prediction equation was not the only one to receive attention. The predictor end received its share, although from the side of management selection rather than that of the rank-and-file employee. In management selection, the growth of interest in assessment center methods eclipsed test research and focused interest on broad-band global techniques such as the In-Basket and the leaderless group discussion.

These and other issues have been prominent in the selection research and practice of the past 3 years. They will be seen, or sometimes only implied, in the review which follows. This review will be organized around the following topics:

- · The Test Fairness Controversy
- · Methodological Developments
- · Criterion Questions
- · Selection Instruments
- · Managerial Selection

THE TEST FAIRNESS CONTROVERSY

An overview.—The personnel selection field has been dominated during the past 3 years, at least as far as the selection of rank-and-file employees is concerned, by the question of the fairness of selection tests to members of disadvantaged groups. Pressure to address this question came from many sources. Paramount among them were the guidelines on testing promulgated by the Equal Employment Opportunity Commission and the Office of Federal Contract Compliance, which carried the threat of legal and economic sanctions against employers who used biased tests. Also of importance was the strong push toward "social responsibility" which many psychologists began to feel more strongly than ever before.

There is no question that many employment practices have been or are being reexamined in response to these forces. For the most part this has been beneficial to all parties concerned. Yet while the social concerns that have prompted a reexamination of personnel selection policies are clearly real and just, responses to the issues concerning test validity per se frequently appear to be ones which retreat rather than progress.

For example, some psychologists assumed, without questioning the assumption, that the typical selection tests used in industry were biased against blacks. These instruments, they reasoned, clearly must be biased because blacks scored so much lower than did whites. What was needed, they seemed to be saying, was not research on possible test bias but different cutting scores for blacks and whites, or recourse to culture-free tests, or an abolition of selection testing altogether. Several writers went to the trouble of pointing out that different mean scores obtained by blacks and whites did not, by themselves, prove test bias.

Implicit in the thinking of some who quickly reached the conclusion that differences in test scores between groups proved that the tests were unfair selection instruments was the conviction that the two groups did not differ in innate potential. Jensen (115) stirred up a storm by challenging this conviction. Not even he, however, would assert that all the between-group differences were inherent in character. Bennett (21) captured the belief of most personnel psychologists by his observation that tests measure the results of deprivation and discrimination, a view affirmed also by the Task Force on Employment Testing of Minority Groups set up by the American Psychological Association (9). The key question turned out to be whether test scores meant the same thing in terms of the prediction of job performance for those who were disadvantaged and those who were not.

While tests have not been the only predictor challenged on the issue of fairness, they have received the greatest attention. On one hand, critics can cite generally low validities reported for many tests; on the other hand, tests may be singled out by writers such as Bennett (21) because "tests yield objective scores which quantify the consequences of disadvantage." Whatever the reason, bias in testing is often singled out as a significant factor creating unfair hurdles for the disadvantaged. Definitions of bias in the selection process by both Anastasi (6) and Kirkpatrick et al (121) refer directly to the use of tests. On the other hand, Einhorn & Bass (68) and Dunnette (64) note that test discrimination refers to the way tests are used in making personnel decisions, rather than a property or a characteristic of the test itself. This is an important distinction that should be kept in mind. Guion's (94) definition of bias succinctly makes the same point. He notes that: "Unfair discrimination exists when persons with equal probabilities of success on the job have unequal probabilities of being hired for the job."

Legal pressures concerning the use of tests and fair employment.—The Civil Rights Act of 1964 gave rise to several fair employment guidelines, OFCC (198) and EEOC (93). The intent of these guidelines is quite clear—to provide equal employment opportunity for minority group workers as well as for other employable groups. To some extent there is probably more activity reported in the federal courts than in the professional literature, a curious indictment of the communications procedures used by psychologists. Several usable references in this area are provided by the National Association of Manufacturers (71), the U.S. Commission on Civil Rights (197), Rosen (167), Champagne & Duncan (41), Barrett (16), Anderson & Rogers (8), and the recent Supreme Court ruling in the Griggs vs Duke Power case (53).

An article by Cooper & Sobol (45) is must reading for anyone concerned with testing. The authors are counsel for several employees in cases involving tests and fair employment practices. They point out that in their view, fair employment practices (in effect, hiring disadvantaged workers) supercede any effects of validity, and they question the use of valid tests when "the predictive value of a 'valid' test is slight in comparison with the discriminatory impact of the test" (p. 1661). Cooper & Sobol go on to suggest approaches for the courts to use in determining "discriminatory impact."

Professional responses to these pressures.—Bennett (21) notes that both the EEOC and the OFCC have placed the burden of proof upon test users. Yet others have responded to the more global problem facing fair employment practices and selection procedures. For example, Enneis (70) describes some of the barriers facing the disadvantaged, which often go beyond the use of tests. He mentions restricted recruiting practices in addition to test related problems such as failing to consider differential validity. Guion (95) points out that the guidelines established by the OFCC and the EEOC are not unrealistic ones, and fall into what he considers some basic orthodoxies concerning personnel testing. Sparks (185), responding to the problems inherent in weighting low validities in relation to fair employment laws, offers some useful, traditional examples designed to increase the size of validity coefficients. A very critical view of the testing establishment is given by Kirkpatrick (120). On the other hand, Ruch (169) forcefully challenges many of the technical assertions made by Cooper & Sobol (45).

More important, however, has been the demand for research. If an employer used a test which rejected a higher percentage of minority group than of majority group applicants, he was suspected of being guilty of discrimination unless he could prove that prediction of job performance was equal for both groups of applicants. This seemed to some to be a reversal of the usual formula of being innocent until proven guilty. In any case, there developed a great demand for data which could help decide the question.

This demand for hard facts has attracted much attention from those working in the personnel selection area. Over one-fifth of all the personnel selection materials reviewed for this 3 year period dealt with the selection and employment of the disadvantaged. Even so, the hard facts have proved elusive. This is almost as true at this writing as it was in 1969 when the APA Task Force agreed that:

... because such studies are few in number and because many methodological inadequacies are unresolved, no firm conclusions can be drawn from them. Faced with inadequate evidence, the need is highlighted for more and better research designed specifically to pinpoint the behavioral interpretations that properly may be attached to scores on aptitude tests, whether obtained by advantaged or disadvantaged members of the population. Lacking such research data, it is impossible to recommend how or whether predictions from test scores should be interpreted differently for different groups.

Some fundamental research problem areas.—Why has progress been so slow, and why were psychologists so ill-prepared to respond to the challenge to selection testing? A basic reason, in the opinion of the reviewers, is that sound validation studies are difficult and expensive. They require, in the first place, the employment of a reasonably large number of white and black applicants for the same job. Not too many years ago this would have been an impossible requirement; it just didn't happen. Small wonder psychologists didn't produce comparative validity studies! Today jobs in which both blacks and whites are employed in good numbers are not rare. Even so, getting a good employment study under way may require special recruiting efforts to attract applicants of both groups with a wide range of test scores.

The desirability of employing those in both groups with both high and low test scores raises another problem. Operating executives in the employing organization may be reluctant to permit the hiring of those with low test scores, of whatever race, fearing that they will acquire a group of mediocre or inept employees.

One other organizational difficulty is in trying to insure that all members of the study group enter upon reasonably equal conditions. If, as is often the case, there is formal training for the job, it should be the same for all hires in the study. It is not unusual for management to decide to introduce new training methods right in the middle of a research undertaking. The researcher must have good control of the employment and training process to produce a sound study, and, unfortunately, not all personnel psychologists have sufficient influence in their organizations to guarantee this.

Perhaps the main impediment, however, to conclusive validation research is the perennial criterion problem. This will be examined in more detail later. An aspect of the criterion which received increased attention because of the test fairness controversy was the relevance of the criterion to the test being validated. Some researchers insisted that aptitude tests are used to predict job task proficiency and that only a measure of task proficiency is an appropriate criterion. They were unwilling to accept attendance or turnover data as relevant to the question of test validity. Since such data were widely used in test fairness studies, it is no wonder that some psychologists asserted that there were many studies showing differential prediction for white and minority groups, while others said they had yet to see one!

The question of criterion relevance turns out to be a major one which should be kept in mind as the following review is read.

Methodological and statistical considerations.—One response of the profession to the test fairness controversy was a characteristic one; it was methodological rather than substantive. One direction which such contributions took was the production of models illustrating the statistical results which could be expected if certain differences between minority and majority groups did, in fact, exist. Such differences might be in test scores, criterion scores, degree of correlation between these scores, etc. Barrett's theoretical scatter plots in the survey supported by the Ford Foundation (15) have become well known and widely quoted. Bartlett & O'Leary (17) present 11 different models representing the interaction between racial groups and validity. They give examples for the following conditions: equal validity and unequal means; differential validity; opposite validity; and no validity in subgroups.

Such models have had the desirable effect of helping researchers to become more sophisticated in handling data derived from other validation studies. On the other hand, there is a tendency to forget that these diagrams and models are essentially theoretical. Even those that come close to representing real data, as in the Bartlett & O'Leary survey, often use data from studies in which some would argue that the criterion is not relevant to the test.

This is not, of course, to argue that separate analyses by race are not mandatory. In addition to the models, which can make such analyses more insightful, other contributions focused on different statistical considerations. Einhorn & Bass (68) point out that it is primarily the difference in the standard error of estimate rather than the differences in validity coefficients which determine fairness for a test.

O'Leary, Farr & Bartlett (152) note that in addition to the criterion problem, the following factors are present which detract from research methodology in this area: sample sizes are too small to determine practical significance; there are few cross-validation studies reported; and differences in sample size exist between black and white samples due to employment practices.

Practices used to determine test fairness vary from simple correlational reporting of validities for subgroups to testing the differences of the slopes and intercepts of the regression lines obtained. A final consideration, which is more closely related to employment policies rather than methodological considerations, has been raised by Dunnette (64) and others. They question whether prediction should be expressed in correlational terms, and they suggest that predictions indicating the individual's chances of doing the job satisfactorily, in the form of expectancy tables, are more realistic outcomes.

Predictors.—Perhaps because the original EEOC guidelines (92) singled out aptitude testing as a prime suspect in employment discrimination, studies of bias in other selection criteria are notable by their absence. The APA Task Force, in indicating other important selection devices such as skill and knowledge tests, biographical data, and interviewer judgments, noted that these might be as subject to unfairness as aptitude tests. This did not produce any rush of investigators to study them.

On the other hand, considerable attention was devoted to developing procedures which would result in similar test performance among racially mixed groups. Generally none of these approaches have proved to be successful. The attempts to assess and compensate for bias in testing procedures have considered the following aspects: developing "culture-fair" tests; using nonverbal tests; providing special test conditions; and providing special test training.

Krug (126) points out the basic problem inherent in developing culture free tests by noting that such a test must have either of these conditions: "All people of all cultures must have both an equal opportunity and an equal motive to learn all of the items on a test; or, all the items possess complete novelty for all people of all cultures." Obviously it is unlikely that any test will ever meet either of these conditions. Davis & Personke (51) point out that prior learnings rather than language are the most critical components of culture fairness.

The culture-fair fad appears over. One factor hastening its demise was the finding that nonverbal tests did not create additional fairness for disadvantaged group members. Nonverbal tests were initially viewed as approximations of culture-fair tests. Yet one of the few findings that consistently emerges in several studies is that nonverbal tests enhance differences. For example, Kirkpatrick et al (121) note that nonverbal tests are neither more accurate or superior with minority groups. O'Leary and his associates (152) point out that nonverbal tests were most frequently (75% of the time) associated with unfairness while perceptual tests were the most fair. Moore et al (147) note that nonverbal measures may be more culturally biased than verbal tests.

Dyer (66) found that practice for blacks did not materially change their test performance despite a special program to teach her subjects "all of the tricks of the trade" in test taking. Her findings raise serious questions concerning the effectiveness of training and coaching programs prior to testing for the disadvantaged. Dubin, Osburn & Winick (61) found that while significant differences existed in aptitude test scores of white and black subjects, providing either extra testing time or extra test practice had no effect in reducing the racial differences associated with testing. These two studies point out that the differences associated with testing are a function of many different factors, none of which appears readily amenable to change.

The Life Office Management Association (132) describes a rather ambitious undertaking for developing a test battery which will attempt to use culturally loaded items that predict behavior. A final approach is noted by Katz (118), who argues for a series of experiments dealing with an understanding of black-white relationships. This may be useful in determining bias effects in testing. The author cites a study of black freshmen given a digit symbol test under conditions suggesting that their test performance would be compared to either white or black norms. This suggestion resulted in different test performances.

Criteria.—The test fairness problem might, hopefully, have pushed selection research in the direction of greatly improved validity studies. Surely a matter of such importance as to lead to federal legislation and court action requires the best scientific effort. The response, unfortunately, has been disappointing. Models and statistical techniques have been well set forth, but rigorous empirical studies to utilize these efforts have not been numerous. This is most disappointing in the case of that touchstone of validity, the criterion.

The APA Task Force (9) underlined the desirability of a good measure of job proficiency as a most appropriate criterion for aptitude tests, since that is the aspect of job performance an aptitude test is used to predict. Direct measures of job proficiency require some effort to construct and use. As a result, researchers continued, for the most part, to rely on supervisory ratings (in which job proficiency is greatly confounded with other factors) or such readily available quantified indices as attendance and turnover, whose relationship to proficiency is questionable. Because so few studies have developed and used convincing criteria, the assertion that test bias has often been proved is open to serious question.

It should be pointed out immediately that a well-designed study using turnover as a criterion which shows different relationships between test scores and termination for black and white groups may well be a study of practical significance. It would obviously have strong implications for the organization hiring and attempting to retain members of both groups. But when the study is said to prove differential validity of the test, then one may object that the criterion is irrelevant.

Although his warning is hardly needed yet, due to the scarcity of studies using job proficiency as a criterion, Whitlock (207) cautions that the measure of proficiency not be too narrow. He argues for an overall proficiency measure, suggesting that we adopt a coefficient of test effectiveness. This would indicate the maximum possible contribution a test could make based on the part of the total job domain the test can reasonably be expected to measure.

Representative research.—Two major surveys of research on test fairness appeared during the period of this review. Both relied on concurrent validity studies, both tended to rely on supervisory ratings as criterion measures, and both suggested that differential validity may exist at different times for different groups in different jobs.

The first survey was that of Kirkpatrick et al (121). This ground-breaking effort, sponsored by the Ford Foundation, covered five studies in which a total of over 1200 current employees were tested, a third being minority group members. The authors' conclusions have had considerable influence on thinking in the field. Two of them are: "No general statement can be made whether tests are fair or unfair from one ethnic group to another." "Separate validity studies must be conducted for disadvantaged and majority groups."

The studies included in the survey suffer from being based on concurrent designs and from inappropriate or weak criteria, such as supervisory ratings. The book does, however, serve the purpose of alerting test researchers to the danger of assuming that correlations of test scores with important post-employment outcomes will be the same for minority and other groups.

A later survey by O'Leary, Farr & Bartlett (152) picks up the approach of Kirkpatrick et al, viewing studies against models of the results of possible group differences on prediction. The seven studies reviewed include over 1700 subjects, one-third being minority group members. One observation which emerges is that the validities of the tests are quite low for all groups. Another strongly supports the contention that separate validity studies must always be done for different ethnic groups; the authors conlcude that equal validity occurs only infrequently. Once again, however, the studies cited are not based on good job proficiency criteria, and so the conclusion is not inescapable. The reviewers found only a few instances in this survey in which there was a significant difference between the validities for the various subgroups based on a job proficiency criterion.

There were quite a few specific studies dealing with test fairness. In general, the results, as noted above, tended to be inconclusive. Interestingly

enough, it seems that as a general rule most studies showing a lack of differential validity have used better than average criterion measures, while
most of the studies supporting differential validity rely on subjective, poorly
defined rating criteria.

For example, Grant & Bray (90) found no differential validity when learning proficiency measures obtained in a Learning Assessment Program were
used to validate aptitude tests. Similarly, Gael & Grant (80), using job
proficiency measures, found no differential validity between ethnic samples.

Wollowick, Greenwood & McNamara (208) found a lack of differential
validity for black and white groups matched on test score, supervisory ratings, and salary. They note that the major variation was in the variability
of the criterion measures used, rather than in the test scores, and point out
the potential danger of looking at only one issue and neglecting other factors
when analyzing differences in job and test performance in racially mixed
groups.

Ruda & Albright (170) found differences when aptitude test performance
was compared to turnover data. While whites scored higher as a group than
did blacks, blacks tended to have less turnover. Moore, MacNaughton &
Osburn (147) matched race, education, and geographic region with test (not
job) performance, and found racial differences, as might be expected.
Campion & Freihoff's (33) article represents many recent studies conducted
using the fairness model. They found different validities for an aptitude measure and job learning ability as a function of subgrouping. Baehr, Furcon &
Froemel (13) demonstrated that Negro patrolmen had higher multiple correlations between test and performance data than did whites. Their approach
used better than average criterion measures such as paired comparison
rankings by multiple observers. Their study is an example of sound psychometric research done in one organization (the Chicago Police Department).
The chapter, Utilization of an Occupational Test Battery for a Racially
Mixed Group, gives an excellent historical and methodological review of the
testing dilemma, and should be read by all concerned with this area.

Cleary's (43) study, made from an educational viewpoint, is worth noting. She related SAT scores for black and white students in three integrated
colleges with predictions of GPA, and reports that in the three colleges studied there was little evidence that SAT is biased as a predictor of college
grades. Stanley's review (186) presents similar findings, arguing that test
scores are the fairest predictors for college success.

What conclusions can be drawn from the considerable amount of effort
expended on the test fairness problem so far? First, there is the strict validity
question which the reviewers would phrase as follows: Do aptitude test
scores, obtained under proper conditions of administration, show significantly different validities for minority and majority group members in predicting a pertinent measure of job proficiency? This question is still open
since there are few such studies. It does appear, however, that the closer the
study design comes to the ideal, the less likelihood there is of finding differential validity.

Next there is the question of whether the relationship of aptitude test scores to job behavior other than task proficiency is different between minority and nonminority employees. Here correlations are often low, although statistically significant, and the correlations are often significantly different between groups.

The above would suggest that progress might be made (both socially and scientifically) by separating the important consideration of the employment of minority group members from the much narrower question of test validity. What is needed is a more inclusive utility view which would encompass training costs, turnover, proficiency, productivity, etc as functions of the total employment process. This point is also noted by Dunnette (64), who suggests that utility considerations, which are broader than the issues of test fairness, be emphasized.

For definitive answers to any of the above questions, however, what is needed is more and better—which means more difficult and expensive—research. The reviewers are not optimistic. It is likely that many organizations will give up testing rather than make a major commitment to such research.

METHODOLOGICAL DEVELOPMENTS

During the period under review there were several noteworthy contributions which emphasized that personnel selection does not take place in a neat unidimensional world and that ultimate job performance is the product of many interacting variables. MacKinney (136) documents effectively the lack of a conceptual framework in job performance prediction and argues forcefully for what he calls "cross domain" studies. Such studies would include variables from the individual, the job, and the organization. Uhlaner's (196) presidential address to the Division of Military Psychology presents a comprehensive and systematic model addressed to the same problem, which he calls the "Systems Measurement Bed." This model, like MacKinney's, would encompass personal characteristics, training, and the organization. Uhlaner points out not only the need for such a systems approach but stresses that even in a single component of such a model, the measurement of individual characteristics, we have neglected measures of noncognitive attributes. He goes on to suggest that simulation may have an important role to play in the measurement of such attributes, a point we shall return to in the discussion of managerial selection.

Bass (18) notes that few of the issues in traditional personnel psychology can really be examined without paying attention to what are usually thought of as problems of organizational psychology. It may be hoped that the recent change in name of Division 14 of the American Psychological Association to the Division of Industrial and Organizational Psychology will reflect a real interrelationship and not just an alliance. There are signs that point in this direction. For example, Schneider & Bartlett (175) document a strategy for assessing individual differences and organizational climate. Byham's (27) review of personnel research activities indicates a growing interest in developmental and placement strategies rather than on selection per se. Holt

(112) emphasizes the necessity of assessing the situation in which behavior occurs as well as the characteristics of the individual in predicting almost any kind of behavior. He does so in the process of adding another chapter, and an important one, in the clinical-actuarial prediction controversy. Holt's analysis is quite convincing that that dispute is far from decided.

Wernimont & Campbell (206) offer an alternative to the traditional psychometric validity model. Their approach outlines a model emphasizing behavioral consistency. They argue that tests and other predictors should be used as samples rather than signs of behavior. In other words, the measures we use to predict should be measures of behavior. This is quite a departure from the implicit, traditional assumption that our predictor and criterion measures need to be different. This assumption, Wernimont & Campbell note, has led to the current situation where "signs" take inappropriate preference over "samples." They point out that: "utilizing the consistency notion confronts the problem directly and forces a consideration of what job behaviors are recurring contributers to effective performance (and therefore predictable) and which are not." The increased availability of computer technology has caused some concern. For example, Rundquist (171) describes how we often attempt to improve our predictions through item analysis, factor analysis, or through the use of moderator techniques. He criticizes such strategies, noting that there is need for less statistical manipulation and need for more thought regarding the diversity of observable performance. Lawshe (128) presents another view in the same vein. He is particularly critical of those who gild the lily through the uncritical and esoteric use of computer technology. The measurements so thoroughly massaged are themselves suspect.

Numerous studies using convergent-discriminant validation techniques have appeared. Articles by Goodman, Furcon & Rose (85) and Evans (72) are representative of how we try to approximate construct validity even when (in the case of Goodman et al) both the predictors and criteria used in determining creative ability seem to be weak. Lykken (135) notes that statistical significance is probably the least important aspect of a research finding, while Fleiss (77) points out that practical significance can be estimated by expressing the magnitude of experimental effects as a correlational type measure of association.

Smith (183) and Dingman (56) direct their remarks to the reproductibility of research findings and argue for more replication, while Popham & Husek (159) argue for more use of criterion-referenced rather than norm-referenced measurement techniques.

While not strictly in the methodological area, an article by Wright (211) raises serious questions concerning the concepts and terms used by the industrial practitioner. Seventy-six active professionals were given standard information and asked to determine mental age classification. Large errors were noted, and if this represents a valid work sample test for this group and this concept (IQ), one must inwardly shudder when even more esoteric terms are applied in industrial practice.

Moderator variables received a great deal of attention as a way of increasing predictive accuracy. A good example is presented by Dodd, Wollowick & McNamara (58). By using subgroups based on training performance they were able to show that the personality measures employed (particularly the Ascendancy score on the Gordon) predicted later performance. Hakel (96) presents a study with similar findings using the Edwards, and suggests that task difficulty might be used as a sequential moderator in the future. The evidence that some groups of subjects are more predictable than others continues to mount. Gorham & Mann (87), for example, suggest that moderators might indicate where a test might be most useful. Klein, Rock & Evans (122) point out that finding a useful moderator may be difficult if moderators are examined one at a time, and they suggest a technique for using a multiple moderator system.

Several authors criticize the techniques used to develop moderators. For example, Abrahams (1) criticizes the quadrant analysis approach outlined by Hobert & Dunnette (111), claiming that mean differences in the predictors are not weighted properly. McNemar (143) raises criticisms based on the correlation between moderator and predictors.

Many microanalytic and theoretical methodological articles have appeared. For example, DuBois (62) notes that the "important thing is to make our tests do what we want them to do" and describes three types of test homogeneity: factorial, scalar, and criterial. Since no single test can exhibit all three types, test construction should be specified concerning these goals. In the same vein, Athanasiou (12) points out that homogeneity is a test rather than subject characteristic.

Hicks (109) suggests that the mathematical and psychometric basis of ipsative measures (such as the Allport Study of Values and the Edwards Personal Preference Schedule) have such limitations in scoring methods used that one should carefully reconsider their use. Scott (177) compares the homogeneity and validity of three ipsative measures in terms of their convergent and discriminant validities. These measures were scored using both normative and ipsative procedures and were compared to both normative (ratings) and ipsative (rankings) criteria. Neither approach was seen to be consistently superior.

Curtis & Alf (49) compared r, r^2, and E as measures of predictive efficiency. They found that r was most linear, while r^2 and E were related in a curvilinear manner. They present tables to show the predictive efficiency as a function of r and the selection ratio. Schlesinger & Guttman (174) present a nonmetric computer-based alternative to factor analysis which is described as "smallest space" analysis. Tryon & Bailey's (195) cluster analysis is another approach. McCornack (142) found that determining a multiple R via computer analysis was possible through an iterative, a gradient as well as the more frequently used stepwise multiple regression. Darlington's (50) review is most helpful for those now using computer technology to obtain Multiple R's. Weiss & Dawis (205) describe the Reciprocal Averages Prediction Technique, a multivariate prediction approach which works best with curviliniar methods of weighting criteria.

A growing awareness of simulational techniques is seen in the methodological articles in this area. Vinacke (199) reviews the literature on experimental games and suggests that field theory approach might be useful to study how task, situational, and personality variables influence behavior. Payne (157) gives us an example of using simulations to predict interview performance in a counseling situation.

CRITERION QUESTIONS

Although, as has been seen, the "criterion problem" was not dealt with very expertly in the test fairness arena, there were some notable advances in other contexts. One of the more impressive analyses was presented by Ronan & Prien (166), who appear to be moving us closer to a theory of criteria. Taking off from the generally accepted formulation that selection methods should be validated against "job performance," they point out the complexities that lie behind such an apparently simple formulation. Their review of the literature demonstrates that it is totally unrealistic to assume that job performance is unidimensional. A single criterion, even a composite one, is often very misleading. It would indeed be surprising if job performance were unidimensional considering that it, as the authors and others such as Uhlaner (196) and MacKinney (136) suggest, results from an interaction of ability, motivational, and situational factors. Ronan & Prien point out that many investigators have not been attentive to the multidimensional nature of job performance. Instead they have too often used existing, readily available organizational indices alleged to be indicative of performance rather than devising measures focused on appropriate behavior. (The reader should note that "job performance" is not the same as "job proficiency," a distinction emphasized in a previous section.) Whitlock's (207) contribution to the development of job performance criterion has been already cited.

Several new approaches are also evident. The retranslation technique suggested by Smith & Kendall (184) received considerable attention by Campbell and associates (31). Crooks (47) presents a rather sophisticated use of this approach in developing criteria used to validate the Admissions Test for Graduate Study in Business. Taylor and co-workers (191) follow a similar type of approach, using behavioral examples to anchor rating scales. They found good agreement among divergent raters and note that this procedure may be helpful when a composite, global criteria is preferred. In a somewhat different vein, Allen (3) presents a multidimensional analysis which attempts to relate synthetic validity and work taxonomy systems. His approach, which emphasizes worker-oriented rather than job-oriented elements, attempts to determine common behavioral elements across jobs.

Factors influencing the performance of judges were also presented. Gordon (86) demonstrated that raters tend to be able to evaluate good performance more effectively than poor performance, a not too suprising finding. Freeberg (79) found similarly that raters were most reliable when they were aware of the relevant criterion to be evaluated. Sharon & Bartlett (179) demonstrated that graphic rating scales, when used for evaluation purposes, are subject to greater distortion (in the form of greater leniency) than when the same judges used similar forms for research purposes. Forced choice formats were less subject to this type of effect, but since graphic scales are far more frequently used, one wonders about the general accuracy of judgments in this most typical and widely used form of criterion measurement.

Obradovic (151) presents a forced choice rating system used in Yugoslavia. His work suggests the complexity of job behaviors as he tested three different types of criteria against three types of jobs, finding, as Ronan & Prien (166) suggest, that different criteria are more reliable for different jobs. Another forced choice system is offered by Prien & Kult (162), who developed a Clerical Performance Review. They point out that scoring keys which were derived from supervisory judgments were as effective as more cumbersome empirically derived keys.

The use of computers to assist in developing criterion measures is also evident. Dudycha (63) presents a technique called JAN (Judgmental Analysis) which groups raters' strategies using a multiple regression model. This, as well as the work cited earlier by Sharon & Bartlett (179), carries the hallmarks of Wherry's influence. Stephenson & Ward (188) suggest one method to correct for the unreliability in our criteria. They describe a multiple-rating, multiple-criteria system in which weights for the multiple criteria were assigned with the assistance of a computer. An interesting point, which should be pursued further, is their suggestion that the process used in assigning weights for their criteria is similar to the way organizational objectives are frequently established.

Scaling procedures which result in a unidimensional approach to criterion development received considerable attention. Lee (129) describes conditional response scaling, a procedure emphasizing the Guttman approach as a method of constructing rating scales. Siegel et al (180) apply scaling theory to obtain criterion-referenced rather than norm-referenced appraisal systems. Alsikafi and associates (4) used a Guttman approach in determining managerial attitudes towards labor unions. All of these approaches show some merit in moving us a step closer to critically examining and scaling behaviors.

Some other approaches noted were Zedeck & Smith's (212) use of the psychophysical Method of Limits to determine salary jnds for several occupational groups; and Roach & Wherry's (164) factorial analysis of criterion measures which argues for the multidimensionality of criteria.

As with other areas reviewed, some studies show uncritical assumptions concerning criterion dynamics which result in less than meaningful and often unwarranted research conclusions. Although not designed with this in mind, an article by Bray & Campbell (24) points this out. In a validity study regarding the use of assessment centers in evaluating sales potential, they used various types of criterion measures, including a field observation of criterion behavior by a trained and independent auditor. The predictors, which included a final rating based on a 2-day assessment center, were correlated with this behavioral sample and with ratings made by trainers and supervisors. Large differences were found, depending on the criterion. The global assessment rating and the individual assessment techniques correlated substantially with the special behavioral observations but not with trainer and supervisor ratings, even though the latter were gathered with more than ordinary care. This study and others, as well as more theoretical analyses, cast further doubt on the already questionable reliance on supervisory ratings as a useful criterion.

What we are saying is that some very serious questions must be raised about the efficacy of the continued and uncritical use of supervisory ratings as *the* criterion measure. Perhaps this is why we have a criterion "problem." It seems clear from the work of Ronan & Prien (166), as well as those investigating the factors of criterion unreliability, that this is a serious problem which must be overcome in a theory of work behavior. A few years ago a moratorium on tests was suggested. Similarly, a moratorium on the uncritical use of supervisory ratings as *the* criterion may also be in order.

SELECTION INSTRUMENTS

There has been considerable activity directed to refining, and sometimes re-refining, selection devices. In this section the focus will be primarily on methods used in selecting rank and file employees. Managerial selection will be covered in the following section.

One area which has always been under-researched is that of "self-selection," the individual's own decision, once he understands what the job entails. Lack of attention to this area continues to be the rule. Pieters, Hundert & Beer (158), however, do present a tantalizing approach which sheds some light on the search process used by job candidates. The authors developed a measure of attractiveness towards an organization related to the preferences of the applicants. While this study was a post hoc analysis, it offers an avenue to the utilization of individual preferences in selection decisions. Cleff & Hecht (44) describe a computer-assisted job match system which they believe has particular relevance to disadvantaged groups. They look at both jobs and job seekers to learn how the preferred activities of applicants, as expressed in past activities, equate to job duties. Their approach is quantitative and analytic. Benson (22) presents a model based on classical economic concepts of marginal utility which may point out to the organization just what skills and qualifications are really required.

Vocational adjustment has also stimulated research on the dynamics of career choice, as can be seen in the work of Dawis, Lofquist & Weiss (52) and Weiss (204). Dolliver (59) presents a forceful argument that we have tended to emphasize test-induced interest patterns (such as from a vocational interest inventory) at the expense of self-expressed interest patterns. His review of the literature suggests that the predictive validity of self-expressed interest reports is at least as great as the predictive validity of the Strong Vocational Interest Blank. Hall (101) hypothesizes that an individual may have several conceptions of himself in various career roles and that these identities are related to career commitment. We may be able to enhance our selection models by identifying these career identities. Sometimes, as noted by Hall, Schneider & Nygren (102), this type of identity may transcend specific jobs and transfer to the purpose of the organization, particularly when service is a major organizational product. Such approaches are some of the challenging interfaces we should and can expect between organizational and personnel psychology.

There is conflicting evidence as to the value of knowledge of an applicant's previous experience. For example, Browning (26) reports that there was no significant correlation between pre-employment ratings of new teachers by practice teaching supervisors and ratings of actual job performance. Brenner (25) found only a slight relationship between high school attendance and job absenteeism, but found, suprisingly, that teacher ratings of student work habits tended to correlate with supervisory ratings of job performance. While Brenner notes that this suggests that the teacher and supervisor tend to agree on similar behaviors, one wonders if either group is assessing important job behaviors. Judy (117) found that self reports describing both the type and extent of education were helpful in predicting technical school performance in the Air Force. In one of the more promising developments in this area, Nash & Carroll (149) describe the development and cross validation of a forced-choice reference check procedure.

Biodata and the application blank.—Considerable interest continues to be shown in developing and using biographical data as a part of the selection process. Although most of the research reported tends to be job or situation specific, there are some interesting exceptions to this trend. Owens (154) describes a method of subgrouping individuals through factoring biodata responses. Once profiles are developed, he suggests that we learn the relevant behavioral correlates of subgroup membership.

Another more general approach is offered by Starry, Raubenheimer & Tesser (187), who use the stability of various biographical characteristics as rated by external judges as classifier variables. In a similar manner Hendel & Weiss (107) point out that individual response patterns can be used as a moderator within the reliability model. Tanofsky, Shepps & O'Neill (190) emphasize pattern analysis as a useful technique for analyzing biographical data. They find distinct biographical patterns useful in predicting success in life insurance selling.

Many representative studies are more specific. Owens (153) shows how biographical data may be useful in developing criterion measures. This is an excellent example of how we can develop predictor and criterion measures which sample similar behaviors. Baehr & Williams (14) present a well-designed psychometric study using a factorially derived biographical measure to predict occupational choice. A series of studies by Schaefer & Anastasi (178) and Anastasi & Schaefer (7) describe the development of biographical information to identify creativity. Dornon (60) uses a weighted application blank to predict turnover with some success when cross validated. McClelland & Rhodes (140) use biographical data as well as the MMPI to select successful hospital aides. Ellison, James & Carron (69) use biographical data to predict scientific and engineering performance.

An interesting example of the use of biodata to solve a difficult selection problem is presented by Appel & Feinberg (10), who show how an objectively scored questionnaire, administered by mail, can select door-to-door salesmen.

The interview.—Despite a long history as an unrewarding research area, there has been considerable resurgence of interest in the interview. The work of Webster (203) and his students concerning perceptions established in the interview situation spawned many studies designed to shed light on the factors contributing to interviewer decisions. The work of both Hakel and Carlson are examples of systematic research designed to investigate some of the biasing factors present in the interview.

Hakel & his associates (97–100) have designed a series of studies which provide information concerning the stereotypes formed and used by interviewers. Similarly, Carlson (35–37) presents a systematic series of studies designed to clarify how situational determinants such as the applicant sample, degree of interviewer experience, and amount of information obtained influence the interviewer. Both types of studies help to establish a working model which will clarify the situational determinants of interviewer outcomes. This may clarify why the interview is not as predictive as it might be, since both the stereotyping and situational factors probably serve to limit the effectiveness of the procedure.

On the other hand, an example of what can be predicted from interview data is presented by Grant & Bray (89). Their study, one in a series relating the contributions of assessment center techniques to the prediction of progress in management, demonstrates that much meaningful, reliable data can be generated from the interview. It should be noted that in their study, ratings of interview variables were made by coders from the interviewer's transcribed summary, not by the interviewer himself. This separation of interviewing from evaluation may be significant.

Several additional efforts are also worth noting. Rychlak & Bray (172) present a method for scoring interviews along thematic dimensions. Carlson, Schwab & Heneman (38) used a convergent-discriminant design to study the merits of structured, semistructured, and unstructured interview formats. While the structured interview format tended to yield higher validities, a trend noted in several studies, there is also the possibility that these different interviewing styles are probably measuring different characteristics, an important point which should be considered in future research. In a separate study, Schwab & Heneman (176) found that structure provided by the use of an application blank resulted in increased interviewer reliability. Fleiss (78) presents a model for estimating the reliability of interviewer data in considering interviewee, interviewer, and situational effects. Marks (138) turns his attention to the recruiter and suggests a system for evaluating the interviewer's effectiveness. Alderfer & McCord (2) emphasize a field theory approach regarding the interviewee's expectations and his perceptions concerning the quality of the interviewer. Howell & Vincent (113) factor analyzed structured interview data and found several factors which were independent of the global rating.

Examples of other studies which typify the wide range of interest in the interview are offered by a number of articles. Logue, Zenner & Gorman (133), on the basis of research conducted in a neuropsychiatric setting, suggest that interviewee coaching may have little effect on interview outcome. Asher (11) notes that interviews recorded on video tape result in the same degree of interviewer reliability as information recorded on audiotape only. He suggests this may imply that the applicant's appearance has little effect on the reliability of interviewer judgment. On the other hand, Carroll (39) points out that recruiters often consider personal appearance as the most important dimension despite the lack of data that this relates to success. Kleinmuntz & McLean (123) propose a computer system for large-scale psychodiagnostic interviews, while Berkhout, Walter & Adey (23) suggest using autonomic response screening for job reassignment. One wonders what implications these procedures have for invasion of privacy issues.

Wright's review (210) of research on the selection interview is worth reading. He is critical of the many microanalytic studies which permeate this area, and argues for more macroanalytic research which lends itself to model building.

Testing.—In the selection test area, under the impact of the fairness issue and systems thinking, fewer simple selection test studies have been reported. Other changes are also apparent. Grant (88) argues that organizational requirements demand predictors of performance which include interpersonal, administrative, and technological abilities. These, he states, will require methods other than paper-and-pencil testing. This viewpoint will be further represented in the following section on managerial selection.

Even when traditional tests are used, some rationale is necessary for their inclusion in a selection program. Far too often tests are selected on the basis of availability or intuition, neither of which are, of course, defensible. A study by Parry (156) points this out. She asked ten experienced industrial psychologists to estimate the validities of several widely used tests. Only one of the group gave estimates which approximated the true figures. In general the

psychologists overestimated the validities, which may explain why many of
our tests, selected on the basis of past performance, do not account for much
new information.

Some interesting approaches have been suggested for the development of
tests and other new predictors. Waters (201) proposes branching programmed tests for more accurate estimation of a person's abilities. Ewen
(73) suggests using unobtrusive measures of performance. Hermans (108)
describes the development of a psychometrically oriented achievement
motivation measure. Peer nominations received renewed attention. Waters
& Waters (202) used this technique to identify higher producing salesmen;
Mayfield (139) found it helpful in management selection; and Amir,
Kovarsky & Sharan (5) show their effectiveness in a setting well suited to
their use, the military.

In a general review, Levy (130) criticizes the trend towards using short-
form intelligence tests, noting that validity is sacrificed at the expense of
testing time. Bemis (20) presents a comprehensive review of over 400 General
Aptitude Test Battery studies that use a concurrent or a predictive design
for either training or proficiency criteria. The review reaffirms that prediction
of success in training is not the same as predicting job performance. The
distinction between job proficiency and job performance, made earlier, is
relevant here.

Stone & Athelstan (189) found that demographic variables were better
predictors of tenure for women than selected SVIB scales. Hall & MacKinnon
(103) studied the relationship between various personality inventories and
ratings of creativity among architects. Raubenheimer (163) presents a validation study conducted on South African clerical workers. Prien (161) studied
bank tellers and used an impressive array of criterion measures. Thumin
(194) reports that no significant differences were noted in personality dimensions measured by the MMPI for different age groups of job applicants.
Carron's (40) study of clerical plant personnel has many desirable psychometric factors despite limited results. Kelleher, Kerr & Melville (119)
made a similar study within the nursing profession.

In concluding this section on our tools of the trade, it appears that we are
in a period of transition. To some extent, some notable advances designed to
measure *behavior* have appeared. To some extent, recent social forces have
caused a reexamination of the way we do things. These are seen as positive
forces for change. What is missing is a unified system that integrates manpower planning, selection, training, and development. Perhaps this will first
occur in other areas such as management selection, a topic we turn to next.

MANAGEMENT SELECTION

The appearance of the book by Campbell and co-workers (31) renders this
section of the review somewhat superfluous. In that volume, which is required reading for anyone in the management personnel field, the authors
bring together not only the relevant literature but much unpublished practice

in management selection and development. Among the dominant themes that emerge from their analysis, one of central importance to the selection area is the need for focusing on actual behavior at both the predictor and criterion end.

This theme is reflected in many other contributions in the period under review. Chowdhry (42) distinguishes between research strategies designed to describe personal qualities of successful managers and approaches aimed at analyzing managerial job demands. Cummings & El Salmi (48) make a similar point in noting many of the dilemmas seen in current studies of managerial evaluation and performance. Ronan (165) points out that different criteria used to evaluate identical managerial performance would lead to different interpretations. Slivinski (181) emphasizes that while describing managerial behavior is no easy task, the alternative of relying on job descriptions is not acceptable. Kraut (125) found no relationship between scores on difficult cognitive tests and high level management performance and suggests using behavioral work-sample measures of performance.

On the predictor side, Lopez's book (134) considers the pending shortage of managers and notes that outmoded notions of managerial identification are inadequate to the demands for identifying management talent. Alternative methods such as assessment centers and simulations are encouraged to meet these demands. Korman's (124) review of predictive validation studies of managerial performance suggests that judgmental predictions seem to be more effective than psychometric predictors, perhaps because judgmental approaches are able to encompass factorially complex behaviors which are more typical of managerial performance.

On the other hand, judgmental approaches must be based on behavior. Miner (145) presents a critical study of the effectiveness of predictions made by psychologists using traditional psychological evaluations. After examining the recommendations made by representatives of several consulting firms, he concludes that their judgments are frequently unrelated to successful behavior. This may not be a function of the judgmental process but of the evaluation tools used. This, in turn, may be a result of an over-reliance on signs rather than samples (Wernimont & Campbell 206).

There are notable examples of systems designed to sample behavior. Laurent's (127) description of the "Laurent Success Index" is worth examining as an example of interrelating complex criterion measures. The in-basket technique has received considerable attention. Crooks (46) presents an interesting and informative description of in-basket development and validation procedures. Meyer (144) found significant and practical relationships between in-basket performance and on-the-job administrative performance. Interestingly, he indicates that the abilities measured by this technique are independent of actual supervisory or administrative experience.

Other predictors have been used with some success. Edel (67) describes the development of a word meaning test designed to elicit success-oriented approaches. Mayfield (139), as noted earlier, used peer nominations to identify sales managers. Johnson & Dunnette (116) and Campbell (29) indicate that managerial preference patterns on the Strong Vocational Interest Blank are related to managerial job effectiveness. Two approaches emphasizing system interrelationships are presented by Gavin & Greenhaus (81) and the Life Insurance Agency Management Association (131).

As usual, many studies are reported which describe characteristics of successful managers. Apart from being either too global or too situation specific, definitions of "success" also vary. The work of Ghiselli (82, 83), Harrell (105, 106), Wainer & Rubin (200), Rowland & Scott (168), Nealey & Owen (150), and Tenopyr (192) represents various attempts to relate individual characteristics to managerial performance. Several serious questions are raised concerning the importance of previous managerial experience as a determinant of success. Campbell et al (31) point out that different initial management selection and management promotion systems may necessitate the use of different predictors. Glickman et al (84) attempted to study those factors which affected advancement to top management by interviewing recently promoted executives as well as their bosses. They found that in general, early identification and continuous visibility were needed for advancement to high levels. On the other hand, a study by Bassett & Meyer (19) demonstrates to some extent that managerial abilities (such as leadership and administrative skills) are often underemphasized in managerial selection. They asked 80 managers in 26 different departments to indicate the procedures used and factors considered in making a recent managerial appointment. As might be expected, the overwhelming majority used reference sources that were well known to each manager. They note that managers may be more concerned with avoiding failures than selecting success, a procedure which results in emphasizing functional knowledge and experience at the expense of abilities. As noted earlier, Meyer (144) reported that in-basket performance is independent of experience. Similarly, Fiedler (74) suggests that leadership behavior and prior supervisory experience also are generally unrelated. This raises serious questions about the importance of prior management experience. Fiedler notes that prior experience may not contribute to a manager's aptitudes, but it probably gives his superiors an opportunity to observe and hopefully make better predictions.

Assessment centers.—The rapid growth in the use of the assessment center technique clearly is one of the major trends seen during the review period. While originally designed by A.T.&T. for use in identifying managerial potential, many varied applications of the basic approach are evident.

Bray & Campbell (24) present a validation study of an assessment center designed to select salesmen. Moses (148) describes an assessment center used for identifying business potential among disadvantaged college applicants. MacKinnon (137) uses the technique to identify and measure creative abilities, while Salas (173) shows how assessment information is used to select applicants for the Royal Military College in Australia. Greenwood &

McNamara (91) and Dodd (57) demonstrate how assessment data can be used as criterion measures.

The major use of the technique, however, has been and still is for identifying managerial abilities. Conservative estimates indicate that over 100,000 individuals have participated in this process, of which 75,000 have been assessed by the Bell System alone.

Several reviews of assessment programs have been published, an indication of the growing professional interest in the technique. Dunnette's (65) review of the research literature summarizes many of the validity studies reported. Campbell et al (31) devote considerable attention to the assessment process itself, as does Lopez (134). Byham (28) reviews the current industrial usage of assessment centers, while Moore (146) presents an historical review of British Assessment procedures dating back to the War Officer Selection Boards of World War II. Finkle & Jones (75) describe how the format was successfully applied at Standard Oil of Ohio. Descriptions of newly developed programs are presented by McConnell (141) and DiCostanzo & Andretta (55).

One attractive feature of the assessment center is its versatility in examining behavior, as seen by the varied applications of the technique. Another attraction is its ability to interface with a variety of organizational needs. For example, Slivinski & Grant (182) list many organizational uses of assessment centers. These range from selection and placement and development systems to manpower planning and utilization, as well as training managers in appraisal.

Research on assessment centers falls into several categories. Byham (28) describes four kinds of validity studies: experimental, predictive, comparative, and follow up. Essentially, however, two types of research are evident—studies concerned with the validity of the process and studies concerned with the interrelationships between various assessment techniques.

Studies dealing with the validity of the process are more prevalent. Two sources of difficulty in these studies relate to the criteria used and the nature of the validation sample. As in other areas, the "criterion problem" is evident. It seems somewhat absurd to relate expensive and high-powered predictors (in the sense of the information generated) to arbitrary and the most easily available criterion measures. The second source of difficulty lies in the nature of the validity sample. Too often it is difficult to get an adequate sample of the poorer performing assessees, since only the better performers are promoted or hired.

A predictive validity study reported by Bray & Campbell (24) and an experimental-control comparison performed by Campbell & Bray (32) indicate that it is possible to conduct this type of research. Studies by Carleton (34), Porritt (160), DeNelsky & McKee (54), Hardesty & Jones (104), and Jaffee, Bender & Calvert (114) all indicate positive relationships between assessment performance and management success.

The question of how much new information is provided by assessment has been studied by several investigators. Hinrichs (110) compared judgments made by an assessment staff with judgments made by managers using traditional evaluative information. While noting that for this sample the managers who reviewed traditional information were almost as effective as the assessment staff for certain judgments, he indicates that the interpersonal behavioral information generated by the assessment process cannot be effectively estimated from traditional personnel records. Thomson (193) demonstrates that simply asking managers to rate subordinates by use of assessment rating forms is no substitute for ratings based on assessment techniques. Not only does his study argue forcefully against uncritical use of assessment ratings by supervisors as criterion measures, but he demonstrates, by use of a convergent-discriminant design, that supervisory ratings are much poorer in quality than assessor judgments.

Studies concerned with the contribution of various assessment techniques conclude that the overall, global assessment rating made as a result of combining all of the assessment data is a better predictor than any single assessment component. Wollowich & McNamara (209) found, for example, that using situational techniques nearly doubled the criterion variance accounted for when compared to pencil-and-paper measures. Grant & Bray (89) report the contribution of interview data to the assessment process and progress in management, while Finley (76) compares ratings made from projective reports and supervisory ratings.

The salient feature of assessment centers is its focus on behavior through the use of simulations. This, as noted, results in an emphasis on samples rather than signs. The importance of this is shown in a study by Greenwood & McNamara (91). They found no relationship between a pencil-and-paper test of leadership behavior and actual leadership behavior in several group exercises. It would seem that the use of simulations is taking us ever closer to observing the characteristics needed for successful job performance.

Conclusions

It is traditional for reviewers to attempt to discern trends and to extrapolate these trends into at least the near future. The present authors find three developments worthy of comment.

At the risk of being resoundingly wrong, the reviewers predict that the controversy centering on the possible differential validity of selection tests for majority and minority groups will abate. Several factors will cause this. More general utility considerations will come into play, and the question of test validity, in the narrow sense, will be put into perspective. Secondly, if governmental agencies and the courts continue to be very exacting in the evidence they will accept before allowing employment tests to be used, many organizations will give up testing due to an inability to perform the required research or an unwillingness to undertake it.

The reviewers expect the emphasis on simple selection models to decrease in favor of a systems approach which will include, on a conceptual level at least, not only the subject's aptitudes, but his motivation, the training afforded him, the nature of the organization's reward system, quality of supervision, etc. Such a model has clear relevance to the question of fair employment, but is, of course, not at all limited to that special problem.

The reviewers expect also that the use of broad-band selection methods such as assessment center techniques will continue to grow, an emphasis on samples rather than signs. Although such methods will be used primarily with management level personnel, their possible applicability to rank-and-file employees will start to be investigated.

The reviewers feel impelled to point out that the above developments imply much more ambitious activity on the part of personnel selection psychologists than has usually been the case. Truly convincing studies of test fairness, the implementation of utility models in employment decisions, systems studies of the multiple determinants of job performance, and assessment center techniques all demand major efforts. Such efforts are "major" not only in requiring much professional expertise. They require organizations to provide significant financial support and to tolerate at least some interference with normal operations. Personnel psychologists have no alternative but to insist on such support if meaningful progress is to take place.

LITERATURE CITED

1. Abrahams, N. M. 1969. Off quadrant comment. *J. Appl. Psychol.* 53: 66–68
2. Alderfer, C. P., McCord, C. G. 1970. Personal and situational factors in the recruitment interview. *J. Appl. Psychol.* 54:377–85
3. Allen, J. C. 1969. Multidimensional analysis of worker-oriented and job-oriented verbs. *J. Appl. Psychol.* 53:73–79
4. Alsikafi, M., Spray, S. L., Jokinen, W. J., Tracy, G. S. 1968. Managerial attitudes toward labor unions in a southern city. *J. Appl. Psychol.* 52:447–53
5. Amir, Y., Kovarsky, Y., Sharan, S. 1970. Peer nominations as a predictor of multistage promotions in a ramified organization. *J. Appl. Psychol.* 54:462–69
6. Anastasi, A. 1968. *Psychological Testing.* New York: Macmillan
7. Anastasi, A., Schaefer, C. E. 1969. Biographical correlates of artistic and literary creativity in adolescent girls. *J. Appl. Psychol.* 53:267–73
8. Anderson, B. R., Rogers, M. P. 1970. *Personnel Testing and Equal Employment Opportunity.* Washington, D. C.: EEOC
9. APA Task Force on Employment Testing of Minority Groups. 1969. Job testing and the disadvantaged. *Am. Psychol.* 24:637–50
10. Appel, V., Feinberg, M. R. 1969. Recruiting door to door salesmen by mail. *J. Appl. Psychol.* 53:362–66
11. Asher, J. J. 1970. How the applicant's appearance affects the reliability and validity of the interview. *Educ. Psychol. Meas.* 30:687–95
12. Athanasiou, R. 1969. The reliability of homogeneity. *Proc. 77th Ann. Conv. APA* 4:119–20
13. Baehr, M. E., Furcon, J. E., Froemel, E. C. 1968. Psychological assessment of patrolman qualification in relation to field performance. *Law Enforcement Assistance Admin.— LEAA Proj. 046*
14. Baehr, M. E., Williams, G. B. 1968. Prediction of sales success from factorially determined dimensions of background data. *J. Appl. Psychol.* 52:98–103
15. Barrett, R. S. 1967. *Correlation Diagrams for Fair Employment Testing* (Mimeo)
16. Barrett, R. S. 1970. Questions for interrogatories or examination of witnesses regarding fair employment practices. *Cent. Urban Educ.* (Mimeo)
17. Bartlett, C. J., O'Leary, B. S. 1969. A differential prediction model to

moderate the effects of heterogeneous groups in personnel selection and classification. *Personnel Psychol.* 22:1–17

18. Bass, B. M. 1968. Interface between personnel and organizational psychology. *J. Appl. Psychol.* 52:81–88

19. Bassett, G. A., Meyer, H. H. 1968. Selecting managers: a study of the personnel selection decision process. *Personnel Pract. Personnel Ind. Relat., General Electric*

20. Bemis, S. E. 1968. Occupational validity of the General Aptitude Test Battery. *J. Appl. Psychol.* 52: 240–44

21. Bennett, G. K. 1969. Factors affecting the value of validation studies. *Personnel Psychol.* 22:265–68

22. Benson, P. H. 1969. Marginal productivity procedure for staff selection. *J. Appl. Psychol.* 53:124–31

23. Berkhout, J., Walter, D. O., Adey, W. R. 1970. Automatic responses during a replicable interrogation. *J. Appl. Psychol.* 54:316–25

24. Bray, D. W., Campbell, R. J. 1968. Selection of salesmen by means of an assessment center. *J. Appl. Psychol.* 52:36–41

25. Brenner, M. H. 1968. Use of high school data to predict work performance. *J. Appl. Psychol.* 52:29–30

26. Browning, R. C. 1968. Validity of reference ratings from previous employers. *Personnel Psychol.* 21:389–93

27. Byham, W. C. 1968. *The Uses of Personnel Research.* New York: Am. Manage. Assoc.

28. Byham, W. C. 1970. Assessment centers for spotting future managers. *Harvard Bus. Rev.* 48:150–64

29. Campbell, D. P. 1969. Managerial orientation scores of outstanding men. *Personnel Psychol.* 22:41–44

30. Campbell, J. P. 1971. Personnel training and development. *Ann. Rev. Psychol.* 22:565–602

31. Campbell, J. P., Dunnette, M. D., Lawler, E. E., Weick, K. E. 1970. *Managerial Behavior, Performance, and Effectiveness.* New York: McGraw

32. Campbell, R. J., Bray, D. W. 1967. Assessment centers: an aid in management selection. *Personnel Admin.* 30:6–13

33. Campion, J. E., Freihoff, E. C. 1970. Unintentional bias when using racially mixed employee samples for test validation. *Exp. Publ. Syst.* 8:MS-285-2

34. Carleton, F. O. 1970. Relationships between follow-up evaluations and information developed in a management assessment center. *Proc. 78th Ann. Conv. APA* 5:565–66

35. Carlson, R. E. 1968. Employment decisions: effects of mode of applicant presentation on some outcome measures. *Personnel Psychol.* 21:193–207

36. Ibid 1969. Relative influence of a photograph vs. factual written information on an interviewer's employment decision. 22:45–56

37. Carlson, R. E. 1970. Effect of applicant sample on ratings of valid information in an employment setting. *J. Appl. Psychol.* 54:217–22

38. Carlson, R. E., Schwab, D. P., Heneman, H. G. 1970. Agreement among styles of selection interviewing. *J. Ind. Psychol.* 5:8–17

39. Carroll, S. J. 1969. Beauty, bias, and business. *Personnel Admin.* 32: 21–25

40. Carron, T. J. 1969. Validity of tests for chemical plant personnel. *Personnel Psychol.* 22:307–12

41. Champagne, J. E., Duncan, G. D. 1970. *Equal Employment Opportunity Under Federal and State Laws.* Houston: Center for Human Resources, Univ. Houston

42. Chowdhry, K. 1969. Selection of executives and administrators: Implications of recent research. *Personnel J.* 48:102–6

43. Cleary, T. A. 1968. Test bias: Prediction of grades of negro and white students in integrated colleges. *J. Educ. Meas.* 5:115–24

44. Cleff, S. H., Hecht, R. M. 1970. Computer man/job match. *Personnel Admin.* 15:3–12

45. Cooper, G., Sobol, R. S. 1969. Seniority and testing under fair employment laws: A general approach to objective criteria of hiring and promotion. *Harvard Law Rev.* 82: 1598- 1679

46. Crooks, L. A. 1968. Issues in the development and validation of in basket exercises for specific objectives. *Res. Memo. 68-23, Educ. Test. Serv.*

47. Crooks, L. A. 1970. The criterion study: Final report. *Educ. Test. Serv.*

48. Cummings, L. L., El Salmi, A. M. 1968. Empirical research on the bases and correlates of managerial motivation: A review of the literature. *Psychol. Bull.* 70:127–44

49. Curtis, E. W., Alf, E. F. 1969. Validity, predictive efficiency and practical significance of selection tests. *J. Appl. Psychol.* 53:327–37

50. Darlington, R. B. 1968. Multiple regression in psychological research and practice. *Psychol. Bull.* 69: 161–82

51. Davis, O. L., Personke, C. R. 1968. Effects of administering the Metropolitan Readiness Test in English and Spanish to Spanish speaking school entrants. *J. Educ. Meas.* 5:231–34

52. Dawis, R. V., Lofquist, L. H., Weiss, D. J. 1968. A theory of work adjustment. *Minn. Stud. Vocat. Rehabil.*: 23 Bull. 47

53. *Decision of Supreme Court of United States in Case of Willis S. Griggs vs. Duke Power Co. 1971.* Bur. Nat. Affairs Daily Labor Rep.

54. DeNelsky, G. Y., McKee, M. G. 1969. Prediction of job performance from assessment reports: Use of a modified Q sort technique to expand prediction and criterion variance. *J. Appl. Psychol.* 53:439–45

55. DiCostanzo, F., Andretta, T. 1970. The supervisory assessment center in the Internal Revenue Service. *Train. Develop. J.* 24:12–15

56. Dingman, H. F. 1969. Scientific method and reproducibility of results. *Multivar. Behav. Res.* 4: 517–22

57. Dodd, W. E. 1970. Will management assessment centers insure selection of the same old types. *Proc. 78th Ann. Conv. APA* 5:569–70

58. Dodd, W. E., Wollowick, H. B., McNamara, W. J. 1970. Task difficulty as a moderator of long range prediction. *J. Appl. Psychol.* 54: 265–70

59. Dolliver, R. H. 1969. Strong Vocational Interest Blank vs. expressed vocational interests: a review. *Psychol. Bull.* 72:95–107

60. Dornon, J. M. 1970. Identification of long-tenure hourly factory workers using a weighted application blank. *Exp. Publ. Syst.* 8.MS 276-2

61. Dubin, J. A., Osburn, H., Winick, D. M. 1969. Speed and practice: effects of Negro and white test performance. *J. Appl. Psychol.* 53: 19–23

62. DuBois, P. H. 1970. Varieties of psychological test homogeneity. *Am. Psychol.* 25:532–36

63. Dudycha, A. L. 1970. A monte carlo evaluation of JAN: A technique for capturing and clustering raters' policies. *Organ. Behav. Hum. Perform.* 5:501–16

64. Dunnette, M. D. 1970. Personnel selection and job placement of the disadvantaged: issues, problems and suggestions. *Off. Nav. Res. Tech. Rep. No. 4001*

65. Dunnette, M. D. 1971. Multiple assessment procedures in identifying and developing managerial talent. In *Advances in Psychological Assessment*, ed. P. McReynolds, Vol. 2. Palo Alto: Science & Behavior Books

66. Dyer, P. J. 1970. *Effects of test conditions on negro-white differences in test scores.* PhD thesis. Columbia Univ., New York

67. Edel, E. C. 1968. Need for success as a predictor of managerial performance. *Personnel Psychol.* 21: 231–40

68. Einhorn, H. J., Bass, A. R. 1971. Methodological considerations relevant to discrimination in employment testing. *Psychol. Bull.* 75: 261–69

69. Ellison, R. L., James, L. R., Carron, T. J. 1970. Prediction of R & D performance criteria with biographical data. *J. Ind. Psychol.* 5:37–57

70. Enneis, W. H. 1970. Minority employment barriers from the EEOC viewpoint. *Prof. Psychol.* 1:435–39

71. Equal Employment Opportunity; Compliance and affirmative action. 1969. *Nat. Assoc. Mfr. Plans for Progress.* Washington, D. C.

72. Evans, M. D. 1969. Convergent and discriminant validities between the Cornell job descriptive index and a measure of goal attainment. *J. Appl. Psychol.* 53:102–6

73. Ewen, R. B. 1969. The GRE Psychology Test as an unobtrusive measure of motivation. *J. Appl. Psychol.* 53:383–87

74. Fiedler, F. E. 1970. Leadership experience and leader performance—another hypothesis shot to hell. *Organ. Behav. Hum. Perform.* 5: 1–14

75. Finkle, R. B., Jones, W. S. 1970. *Assessing Corporate Talent.* New York: Wiley

76. Finley, R. M. Jr. 1970. Evaluation of behavior predictions from projective tests given in a management assessment center. *Proc. 78th Ann. Conv. APA* 5:567–68

77. Fleiss, J. L. 1969. Estimating the mag-

nitude of experimental effects. *Psychol. Bull.* 72:273–76

78. Fleiss, J. L. 1970. Estimating the reliability of interview data. *Psychometrika* 35:143–62

79. Freeberg, N. E. 1969. Relevance of rater-ratee acquaintance in the validity and reliability of ratings. *J. Appl. Psychol.* 53:518–24

80. Gael, S., Grant, D. L. 1971. Validation of a general learning ability test for selecting telephone operators. *Exp. Publ. Syst.* 10:MS351-2

81. Gavin, J. F., Greenhaus, J. 1969. Selecting potential managers. *LOMA Personnel Admin. Rep. No. 40*

82. Ghiselli, E. E. 1968. Some motivational factors in the success of managers. *Personnel Psychol.* 21:431–40

83. Ibid 1969. Prediction of success of stockbrokers. 22:125–30

84. Glickman, A. S., Hahn, C. P., Fleishman, E. A., Baxter, B. 1968. *Top Management Development and Succession.* New York: Macmillan

85. Goodman, P., Furcon, J., Rose, J. 1969. Examinations of creative ability by the multitrait-multimethod matrix. *J. Appl. Psychol.* 53:240–43

86. Gordon, M. E., 1970. The effect of the correctness of the behavior observed on the accuracy of ratings. *Organ. Behav. Hum. Perform.* 5:366–77

87. Gorham, W. A., Mann, W. G. 1970. Validation, moderation and clarification. *Proc. 78th Ann. Conv. APA* 5:139–41

88. Grant, D. L. 1970. Relevance of education to organizational requirements. *Proc. West. Reg. Conf. Test. Probl. ETS*

89. Grant, D. L., Bray, D. W. 1969. Contributions of the interview to assessment of management potential. *J. Appl. Psychol.* 53:24–34

90. Ibid 1970. Validation of employment tests for telephone company installation and repair occupations. 54:7–14

91. Greenwood, J. M., McNamara, W. J. 1969. Leadership styles of structure and consideration and managerial effectiveness. *Personnel Psychol.* 22:141–52

92. *Guidelines on Employment Testing Procedures.* 1966. Washington, D. C.: EEOC

93. Guidelines on Employee Selection Procedures. 1970. *Fed. Regist.* 35:12333–336

94. Guion, R. M. 1966. Employment tests and discriminatory hiring. *Ind. Relat.* 5:20–37

95. Guion, R. M. 1970. *Some orthodoxies in personnel testing.* Presented at 78th Ann. Conv. APA, Miami Beach

96. Hakel, M. D. 1968. Task difficulty and personality test validity. *Psychol. Rep.* 22:502

97. Hakel, M. D., Dobmeyer, T. W., Dunnette, M. D. 1970. Relative importance of three content dimensions in overall suitability ratings of job applicants' resumes. *J. Appl. Psychol.* 54:65–71

98. Hakel, M. D., Dunnette, M. D. 1968. Interpersonal perception in the employment interview. *Ind. Psychol.* 5:30–38

99. Hakel, M. D., Hollmann, T. D., Dunnette, M. D. 1970. Accuracy of interviewers, CPAs and students in identifying the interests of accountants. *J. Appl. Psychol.* 54:115–19

100. Hakel, M. D., Ohnesorge, J. P., Dunnette, M. D. 1970. Interviewer evaluations of job applicants' resumes as a function of the qualifications of the immediately preceding applicants. *J. Appl. Psychol.* 54:27–30

101. Hall, D. T. 1971. A theoretical model of career subidentity development in organizational settings. *Organ. Behav. Hum. Perform.* 6:50–76

102. Hall, D. T., Schneider, B., Nygren, H. T. 1969. Interpersonal factors in organizational identification. *Admin. Sci., Yale Univ.*

103. Hall, W. B., MacKinnon, D. W. 1969. Personality inventory correlates of creativity among architects. *J. Appl. Psychol.* 53:322–26

104. Hardesty, D. L., Jones, W. S. 1968. Characteristics of judged high potential management personnel: The operations of an industrial assessment center. *Personnel Psychol.* 21:85–98

105. Harrell, T. W. 1969. The personality of high earning MBA's in big business. *Personnel Psychol.* 22:457–63

106. Ibid 1970. The personality of high earning MBA's in small business. 23:369–75

107. Hendel, D. D., Weiss, D. J. 1970. Individual inconsistency and reliability of measurement. *Educ. Psychol. Meas.* 30:579–93

108. Hermans, H. J. M. 1970. A questionnaire measure of achievement motivation. *J. Appl. Psychol.* 54:353–63

109. Hicks, L. E. 1970. Some properties of ipsative, normative, and forced-choice normative measures. *Psychol. Bull.* 74:167–84

110. Hinrichs, J. R. 1969. Comparison of "real life" assessments of management potential with situational exercises, paper and pencil ability tests and personality inventories. *J. Appl. Psychol.* 53:425–32

111. Hobert, R., Dunnette, M. D. 1967. Development of moderator variables to enhance the prediction of managerial effectiveness. *J. Appl. Psychol.* 51:50–64

112. Holt, R. R. 1970. Yet another look at clinical and statistical prediction: Or is clinical psychology worthwhile? *Am. Psychol.* 25:337–49

113. Howell, M. A., Vincent, J. W. 1970. Factor analysis of interview data. *J. Appl. Psychol.* 54:313–15

114. Jaffee, C., Bender, J., Calvert, O. L. 1970. The assessment center technique: A validation study. *Manage. Personnel Quart.* 9:9–14

115. Jensen, A. R. 1969. How much can we boost IQ and scholastic achievement? *Harvard Educ. Rev.* 39:1–123

116. Johnson, J. C., Dunnette, M. D. 1968. Validity and test retest stability of the Nash Managerial Effectiveness Scale on the revised form of the Strong Vocational Interest Blank. *Personnel Psychol.* 21:283–93

117. Judy, C. J. 1970. Predictive validity of educational background information attained from entering airmen. *Proc. 78th Ann. Conv. APA* 5:681–83

118. Katz, I. 1970. Experimental studies of negro-white relationships. In *Advances in Experimental Social Psychology*, ed L. Berkowitz. New York: Academic

119. Kelleher, E. J., Kerr, W. A., Melville, N. T. 1968. The prediction of subprofessional nursing success. *Personnel Psychol.* 21:379–88

120. Kirkpatrick, J. J. 1970. *The psychological testing establishment: Vested interest vs. responsibility.* Presented at 78th Ann. Conv. APA, Miami Beach

121. Kirkpatrick, J. J., Ewen, R. B., Barrett, R. S., Katzell, R. A. 1968. *Testing and Fair Employment.* New York Univ. Press

122. Klein, S., Rock, D., Evans, F. 1968. The use of multiple moderators in academic prediction. *J. Educ. Meas.* 5:151–60

123. Kleinmuntz, B., McLean, R. S. 1968. Diagnostic interviewing by digital computer. *Behav. Sci.* 13:75–80

124. Korman, A. K. 1968. The prediction of managerial performance: A review. *Personnel Psychol.* 21:295–322

125. Kraut, A. I. 1969. Intellectual ability and promotional success among high level managers. *Personnel Psychol.* 22:281–90

126. Krug, R. E. 1966. Some suggested approaches for test development and measurement. *Personnel Psychol.* 19:24–34

127. Laurent, H. 1970. Cross cultural cross validation of empirically validated tests. *J. Appl. Psychol.* 54:417–23

128. Lawshe, C. H. 1969. Statistical theory and practice in applied psychology. *Personnel Psychol.* 22:117–23

129. Lee, H. E. 1968. Conditional response scaling. *Behav. Sci.* 13:29-35

130. Levy, P. 1968. Short form tests: A methodological review. *Psychol. Bull.* 69:410–16

131. Life Ins. Agency Manage. Assoc. 1968. Career guidelines in the life insurance industry. *Personnel Psychol.* 21:1–21

132. Life Off. Manage. Assoc. 1970. *Development of a LOMA Selection Test Battery.* Personnel Admin. Res. Div. LOMA (Mimeo)

133. Logue, P. E., Zenner, M., Gorman, G. 1968. Video-tape role playing in the job interview. *J. Couns. Psychol.* 15:436–38

134. Lopez, F. M. 1970. *The Making of a Manager.* New York: Am. Manage. Assoc.

135. Lykken, D. T. 1968. Statistical significance in psychological research. *Psychol. Bull.* 70:151–59

136. MacKinney, A. C. 1967. The assessment of performance change: An inductive example. *Organ. Behav. Hum. Perform.* 2:56–72

137. MacKinnon, D. W. 1968. The identification and development of creative personnel. *Personnel Admin.* 31:9–17

138. Marks, B. K. 1969. A system for evaluating campus recruiters. *Personnel Admin.* 32:30–34

139. Mayfield, E. C. 1970. Management selection: Buddy nominations revisited. *Personnel Psychol.* 23:377–91

140. McClelland, J. N., Rhodes, F. 1969. Prediction of job success for hospital aides and orderlies from MMPI scores and Personal History Data. *J. Appl. Psychol.* 53:49–54

141. McConnell, J. H. 1969. The assess-

ment center in the smaller company. *Personnel* 46:4–46
142. McCornack, R. L. 1970. A comparison of three predictor selection techniques in multiple regression. *Psychometrika* 35:257–71
143. McNemar, Q. 1969. Moderation of a moderator technique. *J. Appl. Psychol.* 53:69–72
144. Meyer, H. H. 1970. The validity of the in basket test as a measure of managerial performance. *Personnel Psychol.* 23:297–307
145. Miner, J. B. 1970. Psychological evaluations as predictors of consulting success. *Personnel Psychol.* 23:393–405
146. Moore, B. N. 1970. *Personnel Assessment Centres in Britain and America.* N.S.W. Pub. Serv. Bd.
147. Moore, C. L., MacNaughton, J. F., Osburn, H. G. 1969. Ethnic differences within an industrial selection battery. *Personnel Psychol.* 22:473–82
148. Moses, J. L. 1969. The use of an assessment center in the Management Career Program. *Ind. Psychol.* 7:24–25
149. Nash, A. N., Carroll, S. J. 1970. Improving the validity of a forced choice reference check with selected rater and job moderators. *Proc. 78th Ann. Conv. APA* 5:577–78
150. Nealey, S. M., Owen, T. W. 1970. A multitrait-multimethod analysis of predictors and criteria of nursing performance. *Organ. Behav. Hum. Perform.* 5:348–65
151. Obradovic, J. 1970. Modification of the forced choice method as a criterion of job proficiency. *J. Appl. Psychol.* 54:228–33
152. O'Leary, B. S., Farr, J. L., Bartlett, C. J. 1970. *Ethnic group membership as a moderator of job performance.* Washington, D. C.: Inst. Res.
153. Owens, W. A. 1969. Cognitive, noncognitive and environmental correlates of mechanical ingenuity. *J. Appl. Psychol.* 53:199–208
154. Owens, W. A. 1970. *A quasi actuarial prospect for individual assessment.* Pres. Add., Div. 14, 78th Ann. APA, Miami Beach
155. Owens, W. A., Jewell, D. O. 1969. Personnel Selection. *Ann. Rev. Psychol.* 20:419–46
156. Parry, M. E. 1968. Ability of psychologists to estimate validities of personnel tests. *Personnel Psychol.* 21:139–47
157. Payne, P. A. 1968. Use of a situation test for predicting counsellor performance. *J. Couns. Psychol.* 15:512–16
158. Pieters, G. R., Hundert, A. T., Beer, M. 1968. Predicting organizational choice: A post hoc analysis. *Proc. 76th Ann. Conv. APA* 3:573–74
159. Popham, W. J., Husek, T. R. 1969. Implications of criterion-referenced measurement. *J. Educ. Meas.* 6:1–9
160. Porritt, D. 1970. *Research evaluation and development responsibilities for the Personnel Assessment Center.* Pub. Serv. Bd., C & R Div., Sydney, Aust.
161. Prien, E. P. 1970. Measuring performance criteria of bank tellers. *J. Ind. Psychol.* 5:29–36
162. Prien, E. P., Kult, M. 1968. Analysis of performance criteria and comparison of a priori and empirically-derived keys for a forced choice scoring. *Personnel Psychol.* 21:505–13
163. Raubenheimer, I. van W. 1970. Influence of group and situational differences on the applicability of personnel test. *J. Appl. Psychol.* 54:214–16
164. Roach, D. E., Wherry, R. J. 1970. Performance dimensions of multi line insurance agents. *Personnel Psychol.* 23:239–50
165. Ronan, W. W. 1970. Evaluation of three criteria of management performance. *J. Ind. Psychol.* 5:18–28
166. Ronan, W. W., Prien, E. P. 1966. *Toward a criterion theory: A review and analysis of research and opinion.* Greensboro, N. C.: Richardson Found.
167. Rosen, D. B. 1970. *Employment Testing and Minority Groups.* Sch. Ind. Labor Relat., Cornell Univ.
168. Rowland, K. M., Scott, W. E. Jr. 1968. Psychological attributes of effective leadership in a formal organization. *Personnel Psychol.* 21:365–77
169. Ruch, F. L. 1970 Critical notes on "Seniority and Testing under Fair Employment Laws" by Cooper & Sobol. *Ind. Psychol.* 7:13–25
170. Ruda, E., Albright, L. E. 1968. Racial differences on selection instruments related to subsequent job performance. *Personnel Psychol.* 21:31–41
171. Rundquist, E. A. 1969. The prediction ceiling. *Personnel Psychol.* 22:109–16

172. Rychlak, J. F., Bray, D. W. 1967. A life-theme method for scoring of interviews in the longitudinal study of young business managers. *Psychol. Rep.* 21:277–326
173. Salas, R. G. 1970. *The WOSB's revisited: An experimental evaluation of the Australian Army version of the War Office Selection Board Procedure.* Aust. Army Psychol. Res. Unit, Melbourne
174. Schlesinger, I. M., Guttman, L. 1969. Smallest space analysis of intelligence and achievement tests. *Psychol. Bull.* 71:95–100
175. Schneider, B., Bartlett, C. J. 1968. Individual differences and organizational climate: 1. The research plan and questionnaire development. *Personnel Psychol.* 21:323–33
176. Schwab, D. P., Heneman, H. G. 1969. Relationship between interview structure and inter-interviewer reliability in an employment situation. *J. Appl. Psychol.* 53:214–17
177. Scott, W. A. 1968. Comparative validities of forced choice and single stimulus tests. *Psychol. Bull.* 70: 231–34
178. Schaefer, C. E., Anastasi, A. 1968. A biographical inventory for identifying creativity in adolescent boys. *J. Appl. Psychol.* 52:42–48
179. Sharon, A., Bartlett, C. J. 1969. Effect of instructional conditions in producing leniency on two types of rating scales. *Personnel Psychol.* 22:251–63
180. Siegel, A. I., Shultz, D. G., Fischl, M. A., Lanterman, R. S. 1968. Absolute scaling of job performance. *J. Appl. Psychol.* 52:313–18
181. Slivinski, L. W. 1970. Investigation into the work of some managers in the public service. *Stud. Personnel Psychol.* 2:27–43
182. Slivinski, L. W., Grant, K. W. 1970. *Assessment Center Proposal.* Personnel Assess. Res. Div., Pub. Serv. Comm. of Canada
183. Smith, N. C. 1970. Replication studies: A neglected aspect of psychological research. *Am. Psychol.* 25: 970–75
184. Smith, P. C., Kendall, L. M. 1963. Retranslation of expectations: An approach to the construction of unambiguous anchors for rating scales. *J. Appl. Psychol.* 47:149–55
185. Sparks, C. P. 1970. Validity of psychological tests. *Personnel Psychol.* 23:39–46
186. Stanley, J. C. 1971. Predicting college success of the educationally disadvantaged. *Science* 171:640–47
187. Starry, A. R., Raubenheimer, I. V., Tesser, A. 1969. Stability ratings as classifiers of life history item retest reliability. *J. Appl. Psychol.* 53:14–18
188. Stephenson, R. W., Ward, J. H. 1970. Computer-assisted discussions to help a policy group assign weights to criterion ratings. *Proc. 78th Ann. Conv. APA* 5:125–26
189. Stone, T. H., Athelstan, G. T. 1969. The SVIB for women and demographic variables in the prediction of occupational tenure. *J. Appl. Psychol.* 53:408–12
190. Tanofsky, R. T., Shepps, R. R., O'Neill, P. J. 1969. Pattern analysis of biographical predictors of success as an insurance salesman. *J. Appl. Psychol.* 53:136–39
191. Taylor, J. B., Haefele, E., Thompson, P., O'Donoghue, C. 1970. Rating scales as measures of clinical judgment: II. The reliability of example anchored scales under conditions of rater heterogeneity and divergent behavior sampling. *Educ. Psychol. Meas.* 30:301–10
192. Tenopyr, M. L. 1969. The comparative validity of selected leadership scales relative to success in production management. *Personnel Psychol.* 22:77–85
193. Thomson, H. A. 1970. Comparison of predictor and criterion judgments of managerial performance using the multitrait-multimethod approach. *J. Appl. Psychol.* 54:495–502
194. Thumin, F. J. 1968. MMPI profiles as a function of chronological age. *Psychol. Rep.* 22:479–82
195. Tryon, R. C., Bailey, D. E. 1970. *Cluster Analysis.* New York: McGraw
196. Uhlaner, J. E. 1970. *Human performance, jobs and systems psychology—The Systems Measurement Bed.* Pres. Add., Div. Mil. Psychol., 78th Ann. Conv. APA, Miami Beach
197. U. S. Commission on Civil Rights. 1969. *Equal Employment Opportunity under Federal Law.* Washington, D. C.: Clearinghouse Publ. No. 17
198. Validation of employment tests by contractors and subcontractors subject to the provisions of executive

order 11246. 1968. *Fed. Regist.* 33:14392–394

199. Vinacke, W. E. 1969. Variables in experimental games. *Psychol. Bull.* 71:293–318

200. Wainer, H. A., Rubin, I. M. 1969. Motivation of research and development entrepreneurs. Determinants of company success. *J. Appl. Psychol.* 53:178–84

201. Waters, C. W. 1970. Comparison of computer simulated conventional and branching tests. *US Army Behav. Sci. Res. Lab. TRN 216*

202. Waters, L. K., Waters, C. W. 1970. Peer nominations as predictors of short term sales performance. *J. Appl. Psychol.* 54:42–44

203. Webster, E. C. 1964. *Decision Making in the Employment Interview.* Montreal: Ind. Relat. Cent., McGill Univ.

204. Weiss, D. J. 1969. Occupational reinforcers, vocational needs and job satisfaction. *Res. Rep. #28, Work Adjustment Proj., Univ. of Minn.*

205. Weiss, D. J., Dawis, R. V. 1968. Multivariate prediction technique for problems involving multifunctional

predictor-criterion relationships. *Proc. 76th Ann. Conv. APA*, 229–30

206. Wernimont, P. F., Campbell, J. P. 1968. Signs, samples and criteria. *J. Appl. Psychol.* 52:372–76

207. Whitlock, G. H. 1970. *Test validity and fair employment.* Presented at 78th Ann. Conv. APA, Miami Beach

208. Wollowick, H. B., Greenwood, J. M., McNamara, W. J. 1969. Psychological testing with a minority group population. *Proc. 77th Ann. Conv. APA*, 609–10

209. Wollowick, H. B., McNamara, W. J. 1969. Relationship of the components of an assessment center to management success. *J. Appl. Psychol.* 53:348–52

210. Wright, O. R. 1969. Summary of research on the selection interview since 1964. *Personnel Psychol.* 22: 391–413

211. Wright, L. 1970. The meaning of IQ scores among professional groups. *Prof. Psychol.* 1:265–69

212. Zedeck, S., Smith, P. C. 1968. A psychophysical determination of equitable payment: A methodological study. *J. Appl. Psychol.* 52:343–47

PROJECTIVE METHODOLOGIES 190

H. Barry Molish

Texas Children's Hospital, Texas Medical Center, Houston, Texas

INTRODUCTION

Eight years ago, the *Annual Review of Psychology* for the first time "included a chapter devoted solely to the projective methodologies" (102). Frank's classic monograph on *Projective Methods* (87) and Bell's first comprehensive review of the literature on projective techniques (23) heralded in some 15 years earlier the beginning influx of tomes of studies concerning projective methodologies. Fisher's review followed in 1967 (78).

These two reviews prepared specifically for the *Annual Review of Psychology* were testament to the growing importance of the literature of projective methodologies. They addressed themselves in great measure to the classical issues of normative data, reliability, validity, etc.

It is of significance that whereas these classical issues still are relevant in any contemporary review, in the relatively short period of almost a decade, one of the core issues is now that of the continuing decline in the importance and application of projective methodologies.

Perhaps the comments by Zubin et al (328, p. 610) that projective techniques have not lived up to their promise were more prophetic than originally realized. Testament to the decline in the application of diagnostic testing in general has been noted with increasing frequency in the literature. Holt (133, p. 1) refers to this decline in no uncertain terms: "Diagnostic testing today is in a *funk.*" He discusses the reasons for this decline as paralleling those changes evolving in the practice of clinical psychology. In the foreword to a one-volume edited revision of what was once a two-volume edition of *Diagnostic Psychological Testing* (246) Holt discusses this issue further.

This decline in the use of projective methodologies, and the practice of psychodiagnostic testing in general, has been a topic of equal concern for others. Two recent past presidents of the Society for Projective Techniques and Personality Assessment (Molish 213, Ames 5) have made this their topic of poignant presidential messages. The title of Hertz's most recent address in accepting the Great Man Award of the Society for Projective Techniques and Personality Assessment (128) bespeaks this concern with as much clarity: "Projective Techniques In Crisis." The "crisis" Hertz refers to only in part concerns the pragmatic theoretical issues of normative, validity, and reliability data. Much of this state of change is certainly related to the "Uncertain future of Clinical Psychology," as described in

577

Albee's recent presidential address to the American Psychological Association (2), in which he describes a "growing cleavage" between scientific and professional psychology (2).

An awareness of the continuing change in the attitude toward projective methodologies is reflected in a most recent decision of the Society for Projective Techniques and Personality Assessment to change its name to the Society for Personality Assessment, deleting "Projective Techniques" (75). When originally founded, the name of the society was "The Society for Projective Techniques and Rorschach Institute." This decision to change the name of the society reflects the attitude that the projective methodologies in themselves are no longer in the unique key position they once enjoyed in the area of personality assessment.

The rise and decline in the use of projective techniques in psychological testing can be evaluated longitudinally from the data of several articles dealing specifically with this topic. Sundberg (291), referring to the *Fourth Mental Measurement Yearbook of 1951*, found "there are more references to projective tests than to intelligence tests, projective tests which were scarcely envisaged in 1917" (291). In a survey a decade later, Sundberg (292) refers to the Rorschach as "the most widely used test." In surveying the frequency of research application of various projective techniques over a 17 year period (1947–1964), Mills (207) found that "the most commonly used techniques in research have remained quite unchanged in the past 17 years; i.e. the Rorschach, the thematic tests, human figure drawings, and sentence completion."

The research use of leading projective techniques reached a peak in 1955, declined markedly in 1956 and 1957, and has remained rather constant since 1965. An emphasis upon application rather than validation has been noted since the peak years were reached (54).

A definite deemphasis of the use of projective techniques in clinical training programs has been reported (298). This has also been described by Molish (213) as a function of the overall change in the training and practice of clinical psychology. Further reference to the decline in the use and significance of projective tests among academic clinical psychologists has been described (3, 206). Other surveys (142, 184) attest to the increasing rejection of projective techniques by academicians.

Molish (213) and Hertz (128) refer to the contemporary influence of the behavior modification emphasis as one challenging both the utility and validity of psychodiagnosis in contemporary practice. Anastasi (6) challenges psychological testing on the basis of its "not adequately assimilating development from the science of behavior."

Shombry & Kelley (275) placed less emphasis upon projective techniques, as noted in programs of graduate departments granting PhDs in clinical psychology, although the older and more traditional graduate programs still continue to emphasize training in psychodiagnostics.

A perspective of the past and current history of the status of projective techniques is afforded by Buros (42) in his 1970 *Personality Tests and Reviews*. Murray (218) aptly points out some of the historical implications in this text concerning the current research status of projective techniques and personality assessment in general, in light of the *Mental Measurement Yearbook* published in 1965. One of the conclusions drawn by Buros, as cited by Murray (218), is of special import. Buros comments particularly on the "sterility of the research and experimental writing on the Rorschach and the MMPI," a sterility "applicable to other personality tests," and wonders that 2274 references have not thrown sufficient light on the MMPI to result in revision or replacement, and that 3747 Rorschach references have "not produced a body of knowledge generally accepted by competent psychologists" (218, p. 529).

The annual statistics of the ratio of objective personality tests to the projectives graphically depict the shift in interest. "These figures reveal an inverse U-curve, going from 20 percent projectives in 1951, and back to 24 percent projectives in 1967" (218, p. 529).

THE SCOPE OF THIS REVIEW

This review surveys the literature from 1966 through 1970. It would be presumptuous to consider this an all-encompassing review of projective techniques. In spite of the reported decline in the emphasis placed upon psychodiagnostics including the projective techniques, the literature still remains voluminous, as attested to by Buros' (42) most recent yearbook. The projective techniques involved in this review are those which still are most frequently used in psychodiagnostic batteries and concomitantly are those primarily reported in the research literature: *inkblots; thematic methods; completion methods* such as *word association* and *sentence completion* techniques; and *projective drawings*, primarily the Draw-a-Person test.

Techniques such as the Bender-Gestalt, and intelligence tests, described by Rabin (245, Part VI) as "extensions of the projective hypothesis," have not been included. A review of other projective techniques such as the Szondi, facial photographs, Lowenfeld mosaic test, the Kahn test of symbol arrangement, and drawing completion techniques (Franck, Horn-Hellensberg) are reported by Campos (43).

The review of *thematic methods* concentrates upon the Thematic Apperception Test and the more recent Children's Apperception Test. Other projective techniques such as the Picture Story test (Symonds), the Michigan picture test, the Make-a-Picture story (Shneidman), the Object Relations test (Phillipson), and the Three-Dimensional Apperception Test (Twitchell-Allen) have been reviewed by Neuringer (226). Doll play and puppetry techniques in their adaptation as projective methods have been described and reviewed by Haworth (125). Kauffman (153) has published a recent review of research studies involving the Bene-Anthony Family Relations Test (7), especially in reference to its validity. Francis-Williams (86) describes this test especially in relation to psychodiagnostic evaluation of children.

A variety of story completion methods and their research application are reviewed by Lansky (165).

The Hand test (35) and the Blacky pictures (27) are afforded some coverage in this review insofar as reference to them is made in studies concerning specific theoretical issues: the Hand test in relation to projection of aggression (38); the Blacky pictures in relation to the studies attempting to validate psychosexual development within a psychoanalytic framework.

A number of new major texts and manuals directly concerning projective methodologies have been published or have appeared in revised form. A majority of these texts are referred to either in relation to their import concerning a specific projective technique or in relation to the general theory and application of projective methodologies.

Murstein's *Handbook* (222) is an edited volume of research studies prior to its publication in 1965, reviewing the current reliability and validity status of the Rorschach, thematic tests, Draw-a-Person, Bender-Gestalt, and Sentence Completion Test. Rabin's edited text (245) is a thorough compendium on the application of projective techniques in personality assessment, reviewing the literature on all of the known projective techniques in use up to its time of publication in 1968. Schafer (267) devotes his entire text to demonstrating the "consistent and controlled application of psychoanalytic ideas in psychodiagnostic investigation" (267). "Projective types" in the development of scales of "mental health potential" is the main theme of Harrower's text (121). The broad application of projective techniques in the interdisciplinary practice of psychological diagnosis is the major emphasis in a text by Pope & Scott (239). Holt (133) devotes the majority of his text to projective techniques, with a heavy emphasis upon the Rorschach and the Thematic Apperception Test. Weiner (314) discusses the Rorschach, Draw-a-Person, and the Wechsler Adult Intelligence Scale as applied to the problems of psychodiagnosis in schizophrenia. A chapter on Scientific and Professional Issues in Psychodiagnosis (314, pp. 487–509) is specifically devoted to the validity of psychodiagnostic test scores and clinical and statistical prediction. Ogdon's *Handbook* (231) includes individual chapters on the Rorschach (pp. 10–38) and on Projective Drawings (pp. 38–58).

Some of the introductory texts on personality measurement still devote an appreciable amount of pagination to projective methodologies. Kleinmuntz's (156) includes two extensive chapters on the Rorschach and Thematic Apperception Tests. Although emphasizing an objective approach to personality assessment, Sarason (262) orients two of his chapters to projective methodologies with specific reference to their implications in affording ambiguous stimuli in personality assessment. Wolman's *Handbook* (325) includes a series of chapters describing the application and research findings of the most frequently used projective techniques. An entire volume devoted to physchodiagnostic procedures emphasizes the importance of projective techniques and their application, especially in contemporary psychiatric and sociocultural issues (216).

Beck & Molish (21) revised Volume 2 of Beck's earlier (1945) edition on

Rorschach's test. Adult and childhood schizophrenic reaction types, including longitudinal studies, as evaluated by the Rorschach test, is the topic of another text by Beck (20). Allen's (4) text on the Rorschach test was published primarily as a manual for the beginning student. Schachtel (266) emphasizes the experimental implications in the Rorschach and devotes an entire chapter (pp. 268–328) to Interpersonal Meaning of the Rorschach Test Situation. A text devoted to the individual and group administration of Zulliger's ("Z test") inkblot test has recently been translated into English (330).

Fisher & Cleveland (80) published a revision of their 1958 classic text on *Body Image and Personality* as evaluated by the Rorschach test. Fisher's most recent text (79), although expanding the theoretical issues concerning body experience and their assessment by objective tests (Body Focus Questionnaire and Body Distortion Questionnaire—appendices pp. 605–36), still prodigiously concerns itself with the Rorschach Barrier and Penetration scoring and gives a replete account of its current research status based upon an extensive review of the literature.

The first text devoted entirely to the Children's Apperception Test (CAT) by Haworth (124) includes a discussion of the human form of the test (CAT-H) developed by Bellak & Hurvich (25), modifying the original animal form of the test. This text offers a compendium of published and unpublished studies of the CAT, including norms, sociocultural variables, sex differences, sociometric factors, etc. The School Apperception Method (SAM) was introduced by Soloman & Starr (284), with exclusive emphasis upon the school environment through use of a series of drawings depicting children in school.

Beck's translation of Beizmann's *Handbook* (22) is a compilation of more than 10,000 Rorschach responses in an attempt to further standardize the scoring of F-plus and F-minus responses, affording standardized norms for French populations of subjects as well. Hertz (127) published a revision of tables for scoring Rorschach responses. Exner (74) describes the history and development of the various Rorschach systems as represented by the "great people of the Rorschach" (74, p. vii).

Two voluminous texts concerning the Rorschach test as applied to studies on the psychological characteristics of medical students, by Thomas, Ross & Freed (300, 301), are innovative in their application of computer methodology in indexing Rorschach data. One of these volumes (300) affords an index of Rorschach responses based on 586 individual Rorschach records. The other volume (301) reports similar data based on 568 group Rorschachs.

Representative of the tomes of literature on Rorschach studies published from 1921–1964 is Lang's *Rorschach Bibliography* (164). A total of 3855 studies are classified according to subject matter in this bibliography.

The proceedings of the Sixth International Congress of Rorschach and Projective Methods (283) have been published in four volumes. A total of 121 studies dealing with the Rorschach TAT, and other projectives are included.[1]

---

[1] For those interested in Lowenfeld's Worlds and Villages Test, a section devoted

Several new major texts concerning *projective drawing techniques* have been published. Koppitz's (162) text on the human figure drawing is a serious effort to restore an objective basis for this technique which has continuously incurred the wrath of researchers who have attacked the technique's lack of validity and reliability. A text by Thomas (299) affords a unique compendium of 870 human figure drawings of medical students. Figure drawings of subjects with a variety of parental histories in regard to coronary disease and other medical conditions are reproduced for visual comparison. No plea is made for the test's validity. Precision scoring was adhered to and based on the criterion established by Witkin et al. (323) and by Jones & Thomas (146).

A text on the house-tree-person technique by Buck & Hammer (39) describes the application of this technique in school settings, criminal courts, geriatrics, etc. A new projective drawing technique is introduced in a text by Burns & Kaufman (41) concerning kinetic factors in figure drawings of family members, in an attempt to provide "more valid and dynamic material." The text merely introduces this new technique without normative data or data concerning reliability and validity.

Projective techniques may be in a state of "crisis" as noted by Hertz (128), their use in clinical practice and their importance in the teaching and training of clinical psychologists may be declining, but the scope of the literature surveyed would certainly suggest that there is still a continuing vigorous effort to further explore their clinical and research application.

It would be rather platitudinous for this reviewer to concentrate on the topics of validity, reliability, and clinical versus statistical prediction as they apply to projective methodologies.[2] Earlier published reviews have already fully documented these deficiencies in projective methodologies. It is more meaningful and contemporarily appropriate that the emphasis of this review be directed to the current status of projective methodologies in the light of current developments which present a challenge to the entire field of contemporary psychology in the assessment of personality.

McReynolds (186, pp. 6–9) describes "current developments . . . representative of the directions characteristic of modern assessment psychology." He discusses the examiner effects and the effects of the testing situation as noted in the well-documented text by Rosenthal (253). The issues of clinical and actuarial prediction continue to be of major concern, especially in relation to projective methodologies. This review will not directly concern itself with this issue, which has been referenced elsewhere in the literature.

---

entirely to this projective technique can be found in Vol. 4, pp. 787–866. Another section (pp. 715–86) includes a series of articles on Rorschach Test Modifications, Behn-Rorschach, and the Z test (Zulliger). Literature published for both these methods are seldom found in American journals.

[2] For a replete evaluation review of the status of predictive validity of projective tests, see: Suinn, R. M., Oskamp, S. 1969. *The Predictive Validity of Projective Measures.* Springfield, Ill.: Thomas.

Key articles discussing this issue and not cited in previous reviews are those of Sines (279), Lindzey (178), and Meehl (199). Sawyer (265), after a critical review and analysis of 45 clinical-statistical prediction studies, concludes that "the clinical-statistical problem is far from being solved . . . " (p. 198). Holt (135) discusses and criticizes the "continued interest in structuring and maintaining such an artificial dichotomy as clinical versus statistical prediction" (p. 348). Atyas (10) discusses a model that would integrate actuarial principles of test construction with experimental methods.

The current trend in the research concerning projective methodologies over the past 4 years has been directed towards developing greater objectivity in scoring. Projective techniques are beginning to be more and more conceptualized within the framework of new theoretical models with attention paid to stimulus functions, the properties of the situation in which the person is being tested, and in general exploring the concepts of generality vs specificity. The generality-specificity issue is one problem inherent in all types of personality assessment in need of further investigation, as described by McReynolds (186).

The sampling of the studies reviewed does indicate that through a diversity of applications of projective methodologies, many sociocultural processes of interaction have been explored. In this respect, the projective methodologies have been applied to a current pressing need for the "emerging discipline of environmental psychology."[3]

This review has been conceptualized in such a way as to attest to the comments of McReynolds (186, p. 8):

> Projective tests, though less widely used now than formerly, are still a major focus of research and practice. In general, projective tests have not shown up well in validity studies, and many psychologists appear ready to reject the approach as inherently unsatisfactory. Such a conclusion however, would not only be highly premature (the evidence is not that good one way or the other) but also unfortunate in that it would tend to stifle further developments in projective technology.

RORSCHACH INKBLOT TESTS

The general viewpoints concerning the current status of the Rorschach with specific reference to its empirical basis has been the subject of reviews by Eron (42, pp. 1297–1300), Dana (42, pp. 1300–6), and by Jensen (42, pp. 1306–14) concentrating on a review of the Rorschach literature between 1964 and 1968. Each of these reviewers attack the test on the basis of inadequate reliability and validity. Klopfer (158, Chap. 7), even in the light of the test's generally poor research image, states that the test "has risen like a phoenix from its ashes" in affording a set of stimuli which can be used in assessing many facets of personality concerning sematic differential, ambiguity of the stimulus, the meaning of content, and experimenter bias by altering the test situation.

[3] See Wohlwill, J. F., on the Emerging Discipline of Environmental Psychology. *The American Psychologist* (1970) 25:303–12. See also Hertz, M. (128).

There is noted in the Rorschach literature, as well as in the other projective techniques as a whole, a trend toward a serious attempt to conceptualize the theory and application of the technique within the framework of a cognitive theory as described by Fulkerson (90), especially related to defining the stimulus and in general emphasizing the "cognitive style and response set" and the "need to attack directly the definition of the stimulus."

Since the issue of experimenter bias effects was emphasized by Rosenthal (253), its implication for projective methodologies has been prodigiously explored. Masling (193, 194) related the theoretical issues involved directly to projective testing. Several key articles dealing with this issue have appeared in the literature with increasing frequency (15, 263). An entire monograph by Barber & Silver (14) is devoted to the "fact and fiction" of the experimenter bias effects of Rosenthal (254, 255).[4]

Rorschach (251, pp. 66–67) recognized factors other than those related to personality which influenced the response to his test in his suggestion of the need for a parallel series of inkblots.

Research studies concerning the role of examiner bias in inkblot techniques have produced inconsistent results. Strauss (288) failed to detect bias effects on the Experiences Balance (EB), inconsistent with the finding of Masling (192), who found the ratio of animal to human responses in Rorschach content altered by the examiner's influence. Even accounting for the effect of the examiner's productivity (R) expectancies of the subject, Strauss & Marwit (289) still found no effect between R and EB expectancies.

The effects of modeling in mediating bias has been the area of investigation in several studies (95, 191). The issues studied here are the examiner as a model, the subject as the imitator, and the interaction of the modeling effects. In one study (191) Rorschach test data was found to be communicated by modeling. An effort was made to meet the criticisms of experimental design raised by Strauss (288) concerning the use of standardized test procedures and making "the experimental procedure closer to the clinical situation" (191, p. 351). In another study (95), hostility as a personality variable and observation of examiner's models as the experimental variable were studied. Observation of various degrees of the hostile model's Rorschach performance did facilitate projection of more hostile Rorschach content for low but not high hostile subjects.[5]

Effects of the examiner's sex upon Rorschach administration and productivity has been demonstrated in several studies. Rorschach productivity was uniquely affected in the male examiner-female subject situation (120, 126), with male examiners eliciting more responses in female than male subjects. Both of these studies, however, have a major limitation insofar

---

[4] A series of articles concerning this issue also can be found in the *Journal of Consulting and Clinical Psychology* (1969) 33:1–17.

[5] The implications of this study for the social dynamics of learning factors of hostile behavior is related to the theoretical issues of social learning theory discussed by Bandura, as cited in (95, p. 302).

as the examiners were all at an internship level of experience. Replication with different populations of subjects and with more experienced clinicians is needed.[6]

General issues relating to the examiner-subject bias, the stimulus value of Rorschach stimuli, and the variables in the testing situation are discussed in relation to "the role of experiential data in personality assessment" (190). Schachtel's entire text (266) is devoted to the multidimensional experiential factors in the Rorschach test.

Factors influencing scoring, interpretation, and general performance in the Rorschach test have been investigated. Verbal reinforcement was found to increase Rorschach productivity (32); errors in Rorschach scoring were found to be related to the personality of the scorer (307); and subjects in a relaxed situation set gave more Rorschach responses, more self references and pathognomonic verbalizations than those administered in group Rorschach under a pressured situation (122).

Lefcourt & Siegel (171), using Barron's Human Movement Inkblots, tested the findings of a series of investigations which concluded that M responses were an index of repressiveness, were given more often to an examiner who was less likely to censure the subject, were correlated positively to active visual scanning and negatively with defensiveness, and in general were negatively related to repression. In another study (170), experimental conditions affecting projection of M responses were noted which indicated that sex differences in both attention and fantasy processes must be considered.

In a study in which the subjects were instructed to fake the Rorschach test, significant changes in Rorschach scores were noted (67). Rorschachs of lower-class subjects were assessed less favorably than those of middle-class subjects (175). Subjects who were exposed to tests emphasizing animal drawings and animal stories prior to the Rorschach administration produced significantly more animal content (187).

THE STIMULUS IN RORSCHACH CARDS

Previous reviews in this series (78, 102) have not discussed Baughman's classical studies on altering the stimulus characteristics of the Rorschach cards, in which variation in the stimuli of the Rorschach cards appreciably affected many of the dependent measures involved in Rorschach responses (17). Russell (258) re-evaluates Baughman's studies, taking issue with the conclusions drawn by Baughman in a later study (16) in which he says "Baughman reversed himself when only 5 of the scores that were part of the earlier 1954 study failed to show significance" (258, p. 22). Baughman (17) replies to Russell's criticism implying the "we are far from a solution to the problem of the stimulus in Rorschach's test" (258, p. 25).

[6] Harris & Masling (120, p. 62) cite an unpublished study by Donofrio (62) in which "no significant differences as a function of the examiner's experience" in TAT stories on self disclosure were found.

The effects of blurring by projecting Rorschach slides out of focus resulted in marked changes in several Rorschach determinants, suggesting that visual acuity should be tested before any group administration of the Rorschach is attempted (113).

The stimulus value of several Rorschach cards has been investigated by a variety of techniques. Studies have made reference to Cards IV and VII as the "father" and "mother" cards respectively. Any reliable selection of a parental card in view of the research evidence is still open to criticism (188). Parental interpretations of Cards IV and VII were not supported in either adjusted or maladjusted groups of subjects (48). In another study (19) a large sample of first to sixth-grade children selected Cards II and III as "mother" and Card I as well as IV as "father." Age is a significant variable in the choice of Cards IV and VII as parental figures, and without regard for the subject's age no such inferences can be made indiscriminantly (46). The symbolic meaning of Card II as representing a sibling has also not been corroborated (47). One study (176) based on a large sample of children does show convincing evidence that boys and girls do respond differently in their preference to Cards IV and VII; this preference varying with age. However, the recognized complexity of variables would not permit any objective conclusions for these findings. The popular human figure in Card III as an index of sexual identification was not corroborated in either normal adults or adults with emotional problems (116).

Two studies (68, 285) explored the symbolic equivalence of Rorschach cards to conceptions of God, especially Card X. In another study (141) the relationship between pathology and ratings on 15 semantic differential scales was obtained by using the Rorschach cards as stimuli. Extreme response of subjects (Japanese college students) was found to be related to the degree of pathology as measured by other objective personality test criteria. In another study (179) significant differences were found in the ratings of the Rorschach responses on 21 semantic differential scales by schizophrenic patients as compared to nonschizophrenic groups. The Rorschach color cards in another study (55) were found to have a connotative import for schizophrenic patients as rated on a 15-scale sematic differential.

OTHER RORSCHACH VARIABLES
CONTENT

Two extensive reviews and critiques of the literature up to 1967 have been published (63a, 114). One of them (114) concerns itself more with a critique of the scoring systems, symbolic meaning of responses, content signs, and validation of content scales. On the basis of this critique, there is more need for research. Overlap between content scales and signs is still dependent upon a host of mediating variables extremely difficult to control. Davis (60) discusses these issues in a critical review of Brar's study (33).

Concerning the more traditional content categories, the specificity of any single content category as unique for diagnosis and personality variables is not valid (63a). Mayman (197), however, in describing an "object-relational" concept of interest content concludes that content is a significant indicator of psychopathology when based on "extensive psychiatric, psychological, and social work interviews" (197, p. 17).

An effort to objectify the meaning of content by an associative technique has been made (155). In another study (217) reliability, normative data, and validity are cited for a system developed earlier by Peebles, which attempts to measure the many mediating variables between Rorschach content and real-life behavior as described in one critique (114). Another study attempts to (144) resolve the psychometric problems in establishing the reliability and validity of content by measuring the congruance-deviance factor in personality.

Oral psychosexual content as compared to anal content was found significantly more frequent in male psychiatric patients (243), and content reflecting narcissism is significantly more frequent in certain psychiatric disorders (73). Projective measures of anxiety and hostility based on content and those derived from objective personality tests were found to represent independent variables (149). Rorschach content as a technique of studying child development does seem to hold some promise (49).

MOVEMENT RESPONSE

Fisher (78), after reviewing the literature on the M response, concluded, "the box score looks favorable for Rorschach's major hypothesis concerning the relationship of M and kinesthesia."

Dana (56) described a construct validation methodology for the empirical interpretation of the M response. M responses are described on the basis of six constructs established by replicated research findings. These six constructs (delay, time sense, intelligence, creativity, fantasy, and interpersonal relations) were explored in a subsequent study (45). Three of the six (fantasy, time sense, and intelligence) were found to be significantly related to M scores.

Electromyographic records to measure the actual change in muscle potential (286) accompanying the projection of M responses failed to demonstrate that increase in muscle potential was significantly related to the production of movement responses (M, FM, and imagined movement). However, the individual differences reported, and the evidence that aggressive content responses resulted in an increase in muscle potential, are still considered indices of the relationship between M and kinesthesia. Hardyck (119), however, using electromyography in comparing high and low-activity groups in perceived movement and personality measures, including the Rorschach and objective personality tests, was unable to replicate results previously reported in the literature.

In another study (232) measuring dream activity by electroencephalography (rapid eye movements—REM), kinesthesia in M responses and dream activity appear to have a common basis.

Lerner (172, 173) discusses Freudian views of the function of dreaming as related to M and kinesthesia. He used the Holtzman inkblots on subjects with drug-induced dream deprivation as compared with controls not dream deprived and found an increase in both the quantity of M responses and changes in their quality. Newton (228) failed to support these findings. Using barrier scores, the amount of physical activity in dreams of paralyzed men were found to be unrelated.

In another study (51), M responses were obtained before and during exercise and were found to increase significantly during exercise. Previous studies in which M responses were determined after rather than during exercise had shown an inverse relationship between M and physical activity.

Prola (241) re-evaluates the motor inhibition-fantasy hypothesis based upon changes in M responses. Previous studies which infer that total fantasy is stimulated by motor inhibition may have been too broad in their conclusions.

The suggestion that M responses are an index of the individual's inhibitory control over impulse is pursued in a study (59) involving a response inhibition task. Whether M implies only inner fantasy or observable social behavior still appears to be a controversial issue, and most of the evidence favors the hypothesis of overt behavior according to one review (312). Singer (280, p. 594) concludes that "evidence linking Rorschach M responses to motor inhibition or delaying capacity, and to measures of imaginativeness seems moderately convincing." One study (65) found the number of M responses to be a reliable index of this trait, although the quality of M responses was not related to creative expression.

There is a significant although weak relationship betwen M and role-taking ability as a function of cognitive development (163). Subjects producing energetic M responses as an index of expansive behavior were found to be challenged more by space exploration than those giving weak M responses (304).

Mayman discusses the role of M responses as an index of "empathic interpersonal relationships" (197, p. 21), citing a review of the literature to support his position. Holt, however, takes issue with this emphasis placed upon M since other influences such as inhibition and constriction make it "hazardous to interpret its absence" (134, p. 30). In successful artists M was found to be related to creativity, but it did not reflect the capacity to utilize the creativity constructively (66).

COLOR AND SHADING

Beck's paper on Emotions and Understanding (20, pp. 93–114) offers a detailed and theoretical framework of interaction between M and color. The extension of Rorschach's *Elebnistypus* into Beck's *Experience Actual* elaborates the concept of experiencing emotions. This new Rorschach variable is elsewhere referred to extensively (21).

Brockmann (37), reviewing past studies concerning psychophysiological correlates of the color-emotion Rorschach hypotheses, refers to the lack of consistent results. Although finding no conclusive validation, his study did show more significant results than others cited in the literature.

Ability to constructively delay response in problem solving was positively correlated with the number of FC responses and negatively with C and CF responses (101). Generalizations concerning personality in relation to differential diagnosis are not warranted on the basis of colors alone in a study using the semantic differential (50).

One study (177) isolated the response sets of color, anxiety, and order effects in relation to color shock. The stimulus of color alone is not important, but a change in the order in which a color is presented is important for the anxious subject.

The relationship of light and dark shading responses as an index of compliancy and aggressiveness in anxiety reactions, as proposed by Piotrowski, has been corroborated (309). Shading used in colored areas occurs more frequently in a sample of hospitalized psychiatric patients who made suicidal attempts (8).

INKBLOT INDICES OF BODY-IMAGE SCORES

Since Cleveland and Fisher introduced in 1958 the concept of Body Image as measured by the Rorschach, there has been a consistent increase in the number of studies investigating this concept and using their methodology. The second revised edition of their text (80) describes in detail the developments of their method from 1958 to 1967, with a replete review of the literature (80, pp. 370–94). Fisher's text (79) also contains a full review of the literature up to 1968. Summarizing the literature, Fisher & Cleveland conclude that: Barrier and Penetration can be scored with a high degree of objectivity; test-retest reliabilities are impressive; female subjects are inclined to obtain larger Barrier scores than men; and Barrier scores are derived from patterns of exterior-interior body experience. That the use of body image scores is significant as measures of response to stress, factors of social interaction, and in differentiating types of psychopathology, has been documented in many studies.

Fisher (79, pp. 168–75) cites a series of new studies designed to test the Barrier score with more acumen. He outlines a number of studies concerning the correlates of Barrier scores with perceptions of body regions, external and internal.

In view of the psychometric advantages of the Holtzman inkblot technique, the majority of the studies in body image have used this series of blots rather than the standard Rorschach. No distinction between studies on this basis will be made, however, since the method has been found equally applicable to both series of inkblots.

Mitchell (211, 212) challenged the concept of "self-steering behavior" (see 80, Chap. 4) in a study in which he found that the Barrier score was not a valid technique for predicting reaction to disability stress. Fisher &

Cleveland answered this criticism, stating that adjustment measures were used which were not "sensitive to the stress effects of body disablement" (82, p. 320). Another study (129) challenged the construct validity of body-boundary perception of body site of disease. The discrepancy of these findings is explained on the basis of difference in subjects used and the body site of symptomatology (81).

The Penetration score is correlated with the focus upon interior body experiences, while the Barrier score is linked with sensation of the exterior body (305). In explaining the psychic dynamics of arthritic patients, outer control is positively related to Barrier scores and inner control is negatively related to Penetration scores (11). Active physical exercise increased Barrier scores in a group of schizophrenic patients (58).

In a series of studies concerned with social behavior, boundary definiteness predicted classroom behavior in normal and emotionally disturbed boys (77). High and low Barrier scores were related to the proximity and distance respectively in social interaction (88).

No significant differences in Penetration or Barrier scores in a group of LSD users as compared with nonusers was found, but broad generalization cannot be made in view of the unique sample of LSD subjects used (123). Stutterers scored higher than other groups of subjects on body boundary dimensions (236). When high and low Barrier score subjects were subjected to conditioning procedures involving galvanic skin response and heart rate (9), more responses at exterior sites and interior sites were given by high Barrier and low Barrier subjects respectively.

HOLTZMAN INKBLOT TECHNIQUE (HIT)

The HIT must now be regarded as having come into its own as a projective technique, and publications concerning its use have increased markedly since the last review (78). Holtzman's review of the research prior to 1968 has already been published (136). Studies indicate that the Rorschach and Holtzman systems compare well as to the underlying meaning of each of their variables. Split-half reliability and re-test stability of variables have been established for many variables. Factor analytic studies of variables across the 22 HIT variables are cited, and studies concerning the test's clinical application, cross-cultural correlates, differential diagnosis, developmental trends, and correlations with behavior and other personality tests measures have now gained a firm position. The HIT, unlike the Rorschach, is minimally effected by situational factors and the examiner is not considered a major factor in the test's variance. Compared to the Rorschach, the HIT is generally regarded as having a psychometric advantage in its use of parallel forms, standardization, and reliability (136). A series of reviews of the HIT (42, pp. 1244–49) concentrate on its psychrometric advantages over the Rorschach.

As with the Rorschach (237, 300, 301), computer systems have been utilized with HIT data. Gorham (106, 108) describes a validated computer scoring system for group administration of the test and 17 of its variables, based on a sample of 5000 subjects including normals, psychiatric patients, and subjects of several cultures. The method has been applied to large samples of Spanish-speaking cultures. Validity and reliability of this computer-based scoring system have been established, and computer-based scores are equal to scores from records administered and scored individually (107). Computer methods have established universal popular responses based on group administration of the HIT in 5 cultures (160).

Noncomputerized-based age norms for a sample of children and adolescents in a clinical setting indicated some differences from established children norms, but the relatively small sample of children used should be considered (214). Evidence for a hierarchical integration of perceptual organization with increasing age as measured by HIT variables was found in a group of children (303), in part replicating other studies concerning developmental analysis of HIT variables. Developmental trends in color scores for a group of children showed an increase in effective integration of color and forms with increase in chronological age (260). The number of human (H) responses varied directly with social interests and functional pathology (76). The modulating effects of anxiety in the interaction between H responses and empathic capacity should be considered in regarding H responses as an absolute measure of empathy (252).

A series of studies explored the stimulus value of the HIT. In one study, destroying the symmetry of the blots had no effect upon the number of M responses projected, suggesting that M is not directly peripherally determined (296). When the stimulus dimensions of color and shading of standardized group slides were altered, no significant differences in scores for shading and color were found (137).

Two studies (174, 257) utilized the HIT and word association tests to investigate the effects of instructional sets in psychopathology, both resulting in changes in some HIT variables. White noise masking increased the number of color responses (138).

Social isolation and confinement as a stress situation were measured by changes produced in HIT variables (294). Pathognomic verbalization and anatomy scores of the HIT are positively correlated with a psychotic reaction profile, but form definiteness and animal and popular scores are not (256). Increase in color score was the only change noted under acute experimental alcohol intoxication (196). None of the HIT variables correlated with the extraversion scales of the Maudsley Personality Inventory, but 6 HIT variables did correlate with the neuroticism scale. Color and shading are not invariably correlated with neuroticism (203).

THEMATIC METHODS: THE THEMATIC APPERCEPTION TEST (TAT)

The criticisms of the TAT raised and discussed in the last review (78) still are noted in the literature. A series of critical reviews (42, pp. 927–34), although referring to it as a "non-standardized assessment technique" with low reliability and validity, still recognize its research possibilities: the examiner-subject interaction, the stimulus properties, the relationship between fantasy and behavior, etc. Its use to the clinician is not challenged: "If the TAT is short on actual validity, it certainly is not lacking in what may be called 'subject validity' " (78, p. 933). Extensive reviews of the TAT will be found in (325, Chap. 22) and in (245, Chap. 3), replete with documented references concerning reliability and validity. One author (325, p. 597) concludes: "The 'test' is still a test of the tester."

NEED ACHIEVEMENT

The problems linked with McClelland's n Ach formulations as described by Fisher (78, p. 177) still attract research interest. A detailed list of these criticisms, documented by research studies, offers an excellent conceptual framework to judge the application of the TAT in this measure of behavior (325, p. 586).

The most recent criticism of the n Ach formulation is that of Weiner: "The model is stimulus bound; it is assumed that this stimulus engages a motive and initiates a cognitive, inferential process" (313, p. 73). The model Weiner suggests parallels that of the "Lewinian and Hull-Spence conceptions of behavior" (313, p. 105). Some of the theoretical issues raised are also discussed by Wallace (310), not only in relation to the TAT, but to projective methodologies in general. Evidence supporting McClelland's theory based on the most critical studies are also referred to by Weiner (313, p. 71).

Terhune (297) takes issue with the scoring system for n Aff, referring to its low test-retest reliability. Klinger (157), in a critical review of the literature, refers to the possibility of the nonmotivational quality of arousal conditions on fantasy in n Ach. The conscious aspects of projection with specific reference to the TAT (132, p. 266) and to the conscious factors in n Ach (131) are noted.

Thematic drive expression as demonstrated in n Ach and n Aff scores have been studied in occupational groups. In one study (185) no consistent results in relating n Ach scores and course grades were noted. N Ach scores were significantly correlated with grade point average for science majors, but male n Ach scores were not affected by achievement or affiliation arousal (233). A special series of TAT cards representing tasks in which the subject regarded himself as competent resulted in higher achievement fantasy (273). Low correlations were found between authors of short stories in n Ach and n Aff scores in their TAT records (40). Verbal fluency was found to influence n Ach scores, but its effect decreased with habituation to the test situation (282).

Dana (57) discusses general problems for personality assessment and for future research centered about the TAT and n Ach, n Aff, and N Power scores.

On the basis of an extensive longitudinal study, consistent relationships between age, sexes, and motives in TAT themes were not found (281). The relationship between TAT fantasy and behavior is discussed in two position papers (169, 182).

STIMULUS EFFECTS, TEST CONDITIONS, AND EFFECTS OF OTHER VARIABLES ON TAT RESPONSES

Dana stresses the need for "a uniform method of determining cue values across needs and across subject populations" (57, p. 205), emphasizing the need to consider transitory states which have a definite influence upon the expression of needs.

Kaplan (151) discusses the need to define and measure the relative ambiguity of the TAT cards and the lack of objectivity in comparing the degree of ambiguity among specific cards. Murstein's (220) rejoinder to Kaplan refers to "methodological flaws which vitiate the significance of his conclusions" (220, p. 483), and these are discussed by Kaplan (152).

Stimulus ambiguity is associated with hesitant and nonfluent speech in verbal behavior in the TAT (276). However, high ambiguity cards are not associated with high GSR scores (277). In evaluating hostility, the stimulus properties of TAT cards are the prime determinant (221). Stimulus variation does effect thematic expression of sexual conflict, but avoidance reactions to structured and not ambiguous stimuli are more provocative (70). Ambiguity is not more favorable in demonstrating the effects of motivational conditions resulting from food deprivation (264). TAT cards with moderate ambiguity provoked more extreme responses than some Rorschach cards (229). Stimulus cues in *personal time* involving the past (*retrotension*) and the future (*protension*) affect TAT responses (324). Situational similarity in TAT cards may effect the amount of projection, but pictorial figures of males and females do not (315).

SPECIAL APPLICATIONS OF THE TAT

Hostility and aggression.—There is significant relationship between arousal of anger and expression of sex motivation in both sexes (169, 182.) Differences in the stimulus pull of TAT cards for evoking anxiety and hostility based on a content analysis scale are discussed (318). TAT cards of single figures having the special stimulus of situational ambiguity and specificity of drive are best suited in singling out dynamics of antisocial boys (270). Special TAT cards evoking anger and aggression produced a defensive response in paranoid schizophrenic men (195). When test instructions suggested an aggressive response, a significant difference in aggressive TAT imagery in women resulted (200). Alienation test scores among college students were not found to correlate with TAT fantasy (242). Aggressive themes to high stimulus pull cards predicted overt aggression in adolescent boys (145). TAT themes in families with emotionally disturbed children were higher in scored hostility than in families with normal and schizo-phrenic children (320).

In evaluating these studies the theoretical issues of a position paper (202) are to be noted. The literature concerning projective measures of aggression and overt aggressive behavior are contraindicatory, because of different scales, and criteria used. Different projective techniques evoke different aspects of aggressive behavior.

Assessment of family interaction.—Conjoint family assessment with the use of the TAT in relation to other methods is described in a review paper (30). Specific scoring methods for family interaction in TAT stories have been improvised (117). Modified TAT pictures scored for three major categories of interaction showed mothers of allergic subjects to be dominant and fathers passive-aggressive (143). TAT stories of mothers of schizophrenic children were more pathogenic than those of mothers of normal children (209, 210). A content analysis of TAT themes significantly differentiated parental groups of normal, delinquent, and schizophrenic children (316). TAT records of maladjusted boys and their parents scored for affiliation, power, and aggression did not support the concept of a core problem as projected in motivational measures (219). TAT themes of child-abusing mothers projected an inability to empathize with the child and to resolve their own frustrated dependency needs (205). In foster-home children, thematic productions indicated concern with affiliation and were suggestive of depression (230). A method of transactional analysis to TAT stories given by the entire family to assess motivational patterns in the family interaction was developed (306). Factors based on conjoint TAT stories are offered as a method of classifying families that is more independent of psychiatric diagnosis (319).

Other broad applications.—Ego and drive variables as projected in TAT themes were utilized in a psychoanalytic study of pubertal growth (235). TAT measures of castration anxiety in treated snake phobics by behavior modification were found significantly lower than for nontreated snake phobics (150). TAT stories scored for openness on the basis of an affect-cognition scale were used to evaluate reactions to drug effect and placebo (225). Assertive and yielding TAT themes suggested reversal of gender roles in male and female schizophrenics (183). Defensive isolation was measured by incorporating a role-taking task in relation to figures seen in TAT cards (180). A modified TAT given to three Guatemalan groups proved to be discriminating for three subcultures involved (69).

CHILDREN'S APPERCEPTION TEST (CAT-A, CAT-H)

Haworth's book (124) is the first major published text devoted entirely to the CAT. The human modification of the test (H) (25, 26) was developed on the basis of its use with older children (MA beyond 10 years) to serve as an intermediary test between the CAT-A and the TAT. The CAT-H does provide an alternate form which can be applied both to research and clinical use. Projection-introjection was more frequent with animal forms, and repression was used more by normal children on the animal form (124, pp. 283–86). In another study (168), differences obtained between both forms were based more on differences of stimulus determinants. In one study (227) with anxious children, results indicated that both forms elicited similar fantasy productions and could be considered as equivalent. Scored for adaptive mechanisms, the CAT-H differentiated a group of stutterers from nonstutterers (240). Criteria based on the CAT fantasies were found to be the best single predictor of dream characteristics (84).

The use of the CAT as a method in evaluating development in normal children is reviewed and discussed in a series of articles concerning objective scoring methods for longitudinal data (322, pp. 406–12), normative data for preschool children (215, pp. 413–19), and test findings in a kibbutz sample of children (244, pp. 420–24). A critique of these studies (24, pp. 425–27) refers to the value of the test in longitudinal research with children.

HUMAN FIGURE DRAWINGS, DRAW-A-PERSON (HFD, DAP)

After almost 100 pages of review of studies utilizing this projective technique (222, Part IV), it was concluded: "It might be interesting to speculate why such a poorly validated instrument has become so popular as to rank only behind the Rorschach and TAT in frequency of usage . . . " (222, p. 609). Another critical review (245, Chap. 12) expressed this same dilemma: "Research studies in the field of projective drawings are by and large so contradictory that the writer finds himself taking a deep breath as he settles down to try to make sense out of the mosaic" (246, p. 383).

Two recent reviews (249, 293) together cover the literature from 1949 to 1967. Swensen (293) revised some of the criticisms of his earlier review (222, Chap. 35), concluding that the "research has improved substantially in quality and sophistication and has produced increased empirical support for the use of the human figure drawings as a clinical tool" (293, p. 20). Three summarial conclusions were offered by Swensen: (a) "global ratings are the most reliable"; (b) "if content and structural signs are assessed, the quality of drawing the particular body part should be taken into account"; and (c) the "use of structural and content signs . . . for use of clinical assessment is not likely to provide any improvement with clinicians' judgmental accuracy" (293, p. 40). Roback (249) still concludes that there is a dire need for scales of standardization and validation for assessing personality structure for human figure drawings, that the relationship between figure drawings and body image is still controversial, and that the multiplicity of variables must be controlled by adequate experimental design.

There has been no noted decline in the use of human figure drawings. The Draw-a-Person test (DAP) still ranks within the three most frequently used projective techniques (with Rorschach and TAT). The studies selected in this review are those subsequent to 1967.

Koppitz's text (162) on figure drawings by children is a serious effort to conceptualize and standardize the technique in terms of developmental items, clinical interpretation, emotional indicators, and special applications of the test. A critical review of this test (112) would agree with Roback (249) as to the tentative reliability and validity of the test except for its application in gross purposes of screening. Another major text (39) discusses advances in the House-Tree-Person technique (HTP), a technique not covered in this review.

The figure drawing test is considered a one-factor test, and its major valid use is in assessing cognitive maturity; psychopathology cannot be inferred when the drawing is primitive and the level of cognitive maturity has to be controlled (1). Validity of clinical judgment based on human figure drawings is critically challenged by Wanderer (311), and Hammer's rejoinder (115) discusses the variables in research studies which result in inconsistent measures of validity. In a scoring system based on Leary's interpersonal diagnostic system, only gross discriminations among subjects were found possible (198). Validity as a measure of body image was not confirmed (189). In a study of measures of suspiciousness, eye and ear emphasis were not discriminatory for degrees of suspiciousness (71).

Studies concerning personality correlates of size of figure drawings reflect the lack of consistent reliability. A series of studies lends no support to the significant relationship between size and depression (110, 259, 261). Alcoholic men draw their male figures smaller than female figures (52). Lack of role empathy in male alcoholics was inferred from self drawings of male alcoholics based on the criterion of height (53). Variables of size in drawings of psychotic patients (44) may be a function of overcontrol (small) or undercontrol (larger). These studies, however, are not sufficiently astute in design to resolve the question of the general lack of reliability of size (293). Retest and interjudge reliabilities for measures of proportionality in male figure drawings were found to be satisfactory (18).

Induced emotional states and their effect upon figure drawings have been explored in several studies. Previous studies would indicate that induced anxiety, fear, or aggression do produce significant changes in figure drawing (293). Criticizing toy buildings of children 4–5 years old resulted in constriction and impoverishment in family drawings including self image; supportive comments had the opposite effect. These findings are related to cognitive-perceptual styles of children in terms of field dependency and field independence (36). In another study, self-esteem and performance on the DAP were changed with the induction of a threatening situation; height of the figure was constricted and compensated for by an increase in athletic qualities (181). Test-produced anxiety (before and after examination) in high school students did not have an effect in accentuating the traditional signs of anxiety in figure drawings as valid predictions of classroom tension (63). Anxiety as measured by the amount of shading in figure drawings was significantly induced by viewing a stressful film, while neutral films did not have this effect (105). A rejoinder to this study (118) emphasizes that the findings of other studies indicate shading decreased under stress, and reviews a series of studies which document this finding. One study (72) in which the design was carefully planned to avoid the usual cited deficits of Human Figure Drawing Test validation, concludes that the test is limited as a clinical measure of test anxiety (induced by solving a puzzle). Both Swensen (293) and Roback (249) state that the hypothesis of shading as an index to anxiety is inconclusive and not supported.

The effect of cultural factors upon emotional indicators, although showing differences between lower and middle class groups of children, resulted in these differences disappearing when groups are matched for age, sex, and IQ (161). Negro and American adolescents both draw white people most often, and Negro subjects more frequently than white describe their subjects as "rich" and "very smart" (Wise 321). These findings corroborate those of Dennis (61). Caution is indicated, especially when evaluating hair emphasis in interpreting human figure drawings of Negroes, if the normative data upon which such interpretations are based exclude data for the Negro group (89).

Sex of the first figures drawn and its relationship to psychosexual indices of behavior has been prodigiously investigated in the past. Significant results have been reported, relating the sex of the first-drawn figure to self-concept and to pathological symptoms in sexual adjustment, but the relationship is still complex and its use as a diagnostic sign in individual cases is not warranted (293, pp. 36–38). Sex-role identity scores are not significantly related to reported sex of figures drawn in a group of preschoolers (308). Normal males with high MMPI Mf scale scores paradoxically drew more same-sex figures than those with low scores, but Mf scores and normal female figure choices were not related (111). Sex of the human figure drawing is a relevant measure in identification of the practicing male homosexual, but inferences are still considered ambiguous (85). Homosexual indices in figure drawings of drug addicts, based on size and sex of first figure drawn, are significantly different for prison vs nonprison populations (97). The use of clothing in human figure drawings is in part an index of emotional adjustment but not necessarily associated with age and sex (248). Cultural rather than pathological factors may be a more parsimonious explanation of the meaning of opposite-sex figure first drawn (204).

Although the use of figure drawings in the study of body image as based on studies of the past decade are somewhat more promising (293), definitive tests of the body-image hypothesis as measured by figure drawings are still lacking. The human figure drawing in body image scales failed to reveal changes in body image as a result of sensory motor training (189). In one study children given a modified DAP test were found equally aware of bodily attributes of both sexes, and the relationship to body image and IQ is discussed (99).

A more quantitative projective technique in studying body image presents the subject with a series of human figure drawings scaled along seven dimensions (109). Another modification, the Figure Drawing Test (FDT), has been used in relation to other measures of field dependency and defense mechanisms as an example of the increasing trend to relate projective techniques to cognitive and behavioral functioning (31).

SENTENCE COMPLETION TEST (SCT)

The SCT is considered "probably the most valid of all projective techniques reported in the literature" (222, p. 777). Goldberg's extensive review of the literature up to 1965 (222, Chap. 49) states that although the SCT has proved to be a valid instrument in the "assessment of psychological adjustment in adults and severity of psychiatric disturbance, it has not fared well in its attempt to measure variables associated with social perception" (222, pp. 811–13). In another review, Goldberg (104) investigated the status of sentence completion methods in the hierarchy of use of other psychodiagnostic procedures, finding its clinical use "slightly below average" and its research use "decidely below average." For purposes of this review references will be made to the general use of sentence completion methods without specific references to the specific form used. [Rotter ISB is the form most commonly used (104, p. 217).]

A concentration of studies concerns problems with which projective techniques have increasingly become involved with—the nature of the stimulus, experimenter-bias effect, and experimental sets. These, among others, are areas of needed research defined by Goldberg (103).

The effect of imposed time pressure upon the amount of ego-alien SCT contents was the subject of one study (278) in which ego-alien content of SCT stems increased under time pressure, more so for anxious than nonanxious subjects. Methods stressing speed are no more effective in "eliciting ego-alien or ego-syntenic affect than instructions requesting the expression of real feeling or those which are essentially neutral" (140, p. 321). Psychiatric patients were asked to express their "real feelings" in one form of a SCT and "the real feelings of an average person of your sex and age" in another form of a SCT. No difference was noted in the effect of these first- and third-person instructions in eliciting dependency, anxiety, and hostility responses (290). The effect of the experimenter as a situational influence on the openness of SCT responses is reviewed by Jourard (147). Three different forms of a SCT, presented with personal pronoun stems, standard nonpersonal stems, and impersonal stems, had an effect upon projection (327). However, tachistoscopic and conventional modes of presenting SCT stems have no significant effect upon scores due to sex, stimulus items sets, or orders of presenting sets (326). Item factors in a SCT revealed factors did not correspond to item content, but rather to stimulus pull, which influences responses in varying degrees depending upon the subject (287).

Based upon content and affect responses in a SCT, verbal conditioning did not result in any persisting behavior change (166). A SCT was used in support of a hypothesis that susceptible subjects instructed to simulate trance showed specific treatment effects based upon change in their SCT performance (274).

A correlation between a SCT and Repression Sensitization Scale (Byrne) contradicted previous findings that highly repressed subjects as defined by this scale are disturbed. Repressors exhibit more behavior which is normal (13). Using a modified SCT, alcoholics under inebriation decreased coping behavior as measured by the SCT, whereas normals showed the opposite pattern (238). Adjustment scores derived from a SCT were found reliable in identification of drug addicts (96). Individuals who report frequent somatic complaints were significantly identified by their adjustment score based on the SCT (100).

Positive and negative attitudes associated with academic performance, using forms of SCT, have failed to be consistent in their results (104, pp. 216, 292). A re-examination of this issue is discussed (167) as a result of a failure to replicate the findings of a previous study (139) which suggested that attitudes as measured by a SCT were associated with academic performance.

WORD ASSOCIATION TESTS

Word association techniques have in general declined in usage, especially in view of the fact that the psychoanalytic, psychodynamic model inherent in the history of this technique seldom attracts the interest of the researcher.

Problems of response set, appropriate norms, and changes in language are among variables which have limited the technique's research value (245, p. 273). However, even research studies using this technique have begun to orient themselves directly to exploring these variables in need of control.

Experiment-subject relationships before testing of warmth vs rebuff had an effect upon word associations in schizophrenics (34). Environmental stress was found to cause a significant decrease in responses (208). Visual imagery for words representing sex, hostility, and family relationships produced increased GSR activity and broke through the defensive barriers much more than mere verbal associations (247). Spontaneity and originality as measured by word association proved that subjects open to experience (not repressed) were more original and less rigid in their thinking (83). Aggressive associations to aggressive words can be indicators of general aggressiveness (98).

Attitudes toward sex as measured by word association tests are reported in a series of studies. Sexual association to double-entendre words can be scored with reliability for content, and the reliability remains stable for a 3-week interval (91); such sex-related responses reflect sex guilt, need for heterosexuality, and social desirability (93). A significant interaction between sexual stimulation and sex guilt was noted when sex associations were given to double-entendre words (92). Subjects with high sex guilt showed better recall for association under controlled conditions; yet under sexual stimulation, low sex-guilt subjects showed better recall (94). Repressor-sensitizer dimensions are related to responsivity on word association, but only when defensiveness is accounted for under the circumstances in which it is being measured, as for example the sex of the examiner (269). In male subjects, repressors showed less sexual responsivity to double-entendre words than sensitizers. Such differences were not found for female subjects, possibly because double-entendre words are based on masculine usage of slang (268).

THE HAND TEST (HT)

A review of the literature up to 1968 (245, pp. 472–81), as well as the original text on this technique (35), refers to the special application of this test to aggressive behavior. Megargee (201, pp. 143–45), after reviewing studies in aggression utilizing the HT, concluded that the HT still has to prove its validity in predicting violence.[7]

In one study (317) acting out and aggression scores derived from HT significantly discriminated delinquent recidivists from nonrecidivists. Interscorer reliability was affected by loosely defined scoring categories in applying the HT to samples of normal and delinquent children (234). Combining scores for the "acting-out ratio" and "maladjustment category" of the HT was found more sensitive in discriminating between juvenile delinquents than the use of the "acting-out ratio" alone (12). Considerable overlap in "acting-out scores" of the HT was noted in another study of the HT indicators of antisocial behavior. Aggressive and nonaggressive schizophrenics showed no significant differences in their HT scores for aggression (64).

Two studies report the effects of experimental set. Instructed to make the "best" and "worst" impressions resulted in successful falsification of acting-out scores of the HT (280). Increases in aggressive and affection scores of the HT occurred when both these emotions were hypothetically induced (130).

Group administration does not appreciably alter HT responses when compared with individual administration (295). An adaptation of the HT in which two hands paired in each photograph has been used to study the friendliness-hostility dimension in conjunction with sociometric ratings (329). Projected interpersonal responses as measured by the HT were found to be related to occupational status (302).

THE BLACKY PICTURES TEST

The current status of this technique is described in detail by Blum (27). Comprehensive annotated bibliographies cite the literature from 1949–1967 (28, 154). The test is one which has been "singled out as one of the few projective devices to have increased research usage during recent years" (27, p. 150). Blum (29) discusses the Blacky pictures in relation to their use in assessing the psychodynamics of unconscious mental content.

The test has been broadened in its horizons in the form of its evaluation of interpersonal dimensions of behavior. Research with the Defense Pref-

---

[7] For the prediction of aggression by the use of responses to incomplete stories, see: Olweus, D. 1969. *Prediction of Aggression* (on the basis of a projective test). Stockholm, Sweden: Scandinavian Test Corp.

erence Inquiry (DPI) has developed an objective scoring system in evaluation of motivational factors behind defense mechanisms. The Blacky Analogies Test (BAT) was designed to evaluate intellectual functioning when confronted with emotionally laden stimuli. A review of studies using these two special methods is described in detail (316, pp. 160–68).

A female form of the Blacky pictures was developed (250). Differences between female subjects and identification with the black dog and the black cat occurred only when the cat was highly feminized (272). In another study using semantic differential ratings of both forms (271), the Black Cat form was found to be a useful alternate for further research.

SUMMARY

"What we call the beginning
is often the end. And to make an end
is to make a beginning. The end is where
we start from . . ."[8]

It is a paradox that in the *beginning*, the theory and practice of projective techniques was rebellion against the accepted position of the so-called objective psychometric approach to personality assessment. As so aptly stated by Murstein (223, p. 228): "Nomotheticists, or individuals concerned with quantitative measurement, had left the individual no place to sit on his continuum—but projective technique adherents attempted to restore the concept of unity of the individual."

A review of the literature concerning projective techniques should be oriented to capture the essence of the commonality of a research theme which transcends the contemporary theory and practice of personality assessment. This review, it is hoped, was conceptualized with just this in mind. Earlier literature concentrated upon and emphasized the unstructured merits of the projective techniques, primarily discussed within a psychoanalytic framework. "The metamorphosis of projective methods," as described by Klopfer, is certainly an appropriate description of the current status of projective techniques. "The theorist of today considers a projective test as a stimulus with known properties, which interacts with a perceiving subject, and produces certain verbal or graphic results" (159, p. 404).

Although projective tests may be less widely used in clinical practice and in academic training curriculums, this review would attest to the fact that they are still a major focus in reorienting their research efforts, paralleling that for objective personality measurement as well as the general field of personality assessment. This reorientation is characterized by concentrating on the nature of the stimulus, greater objectivity in scoring, new theoretical models, the effect of the examiner-subject interaction, and the variables of the experimental situation in general. Masling (194) pinpoints these variables as they apply to projective techniques. The concentrated efforts of research

[8] Eliot, T. S., 1943. *Four Quartets*. New York: Harcourt Brace.

are involved with the stimulus structure of the projective techniques. This interest, for example, is noted in a position paper by Murstein (224) which applies the classical concept of the "levels" hypotheses to five projective techniques and proposes "a new theory of projection of pathology as a function of the stimulus structure tests."

To accomplish the contemporary research status of projective technique in this review, there are recognizably several limitations. The reader will notice a paucity of studies directly concerning clinical applications of the techniques, especially the Rorschach, in relation to diagnosis of psychopathology, prognostic indicators, developmental factors, etc. Over 100 articles were selected for this area of interest, but the majority had to be discarded by the reality of pagination, in addition to the choice of the reviewer in capturing the *Zeitgeist* of the theory and practice of projective techniques. Likewise, the many references to the kaleidoscopic changes in the entire theory, training, and practice of clinical psychology as described influenced the reviewer's decision. A broad overview of the more classical clinical applications of the projective techniques can readily be found in many of the textbooks cited (20, 21, 35, 39, 86, 121, 124, 133, 162, 216, 222, 239, 245, 266, 267, 283, 314, 325).

Is the "end" of this *Zeitgeist* research endeavor *"where we started from"*? Are we attempting to restore the psychometric approach to personality assessment by our current efforts to make projective techniques *tests* in the true sense of the word? Murstein offers some poignant discussion concerning this question: "What then of future prospects for projective techniques? As an examiner-technique instrument for clinic-interpretation, it still seems viable though its efficiency will vary with the skill of the examiner. As a research instrument it is solidly entrenched, particularly as a measure of arousal drive states" (223, p. 231). As McReynolds emphasizes (186, p. 8), further developments in projective technology should not be stifled because of the hue and cry in the quest for their validity. The position expressed by Holt (135, p. 348) concerning the "clinical and statistical prediction" would adhere to this same conclusion.

Are projective techniques in crisis? The crisis facing projective techniques is not more extenuating than that facing all contemporary scientific endeavor: i.e. change, challenge, and choice (213, p. 112).

LITERATURE CITED

1. Adler, P. T. 1970. Evaluation of the figure drawing technique: Reliability, factoral structure, and diagnostic usefulness. *J. Consult. Clin. Psychol.* 35:52–57
2. Albee, G. W. 1970. The uncertain future of clinical psychology. *Am. Psychol.* 25:1071–79
3. Alexander, I. E., Basowitz, H. 1965. *Current Clinical Training Practices. An Overview*, ed. C. N. Zimet,

F. M. Throne, and conf. comm. (preconference materials). *Conf. Prof. Prep. Clin. Psychol.* Washington, D.C.: Am. Psychol. Assoc.
4. Allen, R. M. 1966. *Students Rorschach Manual: An Introduction to Administering, Scoring and Interpreting Rorschach's Psychodiagnostic Inkblot Test.* New York: Int. Univ. Press
5. Ames, L. B. 1970. Projecting the fu-

ture of a projective technique. *J. Proj. Tech. Pers. Assess.* 34:359–65

6. Anastasi, A. 1967. Psychology, psychologists, and psychological testing. *Am. Psychol.* 22:297–306

7. Anthony, J., Bene, E. 1957. A technique for the objective assessment of the child-family relationships. *J. Men Sci.* 103:541–55

8. Appelbaum, S. A., Colson, D. 1968. A reexamination of the color-shading Rorschach test response and suicide attempts. *J. Proj. Tech. Pers. Assess.* 32:160–64

9. Armstrong, H. E. Jr. 1968. Relationship between a dimension of body image and measure of conditioning. *J. Consult. Clin. Psychol.* 32:696–700

10. Atyas, V. 1970. An actuarial-experimental model of personality assessment. *J. Proj. Tech. Pers. Assess.* 34:83–86

11. Azcarate, E. 1969. Body boundary and psychological control in an arthritic population. *J. Proj. Tech. Pers. Assess.* 33:494–500

12. Azcarate, E., Gutierrez, M. 1969. Differentiation of institutional adjustment of juvenile delinquents with the Hand test. *J. Clin. Psychol.* 25:200–3

13. Baker, R. P., King, H. H. 1970. The relationship between the Repression-Sensitization Scale and the Incomplete Sentences Blank. *J. Proj. Tech. Pers. Assess.* 34:492–96

14. Barber, T. X., Silver, M. J. 1968. Fact, fiction, and the experimenter bias effect. *Psychol. Bull. Monogr.* 70: No. 6, pt. 2

15. Barnard, P. G. 1968. Characteristics on a projective test. *J. Consult. Clin. Psychol.* 32:514–21

16. Baughman, E. E. 1959. An experimental analysis of the relationship between stimulus structure and behavior in the Rorschach. *J. Proj. Tech. Pers. Assess.* 23:134–83

17. Baughman, E. E. 1967. The problem of the stimulus in Rorschach's test. *J. Proj. Tech. Pers. Assess.* 31:23–25

18. Beck, M., Hart, L. 1970. Inter-rater and test-retest reliability of proportionality measure for the D-A-P. *Percept. Mot. Skills* 30:89–90

19. Beck, N., Herron, G. 1969. The meaning of the Rorschach cards for children. *J. Proj. Tech. Pers. Assess.* 33:150–53

20. Beck, S. J. 1965. *Psychological Pro-*

cesses in the Schizophrenic Adaptation. New York: Grune and Stratton

21. Beck, S. J., Molish, H. B. 1967. *Rorschach's Test—II. A Variety of Personality Pictures.* New York: Grune and Stratton. Rev. ed.

22. Beizmann, C. 1966. *Handbook for Scorings of Rorschach Responses.* Transl. S. J. Beck. New York: Grune and Stratton

23. Bell, J. E. 1948. *Projective Techniques.* New York: Longmans, Green

24. Bellak, L. 1968. Discussion. Symposium: The CAT: Its use in developmental assessments of normal children. *J. Proj. Tech. Pers. Assess.* 32:425–27

25. Bellak, L., Hurvich, M. S. 1965. *Manual for the CAT-H (Human Modifications of the CAT).* New York: C.P.S. Co.

26. Bellak, L., Hurvich, M. S. 1966. A human modification of the Children's Apperception Test (CAT-H). *J. Proj. Tech. Pers. Assess.* 30:228–42

27. Blum, G. S. 1950. *The Blacky Pictures: Manual of Instructions.* New York: Psychol. Corp.

28. Blum, G. S. 1968. Assessment of psychodynamic variables by the Blacky pictures. See Ref. 186, Chap. 8

29. Blum, G. S. 1966. *Psychodynamics: The Science of Unconscious Mental Forces.* Belmont, Calif.: Wadsworth

30. Boden, A. M. 1968. Conjoint family assessment: An evolving field. See Ref. 186, Chap. 12

31. Bogo, N., Winget, C., Gleser, G. C. 1970. Ego defenses and perceptual styles. *Percept. Mot. Skills* 30:599–605

32. Boulay, M. A. 1969. Verbal reinforcement and Rorschach productivity. *J. Clin. Psychol.* 25:310

33. Brar, H. S. 1970. Rorschach Content responses of East Indian psychiatric patients. *J. Proj. Tech. Pers. Assess.* 34: 88–94

34. Brenner, A. R. 1967. Effects of prior experimenter-subject relationships on responses to the Kent-Rosanoff Word-Association list in schizophrenics. *J. Abnorm. Psychol.* 72: 273–76

35. Bricklin, B., Piotrowski, Z. A., Wagner, E. E. 1962. *The Hand Test.* Springfield, Ill.: Thomas (2nd print. 1970)

36. Britan, S. D. 1970. Effect of manipulation of children's affect on their

family drawings. *J. Proj. Tech. Pers. Assess.* 34:234–37

37. Brockmann, N. C. 1970. A psycho-physiological investigation of the Rorschach color and form determinants. *J. Proj. Tech. Pers. Assess.* 34:98–103

38. Brodsky, S. L., Brodsky, A. M. 1967. Hand test indicators of antisocial behavior. *J. Proj. Tech. Pers. Assess.* 31:36–39

39. Buck, J. N., Hammer, E. F., Eds. 1969. *Advances in the House-Tree-Person Technique: Variations and Applications.* Los Angeles: West. Psychol. Serv.

40. Buirski, P., Kramer, E. 1970. Literature as a projection of the author's personality. *J. Proj. Tech. Pers. Assess.* 34:27–30

41. Burns, R. C., Kaufman, S. H. 1970. *Kinetic Family Drawings (K-F-D): An Introduction to Understanding Children Through Kinetic Drawings.* New York: Brunner/Mazel

42. Buros, O. K., Ed. 1970. *Personality Tests and Reviews.* Highland Park, N.J.: Gryphon

43. Campos, L. P. 1968. Other projective techniques in personality assessment. See Ref. 245, 461–520

44. Clodfelder, D. L., Craddick, R. A. 1970. Variance in size of drawing in a psychotic population. *Percept. Mot. Skills* 30:110

45. Cocking, R. R., Dana, J. A., Dana, R. H. 1969. Six constructs to define Rorschach M: A response. *J. Proj. Tech. Pers. Assess.* 33:322–23

46. Cole, S., Williams, R. L. 1968. Age as a determinant of parental interpretation of Rorschach Cards IV and VII. *Percept. Mot. Skills* 26:55–58

47. Cole, S., Williams, R. L., Bolen, L. 1967. Symbolic meaning of Card II. *Percept. Mot. Skills* 24:66

48. Cole, S., Williams, R. L., Moore, C. H. 1969. Parental interpretation of Rorschach Cards IV and VII among adjusted and maladjusted subjects. *J. Gen. Psychol.* 81:131–35

49. Coleman, J. C. 1968. Rorschach Content as a means of studying child development. *J. Proj. Tech. Pers. Assess.* 32:435–42

50. Cook, B. F. 1967. An approach to use of color on the Rorschach through individual color preferences. *J. Proj. Tech. Pers. Assess.* 31:48–53

51. Cooper, L., Caston, J. 1970. Physical activity and increase in M response. *J. Proj. Tech. Pers. Assess.* 34:295–301

52. Craddick, R. A., Leipold, W. D. 1968. Note on the height of Draw-a-Person figures by male alcoholics. *J. Proj. Tech. Pers. Assess.* 32:486

53. Craddick, R. A., Leipold, W. D., Leipold, V. 1970. Effect of role-empathy on height of human figures drawn by male alcoholics. *Percept. Mot. Skills* 30:747–52

54. Crenshaw, D. A., Bohn, S., Hoffman, M. R., Matheas, J. M., Offenbach, S. G. 1968. The use of projective methods in research: 1947–1965. *J. Proj. Tech. Pers. Assess.* 32:3–9

55. Crumpton, E., Groot, H. 1966. The "meaning" or Rorschach color cards as a function of color. *J. Proj. Tech. Pers. Assess.* 30:359–63

56. Dana, R. H. 1968. Six constructs to defend Rorschach M. *J. Proj. Tech. Pers. Assess.* 32:138–45

57. Ibid. Thematic technique and clinical practice, 204–14

58. Darby, J. A. 1970. Alteration of some body image indexes in schizophrenia. *J. Consult. Clin. Psychol.* 35:116–21

59. Darby, J., Hofman, K., Melnick, B. 1967. Response inhibition and the Rorschach "M" response. *J. Proj. Tech. Pers. Assess.* 31:29–30.

60. Davis, R. W. 1970. Comment on H. S. Brar: Rorschach Content of East Indian psychiatric patients. *J. Proj. Tech. Pers. Assess.* 34:95–97

61. Dennis, W. 1966. *Group Values Through Children's Drawings.* New York: Wiley

62. Donofrio, I. 1968. *The effect of examiner variables on amount of self-disclosure in TAT stories.* PhD thesis. SUNY, Buffalo

63. Doubros, S. G., Mascarenhas, J. 1967. Effect of test-produced anxiety on human figure drawings. *Percept. Mot. Skills* 25:773–75

63a. Draguns, J. G., Haley, E. M., Phillips, L. 1968. Studies of Rorschach content: a review of the research literature. I. Traditional content categories. *J. Proj. Tech. Pers. Assess.* 32:16–32

64. Drummond, F. 1966. A failure in the discrimination of aggressive behavior of undifferential schizophrenics with the Hand test. *J. Proj. Tech. Pers. Assess.* 30:275–79

65. Dudek, S. Z. 1968. Man-active energy system correlating Rorschach "M" with ease of creative expression. *J. Proj. Tech. Pers. Assess.* 32:453–61

66. Dudek, S. Z. 1968. Regression and creativity. A comparison of the Rorschach records of successful vs. unsuccessful painters and writers. *J. Nerv. Ment. Dis.* 147:535–46

67. Easton, K., Feigenbaum, K. 1967. An examination of an experimental set to fake the Rorschach test. *Percept. Mot. Skills* 24:871–74

68. Eisenman, R., Bernard, J. L., Hannon, J. E. 1966. Benevolence, potency, and God. A semantic differential study of the Rorschach. *Percept. Mot. Skills* 22:75–78

69. Eisenman, R., Foulks, E. F. 1970. Usefulness of Mussen's TAT scoring system: I. Differences among Guatemalan Indians, Ladinos, Mengalas on modified TAT: II. Attitudes toward the physically disabled as related to nurturance and deference. *Psychol. Rep.* 27:179–85

70. Eiseler, R. M. 1968. Thematic exposition of sexual conflict under varying stimulus conditions. *J. Consult. Clin. Psychol.* 32:216–20

71. Endicott, N. A., Jortner, S., Abramoff, E. 1969. Objective measures of suspiciousness. *J. Abnorm. Psychol.* 74:26–32

72. Engle, P. L., Suppes, J. S. 1970. The relation between human figure drawings and test anxiety in children. *J. Proj. Tech. Pers. Assess.* 34:223–31

73. Exner, J. E. Jr. 1969. Rorschach responses as an index of narcissism. *J. Proj. Tech. Pers. Assess.* 33:324–30

74. Exner, J. E. Jr. 1969. *The Rorschach Systems.* New York: Grune and Stratton

75. Faberow, N. L., Little, K. E. 1970. Society for personality assessment —Which way to go? *J. Proj. Tech. Pers. Assess.* 34:468–69

76. Fernald, P. S., Linden, J. D. 1966. The Human Content response in the Holtzman Inkblot Technique. *J. Proj. Tech. Pers. Assess.* 30:441–46

77. Fisher, R. L. 1968. Classroom behavior and the body image boundary. *J. Proj. Tech. Pers. Assess.* 32:350–52

78. Fisher, S. 1967. Projective methodologies. *Ann. Rev. Psychol.* 18:165–90

79. Fisher, S. 1970. *Body Experience in Fantasy and Behavior.* New York: Appleton-Century-Crofts

80. Fisher, S., Cleveland, S. E. 1968. *Body Image and Personality.* New York: Dover. 2nd rev. ed.

81. Fisher, S., Cleveland, S. E. 1969. A rejoinder to Hirt & Kurtz, "A re-examination of the relationship between body boundary and site of disease." *J. Abnorm. Psychol.* 74:144–47

82. Fisher, S., Cleveland, S. E. 1969. Rejoinder to Mitchell's "The Body Image Boundary Construct: A study of the Self-Steering Behavior Syndrome." *J. Proj. Tech. Pers. Assess.* 33:318–21

83. Fitzgerald, E. T. 1966. Measurement of openness to experience: A study of regression in the service of the ego. *J. Pers. Soc. Psychol.* 4:655–63

84. Foulkes, D., Pivik, T., Steadman, H. S. 1967. Dreams of the male child. An EEG study. *J. Abnorm. Psychol.* 72:457–67

85. Fraas, L. A. 1970. Sex of figure drawing in identifying practicing male homosexuals. *Psychol. Rep.* 27:172–74

86. Francis-Williams, J. 1968. *Rorschach with Children. A Comparative Study of the Contribution Made by Rorschach and Other Projective Techniques to Clinical Diagnosis in Work with Children.* New York: Pergamon

87. Frank, L. K. 1948. *Projective Methods.* Springfield, Ill.: Thomas

88. Frede, M. C., Gautney, D. B., Allen, D. A. 1968. Relationships between body image boundary and interaction patterns on the MAPS test. *J. Consult. Clin. Psychol.* 32:575–78

89. Frisch, G. R., Handler, L. 1967. Differences in Negro and White drawings: a cultural interpretation. *Percept. Mot. Skills* 24:667–70

90. Fulkerson, S. C. 1967. Some implications of the new cognitive theory for projective tests. *J. Consult. Psychol.* 29:191–97

91. Galbraith, G. G. 1968. Reliability of free association sexual responses. *J. Consult. Clin. Psychol.* 32:622

92. Ibid. Effects of sexual arousal and guilt upon free associative sexual responses, 707–11

93. Galbraith, G. G., Halm, K., Liebeman, H. 1968. Personality correlates of free-associative sex responses to

double-entendre words. *J. Consult. Clin. Psychol.* 32:193–97

94. Galbraith, G. G., Mosher, D. L. 1970. Effects of sex guilt and sexual stimulation on recall of word associations. *J. Consult. Clin. Psychol.* 34:67–71

95. Ganzer, V. J., Sarason, I. G., Green, C. T., Rinke, C. 1970. Effects of model's and observer's hostility on Rorschach, interview and test performance. *J. Proj. Tech. Pers. Assess.* 34:301–15

96. Gardner, J. M. 1967. The adjustment of drug addicts as measured by the Sentence Completion Test. *J. Proj. Tech. Pers. Assess.* 31:28–29

97. Gardner, J. M. 1969. Indicators of homosexuality in the human figure drawings of heroin- and pill-pushing addicts. *Percept. Mot. Skills* 28:705–6

98. Geen, R. G., George, R. 1969. Relationship of manifest aggressiveness to aggressive word associations. *Psychol. Rep.* 25:711–14

99. Gellert, E. 1968. Comparison of children's self-drawings with their drawings of other persons. *Percept. Mot. Skills* 26:123–38

100. Getter, H., Weiss, S. 1968. The Rotter Incomplete Sentences Blank Adjustment Score as an indicator of somatic complaint frequency. *J. Proj. Tech. Pers. Assess.* 32:266

101. Gill, H. S. 1966. Delay of response and reaction to color on the Rorschach. *J. Proj. Tech. Pers. Assess.* 30:545–52

102. Gleser, G. C. 1963. Projective methodologies. *Ann. Rev. Psychol.* 14:391–422

103. Goldberg, P. A. 1965. A review of sentence completion methods in personality assessment. *J. Proj. Tech. Pers. Assess.* 29:12–45

104. Ibid 1968. The current status of sentence completion methods. 32:215–21

105. Goldstein, H. S., Faterson, H. F. 1969. Shading as an index of anxiety in figure drawings. *J. Proj. Tech. Pers. Assess.* 33:454–56

106. Gorham, D. R. 1965. The development of a computer scoring system for inkblot responses. *Proc. 9th Counc. Interam. Soc. Psychol., Miami Beach,* 258–70

107. Gorham, D. R. 1967. Validity and reliability studies of a computer-based scoring system for inkblot responses. *J. Consult. Psychol.* 31:65–70

108. Gorham, D. R., Moseley, E. C., Holtzman, W. H. 1968. Norms for the computer-scored Holtzman inkblot technique. *Percept. Mot. Skills* 26:1279–88

109. Gottesman, E. G., Caldwell, W. E. 1966. The Body Image Identification Test: A quantitative projective technique to study an aspect of body image. *J. Genet. Psychol.* 108:19–33

110. Gravitz, M. A. 1969. Figure drawing size as an index of depression and MMPI depression scores in normal adults. *J. Clin. Psychol.* 25:77–79

111. Ibid. Direction of psychosexual interest and figure drawing choice, 311

112. Gredler, G. R. 1970. Review of E. M. Koppitz (1968). Psychological evaluation of children's figure drawings. *J. Proj. Tech. Pers. Assess.* 34:435–39

113. Griffith, R. M., Dobbs, D. D. 1966. An experimental manipulation of Rorschach form: The effect of making indistinct the ambiguous. *J. Consult. Psychol.* 30:151–57

114. Haley, E. M., Draguns, J. G., Phillips, L. 1967. Studies of Rorschach content: A review of research literature —Part II; non-traditional uses of content indicators. *J. Proj. Tech. Pers. Assess.* 31:3–31

115. Hammer, E. F. 1969. DAP: back against the wall? [reply to Wanderer's study (see 311)]. *J. Consult. Clin. Psychol.* 33:151–56

116. Hammer, M. 1966. A comparison of responses by clinic and normal adults to Rorschach Card III— human figure area. *J. Proj. Tech. Pers. Assess.* 30:161–62

117. Handel, G., Ed. 1967. Analysis of correlative meaning: The TAT in the study of whole families. *The Psychosocial Interior of the Family,* 104–24. Chicago: Aldine

118. Handler, L., Reyher, J. 1970. Comment on "Shading as an Index of Anxiety in Figure Drawings." *J. Proj. Tech. Pers. Assess.* 34:340–41

119. Hardyck, C. D. 1966. Personality characteristics and motor activity: Some empirical evidence. *J. Pers. Soc. Psychol.* 4:181–88

120. Harris, S., Masling, J. 1970. Examiner sex, subject sex, and Rorschach

productivity. *J. Consult. Clin. Psychol.* 34:60–63

121. Harrower, M. 1965. *Psychodiagnostic Testing: An Empirical Approach.* Springfield, Ill.: Thomas

122. Hartung, J. R., McKenna, S. A., Baxter, J. C. 1969. Test taking attitudes and Rorschach pathognomic verbalization. *J. Proj. Tech. Pers. Assess.* 33:146–49

123. Ibid 1970. Body image and defensiveness in an LSD-taking subculture. 34:316–23

124. Haworth, M. R. 1966. *The CAT: Facts About Fantasy.* New York: Grune and Stratton

125. Haworth, M. R. 1968. Doll play and puppetry. See Ref. 245, 327–65

126. Hersen, M. 1970. Sexual aspects of Rorschach administration. *J. Proj. Tech. Pers. Assess.* 34:104–5

127. Hertz, M. R. 1970. *Frequency Tables for Scoring Rorschach Responses.* Cleveland, Ohio: Case Western Reserve Univ. Press

128. Hertz, M. R. 1970. Projective techniques in crisis. *J. Proj. Tech. Pers. Assess.* 34:449–67

129. Hirt, M., Kurtz, R. 1969. A re-examination of the relationship between body boundary and site of disease. *J. Abnorm. Psychol.* 74:67–70

130. Hodge, J. R., Wagner, E. E., Schreiner, F. 1966. Hypnotic validation of two Hand test scoring categories. *J. Proj. Tech. Pers. Assess.* 30:385–86

131. Holmes, D. S., Tyler, J. D. 1968. Direct vs. projective measurement of achievement motivation. *J. Consult. Clin. Psychol.* 32:712–17

132. Holmes, D. S. 1968. Dimensions of projection. *Psychol. Bull.* 69:248–68

133. Holt, R. R. 1967. Diagnostic testing: Present status and future prospects. *J. Nerv. Ment. Dis.* 144:444–65

134. Holt, R. R. 1967. Discussion: On using experiential data in personality assessment. *J. Proj. Tech. Pers. Assess.* 31:25–30

135. Holt, R. R. 1970. Yet another look at clinical and statistical prediction: Or, is clinical psychology worthwhile? *Am. Psychol.* 25:337–49

136. Holtzman, W. H. 1968. Holtzman inkblot technique. See Ref. 245, Chap. 6

137. Holtzman, W. H., Swartz, J. D., Sanders, J. L. 1970. Effects of stimulus variation on responses to the group version of the Holtzman inkblot technique. *J. Consult. Clin. Psychol.* 34:64–66

138. Holzman, P. S., Rousey, C. 1970. Monitoring, activation, and disinhibition: Effects of white noise masking on spoken thought. *J. Abnorm. Psychol.* 75:227–41

139. Irvin, F. S. 1967. Sentence-completion responses and scholastic success or failure. *J. Couns. Psychol.* 14:269–71

140. Irvin, F. S., Johnson, M. L. 1970. Effect of differential instructional set on sentence completion responses. *J. Consult. Clin. Psychol.* 34:319–22

141. Iwawaki, S., Zax, M. 1969. Personality dimensions and extreme response tendency. *Psychol. Rep.* 25:31–34

142. Jackson, C. W., Wohl, J. 1966. A survey of Rorschach teaching in the university. *J. Proj. Tech. Pers. Assess.* 30:115–34

143. Jacobs, M. A. 1966. The use of projective techniques in research design: The Family Interaction Test. See Ref. 216, 3:237–64

144. Jain, K. S. 1969. Measurement of congruence/deviation factor in personality by Rorschach Content Analysis: A contribution to Rorschach methodology. *J. Gen. Psychol.* 81:177–88

145. James, P. B., Mosher, D. L. 1967. Thematic aggression-hostility-guilt and aggressive behavior. *J. Proj. Tech. Pers. Assess.* 31:61–67

146. Jones, L. W., Thomas, C. B. 1965. Studies on figure drawings: Manual of instructions for coding structural and graphic characteristics. *Psychiat. Quart. Suppl.* 39:241, pt. 2

147. Jourard, S. M. 1969. The effects of experimenter's self-disclosure on subject's behavior. In *Current Topics in Clinical and Community Psychology*, ed C. D. Spielberger, 1:109–50. New York: Academic

149. Jurjevich, R. M. 1967. Hostility and anxiety indices on the Rorschach Content Test, Hostility Guilt Index and the MMPI. *Psychol. Rep.* 21:128

150. Kamil, L. J. 1970. Psychodynamic changes through systematic desensitization. *J. Abnorm. Psychol.* 76:199–205

151. Kaplan, M. F. 1969. The ambiguity of TAT ambiguity. *J. Proj. Tech. Pers. Assess.* 33:25–29

152. Ibid. Reply to Murstein's "Comment on the Ambiguity of TAT Ambiguity," 486–88

153. Kauffman, J. M. 1970. Validity of the Family Relations Test: A review of research. *J. Proj. Tech. Pers. Assess.* 34:186–89

154. Kaulbee, E. S., Stenmark, D. E. 1968. The Blacky pictures: A comprehensive annotative and indexed bibliography (1949–1967). *J. Proj. Tech. Pers. Assess.* 32:105–37

155. Kessel, P., Harris, J. E., Slagle, S. J. 1969. An associative technique for analyzing the content of Rorschach test responses. *Percept. Mot. Skills* 29:535–40

156. Kleinmuntz, B. 1967. *Personality Measurement—An Introduction.* Homewood, Ill.: Dorsey

157. Klinger, E. 1966. Fantasy need achievement as a motivational construct. *Psychol. Bull.* 66:291–308

158. Klopfer, W. G. 1968. See Ref. 186, p. 28

159. Klopfer, W. G. 1968. The metamorphosis of projective methods. *J. Proj. Tech. Pers. Assess.* 32:402–4

160. Knudsen, A. K., Gorham, D. R., Moseley, E. C. 1966. Universal popular responses to inkblots in five cultures: Denmark, Germany, Hong Kong, Mexico, and United States. *J. Proj. Tech. Pers. Assess.* 30:135–42

161. Koppitz, E. M. 1969. Emotional indicators on human figure drawings of boys and girls from lower and middle-class backgrounds. *J. Clin. Psychol.* 25:432–34

162. Koppitz, E. M. 1968. *Psychological Evaluation of Children's Human Figure Drawings.* New York: Grune and Stratton

163. Kurz, R. B., Capone, T. A. 1967. Cognitive level, role-taking ability and the Rorschach human movement response. *Percept. Mot. Skills* 24:657–58

164. Lang, A. 1966. *Rorschach Bibliography: 1921–1964.* Bern, Switzerland: Huber

165. Lansky, L. M. 1968. Story completion methods. See Ref. 245, 290–324

166. Lanyon, R. I. 1967. Verbal conditioning: Transfer of training in a therapy-like situation. *J. Abnorm. Psychol.* 72:30–34

167. La Plante, M. J., Irvin, F. S. 1970. Sentence-completion responses and academic performance—re-examined. *J. Proj. Tech. Pers. Assess.* 34:219–22

168. Lawton, M. J. 1966. Animal and human CATS with a school sample. *J. Proj. Tech. Pers. Assess.* 30:243–46

169. Lazarus, R. S. 1966. Story telling and the measurement of motivation. The direct vs. substitutive controversy. *J. Consult. Psychol.* 30:483–87

170. Lefcourt, H. M. 1969. Need for approval and threatened negative evaluation as determinants of expressiveness in a projective test. *J. Consult. Clin. Psychol.* 33:96–102

171. Lefcourt, H. M., Siegel, J. M. 1970. Predisposition to fantasy and situational variations as determinants of attention in reaction time tasks. *J. Consult. Clin. Psychol.* 34:415–24

172. Lerner, B. 1966. Rorschach movement and dreams: A validation study using drug-induced dream deprivation. *J. Abnorm. Psychol.* 71:75–86

173. Ibid 1967. Dream function reconsidered. 72:85–100

174. Levitz, L. S., Allman, L. P. 1969. Manipulation of indications of disturbed thinking in normal subjects. *J. Consult. Clin. Psychol.* 33:633–41

175. Levy, M. R. 1970. Issues in the personality assessment of lower-class patients. *J. Proj. Tech. Pers. Assess.* 34:6–9

176. Levy, N. 1969. Affective preference for Card IV or VII of the Rorschach as related to sex and age. *Percept. Mot. Skills* 28:741–42

177. Lichtenstein, K. R. 1969. Anxiety, "color shock," and order effect on reaction to inkblots. *J. Proj. Tech. Pers. Assess.* 33:353–56

178. Lindzey, G. 1965. Seer versus sign. *J. Exp. Res. Pers.* 1:17–26

179. Loiselle, R. H., Fisher, V., Parrish, C. E. 1968. Stimulus value of Rorschach inkblots and percepts as perceived by children and schizophrenics. *J. Proj. Tech. Pers. Assess.* 32:238–45

180. Lowenherz, L., Feffer, M. 1969. Cognitive level as a function of defensive isolation. *J. Abnorm. Psychol.* 74:352–57

181. Ludwig, D. J. 1969. Self-perception and Draw-a-Person test. *J. Proj. Tech. Pers. Assess.* 33:257–61

182. McClelland, D. C. 1966. Longitudinal

trends in the relation of thought to action. *J. Consult. Psychol.* 30:479–83

183. McClelland, D. C., Watt, N. F. 1968. Sex role alienation in schizophrenia. *J. Abnorm. Psychol.* 73:226–39

184. McCully, R. S. 1965. Current attitudes about projective techniques in APA approved internship centers. *J. Proj. Tech. Pers. Assess.* 29:271–80

185. McKeachie, W. J., Isaacson, R. L., Milholland, J. E., Lin, Y. G. 1968. Student achievement motives, achievement cues, and academic achievement. *J. Consult. Clin. Psychol.* 32:26–29

186. McReynolds, P., Ed. 1968. *Advances in Psychological Assessment.* Palo Alto: Science and Behavior Books

187. Magnussen, M. G. 1967. Effect of test order upon children's Rorschach animal content. *J. Proj. Tech. Pers. Assess.* 31:41–43

188. Magnussen, M. G., Cole, J. K. 1967. Further evidence of the Rorschach card stimulus values for children: A partial replication (and generalizations). *J. Proj. Tech. Pers. Assess.* 31:44–47

189. Maloney, M. P., Payne, L. E. 1969. Validity of the Draw-a-Person test as a measure of body image. *Percept. Mot. Skills* 29:119–22

190. Martin, M., Schachtel, E. G., Lyons, M., Holt, R. 1967. Symposium: The role of experiential data in personality assessment. *J. Proj. Tech. Pers. Assess.* 31:3–30

191. Marwit, S. J. 1969. Communication of tester bias by means of modeling. *J. Proj. Tech. Pers. Assess.* 33:345–52

192. Masling, J. 1965. Differential indoctrination of examiner and Rorschach responses. *J. Consult. Psychol.* 29:198–201

193. Masling, J. 1960. The influence of situational and interpersonal variables in projective testing. *Psychol. Bull.* 57:65–85

194. Masling, J. 1966. Role-related behavior of the subject and psychologist and its effects upon psychological data. In *Nebraska Symposium on Motivation*, ed. D. Levine. Lincoln: Univ. Nebraska Press

195. May, R. 1970. Paranoia and power anxiety. *J. Proj. Tech. Pers. Assess.* 34:412–18

196. Mayfield, D. G. 1968. Holtzman inkblot technique in acute experimental alcohol intoxication. *J. Proj. Tech. Pers. Assess.* 32:491–94

197. Mayman, M. 1967. Object-representations and object-relationships in Rorschach responses. *J. Proj. Tech. Pers. Assess.* 31:17–24

198. Mebane, D. F., Die, J. G. 1970. A scoring system for human figure drawings as a measure of Level III of the Leary Interpersonal Diagnostic System. *Percept. Mot. Skills* 30:385–86

199. Meehl, P. E. 1965. Seer over sign: The first good example. *J. Exp. Res. Pers.* 1:27–32

200. Megargee, E. I. 1967. Hostility on the TAT as a function of defensive inhibition and stimulus situation. *J. Proj. Tech. Pers. Assess.* 31:73–79

201. Megargee, E. I. 1970. The prediction of violence with psychological tests. See Ref. 147, 2:97–156

202. Megargee, E. I., Cook, P. E. 1967. The relation of TAT and Inkblot Aggressive Content Scales with each other and with criteria of overt aggressiveness in juvenile delinquents. *J. Proj. Tech. Pers. Assess.* 31:48–60

203. Megargee, E. I., Swartz, J. D. 1968. Extraversion, neuroticism, and scores on the Holtzman Inkblot technique. *J. Proj. Tech. Pers. Assess.* 32:262–65

204. Melikian, L. H., Wahab, A. Z. 1969. First-drawn picture: A cross-cultural investigation of the DAP. *J. Proj. Tech. Pers. Assess.* 33:539–41

205. Melnick, B., Hurley, J. R. 1969. Distinctive personality attributes of child-abusing mothers. *J. Consult. Clin. Psychol.* 33:746–49

206. Metarazzo, J. D. 1965. *Postdoctoral Residency Program in Clinical Psychology.* Conf. Prof. Prep. Clin. Psychol. Washington, D.C.: Am. Psychol. Assoc.

207. Mills, D. H. 1965. The research use of projective techniques: A 17 year survey. *J. Proj. Tech. Pers. Assess.* 29:513–15

208. Mintz, S. 1969. Effect of actual stress on word associations. *J. Abnorm. Psychol.* 74:293–95

209. Mitchell, K. M. 1968. An analysis of the schizophrenic mother concept by means of the Thematic Apperception Test. *J. Abnorm. Psychol.* 73:571–74

210. Ibid 1969. Concepts of "Pathogenesis" in parents of schizophrenic and normal children. 74:423–24

211. Mitchell, K. R. 1969. The Body Image Boundary Construct—A reply to Fisher & Cleveland. *J. Proj. Tech. Pers. Assess.* 33:470–73

212. Ibid. The Body Image Boundary Construct: A study of the self-steering behavior syndrome, 311–17

213. Molish, H. B. 1969. The quest for charisma. *J. Proj. Tech. Pers. Assess.* 33:103–17

214. Morgan, A. 1968. Some age norms obtained for the Holtzman inkblot technique administered in a clinical setting. *J. Proj. Tech. Pers. Assess.* 32:165–72

215. Moriarty, A. E. 1968. Normal preschoolers' reactions to the CAT: Some implications for later development. *J. Proj. Tech. Pers. Assess.* 32:413–19

216. Muller, J. J., Ed. 1966. *The Clinical Interpretation of Psychological Tests.* Int. Psychiat. Clin. Boston: Little, Brown

217. Murphy, R. F. Jr., Dana, R. H. 1969. Peebles' Rorschach Content Scoring System: Reliability, normative, data, and validity. *J. Proj. Tech. Pers. Assess.* 33:518–25

218. Murray, D. C. 1970. Review. *J. Proj. Tech. Pers. Assess.* 34:528–32

219. Murray, E. J., Seagull, A., Geisinger, D. 1969. Motivational patterns in the families of adjusted and maladjusted boys. *J. Consult. Clin. Psychol.* 33:337–42

220. Murstein, B. I. 1969. Comment on "The Ambiguity of TAT Ambiguity." *J. Proj. Tech. Pers. Assess.* 33:483–85

221. Murstein, B. I. 1968. Effect of stimulus, background, personality, and scoring system on the Manifestation of Hostility on the TAT. *J. Consult. Clin. Psychol.* 32:355–65

222. Murstein, B. I., Ed. 1965. *Handbook of Projective Techniques.* New York: Basic Books

223. Murstein, B. I. 1968. Discussion for current status of some projective techniques. *J. Proj. Tech. Pers. Assess.* 32:229–39

224. Murstein, B. I., Wolf, S. R. 1970. Empirical test of the "levels" hypotheses with five projective techniques. *J. Abnorm. Psychol.* 75:38–44

225. Nash, M. M., Zimring, F. M. 1969. Prediction of reaction to placebo. *J. Abnorm. Psychol.* 74:568–73

226. Neuringer, C. 1968. A variety of thematic methods. See Ref. 245, 222–61

227. Neuringer, C., Livesay, R. C. 1970. Projective fantasy on the CAT and CAT-H. *J. Proj. Tech. Pers. Assess.* 34:487–91

228. Newton, P. M. 1970. Recalled dream content and the maintenance of body image. *J. Abnorm. Psychol.* 76:134–39

229. Norman, R. P. 1969. Extreme response tendency as a function of emotional adjustment and stimulus ambiguity. *J. Consult. Clin. Psychol.* 33:406–10

230. North, G. E., Keiffer, R. S. 1966. Thematic productions of children in foster homes. *Psychol. Rep.* 19:43–46

231. Ogdon, D. P. 1970. *Psychodiagnostics and Personality Assessment: A Handbook.* Los Angeles: West. Psychol. Serv.

232. Orlinsky, D. E. 1966. Rorschach test correlates of dreaming and dream recall. *J. Proj. Tech. Pers. Assess.* 30:250–53

233. Orso, D. P. 1969. Comparison of achievement and affiliation arousal on n Ach. *J. Proj. Tech. Pers. Assess.* 33:230–33

234. Oswald, M. O., Loftus, A. P. 1967. A normative and comparative study of the Hand test with normal and delinquent children. *J. Proj. Tech. Pers. Assess.* 31:62–8

235. Peskin, H. 1967. Pubertal onset and ego functioning. *J. Abnorm. Psychol.* 72:1–15

236. Pienaar, W. D. 1968. Body awareness in certain types of speech defective individuals. *J. Proj. Tech. Pers. Assess.* 32:537–41

237. Piotrowski, Z. A. 1964. Digital-computer interpretation of inkblot test data. *Psychiat. Quart.* 38:1–26

238. Pollack, D. 1966. Coping and avoidance in inebriated alcoholics and normals. *J. Abnorm. Psychol.* 71:417–19

239. Pope, B., Scott, W. H. 1967. *Psychological Diagnosis in Clinical Practice with Application in Medicine, Law, Education, Nursing, and Social Work.* London: Oxford Univ. Press

240. Porterfield, C. L. 1969. Adaptive mechanisms of young disadvantaged stutterers and non-stutterers. *J. Proj. Tech. Pers. Assess.* 33:371–75

241. Prola, M. 1970. A re-evaluation of the motor inhibition—fantasy hypothesis. *J. Proj. Tech. Pers. Assess.* 34:477–83

242. Propper, M. M. 1970. Direct and projective assessment of alienation among affluent adolescent males. *J. Proj. Tech. Pers. Assess.* 34:41–43

243. Pryor, D. B. 1967. A comparison of the occurrence of oral and anal content on the Rorschach. *J. Proj. Tech. Pers. Assess.* 31:26–28

244. Rabin, A. I. 1968. CAT findings with kibbutz and non-kibbutz preschoolers. *J. Proj. Tech. Pers. Assess.* 32:420–24

245. Rabin, A. I., Ed. 1968. *Projective Techniques in Personality Measurement.* New York: Springer

246. Rapaport, D., Gill, M. M., Schafer, R. 1968. *Diagnostic Psychological Testing*, ed. R. R. Holt. New York: Int. Univ. Press

247. Reyher, J., Smeltzer, W. 1968. Uncovering properties of visual imagery and verbal association: A comparative study. *J. Abnorm. Psychol.* 73:218–22

248. Reznikof, M., Dies, F. 1969. The use of clothing in human figure drawings. *J. Clin. Psychol.* 25:80–81

249. Roback, H. B. 1968. Human figure drawings: Their utility in the clinical psychologist's armamentarium for personality assessment. *Psychol. Bull.* 70:1–19

250. Robinson, S. A. 1968. The development of a female form of the Blacky pictures. *J. Proj. Tech. Pers. Assess.* 32:74–80

251. Rorschach, H. 1942. *Psychodiagnostics.* Transl. P. Lemkan, B. Krononberg. Berne: Huber. 2nd ed.

252. Rosenstiel, L. V. 1969. Capacity for empathy: A function of anxiety in the production of H response. *J. Proj. Tech. Pers. Assess.* 33:336–42

253. Rosenthal, R. 1966. *Experimenter Effects of Behavioral Research.* New York: Appleton-Century-Crofts

254. Rosenthal, R. 1968. Experimenter expectancy and the reassuring nature of the null hypothesis decision procedure. *Psychol. Bull. Monogr. Suppl.* (Dec.) 30–47

255. Rosenthal, R. 1969. On not so replicated experiments and not so null results. *J. Consult. Clin. Psychol.* 33:7–10

256. Rosenzweig, S. P., Harford, T. 1970. Correlates of the psychotic reaction profile in an outpatient psychiatric sample. *J. Consult. Clin. Psychol.* 35:244–47

257. Routh, D. K., Schneider, J. M. 1970. Word association and inkblot responses as a function of instructional sets and psychopathology. *J. Proj. Tech. Pers. Assess.* 34:113–20

258. Russell, E. W. 1967. Rorschach stimulus modification. *J. Proj. Tech. Pers. Assess.* 31:20–22

259. Salzman, L. F., Harway, N. I. 1967. Size of figure drawings of psychotically depressed patients. *J. Abnorm. Psychol.* 72:205–7

260. Sanders, J. L., Holtzman, W. H., Swartz, J. D. 1968. Structural changes of the color variable in the Holtzman inkblot technique. *J. Proj. Tech. Pers. Assess.* 32:556–61

261. Sandman, C. A., Cauthen, N. R., Kilpatrick, D. G., Deabler, H. L. 1968. Size of figure drawing in relation to depression. *Percept. Mot. Skills* 27:945–46

262. Sarason, I. G. 1966. *Personality: An Objective Approach.* New York: Wiley

263. Sarason, I. G., Winkel, G. H. 1966. Individual differences among subjects and experimenter and subject self-description. *J. Pers. Soc. Psychol.* 3:448–57

264. Saugstad, P. 1966. Effect of food deprivations on perception and cognition. *Psychol. Bull.* 65:80–90

265. Sawyer, J. 1966. Measurement and prediction, clinical and statistical. *Psychol. Bull.* 66:178–200

266. Schachtel, E. G. 1966. *Experiential Foundations of Rorschach Test.* New York: Basic Books

267. Schafer, R. 1967. *Projective Testing and Psychoanalysis—Selected Papers.* New York: Int. Univ. Press

268. Schill, T. 1969. Repressor-sensitizer differences in free associative sex responses to double-entendre words. *J. Clin. Psychol.* 25:368–69

269. Schill, T., Emanuel, G., Pederson, V., Schneider, L., Wachowiak, D. 1970. Sexual responsibility of defensive and non-defensive sensitizers and repressions. *J. Consult. Clin. Psychol.* 35:44–7

270. Scott, V., Kempler, H. E. 1970. Can systematically scored thematic stories reflect the attributes of the antisocial child syndrome? *J. Proj. Tech. Pers. Assess.* 34:204–11

271. Shaeffer, D. L. 1968. Blacky the CAT. 1. Semantic ratings. *J. Proj. Tech. Pers. Assess.* 32:542–49

272. Ibid. Addenda to an annotated bibliography of the Blacky Test (1949–1967), 550–55

273. Sharble, K., Moulton, R. W. 1968. Achievement fantasy of variations in self-rated competence. *Percept. Mot. Skills* 27:515–28

274. Sheehan, P. 1970. Analysis of the treatment effects of simulation instructions in the application of the real simulating model of hypnosis. *J. Abnorm. Psychol.* 75:98–103

275. Shombry, K., Kelley, S. 1970. Psychodiagnostic training in the academic setting: Past and present. *J. Consult. Clin. Psychol.* 34:205–11

276. Siegman, A. W., Pope, B. 1966. Ambiguity and verbal fluency in the TAT. *J. Consult. Psychol.* 30:239–45

277. Siegman, A. W., Pope, B. 1965. Stimulus factors in the TAT: Effects of ambiguity on verbal fluency, productivity, and GSR. See Ref. 283, 2:223–28

278. Silpola, E. M. 1968. Incongruency of sentence completions under time, pressure and freedom. 1968. *J. Proj. Tech. Pers. Assess.* 32:562–71

279. Sines, J. O. 1966. Actuarial methods in personality assessment. In *Progress in Experimental Personality Research*, ed. B. A. Maher, 3:133–93. New York: Academic

280. Singer, M. M., Dawson, J. G. 1969. Experimental falsification of the Hand test. *J. Clin. Psychol.* 25:204–5

281. Skolnick, A. 1966. Motivational imagery and behavior over 20 years. *J. Consult. Psychol.* 30:463–78

282. Smith, J. M. 1970. A Note on achievement motivation and verbal fluency. *J. Proj. Tech. Pers. Assess.* 34:121–24

283. Societe Francaise du Rorschach et des Methodes Projectives 1966. *Proc. 6th Int. Congr. Rorschach Proj. Methods*, Paris, Vol. 1–4

284. Solomon, I. L., Starr, B. 1968. *School Apperception Method (SAM)*. New York: Springer

285. Stanley, G. 1968. God in the Rorschach. *Percept. Mot. Skills* 26:463–66

286. Steele, N. M., Kahn, M. W. 1969. Kinesthesia and the Rorschach M response. *J. Proj. Tech. Pers. Assess.* 33:5–10

287. Stephens, M. W. 1970. Stimulus pull as a determinant of individual differences in sentence completion responses. *J. Proj. Tech. Pers. Assess.* 34:332–39

288. Strauss, M. E. 1968. Examiner expectancy: Effects on Rorschach Experiences Balance. *J. Consult. Clin. Psychol.* 32:125–29

289. Strauss, M. E., Marwit, S. J. 1970. Expectancy effects in Rorschach testing. *J. Consult. Clin. Psychol.* 34:448

290. Stricker, G., Dawson, D. D. 1966. The effect of first person and third person instructions and stems on sentence completion responses. *J. Proj. Tech. Pers. Assess.* 30:169–71

291. Sundberg, N. D. 1954. A note concerning the history of testing. *Am. Psychol.* 9:150–51

292. Ibid 1961. The practice of psychological testing in clinical services in the United States. *Am. Psychol.* 16:79–83

293. Swensen, C. H. 1968. Empirical evaluation of human figure drawings: 1957–1966. *Psychol. Bull.* 70:20–44

294. Taylor, D. A., Altman, I., Wheeler, L., Kushman, E. N. 1969. Personality factors related to response to social isolation and confinement. *J. Consult. Clin. Psychol.* 33:411–19

295. Taylor, J. F. 1969. Group administration of the Hand test: Effects on card pull and responses. *J. Proj. Tech. Pers. Assess.* 33:243–46

296. Tedford, W. Jr., Lake A. E. III. 1970. Influences of stimulus symmetry on the movement response. *J. Proj. Tech. Pers. Assess.* 34:16–18

297. Terhune, K. W. 1969. A note on Thematic Apperception scoring of needs for achievement. *J. Proj. Tech. Pers. Assess.* 33:364–70

298. Thelen, M. H., Varble, D. L., Johnson, J. 1968. Attitudes of academic clinical psychologists toward projective techniques. *Am. Psychol.* 23:517–21

299. Thomas, C. B. 1966. *An Atlas of Figure Drawings. Studies on the Psychological Characteristics of Medical Stu-*

dents—III. Baltimore: Johns Hopkins Press

300. Thomas, C. B., Ross, D. C., Freed, E. S. 1964. *An Index of Rorschach Responses. Studies on the Psychological Characteristics of Medical Students—I*. Baltimore: Johns Hopkins Press

301. Thomas, C. B., Ross, D. C., Freed, E. S. 1965. *An Index of Responses to the Group Rorschach Test Studies on the Psychological Characteristics of Medical Students—II*. Baltimore: Johns Hopkins Press

302. Thornton, C. L. 1969. Evaluation of Roe's theory using the Hand test. *Percept. Mot. Skills* 28:95–8

303. Thorpe, J. S., Swartz, J. D. 1966. Perceptual organization: A developmental analysis by means of the Holtzman inkblot technique. *J. Proj. Tech. Pers. Assess.* 30:447–51

304. Tolor, A., Breslow, A. K., Brodie, R. E. 1967. Rorschach human movement and attitudes toward space exploration. *Percept. Mot. Skills* 24:787–91

305. Van De Mark, S., Neuringer, C. 1969. Effect of physical and cognitive somatic arousal on Rorschach responses: An experimental test of the assumption that body image influences the perceptual organization of unstructured stimuli. *J. Consult. Clin. Psychol.* 33:458–85

306. Vassiliou, G., Vassiliou, V. 1965. Transactional story sequence analysis: A new procedure on family diagnosis. See Ref. 283, 1:99–108

307. Voigt, W. H. 1966. Personality variables in Rorschach scoring. *J. Proj. Tech. Pers. Assess.* 30:153–57

308. Vroegh, K. 1970. Lack of sex-role differentiation HFD in preschoolers' figure drawings. *J. Proj. Tech. Pers. Assess.* 34:38–40

309. Wagner, E. E., Slemboski, C. A. 1969. Construct validation of Piotrowski's interpretation of the Rorschach shading response. *J. Proj. Tech. Pers. Assess.* 33:343–44

310. Wallace, J. 1966. An abilities conception of personality: Some implication for personality measurement. *Am. Psychol.* 21:132–38

311. Wanderer, Z. W. 1969. Validity of clinical judgments based on human figure drawings. *J. Consult. Clin. Psychol.* 33:143–50

312. Ward, A. J. 1966. The meaning of the

movement response and of its changes during therapy: A review. *J. Proj. Tech. Pers. Assess.* 30:418–28

313. Weiner, B. 1970. New conception in the study of achievement motivation. In *Progress In Experimental Research*. ed. B. A. Maher, 67–109. New York: Academic

314. Weiner, I. B. 1966. *Psychodiagnosis in Schizophrenia*. New York: Wiley

315. Weisskopf, J. E., Wexner, L. B. 1970. Projection as a function of situational and figural similarity. *J. Proj. Tech. Pers. Assess.* 34:397–400

316. Werner, M., Stabenau, J. R., Pollin, W. 1970. Thematic Apperception Test method for the differentiation of families of schizophrenics, delinquents, and "normals." *J. Abnorm. Psychol.* 75:139–45

317. Wetsel, H., Shapiro, R. J., Wagner, E. E. 1967. Prediction of recidivism among juvenile delinquents with the Hand test. *J. Proj. Tech. Pers. Assess.* 31:69–72

318. Winget, C. N., Gleser, G. C., Clements, W. H. 1969. A method of quantifying human relations, hostility, and anxiety applied to TAT productions. *J. Proj. Tech. Pers. Assess.* 33:433–37

319. Winter, W. D., Ferreira, A. J. 1970. A factor analysis of family interaction measures. *J. Proj. Tech. Pers. Assess.* 34:55–63

320. Winter, W. D., Ferreira, A. J., Olson, J. L. 1966. Hostility themes in the family TAT. *J. Proj. Tech. Pers. Assess.* 30:270–74

321. Wise, J. H. 1969. Self-reports by Negro and White adolescents to the Draw-a-Person. *Percept. Mot. Skills* 28:193–94

322. Witherspoon, R. L. 1968. Development of objective scoring methods for longitudinal CAT data. *J. Proj. Tech. Pers. Assess.* 32:406–12

323. Witkin, H. A., Dyk, R. B., Faterson, H. F., Goodenough, D. R., Karp, S. A. 1962. *Psychological Differentiation: Studies of Development*. New York: Wiley

324. Wohlford, P. 1968. Extension of personal time in TAT and sentence completion stories. *J. Proj. Tech. Pers. Assess.* 32:267–79

325. Wolman, B. B., Ed. 1965. *Handbook of Clinical Psychology*. New York: McGraw

326. Wood, F. A. 1967. Tachistoscopic vs. conventional presentation of incomplete sentence stimuli. *J. Proj. Tech. Pers. Assess.* 31:30–31

327. Wood, F. A. 1969. An investigation of methods of presenting incomplete sentence stimuli. *J. Abnorm. Psychol.* 74:71–74

328. Zubin, J., Eron, L. D., Schumer, F. 1965. *An Experimental Approach to Projective Techniques.* New York: Wiley

329. Zucker, K. B., Jordan, D. C. 1968. The Paired Hands Test: A technique for measuring friendliness. *J. Proj. Tech. Pers. Assess.* 32:522–29

330. Zulliger, H. 1969. *The Zulliger Individual and Group Test,* ed. F. Saloman. Transl. D. T. Dubrovsky. New York: Int. Univ. Press

PSYCHOTHERAPEUTIC PROCESSES[1]

KENNETH I. HOWARD

Institute for Juvenile Research and Northwestern University

AND DAVID E. ORLINSKY

Institute for Juvenile Research and the University of Chicago

Our reading of the literature has indicated a need for an enlarged perspective in thinking about psychotherapy. The field has been dominated by an implicit consensus which reflects the local culture—the tacit assumptions and accepted customs of practitioners—more than it does the phenomenon itself. Consequently, we aim to do three things in this review. We shall propose a conceptual framework[2] which makes it possible to organize the accumulated information about psychotherapy, and to ask new and more meaningful questions about the nature of the psychotherapeutic enterprise. Second, we shall review the recent literature on psychotherapy in terms of this conceptual framework. Third, we shall provide a reasonably thorough bibliography of psychotherapy research for the period January 1969 through March 1971.

By most accounts, psychotherapy is a treatment offered by specialists to people with psychological conditions that impair individual functioning or limit well-being. The specialists, of course, disagree about the correct interpretation of problematic conditions, the needs and capabilities of different patient populations, the nature of effective treatment procedures, and the qualifications and preparation necessary for professional practice. Despite these disagreements, it is nevertheless widely assumed that psychotherapy is basically a mode of treatment. The acceptance of this view by researchers as well as practitioners has restricted our conception of psychotherapy and limited the range of questions we have asked about it to the familiar concerns with treatment process and outcome.

The people who write, read, and review the literature on psychotherapy are often engaged in therapeutic practice themselves. While this coincidence is perhaps inevitable, it does not necessarily help to achieve an understanding of what we do. A decade ago, Frank (75) made an heroic attempt to broaden the thinking of contemporary psychotherapists. Opler (182) and Kiev (137)

[1] We gratefully acknowledge support from General Research Support Grant 5 SO1 RRO 5666-04 from the National Institutes of Health, and the help of Barbara Bouton, Virginia Berman, Ora Benton, and Joann Brown.

[2] A more detailed exposition of this conceptual scheme is available in an unpublished paper by D. E. Orlinsky.

contributed major anthologies offering readers an opportunity to gain a comparative perspective on the therapeutic enterprise, but these reports are too often dismissed as concerning more or less curious primitive antecendents to our scientific practices. As participants in a particular social and cultural form of therapeutic enterprise, we are disinclined to accept, to take seriously, or even to recognize, functionally equivalent endeavors in different social and cultural forms. Yet we could learn much about psychotherapeutic processes, and about our mode of using them, if we could achieve a more general comparative perspective.

A SYSTEMS ANALYSIS OF PSYCHOTHERAPY

The simplest general statement that can be made about psychotherapy is that it is a set of recognized activities in which certain members of a community engage. These activities are systematically elaborated in terms of customs, conceptions, and personnel. They constitute a system of action (189) that exists as part of a complex of functionally interdependent action systems. Unfortunately, so broad a formulation applies to any part of any culture. An understanding of psychotherapy in particular requires the study of its specific properties as an action system, and of its functional interrelations with its system context.

In specifying the parameters of the psychotherapeutic system and its context, we follow Parsons' (189) convention of distinguishing between social, cultural, and psychological system features. Thus, the social system of psychotherapy would consist of the *institutionalized normative organization of therapeutic activities*, and the social system context would be formed by the population and institutional structure of the host community. The cultural system of psychotherapy would consist of *symbolic representations of therapeutic action* as conceived by its participants, and the cultural system context would be found in the belief and value orientations of the host culture. Finally, the psychological system of psychotherapy would consist of the *conduct and experience of therapeutic activities*, and the lives and personalities of those who engage in them would be the psychological system context.

The Analytic Framework: System Parameters

Social system.—The social organization of therapeutic activities can be described with reference to four components: role, collectivity, setting, and schedule. In dramaturgic terms, these are elements in the staging of therapeutic encounters. *Role* refers to the dramatis personnae of the therapeutic system, to their expected statuses and performances over time. The key roles in our own system are those of patient and therapist (or client and counselor). Subsidiary actors are sometimes involved as "collaterals," usually kinsmen of the patient. Basic role definitions are fairly standard in our system, though the specific performances expected of patients and therapists vary with therapeutic orientation.

Collectivity refers to the size and role composition of the social unit in which therapeutic performances are staged. The collectivities used as vehicles of therapy in our system range from the familiar dyad of "individual" therapy, through triadic units in "multiple" and "conjoint marital" therapy, to therapy conducted in primary groups and natural social networks.

Setting refers to the physical locale and arrangement of therapeutic encounters, including the scene (private office, public clinic, hospital ward), the props (couch, desk, writing pad, circle of chairs), and appropriate costumes (business suit, laboratory coat, love beads, etc). The setting functions symbolically as nonverbal background communication, indicating to patients and therapists alike something about the nature of their performance.

Schedule refers to the normative temporal patterning of therapeutic encounters: their timing in relation to other socially significant cycles (hour of day, day of week); the duration of sessions; the frequency of sessions; and the form of the course of treatment (time-limited, open-ended, etc).

Cultural system.—Symbolic representations of therapeutic activities correspond to five questions: What are people really like? What should people ideally be like? How do people go wrong? How can people be made right? Who is qualified to help make people right? Answers to these questions, in imagery or explicit doctrine, guide and rationalize therapeutic activity. They imply some conception of *human nature* or personality (the "material" to be worked with), *human fulfillment* (the ideal to be sought), *human vulnerability* (psychopathology), of *therapeutics*, and of the therapeutic *profession*. Taken together, they comprise what we shall call the Therapeutic Belief-Value Complex.

The clinical literature is a major repository of the culture of psychotherapy in our system, and we suggest that it be studied as such. The theories formulated by therapists to guide and legitimate their activities serve pragmatic rather than purely cognitive functions, and often serve them well without being susceptible to the kind of critical verification demanded in scientific research.

Psychological system.—The conduct and experience of psychotherapy can be viewed in terms of the individual psychology of participants and the group psychology of the interpersonal unit which they form. At the individual level, *conduct* can be usefully differentiated into the tasks and techniques assigned to each participant (instrumental conduct), and the behavior of each of the participants towards the other (relational conduct). Observational schemes pertaining to instrumental conduct might include such things as the topics which patients discuss in their sessions, or the techniques which therapists employ. Relational conduct might be studied in terms of interpersonal behavior (12, 148, 223) or in terms of paralinguistic and expressive variables (33, 207, 220).

The *experiences* of participants can be differentiated according to the "inner" or "outer" locus of events with respect to the individual. Among internal experiences are those of ideation, affect, intention, evaluation, and the on-going self-adaptation reflected in self-awareness, self-esteem, self-control, etc. External experiences include the individual's perception of his own conduct, his perceptions of the conduct and apparent experiences of other participants, and his perception of the development of the "social act" (235) in which they are jointly engaged.

Group psychological processes in the interpersonal unit can be studied with reference to their aspects, phases, and dynamics. The salient *aspects* of conjoint phenomena are interactional processes, interexperiential processes, and group (unit) processes. The former involve patterns emergent in the joint conduct of the various participants, such as the flow of verbal and nonverbal communication. Haley (92) has emphasized the theoretical significance of this aspect, and a variety of approaches to its study have been attempted (e.g. 61, 65, 159). Interexperiential processes involve patterns emergent in the joint perceptions and fantasies of the various participants. Laing (144) has argued that the concept of "social interexperience" is a logical complement to that of social interaction, and we (185) have presented a methodology and some findings pertinent to it. Finally, unit processes refer to the group properties of the therapeutic collectivity (e.g. stratification, cohesion, control).

Phases or temporal stages also concern the group psychology of the therapeutic process, as the participants contribute to and are affected by the phenomenon of therapeutic "movement." The *dynamics* of the therapeutic process (contained in the motivational interplay between participants) have obvious relevance in this connection. The development of a phase x aspect matrix for the description of conjoint processes would provide a useful framework within which to consider the subtle factors involved in dynamics.

A summary of the system parameters of psychotherapeutic activities is presented in Table 1.

THE ANALYTIC FRAMEWORK: CONTEXT PARAMETERS

Questions about the determinants and the outcome of psychotherapy concern the functional relationships between the therapeutic action system and its system contexts. The influence of context on system defines system *input*, while the consequences of therapy for its social, cultural, and psychological contexts define system *output*. In this section, context parameters will be discussed with reference to both input and output functions.

Social system.—The population and institutions of the host community comprise the social system context of therapeutic activities. From the *population* there is an input of personnel to the therapeutic action system. These persons can be described in terms of their distinguishing *demographic characteristics*, and in terms of the *career patterns* or routes by which they come

TABLE 1. System Parameters of Therapeutic Activities

A. Social system: the normative organization of therapeutic encounters
  1. Roles
  2. Collectivity
  3. Setting
  4. Schedule
B. Cultural system: the symbolic representation of therapeutic action
  1. Therapist orientations
    a. human nature, or personality
    b. human fulfillment, or ideal person
    c. human vulnerability, or psychopathology
    d. therapeutics
    e. profession
  2. Patient orientations (as in B1)
C. Psychological system: the conduct and experience of participants
  1. Therapist patterns
    a. conduct, instrumental and relational
    b. experience, internal and external
    c. unit patterns, conduct and experience
  2. Patient patterns (as in C1)
  3. Conjoint patterns
    a. aspects (interaction, interexperience, group)
    b. phases
    c. dynamics

to their respective roles. Access to the patient status in our system lies through referral channels; access to the therapist status, through professional training and certification procedures.

The *institutional* context of psychotherapy can be divided into client institutions and sponsor institutions. The *client institutions* in a community are those in which functional problems occur that extend beyond their own social control resources. The input from client institutions consists of the problems which patients bring to therapy (marital problems, school problems, legal problems, etc). *Sponsor institutions* are those which support or make therapy available in the community. Among these in our society are service establishments such as hospitals and clinics, and ancillary organizations such as professional societies, health insurance agencies, and mental health associations.

Social system outputs of the therapeutic system affect both the personnel and the institutions of the host community. The demographic characteristics of personnel may be altered, and their ensuing careers qualified, by their having been patients or therapists. Similarly, the functional problems of client institutions (e.g. the family system) may be resolved or exacerbated by the participation of its members in psychotherapy. Sponsor institutions may be created, changed, or dissolved in response to alterations in the therapeutic system. Thus, representation of therapy as a science-authorized rather than a magical or religious procedure (a change in the cultural system of therapy) led eventually to the development of research activities, institutes, journals, and in 1970 to the founding of the Society for Psychotherapy Research.

Cultural system.—The belief and value systems of the host culture form the cultural system context of therapeutic activities. One component of this context is the set of popular or *lay attitudes* concerning the issues that define the Therapeutic Belief-Value Complex (human nature, ideal fulfillment, etc). This component of the larger culture corresponds directly to the specialized subculture of therapists and patients, though lay and professional belief-value orientations on therapeutic issues may be divergent.

Another component of the larger culture which functions as a context for the therapeutic action system is the set of *other specialty subcultures* whose professional concerns are more or less related to issues constituting the Therapeutic Belief-Value Complex. In our own case, related specialty subcultures include psychology and other social sciences, biomedical sciences, and a number of humanistic disciplines (literature, philosophy, religion, etc). The behaviorist and the existential types of orientation which have recently figured prominently in the psychotherapeutic culture represent significant inputs from the neighboring specialty subcultures of psychology and philosophy, respectively. Conversely, the output of ideas, beliefs, and values that have developed in the therapeutic subculture has exerted great influence in related fields (e.g. personality theory in psychology, the psychological novel in literature, etc).

A third way in which the larger culture functions as a context for the therapeutic action system is through the *general* (i.e. not specifically therapeutic) *belief-value orientations of patients and therapists.* The social, personal, political, religious, and other attitudes held by different classes of patients and therapists may influence, and be influenced by, their specifically therapeutic beliefs and values.

Psychological system.—The lives and personalities of the participants in therapeutic action constitute its psychological system context. This domain may be divided into the role-relevant characteristics of participants (such traits and qualifications as are functions of, or directly pertinent to, their roles in therapy) and the person-relevant characteristics of participants.

Role-relevant characteristics include patients' and therapists' motivations, expectations, and prior experience regarding their therapeutic roles. For patients, *motivation* would include degree of distress and desire for psychotherapy; for therapists, the attractiveness of the patient and specific treatment goals. *Expectations* focus on hopes, fears, and anticipations (e.g. prognosis) concerning therapy. *Prior experience* includes factors such as patients' previous involvement in therapy and therapists' training and time in practice. It is possible, though admittedly not in every case interesting, to view these same categories in relation to the output of therapeutic activities. One of the more interesting of these as an output variable is the patient's degree of distress.

The *person-relevant characteristics* of patients and therapists include particulars of their life situations, their assumptive systems, personal styles, and adaptational resources. *Life status* pertains to the individual's current involvements (and the rewards and costs he sustains in them), his developmental history, and the future options differentially available to him. The person's *assumptive system* (75) includes his images of, and attitudes towards himself, his significant others, and his world. *Personal styles* include cross-situational tendencies to engage in particular patterns of interpersonal behavior, preferential reliance on various modes of ego-defense, characterstic ways of experiencing and evaluating oneself, etc. Finally, *adaptational resources* refer to the abilities, skills, and habits which constitute assets or deficits for the person in coping with social and situational demands. Intelligence, creativity, emotional responsiveness, social competence, communication skills, etc, are examples of adaptational resources.

The circular relationship between the therapeutic action system and its system contexts can be clearly illustrated here, since we are used to thinking of the person-relevant characteristics of patients and therapists both as determinants of therapeutic processes (system inputs) and—for patients, at least—as targets of the impact of therapeutic processes (system outputs). This circularity of functional flow from context to system to context provides the organizational principle for our analysis of the psychotherapy literature. First, we shall examine studies of the social, cultural, and psychological system contexts from the perspective of their potential influence on therapeutic activities (*input studies*). Then we shall examine studies of the social, cultural, and psychological features of the therapeutic action system (*process studies*), and studies of actual input influences on therapeutic activities. Third, we shall examine studies of the social, cultural, and psychological contexts of psychotherapy from the perspective of their responsiveness to the therapeutic action system (*output studies*)—as well as studies of input and process influences on system output. A summary of the context parameters to be considered is presented in Table 2.

INPUT STUDIES

Input studies focus on those aspects of the social, cultural, and psychological contexts of the therapeutic activity system which have functional consequences for system processes. Input, thus, is not simply temporal priority, or what transpires before the first therapy session. It is functional priority, and concerns context effects that may be chronologically concurrent with therapy, as well as those that occur specifically within the pretherapy period.

622   HOWARD & ORLINSKY

TABLE 2. CONTEXT PARAMETERS OF THERAPEUTIC ACTIVITIES

A. Social system: the population and institutions of the host community
  1. Personnel
    a. demographic characteristics of
      (i) patient population
      (ii) therapist population
    b. Careers, or statuses antecedent and subsequent to
      (i) patient status
      (ii) therapist status
  2. Institutions
    a. client institutions
    b. sponsor institutions
      (i) service organizations
      (ii) ancillary organizations
B. Cultural system: the ideologies and ethics of the host culture
  1. Lay attitudes on therapeutic belief-value issues
  2. Other specialty subcultures
  3. General belief-value orientations of participants
    a. therapist groups
    b. patient groups
C. Psychological system: the lives and personalities of the participants
  1. Patient
    a. role-relevant characteristics
      (i) motivation
      (ii) expectation
      (iii) prior experience
    b. person-relevant characteristics
      (i) life status
      (ii) assumptive system
      (iii) personal style
      (iv) adaptational resources
  2. Therapist (as in C1)

SOCIAL SYSTEM INPUTS

The social system context involves questions relating to the personnel who undertake therapeutic activities and the institutional sectors of the community which sponsor and require the performance of therapy. With regard to personnel, the questions are two: Who are the people engaging in therapeutic activities? How do they come to be so engaged? More specifically: What are the distinguishing demographic characteristics (if any) of patients and therapists, and what leads them to their respective roles in therapy?

Demographic characteristics of patients.—Demographic data on adult patients are available directly from two recent studies (124, 217) as well as from somewhat older ones (90, 109, 233), and indirectly from the sample descriptions of large-scale therapy studies. For the most part, these data derive from the Northeastern sector of the country: New York (124, 213, 233); New Haven (109); and Boston (217). Gurin, Veroff & Feld (90) report data based on one of the few, if not the only, national probability samples available. The impression generated by the reports available to us is that there are at least three distinct population groupings recognizable among adults who come to be patients in psychotherapy. We shall sketch descriptive "types" to summarize these data.

Type One, the group which has achieved the greatest visibility, is composed of persons who tend to be young adults in relatively affluent circumstances, generally college educated, more often women than men, more often than not unmarried. They naturally tend to be culturally sophisticated, verbal, and intelligent. They have been found to reside in rather specific urban neighborhoods, to be less seriously psychiatrically impaired, and to positively value psychotherapy as a cultural form and as a means of help. Persons of Jewish cultural background tend to be somewhat over-represented in this group and non-whites are very substantially under-represented. People with this cluster of characteristics approximate the type described by Schofield (221) as the YAVIS syndrome—"youthful, attractive, verbal, intelligent, and successful."

Type Two has come to the awareness of the professional community in recent years, probably due to the impact of the "community mental health" movement. This group is composed of persons who tend to be distinctly less affluent, of working class or lower class status, and more often than not older adults (over 30), women, sometimes married, who for the most part have finished not more and often less than a high school education. This group tends to be less culturally sophisticated, less verbally communicative, to be judged as more seriously impaired, to be less positively oriented to psychotherapy, and to contain those of the non-white population who receive therapeutic treatment. Persons of Catholic cultural background and immigrant status tend to be over-represented in this group. So, too, do the seriously impaired persons who constitute the core of the "mental health problem" in this country.

Type Three has been relatively hidden from the awareness of the mental health profession, no doubt because people of this type most frequently seek and receive help from religious rather than secular sources. Although not highly visible, this is not a small segment of the population. Ryan (217) reports that as many people are counseled by clergymen as by psychiatrists in Boston, and a national survey (90) showed that 42% of Americans who seek professional help for personal problems turn to the clergy. From the data reported for Boston (217) and for applicants to an outpatient Religion and Psychiatry Institute in New York City (124), this group appears to consist of persons who tend to be middle-aged, of various classes but most typically middle class (businessmen and their wives), more often than not women, with families, Protestant, and less frequently college educated.

Three studies reported demographic characteristics of children seen at child-guidance clinics in Chicago (151), Los Angeles (203), and New York (218). The Chicago and Los Angeles clinics served a fairly broad cross section of the population in their metropolitan areas, while the New York clinic served a more restricted Negro and Puerto Rican working class community. One remarkable consistency was that two-thirds of the child patients in each of these areas were male. There was also a consistent tendency for the 11-and-older age group to be over-represented, although the majority of patients in the Chicago and Los Angeles clinics were younger. Approximately 70% came from intact families (36% in New York), among which families of Jewish background tended to be markedly over-represented. Although the IQ distribution of clinic applicants in Chicago and Los Angeles was approximately normal, those children selected for treatment were overwhelmingly of average or above average intelligence. Also, the majority of those selected for outpatient treatment were mildly to moderately, rather than severely, psychologically impaired.

Several points merit immediate comment. A majority of adult patients in psychotherapy are women. This seems to be a function of a more positive attitude in women towards help-seeking, of a greater readiness of women to define personal problems in mental health terms, and of the fact that therapy is simply more available during ordinary business hours (69, 90, 194). One consequence of this is that the men who are patients in psychotherapy tend to be more seriously disturbed (2, 223). In contrast, the majority of child patients are male. This may reflect a cultural pattern which tends to maladapt boys to institutions in which women are the principal authority figures, just as the over-representation of women among adult patients may reflect the restrictiveness of the traditional feminine role in a male-dominated society.

The three different types of adult patients reflect the socioeconomic and cultural stratification of the American population. Patients of each type tend to enter therapy through different referral routes and probably for different reasons, tend to be seen in different settings by therapists of different professional backgrounds, and tend to receive different types of therapeutic treatment. Can "psychotherapy" mean the same thing to these different types of patients? Traditional intensive individual psychotherapy, as offered in metropolitan private office and training-clinic settings, is obviously best adapted to the capacities of, and most available to, the socioeconomically and culturally elite patient of Type One. Patients who are seen in nonmetropolitan university psychiatric clinics (240) and counseling centers (229) tend to approximate this type. While the best psychotherapeutic services are concentrated on this population (no doubt in part for economic reasons), it does not in itself constitute a significant national mental health problem. The question arises as to what functions psychotherapy has for this population.

The important implication for research is that demographic characteristics of patient samples have to be specified in a way which insures generalizability to the appropriate population segment. For example, Goldstein (84) found that techniques successfully applicable to Type One patients failed in application to Type Two patients. What is needed is a periodic, nationally representative demographic census of patient populations as an essential context for the design, evaluation, and application of psychotherapy research.

Demographic characteristics of therapists.—Who are the psychotherapists? What sort of people are they, and where do they come from? The historical development and manpower growth of the mental health professions has been studied and reviewed (8), but until recently little detailed information about the population characteristics of therapists has been available. A most important contribution has been made by Henry, Sims & Spray (103), who surveyed 3990 of the 6629 psychoanalysts, psychiatrists, clinical psychologists, and psychiatric social workers practicing psychotherapy in New York City, Chicago, and Los Angeles, and intensively interviewed almost 300 of these professionals. Another study (82) surveyed a representative national sample of 421 psychotherapists, providing an interesting comparison group.

In New York, Chicago, and Los Angeles, the population of therapists was 42% psychiatrists (18% psychoanalysts), 33% psychologists, and 26% social workers. Seven in ten were men, a finding confirmed in the national sample. The median age of the metropolitan therapists was 46. In terms of cultural origin (103), 26% of the metropolitan therapists came from Protestant backgrounds, 10% Catholic, 52% Jewish, and 12% no religious background. Thus many therapists, and rather a majority in the biggest cities where therapists are concentrated, come from backgrounds which in terms of the majority of the population are culturally marginal.

In terms of the socioeconomic origin of therapists (103), by far the greatest number (42%) were from lower-middle class (Hollingshead Class IV) backgrounds; the next most numerous group (26%) were from intermediate-middle class (Class III) backgrounds, and nearly as many were of lower class (6%) as of upper class origin (8%). Although in the national sample there were proportionately more therapists of upper and upper-middle class backgrounds (and proportionately more Protestants), 54% were still of intermediate-middle or lesser class origin. By virtue of their present occupational and educational status, psychotherapists must be considered to be an upper or upper-middle class group. Thus, upward social mobility is a characteristic of the majority of psychotherapists. In accordance with the general finding that the more established professions attract people of higher social class origin, two studies have found that psychiatrists tended to be of a higher class background than clinical psychologists (103, 171).

There is an abundance of valuable demographic and other data in the excellently designed and executed study reported by Henry, Sims & Spray (103). Our summary impression of psychotherapists as a distinct population is that they are indeed a socioeconomic elite, but an *achieved* elite whose cultural marginality and status mobility tend to create a relativistic rather than Establishment-oriented value perspective. This no doubt helps them to assist their patients, who are also (though perhaps in more personal ways) culturally marginal people. It seems reasonable to suppose that there may be distinct demographic types in the population of therapists, as there are among patients. Indeed, it has been found (109) that "directive-organic" (contrasted with "analytic-psychological") therapists are less socially mobile and less culturally marginal, i.e. from upper or upper-middle class and Protestant backgrounds.

Paths to the patient role.—What are the routes by which people become patients in psychotherapy? On the basis of his study of applicants to psychiatric clinics in New York City, Kadushin (124) described four stages: (*a*) realization of a problem; (*b*) discussion of problems with laymen; (*c*) choosing the type of helping profession; and (*d*) choosing a particular clinic or therapist. Among the wealth of findings bearing on these stages, one of the most interesting is his identification of a "social circle" or loosely knit network of interpersonal contact and influence which he calls "The Friends and Supporters of Psychotherapy." These are people who "tend to know others with similar problems, to have friends who have also gone to psychiatrists, to have asked their friends for a referral to a psychotherapist or clinic, and to have told a few people about their application to the present clinic. Almost three-fourths of the circle of our Friends are also culturally sophisticated." He goes on to note that "high education, high social class, but especially participation in an occupational milieu which emphasizes the artistic and the psychological—such as the health professions, teaching, communications and the arts—are all highly associated with membership in The Friends. Secularism is also important in creating appropriate conditions for membership." One becomes a member by contact with other members known either through general cultural sophistication, or more narrowly through psychiatric sophistication (contacts made through previous experience in therapeutic situations). Membership, however, makes an important difference in the way each of the four stages is negotiated. Members of this social world, for whom therapy is a significant cultural form,

> realize their problems in a different fashion. The Friends tend to be more sensitive to problems of self-value, sex, and interpersonal difficulties. Members of The Friends are somewhat more likely to take the next step and talk to laymen about their problems. More important, at this second stage of decision-making, they are liable to receive support in their self-recognition of problems whereas non-members of The Friends are more likely to be goaded into problem recognition. When it comes to the choice of type of professional to see first, members of The Friends are more likely to try psychiatrists . . . (They) . . . more often seek knowledge actively and get answers, are more likely to know what to expect from therapy, and are less likely to get pushed into it . . . (124)

Other studies of help-seeking attitudes and behavior related to psychotherapy were reported during this period. Armstrong (7) compared patterns of help-seeking between two groups of high-anxious college students, one of which was in therapy at a counseling center, finding that each group had the same number of intimate friends and outside resources, but that those in the clinical group were less likely than those in the control group to approach their mothers (15% vs 22%) or friends (32% vs 37%) for help, and more likely to choose a counselor or psychiatrist (8% vs 2%). A scale to assess willingness to seek professional help was developed (69), and a factor analysis revealed four attitudinal components: 1. recognition of need for psychotherapeutic help; 2. stigma tolerance; 3. interpersonal openness; 4. confidence in mental health practitioners. Women had consistently more positive attitudes than men; both men and women who had experienced psychotherapeutic help had more positive attitudes than those who had not.

However, Ryan's (217) study as well as earlier surveys (90, 233) make it quite clear that only a small minority of people with real need for professional help pass into and through the paths that lead to the role of patient in psychotherapy. The grim reality of its sheer unavailability again raises the question of the functional relevance of psychotherapy as a form of treatment for mental health problems.

Paths to the therapist role.—The routes by which people become psychotherapists have been studied from two complementary perspectives—that of occupational selection and career development, and that of programs and techniques of professional training. A major portion of the study reported by Henry, Sims & Spray (103) focused on the evolution of professional identity and the various stages of professional training undergone by psychoanalysts, psychiatrists, clinical psychologists, and psychiatric social workers. A major conclusion was that

... despite differential points of entry into professional training, and despite some widely varying experiences within particular training routes, these professionals selectively participate in the available experiences and emerge from professional training with views and skills highly similar to those of other therapists who have taken different formal routes. . . . (C)ompared to the activities in which nontherapist members of their professions are engaged, the similarity of work style and of viewpoint among therapists is marked and sets them apart from other nonpsychiatric physicians and other non-clinical social workers or psychologists.

Research on the teaching and learning of psychotherapeutic skills was the subject of a detailed survey (160) covering contributions from the psychoanalytic and client-centered orientations, the teaching of psychotherapy in medical schools, the teaching of techniques of behavior modification, the use of special devices such as training films and videotape equipment, and the training of "nonprofessional" therapists such as lay counselors, school guidance counselors, and rehabilitation counselors. Magoon, Golann & Freeman (157) reported on an experiment in educating a group of previously untrained women to recognize and assist those in need of psychological aid. It was also noted (198) that trainees who were supervised by therapists low on "facilitative conditions" *declined* in their ability to offer these conditions.

Although most training programs, other than the specifically psychoanalytic, do not require personal psychotherapy of their trainees, it is interesting to note that between 74% (103) and 58% (82) of therapists surveyed had psychotherapy. Evidently, one of the functions of psychotherapy is to train (treat) psychotherapists.

Functional inputs on the institutional level.—The system of psychotherapeutic activities is influenced not only by the nature of the people who participate in it and the routes by which they come to their respective roles, but also by the institutional sectors of society which require and which sponsor the performance of psychotherapy.

Those sectors which require the existence of some sort of therapeutic system have been referred to as client institutions. They are the sectors in which the "problems" or "motives" for which therapy is sought are generated, the institutions in which people's role performances most frequently encounter the sort of difficulties for which therapy is thought to be relevant. Identification of the client institutions in a society would clarify the societal functions of the therapeutic activity system. However, surprisingly little research has focused on this issue. The only data which we are aware of were provided by Gurin, Veroff & Feld (90): among the 345 people who had sought professional help for personal problems, out of the 2460 surveyed, by far the largest number (42%) indicated their problems were with their spouse or marriage. Children and other family relationships (with parents, in-laws, etc) accounted for 12% and 5%, respectively, of the problem areas mentioned. Problems with job, school, or vocational choice accounted for 6%, situational problems involving other people accounted for 6%, and nonpsychological situational problems accounted for 8%. Nonjob adjustment problems in the self (general adjustment, specific symptoms, etc) accounted for 18% of the problems mentioned. Although a minority of these people sought or reached help from mental health professionals, this evidence at least suggests that for adults *the American family, and especially its conjugal core, is the principal institutional client of the therapeutic activity system.* For children, the schools are also an important institutional client.

Characteristics of the institutions which sponsor the provision of psychotherapy, such as the organization of private office practice, outpatient clinics, and mental hospitals, also have a functional impact on the performance of therapeutic activities. For example, Kadushin (124) distinguished three types of outpatient clinic in New York City—psychoanalytically oriented, medically oriented, and religiously oriented—and noted that each served a distinctive clientele and provided a distinctive variety of treatment. Edelson (63) proposed an analysis of psychiatric hospital organization and the therapeutic community in terms of a theory of groups that draws on the work of Talcott Parsons. It is clear that the institutional aspect of social system input has received even less study than the demographic and career aspects, and that research in all three areas has been too meager in relation to their significance in understanding the therapeutic enterprise.

CULTURAL SYSTEM INPUTS

The symbolic influences which affect the ideas and values that guide the therapeutic activity system for patients and therapists derive from three sources. One is the complex of images and values pertaining to therapeutic activities prevalent in the community at large. A second is constituted by other specialized cultural subsystems—i.e. other sectors of the "elite" culture—which are perceived to have some bearing on the issues central to the Therapeutic Belief-Value Complex. Yet a third source of symbolic influence derives from the general (extratherapeutic) belief and value commitments of patient and therapist groups themselves. Although not many studies have been directly focused on cultural system inputs, a few examples can be cited to illustrate the range of questions and information appropriate to this topic.

Community therapeutic ideology.—Gurin, Veroff & Feld's (90) survey included questions about methods of handling worries and periods of unhappiness. They found that only 2% cited some sort of *formal* help-seeking, and 20%–26% cited informal help-seeking, as a means of coping with stresses. A large number of people cited some sort of passive reaction as their first response to worries (34%) and periods of unhappiness (23%), while fewer indicated they would seek to actively "do something about it" (other than seeking help); 33% cited prayer as their first response to periods of unhappiness, and 16% cited prayer as a method of handling worries. These methods of handling stress varied with such demographic characteristics as age, sex, education and income, e.g. younger people, and people with better education and income, are more likely to talk to others about their problems. The main import of these data is to emphasize the irrelevance of psychotherapy, as well as other *formal* helping procedures, as a meaningful resource for the great bulk of the American public.

Correlative specialty subcultures.—A very strong current of influence on psychotherapeutic activities in recent years has come from traditionally nonclinical areas of general psychology. A number of technical practices have been developed from and rationalized in terms of the experimental psychology of classical and operant (180) and social (13) learning, and there was a suggestive integration of learning theory and psychodynamic theory proposed (234). Strong (236) provided an analysis in terms of attribution theory, and others (85) have drawn upon general social-psychological principles. The utility of communication theory was emphasized by Weakland (268), while Pesso (193) has gone further afield to draw upon his experience and training in the dance to develop psychomotor techniques and training exercises for use in psychotherapy. In a somewhat different vein, Lasswell (146) has contributed an analysis of political trends in recent American history in terms of their implications for mental health programs. He indicates that the mental health field has benefited substantially from a long-term trend of rising value emphasis on well-being, but that this benefit has probably peaked and in the future ". . . projects of cultural innovation are likely to be supported in the name of other than the ideology of mental health."

Cultural orientations of patients and therapists.—Little study has been devoted to the broader cultural patterns characterizing patient and therapist groups. Kadushin's (124) description of "The Friends and Supporters of Psychotherapy" is partly in cultural terms, and indicates that members of this select clientele are predominantly urban sophisticates who attend concerts, visit museums and art galleries, go to the theater and to cocktail parties. Henry, Sims & Spray (103) analyzed therapists' religious and political orientations—63% identified themselves as of the same religious faith as their parents, 25% were apostates from their parents' religion, 11% were secularized as were their parents, and 2% were converts to religion from parental secularism. However, a very large majority did not maintain church or temple affiliation (except psychiatrists and social workers of Catholic origin), and described themselves as nonreligious in practices and convictions (except psychiatrists and social workers of Prostestant and Catholic background). Politically, 38% of the therapists described themselves as strong liberals, 50% as moderate liberals, and 12% as conservatives. Another part of the value orientation of therapists is suggested by Bednar & Shapiro (18), who surveyed 16,000 psychologists and psychiatrists and found that less than 1% were willing to participate in a large-scale investigation of psychotherapy.

PSYCHOLOGICAL SYSTEM INPUTS

The lives and personalities of the participants in therapy influence (and are in turn influenced by) the therapeutic action system. They constitute the psychological system context of therapy, which we have classified into the descriptive categories of role-relevant and person-relevant characteristics.

Role-relevant characteristics of patients.—The types of psychological characteristics directly relevant to functioning in the patient role are motivation for therapy, expectations of therapy, and prior experience with therapy (e.g. familiarity with the patient role). For example, Krause has presented a cognitive theory of motivation for treatment modeled upon economic utility analysis (141), and has designed a Client Behavior Inventory to assess various behavioral indices of motivation (142). Goldstein (84) and his colleagues (88) continue their important experimental work on the social psychological determinants of personal attraction in psychotherapy. In our own program of research, Hill (105) found five clusters of motives which patients have in therapy: insight; therapist-involvement; catharsis; relief from tension; support. There is some evidence, however, that the motives of individual patients are highly variable over time (246).

Continuance in therapy can also be viewed as an aspect of patient motivation, and a review (78) of this area suggests that middle class, better educated, higher IQ patients tend to be better motivated—but age and diagnosis were not related to continuance. Among other traits found to be related to continuance were sensitization (245), field-independence (128) and lower F, Pa, Sc, and Ma scale scores on the MMPI (110).

The importance of patient expectations in psychotherapy was emphasized in an earlier work (83). The effect of clinic intake procedures on patient expectations was studied by Krause (140) in relation to subsequent motivation. The research group associated with the Phipps Clinic at Johns Hopkins has continued to investigate the effectiveness of role-induction interviews and vicarious pretherapy training as methods for manipulating patient expectations. Personal characteristics of patients have also been found to influence expectations, e.g. among males in a college clinic, type A patients (on the A-B scale) expected to unburden themselves in an active productive manner, while type B patients expected rational guidance and correctives (28).

Perhaps the chief source of prior role-relevant experience for patients, other than those who are themselves therapists, is previous treatment in psychotherapy. Studies of applicants and patients in a number of clinics report a remarkably high percentage have had previous psychotherapy. For example, Kadushin (124) found that 60% of the 1450 patients applying to 10 New York City clinics has previously received some psychotherapy; 60% of the 118 patients studied in a Chicago clinic (114) had had prior therapeutic treatment.

An interesting sidelight on psychological system input is provided by Rice (206), who studied a college clinic population and found that of those who applied for treatment, accepted males differed from nonaccepted males on a number of role-relevant characteristics (more symptoms; problems in the area of emotional functioning; expectations of longer, more frequent therapy; previous therapy experience), while female applicants were evidently screened on a more subjective basis.

Person-relevant characteristics of patients.—Person-relevant characteristics, as a part of the psychological system context of therapy, were classified into four descriptive categories: life status; assumptive systems; personal styles; adaptational resources and deficits. The determination of life status characteristics involves an individualized interpretation of the kind of data discussed, in part, under social system inputs; we have presented an example of such individualized interpretation (116). Assumptive systems, including images of self and significant others as well as more abstract concepts like world-view, have been studied by a variety of techniques such as Q-sorts, the semantic differential, the role-repertory test, and value questionnaires (e.g. 56, 164, 265). With regard to personal styles, two studies were found to be pertinent to psychological system input. One (245) reported that sensitizers in a college population were more likely to seek therapy than were repressers. The other (69) found that internal control and low authoritarianism were related to more positive attitudes towards seeking therapeutic help. In the area of adaptational resources and deficits, it was reported (121) that college clinic patients exhibited significantly more pathology on the MMPI than matched nonclinic students.

The fact that the design of therapy research typically involves contrasts between different patient groups is probably a major reason why little research has been done on the person-relevant characteristics which distinguish patients in therapy from other groups in the general population. Any study involving tests for which population norms have been established could provide evidence of this sort, but in these terms the literature is too extensive to be readily summarized.

Role-relevant characteristics of therapists.—The motivations of therapists for participating in therapeutic activities were studied retrospectively (103) for two choice points in the development of therapists' occupational identity: selection of general field, and selection of professional speciality. Relative to the first choice point, the three most common motivations for entering medicine given by psychoanalysts were to gain an identity, to help people, and to gain professional status. Psychiatrists gave as motivations the desire to gain an identity, to gain professional status, and to meet practical pressures. The most common motivations of psychologists were to understand people, to help people, and to understand and help themselves. Social workers wanted to help people, to achieve affiliation with others, and to understand people. The social workers were particularly distinguished from the other professions by their desire to help and understand society, to help people, to affiliate with others. Psychologists were differentiated by the extent of their desire to understand people; and the desire to gain an identity differentiated both of the medical groups from the nonmedical groups. At the time of selecting a therapeutic speciality, psychoanalysts had increased in their desire to understand people and to help themselves, while psychologists had developed a greater desire to gain professional status.

Hill (105) studied therapists' motivations at the more microscopic level of treatment process goals and empirically defined three clusters: insight; relationship development; and reduction of stress. However, therapists' treatment goals were variable over time (246). Another aspect of therapist motivation which has received some study (107) is the perceived attractiveness of the patient to the therapist.

Therapists' expectations of patients (e.g. diagnosis and prognosis) were investigated by Lee & Temerlin (149), who found that the social class status attributed to a patient seen in a filmed interview tended to influence the judgments of therapists as to severity of disturbance—lower status patients being seen as more seriously disturbed. However, therapists of lower social class backgrounds had a more positive attitude towards accepting lower class patients for therapy, whereas therapists of higher social class backgrounds were more inclined to have such patients hospitalized (171).

Therapists' experience is an input variable that is frequently studied in relation to process and output variables, but rarely in itself. An oft-heard criticism of therapy research studies is the common use of inexperienced therapists. It is interesting to note in this regard that in a national probability sample (82), 84% of practicing therapists had more than 5 years of experience.

Person-relevant characteristics of therapists.—In accordance with the "Law of the Instrument" (125), there continues to be a substantial research investment in the A-B variable. In this period there were three major reviews of the A-B literature (46, 133, 205) and six research reports (5, 31, 59, 108, 132, 134). With all this, it is distressing that so much perplexity remains about the meaning of the A-B variable. The fact that it was originally devised as an empirical index to differentiate between more or less successful therapists, rather than as the measure of a theoretical construct, no doubt has contributed to this situation. We are inclined to place the A-B variable in the descriptive category of measures of personal style. However, in view of the fact that so many other person-relevant characteristics among measures of life status, assumptive systems, and adaptive resources (as well as personal style) exist to be studied, we question the wisdom of continuing so nearly an exclusive concentration on this mysterious measure.

Roe (210) reviewed the fairly meager literature on differential personality characteristics of psychotherapists, noting such findings as the tendency of therapists to score higher on the MF scale of the MMPI, to have less interest in mathematics and more interest in persons, and to have higher aesthetic and theoretical values, than comparable groups in related disciplines.

PROCESS STUDIES

Process studies focus directly upon the characteristics of the therapeutic activity system: the institutionalized ways of "staging" therapeutic encounters (the social system of psychotherapy); the beliefs and values held by the participants concerning their mutual endeavors (the cultural system of psychotherapy); and the conduct and experiences of the participants as they engage in, and live through, their actual involvement (the psychological system of psychotherapy). In this section, we review recent studies of process, as well as studies of the influence of input variables on process.

THE SOCIAL SYSTEM OF PSYCHOTHERAPY

The elements in the "staging" of therapeutic encounters are roles, collectivity, setting, and schedule. Our report on this facet of psychotherapy will be brief. We have discovered no research studies in this period on social system or the influence of input on social system process, though it seems to us that such research (e.g. a survey of the forms of therapy in current use and the formats in which they are practiced) would be of great interest. We are well into a period of extensive clinical experimentation with variants on the traditional psychoanalytic model. In terms of role patterns, this model prescribed a purely verbal interaction between the patient (free association) and the therapist (interpretation). Three main types of experimentation with role patterns may be discerned: the importation of various directive "behavioral" procedures (13, 66, 139); a testing of the uses and limits of nonverbal techniques such as movement (193) and touching (72, 166); and experimentation with mechanical adjuncts such as audiotape and videotape feedback (11). Hurvitz (120), in an analysis of various types of self-help groups composed of people sharing common self-identified problems, goes so far as to question the utility and the necessity of the therapist role altogether.

The traditional dyadic model has long since been augmented by treatment conducted in primary groups composed of several unrelated patients with one or two therapists; Bednar & Lawlis (16) provide a useful review of empirical research on group psychotherapy. The last decade has seen an extension of the collectivity parameter to the treatment of family groups (93, 275) and the group therapy of other natural relationships (e.g. 54)—and, under the concept of "network therapy," the treatment of patients together with such associates in living as family, relatives, and neighbors (231).

The setting of therapeutic practice—traditionally in the private office, clinic or hospital—has also been extended to carry treatment to the people who are not willing or able to follow the middle class pattern of help-seeking. In communities such as Haight-Ashbury and Greenwich Village, there has been the phenomenon of the free clinic: "a place—it may be an apartment, a garage, or a mobile unit—where people come for free medical, dental, or counseling care" (77). The adjunctive procedure of telephone therapy (214) goes far towards abolishing setting entirely as a factor in staging the therapeutic encounter.

Schedules, too, have undergone substantial modification—in the reduction of the standard analytic "hour" from 60 to 50 to 45 minutes or less, and the reduction in frequency of sessions from 5 to 3 to only 1 or 2 times per week. Later variations were introduced with the concept of time-limited therapy (10 to 20 sessions) and brief psychotherapy (1 to 5 sessions). More recently, the effectiveness of massed-time therapeutic contact has been explored using the "marathon" session, primarily with groups (e.g. 267) but also at least once with an individual patient (216). The limit has been approached for this parameter, too, in a paper reporting "no therapy as a method of psychotherapy" (165).

THE CULTURAL SYSTEM OF PSYCHOTHERAPY

The shared symbolic orientations which focus on the cognitive and evaluative issues involved in any kind of therapeutic enterprise constitute the cultural system of psychotherapy. We have suggested five such issues as components of the Therapeutic Belief-Value Complex: 1. basic human nature, or personality; 2. ideal or "fulfilled" human nature; 3. "normal" human frailties, as well as grosser "abnormalities"; 4. therapeutics, or the process and methods by which abnormalities may be corrected and normalities may be perfected; 5. the therapeutic person and profession. For convenience, we shall first review studies of the symbolic orientations of therapists, then of patients, and then of input influence on symbolic orientations.

Therapist orientations.—Few studies of the "Therapeutic Complex" orientations of therapists were reported in this period. Goldman & Mendelsohn (82) asked random samples of psychiatrists, clinical psychologists, and psychiatric social workers to complete an adjective checklist indicating their conceptions of a normal male, a preferred male patient, a cured male patient, and of themselves. Despite the heterogeneity of the sample, there was a remarkably high level of agreement among therapists. The greatest consensus developed about the conception of an adult male "who has a satisfactory adaptation to himself and his environment." This paragon of virtue, who seems more to represent the ideal than the average, was viewed as "reality oriented, socially effective, self-accepting, free of inner conflict, and concerned with the welfare of others." Additionally, in contrast to the other concepts, "the normal is described as more affectively involved in his relationships," as having "a sense of balance between emotion and control."

The "adult male patient who has successfully terminated therapy" (cured) seems closer to the average or social norm, in contrast to the ideal or cultural norm. "There are no indications of psychological disturbance; instead he has acquired self-confidence, contentment, and a measure of tolerance and stability. He is, above all, a good citizen . . ." but ". . . there is little indication he is seen as a freer, more creative, more unique individual." The conception of the cured patient was closer to that of the normal than were either the therapists' self-concept or their concept of the preferred patient, but in contrast to the cured patient the normal is seen as possessing "characteristics which transcend adjustment."

Naturally enough, the preferred patient (defined as "the kind of adult male patient that you work with best") was most dissimilar from the normal, and there was less agreement among therapists in their description of this concept than about any of the others. The preferred patient was seen as "an imaginative, sensitive, curious, well-motivated, but anxious person." The authors note that "aside from the anxiety, there is little indication of pathology or a 'cry for help' " in the preferred patient, and remark that "if anxious were removed from the list of the 25 most descriptive adjectives, the preferred patient would appear to be an unusually productive and creative person." Although this finding reinforces the impression we have already gained of the main clientele of psychotherapy, the result might have been somewhat different if therapists had been asked to describe their typical rather than their preferred patient.

How do therapists see therapists? They describe themselves, like good scouts, as: dependable, capable, conscientious, intelligent, friendly, honest, adaptable, responsible, etc, etc. "The self-portrait which emerges is of a person who is steady, competent and intellectually alert, and concerned with the welfare and feelings of others" (82). In another study of 200 psychiatrists, psychologists, and social workers (232), the "therapeutic qualities of empathy, dependability, interest, sincerity, and respect seem[ed] to be most valued by all psychotherapists."

Therapists' self-concept (82) was differentiated from their concept of the preferred patient on two dimensions—genuine altruism in interpersonal relations, and less psychopathology—although the discrimination was greater on the first dimension than on the second. In comparing the therapists' self-concept with that of the cured person, the authors see the most striking difference in "the greater self-assurance and confidence ascribed to the cured. The tendency of the therapists to describe themselves as prone to conflict and lacking in self-assurance is most evident in the comparison of the self and normal. But the therapists also see themselves as more intellectually open, thoughtful, and affectively responsive than the cured." The authors note ". . . a sense of vitality in the self-description which is lacking in the description of the cured."

As part of their professional qualifications, ministers are supposed to be more moral, and therapists more mentally healthy, than the average person —and perhaps, to some extent, they are. But from their self-descriptions, at least, the average therapist seems to be no more a completely mature, conflict-free well-adjusted person than the average minister is a saint.

The subject of therapists' symbolic orientations cannot be dropped without further comment because the whole of the clinical literature is itself part (and the most explicitly proliferated part) of the contribution of therapists to the culture of psychotherapy. The clinical literature is a multiplex forum in which therapists communicate to one another their experiences, thoughts, and recommendations on issues germane to therapy. *Voices*, a journal of The American Academy of Psychotherapists, is especially interesting in this respect, because of the personal quality of its contents. The output of all such publications must number in the thousands each year, and defies any summary review—although a serious study of what therapists are concerned to communicate to each other (e.g. a content analysis of themes in the literature) would be of substantial interest to the student of psychotherapy.

Among the items which caught our attention were volumes of collected essays by two of the most stinging and instructive gadflies in the therapeutic community, Szasz (243) and Haley (93). Two other excellent volumes of collected papers offer the reader an opportunity to become current with recent developments in Client-Centered therapy (95) and Gestalt therapy (67). These therapeutic traditions, one originating with Carl Rogers and the other with the late Fritz Perls, have been particularly influential in clinical psychology.

Both Rogers and Perls also made contributions of philosophy and technique to the burgeoning "encounter group" movement, and Rogers (211) has brought out a volume of his writings on the subject. Encounter groups, sensitivity and human relations training, continue to be a subject of great interest to therapists, especially as some therapists have expanded their practice to include leading such groups. For these Gibb (81) offers a brief review of practice and research on the effects of human relations training; Golembiewski & Blumberg (86) present a reader on the concepts and applications of sensitivity training and the laboratory approach; Egan (64) has written a thoughtful book exploring encounter groups as a method for facilitating interpersonal growth.

The problem of whether encounter groups are different from therapy groups, and how, adds another note to the growing tendency of therapists to question the ways in which psychotherapy is defined. A number of writers have been actively seeking to reconceptualize the nature of the therapeutic process. Urban & Ford (263), for example, attempt to bring therapy into the paradigm of problem-solving. Rioch (209) and Carkhuff (43) propose that therapy be viewed as education in interpersonal living, with therapists as teachers of interpersonal skills. Two authors, writing from quite different perspectives, regard therapeutic experiences (in one form or another) as necessary ingredients of effective human living, and propose that these be available to people in peer groups on an on-going basis (175), or as professional care on a per-need basis (34).

Patient orientations.—The symbolic orientations of patients to therapeutic issues have been neglected as a subject of study, although some interest has been taken recently in patients' beliefs and value preferences regarding therapeutic procedures and therapist characteristics. For example, two analog studies of college students' preferences for types of therapists indicated that, were they to seek personal counseling, they would choose a high status, committed therapist of their own sex, who conformed to their expectation of being an understanding person (35, 202). In a study of patients' beliefs about therapeutic activities (20), questionnaires administered to clinic applicants led to the identification of two clusters of patients who differed on the amount of anticipated therapist involvement (warmth, activity, etc). The consensus of these prospective patients was that the therapist would probably: start out taking a history; want to hear about childhood experiences; ask the patient to say whatever comes to mind; ask probing personal questions; not accept the patient's definition of his problems; confront the patient's defenses; try to improve the patient's interpersonal functioning; and take different approaches with different patients. There was also a shared belief that patient and therapist would get along on a natural, easy-going basis, and that the patient would learn the causes of his behavior and feelings and develop a new and different self-image.

Input influence on cultural system process.—One interesting study of the effects of social system input on the cultural system of psychotherapy appeared in this review period. Benfari (21) sampled 20 tribal societies from the Human Relations Area File to assess the relationship between socialization practices regarding childhood dependency and the style of patient-healer interaction among adults. He found eight of the ten societies which fostered childhood dependence had person-oriented therapists, whereas only two of the ten with low childhood dependence had such therapists. Clearly, studies of this type provide an important new perspective on psychotherapy, and should be further pursued.

THE PSYCHOLOGICAL SYSTEM OF PSYCHOTHERAPY

The psychological system properties of psychotherapy have been most intensively studied as the main focus of therapy "process" research. We present the work done in this review period under the headings of *Patient processes*, *Therapist processes*, and *Conjoint processes*, and include within each studies of system process and input influences on system process.

Patient processes.—Content analysis has been the principal methodology used in the study of patient conduct and experience in psychotherapy, and a thorough review of this literature from 1954 through 1968 has been made by Marsden (158). Since then, various aspects of patient conduct have been the focus of several studies. Factor-analysis of interview content for single cases has yielded clinically meaningful themes (97, 167). Tokar & Stefflre (247) selected key words of special psychological significance for a patient and investigated their verbal correlates. A similar technique was used by Luborsky & Auerbach (155) to focus on a patient's symptomatic behavior in therapy sessions, in order to elucidate the meaning of these symptoms in relation to their interview context. In our own work based on the reports of patients and therapists (114), the following topics were found to be most frequently (and modally) discussed by female outpatients in their therapy sessions: relations with the opposite sex; hopes or fears about the future; work, career, or education; and mother. Seven content themes representing areas of patients' life-space were identified through factor-analysis, and the appearance of these themes in patients' sessions was found to be more a function of intercurrent events than of individual differences between patients.

Content systems and analyses have been reported for the study of interpersonal behavior as well as verbal behavior. Bierman (32), in a major review, persuasively demonstrated the application of a Leary-type circumplex model of personal interaction to the study of psychotherapeutic process. A similar model was applied to the study of interpersonal themes rated from tapes of therapy sessions (178). A coding system for interaction behavior in group psychotherapy was also proposed (153). A study of interactions in group therapy (99) reported more, and more dynamically meaningful, dimensions of group process in later sessions. Patients and therapists reported more satisfaction with those sessions in which group behavior was more task-oriented (224).

In an analysis of the experiential correlates of patients' and therapists' satisfaction with individual therapy sessions (184), we found that in dialog the "good therapy hour" (i.e. the most satisfying sessions) focused on experiences of the most intimate personal relationships, past and present: early family relations, erotic attachments, and explorations of fantasy and self-experience. These topics were approached with the aims of achieving deeper insight and of resolving emotional conflict. The type of therapeutic relationship which patients found most satisfying was actively collaborative, genuinely warm, and affectively expressive and involving on both sides. Another study, focusing on the problematic concerns which patients experience in therapy sessions (186) reported modal concerns to be: personal identity; self-disclosures, responsibilities; loneliness; loving; and anger. Factor-analysis revealed the following dimensions of patients' concerns: Isolation vs Intimacy; Ego-Identity; Independence vs Dependence; Sex and Guilt; Anger and Fear. Patients' conscious concerns were more reflective of current developmental problems than of infantile conflicts, and were shown to be differentially related to areas of the life-space discussed in the therapeutic dialog.

The affective states typically experienced by patients (117) were: serious; accepted; anxious; confident; relaxed; hopeful; confused; determined; relieved; grateful; likable; pleased; frustrated; and inadequate. This study reported dimensions of patient feelings, the trait vs state characteristics of feelings, and the differential association of feelings with areas of problematic concern. An earlier study (113) utilized factor-analyses of patients' reports of their conduct *and* experience in therapy sessions, and derived 11 clinically meaningful empirical dimensions. These studies give the first descriptive taxonomy of the ways in which their conduct and experience is perceived by patients in psychotherapy.

Input influence on patient processes.—Although most of the studies on the influence of input factors on patient processes have concentrated on psychological system inputs, one report did examine the effects of social system input. Brody (37) observed 99 lower class Brazilian patients being interviewed in a public clinic setting by two young white upper-middle class psychiatrists, and found that patients of relatively higher status were more comfortable in the interview and related to the doctors with less dependency, less hostility, and more open show of symptoms.

Patient role-relevant characteristics were investigated as an influence on patient conduct (191) in an analog study which reported that a client's responses to a counselor who attempts to modify his behavior are contingent upon how personally attracted the client is to his counselor and how congruent their discussion is with the client's prior expectations.

Person-relevant characteristics of patients (life status and history, assumptive systems, personal style, and adaptive resources and deficits) were the focus of several studies. Shapiro (228), in an excellent review of the placebo effect in psychotherapy, cites a considerable body of research on the influence of patient characteristics. Two papers demonstrated the impact of a person's perceived relationship with his parents on his interview conduct—one (177) through a comparison of interpersonal themes in the family and in therapy, and the other (14) in an experimental analog study. We also reported differential patterns of experience in therapy among female outpatients in relation to current life situation, family background, cultural background, and diagnosis (113).

The influence of therapist characteristics on patient experience was studied by Scott & Kemp (225), who found that type B medical student therapists elicited greater depth of self-exploration in neurotic outpatients than did type A therapists.

Several studies were designed to assess the interacting influences of patient and therapist characteristics on patient conduct and experience. For example, a comparison of dyads of varying degrees of compatibility in interpersonal style revealed that patients in high compatibility pairs liked their therapists more than did those in low compatibility pairs (80). Mihalick (164) found that patients whose personal value orientations were closer to those of their therapists at the beginning of therapy tended to remain in treatment longer than did those whose values were further from their therapists. Tosi (248) measured clients and counselors on the Rokeach Dogmatism Scale and obtained reports from clients after the initial interview, finding that dyads in which both were low in dogmatism were judged best, while dyads in which both were high were judged worst. A study of the effect on patient self-disclosure of prior sets to feel trust or distrust towards A and B type interviewers showed that patients given a distrust set were most self-disclosing with type A interviewers, while patients given a trust set were more self-disclosing with type B interviewers (30). Therapists' orientations have no general differential impact on their patients' experience of therapy, but differential impact of therapist orientation does appear when patients are grouped by diagnostic type (118). Finally, a study exploring the joint impact of patients' and therapists' personal life status on patients reported satisfactions in therapy (116) suggests the importance of the personal aspect of the therapeutic relationship, and provides a promising start towards a more empirical rationale for the assignment of patients to therapists.

Therapist processes.—The conduct and experiences of therapists in therapy constitute the focus of studies of therapist processes, and the field is fortunate in having several recent highly detailed reviews of this literature (158, 162, 254). Most of the research effort on therapist processes in the last few years has concentrated on the therapist-offered conditions defined by Carl Rogers—Communicated Authenticity (genuineness), Regard (warmth), and Empathy (understanding) (CARE). In spite of the fact that Rogers emphasized communication to the client, most research in this area has utilized ratings made by nonparticipant observers. In addition to certain psychometric problems inherent in this measurement procedure (49), it has been repeatedly demonstrated that little relationship exists between patients', therapists' and nonparticipant observers' ratings of therapist-offered conditions (36, 41, 44, 70). Since nonparticipant observers are generally asked to rate segments sampled from recordings of therapy sessions, a convergent criticism of this method was reported by Karl & Abeles (126), who showed that these measures are largely a function of the particular segments sampled. Thus, while great effort has been expended in studying therapist conditions, the accumulated literature seems to be seriously weakened by problems of methodology and theoretical relevance.

Some studies have been addressed to the question of whether CARE is a trait of therapists rather than a function of particular patient-therapist interactions (situational states). One research group (51, 100, 176), on the basis of very limited evidence, posited the existence of a "good guy" factor which asserts that these conditions are personal attributes of therapists. However, Garfield & Bergin (79) again demonstrated that the components of CARE are not always positively correlated (genuineness was negatively related to the other two conditions). In a study of empathic ability per se, Wogan (273) concluded that empathy does not appear to be a trait; i.e. there was as much variability over trials as between individuals. The placement of this literature under the heading of therapist processes, rather than therapist input, reflects our conviction that therapists' facilitative conditions are a complex function of persons and interactions.

Correlates of CARE in therapist conduct, as reported during this review period, were: expression of interest or involvement (41); reference to self and to the therapy relationship (52, 170); more, and more experiential, confrontation with patients (4, 169); and, more direct open response to confrontation by patients (4, 52).

In our own work (106), we factor-analyzed a substantial number of reports of their own conduct and experience in therapy from a limited number of therapists, and tentatively defined 11 empirical patterns. Before a representative taxonomy of therapist conduct and experience can be established, however, a much broader sampling will be necessary.

Input influences on therapist processes.—The distribution of studies of input influences on therapist processes was again skewed in the direction of psychological system inputs, concentrating almost exclusively on the effects of various therapist characteristics on therapist conduct and experience. Several studies were at pains to demonstrate the positive effects of training and/or experience on therapist performance. For example, experienced therapists responded with fewer questions, less manipulative, and more communicative statements to a filmed patient (187); experienced therapists responded with more positive regard to a taped patient (19) and were found to be more empathic in interviews (179); inexperienced therapists were found to be more empathic with patients they liked than with those they disliked (179); but were more favorable in their first impressions of patients (38). The training of nonprofessional personnel was found to improve their ability to discriminate and communicate feelings (42); to enhance their capacity to be empathic, respectful, genuine and concrete, even when the training was given in large groups (50); and to improve their functioning in group therapy, in contrast to untrained volunteers whose performance got worse with time (62).

Guild (89) compared analyzed and nonanalyzed therapists who were matched for level of experience, and found that analyzed therapists had more effective relationships with their patients. In comparing patients' and therapists' reports of therapist-offered conditions, he also found more patient-therapist agreement for analyzed therapists.

Other studies concentrated on the person-relevant characteristics of therapists, in contrast to the role-relevant characteristics just mentioned. Thus, in dealing with neurotic patients, type A therapists were found to be more interpretive and negative, while type B therapists were more facilitative and encouraging of self-expression (226)—though no relationship was found between the A-B variable and levels of CARE (225). Bergin & Jasper (25) found a moderate inverse correlation between empathy in graduate student therapists and levels of anxiety and depression measured on the MMPI, but no correlation of empathy with either intelligence or academic achievement. Passons & Olsen (190) found empathic sensitivity in graduate student therapists correlated with cognitive flexibility, but not with dogmatism, willingness to communicate feelings, or self-concept. Again studying graduate student counselors, Foulds (73) correlated ratings of their CARE in interviews with self-actualization as measured by the scales of Shostrom's Personal Orientation Inventory. He found no correlates of warmth, but empathy did correlate positively with: independence and internal direction; growth; flexibility; awareness of own needs; acceptance of own aggressiveness; and ability to develop I-Thou relationships. These scales correlated with genuineness, too, as did the scales measuring openness, self-liking, acceptance of own weaknesses, and a view of opposites in life as meaningfully related. Given the fact that the therapists in these studies were all graduate students, and the previously cited finding that experienced therapists tend to be more empathic than inexperienced therapists (179), we suspect that the effects of these person-relevant characteristics are attenuated by experience.

In another study (57) of the influence of counselor personality on level of functioning, counselees' ratings were correlated with the scales of Cattell's 16PF, finding warmth positively related to scale A (warm-sociable) and genuineness positively related to scales C (emotional-unstable) and I (tough-minded).

In our own work (106), we studied the relationship between patterns of therapist experience and specific therapist characteristics. For this small sample, no differential associations were found with therapists' sex, age, birth order, number of sibs, social class of origin, and experience. However, therapists who were single, as well as those without children, tended to experience Interpreting Resistance (vs Attentive Empathy); Catholic therapists experienced more Erotic Countertransference; therapists who did not have personal therapy experienced more Giving Insight (vs Strengthening Defenses) and more Patient Passive Dependence; therapists who were trained as psychiatric social workers experienced more Effective Movement (vs Depressive Stasis). This study was also the only one to be concerned with the effects of patient characteristics on therapist conduct and experience.

Conjoint processes.—Conjoint processes refer to the psychological system as a whole, taking both the patient and the therapist into account simultaneously. They are consequently complex, and may be usefully considered under the separate analytic headings of (*a*) process aspects, (*b*) process phases, and (*c*) process dynamics. The aspects of conjoint process are *interaction*, focusing on mutual influence in individual patterns of conduct; "*interexperience*," consisting in relations among individual patterns of experience; and *group process*, subsuming unit patterns present in the collectivity.

The practice of holding "alternate" (leaderless) sessions in group psychotherapy provided an opportunity to test the differential effect of therapist presence or absence in two studies (15, 227), where therapist presence in the group was found related to greater task-orientation, fewer statements, more questions, more confrontation, and less continuity and conventionality in conversation. Audiotape self-confrontation in group psychotherapy was reported to produce more verbal interchange than found in standard group sessions (10), while the use of videotape feedback in interviews was reported to stimulate more honest and open communication (188).

At a more complex level, Mueller (177) studied interactions between clients and therapists and found clients' competitiveness and hostility related to passivity or hostility in therapists, while therapists responded in a nurturant fashion when clients asked for help in more role-appropriate ways. Also, Bierman (32) reported a consistent finding of a positive correlation between therapist activity and patient activity. Moos and his colleagues

(111, 173) extended their research into the mutual influences of patients' and therapists' conduct with respect to such variables as empathy, problem exploration, reinforcement, activity, use of feeling and action words, etc. Their general finding was that these variables were most influenced by the interaction of patient, therapist, and session, and that the influence of patient conduct was stronger than the influence of therapist conduct. The one identified area in which therapists' influence was predominant was the selection of topics in the therapeutic dialog.

Several studies focused on the relationship between therapist conduct and client experience. Depth of self-exploration in clients was found to be positively related to therapist-offered CARE (3, 4), and to be more strongly elicited by therapist conflict attention than by either nondirective reflection or nonresponse (196). Truax (252) also found that therapist genuineness facilitated negative transference in group psychotherapy.

Part of our own work has been concerned with therapeutic "interexperience," or relationships among individual patterns of experience. The affective tone of sessions tended to be shared and mutually perceived (117). Further analyses relating to the direction of causal influence in the affective process (112) showed that therapists' experiencing negative feelings (e.g. uncertain, demanding) was *sufficient* to elicit negative feelings (e.g. depressed, inhibited, anxious) in patients, but that patients' negative feelings did not so affect therapists. The same pattern held with respect to positive feelings for experienced therapists. However, for inexperienced therapists, patients' experiencing positive feelings (e.g. relieved, confident) was *sufficient* to elicit positive feelings (e.g. expansive confidence) in therapists. In another study (115), we demonstrated some of the ways in which therapists' feelings were responsive to qualities of their patients' participation in therapy, and suggested conditions under which therapists might use their own feelings as clues to patient processes.

Two studies showed concordance between patients' and therapists' evaluations of their sessions: a P-analysis of reports from individual therapy sessions (184), and an R-analysis of data from group psychotherapy (224).

Four dimensions of individual's participation in therapy were derived from a factor-analysis of ratings of therapy tapes (168). Analyses of variance showed significant differences between therapists on Optimal Empathic Relationship, though there were also significant differences in this between patients of the same therapist. Individual differences among patients accounted for 77% of the variance on Patient Health vs Distress, while patients and therapists contributed equal amounts of variance for Directive Mode, and Interpretive Mode with Receptive Patient.

In one of our early studies (185) we factor-analyzed patterns of conduct and experience of both patients and therapists together. This resulted in the empirical definition of seven dimensions, five of which reflected conjoint group processes in the dyad: Conflictual Erotization vs Quasi-Parental Support; Collaborative Analytic Progress vs Obstructive Defensive Impasse; Ambivalent Nurturance-Dependence vs Mutual Personal Openness; Critical

Depressive Stasis vs Sympathetic Responsiveness; and Healing Magic (Positive Transference). Two other factors were defined predominantly by patients (Intrusive Contact-Seeking vs Passive Contact-Waiting) or by therapists (Reagency vs Catalysis).

These studies (168, 185) are initial efforts based upon limited samples, and their findings must be regarded as tentative. However, they emphasize the importance of viewing individual patient and therapist processes as components of conjoint processes in the psychological system, and reveal emergent patterns not readily apparent from the examination of either patient or therapist separately.

Change over time in the conduct and experience of therapy represents another facet of psychological system process. Mihalick (164), for example, demonstrated a growing similarity of patients' values to those of their therapists, and Chessick & Bassan (48) showed an interesting convergence in physiological signs in patients and therapists over time, within sessions as well as over sessions. Smeltzer (230) rated tapes of sessions and noted that the temporal focus of patients' dialog shifted from past to present as therapy progressed. Finally, Mueller (177) presented an interesting body of research showing that, as therapy progresses, patients treat their therapists more like they treat their parents, while therapists tend to treat patients more like patients' parents do. Perhaps the most challenging problem for research in this area is the empirical definition of phases of therapeutic process, but in this review period there was no advance over work previously done.

OUTPUT STUDIES

No area of psychotherapy has suffered so much from simplistic thinking in the guise of tough-minded pragmatism as has research on therapy outcome. The insistent demand to know if therapy "works" has obscured the extreme subtlety of the question, and a number of commentators recently have been recommending that a more differentiated approach be taken (e.g. 27, 135, 136, 238). Such an approach, we feel, follows from the conceptual scheme presented in this chapter.

Any system of psychotherapeutic activities has some functional consequences simply by virtue of its existence and operation. These functional consequences are to be sought in the action systems environment of the therapeutic activity system: the population and institutional structure of the host community (social system context); the symbolic belief and value patterns of the host culture (cultural system context); and the lives and personalities of the persons who participate in it (psychological system context). However, the problem goes beyond merely specifying the output of therapeutic activities for each of these system contexts. Evaluative judgments must also be made if we are to conclude that the changes attributable to psychotherapy are desirable or undesirable, significant or trivial. Evaluative judgments can only be made in relation to value criteria, and if the judgments are to be public and rational (a value criterion posited in our scientific activities system), then the values we hold must be explicitly defined. Thus, the evaluation of outcome is not only complex but also rests ultimately upon subjective commitments.

The traditional model of outcome evaluation has operated with the assumption that psychotherapy is a treatment for mental or emotional illness or behavior disorder, consisting of technical procedures applied by trained personnel to persons manifesting the illness. The outcome question has focused on the curative efficacy of the technical procedures, and the target for such evaluation has naturally been the mental or emotional or behavioral functioning of the patient. The sick patient entering treatment has been viewed as a kind of inert raw material, the treatment techniques as a process to which it is subjected, and the patient who has completed treatment as a more or less stable finished product. This model suggests that the appropriate time for evaluation of outcome is the termination of treatment, and that follow-up evaluations are desirable to test the stability of the treatment effect. The value criterion most persuasively employed has been the reduction of manifestations of the pathological condition in the patient, though more recently arguments have been made for use of signs of positive mental health as a supplementary or an alternative criterion. When determinants of outcome (other than treatment techniques) have been studied, these have focused on the nature of the raw material (person-relevant characteristics of patients) and the skill of the processor (role-relevant characteristics of therapists).

The model of outcome evaluation suggested by our conceptual scheme substantially modifies and expands the traditional approach. It is not committed to the assumption that psychotherapy is a treatment for some sort of illness. Whether therapeutic activities are conceptualized as a medical process of curing, or a religious process of redemption, or an educational process of remedial or advanced instruction, etc, is itself a system variable. Relieved of this assumption, the model suggests that the target of outcome evaluation need not be limited to the psychological system characteristics of the patient, but should be widened to encompass all of the system contexts that may show the functional impact of therapeutic activities—the social system context parameters, the cultural system context parameters, and even the therapist or "collaterals" as the other components of the psychological system context.

In addition, this model's treatment of the psychological system context makes no assumptions about "personality" as a substantive entity, inert or plastic or otherwise. Instead it is data-oriented, seeking for heuristic reasons to distinguish the main categories of variables pertinent to the lives and persons of individuals. The researcher is free to examine interindividual and intraindividual (situational and temporal) variability of constructs in this domain. The design employed by Wessman & Ricks (271) fits this perspective and could provide a useful approach for studying psychological system output.

Furthermore, the model suggests that outputs are primarily *functional* rather than *temporal* sequelae of therapeutic activities, and thus might be meaningfully measured as soon as the therapeutic system is activated. There is no necessity to await the termination of therapeutic contacts to evaluate their social, cultural, and psychological consequences, nor is there anything to suggest that the time of termination has more importance than other times as an occasion for assessment. Thus, if initial contact with a professional helper, or even placement on a clinic waiting list, is sufficient to arouse a hopeful expectation in the patient, and if that expectation is a factor productive of therapeutic change, then a finding that patients improve even before the application of what therapists regard as treatment is not an embarrassment but a valuable conclusion.

Another way this new conceptualization expands the traditional model of outcome evaluation is with respect to value criteria. The "medical" assumption that psychotherapy is a treatment for some kind of illness commits evaluation to a health-illness value criterion, and relegates other possible value criteria to a distinctly secondary status, or to oblivion. Suspension of this assumption leads to a consideration of the variety of value criteria which might be persuasive to us. We are also led by our conceptual scheme to consider the different value criteria which are appropriate for evaluating the social, the cultural, and the psychological outputs of psychotherapy.

SOCIAL SYSTEM OUTPUT

The output of the therapeutic activity system to its social system context should be sought in changes in the personnel and institutions of the host community. Personnel changes might occur in the demographic characteristics of patient and therapist populations, and in the further careers (i.e. subsequent statuses) normatively or customarily following participation in the patient or in the therapist role. The functional consequences of the therapeutic activity system for institutions might occur in sponsoring institutions (service organizations such as clinics, and ancillary organizations such as professional societies) or, perhaps more interestingly, in client institutions. Client institutions, it will be recalled, are those sectors of the social system in which the "problems" of patients are generated (i.e. in which people have difficulty functioning).

Even fewer studies of social system output have been done than of social system input, although outcome studies sometimes use variables which have social system implications. One such is the length of time that patients are removed from participation in community life roles (family, work, etc) through hospitalization, though in this perspective it is not the effect on the life and personality of the patient that counts but rather the effect on the collectivities in which he participates (family disruption, manpower time lost, public hospitalization costs, etc). A good example of social system output is provided by Targow & Zweber (244), who found that treatment in a married couples' group improved communication between marital partners.

The fact that functioning of the marital dyad was improved makes this an output to a client institution (the kinship system).

The value criteria by which social system functioning may be judged have been traditionally more the province of the social and political philosopher than of the mental health professional. A purely instrumental value, but one which has gained some currency in mental health policy planning, is the effective use of scarce resources. In this connection, Klarman (138) provides a useful discussion of cost-benefit analysis and its application to the evaluation of mental health services and manpower utilization. The effects of the therapeutic activity system also have recently received salutary attention in relation to values like individual liberty (243) and social progress (94), although such discussion has not yet passed from the stage of argument to that of investigation. Perhaps the cardinal social value in Western culture—from Plato and the Prophets to modern writers like Marx, Dewey, and Tillich— is that of justice. Freedom, equality, and community are general value criteria which also have compelling force in our culture. The task of phrasing these with sufficient specificity and exploring their relation to the social system output of psychotherapy is a major challenge that has only recently been addressed.

CULTURAL SYSTEM OUTPUT

Contact between the system of therapeutic activities and the larger culture occurs in three specific areas: the beliefs and values concerning specifically "therapeutic" issues shared in the community; the subcultural systems adjacent to the therapeutic system which are shared by specialized cultural elites; and the full range of extratherapeutic beliefs and values that are shared particularly by those who participate directly in psychotherapy.

Although there is manifest cultural output from therapeutic activity in these areas, there are no studies which document it. Rieff (208) has provocatively discussed the impact of Freud and other therapists on some of the core symbolic categories of the general culture. Rogow (212) has emphasized the cultural influence which therapeutic conceptions and values gain by virtue of the fact that social and cultural elites comprise such an important segment of the clientele of psychotherapists. However, Halleck (94) warns that psychotherapy, by emphasizing individual "adjustment," can have the effect of encouraging social and cultural conformity.

It is clear that the therapeutic activity system has been a major source of speculation and hypotheses concerning the nature of human personality and relationships (as well as the major "natural laboratory" for testing such hypotheses). It is also clear that the concerns and values characteristic of the culture of psychotherapy have penetrated and stimulated the literary and artistic subcultures. The general value criteria pertinent to these cultural outputs are truth and beauty. The truth of these hypotheses, and the beauty of these works of art, may prove in historical perspective as relevant to the evaluation of our therapeutic action system as change in the psychological functioning of patients.

PSYCHOLOGICAL SYSTEM OUTPUT

The psychological system context of psychotherapy consists of the lives and personalities of the individuals who participate in it—in our system as patients, as therapists, and at times as "collaterals" of patients. Our analysis of the psychological system context focused on the two main classes of participants, and distinguished between their role-relevant characteristics and their person-relevant characteristics. The major focus of research has been on the person-relevant characteristics of patients, dealing with variables in the categories we have defined as life status, assumptive systems, personal styles, and adaptational resources and deficits.

The problem of evaluating the psychological system effects of psychotherapy has been greatly complicated by the felt value prohibition against making value-judgments which has been current in the scientific subculture. Because of the conflict this implicitly generates for those who would evaluate therapy outcome, researchers have often described the subject of study as personality "change." But this is logically insupportable, however understandable it may be that few researchers would want to propound criteria by which to judge the "good" life or the "good" person. In fact, studies often report improvement or success on specific measures, leaving their value criteria implicit. The recent discussion of deteriorative effects (23) forces us to confront the fact that it is improvement or its opposite, in reference to *some* value criterion, which really interests us, and with which we must deal.

There are a variety of value criteria or norms which might be, and no doubt in some studies have been, applied singly or in combination in the assessment of personal functioning. Viewing the person as an individual organism, there are norms of somatic functioning (health vs sickness), affective functioning (happiness vs unhappiness), and ideational functioning (sanity vs insanity). These correspond to a more global dimension of "individual well-being." On the other hand, viewed as a member of his community, the social conduct of a person can be judged with reference to an instrumental norm (competence vs incompetence), a situational norm (propriety vs impropriety), and a political-legal norm (lawfulness vs criminality). These reflect a set of standards that are often implied by the more global criterion of "social adjustment." Finally, viewing the person as an embodiment of his culture, his character may be evaluated with reference to a developmental norm (maturity vs immaturity), an esthetic norm (creativity vs banality), and a moral norm (virtue vs sin). These may be part of the more global dimension which has come to be called "self-actualization."

It would be interesting and instructive to study the content of measures that have been used in outcome research, to determine the kinds of value criteria embodied in them. Although it is beyond the scope of this review to attempt such an analysis, two papers have some relevance to this issue. In one study (68), counselors' judgments of the extent to which certain events indicate successful therapy were subjected to factor-analysis, and six evaluative dimensions were identified. Krause (143), in a theoretical discussion of the problem, drew a useful distinction between four "publics" or reference groups for which the evaluation of therapy has some importance—those who receive therapy (patients), those who benefit from the patient's receipt of therapy (clients), those who do therapy (therapists), and those who organize and underwrite the provision of therapy (sponsors)—and noted that these publics are likely to favor different value criteria in making such evaluations. It is quite conceivable that, in any particular case, psychotherapy may have positive effects by some, negative effects by others, and negligible effects with reference to yet other value criteria.

Output studies.—The literature on outcome has been dominated to date by the simplistic question, "Does psychotherapy work?" Evaluative criteria have been limited to very general conceptions of improvement or success. Within this context, there were in this period three major attempts to assess the outcome literature on individual psychotherapy with adults. By far the most careful and scholarly analysis of the issues and data was provided by Bergin (23), who concluded that ". . . psychotherapy, as practiced over the past 40 years, has had an average effect that is modestly positive. . . . While we have more assurance than before that there are efficacious influences present in traditional therapy, the weakness of the average effects implies that only some methods or some therapists are especially effective." In a highly biased and limited review, Stuart (241) contends that patients in psychotherapy expose themselves to a marked risk of deterioration or wasteful stagnation. Meltzoff & Kornreich (162), in an extensive and oppositely biased review, spend several chapters documenting the effectiveness of therapy—though they seem willing to call virtually any intervention "psychotherapy." Bergin's (23) work, however, should lay the issue to a long overdue rest. The field can only profit now from research on more differentiated questions.

With respect to the problem of spontaneous remission, both Bergin (23) and Subotnik (242) produced important analyses concluding that different clinical syndromes show different spontaneous remission rates. Jurjevich (123) also cited evidence of symptomatic remission with the passage of time, and showed different rates for different syndromes.

In contrast to positive changes occurring in the absence of therapy, a number of writers have shown that therapy can be harmful to patients (6, 22, 23, 213, 215, 219, 240, 241, 270), but estimates of this deterioration effect vary greatly, hovering around 15%.

There were also several new studies of outcome during this period. Among those with controls, Verinis (266) and Goodstein (87) both found more constructive change in treated patients than in a no-treatment group. Coons & Peacock (53) reported similar results for group therapy as compared to a (no-treatment) control of normal ward interaction. Varble & Landfield (265) found a greater increase in congruence between self and ideal-self (patients' assumptive system) for treated as compared with untreated subjects. Two controlled studies reported the beneficial effects on hospitalized patients of minimal supportive contact with volunteers, using recidivism (130) and ward adjustment (39) as outcome indicators. Gassner (80), on the other hand, using pastoral counseling trainees as therapists, found no differential effect of treatment (vs no-treatment) on patients' ward behavior.

The effectiveness of the initial interview in reducing symptomatic distress (a role-relevant motivational variable) has again been documented (200, 260).

Some tentative evidence was provided (272) that improvement in one area of a patient's functioning is accompanied by improvement in other areas. A significant increase in IQ (patients' adaptational resource) was also reported (6) to be a function of psychotherapy, and correlates of IQ change (ego-strength, patterning of defenses, etc) indicated some generality of effect.

A further result of therapy which bears mention is an apparent tendency on the part of patients to want even more therapy (a role-relevant characteristic)—what may be called the "salted peanut effect." In one report (240), 44% of treated patients indicated a "considerable" to "earnest" desire for further help (though only 11% of the patients reported no improvement), while Henry, Sims & Spray (103) found that 33% of the therapists they studied were not yet satisfied with the results of the personal therapy they had received, even after as many as three separate courses of treatment.

Input influences on psychological system output.—The great majority of studies of input influences on therapy outcome have concerned psychological input characteristics, to the neglect of social and cultural system inputs. Meltzoff & Kornreich (162), in a 17-chapter comprehensive review of research in psychotherapy, take only part of one chapter to summarize studies pertaining to the influence of social system inputs on therapy outcome, while the better part of four chapters are devoted to summarizing the influence of psychological system inputs. With respect to the latter, readers are also advised to consult the more specialized reviews of patient variables (78), psychoanalytic therapy (156), placebo effects (228), and child psychotherapy (152) which appear in Bergin & Garfield's (24) monumental *Handbook of Psychotherapy and Behavior Change*.

A few papers published in this period focused on patients' role-relevant characteristics in relation to outcome. Good motivation for change was found positively related to outcome in psychoanalytic therapy (9). It was also reported that a high initial level of symptomatology, presumably reflecting patient distress, related positively to improvement in time-limited therapy, (98) and even to improvement with the initial interview (260), though these results may be attributable to statistical regression. It was also found that patients who score as terminators on the Terminator-Remainer Scale fare better in time-limited therapy, while those who score as remainers do worse (98). The effect of patients' expectations of change on the impact of the initial interview was assessed, with a negative finding reported (200). More positive was the report (204) indicating that experienced patients did better in group therapy than patients involved in their first course of treatment. Also concerned with the factor of prior experience was a study showing the beneficial effect of vicarious therapy pretraining in group psychotherapy (255). Even pretesting of patients was found to have a positive influence on outcome (91).

The influence of patients' person-relevant characteristics on outcome was the focus of several studies. Patient "attractiveness" (reflecting the life-status variable of youth, education, and high occupation) related positively to judgments of outcome in a 10-year follow-up study (107). Two other studies examined patients' assumptive systems, finding good outcome predicted by low initial discrepancy between self and ideal-self concepts (265) but high discrepancy between self-description and description by spouse (181). The personal style variable of persuasibility was also investigated, with the finding that highly persuasible patients received more benefit from treatment (17). However, more research interest was concentrated on the category of patients' adaptational resources and deficits, generally reconfirming the finding that patients with better personality resources gain more from psychotherapy (107, 219, 272). Saenger (219), however, showed that patients with good prognoses do even better without than with treatment, while patients with poor prognoses profit more from treatment than from nontreatment.

In one study of therapists' role-relevant characteristics, therapists were given optimistic or guarded expectancies of patient improvement, but with no discernible influence on outcome (266). The effects of experience were assessed in another study (96) wherein student nurses were trained to treat hospitalized chronic schizophrenics with reinforcement therapy and with traditional psychotherapy. The fact that they were more effective with the reinforcement treatment, however, may only indicate that inexperienced therapists do better with techniques that are easier to learn. Inexperienced therapists were also found to be more satisfied than experienced therapists with the outcome of their cases (38).

Some attention was also given to the effects of therapists' person-relevant characteristics on outcome. In a study of patients' retrospective reports (240), important aspects of perceived change were found to be related to a view of the therapist as a capable, involved, accepting person. Another study found that therapists scoring higher on "neuroticism" (presumably an adaptational deficit) achieved more change in patients, though they elicited less change in patients' values (164). A "pathogenesis" score for therapists, reflecting personal style, was derived from the TAT in another study (264). Therapists with higher scores were found to have poorer treatment results. These studies have particular interest in light of the growing concern with the deterioration effect, and may help us to understand which therapist characteristics, alone or in combination with given patient characteristics, contribute harmful or beneficial results.

Two studies investigated the effects of matching therapist and patient on personal style variables (scores on the FIRO-B inventory), one finding this matching to have no effect on outcome (80), while the other (163) found no effect for males but a positive relation to outcome for female patients. Also reported was an approach to matching patients and therapists in one clinic by comparing the differential effectiveness of staff therapists with patients having different initial reports of symptoms and expectations (29) The finding of empirical criteria for guiding case assignments suggests a promising avenue for exploration by clinic administrators.

Process influence on psychological system output.—Excellent reviews of this extensive literature are now available in Meltzoff & Kornreich (162) and various chapters of Bergin & Garfield's (24) *Handbook.* Current literature contains a number of studies pertinent to the effects of the social and cultural systems of psychotherapy on psychological output, as well as studies focusing on the influence of psychological system processes.

In line with the general conception of psychotherapy as a treatment for mental or emotional illness, considerable interest has been shown in the comparative effectiveness of different technical procedures available to therapists. These procedures constitute parts of the therapist role—a parameter of social system process. In one study (197), patients were trained directly in facilitative interpersonal functioning with results found to be superior to both group and individual therapy. For brief group therapy, assertion training was reported to be better than insight orientation in treating hospitalized nonpsychotic patients (154). The use of psychotherapy by inexperienced therapists without concomitant medication for schizophrenic inpatients was found to result in longer hospitalization, but more change on a measure of thought disorder, than the combined use of drugs and therapy (127). Two general reviews on the effects of combining psychotherapy and pharmacotherapy appeared in this period (161, 261). Several investigators during this period have also experimented with various forms of audio and video playback as a technical procedure, though reports of results thus far are mixed (10, 129, 188). The absence of studies dealing with the patient role may be partly explained by the fact that, with some exceptions (e.g. free association), the technical procedures used in therapy form part of the therapist role.

With respect to other parameters of social system process, the element of collectivity was varied in a study (104) reporting the efficacy of including well-adjusted boys (nonpatients) in group therapy with disturbed boys (patients). Two studies reported the superiority of group over individual therapy for experienced patients (204), and as a way of improving patients' interpersonal relationships (174). Some renewed attention was also paid to the effects of schedule on outcome. With brief (time-limited) psychotherapy, one study using experienced therapists reported no effects (222), while another reported a 45% no-improvement rate (213). A small-scale study of different frequencies of contact found no difference in outcome between once-weekly and four times a week psychoanalytic therapy with boys, but did find

significant differences favoring the more frequent treatment at follow-up
(101).

Cultural system processes have been examined mostly with regard to the
effects of different theoretical orientations on outcome. In one study (17),
recruited "patients" were assigned to programmed rational-emotive and
expressive therapies, leading the former to change in directions emphasizing
control and thinking while the latter changed in directions emphasizing expression and feelings. Another study (60) compared the effects of psychoanalytic, medical (drug), and supportive treatments on Rorschach test
measures of patients, finding that psychoanalytic therapy resulted in liberation of fantasy and libido and in greater awareness, medical therapies resulted in better reality contact but with greater personality constriction,
while maintenance therapies resulted in no basic personality changes in both
neurotic and schizophrenic patients. Perhaps the most interesting result
relating to outcome is the consistent finding that the more patients and
therapists agree in their orientations, the better are the outcomes of therapy
(119, 122, 222).

The impact of psychological system processes has been studied in an unbalanced fashion during this period. Only five reports focused on patients'
conduct and experiences in relation to outcome. The most elaborate was a
factor-analytic study of ratings from therapy tapes (168), in which female
patients who scored high on health and low on distress in early sessions, and
who were capable of expressing hostility, were found to have better outcomes.
The expression of negative feelings in group psychotherapy was also found
to facilitate improvement (252). Another study (272) showed that changes
in verbal behavior in therapy are accompanied by changes in other behaviors
as well. Paradoxically, Truax and his associates reported that patients'
depth of self-exploration in group therapy was related to positive outcome
(255) and was not related to outcome (256).

There were 17 studies reporting information relating therapist processes
to therapy outcome, but this literature is confused by the overlapping operational definitions of different constructs and the tendency of some investigators to report in separate papers confounded analyses of the same data. To
add to the confusion, for virtually any effect studied more than once there
was a contrary report. Most often studied were the "facilitative conditions"
—CARE—showing promising relations with outcome in some studies (179,
250, 252, 256, 258, 259) and no relation to outcome in others (25, 58, 79,
251). Brown (38) reported that counselor liking (first impression of patient)
was related to good outcome, but Mullen & Abeles (179) found no relationship between these two variables. Truax & Wittmer (258) found amount of
therapist personal reference to be related to good outcome in individual
therapy, but Dickenson (55) found a similar variable (self-disclosure of
therapist) to not relate to outcome in individual therapy (although it did
relate to outcome in group therapy for schizophrenic patients). Unreplicated
therapist conduct variables which were related to positive therapeutic out-

come were: facilitative responsibility (199); small number of evaluative statements (249); greater amount of talk (250); persuasiveness (253); and focus on source of patient's anxiety (257).

If there has yet been no consistent confirmation of the kind of therapist participation which is necessary or sufficient for successful outcome, there has nevertheless been a theme running through the literature suggesting that therapists who are low on many of the "facilitative conditions" may actually harm their patients. For example, Truax (251) found no general relationship between CARE and outcome, but found that patients of therapists who were particularly low on these conditions tended to deteriorate. One plausible explanation of these results might be that therapists can show too much as well as too little warmth, empathy, etc. A curvilinear relationship may obtain between facilitative conditions and outcome, such that a therapist's characteristic level of response may exceed or fall short of the *optimum* level of conditions for a given patient. Too much warmth or genuineness in a therapist can obviously threaten a patient.

Joint input and process influences on psychological system output.—Every major reviewer of psychotherapy research has emphasized the need to investigate the joint effects of input and process characteristics on therapy outcome, yet in the present period only three studies attempted such analyses. One empirically distinguished several types of depression in patients and found that these were differentially responsive to different treatments (269). Another found no interaction effect between patient characteristics (persuasibility and expectation) and therapeutic orientations (rational-emotive and expressive treatments) in determining outcome (17). Finally, Goodstein (87) assigned an equal number of "neurotic" and "adolescent reaction" patients to nondirective and psychoanalytic therapy, using a variety of assessment techniques to examine outcome. He found that "neurotics" did better with psychoanalytic treatment (those who received nondirective treatment actually deteriorated over 30 sessions), and some support for the conclusion that nondirective therapy was more effective with "adolescent reactions." Many studies of this sort remain to be done before we begin to find optimal combinations of patients, therapists, situations, and techniques.

CONCLUDING COMMENTS

The conceptual model of the therapeutic activity system and its social, cultural, and psychological system contexts, has been introduced in this chapter with the thought that it might help to distill a certain amount of cumulative knowledge from the mass of published research, and perhaps direct attention to areas in which further data might be fruitfully gathered. From the knowledge that has accrued, we offer some concluding reflections directed to these two questions: What is the state of the art in psychotherapy research, and how might it be improved? What do we know of the psychotherapeutic enterprise and its functions in our society?

The State of the Art in Psychotherapy Research

This review period has included a veritable explosion of critical reviews and methodological suggestions. Strupp and Bergin (26, 27, 238, 239) have provided the most comprehensive review of the research literature, and have presented a number of recommendations for the guidance of future research. The volume by Meltzoff & Kornreich (162) is another important bibliographic resource for students in this field. The single most valuable contribution is probably the *Handbook* edited by Bergin & Garfield (24), containing chapters on virtually every substantive, technical, and methodological issue in psychotherapy research, with the major exception of research on the experience of psychotherapy. Beyond these works, however, several issues deserve special mention.

Sampling.—Sampling of personnel in psychotherapy is greatly hampered by an inadequate specification of the population. In principle, such a specification would include all people who ever were or ever will be patients or therapists (a problem in any field of human psychology), but even more limited specification would be helpful. Important beginnings have been made by Kadushin (124) and Ryan (217) with respect to patient demography, and by Henry, Sims & Spray (103) and Goldman & Mendelsohn (82) with respect to therapists; but this work needs to be extended and utilized.

Other sampling problems concern setting and treatment segments. Wolff (274) noted that in the past 25 years only 15 studies have employed the private practice setting, certainly a major locus of therapeutic activity. With regard to treatment segment, many investigators have shown measures to be a function of the particular sessions and of segments of sessions sampled. We need to attend more to problems of generalizability of findings, and sampling is the crucial issue.

Single case designs.—There has been a renewed interest in research on the single case in psychotherapy—a scientific counterpart to the clinical case study. Lazarus & Davison (147) discussed the kinds of inferences which can be drawn from this approach. Other methods proposed during the present review period were: a simplified clinical record of change (215); repeated assessment of symptomotology (172); P-factor analysis of patient reports (56); and dream characteristics (76). The basic methodology of single case (intensive) design proposed by Chassan (47) has yet to be applied to psychotherapy research.

Observational perspectives.—Studies of psychotherapy have characteristically relied on third-person (nonparticipant) observation. The wealth of data advantageously or uniquely available from first- and second-person perspectives (participant observation) has for the most part been neglected. Yet most theories of psychotherapy emphasize constructs which are embedded in the experiences of patients and therapists—insight, experienced empathy, fear reduction, etc. In our own work we have tried to show how patients' and therapists' experiences can be objectively and quantitatively studied. In the main, little convergence has been demonstrated for measures of the same construct based on different perspectives (36, 41, 44, 45, 70). This argues the necessity of studying therapeutic phenomena from *each* of the relevant perspectives.

General design issues.—Nine papers directly pertained to the design of psychotherapy research. Two attempted to specify the conditons under which an analog approach would be useful (102, 237); one discussed the utility of psychophysiological measures (145); and another considered the methodology of research based on retrospective reports (74). Others presented general discussions of research strategy (27, 71, 131, 136, 192).

Bergin & Strupp (27) offered 21 conclusions based on their survey of the field; and although we do not agree with some of these (indeed the two authors didn't agree on all), they provide a useful resource for investigators. A report from a task force (71) which devoted considerable energy to the analysis of technical and methodological issues in psychotherapy research provides an outline of items to be considered in designing a study. Along with the design books by Chassan (47) and Campbell & Stanley (40), these will be valuable to investigators. One team (131) actually applied the Campbell-Stanley system to the evaluation of designs of published studies. Of course, they concluded that there is a lot of poor research in the area; but, more importantly, they used the system to indicate directions for improvement. As in other areas of psychology, the technical and methodological sophistication available has not been consistently applied, nor have the problems of interest always been adequately conceptualized.

THE FUNCTIONS OF PSYCHOTHERAPY

Psychotherapy in our society is generally viewed as a treatment for mental or emotional illness, but a number of facts cast serious doubt on this notion. The overwhelming majority of severely distressed people—those whose functional incapacity most resembles the incapacity of the physically ill, and who comprise this nation's "mental health problem"—never receive professional psychotherapeutic attention. There are not nearly enough trained professional psychotherapists to treat them, nor are there ever likely to be enough. The strata of our population from which most "mental patients" are recruited are those for which psychotherapy is least *meaningful* as an idea or as a helping procedure, and they comprise the least preferred group of clients among those whom therapists see. Moreover, psychotherapy is generally found to be least effective for those who have the severest adaptational deficits. The preferred client, the one who seeks psychotherapy as a meaningful experience and who stands to profit most from participation in our therapeutic activity system, is the Type One or YAVIS person—distressed, no doubt, but not incapacitated.

Why does the conception of psychotherapy as a form of treatment continue to prevail? The answer, we think, lies partly in history and partly in professional politics. Our modern system of therapeutic activities had its origin at the close of the last century in a medical context, dealing with pseudoneurological manifestations ("psychoneuroses"). The medical profession was by that time also in a position to lend the cultural authority of science to its psychotherapeutic activities—an advantage which older, competing religious, moral, and spiritualistic therapeutic practitioners did not share. This advantage was decisive with respect to that segment of the population for whom reality is defined in terms of a secular, rational, naturalistic world view—the urbanized, higher-educated, nontraditional new generation of upper-middle class people. The growth of this cultural orientation through the first half of our century, of the classes which hold to it, and of the social structural stresses with which they must cope, has created a demand for psychotherapeutic services exceeding the supply of medical psychotherapists, calling new professional groups into the field. The now traditional view of psychotherapy as a medical or paramedical treatment serves to give the psychiatric profession an hegemony over the field of therapeutic practice in which it no longer has an effective monopoly (1). The insurgence of psychologists, first as lay analysts and then with their "own" therapeutic orientation (e.g. Carl Rogers), culminated in the 1960s with the behavior therapy movement which claims to operate under the aegis of its "own" science (201, 262). If the social work profession liberates itself from its group image as an ancillary profession and renews its ties with the discipline of scientific sociology, it too may advance a claim to independent operational authority.

How then do we view our present society's system of psychotherapeutic activities? In terms of the available evidence relating to social system input (especially patient demography and client institutions), it begins to appear that the major de facto function of our therapeutic activity system is *as a kind of "higher education" in the development of interpersonal skills and emotional capacities* (42, 209, 240). It parallels the function of collegiate education, in which occupational skills and instrumental capacities are developed to the high level required by our socioeconomic system. Those who have higher education in the latter sphere frequently also find a need for it in the former. Personal distress is still a critical factor in determining a person's becoming a patient in psychotherapy, but it is distress (or aberrant reactions to stress) occasioned by experienced frustration or failure in social-emotional functioning, rather than distress occasioned by (somatic) illness. Psychotherapeutic "education" is tutorial in form, and often requires remedial work to correct dysfunctional interpersonal and emotional patterns learned in the course of family and peer group socialization, but it characteristically includes more advanced work as well (intimacy, spontaneity, self-disclosure, etc).

The people who most frequently find themselves in need of psychotherapeutic education in our society are those whose major life roles require highly developed interpersonal skills and emotional capacities for successful functioning: middle and upper-middle class women involved in the very taxing work of maintaining "fulfilling" marriages and rearing personable, independent, achievement-oriented children; men and women engaged in professions which involve intensive work with people and/or personal creativity (psychotherapists, teachers, ministers, administrators, service and sales personnel of various kinds, writers, advertising men, entertainers, etc). To this list must be added those young people whose socioeconomic and educational advantages give them such a range of choice in shaping their lives that they have both the privilege and the problem of "finding themselves."

As the validity and importance of social-emotional education (once called "moral education") for effective functioning in the kinship and occupational institutions of our society become more widely recognized, the need for people to wait until they are distressed before they enroll may tend to vanish. Human relations training, experimental programs of sensitivity training in schools and organizations, and the rapid development of formal and informal encounter groups among married couples in many communities suggest that the first steps have already been taken in moving psychotherapeutic education from its clinical context.

Probably the clinical function of psychotherapeutic education will remain, however—as a means of alleviating personal distress, and as remedial socialization—for those with adaptational deficits in the interpersonal-emotional sphere. The available evidence concerning therapeutic processes and their psychological system output suggests to us, and in some respects to many others (32, 34, 150, 175, 180, 201, 228, 240), that *psychotherapies of all types involve the symbolic communication—through language, gestures, and actions that the patient understands and believes—of benevolent care from a person or agency of respected influence.*

People develop, as Piaget (195) has suggested, through phases of sensorimotor, symbolic, and rational functioning—but this is a cumulative development, in which each successive stage adds to and modifies, but does not abolish what came before it. Insight therapies of all types address themselves to the rationality of the patient, and behavioral therapies direct their operations to the sensorimotor level, but all therapies work through the medium of an actual or implied human relationship whose manifest and convincing purpose must be to help the patient. The insight and the conditioning given the patient are, under various and as yet imperfectly understood conditions, evidently effective, but the medium cannot itself fail to be an important part of the message. Perhaps, as Opler (183) proposed, the time has come when professional therapists will finally realize that they must learn ways to communicate this message to patients who [unlike "The Friends and Supporters of Psychotherapy" (124)] have cultural orientations that differ markedly from their own. When we can rationally design our therapies to communicate effectively with different segments of the patient population, then we shall have a psychotherapeutic system that is really scientific, rather than one that is merely cloaked in the impressive imagery of science.

LITERATURE CITED

1. Albee, G. W. 1969. The relation of conceptual models of disturbed behavior to institutional and manpower requirements. In *Manpower for Mental Health*, ed. F. N. Arnhoff, E. A. Rubinstein, J. C. Speisman, 93–112. Chicago: Aldine. 204 pp.

2. Alexander, J. F., Abeles, N. 1969. Psychotherapy process: sex differences and dependency. *J. Couns. Psychol.* 16:191–96

3. Anderson, S. C. 1969. Effects of confrontation by high- and low-functioning therapists on high- and low-functioning clients. *J. Couns. Psychol.* 16:299–302

4. Anthony, W. A. 1971. A methodological investigation of the "minimally facilitative level of interpersonal functioning." *J. Clin. Psychol.* 27:156–57

5. Anzel, A. S. 1970. A–B typing and patient socioeconomic and personality characteristics in a quasi-therapeutic situation. *J. Consult. Clin. Psychol.* 35:102–15

6. Appelbaum, S. A., Coyne, L., Siegal, R. S. 1970. Routes to change in IQ during and after long term psychotherapy. *J. Nerv. Ment. Dis.* 151:310–15

7. Armstrong, J. C. 1969. Perceived intimate friendship as a quasi-therapeutic agent. *J. Couns. Psychol.* 16:137–41

8. Arnhoff, F. N., Rubinstein, E. A., Shriver, B. M., Jones, D. R. 1969. The mental health fields: an overview of manpower growth and development. See Ref. 1, 1–38

9. Aronson, H., Weintraub, W. 1969. Certain initial variables as predictors of change with classical psychoanalysis. *J. Abnorm. Psychol.* 74:490–97

10. Bailey, K. G. 1970. Audiotape self-confrontation in group psychotherapy. *Psychol. Rep.* 27:439–44

11. Bailey, K. G., Sowder, W. T. 1970. Audiotape and videotape self-confrontation in psychotherapy. *Psychol. Bull.* 74:127–37

12. Bales, R. F. 1950. *Interaction Process Analysis.* Cambridge: Addison-Wesley. 203 pp.

13. Bandura, A. 1971. Psychotherapy based upon modeling principles. See Ref. 24, 653–708

14. Baugh, J. R., Pascal, G. R., Cottrell, T. B. 1970. Relationship of reported memories of early experiences with parents on interview behavior. *J. Consult. Clin. Psychol.* 35:23–29

15. Becker, R. E., Harrow, M., Astrachan, B. 1970. Leadership and content in group psychotherapy. *J. Nerv. Ment. Dis.* 150:346–53

16. Bednar, R. L., Lawlis, G. F. 1971. Empirical research in group psychotherapy. See Ref. 24, 812–38

17. Bednar, R. L., Parker, C. A. 1969. Client susceptibility to persuasion and counseling outcome. *J. Couns. Psychol.* 16:415–20

18. Bednar, R. L., Shapiro, J. G. 1970. Professional research commitment: a symptom or a syndrome. *J. Consult. Clin. Psychol.* 34:323–26

19. Beery, J. W. 1970. Therapists' responses as a function of level of therapist experience and attitude of the patient. *J. Consult. Clin. Psychol.* 34:239–43

20. Begley, C. E., Lieberman, L. R. 1970. Patient expectations of therapists' techniques. *J. Clin. Psychol.* 26:113–16

21. Benfari, R. C. 1969. Relationship between early dependence training and patient-therapist dyad. *Psychol. Rep.* 25:552–54

22. Bergin, A. E. 1970. The deterioration effect: a reply to Braucht. *J. Abnorm. Psychol.* 75:300–2

23. Bergin, A. E. 1971. The evaluation of therapeutic outcomes. See Ref. 24, 217–71

24. Bergin, A. E., Garfield, S. L., Eds. 1971. *Handbook of Psychotherapy and Behavior Change: An Empirical Analysis.* New York: Wiley. 957 pp.

25. Bergin, A. E., Jasper, L. G. 1969. Correlates of empathy in psychotherapy: a replication. *J. Abnorm. Psychol.* 74:477–81

26. Bergin, A. E., Strupp, H. H. 1969. The last word (?) on psychotherapy research: a reply. *Int. J. Psychiat.* 7:160–68

27. Bergin, A. E., Strupp, H. H. 1970. New directions in psychotherapy research. *J. Abnorm. Psychol.* 75:13–26

28. Berzins, J. I., Friedman, W. H., Seidman, E. 1969. Relationship of the A–B variable to patient symptomatology and psychotherapy expectancies. *J. Abnorm. Psychol.* 74:119–25

29. Berzins, J. I., Friedman, W. H.,

Seidman, E. 1970. An approach to matching patients with therapists in short-term psychotherapy. *J. Am. Coll. Health Assoc.* 18:245–50

30. Berzins, J. I., Ross, W. F., Cohen, D. I. 1970. Relation of the A–B distinction and trust-distrust sets to addict patients' self-disclosures in brief interviews. *J. Consult. Clin. Psychol.* 34:289–96

31. Berzins, J. I., Seidman, E. 1969. Differential therapeutic responding of A and B quasi-therapists to schizoid and neurotic communications. *J. Consult. Clin. Psychol.* 33:279–86

32. Bierman, R. 1969. Dimensions of interpersonal facilitation in psychotherapy and child development. *Psychol. Bull.* 72:338–52

33. Birdwhistell, R. L. 1970. *Kinesics and Context: Essays on Body Motion and Communication.* Philadelphia: Univ. Pennsylvania Press. 338 pp.

34. Boris, H. 1971. Treatment or treat. *Psychiat. Soc. Sci. Rev.* 5:20–24

35. Boulware, D. W., Holmes, D. S. 1970. Preferences for therapists and related expectancies. *J. Consult. Clin. Psychol.* 35:269–77

36. Bozarth, J. D., Grace, D. P. 1970. Objective ratings and client perceptions of therapeutic conditions with university counseling center clients. *J. Clin. Psychol.* 26:117–18

37. Brody, E. B. 1968. Status and role influence on initial interview behavior in psychiatric patients. In *An Evaluation of the Results of the Psychotherapies,* ed. S. Lesse, 269–79. Springfield, Ill.: Thomas. 351 pp.

38. Brown, R. D. 1970. Experienced and inexperienced counselors' first impressions of clients and case outcomes: are first impressions lasting? *J. Couns. Psychol.* 17:550–58

39. Buckley, H. M., Muench, G. A., Sjoberg, B. M. 1970. Effects of a college student visitation program on a group of chronic schizophrenics. *J. Abnorm. Psychol.* 75:242–44

40. Campbell, D. T., Stanley, J. C. 1966. *Experimental and Quasiexperimental Designs for Research.* Chicago: Rand McNally. 84 pp.

41. Caracena, P. F., Vicory, J. R. 1969. Correlates of phenomenological and judged empathy. *J. Couns. Psychol.* 16:510–15

42. Carkhuff, R. R. 1969. Helper communication as a function of helpee affect and content. *J. Couns. Psychol.* 16:126–32

43. Ibid 1971. Training as a preferred mode of treatment. 18:123–31

44. Carkhuff, R. R., Burstein, J. W. 1970. Objective therapist and client ratings of therapist-offered facilitative conditions of moderate to low functioning therapists. *J. Clin. Psychol.* 26:394–95

45. Carr, J. E., Whittenbaugh, J. 1969. Sources of disagreement in the perception of psychotherapy outcomes. *J. Clin. Psychol.* 25:16–21

46. Chartier, G. M. 1971. A–B therapist variable: real or imagined? *Psychol. Bull.* 75:22–33

47. Chassan, J. B. 1967. *Research Design in Clinical Psychology and Psychiatry.* New York: Appleton-Century-Crofts. 280 pp.

48. Chessick, R. D., Bassan, M. 1968. Experimental approaches to the concept of empathy in psychotherapy. See Ref. 37, 49–69

49. Chinsky, J. M., Rappaport, J. 1970. Brief critique of the meaning and reliability of "accurate empathy" ratings. *Psychol. Bull.* 73:379–82

50. Collingwood, T. R. 1969. The effects of large group training on facilitative interpersonal communication. *J. Clin. Psychol.* 25:461–62

51. Collingwood, T. R., Hefele, T. J., Muehlberg, N., Drasgow, J. 1970. Toward identification of the therapeutically facilitative factor. *J. Clin. Psychol.* 26:119–20

52. Collingwood, T. R., Renz, L. 1969. The effects of client confrontations upon levels of immediacy offered by high and low functioning counselors. *J. Clin. Psychol.* 25:224–26

53. Coons, W. H., Peacock, E. P. 1970. Interpersonal interaction and personality change in group psychotherapy. *Can. Psychol. Assoc. J.* 15:347–55

54. Crabtree, L. H., Graller, J. L. 1971. The group psychotherapy of natural relationships. *Psychother. Theory Res. Pract.* 8:55–58

55. Dickenson, W. A. 1969. Therapist self-disclosure as a variable in psychotherapeutic process and outcome. *Diss. Abstr. Int.* 30:2434B

56. Dingman, H. F., Paulson, M. J., Eyman, R. K., Miller, C. R. 1969. The semantic differential as a tool for measuring progress in therapy. *Psychol. Rep.* 25:271–79

57. Donnan, H. H., Harlan, G. E., Thompson, S. A. 1969. Counselor personality and level of functioning as perceived by counselees. *J. Couns. Psychol.* 16:482–85

58. Donofrio, D. S. 1969. The effect of therapist variables on parents and

their children as a function of work with parent counseling groups. *Diss. Abstr. Int.* 30:2904B

59. Dublin, J. E., Elton, C. F., Berzins, J. I. 1969. Some personality and aptitudinal correlates of the "A-B" therapist scale. *J. Consult. Clin. Psychol.* 33:739–45

60. Dudek, S. Z. 1970. Effects of different types of therapy on the personality as a whole. *J. Nerv. Ment. Dis.* 150: 329–45

61. Duncan, S. Jr. 1969. Nonverbal communication. *Psychol. Bull.* 72:118–37

62. Ebersole, G. O., Leiderman, P. H., Yalom, I. D. 1969. Training the nonprofessional group therapist. *J. Nerv. Ment. Dis.* 149:294–302

63. Edelson, M. 1970. *Sociotherapy and Psychotherapy.* Univ. Chicago Press. 266 pp.

64. Egan, G. 1970. *Encounter: Group Processes for Interpersonal Growth.* Belmont, Calif: Brooks/Cole. 424 pp.

65. English, O. S., Scheflen, A. E., Hampe, W. W., Auerbach, A. H. 1965. *Strategy and Structure in Psychotherapy,* ed. O. S. English. Philadelphia: East. Pa. Psychiat. Inst. 124 pp.

66. Eysenck, H. J., Beech, H. R. 1971. Counterconditioning and related methods. See Ref. 24, 543–611

67. Fagan, J., Shepherd, I. L. 1970. *Gestalt Therapy Now.* New York: Harper Colophon Books. 328 pp.

68. Farnsworth, K. E., Lewis, E. C., Walsh, J. A. 1971. Counseling outcome and the question of dimensionality. *J. Clin. Psychol.* 27: 143–45

69. Fischer, E. H., Turner, J. LeB. 1970. Orientations to seeking professional help: development and research utility of an attitude scale. *J. Consult. Clin. Psychol.* 35:79–90

70. Fish, J. M. 1970. Empathy and the reported emotional experiences of beginning psychotherapists. *J. Consult. Clin. Psychol.* 35:64–69

71. Fiske, D. W. et al 1970. Planning of research on effectiveness of psychotherapy. *Arch. Gen. Psychiat.* 22: 22–32

72. Forer, B. R. 1969. The taboo against touch in psychotherapy. *Psychother. Theory Res. Pract.* 6:229–31

73. Foulds, M. L. 1969. Self-actualization and the communication of facilitative conditions during counseling. *J. Couns. Psychol.* 16:132–36

74. Fox, R. E., Strupp, H. H., Lessler, K.

1968. The psychotherapy experience in retrospect: problems and potentials of an approach. See Ref. 37, 38–48

75. Frank, J. D. 1961. *Persuasion and Healing.* Baltimore: Johns Hopkins Press. 282 pp.

76. Freedman, A., Luborsky, L., Harvey, R. B. 1970. Dream time (REM) and psychotherapy. *Arch. Gen. Psychiat.* 22:33–39

77. Freudenberger, H. J. 1971. New psychotherapy approaches with teenagers in a new world. *Psychother. Theory Res. Pract.* 8:38–43

78. Garfield, S. L. 1971. Research on client variables in psychotherapy. See Ref. 24, 271–98

79. Garfield, S. L., Bergin, A. E. 1971. Therapeutic conditions and outcome. *J. Abnorm. Psychol.* 77:108–14

80. Gassner, S. M. 1970. Relationship between patient-therapist compatibility and treatment effectiveness. *J. Consult. Clin. Psychol.* 34:408–14

81. Gibb, J. R. 1971. The effects of human relations training. See Ref. 24, 839–62

82. Goldman, R. K., Mendelsohn, G. A. 1969. Psychotherapeutic change and social adjustment: a report of a national survey of psychotherapists. *J. Abnorm. Psychol.* 74: 164–72

83. Goldstein, A. P. 1962. *Therapist-Patient Expectancies in Psychotherapy.* New York: Pergamon. 141 pp.

84. Goldstein, A. P. 1971. *Psychotherapeutic Attraction.* Elmsford, NY: Pergamon. 250 pp.

85. Goldstein, A. P., Simonson, N. R. 1971. Social psychological approaches to psychotherapy research. See Ref. 24, 154–95

86. Golembiewski, R. T., Blumberg, A., Eds. 1970. *Sensitivity Training and the Laboratory Approach.* Itasca, Ill.: Peacock. 515 pp.

87. Goodstein, M. A. 1969. The relationship of personality change to therapeutic system and diagnosis. *Diss. Abstr. Int.* 30:2419B

88. Greenberg, R. P., Goldstein, A. P., Perry, M. A. 1970. The influence of referral information upon patient perception in a psychotherapy analogue. *J. Nerv. Ment. Dis.* 150: 31–36

89. Guild, M. 1969. Therapeutic effectiveness of analyzed and non-analyzed therapists. *Diss. Abstr. Int.* 30: 1869B

90. Gurin, G., Veroff, J., Feld, S. 1960. *Americans View Their Mental Health*. New York: Basic Books. 444 pp.

91. Haase, R. F., Ivey, A. E. 1970. Influence of client pretesting on counseling outcome. *J. Consult. Clin. Psychol.* 34:128

92. Haley, J. 1963. *Strategies of Psychotherapy*. New York: Grune & Stratton. 204 pp.

93. Haley, J. 1971. *The Power Tactics of Jesus Christ and Other Essays*. New York: Avon. 176 pp.

94. Halleck, S. L. 1971. Therapy is the handmaiden of the status quo. *Psychol. Today* 4:30

95. Hart, J. T., Tomlinson, T. M., Eds. 1970. *New Directions in Client-Centered Therapy*. Boston: Houghton Mifflin. 619 pp.

96. Hartlage, L. C. 1970. Subprofessional therapists' use of reinforcement versus traditional psychotherapeutic techniques with schizophrenics. *J. Consult. Clin. Psychol.* 34:181–83

97. Harway, N. I., Iker, H. P. 1969. Content analysis and psychotherapy. *Psychother. Theory Res. Pract.* 6: 97–104

98. Haskell, D., Pugatch, D., McNair, D. M. 1969. Time-limited psychotherapy for whom. *Arch. Gen. Psychiat.* 21:546–51

99. Heckel, R. V., Holmes, G. R., Rosecrans, C. J. 1971. A factor analytic study of process variables in group therapy. *J. Clin. Psychol.* 27:146–50

100. Hefele, T. J., Collingwood, T. R., Drasgow, J. 1970. Therapeutic facilitativeness as a dimension of effective living: a factor analytic study. *J. Clin. Psychol.* 26:121–23

101. Heinicke, C. M. 1969. Frequency of psychotherapeutic session as a factor affecting outcome: analysis of clinical ratings and test results. *J. Abnorm. Psychol.* 74:553–60

102. Heller, K. 1971. Laboratory interview research as an analogue to treatment. See Ref. 24, 36–74

103. Henry, W. E., Sims, J. H., Spray, S. L. 1971. *The Fifth Profession*. San Francisco: Jossey-Bass. 221 pp.

104. Hilgard, J. R., Straight, D. C., Moore, U. S. 1969. Better adjusted peers as resources in group therapy with adolescents. *J. Psychol.* 73:75–100

105. Hill, J. A. 1969. Therapist goals, patient aims and patient satisfaction in psychotherapy. *J. Clin. Psychol.* 25:455–59

106. Hill, J. A., Howard, K. I., Orlinsky, D. E. 1970. The therapist's experience of psychotherapy: some dimensions and determinants. *Multivar. Behav. Res.* 5:435–51

107. Hoehn-Saric, R., Frank, J. D., Stone, A. R., Imber, S. D. 1969. Prognosis in psychoneurotic patients. *Am. J. Psychother.* 23:252–59

108. Hoffnung, R. J., Stein, L. S. 1970. Responses of A and B subjects to normal, neurotic, schizophrenic, and ambiguous communications. *J. Consult. Clin. Psychol.* 34:327–32

109. Hollingshead, A. deB., Redlich, F. C. 1958. *Social Class and Mental Illness*. New York: Wiley. 442 pp.

110. Horton, M., Kriauciunas, R. 1970. Minnesota Multiphasic Personality Inventory differences between terminators and continuers in youth counseling. *J. Couns. Psychol.* 17: 98–101

111. Houts, P. S., MacIntosh, S., Moos, R. H. 1969. Patient-therapist interdependence: cognitive and behavioral. *J. Consult. Clin. Psychol.* 33:40–45

112. Howard, K. I., Krause, M. S., Orlinsky, D. E. 1969. Direction of affective influence in psychotherapy. *J. Consult. Clin. Psychol.* 33: 614–20

113. Howard, K. I., Orlinsky, D. E., Hill, J. A. 1968. The patient's experience of psychotherapy: some dimensions and determinants. *Multivar. Behav. Res.* Special Issue: 55–72

114. Howard, K. I., Orlinsky, D. E., Hill, J. A. 1969. Content of dialogue in psychotherapy. *J. Couns. Psychol.* 16:396–404

115. Howard, K. I., Orlinksy, D. E., Hill, J. A. 1969. The therapist's feelings in the therapeutic process. *J. Clin. Psychol.* 25:83–93

116. Howard, K. I., Orlinsky, D. E., Hill, J. A. 1970. Patient satisfactions as a function of patient-therapist pairing. *Psychother. Theory Res. Pract.* 7:130–34

117. Howard, K. I., Orlinsky, D. E., Hill, J. A. 1970. Affective experience in psychotherapy. *J. Abnorm. Psychol.* 75:267–75

118. Howard, K. I., Orlinsky, D. E., Trattner, J. H. 1970. Therapist orientation and patient experience in psychotherapy. *J. Couns. Psychol.* 17:263–70

119. Hurst, J. C., Weigel, R. G., Thatcher, R., Nyman, A. J. 1969. Counselor-client diagnostic agreement and perceived outcomes of counseling. *J. Couns. Psychol.* 16:421–26

120. Hurvitz, N. 1970. Peer self-help psy-

chotherapy groups and their implication for psychotherapy. *Psychother. Theory Res. Pract.* 7:41–49

121. Jansen, D. G., Robb, G. P. 1970. Differences between counseled and non-counseled students on the MMPI. *J. Clin. Psychol.* 26:391–93

122. Johnson, F. L. 1970. The importance of the psychotherapist: patient and therapist conceptions. *Diss. Abstr. Int.* 30:4373B

123. Jurjevich, R. M. 1968. Changes in psychiatric symptoms without psychotherapy. See Ref. 37, 190–200

124. Kadushin, C. 1969. *Why People Go To Psychiatrists.* New York: Atherton. 373 pp.

125. Kaplan, A. 1964. *The Counduct of Inquiry.* San Francisco: Chandler. 428 pp.

126. Karl, N. J., Abeles, N. 1969. Psychotherapy process as a function of the time segment sampled. *J. Consult. Clin. Psychol.* 33:207–12

127. Karon, B. P., Vandenbos, G. R. 1970. Experience, medication, and the effectiveness of psychotherapy with schizophrenics. *Brit. J. Psychiat.* 116:427–28

128. Karp, S. A., Kissin, B., Hustmyer, F. E. 1970. Field dependence as a predictor of alcoholic therapy dropouts. *J. Nerv. Ment. Dis.* 150:77–83

129. Kaswan, J., Love, L. R. 1969. Confrontation as a method of psychological intervention. *J. Nerv. Ment. Dis.* 148:224–37

130. Katkin, S., Ginsburg, M., Rifkin, M. J., Scott, J. T. 1971. Effectiveness of female volunteers in the treatment of outpatients. *J. Couns. Psychol.* 18:97–100

131. Kelley, J., Smits, S. J., Leventhal, R., Rhodes, R. 1970. Critique of the designs of process and outcome research. *J. Couns. Psychol.* 17:337–41

132. Kemp, D. E. 1969. The AB scale and attitudes toward patients: studies of a disappearing phenomenon. *Psychother. Theory Res. Pract.* 6:223–29

133. Kemp, D. E. 1970. Routinizing art: implications of research with the A-B scale for the practice of psychotherapy. *J. Am. Coll. Health Assoc.* 18:238–40

134. Kemp, D. E., Stephens, J. H. 1971. Which AB scale? a comparative analysis of several versions. *J. Nerv. Ment. Dis.* 152:23–30

135. Kiesler, D. J. 1966. Some myths of psychotherapy research and the search for a paradigm. *Psychol. Bull.* 65:110–36

136. Kiesler, D. J. 1971. Experimental designs in psychotherapy research. See Ref. 24, 36–74

137. Kiev, A., Ed. 1964. *Magic, Faith, and Healing.* Glencoe, Ill.: Free Press. 475 pp.

138. Klarman, H. E. 1969. Economic aspects of mental health manpower. See Ref. 1, 67–92

139. Krasner, L. 1971. The operant approach in behavior therapy. See Ref. 24, 612–52

140. Krause, M. S. 1966. Comparative effects on continuance of four experimental intake procedures. *Soc. Casework* 47:515–19

141. Krause, M. S. 1966. A cognitive theory of motivation for treatment. *J. Gen. Psychol.* 75:9–19

142. Krause, M. S. 1967. Behavioral indices of motivation for treatment. *J. Couns. Psychol.* 14:426–35

143. Krause, M. S. 1969. Construct validity for the evaluation of therapy outcomes. *J. Abnorm. Psychol.* 74:524–30

144. Laing, R. D. 1967. *The Politics of Experience.* New York: Pantheon. 138 pp.

145. Lang, P. J. 1971. The application of psychophysiological methods to the study of psychotherapy and behavior modification. See Ref. 24, 75–125

146. Lasswell, H. D. 1969. The politics of mental health objectives and manpower assets. See Ref. 1, 53–66

147. Lazarus, A. A., Davison, G. C. 1971. Clinical innovation in research and practice. See Ref. 24, 196–213

148. Leary, T. F. 1957. *Interpersonal Diagnosis of Personality.* New York: Ronald. 518 pp.

149. Lee, S. D., Temerlin, M. K. 1970. Social class, diagnosis, and prognosis for psychotherapy. *Psychother. Theory Res. Pract.* 7:181–85

150. Lennard, H. L., Bernstein, A. 1969. *Patterns in Human Interaction.* San Francisco: Jossey-Bass. 224 pp.

151. Lessing, E. E., Schilling, F. H. 1966. Relationship between treatment selection variables and treatment outcome in a child guidance clinic: an application of data-processing methods. *J. Am. Acad. Child Psychiat.* 5:313–48

152. Levitt, E. E. 1971. Research on psychotherapy with children. See Ref. 24, 474–95

153. Lewinsohn, P. M., Weinstein, M. S., Alper, T. 1970. A behavioral ap-

proach to the group treatment of depressed persons: a methodological contribution. *J. Clin. Psychol.* 26:525–32

154. Lomont, J. F., Gilner, F. H., Spector, N. J., Skinner, K. K. 1969. Group assertion training and group insight therapies. *Psychol. Rep.* 25:463–70

155. Luborsky, L., Auerbach, A. H. 1969. The symptom-context method. *J. Am. Psychoanal. Assoc.* 17:68–99

156. Luborsky, L., Spence, D. P. 1971. Quantitative research on psychoanalytic treatment. See Ref. 24, 403–38

157. Magoon, T. M., Golann, S. E., Freeman, R. W. 1969. *Mental Health Counselors at Work.* Elmsford, NY: Pergamon. 219 pp.

158. Marsden, G. 1971. Content analysis studies of psychotherapy: 1954 through 1968. See Ref. 24, 345–407

159. Matarazzo, J. D., Wiens, A. N., Matarazzo, R. G., Saslow, G. 1968. Speech and silence behavior in clinical psychotherapy and its laboratory correlates. In *Research in Psychotherapy*, ed. J. M. Shlien, 3:347–94. Washington, D. C.: Am. Psychol. Assoc. 618 pp.

160. Matarazzo, R. G. 1971. Research on the teaching and learning of psychotherapeutic skills. See Ref. 24, 895–924

161. May, P. R. A. 1971. Psychotherapy and ataraxic drugs. See Ref. 24, 495–540

162. Meltzoff, J., Kornreich, M. 1970. *Research in Psychotherapy.* New York: Atherton. 561 pp.

163. Mendelsohn, G. A., Rankin, N. O. 1969. Client-counselor compatibility and the outcome of counseling. *J. Abnorm. Psychol.* 74:157–63

164. Mihalick, R. E. 1970. Values and psychotherapy. *Diss. Abstr. Int.* 30: 4377B

165. Miller, R. L., Bloomberg, L. I. 1969. No therapy as a method of psychotherapy. *Psychother. Theory Res. Pract.* 6:49

166. Mintz, E. E. 1969. On the rationale of touch in psychotherapy. *Psychother. Theory Res. Pract.* 6:232–34

167. Mintz, J., Luborsky, L. 1970. P-technique factor analysis in psychotherapy: an illustration of a method. *Psychother. Theory Res. Pract.* 7:13–18

168. Mintz, J., Luborsky, L., Auerbach, A. H. 1971. Dimensions of psychotherapy: a factor-analytic study of ratings of psychotherapy sessions. *J. Consult. Clin. Psychol.* 36:106–20

169. Mitchell, K. M., Berenson, B. G. 1970. Differential use of confrontation by high and low facilitative therapists. *J. Nerv. Ment. Dis.* 151:303–9

170. Mitchell, K. M., Mitchell, R. M., Berenson, B. G. 1970. Therapist focus on client's significant others in psychotherapy. *J. Clin. Psychol.* 26:533–36

171. Mitchell, K. M., Namenek, T. M. 1970. A comparison of therapist and client social class. *Prof. Psychol.* 1:225–30

172. Mitchell, K. R. 1969. Repeated measures and the evaluation of change in the individual client during counseling. *J. Couns. Psychol.* 16:522–27

173. Moos, R. H., MacIntosh, S. 1970. Multivariate study of the patient-therapist system: a replication and extension. *J. Consult. Clin. Psychol.* 35:298–307

174. Mordock, J. B., Ellis, M. H., Greenstone, J. L. 1969. The effects of group and individual therapy on sociometric choice of disturbed institutionalized adolescents. *Int. J. Group Psychother.* 19:510–17

175. Mowrer, O. H. 1971. Peer groups and medication, the best "therapy" for professionals and laymen alike. *Psychother. Theory Res. Pract.* 8:44–54

176. Muehlberg, N., Pierce, R. M., Drasgow, J. 1969. A factor analysis of therapeutically facilitative conditions. *J. Clin. Psychol.* 25:93–95

177. Mueller, W. J. 1969. Patterns of behavior and their reciprocal impact in the family and in psychotherapy. *J. Couns. Psychol. Monogr.* 16:1–25

178. Mueller, W. J., Dilling, C. A. 1969. Studying interpersonal themes in psychotherapy research. *J. Couns. Psychol.* 16:50–58

179. Mullen, J., Abeles, N. 1971. Relationship of liking, empathy, and therapist's experience to outcome of therapy. *J. Couns. Psychol.* 18:39–43

180. Murray, E. J., Jacobson, L. I. 1971. The nature of learning in traditional and behavior psychotherapy. See Ref. 24, 709–47

181. Murrell, S. A. 1970. Intrafamily variables and psychotherapy outcome research. *Psychother. Theory Res. Pract.* 7:19–22

182. Opler, M. K. 1959. *Culture and Mental Health.* New York: Macmillan. 533 pp.

183. Opler, M. K. 1968. The social and cultural nature of mental illness

and its treatment. See Ref. 37, 280–91

184. Orlinsky, D. E., Howard, K. I. 1967. The good therapy hour. *Arch. Gen. Psychiat.* 16:621–32

185. Orlinsky, D. E., Howard, K. I. 1967. Dimensions of conjoint experience in psychotherapy relationships. *Proc. 75th Ann. Conv. APA*, 251–52

186. Orlinsky, D. E., Howard, K. I., Hill, J. A. 1970. The patient's concerns in psychotherapy. *J. Clin. Psychol.* 26:104–11

187. Ornston, P. S., Cicchetti, D. V., Towbin, A. P. 1970. Reliable changes in psychotherapy behavior among first-year psychiatric residents. *J. Abnorm. Psychol.* 75:7–11

188. Paredes, A., Gottheil, E., Tausig, T. N., Cornelison, F. S. 1969. Behavioral changes as a function of repeated self-observation. *J. Nerv. Ment. Dis.* 148:287–99

189. Parsons, T. 1951. *The Social System.* Glencoe, Ill.: Free Press. 575 pp.

190. Passons, W. R., Olsen, L. C. 1969. Relationship of counselor characteristics and empathic sensitivity. *J. Couns. Psychol.* 16:440–45

191. Patton, M. J. 1969. Attraction, discrepancy, and response to psychological treatment. *J. Couns. Psychol.* 16:317–24

192. Paul, G. L. 1969. Behavior modification research: design and tactics. In *Behavior Therapy: Appraisal and Status,* ed. C. M. Franks, 29–62. New York: McGraw. 730 pp.

193. Pesso, A. 1969. *Movement in Psychotherapy.* New York Univ. Press. 221 pp.

194. Phillips, D. L., Segal, B. E. 1969. Sexual status and psychiatric symptoms. *Am. Sociol. Rev.* 34:58–72

195. Piaget, J., Inhelder, B. 1969. *The Psychology of the Child.* New York: Basic Books. 173 pp.

196. Pierce, R. M., Drasgow, J. 1969. Nondirective reflection vs. conflict attention: an empirical evaluation. *J. Clin. Psychol.* 25:341–42

197. Pierce, R. M., Drasgow, J. 1969. Teaching facilitative interpersonal functioning to psychiatric inpatients. *J. Couns. Psychol.* 16:295–98

198. Pierce, R. M., Schauble, P. G. 1970. Graduate training of facilitative counselors: the effects of individual supervision. *J. Couns. Psychol.* 17:210–15

199. Pierce, R. M., Schauble, P. G. 1970. A note on the role of facilitative responsibility in the therapeutic relationship. *J. Clin. Psychol.* 26:250–52

200. Piper, W. E., Wogan, M. 1970. Placebo effect in psychotherapy. *J. Consult. Clin. Psychol.* 34:447

201. Portes, A. 1971. On the emergence of behavior therapy in modern society. *J. Consult. Clin. Psychol.* 36:303–13

202. Price, L. Z., Iverson, M. A. 1969. Students' perceptions of counselors with varying statuses and role behaviors in the initial interview. *J. Couns. Psychol.* 16:469–75

203. Ramsey-Klee, D. M., Eiduson, B. T. 1969. A comparative study of two child guidance clinic populations. *J. Am. Acad. Child Psychiat.* 8:493–516

204. Ravid, R. S. 1969. Effect of group therapy on long term individual patients. *Diss. Abstr. Int.* 30:2427B

205. Razin, A. M. 1971. A-B variable in psychotherapy: a critical review. *Psychol. Bull.* 75:1–21

206. Rice, D. G. 1969. Patient sex differences and selection for individual psychotherapy. *J. Nerv. Ment. Dis.* 148:124–33

207. Rice, L. N. 1965. Therapist's style of participation and case outcome. *J. Consult. Psychol.* 29:155–60

208. Rieff, P. 1968. *The Triumph of the Therapeutic.* New York: Harper & Row. 274 pp.

209. Rioch, M. J. 1970. Should psychotherapists do therapy? *J. Contemp. Psychother.* 3:61–64

210. Roe, A. 1969. Individual motivation and personal factors in career choice. See Ref. 1, 131–48

211. Rogers, C. R. 1970. *Carl Rogers on Encounter Groups.* New York: Harper & Row. 172 pp.

212. Rogow, A. A. 1970. *The Psychiatrists.* New York: Putnam. 317 pp.

213. Rosenberg, S., Prola, M., Meyer, E. J., Zuckerman, M., Bellak, L. 1968. Factors related to improvement in brief psychotherapy. See Ref. 37, 82–100

214. Rosenblum, L. 1969. Telephone therapy. *Psychother. Theory Res. Pract.* 6:241–42

215. Rosenfeld, E., Frankel, N., Esman, A. H. 1969. A model of criteria for evaluating progress in children undergoing psychotherapy. *J. Am. Acad. Child Psychiat.* 8:193–228

216. Roth, R. M., Berenbaum, H. L., Garfield, S. J. 1969. Massed time limit therapy. *Psychother. Theory Res. Pract.* 6:54–56

217. Ryan, W., Ed. 1969. *Distress in the City.* Cleveland: Case Western Reserve Univ. Press. 270 pp.

218. Sabot, L. M., Peck, R., Raskin, J. 1969. The waiting room society. *Arch. Gen. Psychiat.* 21:25–32

219. Saenger, G. 1970. Patterns of change among "treated" and "untreated" patients seen in psychiatric community mental health clinics. *J. Nerv. Ment. Dis.* 150:37–50

220. Scheflen, A. E. 1965. Quasi-courtship behavior in psychotherapy. *Psychiatry* 28:245–57

221. Schofield, W. 1964. *Psychotherapy: The Purchase of Friendship.* Englewood Cliffs, N. J.: Prentice-Hall. 186 pp.

222. Schonfield, J., Stone, A. R., Hoehn-Saric, R., Imber, S. D., Pande, S. K. 1969. Patient-therapist convergence and measures of improvement in short-term psychotherapy. *Psychother. Theory Res. Pract.* 6:267–73.

223. Schutz, W. C. 1958. *FIRO: A Three Dimensional Theory of Interpersonal Behavior.* New York: Rinehart. 267 pp.

224. Schwartz, A. H. et al 1970. Influence of therapeutic task orientation on patient and therapist satisfaction in group psychotherapy. *Int. J. Group Psychother.* 20:460–69

225. Scott, R. W., Kemp, D. E. 1971. The A-B scale and empathy, warmth, genuineness, and depth of self-exploration. *J. Abnorm. Psychol.* 77:49–51

226. Segal, B. 1970. A-B distinction and therapeutic interaction. *J. Consult. Clin. Psychol.* 34:442–46

227. Seligman, M., Sterne, D. M. 1969. Verbal behavior in therapist-led, leaderless, and alternating group psychotherapy sessions. *J. Couns. Psychol.* 16:325–28

228. Shapiro, A. K. 1971. Placebo effects in medicine, psychotherapy, and psychoanalysis. See Ref. 24, 439–73

229. Sharp, W. H., Marra, H. A. 1971. Factors related to classification of client problem, number of counseling sessions, and trends of client problems. *J. Couns. Psychol.* 18:117–22

230. Smeltzer, W. 1969. Time orientation and time perspective in psychotherapy. *Diss. Abstr. Int.* 29:3922B

231. Speck, R. V., Rueveni, U. 1969. Network therapy—a developing concept. *Fam. Proc.* 8:182–91

232. Spilken, A. Z., Jacobs, M. A., Muller, J. J., Knitzer, J. 1969. Personality characteristics of therapists: description of relevant variables and examination of conscious prefer-ences. *J. Consult. Clin. Psychol.* 33:317–26

233. Srole, L. et al 1962. *Mental Health in the Metropolis.* New York: McGraw. 428 pp.

234. Stampfl, T. G., Lewis, D. J. 1969. Learning theory: an aid to dynamic therapeutic practice. In *The Relation of Theory to Practice in Psychotherapy,* ed. L. D. Eron, R. Callahan, 85–114. Chicago: Aldine. 176 pp.

235. Strauss, A. L., Ed. 1956. *The Social Psychology of George Herbert Mead.* Univ. Chicago Press. 296 pp.

236. Strong, S. R. 1970. Causal attribution in counseling and psychotherapy. *J. Couns. Psychol.* 17:388–99

237. Ibid 1971. Experimental laboratory research in counseling. 18:106–10

238. Strupp, H. H., Bergin, A. E. 1969. Some empirical and conceptual bases for coordinated research in psychotherapy. *Int. J. Psychiat.* 7:18–90

239. Strupp, H. H., Bergin, A. E. 1969. *A Bibliography of Research in Psychotherapy: A Critical Review of Issues, Trends, and Evidence.* Washington, D. C.: Nat. Inst. Ment. Health. 167 pp.

240. Strupp, H. H., Fox, R. E., Lessler, K. 1969. *Patients View Their Psychotherapy.* Baltimore: Johns Hopkins Press. 220 pp.

241. Stuart, R. B. 1970. *Trick or Treatment: How and When Psychotherapy Fails.* Champaign, Ill.: Research Press. 201 pp.

242. Subotnik, L. 1971. Spontaneous remission: fact or artifact? *Psychol. Bull.* 75. In press

243. Szasz, T. S. 1970. *Ideology and Insanity.* Garden City, NY: Doubleday. 265 pp.

244. Targow, J. G., Zweber, R. B. 1969. Participants' reactions to treatment in married couples' group. *Int. J. Group Psychother.* 19:221–25

245. Thelen, M. H. 1969. Repression-sensitization: its relation to adjustment and seeking psychotherapy among college students. *J. Consult. Clin. Psychol.* 33:161–65

246. Thompson, A., Zimmerman, R. 1969. Goals of counseling: whose? when? *J. Couns. Psychol.* 16:121–25

247. Tokar, J. T., Stefflre, V. 1969. A technique for studying an individual and his language: part I. Techniques for eliciting patterns of use of an individual's key words. *Psychother. Theory Res. Pract.* 6:105–8

248. Tosi, D. J. 1970. Dogmatism within the counselor-client dyad. *J. Couns. Psychol.* 17:284–89
249. Truax, C. B. 1970. Therapist's evaluative statements and patient outcome in psychotherapy. *J. Clin. Psychol.* 26:536–38
250. Ibid. Length of therapist response, accurate empathy and patient improvement, 539–41
251. Truax, C. B. 1970. Effects of client-centered psychotherapy with schizophrenic patients: nine years pretherapy and nine years posttherapy hospitalization. *J. Consult. Clin. Psychol.* 35:417–22
252. Truax, C. B. 1971. Degree of negative transference occurring in group psychotherapy and client outcome in juvenile delinquents. *J. Clin. Psychol.* 27:132–36
253. Truax, C. B., Lister, J. L. 1970. Effects of therapist persuasive potency in group psychotherapy. *J. Clin. Psychol.* 26:396–97
254. Truax, C. B., Mitchell, K. M. 1971. Research on certain therapist interpersonal skills in relation to process and outcome. See Ref. 24, 299–344
255. Truax, C. B., Wargo, D. G. 1969. Effects of vicarious therapy pretraining and alternate sessions on outcome in group psychotherapy with outpatients. *J. Consult. Clin. Psychol.* 33:440–47
256. Truax, C. B., Wargo, D. G., Volksdorf, N. R. 1970. Antecedents to outcome in group counseling with institutionalized juvenile delinquents: effects of therapeutic conditions, patient self-exploration, alternate sessions, and vicarious therapy pretraining. *J. Abnorm. Psychol.* 76:235–42
257. Truax, C. B., Wittmer, J. 1971. The effects of therapist focus on patient anxiety source and the interaction with therapist level of accurate empathy. *J. Clin. Psychol.* 27: 297–99
258. Ibid. Patient non-personal reference during psychotherapy and therapeutic outcome, 300–2
259. Truax, C. B., Wittmer, J., Wargo, D. G. 1971. Effects of the therapeutic conditions of accurate empathy, non-possessive warmth, and genuineness on hospitalized mental patients during group therapy. *J. Clin. Psychol.* 27:137–42
260. Uhlenhuth, E. H., Covi, L. 1969. Subjective change with the initial

261. Uhlenhuth, E. H., Lipman, R. S., Covi, L. 1969. Combined pharmacotherapy and psychotherapy. *J. Nerv. Ment. Dis.* 148:52–64
262. Ullman, L. P. 1969. Behavior therapy as a social movement. See Ref. 192, 495–523
263. Urban, H. B., Ford, D. H. 1971. Some historical and conceptual perspectives on psychotherapy and behavior change. See Ref. 24, 3–35
264. Vandenbos, G. R., Karon, B. P. 1971. Pathogenesis: a new therapist personality dimension related to therapeutic effectiveness. *J. Pers. Assess.* 35:252–60
265. Varble, D. L., Landfield, A. W. 1969. Validity of the self-ideal discrepancy criterion measure for success in psychotherapy—a replication. *J. Couns. Psychol.* 16:150–56
266. Verinis, J. S. 1970. Therapeutic effectiveness of untrained volunteers with chronic patients. *J. Consult. Clin. Psychol.* 34:152–55
267. Vernallis, F. F., Shipper, J. C., Butler, D. C., Tomlinson, T. M. 1970. Saturation group psychotherapy in a weekend clinic: an outcome study. *Psychother. Theory Res. Pract.* 7: 144–52
268. Weakland, J. H. 1969. Anthropology, psychiatry, and communication. *Am. Anthropol.* 71:880–88
269. Weckowicz, T. E., Yonge, K. A., Cropley, A. J., Muir, W. 1971. Objective therapy predictors in depression: a multivariate approach. *J. Clin. Psychol.* 27:3–29
270. Weintraub, W., Aronson, H. 1969. Is classical psychoanalysis a dangerous procedure? *J. Nerv. Ment. Dis.* 149:224–28
271. Wessman, A. E., Ricks, D. F. 1966. *Mood and Personality.* New York: Holt, Rinehart & Winston. 317 pp.
272. White, A. M., Fichtenbaum, L., Dollard, J. 1969. Measurement of what the patient learns from psychotherapy. *J. Nerv. Ment. Dis.* 149:281–93
273. Wogan, M. 1969. Investigation of a measure of empathic ability. *Psychother. Theory Res. Pract.* 6:109–13
274. Wolff, W. M. 1970. Private practice research. *J. Consult. Clin. Psychol.* 34:281–86
275. Zuk, G. H. 1971. Family therapy during 1964–1970. *Psychother. Theory Res. Pract.* 8:90–97

interview. *Am. J. Psychother.* 23: 415–27

ESTHETICS 192

Irvin L. Child

Department of Psychology, Yale University

Psychological esthetics, broadly defined, is so diverse that major progress in the 11 years since Pratt's review (118) is hard to summarize briefly. A handbook chapter I wrote midway in this period (13) I have taken as sufficient coverage of the years before 1965. I have taken advantage, too, of D. E. Berlyne's kindness in letting me read the manuscript of his book on *Aesthetics and Psychobiology* (6), scheduled for publication a few months earlier than this article. While the book is first of all an original contribution to theory, and deals with research primarily as it is relevant to that contribution, it describes much of the most significant work in experimental esthetics. Therefore, quite against the bias associated with some of my own research, I have almost totally neglected experimental esthetics in order to expand here on other kinds of recent work to which Berlyne's book does not give so much attention. Moreover, I have included and described more fully work I thought likely to be novel to many readers of this article, altogether omitting or alluding only briefly to much work of equal importance already widely known by American psychologists or easily located through *Psychological Abstracts*. For an up-to-date report of other recent work, see Lindauer's forthcoming review (83a) of the current broadening of experimental esthetics and its possible effects on general psychology.

For readers of French, a brief but excellent introduction to psychological esthetics has been provided by Francès (37). It includes developmental studies and research on personality correlates of response to art, as well as experimental esthetics. Nothing of equal breadth seems to have appeared in English during this period, but several important general publications should be mentioned here at the outset. Two meetings of the International Society for Empirical Aesthetics have been followed by publication of the papers presented—for the 1965 meeting, in French (35), and for the 1966 meeting, in Italian (49). Arnheim (1) has brought together a diversified volume of his papers—with principal emphasis on problems of visual art, as might be expected, but with a wide range of more general discussion. Burnshaw (8) has offered a philosophy of the arts—addressed mostly to literature but intended to have broader application—which is based largely on ideas from biology, psychology, and the social sciences. Machotka (90), in discussing educational techniques that might help stimulate esthetic sensitivity, argues for the practical relevance of the findings of psychological esthetics. Although

669

these findings suggest that direct efforts to increase esthetic sensitivity may be unsuccessful, Machotka derives a number of ingenious ideas for indirect approaches that seem much more likely to succeed. Gardner has published a series of papers on general issues in psychology of the arts. In one (41) he finds in Erikson's concepts of mode and vector the basis for a very provocative consideration of all the arts in relation to developmental psychology. In a general psychological consideration of style in the arts (44), he compares across various art forms the stylistic aspect of creating art with the perception of style in art, concluding that the centrality of style and the methods appropriate for measuring sensitivity to style vary from one art form to another. In a third paper (45), Gardner argues very lucidly the thesis that differences between problem solving in art and in science lie in relative emphasis on execution vs conceptualization, and discusses the implications of this thesis for educational practices in art and science.

PROBLEMS IN THE COGNITIVE PSYCHOLOGY OF ART
VISUAL ART

Perception and cognition of visual art.—In his book setting forth a new framework for understanding perception, Gibson (51) includes a chapter on perception of visual art. He views perception as an activity of the whole organism, obtaining information about the world by detecting invariances of texture, form, energy gradients, etc. This is an enormously clarifying replacement for the older view of perception as a separate process of inference, for each modality, from sensation. His view makes clear why a painter must learn, often with difficulty, what colors and brightnesses will serve to create the illusions he wishes; perception is based on complex relationships, whereas the painter must work directly with single brush strokes. The older view of perception as based on sensation, Gibson in effect argues, could have arisen only in a culture with a tradition of representational painting; it is a product of reflections on the technique of painting, not of reflections on visual experience. In a subsequent paper (52), Gibson has considered further, and with the same clarity, the implications his general theory of perception has for understanding the perception of pictures. He has not attempted, however, to carry his account beyond the problem of iconic representation; consideration of noniconic aspects of the meaning of visual art in relation to this new view of iconic aspects remains for the future.

A Gibsonian approach provides the theoretical base for a program of research by Kennedy on picture perception, which is just beginning to reach publication (73). For the old idea that in perceiving incomplete pictures (as in the Street test) the viewer "fills in" the gaps, Kennedy is able even in this first paper to substitute solid understanding. An aspect of picture perception first studied long ago—the temporal aspect indexed by eye fixation—has received renewed and fruitful attention in recent years from Molnar (104) and from Mackworth & Morandi (92).

Arnheim (2) draws from psychology of art suggestions for modifying aspects of general psychology. In this as in his previous writings on visual art, he argues for viewing perception as laden with meaning—as including, for example, recognition of an abstraction represented in concrete visual form. Here he generalizes the implications of this analysis, correcting the exaggerated dichotomy psychology has inherited from philosophy, between the supposed concrete specificity of perceptual experience and the supposed abstract generality of thought. His account of visual thinking contributes importantly to general psychology and also provides a base for further exploration of the thinking of artists in creating visual art.

Several lines of research on visual perception and memory require notice because of their special relevance, direct or indirect, to psychology of visual art:

1. A series of studies have shown that people have an astonishingly large capacity to remember pictures. Several thousand pictures, viewed for only a few seconds each, can later be recognized as familiar, with a low frequency of error (Standing, Conezio & Haber 134). Applying this method to memory of faces and of their expression, Galper & Hochberg (39) use it as a means of studying how faces are perceived.

2. A variety of techniques from experimental psychology have been adapted to exploring the problem of how pictures are perceived; Kolers (78) describes and discusses several of them. In an experiment on apparent motion where the two successive stimuli are of different shape, Kolers & Pomerantz (79) show that the visual system has a very important creative aspect even at a relatively simple level of functioning.

3. Walk (140) and Tighe (136) have shown that recognition of distinctions of style among artists of a single school can be learned rapidly by college students in experiments of the standard concept-formation pattern.

Working with children 4 years of age and older, Walk et al (141) conducted similar experiments in response to art more diversified in style, and with training reduced to merely calling attention to the similarity of three diverse pictures by each artist. On this relatively easy task, they found that the greatest improvement in ability to discriminate style comes between ages 4 and 6, while the greatest improvement in ability to describe the discriminated styles comes between 6 and 8.

On a more difficult task of discriminating artistic styles, Gardner (40) found no significant improvement from age 6 to 8, or even to 11, but marked improvement from age 11 to 14. In another experiment with subjects about 6, 11, and 19 years of age, Gardner & Gardner (46) found very little evidence of increase in spontaneous groupings by style rather than subject matter where both choices were available. This result agrees with and extends what Frechtling & Davidson (38) found in studying the span from 5 to 12 years of age. It is the ability to group by style when instructed to do so that increases with age, according to Gardner & Gardner. In this instance, they found a larger increase in sensitivity between ages 6 and 11 than between 11 and 19. Evidently the course of development here is influenced by a number of variables which need to be disentangled before sensitivity to style can be confidently related to general principles of cognitive development.

Individual differences in sensitivity to art style were measured by a set of materials devised by Maslow; a preliminary study of this measure, exploring its relation to personality variables and obtaining rather inconclusive results with a small sample, has been reported by Morant & Maslow (105). Nidorf & Argabrite (106) have found individual differences in understanding pictures positively correlated with two other variables—accuracy of physiognomic perception, and a measure of cognitive complexity.

Meaning of elements used in visual art.—A number of studies have been concerned with the connotative meaning of colors. As the studies have been directed at a variety of specific problems, and have thus used highly diverse materials, their details are not easily compared. Williams, Morland & Underwood (147), with special interest in the meaning of color words used to identify human races, have used ten names of colors (an earlier study in the same series had found close agreement between judgments for names and judgments for corresponding color samples). Hogg (57), Tannenbaum (135), and Oyama, Tanaka & Chiba (111) have all used color samples, but not a consistent set. Smets (132) seems to be the only recent student of color meanings whose interest directly grows out of problems of art. She has investigated simultaneously the connotative meaning of the six principal colors (maximally saturated), six geometrical figures, and six concepts which certain artistic traditions have asserted to be matched, each one with a particular color and figure. A hundred university students judged the 18 stimuli on 30 semantic-differential scales derived from art students' associations. Some of the traditional associations of meaning were strongly confirmed, and others failed to appear. The results are presented in great detail, so that various specific questions can be answered by consulting her tables.

Despite the diversity, some broad comparisons can be made. These studies add to previous evidence that connotative meanings of colors are not entirely arbitrary conventions, for uniformities in them appear among people of varied background and age in diverse countries (including Japan, China, and India, as well as several Western countries). Which connotative meanings do vary with exactly which variables of artistic or general culture, and the significance of these issues for understanding art, will not be resolved unless future research involves much more uniformity of approach and more guidance by distinctive interest in esthetics than has characterized the work done up to now.

Recent years have also seen the beginning of systematic study of posture and movement, a visual component of the language of drama and dance as well as of the completely visual arts. Knapp (75) has explored the meaning of variations in the relative position and posture of two silhouetted figures. Hays (56) has studied the effects on meaning of experimental variations in the speed of showing a single film of dance. Lomax, Bartenieff & Paulay (86, pp. 222–73) have developed a system of analyzing dance style especially for cross-cultural comparisons; in their account of the system and of the relation of dance style to song style are many suggestions about the meanings conveyed by posture and movement. In developing a general account of the expressive meaning of bodily movement and position, Spiegel & Machotka (133) report on college students' interpretations of these aspects of several well-known paintings, and also on the effects of systematically varying posture and gaze in outline drawings of single figures and groups.

Meaning of works of visual art.—Psychological study of problems in the meaning of visual art has continued to be largely directed at determining whether artistically naive viewers show any agreement among themselves in judging meaning, and whether their judgments correspond with the artist's intent. Lindauer (83) has tested these issues by asking college students to match abstract paintings with possible titles. Some agreement emerges among the viewers, clearly indicating some uniformity of meaning, but he finds no tendency for naive viewers to pick the title assigned by the painter. Siddiqi & Thieme (129), using various types of painting, obtained semantic-differential judgments from the artists themselves, from art students, and from psychology students; the latter two groups showed substantial agreement with each other and little with judgments by those who painted the pictures. (Some of this difference, at least, can be ascribed to the fact that one person's judgments are less stable than the pooled judgments of a large group.) These and other similar studies demonstrate that communication of connotative meaning from artist to viewer is far less dependable and complete than some people might suppose; they do not suggest that such communication is absent. Indirect support for such a view comes in a further experiment reported by Siddiqi & Thieme in the same article. Though naive students, when asked for associations to paintings, give few that are formal (i.e. referring to color, form, or composition), they are able, when presented with the art students' formal associations, to match them appropriately with the paintings. (This fact is reminiscent of Gardner & Gardner's finding cited earlier that with increasing age people may not increase in tendency to sort art by style, yet do increase in ability to sort by style when instructed to do so.)

The problem here in comparing artist (or expert) with naive viewer lies partly, as Siddiqi & Thieme point out, in the naive viewer's lack of command over an appropriate technical vocabulary. The use in art psychology of a technique which might avoid this problem has been pointed out by Mirels & Efland (103). They had subjects sort abstract paintings freely into sets; from the 2-point scale for pair similarity implied by each subject's sorting (i.e. a pair either were or were not placed in the same group), they proceeded with multidimensional scaling. Thus completely nonverbal procedures can yield measures of the meaning found in pictures, permitting comparison among individuals or among groups. This nonverbal approach, applying multidimensional scaling to judgments of undefined similarity-dissimilarity of paired works, has been applied to representational painting by Skager, Schultz & Klein (130) and by Goude, Lindén & Lundström (53), identifying dimensions of meaning which can then be interpreted. Only a little more demanding of the judges' vocabulary is the technique of having works rated or judged on semantic-differential or other similar scales. Choynowski (17) and Kapp (76) have recently applied this technique to paintings, and Knapp has used it to obtain an objective characterization of style change through the productive years of two single artists, Cézanne and Picasso. In the one test so far available—concerned with music rather than visual art—these two approaches to identifying dimensions seem to yield similar results (Nordenstreng 107).

MUSIC

Perception and cognition of music.—English and American psychologists have given relatively little attention recently to music perception. Shuter (128), in a book principally on musical ability and its measurement, reviews some of the earlier research on music perception. Fundamental problems have been considered in two recent American articles. Deutsch (28) has suggested a neural mechanism that could account for the specific processes of abstraction required in music perception. Creel, Boomsliter & Powers (19) have presented a variety of evidence that perception of a tone is an active construction, dependent upon expectation and recurrence, and they argue that such a view is essential to progress in understanding musical perception and auditory perception in general. At a higher level of complexity, meanwhile, the musicologist Meyer has continued to work toward psychological understanding of musical perception and cognition, notably in several chapters of his recent book (99).

The tradition of distinguished pioneering work in France on perception of music, established earlier by Francès (34), has been continued in recent developmental research by Zenatti (150) and by Imberty (62, 63).

Zenatti's research (150) falls into three parts. 1. Polyphonic perception. Polyphonic passages in two, three, or four voices, played on an organ, were recorded; as a child heard them, he was to signal to the experimenter when he could identify a melody. Melodies of higher voice were the more often and the more speedily recognized, and the difference increased with the number of voices. Subjects aged 7 to 8 were already able to recognize melodies; but those $8\frac{1}{2}$ to 10 were much better, and those 10 to 12 somewhat better still. With increasing age through these years, the advantage of higher voices in speed of melody detection became smaller but did not disappear. 2. Melody perception and acculturation in tonality. Despite care in adapting procedures to age, attempts to discriminate between slight change and exact repetition of a melody did not reliably exceed chance until above the age of 8. At all ages where performance was above chance, it was better if the melody was probable within our tonal system than if improbable; acculturation in tonality thus seems to be effective early. 3. Intensive study of musical perception in a dozen 6-year-olds. Clear evidence was found of perception of pitch, harmony, and rhythm, and a strong suggestion of large individual differences already at this age. Zenatti places her findings in a Piagetian framework and argues that a developmental understanding of musical perception has important implications for musical education.

In children 7 to 12 and in college students, Imberty (62) has studied response both to a variety of musical intervals and to differing harmonized versions of a melody. He concludes that physically different patterns of sound are recognized early, but that any concept like consonance is from the start a syntactic concept dependent upon acquaintance with a musical tradition. Interpreting his findings in relation to general cognitive development, he sees the child's musical perception dominated by melody—i.e. changes in the total pattern of sound from one moment to another—with a concept of harmony emerging only when separate components of momentary sound are differentiated. In a monograph which I have not yet seen but am familiar with through a summary, Imberty (63) carries further this developmental interpretation of the child's gradual acquisition of tonal structure, presenting it as a realistic substitute for the old tendency to consider consonance either biologically or socially determined; it is an individual attainment influenced by both kinds of factors.

Gardner (43) has pursued a developmental approach in studying sensitivity to musical style. A subject listened to two 15-second extracts of music and then judged whether they were from the same piece of music. By a carefully prepared plan, they were actually sometimes from the same piece, sometimes from a single historical period, and sometimes from differing periods. The youngest subjects were 6 years old, and even they showed some discrimination; the largest improvement seemed to come between 8 and 11. In a simpler task relevant to music, that of immediately reproducing a rhythmic pattern of tapping, Gardner (42) found the largest improvement between ages 6 and 8, with a sizeable improvement also between 8 and 11.

Meaning of music —This period has seen the publication of two general reviews of theory and research on musical meaning guided by psychoanalytic theory. One by Michel (100), published in French, attends almost exclusively to psychoanalytic writings; the other, by Noy (108), attempts more integration with other psychological approaches. Similar integration characterizes the passages on music in Ehrenzweig's strikingly original work (32) on artistic perception and creation. Tension in music is the specific topic of a psychoanalytic paper by Miller (101); its treatment shows some similarities to Leonard Meyer's more cognitive approach, but adds psychodynamic elements.

Some of the psychodynamic meaning of music may derive from the words sung to the music. A notable earlier paper by Hannett (55) had elaborated this point with clinical examples and with content analysis of lyrics from the most popular songs in the United States between 1900 and 1950. Recently Rockland (122) has demonstrated the validity of this argument with details from the therapy record of one patient. A content analysis by Carey (11) extends the historical treatment to the lyrics of rock music.

Allied to a cognitive rather than to a psychodynamic theory is recent research by Jakobovits (67) and by Bush & Pease (10) on generation and satiation of meaning as a basis for changed liking for music on repeated hearing. Other recent research on musical meaning has been less theoretical. White & Butler (144), for example, have demonstrated that the semantic-differential technique may be used in assessing the meaning for nonexperts of brief musical extracts. Using the same technique, Edmonston (31) provides some direct evidence that recognition of connotative meaning in music is to some extent cross-cultural and independent of specific training. Playing to various U.S. groups two versions of an Indian kriti, he found judgments of potency and activity were significantly different for the two versions and that this differentiation did not significantly differ according to musical training or familiarity with Indian music. Without hearing the particular music, I cannot tell whether to be surprised by this very specific finding; it does at least refute possible extremes of cultural relativism and argue for the value of detailed study of how much universality is to be found in musical meaning.

A considerable degree of transcultural uniformity in emotional meaning is also expected from a view of music as temporal forms resembling the forms of emotional experience. This view, and the implied expectation of some degree of universality, have been stated by Pratt in the introduction written for a new edition (119) of his classic work on the meaning of music. New developments in measurement techniques may offer opportunity for expanding and testing the implications of this view. Clynes (18) describes a way of distinguishing among thoughts of the various emotions by having a subject express an emotion in finger pressure, and finds the technique useful in studying the emotional meaning of music. He claims, for instance, that the general patterns of different composers' work as one person understands them, or different persons' interpretations of a single composition, can be distinguished by measurements obtained in this way.

LITERATURE

Perception and cognition of literature and of its elements.—Olson (110) views the understanding of language as a process of perception rather than of response. The meaning of a word is the percept of the intended referent relative to a set of alternatives, he says, and "understanding a sentence causes the restructuring of one's perceptual information." This view is allied to Gibson's interpretation of perception, placing similar emphasis on detection of what is given from outside rather than on construction by the knower. The stress on possible alternatives is parallel to Garner's similar stress (48) in dealing with goodness of patterns, visual and auditory. Olson, Gibson, and Garner seem to be ranged here against Osgood's response theory of meaning, and against Arnheim's view of perception as itself a process of construction rather than detection. In their very different ways, the views of Osgood and of Arnheim have influenced thinking and research in art psychology. The future will show whether these perceptual interpretations of meaning will have a similar fruitfulness.

Meaning of literature and of its elements.—Even closer to immediate relevance to esthetics is Wickens' account (145) of applying to the problem of meaning techniques of laboratory study of memory. When sets of words sharing some features of form or meaning are successively memorized, performance declines. If a set lacking one of these features is next memorized, performance may or may not improve; where this release from proactive inhibition does occur, it provides objective evidence that the given feature had been employed in encoding words of the previous sets. Since the encoding process is mostly not conscious, the attempt to study it by introspection led to frustration a half century ago; today pursuit can be resumed. The methods Wickens describes most obviously lend themselves to studying dimensions of meaning in single words, and the findings of such research may have relevance for esthetics. If similar methods can be adapted to study words in context, or to study larger units, then they should be extremely valuable in research on literary meaning.

Charles Mauron's series of major publications in the psychoanalytic study of literature continued with the posthumous publication of a detailed study of Racine's *Phèdre* (96), a demonstration that psychocriticism (as Mauron termed it) can enrich our understanding of a single text. Psychologists are—at least as psychologists—likely to be more excited by Mauron's earlier works, directed at attacking general issues through methods of systematic comparison familiar to clinical psychologists. Mauron's approach is similar to that of McCurdy's several earlier studies of single authors, but Mauron is less concerned with objectification of method and uses psychoanalytic theory more. He compares the various works of an author, looking behind the superficial specificities for underlying recurrences of image, character type, and theme. He arrives both at a notion of fundamental similarity in the works of an author and at a picture of development through the author's years of writing. His subjects have been French dramatists of the 17th century and French poets of the last century. He is reluctant to venture generalizations, but those the reader tentatively extracts are likely to be of great interest for the psychology of art. Only one of Mauron's books (95), unfortunately, has thus far been translated into English. For readers of French, an excellent account of his work and of its origins in Freud has recently been published by Mehlman (98).

Norman Holland, who had earlier published an exhaustive, balanced, and synthesizing account of psychoanalytic writings on Shakespeare and his works (58), has now published a general psychological treatise on *The Dynamics of Literary Response* (59), based on psychoanalytic theory. His argument develops from a succession of careful analyses of well-known texts (supplemented by a few analyses of cinema). He goes far beyond the usual application of psychoanalytic theory to interpretation of themes and characters, applying it also to clarifying problems of literary form and of word meaning in relation to theme and form. He pushes on, finally, to speculation about long-range effects on personality of the reading of literature. The book is richly suggestive of possible, though difficult, research that might in the future be done to test the validity of the views put forth about interaction between reader and literature.

In many psychiatric and psychoanalytic journals, the application of psychodynamics to the interpretation of literature and drama has continued in numerous articles on particular authors or works and occasional articles of greater breadth. I have the impression that this work tends to be better than in earlier years—perhaps because there is no longer need to demonstrate the relevance of psychodynamics, and writers are therefore freer to devote their energies to setting a psychodynamic view in a fuller context. Meanwhile the use of psychodynamic ideas in the journals of literary criticism has continued; one journal, for example, *Literature and Psychology*, is largely devoted to it. To the earlier anthologies of psychoanalytic criticism have been added two new volumes (21, 93), and one (21) begins with an excellent general essay by Crews, who seems to be as skilled at practicing as he is at parodying psychoanalytic criticism (20). From the small sample I have read of the numerous analyses by members of the critical and the psychological professions, I can only select a few examples to illustrate some of the recent developments.

1. Psychodynamic interpretation of form, conspicuous in the Holland book already mentioned, is the topic of a paper by Bush (9). He reviews efforts by psychoanalysts, beginning with Freud, to apply psychodynamic principles to artistic form rather than to content alone, and finds modern ego psychology especially helpful.

2. As psychodynamic theory itself changes, so—with a time lag—does psychodynamic interpretation of literature. H. R. Wolf (148) brings to a recent interpretation of E. A. Robinson's poetry, for instance, not only ideas from orthodox analysis but also from recent ego-oriented analysis and from existentialist psychiatry. In a book by van Kaam & Healy (137), existentialist thought is brought to bear on understanding five fictional characters—from Shakespeare's Angelo in *Measure for Measure* to Graham Greene's Querry in *A Burnt-out Case*. The authors also consider the influence of literature on the reader. An existentialist approach to the never-ending task of interpreting Shakespeare's *Hamlet* leads Varga & Fye (138) to some surprising and interesting new points.

3. Litowitz & Newman (84) find that many characters in theatre of the

absurd closely parallel the diagnostic category of borderline personality. They argue—as have others in the past, interpreting other literary movements—that the playwrights are thus presenting forms of psychopathology especially common in their time.

PSYCHOLOGY OF THE ARTIST
The Process of Artistic Creation

Ehrenzweig (32) has continued his earlier analysis of the creative activity of artists, drawing on both psychoanalytic and Gestalt theory. He modifies Gestalt theory by stressing that structured perception is not innately given but is a gradual development, that the achieved differentiation is open to dedifferentiation, and that it is possible to perceive and to think at several different levels of structured differentiation more or less simultaneously. He modifies psychoanalytic theory in ways related to this. What is unconscious is based not just on censorship but on degree of differentiation. We are aware of differentiated structure, including bizarre elements coming from the unconscious and dedifferentiated structure, but not of the dedifferentiated structure itself. Ehrenzweig views primary process in the adult as a much more active and regular participant than is suggested by the concept of regression in the service of the ego. Creative activity "does not merely control the regression towards the primary process, but also the work of the primary process itself," and this is so intrinsic in Ehrenzweig's view of the autonomous rhythm of ego activity that he does not consider "regression" an apt term. Ehrenzweig considers his ideas the key to further progress in understanding artistic creativity and the perception of art. He is little oriented toward the problem of observational test, but cites Charles Fisher's experiments on effects of subliminal visual stimulation as an example of evidence favoring his views.

Criticism of Kris' theory of artistic creativity as regression in the service of the ego is also part of Weissman's psychoanalytic account of creativity (142, 143). He too doubts that the term "regression" is appropriate, and he considers Kris' concept insufficient in not making explicit the ego functions involved. He attempts to repair this insufficiency with the concept of dissociative function, following earlier suggestions by Glover and Greenacre. The dissociative function is "the ego's capacity to dissociate itself from its established object relationships and responses to specific id derivatives and superego demands." Weissman considers the creative person's tendency toward traits of oddness, eccentricity, rebelliousness, and obstinacy as outgrowths of great strength, even at early ages, of the dissociative function. In everyone Weissman sees some degree of dissociative function as essential in development through childhood and adolescence; it is a necessary preliminary to moving on from one stage of ego functioning to the next. In a noncreative person the dissociative function continues to serve only this purpose of achieving greater maturity, while in a creative person it also becomes the preliminary to a variety of new syntheses. If this view, like Ehrenzweig's, does not immediately lend itself to obvious empirical test, it has the great interest of being extremely close to Piaget's theory of cognitive development and of suggesting to psychologists that that theory is a long-neglected resource for the exploration of adult creativity.

While the concept of regression in the service of the ego has thus been challenged, its potential productivity in research has been shown by Wild (146). Applying Kris' concept, she prepared tests specifically requiring the subject to shift from usual to less regulated modes of thought, and found art students more capable of such changes than were control subjects. Wild also found that many other aspects of the artistic subjects' responses fit well the concept of regression in the service of the ego.

Additional emergents from psychoanalytic theory appear in recent work by Rothenberg, beginning with a detailed study (123) of Eugene O'Neill's creative activity when writing *The Iceman Cometh*. Rothenberg studied the biographical antecedents of the characters and events of the play, facts about O'Neill's life during the period of composition, and the textual changes to be found in the successive manuscript versions of the play. His analysis led him to five hypotheses descriptive of this particular instance of creativity and possibly generalizable. Two of these hypotheses—that the simultaneous conceptualization and the integration of opposites are especially characteristic of the creative process—Rothenberg has begun to test in other contexts, and he has included a preliminary report of the outcome in a general account (124) of what he earlier called oppositional thinking and now calls *Janusian thinking*. One source of evidence consists of interviews with creative writers about their work and parallel interviews with noncreative people about attempts at creative writing. Janusian thinking—simultaneous consideration and integration of opposites—often appears, Rothenberg reports, in the creative but never in the noncreative interviewees. The second source of evidence, pertaining to the consideration of opposites and not directly to their integration, comes from use of word-association tests; more creative people are found to respond with opposites more frequently than do less creative people, and to show especially low reaction time for their opposite responses.

In another paper (125), Rothenberg has given a more general account of the literary creative process as he has learned about it through a series of interviews with poets. He explores in considerable detail the parallel between the process of poetic creation and the process of psychotherapy. Without implying that poetic creation is in any way pathological, he finds that the parallel helps in understanding both processes. One of the parallel elements—that both successful psychotherapy and poetic creation end with some kind of increased freedom—is also useful, he suggests, in understanding the reader's response to poetry.

Rothenberg's account stresses the elaboration rather than the inspiration phase of literary creation. The opposite is true of a rather narrower inquiry by Durr (30), comparing recent descriptions of psychedelic experiences with earlier literary texts. He shows close parallels between the mystical experience or trance state reported by some users of psychedelic drugs and the similar experiences reported by many poets without use of drugs. He concentrates on certain romantic, mystical, or visionary poets—especially Vaughan, Traherne, Blake, Wordsworth, and Whitman. The vivid and direct sense of mystic union described in their poetry is, Durr argues directly, intrinsic to their mode of poetic creation. Less directly he seems to suggest that similar visionary experiences may be involved in some other literary creation, though he makes no claim that they are characteristically present. He makes a comparison with mystic experiences outside the literary and drug contexts, too; the implicit lesson may well be that understanding of creativity has much to gain from improved knowledge of altered states of consciousness. This argument seems to be quite independent of the question of whether drug-induced alterations of consciousness are more likely to be favorable or unfavorable to artistic creativity.

From the Berkeley studies comparing more and less creative groups in several professions have come during this period further publications on writers and architects. In chapters in two different books (4, 5), Barron has reported briefly on the study of writers. MacKinnon (91) has discussed the study of architects in relation to Otto Rank's theory of creativity. Many aspects of the empirical results, he indicates, support Rank's picture of how creative potential develops and is realized. Hall & MacKinnon (54) have divided the 124 architects of the study in random halves, determined on one half the best three scales from each of several personality tests for predicting creativity rating by peers, and then cross-validated the predictions on the other half. The cross-validated coefficients reach as high as .55, indicating very substantial correlations between architectural creativity and personality-test variables.

Several more empirical studies of artists are of special interest. Cross, Cattell & Butcher (22) gave the 16PF personality questionnaire to 63 visual artists and 28 craft students, and to a control group of nonartists. They compare the results with those of some earlier studies of artists and of other creative groups and find a good deal of stability in the pictures that emerge. A similar conclusion is reached in the much more extensive review by Dellas & Gaier (24) of research on creativity in relation to personality. Dennis (25) has compared artists with other creative groups in the way their creative productivity varies with age. Where an earlier decline of productivity occurs among artists, he suggests, it may result from the greater dependence upon individual creativity established by the conditions of their work. Pickford has published a series of studies of artists and art students with defective color vision; the latest (117) provides references to the others. He finds no evidence that color deficiencies are less frequent among art students than elsewhere, and some art students are not aware of their deficiency; various adaptations to color defect occur, and the defect does not necessarily constitute a great handicap.

The process of creating a work of art has been studied directly in students in art schools. Csikszentmihalyi & Getzels (23) interviewed each student after he had drawn a still life especially for their research, and the drawings were later assessed for esthetic value, originality, and craftsmanship. These assessments were related to interview evidence of "concern for discovery," an attitude of starting the work without a preconceived solution, of expecting to discover a problem and its solution in the course of work. This attitudinal variable was positively related to the assessments of the drawings, most strongly to the ratings of esthetic value and next to the ratings of originality. In a series of studies (80, 81, 115) Lansky & Peterson have analyzed the work of freshman architecture students instructed to carve an abstract sculpture, starting from a 6-inch wood cube and observing certain restraints; the uniformity of esthetic task here facilitates the classification and comparison of strategies employed in its solution.

Art teachers are, of course, constantly observing artistic creation in their students—sometimes in children not selected for artistic promise and, at other times, in students in professional schools among whom are many already competent artists. The professional literature of art education contains extended discussion of artistic creation at one level or another and of how it may be facilitated or influenced. An introduction to this literature, possibly useful to psychological estheticians, is available in two recent books of readings, one edited by Eisner & Ecker (33) and the other by Pappas (112). Both books also include a number of papers from outside art education. A few scholars in art education have applied the methods and concepts of psychology to the study of problems arising in art education, and in doing so have developed ideas and findings of general interest for psychological esthetics. The papers by Kenneth Beittel in both these volumes are especially valuable; Beittel carries the themes of these papers further in a forthcoming book.

ART PRODUCED BY PSYCHIATRIC PATIENTS

The study of imaginative productions by psychiatric patients is extremely diverse but thus far more in the tradition of case study than of systematic research, and I will do no more here than cite several recent publications which can serve as an introduction to this diversity. Many authors have contributed varied papers to the published proceedings (65, 66) of two international meetings on art and psychopathology. Pickford, through a number of years, has presented both case studies and theoretical accounts of visual art produced by psychiatric patients, and a recent book (116) brings these various papers together. An unusually rich case study has been published by Milner (102)—a long account of many years of therapy with a patient who used drawings as one way to communicate with the therapist and gain insight into herself. Finally, a number of fine colored reproductions of art by psychiatric patients have been published (120), providing an important resource for research and teaching.

ART PRODUCED BY CHILDREN

Artistic production by children has of late begun to be studied in arts other than visual. A poet, Kenneth Koch (77), has described his experience in teaching grade-school children to write poetry, as an introduction to an extensive anthology of the poems that have resulted. For use in future research, Duffy (29) has developed a rating scale to evaluate children's poetry. Gardner & Gardner (47) have explored literary competence and creativity in children of four ages (group modes of 6, 8, $11\frac{1}{2}$, and $14\frac{1}{2}$) through a story-completion task; their findings clearly indicate growth up through the third age group but suggest a decline afterwards, attendant upon the development of formal operations.

Major work on children's visual art has been published during this period by Kellogg and by Dennis—the former concerned with some universals of development and the latter with cultural influences, but nicely complementing each other in bringing out the diversity of factors which unite to influence imaginative productions.

Kellogg continues the stress of her earlier work on cognitive and motor development as underlying sequential change in children's drawing. She has recently published two books: one (72) has a brief and journalistic text, and I mention it only to call attention to its many colored plates illustrating points made in the black-and-white book (71) whose text is of much greater interest to psychologists. Here she works out with considerable care the fairly uniform sequence through which the early drawing of children seems to develop. Her account is fascinating and reasonably convincing, even though not based on the meticulous evaluation of evidence required for complete confidence. One point of special interest Kellogg argues for is the notion that school art training, by introducing aims and criteria irrelevant to the child's own imaginative production, often interferes with further development and leads to poorer quality of work. Some evidence in support of this view may be found in a study by Voillaume (139). Children's paintings were evaluated by artists, who found excellence as often in those by children of 5 to 6 as in those by children of any later age. Noteworthy was the fact that general cultural level of family was negatively correlated with quality of production; the kind of contract it implies with an adult approach to art appears on balance to hinder a child's own esthetic productivity.

Dennis's research (26) is concerned with the subject matter of children's drawings interpreted as an expression of social values. Children in school classrooms in several countries were each asked to draw a man. Various aspects of what they drew are analyzed—e.g. race, clothing, expression, emphasis on masculinity—to show agreement and variation among different groups of children. Dennis brings the various results together to support the general thesis that children draw what they and their elders admire. This thesis is extended to college students in a supplementary study (27) of social change. Dennis obtained drawings of a man from comparable college classes in the United States in 1957 and 1967. No drawings by blacks in 1957 clearly presented black racial characteristics; in 1967, 18% did. The change is consonant with shifts in value during those years in black Americans.

Though Kellogg's particular research is concerned with universals of development and Dennis's with cultural influences, both authors are clearly aware that biological and social factors interact in leading to the art productions of children as well as of adult artists. This interaction is illustrated in Olson's distinguished work on the child's acquisition of diagonality (109). Ability to construct a diagonal is one component of drawing skill and also a component of other skills. Isolating it for study, both developmental and experimental, Olson arrives at conclusions equally pertinent to the value of childhood art education and to general theory of cognitive development. Performatory acts, he holds, are basic to perceptual development because they provide the occasion for noticing cues necessary for the particular performance which may otherwise go unnoticed. The medium in which one will come to perceive well, and the discriminations one makes within it and elsewhere, will therefore be influenced by the choice of media in which to pursue performatory practice. On these considerations Olson bases a very illuminating discussion of the effects on man of the historically shifting predominance of various media.

PSYCHOLOGY IN RELATION TO HISTORY AND CROSS-CULTURAL COMPARISONS IN ART

The art characteristic of a society (or of its leading artistic innovators) may be considered in relation to psychological hypotheses even when there is no direct study of individuals. Should the art then be thought to express shared personal characteristics of the artists producing it or should the art be thought to indicate what the audience or viewers demand that their artists supply? On the latter assumption, studies of this sort would belong in the section that follows, on response to art; on the former assumption, they belong here. Since the former assumption is the one most often used, I will discuss such studies here. There is, however, no strong reason for arguing for either assumption to the exclusion of the other, and many writers use both together; in general, with some exceptions, references to artist and to audience are likely to lead to similar and mutually reinforcing interpretations.

One form this application of psychological ideas takes is the study of the single case—a psychological interpretation of why a particular society at a particular time creates or enjoys particular kinds of art. Where research goes beyond the single case study, it can emphasize either of two possible patterns: historical, applying psychology to understanding the sequence of art in a society through time; or cross-cultural, applying psychology to understanding why various societies, each studied at some definite time, have the kinds of art they do.

The historical emphasis predominates in the writings of Peckham (113, 114), a literary critic and historian of the arts who draws from behavioral and perceptual psychology a framework of ideas for interpreting social change. In *Man's Rage for Chaos* (113) he worked out, with examples from the history of Western culture, the thesis that art has the biological function of preparing the individual for adjusting to change. In *Art and Pornography* (114) he restates this thesis and applies it (with a diversity of other stimulating ideas as well) to an analysis of pornography. He draws on the Japanese and Chinese as well as the Western traditions, having studied materials from all three in the collections of the Institute for Sex Research at Indiana University. He sees pornography as an art form especially well suited for ideational practice of innovation, serving often as a step toward transcendence of cultural limitations, and therefore highly developed in periods characterized by high rate of innovation. His interpretation of pornography is one which thus gives little weight to specifically sexual components; indeed in the course of the argument he presents a largely nonsexual interpretation of sexual interests generally, different from but parallel to some of the arguments for de-emphasis of sexual "drive" that have developed in clinical and experimental psychology.

Not only the ideas but also the methods of psychology may be applied in studying artistic history, as is well demonstrated by the psychologist Martindale (94). His theory holds that effort to be ever more original is of prime importance among forces making for artistic change, and that it tends to produce movement toward deeper regression of content and lesser elaboration of style—except that when regression has reached a limit, acceleration of style change permits a reversal of regression. He applies the theory to studying the course of English poetry from 1700 to 1840 and of French poetry from 1800 to 1940, controlling carefully the selection and especially the analysis of texts. The outcome is a highly objective demonstration of remarkable regularities of change within each historical sequence, and of some remarkable agreements between the two.

Cross-cultural comparison has a major, but not exclusive, part in the sociological approach of Kavolis (69). Considering the dependence of art style on economy, politics, social structure, and social values, his interpretations often imply psychological assumptions and may suggest inferences about sources of an individual artist's style in his personality and life history. In a subsequent article (70) Kavolis has again drawn on both historical and cross-cultural comparisons, this time to consider social influences on creativity; his discussion in this instance is more thoroughly at a social level.

Cross-cultural comparisons are made in many studies of art in tribal societies. In a symposium edited by Biebuyck (7), several anthropologists and art historians have come together, drawing on field observations of behavior and on interviews with tribal artists, to discuss whether the category "art" exists in various cultures, and how to consider and to evaluate the products and processes observed in other societies that parallel those in our society which we categorize as art and artistic creativity. Similar concerns and sources of evidence are reflected in the more numerous and varied collection of anthropological papers brought together by Jopling (68).

Cross-cultural hypothesis testing, where single cultures are the units on which variables are assessed and the intercorrelations among variables are then determined, has been applied to studying problems of esthetics. Marginal to esthetics are two studies of alcohol usage (3, 97) and two studies of homicide and suicide (82, 127). They establish theoretically meaningful correlations between variables of literature and other aspects of culture, adding to previous evidence that literature expresses personality trends common in a society. The studies of homicide and suicide are especially pertinent to this methodological point in obtaining closely similar results from very diverse materials.

More central to psychology of art is Wolfe's direct attack (149) on the question of why some societies produce more and better art than do other societies. He began with the hypothesis, suggested both by esthetic theory and by his initial observation, that "High development of graphic and plastic arts is associated with social structural features that set up barriers between males in local communities"; the association is predicted on the assumption that art is a medium for communication of emotion. He dealt only with African societies because their artistic achievements could be and were reliably evaluated by a large number of qualified experts. The art ratings were then tested for association with variables of social structure, and the prediction was strikingly confirmed. Wolfe's research points the way to further cross-cultural study of problems central to esthetics. Of special value in his paper is its conclusion with comments on his research by a number of other specialists, and his reply. This discussion brings out some of the important alternative interpretations and raises questions about how evidence can be otained to decide among them.

For a sample of preliterate societies, Robbins (121) tested the correlation between curvilinearity of house shape and curvilinearity of visual art and found a strong negative correlation. Regarding house form as determined by materials and technology, he suggests that art tends to introduce forms which in relation to this major man-made feature of the environment will provide visual novelty. He interprets the suggestion by adopting Berlyne's view, based on experimental research, of the role of collative variables in esthetic satisfaction. There is a real convergence here of ideas diverse in origin, for Robbins's finding is also strikingly consistent with Peckham's theory mentioned above, derived from considering the history of style in Western European culture.

These years have seen continued publication of results obtained in the Cantometrics Project directed by Alan Lomax, a cross-cultural analysis of folk song style considered in relation to other cultural characteristics in more than 200 societies. An article in 1967 (85) provides a summary of the methods and findings. A later book (86) gives a more detailed review of the project. The system of analysis of musical features is first described in detail and the reliability of judgments established. The correlation of song style with features of economy, social structure, and child training is then explored, and many very striking relationships are reported. The results offer, in general, pan-human evidence that music gives symbolic expression to feelings about impulse, inhibition, and social structure. The book also includes a preliminary account of a similar analysis of dance style, which is said to express dynamic components of the interaction patterns characterizing a culture, and of song texts, which indicate more concretely the values embodied in a culture.

RESPONSE TO ART AND TO COMPONENTS AND ANALOGS OF ART

In a general book on psychological esthetics (6), Berlyne contributes much to topics discussed in the first two sections of this article as well as in this third section. He sets his contribution in the framework of the history of experimental esthetics, and draws primarily on experimental research both in esthetics and in general psychology. The research he reviews is mostly, though not exclusively, on the topics of this third section—response to art and to its components and analogs. The responses he considers especially important are changes in arousal and various verbal and other responses that may be thought to index arousal changes. The antecedent variables he distinguishes are classified into psychophysical variables (characteristic of the older experimental esthetics), ecological variables, and collative variables (characteristic of the newer experimental esthetics of which Berlyne is a leader). The systematic research of recent years on these topics exceeds by far that on all the rest of psychological esthetics, and only by referring the reader to Berlyne's book have I felt justified in omitting that research here in order to review the rest of psychological esthetics, including a number of publications from outside the stream of systematic psychological research.

Anxious to ground psychological esthetics firmly in rigorously established evidence, Berlyne goes further than I feel necessary or desirable toward restricting it to study of especially pertinent aspects of general psychology rather than directing it also immediately toward the arts and including consideration of what may be distinctive of the arts. Most of the research he reviews—and it is in this respect representative of experimental esthetics—deals not with the arts but with simplified analogs, studying, for instance, response to polygons rather than response to geometric paintings. Unlike some critics of experimental esthetics, I feel this study of simple analogs is of great value. But to me it does not seem sufficient even for the present, so I would like to refer briefly to additional research concerned directly with response to the arts.

As I have argued elsewhere (12), evaluative judgments can be studied scientifically, and their study is essential to progress on some of the major issues in esthetics. Recent research on evaluative judgments has added to earlier evidence of some degree of transcultural agreement among participants in different artistic traditions (Iwao, Child & Garcia 64); it also suggests that an esthetic orientation, as measured by tendency to share the judgments of experts, has similar personality correlates in different cultures (Child & Iwao 16). Within our culture, the range of personality variables to which an esthetic orientation is known to be related has been expanded (Child, Cooperman & Wolowitz 15).

Esthetic judgments by experts and nonexperts have been compared by Getzels & Csikszentmihalyi (50) and by Voillaume (139), the former using art students' work and the latter using children's. They agree in finding originality or freedom a more important determinant of experts' judgments. Variation between different groups of experts is demonstrated and used to characterize major variations in style by Skager, Schultz & Klein (131) and by Klein & Skager (74). Reasons given in justification of like or dislike have been studied by Hussain (60). He finds the same categories applicable to response to music, poems, and several types of visual art, with small but genuine differences in relative frequencies according to art form and kind of judge. In another publication Hussain (61) sets the psychological study of esthetic judgment in a philosophical background, suggesting that much research has naively neglected the specific and varying psychological matrix in which each judgment necessarily arises.

In everyday life people are constantly indicating their attitudes to art in their spontaneous choices of how to spend their leisure time. Roubertoux (126) has begun psychological study of how these choices relate to personality. Parisian high-school students answered questionnaires about their contact with the arts, and three groups were selected for study: those who frequently attend the theater, those who frequently visit art museums, and those who do neither. On a number of personality scales, the two groups with artistic interests generally differed in a single direction from the control group, yet they often differed significantly from each other. Different artistic interests seem to be related both to some common and to some distinctive aspects of personality.

Of special significance, because it originated in esthetic theory rather than as the purely empirical exploration so common in this area, is a series of studies by Machotka (88, 89) on preferred degree of distortion of nude pictures. The research was designed to test the arousal-control hypothesis that the greater the sexual arousal value of an object, the greater the degree of disguise required for a representation of the object to be considered esthetically pleasing. The studies provide no simple confirmation or rejection of the hypothesis; while indicating that the hypothesis identifies pertinent variables, the outcome suggests they interact in complex fashion with personality and situational variables. Machotka's work argues strongly for the value of such coordinated programs of research in this area and for giving only the most tentative credence to conclusions from single isolated experiments.

Developmental study of art preference has continued to be pursued in recent years, and with closer relation than before to general developmental theory (Machotka 87; Francès 36; Child 14). A coming step perhaps is the more integrated developmental study of understanding, creating, and responding to art.

LITERATURE CITED

1. Arnheim, R. 1966. *Toward a Psychology of Art: Collected Essays.* Berkeley: Univ. California Press. 369 pp.
2. Arnheim, R. 1969. *Visual Thinking.* Berkeley: Univ. California Press. 345 pp.
3. Bacon, M. K., Barry, H. III, Child, I. L. 1965. A cross-cultural study of drinking: II. Relations to other features of culture. *Quart. J. Stud. Alc.*, Suppl. No. 3: 29–48
4. Barron, F. 1968. *Creativity and Personal Freedom.* Princeton: Van Nostrand. 322 pp.
5. Barron, F. 1969. *Creative Person and Creative Process.* New York: Holt, Rinehart & Winston. 312 pp.
6. Berlyne, D. E. 1971. *Aesthetics and Psychobiology.* New York: Appleton-Century-Crofts. In press
7. Biebuyck, D. P., Ed. 1969. *Tradition and Creativity in Tribal Art.* Berkeley: Univ. California Press. 236 pp.
8. Burnshaw, S. 1970. *The Seamless Web.* New York: Braziller. 320 pp.
9. Bush, M. 1967. The problem of form in the psychoanalytic theory of art. *Psychoanal. Rev.* 54:5–35
10. Bush, P. A., Pease, K. G. 1968. Pop records and connotative satiation: Test of Jakobovits' theory. *Psychol. Rep.* 23:871–75
11. Carey, J. T. 1969. The ideology of autonomy in popular lyrics: A content analysis. *Psychiatry* 32: 150–64
12. Child, I. L. 1966. The problem of objectivity in esthetic value. *Penn. State Papers in Art Education*, no. 1. 25 pp. Reprinted in Ref. 112, 390–404
13. Child, I. L. 1969. Esthetics. In *The Handbook of Social Psychology*, ed. G. Lindzey, E. Aronson, 3: 853–916. Reading, Mass.: Addison-Wesley. 2nd ed. 978 pp.
14. Child, I. L. 1970. Aesthetic judgment in children. *Transaction* 7(7):45–51
15. Child, I. L., Cooperman, M., Wolowitz, H. M. 1969. Esthetic preference and other correlates of active versus passive food preference. *J. Pers. Soc. Psychol.* 11:75–84
16. Child, I. L., Iwao, S. 1968. Personality and esthetic sensitivity: Extension of findings to younger age and to different culture. *J. Pers. Soc. Psychol.* 8:308–12

17. Choynowski, M. 1967. Dimensions of painting. *Percept. Mot. Skills* 25: 128
18. Clynes, M. 1970. Toward a view of man. In *Biomedical Engineering Systems*, ed. M. Clynes, J. H. Milsum, 272–358. New York: McGraw. 665 pp.
19. Creel, W., Boomsliter, P. C., Powers, S. R. Jr. 1970. Sensations of tone as perceptual forms. *Psychol. Rev.* 77:534–45
20. Crews, F. C. 1963. *The Pooh Perplex.* New York: Dutton. 150 pp.
21. Crews, F., Ed. 1970. *Psychoanalysis and Literary Process.* Cambridge, Mass.: Winthrop. 296 pp.
22. Cross, P. G., Cattell, R. B., Butcher, H. J. 1967. The personality pattern of creative artists. *Brit. J. Educ. Psychol.* 37:292–99
23. Csikszentmihalyi, M., Getzels, J. W. 1970. Concern for discovery: An attitudinal component of creative production. *J. Pers.* 38:91–105
24. Dellas, M., Gaier, E. L. 1970. Identification of creativity: The individual. *Psychol. Bull.* 73:55–73
25. Dennis, W. 1966. Creative productivity between ages of 20 and 80 years. *J. Gerontol.* 21:1–8
26. Dennis, W. 1966. *Group Values Through Children's Drawings.* New York: Wiley. 211 pp.
27. Dennis, W. 1968. Racial change in Negro drawings. *J. Psychol.* 69: 129–30
28. Deutsch, D. 1969. Music recognition. *Psychol. Rev.* 76:300–7
29. Duffy, G. G. 1968. The construction and validation of an instrument to measure poetry writing performance. *Educ. Psychol. Meas.* 28: 1233–36
30. Durr, R. A. 1970. *Poetic Vision and the Psychedelic Experience.* Syracuse Univ. Press. 275 pp.
31. Edmonston, W. E. Jr. 1969. Familiarity and musical training in the esthetic evaluation of music. *J. Soc. Psychol.* 79:109–11
32. Ehrenzweig, A. 1967. *The Hidden Order of Art: A Study in the Psychology of Artistic Imagination.* Berkeley: Univ. California Press. 306 pp.
33. Eisner, E. W., Ecker, D. W., Eds. 1966. *Readings in Art Education.* Waltham, Mass.: Blaisdell. 468 pp.

34. Francès, R. 1958. *La Perception de la Musique*. Paris: Vrin. 408 pp.
35. Francès, R. 1966. Actes du Premier Colloque d'Esthétique Expérimentale. *Sciences de l'Art* 3:1–184
36. Ibid. Variations génétiques et différentielles des critères du jugement pictural, 119–35
37. Francès, R. 1968. *Psychologie de l'Esthétique*. Paris: P.U.F. 204 pp.
38. Frechtling, J. A., Davidson, P. W. 1970. The development of the concept of artistic style: A free classification study. *Psychon. Sci.* 18: 79–81
39. Galper, R. E., Hochberg, J. 1972. Recognition memory for facial expression. In press
40. Gardner, H. 1970. Children's sensitivity to artistic styles. *Child Develop.* 41:813–21
41. Gardner, H. 1970. From mode to symbol: Thoughts on the genesis of the arts. *Brit. J. Aesthet.* 10:359–75
42. Gardner, H. 1971. Children's duplication of rhythmic patterns. *J. Res. Music Educ.*
43. Gardner, H. 1971. Children's sensitivity to musical styles. *Harvard Proj. Zero Tech. Rep. No. 4*
44. Gardner, H. 1971. The development of sensitivity to artistic styles. *J. Aesthet. Art Criticism* 29:515–27
45. Gardner, H. 1971. Problem-solving in the arts. *J. Aesthet. Educ.* 5:92–113
46. Gardner, H., Gardner, J. 1970. Developmental trends in sensitivity to painting style and subject matter. *Stud. Art Educ.* 12:11–16
47. Gardner, H., Gardner, J. 1971. Children's literary skills. *J. Exp. Educ.* 39:42–46
48. Garner, W. R. 1970. Good patterns have few alternatives. *Am. Sci.* 58:34–42
49. Genovese, C., Dasi, G. F., Eds. 1969. *Gli Incontri di Verucchio: Estetica Sperimentale*. Bologna: Cappelli. 281 pp.
50. Getzels, J. W., Csikszentmihalyi, M. 1969. Aesthetic opinion: An empirical study. *Pub. Opin. Quart.* 33: 34–45
51. Gibson, J. J. 1966. *The Senses Considered as Perceptual Systems*. Boston: Houghton Mifflin. 335 pp.
52. Gibson, J. J. 1971. The information available in pictures. *Leonardo* 4: 27–35
53. Goude, G., Lindén, G., Lundström, L. 1966. An experimental psychological technique for the construction of a characterizing system of art painting and an attempt at physiological validation. Dep. Psychol., Univ. Uppsala, Rep. 33. 28 pp.
54. Hall, W. B., MacKinnon, D. W. 1969. Personality inventory correlates of creativity among architects. *J. Appl. Psychol.* 53:322–26
55. Hannett, F. 1964. The haunting lyric: The personal and social significance of American popular songs. *Psychoanal. Quart.* 33:226–69
56. Hays, J. C. 1967. Effect of two regulated changes of tempo upon emotional connotations in dance. *Res. Quart.* 38:389–97
57. Hogg, J. 1969. A principal components analysis of semantic differential judgments of single colors and color pairs. *J. Gen. Psychol.* 80:129–40
58. Holland, N. N. 1966. *Psychoanalysis and Shakespeare*. New York: McGraw. 412 pp.
59. Holland, N. N. 1968. *The Dynamics of Literary Response*. New York: Oxford Univ. Press. 378 pp.
60. Hussain, F. 1966. L'unité des critères de jugement esthétique: Enquête expérimentale sur la correspondance des arts. *Psychol. Franc.* 11: 285–98
61. Hussain, F. 1967. *Le Jugement Esthétique: Inventaire des Théories, Essai de Méthodologie*. Paris: Minard. 145 pp.
62. Imberty, M. 1968. Recherche sur la genèse du sentiment de consonance. *Sciences de l'Art* 5:29–44
63. Imberty, M. 1969. *L'Acquisition des Structures Tonales chez l'Enfant*. Paris: Klincksieck
64. Iwao, S., Child, I. L., Garcia, M. 1969. Further evidence of agreement between Japanese and American esthetic evaluations. *J. Soc. Psychol.* 78:11–15
65. Jakab, I., Ed. 1968. *Psychiatry and Art. Proc. 4th Int. Colloq. Psychopathol. Expression*. Basel & New York: Karger. 211 pp.
66. Jakab, I., Ed. 1969. *Psychiatry and Art*, Vol. 2. *Proc. 5th Int. Colloq. Psychopathol. Expression*. Basel & New York: Karger. 257 pp.
67. Jakobovits, L. A. 1966. Studies of fads: I. The "Hit Parade." *Psychol. Rep.* 18:443–50
68. Jopling, C. F., Ed. 1971. *Art and Aesthetics in Primitive Societies*. New York: Dutton
69. Kavolis, V. 1968. *Artistic Expression:*

A Sociological Analysis. Ithaca:
Cornell Univ. Press. 272 pp.

70. Kavolis, V. 1969. Social evolution, the organization of the artistic enterprise, and creativity. *Aris* 2:1–8

71. Kellogg, R. 1969. *Analyzing Children's Art.* Palo Alto: National Press. 308 pp.

72. Kellogg, R., O'Dell, S. 1967. *The Psychology of Children's Art.* San Diego: CRM. 112 pp.

73. Kennedy, J. M. 1971. Incomplete pictures and detection of features. *J. Struct. Learn.* 1

74. Klein, S. P., Skager, R. W. 1967. "Spontaneity vs deliberateness" as a dimension of esthetic judgment. *Percept. Mot. Skills* 25:161–68

75. Knapp, R. H. 1965. The language of postural interpretation. *J. Soc. Psychol.* 67:371–77

76. Knapp, R. H. 1969. Une comparaison stylistique de Picasso et de Cézanne. *Sciences de l'Art* 6:6–11

77. Koch, K., the Students of P. S. 61 in New York City. 1970. *Wishes, Lies, and Dreams: Teaching Children to Write Poetry.* New York: Chelsea. 309 pp.

78. Kolers, P. A. 1970. The role of shape and geometry in picture recognition. *Picture Processing and Psychopictorics,* ed. B. S. Lipkin, A. Rosenfeld, 181–202. New York: Academic

79. Kolers, P. A., Pomerantz, J. R. 1971. Figural change in apparent motion. *J. Exp. Psychol.* 87:99–108

80. Lansky, L. M., Peterson, J. M. 1966. Effect of instructions on a creative task: Discipline and form in hand sculptures. *Percept. Mot. Skills* 22:943–50

81. Ibid 1968. Stimulus complexity and the cube: Mass and space in a handcarving. 27:967–74

82. Lester, D. 1968. National motives and psychogenic death rates. *Science* 161:1260

83. Lindauer, M. S. 1970. Physiognomic properties of abstract art and titles. *Proc. 78th Ann. Conv. APA* 5:402–3

83a. Lindauer, M. S. 1972. Toward a liberalization of experimental esthetics. *J. Aesthet. Art Criticism.* In press

84. Litowitz, N. S., Newman, K. M. 1967. Borderline personality and the theatre of the absurd. *Arch. Gen. Psychiat.* 16:268–80

85. Lomax, A. 1967. Special features of the sung communication. *Essays on the Verbal and Visual Arts,* ed. J. Helm, 109–27. Proc. 1966 Ann. Spring Meet. Am. Ethnol. Soc. Seattle: Univ. Washington Press

86. Lomax, A., Ed. 1968. *Folk Song Style and Culture.* Washington, D. C.: AAAS Publ. No. 88. 373 pp.

87. Machotka, P. 1966. Aesthetic criteria in childhood: Justifications of preference. *Child Develop.* 37:877–85

88. Machotka, P. 1967. Defensive style and esthetic distortion. *J. Pers.* 35:600–22

89. Ibid 1970. Ego defense and aesthetic distortion: Experimenter effects. 38:560–80

90. Machotka, P. 1970. Visual aesthetics and learning. *J. Aesthet. Educ.* 4:117–30

91. MacKinnon, D. W. 1965. Personality and the realization of creative potential. *Am. Psychol.* 20:273–81

92. Mackworth, N. H., Morandi, A. J. 1967. The gaze selects informative details within pictures. *Percept. Psychophys.* 2:547–52

93. Manheim, L., Manheim, E., Eds. 1966. *Hidden Patterns: Studies in Psychoanalytic Literary Criticism.* 310 pp.

94. Martindale, C. 1972. *The Romantic Progression: On the Psychology of Literary Change.* Philadelphia: Temple Univ. Press. In press

95. Mauron, C. 1963. *Introduction to the Psychoanalysis of Mallarmé.* Berkeley: Univ. California Press. 280 pp.

96. Mauron, C. 1968. *Phèdre.* Paris: Jose Corti. 188 pp.

97. McClelland, D. C., Davis, W., Wanner, E., Kalin, R. 1966. A cross-cultural study of folk-tale content and drinking. *Sociometry* 29:308–33

98. Mehlman, J. 1970. Entre psychanalyse et psychocritique. *Poétique* 365–85

99. Meyer, L. B. 1967. *Music, the Arts, and Ideas: Patterns and Prediction in Twentieth-Century Culture.* Univ. Chicago Press. 342 pp.

100. Michel, A. 1965. *L'Ecole Freudienne devant la Musique.* Paris: Editions du Scorpion. 511 pp.

101. Miller, M. D. 1967. Music and tension. *Psychoanal. Rev.* 54:141–56

102. Milner, M. 1969. *The Hands of the Living God: An Account of a Psychoanalytic Treatment.* London: Hogarth. 444 pp.

103. Mirels, H. L., Efland, A. D. 1970. *A cognitive approach to the assessment of esthetic responses.* Final Rep., Proj. No. 9-0047, U.S. Off. Educ. Columbus: Ohio State Univ. 49 pp.

104. Molnar, F. 1966. Aspect temporel de la perception de l'oeuvre picturale. *Sciences de l'Art* 3:136–46

105. Morant, R. B., Maslow, A. H. 1965. Art judgment and the judgment of others: A preliminary study. *J. Clin. Psychol.* 21:389–91

106. Nidorf, L. J., Argabrite, A. H. 1970. Aesthetic communication: I. Mediating organismic variables. *J. Gen. Psychol.* 82:179–93

107. Nordenstreng, K. 1968. A comparison between the semantic differential and similarity analysis in the measurement of musical experience. *Scand. J. Psychol.* 9:89–96

108. Noy, P. 1966–67. The psychodynamic meaning of music. *J. Music Ther.* 3:126–34; 4:7–23, 45–51, 81–94

109. Olson, D. R. 1970. *Cognitive Development: The Child's Acquisition of Diagonality.* New York: Academic. 220 pp.

110. Olson, D. R. 1970. Language and thought: Aspects of a cognitive theory of semantics. *Psychol. Rev.* 77:274–81

111. Oyama, T., Tanaka, Y., Chiba, Y. 1962. Affective dimensions of colors: A cross-cultural study. *Jap. Psychol. Res.* 4:78–91

112. Pappas, G., Ed. 1970. *Concepts in Art and Education: An Anthology of Current Issues.* New York: Macmillan. 473 pp.

113. Peckham, M. 1965. *Man's Rage for Chaos: Biology, Behavior and the Arts.* Philadelphia: Chilton. 339 pp.

114. Peckham, M. 1969. *Art and Pornography: An Experiment in Explanation.* New York: Basic Books. 306 pp.

115. Peterson, J. M., Lansky, L. M. 1970. Effect of design strategies on handcarvings: Order in mass and space. *Proc. Ann. Conv. APA* 5:497–98

116. Pickford, R. W. 1967. *Studies in Psychiatric Art.* Springfield, Ill.: Thomas. 340 pp.

117. Pickford, R. W. 1969. The frequency of colour vision defective students in a school of art and the influence of their defects. *J. Biosoc. Sci.* 1:3–13

118. Pratt, C. C. 1961. Aesthetics. *Ann. Rev. Psychol.* 12:71–92

119. Pratt, C. C. 1968. *The Meaning of Music: A Study in Psychological Aesthetics.* New York: Johnson Reprint Corp. 253 pp.

120. *Psychopathology and Pictorial Expression: An International Iconographical Collection.* 1966. Basel & New York: Karger. 2 vols.

121. Robbins, M. C. 1966. Material culture and cognition. *Am. Anthropol.* 68:745–48

122. Rockland, L. H. 1970. "What Kind of Fool Am I?": A study of popular songs in the analysis of a male hysteric. *Psychiatry* 33:516–25

123. Rothenberg, A. 1969. The iceman changeth: Toward an empirical approach to creativity. *J. Am. Psychoanal. Assoc.* 17:549–607

124. Rothenberg, A. 1971. The process of Janusian thinking in creativity. *Arch. Gen. Psychiat.* 24:195–205

125. Rothenberg, A. 1971. Poetic process and psychotherapy. *Am. J. Psychother.* In press

126. Roubertoux, P. 1970. Personality variables and interest in art. *J. Pers. Soc. Psychol.* 16:665–68

127. Rudin, S. A. 1968. National motives predict psychogenic death rates 25 years later. *Science* 160:901–3

128. Shuter, R. 1968. *The Psychology of Musical Ability.* London: Methuen. 347 pp.

129. Siddiqi, J. A., Thieme, T. 1969. Die verlorenen Botschaften. *Z. Exp. Angew. Psychol.* 16:507–18

130. Skager, R. W., Schultz, C. B., Klein, S. P. 1966. The multidimensional scaling of a set of artistic drawings: Perceived structure and scale correlates. *Multivar. Behav. Res.* 1:425–36

131. Skager, R. W., Schultz, C. B., Klein, S. P. 1966. Points of view about preference as tools in the analysis of creative products. *Percept. Mot. Skills* 22:83–94

132. Smets, G. 1969. Etude expérimentale des réactions entre les qualités expressives des couleurs et des figures géométriques. *Sciences de l'Art* 6:17–24

133. Spiegel, J. P., Machotka, P. 1971. *Movement and Message.* Cambridge: Harvard Univ. Press. In press

134. Standing, L., Conezio, J., Haber, R. N. 1970. Perception and memory for pictures: Single-trial learning of 2500 visual stimuli. *Psychon. Sci.* 19:73–74

135. Tannenbaum, P. H. 1961. Semantic judgments of color. *Acta Psychol.* 19:698 (*Proc. 16th Int. Congr. Psychol.*)

136. Tighe, T. J. 1968. Concept formation and art: Further evidence on the applicability of Walk's technique. *Psychon. Sci.* 12:363–64

137. van Kaam, A., Healy, K. 1967. *The Demon and the Dove: Personality Growth Through Literature.* Duquesne Univ. Press. 308 pp.

138. Varga, L., Fye, B. 1966. Ghost and antic disposition: an existential and psychoanalytic interpretation of Shakespeare's 'Hamlet'. *Psychiat. Quart.* 40:607–27

139. Voillaume, H. 1965. Les activités picturales des enfants et les réactions comparées des enfants et des adultes devant les oeuvres d'enfants. *Psychol. Franç.* 10:178–87

140. Walk, R. D. 1967. Concept formation and art: Basic experiment and controls. *Psychon. Sci.* 9:237–38

141. Walk, R. D., Karusaitis, K., Lebowitz, C., Falbo, T. 1971. Artistic style as concept formation for children and adults. *Merrill-Palmer Quart.* In press

142. Weissman, P. 1967. Theoretical considerations of ego regression and ego function in creativity. *Psychoanal. Quart.* 36:37–50

143. Weissman, P. 1968. Psychological concomitants of ego functioning. *Int. J. Psychoanal.* 49:464–70

144. White, W. F., Butler, J. H. 1968. Classifying meaning in contemporary music. *J. Psychol.* 70:261–66

145. Wickens, D. D. 1970. Encoding categories of words: An empirical approach to meaning. *Psychol. Rev.* 77:1–15

146. Wild, C. 1965. Creativity and adaptive regression. *J. Pers. Soc. Psychol.* 2:161–69

147. Williams, J. E., Morland, J. K., Underwood, W. L. 1970. Connotations of color names in the United States, Europe, and Asia. *J. Soc. Psychol.* 82:3–14

148. Wolf, H. R. 1970. E. A. Robinson and the integration of self. In *Modern American Poetry: Essays in Criticism*, ed. J. Mazzaro, 40–59. New York: McKay. 368 pp.

149. Wolfe, A. W. 1969. Social structural bases of art. *Current Anthropol.* 10:3–44

150. Zenatti, A. 1969. *Le Développement Génétique de la Perception Musicale.* Paris: Cent. Nat. Rech. Sci. 110 pp. (Monogr. Franc. Psychol. 17)

PSYCHOLOGY IN JAPAN 193

Yoshihisa Tanaka[1]

Department of Psychology, University of Tokyo, Tokyo, Japan

and George W. England[2]

Industrial Relations Center, University of Minnesota, Minneapolis, Minnesota

INTRODUCTION

The purpose of this chapter is twofold. First, it continues and supplements the previous review of Japanese psychology which appeared in Volume 17 of the *Annual Review of Psychology* (193). Second, it will give readers an overview of psychological work in Japan in several subspecialty fields. Due to limitations of time and space, a number of areas are omitted where active research is in progress. We have chosen to review work in the following areas: sensation and perception; conceptual learning; physiological, comparative, and mathematical psychology. The reader will find differences in coverage in various parts of the review. Only general information is presented for some areas, while more detailed reviews are made in other areas. In addition, brief surveys of research areas in social and personality psychology will be given in Tables 3 and 4 at the end of the chapter.

Educational system.—The educational system in Japan is quite similar to that of the United States, and psychologists are trained in approximately the same way in both countries. There has been an enormous increase in the number of colleges and universities, as well as in the number of students studying in these institutions, during the past 7 years. The number of national universities increased from 72 (29 graduate schools) in 1962 to 75 (58 graduate schools) in 1969. The large increase has occurred primarily at the graduate level where nearly 80 percent of the national universities currently provide graduate programs.

There has been little growth in the number of public universities, that is, those established by local governments. There were 34 (16 graduate schools) in 1962 and 34 (17 graduate schools) in 1969; just half of the public institutions provide graduate programs.

[1] The authors are greatly indebted to Dr. Juji Misumi at Kyushu University and Dr. Giyo Hatano at Dokkyo University for their help in preparation of the original draft. Thanks are also due to Dr. Goro Imamura and Dr. Shuko Torii at the University of Tokyo for their assistance in preparation of this chapter.

[2] Preparation of this review was aided by a grant from the American Psychological Foundation.

The number of private colleges and universities has substantially increased from 164 (58 graduate schools) in 1962 to 270 (100 graduate schools) in 1969. About 37 percent of these private institutions currently provide graduate programs.

There were about 290 junior colleges in 1962, but now there are 533 (including Kōhtō Senmon Gakko, a combined senior high school and junior college). Some of these junior colleges provide courses related to the application of psychology, such as training for social or child welfare workers. The total number of institutions for higher education in Japan is 912 (the number was 560 in 1962). The report of the Ministry of Education indicates that the number of students studying at these institutions was 1,659,826 in 1969 compared with 916,392 in 1962.

Government reports show the total number of full-time teachers at these institutions to be as follows: national universities, 36,274 faculty members; public universities, 5,272 faculty members; and 33,060 faculty members in private universities. The total of faculty members teaching at universities and colleges is 74,796, while the total teaching staff for junior colleges numbers 18,526.

Although there are 175 universities which provide graduate schools, only 20 universities offer specialized programs in the psychological sciences. Table 1 lists the names of these 20 universities and some of the professors of psychology.

Research emphases in Japanese psychology.—The nature of the current research emphasis in Japanese psychology may be represented by the number of free papers presented before meetings of the annual conventions of the Japanese Psychological Association (JPA). JPA usually has a convention annually in Tokyo or one of the other large cities. The number and percentage representation of papers appearing in the programs of JPA conventions during the past 5 years are shown in Table 2 for each of the 12 divisions. It is obvious from this table that studies on perception, learning, and development are popular in Japan. Social and clinical psychology, relatively new areas in Japan, have also attracted the interest of many researchers. The impact of student unrest can be seen in the lower number of papers in the 1967 and 1969 conventions which were held in Tokyo.

SENSATION AND PERCEPTION
VISION

Eye movement.—Almost all research on eye movement in Japan has been done by photographic camera (128), TV camera, or by the electro-oculography (EOG) method (153, 154). A new type of ophthalmograph which enables one to correct for optical system biases has been devised by Osaka (158) at the Kyoto University Audiovisual Communication Laboratory. By using such improved apparatus, both horizontal and vertical eye movements have

TABLE 1. Universities Offering Graduate Programs in Psychology (1969)

University	Location	Courses	Faculty[a]
NATIONAL			
Hokkaido Univ.	Sapporo	Psychology	Y. Umeoka, M. Toda
Tohoku Univ.	Sendai	Psychology	S. Kitamura, J. Abe
		Educ. Psychol.	T. Tsukada, T. Miyagawa
Univ. Tokyo	Tokyo	Psychology	B. Yagi, Y. Tanaka
		Educ. Psychol.	Y. Miki, T. Hidano
Tokyo Univ. Educ.	Tokyo	Exp. Psychol.	S. Nagashima, S. Iwahara
		Educ. Psychol.	S. Kamitake, H. Katsura
Nagoya Univ.	Nagoya	Psychology	Z. Yokose, H. Maeda
		Educ. Psychol.	A. Tsuzuki, Y. Shioda
Kyoto Univ.	Kyoto	Psychology	T. Sonohara, S. Kakizaki
		Educ. Psychol.	S. Kuraishi, R. Osaka
Osaka Univ.	Osaka	Psychology	Y. Maeda, T. Tashiro
Hiroshima Univ.	Hiroshima	Psychology	G. Hagino
		Educ. Psychol.	I. Koura
Kyushu Univ.	Fukuoka	Psychology	T. Funatsu
		Educ. Psychol.	T. Endo, J. Misumi
PUBLIC			
Tokyo Metrop. Univ.	Tokyo	Psychology	Y. Wada, S. Tsuji
Osaka City Univ.	Osaka	Psychology	K. Ohnishi, S. Ohno
PRIVATE			
Aoyama Gakuin Univ.	Tokyo	Psychology	Y. Ushijima
Keio Univ.	Tokyo	Psychology	Y. Ogawa, T. Indow
Komazawa Univ.	Tokyo	Psychology	Y. Akishige, J. Ogasawara
Nihon Univ.	Tokyo	Psychology	S. Ito, K. Ando
Rikkyo Univ.	Tokyo	Psychology	T. Toyohara, K. Moriwaki
Waseda Univ.	Tokyo	Psychology	Y. Togawa, H. Motoaki
		Educ. Psychol.	J. Mishima
Doshisha Univ.	Kyoto	Psychology	O. Endo, Y. Matsuyama
Ritsumeikan Univ.	Kyoto	Psychology	C. Hasuo
Kwansei Gakuin Univ.	Nashinomiya	Psychology	Y. Kotake, I. Ishihara
International Christian Univ.[b]	Tokyo	Psychology	H. Tsuru

[a] Staff members at each institution are presented for the purpose of correspondence and do not necessarily include all professors.

[b] International Christian University provides a one-year postgraduate course in psychology.

been recorded more precisely than before. Yuki (259) has pointed out that the role of eye movements in perceiving objects is to trace the features of the objects, comparable to the role of a finger in touching objects.

Electrophysiological study on "flick" (saccade) eye movements during monocular fixation on a small target was done by Yamazaki (241). The horizontal component of flick was recorded by means of two silicon photo-electric detectors for five normal subjects and three pathological cases. The records in the normal eyes showed that excursion of the flicks was 3'–45' arc (average, 19' arc), and the interval between the flicks was 0.1–9.8 sec (average, 1.5 sec). In contrast to the normal flicks, those from the three patients whose fixations were unstable showed higher amplitude and increased frequency. According to Yamazaki (242), when patients suffering from neuro-

TABLE 2. Divisional Representation of Papers Presented at JPA Annual Conventions

Year Location	1966 Nagoya	1967 Tokyo	1968 Kyoto	1969 Tokyo	1970 Sendai	Total
Division I (theories and methods)	4[a]	3	4	4	4	4
Division II (physiological)	4	2	11	8	6	6
Division III (sensation & perception)	13	15	14	15	15	14
Division IV (behavior & behavior theory)	5	7	5	6	5	6
Division V (developmental)	10	9	11	10	11	10
Division VI (learning & memory)	11	14	11	13	14	13
Division VII (educational)	10	11	7	10	8	9
Division VIII (personality)	6	8	5	8	7	7
Division IX (clinical)	13	9	10	10	9	10
Division X (criminal)	3	3	2	1	2	2
Division XI (social)	13	10	11	10	10	11
Division XII (industrial)	8	9	9	5	9	8
Total number of papers	513	392	522	411	580	2418

[a] Percentage of total papers presented each year (rounded to closest whole number).

logical disorders were asked to follow an object moving sinusoidally by an excursion of 5°, the frequency varied from 0.05 to 1.0 cps.

Inaba & Ishikawa (51) conducted electrophysiological studies of the smooth pursuit movement of the eyes. They recorded movement by electro-oculography (EOG) with simultaneous recording of the electromyography (EMG) of the horizontal trace to determine the reason why the smooth pursuit movement was impaired from innervational aspects in patients suffering from multiple sclerosis.

Pupillary movement.—Modern television systems are able not only to record quick pupillary movement but also to provide visual monitoring of the pupil, which permits accurate calibration of pupillary size. Asano & Stark (17) used an image orthicon tube and an infrared image converter, thus requiring an expensive device and a high voltage source. An advanced technique was developed by Green & Maaseidvaag (30), who used an infrared-sensitive, closed circuit television camera of electromagnetic vidicon type. Using an instrument similar in principle to that designed by Asano & Stark, Kurioka (96) observed the pupillary light reflex after administration of drugs which act on pupillary muscles. Ishikawa et al (60) constructed a new instrument which measures instantaneous area changes of the pupil, the minimum measurable area being 0.002 mm² and the linearity better than 1% up to the area of 150 mm². Funatsu (27) measured pupil size during various kinds of mental activity.

Color sensation and perception.—Since Rushton's measurements in chlorolabe are in general agreement with Stiles' green (π_4) mechanism, and since those on erythrolabe agree with Stiles' red (π_5) mechanism, it may be assumed that Stiles' experiments would provide an effective method of determining the absorption spectra of red, green, and blue cone pigments. A fundamental assumption, however, is that the different color mechanisms are independent of one another at threshold. This assumption has been examined by Boynton et al (19). Further study on the interactions among Stiles' π mechanisms was done by Ikeda et al (48).

In the after-flash situation, however, it was found that the mechanisms are completely independent of one another (10). The technique of after-flash (9) was used to measure the size of rod signal by Alpern et al (11). The signal was found to be directly proportional to flash energy over a range of some 4 log units, while the signal began to saturate above this level and followed the same saturation curve as electrical signals recorded intracellularly from receptors (205) or S-potentials (131). Alpern et al (12) studied π_4 and π_5 by after-flash technique and found them both to be very similar to rods in their response to flash energy, except that all light quantities must be some hundredfold greater in cones than in rods for the same effect.

Takasaki & Hioki (190) were concerned with methods of measuring human luminosity. The luminosity of a normal person was measured by several methods. Alpern & Torii (13, 14) measured threshold spectral sensitivities and luminosity curves for protanopes, protanomalous, deuteranopes, and deuteranomalous and found slight differences in luminosity curves. They inferred that these differences are due (at least in part) to contributions of cones containing the protanomalous or deuteranomalous pigments which are missing from the protanopes' or deuteranopes' eyes, respectively.

Emori (22) attempted to measure the spectral sensitivity based on threshold for detecting the gap in Landolt rings and reported that several maxima and minima were observed on the curve.

Yonemura & Kasuya (249) reported that color discrimination for normal eyes deteriorated in a manner similar to that observed for tritanopic vision, under reduced visual conditions of small area and low luminance. Hasegawa (32) reported that shift of color on the chromaticity diagram (measured by means of binocular color match) was seen under the reduced visual condition (short duration of stimulus, 0.6 to 150 msec). Based on data concerning the effect of color adaptation (530 nm, about 250 troland) on appearance of colored test stimuli, Kambe (71) examined a law of coefficients put forward by von Kries. Apparent change in colored light under peripheral vision was reported by Minato (112).

Indow & Takagi (58) plotted 12 sets of directly obtained hue-discrimination thresholds (from König up to Weale) in a figure and determined a representative curve as a function of wavelength. The following three sets of theoretical thresholds were compared: one derived from multidimensional scaling by Shepard with Ekman's data; one from Shepard and Carroll with

Boynton and Gordon's data; and the third from opponent-color theory by Hurvich and Jameson. Except for a few points, those indirectly obtained thresholds were in good agreement with the representative curve.

Akita et al (6) had subjects make wavelength settings for various hues by an absolute method in the presence of surround-field colors or darkness. The subject's compensatory shift in setting for the maintenance of a test color was taken to be the difference between his wavelength setting for the test color in the presence of the surround-field color and the wavelength setting for the test color with a dark surround. The compensatory shift in wavelength setting always occurred in the direction of the background wavelength. Akita & Graham (5) further studied changes in test wavelength required to compensate for a contrast effect in the presence of different background colors. Ratio of test-to-background luminance has an "imprecisely specifiable influence" on compensatory wavelength changes in the test area. Oyama & Hsia (161) used a similar procedure and obtained analogous results. Akita (4) analyzed distribution of wavelength settings for various hues which had been obtained from his results and found them to be the normal distribution, unchanged in the presence of various background colors and absence of colors. Induced colors were made observable on the central white area. The subjects were asked to detect changes of chromaticity of induced color by increasing luminance of a superimposed test light of wavelength (cf 206). Takasaki (189) showed that an empirical formula derived from lightness contrast predicted color contrast effect with reasonable success in his study of quantitative determination of the contrast effect using Munsell color samples.

A rapid desaturation process of color sensation which takes place within a fraction of a second of the retinal stimulation was studied by Kaneko (72). In terms of color difference on the Adams chromance scale, the desaturation was found to be large in the hues of yellow, red, and purple (reacting nearly 2 Munsell chroma steps), while it was small in blue-green. Hue was found to recede quickly from red toward yellow or toward purple, red being invariant. Blue-green appeared to be another invariant.

Affective values of color have been studied by many investigators. Nayatani (134) summarized recent work on color harmony. A review article on the affective value of color has been presented by Tomiie (204). Oyama et al (163) conducted a cross-cultural study on affective dimension of colors. Attractiveness of colored light was investigated by Kansaku (75). Based on cinematographic records of eye movements and verbal reports of 10 subjects, he obtained the order of attractiveness in the situation of paired presentation of colored lights. When the luminance was held constant (64 nit) and high purity colors were used, the attractiveness order of colored light was red, blue, yellow, green, and white.

Although Chow (20) failed to demonstrate changes in the visual system of monkeys kept in darkness or in colored light, Mitarai et al (115) found a great suppression of the evoked potential from the optic tectum under long periods of exposure to monochromatic light for goldfish. Mori et al (119) observed changes in acquisition and extinction of color-discrimination learning by using four pigeons kept in green light (549 nm, 140 lux) for 5 months. A significant decrease in learning ability for discrimination between green (538 nm) and red (633 nm) light was shown.

Sensitivity.—The effects of intensity or duration or preadapting light upon the adaptation process in the darkness were examined by Nakamura (132). Especially measured was the adaptation time after a change from a certain intensity of light (preadapting light) to less intensity (adapting light). When the intensity of preadapting or adapting light was kept constant, the adaptation time increased as the amount of change in intensity increased.

Effects of spatially adjoining retinal regions upon the test threshold luminance have been of two kinds. The first is shown by a decrease in the test threshold luminance (208). The second (sensitizing effect) manifests itself in an increased sensitivity of a retinal area when an adjoining region is steadily illuminated. Y. Tanaka et al (196) found that the foveal luminance threshold of a test patch (surrounded by a contiguous annular inducing field) increased in sensitivity under various combinations of luminance and area of the inducing field. M. Takahashi & Uemura (188) confirmed that a similar effect exists, even when there was some separation between the test and inducing fields (cf 62, 63, 176).

Yokose and his co-workers have continued studies based on a theory of potential field proposed by Yokose (244). Ichikawa (47) measured the figure effect in the third dimension by a light threshold method. A small luminous point was presented at various positions in front and to the rear of the figure (two parallel lines) and threshold for the test point was measured. Threshold was found to be gradually higher as the distance between the figure and the spot was increased; and at a certain place far from the figure, it became highest.

The so-called figure effect has been investigated most often by using simple geometrical figures. However, when compound figures were used, their appearances changed readily according to the observer's attitude in grasping the form. Yokose & Ito (248) measured the threshold of a test spot presented inside the reversible figure-ground patterns under two kinds of subject attitudes. In one condition, the subject was required to grasp one part of the pattern as figure, while in the second condition, another part of the pattern was grasped as figure. The manner and the extent of attitude influence on the light threshold was analyzed quantitatively according to Yokose's potential theory.

Motokawa & Ogawa (127), on the other hand, devised a method to record the potential difference between inner and outer positions of the stimulus figure projected on the isolated retina of the carp. The form of electrophysiological potential distribution around stimulus figure (e.g. Müller-Lyer figure) and the psychological potential distribution calculated by Yokose's theoretical formula are surprisingly similar.

To separate the influence of physical factors, such as diffracted rays and

stray light, from that of inducing figure upon the test light, Komatsu (88)
presented the inducing figure and the test figure to subjects along two separate optical paths. It was seen that the greater the apparent distance between them, the smaller the influence of the inducing figure upon the test
light. The theoretical formulas of Yokose were found to fit the data obtained.

Werner (237) found that when two figures are presented in succession
for brief durations, the first figure (black disk) disappears at a certain duration of the pause between them. Wake (233, 234) measured a critical pause
threshold (CPT) at which the first figure can just be seen, keeping the duration of first and second figures constant. CPT tended to decrease with increased width of the second figure (ring), and CPT increased with a decrease
of the reflectance of the first figure. The spatial relationships between the
first and the second figures seemed to be important. An optimal overlap
between the two figures was found to have an effect upon CPT (cf 29).

Brightness perception and contrast.—Aiba & Stevens (1) studied the influence of light and dark adaptation on brightness matches when the test
stimuli were presented to one eye and the matching stimulus to the other.
Matches obtained under dark-adapted conditions no longer held when the
eyes were light adapted, a result indicating a nonlinear effect of light adaptation upon whatever processes are involved in determining the matches. The
question of how apparent brightness varies with area was investigated by
Ogawa et al (147), with special emphasis on stimuli which were well above
threshold. Size had more effect on apparent brightness at low luminances
than at high luminances. The results showed that the apparent brightness
varied not only with visual angles but also with observation distance. Sato
(168) reported that an apparent brightness of flickering target is seen to be
enhanced at low frequency ranges.

Torii & Uemura (209) investigated the effects of varying the areas of
an annular surround upon the brightness of the enclosed test field. A contrast effect was found at all levels of test field luminance; on the whole, the
larger the surround area, the greater the effect at a given test field luminance.
The opposite effect, an enhancement, also was found by Torii & Uemura,
the usual result being that the lower the luminance and the smaller the area,
the larger the amount of the effect.

Kato examined the influence of figure configuration upon brightness contrast by studying changes in the phenomenal brightness of a small gray
patch presented inside or outside of the figure with (a) differences in configuration, and (b) location of the small patch, when brightness contrast between
figure and background is kept constant (77). The phenomenal brightness of
the gray patch changed in proportion to the field force. Von Bezold type of
assimilation was observed by T. Kozaki (92) under various conditions in
which the widths of line and space and the reflectances of line, space, and
background were varied systematically. According to the author's conclusion

the results confirmed the "differential stimulation" and "area luminance" hypotheses proposed by Helson (39).

Psychophysical measurement of the spatial sine-wave responses have been carried out by Watanabe et al in the Broadcasting Science Research Laboratory (120, 235). By using a grid pattern consisting of bands sinusoidally modulated in brightness, they measured the threshold value of ΔB (the amplitude of the sinusoidal change of brightness).

Optical illusions.—Morinaga (123) pointed out that displacement measured in distance does not necessarily coincide with that measured in direction, even when the same figure is used (cf 180). This contradictory effect was called "paradox of displacement" in geometrical illusion. Morinaga & Ikeda (124) confirmed that the displacement in direction differed from that in distance by using modifications of Zöllner, Hering, and Müller-Lyer figures. This finding seems important from a methodological point of view. It has been known that "assimilation" and "contrast" illusions can be seen in a concentric circle figure (Delboeuf illusion). Wada (229), however, proposed that the terms of "assimilation" and "contrast" are not adequate to use since they are presumably irrelevant to the mechanism of the illusion.

Ogasawara (145) has measured the deflection of line under various angular separations ($\theta = 5°$ to $90°$) between two lines presented obliquely on a frontal parallel plane. The relationship between the amount of deflection and θ was shown by a convex curve having the maxima around $20°-30°$. As θ got smaller (less than $5°$), deflection decreased and began to be negative. Ogasawara also found that this amount of deflection was a function of the position of intersection between lines. The maximum deflection was obtained when the intersecting point was near the vertex. Following studies on the Lipps illusion, Imai (50) examined the effect of distance (d) between the parallel main lines upon the Zöllner illusion and found that the amount of illusion decreased as d got smaller. Effect of the slope ϕ of the parallelogram composed of parallel main lines was also investigated; it was found that as ϕ approached the rectangle-like shape ($\phi = 90°$) the amount of illusion decreased. Determinants found in Lipps illusion are considered to have an analogous effect on Zöllner illusion.

Wada (226) studied the effect of brightness difference between figure and ground and that of width of lines of the Delboeuf illusion and the illusion of divided extent. When the brightness difference was large, the amount of illusion was correspondingly large. The width of lines had an analogous effect to that of brightness difference on the Delboeuf illusion (227). As the width of the inner circle increased (0.2 to 1.2 mm) overestimation of the inner circle decreased and the underestimation of the outer circle increased. Increased width of the outer circle resulted in increased overestimation of the inner circle and decreased underestimation of the outer circle. A similar effect of brightness difference was observed on the modified Zöllner illusion. An effect of width of line also was seen in the modified Zöllner illusion, Poggendorff illusion, and Müller-Lyer illusion (228).

To interpret these findings, Wada assumed two kinds of forces: cohesive force ($\overline{C}$) and the restraining force ($\overline{R}$) proposed by Orbison (157). Based on this assumption, Wada predicted that as the difference between figure and ground became larger, not only $\overline{R}$ but also $\overline{C}$ would get stronger; on the other hand, increase in the width of lines would result in increased $\overline{R}$ and $\overline{C}$, although increase in $\overline{R}$ would be more prominent than that of $\overline{C}$. Illusion of divided extent, however, could not be explained merely by assuming $\overline{C}$ and $\overline{R}$. Wada therefore proposed the diffusive force $\overline{D}$, by which a figure expands as a whole (225). He predicted that while $\overline{C}$ would be relatively strong in the figure of cohesive configurations, in the figure of expanding configurations, $\overline{D}$ would be relatively strong (230). This prediction was confirmed by comparing the distance between parallel discontinuous lines with that between parallel solid lines. That is, the former (strong $\overline{D}$) was seen as longer than the latter.

A theory of vector field was derived from the theory of potential field by Yokose (244; cf 245, 246). The theoretical formula of the rectilinear figures was found applicable to estimate the vector field of the curved figures (247). A small test point was seen to be displaced when presented at various positions away from the center of a circle and circular arcs. Such displacement can be seen in the frontal plane and in the third dimension. Ichikawa (46) found that at a large distance from the figure, a test point was so displaced as to be away from the figure in the third dimension.

After-effects.—Nozawa (141) studied the process of growth and decay of the figural after-effect by the threshold measurement of light spot and confirmed that it was based on the same process as that measured by the displacement of the test figure. Nozawa (142) also examined the experiment conducted by Bevan (18) by means of the same method. He reported that the after-effect of vertical line (as inspection figure) decreased when the separation from the figure was increased, and that the phenomenon based on distance paradox could not be observed.

The effect of an interpolated circle on successive comparison of two circles of equal size was studied by Morikawa (121, 122). When the standard stimulus (S_1) and comparison stimulus (S_2) were presented on the right and left side respectively of a fixation point, results which could be expected from figural after-effect of an interpolated stimulus (S_i) on S_2 were obtained, as long as S_i was presented at the same place where S_2 was presented. However, when S_i was presented at the same place where S_1 was presented, no clear finding could be obtained.

Constancy phenomena.—Akishige's review (3) has covered most of the studies on constancy which were conducted from 1959 to 1966. Since his article was written in English, the studies reviewed in it will be omitted here, with a few exceptions.

Methodological problems on size constancy have been discussed by Makino (103), Ogasawara (144), Ogasawara & Mori (146), and others. Since they were concerned with how to express the degree of size constancy, attention has been focused mainly on the Thouless ratio. To study the effects of such stimulus variables as convergence, binocular disparity, and luminance on size constancy, Oyama & Sato (162) measured apparent size ratio between two disks seen in their stereoscopic apparatus. They were thus able to control these variables independently. The logarithm of the matched size ratio was found to increase linearly as the binocular disparity decreased $+1.09$ to -1.90. An imbalance in luminance between the stimuli presented to the two eyes reduced the linear relation, while neither the level of convergence nor the level of luminance affected this relation.

An experiment on size constancy under reduced conditions was carried out by Yoshioka (257). Two pairs of luminous points were exposed in a dark room. Subjects were required to match the apparent lateral distance between the nearer two points with that of the farther one (standard stimulus). The indices of constancy were found to range from 0.343 to 0.608.

Kuroda (97–99) set up several stages in the transition from the homogeneous to the normal state of space and found that a continuous surface, gradient of the texture, binocular cues, and a visual field correspondingly increased size and distance constancies, while in the homogeneous space this correspondence depended upon the size of the stimulus. Akishige (2) maintained that, according to his law of conservation of perceptual information, apparent size and apparent distance mutually act as determinant to each other.

Noguchi (140) examined the problem of size constancy in terms of the system of reference (Bezugssystem) which is closely related to Helson's (39) adaptation level (111, 125). He concluded that size constancy can be explained in terms of transformation in the system of reference which corresponds to changes either in the distance of object or in the size and texture of background.

Developmental studies on size constancy were carried out by K. Tanaka (192), in which the central tendency of judgment as well as the degree of size constancy were considered. It was concluded that both depend upon the experimental situation in which they are measured. On the other hand, Makino (104) attempted to demonstrate experimentally the artifacts involved in size constancy by the method of two stimulus comparisons. He concluded that the developmental problems of size constancy can be reduced to the problems of grasping or perceiving the range of the comparison stimulus series. It was emphasized that the variation of size constancy with age is not due to the variations of perceived size, but to the different effects of the comparison stimulus series according to age.

In Okada's (155, 156) experiments (in which various fan shapes were used as the standard stimulus), a linear function was found between the cosine of the physical angle of slant and apparent shape. Also, it was found that there exists a linear function between the physical angle of slant and the logarithm of apparent slant. In ordinary lighted space, subjects generally judged the slant of the object by using the ceiling, floor, and side walls as the cues, whereas in the dark they judged slant by the assumed ceiling and walls.

Factors which have effects on brightness constancy have been investigated. Yuki & Hashimoto (260) found that under the condition by which the perception of contour was made difficult, the brightness constancy became lower in degree. A. Kozaki (91) conducted experiments on the effects of the reflectance and size of the inducing and test fields and interpreted her results as being inconsistent with the "contrast hypothesis" of brightness constancy. In Oyama's experiment (160), simultaneous approach to brightness constancy and to the perception of illumination were made in a Hsia-type experimental situation where the immediate surround of the standard disk was kept at a constant low luminance. A log-log relation ($\log Lc = \log a + b \log Es$) was found between the illuminance on the standard disk (Es) and the matched luminance (Lc).

T. Ohmura (152) defined operationally the concepts of whiteness constancy and illumination constancy, and observed that subjects giving high whiteness constancy responded with lower illumination constancy. According to H. Ohmura (151), even if the retinal illuminance was the same, the phenomenal enhancement of the illumination in question was larger when the intensity of the illumination background was lower than when it was higher. Illumination constancy could be noticed only when the visual field had diversity in terms of both illuminance and surface reflectance.

Toshima (210) attempted to examine the relation between constancy and transposition of velocity. From the experimental equation of velocity constancy (which can be expressed in general by a power function), the invariant function of stimulus factors is deduced, which is represented by the form of a particular stimulus ratio. The invariant function is applied satisfactorily to the experimental equations of velocity transposition phenomena, and its experimental equations were found to be expressed also by power functions. It was shown, therefore, that both equations of constancy and transposition are of the same functional form. Moreover, the degree of agreement between their exponents is rather high if conditions of both visual fields are similar.

Sonoda (177) examined the effect of lightness gradient upon perceived size and found that the apparent size is determined not by the lightness gradient but by the cues of relative height.

Research on constancy of loudness within the range of 0 to 60 m in outdoor space was done by Shigenaga (169). Requirements in constructing the auditory space necessary to maintain the constancy in an auditorium and the like were discussed. He also studied the constancy of acoustic distance in three kinds of test field with different structures of sound space and obtained results which showed that the shorter the distance, the higher the degree of constancy of acoustic distance.

Ueda (213) reported that in two cases of congenitally blind subjects, perceptual constancies were observed even immediately after their sight-gaining operations. In the near space within one meter from their bodies, a rather high degree of constancy was seen. Nevertheless, according to observations on one case made immediately after operation, after 3 months, 12 months, and 7 years, the degree of constancy had gradually increased.

Perception of shape and form.—A series of experiments conducted by Umezu and associates confirmed in a general way the conclusion drawn by Senden. According to Umezu & Torii (221), congenitally blind subjects who have recovered sight by operation require considerable time to discriminate by sight whether a patch of black paper on a sheet of white paper is, for example, a triangle or a circle, although they easily recognize the shape by touch. Without movement of the head or the figure, recognition of figures by sight was very difficult in the first stage. A circle and a square were most often confused, whereas a triangle was quickly selected from other figures. An inverted triangle, however, was frequently confused with a rectangle. Size of the figures was an important factor, a very small figure being recognized merely as "something." Progress in recognizing figures differed from one patient to another.

Umezu & Torii (222) tested congenitally blind subjects with compound stimulus figures in which two kinds of geometrical contour figure (e.g. square and triangle) overlapped, having subjects perceive by touch. As Metzger (110) has pointed out, tactual perception of such overlapping figures is most often determined by a factor of closure, and such was seen typically to be the case for congenitally blind persons. For instance, when a figure such as one consisting of two overlapping contour circles was presented, subjects reported it as being "oval-like envelopes with a small core" (or according to Metzger as "Kern-Mantel Gliederung").

Torii & Kimura (207) found that normal sighted children, 6 to 7 years old or younger, perceived such figures in a similar manner to the congenitally blind. In general, as they become older, the factor of good continuation instead of closure seems to become gradually dominant. It was also found that the factor of closure exclusively determined one patient's (T.M.) visual and tactual perceiving of the overlapped figures. During the following half year, she was trained to discriminate figures visually. Surprisingly, the factor of closure was gradually replaced by the factor of good continuation in her perceiving of overlapped figures by both touch and sight. On the other hand, another subject (M.M.) continued to perceive the overlapped figures tactually as she had in the first stage. For M.M. the factor of closure was still a determinant even after 3 years (223). Following this investigation, M.M. successfully learned to discriminate horizontal and vertical lines systematically (220). Then M.M. successfully learned to discriminate two kinds of tilted lines.

Under ordinary circumstances, geometrical figures are identified insufficiently and less immediately by children. Katori (78) attempted to explore the essential conditions for such differences between adults and children when identifying figures. He observed how adults and children perceived the stimulus figures under the following conditions: (*a*) when the stimulus pattern is composed of luminous dots; (*b*) when points constructing a form are presented successively; and (*c*) when the range of the viewing field is restricted by covering the stimulus figures with a circular board 40 cm in diameter, which has a small hole 2 cm in diameter. An optimal sequence of presentation of a figure segment, which differs because of the nature of the figures used, is found when adults identify the figures, but such a sequence is not found with children under 4 years of age.

Distortion of form due to prism wearing and adapting processes to such a prismatic condition were described by Tashiro (199). His main experiment was concerned with distortion of a physically straight line during 60 min in which the subject wore a wedge-type prism.

Ueno & Nakaseko (216) applied a stochastic model to describe random fluctuations of the latency consumed by the scanner when he is required to recognize tactually the capital letters of the alphabet with his right finger tip. The model satisfactorily accounts for the main portion of the data in the experiment. To account for random fluctuations of the time that the subject consumed when he was asked to search for a single target number, or one of two or three target numbers through the sets of small two-digit numbers randomly distributed on a white square, Ueno (215) used two stochastic latency models: McGill's two-step serial processing model, and the parallel processing model.

Umezu (219) attempted to make deaf-blind children acquire the habit of communication by touch and by speech. One of his subjects was a boy, born in 1944, who totally lost both sight and hearing from an unnamed fever at the age of 1 year and 9 months. The second, a girl, born in 1943, became totally deaf and blind after suffering from pneumonia and measles at the age of 1 year and 3 months. Umezu and his colleagues started in 1952 to have them discriminate very simple geometrical forms (circle, equilateral triangle, square, and regular pentagon) by manipulating a wooden form board. Simple geometrical figures drawn (embossed) on paper were also used. After discrimination learning of the position of dots in a definite frame was completed, the following training procedures were attempted in sequence: discrimination of the Braille letter groups containing two or three units; association of words written in Braille with things and behaviors; and association of sentence paragraphs written in Braille with behavior sequences. Since 1953, basic learning of communication by speech has been systematically conducted in the following sequence: discrimination of intensity of vibrations generated by vibrators; association of other's speech received by touch with things; utterance of vowels; and utterance of fundamental syllables other than vowel syllables. Thus through basic learning of communication by manual alphabet (since 1957) and learning of categorizing through language symbols (since 1958), these deaf-blind children have acquired the habit of using language or symbols.

Katori & Natori (79) found the manner of touch to be a determinant of the immediate reproduction of tactually perceived geometrical figures. First, effects of active and passive touch were compared, and it was shown that figures were perceived relatively well through active touch. Analysis of the touching process revealed that the function of active motion and the increase in tactual surface provided higher chances of performing some operation which would identify prominent component features of a figure.

Space perception.—Osaka & Iwawaki (159) reported data obtained from experiments on visual size perception in the parachute-hanging situation in the air. Visual size perception under the downward viewing condition might be regarded as a new problem for investigation (cf 149).

To study the significance of the horopter in visual space Shigeoka (170) attempted to plot the subjective correlates of horopter-torus with three kinds of visual planes (horizontal, upward-inclined, and downward-inclined) under the conditions of median plane fixation of straight-in-frontness and free vision. He found that under the condition of fixation the loci of the correlates approximate the torus in the vicinity of the median plane, while under free vision the loci deviate from the horopter-torus.

Ogasawara (143) presented three main formulas on the density gradient which are more precise and more convenient than Gibson's scale (28). The Ogasawara formulas enable one to draw both the expected and the exact density-gradient picture.

Two test stimuli provided for stereoscopic depth perception (S_1 and S_2) were exposed successively to their corresponding eyes in an experiment by Ki. Maruyama & Tsukahara (106). Even when there was no temporal overlapping between exposures of the two stimuli, the usual stereoscopic depth was perceived as long as the duration of S_1 was less than 375 msec. Nearly 30 msec overlapping of the trial of S_1 and the top of S_2 was needed for stereoscopic depth perception (cf 105).

Kume and her co-workers (95) studied the development of depth perception in human infants by means of a "visual cliff." Thirty-six infants were randomly sampled as subjects. Response latency to deep side (60 cm in height) was compared to that with shallow side (18 cm in height). It was found that infants over a year old avoided the deep side. From observation of two infants whom the author studied continuously, it was noted that they began to avoid a cliff given visually some months after they began to locomote. The authors concluded that avoidance of the visual cliff is not innate.

Ishii (59) studied the correlations between various perceptual constancies and pointed out that a significant correlation occurs between size and shape constancy phenomena. Further, he showed that this finding could be explained by the two personal constants in Luneberg's theory, σ and κ.

A new approach was tried to determine the extent to which visual space is approximated by Euclidean space through the application of a multidimensional scaling method. Since 1962, Indow and his collaborators have attempted to construct Euclidean representations of perceived configurations corresponding to various stimulus configurations, such as configurations of small light points in two- or three-dimensional arrangement in a dark room, and configuration of real stars of equal brightness in the night sky (55, 56). Almost all the data showed that the perceived configurations could be accounted for by the Euclidean representation with sufficient accuracy (108, 139).

Perception of movement.—Apparent movement of a luminous spot presented in a dark room was studied by Kano (73). When a luminous spot, body, or both were moved objectively, apparent movement of the luminous spot was seen more vividly than that of body. The interpretation was that the body has a tendency to be stationary as the system of reference (Bezugssystem).

An investigation of the path of seen motion and motion after-effect was conducted by Sumi (179). When two small light spots moved successively and independently in straight lines, the apparent path of the second light was seen as curving in a direction opposite to that of the motion of the first light.

To test effects of bodily (systemic) condition, which is related to musculature, upon the apparent movement, Nagatsuka (130) tried to vary a tonic stimulation by means of (*a*) restriction of bodily actions, and (*b*) motor enhancement. Under condition *a*, subjects reported the apparent movement with ease; even when the interval between the two lights was longer than in normal condition, an optimal movement could be seen. Under condition *b*, the apparent movement seemed inhibited.

Kano (74) examined whether or not thresholds for moving objects would change in proportion to varying the retinal or the objective size of the objects. The condition of constant retinal size of the objects was produced by enlargement of the size of the objects proportional to the distance from the subjects. Her results showed that thresholds corresponded neither to the predicted values from the retinal sizes, nor to those from the objective sizes of the stimuli; they were found to be between those two predicted values.

Suzumura and his co-workers in the Research Institute of Environmental Medicine at Nagoya University have conducted a series of studies on kinetic visual acuity. Suzumura (183) reported that flickering light presented at the peripheral region of the visual field resulted in increased or decreased kinetic visual acuity, depending on the size and frequency of flickering light. Further, Suzumura & Miwa (184) examined the influence of moving stimuli at the peripheral region upon the central vision.

OTHER SENSES

Hearing.—Teranishi & Takekawa (202) attempted to measure reaction time needed to discriminate two pure tones as a function of pitch difference. They were interested in examining Takada's hypothesis (185) which had been proposed from an information theory point of view. The relation between reaction time (Rt in msec) and the transmitted information (It) could be predicted from the equation $Rt = a\ It + b$ (where a and b are constants). The amount of information transmitted by stimulus patterns consisting of two tones was calculated from the absolute pitch differences in log mel, using the following equation: $It = \log_2 M - \log_2 \Delta m$, where M is the maximum range of pitch in mel and Δm is the pitch difference in mel between the standard and the comparison tones.

Differential sensitivity in auditory flutter was measured by Suzuki & Maruyama (182), using two different psychological methods. It was suggested that the constant method is not proper for measuring the psychophysical constants of flutter. As to the method of just noticeable differences, the ascending series was shown to be preferable to the descending for determination of differential limens. The Weber ratios were approximately constant over the range of noise from 20 to 320 intermissions per second (ips), but turned suddenly upward at 500 ips.

Kuroki (100) reported that the perception of acoustic distance was based not on binaural time difference but on the changes in the intensity and timbre of a sound stimulus. Thus, in listening to a radio drama, one can tell the change in the distance of the sound source but not its lateral movement. Although the changes in standing wave can be expected to serve as an essential cue for the perception of the acoustic distance in the median plane, factors such as binaural time difference, intensity difference, and phase difference seem to be ineffectual as cues.

Dimensions of sensory impressions.—In order to determine the principal dimensions of surface touch, Yoshida (250) applied haptic differential rating scales to 50 samples of various texture, shape, size, and material. The correlations among these scales were factor analyzed. The most important dimensions of tactual impressions were found to be heaviness and coldness, wetness and smoothness, and hardness. In a later study (251), similarity among 25 samples of various materials was directly estimated with actual touch, with vision only, and with concepts only. Additionally, a measure of similarity was indirectly scaled from semantic differential ratings. The results of the three direct estimation procedures were very similar.

Ninomiya et al (138) used various amino acids in water solution or in powdery state and had 100 subjects judge the taste in numerical terms. Their results showed a triangular pattern on a two-dimensional plane; sweet, sour, and bitter were at the apices, while no salty apex was found. Yoshida & Saito (256) confirmed these findings and further constructed the distance matrix from the direct judgment of similarity among pairs of amino acids and NaCl.

Perceptual judgment.—Morikawa (122) observed that the positive time-order error decreased with an increased time interval between the first circle and the second. Wada (231) reported an experiment on the relationship between indifference level and time-order errors by means of pitch discrimination. It was found that negative time-order errors increased (or positive time-order errors decreased) as the interval between the first and second stimulus increased, irrespective of the height of pitch compared with tones at the indifferent level. This tendency is inconsistent with Woodrow's theory on mechanism of time-error.

Kakizaki (68) reviewed the studies upon absolute judgment, including his own experiments. Further, Kakizaki (69) has been concerned with the problem of semantic effects on perceptual judgment. He has challenged the troublesome problem concerning the dichotomous relation of perception vs response. Most often they can be separated from each other, although they must be more or less interrelated. He therefore attempted, through manipulation of different variables, to analyze characteristics and to infer some invariable properties of the perception and judgment systems.

Kakizaki & Morikiyo (70) set up two kinds of experiments and procedures. They found that the magnitude estimates of weights fit a power function fairly well: $V = kW^{1.45}$, where V refers to estimate magnitude, W to physical weight in grams, and k is a constant. The gram estimation, however, revealed a significant curvilinearity in the log-log plots. In Yoshitake's experiments (258), lengths of white lines projected on a screen were judged. Subjects in one group were required to make judgments by the centimeter scale, while another group judged by a nine-category scale. The author concluded that it is an oversimplification to consider the centimeter scale as representing perceptual factors and the category scale as representing semantic factors. Namba et al (133) had subjects judge the point of half-loudness of the standard or judge the absolute loudness using seven categories, and found that stimulus context had an effect on loudness judgment in both experiments.

To test the explanation where shifts due to anchor stimuli using absolute judgments have been ascribed to "semantic" and "scale modulus" changes, Helson & A. Kozaki (40) exposed random dot patterns for 0.30 sec with anchors preceding each of the stimuli. Numerical estimates of the number of dots increased with small anchor, decreased with large anchor, and did not significantly change with anchor in the vicinity of adaptation level. These results exactly paralleled those found by using methods of absolute and comparative ratings and hence cannot be ascribed to semantic shifts. The anchor effects are significant but not so large that they can be ascribed to scale modulus. Two experiments dealing with the effects of duration of series and anchor stimuli on estimates of perceived size also were reported by Helson & T. Kozaki (41).

CONCEPTUAL LEARNING

As pointed out earlier, "learning and memory" is an attractive area for Japanese psychological research. Recently, more and more researchers have been concerned with human as opposed to animal learning. For example, the *Proceedings* of the JPA meetings in 1961 and 1962 included 44 papers using animal subjects (40%) out of a total of 106 papers in the category of "learning." In 1969 and 1970, however, of 128 papers dealing with learning only 34 (27%) were on animal studies. In addition to traditional learning research, many studies in cognitive development have been concerned with behavioral change induced by systematic experience. Even when dealing with developmental conceptions and using children as subjects, these studies involve general learning-psychological questions.

Because of space limitations, we have excluded research on elementary forms of human learning such as perceptual and discrimination learning, language acquisition, and rote verbal learning. Even in conceptual learning, only selected topics will be considered.

Classification and concept.—Kuhara & Hatano (93) investigated developmental changes in concept formation using a modified and objectively defined procedure of Vygotsky. Subjects were asked to classify a set of 22 cardboard figures having one of four different names according to their area and the presence or absence of a border irrespective of form or color. Misclassifications were corrected by showing names without any explanation. Ninety-five subjects, in age ranges of 5–6, 7–8, 9–10, 11–12, 13–15, and 20 and above, were tested individually. Three developmental stages were distinguished according to structural characteristics of first and second classifications and the level of verbalization of concept intention. Subjects belonging to Stage I, who were mostly kindergarten children, could not classify a set of figures with any discernible principle. Stage II subjects, mainly second to eighth graders, could identify the concept intention inductively and apply it to other stimuli. Subjects at Stage III classified figures according to hypothetical, deductively selected criteria from the start.

Miura (117) studied children's classifying behavior. Each subject was asked to classify a set of blocks or cards into two, four, or eight groups. There was clear developmental increase in ability to classify, and the task became more and more difficult when subject had to consider several dimensions at a time. Shinomiya (174) studied children's ability to abstract, i.e. to find similarities between two among three objects, or to classify the two as equivalent. Perceptual equivalence, errors, and no answers declined as the child grew older, while conceptual equivalence correspondingly increased.

Mishima & M. Tanaka (113), using subjects 6, 10, and 14 years of age, found positive correlations between measured intelligence and ability to learn to conceptualize direction, number, and movement. The hypothesis-testing procedure effectively used in concept learning was characteristic not only of high IQ children, but also of less intelligent but mature children.

Shimizu (171) compared feeble-minded and normal children (mental age 4–9 years) on the task of free classification and verbalization of principle for 20 picture cards of familiar objects. Responses at the conceptual level increased in both groups. However, the feeble-minded also employed more immature criteria such as similarity in color and connection by inventing a story. Shimizu (172) also analyzed classifying behavior of highly intelligent children under the same experimental conditions and found a similar but faster increase in conceptual responses.

Kuhara & Hatano (94) found that mental age, not IQ, is critical in concept learning. They also clearly showed the inhibitive effect of an increased number of irrelevant dimensions, regardless of the degree of intellectual development. The facilitative effect of "intuitive conspicuousness" of the relevant dimensions was not uniform, being smaller among highly intelligent and older subjects.

The studies described above were all "static" or cross-sectional in nature, i.e. no attempt was made to improve subject's performance. A related question is: Can we change performance by revising the experimental procedure to be more "educational"? H. Sasaki (165) examined children's classificatory behavior *with* and *without* teaching of class-defining attributes. Preschool children were given a set of 16 cards of animals, which they were allowed to classify freely on the first trial; then they were required to classify only into the four categories of fish, bird, insect, and beast. Before the first trial the experimental group was shown a picture book with a verbal definition for each class of animal. The experimental group showed better performance than the control group who had received no information in advance.

H. Sasaki (101) compared the effectiveness of teaching methods. Preschool children were given sets of blocks which could be classified into four categories according to their height and size of top area, irrespective of color and shape. When the set used for demonstration could be classified in terms of color or shape, most children failed to classify the test set. They adhered to the "conspicuous" aspects—color and shape—even after the correct criterion was transmitted verbally. Almost no subject could find the correct criterion inductively. However, the demonstration method, using a set which could not be classified according to color or shape, worked well. A more analytic method, asking subject to choose blocks belonging to each category defined successively, was also effective.

Moriya (126) also has emphasized the role of language in categorization. Using a set of blocks varying in color and shape, half with a white stripe, she examined use of "lack of quality" as the basis for equivalence. Subjects were required to choose blocks similar to the model presented. When the model had the stripe, 90% of young children could use its presence or absence as the basis of equivalence. Only 10% could do so when the model didn't have a stripe. However, the experimenter's verbal description of the model in terms of lack of the stripe facilitated its use on the following trials.

Relevant dimensions have not been defined nor explained verbally to subjects in most traditional concept-learning experiments. However, as is clearly demonstrated in Sasaki's and Moriya's studies, ability for identifying classification principles inductively is quite limited, especially in young children. Thus we have to be concerned with more efficient methods of transmission, including verbal explanation, to deal with more complex concepts and to develop procedures for teaching concepts in the classroom. In fact, Hosoya (45) succeeded in teaching fourth-graders to correctly identify a group of figures such as triangles and tetragons by verbally defining their attributes at the beginning of instruction.

Learning studies of concrete operations.—Conceptions used in daily life have been investigated in a neo-Piagetian framework. The studies concerning number and spatial concept acquisition are summarized below.

Fujinaga et al (23) attempted to clarify the acquisition process of number concept in children by the "method of experimental education." According to their pretraining survey, number abilities of preschool children were generally higher than ordinarily expected, especially in counting and calculation. However, identification and comparison of numbers of collections were far more difficult for them. Fujinaga et al asserted that this apparent inconsistency could be attributed to parents' emphasis on the former type of ability in their number teaching at home. In their first experimental program, lasting 16 months, children were taught by using dice-pattern symbols (1 to 5) as representative of sets of concrete objects and simultaneously of abstract cardinal numbers, or by using counting and counting-produced ordinal numbers as mediators. Though findings were not conclusive, they were promising for constructing effective training programs even for children 3 years of age.

Another series of studies on number conception started with the preliminary work by Y. Ito (64). Here it was shown that most young children's comparative judgment of two sets was easily dominated by irrelevant perceptual cues, even when they could count and assign a numeral correctly. Ito also tried experimental education of eight or nine sessions and found mediating numerals were effectively used in comparative judgment of two sets only when they had clear meaning or images. Acquisition of number conservation was facilitated by the comprehension of internumber relationships. These findings suggest that a developmental sequence of number conception can be divided into at least three phases. In the first, counting is only a mechanical recitation; in the second, numerals produced by counting have corresponding images of quantities and can be used reliably in numerical comparison; and in the final stage, various numerals are coordinated and inferences concerning invariance and change can be made through the comprehension of the structure of numbers. In fact, Ito & Hatano (65) confirmed this sequence by scalogram analysis. Number conservation could be acquired easily by those who had attained the step just below in the sequence. Moreover, training of comprehension of internumber relationships facilitated not only comparative judgment of two sets by counting, but also those tasks without counting, i.e. number conservation (cf 164).

Terada (200) compared the development of number concept in retarded children with that in normal children having the same mental age. While they were on the same level in counting and one-to-one correspondence, the retarded child was inferior in assigning numerals and conserving the number. Terada (201) also found that while the retarded child was easily dominated by perceptual cues without spontaneously counting, it was possible to teach conservation when there was sufficient learning experience in mathematics.

Several other training experiments have been conducted concerning the development of spatial abilities. Yoshiko Tanaka (197) studied chil-

dren's representation of spatial transformations by using the "three-moun-
tain problem" and its simplified versions. According to her, children could
represent all types of transformations correctly by 9 or 10 years of age
in the case of one dimension. However, they needed to be 2 or 3 years older
when two dimensions were involved. The effect of experience (actual confirmation of sight by walking to different side) was not large initially but
became larger in older children. In her second study (198), Tanaka tried to
identify mediators by which actual confirmation became effective. Ability
for using left-right cues seemed to be significant, while verbal labels were
irrelevant.

Akiyama (7) examined the development of children's water surface
representation. He used not only the traditional Piagetian "tilted bottle
on the horizontal table" but also "tilted bottle on the 22.5° tilted stand."
Five stages were distinguished. The first stage, in which the water surface
is drawn horizontally in all cases, was achieved only by two-thirds of ninth-
graders. However, his results revealed that training in which the child
observed the actual water surface in a tilted bottle, supplemented by the
experimenter's hints, was effective, three-fourths of the trainees attaining
the stage higher than the one at which each had started. Akiyama (8) also
tried to determine what type of child could profit from observation. He
found that a certain measurable cognitive style was related to learning
efficiency by observation, and teaching the use of coordinates was effective
even for children inferior in their image-manipulating capacity. The effectiveness of training on this representation was also confirmed by H. Watanabe (236). He asserted that the most efficient way of teaching is to lead
children to conceptualize the water surface with reference to a vertical line.

As in neo-Piagetian research done elsewhere, there have been two
conflicting tendencies in Japanese learning studies of concrete operations,
i.e. seeking scientific rigor and educational efficiency. Integration of findings
from "complex and flexible educational programs" and "simple and ob-
jectified training programs" is yet to be attempted.

Strategy in conceptual and memory tasks.—The total overt and covert
responses of an individual subject in a learning situation present complicated sequences of information processing. As Bruner and associates showed
in concept learning, a series of responses for a subject was determined by his
program—or strategy.

Teraoka (203) criticized Bruner and tried to develop a behavioristic
theory of strategy. Bruner's four selection strategies could not always be
distinguished from each other, not could they be readily identified from
subject's selections of instances. Moreover, Bruner didn't consider the
possibility of shift of strategy during learning. Teraoka calculated the probabilities in which a selection would be positive or negative under a set of
possible alternatives and logically distinguished four stages of his own.

Shimizu & Kamei (173) also pursued strategy from the behavioristic
point of view. They gave two sets of instructions for information processing

when four positive instances were presented, and the subject was asked to identify the concept "intention." One of them was to check dimensions having different values from those of the preceding instances, and another was to eliminate hypotheses which proved to be false from the set of possible alternatives.

Another approach to strategy was developed by Suzuki & Indow (181), who examined hypothesis-testing strategy in concept learning. Subjects were presented a series of stimuli consisting of five letters out of a possible ten, were asked to decide whether it was positive (having a certain letter) or negative (lacking that letter), and were required to explain their decisions. The investigators distinguished two main strategies: focusing or all-letter strategy, and scanning or one-letter strategy. Although psychological processes differed radically between the two strategies or programs, the mathematical model of Bower and Trabasso fit both sets of data with only an adjustment of parameters.

Strategies in a broad sense have been studied in verbal learning and related memory tasks. According to Umemoto (217), the following problems should be considered concerning strategy in memory: selection of information to be memorized; division and ordering of items of information; "coding" or transforming presented information into different forms which are convenient for retention; and utilization of position cues. Naturalistic observations and experimental and instructional elicitations of strategy on memory tasks are currently under study by many investigators.

Komori (89) has been concerned with unification and labeling. He showed that subjects in free recall learning tried to form higher order units in order to reduce memory load. Grouping of items different from each subject's "familiar" organization was found to inhibit retention.

Wakai (232), using several digit series and two-letter nonsense syllables, examined effects of methods of presentation and solution-orienting instructions on serial memory. Subjects were required not to reproduce the series but to answer several items by simple information processing. Wakai's main findings were that subjects performed better when the series became monotonously longer, and instruction facilitated performance.

Kitao (86) examined effects of contextual experiences which involved stimulus word (S) in relation to response word (R) on paired-associate learning. His findings were as follows: composition of a sentence including both S and R was the most effective; reading the sentence was second most facilitative; while reading S and R separately had no effect. No examination was made, however, concerning whether or not these experiences induced subjects to make sentences in later paired-associate learning with no special instructions. In his study of the transfer effect of mediated association with the paradigm A–B, B–C, A–C, Kitao (87) also revealed that mediative instructions suggesting relevance of prior learning to the final learning increased the effect.

Cognitive motivation and curiosity.—The concern with cognitive or conceptual behavior and learning has been accompanied by an emphasis on cognitive motivation. Hatano & Ito (35) applied Smedslund's procedure to conservation of area. They found that some children did not respond correctly to conflict situations because they judged the area in terms of vertical or horizontal length of the figure. An auxiliary step, differentiating the conception of area by practicing area comparison, was needed before Smedslund's procedure worked well. This implies that cognitive motivation may be necessary but not sufficient for conservation acquisition.

Hatano & Suga (36) also examined the effectiveness of Smedslund's training program in the acquisition of number conservation. While practice in conflict situations could facilitate the acquisition with reinforcement, it was not effective without reinforcement unless subjects had been able to respond correctly to conflict situations before the training.

Ando (15) hypothesized that training without external reinforcement should have the greater transfer effect for subjects of high intelligence because "the effect of intrinsic reinforcement would be stronger." Subjects were given a series of ten problems of number conservation. With reinforcement, almost all subjects of both high and average intelligence groups attained the success criterion of five consecutive correct responses, although those of average intelligence needed more trials. Without reinforcement, however, fewer of the average intelligence subjects attained the criterion, while subjects of high intelligence performed nearly as well as with reinforcement.

These studies demonstrate that certain concepts like conservation may be acquired without external reinforcement and suggest that it is cognitive conflict and its reduction which produce learning. Inagaki (52–54) has studied the effects of cognitive conflict and its reduction on classroom learning of weight conservation. She extended her scheme of research to verbal transmissions. Fifth-graders were taught information about the classification of animals. Experimental group subjects were presented "positive infirming" instances which were discrepant with children's prior intentions, while control group subjects were presented confirming instances. The experimental subjects used information that followed telling classification principles for animals more flexibly and in a wider range than the control subjects. Moreover, information describing infirming instances was evaluated as more interesting than that of confirming instances.

It often has been asserted that cognitive or intrinsic motivation can be used and fostered in "discovery" methods of instruction. Although there has been no direct evidence concerning arousal of cognitive motivation in discovery learning, Miura's study (116) suggested that discovery learning could produce stable "knowledge." Dealing with a formula for calculation of the sum of arithmetic progression, he found that knowledge by discovery learning showed only a slight decline even 8 weeks after the instruction. However, Matsuura (109) did not find discovery learning superior in transfer tasks. In his series of experiments, "expository and guided discovery methods had the greatest effects on retention of rules."

More efficient use of cognitive motivation in the classroom presupposes measurement of individual differences in curiosity as a trait. Two studies should be noted in this connection. Miyamoto et al (118), using a set of 11 pictures representing various areas of children's intellectual interest, asked third-graders to tell "what they knew about" and "what they wanted to know about" and described patterns of interest in terms of these protocols. A. Ohmura (150), following Heath, constructed a Cognitive Preference Test, and found that cognitive preference differed significantly among students who liked certain school subjects. Students tended to score higher in achievement areas corresponding to their cognitive preferences.

PHYSIOLOGICAL PSYCHOLOGY

While Kotake and his collaborators at Kwansei Gakuin University have conducted a series of investigations on the human conditioned reflex since the 1940s (90), it is only recently that young researchers in this field have grown in number. Neurophysiologists like Tokizane at the University of Tokyo, Yoshii at Osaka University, and others have contributed heavily to this growth in physiological psychological research.

In recent years, researchers who group themselves around Iwahara at Tokyo University of Education have conducted a series of studies on EEG (electroencephalograph) during sleep (24), dreaming in activated sleep (25), and effects of various psychotropic drugs on behavior (66, 67).

Studies of the relationships between brain wave and behavior have been conducted by many investigators: among these the electrographic study of Zen meditation (Zazen) is perhaps unique in Japan. Kasamatsu & Hirai (76) recorded EEGs of 48 priests and disciples of Zen sects of Buddhism and found that alpha waves appeared and increased in amplitude, without regard to opened eyes, within 50 seconds after the beginning of Zen meditation. As Zen meditation progressed, the decrease of the alpha frequency was gradually manifested, and the rhythmical theta train was observed in records of some priests.

Experimental studies on sensory deprivation and those on overloading have been carried out by Kitamura and collaborators at Tohoku University since 1962 (84, 85). Various changes in terms of EEG and in perceptual experiences during sensory deprivation have been described by Sugimoto et al (178) at the Research Institute of Environmental Medicine, Nagoya University.

Niimi and others at Waseda University have systematically studied GSR (galvanic skin response) conditioning and have compared GSR during waking with that during sleeping. Characteristics of GSR during paradoxical sleep also have been described. Their findings were published in a book on *Psychogalvanic Responses* (135).

The effects of ablation of a particular part of the brain upon behavior have been investigated. Niki (136, 137) studied the effects of hippocampal ablation upon the inhibitory control of operant behavior and concluded that they were based on blocking of internal inhibition. Using rats and cats, Hirano (42, 43) tested the effects of functional disturbances of the limbic system upon memory consolidation. He established that seizure discharges are localized within the limbic system and thus do not have marked blocking effects upon the consolidation process.

COMPARATIVE PSYCHOLOGY

Among the well-known studies in the field of comparative psychology in Japan are those concerned with the behavior of Japanese monkeys. Since 1948, Imanishi and his co-workers in the Primate Research group at Kyoto University have conducted a series of field surveys on wild troops of monkeys that live in various parts of Japan, and have published their findings in *Primates: A Journal of Primatology* and others (61, 80). Their method of baiting made observation much easier and enabled them to identify all members of a troop. They have been interested in social behavior, social organization, personality and the process of its formation, and development and growth of infants.

Maeda and his colleagues at Osaka University have performed similar studies on monkeys since the latter half of the 1950s. Results from their field surveys and laboratory observations of behavior have been summarized by Maeda (102).

Since 1940, experimental studies on the behavior of Japanese monkeys have been carried out by Takagi at the University of Tokyo. Following him at the same institution, Yagi has conducted various experiments on intelligence and learning in Japanese monkeys, and has found that they are high in intelligence as compared to other kinds of monkeys (238, 239).

Another approach to behavior of Japanese monkeys has been pursued by Asami (16), who studied the development of behavior, and by Itoigawa, who has investigated the process of fixation behavior in individuals bred in isolation.

Other than monkeys, rats have been most frequently used as experimental animals by investigators. A recent study on the effect of stimulus adaptation on exploratory behavior in the rat was conducted by Fujita & Ibuka (26). Umeoka et al (218a) studied the detailed structure of rats' general activity through factor analysis techniques.

Experimental studies on learning in rats have been conducted by many investigators; for instance, Hirai (41a) has been concerned with the problems of generalization as well as extinction in avoidance behavior, and Haruki (31) has studied discrimination of avoidance conditioning in the white rat. Imada & Shikano (49) investigated the fixation of avoidance response and suggested that fear-motivated avoidance responses produce abnormal fixation.

M. Sasaki (166, 167) studied species differences in discrimination reversal learning. In rats, prereversal experience which consisted of extinction of the positive response in original learning facilitates the reversal learning. In kindergarten children, on the other hand, reinforcement of the original negative response facilitated the reversal. Further, Japanese monkeys were found to utilize both kinds of prereversal experiences equally well.

Studies on social structure and social behavior in domestic fowl have been conducted by Ohba (148); on formation of classical conditioned responses in the eel by Umeoka and his co-workers (218); and on fighting behavior of the guppy, *Lebistes reticulatas*, by Uematsu (214).

MATHEMATICAL PSYCHOLOGY

Although mathematical psychology is a new field in Japan, there are now several groups actively engaged in research. One group is at Hokkaido University, where Umeoka and Toda are active leaders. They are concerned with game theories and mathematical models for social processes. The second group is at Keio University, where Indow is the leader. They are concerned with scaling and mathematical models of space perception. Indow edited a new book, *Mathematical Psychology* (57), in the Psychology Series edited by Yagi. There are several people who are concerned with the problems of psychometrics and psychological scaling at the University of Tokyo. Tanaka edited a book on *Psychometrics* (195) in the same series as Indow's. Shiba and Nakatani represent the younger generation in this field. Hidano and Azuma at the University of Tokyo have been concerned with test theories. Takada at the Tokyo Christian Woman's College has done work in information theory and is now concerned with problems of language.

A group at Hiroshima University, under the leadership of Ono, is concerned with mathematical learning theory. There are several other psychologists working in the field of perceptual studies who have an interest in mathematical theories. Akishige in the field of perceptual constancy, Yokose in figural induction, and Hagino in space perception are examples.

Application of semantic differential methods is now very popular, and factor analysis has been widely used. Kashiwagi suggested several new developments in factor analysis. Hayashi at the National Institute of Statistical Mathematics has proposed many new methods which are relevant for psychological studies. His theory of quantification, for example, which unfortunately is not well known outside of Japan, deserves careful attention (37). This technique has a wide range of application in the behavioral sciences. He also suggested a new method of estimating errors in classification. Some of the biases which may appear in classification were analyzed by Tanaka (194), based on Torgerson's model of categorical judgment. Hayashi suggested a new method of estimating the amount of errors (38), and application of the method to data has been done by Maruyama & Hayashi (107).

TABLE 3. RESEARCH ACTIVITIES OF JAPANESE SOCIAL PSYCHOLOGISTS AS REPORTED AT PROFESSIONAL MEETINGS OR IN PUBLICATIONS[a,b]

Topic	Investigators	Institution[c,d]
Interpersonal Relations		
Interpersonal relations	Kikuchi, A.	Fukushima Univ.
Formation of interpersonal impression	Hashimoto, H.	Waseda Univ., Tokyo
Interpersonal attitudes	Tsuji, S.	Tokyo Metropolitan Univ.
Interpersonal cognizance structure	Fujiwara, T.	Niigata Univ.
Social power in hospitals	Takeda, T.	Fukuoka Univ.
Sensitivity training	Maeda, S., Ando, N. & Murayama, S.	Kyushi Univ., Fukuoka
Person perception	Ogawa, K.	Hiroshima Univ.
Personality and person perception	Hamana, T.	Hiroshima Univ.
Person perception	Aoyagi, Y.	Nat. Educ. Res. Inst., Tokyo
Person perception	Osada, M.	Gifu Univ.
Role and personality	Nagashima, S.	Tokyo Univ. of Educ.
Person cognizance	Agarie, N.	Ryukyu Univ., Naha, Okinawa
Group Dynamics		
Group dynamics	Suenaga, T.	Univ. of Tokyo
Group formation by schizophrenics	Utena, H., Hirao, T.	Univ. of Tokyo
Group dynamics in the classroom	Shiota, Y.	Nagoya Univ.
Human relations in the classroom	Ohashi, M.	Nagoya Univ.
Group norms	Sasaki, K.	Kwansei Gakuin Univ., Nishino-miya
Group functions	Hachiya, Y.	Kyoto Prefectural Univ.
Human relations between students and teacher	Kishida, M.	Tokushima Univ.
Least preferred co-workers	Okamura, N., Shirakashi, S.	Fukuoka Educ. Univ.
Group structure and behavior	Kano, S.	Kyushu Univ., Fukuoka
Group dynamics	Tasaki, T.	Saga Univ.
Cooperation and competition	Furuhata, K.	Int. Christian Univ., Tokyo
Attitudes—Values—Morale		
Religious attitudes and reference groups	Ando, N.	Kyushu Univ., Fukuoka
Cognitive dissonance	Sugita, C.	Kyoto Univ.
Value consciousness	Nanjo, M.	Okayama Univ.
Attitude surveys	Tanaka, K.	Kwansei Gakuin Univ., Nishino-miya
Social attitudes by region	Akiyama, T.	Tokyo Inst. Technol.
Social attitudes among Japanese and Westerners	Ushijima, Y.	Aoyama Gakuin Univ., Tokyo
Morale surveys	Sano, K., Sekimoto, M.	Keio Univ., Tokyo
Political attitudes	Ito, Y.	Waseda Univ., Tokyo
Cognitive structure of attitude	Mizuhara, T.	Univ. of Tokyo
Sex differences in attitude and opinion change	Nakamura, H.	Tokyo Christian Woman's College
Value and meaning	Yoshida, M.	Chuo Univ., Tokyo
Attitude change	Haraoka, K.	Saga Univ.
Cognitive dissonance	Sato, S.	Kumamoto Univ.

[a] Detailed information on social psychology in Japan can be obtained by addressing inquiries as follows: Dr. Juji Misumi, Department of Group Dynamics, Faculty of Education, Kyushu University, Fukuoka, 810 Japan.

[b] See also Hirota (44), Kirihara (83), Misumi (114).

[c] Institution of first-listed investigator is given.

[d] Name of the city is indicated where this is not clear from the name of the institution.

TABLE 3.—*Continued*

Topic	Investigators	Institution[c,d]
Leadership		
Mass communication and political behavior	Ikeuchi, H.	Univ. of Tokyo
Student leadership	Nagata, Y.	Osaka Women's College
Leadership and accidents	Shinohara, H.	Japan Inst. Group Dyn., Fukuoka
Personal values and leadership	Shinohara, H.	Japan Inst. Group Dyn., Fukuoka
Need for achievement and leadership	Seki, F.	Japan Inst. Group Dyn., Fukuoka
Physiological indices and leadership	Ogawa, N., Kawazu, Y.	Kyushu Univ., Fukuoka
Leadership patterns and group behavior	Misumi, J.	Kyushu Univ., Fukuoka
Leadership function and group size	Kurokawa, M.	Kyushu Univ., Fukuoka
Political and Social Behavior		
Industrial elite	Mannari, H.	Kwansei Gakuin Univ., Nishinomiya
Consumer behavior	Kojima, S.	Doshisha Univ., Kyoto
Voting behavior	Kinoshita, T.	Kyoto Univ.
Decision-making process	Toda, M.	Hokkaido Univ., Sapporo
Prediction of social phenomena	Hayashi, C.	Inst. Math. Statist., Tokyo
Response to suggestions	Suzuki, K.	Kumamoto Univ.
Ecological psychology	Funatsu, T.	Kyushu Univ., Fukuoka
Juvenile delinquency	Endo, T.	Kyushu Univ., Fukuoka
Psychology of divorce	Ito, Y.	Waseda Univ., Tokyo
Psychological characteristics of alcoholics and schizophrenics	Aiba, H.	Waseda Univ., Tokyo
Behavioral science	Kitagawa, T.	Kyushu Univ., Fukuoka
Structure and Class		
Social structure and social class	Abe, J.	Tohoku Univ., Sendai
National stereotypes	Tanaka, Y.	Gakushuin Univ., Tokyo
Sociometry and social structure	Nishiyama, M.	Kansai Univ., Suita, Osaka
Cultural psychology	Tsukishima, K.	Univ. of Tokyo
Comparative		
Comparative studies of moral education, personality formation and sociocultural change	Ino, M., Ayabe, T.	Kyushu Univ., Fukuoka
Creativity by region	Akiyama, T.	Tokyo Inst. Technol.
Esthetic taste and personality of Japanese and American students	Iwao, S.	Keio Univ., Tokyo
Communication		
Communication problems of Japanese people	Inui, T., Sera, M.	Hosei Univ., Tokyo
Japanese communication	Mashiori, M.	Chiba Univ.
Other		
Authoritarian personality inventory	Hamada, T.	Kyushu Univ., Fukuoka
Architectural design & group activities	Kato, T.	Kyushu Univ., Fukuoka
Japanese personality	Sofue, T., Hoshino, M.	Meiji Univ., Tokyo
Psychology of ego	Kitamura, S.	Tohoku Univ., Sendai
Questionnaire methodology	Tsuzuki, A.	Nagoya Univ.

TABLE 4. PERSONALITY STUDIES BY JAPANESE INVESTIGATORS AS REPORTED AT PROFESSIONAL MEETINGS OR IN PUBLICATIONS

Topic	Investigator	Institution[a, b]
Analysis of moral concepts "on"[e] and "giri"[d]	Yoshida et al (252–254)	Chuo Univ., Tokyo
Mothers' opinions towards filial duty of children	Hatano & Eguchi (34)	Dokkyo Univ., Soka, Saitama
Determinates of feudalistic authoritarianism	Muramatsu (129)	Nagoya Univ.
Japanese concept structure of authority	Yoshida (255)	Chuo Univ., Tokyo
Cross-cultural survey of character formation and child-rearing opinions	Ushijima et al (224)	Aoyama Gakuin Univ., Tokyo
Comparison of Japanese and American tendency to make extreme Rorschach responses	Zax & Takahashi (261, 262)	Kagawa Univ., Takamatsu
Comparison of Japanese and American personality through a Sentence Completion Test	Sofue (175)	Meiji Univ., Tokyo
Japanese child-rearing practices	Takahashi et al (187)	Kunitachi Music Coll., Tokyo
Most preferred family member	Tsuji (211)	Tokyo Metropolitan Univ.
Most preferred family member	Tsuji & Kato (212)	Tokyo Metropolitan Univ.
Development of dependency in female adolescents	Takahashi (186)	Kunitachi Music Coll., Tokyo
Analysis of "amae"[e]	Doi (21)	St. Luke Hospital, Tokyo
Development of "amae"	Yamamura (240)	Saitama Univ., Urawa
Personality differences in children by sex and birth order	Yoda & Fukatsu (243)	Yokohama National Univ.
Personality differences in kindergarten children by sex and birth order	Takuma & Yoda (191)	Tokyo Metropolitan Univ.
Analysis of images of child personality	Hatano (33)	Dokkyo Univ., Soka, Saitama
Family as a model for social organization	Kawashima (81)	Univ. of Tokyo
Interpersonal relations among Japanese	Kikuchi (82)	Fukushima Univ.

[a] Institution of first-listed investigator is given.
[b] Name of the city is indicated where this is not clear from the name of the institution.
[e] One's debt or obligation to other(s) who bestowed favors on the person.
[d] A debt of gratitude.
[e] Presume upon another's love (and behave like a child); take advantage of another's kindness.

LITERATURE CITED

1. Aiba, T. S., Stevens, S. S. 1964. Relation of brightness to duration and luminance under light- and dark-adaptation. *Vision Res.* 4:391–401

2. Akishige, Y. 1965. Perceptual constancy and the law of conservation of perceptual information. *Bull. Fac. Lit. Kyushu Univ.* 9:1–48

3. Akishige, Y. 1968. Studies on constancy problem in Japan. *Psychologia* 11:43–55, 127–38

4. Akita, M. 1967. Some quantitative aspects of simultaneous color contrast. *Psychologia* 10:197–209

5. Akita, M., Graham, C. H. 1966. Maintaining an absolute test hue in the presence of different background colors and luminance ratios. *Vision Res.* 6:315–23

6. Akita, M., Graham, C. H., Hsia, Y. 1964. Maintaining an absolute hue in the presence of different background colors. *Vision Res.* 4:539–56

7. Akiyama, M. 1969. A developmental study of conception of the horizontality of water surface. *Jap. J. Educ. Psychol.* 17:79–89

8. Akiyama, M. 1970. A study of cognitive styles in the development of water surface representation. *Proc. 12th Ann. Conv. Jap. Assoc. Educ. Psychol.*, 62–63

9. Alpern, M. 1965. Rod-cone independence in the after-flash effect. *J. Physiol.* 176:462–72

10. Alpern, M., Rushton, W.A.H. 1965. The specificity of the cone interaction in the after-flash effect. *J. Physiol.* 176:473–82

11. Alpern, M., Rushton, W.A.H., Torii, S. 1970. The size of rod signals. *J. Physiol.* 206:193–208

12. Ibid 1970. Signals from cones. 207: 463–75

13. Alpern, M., Torii, S. 1968. The luminosity curve of the protanomalous fovea. *J. Gen. Physiol.* 52:717–37

14. Ibid. The luminosity curve of the deuteranomalous fovea, 738–49

15. Ando, T. 1967. The relationship between intelligence level and training effect in the concept formation in children. *Jap. J. Psychol.* 37:331–41

16. Asami, C. 1964. Comparative psychology of personality. I. Development of behavior in the Japanese monkeys. *Ochanomizu Univ. Stud. Arts Cult.* 17:115–43

17. Asano, S., Stark, L. 1962. Pupillometry. *Mass. Inst. Technol. Quart. Progr. Rep. Electron.* 66:404–12

18. Bevan, W. Jr. 1951. The influence of figural after-effects upon visual intensity thresholds. *J. Gen. Psychol.* 45:189–207

19. Boynton, R. M., Ikeda, M., Stiles, W. S. 1964. Interactions among chromatic mechanisms as inferred from positive and negative increment thresholds. *Vision Res.* 4:87–117

20. Chow, K. L. 1955. Failure to demonstrate changes in the visual system of monkeys kept in darkness or in colored light. *J. Comp. Neurol.* 102: 597–606

21. Doi, T. 1971. *Structure of "Amae."* Tokyo: Kobundo

22. Emori, Y. 1969. The effect of acuity and contrast on the spectral visual sensitivity. *Jap. J. Clin. Ophthalmol.* 23:899–902

23. Fujinaga, T., Saiga, H., Hosoya, J. 1963–1964. The developmental study of the number concept by the method of experimental education. I. II. III. *Jap. J. Educ. Psychol.* 11: 18–26, 75–85; 12:44–53

24. Fujisawa, K. 1960. The psycho-physiological studies of sleep. *Jap. Psychol. Res.* 2:120–34

25. Fujisawa, K. 1970. A study of dreaming in the activated sleep (1). *Jap. J. Psychol.* 41:131–41

26. Fujita, O., Ibuka, N. 1967. The effect of stimulus adaptation upon exploratory behavior in the rat. *Ann. Anim. Psychol.* 17:65–77

27. Funatsu, T. 1969. Pupillary response as an index of load on mental task. *Bull. Fac. Lit. Kyushu Univ.* 28: 67–102

28. Gibson, J. J. 1950. *The Perception of the Visual World.* Boston: Houghton Mifflin

29. Goryo, K. 1969. The effect of past experience upon the binocular rivalry. *Jap. Psychol. Res.* 11:46–53

30. Green, D. G., Maaseidvaag, F. 1967. Closed-circuit television pupillometer. *J. Opt. Soc. Am.* 57:830–33

31. Haruki, Y. 1966. On the discrimination of avoidance conditioning in the white rat. *Jap. J. Psychol.* 37: 278–86

32. Hasegawa, T. 1969. Effects of temporal factors upon color perception. *Proc. 33rd Ann. Conv. JPA*, 25

33. Hatano, G. 1970. Differences in social expectations according to siblings sex and order of birth. Tokyo: Nihon Jido Kenkyujo

34. Hatano, G., Eguchi, K. 1965. Old and new conceptions of a "good child." *Jap. Ann. Soc. Psychol.* 6:89–99

35. Hatano, G., Ito, Y. 1966. The acquisition of conservation of area in second-graders. *Jap. J. Psychol.* 37: 185–94

36. Hatano, G., Suga, Y. 1969. Equilibration and external reinforcement in the acquisition of number conservation. *Jap. Psychol. Res.* 11:17–31

37. Hayashi, C. 1961. Sample survey and theory of quantification. *Bull. Int. Statist. Inst.* 38:505–14

38. Hayashi, C., Higuchi, I., Komazawa, T. 1970. *Information Processing and Mathematical Statistics.* Tokyo: Sangyotosyo

39. Helson, H. 1964. *Adaptation-Level Theory.* New York: Harper & Row

40. Helson, H., Kozaki, A. 1968. Anchor effects using numerical estimates of simple dot patterns. *Percept. Psychophys.* 4:163–64

41. Helson, H., Kozaki, T. 1968. Effects of duration of series and anchor-stimuli on judgments of perceived size. *Am. J. Psychol.* 81:291–302

41a. Hirai, H. 1967. An analysis of avoidance behavior. *Jap. Psychol. Monogr.* No. 3

42. Hirano, T. 1965. Effects of functional disturbances of the limbic system

on the memory consolidation. *Jap. Psychol. Res.* 7:171–82

43. Hirano, T. 1966. Effect of limbic seizure on memory consolidation. *Jap. J. Psychol.* 37:11–22

44. Hirota, K. 1959. Development of social psychology in Japan. *Psychologia* 2:216–28

45. Hosoya, J. 1967. The effect of between-dimensional differentiation on the acquisition of a classification system of figures. *Proc. 9th Ann. Conv. Jap. Assoc. Educ. Psychol.*, 120–21

46. Ichikawa, N. 1966. A study on figural effects in the third dimension—The displacement effects in the front visual space of a figure. *Jap. J. Psychol.* 37:268–77

47. Ibid 1967. The measurement of the figure-effect in the third dimension by the light threshold method. 38:274–83

48. Ikeda, M., Uetsuki, T., Stiles, W. S. 1970. Interrelations among Stiles' mechanisms. *J. Opt. Soc. Am.* 60:406–15

49. Imada, H., Shikano, T. 1968. Studies on rigidity and crystalization of behavior: I. Preliminary report on the rigidity of fear-motivated behavior in the rat. *Jap. Psychol. Res.* 10:138–45

50. Imai, S. 1970. The effects of parallel lines and forms on Zöllner figure. *Jinbun Gakuho* 77:8–16

51. Inaba, K., Ishikawa, S. 1968. EMG study of the smooth pursuit movement of the eye in patients with multiple sclerosis. *Jap. J. Ophthalmol.* 12:103–11

52. Inagaki, K. 1970. The effect of cognitive motivation on receiving and gathering of information. *Jap. J. Educ. Psychol.* 18:14–25

53. Inagaki, K., Hatano, G. 1968. Motivational influences on epistemic observation. *Jap. J. Educ. Psychol.* 16:191–202

54. Ibid 1971. The effect of cognitive motivation aroused by position infirming instances. In press

55. Indow, T. 1967. Two interpretations of binocular visual space: Hyperbolic and Euclidean. *Ann. Jap. Assoc. Phil. Sci.* 3:51–64

56. Indow, T. 1968. Multidimensional mapping of visual space with real and simulated stars. *Percept. Psychophys.* 3:45–53

57. Indow, T., Ed. 1969. *Mathematical Psychology.* Tokyo: Univ. of Tokyo Press

58. Indow, T., Takagi, C. 1968. Hue-discrimination threshold and hue-co-efficients—Comparison among data. *Jap. Psychol. Res.* 10:179–90

59. Ishii, K. 1965. Studies on the correlations between various perceptual constancies. II. Particularly in relation to Luneburg's theory of binocular visual space. *Bull. Fac. Lit. Kyushu Univ.* 9:335–62

60. Ishikawa, S., Naito, M., Inaba, K. 1970. A new videopupillography. *Ophthalmologica* 160:248–59

61. Itani, J., Ikeda, J., Tanaka, T., Eds. 1964. *Wild Japanese Monkeys in Takasakiyama. Report of the General Investigation Held 10 Years After Feeding.* Tokyo: Keiso Shobo

62. Ito, M. 1966. On a factor of luminance in the field of vision (3). *J. Fac. Lit. Nagoya Univ.* 42:45–57

63. Ito, M. 1969. A factor of luminance in the "field" of vision: The interaction between the luminance and the area of the figure. *Kiyo Tokushima Univ.* 4:1–21

64. Ito, Y. 1963. An experimental study of children's conception of number: The conception of equivalence of sets and conservation of number. *Jap. J. Educ. Psychol.* 11:157–67

65. Ito, Y., Hatano, G. 1963. An experimental education of number conservation. *Jap. Psychol. Res.* 5:161–70

66. Iwahara, S., Iwasaki, T. 1969. Effect of chlordiazepoxide upon food intake and spontaneous motor activity of the rat as a function of hours of food deprivation. *Jap. Psychol. Res.* 11:117–28

67. Iwahara, S., Sugimura, T. 1970. Effects of chlordiazepoxide on black-white discrimination acquisition and reversal in white rats. *Jap. J. Psychol.* 41:142–50

68. Kakizaki, S. 1966. Context effects in psychophysical judgments. *Jap. J. Psychol.* 37:235–46

69. Kakizaki, S. 1967. Semantic effects in perceptual judgments. *Psychologia* 10:187–96

70. Kakizaki, S., Morikiyo, Y. 1961. Sensory magnitude and linguistic frame of reference. *Proc. 25th Ann. Conv. JPA*, 105

71. Kambe, N. 1969. Effect of chromatic adaptation upon appearance of colored stimulus. *Proc. 33rd Ann. Conv. JPA*, 24

72. Kaneko, T. 1965. A study on rapid declining processes of color sensation. *Acta Chromatica* 1:156–63

73. Kano, C. 1967. Die induzierte Bewe-

gung zwischen dem Körper und dem Objekt. *Jap. Psychol. Res.* 9:135–51

74. Kano, C. 1970. Die Wirkung der anschaulichen Grössenunterschiede auf die Bewegungsschwelle bei übereinstimmender Grösse der gereizten Netzhaut Areale. *Psychol. Forsch.* 33:242–53

75. Kansaku, H. 1967. Attractiveness of colored lights. *J. Illum. Eng. Inst. Jap.* 51:684–90

76. Kasamatsu, A., Hirai, T. 1969. An electrographic study of the Zen meditation (Zazen). *Psychologia* 12:205–25

77. Kato, K. 1964. The influence of the figure configuration upon the lightness contrast. *Jap. J. Psychol.* 35:18–26

78. Katori, H. 1968. The genetic conditions for pattern cognition: An experimental analysis of the subjective factors sustaining the identification of geometrical figures. *Jap. Psychol. Monogr.* 7

79. Katori, H., Natori, K. 1967. The immediate reproduction of tactually perceived figures and the drawing process in reproducing the figures. *Jap. J. Psychol.* 38:121–36

80. Kawamura, S., Itani, J., Eds. 1965. *Monkeys and Apes—Sociological Studies.* Tokyo: Chuokoronsha

81. Kawashima, T. 1957. *Family Institution as Ideology.* Tokyo: Iwanami-shoten

82. Kikuchi, A. 1964. Survey of Japanese interpersonal values. *Jap. Ann. Soc. Psychol.* 5:161–77

83. Kirihara, S. 1959. Development of industrial psychology in Japan. *Psychologia* 2:206–15

84. Kitamura, S., Tada, H. 1970. Studies on sensory overload: I. General method and problem. *Tohoku Psychol. Folia* 28:69–72

85. Kitamura, S., Tada, H., Kato, T. 1969. Studies on sensory deprivation: VII. *Tohoku Psychol. Folia* 27:67–73

86. Kitao, N. 1965. The effect of contextual experiences on verbal memory in children. *Jap. J. Educ. Psychol.* 13:154–60

87. Kitao, N. 1967. Effects of mediated association on paired-associated learning: VIII. About the degree of prior-learning and instruction. *Jap. J. Psychol.* 38:137–47

88. Komatsu, H. 1968. The measurement of the field-strength near a segmental line and a ring in binocular vision. *Tohoku Psychol. Folia* 27:32–49

89. Komori, T. 1968. The role of encoding in memory. *Bull. Fac. Educ. Kyoto Univ.* 14:89–90

90. Kotake, Y., Miyata, Y. 1958. Our 17 years of research on conditioned responses in man. *Psychologia* 1:158–66

91. Kozaki, A. 1965. The effect of co-existent stimuli other than test stimulus on brightness constancy. *Jap. Psychol. Res.* 7:138–47

92. Kozaki, T. 1970. Effect of background lightness on contrast and assimilation. *Jap. J. Psychol.* 12:75–81

93. Kuhara, K., Hatano, G. 1967. A developmental study of concept formation. *Jap. J. Educ. Psychol.* 15:226–35

94. Ibid 1968. Concept learning and intelligence: Effect of task complexity and intuitiveness of the relevant dimension. 16:65–71.

95. Kume, K., Nakamura, S., Kikuta, S., Sugekawa, S. 1968. Development of depth perception in infants: A study by means of visual cliff. *Ningen Kenkyu* 6:1–41

96. Kurioka, Y. 1968. Automatic recording of pupillary reflex. *Bull. Electrotech. Lab.* 32:958–66

97. Kuroda, T. 1961. Experimental studies on size constancy. *Bull. Fac. Lit. Kyushu Univ.* 7:60–102

98. Ibid 1965. Methodological and experimental studies on size constancy. 9:49–96

99. Kuroda, T. 1966. Size constancy and distance constancy. *Rep. 18th Int. Congr. Psychol. Moscow* 19:49–54

100. Kuroki, S. 1957. *Psychology of Hearing.* Tokyo: Kyoritsu Shuppan

101. Kushida, H. (Sasaki) 1967. Some remarks on methodology for the study of thinking: Experimental studies of children's concept formation. *Jap. J. Educ. Psychol.* 15:1–10

102. Maeda, Y., Ed. 1967. *Behavior Study of Japanese Macaques: Focusing on the Wild Troop of Chugoku-Katsuyama, Okayama Prefecture.* Dept. Psychol., Osaka Univ.

103. Makino, T. 1965. Problems on indices of size constancy. *Jap. Psychol. Rev.* 9:47–162

104. Makino, T. 1965. Developmental problems of size constancy. *Jap. Psychol. Res.* 7:15–19

105. Maruyama, Ki. 1961. "Contralateral relationship" between the ears and

the halves of visual field in the sensory interaction. *Tohoku Psychol. Folia* 19:81–92

106. Maruyama, Ki., Tsukahara, S. 1968. Stereoscopic depth perception under successive exposure of test stimuli to the two eyes. *Tohoku Psychol. Folia* 27:9–21

107. Maruyama, Ku., Hayashi, C. 1968. Data analysis with response errors. *Jap. J. Psychol.* 38:297–310

108. Matsushima, K., Noguchi, H. 1967. Multidimensional representation of binocular visual space. *Jap. Psychol. Res.* 9:85–94

109. Matsuura, H. 1970. The study of the expository method and discovery method in rule learning. *Jap. J. Educ. Psychol.* 18:129–38

110. Metzger, W. 1953. *Gesetze des Sehens.* Frankfurt am Main: Kramer

111. Metzger, W. 1954. *Psychologie.* Darmstadt: Steinkopff. 2nd ed.

112. Minato, Y. 1969. Color sensation in the perceptual visual field. *Proc. 33rd Ann. Conv. JPA*, 26

113. Mishima, J., Tanaka, M. 1966. The role of age and intelligence in concept formation of children. *Jap. Psychol. Res.* 8:30–37

114. Misumi, J. 1959. Experimental studies on "Group Dynamics" in Japan. *Psychologia* 2:229–35

115. Mitarai, G., Takagi, S., Muroga, T. 1968. Changes of color coding system in the goldfish under long period of exposure to monochromatic light. *Ann. Rep. Res. Inst. Environ. Med. Nagoya Univ.* 20:62–67

116. Miura, K. 1964. An experimental study of "discovery" learning. *Jap. J. Educ. Psychol.* 12:202–15

117. Ibid 1967. The developmental study of classification behavior: I. 15:65–74

118. Miyamoto, M., Fukuoka, R., Iwasaki, Y., Kizaki, T., Nakamura, M. 1964. Qualitative analysis of children's intellectual interests. *Jap. J. Educ. Psychol.* 12:139–51

119. Mori, S., Mitarai, G., Mori, S. 1969. Effect of monochromatic light environment on color discrimination learning in pigeons. *Ann. Rep. Res. Inst. Environ. Med. Nagoya Univ.* 17:35–43

120. Mori, T., Watanabe, A., Yamaguchi, Y. 1966. Spatial sine-wave response of the visual system. *Tech. J. Jap. Broadcasting Corp.* 18:79–93

121. Morikawa, Y. 1964. Successive comparison of visual size. II. On the effect of interpolated circle. *Jap. J. Psychol.* 35:117–25

122. Morikawa, Y. 1965. A study on successive comparison of size of circles. *Res. Rep. Fac. Educ. Waseda Univ.* 14:11–22

123. Morinaga, S. 1954. Paradox of displacement in geometrical illusion. *Proc. 18th Ann. Conv. JPA*

124. Morinaga, S., Ikeda, H. 1965. Paradox of displacement in geometrical illusion and the problem of dimensions: A contribution to the study of space perception. *Jap. J. Psychol.* 36:231–38

125. Morinaga, S., Noguchi, K. 1966. The perceptual constancy and the system of reference. *Psychol. Forsch.* 29:149–60

126. Moriya, K. 1970. The role of speech in cognitive process: On the verbalization as objectification. *Jap. J. Educ. Psychol.* 18:26–32

127. Motokawa, K., Ogawa, T. 1962. The electrical field in the retina and pattern vision. *Tohoku J. Exp. Med.* 77:209–21

128. Mugishima, F. 1969. Eye movements. *Handbook of Sensation and Perception*, ed. Y. Wada, T. Oyama, S. Imai, 670–81. Tokyo: Seishin Shobo

129. Muramatsu, T., Ed. 1962. *Japanese: An Empirical Study of Culture and Personality.* Nagoya: Reimei Shobo

130. Nagatsuka, Y. 1960. On the effects of observing body condition upon visuo-spatial perception. The effects upon "apparent movement." *Tohoku Psychol. Folia* 19:37–47

131. Naka, K. I., Rushton, W. A. H. 1966. S-potentials from luminosity units in the retina of fish (*Cyprinidae*). *J. Physiol.* 185:587–99

132. Nakamura, A. 1968. The relation between the adaptation time in the eye and the rate of variation in the luminance. *Stud. Hum., Fac. Arts Shinshu Univ.* 3:11–19

133. Namba, S., Yoshikawa, T., Kuwano, S. 1968. Context effects in loudness judgment. *Jap. J. Psychol.* 39:191–99

134. Nayatani, Y. 1968. On recent works on color harmony. *Jap. Psychol. Rev.* 11:156–70

135. Niimi, Y., Shirafuji, Y. 1969. *Psychogalvanic Responses.* Tokyo: Ishiyaku Shuppan

136. Niki, H. 1965. The effects of hippocampal ablation on the inhibitory control of operant behavior in the rat. *Jap. Psychol. Res.* 7:126–37

137. Ibid 1966. Response perseveration following the hippocampal ablation in the rat. 8:1–9

138. Ninomiya, T., Ikeda, S., Yamaguchi, S., Yoshikawa, T. 1966. Studies on the taste of various amino acids. *Rep. 7th Sensory Eval. Symp. JUSE*, 109–23

139. Nishikawa, Y. 1967. Euclidean interpretation of binocular visual space. *Jap. Psychol. Res.* 9:191–98

140. Noguchi, K. 1969. Effects of the size and texture of background upon size constancy. *Jap. Psychol. Res.* 11:198–207

141. Nozawa, S. 1961. Studies on figural after-effects by the measurement of field strength. *Proc. 25th Ann. Conv. JPA*, 91

142. Nozawa, S. 1961. Studies on figural after-effects by the measurement of field strength and the factor of spatial distance. *Seishin Studies* 16:111–40

143. Ogasawara, J. 1966. Three formulae for the density-gradient of stimuli in depth perception. *Percept. Mot. Skills* 23:1086

144. Ogasawara, J. 1968. On Thouless' Z as an index of constancy. *Jap. Psychol. Rev.* 11:217–30

145. Ogasawara, J. 1969. Visual deflexion of the line obliquely laid to another line II. *Proc. Dept. Hum., Coll. Gen. Educ., Univ. Tokyo* XLIX:1–24

146. Ogasawara, J., Mori, T. 1966. Short article on Thouless constancy ratios. *Jap. Psychol. Rev.* 10:186–96

147. Ogawa, T., Kozaki, T., Takano, Y., Okayama, K. 1966. Effect of area on apparent brightness. *Rep. Psychol. Lab. Keio Univ.* 2:1–15

148. Ohba, K. 1971. Social order in the domestic fowl. *Kagaku Asahi* 31: 78–84

149. Ohba, S. 1966. Changes of perceived size of the object in the downward viewing condition to the ground. *Psychologia* 9:95–101

150. Ohmura, A. 1966. Cognitive preferences in high school physics. *Jap. J. Educ. Psychol.* 14:1–8

151. Ohmura, H. 1967. Illumination constancy and illumination contrast: I. Relation to whiteness constancy. *Bull. Fac. Lit. Kyushu Univ.* 10: 39–76

152. Ohmura, T. 1965. Whiteness constancy and illumination constancy. *Bull. Fac. Lit. Kyushu Univ.* 9:97–158

153. Ohtani, A. 1968. Temporal character-

istics of the eye movements. *Jap. J. Ergonom.* 4:29–36

154. Ohtani, A. 1970. An analysis of eye movements during visual task. *Ergonomics.* In press

155. Okada, T. 1961. Experimental studies on shape constancy. *Bull. Fac. Lit. Kyushu Univ.* 7:163–97

156. Ibid 1965. Shape constancy and slant constancy. 19:159–87

157. Orbison, W. B. 1939. Shape as a function of vector-field. *Am. J. Psychol.* 52:31–45

158. Osaka, R. 1966. The ophthalmograph and oculo-optical switch. *Psychologia* 9:125–30

159. Osaka, R., Iwawaki, S. 1965. Visual perception toward the ground and head movement. *Proc. 29th Ann. Conv. JPA*, 99

160. Oyama, T. 1968. Stimulus determinants of brightness constancy and the perception of illumination. *Jap. Psychol. Res.* 10:146–55

161. Oyama, T., Hsia, Y. 1966. Compensatory hue shift in simultaneous color contrast as a function of separation between inducing and test fields. *J. Exp. Psychol.* 71:405–13

162. Oyama, T., Sato, F. 1967. Perceived size-ratio in stereoscopic vision as a function of convergence, binocular disparity and luminance. *Jap. Psychol. Res.* 9:1–13

163. Oyama, T., Tanaka, Ya., Chiba, Y. 1962. Affective dimensions of colors: A cross-cultural study. *Jap. Psychol. Res.* 4:78–91

164. Samejima, Y., Hatano, G. 1965. The acquisition of counting as a method of quantification. *Jap. J. Educ. Psychol.* 13:234–46

165. Sasaki, H. 1970. Some experimental remarks on logical thinking of preschool children. *Jap. J. Educ. Psychol.* 18:193–203

166. Sasaki, M. 1968. The influence of prereversal experience on reversal learning in Japanese monkeys (*Macaca fuscata Yakui*) and children. *Ann. Anim. Psychol.* 18:75–88

167. Ibid 1969. The influence of prereversal experience on reversal learning in white rats. 19:17–28

168. Sato, A. 1969. Brightness enhancement of flicker and response variability. *Jap. J. Psychol.* 40:267–72

169. Shigenaga, S. 1965. The constancy of loudness and of acoustic distance. *Bull. Fac. Lit. Kyushu Univ.* 9:290–333

170. Shigeoka, K. 1965. Experimental stud-

ies on position constancy. *Bull. Fac. Lit. Kyushu Univ.* 9:189–228

171. Shimizu, M. 1962. An experimental study of the developmental process of conceptualization: The interrelationship of conceptualization and intelligence. *Jap. J. Psychol.* 33:71–83

172. Ibid 1963. An experimental study of developmental process of conceptualization: The interrelationship of conceptualization and intelligence. 33:299–304

173. Shimizu, M., Kamei, S. 1966. Analysis of the process of concept learning by manipulating easiness of retention of information concerning instances, dimensions or hypotheses. *Proc. 30th Ann. Conv. JPA*, 159–60

174. Shinomiya, A. 1967. A developmental study of the child's ability of abstraction in verbal thinking: I. On the functional levels of abstraction. *Jap. J. Educ. Psychol.* 15:161–73

175. Sofue, T. 1969. Some aspects of the Japanese personality as seen through the Sentence Completion Test. *Jap. J. Clin. Psychol.* 8:65–77

176. Somiya, T. 1967. Measurements of on-and-off responses in the human fovea by means of psychophysical technique: An explanation for some contradictions between sensitivities measured in terms of light threshold and of CFF. *Jap. J. Psychol.* 38:1–13

177. Sonoda, G. 1965. Perceptual transformation of objects in picture-plane. *Bull. Fac. Lit. Kyushu Univ.* 9:229–58

178. Sugimoto, S., Kida, M., Teranishi, T. 1969. Frequency changes of alpha brain waves during 3 days of sensory deprivation. *Ann. Rep. Res. Inst. Environ. Med. Nagoya Univ.* 17:73–78

179. Sumi, S. 1966. Paths of seen motion and motion aftereffect. *Percept. Mot. Skills* 23:1003–8

180. Suzuki, M. 1964. On the relationships between displacement-effect and figure-ground reversal of concentric circles: I. *Jap. J. Psychol.* 35:133–39

181. Suzuki, S., Indow, T. 1970. Strategy in the process of concept learning. *Proc. 34th Ann. Conv. JPA*, 296–97

182. Suzuki, Y., Maruyama, K. 1967. Differential sensitivity in auditory flutter measured by the constant method and the method of just noticeable difference. *Tohoku Psychol. Folia* 25:65–80

183. Suzumura, A. 1965. Studies on kinetic visual acuity. *Ann. Rep. Res. Inst. Environ. Med. Nagoya Univ.* 17:70–78

184. Suzumura, A., Miwa, T. 1967. Studies on the kinetic visual acuity: On the influence of the moving stimuli at the peripheral part upon the central vision. *Ann. Rep. Res. Inst. Environ. Med. Nagoya Univ.* 19:29–35

185. Takada, Y. 1960. Reaction time and information in the discrimination of length of lines. *Jap. Psychol. Res.* 9:14–24

186. Takahashi, K. 1968–1970. The dependent behavior in female adolescents: I, II, III. *Jap. J. Educ. Psychol.* 16:7–16, 216–26; 18:65–75

187. Takahashi, K., Ishikawa, S., Ishizone, M., Shioda, T., Hatano, G. 1969 *Content Analysis of Parental Guidebooks on Child-rearing.* Tokyo: Nihon Jido Kenkyujo

188. Takahashi, M., Uemura, Y. 1967. Test-threshold luminance under various luminance and area conditions of a ring-shaped inducing field. *Jap. Psychol. Res.* 9:199–204

189. Takasaki, H. 1967. Chromatic changes induced by changes in chromaticity of background of constant lightness. *J. Opt. Soc. Am.* 57:93–96

190. Takasaki, H., Hioki, R. 1962. Some studies on human visibility. *Rep. Dep. Technol. Shizuoka Univ.* 13:26–40

191. Takuma, T., Yoda, A. Jr. 1961. Child personality and cultural background. *Jap. J. Educ. Psychol.* 9:75–83

192. Tanaka, K. 1967. Developmental studies on size constancy. *Bull. Fac. Lit. Kyushu Univ.* 10:99–128

193. Tanaka, Y. 1966. Status of Japanese experimental psychology. *Ann. Rev. Psychol.* 17:233–72

194. Tanaka, Y. 1967. Analysis of errors in classification. *Jap. Psychol. Res.* 9:20–27

195. Tanaka, Y., Ed. 1969. *Psychometrics.* Tokyo: Univ. of Tokyo Press

196. Tanaka, Y., Uemura, Y., Torii, S. 1967. Decrease and increase in test-threshold luminance induced by a contiguous annular field. *Percept. Mot. Skills* 24:1319–26

197. Tanaka, Yo. 1968. Children's representation of spatial transformation. *Jap. J. Educ. Psychol.* 16:87–99

198. Tanaka, Yo. 1971. The role of mediators in the epistemic observation: especially on spatial representation. *Jap. J. Educ. Psychol.* In press

199. Tashiro, T. 1970. Perceptual adaptation to prismatic distortion of form. *Stud. Hum., Osaka City Univ.* 21: 1043–61

200. Terada, A. 1967. An experimental study on the development of number concept in mentally retarded children. *Jap. J. Educ. Psychol.* 15:11–20

201. Ibid 1969. An experimental study on the development of number concept in mentally retarded children: II. 17:102–17

202. Teranishi, R., Takekawa, T. 1965. Reaction time and information processing in pitch discrimination. *Jap. J. Psychol.* 36:103–11

203. Teraoka, T. 1965. On selection strategies in concept formation: A behavioral approach. *Jap. Psychol. Rev.* 9:16–43

204. Tomiie, T. 1969. Study on an affective value of color (I). *Ronso Seishin Woman's College* 31 & 32:65–98

205. Tomita, T. 1968. Electrical responses of single photoreceptors. *Proc. IEEE* 56:1015–23

206. Tone, T. 1967. Psychological studies on the Land effect. *Bull. Fac. Lit. Kyushu Univ.* 10:77–98

207. Torii, S., Kimura, M. 1965. Tactual form perception in the congenitally blinds and the children with normal sight. *Proc. 29th Ann. Conv. JPA*, 71

208. Torii, S., Uemura, Y. 1965. Effects of inducing luminance and area on test-threshold luminance. *Percept. Mot. Skills* 21:779–82

209. Torii, S., Uemura, Y. 1965. Effects of inducing luminance and area upon the apparent brightness of the test field. *Jap. Psychol. Res.* 7:86–100

210. Toshima, Y. 1969. Velocity constancy and its transposition principle. *Jap. Psychol. Res.* 11:91–102

211. Tsuji, S. 1960. A psychological analysis of family relationship. *Festschr. 10th anniv. of establishment of Tokyo Metropolitan Univ.*, 105–79

212. Tsuji, S., Kato, N. 1966. Some investigations of parental preference in early childhood: An attempt to obtain a correspondence of verbally expressed preference with projectively expressed preference. *Jap. Psychol. Res.* 8:10–17

213. Ueda, T. 1967. Comparative and developmental studies on perceptual constancies. *Bull. Fac. Lit. Kyushu Univ.* 10:151–76

214. Uematsu, T. 1964. Fighting behavior of the guppy, *Lebistes reticulatus. Ann. Anim. Psychol.* 14:41–47

215. Ueno, T. 1968. Visual search time based on stochastic serial and parallel processing. *Percept. Psychophys.* 3(3B):229–32

216. Ueno, T., Nakaseko, M. 1967. A serial processing model for tactile scanning. *Jap. Psychol. Res.* 9:62–69

217. Umemoto, T. 1969. Strategy in memory. *Proc. 33rd Ann. Conv. JPA*, 33–34

218. Umeoka, Y., Iwamoto, T., Matsumune, K. 1968. Formation of classical conditional responses in the eel. *Ann. Anim. Psychol.* 18:42–43

218a. Umeoka, Y., Iwamoto, T., Suzuki, N. 1967. Microstructure of general activities in rat. I. Analysis of restless activity by spring-mounted cage. *Ann. Anim. Psychol.* 17:39–40

219. Umezu, H. 1960. Studies in the learning of language communications by the deaf-blind. *Jap. Sci. Rev. Hum. Stud.* 11:108–12

220. Umezu, H., Nakatani, K., Uemura, Y. 1967. Visual discrimination in the congenitally blind after operation (II). *Proc. 31st Ann. Conv. JPA*, 27

221. Umezu, H., Torii, S. 1964. Perception of form in the congenitally blind after operation. *Proc. 28th Ann. Conv. JPA*, 85

222. Umezu, H., Torii, S. 1965. Tactual form perception in the congenitally blinds. *Proc. 29th Ann. Conv. JPA*, 70

223. Umezu, H., Torii, S. 1966. Visual discrimination in the congenitally blind after operation. *Proc. 30th Ann. Conv. JPA*, 54

224. Ushijima, Y. 1961. *Personality Formation in Western Europe and Japan.* Tokyo: Kanekoshobo

225. Wada, Y. 1960. Expansion effect in the geometrical illusion. *Jinbun Gakuho* 23:33–53

226. Ibid 1962. Effect of brightness difference on geometrical illusions. 27: 9–22

227. Ibid 1963. Effect of width of lines on Delboeuf illusion. 37:13–23

228. Ibid 1965. Effect of brightness difference and of width of lines on geometrical illusions. 50:1–11

229. Wada, Y. 1968. Assimilation and contrast in perception. *Gendai Shinrigaku Ronshu, Meisei Univ.*, 32–43

230. Wada, Y. 1968. Perception of distance between parallel discontinuous lines. *Jinbun Gakuho* 62:1–11

231. Ibid 1970. A preliminary experiment on the relationship between the in-

difference level and the time-errors. 77:1–7

232. Wakai, K. 1968. Memory and problem solving. *Jap. J. Educ. Psychol.* 16: 17–25

233. Wake, T. 1965. Visual effect of the ring upon critical pause threshold of the disk in disk-ring sequence. *Jap. Psychol. Res.* 7:110–19

234. Ibid 1967. The effect of separation and overlap between the disk and the ring upon the contour effect. 9: 35–41

235. Watanabe, A., Mori, T., Nagata, S., Hiwatashi, K. 1968. Spatial sine-wave responses of the human visual system. *Vision Res.* 8:1245–63

236. Watanabe, H. 1970. The acquisition process of knowledge in children. *Jap. J. Educ. Psychol.* 18:65–128

237. Werner, H. 1935. Studies on contour: I. Qualitative analysis. *Am. J. Psychol.* 47:40–64

238. Yagi, B. 1964. Solution of patterned string problems by Japanese monkeys (*Macaca fuscata Yakui*). *Ann. Anim. Psychol.* 14:73–81

239. Yagi, B., Shinohara, S., Shinoda, A. 1969. A study of delayed response in Japanese monkeys (*Macaca fuscata Yakui*). *Ann. Anim. Psychol.* 19:65–71

240. Yamamura, Y. 1969. Emotional aspects of group and mother-child relationship in Japan. *Jap. Soc. Rev.* 19–4:54–63

241. Yamazaki, A. 1968. Electrophysiological study on "flick" eye movements during fixation. *Acta Soc. Ophthalmol. Japan* 72:2446–59

242. Ibid 1970. Electrophysiological study on saccades during fixation and small smooth pursuit movement in neurological disorders. 74:882–90

243. Yoda, A. Jr., Fukatsu, C. 1963. Ordinal position and personality. *Jap. J. Educ. Psychol.* 11:239–46

244. Yokose, Z. 1956. *Psychology of Visual Perception.* Tokyo: Kyoritsu

245. Yokose, Z. 1966. Pattern recognition and reading of characters by machine. *Jap. J. Ergonom.* 2:10–16

246. Yokose, Z. 1970. A study on character patterns based upon the theory of psychological potential field. *Jap. Psychol. Res.* 12:18–25

247. Yokose, Z., Goto, T. 1965. The measurement of the magnitude of the field-force of a circle and circular arcs. *Jap. Psychol. Res.* 7:101–9

248. Yokose, Z., Ito, M. 1968. A quantitative analysis of the influence of the subject's attitude on the light threshold of a small test patch projected inside various compound figures. *Jap. J. Psychol.* 39:171–80

249. Yonemura, G. T., Kasuya, M. 1969. Color discrimination under reduced angular subtense and luminance. *J. Opt. Soc. Am.* 59:131–35

250. Yoshida, M. 1968. Dimensions of tactual impressions (1). *Jap. Psychol. Res.* 10:123–37

251. Ibid. Dimensions of tactual impressions (2), 157–73

252. Yoshida, M., Fujii, K., Kurita, J. 1966. Structure of a moral concept "on" in the Japanese mind: I. *Jap. J. Psychol.* 37:74–85

253. Ibid. Structure of a moral concept "on" in the Japanese mind: II. 195–203

254. Yoshida, M., Iiyoshi, S., Koike, M. 1969. Structure of a moral concept "giri" in the Japanese mind. *Jap. Psychol. Rev.* 12:108–32

255. Yoshida, M., Moriyama, M., Tamai, C. 1962. Structure of authority in the Japanese mind. *Jap. J. Psychol.* 32:353–66

256. Yoshida, M., Saito, S. 1969. Multidimensional scaling of the taste of amino acids. *Jap. Psychol. Res.* 11:149–66

257. Yoshioka, I. 1966. A note on size constancy under reduced stimulus condition. *Bull. Fac. Educ. Hiroshima Univ.* 15:83–92

258. Yoshitake, H. 1968. Context effects and response languages in the judgment of visual length. *Jap. J. Psychol.* 39:49–56

259. Yuki, K. 1968. "Seeing" and "Movement." *Proc. 32nd Ann. Conv. JPA,* 99

260. Yuki, K., Hashimoto, M. 1964. Contour and brightness constancy. *Proc. 28th Ann. Conv. JPA,* 61

261. Zax, M., Takahashi, S. 1967. Response styles among Japanese and American children. *Jap. Psychol. Res.* 9:58–61

262. Zax, M., Takahashi, S. 1967. Cultural influences on response style: Comparisons of Japanese and American college students. *J. Soc. Psychol.* 71:3–10

AUTHOR INDEX

733

Berberich, J. P., 257
Berch, D. B., 16
Bereiter, C., 12, 180, 221, 222, 223, 227
Berenbaum, H. L., 389, 634
Berendes, J., 313
Berenson, B. G., 641
Berger, B. D., 475
Berger, S. E., 397
Berger, W. G., 497
Bergin, A. E., 641, 642, 645, 649, 650, 651, 653, 654, 655, 656, 657
Berkhout, J., 563
Berkowitz, L., 386, 487, 511, 531
Berkowitz, N. N., 488, 517
Berland, O., 315
Berlin, C. I., 333
Berlucchi, G., 417
Berlyne, D. E., 669, 687
Berman, P. W., 31
Bernard, J. L., 586
Bernhard, C. G., 365
Bernstein, A., 659
Bernstein, I. S., 302, 303
Berry, F. M., 21
Berscheid, E., 487
Berson, E. L., 348
Berzins, J. I., 631, 633, 640, 653
Best, P. J., 431
Bettinger, L. A., 74
Bevan, W. Jr., 704
Bever, T. G., 32, 33, 197
Bezembinder, T. G. G., 134, 135, 140
Bhargava, R. P., 365
Bianchi, C., 469
Biblow, E., 387, 390
Bickford, R. G., 328, 329, 459
Bidder, T. G., 459
Biebuyck, D. P., 686
Biedenbach, M. A., 421
Biener, L., 497
Bierman, R., 638, 643, 659
Bignall, K. E., 415, 426
Bilger, R. C., 336
Biller, H. B., 397
Bilstrom, D. E., 435
Bindra, D., 52, 54
Birch, H., 74
Birch, H. G., 7, 196
Birch, L. M., 333
Birdsall, T. G., 162, 163
Birdwhistell, R. L., 617
Birkimer, J. C., 57
Bis, J., 255
Bisbicos, E., 258
Bishop, D. W., 495, 515
Bishop, P. O., 413, 414, 416, 417

Bissell, J. S., 183
Bitterman, M. E., 52, 53, 86
Bizzi, E., 429
Black, A. H., 65
Blackwell, H. R., 356, 363
Blackwell, O. M., 356, 363
Blaine, D. D., 121
Blake, B. F., 510
Blake, R. R., 507, 530, 531
Blakemore, C., 413-56; 417, 418, 422
Blalock, H. M. Jr., 490
Blanchard, E. B., 494, 496, 529, 531
Blank, M., 18, 184, 220, 221, 228
Blasdell, R., 33
Blegvad, B., 337
Block, K. K., 108, 109
Bloom, B.S., 229, 263
Bloom, L., 32
Bloom, R. D., 260
Bloomberg, L. I., 635
Bloomfield, S., 430
Blue, C. M., 19
Blue, S., 333
Blum, G. S., 580, 600
Blumberg, A., 637
Blumberg, E. L., 15
Blumenkrantz, J., 196
Blumer, D., 459
Bock, R. D., 148
Boden, A. M., 594
Boeihenga, J., 437
Boerger, G., 330
Boersma, F. J., 185
Boëthius, J., 365
Bogen, J. E., 440, 441
Bogo, N., 598
Bohdanecka, M., 464
Bohdanecky, Z., 460, 461, 464, 471
Bohn, S., 578
Bohus, B., 470
Bolen, L., 586
Boller, F., 442, 443
Bolles, R. C., 51-72; 52, 53, 56, 59, 61, 62, 63, 64, 65
Bond, M. H., 505, 506
Bonoma, T., 397
Boomsliter, P. C., 674
Boozer, R., 212, 224
Borden, R., 488, 498, 518, 520, 522
Boris, H., 637, 659
Borns, J. F., 338
Boroto, D. R., 397
Bossema, I., 299
Bossom, J., 432
Bothe, G. G., 336
Bouchard, T. J. Jr., 179
Boucher, J., 514
Boucher, R., 428

Boudreau, J. C., 327, 419, 420
Boulay, M. A., 585
Boulware, D. W., 637
Bouma, H., 355
Bouman, M. A., 349, 356, 357, 358, 361
Bourne, L. E. Jr., 105-30; 28, 31, 106, 108, 109, 110, 112, 113, 117, 118, 119, 120, 121, 122, 123
Bouvier, G., 428
Bovet, M. C., 240
Bowen, F. P., 432
Bowen, J., 142, 143, 144
Bower, A. C., 115, 118
Bower, G., 54, 57, 63, 107, 108, 121, 122
Bower, G. H., 245
Bower, T. G. R., 5
Bowers, J., 185
Bowers, K. S., 186, 392
Bowlby, J., 277
Bowles, S., 400
Bowman, R. E., 477
Boyle, A. J., 322
Boyle, M., 350
Boynton, R. M., 348, 355, 360, 699
Bozarth, J. D., 641, 657
Bracchitta, H., 79
Bracht, G. H., 243
Brackbill, Y., 7, 8
Bradford, J. P., 469
Bradley, P. A., 189
Brady, J. V., 460, 474
Bragg, B. W., 402
Bragg, V. C., 333
Brahlek, J. A., 53
Brain, C. K., 299
Brainerd, C. J., 27, 233, 234, 235
Bramos, I., 190
Brar, H. S., 586
Bratfisch, O., 189
Braunstein, M. L., 149, 150
Brawley, E. R., 254
Bray, D. W., 545-76; 190, 560, 562, 566, 567, 568
Bredberg, G., 321
Brehm, J. W., 493, 524, 526
Brenner, A. R., 599
Brenner, M. H., 561
Bresler, J. B., 12
Breslow, A. K., 588
Brethower, D., 254
Brewer, B. A., 223, 227
Brewer, M. B., 518, 522
Brewer, W. F., 442
Breznitz, S., 503
Brian, D., 217, 263
Bricklin, B., 580, 600, 602
Bridges, C. D. B., 348
Briese, E., 467

SUBJECT INDEX

CUMULATIVE INDEXES

VOLUMES 19 - 23

INDEX OF CONTRIBUTING AUTHORS

INDEX OF CHAPTER TITLES

VOLUMES   19-23